Contents
Table des matières

Editor/Rédactrice
Kate Nicholson

Publishing Manager/Direction éditoriale
Anna Stevenson

Prepress/Prépresse
Andrew Butterworth
Nicolas Echallier
Helen Hucker

Preface

This new *Harrap's Everyday French and English Dictionary* aims to provide students of French at beginner and intermediate level with a reliable and user-friendly dictionary in a compact form. The clear, systematic presentation makes the dictionary an easy-to-use tool and its broad coverage should ensure that it becomes an invaluable resource.

With over 30,000 references, this little book covers all the words and phrases needed for everyday situations and travels in French-speaking countries. It includes colloquial and idiomatic expressions as well as vocabulary from a range of different fields.

The middle supplement provides extra help with both English and French irregular verbs, while pronunciation tips can be found at the start of the book, making it an essential pocket resource.

Préface

Ce nouveau *Harrap's Everyday French and English Dictionary* a pour but de fournir aux apprenants d'anglais de niveau débutant ou intermédiaire un dictionnaire fiable et pratique sous forme compact. La présentation claire et systématique en fait un outil d'usage facile, et grâce à son traitement du vocabulaire, il devrait s'avérer une aide précieuse pour l'utilisateur.

Avec plus de 30,000 références, ce petit livre traite tous les mots et expressions utiles pour les situations courantes et les voyages aux pays anglo-saxons. Il contient des expressions familiers et idiomatiques ainsi que des termes issus de domaines variés.

Le supplément au centre de l'ouvrage contient des informations sur les verbes irréguliers anglais et français, et des tableaux de prononciation se trouvent au début de livre pour en faire une ressource de poche essentielle.

Abbreviations · Abréviations

gloss	=	glose
[introduces an explanation]		[introduit une explication]
cultural equivalent	≃	équivalent culturel
[introduces a translation		[introduit une traduction
which has a roughly		dont les connotations dans
equivalent status		la langue cible sont
in the target language]		comparables]
abbreviation	*abbr, abrév*	abréviation
adjective	*adj*	adjectif
adverb	*adv*	adverbe
agriculture	*Agr*	agriculture
American English	*Am*	anglais américain
anatomy	*Anat*	anatomie
architecture	*Archit*	architecture
slang	*Arg*	argot
astrology	*Astrol*	astrologie
cars	*Aut*	automobile
auxiliary	*aux*	auxiliaire
aviation	*Aviat*	aviation
Belgian French	*Belg*	belgicisme
biology	*Biol*	biologie
botany	*Bot*	botanique
British English	*Br*	anglais britannique
Canadian French	*Can*	canadianisme
chemistry	*Chem, Chim*	chimie
cinema	*Cin*	cinéma
commerce	*Com*	commerce
computing	*Comptr*	informatique
conjunction	*conj*	conjonction
cooking	*Culin*	cuisine
economics	*Econ, Écon*	économie
electricity, electronics	*El, Él*	électricité, électronique
exclamation	*exclam*	exclamation
feminine	*f*	féminin
familiar	*Fam*	familier
figurative	*Fig*	figuré
finance	*Fin*	finance
geography	*Geog, Géog*	géographie
geology	*Geol, Géol*	géologie
grammar	*Gram*	grammaire
gymnastics	*Gym*	gymnastique
history	*Hist*	histoire

humorous	*Hum*	humoristique
invariable	*inv*	invariable
journalism	*Journ*	journalisme
law	*Jur*	droit
linguistics	*Ling*	linguistique
masculine	*m*	masculin
mathematics	*Math*	mathématique
medicine	*Med, Méd*	médecine
military	*Mil*	militaire
music	*Mus*	musique
noun	*n*	nom
shipping	*Naut*	nautisme
feminine noun	*nf*	nom féminin
feminine plural noun	*nfpl*	nom féminin pluriel
masculine noun	*nm*	nom masculin
masculine and feminine noun	*nmf*	nom masculin et féminin
masculine plural noun	*nmpl*	nom masculin pluriel
plural noun	*npl*	nom pluriel
computing	*Ordinat*	ordinateurs, informatique
pejorative	*Pej, Péj*	péjoratif
philosophy	*Phil*	philosophie
photography	*Phot*	photographie
physics	*Phys*	physique
plural	*pl*	pluriel
politics	*Pol*	politique
past participle	*pp*	participe passé
prefix	*pref, préf*	préfixe
preposition	*prep, prép*	préposition
pronoun	*pron*	pronom
past tense	*pt*	prétérit
something	*qch*	quelque chose
registered trademark	®	marque déposée
rail	*Rail*	chemin de fer
religion	*Rel*	religion
somebody	*sb*	quelqu'un
school	*Sch, Scol*	domaine scolaire
Scottish English	*Scot*	anglais d'Écosse
singular	*sing*	singulier
something	*sth*	quelque chose
suffix	*suff*	suffixe
technology	*Tech*	technologie
telecommunications	*Tel, Tél*	télécommunications
theatre	*Theat, Théât*	théâtre
television	*TV*	télévision

typography, printing	*Typ*	typographie, imprimerie
university	*Univ*	domaine universitaire
verb	*v*	verbe
intransitive verb	*vi*	verbe intransitif
reflexive verb	*vpr*	verbe pronominal
transitive verb	*vt*	verbe transitif
inseparable transitive verb	*vt insep*	verbe transitif à particule inséparable [par ex.: **he looks after the children** il s'occupe des enfants]
separable transitive verb	*vt sep*	verbe transitif à particule séparable [par ex.: **she sent the present back** *or* **she sent back the present** elle a rendu le cadeau]

All other labels are written in full.
Toutes les autres indications d'usage sont données en entier.

Prononciation de l'anglais

Pour indiquer la prononciation anglaise, nous avons utilisé dans ce dictionnaire les symboles de l'API (Alphabet phonétique international). Pour chaque son anglais, vous trouverez dans le tableau ci-dessous des exemples de mots anglais, suivis de mots français présentant un son similaire. Une explication est donnée lorsqu'il n'y a pas d'équivalent en français.

Caractère API	Exemple en anglais	Exemple en français
Consonnes		
[b]	**b**a**bb**le	**b**é**b**é
[d]	**d**ig	**d**ent
[dʒ]	**g**iant, **j**ig	**j**ean
[f]	**f**it, **ph**ysics	**f**ace
[g]	**g**rey, bi**g**	**g**a**g**
[h]	**h**appy	h aspiré : à quelques rares exceptions près, il est toujours prononcé en anglais
[j]	**y**ellow	**y**aourt
[k]	**c**lay, **k**i**ck**	**c**ar
[l]	**l**ip, pi**ll**	**l**i**l**as
[m]	**m**u**mm**y	**m**a**m**an
[n]	**n**ip, pi**n**	**n**é
[ŋ]	si**ng**	parki**ng**
[p]	**p**i**p**	**p**a**p**a
[r]	**r**ig, **wr**ite	Pas d'équivalent français : se prononce en plaçant le bout de la langue au milieu du palais
[(r)]		Seulement prononcé en cas de liaison avec la voyelle qui suit comme dans : fa**r** away; the ca**r** is blue
[s]	**s**ick, **sc**ience	**s**ilen**c**e
[ʃ]	**sh**ip, na**t**ion	**ch**èvre
[t]	**t**ip, bu**tt**	**t**ar**t**ine
[tʃ]	**ch**ip, ba**tch**	a**tch**oum
[Ɵ]	**th**ick	Son proche du /s/ français, il se prononce en plaçant le bout de la langue entre les dents du haut et celles du bas

x

Caractère API	Exemple en anglais	Exemple en français
[ð]	**th**is	Son proche du /z/ français, il se prononce en plaçant le bout de la langue entre les dents du haut et celles du bas
[v]	**v**ague, gi**v**e	**v**ie
[w]	**w**it, **wh**y	**wh**isky
[z]	**z**ip, phy**s**ics	ro**s**e
[ʒ]	plea**s**ure	**j**e
[χ]	lo**ch**	Existe seulement dans certains mots écossais. Pas d'équivalent français : se prononce du fond de la gorge, comme Ba**ch** en allemand ou la 'jota' espagnole.

Voyelles

[æ]	r**a**g	n**a**tte
[ɑː]	l**ar**ge, h**al**f	p**â**te
[e]	s**e**t	/e/ moins ouvert que le [ɛ] français
[ɜː]	c**ur**tain, w**ere**	h**eu**re
[ə]	utt**er**	**che**val
[ɪ]	b**i**g, wom**e**n	/i/ bref, à mi-chemin entre les sons [ɛ] et [i] français (plus proche de 'net' que de 'vite')
[iː]	l**ea**k, w**ee**	/i/ plus long que le [i] français
[ɒ]	l**o**ck	b**o**nne – mais plus ouvert et prononcé au fond du palais
[ɔː]	w**a**ll, c**or**k	b**au**me – mais plus ouvert et prononcé au fond du palais
[ʊ]	p**u**t, l**oo**k	Son à mi-chemin entre un /ou/ bref et un /o/ ouvert
[uː]	m**oo**n	Son /ou/ prolongé
[ʌ]	c**u**p	À mi-chemin entre un /a/ et un /e/ ouverts

Diphtongues

Elles sont rares en français et sont la combinaison de deux sons.

[aɪ]	wh**y**, h**igh**, l**ie**	**aï**e
[aʊ] comme	h**ow**	mi**aou**, **aoû**tat – mais se prononce un seul son
[eə]	b**ear**, sh**are**, wh**ere**	fl**air**
[eɪ]	d**ay**, m**a**ke, m**ai**n	merv**eille**
[əʊ]	sh**ow**, g**o**	Combinaison d'un /o/ fermé et d'un /ou/

[ɪə]	h**ere**, g**ear**	Combinaison d'un /i/ long suivi d'un /e/ ouvert bref
[ɔɪ]	b**oy**, s**oil**	langue d'**oïl**
[ʊə]	s**ure**	Combinaison d'un son /ou/ suivi d'un /e/ ouvert bref

Prononciation de l'anglais américain

L'accent américain est différent de l'accent anglais : il est facile de le constater dans la prononciation du mot **tomato** qui se dit [təˈmeɪtəʊ] en anglais américain et [təˈmɑːtəʊ] en anglais britannique. Le r, qui disparaît souvent en anglais, est toujours prononcé en américain : **mother** se dit [ˈmʌðər] aux États-Unis et [ˈmʌðə] en Grande-Bretagne.

Quelques exemples :

	Prononciation américaine	*Prononciation anglaise*
advertisement	[ædvəˈtaɪzmənt]	[ədˈvɜːtɪsmənt]
clerk	[klɜːk]	[klɑːk]
derby	[ˈdɜːbɪ]	[ˈdɑːbɪ]
leisure	[ˈliːʒər]	[ˈleʒə]
privacy	[ˈpraɪvəsɪ]	[ˈprɪvəsɪ]
schedule	[ˈskedjʊl]	[ˈʃedjuːl]
tube	[tuːb]	[tjuːb]
vase	[veɪz]	[vɑːz]
z	[ziː]	[zed]

L'accent tonique est souvent différent : **distribute** se prononce [dɪsˈtrɪbjuːt] aux États-Unis et [ˈdɪstrɪbjuːt] en Grande-Bretagne ; **ballet** se dit [bæˈleɪ] en américain et [ˈbæleɪ] en anglais britannique.

Autres exemples :

	Prononciation américaine	*Prononciation anglaise*
Birmingham	[bɜːmɪŋˈhæm]	[ˈbɜːmɪŋəm]
laboratory	[ˈlæbrətərɪ]	[ləˈbɒrətərɪ]
fillet	[fɪˈleɪ]	[ˈfɪlɪt]
garage	[gəˈrɑːʒ]	[ˈgærɪdʒ]
pecan	[pɪˈkæn]	[ˈpiːkæn]

French Pronunciation

French pronunciation is shown in this dictionary using the symbols of the IPA (International Phonetic Alphabet). In the table below, examples of French words using these sounds are given, followed by English words which have a similar sound. Where there is no equivalent in English, an explanation is given.

IPA symbol	French example	English example
Consonants		
[b]	**bé**bé	**b**ut
[d]	**d**onner	**d**oor
[f]	**f**orêt	**f**ire
[g]	**g**are	**g**et
[ʒ]	**j**our	plea**s**ure
[k]	**c**arte	**k**itten
[l]	**l**ire	**l**onely
[m]	**m**a**m**an	**m**at
[n]	**n**i	**n**ow
[ŋ]	parki**ng**	si**ng**ing
[ɲ]	campa**gn**e	ca**ny**on
[p]	**p**atte	**p**at
[r]	**r**are	Like an English /r/ but pronounced at the back of the throat
[s]	**s**oir	**s**it
[ʃ]	**ch**ose	**sh**am
[t]	**t**able	**t**ap
[v]	**v**aleur	**v**alue
[z]	**z**éro	**z**ero
Vowels		
[a]	ch**a**t	c**a**t
[ɑ]	**â**ge	g**a**sp
[e]	**é**t**é**	b**ay**
[ɛ]	p**è**re	b**e**d
[ə]	l**e**	**a**mend
[ø]	d**eu**x	Does not exist in English: [e] pronounced with the lips rounded

[œ]	seul	curtain
[i]	vite	bee – not quite as long as the English [i:]
[ɔ]	donner	cot – slightly more open than the English /o/
[o]	chaud	daughter – but higher than its English equivalent
[u]	tout	you – but shorter than its English equivalent
[y]	voiture	Does not exist in English: [i] with lips rounded
[ɑ̃]	enfant	Nasal sound pronounced lower and further back in the mouth than [ɔ̃]

Vowels

[ɛ̃]	vin	Nasal sound: /a/ sound pronounced letting air pass through the nose
[ɔ̃]	bonjour	Nasal sound: closed /o/ sound pronounced letting air pass through the nose
[œ̃]	un	Nasal sound: like [ɛ̃] but with lips more rounded

Semi-vowels

[w]	voir	week
[j]	yoyo, paille	yard
[ɥ]	nuit	Does not exist in English: the vowel [y] elided with the following vowel

English-French
Anglais-Français

Aa

A, a¹ [eɪ] *n* (**a**) A, a *m inv*; **5A** *(in address, street number)* 5 bis; **to go from A to B** aller du point A au point B (**b**) *Sch (grade)* **to get an A in French** = avoir une très bonne note en français, ≃ avoir entre 16 et 20 en français (**c**) *(street atlas)* **an A to Z of London** un plan de Londres

a² [ə, *stressed* eɪ]

a devient **an** [ən, *stressed* æn] devant voyelle ou h muet.

indefinite article (**a**) *(in general)* un, une; **a man** un homme; **an apple** une pomme; **an hour** une heure (**b**) *(definite article in French)* 60 **pence a kilo** 60 pence le kilo; **50 km an hour** 50 km à l'heure; **I have a broken arm** j'ai le bras cassé (**c**) *(article omitted in French)* **he's a doctor/a father** il est médecin/père; **Caen, a town in Normandy** Caen, ville de Normandie; **what a man!** quel homme!; **a hundred** cent (**d**) *(a certain)* **a Mr Smith** un certain M. Smith (**e**) *(time)* **twice a month** deux fois par mois

abandon [ə'bændən] *vt* abandonner

abbey ['æbɪ] *(pl* **-eys**) *n* abbaye *f*

abbreviation [əbriːvɪ'eɪʃən] *n* abréviation *f*

abduct [æb'dʌkt] *vt* enlever

able ['eɪbəl] *adj* capable; **to be a. to do sth** être capable de faire qch, pouvoir faire qch; **to be a. to**

swim/drive savoir nager/conduire
● **ability** [ə'bɪlətɪ] *(pl* **-ies**) *n* capacité *f* (**to do** de faire); **to the best of my a.** de mon mieux

abnormal [æb'nɔːməl] *adj* anormal

aboard [ə'bɔːd] **1** *adv (on ship, plane)* à bord; **to go a.** monter à bord **2** *prep* **a. the ship/plane** à bord du navire/de l'avion; **a. the train** dans le train

abolish [ə'bɒlɪʃ] *vt* abolir

abortion [ə'bɔːʃən] *n* avortement *m*; **to have an a.** se faire avorter

about [ə'baʊt] **1** *adv* (**a**) *(approximately)* à peu près, environ; **at a. two o'clock** vers deux heures (**b**) *(here and there)* çà et là, ici et là; **to look a.** regarder autour de soi; **to follow sb a.** suivre qn partout **2** *prep* (**a**) *(around)* **a. the garden** autour du jardin (**b**) *(near to)* **a. here** par ici (**c**) *(concerning)* au sujet de; **to talk a. sth** parler de qch; **a book a. sth** un livre sur qch; **what's it (all) a.?** de quoi s'agit-il? (**d**) *(+ infinitive)* **a. to do** sur le point de faire; **I was a. to say…** j'étais sur le point de dire…

above [ə'bʌv] **1** *adv* au-dessus; *(in book)* ci-dessus; **from a.** d'en haut; **the floor a.** l'étage *m* du dessus **2** *prep* (**a**) *(in height, hierarchy)* au-dessus de; **he's a. me** *(in rank)* c'est mon supérieur; **he's not a. asking** il n'est pas trop

fier pour demander; **a. all** surtout
(b) *(with numbers)* plus de

abroad [ə'brɔːd] *adv* à l'étranger

abrupt [ə'brʌpt] *adj (sudden)*
brusque, soudain; *(rude)* brusque

absent ['æbsənt] *adj* absent (**from**
de) • **absent-minded** *adj* distrait

absolute ['æbsəluːt] *adj* absolu;
he's an a. fool! il est complètement idiot!; **it's an a. disgrace!**
c'est une honte! • **absolutely** *adv*
absolument; **you're a. right** tu as
tout à fait raison

absorb [əb'zɔːb] *vt (liquid)* absorber; *(shock)* amortir; **to be ab-
sorbed in sth** être plongé dans qch

abstract ['æbstrækt] *adj* abstrait

absurd [əb'sɜːd] *adj* absurde

abuse 1 [ə'bjuːs] *n (of child)*
mauvais traitements *mpl*; *(insults)*
injures *fpl* **2** [ə'bjuːz] *vt (misuse)*
abuser de; *(ill-treat)* maltraiter;
(insult) injurier

academic [ækə'demɪk] *adj* **(a)**
(year) (of school) scolaire; *(of university)* universitaire **(b)** *(scholarly)*
intellectuel, -elle • **academy**
[ə'kædəmɪ] *(pl* **-ies)** *n* académie *f*

accelerate [ək'seləreɪt] accélérer
• **accelerator** *n* accélérateur *m*

accent ['æksənt] *n* accent *m*

accept [ək'sept] *vt* accepter •
acceptable *adj* acceptable

access ['ækses] **1** *n* accès *m* (**to
sth** à qch; **to sb** auprès de qn) **2**
vt accéder à

accessories [ək'sesərɪz] *npl*
accessoires *mpl*

accident ['æksɪdənt] *n* accident
m; **by a.** accidentellement; *(by
chance)* par hasard • **accidentally**
adv accidentellement; *(by chance)*
par hasard

accommodation [əkɒmə'deɪʃən]
(*Am* **accommodations**) *n (lodg-*

ing) logement *m*; *(rented room(s))*
chambre(s) *f(pl)*

accompany [ə'kʌmpənɪ] (*pt & pp*
-ied) *vt* accompagner

accomplish [ə'kʌmplɪʃ] *vt (task,
duty)* accomplir; *(aim)* atteindre
• **accomplishment** *n (of task,
duty)* accomplissement *m*; *(thing
achieved)* réalisation *f*

accord [ə'kɔːd] *n* accord *m*; **of
my own a.** de mon plein gré •
according to *prep* selon, d'après

account [ə'kaunt] **1** *n* **(a)** *(with
bank)* compte *m* **(b)** *(report)*
compte rendu *m*; *(explanation)*
explication *f* **(c)** *(expressions)* **by
all accounts** au dire de tous;
on a. of à cause de; **on no a.**
en aucun cas; **to take sth into
a.** tenir compte de qch **2** *vi* **to
a. for** *(explain)* expliquer; *(give
reckoning of)* rendre compte de
• **accountant** *n* comptable *mf* •
accounting *n* comptabilité *f*

accumulate [ə'kjuːmjʊleɪt] **1** *vt*
accumuler **2** *vi* s'accumuler

accurate ['ækjʊrət] *adj* exact,
précis

accuse [ə'kjuːz] *vt* **to a. sb (of
sth/of doing sth)** accuser qn (de
qch/de faire qch)

accustomed [ə'kʌstəmd] *adj* **to
be a. to sth/to doing sth** être
habitué à qch/à faire qch; **to get
a. to sth/to doing sth** s'habituer
à qch/à faire qch

ace [eɪs] *n (card, person)* as *m*

ache [eɪk] **1** *n* douleur *f* **2** *vi* faire
mal; **my head aches** j'ai mal à
la tête

achieve [ə'tʃiːv] *vt (result)*
obtenir; *(aim)* atteindre; *(ambition)*
réaliser; **to a. success** réussir •
achievement *n (success)* réussite
f; *(of ambition)* réalisation *f*

acid ['æsɪd] *adj & n* acide *(m)*

acknowledge [ək'nɒlɪdʒ] *vt* reconnaître (**as** pour); *(greeting)* répondre à ● **acknowledg(e)ment** *n (of letter)* accusé *m* de réception; *(confession)* aveu *m* (**of** de)

acne ['æknɪ] *n* acné *f*

acoustics [ə'kuːstɪks] *npl* acoustique *f*

acquaint [ə'kweɪnt] *vt* **to be acquainted with** *(person)* connaître ● **acquaintance** *n (person)* connaissance *f*

acquire [ə'kwaɪə(r)] *vt* acquérir; *(taste)* prendre (**for** à)

acre ['eɪkə(r)] *n* ≃ demi-hectare *m*, acre *f*

acrobat ['ækrəbæt] *n* acrobate *mf* ● **acrobatics** *npl* acrobaties *fpl*

acronym ['ækrənɪm] *n* sigle *m*

across [ə'krɒs] **1** *prep (from side to side of)* d'un côté à l'autre de; *(on the other side of)* de l'autre côté de; *(crossways)* en travers de; **a bridge a. the river** un pont sur la rivière; **to walk** *or* **go a.** *(street, lawn)* traverser; **to run/swim a.** traverser en courant/à la nage **2** *adv* **to get sth a. to sb** faire comprendre qch à qn

acrylic [ə'krɪlɪk] *adj (paint, fibre)* acrylique; *(garment)* en acrylique

act [ækt] **1** *n* (**a**) *(deed)* acte *m*; **caught in the a.** pris sur le fait (**b**) *Theatre (part of play)* acte *m*; *Fig* **to get one's a. together** se secouer; *Fam* **in on the a.** dans le coup **2** *vt (part)* jouer; **to a. the fool** faire l'idiot **3** *vi* (**a**) *(take action, behave)* agir; **it's time to a.** il est temps d'agir; **to a. as secretary/ etc** faire office de secrétaire/*etc*; **to a. on behalf of sb** représenter qn (**b**) *(in play, film)* jouer; *(pretend)* jouer la comédie ● **acting** *n (of play)* représentation *f*; *(art)* jeu *m*; *(career)* théâtre *m*

action ['ækʃən] *n* action *f*; **to take a.** prendre des mesures; **to put into a.** *(plan)* exécuter; **out of a.** *(machine)* hors service; *(person)* hors de combat

active ['æktɪv] **1** *adj* actif, -ive **2** *n Gram* actif *m* ● **activity** *(pl* **-ies**) *n* activité *f*; *(in street)* animation *f*

actor ['æktə(r)] *n* acteur *m* ● **actress** *n* actrice *f*

actual ['æktʃuəl] *adj* réel *(f* réelle); *(example)* concret, -ète; **the a. book** le livre même; **in a. fact** en réalité ● **actually** *adv (truly)* réellement; *(in fact)* en fait

acute [ə'kjuːt] *adj (pain, angle)* aigu *(f* aiguë); *(anxiety, emotion)* vif *(f* vive); *(shortage)* grave

AD [eɪ'diː] *(abbr* **anno Domini**) apr. J.-C.

ad [æd] *n Fam (on radio, TV)* pub *f*; *(private, in newspaper)* annonce *f*; *Br* **small ad,** *Am* **want ad** petite annonce *f*

adapt [ə'dæpt] **1** *vt* adapter (**to** à) **2** *vi* s'adapter ● **adapter, adaptor** *n (for use abroad)* adaptateur *m*; *(for several plugs)* prise *f* multiple

add [æd] **1** *vt* ajouter (**to/that** à/que); **to a. (up** *or* **together)** *(numbers)* additionner; **to a. in** inclure **2** *vi* **to a. to** *(increase)* augmenter; **to a. up to** *(total)* s'élever à; *(mean)* signifier

addict ['ædɪkt] *n* **drug a.** toxicomane *mf*, drogué, -e *mf*; **TV a.** fana(tique) *mf* de la télé ● **addicted** *adj* **to be a. to drugs** être toxicomane; **to be a. to cigarettes** ne pas pouvoir se passer de tabac ● **addictive** *adj (drug, TV)* qui crée une dépendance

addition [ə'dɪʃən] *n* addition *f*; *(increase)* augmentation *f*; **in a.** de plus; **in a. to** en plus de ● **additional** *adj* supplémentaire

additive ['ædɪtɪv] n additif m

address 1 [Br ə'dres, Am 'ædres] n adresse f **2** [ə'dres] vt (person, audience) s'adresser à; (words, speech) adresser (**to** à); (letter) mettre l'adresse sur

adequate ['ædɪkwət] adj (enough) suffisant; (acceptable) convenable; (performance) acceptable ● **adequately** adv (sufficiently) suffisamment; (acceptably) convenablement

adhere [əd'hɪə(r)] vi **to a. to** adhérer à ● **adhesive** [-'hiːsɪv] adj & n adhésif (m)

adjacent [ə'dʒeɪsənt] adj (house, angle) adjacent (**to** à)

adjective ['ædʒɪktɪv] n adjectif m

adjourn [ə'dʒɜːn] vt (postpone) ajourner; (session) suspendre

adjust [ə'dʒʌst] vt (machine) régler; (clothes) rajuster; **to a. to sth** s'adapter à qch

administration [ədmɪnɪ'streɪʃən] n administration f; (government) gouvernement m ● **administrator** n administrateur, -trice mf

admire [əd'maɪə(r)] vt admirer (**for sth** pour qch; **for doing sth** de faire qch)

admit [əd'mɪt] (pt & pp -tt-) **1** vt (acknowledge) reconnaître, admettre (**that** que); (to hospital, college) admettre **2** vi **to a. to sth** avouer qch; (mistake) reconnaître qch ● **admission** n (acknowledgement) aveu m; (to theatre) entrée f (**to** à ou de); (to club, school) admission f; **a. (charge)** (prix m d')entrée f

adolescent [ædə'lesənt] n adolescent, -e mf

adopt [ə'dɒpt] vt adopter ● **adopted** adj (child) adopté; (son, daughter) adoptif, -ive

adore [ə'dɔː(r)] vt adorer (**doing** faire) ● **adorable** adj adorable

adult ['ædʌlt, ə'dʌlt] **1** n adulte mf **2** adj (animal) adulte; **a. class/film** classe f/film m pour adultes

advance [əd'vɑːns] **1** n (movement, money) avance f; (of science) progrès mpl; **in a.** (book, inform, apply) à l'avance; (pay) d'avance; (arrive) en avance **2** adj (payment) anticipé; **a. booking** réservation f **3** vi (go forward, progress) avancer; **to a. towards sb** s'avancer ou avancer vers qn ● **advanced** adj avancé

advantage [əd'vɑːntɪdʒ] n avantage m (**over** sur); **to take a. of** (situation) profiter de; (person) exploiter; **a. Williams** (in tennis) avantage Williams

adventure [əd'ventʃə(r)] **1** n aventure f **2** adj (film, story) d'aventures ● **adventurous** adj aventureux, -euse

adverb ['ædvɜːb] n adverbe m

advert ['ædvɜːt] n Br pub f; (private, in newspaper) annonce f

advertise ['ædvətaɪz] **1** vt (commercially) faire de la publicité pour; (privately) passer une annonce pour vendre **2** vi faire de la publicité; (privately) passer une annonce (**for** pour trouver) ● **advertisement** [Br əd'vɜːtɪsmənt, Am ædvər'taɪzmənt] n publicité f; (private or in newspaper) annonce f; (poster) affiche f; TV **the advertisements** la publicité ● **advertising** n publicité f; **a. campaign** campagne f de publicité

advise [əd'vaɪz] vt (counsel) conseiller; (recommend) recommander; **to a. sb to do sth** conseiller à qn de faire qch; **to a. sb against doing sth** déconseiller à qn de faire qch ● **advice** n conseil(s) *m(pl)*; **a piece of a.** un conseil; **to ask sb's a.** demander conseil à qn; **to take sb's a.** suivre les conseils de qn • **adviser, advisor** *n* conseiller, -ère *mf*

aerial ['eərɪəl] *n Br* antenne *f*

aerobics [eə'rəʊbɪks] *npl* aérobic *m*

aeroplane ['eərəpleɪn] *n Br* avion *m*

aerosol ['eərəsɒl] *n* aérosol *m*

affair ['əfeə(r)] *n (matter, concern)* affaire *f*; **(love) a.** liaison *f*; **state of affairs** situation *f*

affect [ə'fekt] *vt (concern)* concerner; *(move)* affecter; *(harm)* nuire à; *(influence)* influer sur • **affection** *n* affection *f* (**for** pour) • **affectionate** *adj* affectueux, -euse

afford [ə'fɔːd] *vt (pay for)* **I can't a. it/a new car** je n'ai pas les moyens de l'acheter/d'acheter une nouvelle voiture; **I can a. to wait** je peux me permettre d'attendre • **affordable** *adj (price)* abordable

afloat [ə'fləʊt] *adv (ship, swimmer, business)* à flot

afraid [ə'freɪd] *adj* **to be a.** avoir peur (**of** de); **to be a. to do** *or* **of doing sth** avoir peur de faire qch; **I'm a. (that) he'll fall** j'ai peur qu'il (ne) tombe; **I'm a. he's out** je regrette, il est sorti

afresh [ə'freʃ] *adv* **to start a.** recommencer

Africa ['æfrɪkə] *n* l'Afrique *f* • **African 1** *adj* africain **2** *n* Africain, -e *mf*

after ['ɑːftə(r)] **1** *adv* après; **soon/long a.** peu/longtemps après; **the day a.** le lendemain **2** *prep* après; **a. three days** au bout de trois jours; **the day a. the battle** le lendemain de la bataille; **a. eating** après avoir mangé; **day a. day** jour après jour; **a. all** après tout; *Am* **ten a. four** quatre heures dix; **to be a. sb/sth** *(seek)* chercher qn/qch **3** *conj* après que; **a. he saw you** après qu'il t'a vu • **aftershave** *n* (lotion *f*) après-rasage *m* • **afterthought** *n* réflexion *f* après coup; **to say sth as an a.** dire qch après coup • **afterward(s)** *adv* après, plus tard

afternoon [ɑːftə'nuːn] *n* après-midi *m ou f inv*; **in the a.** l'après-midi; **at three in the a.** à trois heures de l'après-midi; **every Monday a.** tous les lundis après-midi; **good a.!** bonjour!

again [ə'gen] *adv* de nouveau, encore une fois; *(furthermore)* en outre; **to go down/up a.** redescendre/remonter; **she won't do it a.** elle ne le fera plus; **never a.** plus jamais; **a. and a.** bien des fois; **what's his name a.?** comment s'appelle-t-il déjà?

against [ə'genst, ə'geɪnst] *prep* contre; **to lean a. sth** s'appuyer contre qch; **to go** *or* **be a. sth** s'opposer à qch; **a. the law** illégal

age [eɪdʒ] **1** *n* âge *m*; **(old) a.** vieillesse *f*; **what a. are you?** quel âge as-tu?; **five years of a.** âgé de cinq ans; *Fam* **to wait (for) ages** attendre une éternité; **a. limit** limite *f* d'âge **2** *vti (pres p ag(e)ing)* vieillir • **aged** *adj* **a. ten** âgé de dix ans

agenda [ə'dʒendə] *n* ordre *m* du jour

agent ['eɪdʒənt] *n* agent *m* • **agency** *n* agence *f*

aggravate ['ægrəveɪt] *vt (make worse)* aggraver; *Fam (annoy)* exaspérer

aggressive [ə'gresɪv] *adj* agressif, -ive

agile [*Br* 'ædʒaɪl, *Am* 'ædʒəl] *adj* agile

agitated ['ædʒɪteɪtɪd] *adj* agité

ago [ə'gəʊ] *adv* **a year a.** il y a un an; **long a.** il y a longtemps; **a short time a.** il y a peu de temps

agony ['ægənɪ] (*pl* **-ies**) *n (pain)* douleur *f* atroce; *(anguish)* angoisse *f*; **to be in a.** être au supplice

agree [ə'griː] **1** *vi (come to an agreement)* se mettre d'accord; *(be in agreement)* être d'accord (**with** avec); *(of facts, dates)* concorder; **to a. (up)on** *(decide)* convenir de; **to a. to sth/to doing sth** consentir à qch/à faire qch **2** *vt (plan)* se mettre d'accord sur; *(date, price)* convenir de; *(approve)* approuver; **to a. to do sth** accepter de faire qch; **to a. that...** admettre que... ● **agreement** *n (contract, assent)* accord *m* (**with** avec); **to come to an a.** se mettre d'accord

agriculture ['ægrɪkʌltʃə(r)] *n* agriculture *f*

ahead [ə'hed] *adv (in space)* en avant; *(leading)* en tête; *(in the future)* à l'avenir; **a. of** *(in space)* devant; *(in time)* avant; **one hour/etc a. (of)** une heure/*etc* d'avance (sur); **to be a. of schedule** être en avance; **to go a.** *(advance)* avancer; *(continue)* continuer; *(start)* commencer; **go a.!** allez-y!

aid [eɪd] **1** *n (help)* aide *f*; *(device)* accessoire *m*; **with the a. of sb** avec l'aide de qn; **with the a. of sth** à l'aide de qch; **in a. of** *(charity)* au profit de **2** *vt* aider (**sb to do** qn à faire)

AIDS [eɪdz] *(abbr* **Acquired Immune Deficiency Syndrome)** *n* SIDA *m*

aim [eɪm] **1** *n* but *m*; **to take a. (at)** viser; **with the a. of** dans

le but de **2** *vt (gun)* braquer (**at** sur); *(stone)* lancer (**at** à *ou* vers); *(remark)* décocher (**at** à) **3** *vi* viser; **to a. at sb** viser qn; **to a. to do sth** avoir l'intention de faire qch ● **aimless** *adj (existence)* sans but

air [eə(r)] **1** *n* (a) *(atmosphère)* air *m*; **in the open a.** en plein air; **to be** *or* **go on (the) a.** *(of person)* passer à l'antenne; *(of programme)* être diffusé; **to throw sth in(to) the a.** jeter qch en l'air; *Aut* **a. bag** airbag *m*; **a. bed** matelas *m* pneumatique; **a. fare** prix *m* du billet d'avion; **a. force** armée *f* de l'air; **a. freshener** désodorisant *m (pour la maison)* (b) *(appearance, tune)* air *m*; **to put on airs** se donner des airs; **with an a. of sadness** d'un air triste **2** *vt (room)* aérer ● **air-conditioning** *n* climatisation *f* ● **aircraft** *n inv* avion *m* ● **airline** *n* compagnie *f* aérienne ● **airmail** *n* poste *f* aérienne; **by a.** par avion ● **airplane** *n Am* avion *m* ● **airport** *n* aéroport *m* ● **airtight** *adj* hermétique

aisle [aɪl] *n (in supermarket, cinema)* allée *f*; *(in plane)* couloir *m*; *(in church)* allée *f* centrale

ajar [ə'dʒɑː(r)] *adj & adv (door)* entrouvert

alarm [ə'lɑːm] **1** *n (warning, fear, device)* alarme *f*; **false a.** fausse alerte *f*; **a. clock** réveil *m* **2** *vt (frighten)* alarmer; *(worry)* inquiéter; **they were alarmed at the news** la nouvelle les a beaucoup inquiétés

album ['ælbəm] *n (book, record)* album *m*

alcohol ['ælkəhɒl] *n* alcool *m* ● **alcoholic 1** *adj (person)* alcoolique; **a. drink** boisson *f* alcoolisée **2** *n (person)* alcoolique *mf*

ale [eɪl] n bière f
alert [ə'lɜ:t] adj (watchful) vigilant; (lively) éveillé
A level ['eɪlevəl] n Br (exam) ≃ épreuve f de baccalauréat
Algeria [æl'dʒɪərɪə] n l'Algérie f • **Algerian 1** adj algérien, -enne **2** n Algérien, -enne mf
alias ['eɪlɪəs] adv alias
alibi ['ælɪbaɪ] n alibi m
alien ['eɪlɪən] n (from outer space) extraterrestre mf; Formal (foreigner) étranger, -ère mf
alight [ə'laɪt] adj **to set sth a.** mettre le feu à qch
align [ə'laɪn] vt aligner
alike [ə'laɪk] **1** adj (people, things) semblables, pareils, -eilles; **to look a.** se ressembler **2** adv de la même manière; **summer and winter a.** été comme hiver
alive [ə'laɪv] adj vivant, en vie; **a. and well** bien portant

all [ɔ:l] **1** adj tout, toute, pl tous, toutes; **a. day** toute la journée; **a. men** tous les hommes; **a. the girls** toutes les filles; **a. four of them** tous les quatre; **for a. his wealth** malgré toute sa fortune **2** pron (everyone) tous mpl, toutes fpl; (everything) tout; **my sisters are a. here** toutes mes sœurs sont ici; **he ate it a., he ate a. of it** il a tout mangé; **take a. of it** prends (le) tout; **a. of us** nous tous; **a. together** tous ensemble; **a. (that) he has** tout ce qu'il a; **a. in a.** dans l'ensemble; **anything at a.** quoi que ce soit; **nothing at a.** rien du tout; **not at a.** pas du tout; (after 'thank you') il n'y a pas de quoi **3** adv tout; **a. alone** tout seul; **a. over** (everywhere) partout; (finished) fini; Sport **six a.** six partout • **all-night** adj (party)

qui dure toute la nuit; (shop) ouvert toute la nuit • **all-round** adj (knowledge) approfondi; (athlete) complet, -ète • **all-time** adj (record) jamais battu; **to reach an a. low/high** arriver à son point le plus bas/le plus haut

allegation [ælə'geɪʃən] n accusation f • **alleged** [ə'ledʒd] adj (crime, fact) prétendu; (author, culprit) présumé; **he is a. to be...** on prétend qu'il est...
allergy ['ælədʒɪ] (pl -ies) n allergie f (to à) • **allergic** [ə'lɜ:dʒɪk] adj allergique (to à)
alley ['ælɪ] (pl -eys) n ruelle f; Fam **that's (right) up my a.** c'est mon rayon
alligator ['ælɪgeɪtə(r)] n alligator m
allocate ['æləkeɪt] vt (assign) affecter (to à); (distribute) répartir
allow [ə'laʊ] **1** vt permettre (sb sth qch à qn); (give, grant) accorder (sb sth qch à qn); (request) accéder à; **to a. sb to do** permettre à qn de faire; **to a. an hour/a metre/etc** prévoir une heure/un mètre/etc; **it's not allowed** c'est interdit; **you're not allowed to go** on vous interdit de partir **2** vi **to a. for sth** tenir compte de qch • **allowance** n allocation f; (for travel, housing) indemnité f; **to make allowances for** (person) être indulgent envers; (thing) tenir compte de
all right [ɔ:l'raɪt] **1** adj (satisfactory) bien inv; (unharmed) sain et sauf (f saine et sauve) intact; (without worries) tranquille; **it's a.** ça va; **are you a.?** ça va?; **I'm a.** je vais bien; **to be a. at maths** se débrouiller en maths **2** adv (well) bien; **a.!** (in agreement) d'accord!;

is it a. if I smoke? ça ne vous dérange pas si je fume?

ally ['ælaɪ] (*pl* **-ies**) *n* allié, -e *mf*

almighty [ɔːl'maɪtɪ] *adj* (*powerful*) tout-puissant (*f* toute-puissante); *Fam* (*enormous*) terrible, formidable

almond ['ɑːmənd] *n* amande *f*

almost ['ɔːlməʊst] *adv* presque; **he a. fell** il a failli tomber

alone [ə'ləʊn] *adj & adv* seul; **I did it (all) a.** je l'ai fait (tout) seul; **to leave a.** (*person*) laisser tranquille; (*thing*) ne pas toucher à; **I can't afford a bike, let a. a car!** je n'ai pas les moyens de m'acheter un vélo, encore moins une voiture!

along [ə'lɒŋ] **1** *prep* (*all*) **a.** (tout) le long de; **to walk a. the shore** marcher le long du rivage; **to walk a. the street** marcher dans la rue; **a. here** par ici; *Fig* **somewhere a. the way** à un moment donné **2** *adv* **to move a.** avancer; **I'll be** *or* **come a. shortly** je viendrai tout à l'heure; **come a.!** venez donc!; **to bring sth a.** apporter qch; **to bring sb a.** amener qn; **all a.** (*all the time*) dès le début; (*all the way*) d'un bout à l'autre; **a. with** ainsi que ● **alongside** [-'saɪd] *prep & adv* à côté (de)

aloof [ə'luːf] *adj* distant

aloud [ə'laʊd] *adv* à haute voix

alphabet ['ælfəbet] *n* alphabet *m* ● **alphabetical** *adj* alphabétique

Alps [ælps] *npl* **the A.** les Alpes *fpl*

already [ɔːl'redɪ] *adv* déjà

alright [ɔːl'raɪt] *adv Fam* = **all right**

also ['ɔːlsəʊ] *adv* aussi, également; (*moreover*) de plus

altar ['ɔːltə(r)] *n* autel *m*

alter ['ɔːltə(r)] **1** *vt* changer; (*clothing*) retoucher **2** *vi* changer

alteration *n* changement *m* (**in** de); (*of clothing*) retouche *f*

alternate 1 [ɔːl'tɜːnət] *adj* alterné; **on a. days** tous les deux jours **2** ['ɔːltəneɪt] *vt* faire alterner **3** ['ɔːltəneɪt] *vi* alterner (**with** avec)

alternative [ɔːl'tɜːnətɪv] **1** *adj* (*other*) de remplacement; **an a. way** une autre façon; **2** *n* (*choice*) alternative *f*; **she had no a. but to obey** elle n'a pas pu faire autrement que d'obéir ● **alternatively** *adv* (**or**) **a.** ou alors, ou bien

although [ɔːl'ðəʊ] *adv* bien que (+ *subjunctive*)

altogether [ɔːltə'geðə(r)] *adv* (*completely*) tout à fait; (*on the whole*) somme toute; **how much a.?** combien en tout?

aluminium [*Br* ælju'mɪnɪəm] (*Am* **aluminum** [ə'luːmɪnəm]) *n* aluminium *m*

always ['ɔːlweɪz] *adv* toujours; **he's a. criticizing** il est toujours à critiquer; **as a.** comme toujours

am [æm, *unstressed* əm] *see* **be**

a.m. [eɪ'em] *adv* du matin

amateur ['æmətə(r)] **1** *n* amateur *m* **2** *adj* (*interest, sports, performance*) d'amateur; **a. painter/actress** peintre *m*/actrice *f* amateur

amaze [ə'meɪz] *vt* stupéfier ● **amazed** *adj* stupéfait (**at sth** de qch); (*filled with wonder*) émerveillé ● **amazing** *adj* (*surprising*) stupéfiant; (*incredible*) extraordinaire

ambassador [æm'bæsədə(r)] *n* ambassadeur, -drice *mf*

ambiguous [æm'bɪgjʊəs] *adj* ambigu (*f* ambiguë)

ambition [æm'bɪʃən] *n* ambition *f* ● **ambitious** *adj* ambitieux, -euse

ambulance ['æmbjʊləns] *n* ambulance *f*; **a. driver** ambulancier, -ère *mf*

ambush ['æmbʊʃ] *vt* tendre une embuscade à

amend [ə'mend] *vt (text)* modifier; *Pol (law)* amender • **amends** *npl* **to make a.** se racheter

America [ə'merıkə] *n* l'Amérique *f*; **North/South A.** l'Amérique *f* du Nord/du Sud • **American 1** *adj* américain **2** *n* Américain, -e *mf*

among(st) [ə'mʌŋ(st)] *prep (amidst)* parmi; *(between)* entre; **a. the crowd/books/etc** parmi la foule/les livres/*etc*; **a. friends** entre amis; **a. other things** entre autres (choses)

amount [ə'maʊnt] **1** *n* quantité *f*; *(sum of money)* somme *f*; *(total figure)* montant *m* **2** *vi* **to a. to** *(bill)* s'élever à; *Fig* **it amounts to the same thing** ça revient au même

ample ['æmpəl] *adj* abondant

amplifier ['æmplıfaıə(r)] *n* amplificateur *m*

amputate ['æmpjʊteıt] *vt* amputer; **to a. sb's hand/etc** amputer qn de la main/*etc*

amuse [ə'mjuːz] *vt* amuser; **to keep sb amused** distraire qn • **amusement** *n* divertissement *m*; *(pastime)* distraction *f*; **a. arcade** salle *f* de jeux; **a. park** parc *m* d'attractions

an [æn, *unstressed* ən] *see* **a**

an(a)esthetic [ænəs'θetık] *n (substance)* anesthésique *m*; **under a.** sous anesthésie

analyse ['ænəlaız] *vt* analyser • **analysis** (*pl* **-yses** [-əsiːz]) *n* analyse *f*

anarchy ['ænəkı] *n* anarchie *f* • **anarchist** *n* anarchiste *mf*

anatomy [ə'nætəmı] *n* anatomie *f*

ancestor ['ænsestə(r)] *n* ancêtre *m*

anchor ['æŋkə(r)] *n* ancre *f*

anchovy [*Br* 'æntʃəvı, *Am* æn'tʃəʊvı] (*pl* **-ies**) *n* anchois *m*

ancient ['eınʃənt] *adj* ancien, -enne; *(pre-medieval)* antique

and [ænd, *unstressed* ən(d)] *conj* et; **a knife a. fork** un couteau et une fourchette; **my mother a. father** mon père et ma mère; **two hundred a. two** deux cent deux; **four a. three quarters** quatre trois quarts; **nice a. warm** bien chaud; **better a. better** de mieux en mieux; **she can read a. write** elle sait lire et écrire; **go a. see** va voir

anesthetic [ænəs'θetık] *n* = **anaesthetic**

angel ['eındʒəl] *n* ange *m*

anger ['æŋgə(r)] *n* colère *f*

angle ['æŋgəl] *n* angle *m*; **at an a.** en biais

Anglo- ['æŋgləʊ] *pref* anglo- • **Anglo-Saxon** *adj & n* anglo-saxon, -onne *(mf)*

angry ['æŋgrı] (**-ier, -iest**) *adj (person)* en colère, fâché; *(look)* furieux, -euse; **an a. letter** une lettre indignée; **to get a. (with)** se fâcher (contre)

animal ['ænıməl] *n* animal *m*

animation [ænı'meıʃən] *n (liveliness) & Cin* animation *f*

aniseed ['ænısiːd] *n* anis *m*

ankle ['æŋkəl] *n* cheville *f*

annex, *Br* **annexe** ['æneks] *(building)* annexe *f*

anniversary [ænı'vɜːsərı] (*pl* **-ies**) *n (of event)* anniversaire *m*

announce [ə'naʊns] *vt* annoncer; *(birth, marriage)* faire part de • **announcement** *n (statement)* annonce *f*

annoy [ə'nɔı] *vt (inconvenience)* ennuyer; *(irritate)* agacer • **annoyed** *adj* fâché; **to get**

a. (with) se fâcher (contre) •
annoying *adj* ennuyeux, -euse
annual ['ænjʊəl] **1** *adj* annuel,
-elle **2** *n (book)* album *m*
anonymous [ə'nɒnɪməs] *adj*
anonyme
anorak ['ænəræk] *n* anorak *m*
anorexic [ænə'reksɪk] *adj*
anorexique
another [ə'nʌðə(r)] *adj & pron*
un(e) autre; **a. man** *(different)*
un autre homme; **a. month**
(additional) encore un mois; **a. ten**
encore dix; **one a.** l'un(e) l'autre,
pl les un(e)s les autres; **they love
one a.** ils s'aiment
answer ['ɑːnsə(r)] **1** *n* réponse
f; *(to problem)* solution *f* (**to** de);
in a. to your letter en réponse
à votre lettre **2** *vt (person, question,
letter)* répondre à; *(prayer, wish)*
exaucer; **to a. the door** ouvrir
la porte; **to a. the phone** répondre
au téléphone **3** *vi* répondre •
answering machine *n* répondeur
m
ant [ænt] *n* fourmi *f*
Antarctic [æn'tɑːktɪk] *n* **the A.**
l'Antarctique *m*
antenna [æn'tenə] *n* **(a)** *(pl* **-ae**
[-iː])* *(of insect)* antenne *f* **(b)** *(pl*
-as) *Am (for TV, radio)* antenne *f*
anthem ['ænθəm] *n* **national a.**
hymne *m* national
anthology [æn'θɒlədʒɪ] *(pl* **-ies)**
n anthologie *f*
anti- [*Br* 'æntɪ, *Am* 'æntaɪ]
pref anti- • **antibiotic** *adj & n*
antibiotique *(m)* • **anticlockwise**
adv Br dans le sens inverse
des aiguilles d'une montre •
antiseptic *adj & n* antiseptique
(m) • **antisocial** *adj (unsociable)*
peu sociable
anticipate [æn'tɪsɪpeɪt] *vt (foresee)* anticiper; *(expect)* s'attendre

à, prévoir • **anticipation** *n*
(expectation) attente *f*; *(foresight)*
prévision *f*; **in a. of** en prévision
de; **in a.** *(thank, pay)* d'avance
antique [æn'tiːk] **1** *adj (furniture)*
ancien, -enne; *(of Greek or
Roman antiquity)* antique objet *m*
d'époque; **2** *n* antiquité *f*, **a. shop**
magasin *m* d'antiquités
anxiety [æŋ'zaɪətɪ] *(pl* **-ies)** *n*
(worry) inquiétude *f* (**about** au
sujet de); *(eagerness)* désir *m* (**to
do** de faire; **for sth** de qch)
anxious ['æŋkʃəs] *adj (worried)*
inquiet, -ète (**about** pour); *(eager)*
impatient (**to do** de faire)

any ['enɪ] **1** *adj* **(a)** *(in questions)*
du, de la, des; **have you a.
milk/tickets?** avez-vous du lait/
des billets? **(b)** *(in negatives)* de;
(the slightest) aucun; **he hasn't
got a. milk/tickets** il n'a pas
de lait/de billets; **there isn't a.
doubt/problem** il n'y a aucun
doute/problème **(c)** *(no matter
which)* n'importe quel; **ask a.
doctor** demande à n'importe
quel médecin **(d)** *(every)* tout; **at
a. moment** à tout moment; **in a.
case, at a. rate** de toute façon **2**
pron **(a)** *(no matter which one)*
n'importe lequel; *(somebody)*
quelqu'un; **if a. of you...** si l'un
d'entre vous..., si quelqu'un parmi
vous... **(b)** *(quantity)* en; **have
you got a.?** en as-tu?; **I don't
see a.** je n'en vois pas **3** *adv* **not
a. further/happier** pas plus loin/
plus heureux, -euse; **I don't see
him a. more** je ne le vois plus;
a. more tea? encore un peu de
thé?; **I'm not a. better** je ne vais
pas mieux • **anybody** *pron* **(a)**
(somebody) quelqu'un; **do you
see a.?** tu vois quelqu'un?; **more**

than a. plus que tout autre (b) *(in negatives)* personne; **he doesn't know a.** il ne connaît personne (c) *(no matter who)* n'importe qui; **a. would think that...** on croirait que... • **anyhow** *adv (at any rate)* de toute façon; *Fam (badly)* n'importe comment • **anyone** *pron* = **anybody** • **anyplace** *adv Am* = **anywhere** • **anything** *pron* (a) *(something)* quelque chose; **can you see a.?** tu vois quelque chose? (b) *(in negatives)* rien; **he doesn't do a.** il ne fait rien; **without a.** sans rien (c) *(everything)* tout; **a. you like** tout ce que tu veux • **anyway** *adv (in any case)* de toute façon • **anywhere** *adv* (a) *(no matter where)* n'importe où (b) *(everywhere)* partout; **a. you go** où que vous alliez, partout où vous allez; **a. you like** (là) où tu veux (c) *(somewhere)* quelque part; **is he going a.?** va-t-il quelque part? (d) *(in negatives)* nulle part; **he doesn't go a.** il ne va nulle part; **without a. to put it** sans un endroit où le/la mettre

apart [ə'pɑːt] *adv* (a) *(separated)* **we kept them a.** nous les tenions séparés; **two years a.** à deux ans d'intervalle; **they are a metre a.** ils se trouvent à un mètre l'un de l'autre; **to come a.** *(of two objects)* se séparer; **to tell two things/people a.** distinguer deux choses/personnes (l'une de l'autre) (b) *(to pieces)* **to tear a.** mettre en pièces; **to take a.** démonter (c) *(to one side)* à part; **a. from** *(except for)* à part

apartment [ə'pɑːtmənt] *n* appartement *m; Am* **a. building** immeuble *m* (d'habitation)

ape [eɪp] *n* grand singe *m*

apology [ə'pɒlədʒɪ] *(pl* **-ies)** *n* excuses *fpl* • **apologetic** [-'dʒetɪk] *adj (letter)* plein d'excuses; *(smile)* d'excuse; **to be a. (about)** s'excuser (de) • **apologize** *vi* s'excuser **(for** de); **he apologized for being late** il s'est excusé de son retard; **to a. to sb (for)** faire ses excuses à qn (pour)

apostrophe [ə'pɒstrəfɪ] *n* apostrophe *f*

appalled [ə'pɔːld] *adj* **to be a. (at)** être horrifié (par) • **appalling** *adj* épouvantable

apparent [ə'pærənt] *adj (seeming)* apparent; *(obvious)* évident; **it's a. that...** il est clair que... • **apparently** *adv* apparemment; **a. she's going to Venice** il paraît qu'elle va à Venise

appeal [ə'piːl] **1** *n (charm)* attrait *m; (call)* appel *m; (to a court)* appel *m* **2** *vi* (a) *(in court)* faire appel (b) **to a. to sb** *(attract)* plaire à qn; *(ask for help)* faire appel à qn; **to a. to sb for sth** demander qch à qn; **to a. to sb to do sth** supplier qn de faire qch • **appealing** *adj (offer, idea)* séduisant

appear [ə'pɪə(r)] *vi (become visible)* apparaître; *(seem)* paraître; **it appears that...** *(it seems that)* il semble que... *(+ subjunctive or indicative)*; *(it is rumoured that)* il paraît que... *(+ indicative)* • **appearance** *n (act)* apparition *f; (look)* apparence *f;* **to keep up appearances** sauver les apparences

appendix [ə'pendɪks] *(pl* **-ixes** [-ɪksɪz] *or* **-ices** [-ɪsiːz]) *n (in book, body)* appendice *m;* **to have one's a. out** se faire opérer

de l'appendicite • **appendicitis** [əpendɪ'saɪtɪs]*n* appendicite *f*
appetite ['æpɪtaɪt] *n* appétit *m* • **appetizer** *n* amuse-gueule *m inv* • **appetizing** *adj* appétissant
applaud [ə'plɔːd] *vti* applaudir • **applause** *n* applaudissements *mpl*
apple ['æpəl] *n* pomme *f*; **a. core** trognon *m* de pomme; **a. pie** tarte *f* aux pommes; **a. sauce** compote *f* de pommes
appliance [ə'plaɪəns] *n* appareil *m*
applicable [ə'plɪkəbəl] *adj (rule)* applicable (**to** à)
application [æplɪ'keɪʃən] *n (request)* demande *f* (**for** de); *(for job)* candidature *f* (**for** de); **a. (form)** *(for job)* formulaire *m* de candidature; *(for club)* formulaire *m* d'inscription • **applicant** ['æplɪkənt] *n* candidat, -e *mf* (**for** à)
apply [ə'plaɪ] *(pt & pp* **-ied)** **1** *vt (put on, carry out)* appliquer **2** *vi (be relevant)* s'appliquer (**to** à); **to a. for** *(job)* poser sa candidature à
appoint [ə'pɔɪnt] *vt (person)* nommer (**to a post** à un poste; **to do** pour faire); *(time, place)* fixer; **the appointed time** l'heure dite • **appointment** *n* nomination *f*; *(meeting)* rendez-vous *m inv*; *(post)* situation *f*; **to make an a. with** prendre rendez-vous avec
appraisal [ə'preɪzəl] *n* évaluation *f*
appreciate [ə'priːʃɪeɪt] *vt (enjoy, value)* apprécier; *(understand)* comprendre; *(be grateful for)* être reconnaissant de • **appreciation** *n (gratitude)* reconnaissance *f*
apprehensive [æprɪ'hensɪv] *adj*

inquiet, -ète (**about** de *ou* au sujet de); **to be a. of** appréhender
apprentice [ə'prentɪs] *n* apprenti, -e *mf* • **apprenticeship** *n* apprentissage *m*
approach [ə'prəʊtʃ] **1** *n (method)* façon *f* de s'y prendre; *(path, route)* voie *f* d'accès; *(of winter, vehicle)* approche *f* **2** *vt (draw near to)* s'approcher de; *(go up to, tackle)* aborder; **to a. sb about sth** parler à qn de qch; **he's approaching forty** il va sur ses quarante ans **3** *vi (of person, vehicle)* s'approcher; *(of date)* approcher
appropriate [ə'prəʊprɪət] *adj (place, clothes, means)* approprié (**to** à); *(remark, time)* opportun; **a. to** *or* **for** qui convient à
approve [ə'pruːv] *vt* approuver; **to a. of** *(conduct, decision, idea)* approuver; **I don't a. of him** il ne me plaît pas • **approval** *n* approbation *f*
approximate [ə'prɒksɪmət] *adj* approximatif, -ive
apricot ['eɪprɪkɒt] *n* abricot *m*
April ['eɪprəl] *n* avril *m*; **A. fool!** poisson d'avril!
apron ['eɪprən] *n* tablier *m*
apt [æpt] *adj (word, name)* bien choisi; **to be a. to do sth** avoir tendance à faire qch
aquarium [ə'kweərɪəm] *n* aquarium *m*
Aquarius [ə'kweərɪəs] *n (sign)* le Verseau
Arab ['ærəb] **1** *adj* arabe **2** *n* Arabe *mf* • **Arabic** *adj & n (language)* arabe *(m)*
arbitrary ['ɑːbɪtrərɪ] *adj* arbitraire
arc [ɑːk] *n (of circle)* arc *m*
arcade [ɑː'keɪd] *n (for shops) (small)* passage *m* couvert; *(large)* galerie *f* marchande
arch [ɑːtʃ] **1** *n (of bridge)* arche

f; *(of building)* voûte *f*, arc *m*; *(of foot)* cambrure *f* **2** *vt* **to a. one's back** *(inwards)* se cambrer; *(outwards)* se voûter

arch- [ɑːtʃ] *pref* **a.-enemy** ennemi *m* juré; **a.-rival** grand rival *m*

arch(a)eology [ɑːkɪ'ɒlədʒɪ] *n* archéologie *f* • **arch(a)eologist** *n* archéologue *mf*

architect ['ɑːkɪtekt] *n* architecte *mf* • **architecture** *n* architecture *f*

archives ['ɑːkaɪvz] *npl* archives *fpl*

Arctic ['ɑːktɪk] *n* **the A.** l'Arctique *m*

are [ɑː(r)] *see* **be**

area ['eərɪə] *n (of country)* région *f*; *(of town)* quartier *m*; *(surface)* superficie *f*; *Fig (of knowledge)* domaine *m*; **play a.** aire *f* de jeux; *Am Tel* **a. code** indicatif *m*

arena [ə'riːnə] *n* arène *f*

aren't [ɑːnt] = **are not**

Argentina [ɑːdʒən'tiːnə] *n* l'Argentine *f*

argue ['ɑːgjuː] **1** *vi (matter)* discuter (de); *(position)* défendre; **to a. that...** soutenir que... **2** *vi (quarrel)* se disputer (**with/about** avec/au sujet de); *(reason)* raisonner (**with/about** avec/sur) • **argument** *n (quarrel)* dispute *f*; *(debate)* discussion *f*; *(point)* argument *m*; **to have an a.** *(quarrel)* se disputer (**with** avec)

Aries ['eəriːz] *n (sign)* le Bélier

arise [ə'raɪz] *(pt* **arose,** *pp* **arisen** [ə'rɪzən]) *vi (problem, opportunity)* se présenter; *(result)* provenir (**from** de)

aristocrat [*Br* 'ærɪstəkræt, *Am* ə'rɪstəkræt] *n* aristocrate *mf*

arithmetic [ə'rɪθmətɪk] *n* arithmétique *f*

ark [ɑːk] *n* **Noah's a.** l'arche *f* de Noé

arm¹ [ɑːm] *n* bras *m*; **a. in a.** bras dessus bras dessous • **armchair** *n* fauteuil *m* • **armpit** *n* aisselle *f*

arm² [ɑːm] *vt (with weapon)* armer (**with** de) • **arms** *npl (weapons)* armes *fpl*

armour ['ɑːmə(r)] *n* armure *f*

army ['ɑːmɪ] *(pl* **-ies**) *n* armée *f*; **to join the a.** s'engager

A road ['eɪrəʊd] *n Br* ≃ route *f* nationale

aroma [ə'rəʊmə] *n* arôme *m* • **aromatic** [ærəʊ'mætɪk] *adj* aromatique

arose [ə'rəʊz] *pt of* **arise**

around [ə'raʊnd] **1** *prep* autour de; *(approximately)* environ; **to travel a. the world** faire le tour du monde **2** *adv* autour; **all a.** tout autour; **a. here** par ici; **to follow sb a.** suivre qn partout; **to rush a.** courir dans tous les sens; **is Jack a.?** est-ce que Jack est dans le coin?; **he's still a.** il est encore là

arouse [ə'raʊz] *vt (suspicion, anger, curiosity)* éveiller

arrange [ə'reɪndʒ] *vt* arranger; *(time, meeting)* fixer; **to a. to do sth** s'arranger pour faire qch • **arrangement** *n (layout, agreement)* arrangement *m*; **arrangements** *(preparations)* préparatifs *mpl*; *(plans)* projets *mpl*; **to make arrangements to do sth** prendre des dispositions pour faire qch

arrest [ə'rest] **1** *vt (criminal)* arrêter **2** *n (of criminal)* arrestation *f*; **under a.** en état d'arrestation

arrive [ə'raɪv] *vi* arriver; **to a. at** *(conclusion, decision)* arriver à, parvenir à • **arrival** *n* arrivée *f*; **on my a.** à mon arrivée

arrogant ['ærəgənt] *adj* arrogant

arrow ['ærəʊ] *n* flèche *f*

art [ɑːt] *n* art *m*; **faculty of arts** faculté *f* des lettres; **a. exhibition** exposition *f* d'œuvres d'art; **a. gall-**

ery *(museum)* musée *m* d'art; **a. school** école *f* des beaux-arts

artery [ˈɑːtərɪ] *(pl* **-ies)** *n* artère *f*

artichoke [ˈɑːtɪtʃəʊk] *n* artichaut *m*

article [ˈɑːtɪkəl] *n* article *m*; **a. of clothing** vêtement *m*

articulate 1 [ɑːˈtɪkjʊlət] *adj (person)* qui s'exprime clairement; *(speech)* clair **2** [ɑːˈtɪkjʊleɪt] *vti (speak)* articuler

artificial [ɑːtɪˈfɪʃəl] *adj* artificiel, -elle

artist [ˈɑːtɪst] *n* artiste *mf* ● **artistic** *adj (pattern, treasure)* artistique; *(person)* artiste

as [æz, *unstressed* əz] **1** *adv* **(a)** *(with manner)* comme; **as promised/planned** comme promis/prévu; **as you like** comme tu veux; **such as** comme, tel que; **as much as I can** (au)tant que je peux; **as it is** *(this being the case)* les choses étant ainsi; **to leave sth as it is** laisser qch comme ça *ou* tel quel; **as if, as though** comme si; **you look as if** *or* **as though you're tired** tu as l'air fatigué **(b)** *(comparison)* **as tall as you** aussi grand que vous; **as white as a sheet** blanc (*f* blanche) comme un linge; **as much as you** autant que vous; **as much money as** autant d'argent que; **as many people as** autant de gens que; **twice as big as** deux fois plus grand que; **the same as** le même que **2** *conj* **(a)** *(expressing time)* **as always** comme toujours; **as I was leaving, as I left** comme je partais; **as one grows older** à mesure que l'on vieillit; **as he slept** pendant qu'il dormait; **one day as...** un jour que...; **as from, as of** *(time)* à partir de **(b)** *(expressing reason)*

puisque, comme; **as it's late...** puisqu'il est tard..., comme il est tard... **(c)** *(though)* **(as) clever as he is...** si intelligent qu'il soit... **(d)** *(concerning)* **as for that** quant à cela **(e)** *(+ infinitive)* **so as to...** de manière à...; **so stupid as to...** assez bête pour... **3** *prep* comme; **she works as a cashier** elle est caissière, elle travaille comme caissière; **dressed as a clown** déguisé en clown

ash [æʃ] *n (of cigarette, fire)* cendre *f* ● **ashtray** *n* cendrier *m*

ashamed [əˈʃeɪmd] *adj* **to be/ feel a. (of sb/sth)** avoir honte (de qn/qch); **to be a. of oneself** avoir honte

Asia [ˈeɪʃə, ˈeɪʒə] *n* l'Asie *f* ● **Asian 1** *adj* asiatique; *Br (from Indian sub-continent)* = du sous-continent indien **2** *n* Asiatique *mf*; *Br (from Indian sub-continent)* = personne originaire du sous-continent indien

aside [əˈsaɪd] *adv* de côté; **to step a.** s'écarter

ask [ɑːsk] **1** *vt (request, inquire about)* demander; *(invite)* inviter **(to sth** à qch); **to a. sb sth** demander qch à qn; **to a. sb about sb/sth** interroger qn sur qn/qch; **to a. (sb) a question** poser une question (à qn); **to a. sb the time/way** demander l'heure/son chemin à qn; **to a. sb for sth** demander qch à qn; **to a. sb to do** *(request)* demander à qn de faire; **to a. to leave/etc** demander à partir/etc **2** *vi (inquire)* se renseigner **(about** sur); *(request)* demander; **to a. for sb/sth** demander qn/qch; **to a. after** *or* **about sb** demander des nouvelles de qn; **the asking price** le prix demandé

asleep [əˈsliːp] *adj* endormi; **to be a.** dormir; **to fall a.** s'endormir

asparagus [əˈspærəgəs] *n* asperges *fpl*

aspect [ˈæspekt] *n* aspect *m*

aspire [əˈspaɪə(r)] *vi* **to a. to** aspirer à

aspirin [ˈæsprɪn] *n* aspirine *f*

assassinate [əˈsæsɪneɪt] *vt* assassiner • **assassination** *n* assassinat *m*

assault [əˈsɔːlt] **1** *n* agression *f* **2** *vt* agresser; **to be sexually assaulted** être victime d'une agression sexuelle

assemble [əˈsembəl] **1** *vt* (*objects, ideas*) assembler; (*people*) rassembler; (*machine*) monter **2** *vi* se rassembler • **assembly** *n* (*meeting*) assemblée *f*; (*of machine*) montage *m*; (*in school*) rassemblement *m* (*avant les cours*)

assert [əˈsɜːt] *vt* affirmer (**that** que); **to a. oneself** s'affirmer • **assertive** *adj* (*tone, person*) affirmatif, -ive

assess [əˈses] *vt* (*value, damage*) évaluer; (*situation*) analyser; (*person*) juger • **assessment** *n* (*of value, damage*) évaluation *f*; (*of situation*) analyse *f*; (*of person*) jugement *m*

asset [ˈæset] *n* (*advantage*) atout *m*

assign [əˈsaɪn] *vt* (*give*) attribuer; (*appoint*) nommer • **assignment** *n* (*task*) mission *f*; (*for student*) devoir *m*

assist [əˈsɪst] *vti* aider (**in doing** *or* **to do** à faire) • **assistance** *n* aide *f*; **to be of a. to sb** aider qn • **assistant** *n* assistant, -e *mf*; *Br* (*in shop*) vendeur, -euse *mf*

associate [əˈsəʊʃɪeɪt] **1** *vt* associer (**with sth** à *ou* avec qch;

with sb à qn) **2** *vi* **to a. with sb** (*mix socially*) fréquenter qn • **association** [-ˈeɪʃən] *n* association *f*

assorted [əˈsɔːtɪd] *adj* (*different*) variés; (*foods*) assortis • **assortment** *n* assortiment *m*; **an a. of people** des gens de toutes sortes

assume [əˈsjuːm] *vt* (**a**) (*suppose*) supposer (**that** que); **let us a. that...** supposons que... (+ *subjunctive*) (**b**) (*take on*) (*responsibility, role*) assumer; (*attitude, name*) adopter

assure [əˈʃʊə(r)] *vt* assurer • **assurance** *n* assurance *f*

asterisk [ˈæstərɪsk] *n* astérisque *m*

asthma [ˈæsmə] *n* asthme *m*

astonish [əˈstɒnɪʃ] *vt* étonner; **to be astonished (at sth)** s'étonner (de qch) • **astonishing** *adj* étonnant

astound [əˈstaʊnd] *vt* stupéfier • **astounding** *adj* stupéfiant

astray [əˈstreɪ] *adv* **to go a.** s'égarer; **to lead a.** détourner du droit chemin

astrology [əˈstrɒlədʒɪ] *n* astrologie *f*

astronaut [ˈæstrənɔːt] *n* astronaute *mf*

astronomy [əˈstrɒnəmɪ] *n* astronomie *f*

asylum [əˈsaɪləm] *n* asile *m*

at [æt, *unstressed* ət] *prep* (**a**) à; **at the end** à la fin; **at school** à l'école; **at work** au travail; **at six (o'clock)** à six heures; **at Easter** à Pâques; **to drive at 10 mph** rouler à ≈ 15 km; **to buy/sell at 10 euros a kilo** acheter/vendre (à) 10 euros le kilo (**b**) chez; **at the doctor's** chez le médecin; **at home** chez soi, à la maison (**c**) en; **at sea** en mer; **at war** en guerre; **good at maths** fort en maths (**d**) contre; **angry at** fâché contre (**e**) sur; **to shoot at** tirer sur; **at my request** sur ma demande (**f**) de; **to laugh at sb/sth** rire de qn/qch; **surprised at sth** surpris de qch (**g**) (au)près de; **at the window** près de la fenêtre (**h**) par; **six at a time** six par six (**i**) *(phrases)* **at night** la nuit; **to look at** regarder; **while you're at it** tant que tu y es

ate [eɪt] *pt of* eat

Athens ['æθənz] *n* Athènes *m ou f*

athlete ['æθliːt] *n* athlète *mf* • **athletic** *adj* athlétique • **athletics** *npl Br* athlétisme *m*; *Am* sport *m*

Atlantic [ət'læntɪk] *n* **the A.** l'Atlantique *m*

atlas ['ætləs] *n* atlas *m*

atmosphere ['ætməsfɪə(r)] *n* atmosphère *f*

atrocious [ə'trəʊʃəs] *adj* atroce

attach [ə'tætʃ] *vt* attacher (**to** à); *(document)* joindre (**to** à); **attached to sb** *(fond of)* attaché à qn • **attachment** *n* (**a**) *(affection)* attachement *m* (**to sb** à qn) (**b**) *(to e-mail)* fichier *m* joint

attack [ə'tæk] **1** *n* *(military)* attaque *f* (**on** contre); *(of illness)* crise *f* **2** *vt* attaquer; *(problem, plan)* s'attaquer à • **attacker** *n* agresseur *m*

attempt [ə'tempt] **1** *n* tentative *f*; **to make an a. to do** tenter de faire **2** *vt* tenter; *(task)* entreprendre; **to a. to do** tenter de faire; **attempted murder** tentative *f* d'assassinat

attend [ə'tend] **1** *vt* *(meeting)* assister à; *(school, church)* aller à **2** *vi* assister; **to a. to** *(take care of)* s'occuper de

attention [ə'tenʃən] *n* attention *f*; **to pay a.** faire *ou* prêter attention

(**to** à); **for the a. of** à l'attention de • **attentive** *adj* attentif, -ive (**to** à)

attic ['ætɪk] *n* grenier *m*

attitude ['ætɪtjuːd] *n* attitude *f*

attorney [ə'tɜːnɪ] (*pl* **-eys**) *n Am (lawyer)* avocat *m*

attract [ə'trækt] *vt* attirer • **attraction** *n (charm)* attrait *m*; *(place)* attraction *f*; *(between people)* attirance *f* • **attractive** *adj (house, room, person)* beau (*f* belle); *(price, offer)* intéressant

aubergine ['əʊbəʒiːn] *n Br* aubergine *f*

auburn ['ɔːbən] *adj (hair)* auburn *inv*

auction ['ɔːkʃən] **1** *n* vente *f* aux enchères **2** *vt* **to a. (off)** vendre aux enchères

audible ['ɔːdɪbəl] *adj* audible

audience ['ɔːdɪəns] *n (at concert, play)* public *m*; *(of radio broadcast)* auditeurs *mpl*; **TV a.** téléspectateurs *mpl*

audit ['ɔːdɪt] *vt (accounts)* vérifier

audition [ɔː'dɪʃən] **1** *n* audition *f* **2** *vi* auditionner

auditorium [ɔːdɪ'tɔːrɪəm] *n (of theatre, concert hall)* salle *f*

August ['ɔːgəst] *n* août *m*

aunt [ɑːnt] *n* tante *f* • **auntie, aunty** (*pl* **-ies**) *n Fam* tata *f*

au pair [əʊ'peə(r)] *n* **a. (girl)** jeune fille *f* au pair

Australia [ɒ'streɪlɪə] *n* l'Australie *f* • **Australian 1** *adj* australien, -enne **2** *n* Australien, -enne *mf*

Austria ['ɒstrɪə] *n* l'Autriche *f* • **Austrian 1** *adj* autrichien, -enne **2** *n* Autrichien, -enne *mf*

authentic [ɔː'θentɪk] *adj* authentique

author ['ɔːθə(r)] *n* auteur *m*

authority [ɔː'θɒrɪtɪ] (*pl* **-ies**) *n* autorité *f*; **to be in a.** *(in charge)* être

responsable • **authoritarian** *adj &*
n autoritaire *(mf)* • **authoritative**
adj (report, book) qui fait autorité;
(tone, person) autoritaire
authorize ['ɔːθəraɪz] *vt* autoriser
(**to do** à faire) • **authorization**
[-'zeɪʃən] *n* autorisation *f* (**to do**
de faire)
autobiography [ɔːtəʊbaɪ'ɒgrəfɪ]
(*pl* **-ies**) *n* autobiographie *f*
autograph ['ɔːtəgrɑːf] **1** *n*
autographe *m*; **a. book** album *m*
d'autographes **2** *vt* dédicacer (**for
sb** à qn)
automatic [ɔːtə'mætɪk] *adj*
automatique
autonomous [ɔː'tɒnəməs] *adj*
autonome
autumn ['ɔːtəm] *n* automne *m*; **in
a.** en automne
auxiliary [ɔːg'zɪljərɪ] (*pl* **-ies**)
adj & n auxiliaire *(mf)*; **a. (verb)**
(verbe *m*) auxiliaire *m*
available [ə'veɪləbəl] *adj*
disponible; **tickets are still a.** il
reste des tickets; **a. in black or
green** existe en noir et en vert •
availability *n* disponibilité *f*
avalanche ['ævəlɑːnʃ] *n* avalanche *f*
Ave (*abbr* **Avenue**) av.
avenge [ə'vendʒ] *vt* venger; **to a.
oneself (on)** se venger (de)
avenue ['ævənjuː] *n* avenue *f*
average ['ævərɪdʒ] **1** *n* moyenne
f; **on a.** en moyenne; **above/
below a.** au-dessus/au-dessous de
la moyenne **2** *adj* moyen, -enne
avert [ə'vɜːt] *vt (prevent)* éviter;
to a. one's eyes (from) *(turn
away)* détourner les yeux (de)
avocado [ævə'kɑːdəʊ] (*pl* **-os**) *n*
avocat *m*

avoid [ə'vɔɪd] *vt* éviter; **to a.
doing** éviter de faire
await [ə'weɪt] *vt* attendre
awake [ə'weɪk] **1** *adj* réveillé,
éveillé; **he's still a.** il ne dort pas
encore
award [ə'wɔːd] **1** *n* prix *m*,
récompense *f* **2** *vt (prize)* décerner
aware [ə'weə(r)] *adj* **to be a.
of** *(conscious)* être conscient de;
(informed) être au courant de;
(realize) se rendre compte de;
to become a. of/that se rendre
compte de/que • **awareness** *n*
conscience *f*

away [ə'weɪ] *adv* **(a)** *(distant)*
loin; **5 km a.** à 5 km (de distance)
(b) *(in time)* **ten days a.** dans dix
jours **(c)** *(absent, gone)* absent;
to drive a. partir (en voiture); **to
fade/melt a.** disparaître/fondre
complètement **(d)** *(to one side)* **to
look** *or* **turn a.** détourner les yeux
(e) *(continuously)* **to work/talk
a.** travailler/parler sans arrêt

awe [ɔː] *n* **to be in a. of sb** être
impressionné(e) par qn • **awesome**
adj (impressive) impressionnant;
Fam (excellent) super *inv*
awful ['ɔːfəl] *adj* affreux, -euse;
Fam **an a. lot (of)** énormément
(de); **I feel a. (about it)** j'ai
vraiment honte • **awfully** *adv*
(very) (good, pretty) extrêmement;
(bad, late) affreusement
awkward ['ɔːkwəd] *adj* **(a)**
(clumsy) maladroit **(b)** *(difficult)*
difficile; *(cumbersome)* gênant;
(time) mal choisi; *(silence)* gêné
axe [æks] *(Am* **ax)** **1** *n* hache *f* **2** *vt*
(costs) réduire; *(job)* supprimer

Bb

B, b [biː] *n* B, b *m inv*; **2B** *(number)*
2 ter

BA [biːˈeɪ] *(abbr* **Bachelor of Arts)**
n **to have a BA in history** ≃ avoir
une licence en histoire

baby [ˈbeɪbɪ] *(pl* **-ies)** *n* bébé *m*; **b.
boy** petit garçon *m*; **b. girl** petite
fille *f*; **b. tiger/etc** bébé-tigre/*etc
m*; **b. clothes/toys/etc** vêtements
mpl/jouets *mpl*/etc de bébé; *Am* **b.
carriage** landau *m* • **baby-sit** *(pt
& pp* **-sat,** *pres p* **-sitting)** *vi* faire
du baby-sitting • **baby-sitter** *n*
baby-sitter *mf*

bachelor [ˈbætʃələ(r)] *n* **(a)** *(not
married)* célibataire *m* **(b)** *Univ*
B. of Arts/of Science *(person)*
≃ licencié, -e *mf* ès lettres/ès
sciences; *(qualification)* ≃ licence
f de lettres/de sciences

back [bæk] **1** *n (of person, animal)*
dos *m*; *(of chair)* dossier *m*; *(of
house, vehicle)* arrière *m*; *(of room)*
fond *m*; *(of page)* verso *m*; **at the
b. of the book** à la fin du livre; **at
the b. of one's mind** derrière la
tête; **b. to front** devant derrière, à
l'envers **2** *adj (wheel, seat)* arrière
inv; **b. door** porte *f* de derrière; **b.
street** rue *f* écartée **3** *adv (behind)*
en arrière; **far b., a long way b.**
loin derrière; **a month b.** il y a un
mois; **to go b. and forth** aller et
venir; **to come b.** revenir; **he's b.**
il est de retour, il est revenu; **the
journey there and b.** le voyage
aller et retour **4** *vi* **to b. out**
(withdraw) se retirer; *(of vehicle)*

sortir en marche arrière; **to b. on
to** *(of house)* donner par derrière
sur • **backbone** *n* colonne *f*
vertébrale • **background** *n* fond
m, arrière-plan *m*; *(circumstances)*
contexte *m*; **b. music** musique
f de fond • **backpack** *n* sac *m* à
dos • **backside** *n Fam (buttocks)*
derrière *m* • **backstage** *adv*
dans les coulisses • **backstroke**
n (in swimming) dos *m* crawlé
• **backward(s)** *adv* en arrière;
(walk) à reculons; **to go** *or* **move
b.** reculer • **backyard** *n Br
(enclosed area)* arrière-cour *f; Am
(garden)* jardin *m* de derrière

▶**back up** *vt sep (support)* appuyer;
Comptr sauvegarder

bacon [ˈbeɪkən] *n* bacon *m*; **b.
and eggs** œufs *mpl* au bacon

bacteria [bækˈtɪərɪə] *npl* bactéries
fpl

bad [bæd] **(worse, worst)** *adj*
mauvais; *(wicked)* méchant; *(accident, wound)* grave; **b. language**
gros mots *mpl*; **to feel b.** *(ill)* se
sentir mal; **to be b. at maths** être
mauvais en maths; **it's not b.** ce
n'est pas mal; **to go b.** *(of fruit,
meat)* se gâter; *(of milk)* tourner;
too b.! tant pis! • **badly** *adv* mal;
(hurt) grièvement; **b. off** dans la
gêne; **to want sth b.** avoir grande
envie de qch • **bad-tempered** *adj*
grincheux, -euse

badge [bædʒ] *n (plastic)* badge *m*;
(metal) pin's *m*

badger [ˈbædʒə(r)] *n* blaireau *m*

badminton ['bædmɪntən] *n* badminton *m*

baffle ['bæfəl] *vt* laisser perplexe

bag [bæg] *n* sac *m*; **bags** *(luggage)* bagages *mpl*

baggage ['bægɪdʒ] *n* bagages *mpl*; *Am* **b. room** consigne *f*

baggy ['bægɪ] **(-ier, -iest)** *adj (garment) (out of shape)* déformé; *(by design)* large

bail [beɪl] *n Law* caution *f*; **on b.** sous caution

bait [beɪt] *n* appât *m*

bake [beɪk] **1** *vt* (faire) cuire au four **2** *vi (make cakes)* faire de la pâtisserie; *(of food)* cuire (au four); ● **baked** *adj (potatoes, apples)* au four; **b. beans** haricots *mpl* blancs à la tomate ● **baker** *n* boulanger, -ère *mf* ● **bakery** *n* boulangerie *f* ● **baking** *n* cuisson *f*; **b. powder** levure *f* chimique; **b. tin** moule *m* à pâtisserie

balaclava [bælə'klɑːvə] *n Br* passe-montagne *m*

balance ['bæləns] **1** *n (equilibrium)* équilibre *m*; *(of account)* solde *m*; *(remainder)* reste *m*; **to lose one's b.** perdre l'équilibre; **on b.** à tout prendre **2** *vt* maintenir en équilibre (**on** sur); *(budget)* équilibrer **3** *vi (of person)* se tenir en équilibre; *(of accounts)* être en équilibre, s'équilibrer; **to b. (out)** *(even out)* s'équilibrer

balcony ['bælkənɪ] **(pl -ies)** *n* balcon *m*

bald [bɔːld] **(-er, -est)** *adj* chauve

ball¹ [bɔːl] *n* balle *f*; *(for football, rugby)* ballon *m*; *(for snooker, pool)* bille *f*; *(of string, wool)* pelote *f*; *(sphere)* boule *f*; *Am* **b. game** match *m* de base-ball

ball² [bɔːl] *n (dance)* bal *m* (*pl* bals)

ballad ['bæləd] *n (poem)* ballade *f*; *(song)* romance *f*

ballet ['bæleɪ] *n* ballet *m* ● **ballerina** [bælə'riːnə] *n* ballerine *f*

balloon [bə'luːn] *n* ballon *m*

ballot ['bælət] *n (voting)* scrutin *m*; **b. paper** bulletin *m* de vote; **b. box** urne *f*

ballpoint (pen) ['bɔːlpɔɪnt(pen)] *n* stylo *m* à bille

ballroom ['bɔːlruːm] *n* salle *f* de danse

bamboo [bæm'buː] *n* bambou *m*

ban [bæn] **(pt & pp -nn-)** *vt* interdire; **to b. sb from doing sth** interdire à qn de faire qch; **to b. sb from** *(club)* exclure qn de

banana [bə'nɑːnə] *n* banane *f*

band [bænd] *n* **(a)** *(strip)* bande *f*; **rubber** *or* **elastic b.** élastique *m* **(b)** *(group of people)* bande *f*; *(pop group)* groupe *m*

bandage ['bændɪdʒ] **1** *n* bandage *m* **2** *vt* **to b. (up)** *(arm, leg)* bander; *(wound)* mettre un bandage sur; **to b. sb's arm** bander le bras à qn

Band-aid® ['bændeɪd] *n Am* pansement *m* adhésif

B and B, B & B [biːənd'biː] *(abbr* **bed and breakfast)** *n* ≃ chambre *f* d'hôte

bang [bæŋ] **1** *n (blow, noise)* coup *m* (violent); *(of gun)* détonation *f*; *(of door)* claquement *m* **2** *vt (hit)* cogner, frapper; *(door)* (faire) claquer; **to b. one's head** se cogner la tête **3** *vi* cogner, frapper; *(of door)* claquer; **to b. into sb/sth** heurter qn/qch **4** *exclam* vlan!, pan! **5** *adv Br Fam (exactly)* exactement; **b. in the middle** en plein milieu; **b. on six** à six heures tapantes

banger ['bæŋə(r)] *n Br* **(a)** *Fam (sausage)* saucisse *f* **(b)** *(firecracker)* pétard *m*

bangs [bæŋz] *npl Am (of hair)* frange *f*

banish ['bænɪʃ] *vt* bannir

banister ['bænɪstə(r)] *n* **banister(s)** rampe *f* (d'escalier)

bank¹ [bæŋk] *n (of river)* rive *f*

bank² [bæŋk] *n (for money)* banque *f*; **b. account** compte *m* en banque; *Br* **b. holiday** jour *m* férié; *Br* **b. note** billet *m* de banque • **bankrupt** *adj* **to go b.** faire faillite

bank³ [bæŋk] *vi* **to b. on sb/sth** *(rely on)* compter sur qn/qch

banner ['bænə(r)] *n* banderole *f*

banquet ['bæŋkwɪt] *n* banquet *m*

baptize [bæp'taɪz] *vt* baptiser

bar [bɑː(r)] **1** *n* **(a)** *(of metal)* barre *f*; *(of chocolate)* tablette *f*; *(on window)* barreau *m*; **behind bars** *(criminal)* sous les verrous; **b. code** code-barres *m* **(b)** *(pub)* bar *m*; *(counter)* bar *m*, comptoir *m* **2** *(pt & pp* **-rr-**) *vt* **(a)** **to b. sb's way** barrer le passage à qn **(b)** *(prohibit)* interdire (**sb from doing** à qn de faire); *(exclude)* exclure (**from** à) • **barmaid** *n Br* serveuse *f* (de bar) • **barman** *(pl* **-men**) *n Br* barman *m* • **bartender** *n Am* barman *m*

barbecue ['bɑːbɪkjuː] **1** *n* barbecue *m* **2** *vt* cuire au barbecue

barbed wire [bɑːbd'waɪə(r)] *n (fence)* barbelés *mpl*

barber ['bɑːbə(r)] *n* coiffeur *m* pour hommes

bare [beə(r)] (**-er, -est**) *adj* nu; *(tree)* dénudé; *(room, cupboard)* vide; **the b. necessities** le strict nécessaire; **with his b. hands** à mains nues • **barefoot 1** *adv* nu-pieds **2** *adj* aux pieds nus

barely ['beəlɪ] *adv (scarcely)* à peine; **b. enough** tout juste assez

bargain ['bɑːgɪn] **1** *n (deal)* marché *m*; **a b.** *(good buy)* une bonne affaire **2** *vi (negotiate)* négocier; *(haggle)* marchander; **to b. for** *or* **on sth** *(expect)* s'attendre à qch

barge [bɑːdʒ] **1** *n* péniche *f* **2** *vi* **to b. in** *(enter room)* faire irruption

bark [bɑːk] *vi* aboyer

barn [bɑːn] *n* grange *f*

barometer [bə'rɒmɪtə(r)] *n* baromètre *m*

baron ['bærən] *n* baron *m* • **baroness** *n* baronne *f*

barrel ['bærəl] *n (cask)* tonneau *m*; *(of oil)* baril *m*

barricade ['bærɪkeɪd] *vt* barricader; **to b. oneself (in)** se barricader (dans)

barrier ['bærɪə(r)] *n also Fig* barrière *f*; **sound b.** mur *m* du son

barrister ['bærɪstə(r)] *n Br* ≃ avocat *m*

base [beɪs] **1** *n (bottom, main ingredient)* base *f*; *(of tree, lamp)* pied *m* **2** *vt* baser, fonder (**on** sur); **based in London** *(person, company)* basé à Londres • **baseball** *n* base-ball *m* • **basement** *n* sous-sol *m*

bash [bæʃ] *vt (hit)* cogner; **to b. in** *or* **down** *(door, fence)* défoncer

basic ['beɪsɪk] **1** *adj* essentiel, -elle, de base; *(elementary)* élémentaire; *(room, house, meal)* tout simple **2** *n* **the basics** l'essentiel *m* • **basically** *adv (on the whole)* en gros; *(fundamentally)* au fond

basil [*Br* 'bæzəl, *Am* 'beɪzəl] *n* basilic *m*

basin ['beɪsən] *n (plastic)* bassine *f*; *(sink)* lavabo *m*

basis ['beɪsɪs] *(pl* **-ses** [-siːz]) *n (for discussion)* base *f*; *(for opinion)* fondement *m*; **on the b. of** d'après; **on a weekly b.** chaque semaine

basket ['bɑːskɪt] *n* panier *m*; *(for*

bread, laundry, litter) corbeille *f* •
basketball *n* basket(-ball) *m*
Basque [bæsk] **1** *adj* basque **2** *n*
Basque *mf*
bass [beɪs] *n Mus* basse *f*
bat¹ [bæt] *n (animal)* chauve-
souris *f*
bat² [bæt] **1** *n (for cricket, baseball)*
batte *f; (for table-tennis)* raquette *f*
2 *(pt & pp* -**tt**-*) vt (ball)* frapper
batch [bætʃ] *n (of people)* groupe
m; (of loaves) fournée *f; (of
papers)* liasse *f*
bath [bɑːθ] *(pl* **baths** [bɑːðz])
n bain *m; (tub)* baignoire *f;* **to
have** *or* **take a b.** prendre un
bain; **b. towel** serviette *f* de bain
• **bathrobe** *n Br* peignoir *m* de
bain, *Am* robe *f* de chambre •
bathroom *n* salle *f* de bain(s); *Am
(toilet)* toilettes *fpl* • **bathtub** *n*
baignoire *f*
bathe [beɪð] *vi (swim)* se baigner;
(have a bath) prendre un bain •
bathing *n* baignades *fpl;* **b. suit,**
Br **b. costume** maillot *m* de bain
baton [*Br* 'bætən, *Am* bə'tɒn]
n (of conductor) baguette *f; (of
majorette)* bâton *m*
batter ['bætə(r)] **1** *n* pâte *f* à frire
2 *vt (strike)* cogner sur; *(person)*
frapper; **to b. down** *(door)*
défoncer • **battered** *adj (car, hat)*
cabossé; **b. wife** femme *f* battue
battery ['bætərɪ] *(pl* -**ies**) *n (in
vehicle)* batterie *f; (in appliance)*
pile *f;* **b. hen** poule *f* de batterie
battle ['bætəl] *n* bataille *f;
(struggle)* lutte *f*
bawl [bɔːl] *vti* brailler
bay¹ [beɪ] *n (a) (part of coastline)*
baie *f* **(b) b. window** bow-
window *m*
bay² [beɪ] *n* **b. leaf** feuille *f* de
laurier

bazaar [bə'zɑː(r)] *n (market)* bazar
m; (charity sale) vente *f* de charité
BC [biː'siː] *(abbr* **before Christ**)
av. J.-C.

be [biː] *(present tense* **am, are,
is;** *past tense* **was, were;** *pp*
been; *pres p* **being**) **1** *vi* **(a)** *(gen)*
être; **it is green/small/***etc* c'est
vert/petit/*etc;* **he's a doctor** il est
médecin; **he's an Englishman**
c'est un Anglais; **it's him** c'est lui;
it's them ce sont eux; **it's three
(o'clock)** il est trois heures; **it's
the sixth of May,** *Am* **it's May
sixth** nous sommes le six mai;
to be hot/lucky avoir chaud/de
la chance; **my feet are cold** j'ai
froid aux pieds **(b)** *(with age,
height)* avoir; **to be 20** *(age)* avoir
20 ans; **to be two metres high**
avoir deux mètres de haut; **to be
six feet tall** ≃ mesurer 1,80 m **(c)**
(with health) aller; **how are you?**
comment vas-tu?; **I'm well/not
well** je vais bien/mal **(d)** *(with
place, situation)* se trouver, être;
she's in York elle se trouve *ou* elle
est à York **(e)** *(exist)* être; **the best
painter there is** le meilleur peintre
qui soit **(f)** *(go, come)* **I've been
to see her** je suis allé la voir; **he's
(already) been** il est (déjà) venu
(g) *(with weather, calculations)*
faire; **it's nice** il fait beau; **it's
foggy** il y a du brouillard; **two
and two are four** deux et deux
font quatre **(h)** *(cost)* coûter, faire;
it's 20 pence ça coûte 20 pence;
how much is it? ça fait combien?,
c'est combien? **2** *v aux* **(a)** **I am
going** je vais; **I was going** j'allais;
I'll be staying je vais rester; **I'm
listening to the radio** je suis en
train d'écouter la radio; **what has
she been doing?** qu'est-ce qu'elle

a fait?; **she's been there some time** elle est là depuis un moment; **he was killed** il a été tué; **I've been waiting (for) two hours** j'attends depuis deux heures; **it is said** on dit **(b)** *(in questions and answers)* **isn't it?/aren't you?/***etc* n'est-ce pas?, non?; **she's ill, is she?** *(in surprise)* alors, comme ça, elle est malade?; **he isn't English, is he?** il n'est pas anglais, si? **(c)** *(+ infinitive)* **he is to come at once** *(must)* il doit venir tout de suite **(d) there is/are** il y a; *(pointing)* voilà; **here is/are** voici; **there she is** la voilà; **here they are** les voici

beach [bi:tʃ] *n* plage *f*

bead [bi:d] *n* perle *f*; **(string of) beads** collier *m*

beak [bi:k] *n* bec *m*

beaker ['bi:kə(r)] *n* gobelet *m*

beam [bi:m] **1** *n* **(a)** *(of wood)* poutre *f* **(b)** *(of light, sunlight)* rayon *m*; *(of torch)* faisceau *m* (lumineux) **2** *vi* *(of light)* rayonner; *(of sun, moon)* briller; *(smile)* sourire largement

bean [bi:n] *n* haricot *m*; *(of coffee)* grain *m*; *Fam* **to be full of beans** être plein d'énergie

bear¹ [beə(r)] *n* *(animal)* ours *m*

bear² [beə(r)] *(pt* **bore,** *pp* **borne)** *vt* *(carry, show)* porter; *(endure)* supporter; **I can't b. him/it** je ne peux pas le supporter/supporter ça; **to b. sth in mind** *(remember)* se souvenir de qch; *(take into account)* tenir compte de qch ● **bearable** *adj* supportable

beard [bɪəd] *n* barbe *f*; **to have a b.** porter la barbe

beast [bi:st] *n* bête *f*

beat [bi:t] **1** *n* *(of heart, drum)* battement *m*; *(in music)* rythme *m* **2** *(pt* **beat,** *pp* **beaten** [bi:tən]) *vt*

battre; **to b. sb to it** devancer qn; **to b. sb up** tabasser qn **3** *vi* battre; *Fam* **to b. about** *or* **around the bush** tourner autour du pot ● **beating** *n* *(blows, defeat)* raclée *f*; *(of heart, drums)* battement *m*

beauty ['bju:tɪ] *(pl* **-ies)** *n* beauté *f*; **b. parlour** *or* **salon** institut *m* de beauté; **b. spot** *(on skin)* grain *m* de beauté ● **beautician** [-'tɪʃən] *n* esthéticienne *f* ● **beautiful** *adj* (très) beau *(f* belle); *(superb)* merveilleux, -euse

beaver ['bi:və(r)] *n* castor *m*

became [bɪ'keɪm] *pt of* **become**

because [bɪ'kɒz] *conj* parce que; **b. of** à cause de

beckon ['bekən] *vti* **to b. to sb (to do sth)** faire signe à qn (de faire qch)

become [bɪ'kʌm] *(pt* **became,** *pp* **become)** *vi* devenir; **to b. a painter** devenir peintre; **to b. thin** maigrir; **what has b. of her?** qu'est-elle devenue?

bed [bed] *n* lit *m*; **to go to b.** (aller) se coucher; **to put sb to b.** coucher qn; **in b.** couché; **to get out of b.** se lever; **to make the b.** faire le lit; **b. and breakfast** *(in hotel)* chambre *f* avec petit déjeuner; ● **bedclothes** *npl,* **bedding** *n* couvertures *fpl* et draps *mpl* ● **bedroom** *n* chambre *f* à coucher ● **bedside** *adj* **b. lamp/table** lampe *f*/table *f* de chevet ● **bedsit** *n* *Br* studio *m* ● **bedtime** *n* heure *f* du coucher; **b. story** histoire *f* *(pour endormir les enfants)*

bee [bi:] *n* abeille *f* ● **beehive** *n* ruche *f*

beef [bi:f] *n* bœuf *m*

been [bi:n] *pp of* **be**

beer [bɪə(r)] *n* bière *f*

beet [bi:t] *n* *Am* betterave *f*

beetle ['biːtəl] *n* scarabée *m*

beetroot ['biːtruːt] *n Br* betterave *f*

before [bɪ'fɔː(r)] **1** *adv* avant; *(already)* déjà; *(in front)* devant; **the day b.** la veille; **I've seen it b.** je l'ai déjà vu; **I've never done it b.** je ne l'ai (encore) jamais fait **2** *prep (time)* avant; *(place)* devant; **the year b. last** il y a deux ans; **b. my eyes** sous mes yeux **3** *conj* avant que (ne) (+ *subjunctive)*, avant de (+ *infinitive)*; **b. he goes** avant qu'il (ne) parte; **b. going** avant de partir

beg [beg] **1** (*pt & pp* **-gg-**) *vt* **to b. (for)** *(favour, help)* demander; *(bread, money)* mendier; **to b. sb to do sth** supplier qn de faire qch **2** *vi (in street)* mendier; *(ask earnestly)* supplier • **beggar** *n* mendiant, -e *mf*

begin [bɪ'gɪn] **1** (*pt* **began,** *pp* **begun,** *pres p* **beginning**) *vt* commencer; *(campaign)* lancer; *(conversation)* engager; **to b. doing** *or* **to do sth** commencer *ou* se mettre à faire qch; **he began laughing** il s'est mis à rire **2** *vi* commencer (**with** par; **by doing** par faire); **to b. with** *(first of all)* d'abord • **beginner** *n* débutant, -e *mf* • **beginning** *n* commencement *m*, début *m*; **in** *or* **at the b.** au début, au commencement

behalf [bɪ'hɑːf] *n* **on b. of sb, on sb's b.** *(representing)* au nom de qn, de la part de qn; *(in the interests of)* en faveur de qn

behave [bɪ'heɪv] *vi* se conduire; **to b. (oneself)** se tenir bien; *(of child)* être sage • **behaviour** (*Am* **behavior**) *n* conduite *f*, comportement *m*; **to be on one's best b.** se tenir particulièrement bien

behind [bɪ'haɪnd] **1** *prep* derrière; *(in terms of progress)* en retard sur **2** *adv* derrière; *(late)* en retard; **to be b. with one's work** avoir du travail en retard

beige [beɪʒ] *adj & n* beige *(m)*

Beijing [beɪ'dʒɪŋ] *n* Beijing *m ou f*

belated [bɪ'leɪtɪd] *adj* tardif, -ive

belch [beltʃ] *vi (of person)* roter

Belgium ['beldʒəm] *n* la Belgique • **Belgian 1** *adj* belge **2** *n* Belge *mf*

belief [bɪ'liːf] *n* croyance *f* (**in sb** en qn; **in sth** à *ou* en qch)

believe [bɪ'liːv] **1** *vt* croire; **I don't b. it!** c'est pas possible!; **I b. I'm right** je crois avoir raison, je crois que j'ai raison **2** *vi* croire (**in sth** à qch); **to b. in God** croire en Dieu; **I b. so/not** je crois que oui/que non; **to b. in doing sth** croire qu'il faut faire qch

bell [bel] *n (large) (of church)* cloche *f*; *(small)* clochette *f*; *(on door, bicycle)* sonnette *f*

belly ['belɪ] (*pl* **-ies**) *n* ventre *m*; *Fam* **b. button** nombril *m*

belong [bɪ'lɒŋ] *vi* appartenir (**to** à); **to b. to a club** être membre d'un club; **that book belongs to me** ce livre m'appartient *ou* est à moi; **that cup belongs here** cette tasse se range ici • **belongings** *npl* affaires *fpl*

below [bɪ'ləʊ] **1** *prep (lower than)* au-dessous de; *(under)* sous; *(with numbers)* moins de **2** *adv* en dessous; *(in text)* ci-dessous; **on the floor b.** à l'étage du dessous

belt [belt] *n* ceinture *f*

bench [bentʃ] *n (seat)* banc *m*; *(work table)* établi *m*

bend [bend] **1** *n* courbe *f*; *(in road)* virage *m* **2** (*pt & pp* **bent**) *vt* courber; *(leg, arm)* plier; **to b. one's head** baisser la tête; **to b. the rules** faire une entorse au

règlement **3** *vi (of branch)* plier; *(of road)* tourner; **to b. (down)** *(stoop)* se courber; **to b. (over** *or* **forward)** se pencher
beneath [bɪ'niːθ] **1** *prep* sous; *(unworthy of)* indigne de **2** *adv* (au-)dessous
benefit ['benɪfɪt] **1** *n (advantage)* avantage *m*; *(money)* allocation *f*; **benefits** *(of science, education)* bienfaits *mpl*; **for your (own) b.** pour vous, pour votre bien **2** *vt* faire du bien à; *(be useful to)* profiter à **3** *vi* **to b. from doing sth** gagner à faire qch ● **beneficial** [-'fɪʃəl] *adj* bénéfique
bent [bent] **1** *pt & pp of* **bend 2** *adj (nail, mind)* tordu; **b. on doing sth** résolu à faire qch
beret [*Br* 'bereɪ, *Am* bə'reɪ] *n* béret *m*
berry ['berɪ] *(pl* **-ies)** *n* baie *f*
berserk [bə'zɜːk] *adj* **to go b.** devenir fou furieux *(f* folle furieuse)
berth [bɜːθ] *n* **(a)** *(in ship, train)* couchette *f* **(b)** *Fig* **to give sb a wide b.** éviter qn comme la peste
beside [bɪ'saɪd] *prep* à côté de; **that's b. the point** ça n'a rien à voir ● **besides 1** *prep (in addition to)* en plus de; *(except)* excepté; **there are ten of us b. Paul** nous sommes dix sans compter Paul **2** *adv (in addition)* en plus; *(moreover)* d'ailleurs
best [best] **1** *adj* meilleur; **my b. dress** ma plus belle robe; **the b. thing is to accept** le mieux c'est d'accepter; **'b. before...'** *(on product)* 'à consommer avant...'; **b. man** *(at wedding)* témoin *m* **2** *n* **the b. (one)** le meilleur, la meilleure; **it's for the b.** c'est pour le mieux; **at b.** au mieux; **to do one's b.** faire de son mieux; **to**

the b. of my knowledge autant que je sache; **to make the b. of sth** *(accept)* s'accommoder de qch; **all the b.!** *(when leaving)* prends bien soin de toi!; *(good luck)* bonne chance!; *(in letter)* amicalement **3** *adv* **(the) b.** *(play, sing)* le mieux; **to like sb/sth (the) b.** aimer qn/qch le plus; **I think it b. to wait** je juge prudent d'attendre ● **best-seller** *n (book)* best-seller *m*
bet [bet] **1** *n* pari *m* **2** *(pt & pp* **bet** *or* **betted,** *pres p* **betting)** *vt* parier **(on** sur; **that** que); *Fam* **you b.!** tu parles!
betray [bɪ'treɪ] *vt (person, secret)* trahir ● **betrayal** *n (disloyalty)* trahison *f*
better ['betə(r)] **1** *adj* meilleur **(than** que); **I need a b. car** j'ai besoin d'une meilleure voiture; **that's b.** c'est mieux; **she's (much) b.** *(in health)* elle va (beaucoup) mieux; **to get b.** *(recover)* se remettre; *(improve)* s'améliorer; **it's b. to go** il vaut mieux partir **2** *adv* mieux **(than** que); **b. and b.** de mieux en mieux; **so much the b., all the b.** tant mieux **(for** pour); **I'd b. go** il vaut mieux que je parte
between [bɪ'twiːn] **1** *prep* entre; **in b.** entre **2** *adv* **in b.** *(space)* au milieu; *(time)* dans l'intervalle
beware [bɪ'weə(r)] *vi* se méfier **(of** de); **b.!** attention!; **'b. of the dog!'** 'attention, chien méchant!'
bewildered [bɪ'wɪldəd] *adj* perplexe
beyond [bɪ'jɒnd] **1** *prep* au-delà de; **b. reach/doubt** hors de portée/de doute; **b. belief** incroyable; **it's b. me** ça me dépasse **2** *adv* au-delà
bias(s)ed ['baɪəst] *adj* partial; **to**

be b. **against** avoir des préjugés contre

bib [bɪb] *n (for baby)* bavoir *m*

Bible ['baɪbəl] *n* **the B.** la Bible

bicycle ['baɪsɪkəl] *n* bicyclette *f*; **by b.** à bicyclette

bid [bɪd] **1** *n (offer)* offre *f*; *(at auction)* enchère *f* (**for** pour) **2** *(pt & pp* bid, *pres p* **bidding**) *vi* faire une offre (**for** pour); *(at auction)* faire une enchère (**for** sur)

big [bɪg] (**bigger, biggest**) *adj (tall, large)* grand; *(fat)* gros (*f* grosse); *(drop, increase)* fort; **to get big(ger)** *(taller)* grandir; *(fatter)* grossir; **my b. brother** mon grand frère; **b. toe** gros orteil *m*

bike [baɪk] *n Fam* vélo *m*

bikini [bɪ'kiːnɪ] *n* bikini® *m*

bilingual [baɪ'lɪŋgwəl] *adj* bilingue

bill [bɪl] *n* (a) *(invoice)* facture *f*; *(in restaurant)* addition *f*; *(in hotel)* note *f* (b) *Am (banknote)* billet *m* (c) *Pol* projet *m* de loi ● **billboard** *n* panneau *m* d'affichage

billion ['bɪljən] *n* milliard *m*

bin [bɪn] *n (for litter)* poubelle *f*

bind [baɪnd] *(pt & pp* **bound**) *vt (fasten)* attacher; *(book)* relier; *(unite)* lier; **to be bound by sth** être lié par qch

bingo ['bɪŋgəʊ] *n* ≃ loto *m*

binoculars [bɪ'nɒkjʊləz] *npl* jumelles *fpl*

biodegradable [baɪəʊdɪ'greɪdə-bəl] *adj* biodégradable

biography [baɪ'ɒgrəfɪ] *(pl* -ies) *n* biographie *f*

biology [baɪ'ɒlədʒɪ] *n* biologie *f* ● **biological** *adj* biologique;

bird [bɜːd] *n* oiseau *m*

birth [bɜːθ] *n* naissance *f*; **to give b. to** donner naissance à; **from b.** *(blind, deaf)* de naissance; **b. certificate** acte *m* de naissance ●

birthday *n* anniversaire *m*; **happy b.!** joyeux anniversaire!; **b. party** fête *f* d'anniversaire ● **birthmark** *n* tache *f* de naissance ● **birthplace** *n* lieu *m* de naissance

biscuit ['bɪskɪt] *n Br* biscuit *m*, petit gâteau *m*; *Am* petit pain *m* au lait

bishop ['bɪʃəp] *n* évêque *m*

bit[1] [bɪt] *n (of string, time)* bout *m*; **a b.** *(a little)* un peu; **b. by b.** petit à petit

bit[2] [bɪt] *pt of* bite

bite [baɪt] **1** *n* (a) *(wound)* morsure *f*; *(from insect)* piqûre *f* (b) *(mouthful)* bouchée *f*; **to have a b. to eat** manger un morceau **2** *(pt* bit, *pp* **bitten** ['bɪtən]) *vt* mordre; *(of insect)* piquer; **to b. one's nails** se ronger les ongles **3** *vi* mordre; *(of insect)* piquer; **to b. into sth** mordre dans qch

bitter ['bɪtə(r)] *adj (person, taste, irony)* amer, -ère; *(cold, wind)* glacial; **to feel b. (about sth)** être plein d'amertume (à cause de qch) ● **bitterly** *adv* **b. disappointed** cruellement déçu; **it's b. cold** il fait un froid de canard

bizarre [bɪ'zɑː(r)] *adj* bizarre

black [blæk] **1** (-er, -est) *adj* noir; **b. eye** œil *m* au beurre noir; *Br* **b. ice** verglas *m* **2** *n (colour)* noir *m*; *(person)* Noir, -e *mf* ● **blackberry** *(pl* -ies) *n* mûre *f* ● **blackboard** *n* tableau *m* (noir) ● **blackcurrant** *n* cassis *m* ● **blackmail 1** *n* chantage *m* **2** *vt* faire chanter; **to b. sb into doing sth** faire chanter qn pour qu'il/elle fasse qch

bladder ['blædə(r)] *n* vessie *f*

blade [bleɪd] *n* lame *f*; **b. of grass** brin *m* d'herbe

blame [bleɪm] **1** *n* responsabilité *f*; **to take the b. for sth** endosser la responsabilité de qch **2** *vt* rendre responsable, faire porter la responsabilité à (**for** de); **to b. sb for doing sth** reprocher à qn d'avoir fait qch; **you're to b.** c'est de ta faute

bland [blænd] (**-er, -est**) *adj (person)* terne; *(food)* insipide

blank [blæŋk] **1** *adj (paper, page)* blanc (*f* blanche), vierge; *(cheque)* en blanc; *(look, mind)* vide **2** *n (space)* blanc *m*

blanket ['blæŋkɪt] *n (on bed)* couverture *f*

blare [bleə(r)] *vi* **to b. (out)** *(of radio)* beugler; *(of music)* retentir

blast [blɑːst] *n* explosion *f*; *(of trumpet)* sonnerie *f*; **(at) full b.** *(loud)* à fond

blaze [bleɪz] **1** *n (fire)* feu *m*; *(large)* incendie *m*; **a b. of colour** une explosion de couleurs **2** *vi (of fire, sun)* flamboyer; *(of light, eyes)* être éclatant

blazer ['bleɪzə(r)] *n* blazer *m*

bleach [bliːtʃ] **1** *n (household)* (eau *f* de) Javel *f*; *(for hair)* décolorant *m* **2** *vt (clothes)* passer à l'eau de Javel; *(hair)* décolorer

bleak [bliːk] (**-er, -est**) *adj (landscape, weather)* morne; *(prospect)* peu encourageant

bleed [bliːd] (*pt & pp* **bled** [bled]) *vi* saigner; **her nose is bleeding** elle saigne du nez

blemish ['blemɪʃ] *n (fault)* défaut *m*; *(mark)* marque *f*

blend [blend] **1** *n* mélange *m* **2** *vt* mélanger (**with** à *ou* avec) • **blender** *n* mixer *m*

bless [bles] *vt* bénir; **to be blessed with sth** être doté de qch; **b. you!** *(when sneezing)* à vos souhaits! • **blessing** *n Rel* bénédiction *f*; *(benefit)* bienfait *m*; **it was a b. in disguise** finalement, ça a été une bonne chose

blew [bluː] *pt of* **blow²**

blind¹ [blaɪnd] **1** *adj* aveugle; **b. person** aveugle *mf*; *Fig* **to be b. to sth** ne pas voir qch; **b. alley** impasse *f*; **b. date** = rencontre arrangée avec quelqu'un qu'on ne connaît pas **2** *npl* **the b.** les aveugles *mpl* **3** *vt (dazzle, make blind)* aveugler • **blindfold 1** *n* bandeau *m* **2** *vt* bander les yeux à • **blindly** *adv Fig* aveuglément

blind² [blaɪnd] *n Br (on window)* store *m*

blink [blɪŋk] *vi (of person)* cligner des yeux; *(of eyes)* cligner

blissful ['blɪsfʊl] *adj (wonderful)* merveilleux, -euse; *(very happy)* aux anges • **blissfully** *adv (happy)* merveilleusement; **to be b. unaware that...** ne pas se douter le moins du monde que...

blister ['blɪstə(r)] *n* ampoule *f*

blizzard ['blɪzəd] *n* tempête *f* de neige

bloated ['bləʊtɪd] *adj* gonflé

blob [blɒb] *n (of ink, colour)* tache *f*

block [blɒk] **1** *n (of stone)* bloc *m*; *(of buildings)* pâté *m* de maisons; **b. of flats** immeuble *m*; *Am* **a b. away** une rue plus loin; **b. capitals** majuscules *fpl* **2** *vt (obstruct)* bloquer; *(pipe)* boucher; *(view)* cacher; **to b. up** *(pipe, hole)* boucher • **blockbuster** *n (film)* film *m* à grand spectacle

bloke [bləʊk] *n Br Fam* type *m*

blond [blɒnd] *adj & n* blond (*m*) • **blonde** *adj & n* blonde (*f*)

blood [blʌd] *n* sang *m*; **b. donor** donneur, -euse *mf* de sang; **b. group** groupe *m* sanguin; **b. pressure** tension *f* artérielle; **to have high b. pressure** avoir de la tension; **b. test** prise *f* de sang

bloody ['blʌdɪ] **1** (**-ier, -iest**) *adj*

(a) *(covered in blood)* ensanglanté **(b)** *Br very Fam* foutu; **a b. liar** un sale menteur **2** *adv Br very Fam (very)* vachement; **it's b. hot!** il fait une putain de chaleur!

bloom [bluːm] *vi (of tree, flower)* fleurir; *Fig (of person)* s'épanouir

blossom ['blɒsəm] **1** *n* fleurs *fpl* **2** *vi (of tree, flower)* fleurir; *Fig (of person)* s'épanouir

blot [blɒt] **1** *n* tache *f* **2** *(pt & pp -tt-) vt (stain)* tacher; *(dry)* sécher; **to b. sth out** *(obliterate)* effacer qch

blotchy [blɒtʃɪ] **(-ier, -iest)** *adj* couvert de taches; *(skin)* marbré

blouse [blauz] *n* chemisier *m*

blow¹ [bləu] *n (hit, setback)* coup *m*

blow² [bləu] **1** *(pt* **blew,** *pp* **blown)** *vt (of wind)* pousser; *(of person) (smoke)* souffler; *(bubbles)* faire; **to b. one's nose** se moucher; **to b. a whistle** donner un coup de sifflet **2** *vi (of wind, person)* souffler; *(of fuse)* sauter; *(of papers) (in wind)* s'éparpiller • **blow-dry** *(pt & pp* **blow-dried)** *vt* **to b. sb's hair** faire un brushing® à qn

▶**blow away 1** *vt sep (of wind)* emporter **2** *vi (of hat, paper)* s'envoler

▶**blow out** *vt sep (candle)* souffler; *(cheeks)* gonfler

▶**blow up 1** *vt sep (building)* faire sauter; *(pump up)* gonfler; *(photo)* agrandir **2** *vi (explode)* exploser

blue [bluː] **1** **(-er, -est)** *adj* bleu; *Fam* **to feel b.** avoir le cafard **2** *n* bleu *m*; **blues** *(music)* le blues; *Fam* **the blues** *(depression)* le cafard; **out of the b.** *(unexpectedly)* sans crier gare • **blueberry** *(pl* **-ies)** *n* airelle *f*

blunder ['blʌndə(r)] *n* gaffe *f*

blunt [blʌnt] **(-er, -est)** *adj (edge)* émoussé; *(pencil)* mal taillé; *(question, statement)* direct

blur [blɜː(r)] **1** *n* tache *f* floue **2** *(pt & pp -rr-) vt (outline)* brouiller • **blurred** *adj (image, outline)* flou

blurb [blɜːb] *n* notice *f* publicitaire

blurt [blɜːt] *vt* **to b. (out)** *(secret)* laisser échapper

blush [blʌʃ] *vi* rougir **(with** de)

boar [bɔː(r)] *n* **(wild) b.** sanglier *m*

board¹ [bɔːd] **1** *n (piece of wood)* planche *f*; *(for notices)* panneau *m*; *(for games)* tableau *m*; **on b. (a ship/plane)** à bord (d'un navire/avion) **2** *vt (ship, plane)* monter à bord de; *(bus, train)* monter dans; **to b. up** *(door)* condamner **3** *vi* **flight Z001 is now boarding** vol Z001, embarquement immédiat • **boarding** *n (of passengers)* embarquement *m*; **b. pass** carte *f* d'embarquement

board² [bɔːd] *n (committee)* conseil *m*; **b. (of directors)** conseil *m* d'administration; **b. room** salle *f* du conseil

board³ [bɔːd] **1** *n (food)* pension *f*; **b. and lodging,** *Br* **full b.** pension *f* complète; *Br* **half b.** demi-pension *f* **2** *vi (lodge)* être en pension **(with** chez); **boarding house** pension *f* de famille; **boarding school** pensionnat *m*

boast [bəust] **1** *vt* se glorifier de **2** *vi* se vanter **(about** *or* **of** de)

boat [bəut] *n* bateau *m*; **by b.** en bateau; *Fig* **in the same b.** logé à la même enseigne

body ['bɒdɪ] **(pl -ies)** *n* corps *m*; *(institution)* organisme *m*; **(dead) b.** cadavre *m* • **bodyguard** *n* garde *m* du corps

bog [bɒg] **1** *n (swamp)* marécage *m* **2** *(pt & pp -gg-) vt* **to get**

bogged down in *(mud, work)* s'enliser *(dans)*; *(details)* se perdre *(dans)*

boil [bɔɪl] **1** *n* **to bring sth to the b.** amener qch à ébullition **2** *vt* **to b. (up)** faire bouillir; **to b. the kettle** mettre de l'eau à chauffer **3** *vi* bouillir; **to b. over** *(of milk)* déborder • **boiled** *adj* bouilli; **b. egg** œuf *m* à la coque • **boiler** *n* chaudière *f*; *Br* **b. suit** bleus *mpl* de chauffe • **boiling 1** *n* ébullition *f*; **to be at b. point** *(of liquid)* bouillir **2** *adj* **b. (hot)** bouillant; **it's b. (hot)** *(weather)* il fait une chaleur infernale

boisterous ['bɔɪstərəs] *adj (child)* turbulent; *(meeting)* houleux, -euse

bold [bəʊld] **(-er, -est)** *adj* hardi

bolt [bəʊlt] **1** *n* **(a)** *(on door)* verrou *m*; *(for nut)* boulon *m* **(b) b. of lightning** éclair *m* **2** *adv* **b. upright** tout droit **3** *vt* **(a)** *(door)* verrouiller **(b)** *(food)* engloutir

bomb [bɒm] **1** *n* bombe *f*; **b. scare** alerte *f* à la bombe **2** *vt (from the air)* bombarder; *(of terrorist)* faire sauter une bombe dans *ou* à • **bombshell** *n* **to come as a b.** faire l'effet d'une bombe

bombard [bɒm'bɑːd] *vt (with bombs, questions)* bombarder **(with** de)

bond [bɒnd] **1** *n (link)* lien *m*; *(agreement)* engagement *m* **2** *vi (form attachment)* créer des liens affectifs **(with** avec)

bone [bəʊn] *n* os *m*; *(of fish)* arête *f* • **bone-dry** *adj* complètement sec *(f* sèche)

bonfire ['bɒnfaɪə(r)] *n (for celebration)* feu *m* de joie; *Br (for dead leaves)* feu *m* (de jardin)

bonkers ['bɒŋkəz] *adj Br Fam* dingue

bonnet ['bɒnɪt] *n (hat)* bonnet *m*; *Br (of vehicle)* capot *m*

bonus ['bəʊnəs] **(pl -uses** [-əsɪz]) *n* prime *f*

boo [buː] **1** *exclam (to frighten)* hou! **2** *n* boos huées *fpl* **3** *(pt & pp* **booed)** *vti* huer

book [bʊk] **1** *n* livre *m*; *(of tickets)* carnet *m*; *(for writing in)* cahier *m*; **b. club** club *m* du livre **2** *vt (seat)* réserver; **fully booked** *(hotel)* complet, -ète **3** *vi* **to b. (up)** réserver des places; **to b. in** *(to hotel)* signer le registre; **to b. into a hotel** prendre une chambre dans un hôtel • **bookcase** *n* bibliothèque *f* • **booking** *n* réservation *f*; **b. office** bureau *m* de location • **booklet** *n* brochure *f* • **bookmark** *n* marque-page *m* • **bookshelf** *n* étagère *f* • **bookshop** (*Am* **bookstore**) *n* librairie *f*

boom [buːm] **1** *n* **(a)** *(noise)* grondement *m* **(b)** *(economic)* boom *m* **2** *vi* **(a)** *(of thunder, gun)* gronder **(b)** *(of business, trade)* être florissant

boost [buːst] *vt (increase)* augmenter; *(economy)* stimuler; **to b. sb's morale** remonter le moral à qn

boot [buːt] **1** *n* **(a)** *(footwear)* botte *f*; **(ankle) b.** bottillon *m*; **(knee) b.** bottine *f* **(b)** *Br (of vehicle)* coffre *m* **2** *vt Fam (kick)* donner un coup/ des coups de pied à; **to b. sb out** mettre qn à la porte

booth [buːθ, buːð] *n (for phone, in language lab)* cabine *f*

booze [buːz] *n Fam* alcool *m*

border ['bɔːdə(r)] **1** *n (of country)* & *Fig* frontière *f*; *(edge)* bord *m* **2** *vt (street)* border; **to b. (on)** *(country)* avoir une frontière commune avec; *(resemble, verge on)* être voisin de

bore[1] [bɔː(r)] **1** vt (weary) ennuyer; **to be bored** s'ennuyer **2** n (person) raseur, -euse mf; **it's a b.** c'est ennuyeux ou rasoir ● **boredom** n ennui m ● **boring** adj ennuyeux, -euse

bore[2] [bɔː(r)] pt of **bear**[2]

born [bɔːn] adj né; **to be b.** naître; **he was b. in Paris/in 1980** il est né à Paris/en 1980

borne [bɔːn] pp of **bear**[2]

borrow ['bɒrəʊ] vt emprunter (**from** à)

bosom ['bʊzəm] n (chest, breasts) poitrine f; (breast) & Fig sein m

boss [bɒs] **1** n patron, -onne mf **2** vt **to b. sb around** or **about** donner des ordres à qn ● **bossy** (-ier, -iest) adj Fam autoritaire

both [bəʊθ] **1** adj les deux; **b. brothers** les deux frères **2** pron tous/toutes (les) deux; **b. of the boys** les deux garçons; **b. of us** tous les deux; **b. of them died** ils sont morts tous les deux **3** adv (at the same time) à la fois; **b. in England and in France** en Angleterre comme en France; **b. you and I know that...** vous et moi, nous savons que...

bother ['bɒðə(r)] **1** n (trouble) ennui m; (effort) peine f; (inconvenience) dérangement m **2** vt (annoy, worry) ennuyer; (disturb) déranger; (hurt, itch) (of foot, eye) gêner; **to b. doing** or **to do sth** se donner la peine de faire qch; **I can't be bothered** ça ne me dit rien **3** vi **to b. about** (worry about) se préoccuper de; (deal with) s'occuper de; **don't b.!** ce n'est pas la peine!

bottle ['bɒtəl] n bouteille f; (for perfume) flacon m; (for baby) biberon m; **b. bank** conteneur m pour verre usagé; **b. opener** ouvre-bouteilles m inv

bottom ['bɒtəm] **1** n (of sea, box) fond m; (of page, hill) bas m; (buttocks) derrière m; **to be (at the) b. of the class** être le dernier/la dernière de la classe **2** adj (shelf) inférieur, du bas; **b. part** or **half** partie f inférieure

bought [bɔːt] pt & pp of **buy**

bounce [baʊns] vi (of ball) rebondir (**off** contre); (of person) faire des bonds; Fam (of cheque) être sans provision

bouncer ['baʊnsə(r)] n Fam (doorman) videur m

bound[1] [baʊnd] **1** pt & pp of **bind** **2** adj **b. to do** (obliged) obligé de faire; (certain) sûr de faire; **it's b. to snow** il va sûrement neiger

bound[2] [baʊnd] **1** n (leap) bond m **2** vi bondir

boundary ['baʊndərɪ] (pl -ies) n limite f

bouquet [bʊ'keɪ] n (of flowers) bouquet m

bout [baʊt] n (of fever, coughing) accès m; (of asthma) crise f; **a b. of flu** une grippe

boutique [buː'tiːk] n boutique f (de mode)

bow[1] [bəʊ] n (weapon) arc m; (of violin) archet m; (knot) nœud m; **b. tie** nœud m papillon

bow[2] [baʊ] **1** n (with knees bent) révérence f; (nod) salut m **2** vt **to b. one's head** incliner la tête **3** vi s'incliner (**to** devant); (nod) incliner la tête (**to** devant); **to b. down (to)** (submit) s'incliner (devant)

bowels ['baʊəlz] npl intestins mpl

bowl [bəʊl] n bol m

bowling ['bəʊlɪŋ] n (tenpin) **b. bowling** m; **b. alley** bowling m; **b. ball** boule f de bowling

box 30 **break**

box [bɒks] **1** *n* boîte *f*; *(larger)* caisse *f*; *(cardboard)* carton *m*; *(in theatre)* loge *f*; **b. office** bureau *m* de location; *Br* **b. room** débarras *m* **2** *vi* boxer ● **boxer** *n* boxeur *m* ● **boxing** *n* (a) *(sport)* boxe *f*; **b. gloves/match** gants *mpl*/combat *m* de boxe (b) *Br* **B. Day** le lendemain de Noël

boy [bɔɪ] *n* garçon *m* ● **boyfriend** *n* petit ami *m*

boycott ['bɔɪkɒt] *vt* boycotter

bra [brɑː] *n* soutien-gorge *m*

brace [breɪs] **1** *n* *(dental)* appareil *m* dentaire; *(on leg, back)* appareil *m* orthopédique; *Br* **braces** *(for trousers)* bretelles *fpl* **2** *vt* **to b. oneself for sth** *(news, shock)* se préparer à qch

bracelet ['breɪslɪt] *n* bracelet *m*

bracket ['brækɪt] *n* *(for shelves)* équerre *f*; *(in writing)* parenthèse *f*; **in brackets** entre parenthèses

brag [bræg] *(pt & pp* **-gg-)** *vi* se vanter (**about** *or* **of sth** de qch; **about doing sth** de faire qch)

braid [breɪd] **1** *n (of hair)* tresse *f* **2** *vt (hair)* tresser

Braille [breɪl] *n* braille *m*; **in B.** en braille

brain [breɪn] *n* cerveau *m*; *(of animal)* cervelle *f*; *Fam* **to have brains** être intelligent; *Fam* **to have sth on the b.** être obsédé par qch ● **brainwash** *vt* faire un lavage de cerveau à ● **brainwave** *n* idée *f* géniale ● **brainy** (**-ier, -iest**) *adj Fam* intelligent

brake [breɪk] **1** *n* frein *m*; **b. light** (feu *m* de) stop *m* **2** *vi* freiner

branch [brɑːntʃ] **1** *n* branche *f*; *(of shop)* succursale *f*; *(of bank)* agence *f* **2** *vi* **to b. out** *(of company, person)* étendre ses activités

brand [brænd] **1** *n (on product)* marque *f*; **b. name** marque *f* **2** *vt (mark)* marquer; *Fig* **to be branded a liar/coward** avoir une réputation de menteur/lâche ● **brand-new** *adj* tout neuf (*f* toute neuve)

brandy ['brændɪ] *(pl* **-ies)** *n* cognac *m*

brass [brɑːs] *n* cuivre *m*

brat [bræt] *n Pej (child)* sale gosse *mf*

brave [breɪv] (**-er, -est**) *adj* courageux, -euse ● **bravery** *n* courage *m*

brawl [brɔːl] *n (fight)* bagarre *f*

Brazil [brə'zɪl] *n* le Brésil ● **Brazilian 1** *adj* brésilien, -enne **2** *n* Brésilien, -enne *mf*

bread [bred] *n* pain *m*; **loaf of b.** pain *m*; **brown b.** pain *m* bis; **b. knife** couteau *m* à pain ● **breadcrumb** *n* miette *f* de pain; **breadcrumbs** *(in cooking)* chapelure *f*

breadth [bredθ] *n* largeur *f*

break [breɪk] **1** *n* cassure *f*; *(rest)* repos *m*; *(in activity)* pause *f*; *(at school)* récréation *f*; *(holidays)* vacances *fpl* **2** *(pt* **broke,** *pp* **broken)** *vt* casser; *(into pieces)* briser; *(silence)* rompre; *(promise)* manquer à; *(law)* violer; *(record)* battre; *(journey)* interrompre; *(news)* annoncer (**to** à); **to b. one's arm** se casser le bras; **to b. sb's heart** briser le cœur à qn; **3** *vi* se casser; *(into pieces, of heart)* se briser; *(of news)* éclater; **to b. in two** se casser en deux; **to b. free** se libérer ● **breakable** *adj* fragile ● **breakdown** *n (of machine)* panne *f*; *(of person)* dépression *f*; *Br* **b. lorry** *or* **van** dépanneuse *f* ● **break-in** *n* cambriolage *m* ● **breakthrough** *n (discovery)* découverte *f* fondamentale

▶**break away** *vi* se détacher

►**break down 1** *vt sep (door)* enfoncer; *(argument, figures)* analyser **2** *vi (of machine)* tomber en panne; *(of person) (have nervous breakdown)* craquer; *(start crying)* éclater en sanglots

►**break in** *vi (of burglar)* entrer par effraction; *(interrupt)* interrompre

►**break into** *vt insep (house)* entrer par effraction; *(safe)* forcer; **to b. into song/a run** se mettre à chanter/courir

►**break out** *vi (of war, fire)* éclater; *(escape)* s'échapper **(of** de); **to b. out in a rash** se couvrir de boutons

►**break through 1** *vi (of sun, army)* percer **2** *vt insep (defences)* percer; *(barrier)* forcer

►**break up 1** *vt sep (reduce to pieces)* mettre en morceaux; *(marriage)* briser; *(fight)* mettre fin à **2** *vi (end)* prendre fin; *(of group)* se disperser; *(of marriage)* se briser; *(from school)* partir en vacances

breakfast ['brekfəst] *n* petit déjeuner *m*; **to have b.** prendre le petit déjeuner

breast [brest] *n (of woman)* sein *m*; *(chest)* poitrine *f*; *(of chicken)* blanc *m* ● **breastfeed** *(pt & pp -fed) vt* allaiter ● **breaststroke** *n (in swimming)* brasse *f*

breath [breθ] *n* souffle *m*; **bad b.** mauvaise haleine *f*; **out of b.** à bout de souffle; **to hold one's b.** retenir son souffle; **under one's b.** tout bas ● **breathless** *adj* hors d'haleine ● **breathtaking** *adj* à couper le souffle

breathe [briːð] **1** *vi* respirer; **to b. in** inhaler; **to b. out** expirer **2** *vt* respirer; **to b. a sigh of relief** pousser un soupir de soulagement ● **breathing** *n* respiration *f*

breed [briːd] **1** *n* race *f* **2** *(pt & pp* **bred)** *vt (animals)* élever; *Fig (hatred, violence)* engendrer **3** *vi (of animals)* se reproduire

breeze [briːz] *n* brise *f* ● **breezy** **(-ier, -iest)** *adj (weather, day)* frais *(f* fraîche), venteux, -euse

brew [bruː] **1** *vt (beer)* brasser; *Fig (trouble, plot)* préparer **2** *vi (of beer)* fermenter; *(of tea)* infuser; *Fig (of storm)* se préparer ● **brewery** *(pl -ies) n* brasserie *f*

bribe [braɪb] **1** *n* pot-de-vin *m* **2** *vt* acheter, soudoyer; **to b. sb into doing sth** soudoyer qn pour qu'il fasse qch ● **bribery** *n* corruption *f*

brick [brɪk] *n* brique *f*; **b. wall** mur en briques

bride [braɪd] *n* mariée *f*; **the b. and groom** les mariés *mpl* ● **bridegroom** *n* marié *m* ● **bridesmaid** *n* demoiselle *f* d'honneur

bridge[1] [brɪdʒ] **1** *n* pont *m* **2** *vt* **to b. a gap** combler une lacune

bridge[2] [brɪdʒ] *n (game)* bridge *m*

brief[1] [briːf] **(-er, -est)** *adj* bref *(f* brève); **in b.** en résumé ● **briefly** *adv (say)* brièvement; *(hesitate, smile)* un court instant

brief[2] [briːf] **1** *n (instructions)* instructions *fpl* **2** *vt* donner des instructions à; *(inform)* mettre au courant **(on** de)

briefcase ['briːfkeɪs] *n* mallette *f*

briefs [briːfs] *npl (underwear)* slip *m*

brigade [brɪ'geɪd] *n* brigade *f*

bright [braɪt] **1** **(-er, -est)** *adj (star, eyes)* brillant; *(light, colour)* vif *(f* vive); *(weather, room)* clair; *(clever)* intelligent; *(idea)* génial **2** *adv* **b. and early** de bon matin ● **brighten 1** *vt* **to b. (up)** *(room)* égayer **2** *vi* **to b. (up)** *(of weather)* s'éclaircir; *(of person)* s'égayer • **brightly** *adv (shine)* avec éclat

brilliant ['brɪljənt] *adj (light)* éclatant; *(person, idea, career)* brillant; *Br Fam (fantastic)* super *inv*

brim [brɪm] *n (of hat)* bord *m*

bring [brɪŋ] *(pt & pp* **brought)** *vt (person, animal, car)* amener; *(object)* apporter; *(cause)* provoquer; **it has brought me great happiness** cela m'a procuré un grand bonheur; **to b. sth to sb's attention** attirer l'attention de qn sur qch

▶**bring about** *vt sep* provoquer

▶**bring back** *vt sep (person)* ramener; *(object)* rapporter; *(memories)* rappeler

▶**bring down** *vt sep (object)* descendre; *(reduce)* réduire

▶**bring in** *vt sep (object)* rentrer; *(person)* faire entrer; *(introduce)* introduire

▶**bring out** *vt sep (object)* sortir; *(book)* publier; *(product)* lancer

▶**bring up** *vt sep (object)* monter; *(child)* élever; *(question)* soulever; *(subject)* mentionner

brisk [brɪsk] (**-er, -est**) *adj (lively)* vif *(f* vive); **at a b. pace** vite; **business is b.** les affaires marchent bien

bristle ['brɪsəl] *n* poil *m*

Britain ['brɪtən] *n* la Grande-Bretagne • **British 1** *adj* britannique; **the B. Isles** les îles *fpl* Britanniques **2** *npl* **the B.** les Britanniques *mpl* • **Briton** *n* Britannique *mf*

Brittany ['brɪtənɪ] *n* la Bretagne

brittle ['brɪtəl] *adj* cassant

broad [brɔːd] (**-er, -est**) *adj (wide)* large; *(accent)* prononcé; **in b. daylight** en plein jour; **b. bean** fève *f*; *Am Sport* **b. jump** saut *m* en longueur • **broad-minded** *adj (person)* à l'esprit large • **broaden** *vt* élargir • **broadly** *adv* **b. (speaking)** en gros

broadcast ['brɔːdkɑːst] **1** *n* émission *f* **2** *(pt & pp* **broadcast)** *vt* diffuser

broccoli ['brɒkəlɪ] *n inv* brocolis *mpl*

brochure ['brəʊʃə(r)] *n* brochure *f*

broil [brɔɪl] *vti Am* griller

broke [brəʊk] **1** *pt of* **break 2** *adj Fam (penniless)* fauché • **broken 1** *pp of* **break 2** *adj (line voice)* brisé; **b. English** mauvais anglais

bronze [brɒnz] *n* bronze *m*

brooch [brəʊtʃ] *n* broche *f*

brood [bruːd] **to b. over sth** *(of person)* ruminer qch

broom [bruːm] *n* balai *m*

broth [brɒθ] *n (thin)* bouillon *m*; *(thick)* potage *m*

brother ['brʌðə(r)] *n* frère *m* • **brother-in-law** *(pl* **brothers-in-law)** *n* beau-frère *m*

brought [brɔːt] *pt & pp of* **bring**

brow [braʊ] *n (forehead)* front *m*

brown [braʊn] **1** (**-er, -est**) *adj* marron *inv*; *(hair)* châtain; *(tanned)* bronzé **2** *n* marron *m*

Brownie ['braʊnɪ] *n (girl scout)* ≃ jeannette *f*

brownie ['braʊnɪ] *n (cake)* brownie *m*

browse [braʊz] **1** *vt Comptr* **to b. the Web** naviguer sur le Web **2** *vi (in shop)* regarder; **to b. through** *(book)* feuilleter

bruise [bruːz] **1** *n* bleu *m* **2** *vt* **to b. one's knee/hand** se faire un bleu au genou/à la main

brunch [brʌntʃ] *n* brunch *m*

brush [brʌʃ] **1** *n* brosse *f* **to give sth a b.** donner un coup de brosse à qch **2** *vt (teeth, hair)* brosser; **to b. sb/sth aside** écarter qn/qch; **to b. sth away** *or* **off** enlever

qch; **to b. up (on) one's French**
se remettre au français **3** *vi* **to b.**
against sb/sth effleurer qn/qch
brusque [bruːsk] *adj* brusque
Brussels ['brʌsəlz] *n* Bruxelles *m*
ou f; **B. sprouts** choux *mpl* de
Bruxelles
brute [bruːt] **1** *n (person)* brute *f*
2 *adj* **by b. force** par la force ●
brutal *adj* brutal; *(attack)* sauvage
BSc [biːes'siː] *(Am* **BS** [biː'es])
(abbr **Bachelor of Science)**
(person) ≃ licencié, -e *mf* ès
sciences; *(qualification)* ≃ licence
f de sciences
bubble ['bʌbəl] **1** *n (of air, soap)*
bulle *f*; **b. bath** bain *m* moussant;
b. gum chewing-gum *m* **2** *vi (of*
liquid) bouillonner ● **bubbly** *adj*
(liquid) plein de bulles; *(person)*
débordant de vitalité
buck [bʌk] *Fam* **1** *n Am* dollar *m* **2**
vt **to b. sb up** remonter le moral à
qn **3** *vi* **to b. up** *(become livelier)*
reprendre du poil de la bête
bucket ['bʌkɪt] *n* seau *m*
buckle ['bʌkəl] **1** *n* boucle *f* **2** *vt*
(fasten) boucler
bud [bʌd] *n (on tree)* bourgeon *m*;
(on flower) bouton *m* ● **budding**
adj (talent) naissant; *(actor)* en
herbe
Buddhist ['budɪst] *adj & n*
bouddhiste *(mf)*
buddy ['bʌdɪ] *(pl* -ies) *n Am Fam*
pote *m*
budge [bʌdʒ] *vi* bouger
budget ['bʌdʒɪt] **1** *n* budget *m* **2**
vi dresser un budget; **to b. for sth**
inscrire qch au budget
budgie ['bʌdʒɪ] *n Br* perruche *f*
buff [bʌf] *n Fam* **film b.** fanatique
mf de cinéma
buffet ['bufeɪ] *n (meal, café)*
buffet *m*; *Br* **b. car** *(on train)*
wagon-restaurant *m*

bug [bʌg] **1** *n (insect)* bestiole *f*;
Fam (germ) microbe *m* **2** *(pt & pp*
-gg-) *vt Fam (nag)* embêter
buggy ['bʌgɪ] *(pl* -ies) *n Br* **(baby)**
b. *(pushchair)* poussette *f*
build [bɪld] *(pt & pp* **built**) **1** *vt*
construire; **to b. sth up** *(increase)*
augmenter qch; *(business)* monter
qch **2** *vi* **to b. up** *(of tension,*
pressure) augmenter; *(of dust,*
snow, interest) s'accumuler ●
builder *n (skilled)* maçon *m*;
(unskilled) ouvrier *m* ● **building**
n bâtiment *m*; *(flats, offices)*
immeuble *m*; *(action)* construction
f; **b. site** chantier *m*; *Br* **b. society**
≃ société *f* de crédit immobilier
bulb [bʌlb] *n (of plant)* bulbe *m*;
(of lamp) ampoule *f*
bulge [bʌldʒ] *vi* **to b. (out)**
bomber; *(of eyes)* sortir de la tête
● **bulging** *adj* bombé; *(eyes)*
protubérant; **to be b. (with)** *(of*
bag, pocket) être bourré (de)
bulk [bʌlk] *n inv* volume *m*; **the b.**
of sth la majeure partie de qch ●
bulky (-ier, -iest) *adj* volumineux,
-euse
bull [bʊl] *n* taureau *m* ● **bulldozer**
n bulldozer *m* ● **bullfight** *n*
corrida *f* ● **bull's-eye** *n* **to hit the**
b. mettre dans le mille
bullet ['bʊlɪt] *n* balle *f* ●
bulletproof *adj (glass)* blindé;
Br **b. jacket,** *Am* **b. vest** gilet *m*
pare-balles *inv*
bulletin ['bʊlətɪn] *n* bulletin *m*; *Am*
b. board panneau *m* d'affichage
bully ['bʊlɪ] **1** *(pl* -ies) *n* terreur
f **2** *(pt & pp* -ied) *vt (ill-treat)*
maltraiter
bum [bʌm] *Fam n* **(a)** *(loafer)*
clochard, -e *mf* **(b)** *Br (buttocks)*
derrière *m*; **b. bag** banane *f*
bump [bʌmp] **1** *n (impact)* choc
m; *(jerk)* secousse *f*; *(on road,*

head) bosse *f* **2** *vt (of car)* heurter; **to b. one's head/knee** se cogner la tête/le genou; **to b. into** *(of person)* se cogner contre; *(of car)* rentrer dans; *(meet)* tomber sur • **bumper** *n (of car)* pare-chocs *m inv* • **bumpy** (**-ier, -iest**) *adj (road, ride)* cahoteux, -euse

bun [bʌn] *n* (**a**) *(cake)* petit pain *m* au lait (**b**) *(of hair)* chignon *m*

bunch [bʌntʃ] *n (of flowers)* bouquet *m; (of keys)* trousseau *m; (of bananas)* régime *m; (of grapes)* grappe *f; (of people)* bande *f*

bundle ['bʌndəl] **1** *n* paquet *m; (of papers)* liasse *f* **2** *vt (put)* fourrer (**into** dans); *(push)* pousser (**into** dans); **to b. up** *(newspapers, letters)* mettre en paquet

bungalow ['bʌŋgələʊ] *n* pavillon *m* de plain-pied

bunk [bʌŋk] *n (in ship, train)* couchette *f;* **b. beds** lits *mpl* superposés

bunny ['bʌnɪ] (*pl* **-ies**) *n Fam* **b. (rabbit)** petit lapin *m*

buoy [bɔɪ] *n* bouée *f*

burden ['bɜːdən] **1** *n* fardeau *m* **2** *vt* charger (**with** de); *Fig* accabler (**with** de)

bureau ['bjʊərəʊ] (*pl* **-eaux** [-əʊz]) *n (office)* bureau *m; Br (desk)* secrétaire *m; Am (chest of drawers)* commode *f* • **bureaucracy** [-'rɒkrəsɪ] *n* bureaucratie *f*

burger ['bɜːgə(r)] *n* hamburger *m*

burglar ['bɜːglə(r)] *n* cambrioleur, -euse *mf;* **b. alarm** alarme *f* antivol • **burgle** (*Am* **burglarize**) *vt Br* cambrioler

burn [bɜːn] **1** *n* brûlure *f* **2** (*pt & pp* **burned** *or* **burnt**) *vt* brûler; **to b. sth down** incendier qch **3** *vi* brûler; **to b. down** *(of house)* être détruit par les flammes; *(of fuse)* sauter • **burner** *n Fig* **to put**

sth on the back b. remettre qch à plus tard • **burning 1** *adj* en feu; *(fire)* allumé **2** *n* **a smell of b.** une odeur de brûlé

burp [bɜːp] *vi Fam* roter

burst [bɜːst] **1** (*pt & pp* **burst**) *vt (bubble, balloon)* crever; *(tyre)* faire éclater; **to b. open** *(door)* ouvrir brusquement **2** *vi (of bubble, balloon, tyre)* crever; *(with force) (of boiler, tyre)* éclater; **to b. into a room** faire irruption dans une pièce; **to b. into flames** prendre feu; **to b. into tears** fondre en larmes; **to b. out laughing** éclater de rire; **to b. open** *(of door)* s'ouvrir brusquement

bury ['berɪ] (*pt & pp* **-ied**) *vt (body)* enterrer; *(hide)* enfouir

bus [bʌs] (*pl* **buses** *or* **busses**) *n* autobus *m*, bus *m; (long-distance)* autocar *m*, car *m;* **by b.** en bus/en car; **b. driver** chauffeur *m* de bus/car; **b. station** gare *f* routière; **b. stop** arrêt *m* de bus

bush [bʊʃ] *n* buisson *m* • **bushy** (**-ier, -iest**) *adj (hair, tail)* touffu

business ['bɪznɪs] **1** *n* affaires *fpl,* commerce *m; (shop)* commerce *m; (company, concern, matter)* affaire *f;* **the textile/construction b.** l'industrie *f* du textile/de la construction; **to go out of b.** *(stop trading)* fermer; **that's none of your b.!, mind your own b.!** ça ne vous regarde pas! **2** *adj* commercial; *(meeting, trip, lunch)* d'affaires; **b. card** carte *f* de visite; **b. school** école *f* de commerce • **businessman** (*pl* **-men**) *n* homme *m* d'affaires • **businesswoman** (*pl* **-women**) *n* femme *f* d'affaires

bust [bʌst] **1** *n (statue)* buste *m; (of woman)* poitrine *f* **2** *adj Fam (broken)* fichu; **to go b.** *(bankrupt)* faire faillite **3** (*pt & pp*

bust or **busted**) vt Fam (break) bousiller; (arrest) coffrer

bustle ['bʌsəl] vi **to b. (about)** s'affairer

busy ['bɪzɪ] (**-ier, -iest**) adj occupé; (day) chargé; (street) animé; Am (phone, line) occupé; **to be b. doing** (in the process of) être occupé à faire; **to keep oneself b.** s'occuper; **the shops were very b.** il y avait plein de monde dans les magasins; Am **b. signal** sonnerie f 'occupé'

but [bʌt, unstressed bət] **1** conj mais **2** prep (except) sauf; **b. for him** sans lui; **no one b. you** personne d'autre que toi; **the last b. one** l'avant-dernier, -ère mf

butcher ['bʊtʃə(r)] n boucher, -ere mf; **b.'s (shop)** boucherie f

butler ['bʌtlə(r)] n maître m d'hôtel

butt [bʌt] **1** n (of cigarette) mégot m; Am Fam (buttocks) derrière m **2** vt (with head) donner un coup de tête à **3** vi **to b. in** intervenir

butter ['bʌtə(r)] **1** n beurre m **2** vt beurrer

butterfly ['bʌtəflaɪ] (pl **-ies**) n papillon m; Fam **to have butterflies** avoir l'estomac noué; **b. stroke** (in swimming) brasse f papillon

buttock ['bʌtək] n fesse f

button ['bʌtən] **1** n bouton m; (of phone) touche f; Am (badge) badge m **2** vt **to b. (up)** boutonner

buy [baɪ] **1** n **a good b.** une bonne affaire **2** (pt & pp **bought**) vt acheter (**from sb** à qn; **for sb** à ou pour qn)

buzz [bʌz] vi bourdonner •
buzzer n (for entry) Interphone® m; (of bell, clock) sonnerie f

by [baɪ] **1** prep (a) (agent) par, de; **hit/chosen by** frappé/choisi par; **surrounded/followed by** entouré/suivi de; **a book/painting by…** un livre/tableau de… (b) (manner, means) par, en, à, de; **by sea** par mer; **by mistake** par erreur; **by car/train** en voiture/train; **by bicycle** à bicyclette; **by moonlight** au clair de lune; **by doing** en faisant; **one by one** un à un; **day by day** de jour en jour; **by sight/day** de vue/jour; **(all) by oneself** tout seul (c) (next to) à côté de; (near) près de; **by the lake/sea** au bord du lac/de la mer (d) (before in time) avant; **by Monday** avant lundi, d'ici lundi; **by now** à cette heure-ci (e) (amount, measurement) à; **by the kilo** au kilo; **taller by a metre** plus grand d'un mètre; **paid by the hour** payé à l'heure (f) (according to) à, d'après; **it's fine by me** je n'y vois pas d'objection **2** adv **close by** tout près; **to go** or **pass by** passer; **by and large** en gros • **bypass 1** n rocade f; **(heart) b. operation** pontage m **2** vt (town) contourner

bye(-bye) ['baɪ('baɪ)] exclam Fam salut!, au revoir!

Cc

C, c¹ [siː] n C, c m inv

c² (abbr **cent(s)**) ct

cab [kæb] n taxi m

cabbage ['kæbɪdʒ] n chou m (pl choux)

cabin ['kæbɪn] n (on ship) cabine f; (hut) cabane f; Aviat **c. crew** équipage m

cabinet ['kæbɪnɪt] n (a) (cupboard) armoire f; (for display) vitrine f; **(filing) c.** classeur m (meuble) (b) Pol gouvernement m

cable ['keɪbəl] n câble m; **c. car** téléphérique m; **c. television** la télévision par câble

cactus ['kæktəs] (pl **-ti** [-taɪ] or **-tuses** [-təsɪz]) n cactus m

café ['kæfeɪ] n café m

caffeine ['kæfiːn] n caféine f

cage [keɪdʒ] n cage f

cake [keɪk] n gâteau m; (small) pâtisserie f

calculate ['kælkjʊleɪt] vti calculer; **to c. that...** (estimate) calculer que... • **calculation** [-'leɪʃən] n calcul m • **calculator** n calculatrice f

calendar ['kælɪndə(r)] n calendrier m

calf [kɑːf] (pl **calves**) n (a) (animal) veau m (b) (part of leg) mollet m

call [kɔːl] 1 n (shout) cri m; (visit) visite f; (telephone) **c.** appel m (téléphonique); **to make a c.** téléphoner (**to** à); **to give sb a c.** téléphoner à qn; **c. centre** centre m d'appels 2 vt (phone) appeler; (shout to) crier; **he's called David** il s'appelle David; **to c. sb a liar** traiter qn de menteur 3 vi appeler; (cry out) crier; (visit) passer • **caller** n visiteur, -euse mf; (on phone) correspondant, -e mf

► **call back** vt sep & vi rappeler

► **call for** vt insep (require) demander; (collect) passer prendre

► **call in** vi **to c. in (on sb)** (visit) passer (chez qn)

► **call off** vt sep (cancel) annuler; (strike) mettre fin à

► **call on** vt insep (visit) passer voir; **to c. on sb to do** (urge) sommer qn de faire

► **call out 1** vt sep (shout) crier **2** vi (shout) crier; **to c. out to sb** interpeller qn

► **call up** vt sep (phone) appeler

calm [kɑːm] 1 (**-er, -est**) adj calme, tranquille; **keep c.!** restez calme! **2** n calme m **3** vt **to c. (down)** calmer **4** vi **to c. down** se calmer • **calmly** adv calmement

calorie ['kælərɪ] n calorie f

calves [kɑːvz] pl of **calf**

camcorder ['kæmkɔːdə(r)] n caméscope® m

came [keɪm] pt of **come**

camel ['kæməl] n chameau m

camera ['kæmrə] n appareil photo m; (for film, video) caméra f

camouflage ['kæməflɑːʒ] vt also Fig camoufler

camp [kæmp] **1** n camp m, campement m; **c. bed** lit m de camp **2** vi **to c. (out)** camper

● **camping** n camping m ●
campsite n camping m
campaign [kæm'peɪn] **1** n
(political) campagne f; **publicity
c.** campagne f de publicité **2**
vi faire campagne (**for/against**
pour/contre)
campus ['kæmpəs] n campus m

can¹ [kæn, unstressed kən] (pt
could)

Le verbe **can** n'a ni infinitif,
ni gérondif, ni participe. Pour
exprimer l'infinitif ou le participe,
on aura recours à la forme
correspondante de **be able to**
(he wanted to be able to speak
English; she has always been able
to swim). La forme négative est
can't, qui s'écrit **cannot** dans la
langue soutenue.

v aux (be able to) pouvoir; (know
how to) savoir; **he couldn't help
me** il ne pouvait pas m'aider;
she c. swim elle sait nager; **he
could do it tomorrow** il pourrait
le faire demain; **he could have
done it** il aurait pu le faire; **you
could be wrong** (possibility) tu as
peut-être tort; **he can't be dead**
(probability) il ne peut pas être
mort; **c. I come in?** (permission)
puis-je entrer?; **yes, you c.!** oui!

can² [kæn] n (for food) boîte f; (for
beer) can(n)ette f ● **canned** adj
en boîte, en conserve; **c. food**
conserves fpl ● **can-opener** n
ouvre-boîtes m inv
Canada ['kænədə] n le Canada ●
Canadian 1 adj canadien, -enne **2**
n Canadien, -enne mf
canal [kə'næl] n canal m
canary [kə'neəri] (pl **-ies**) n canari
m
cancel ['kænsəl] (Br **-ll-**, Am **-l-**)
vt (appointment) annuler; (goods)

décommander; (train) supprimer
● **cancellation** [-'leɪʃən] n annulation f
cancer ['kænsə(r)] n cancer
m; **lung/skin c.** cancer m du
poumon/de la peau
candidate ['kændɪdeɪt] n candidat, -e mf (**for** à)
candle ['kændəl] n (made of wax)
bougie f; (in church) cierge m ●
candlelight n **to have dinner by
c.** dîner aux chandelles
candy ['kændɪ] (pl **-ies**) n Am
bonbon m; (sweets) bonbons mpl;
c. store confiserie f ● **candyfloss**
n Br barbe f à papa
cane [keɪn] n (stick) canne f; (for
punishment) baguette f
cannabis ['kænəbɪs] n cannabis m
cannon ['kænən] (pl **-s** or **cannon**)
n canon m
cannot ['kænɒt] = **can not**
canoe [kə'nuː] n canoë m ●
canoeing n **to go c.** faire du
canoë-kayak
can't [kɑːnt] = **can not**
canteen [kæn'tiːn] n cantine f
canvas ['kænvəs] n (cloth) toile f;
(for embroidery) canevas m
canyon ['kænjən] n canyon m
cap [kæp] n (**a**) (hat) casquette f;
(for shower, of sailor) bonnet m (**b**)
(of bottle) capsule f
capable ['keɪpəbəl] adj (person)
capable (**of sth** de qch; **of doing
sth** de faire qch) ● **capacity**
[kə'pæsɪtɪ] (pl **-ies**) n capacité f
cape [keɪp] n cape f
capital ['kæpɪtəl] **1** adj (letter)
majuscule; **c. punishment** peine f
capitale **2** n (letter) majuscule f; **c.
(city)** capitale f ● **capitalist** adj &
n capitaliste (mf)
capsize [kæp'saɪz] vi chavirer
capsule [Br 'kæpsjuːl, Am

'kæpsəl] n (of medicine) gélule f;
(space) c. capsule f spatiale
captain ['kæptɪn] n capitaine m
caption ['kæpʃən] n (of illustration)
légende f
captivate ['kæptɪveɪt] vt captiver
captive ['kæptɪv] n captif, -ive mf
capture ['kæptʃə(r)] vt (person,
animal) capturer; (escaped
prisoner or animal) reprendre
car [kɑː(r)] n voiture f, automobile f;
c. insurance/industry assurance f
/industrie f automobile; **c. crash**
accident m de voiture; **c. door**
portière f; Br **c. park** parking m;
c. radio autoradio m; **c. wash**
(machine) = station de lavage
automatique pour voitures
caramel ['kærəməl] n caramel m
caravan ['kærəvæn] n caravane f
carbon ['kɑːbən] n carbone m; **c.
dioxide** gaz m carbonique
card [kɑːd] n carte f; (cardboard)
carton m; **to play cards** jouer aux
cartes ● **cardboard** n carton m; **c.
box** boîte f en carton, carton m
cardigan ['kɑːdɪgən] n cardigan m
care [keə(r)] **1** n (attention) soin
m; (protection) soins mpl; (worry)
souci m; **to take c. to do** veiller
à faire; **to take c. not to do** faire
attention à ne pas faire; **to take c.
of sb/sth** s'occuper de qn/qch; **to
take c. of oneself** (keep healthy)
faire bien attention à soi; **take
c.!** (goodbye) au revoir!; **'c. of'**
(on envelope) 'chez' **2** vt **I don't
c. what he says** peu m'importe
ce qu'il en dit **3** vi **I don't c.** ça
m'est égal; **who cares?** qu'est-ce
que ça peut faire?; **to c. about**
(feel concern about) se soucier de;
to c. about or **for sb** (be fond of)
avoir de la sympathie pour qn;
to c. for sb (look after) soigner
qn ● **carefree** adj insouciant ●

caretaker n gardien, -enne mf,
concierge mf
career [kə'rɪə(r)] n carrière f
careful ['keəfəl] adj (exact,
thorough) soigneux, -euse (**about**
de); (cautious) prudent; **to be
c. of** or **with sth** faire attention
à qch; **be c.!** (fais) attention! ●
carefully adv (thoroughly) avec
soin; (cautiously) prudemment ●
careless adj négligent; **c. mistake**
faute f d'étourderie
caress [kə'res] vt caresser
cargo ['kɑːgəʊ] (pl -oes or -os) n
cargaison f; **c. ship** cargo m
Caribbean [Br kærɪ'biːən, Am
kə'rɪbɪən] **1** adj caraïbe **2** n **the C.**
les Antilles fpl
caricature ['kærɪkətʃʊə(r)] n
caricature f
carnival ['kɑːnɪvəl] n carnaval m
(pl -als)
carol ['kærəl] n chant m de Noël
carpenter ['kɑːpɪntə(r)] n (for
house building) charpentier m; (for
light woodwork) menuisier m
carpet ['kɑːpɪt] n (rug) tapis m;
(fitted) moquette f
carriage ['kærɪdʒ] n Br (of train,
with horses) voiture f
carrot ['kærət] n carotte f
carry ['kærɪ] (pt & pp -ied) vt
porter; (goods, passengers) transporter; (gun, money) avoir sur soi
►**carry away** vt sep emporter; **to
be** or **get carried away** (excited)
s'emballer
►**carry on 1** vt sep (continue)
continuer (**doing** à faire);
(conversation) poursuivre **2** vi
(continue) continuer; **to c. on
with sth** continuer qch
►**carry out** vt sep (plan, promise)
mettre à exécution; (order)
exécuter; (repair, reform) effectuer;
Am (meal) emporter

cart [kɑːt] **1** *n (horse-drawn)*
charrette *f*; *Am (in supermarket)*
Caddie® *m* **2** *vt Fam* **to c.**
(around) trimbaler

carton ['kɑːtən] *n (box)* carton *m*;
(of milk, fruit juice) brique *f*; *(of*
cigarettes) cartouche *f*

cartoon [kɑː'tuːn] *n (in*
newspaper) dessin *m* humoristique;
(film) dessin *m* animé; **c. (strip)**
bande *f* dessinée

cartridge ['kɑːtrɪdʒ] *n* cartouche *f*

carve [kɑːv] *vt (cut)* tailler (**out of**
dans); *(name)* graver; **to c. (up)**
(meat) découper • **carving** *adj* **c.**
knife couteau *m* à découper

case¹ [keɪs] *n (instance, situation)*
cas *m*; *Law* affaire *f*; *Fig (argu-*
ments) arguments *mpl*; **in any c.**
en tout cas; **in c. it rains** au cas
où il pleuvrait; **in c. of** en cas de

case² [keɪs] *n (bag)* valise *f*; *(for*
glasses, camera, violin) étui *m*

cash [kæʃ] **1** *n (coins, banknotes)*
liquide *m*; *Fam (money)* sous *mpl*;
to pay (in) c. payer en liquide; *Br*
c. desk caisse *f*; **c. dispenser** *or*
machine distributeur *m* de billets;
c. register caisse *f* enregistreuse **2**
vt **to c. a cheque** *or Am* **check** *(of*
person) encaisser un chèque; *(of*
bank) payer un chèque • **cashier**
n caissier, -ère *mf*

cashew ['kæʃuː] *n* **c. (nut)** noix *f*
de cajou

casino [kə'siːnəʊ] *(pl* **-os)** *n* casino
m

casserole ['kæsərəʊl] *n (covered*
dish) cocotte *f*; *(stew)* ragoût *m*

cassette [kə'set] *n (audio, video)*
cassette *f*; **c. player** lecteur *m* de
cassettes

cast [kɑːst] **1** *n (actors)* acteurs
mpl; *Med* **in a c.** dans le plâtre **2** *(pt*
& pp **cast)** *vt (throw)* jeter; *(light,*

shadow) projeter; **to c. doubt on**
sth jeter le doute sur qch

castle ['kɑːsəl] *n* château *m*

casual ['kæʒjʊəl] *adj (remark)*
en passant; *(relaxed, informal)*
décontracté; *(clothes)* sport *inv*;
(employment, worker) temporaire
• **casually** *adv (remark)* en
passant; *(informally)* avec décontraction; *(dress)* sport

casualty ['kæʒjʊəltɪ] *(pl* **-ies)** *n*
victime *f*; *Br* **c. (department)** *(in*
hospital) (service *m* des) urgences
fpl

cat [kæt] *n* chat *m*

catalogue ['kætəlɒg] *(Am*
catalog) *n* catalogue *m*

catapult ['kætəpʌlt] **1** *n (toy)*
lance-pierres *m inv* **2** *vt* catapulter

catastrophe [kə'tæstrəfɪ] *n*
catastrophe *f*

catch [kætʃ] *(pt & pp* **caught)**
1 *vt (ball, thief, illness)* attraper;
(fish, train, bus) prendre; *(grab)*
prendre, saisir; **to c. sb's eye** *or*
attention attirer l'attention de qn;
to c. sight of sb/sth apercevoir
qn/qch; **to c. fire** prendre feu; **to**
c. sb doing surprendre qn à faire;
to c. sb up rattraper qn **2** *vi* **her**
skirt (got) caught in the door sa
jupe s'est prise dans la porte; **to c.**
up with sb rattraper qn • **catchy**
(-ier, -iest) *adj (tune, slogan)* facile
à retenir

category ['kætɪgərɪ] *(pl* **-ies)** *n*
catégorie *f*

cater ['keɪtə(r)] *vi (provide food)*
s'occuper des repas (**for** pour);
to c. to, *Br* **to c. for** *(need, taste)*
satisfaire • **catering** *n* restauration
f

caterpillar ['kætəpɪlə(r)] *n*
chenille *f*

cathedral [kə'θiːdrəl] *n* cathédrale
f

Catholic ['kæθlɪk] *adj & n* catholique *(mf)*

cattle ['kætəl] *npl* bétail *m*

caught [kɔːt] *pt & pp of* **catch**

cauliflower ['kɒlɪflauə(r)] *n* chou-fleur *m*

cause [kɔːz] **1** *n (origin, ideal)* cause *f; (reason)* raison *f,* motif *m* **(of** de) **2** *vt* causer, occasionner; **to c. trouble for sb** créer *ou* causer des ennuis à qn

caution ['kɔːʃən] *n (care)* prudence *f* • **cautious** *adj* prudent

cave [keɪv] *n* grotte *f*

CD [siː'diː] *(abbr* **compact disc)** *n* CD *m inv;* **CD player** lecteur *m* de CD

CD-ROM [siːdiː'rɒm] *(abbr* **compact disc read-only memory)** *n Comptr* CD-ROM *m inv*

cease [siːs] *vti* cesser **(doing** de faire)

ceiling ['siːlɪŋ] *n (of room) & Fig (limit)* plafond *m*

celebrate ['selɪbreɪt] **1** *vt* célébrer, fêter **2** *vi* faire la fête • **celebration** [-'breɪʃən] *n (event)* fête *f;* **the celebrations** les festivités *fpl*

celebrity [sə'lebrətɪ] *(pl* **-ies)** *n* célébrité *f*

celery ['selərɪ] *n* céleri *m*

cell [sel] *n* cellule *f*

cellar ['selə(r)] *n* cave *f*

cello ['tʃeləu] *(pl* **-os)** *n* violoncelle *m*

cellphone ['selfəun] *n Am* (téléphone *m*) portable *m*

cement [sɪ'ment] *n* ciment *m;* **c. mixer** bétonnière *f*

cemetery ['semətrɪ] *(pl* **-ies)** *n* cimetière *m*

censor ['sensə(r)] *vt* censurer

census ['sensəs] *n* recensement *m*

cent [sent] *n (coin)* cent *m*

center ['sentə(r)] *n Am* = **centre**

centigrade ['sentɪgreɪd] *adj* centigrade

centimetre ['sentɪmiːtə(r)] *n* centimètre *m*

central ['sentrəl] *adj* central; **C. London** le centre de Londres; **c. heating** chauffage *m* central

centre ['sentə(r)] *(Am* **center)** *n* centre *m*

century ['sentʃərɪ] *(pl* **-ies)** *n* siècle *m;* **in the twenty-first c.** au vingt-et-unième siècle

ceramic [sə'ræmɪk] *adj (tile)* en céramique

cereal ['sɪərɪəl] *n* céréale *f;* **(breakfast) c.** céréales *fpl*

ceremony ['serɪmənɪ] *(pl* **-ies)** *n (event)* cérémonie *f*

certain ['sɜːtən] *adj* **(a)** *(sure)* certain **(that** que); **she's c. to come, she'll come for c.** c'est certain qu'elle viendra; **to be c. of sth** être certain *ou* sûr de qch; **for c.** *(say, know)* avec certitude **(b)** *(particular, some)* certain; **c. people** certaines personnes • **certainly** *adv (undoubtedly)* certainement; *(yes)* bien sûr

certificate [sə'tɪfɪkɪt] *n* certificat *m; (from university)* diplôme *m*

chain [tʃeɪn] *n (of rings, mountains)* chaîne *f; (of events)* suite *f; (of toilet)* chasse *f* d'eau; **c. saw** tronçonneuse *f;* **c. store** magasin *m* à succursales multiples

chair [tʃeə(r)] **1** *n* chaise *f; (armchair)* fauteuil *m;* **c. lift** télésiège *m* **2** *vt (meeting)* présider • **chairman** *(pl* **-men), chairperson** *n* président, -e *mf*

chalet ['ʃæleɪ] *n* chalet *m*

chalk [tʃɔːk] *n* craie *f*

challenge ['tʃælɪndʒ] **1** *n* défi *m; (task)* challenge *m,* gageure *f* **2** *vt* défier **(sb to do** qn de faire); *(question, dispute)* contester

chamber ['tʃeɪmbə(r)] *n (room, assembly)* chambre *f* • **chambermaid** *n* femme *f* de chambre
champagne [ʃæm'peɪn] *n* champagne *m*
champion ['tʃæmpɪən] *n* champion, -onne *mf*; **c. skier, skiing c.** champion, -onne *mf* de ski • **championship** *n* championnat *m*
chance [tʃɑːns] *n (luck)* hasard *m*; *(possibility)* chance *f*; *(opportunity)* occasion *f*; **by c.** par hasard; **to have the c. to do sth** *or* **of doing sth** avoir l'occasion de faire qch; **to give sb a c.** donner une chance à qn; **to take a c.** tenter le coup
chancellor ['tʃɑːnsələ(r)] *n Pol* chancelier *m*
change [tʃeɪndʒ] **1** *n* changement *m*; *(money)* monnaie *f*; **for a c.** pour changer; **a c. of clothes** des vêtements de rechange **2** *vt (modify)* changer; *(exchange)* échanger (**for** pour *ou* contre); *(money)* changer (**into** en); *(transform)* changer, transformer (**into** en); **to c. trains/colour/one's skirt** changer de train/de couleur/de jupe; **to c. gear** *(in vehicle)* changer de vitesse; **to c. the subject** changer de sujet; **to get changed** *(put on other clothes)* se changer **3** *vi (alter)* changer; *(change clothes)* se changer; **to c. into sth** *(be transformed)* se changer *ou* se transformer en qch; **she changed into a dress** elle a mis une robe; **to c. over** passer (**from** de; **to** à) • **changing** *n* **c. room** vestiaire *m*; *(in shop)* cabine *f* d'essayage
channel ['tʃænəl] *n (on television)* chaîne *f*; *(of communication, distribution)* canal *m*; *Geog* **the C.** la Manche; **the C. Islands** les îles Anglo-Normandes; **the C. Tunnel** le tunnel sous la Manche
chant [tʃɑːnt] **1** *vt (slogan)* scander **2** *vi (of demonstrators)* scander des slogans
chaos ['keɪɒs] *n* chaos *m* • **chaotic** *adj (situation, scene)* chaotique
chapel ['tʃæpəl] *n* chapelle *f*
chapped ['tʃæpt] *adj (hands, lips)* gercé
chapter ['tʃæptə(r)] *n* chapitre *m*
character ['kærɪktə(r)] *n (of person, place)* caractère *m*; *(in book, film)* personnage *m*; *(unusual person)* personnage *m* • **characteristic** *adj & n* caractéristique *(f)*
charge¹ [tʃɑːdʒ] **1** *n* **to take c. of sth** prendre qch en charge; **to be in c. of** être responsable de **2** *vt (battery)* charger; *Law (accuse)* inculper (**with** de) • **charger** *n (for battery)* chargeur *m*
charge² [tʃɑːdʒ] **1** *n (cost)* prix *m*; **charges** *(expenses)* frais *mpl* **2** *vt (amount)* demander (**for** pour); **to c. sb** faire payer qn
charity ['tʃærɪtɪ] *(pl* **-ies)** *n (kindness, money)* charité *f*; *(society)* œuvre *f* de charité
charm [tʃɑːm] *n (attractiveness)* charme *m*; *(trinket)* breloque *f* • **charming** *adj* charmant
chart [tʃɑːt] *n (map)* carte *f*; *(table)* tableau *m*; *(graph)* graphique *m*; **(pop) charts** hit-parade *m*
chase [tʃeɪs] **1** *vt* poursuivre; **to c. sb away** chasser qn **2** *vi* **to c. after sb/sth** courir après qn/qch
chat [tʃæt] **1** *n* petite conversation *f*; **to have a c.** causer (**with** avec); *Comptr* **c. room** site *m* de bavardage **2** *(pt & pp* **-tt-)** *vi* causer (**with** avec); *Comptr* bavarder **3** *vt Br Fam* **to c. sb up** draguer qn • **chatty** *(*-ier, -iest*) adj* bavard
chatter ['tʃætə(r)] *vi (of person)*

bavarder; **his teeth were chattering** il claquait des dents

chauffeur ['∫əʊfə(r)] *n* chauffeur *m*

cheap [t∫i:p] **1** (**-er, -est**) *adj* bon marché *inv*, pas cher (*f* pas chère); *(rate, fare)* réduit; *(worthless)* sans valeur; **cheaper** meilleur marché *inv*, moins cher (*f* moins chère) **2** *adv (buy)* (à) bon marché, au rabais • **cheaply** *adv* (à) bon marché

cheat [t∫i:t] **1** *n* tricheur, -euse *mf* **2** *vi* tricher

check [t∫ek] **1** *n* vérification *f* (**on** de); *(inspection)* contrôle *m*; *Am (restaurant bill)* addition *f*; *Am (cheque)* chèque *m* **2** *vt (examine)* vérifier; *(inspect)* contrôler; *Am (baggage)* mettre à la consigne **3** *vi* vérifier; **to c. on sth** vérifier qch; **to c. on sb** surveiller qn • **checkbook** *n Am* carnet *m* de chèques • **check-in** *n (at airport)* enregistrement *m* (des bagages) • **checklist** *n* liste *f* de contrôle • **checkout** *n (in supermarket)* caisse *f* • **checkup** *n (medical)* bilan *m* de santé; **to have a c.** faire un bilan de santé

►**check in 1** *vt sep (luggage)* enregistrer **2** *vi (arrive)* arriver; *(sign in)* signer le registre; *(at airport)* se présenter à l'enregistrement

►**check out 1** *vt sep (confirm)* confirmer **2** *vi (at hotel)* régler sa note

checked [t∫ekt] *adj* à carreaux

checkers ['t∫ekərz] *npl Am* jeu *m* de dames

cheddar ['t∫edə(r)] *n* cheddar *m*

cheek [t∫i:k] *n* (**a**) *(of face)* joue *f* (**b**) *Br (impudence)* culot *m* • **cheeky** (**-ier, -iest**) *adj Br (person, reply)* insolent

cheer [t∫ɪə(r)] **1** *n* **cheers** *(shouts)* acclamations *fpl*; *Fam* **cheers!** *(when drinking)* à votre santé!; *(thanks)* merci! **2** *vt (applaud)* acclamer; **to c. sb up** *(comfort)* remonter le moral à qn; *(amuse)* faire sourire qn **3** *vi* applaudir; **to c. up** reprendre courage; **c. up!** (du) courage! • **cheerful** *adj* gai

cheerio [t∫ɪərɪ'əʊ] *exclam Br Fam* salut!, au revoir!

cheese [t∫i:z] *n* fromage *m* • **cheeseburger** *n* cheeseburger *m* • **cheesecake** *n* cheesecake *m*, tarte *f* au fromage blanc

chef [∫ef] *n* chef *m* (cuisinier)

chemical 1 *adj* chimique **2** *n* produit *m* chimique

chemist ['kemɪst] *n Br (pharmacist)* pharmacien, -enne *mf*; *(scientist)* chimiste *mf*; *Br* **c.'s (shop)** pharmacie *f* • **chemistry** *n* chimie *f*

cheque [t∫ek] *n Br* chèque *m* • **chequebook** *n Br* carnet *m* de chèques

cherry ['t∫erɪ] (*pl* **-ies**) *n* cerise *f*

chess [t∫es] *n* échecs *mpl* • **chessboard** *n* échiquier *m*

chest [t∫est] *n* (**a**) *(part of body)* poitrine *f* (**b**) *(box)* coffre *m*; **c. of drawers** commode *f*

chestnut ['t∫estnʌt] *n (nut)* châtaigne *f*; *(cooked)* marron *m*

chew [t∫u:] **1** *vt* **to c. (up)** mâcher **2** *vi* mastiquer • **chewing gum** *n* chewing-gum *m*

chicken ['t∫ɪkɪn] *n* poulet *m* • **chick** *n (chicken)* poussin *m* • **chickenpox** *n* varicelle *f*

chickpea ['t∫ɪkpi:] *n* pois *m* chiche

chief [t∫i:f] **1** *n* chef *m* **2** *adj Com* **c. executive** directeur *m* général

child [t∫aɪld] (*pl* **children**) *n* enfant *mf*; **c. care** *(for working parents)* garde *f* d'enfants; *Br* **c. minder** nourrice *f* • **childhood** *n* enfance *f* • **childish** *adj* puéril • **childlike** *adj* enfantin • **childproof** *adj* *(lock, bottle)* que les enfants ne peuvent pas ouvrir

chill [tʃɪl] *vt (wine, melon)* mettre au frais • **chilly (-ier, -iest)** *adj* froid; **it's c.** il fait (un peu) froid

chilli ['tʃɪlɪ] *(pl* -**is** *or* -**ies**) *n (vegetable)* piment *m; (dish)* chili *m* con carne; **c. powder** ≈ chili *m*

chimney ['tʃɪmnɪ] *(pl* -**eys**) *n* cheminée *f*

chimpanzee [tʃɪmpæn'ziː] *n* chimpanzé *m*

chin [tʃɪn] *n* menton *m*

China ['tʃaɪnə] *n* la Chine • **Chinese 1** *adj* chinois **2** *n inv (person)* Chinois, -e *mf; (language)* chinois *m*

china ['tʃaɪnə] **1** *n inv* porcelaine *f* **2** *adj* en porcelaine

chip [tʃɪp] **1** *n (splinter)* éclat *m; (break)* ébréchure *f; Comptr* puce *f*; **chips** *Br (French fries)* frites *fpl; Am (crisps)* chips *fpl; Br* **c. shop** = ̶b̶o̶u̶t̶i̶q̶u̶e̶ ̶o̶ù̶ ̶l̶'̶o̶n̶ ̶v̶e̶n̶d̶ ̶d̶u̶ ̶p̶o̶i̶s̶s̶o̶n̶ pané et des frites **2** *(pt & pp* -**pp**-) *vt (cup)* ébrécher; *(paint)* écailler

chisel ['tʃɪzəl] *n* ciseau *m*

chives [tʃaɪvz] *npl* ciboulette *f*

chlorine ['klɔriːn] *n* chlore *m*

chocolate ['tʃɒklɪt] **1** *n* chocolat *m*; **hot c.** chocolat *m* chaud; **plain c.** chocolat *m* noir **2** *adj (made of chocolate)* en chocolat; *(chocolate-flavoured)* au chocolat

choice [tʃɔɪs] *n* choix *m*; **to make a c.** choisir

choir ['kwaɪə(r)] *n* chœur *m*

choke [tʃəʊk] **1** *vt* étrangler **2** *vi* **she choked on a fishbone** elle a failli s'étouffer avec une arête

choose [tʃuːz] **1** *(pt* **chose**, *pp* **chosen)** *vt* choisir; **to c. to do sth** choisir de faire qch **2** *vi* choisir

chop [tʃɒp] **1** *n (of lamb, pork)* côtelette *f* **2** *(pt & pp* -**pp**-) *vt (wood)* couper (à la hache); *(food)* couper en morceaux; *(finely)* hacher; **to c. down** *(tree)* abattre; **to c. off** *(branch, finger)* couper; **to c. up** couper en morceaux

chopsticks ['tʃɒpstɪks] *npl* baguettes *fpl (pour manger)*

chord [kɔːd] *n Mus* accord *m*

chore [tʃɔː(r)] *n* corvée *f*; **(household) chores** travaux *mpl* ménagers

chorus ['kɔːrəs] *n (of song)* refrain *m*

chose [tʃəʊz] *pt of* **choose** • **chosen** ['tʃəʊzən] *pp of* **choose**

Christ [kraɪst] *n* le Christ • **Christian** ['krɪstʃən] *adj & n* chrétien, -enne *(mf)*; **C. name** prénom *m*

christen ['krɪsən] *vt* baptiser • **christening** *n* baptême *m*

Christmas ['krɪsməs] **1** *n* Noël *m*; **at C. (time)** à Noël; **Merry** *or* **Happy C.!** Joyeux Noël! **2** *adj (tree, card, Day, party)* de Noël

chronic ['krɒnɪk] *adj* chronique

chubby ['tʃʌbɪ] **(-ier, -iest)** *adj (person)* potelé; *(cheeks)* rebondi

chuck [tʃʌk] *vt Fam (throw)* lancer; *(boyfriend, girlfriend)* plaquer; *Br* **to c. in** *(give up)* laisser tomber; **to c. out** *(throw away)* balancer; *(from house, school, club)* vider

chuckle ['tʃʌkəl] *vi* rire tout bas

chunk [tʃʌŋk] *n* (gros) morceau *m*

church [tʃ3ːtʃ] *n* église *f*; **to go to c.** aller à l'église; **c. hall** salle *f* paroissiale • **churchyard** *n* cimetière *m*

churn [tʃ3ːn] *vt Pej* **to c. out** produire en série

chute [ʃuːt] *n Br (in pool, playground)* toboggan *m; (for rubbish)* vide-ordures *m inv*

cider ['saɪdə(r)] *n* cidre *m*

cigar [sɪ'gɑː(r)] *n* cigare *m*
cigarette [sɪgə'ret] *n* cigarette *f*; **c. end** mégot *m*
cinema ['sɪnəmə] *n (art)* cinéma *m*; *Br (place)* cinéma; *Br* **to go to the c.** aller au cinéma
cinnamon ['sɪnəmən] *n* cannelle *f*
circle ['sɜːkəl] *n (shape, group, range)* cercle *m*; *Theatre* balcon *m* • **circular** *adj* circulaire
circuit ['sɜːkɪt] *n (electrical, route for motor racing)* circuit *m*
circulate ['sɜːkjʊleɪt] **1** *ut* faire circuler **2** *vi* circuler • **circulation** [-'leɪʃən] *n (of air, blood)* circulation *f*; *(of newspaper)* tirage *m*
circumstance ['sɜːkəmstæns] *n* circonstance *f*; **in** or **under the circumstances** étant donné les circonstances
circus ['sɜːkəs] *n* cirque *m*
citizen ['sɪtɪzən] *n* citoyen, -enne *mf*
citrus ['sɪtrəs] *adj* **c. fruit(s)** agrumes *mpl*
city ['sɪtɪ] *(pl* **-ies)** *n* (grande) ville *f*, cité *f*; **c. centre** centre-ville *m*; *Am* **c. hall** hôtel *m* de ville
civil ['sɪvəl] *adj* **(a)** *(rights, war)* civil; **c. servant** fonctionnaire *mf*; **c. service** fonction *f* publique **(b)** *(polite)* civil • **civilian** [-'vɪlɪən] *adj & n* civil, -e *(mf)* • **civilization** [-'zeɪʃən] *n* civilisation *f*
claim [kleɪm] *ut (as a right)* réclamer, revendiquer; *(payment, benefit)* demander à bénéficier de; **to c. that...** *(assert)* prétendre que...
clam [klæm] *n* palourde *f*
clamp [klæmp] **1** *n (clip-like)* pince *f*; **(wheel) c.** *(for vehicle)* sabot *m* (de Denver) **2** *ut* serrer; *(vehicle)* mettre un sabot à **3** *vi* **to c. down on** sévir contre
clan [klæn] *n also Fig* clan *m*

clap [klæp] *(pt & pp* **-pp-)** *vti* **to c. (one's hands)** applaudir
clarify ['klærɪfaɪ] *(pt & pp* **-ied)** *ut* clarifier
clarinet [klærɪ'net] *n* clarinette *f*
clarity ['klærətɪ] *n (of argument)* clarté *f*; *(of sound)* pureté *f*
clash [klæʃ] **1** *n (of interests)* conflit *m*; *(of events)* coïncidence *f* **2** *vi (of objects)* s'entrechoquer; *(of interests)* s'affronter; *(of colours)* jurer (**with** avec); *(coincide)* tomber en même temps (**with** que)
clasp [klɑːsp] *ut (hold)* serrer; **to c. one's hands** joindre les mains
class [klɑːs] **1** *n* classe *f*; *(lesson)* cours *m* **2** *ut* classer (**as** comme) • **classmate** *n* camarade *mf* de classe • **classroom** *n* (salle *f* de) classe *f*
classic ['klæsɪk] **1** *adj* classique **2** *n (writer, work)* classique *m* • **classical** *adj* classique
classify ['klæsɪfaɪ] *(pt & pp* **-ied)** *ut* classer • **classification** *n* classification *f* • **classified** *adj (information)* confidentiel, -elle; **c. advertisement** petite annonce *f*
classy ['klɑːsɪ] *(-ier, -iest) adj Fam* chic *inv*
clause [klɔːz] *n (in sentence)* proposition *f*; *(in contract)* clause *f*
claustrophobic [klɔːstrə'fəʊbɪk] *adj (person)* claustrophobe; *(room, atmosphere)* oppressant
claw [klɔː] *n (of crab)* pince *f*; *(of cat, sparrow)* griffe *f*; *(of eagle)* serre *f*
clay [kleɪ] *n* argile *f*
clean [kliːn] **1** *(-er, -est) adj* propre; **to come c.** tout avouer **2** *adv (utterly)* complètement **3** *ut* nettoyer; *(wash)* laver; **to c. one's teeth** se brosser *ou* se laver les dents; **to c. out** *(room)* nettoyer à fond; *(empty)* vider; **to**

c. up nettoyer 4 *vi* **to c. (up)** faire le nettoyage • **cleaner** *n* femme *f* de ménage; **(dry) c.** teinturier, -ère *mf* • **cleaning** *n* nettoyage *m*; *(housework)* ménage *m*; **c. lady** femme *f* de ménage

cleanse [klenz] *vt (wound, skin)* nettoyer

clear [klɪə(r)] **1** (**-er, -est**) *adj (sky, water, sound, thought)* clair; *(glass)* transparent; *(outline, photo, skin)* net (*f* nette); *(road)* libre; *(obvious)* évident, clair; **to make oneself c.** se faire comprendre; **it is c. that...** il est évident *ou* clair que... **2** *adv* **to steer c. of** se tenir à l'écart de; **to get c. of** *(away from)* s'éloigner de **3** *vt (table)* débarrasser; *(road, area)* dégager; **to c. one's throat** s'éclaircir la gorge • **clearly** *adv (explain, write)* clairement; *(see, understand)* bien; *(obviously)* évidemment

▶**clear away** *vt sep (remove)* enlever

▶**clear off** *vi Fam (leave)* filer

▶**clear out** *vt sep (empty)* vider; *(remove)* enlever

▶**clear up 1** *vt sep (mystery)* éclaircir; *(room)* ranger **2** *vi (of weather)* s'éclaircir; *(tidy)* ranger

clench [klentʃ] *vt* **to c. one's fist/teeth** serrer le poing/les dents

clergy ['klɜːdʒɪ] *n* clergé *m*

clerk [*Br* klɑːk, *Am* klɜːk] *n* employé, -e *mf* de bureau; *Am (in store)* vendeur, -euse *mf* • **clerical** ['klerɪkəl] *adj (work)* de bureau

clever ['klevə(r)] (**-er, -est**) *adj* intelligent; *(shrewd)* astucieux, -euse; *(skilful)* habile (**at sth à** qch; **at doing** à faire); *(ingenious)* *(machine, plan)* ingénieux, -euse • **cleverly** *adv* intelligemment; *(ingeniously)* astucieusement; *(skilfully)* habilement

cliché ['kliːʃeɪ] *n* cliché *m*

click [klɪk] **1** *n* bruit *m* sec **2** *vi* faire un bruit sec; *Fam* **it suddenly clicked** ça a fait tilt

client ['klaɪənt] *n* client, -e *mf*

cliff [klɪf] *n* falaise *f*

climate ['klaɪmɪt] *n* climat *m*

climax ['klaɪmæks] *n* point *m* culminant

climb [klaɪm] **1** *vt* **to c. (up)** *(steps, hill)* gravir; *(mountain)* faire l'ascension de; *(tree, ladder)* grimper à; **to c. (over)** *(wall)* escalader; **to c. down (from)** *(wall, tree)* descendre de; *(hill)* descendre **2** *vi* **to c. (up)** *(steps, tree, hill)* monter; **to c. down** descendre • **climber** *n (mountaineer)* alpiniste *mf*; *(on rocks)* varappeur, -euse *mf* • **climbing** *n* **(mountain) c.** alpinisme *m*; **(rock-)c.** varappe *f*

cling [klɪŋ] (*pt & pp* **clung**) *vi* s'accrocher (**to à**)

clinic ['klɪnɪk] *n Br (private)* clinique *f*; *(part of hospital)* service *m*

clip [klɪp] **1** *n* (**a**) *(for paper)* trombone *m*; *(fastener)* attache *f*; *(for hair)* pince *f* (**b**) *(of film)* extrait *m* **2** (*pt & pp* **-pp-**) *vt (paper)* attacher *(avec un trombone)*; *(cut)* couper; **to c. (on)** *(attach)* attacher (**to à**) **3** *vi* **to c. together** s'emboîter • **clipping** *n (from newspaper)* coupure *f*

clique [kliːk] *n Pej* clique *f*

cloak [kləʊk] *n* cape *f* • **cloakroom** *n* vestiaire *m*; *Br (toilets)* toilettes *fpl*

clock [klɒk] *n (large)* horloge *f*; *(small)* pendule *f*; **round the c.** vingt-quatre heures sur vingt-quatre; **to put the clocks forward/back** *(in spring, autumn)* avancer/retarder les pendules; **c. radio** radio-réveil *m* • **clockwise** *adv* dans le sens des aiguilles d'une montre • **clockwork 1** *adj* *(toy)* mécanique **2** *n* **to go like c.** marcher comme sur des roulettes

clog [klɒg] **1** *n (shoe)* sabot *m* **2** *(pt & pp* -gg-*) vt* **to c. (up)** *(obstruct)* boucher

close¹ [kləʊs] **1** (-er, -est) *adj (in distance, time, relationship)* proche; *(collaboration, resemblance, connection)* étroit; *(friend)* intime; *(contest)* serré; *Br* **it's c.** *(of weather)* il fait lourd; **c. to** *(near)* près de, proche de; **that was a c. shave** *or* **call** il s'en est fallu de peu **2** *adv* **c. (by)** tout près; **we sat c. together** nous étions assis serrés les uns contre les autres; **to follow c. behind** suivre de près • **close-fitting** *adj (clothes)* ajusté • **close-up** *n* gros plan *m*

close² [kləʊz] **1** *vt (door, shop, account, book, eye)* fermer; *(road)* barrer; *(gap)* réduire **2** *vi (of door)* se fermer; *(of shop)* fermer • **closed** *adj (door, shop)* fermé; **c.-circuit television** télévision *f* en circuit fermé • **closing 1** *n* fermeture *f* **2** *adj (remarks)* dernier, -ère; **c. date** *(for application)* date *f* limite; **c. time** heure *f* de fermeture

►**close down** *vt sep & vi (business, factory)* fermer (définitivement)

closet [klɒzɪt] *n Am (cupboard)* placard *m*; *(wardrobe)* penderie *f*

cloth [klɒθ] *n* tissu *m*; *(for dusting)* chiffon *m*; *(for dishes)* torchon *m*

clothes [kləʊðz] *npl* vêtements *mpl*; **to put one's c. on** s'habiller; **to take one's c. off** se déshabiller; **c. line** corde *f* à linge; *Br* **c. peg**, *Am* **c. pin** pince *f* à linge; **c. shop** magasin *m* de vêtements • **clothing** *n* vêtements *mpl*

cloud [klaʊd] *n* nuage *m* • **cloudy** (-ier, -iest) *adj (weather, sky)* nuageux, -euse; *(liquid)* trouble

clove [kləʊv] *n (spice)* clou *m* de girofle; **c. of garlic** gousse *f* d'ail

clover ['kləʊvə(r)] *n* trèfle *m*

clown [klaʊn] **1** *n* clown *m* **2** *vi* **to c. around** *or* **about** faire le clown

club [klʌb] **1** *n* **(a)** *(society)* club *m* **(b)** *(nightclub)* boîte *f* de nuit **(c)** *(weapon)* massue *f*; *(in golf)* club *m* **(d)** **clubs** *(in cards)* trèfle *m* **2** *(pt & pp* -bb-*) vi Br* **to c. together** se cotiser **(to buy** pour acheter)

clue [kluː] *n* indice *m*; *(of crossword)* définition *f*; *Fam* **I haven't a c.** je n'en ai pas la moindre idée

clumsy ['klʌmzɪ] (-ier, -iest) *adj* maladroit

clung [klʌŋ] *pt & pp of* **cling**

cluster ['klʌstə(r)] **1** *n* groupe *m* **2** *vi* se grouper

clutch [klʌtʃ] **1** *n (in car)* embrayage *m*; *(pedal)* pédale *f* d'embrayage **2** *vt* tenir fermement

clutter ['klʌtə(r)] **1** *n (objects)* désordre *m* **2** *vt* **to c. (up)** *(room, table)* encombrer **(with** de)

cm *(abbr* **centimetre(s))** cm

Co *(abbr* **company)** Cie

co- [kəʊ] *pref* co-

c/o *(abbr* **care of)** *(on envelope)* chez

coach [kəʊtʃ] **1** *n* **(a)** *Br (train carriage)* voiture *f*, wagon *m*; *Br (bus)* car *m*; *(horse-drawn)* carrosse *m* **(b)** *(for sports)* entraîneur, -euse *mf* **2** *vt (athlete, team)* entraîner

coal [kəʊl] *n* charbon *m* • **coalmine** *n* mine *f* de charbon

coarse [kɔːs] (-er, -est) *adj (person, manners)* grossier, -ère, vulgaire; *(surface, fabric)* grossier, -ère

coast [kəʊst] *n* côte *f*

coat [kəʊt] **1** *n* manteau *m*; *(of animal)* pelage *m*; *(of paint)* couche *f*; **c. hanger** cintre *m* **2**

vt couvrir (**with** de) • **coating** *n* couche *f*

coax [kəʊks] *vt* **to c. sb to do** *or* **into doing sth** amener qn à faire qch par des cajoleries

cobbled ['kɒbəld] *adj (street)* pavé

cobweb ['kɒbweb] *n* toile *f* d'araignée

cock [kɒk] *n (rooster)* coq *m* • **cockerel** *n* jeune coq *m*

cockney ['kɒknɪ] *adj & n* cockney *(mf) (natif des quartiers est de Londres)*

cockpit ['kɒkpɪt] *n (of aircraft)* cabine *f* de pilotage, cockpit *m*

cockroach ['kɒkrəʊtʃ] *n* cafard *m*

cocktail ['kɒkteɪl] *n* cocktail *m*; **c. party** cocktail *m*

cocky ['kɒkɪ] **(-ier, -iest)** *adj Fam* culotté

cocoa ['kəʊkəʊ] *n* cacao *m*

coconut ['kəʊkənʌt] *n* noix *f* de coco

cod [kɒd] *n* cabillaud *m*

code [kəʊd] *n* code *m*; **in c.** *(letter, message)* codé

coffee ['kɒfɪ] *n* café *m*; **c. with milk,** *Br* **white c.** café *m* au lait; **black c.** café *m* noir; *Br* **c. bar, c. house** café *m*; **c. break** pause-café *f*; **c. table** table *f* basse

coffin ['kɒfɪn] *n* cercueil *m*

coherent [kəʊ'hɪərənt] *adj (logical)* cohérent; *(way of speaking)* compréhensible, intelligible

coil [kɔɪl] *n (of rope)* rouleau *m*

coin [kɔɪn] *n* pièce *f* (de monnaie)

coincidence [kəʊ'ɪnsɪdəns] *n* coïncidence *f*

colander ['kʌləndə(r)] *n (for vegetables)* passoire *f*

cold [kəʊld] **1 (-er, -est)** *adj* froid; **to be** *or* **feel c.** *(of person)* avoir froid; **my hands are c.** j'ai froid aux mains; **it's c.** *(of weather)* il

fait froid; **to get c.** *(of weather)* se refroidir; *(of food)* refroidir; *Br* **c. meats,** *Am* **c. cuts** viandes *fpl* froides **2** *n* **(a)** *(temperature)* froid *m* **(b)** *(illness)* rhume *m*; **to have a c.** être enrhumé; **to get a c.** s'enrhumer

collaborate [kə'læbəreɪt] *vi* collaborer **(on** à**)** • **collaboration** [-'reɪʃən] *n* collaboration *f*

collapse [kə'læps] *vi (of building)* s'effondrer; *(faint)* s'évanouir; *(of government)* tomber

collar ['kɒlə(r)] *n (on garment)* col *m*; *(of dog)* collier *m*

colleague ['kɒliːg] *n* collègue *mf*

collect [kə'lekt] **1** *vt (pick up)* ramasser; *(gather)* rassembler; *(stamps)* collectionner; **to c. sb** *(pick up)* passer prendre qn **2** *adv Am* **to call sb c.** téléphoner à qn en PCV • **collection** *n (of objects, stamps)* collection *f* • **collector** *n (of objects, stamps)* collectionneur, -euse *mf*

college ['kɒlɪdʒ] *n Br (of further education)* établissement *m* d'enseignement supérieur; *Am (university)* université *f*; **to be at c.** être étudiant

collide [kə'laɪd] *vi* entrer en collision **(with** avec**)** • **collision** *n* collision *f*

colloquial [kə'ləʊkwɪəl] *adj* familier, -ère

colon ['kəʊlən] *n (punctuation mark)* deux-points *m*

colonel ['kɜːnəl] *n* colonel *m*

colony ['kɒlənɪ] **(pl -ies)** *n* colonie *f*

colour ['kʌlə(r)] *(Am* **color) 1** *n* couleur *f* **2** *adj (photo, television)* en couleurs **3** *vt* colorer; **to c. (in)** *(drawing)* colorier • **colour-blind** *(Am* **color-blind)** *adj* daltonien, -enne • **coloured** *(Am* **colored)**

adj (person, pencil) de couleur; *(glass)* coloré • **colourful** *(Am* **colorful)** *adj (crowd, story)* coloré; *(person)* pittoresque • **colouring** *(Am* **coloring)** *n (shade, effect)* coloris *m*; **c. book** album *m* de coloriages

column ['kɒləm] *n* colonne *f*; *(newspaper feature)* rubrique *f*

coma ['kəʊmə] *n* **in a c.** dans le coma

comb [kəʊm] **1** *n* peigne *m* **2** *vt* **to c. one's hair** se peigner

combat ['kɒmbæt] *n* combat *m*

combine [kəm'baɪn] *vt (activities, qualities, elements, sounds)* combiner; *(efforts)* joindre, unir • **combination** [kɒmbɪ'neɪʃən] *n* combinaison *f*; **c. lock** serrure *f* à combinaison

come [kʌm] *(pt* **came,** *pp* **come)** *vi* venir **(from** de; **to** à); **to c. home** rentrer (à la maison); **to c. first** *(in race, exam)* se classer premier; **c. and see me** viens me voir; **to c. near** *or* **close to doing sth** faillir faire qch • **comeback** *n* **to make a c.** *(of actor, athlete)* faire un come-back • **coming 1** *adj (future) (years, election)* à venir; **the c. days** les prochains jours **2** *n* **comings and goings** allées *fpl* et venues *fpl*

▶**come about** *vi (happen)* arriver

▶**come across 1** *vi* **to c. across well/badly** bien/mal passer **2** *vt insep (find)* tomber sur

▶**come along** *vi* venir **(with** avec); *(progress)* avancer

▶**come back** *vi* revenir; *(return home)* rentrer

▶**come down 1** *vi* descendre; *(of rain, temperature, price)* tomber **2** *vt insep (stairs, hill)* descendre

▶**come down with** *vt insep (illness)* attraper

▶**come forward** *vi (make oneself known, volunteer)* se présenter

▶**come in** *vi (enter)* entrer; *(of train)* arriver; **to c. in useful** être bien utile

▶**come off 1** *vi (of button)* se détacher **2** *vt insep (fall from)* tomber de; *(get down from)* descendre de

▶**come on** *vi (make progress)* avancer; **c. on!** allez!

▶**come out** *vi* sortir; *(of sun, book)* paraître; *(of photo)* réussir

▶**come over** *vi (visit)* passer **(to** chez); **to c. over to** *(approach)* s'approcher de

▶**come round** *vi (visit)* passer **(to** chez); *(regain consciousness)* revenir à soi

▶**come to 1** *vi (regain consciousness)* revenir à soi **2** *vt insep (amount to)* revenir à; **to c. to a conclusion** arriver à une conclusion

▶**come up 1** *vi (rise)* monter; *(of question, job)* se présenter **2** *vt insep (stairs)* monter

▶**come upon** *vt insep (book, reference)* tomber sur

▶**come up to** *vt insep (reach)* arriver jusqu'à; *(approach)* s'approcher de

▶**come up with** *vt insep (idea, money)* trouver

comedy ['kɒmɪdɪ] *(pl* **-ies)** *n* comédie *f* • **comedian** [kə'miːdɪən] *n* comique *mf*

comet ['kɒmɪt] *n* comète *f*

comfort ['kʌmfət] **1** *n (ease)* confort *m*; *(consolation)* réconfort *m*, consolation *f* **2** *vt* consoler • **comfortable** *adj (chair, house)* confortable; *(rich)* aisé • **com-**

fortably *adv (sit)* confortablement; *(win)* facilement; **c. off** *(rich)* à l'aise financièrement

comic ['kɒmɪk] *n Br (magazine)* bande *f* dessinée, BD *f*; **c. strip** bande *f* dessinée • **comical** *adj* comique

comma ['kɒmə] *n* virgule *f*

command [kə'mɑːnd] **1** *n (order)* ordre *m*; *(authority)* commandement *m*; *(mastery)* maîtrise *f* (**of** de) **2** *vt (order)* commander (**sb to do** à qn de faire)

commemorate [kə'meməreɪt] *vt* commémorer • **commemoration** [-'reɪʃən] *n* commémoration *f*

comment ['kɒment] **1** *n* commentaire *m* (**on** sur) **2** *vi* faire des commentaires (**on** sur); **to c. on** *(text, event, news item)* commenter; **to c. that...** remarquer que... • **commentary** *(pl* **-ies)** *n* commentaire *m*; **live c.** *(on TV or radio)* reportage *m* en direct • **commentator** *n* commentateur, -trice *mf* (**on** de)

commercial [kə'mɜːʃəl] **1** *adj* commercial **2** *n (advertisement)* publicité *f*; **the commercials** la publicité

commiserate [kə'mɪzəreɪt] *vi* **to c. with sb** être désolé pour qn

commission [kə'mɪʃən] *n (fee, group)* commission *f*; *(order for work)* commande *f*

commit [kə'mɪt] *(pt & pp* **-tt-)** *vt (crime)* commettre; *(bind)* engager; **to c. suicide** se suicider; **to c. oneself** *(make a promise)* s'engager (**to** à) • **commitment** *n (duty, responsibility)* obligation *f*; *(promise)* engagement *m*; *(devotion)* dévouement *m* (**to** à)

committee [kə'mɪtɪ] *n* comité *m*

common ['kɒmən] **(-er, -est)**

adj (shared, vulgar) commun; *(frequent)* courant, commun; **in c.** *(shared)* en commun (**with** avec); **to have nothing in c.** n'avoir rien de commun (**with** avec); **c. room** *(for students)* salle *f* commune; *(for teachers)* salle *f* des professeurs; **c. sense** sens *m* commun, bon sens *m* • **Commonwealth** *n Br* **the C.** le Commonwealth

commotion [kə'məʊʃən] *n (disruption)* agitation *f*

communal [kə'mjuːnəl] *adj (shared) (bathroom, kitchen)* commun; *(of the community)* communautaire

communicate [kə'mjuːnɪkeɪt] **1** *vt* communiquer **2** *vi (of person)* communiquer (**with** avec) • **communication** [-'keɪʃən] *n* communication *f*

Communion [kə'mjuːnjən] *n* **(Holy) C.** communion

communist ['kɒmjʊnɪst] *adj & n* communiste *(mf)*

community [kə'mjuːnɪtɪ] **1** *(pl* **-ies)** *n* communauté *f*; **the student c.** les étudiants *mpl* **2** *adj (life, spirit)* communautaire; **c. centre** centre *m* socioculturel

commute [kə'mjuːt] *vi* **to c. (to work)** faire la navette entre son domicile et son travail • **commuter** *n* banlieusard, -e *mf*; **c. train** train *m* de banlieue

compact [kəm'pækt] *adj (car, crowd, substance)* compact; **c. disc** ['kɒmpækt] disque *m* compact

companion [kəm'pænjən] *n (person)* compagnon *m*, compagne *f*

company ['kʌmpənɪ] *(pl* **-ies)** *n (companionship)* compagnie *f*; *(guests)* invités *mpl*; *(business)* société *f*, compagnie *f*; **to keep sb c.** tenir compagnie à qn; **c. car** voiture *f* de société

compare [kəm'peə(r)] *vt* comparer (**with** *or* **to** à); **compared to** *or* **with** en comparaison de • **comparison** [-'pærɪsən] *n* comparaison *f* (**between** entre; **with** avec); **by** *or* **in c.** en comparaison

compartment [kəm'pɑːtmənt] *n* compartiment *m*

compass ['kʌmpəs] *n* (a) *(for direction)* boussole *f* (b) **(pair of) compasses** compas *m*

compassion [kəm'pæʃən] *n* compassion *f*

compatible [kəm'pætɪbəl] *adj* compatible

compensate ['kɒmpənseɪt] **1** *vt* **to c. sb** *(with payment, reward)* dédommager qn (**for** de) **2** *vi* compenser; **to c. for sth** *(make up for)* compenser qch • **compensation** [-'seɪʃən] *n (financial)* dédommagement *m*; *(consolation)* compensation *f*

compete [kəm'piːt] *vi (take part in race)* concourir (**in** à); **to c.** **(with sb)** rivaliser (avec qn); *(in business)* faire concurrence (à qn); **to c. for sth** se disputer qch

competent ['kɒmpɪtənt] *adj* *(capable)* compétent (**to do** pour faire)

competition [kɒmpə'tɪʃən] *n* (a) *(rivalry)* rivalité *f*; *(between companies)* concurrence *f* (b) *(contest)* concours *m*; *(in sport)* compétition *f* • **competitive** [kəm'petɪtɪv] *adj (price, market)* compétitif, -ive; *(person)* qui a l'esprit de compétition • **competitor** [kəm'petɪtə(r)] *n* concurrent, -e *mf*

compile [kəm'paɪl] *vt (list)* dresser; *(book, documents)* compiler

complain [kəm'pleɪn] *vi* se plaindre (**to sb** à qn; **of** *or* **about**

sb/sth de qn/qch; **that** que) • **complaint** *n* plainte *f*; *(in shop)* réclamation *f*; *(illness)* maladie *f*

complement ['kɒmplɪment] *vt* compléter

complete [kəm'pliːt] **1** *adj* *(whole)* complet, -ète; *(utter)* total; *(finished)* achevé **2** *vt (finish)* achever; *(form)* compléter • **completely** *adv* complètement

complex ['kɒmpleks] **1** *adj* complexe **2** *n (feeling, buildings)* complexe *m* • **complexion** [kəm'plekʃən] *n (of face)* teint *m*

complicate ['kɒmplɪkeɪt] *vt* compliquer • **complication** *n* complication *f*

compliment 1 ['kɒmplɪmənt] *n* compliment *m*; **to pay sb a c.** faire un compliment à qn **2** ['kɒmplɪment] *vt* **to c. sb on sth** *(bravery)* féliciter qn de qch; *(dress, haircut)* faire des compliments à qn sur qch • **complimentary** [-'mentərɪ] *adj* (a) *(praising)* élogieux, -euse (b) *(free)* gratuit; **c. ticket** billet *m* de faveur

compose [kəm'pəʊz] *vt* composer; **to c. oneself** se calmer • **composed** *adj* calme • **composer** *n (of music)* compositeur, -trice *mf*

compost ['kɒmpɒst] *n* compost *m*

compound ['kɒmpaʊnd] *n (word, substance)* composé *m*; *(area)* enclos *m*

comprehend [kɒmprɪ'hend] *vt* comprendre • **comprehensive 1** *adj* complet, -ète; *(study)* exhaustif, -ive; *(insurance)* tous risques *inv* **2** *adj & n Br* **c. (school)** ≃ établissement *m* d'enseignement secondaire *(n'opérant pas de sélection à l'entrée)*

compress [kəm'pres] *vt (gas, air)* comprimer

compromise [ˈkɒmprəmaɪz] **1** n compromis m **2** vt (person, security) compromettre **3** vi transiger (**on** sur)

compulsory [kəmˈpʌlsərɪ] adj obligatoire

computer [kəmˈpjuːtə(r)] **1** n ordinateur m **2** adj (program, system) informatique; (course, firm) d'informatique; **c. game** jeu m électronique; **c. science** informatique f • **computerized** adj informatisé • **computing** n informatique f

con [kɒn] Fam **1** n arnaque f; **c. man** arnaqueur m **2** (pt & pp -nn-) vt arnaquer; **to be conned** se faire arnaquer

conceal [kənˈsiːl] vt (hide) (object) dissimuler (**from sb** à qn); (plan, news) cacher (**from sb** à qn)

conceited [kənˈsiːtɪd] adj vaniteux, -euse

conceive [kənˈsiːv] **1** vt (idea, child) concevoir **2** vi (of woman) concevoir, **to c. of sth** concevoir qch

concentrate [ˈkɒnsəntreɪt] **1** vt concentrer (**on** sur) **2** vi se concentrer (**on** sur); **to c. on doing sth** s'appliquer à faire qch • **concentration** [-ˈtreɪʃən] n concentration f; **c. camp** camp m de concentration

concept [ˈkɒnsept] n concept m

concern [kənˈsɜːn] **1** n (matter) affaire f; (worry) inquiétude f; **his c. for** son souci de **2** vt concerner; **to be concerned about** (be worried) s'inquiéter de; **as far as I'm concerned...** en ce qui me concerne... • **concerned** adj (anxious) inquiet, -ète (**about/at** au sujet de); **the person c.** (in question) la personne dont il s'agit; (involved) la personne concernée

• **concerning** prep en ce qui concerne

concert [ˈkɒnsət] n concert m; **c. hall** salle f de concert

concise [kənˈsaɪs] adj concis

conclude [kənˈkluːd] **1** vt (end, settle) conclure; **to c. that...** (infer) conclure que... **2** vi (of event) se terminer (**with** par); (of speaker) conclure • **conclusion** n conclusion f

concoction [kənˈkɒkʃən] n (dish, drink) mixture f

concrete [ˈkɒŋkriːt] n béton m; **c. wall** mur m en béton

concussion [kənˈkʌʃən] n (injury) commotion f cérébrale

condemn [kənˈdem] vt condamner (**to** à); (building) déclarer inhabitable

condensation [kɒndenˈseɪʃən] n (mist) buée f

condition [kənˈdɪʃən] n (stipulation, circumstance) condition f; (state) état m, condition f; (disease) maladie f; **on the c. that...** à la condition que... (+ subjunctive); **in good c.** en bon état • **conditional** adj conditionnel, -elle • **conditioner** n (for hair) après-shampooing m

condo [ˈkɒndəʊ] (pl **-os**) n Am = **condominium**

condolences [kənˈdəʊlənsɪz] npl condoléances fpl

condom [ˈkɒndɒm] n préservatif m

condominium [kɒndəˈmɪnɪəm] n Am (building) immeuble m en copropriété; (apartment) appartement m en copropriété

condone [kənˈdəʊn] vt (overlook) fermer les yeux sur; (forgive) excuser

conduct 1 [ˈkɒndʌkt] n (behaviour, directing) conduite f **2** [kənˈdʌkt] vt (campaign, inquiry,

experiment) mener; *(orchestra)* diriger; **to c. oneself** se conduire
• **conductor** [-'dʌktə(r)] *n (of orchestra)* chef *m* d'orchestre; *Br (on bus)* receveur *m; Am (on train)* chef *m* de train
cone [kəʊn] *n* cône *m; (for ice cream)* cornet *m; Br* **traffic c.** cône de chantier
confectionery [kən'fekʃənərɪ] *n (sweets)* confiserie *f; (cakes)* pâtisserie *f*
conference ['kɒnfərəns] *n* conférence *f*; **press** or **news c.** conférence *f* de presse
confess [kən'fes] **1** *vt* avouer, confesser **(that** que; **to sb** à qn) **2** *vi* avouer; **to c. to sth** *(crime)* avouer *ou* confesser qch • **confession** *n* aveu *m*, confession *f; Rel* confession *f*; **to go to c.** aller à confesse
confetti [kən'fetɪ] *n* confettis *mpl*
confide [kən'faɪd] *vi* **to c. in sb** se confier à qn • **confidential** [kɒnfɪ'denʃəl] *adj* confidentiel, -elle
confidence ['kɒnfɪdəns] *n* confiance *f* **(in** en); **(self-)c.** confiance *f* en soi; **in c.** en confidence • **confident** *adj (smile, exterior)* confiant; **(self-)c.** sûr de soi
confine [kən'faɪn] *vt* **(a)** *(limit)* limiter **(to** à) **(b)** *(keep prisoner)* enfermer **(to/in** dans) • **confined** *adj (space)* réduit; **c. to bed** alité
confirm [kən'fɜːm] *vt* confirmer **(that** que) • **confirmation** [kɒnfə'meɪʃən] *n also Rel* confirmation *f*
confiscate ['kɒnfɪskeɪt] *vt* confisquer **(from** à)
conflict 1 ['kɒnflɪkt] *n* conflit *m* **2** [kən'flɪkt] *vi (of statement)* être en contradiction **(with** avec);

(of dates, events, programmes) tomber en même temps **(with** que) • **conflicting** *adj (views, evidence)* contradictoire; *(dates)* incompatible
conform [kən'fɔːm] *vi (of person)* se conformer **(to** or **with** à); *(of ideas, actions)* être en conformité **(to** with)
confront [kən'frʌnt] *vt (danger)* affronter; *(problem)* faire face à; **to c. sb** *(be face to face with)* se trouver en face de qn; *(oppose)* s'opposer à qn; **to c. sb with sth** mettre qn en face de qch • **confrontation** [kɒnfrʌn'teɪʃən] *n* confrontation *f*
confuse [kən'fjuːz] *vt (make unsure)* embrouiller; **to c. sb/sth with** *(mistake for)* confondre qn/qch avec • **confused** *adj (situation, noises, idea)* confus; **to get c.** s'embrouiller • **confusing** *adj* déroutant • **confusion** [-ʒən] *n (bewilderment)* perplexité *f; (disorder, lack of clarity)* confusion *f*
congestion [kən'dʒestʃən] *n (traffic)* encombrements *mpl*
congratulate [kən'grætʃuleɪt] *vt* féliciter **(sb on sth** qn de qch; **sb on doing sth** qn d'avoir fait qch) • **congratulations** [-'leɪʃənz] *npl* félicitations *fpl* **(on** pour)
congregation [kɒŋgrɪ'geɪʃən] *n (worshippers)* fidèles *mpl*
Congress ['kɒŋgres] *n Am Pol* le Congrès *(assemblée législative américaine)*
conjunction [kən'dʒʌŋkʃən] *n* **in c. with** conjointement avec
connect [kə'nekt] *vt* relier **(with** or **to** à); *(telephone, washing machine)* brancher; **to c. sb with sb** *(on phone)* mettre qn en communication avec qn; **to c. sb/sth with sb/sth** établir

un lien entre qn/qch et qn/qch ● **connected** *adj (facts, events)* lié; **to be c. with** *(have to do with, relate to)* avoir un lien avec ● **connection** *n (link)* rapport *m*, lien *m* (**with** avec); *(train, bus)* correspondance *f*; *(electrical)* contact *m*; **connections** *(contacts)* relations *fpl*; **to have no c. with** n'avoir aucun rapport avec; **in c. with** à propos de

connotation [kɒnə'teɪʃən] *n* connotation *f*

conquer ['kɒŋkə(r)] *vt (country)* conquérir; *(enemy, difficulty)* vaincre

cons [kɒnz] *npl* **the pros and c.** le pour et le contre

conscience ['kɒnʃəns] *n* conscience *f*

conscientious [kɒnʃɪ'enʃəs] *adj* consciencieux, -euse

conscious ['kɒnʃəs] *adj (awake)* conscient; **c. of sth** *(aware)* conscient de qch ● **consciously** *adv (knowingly)* consciemment ● **consciousness** *n* **to lose/regain c.** perdre/reprendre connaissance

consecutive [kən'sekjʊtɪv] *adj* consécutif, -ive

consent [kən'sent] **1** *n* consentement *m* **2** *vi* consentir (**to** à)

consequence ['kɒnsɪkwəns] *n (result)* conséquence *f* ● **consequently** *adv* par conséquent

conservation [kɒnsə'veɪʃən] *n (of nature)* protection *f* de l'environnement

conservative [kən'sɜːvətɪv] **1** *adj (estimate)* modeste; *(view, attitude)* traditionnel, -elle; *(person)* traditionaliste; *Br Pol* conservateur, -trice **2** *n Br Pol* conservateur, -trice *mf*

conservatory [kən'sɜːvətrɪ] *(pl -ies) n Br (room)* véranda *f*

consider [kən'sɪdə(r)] *vt (think*

over) considérer; *(take into account)* tenir compte de; *(an offer)* étudier; **to c. doing sth** envisager de faire qch; **to c. that...** considérer que...; **I c. her (as) a friend** je la considère comme une amie; **considering (that)...** étant donné (que)... ● **considerable** *adj (large)* considérable; *(much)* beaucoup de ● **considerably** *adv* considérablement ● **considerate** *adj* attentionné (**to** à l'égard de) ● **consideration** [-'reɪʃən] *n* considération *f*; **to take sth into c.** prendre qch en considération

consist [kən'sɪst] *vi* consister (**of** en; **in** en; **in doing** à faire)

consistent [kən'sɪstənt] *adj (quality, results)* constant ● **consistency** *n (of substance)* consistance *f*

console¹ [kən'səʊl] *vt* consoler ● **consolation** *n* consolation *f*; **c. prize** lot *m* de consolation

console² ['kɒnsəʊl] *n (control desk)* console *f*

consonant ['kɒnsənənt] *n* consonne *f*

conspicuous [kən'spɪkjʊəs] *adj (noticeable)* bien visible; *(striking)* manifeste; *(showy)* voyant

conspiracy [kən'spɪrəsɪ] *(pl -ies) n* conspiration *f*

constable ['kɒnstəbəl] *n Br* **(police) c.** agent *m* de police

constant ['kɒnstənt] *adj (frequent)* incessant; *(unchanging)* constant ● **constantly** *adv* sans cesse

constellation [kɒnstə'leɪʃən] *n* constellation *f*

constipated ['kɒnstɪpeɪtɪd] *adj* constipé

constituency [kən'stɪtjʊənsɪ] *(pl -ies) n Pol* circonscription *f* électorale

constitution [kɒnstɪˈtjuːʃən] *n* constitution *f*

construct [kənˈstrʌkt] *vt* construire • **construction** *n* (building, structure, in grammar) construction *f*; **c. site** chantier *m* • **constructive** *adj* constructif, -ive

consulate [ˈkɒnsjʊlət] *n* consulat *m*

consult [kənˈsʌlt] *vt* consulter • **consultant** *n* (adviser) consultant *m*; *Br* (doctor) spécialiste *mf* • **consultation** [kɒnsəlˈteɪʃən] *n* consultation *f*

consume [kənˈsjuːm] *vt* consommer • **consumer** *n* consommateur, -trice *mf* • **consumption** [-ˈsʌmpʃən] *n* consommation *f*

contact [ˈkɒntækt] **1** *n* (act of touching) contact *m*; (person) relation *f*; **in c. with** en contact avec; **c. lenses** lentilles *fpl* de contact **2** *vt* contacter

contagious [kənˈteɪdʒəs] *adj* (disease) contagieux, -euse

contain [kənˈteɪn] *vt* (enclose, hold back) contenir • **container** *n* (box, jar) récipient *m*

contaminate [kənˈtæmɪneɪt] *vt* contaminer

contemplate [ˈkɒntəmpleɪt] *vt* (look at) contempler; (consider) envisager (**doing** de faire)

contemporary [kənˈtempərərɪ] *adj* contemporain (**with** de); (style) moderne

contempt [kənˈtempt] *n* mépris *m*

contend [kənˈtend] *vi* **to c. with** (problem) faire face à

content¹ [kənˈtent] *adj* (happy) satisfait (**with** de) • **contented** *adj* satisfait

content² [ˈkɒntent] *n* (of book, text, film) (subject matter) contenu *m*; **contents** contenu *m*; (in book) table *f* des matières

contest [ˈkɒntest] *n* concours *m* • **contestant** [kənˈtestənt] *n* concurrent, -e *mf*

context [ˈkɒntekst] *n* contexte *m*; **in/out of c.** en/hors contexte

continent [ˈkɒntɪnənt] *n* continent *m*; **the C.** l'Europe *f* continentale; **on the C.** en Europe • **continental** [-ˈnentəl] *adj* (of Europe) européen, -enne; **c. breakfast** petit déjeuner *m* à la française

contingency [kənˈtɪndʒənsɪ] (pl -ies) *n* éventualité *f*; **c. plan** plan *m* d'urgence

continue [kənˈtɪnjuː] **1** *vt* continuer (**to do** or **doing** à ou de faire); **to c. (with)** (work, speech) poursuivre; (resume) reprendre **2** *vi* continuer; (resume) reprendre • **continuous** *adj* continu; *Sch & Univ* **c. assessment** contrôle *m* continu des connaissances • **continuously** *adv* sans interruption

contour [ˈkɒntʊə(r)] *n* contour *m*

contraception [kɒntrəˈsepʃən] *n* contraception *f* • **contraceptive** *n* contraceptif *m*

contract¹ [ˈkɒntrækt] *n* contrat *m*

contract² [kənˈtrækt] *vi* (shrink) se contracter

contradict [kɒntrəˈdɪkt] *vt* (person, statement) contredire; (deny) démentir; **to c. oneself** se contredire • **contradictory** *adj* contradictoire

contraption [kənˈtræpʃən] *n* *Fam* machin *m*

contrary [ˈkɒntrərɪ] **1** *adv* **c. to** contrairement à **2** *n* contraire *m*; **on the c.** au contraire; **unless you/I/etc hear to the c.** sauf avis contraire

contrast 1 [ˈkɒntrɑːst] *n* contraste *m*; **in c. to** par opposition à **2** [kənˈtrɑːst] *vt* mettre en contraste

3 [kən'trɑːst] *vi* contraster (**with** avec)

contribute [kən'trɪbjuːt] **1** *vt* *(time, clothes)* donner (**to** à); *(article)* écrire (**to** pour); **to c. money to** verser de l'argent à **2** *vi* **to c. to** contribuer à; *(publication)* collaborer à; *(discussion)* prendre part à; *(charity)* donner à • **contribution** [kɒntrɪ'bjuːʃən] *n* contribution *f* • **contributor** *n (to newspaper)* collaborateur, -trice *mf*; *(of money)* donateur, -trice *mf*

contrive [kən'traɪv] *vt* **to c. to do sth** trouver moyen de faire qch

control [kən'trəʊl] **1** *n* contrôle *m*; *(authority)* autorité *f* (**over** sur); (**self-)c.** la maîtrise (de soi); **the situation** *or* **everything is under c.** je/il/*etc* contrôle la situation; **to lose c. of** *(situation, vehicle)* perdre le contrôle de; **out of c.** *(situation, crowd)* difficilement maîtrisable **2** *(pt & pp -ll-) vt (business, organization)* diriger, *(prices, quality)* contrôler; *(emotion, reaction)* maîtriser; *(disease)* enrayer; **to c. oneself** se contrôler

controversial [kɒntrə'vɜːʃəl] *adj* controversé

convenience [kən'viːnɪəns] *n* commodité *f*; **c. food(s)** plats *mpl* tout préparés • **convenient** *adj* commode, pratique; **to be c. (for)** *(suit)* convenir (à) • **conveniently** *adv* **c. situated** bien situé

convention [kən'venʃən] *n (custom)* usage *m*; *(agreement)* convention *f*; *(conference)* convention *f*, congrès *m* • **conventional** *adj* conventionnel, -elle

conversation [kɒnvə'seɪʃən] *n* conversation *f* (**with** avec)

convert [kən'vɜːt] *vt (change)* convertir (**into** *or* **to** en);

(building) aménager (**into** *or* **to** en); *Rel* **to c. sb** convertir qn (**to** à) • **conversion** *n* conversion *f*; *(of building)* aménagement *m*

convertible [kən'vɜːtəbəl] *n Aut* décapotable *f*

conveyor [kən'veɪə(r)] *n* **c. belt** tapis *m* roulant

convict 1 ['kɒnvɪkt] *n* détenu, -e *mf* **2** [kən'vɪkt] *vt* déclarer coupable (**of** de) • **conviction** [kən'vɪkʃən] *n (for crime)* condamnation *f*; *(belief)* conviction *f* (**that** que)

convince [kən'vɪns] *vt* convaincre (**of sth** de qch; **sb to do sth** qn de faire qch) • **convincing** *adj* *(argument, person)* convaincant

cook [kʊk] **1** *n (person)* cuisinier, -ère *mf* **2** *vt (meal)* préparer; *(food)* (faire) cuire **3** *vi (of food)* cuire; *(of person)* faire la cuisine • **cookbook** *n* livre *m* de cuisine • **cooker** *n Br (stove)* cuisinière *f* • **cookery** *n* cuisine *f*; *Br* **c. book** livre *m* de cuisine • **cooking** *n* *(activity, food)* cuisine *f*; *(process)* cuisson *f*; **to do the c.** faire la cuisine

cookie ['kʊkɪ] *n Am* biscuit *m*

cool [kuːl] **1** (**-er, -est**) *adj* *(weather, place, wind)* frais (*f* fraîche); *(tea, soup)* tiède; *(calm)* calme; *Fam (good)* cool *inv*; *Fam (fashionable)* branché; **a (nice) c. drink** une boisson (bien) fraîche; **the weather is c., it's c.** il fait frais; **to keep sth c.** tenir qch au frais **2** *vt* **to c. (down)** refroidir, rafraîchir **3** *vi* **to c. (down** *or* **off)** *(of hot liquid)* refroidir; *(of enthusiasm)* se refroidir; *(of angry person)* se calmer; **to c. off** *(by drinking, swimming)* se rafraîchir

cooperate [kəʊ'ɒpəreɪt] *vi*

coopérer (**in** à; **with** avec) •
cooperation n coopération f
coordinate [kəʊ'ɔːdɪneɪt] vt
coordonner • **coordination**
[-'neɪʃən] n coordination f
cop [kɒp] n Fam (policeman) flic m
cope [kəʊp] vi **to c. with** (problem,
demand) faire face à
copper ['kɒpə(r)] n cuivre m
copy ['kɒpɪ] **1** (pl **-ies**) n (of letter,
document) copie f; (of book,
magazine) exemplaire m; (of
photo) épreuve f **2** (pt & pp **-ied**)
vt copier; **to c. out** or **down** (text,
letter) copier
coral ['kɒrəl] n corail m
cord [kɔːd] n (**a**) (of curtain, bell)
cordon m; (electrical) cordon
électrique (**b**) **cords** (trousers)
pantalon m en velours côtelé •
cordless adj (phone) sans fil
corduroy ['kɔːdərɔɪ] n velours m
côtelé
core [kɔː(r)] n (of apple) trognon
m; (group of people) noyau m
cork [kɔːk] n (material) liège m;
(stopper) bouchon m • **corkscrew**
n tire-bouchon m
corn¹ [kɔːn] n Br (wheat) blé m;
Am (maize) maïs m
corn² [kɔːn] n (on foot) cor m
corner ['kɔːnə(r)] n (of street,
room, page, screen) coin m; (bend
in road) virage m; (in football)
corner m; **it's just round the c.**
c'est juste au coin; **c. shop** épicerie
f du coin
corny ['kɔːnɪ] (**-ier, -iest**) adj Fam
(joke) nul (f nulle); (film) tarte
corps [kɔː(r), pl kɔːz] n inv Mil &
Pol corps m
corpse [kɔːps] n cadavre m
correct [kə'rekt] **1** adj (accurate)
exact; (proper) correct; **he's c.**
il a raison; **the c. time** l'heure

exacte **2** vt corriger • **correction**
n correction f
correspond [kɒrɪ'spɒnd] vi
correspondre • **correspondence**
n correspondance f; **c. course**
cours m par correspondance •
corresponding adj (matching)
correspondant; (similar) semblable
corridor ['kɒrɪdɔː(r)] n couloir m
corrupt [kə'rʌpt] **1** adj corrompu
2 vt corrompre • **corruption** n
corruption f
Corsica ['kɔːsɪkə] n la Corse
cosmetic [kɒz'metɪk] **1** adj **c.
surgery** chirurgie f esthétique **2** n
produit m de beauté
cosmopolitan [kɒzmə'pɒlɪtən]
adj cosmopolite
cost [kɒst] **1** n coût m; **the c. of
living** le coût de la vie; **at any c.,
at all costs** à tout prix **2** (pt & pp
cost) vti coûter; **how much does
it c.?** ça coûte combien?
costume ['kɒstjuːm] n costume
m; Br (**swimming**) **c.** maillot m
de bain
cosy ['kəʊzɪ] (**-ier, -iest**) adj
Br (house) douillet, -ette;
(atmosphere) intime
cot [kɒt] n Br (for child) lit m
d'enfant; Am (camp bed) lit m de
camp
cottage ['kɒtɪdʒ] n petite maison
f de campagne; **c. cheese** fromage
m blanc (maigre)
cotton ['kɒtən] n coton m; (yarn)
fil m de coton; Br **c. wool,** Am
absorbent c. coton m hydrophile,
ouate f; Am **c. candy** barbe f à
papa
couch [kaʊtʃ] n (sofa) canapé m;
(for doctor's patient) lit m
cough [kɒf] **1** n toux f; **c. syrup** or
medicine, Br **c. mixture** sirop m
pour la toux **2** vi tousser
could [kʊd, unstressed kəd] pt

of **can¹** • **couldn't** [ˈkʊdənt] = **could not**

council [ˈkaʊnsəl] *n* **(town/city) c.** conseil *m* municipal; *Br* **c. flat/house** ≃ HLM *f*; *Br* **c. tax** = impôt regroupant taxe d'habitation et impôts locaux • **councillor** *n* **(town) c.** conseiller *m* municipal

count [kaʊnt] **1** *vt (find number of, include)* compter; *(consider)* considérer; **c. me in!** j'en suis!; **c. me out!** ne compte pas sur moi! **2** *vi* compter; **to c. on sb/sth** *(rely on)* compter sur qn/qch; **to c. on doing sth** compter faire qch • **countdown** *n* compte *m* à rebours

counter [ˈkaʊntə(r)] *n* **(a)** *(in shop, bar)* comptoir *m*; *(in bank)* guichet *m* **(b)** *(in games)* jeton *m*

counter- [ˈkaʊntə(r)] *pref* contre-**counterclockwise** [kaʊntə-ˈklɒkwaɪz] *adj & adv Am* dans le sens inverse des aiguilles d'une montre

counterfeit [ˈkaʊntəfɪt] *adj* faux (*f* fausse)

counterpart [ˈkaʊntəpɑːt] *n (thing)* équivalent *m*; *(person)* homologue *mf*

countless [ˈkaʊntlɪs] *adj* innombrable

country [ˈkʌntrɪ] (*pl* **-ies**) **1** *n* pays *m*; *(opposed to town)* campagne *f*; **in the c.** à la campagne **2** *adj (house, road)* de campagne; **c. (and western) music** country *f* • **countryside** *n* campagne *f*; **in the c.** à la campagne

county [ˈkaʊntɪ] (*pl* **-ies**) *n* comté *m*

coup [kuː, *pl* kuːz] *n Pol* coup *m* d'État

couple [ˈkʌpəl] *n (of people)* couple *m*; **a c. of** deux ou trois; *(a few)* quelques

coupon [ˈkuːpɒn] *n (for discount)* bon *m*; *(form)* coupon *m*

courage [ˈkʌrɪdʒ] *n* courage *m*

courgette [kʊəˈʒet] *n Br* courgette *f*

courier [ˈkʊrɪə(r)] *n (for tourists)* guide *mf*; *(messenger)* messager *m*

course [kɔːs] **1** *n* **(a)** *(of river, time, events)* cours *m*; **c. of action** ligne *f* de conduite; **in due c.** en temps utile **(b)** *(lessons)* cours *m* **(c)** *(of meal)* plat *m*; **first c.** entrée *f* **(d)** *(for race)* parcours *m*; *(for golf)* terrain *m* **2** *adv* **of c.!** bien sûr!; **of c. not!** bien sûr que non!

court [kɔːt] *n Law* cour *f*, tribunal *m*; *(for tennis)* court *m*; **to go to c.** aller en justice; **to take sb to c.** poursuivre qn en justice • **courtyard** *n* cour *f*

courtesy [ˈkɜːtəsɪ] (*pl* **-ies**) *n* politesse *f*, courtoisie *f*; **c. car** = voiture mise à la disposition d'un client par un hôtel, un garage etc

cousin [ˈkʌzən] *n* cousin, -e *mf*

cover [ˈkʌvə(r)] **1** *n (lid)* couvercle *m*; *(of book)* couverture *f*; *(for furniture, typewriter)* housse *f*; **to take c.** se mettre à l'abri; **under c.** *(sheltered)* à l'abri **2** *vt* couvrir **(with** *or* **in** de); *(include)* englober; *(treat)* traiter; *(distance)* parcourir; **to c. up** recouvrir; *(scandal)* étouffer • **coverage** *n (on TV, in newspaper)* couverture *f* médiatique • **covering** *adj* **c. letter** lettre *f* jointe • **cover-up** *n* **there was a c.** on a étouffé l'affaire

cow [kaʊ] *n* vache *f* • **cowboy** *n* cow-boy *m*

coward [ˈkaʊəd] *n* lâche *mf*

cozy [ˈkəʊzɪ] *adj Am* = **cosy**

crab [kræb] *n* crabe *m*

crack [kræk] **1** *n (split)* fente *f*; *(in glass, china, bone)* fêlure *f*; *(noise)* craquement *m* **2** *vt (glass, ice)* fêler; *(nut)* casser; *(code)* déchiffrer **3** *vi* se fêler; *(of branch, wood)* craquer; **to c. down on** prendre des mesures énergiques en matière de

cracker ['krækə(r)] *n* **(a)** *(biscuit)* biscuit *m* salé **(b)** *(firework)* pétard *m*; **Christmas c.** diablotin *m*

crackle ['krækəl] *vi (of fire)* crépiter; *(of radio)* crachoter

cradle ['kreɪdəl] *n* berceau *m*

craft [krɑːft] *n (skill)* art *m*; *(job)* métier *m* • **crafty (-ier, -iest)** *adj* rusé

cram [kræm] *(pt & pp* **-mm-)** **1** *vt* **to c. sth into** *(force)* fourrer qch dans; **to c. with** *(fill)* bourrer de **2** *vi* **to c. into** *(of people)* s'entasser dans

cramp [kræmp] *n (pain)* crampe *f* (**in** à) • **cramped** *adj (surroundings)* exigu *(f* exiguë)

crane [kreɪn] **1** *n* grue *f* **2** *vt* **to c. one's neck** tendre le cou

crash [kræʃ] **1** *n (accident)* accident *m*; *(noise)* fracas *m*; **c. course/diet** cours *m*/régime *m* intensif; **c. helmet** casque *m*; **c. landing** atterrissage *m* en catastrophe **2** *exclam (of fallen object)* patatras! **3** *vt (car)* avoir un accident avec **4** *vi (of car, plane)* s'écraser; **to c. into** rentrer dans

crate [kreɪt] *n (large)* caisse *f*; *(small)* cageot *m*; *(for bottles)* casier *m*

craving ['kreɪvɪŋ] *n* envie *f* (**for** de)

crawl [krɔːl] **1** *n (swimming stroke)* crawl *m* **2** *vi (of animal)* ramper; *(of baby)* marcher à quatre pattes

crayon ['kreɪən] *n (wax)* crayon *m* gras

crazy ['kreɪzɪ] **(-ier, -iest)** *adj* fou *(f* folle) (**about** de); **to drive sb c.**

rendre qn fou; **to run/work like c.** courir/travailler comme un fou

creak [kriːk] *vi (of hinge)* grincer; *(of floor, timber)* craquer

cream [kriːm] *n (of milk, lotion)* crème *f*; **c. of tomato soup** crème *f* de tomates; **c. cake** gâteau *m* à la crème; **c. cheese** fromage *m* à tartiner • **creamy (-ier, -iest)** *adj* crémeux, -euse

crease [kriːs] **1** *n* pli *m* **2** *vi* se froisser

create [kriːˈeɪt] *vt* créer • **creation** *n* création *f* • **creative** *adj (person, activity)* créatif, -ive

creature ['kriːtʃə(r)] *n (animal)* bête *f*; *(person)* créature *f*

crèche [kreʃ] *n Br (nursery)* crèche *f*

credit ['kredɪt] **1** *n (financial)* crédit *m*; *(merit)* mérite *m*; **credits** *(of film)* générique *m*; **to be in c.** *(of account)* être créditeur; *(of person)* avoir un solde positif; **c. card** carte *f* de crédit **2** *vt (of bank)* créditer (**sb with sth** qn de qch)

creek [kriːk] *n (bay)* crique *f*; *Am (stream)* ruisseau *m*

creep [kriːp] **1** *n Fam* **it gives me the creeps** ça me fait froid dans le dos **2** *(pt & pp* **crept)** *vi (silently)* se glisser *(furtivement)*; *(slowly)* avancer lentement • **creepy (-ier, -iest)** *adj Fam* sinistre

cremation [krɪˈmeɪʃən] *n* crémation *f* • **crematorium** [kremə'tɔːrɪəm] *(pl* **-ia** [-ɪə]), *Am* **crematory** ['kriːmətɔːrɪ] *(pl* **-ies)** *n* crématorium *m*

crept [krept] *pt & pp of* **creep**

crescent ['kresənt] *n (shape)* croissant *m*; *Br Fig (street)* rue *f* en demi-lune

crevice ['krevɪs] *n (crack)* fente *f*

crew [kruː] *n (of ship, plane)*

équipage *m*; **c. cut** coupe *f* en brosse

crib [krɪb] *n Am (cot)* lit *m* d'enfant; *(cradle)* berceau *m*

cricket¹ ['krɪkɪt] *n (game)* cricket *m*

cricket² ['krɪkɪt] *n (insect)* grillon *m*

crime [kraɪm] *n* crime *m*; *Law* délit *m*; *(criminal activity)* criminalité *f*

criminal ['krɪmɪnəl] *adj & n* criminel, -elle *(mf)*; **c. record** casier *m* judiciaire

crimson ['krɪmzən] *adj & n* cramoisi *(m)*

cringe [krɪndʒ] *vi (show fear)* avoir un mouvement de recul; *(be embarrassed)* avoir envie de rentrer sous terre

crisis ['kraɪsɪs] *(pl* **crises** ['kraɪsiːz]) *n* crise *f*

crisp [krɪsp] **1** (**-er, -est**) *adj (biscuit)* croustillant; *(apple)* croquant **2** *npl Br* **crisps** chips *fpl*

criterion [kraɪ'tɪərɪən] *(pl* **-ia** [-ɪə]) *n* critère *m*

critic ['krɪtɪk] *n (reviewer)* critique *mf*; *(opponent)* détracteur, -trice *mf* • **critical** *adj* critique • **critically** *adv (examine)* en critique; **to be c. ill** être dans un état critique • **criticism** [-sɪzəm] *n* critique *f* • **criticize** [-saɪz] *vti* critiquer

croak [krəʊk] *vi (of frog)* croasser

crockery ['krɒkərɪ] *n* vaisselle *f*

crocodile ['krɒkədaɪl] *n* crocodile *m*

crook [krʊk] *n (thief)* escroc *m* • **crooked** [-ɪd] *adj (hat, picture)* de travers; *(deal, person)* malhonnête

crop [krɒp] **1** *n (harvest)* récolte *f*; *(produce)* culture *f* **2** *(pt & pp* **-pp-**) *vt (hair)* couper ras **3** *vi* **to c. up** *(of issue)* survenir; *(of opportunity)* se présenter

cross¹ [krɒs] **1** *n* croix *f*; **a c. between** *(animal)* un croisement entre **2** *vt (street, room)* traverser; *(barrier, threshold)* franchir; *(legs)* croiser; **to c. off** *or* **out** *(word, name)* rayer; **to c. over** *(road)* traverser **3** *vi (of paths)* se croiser; **to c. over** traverser • **cross-country** *adj* **c. runner** coureur, -euse *mf* de fond • **crossing** *n (of sea, river)* traversée *f*; *Br* **(pedestrian) c.** passage *m* clouté • **cross-legged** *adj & adv* **to sit c.** être assis en tailleur • **crossroads** *n* carrefour *m* • **crossword (puzzle)** *n* mots *mpl* croisés

cross² [krɒs] *adj (angry)* fâché **(with** contre); **to get c.** se fâcher **(with** contre)

crotch [krɒtʃ] *n (of garment, person)* entrejambe *m*

crouch [kraʊtʃ] *vi* **to c. (down)** *(of person)* s'accroupir; *(of animal)* se tapir

crow [krəʊ] *n* corbeau *m*; **as the c. flies** à vol d'oiseau

crowbar ['krəʊbɑː(r)] *n* levier *m*

crowd [kraʊd] **1** *n* foule *f*; *Fam (group of people)* bande *f*; **there was quite a c.** il y avait beaucoup de monde **2** *vt (street)* envahir **3** *vi* **to c. round sb/sth** se presser autour de qn/qch • **crowded** *adj* plein **(with** de); *(train, room)* bondé; **it's very c.** il y a beaucoup de monde

crown [kraʊn] **1** *n* couronne *f* **2** *vt* couronner

crucial ['kruːʃəl] *adj* crucial

crucifix ['kruːsɪfɪks] *n* crucifix *m*

crude [kruːd] (**-er, -est**) *adj (manners, person)* grossier, -ère; *(painting, work)* rudimentaire; **c. oil** pétrole *m* brut

cruel [krʊəl] (**crueller, cruellest**) *adj* cruel, -elle • **cruelty** *n* cruauté *f*

cruise [kruːz] *n* croisière *f*; **to go on a c.** partir en croisière; **c. ship** bateau *m* de croisière

crumb [krʌm] *n* miette *f* •
crumble *vi (of bread)* s'émietter;
(collapse) s'effondrer

crumple ['krʌmpəl] **1** *vt* froisser **2**
vi se froisser

crunch [krʌntʃ] *vt (food)* croquer

crusade [kruːˈseɪd] *n Hist & Fig*
croisade *f*

crush [krʌʃ] **1** *n (crowd)* foule
f; *Fam* **to have a c. on sb** en
pincer pour qn **2** *vt* écraser; *(cram)*
entasser (**into** dans)

crust [krʌst] *n* croûte *f* • **crusty** (-
ier, -iest) *n (bread)* croustillant

crutch [krʌtʃ] *n (for walking)*
béquille *f*

cry [kraɪ] **1** *(pl* **cries)** *n (shout)* cri
m **2** *(pt & pp* **cried)** *vt* **to c. (out)**
(shout) crier **3** *vi (weep)* pleurer;
to c. (out) pousser un cri; **to c.
for help** appeler au secours; **to c.
over sb/sth** pleurer qn/qch

crystal ['krɪstəl] *n* cristal *m*; **c.
vase** vase *m* en cristal

cub [kʌb] *n (of animal)* petit *m*

cube [kjuːb] *n* cube *m*; *(of meat,
vegetables)* dé *m*; *(of sugar)*
morceau *m*

cubicle ['kjuːbɪkəl] *n (for changing
clothes)* cabine *f*

cuckoo ['kʊkuː] *(pl* **-oos)** *n (bird)*
coucou *m*

cucumber ['kjuːkʌmbə(r)] *n*
concombre *m*

cuddle ['kʌdəl] **1** *n* câlin *m*; **to
give sb a c.** faire un câlin à qn **2** *vt
(hug)* serrer dans ses bras; *(caress)*
câliner • **cuddly (-ier, -iest)** *adj
(person)* mignon, -onne à croquer;
c. toy peluche *f*

cue¹ [kjuː] *n (in theatre)* réplique *f*;
(signal) signal *m*

cue² [kjuː] *n* **(billiard) c.** queue *f*
de billard

cuff [kʌf] *n (of shirt)* poignet *m*;
Am (of trousers) revers *m*

cul-de-sac ['kʌldəsæk] *n Br*
impasse *f*

culprit ['kʌlprɪt] *n* coupable *mf*

cult [kʌlt] *n* culte *m*; **c. film** film
m culte

cultivate ['kʌltɪveɪt] *vt (land,
mind)* cultiver • **cultivated** *adj*
cultivé

culture ['kʌltʃə(r)] *n* culture *f*
• **cultural** *adj* culturel, -elle •
cultured *adj (person)* cultivé

cunning ['kʌnɪŋ] *adj (ingenious)*
astucieux, -euse; *(devious)* rusé

cup [kʌp] *n* tasse *f*; *(prize)* coupe
f; **c. final** *(in football)* finale *f* de
la coupe

cupboard ['kʌbəd] *n Br* armoire *f*;
(built into wall) placard *m*

curb [kɜːb] *n Am* = **kerb**

cure ['kjʊə(r)] **1** *n* remède *m* (**for**
contre) **2** *vt (person, illness)* guérir;
to c. sb of guérir qn de

curious ['kjʊərɪəs] *adj* curieux,
-euse (**about** de); **to be c. to
know/see** être curieux de savoir/
voir • **curiosity** *(pl* **-ies)** *n* curiosité
f (**about** de)

curl [kɜːl] **1** *n (in hair)* boucle *f* **2** *vti
(hair)* boucler **3** *vi* **to c. up** *(shrivel)*
se racornir • **curler** *n* bigoudi *m* •
curly (-ier, -iest) *adj (hair)* bouclé;
(with tight curls) frisé

currant ['kʌrənt] *n (dried grape)*
raisin *m* de Corinthe

currency ['kʌrənsɪ] *(pl* **-ies)** *n
(money)* monnaie *f*; **(foreign) c.**
devises *fpl* (étrangères)

current ['kʌrənt] **1** *adj (fashion,
trend)* actuel, -elle; *(opinion, use)*
courant; **c. account** *(in bank)*
compte *m* courant; **c. affairs**
questions *fpl* d'actualité **2** *n (of
river, air, electricity)* courant *m* •
currently *adv* actuellement

curriculum [kəˈrɪkjʊləm] *(pl* **-la**

[-lə]) *n* programme *m* scolaire; *Br* **c. vitae** curriculum vitae *m inv*

curry ['kʌrɪ] (*pl* **-ies**) *n* (*dish*) curry *m*

curse [kɜːs] **1** *n* malédiction *f*; (*swearword*) juron *m* **2** *vt* maudire; **cursed with sth** affligé de qch **3** *vi* (*swear*) jurer

curt [kɜːt] *adj* brusque

curtain ['kɜːtən] *n* rideau *m*; **to draw the curtains** (*close*) tirer les rideaux

curve [kɜːv] **1** *n* courbe *f*; (*in road*) virage *m* **2** *vi* se courber; (*of road*) faire une courbe ● **curved** *adj* (*line*) courbe

cushion ['kʊʃən] *n* coussin *m*

custard ['kʌstəd] *n* crème *f* anglaise; (*solid*) crème *f* renversée

custody ['kʌstədɪ] *n* (*of child*) garde *f*

custom ['kʌstəm] *n* coutume *f* ● **customary** *adj* habituel, -elle; **it is c. to...** il est d'usage de...

customer ['kʌstəmə(r)] *n* client, -e *mf*

customs ['kʌstəmz] *npl* **(the) c.** la douane; **to go through c.** passer la douane; **c. officer** douanier, -ère *mf*

cut [kʌt] **1** *n* (*mark*) coupure *f* (*of clothes, hair*) coupe *f*; (*in prices*) réduction *f* **2** (*pt & pp* **cut**, *pres p* **cutting**) *vt* couper; (*meat*) découper; (*glass, tree*) tailler; (*salary, prices, profits*) réduire; **to c. sb's hair** couper les cheveux à qn; **to c. sth open** ouvrir qch avec un couteau/des ciseaux/*etc*; **to c.**

sth short (*visit*) écourter qch **3** *vi* (*of knife, scissors*) couper ● **cut-price** *adj* à prix réduit

▶**cut back** *vt sep & vi* réduire

▶**cut down 1** *vt sep* (**a**) (*tree*) abattre (**b**) (*reduce*) réduire **2** *vi* réduire

▶**cut off** *vt sep* (*piece, hair*) couper; (*isolate*) isoler

▶**cut out** *vt sep* (*article*) découper; (*remove*) enlever; (*eliminate*) supprimer; **to c. out drinking** s'arrêter de boire; *Fam* **c. it out!** ça suffit!; **c. out to be a doctor** fait pour être médecin

▶**cut up** *vt sep* couper en morceaux; (*meat*) découper

cute [kjuːt] (**-er**, **-est**) *adj Fam* (*pretty*) mignon, -onne

cutlery ['kʌtlərɪ] *n* couverts *mpl*

cutting ['kʌtɪŋ] *n* (*from newspaper*) coupure *f*

CV [siːˈviː] (*abbr* **curriculum vitae**) *n Br* CV *m*

cycle[1] ['saɪkəl] **1** **c. path** piste *f* cyclable **2** *vi* aller à bicyclette (**to** à); (*as activity*) faire de la bicyclette ● **cyclist** *n* cycliste *mf*

cycle[2] ['saɪkəl] *n* (*series, period*) cycle *m*

cylinder ['sɪlɪndə(r)] *n* cylindre *m*

cymbal ['sɪmbəl] *n* cymbale *f*

cynical ['sɪnɪkəl] *adj* cynique

Cyprus ['saɪprəs] *n* Chypre *f*

Czech [tʃek] **1** *adj* tchèque; **the C. Republic** la République tchèque **2** *n* (*person*) Tchèque *mf*; (*language*) tchèque *m*

Dd

D, d [diː] n D, d m inv
dab [dæb] (pt & pp -bb-) vt (wound, brow) tamponner
dad [dæd] n Fam papa m • **daddy** (pl -ies) n Fam papa m
daft [dɑːft] (-er, -est) adj Fam bête
dagger ['dægə(r)] n dague f
daily ['deɪlɪ] 1 adj quotidien, -enne 2 adv chaque jour; **twice d.** deux fois par jour 3 (pl -ies) n (newspaper) quotidien m
dainty ['deɪntɪ] (-ier, -iest) adj délicat
dairy ['deərɪ] 1 (pl -ies) n laiterie f 2 adj **d. produce** produits mpl laitiers
daisy ['deɪzɪ] (pl -ies) n pâquerette f; (bigger) marguerite f
dam [dæm] n (wall) barrage m
damage ['dæmɪdʒ] 1 n dégâts mpl; (harm) préjudice m; **damages** (in court) dommages-intérêts mpl 2 vt (object) endommager, abîmer; (health) nuire à; (plans, reputation) compromettre
damn [dæm] 1 n Fam **he doesn't give a d.** il s'en fiche pas mal 2 adj Fam fichu 3 adv Fam (very) vachement 4 exclam Fam **d. (it)!** mince!
damp [dæmp] 1 (-er, -est) adj humide; (skin) moite 2 n humidité f • **damp(en)** vt humecter
dance [dɑːns] 1 n danse f; (social event) bal m (pl bals) 2 vi danser • **dancing** n danse f

dandelion ['dændɪlaɪən] n pissenlit m
dandruff ['dændrʌf] n pellicules fpl
Dane [deɪn] n Danois, -e mf
danger ['deɪndʒə(r)] n danger m (**to** pour); **in d.** en danger; **out of d.** hors de danger; **to be in d. of doing sth** risquer de faire qch • **dangerous** adj dangereux, -euse (**to** pour)
dangle ['dæŋgəl] 1 vt balancer 2 vi (hang) pendre; (swing) se balancer
Danish ['deɪnɪʃ] 1 adj danois 2 n (language) danois m
dare [deə(r)] vt **to d. (to) do sth** oser faire qch; **I d. say he tried** il a essayé, c'est bien possible; **to d. sb to do sth** défier qn de faire qch • **daring** adj audacieux, -euse
dark [dɑːk] 1 (-er, -est) adj (room, night) & Fig sombre; (colour, skin, hair, eyes) foncé; **it's d. at six** il fait nuit à six heures; **d. glasses** lunettes fpl noires 2 n obscurité f; **after d.** une fois la nuit tombée • **darken** 1 vt assombrir; (colour) foncer 2 vi s'assombrir; (of colour) foncer • **dark-haired** adj aux cheveux bruns • **darkness** n obscurité f • **dark-skinned** adj (person) à peau brune
darling ['dɑːlɪŋ] n **(my) d.** (mon) chéri/(ma) chérie
darn [dɑːn] vt (mend) repriser
dart [dɑːt] 1 n (in game) fléchette

f; **darts** *(game)* fléchettes *fpl* **2** *vi* *(dash)* se précipiter (**for** vers)

dash [dæʃ] **1** *n* (**a**) *(run, rush)* ruée *f* (**b**) *(handwritten stroke)* trait *m*; *(punctuation sign)* tiret *m* **2** *vi* *(rush)* se précipiter; **to d. in/out** entrer/sortir en vitesse; **to d. off** *or* **away** filer • **dashboard** *n (of vehicle)* tableau *m* de bord

data ['deɪtə] *npl* informations *fpl*; *Comptr* données *fpl*; • **database** *n* base *f* de données

date¹ [deɪt] **1** *n (day)* date *f*; *Fam (meeting)* rendez-vous *m inv*; **d. of birth** date *f* de naissance; **up to d.** *(in fashion)* à la mode; *(information)* à jour; *(well-informed)* au courant (**on** de); **out of d.** *(old-fashioned)* démodé; *(expired)* périmé **2** *vt (letter)* dater; *Fam (girl, boy)* sortir avec **3** *vi (go out of fashion)* dater; **to d. back to, to d. from** dater de • **dated** *adj* démodé

date² [deɪt] *n (fruit)* datte *f*

daughter ['dɔːtə(r)] *n* fille *f* • **daughter-in-law** (*pl* **daughters-in-law**) *n* belle-fille *f*

dawdle ['dɔːdəl] *vi* traînasser

dawn [dɔːn] **1** *n* aube *f*; **at d.** à l'aube **2** *vi* **it dawned on him that...** il s'est rendu compte que...

day [deɪ] *n (period of daylight, 24 hours)* jour *m*; *(referring to duration)* journée *f*; **all d. (long)** toute la journée; **what d. is it?** quel jour sommes-nous?; **the following** *or* **next d.** le lendemain; **the d. before** la veille; **the d. before yesterday** avant-hier; **the d. after tomorrow** après-demain; **in those days** en ce temps-là; **these days** de nos jours • **daydream 1** *n* rêverie *f* **2** *vi* rêvasser • **daylight** *n (lumière f du)* jour *m* • **daytime** *n* journée *f*, jour *m*

daze [deɪz] *n* **in a d.** étourdi

dazzle ['dæzəl] *vt* éblouir

dead [ded] **1** *adj* mort; **d. end** *(street)* & *Fig* impasse *f*; **a d. stop** un arrêt complet **2** *npl* **the d.** les morts *mpl* **3** *adv (completely)* totalement; **to stop d.** s'arrêter net • **deadline** *n* date *f* limite; • **deadly 1** (**-ier, -iest**) *adj (poison, blow)* mortel, -elle; **d. weapon** arme *f* meurtrière **2** *adv (pale, boring)* mortellement

deaf [def] **1** *adj* sourd **2** *npl* **the d.** les sourds *mpl* • **deafen** *vt* assourdir

deal¹ [diːl] *n* **a good** *or* **great d. (of)** *(a lot)* beaucoup (de)

deal² [diːl] *n* **1** *(in business)* marché *m*, affaire *f*; **to make** *or* **do a d. (with sb)** conclure un marché (avec qn); **it's a d.!** d'accord!; *Ironic* **big d.!** la belle affaire! **2** (*pt & pp* **dealt** [delt]) *vt* **to d. (out)** *(cards, money)* distribuer **3** *vi* **to d. with** *(take care of)* s'occuper de; *(concern) (of book)* traiter de, parler de • **dealer** *n* marchand, -e *mf* (**in** de); *(for cars)* concessionnaire *mf*; *(in drugs)* revendeur, -euse *mf*; *(in card games)* donneur, -euse *mf*

dear [dɪə(r)] **1** (**-er, -est**) *adj (loved, precious, expensive)* cher (*f* chère); **D. Madam** *(in letter)* Madame; **D. Sir** Monsieur; **D. Jane** chère Jane; **oh d.!** oh là là! **2** *n (my)* **d.** *(darling)* (mon) chéri/(ma) chérie; *(friend)* mon cher/ma chère

death [deθ] *n* mort *f*; **to be bored to d.** s'ennuyer à mourir; **to be scared to d.** être mort de peur; **to be sick to d. of** en avoir vraiment marre de; **d. penalty** peine *f* de mort • **deathly** *adj (silence, paleness)* de mort

debate [dɪ'beɪt] **1** *n* débat *m* **2** *vti* discuter

debit ['debɪt] *vt* débiter (**sb with sth** qn de qch)

debris ['debriː] *n (of building)* décombres *mpl*; *(of plane, car)* débris *mpl*

debt [det] *n* dette *f*; **to be in d.** avoir des dettes; **to run** *or* **get into d.** faire des dettes

decade ['dekeɪd] *n* décennie *f*

decaffeinated [diː'kæfɪneɪtɪd] *adj* décaféiné

decay [dɪ'keɪ] **1** *n (rot)* pourriture *f*; *(of tooth)* carie *f*; **to fall into d.** *(of building)* tomber en ruine **2** *vi (go bad)* se gâter; *(rot)* pourrir; *(of tooth)* se carier

deceased [dɪ'siːst] **1** *adj* décédé **2** *n* **the d.** le défunt/la défunte

deceive [dɪ'siːv] *vti* tromper; **to d. oneself** se faire des illusions ● **deceit** *n* tromperie *f*

December [dɪ'sembə(r)] *n* décembre *m*

decent ['diːsənt] *adj (respectable)* convenable; *(good)* bon *(f* bonne); *(kind)* gentil, -ille

deception [dɪ'sepʃən] *n* tromperie *f*

decide [dɪ'saɪd] **1** *vt (outcome, future)* décider de; *(question, matter)* régler; **to d. to do sth** décider de faire qch; **to d. that...** décider que... **2** *vi (make decisions)* décider; *(make up one's mind)* se décider (**on doing** à faire); **to d. on sth** décider de qch; *(choose)* choisir qch

decimal ['desɪməl] **1** *adj* décimal; **d. point** virgule *f* **2** *n* décimale *f*

decipher [dɪ'saɪfə(r)] *vt* déchiffrer

decision [dɪ'sɪʒən] *n* décision *f*

deck [dek] *n* (**a**) *(of ship)* pont *m*; **top d.** *(of bus)* impériale *f* (**b**) **d. of cards** jeu *m* de cartes (**c**) *(of record player)* platine *f* ● **deckchair** *n* chaise *f* longue

declare [dɪ'kleə(r)] *vt* déclarer (**that** que); *(result)* proclamer ● **declaration** *n* déclaration *f*

decline [dɪ'klaɪn] **1** *n* déclin *m*; *(fall)* baisse *f* **2** *vt (offer)* décliner; **to d. to do sth** refuser de faire qch **3** *vi (become less)* être en baisse; *(deteriorate)* décliner; *(refuse)* refuser

decode [diː'kəʊd] *vt (message)* décoder

decor ['deɪkɔː(r)] *n* décor *m*

decorate ['dekəreɪt] *vt (cake, house, soldier)* décorer (**with** de); *(hat, skirt)* orner (**with** de); *(paint)* peindre; *(wallpaper)* tapisser ● **decoration** *n* décoration *f* ● **decorator** *n Br (house painter)* peintre *m* décorateur; **(interior) d.** décorateur, -trice *mf*

decrease 1 ['diːkriːs] *n* diminution *f* (**in** de) **2** [dɪ'kriːs] *vti* diminuer

dedicate ['dedɪkeɪt] *vt (devote)* consacrer (**to** à); *(book)* dédier (**to** à); **to d. oneself to sth** se consacrer à qch ● **dedicated** *adj (teacher)* consciencieux, -euse ● **dedication** *n (in book)* dédicace *f*; *(devotion)* dévouement *m*

deduce [dɪ'djuːs] *vt (conclude)* déduire (**from** de; **that** que)

deduct [dɪ'dʌkt] *vt* déduire (**from** de) ● **deduction** *n* déduction *f*

deed [diːd] *n* action *f*, acte *m*

deep [diːp] **1** (**-er, -est**) *adj* profond; *(snow)* épais *(f* épaisse); *(voice)* grave; **to be six metres d.** avoir six mètres de profondeur; **d. in thought** plongé dans ses pensées; **d. red** rouge foncé **2** *adv* profondément ● **deepen 1** *vt* approfondir **2** *vi (of river)* devenir plus profond; *(of mystery)* s'épaissir; *(of voice)* devenir plus grave ● **deeply** *adv* profondément

deer [dɪə(r)] *n inv* cerf *m*
default [dɪ'fɔːlt] *n* **by d.** par défaut
defeat [dɪ'fiːt] **1** *n* défaite *f* **2** *vt* *(opponent, army)* vaincre; **that defeats the purpose** *or* **object** ça va à l'encontre du but recherché
defect ['diːfekt] *n* défaut *m* • **defective** [dɪ'fektɪv] *adj* *(machine)* défectueux, -euse
defend [dɪ'fend] *vti* défendre • **defence** (*Am* **defense**) *n* défense *f* (**against** contre); **in his d.** à sa décharge • **defensive** *adj* défensif, -ive; **to be d.** être sur la défensive
defiant [dɪ'faɪənt] *adj* *(person)* provocant
deficient [dɪ'fɪʃənt] *adj* *(not adequate)* insuffisant; *(faulty)* défectueux, -euse; **to be d. in** manquer de • **deficiency** (*pl* **-ies**) *n* *(shortage)* manque *m*; *(in vitamins, minerals)* carence *f* (**in** de); *(flaw)* défaut *m*
definite ['defɪnɪt] *adj* *(exact)* *(date, plan, answer)* précis; *(clear)* *(improvement, advantage)* net (*f* nette); *(firm)* *(offer, order)* ferme; *(certain)* certain; **he was quite d.** il a été tout à fait formel; **d. article** *(in grammar)* article *m* défini • **definitely** *adv* certainement; *(improved, superior)* nettement
definition [defɪ'nɪʃən] *n* définition *f*
deformed [dɪ'fɔːmd] *adj* *(body)* difforme
defrost [diː'frɒst] *vt* *(fridge)* dégivrer; *(food)* décongeler
defuse [diː'fjuːz] *vt* *(bomb, conflict)* désamorcer
degenerate [dɪ'dʒenəreɪt] *vi* dégénérer (**into** en)
degrading [dɪ'greɪdɪŋ] *adj* dégradant

degree [dɪ'griː] *n* (**a**) *(of angle, temperature, extent)* degré *m*; **it's 20 degrees** *(temperature)* il fait 20 degrés; **to some d., to a certain d.** jusqu'à un certain point; **to such a d.** à tel point (**that** que) (**b**) *(from university)* diplôme *m*; *(Bachelor's)* ≃ licence *f*; *(Master's)* ≃ maîtrise *f*; *(PhD)* ≃ doctorat *m*
dehydrated [diːhaɪ'dreɪtɪd] *adj* déshydraté; **to get d.** se déshydrater
de-ice [diː'aɪs] *vt* dégivrer
delay [dɪ'leɪ] **1** *n* *(lateness)* retard *m*; *(waiting period)* délai *m*; **without d.** sans tarder **2** *vt* retarder; *(payment)* différer; **to d. doing sth** tarder à faire qch; **to be delayed** avoir du retard **3** *vi* *(be slow)* tarder (**in doing** à faire)
delegate 1 ['delɪgət] *n* délégué, -e *mf* **2** ['delɪgeɪt] *vt* déléguer (**to** à)
delete [dɪ'liːt] *vt* supprimer
deliberate [dɪ'lɪbərət] *adj* *(intentional)* délibéré; *(slow)* mesuré • **deliberately** *adv* *(intentionally)* délibérément
delicate ['delɪkət] *adj* délicat • **delicacy** (*pl* **-ies**) *n* *(quality)* délicatesse *f*; *(food)* mets *m* délicat
delicatessen [delɪkə'tesən] *n* *(shop)* épicerie *f* fine
delicious [dɪ'lɪʃəs] *adj* délicieux, -euse
delight [dɪ'laɪt] *n* *(pleasure)* plaisir *m*, joie *f* • **delighted** *adj* ravi (**with sth** de qch; **to do** de faire; **that** que) • **delightful** *adj* charmant; *(meal, perfume, sensation)* délicieux, -euse
delinquent [dɪ'lɪŋkwənt] *adj & n* délinquant, -e *(mf)*
delirious [dɪ'lɪrɪəs] *adj* délirant; **to be d.** délirer
deliver [dɪ'lɪvə(r)] *vt* (**a**) *(goods)* livrer; *(letters)* distribuer; *(hand over)* remettre (**to** à) (**b**) **to d. a**

woman's baby accoucher une femme (**c**) *(speech)* prononcer • **delivery** *(pl* **-ies**) *n* (**a**) *(of goods)* livraison *f; (of letters)* distribution *f* (**b**) *(birth)* accouchement *m*

delusion [dɪ'luːʃən] *n* illusion *f*

demand [dɪ'mɑːnd] **1** *n* exigence *f; (claim)* revendication *f; (for goods)* demande *f* (**for** pour); **to be in (great) d.** être très demandé; **to make demands on sb** exiger beaucoup de qn **2** *vt* exiger (**sth from sb** qch de qn); *(rights, pay)* revendiquer; **to d. that...** exiger que... • **demanding** *adj* exigeant

demo ['deməʊ] *(pl* **-os**) *n Fam (demonstration)* manif *f*

democracy [dɪ'mɒkrəsɪ] *(pl* **-ies**) *n* démocratie *f* • **democratic** *adj* démocratique

demolish [dɪ'mɒlɪʃ] *vt* démolir

demon ['diːmən] *n* démon *m*

demonstrate ['demənstreɪt] **1** *vt* démontrer; *(machine)* faire une démonstration de; **to d. how to do sth** montrer comment faire qch **2** *vi (protest)* manifester • **demonstration** [-'streɪʃən] *n* démonstration *f; (protest)* manifestation *f*

den [den] *n* antre *m*

denial [dɪ'naɪəl] *n (of rumour, allegation)* démenti *m*

denim ['denɪm] *n* denim *m*

Denmark ['denmɑːk] *n* le Danemark

dense [dens] (**-er, -est**) *adj* dense

dent [dent] **1** *n (in car, metal)* bosse *f* **2** *vt* cabosser

dentist ['dentɪst] *n* dentiste *mf;* **to go to the d.** aller chez le dentiste

deny [dɪ'naɪ] *(pt & pp* **-ied**) *vt* nier (**doing** avoir fait; **that** que); *(rumour)* démentir; **to d. sb sth** refuser qch à qn

deodorant [diː'əʊdərənt] *n* déodorant *m*

depart [dɪ'pɑːt] *vi* partir; *(deviate)* s'écarter (**from** de) • **departure** [-tʃə(r)] *n* départ *m;* **d. lounge** *(in airport)* salle *f* d'embarquement

department [dɪ'pɑːtmənt] *n* département *m; (in office)* service *m; (in shop)* rayon *m; (of government)* ministère *m;* **d. store** grand magasin *m*

depend [dɪ'pend] *vi* dépendre (**on or upon** de); **to d. (up)on** *(rely on)* compter sur (**for sth** pour qch) • **dependent** *adj (relative, child)* à charge; **to be d. (up)on** dépendre de; **to be d. on sb** *(financially)* être à la charge de qn

deposit [dɪ'pɒzɪt] **1** *n (in bank)* dépôt *m; (part payment)* acompte *m; (returnable)* caution *f* **2** *vt (object, money)* déposer

depot [*Br* 'depəʊ, *Am* 'diːpəʊ] *n (for goods)* dépôt *m; Am (railroad station)* gare *f;* (**bus**) **d.** gare *f* routière

depressed [dɪ'prest] *adj* déprimé; **to get d.** se décourager • **depression** [-ʃən] *n* dépression *f*

deprive [dɪ'praɪv] *vt* priver (**of** de) • **deprived** *adj (child)* défavorisé

depth [depθ] *n* profondeur *f;* **in the depths of** *(forest, despair)* au plus profond de; *(winter)* au cœur de; **in d.** en profondeur

deputy ['depjʊtɪ] *(pl* **-ies**) *n (replacement)* remplaçant, -e *mf; (assistant)* adjoint, -e *mf*

derelict ['derɪlɪkt] *adj (building)* abandonné

derive [dɪ'raɪv] *vi* **to d. from** provenir de

descend [dɪ'send] **1** *vt (stairs, hill)* descendre; **to be descended from** descendre de **2** *vi* descendre (**from** de); **to d. upon** *(attack)* faire une descente sur; **in descending order** en ordre décrois-

sant • **descendant** *n* descendant,
-e *mf* • **descent** *n* descente *f*
describe [dɪ'skraɪb] *vt* décrire
• **description** [dɪ'skrɪpʃən] *n*
description *f*
desert¹ ['dezət] *n* désert *m*; **d.
island** île *f* déserte
desert² [dɪ'zɜːt] *vt* (person) abandonner; (place, cause) déserter •
deserted *adj* désert
deserve [dɪ'zɜːv] *vt* mériter (**to
do** de faire)
design [dɪ'zaɪn] **1** *n* (pattern)
motif *m*; (sketch) plan *m*; (of
dress) modèle *m* **2** *vt* (dress) créer;
(building) concevoir; **designed to
do sth/for sth** conçu pour faire
qch/pour qch • **designer** *n*
(artistic) dessinateur, -trice *mf*; (of
clothes) styliste *mf*; (well-known)
couturier *m*; **d. clothes** vêtements
mpl de marque
desire [dɪ'zaɪə(r)] **1** *n* désir *m* **2** *vt*
désirer (**to do** faire) • **desirable**
adj désirable
desk [desk] *n* (in school) table *f*; (in
office) bureau *m*; (reception) **d.**
(in hotel) réception *f*; *Am* **d. clerk**
(in hotel) réceptionniste *mf*
desktop ['desktɒp] *n* **d. computer** ordinateur *m* de bureau; **d.
publishing** publication *f* assistée
par ordinateur
desolate ['desələt] *adj* (deserted)
désolé; (bleak) morne, triste
despair [dɪ'speə(r)] **1** *n* désespoir
m; **to be in d.** être au désespoir
2 *vi* désespérer (**of sb** de qn; **of
doing** de faire)
desperate ['despərət] *adj* désespéré; **to be d. for** (money, love)
avoir désespérément besoin de;
(baby) mourir d'envie d'avoir •
desperately *adv* (ill) gravement
despise [dɪ'spaɪz] *vt* mépriser
despite [dɪ'spaɪt] *prep* malgré

dessert [dɪ'zɜːt] *n* dessert *m*
destination [destɪ'neɪʃən] *n*
destination *f*
destiny ['destɪnɪ] (*pl* **-ies**) *n* destin
m, destinée *f*
destroy [dɪ'strɔɪ] *vt* détruire
• **destruction** [-'strʌkʃən] *n*
destruction *f*
detach [dɪ'tætʃ] *vt* détacher (**from**
de) • **detached** *adj* *Br* **d. house**
maison *f* individuelle
detail ['diːteɪl] *n* détail *m*; **in d.** en
détail; **to go into d.** entrer dans
les détails • **detailed** *adj* (account)
détaillé
detect [dɪ'tekt] *vt* détecter •
detective *n* (police officer) ≃
inspecteur *m* de police; (private)
détective *m* privé; **d. film/novel**
film *m*/roman *m* policier
detention [dɪ'tenʃən] *n* (at
school) retenue *f*
detergent [dɪ'tɜːdʒənt] *n*
détergent *m*
deteriorate [dɪ'tɪərɪəreɪt] *vi* se
détériorer
determine [dɪ'tɜːmɪn] *vt* (cause,
date) déterminer; **to d. to do sth**
décider de faire qch • **determined**
adj (look, person) déterminé; **to
be d. to do sth** être décidé à
faire qch
detest [dɪ'test] *vt* détester (**doing**
faire)
detonate ['detəneɪt] *vt* faire
exploser
detour ['diːtʊə(r)] *n* détour *m*; **to
make a d.** faire un détour
devastate ['devəsteɪt] *vt* (person)
anéantir • **devastating** *adj* (news,
results) accablant
develop [dɪ'veləp] **1** *vt* (theory)
développer; (area, land) mettre
en valeur; (habit) contracter;
(photo) développer **2** *vi* (grow) se
développer; (of event) se produire;

(of talent, illness) se manifester; **to d. into** devenir • **developing** *adj* **d. country** pays *m* en voie de développement • **development** *n (growth, progress)* développement *m;* **(housing) d.** lotissement *m*

device [dɪ'vaɪs] *n (instrument, gadget)* dispositif *m;* **left to one's own devices** livré à soi-même

devil ['devəl] *n* diable *m*

devious ['diːvɪəs] *adj (mind, behaviour)* tortueux, -euse

devise [dɪ'vaɪz] *vt* imaginer; *(plot)* ourdir

devote [dɪ'vəʊt] *vt* consacrer **(to** à) • **devoted** *adj* dévoué; *(admirer)* fervent

devour [dɪ'vaʊə(r)] *vt* dévorer

devout [dɪ'vaʊt] *adj* dévot

dew [djuː] *n* rosée *f*

diabetes [daɪə'biːtiːz] *n* diabète *m* • **diabetic** [-'betɪk] *adj & n* diabétique *(mf)*

diagnose [daɪəg'nəʊz] *vt* diagnostiquer • **diagnosis** [-'nəʊsɪs] *(pl* -**oses** [-əʊsiːz]) *n* diagnostic *m*

diagonal [daɪ'ægənəl] *adj* diagonal

diagram ['daɪəgræm] *n* schéma *m*

dial ['daɪəl] **1** *n* cadran *m; Am* **d. tone** tonalité *f* **2** *(Br* -**ll-,** *Am* -**l-**) *vt (phone number)* composer

dialect ['daɪəlekt] *n* dialecte *m*

dialogue ['daɪəlɒg] *(Am* **dialog)** *n* dialogue *m*

diamond ['daɪəmənd] *n* **(a)** *(stone)* diamant *m;* **(shape)** losange *m;* **d. necklace** rivière *f* de diamants **(b)** **diamond(s)** *(in cards)* carreau *m*

diaper ['daɪpər] *n Am* couche *f*

diarrh(o)ea [daɪə'riːə] *n* diarrhée *f;* **to have d.** avoir la diarrhée

diary ['daɪərɪ] *(pl* -**ies**) *n Br (for appointments)* agenda *m; (private)* journal *m* (intime)

dice [daɪs] *n inv* dé *m*

dictate [dɪk'teɪt] *vt (letter, conditions)* dicter **(to** à) • **dictation** *n* dictée *f* • **dictator** *n* dictateur *m*

dictionary ['dɪkʃənərɪ] *(pl* -**ies**) *n* dictionnaire *m*

did [dɪd] *pt of* **do**

die [daɪ] *(pt & pp* **died,** *pres p* **dying)** *vi* mourir *(of or from* de); *Fig* **to be dying to do sth** mourir d'envie de faire qch; **to be dying for sth** avoir une envie folle de qch; **to d. down** *(of storm)* se calmer; **to d. out** *(of custom)* mourir

diesel ['diːzəl] *adj & n* **d. (engine)** (moteur *m)* diesel *m;* **d. (oil)** gazole *m*

diet ['daɪət] *n (usual food)* alimentation *f; (restricted food)* régime *m;* **to go on a d.** faire un régime

difference ['dɪfərəns] *n* différence *f* **(in** de); **it makes no d.** ça n'a pas d'importance • **different** *adj* différent **(from** de); *(another)* autre; *(various)* divers • **differently** *adv* différemment **(from** de)

difficult ['dɪfɪkəlt] *adj* difficile **(to do** à faire) • **difficulty** *(pl* -**ies**) *n* difficulté *f;* **to have d. doing sth** avoir du mal à faire qch

dig [dɪg] *(pt & pp* **dug,** *pres p* **digging**) **1** *vt (ground, garden)* bêcher; *(hole, grave)* creuser **to d. up** *(from ground)* déterrer; *(road)* excaver; *Fam (find)* dénicher **2** *vi (dig a hole)* creuser

digest [daɪ'dʒest] *vti* digérer • **digestion** *n* digestion *f*

digit ['dɪdʒɪt] *n (number)* chiffre *m* • **digital** *adj (camera, television)* numérique

dignified ['dɪgnɪfaɪd] *adj* digne • **dignity** *n* dignité *f*

dilemma [daɪ'lemə] *n* dilemme *m*

diligent ['dɪlɪdʒənt] *adj* appliqué

dilute [daɪ'luːt] *vt* diluer

dim [dɪm] (**dimmer, dimmest**) *adj* (*light*) faible; (*memory*) vague; (*person*) stupide

dime [daɪm] *n Am* (pièce *f* de) dix cents *mpl*

dimension [daɪ'menʃən] *n* dimension *f*

diminish [dɪ'mɪnɪʃ] *vti* diminuer

dimple ['dɪmpəl] *n* fossette *f*

dine [daɪn] *vi* dîner (**on** *or* **off** de) • **diner** *n* (*person*) dîneur, -euse *mf*; *Am* (*restaurant*) petit restaurant *m* • **dining** *n* **d. car** (*on train*) wagon-restaurant *m*; **d. room** salle *f* à manger

dinghy ['dɪŋgɪ] (*pl* **-ies**) *n* petit canot *m*; (**rubber**) **d.** canot *m* pneumatique

dingy ['dɪndʒɪ] (**-ier, -iest**) *adj* (*room*) minable; (*colour*) terne

dinner ['dɪnə(r)] *n* (*evening meal*) dîner *m*; (*lunch*) déjeuner *m*; **to have d.** dîner; **d. jacket** smoking *m*; **d. party** dîner *m*; **d. service**, **d. set** service *m* de table

dinosaur ['daɪnəsɔː(r)] *n* dinosaure *m*

dip [dɪp] **1** *n* (*in road*) petit creux *m*; *Fam* **to go for a d.** (*swim*) faire trempette **2** (*pt & pp* **-pp-**) *vt* plonger **3** *vi* (*of road*) plonger; **to d. into** (*pocket, savings*) puiser dans; (*book*) feuilleter

diploma [dɪ'pləʊmə] *n* diplôme *m*

diplomat ['dɪpləmæt] *n* diplomate *mf* • **diplomatic** *adj* diplomatique

dire ['daɪə(r)] *adj* (*situation*) affreux, -euse; (*consequences*) tragique; (*poverty, need*) extrême

direct [daɪ'rekt] **1** *adj* (*result, flight, person*) direct; *Br* **d. debit** prélèvement *m* automatique **2** *adv* directement **3** *vt* (*gaze, light, attention*) diriger (**at** sur); (*traffic*) régler; (*letter, remark*) adresser (**to** à); (*film*) réaliser; (*play*) mettre en scène; **to d. sb to** (*place*) indiquer à qn le chemin de; **to d. sb to do sth** charger qn de faire qch • **directly** *adv* (*without detour*) directement; (*exactly*) juste; (*at once*) tout de suite; **d. in front** juste devant

direction [daɪ'rekʃən] *n* direction *f*, sens *m*; **directions** (*orders*) indications *fpl*; (*for use*) mode *m* d'emploi

director [daɪ'rektə(r)] *n* directeur, -trice *mf*; (*of film*) réalisateur, -trice *mf*; (*of play*) metteur *m* en scène

directory [daɪ'rektərɪ] (*pl* **-ies**) *n* répertoire *m*; **telephone d.** annuaire *m* du téléphone; *Br* **d. enquiries** renseignements *mpl* téléphoniques

dirt [dɜːt] *n* saleté *f* • **dirty** (**-ier, -iest**) *adj* sale; (*job*) salissant; (*word*) grossier, -ère; **to get d.** se salir; **to get sth d.** salir qch; **a d. joke** une histoire cochonne; **a d. trick** un sale tour

disabled [dɪ'seɪbəld] **1** *adj* handicapé **2** *npl* **the d.** les handicapés *mpl* • **disability** [dɪsə'bɪlɪtɪ] (*pl* **-ies**) *n* (*injury*) infirmité *f*; (*condition*) invalidité *f*

disadvantage [dɪsəd'vɑːntɪdʒ] *n* désavantage *m*

disagree [dɪsə'griː] *vi* ne pas être d'accord (**with** avec); **to d. with sb** (*of food, climate*) ne pas réussir à qn • **disagreement** *n* désaccord *m*; (*quarrel*) différend *m*

disappear [dɪsə'pɪə(r)] *vi* disparaître

disappoint [dɪsə'pɔɪnt] *vt* décevoir • **disappointing** *adj* décevant • **disappointment** *n* déception *f*

disapprove [dɪsə'pruːv] *vi* **to d. of sb/sth** désapprouver qn/qch • **disapproval** *n* désapprobation *f*

disaster [dɪ'zɑːstə(r)] n désastre m, catastrophe f; **d. area** région f sinistrée • **disastrous** adj désastreux, -euse

disbelief [dɪsbə'liːf] n incrédulité f

disc [dɪsk] (Am **disk**) n disque m; **d. jockey** disc-jockey m

discard [dɪs'kɑːd] vt (get rid of) se débarrasser de; (plan) abandonner

discipline ['dɪsɪplɪn] n discipline f

disclose [dɪs'kləʊz] vt révéler

disco ['dɪskəʊ] (pl **-os**) n discothèque f

discolour [dɪs'kʌlə(r)] (Am **discolor**) vt décolorer

discomfort [dɪs'kʌmfət] n petite douleur f

disconcerting [dɪskən'sɜːtɪŋ] adj déconcertant

disconnect [dɪskə'nekt] vt (unplug) débrancher; (gas, telephone, electricity) couper

discount ['dɪskaʊnt] n réduction f

discourage [dɪs'kʌrɪdʒ] vt décourager (**sb from doing** qn de faire)

discover [dɪs'kʌvə(r)] vt découvrir (**that** que) • **discovery** (pl **-ies**) n découverte f

discreet [dɪ'skriːt] adj discret, -ète

discrepancy [dɪ'skrepənsɪ] (pl **-ies**) n décalage m (**between** entre)

discriminate [dɪ'skrɪmɪneɪt] vi to **d. against** faire de la discrimination envers; **to d. between** distinguer entre • **discrimination** [-'neɪʃən] n (bias) discrimination f

discuss [dɪ'skʌs] vt discuter de • **discussion** n discussion f

disdain [dɪs'deɪn] n dédain m

disease [dɪ'ziːz] n maladie f

disembark [dɪsɪm'bɑːk] vti débarquer

disfigured [dɪs'fɪgə(r)] adj défiguré

disgrace [dɪs'greɪs] n (shame) honte f (**to** à) • **disgraceful** adj honteux, -euse

disgruntled [dɪs'grʌntəld] adj mécontent

disguise [dɪs'gaɪz] **1** n déguisement m; **in d.** déguisé **2** vt déguiser (**as** en)

disgust [dɪs'gʌst] **1** n dégoût m (**for** or **at** or **with** de) **2** vt dégoûter • **disgusted** adj dégoûté (**at** or **by** or **with** de); **to be d. with sb** (annoyed) être fâché contre qn • **disgusting** adj dégoûtant

dish [dɪʃ] **1** n (container, food) plat m; **to do the dishes** faire la vaisselle **2** vt **to d. out** or **up** (food) servir • **dishcloth** n (for washing) lavette f; (for drying) torchon m • **dishwasher** n (machine) lave-vaisselle m inv

dishevelled [dɪ'ʃevəld] (Am **disheveled**) adj (person, hair) ébouriffé

dishonest [dɪs'ɒnɪst] adj malhonnête • **dishonesty** n malhonnêteté f

disillusioned [dɪsɪ'luːʒənd] adj **to be d.** être déçu (**with** de)

disinfect [dɪsɪn'fekt] vt désinfecter • **disinfectant** n désinfectant m

disintegrate [dɪs'ɪntɪgreɪt] vi se désintégrer

disinterested [dɪs'ɪntrɪstɪd] adj (impartial) désintéressé

disk [dɪsk] n (a) Am = **disc** (b) Comptr disque m; (floppy) disquette f; **d. drive** unité f de disques

dislike [dɪs'laɪk] vt ne pas aimer (**doing** faire)

dislocate ['dɪsləkeɪt] vt (limb) démettre; **to d. one's shoulder** se démettre l'épaule

dislodge [dɪs'lɒdʒ] *vt* faire bouger, déplacer; *(enemy)* déloger

dismal ['dɪzməl] *adj* lugubre

dismantle [dɪs'mæntəl] *vt* *(machine)* démonter

dismay [dɪs'meɪ] *n* consternation *f*

dismiss [dɪs'mɪs] *vt* *(from job)* renvoyer (**from** de); *(thought, suggestion)* écarter

disobey [dɪsə'beɪ] 1 *vt* désobéir à 2 *vi* désobéir • **disobedient** [dɪsə'biːdɪənt] *adj* désobéissant

disorder [dɪs'ɔːdə(r)] *n (confusion)* désordre *m*; *(illness, riots)* troubles *mpl* • **disorderly** *adj (behaviour)* désordonné; *(meeting, crowd)* houleux, -euse

disorganized [dɪs'ɔːgənaɪzd] *adj* désorganisé

disorientate [dɪs'ɔːrɪənteɪt] *(Am* **disorient** [dɪs'ɔːrɪənt]) *vt* désorienter

dispense [dɪ'spens] 1 *vt (give out)* distribuer; *(medicine)* préparer 2 *vi* **to d. with** *(do without)* se passer de

disperse [dɪ'spɜːs] 1 *vt* disperser 2 *vi* se disperser

displace [dɪs'pleɪs] *vt (shift)* déplacer; *(replace)* supplanter

display [dɪ'spleɪ] 1 *n (in shop)* étalage *m*; *(of paintings, crafts)* exposition *f*; **on d.** exposé 2 *vt (goods)* exposer; *(sign, notice)* afficher; *(emotion)* manifester; *(talent, concern)* faire preuve de

dispose [dɪ'spəuz] *vi* **to d. of** *(get rid of)* se débarrasser de; *(throw away)* jeter • **disposable** *adj Br* jetable • **disposal** *n (of waste)* évacuation *f*; **at sb's d.** à la disposition de qn

dispute [dɪ'spjuːt] *n* dispute *f*

disqualify [dɪs'kwɒlɪfaɪ] *(pt & pp*

-**ied**) *vt (make unfit)* rendre inapte (**from** à); *Sport* disqualifier

disregard [dɪsrɪ'gɑːd] 1 *n* mépris *m* (**for** de) 2 *vt* ne tenir aucun compte de

disrepute [dɪsrɪ'pjuːt] *n* **to bring sb/sth into d.** discréditer qn/qch

disrespectful [dɪsrɪ'spektful] *adj* irrespectueux, -euse (**to** envers)

disrupt [dɪs'rʌpt] *vt (traffic, class)* perturber; *(communications)* interrompre; *(plan)* déranger • **disruption** *n* perturbation *f* • **disruptive** *adj* perturbateur, -trice

dissatisfied [dɪ'sætɪsfaɪd] *adj* mécontent (**with** de)

dissertation [dɪsə'teɪʃən] *n* mémoire *m*

dissolve [dɪ'zɒlv] *vi* se dissoudre

distance ['dɪstəns] *n* distance *f*; **in the d.** au loin; **from a d.** de loin; **to keep one's d.** garder ses distances • **distant** *adj* lointain; *(relative)* éloigné; *(reserved)* distant

distinct [dɪ'stɪŋkt] *adj* **(a)** *(clear)* clair; *(preference, improvement, difference)* net *(f* nette) **(b)** *(different)* distinct (**from** de) • **distinctly** *adv (see, hear)* distinctement; *(remember)* très bien; *(better, easier)* nettement • **distinction** *n* distinction *f*; *(in exam)* mention *f* bien • **distinctive** *adj* distinctif, -ive

distinguish [dɪ'stɪŋgwɪʃ] *vti* distinguer (**from** de; **between** entre); **to d. oneself** se distinguer (**as** en tant que) • **distinguished** *adj* distingué

distort [dɪ'stɔːt] *vt* déformer

distract [dɪ'strækt] *vt* distraire (**from** de) • **distracted** *adj* préoccupé • **distraction** *n* distraction *f*

distraught [dɪ'strɔːt] *adj* éperdu

distress [dɪ'stres] 1 *n (mental)*

détresse *f*; *(physical)* douleur *f* **2**
vt bouleverser • **distressing** *adj*
bouleversant

distribute [dɪ'strɪbjuːt] *vt (give
out)* & *Com (supply)* distribuer;
(spread evenly) répartir • **distribution** [-'bjuːʃən] *n* distribution *f*

district ['dɪstrɪkt] *n* région *f*; *(of
town)* quartier *m*; *(administrative)*
district *m*

distrust [dɪs'trʌst] **1** *n* méfiance *f*
(**of** à l'égard de) **2** *vt* se méfier de

disturb [dɪ'stɜːb] *vt (sleep, water)*
troubler; *(papers, belongings)*
déranger; **to d. sb** *(bother)* déranger qn; *(worry, alarm)* troubler qn •
disturbing *adj (worrying)* inquiétant; *(annoying)* gênant

ditch [dɪtʃ] *n* fossé *m*

ditto ['dɪtəʊ] *adv* idem

dive [daɪv] **1** *n (of swimmer,
goalkeeper)* plongeon *m* **2** *(pt
dived, Am dove) vi* plonger •
diver *n* plongeur, -euse *mf*; *(deep-
sea)* scaphandrier *m*

diverse [daɪ'vɜːs] *adj* divers •
diversity *n* diversité *f*

divert [daɪ'vɜːt] *vt (attention,
river, plane)* détourner; *Br
(traffic)* dévier; *(amuse)* divertir •
diversion *n Br (on road)* déviation *f*; *(amusement)* distraction *f*;
to create a d. faire diversion

divide [dɪ'vaɪd] *vt Math* diviser
(**into** en; **by** par); *(food, money,
time)* partager (**between** or
among entre); **to d. sth up** *(share
out)* partager qch

divine [dɪ'vaɪn] *adj* divin

diving ['daɪvɪŋ] *n (underwater)*
plongée *f* sous-marine; **d. board**
plongeoir *m*

division [dɪ'vɪʒən] *n* division *f*;
(distribution) partage *m*

divorce [dɪ'vɔːs] **1** *n* divorce *m* **2**
vt (husband, wife) divorcer de •

divorced *adj* divorcé (**from** de);
to get d. divorcer • **divorcee**
[dɪvɔː'siː, *Am* dɪvɔːr'seɪ] *n*
divorcé, -e *mf*

DIY [diːaɪ'waɪ] *(abbr* **do-it-
yourself)** *n Br* bricolage *m*

dizzy ['dɪzɪ] **(-ier, -iest)** *adj* **to be
or feel d.** avoir le vertige; **to make
sb (feel) d.** donner le vertige à qn

DJ ['diːdʒeɪ] *(abbr* **disc-jockey)** *n*
disc-jockey *m*

do [duː]

Les formes négatives sont **don't/
doesn't** et **didn't**, qui deviennent
do not/does not et **did not**
dans un style plus soutenu.

1 *(3rd person sing present tense*
does, *pt* **did,** *pp* **done,** *pres p*
doing) *v aux* **do you know?**
savez-vous?, est-ce que vous
savez?; **I do not** or **don't see** je ne
vois pas; **he did say so** *(emphasis)*
il l'a bien dit; **do stay** reste donc;
you know him, don't you? tu le
connais, n'est-ce pas?; **you know
him better than I do** tu le connais
mieux que moi; **so do I** moi aussi;
don't! non! **2** *vt* faire; **what does
she do?** *(in general)* qu'est-ce
qu'elle fait?, que fait-elle?; **what
is she doing?** *(now)* qu'est-ce
qu'elle fait?, que fait-elle?; **what
have you done (with...)?**
qu'as-tu fait *(de...)?*; **well done**
(congratulations) bravo; *(steak)*
bien cuit; **it's over and done
(with)** c'est fini; **to do up** *(coat,
buttons)* boutonner; *(zip)* fermer;
(house) refaire **3** *vi* **do as you're
told** fais ce qu'on te dit; **that will
do** *(be OK)* ça ira; *(be enough)*
ça suffit; **to do well/badly** *(of
person)* bien/mal se débrouiller;
business is doing well les
affaires marchent bien; **how are**

you doing? (comment) ça va?; **how do you do** (introduction) enchanté; (greeting) bonjour; **to make do** se débrouiller; **to do away with sb/sth** supprimer qn/qch; **I could do with a coffee** (need, want) je prendrais bien un café; **it has to do with...** (relates to) cela a à voir avec...; (concerns) cela concerne... **4** n (pl **dos**) Br Fam (party) fête f

docile ['dəʊsaɪl] adj docile

dock [dɒk] n (**a**) (for ship) dock m (**b**) (in court) banc m des accusés

doctor ['dɒktə(r)] n médecin m, docteur m

document ['dɒkjʊmənt] n document m ● **documentary** [-'mentəri] (pl **-ies**) n (film) documentaire m

dodge [dɒdʒ] vt (question) esquiver; (person) éviter ● **dodgy** (**-ier, -iest**) adj Fam (suspect) louche; (not working properly) en mauvais état; (risky) risqué

does [dʌz] see **do** ● **doesn't** ['dʌzənt] = **does not**

dog [dɒg] n chien m

do-it-yourself [duːɪtjə'self] n Br bricolage m

dole [dəʊl] n Br **d. (money)** allocation f de chômage; **to go on the d.** s'inscrire au chômage

doll [dɒl] n poupée f; Br **doll's house,** Am **dollhouse** maison f de poupée

dollar ['dɒlə(r)] n dollar m

dollop ['dɒləp] n (of cream, purée) grosse cuillerée f

dolphin ['dɒlfɪn] n dauphin m

domain [dəʊ'meɪn] n (land, sphere) domaine m

dome [dəʊm] n dôme m

domestic [də'mestɪk] adj (appli-ance, tasks) ménager, -ère; (animal) domestique; (policy, flight) intérieur

dominate ['dɒmɪneɪt] vti dominer

domino ['dɒmɪnəʊ] (pl **-oes**) n domino m; **dominoes** (game) dominos mpl

donate [dəʊ'neɪt] vt faire don de; (blood) donner ● **donation** n don m

done [dʌn] pp of **do**

donkey ['dɒŋkɪ] (pl **-eys**) n âne m

donor ['dəʊnə(r)] n donneur, -euse mf

don't [dəʊnt] = **do not**

donut ['dəʊnʌt] n Am beignet m

doom [duːm] vt condamner (**to** à); **to be doomed (to failure)** (of project) être voué à l'échec

door [dɔː(r)] n porte f; (of vehicle, train) portière f; **d. handle** poignée f de porte ● **doorbell** n sonnette f ● **doorknob** n poignée f de porte ● **doormat** n paillasson m ● **doorstep** n seuil m ● **door-to-door** adj **d. salesman** démarcheur m ● **doorway** n **in the d.** dans l'embrasure de la porte

dope [dəʊp] n Fam (**a**) (drugs) drogue f (**b**) (idiot) andouille f

dormitory [Br 'dɔːmɪtrɪ, Am 'dɔːrmɪtɔːrɪ] (pl **-ies**) n dortoir m; Am (university residence) résidence f universitaire

dose [dəʊs] n dose f

dot [dɒt] n point m; Fam **on the d.** à l'heure pile ● **dotted** adj **d. line** pointillé m

double ['dʌbəl] **1** adj double; **a d. bed** un grand lit; **a d. room** une chambre pour deux personnes; **d. 's'** deux 's'; **d. three four two** (phone number) trente-trois quarante-deux **2** adv (twice) deux fois; (fold) en deux; **he earns d.**

what I do il gagne le double de moi **3** *n* double *m*; *(person)* double *m*, sosie *m*; *(stand-in in film)* doublure *f* **4** *vti* doubler ● **double-bass** *n Br* contrebasse *f* ● **double-check** *vti* revérifier ● **double-decker** *n* **d. (bus)** autobus *m* à impériale ● **double-glazing** *n (window)* double vitrage *m*

doubt [daʊt] **1** *n* doute *m*; **I have no d. about it** je n'en doute pas; **no d.** *(probably)* sans doute; **in d.** *(result, career)* dans la balance **2** *vt* douter de; **to d. whether** *or* **that** *or* **if...** douter que... *(+ subjunctive)* ● **doubtful** *adj (person, future, success)* incertain; **to be d. (about sth)** avoir des doutes (sur qch); **it's d. whether** *or* **that** *or* **if...** il n'est pas certain que... *(+ subjunctive)*

doughnut ['dəʊnʌt] *n* beignet *m*

dove¹ [dʌv] *n* colombe *f*

dove² [dəʊv] *Am pt of* **dive**

down [daʊn] **1** *adv* en bas; *(to the ground)* à terre; **d. there** *or* **here** en bas; *Fam* **to feel d.** *(depressed)* avoir le cafard; **d. to** *(in series, numbers, dates)* jusqu'à **2** *prep (at bottom of)* en bas de; *(from top to bottom of)* du haut en bas de; *(along)* le long de; **to go d.** *(hill, street, stairs)* descendre; **to live d. the street** habiter plus loin dans la rue ● **down-hearted** *adj* découragé ● **downhill** *adv* en pente; **to go d.** descendre; *(of sick person, business)* aller de plus en plus mal ● **downpour** *n* averse *f* ● **downright** *adv (rude, disagreeable)* franchement ● **downstairs 1** ['daʊnsteəz] *adj (room, neighbours) (below)* d'en bas; *(on the ground floor)* du rez-de-chaussée **2** [daʊn'steəz] *adv*

en bas; *(to the ground floor)* au rez-de-chaussée; **to come** *or* **go d.** descendre l'escalier ● **down-to-earth** *adj* terre-à-terre *inv* ● **downtown** *adv Am* en ville; **d. Chicago** le centre de Chicago ● **downward** *adj* vers le bas; *(path)* qui descend; *(trend)* à la baisse ● **downward(s)** *adv* vers le bas

doze [dəʊz] *vi* sommeiller; **to d. off** s'assoupir

dozen ['dʌzən] *n* douzaine *f*; **a d. books/eggs** une douzaine de livres/d'œufs; *Fig* **dozens of** des dizaines de

Dr *(abbr* **Doctor)** Docteur

drab [dræb] *adj* terne

draft¹ [drɑːft] **1** *n (letter)* brouillon *m* **2** *vt (letter)* faire le brouillon de

draft² [drɑːft] *n Am =* **draught** ● **drafty** ['drɑːftɪ] **(-ier, -iest)** *adj Am =* **draughty**

drag [dræg] **1** *n Fam* **it's a d.!** *(boring)* c'est la barbe! **2** *(pt & pp* **-gg-)** *vt* traîner; **to d. sb/sth along** (en)traîner qn/qch; **to d. sb away from** arracher qn à; **to d. sb into** entraîner qn dans **3** *vi* traîner; **to d. on** *or* **out** *(of film, day)* traîner en longueur

dragon ['drægən] *n* dragon *m*

drain [dreɪn] **1** *n (sewer)* égout *m*; *(in street)* bouche *f* d'égout **2** *vt (glass, tank)* vider; *(vegetables)* égoutter; **to d. (off)** *(liquid)* faire écouler; **to feel drained** être épuisé ● **draining** *n* **d. board** égouttoir *m* ● **drainpipe** *n* tuyau *m* d'évacuation

drama ['drɑːmə] *n (event)* drame *m*; *(dramatic art)* théâtre *m* ● **dramatic** *adj* dramatique; *(very great, striking)* spectaculaire

drank [dræŋk] *pt of* **drink**

drape [dreɪp] *vt (person, shoul-*

ders) draper (**with** de) • **drapes**
npl Am (curtains) rideaux mpl
drastic ['dræstɪk] adj (change,
measure) radical; (remedy) puissant
draught [drɑ:ft] (Am **draft**) n
(**a**) (wind) courant m d'air (**b**)
Br **draughts** (game) dames fpl
(**c**) **d. beer** bière f (à la) pression
• **draughty** (Am **drafty**) (**-ier,
-iest**) adj (room) plein de cour-
ants d'air
draw[1] [drɔ:] **1** n Sport match m
nul; (of lottery) tirage m au sort
2 (pt **drew,** pp **drawn**) vt (**a**)
(pull) tirer; **to d. up** (contract, list,
plan) dresser, rédiger (**b**) (extract)
retirer; Fig (strength, comfort)
retirer, puiser (**from** de) **3** vi
Sport faire match nul; **to d. near
(to)** s'approcher (de); (of time)
approcher (de); **to d. back** (go
backwards) reculer • **drawback** n
inconvénient m
draw[2] [drɔ:] **1** (pt **drew,** pp
drawn) vt (picture) dessiner; (circle) tracer; Fig (parallel, distinction) faire (**between** entre) **2** vi
dessiner • **drawing** n dessin m;
Br **d. pin** punaise f
drawer [drɔ:(r)] n tiroir m
drawn [drɔ:n] pp of **draw**[1,2]
dread [dred] vt (exam) appréhender; **to d. doing sth** appréhender
de faire qch • **dreadful** adj épouvantable; **I feel d.** (ill) je ne me
sens vraiment pas bien; **I feel d.
about it** j'ai vraiment honte •
dreadfully adv terriblement; **to
be d. sorry** regretter infiniment
dream [dri:m] **1** n rêve m; **to have
a d.** faire un rêve (**about** de); **a
d. world** un monde imaginaire
2 (pt & pp **dreamed** or **dreamt**
[dremt]) vt rêver (**that** que); **I
never dreamt that...** (imagined)

je n'aurais jamais songé que... **3** vi
rêver (**of** or **about sb/sth** de qn/
qch; **of** or **about doing** de faire)
dreary ['drɪərɪ] (**-ier, -iest**) adj
morne
drench [drentʃ] vt tremper; **to
get drenched** se faire tremper
(jusqu'aux os)
dress [dres] **1** n (garment) robe
f; (style of dressing) tenue f; **d.
rehearsal** (in theatre) répétition f
générale **2** vt (person) habiller;
(wound) panser; (salad) assaisonner; **to get dressed** s'habiller **3**
vi s'habiller; **to d. up** (smartly)
bien s'habiller; (in disguise) se
déguiser (**as** en) • **dressing** n (for
wound) pansement m; (for salad)
assaisonnement m; Br **d. gown**
robe f de chambre; **d. room** (in
theatre) loge f; (in shop) cabine f
d'essayage; **d. table** coiffeuse f
drew [dru:] pt of **draw**[1,2]
dribble ['drɪbəl] vi (**a**) (of baby)
baver (**b**) Sport dribbler
dried [draɪd] adj (fruit) sec (f
sèche); (flowers) séché
drier ['draɪə(r)] n = **dryer**
drift [drɪft] vi (of ship) dériver; Fig
(of person) aller à la dérive
drill [drɪl] **1** n (**a**) (tool) perceuse f
(**b**) (exercise) exercice m; (correct
procedure) marche f à suivre **2** vt
percer
drink [drɪŋk] **1** n boisson f; **to
have a d.** boire quelque chose;
(alcoholic) prendre un verre **2**
(pt **drank,** pp **drunk**) vt boire **3**
vi boire (**out of** dans) • **drink-
driving** n Br conduite f en état
d'ivresse • **drinking** n **d. water**
eau f potable
drip [drɪp] **1** n (drop) goutte f; Med
to be on a d. être sous perfusion
2 (pt & pp **-pp-**) vi (of water, rain)
goutter; (of tap) fuir

drive [draɪv] **1** *n* *(in car)* promenade *f* en voiture; *(path to house)* allée *f*; *Comptr* lecteur *m*; **an hour's d.** une heure de voiture **2** *(pt* **drove**, *pp* **driven** ['drɪvən]) *vt* *(vehicle, train, passenger)* conduire (**to** à); *(machine)* actionner; **to d. sb to do sth** pousser qn à faire qch; **to d. sb mad** *or* **crazy** rendre qn fou/folle; **he drives a Ford** il a une Ford **3** *vi* *(drive a car)* conduire; *(go by car)* rouler; **to d. on the left** rouler à gauche; **to d. to Paris** aller en voiture à Paris; **to d. to work** aller au travail en voiture ● **drive-in** *adj* *Am* **d. (movie theater)** drive-in *m* *inv*; **d. (restaurant)** = restaurant où l'on est servi dans sa voiture ● **driver** *n* *(of car)* conducteur, -trice *mf*; *(of taxi, truck)* chauffeur *m*; **(train** *or* **engine) d.** mécanicien *m*; **she's a good d.** elle conduit bien; *Am* **d.'s license** permis *m* de conduire ● **driveway** *n* *(path to house)* allée *f* ● **driving** *n* *(in car)* conduite *f*; **d. lesson** leçon *f* de conduite; *Br* **d. licence** permis *m* de conduire; **d. school** auto-école *f*; **d. test** examen *m* du permis de conduire

▶**drive along** *vi* *(in car)* rouler

▶**drive away 1** *vt sep* *(chase away)* chasser **2** *vi* *(in car)* partir (en voiture)

▶**drive off** *vi* *(in car)* partir (en voiture)

drizzle ['drɪzəl] *vi* bruiner

droop [druːp] *vi* *(of flower)* se faner; *(of head)* pencher; *(of eyelids, shoulders)* tomber

drop [drɒp] **1** *n* **(a)** *(of liquid)* goutte *f*; **eye drops** gouttes *fpl* pour les yeux **(b)** *(fall)* baisse *f*, chute *f* **(in** de); *(distance of fall)* hauteur *f* de chute; *(slope)* descente *f* **2** *(pt & pp* **-pp-**) *vt* laisser tomber; *(price, voice)* baisser; *(bomb)* larguer;

(passenger) déposer; *(leave out)* omettre; *(get rid of)* supprimer; **to d. sb off** *(from vehicle)* déposer qn; **to d. sb a line** écrire un petit mot à qn **3** *vi* *(fall)* tomber; **to d. back** *or* **behind** rester en arrière; **to d. by** *or* **in** *(visit sb)* passer; **to d. off** *(fall asleep)* s'endormir; *(fall off)* tomber; **to d. out** *(fall out)* tomber; *(withdraw)* se retirer; *(of student)* laisser tomber ses études ● **dropout** *n* marginal, -e *mf*; *(student)* étudiant, -e *mf* qui abandonne ses études

drought [draʊt] *n* sécheresse *f*

drove [drəʊv] *pt of* **drive**

drown [draʊn] **1** *vt* noyer **2** *vi* se noyer

drowsy ['draʊzɪ] (**-ier**, **-iest**) *adj* **to be** *or* **feel d.** avoir sommeil

drug [drʌg] **1** *n* *(medical)* médicament *m*; *(narcotic)* drogue *f*; **drugs** *(narcotics in general)* la drogue; **to be on drugs, to take drugs** se droguer; **d. addict** drogué, -e *mf*; **d. dealer** *(large-scale)* trafiquant *m* de drogue; *(small-scale)* dealer *m* **2** *(pt & pp* **-gg-**) *vt* droguer ● **drugstore** *n Am* drugstore *m*

drum [drʌm] *n Mus* tambour *m*; **the drums** *(of rock group)* la batterie ● **drummer** *n* tambour *m*; *(in rock group)* batteur *m* ● **drumstick** *n* *(for drum)* baguette *f* de tambour; *(of chicken)* pilon *m*

drunk [drʌŋk] **1** *pp of* **drink 2** *adj* ivre; **to get d.** s'enivrer ● **drunken** *adj* *(driver)* ivre; *(quarrel, brawl)* d'ivrognes

dry [draɪ] **1** (**drier, driest**) *adj* sec *(f* sèche); *(well, river)* à sec; *(day)* sans pluie; *(subject, book)* aride; **to wipe sth d.** essuyer qch **2** *vt* sécher; *(by wiping)* essuyer; *(clothes)* faire sécher; **to d. the**

dishes essuyer la vaisselle; **to d. sth off** or **up** sécher qch **3** *vi* sécher; **to d. off** sécher; **to d. up** sécher; *(dry the dishes)* essuyer la vaisselle; *(of stream)* se tarir • **dry-clean** *vt* nettoyer à sec • **dry-cleaner** *n* **the d.'s** *(shop)* le pressing, la teinturerie • **dryer** *n* *(for hair, clothes)* séchoir *m*

dual ['djuːəl] *adj* *Br* **d. carriageway** route *f* à deux voies

dub [dʌb] *(pt & pp* **-bb-***)* *vt* *(film)* doubler (**into** en)

dubious ['djuːbɪəs] *adj* douteux, -euse; **I'm d. about going** or **about whether to go** je me demande si je dois y aller

duchess ['dʌtʃɪs] *n* duchesse *f*

duck [dʌk] **1** *n* canard *m* **2** *vi* se baisser • **duckling** *n* caneton *m*

due [djuː] *adj* *(money, sum)* dû *(f* due) **(to** à); *(rent, bill)* à payer; *(fitting, proper)* qui convient; **he's d. (to arrive)** il doit arriver d'un moment à l'autre; **in d. course** *(when appropriate)* en temps voulu; *(eventually)* le moment venu; **d. to** par suite de, en raison de

duet [djuːˈet] *n* duo *m*

duffel, duffle ['dʌfəl] *adj* **d. coat** duffel-coat *m*

dug [dʌg] *pt & pp of* **dig**

duke [djuːk] *n* duc *m*

dull [dʌl] (**-er, -est**) *adj* *(boring)* ennuyeux, -euse; *(colour, character)* terne; *(weather)* maussade

dumb [dʌm] (**-er, -est**) *adj* muet *(f* muette); *Fam (stupid)* bête

dummy ['dʌmɪ] *(pl* **-ies***)* *n* *Br (of baby)* tétine *f*; *(for clothes)* mannequin *m*

dump [dʌmp] **1** *n* *(for refuse)* décharge *f*; *Fam Pej (town)* trou *m* **2** *vt* *(rubbish)* déposer; *Fam* **to d. sb** plaquer qn

dumpling ['dʌmplɪŋ] *n* *(in stew)* boulette *f* de pâte

dune [djuːn] *n* **(sand) d.** dune *f*

dungarees [dʌngəˈriːz] *npl* *(of child, workman)* salopette *f*

dunk [dʌŋk] *vt* tremper

dupe [djuːp] *vt* duper

duplex ['duːpleks] *n* *Am* *(apartment)* duplex *m*

duplicate ['djuːplɪkeɪt] *vt* *(key, map)* faire un double de; *(on machine)* photocopier

duration [djʊəˈreɪʃən] *n* durée *f*

during ['djʊərɪŋ] *prep* pendant

dusk [dʌsk] *n* crépuscule *m*

dust [dʌst] **1** *n* poussière *f* **2** *vt* *(furniture)* dépoussiérer **3** *vi* faire la poussière • **dustbin** *n* *Br* poubelle *f* • **duster** *n* chiffon *m* • **dustman** *(pl* **-men***)* *n* *Br* éboueur *m* • **dusty** (**-ier, -iest**) *adj* poussiéreux, -euse

Dutch [dʌtʃ] **1** *adj* hollandais **2** *n* **(a) the D.** *(people)* les Hollandais *mpl* **(b)** *(language)* hollandais *m*

duty ['djuːtɪ] *(pl* **-ies***)* *n* devoir *m*; *(tax)* droit *m*; **duties** *(responsibilities)* fonctions *fpl*; **to be on/off d.** être/ne pas être de service • **duty-free** *adj* *(goods, shop)* hors taxe *inv*

duvet ['duːveɪ] *n* *Br* couette *f*

DVD [diːviːˈdiː] *(abbr* **Digital Versatile Disk, Digital Video Disk***)* *n* *Comptr* DVD *m inv*

dwarf [dwɔːf] *n* nain, -e *mf*

dwell [dwel] *(pt & pp* **dwelt** [dwelt]*)* *vi* demeurer; **to d. (up)on** *(think about)* penser sans cesse à

dye [daɪ] **1** *n* teinture *f* **2** *vt* teindre; **to d. sth blue** teindre qch en bleu

dynamic [daɪˈnæmɪk] *adj* dynamique

dynamite ['daɪnəmaɪt] *n* dynamite *f*

dyslexic [dɪsˈleksɪk] *adj & n* dyslexique *(mf)*

Ee

E, e [i:] *n (letter)* E, e *m inv*

each [i:tʃ] **1** *adj* chaque; **e. one** chacun, -e; **e. one of us** chacun d'entre nous **2** *pron* chacun, -e; **e. other** l'un(e) l'autre, *pl* les un(e)s les autres; **to see/greet e. other** se voir/se saluer; **e. of us** chacun, -e d'entre nous

eager ['i:gə(r)] *adj (impatient)* impatient (**to do** de faire); *(enthusiastic)* plein d'enthousiasme • **eagerly** *adv (do)* avec enthousiasme; *(await)* avec impatience

eagle ['i:gəl] *n* aigle *m*

ear [ɪə(r)] *n* oreille *f*; **to play it by e.** improviser • **earache** *n* mal *m* d'oreille • **earphones** *npl* écouteurs *mpl* • **earplug** *n* boule *f* Quiès® • **earring** *n* boucle *f* d'oreille

early ['ɜ:lɪ] **1** (**-ier, -iest**) *adj (first)* premier, -ère; *(death)* prématuré; *(age)* jeune; *(retirement)* anticipé; **it's e.** *(on clock)* il est tôt; *(referring to meeting, appointment)* c'est tôt; **to be e.** *(ahead of time)* être en avance; **in the e. 1990s** au début des années 90; **to be in one's e. fifties** avoir à peine plus de cinquante ans **2** *adv* tôt, de bonne heure; *(ahead of time)* en avance; *(die)* prématurément; **earlier (on)** plus tôt; **at the earliest** au plus tôt

earn [ɜ:n] *vt* gagner; *(interest)* rapporter; **to e. one's living** gagner sa vie • **earnings** *npl* *(wages)* salaire *m*; *(profits)* bénéfices *mpl*

earnest ['ɜ:nɪst] **1** *adj (serious)* sérieux, -euse **2** *n* **in e.** sérieusement

earth [ɜ:θ] *n (ground)* sol *m*; *(soil)* terre *f*; *Br (electrical wire)* terre *f*, masse *f*; **the E.** *(planet)* la Terre; **where/what on e....?** où/que diable...? • **earthquake** *n* tremblement *m* de terre

ease [i:z] **1** *n (facility)* facilité *f*; **with e.** facilement; **to be at e./ ill at e.** être à l'aise/mal à l'aise **2** *vt (pain)* soulager; *(mind)* calmer; *(tension)* réduire; *(restrictions)* assouplir **3** *vi* **to e. (off** *or* **up)** *(of pressure)* diminuer; *(of demand)* baisser; *(of pain)* se calmer • **easily** *adv* facilement

east [i:st] **1** *n* est *m*; **(to the) e. of** à l'est de; **the E.** *(Eastern Europe)* l'Est *m*; *(the Orient)* l'Orient *m* **2** *adj (coast)* est *inv*; *(wind)* d'est; **E. Africa** l'Afrique *f* orientale **3** *adv* à l'est; *(travel)* vers l'est • **eastern** *adj (coast)* est *inv*; **E. France** l'est *m* de la France; **E. Europe** l'Europe *f* de l'Est

Easter ['i:stə(r)] *n* Pâques *fpl*; **Happy E.!** joyeuses Pâques!; **E. egg** œuf *m* de Pâques

easy ['i:zɪ] **1** (**-ier, -iest**) *adj (not difficult)* facile; *(solution)* simple **2** *adv* doucement; **take it e.** *(rest)* repose-toi; *(work less)* ne te fatigue pas; *(calm down)* calmetoi • **easygoing** *adj (carefree)* insouciant; *(easy to get along with)* facile à vivre

eat [iːt] *(pt* **ate** *[Br* et, eɪt, *Am* eɪt], *pp* **eaten** ['iːtən]) **1** *vt* manger; *(meal)* prendre; **to e. sth up** *(finish)* finir qch **2** *vi* manger; **to e. out** aller au restaurant

eavesdrop ['iːvzdrɒp] *(pt & pp* **-pp-)** *vti* **to e. (on)** écouter avec indiscrétion

eccentric [ɪk'sentrɪk] *adj & n* excentrique *(mf)*

echo ['ekəʊ] **1** *(pl* **-oes)** *n* écho *m* **2** *(pt & pp* **echoed)** *vi* résonner **(with** de)

eclipse [ɪ'klɪps] *n (of sun, moon)* éclipse *f*

ecological [iːkə'lɒdʒɪkəl] *adj* écologique

economy [ɪ'kɒnəmɪ] *(pl* **-ies)** *n* économie *f; Aviat* e. **class** classe *f* économique ● **economic** [iːkə'nɒmɪk] *adj* économique ● **economical** [iːkə'nɒmɪkəl] *adj* économique ● **economics** [iːkə'nɒmɪks] *n* économie *f* ● **economize** [ɪ'kɒnəmaɪz] *vti* économiser **(on** sur)

ecstasy ['ekstəsɪ] *(pl* **-ies)** *n (state)* extase *f; (drug)* ecstasy *f*

edge [edʒ] *n* bord *m; (of town)* abords *mpl; (of page)* marge *f; (of knife, blade)* tranchant *m* ● **edgeways** *(Am* **edgewise)** *adv* de côté; *Fam* **I can't get a word in e.** je ne peux pas en placer une

edible ['edɪbəl] *adj (safe to eat)* comestible; *(fit to eat)* mangeable

Edinburgh ['edɪnbərə] *n* Édimbourg *m ou f*

edit ['edɪt] *vt (newspaper)* diriger; *(article)* corriger; *(film)* monter ● **edition** [ɪ'dɪʃən] *n* édition *f* ● **editor** *n (of newspaper)* rédacteur, -trice *mf* en chef; *(of film)* monteur, -euse *mf*

educate ['edjʊkeɪt] *vt (bring up)* éduquer; *(in school)* instruire ● **educated** *adj* **(well-)e.** *(person)* instruit ● **education** [-'keɪʃən] *n* éducation *f; (teaching)* enseignement *m; (university subject)* pédagogie *f* ● **educational** [-'keɪʃənəl] *adj (qualification)* d'enseignement; *(method, content)* pédagogique; *(game, film, system)* éducatif, -ive

eel [iːl] *n* anguille *f*

eerie ['ɪərɪ] **(-ier, -iest)** *adj* sinistre

effect [ɪ'fekt] *n (result, impression)* effet *m* **(on** sur); **in e.** en fait; **to come into e., to take e.** *(of law)* entrer en vigueur ● **effective** *adj (efficient)* efficace; *(actual)* réel *(f* réelle); **to become e.** *(of law)* prendre effet ● **effectively** *adv (efficiently)* efficacement; *(in fact)* effectivement

efficient [ɪ'fɪʃənt] *adj* efficace; *(productive)* performant ● **efficiently** *adv* efficacement

effort ['efət] *n* effort *m;* **to make an e.** faire un effort **(to** pour)

e.g. [iː'dʒiː] *(abbr* **exempli gratia)** p. ex.

egg [eg] *n* œuf *m;* **e. timer** sablier *m* ● **eggplant** *n Am* aubergine *f*

ego ['iːgəʊ] *(pl* **-os)** *n* **to have a big e.** avoir une haute opinion de soi-même

Egypt ['iːdʒɪpt] *n* l'Égypte *f* ● **Egyptian** [ɪ'dʒɪpʃən] **1** *adj* égyptien, -enne **2** *n* Égyptien, -enne *mf*

eight [eɪt] *adj & n* huit *(m)* ● **eighth** *adj & n* huitième *(mf);* **an e.** *(fraction)* un huitième

eighteen [eɪ'tiːn] *adj & n* dix-huit *(m)* ● **eighteenth** *adj & n* dix-huitième *(mf)*

eighty ['eɪtɪ] *adj & n* quatre-vingts *(m);* **e.-one** quatre-vingt-un; **in**

the eighties dans les années 80 • **eightieth** *adj & n* quatre-vingtième *(mf)*

either ['aɪðə(r), i:ðə(r)] **1** *adj & pron (one or other)* l'un(e) ou l'autre; *(with negative)* ni l'un(e) ni l'autre; *(each)* chaque; **on e. side** des deux côtés **2** *adv* **she can't swim e.** elle ne sait pas nager non plus; **I don't e.** (ni) moi non plus **3** *conj* **e.... or...** ou... ou..., soit... soit...; *(with negative)* ni... ni...

eject [ɪ'dʒekt] *vt (from machine)* éjecter

elaborate 1 [ɪ'læbərət] *adj (meal)* élaboré; *(scheme)* compliqué; *(description)* détaillé; *(style)* recherché **2** [ɪ'læbəreɪt] *vi* entrer dans les détails **(on** de)

elapse [ɪ'læps] *vi* s'écouler

elastic [ɪ'læstɪk] **1** *adj* élastique; *Br* **e. band** élastique *m* **2** *n (fabric)* élastique *m*

elbow ['elbəʊ] *n* coude *m*

elder ['eldə(r)] *adj & n (of two people)* aîné, -e *(mf)* • **elderly 1** *adj* âgé **2** *npl* **the e.** les personnes *fpl* âgées • **eldest** *adj & n* aîné, -e *(mf)*; **his/her e. brother** l'aîné de ses frères

elect [ɪ'lekt] *vt (by voting)* élire **(to** à) • **election** [-ʃən] **1** *n* élection *f*; **general e.** élections *fpl* législatives **2** *adj (campaign)* électoral; *(day, results)* des élections

electric [ɪ'lektrɪk] *adj* électrique; **e. shock** décharge *f* électrique • **electrical** *adj* électrique • **electrician** [-'trɪʃən] *n* électricien *m* • **electricity** [-'trɪsɪtɪ] *n* électricité *f*

electronic [ɪlek'trɒnɪk] *adj* électronique • **electronics** *n (subject)* électronique *f*

elegant ['elɪgənt] *adj* élégant • **elegantly** *adv* avec élégance

element ['eləmənt] *n (component, chemical, person)* élément *m*; *(of heater, kettle)* résistance *f*; **the elements** *(bad weather)* les éléments *mpl*; **to be in one's e.** être dans son élément

elementary [elɪ'mentərɪ] *adj* élémentaire; *Am (school)* primaire

elephant ['elɪfənt] *n* éléphant *m*

elevator ['elɪveɪtə(r)] *n Am* ascenseur *m*

eleven [ɪ'levən] *adj & n* onze *(m)* • **eleventh** *adj & n* onzième *(mf)*

eligible ['elɪdʒəbəl] *adj (for post)* admissible **(for** à); **to be e. for sth** *(entitled to)* avoir droit à qch

eliminate [ɪ'lɪmɪneɪt] *vt* éliminer

elite [eɪ'li:t] *n* élite *f* **(of** de)

elope [ɪ'ləʊp] *vi (of lovers)* s'enfuir **(with** avec)

eloquent ['eləkwənt] *adj* éloquent

else [els] *adv* d'autre; **somebody/anybody e.** quelqu'un/n'importe qui d'autre; **everybody e.** tous les autres; **something e.** autre chose; **anything e.?** *(in shop)* est-ce qu'il vous faut autre chose?; **somewhere e.,** *Am* **someplace e.** ailleurs, autre part; **nowhere e.** nulle part ailleurs; **who e.?** qui d'autre?; **or e.** ou bien, sinon • **elsewhere** *adv* ailleurs

e-mail ['i:meɪl] **1** *n* courrier *m* électronique, e-mail *m*; **e. address** adresse *f* électronique **2** *vt* envoyer un courrier électronique *ou* un e-mail à

embankment [ɪm'bæŋkmənt] *n (of path)* talus *m*; *(of river)* berge *f*

embargo [ɪm'ba:gəʊ] *(pl* -**oes)** embargo *m*

embark [ɪm'ba:k] *vi* (s')embarquer; **to e. on sth** s'embarquer dans qch

embarrass [ɪm'bærəs] *vt*

embarrasser • **embarrassing** *adj*
embarrassant
embassy ['embəsɪ] (*pl* **-ies**) *n*
ambassade *f*
embellish [ɪm'belɪʃ] *vt* embellir
embezzle [ɪm'bezəl] *vt (money)*
détourner
emblem ['embləm] *n* emblème *m*
embrace [ɪm'breɪs] **1** *n* étreinte *f*
2 *vt (person)* étreindre; *Fig (belief)*
embrasser **3** *vi* s'étreindre
embroider [ɪm'brɔɪdə(r)] *vt*
broder • **embroidery** *n* broderie *f*
embryo ['embrɪəʊ] (*pl* **-os**) *n*
embryon *m*
emerald ['emərəld] *n* émeraude *f*
emerge [ɪ'mɜːdʒ] *vi* apparaître
(**from** de); *(from hole)* sortir; *(from
water)* émerger
emergency [ɪ'mɜːdʒənsɪ] **1** (*pl*
-ies) *n (situation, case)* urgence *f*;
in an e. en cas d'urgence **2** *adj
(measure, operation, services)*
d'urgence; **e. exit** sortie *f* de
secours; **e. landing** atterrissage
m forcé
emigrate ['emɪɡreɪt] *vi* émigrer
emit [ɪ'mɪt] (*pt & pp* **-tt-**) *vt (gas,
heat)* émettre • **emission** [-ʃən] *n
(of gas, light)* émission *f*
emotion [ɪ'məʊʃən] *n (strength
of feeling)* émotion *f*; *(individual
feeling)* sentiment *m* • **emotional**
adj (person, reaction) émotif, -ive;
(speech, plea) émouvant
empathy ['empəθɪ] *n* compassion
f
emperor ['empərə(r)] *n* empereur
m
emphasize ['emfəsaɪz] *vt
(importance)* souligner; *(word,
fact)* insister sur, souligner;
(syllable) appuyer sur; **to e. that...**
souligner que... • **emphasis** *n
(in word or phrase)* accent *m*;
(insistence) insistance *f*

empire ['empaɪə(r)] *n* empire *m*
employ [ɪm'plɔɪ] *vt (person,
means)* employer • **employee**
[em'plɔɪiː] *n* employé, -e *mf* •
employer *n* patron, -onne *mf*
• **employment** *n* emploi *m*; **e.
agency** bureau *m* de placement
empty ['emptɪ] **1** (**-ier, -iest**)
adj vide; *(threat, promise)* vain;
on an e. stomach à jeun **2** (*pt
& pp* **-ied**) *vt* **to e. (out)** *(box,
pocket, liquid)* vider; *(objects from
box)* sortir (**from** or **out of** de)
3 *vi (of building, tank)* se vider •
emptiness *n* vide *m* • **empty-
handed** *adv* **to return e.** revenir
les mains vides
enable [ɪ'neɪbəl] *vt* **to e. sb to do
sth** permettre à qn de faire qch
enamel [ɪ'næməl] **1** *n* émail *m* (*pl*
émaux) **2** *adj* en émail
enclose [ɪn'kləʊz] *vt (send with
letter)* joindre (**in** or **with** à);
(fence off) clôturer • **enclosed**
adj (receipt, document) ci-joint;
please find e.... veuillez trouver
ci-joint... • **enclosure** [-ʒə(r)] *n
(in letter)* pièce *f* jointe; *(place)*
enceinte *f*
encore ['ɒŋkɔː(r)] *exclam & n*
bis *(m)*
encounter [ɪn'kaʊntə(r)] *vt
(person, resistance)* rencontrer
encourage [ɪn'kʌrɪdʒ] *vt* encourager (**to do** à faire) • **encouragement** *n* encouragement
m
encyclop(a)edia [ɪnsaɪklə'piːdɪə]
n encyclopédie *f*
end [end] **1** *n (extremity)* bout *m*,
extrémité *f*; *(of month, meeting,
book)* fin *f*; *(purpose)* but *m*; **at an
e.** *(discussion, war)* fini; *(period of
time)* écoulé; **in the e.** à la fin; **to
come to an e.** prendre fin; **for
days on e.** pendant des jours et

des jours **2** *vt* finir, terminer (**with** par); *(rumour, speculation)* mettre fin à **3** *vi* finir, se terminer; **to e. up doing sth** finir par faire qch; **he ended up in prison/a doctor** il a fini en prison/médecin • **ending** *n* fin *f*; *(of word)* terminaison *f* • **endless** *adj (speech, series, list)* interminable; *(countless)* innombrable

endanger [ɪn'deɪndʒə(r)] *vt* mettre en danger; **endangered species** espèce *f* menacée

endeavour [ɪn'devə(r)] *(Am* **endeavor)** *vi* s'efforcer (**to do** de faire)

endure [ɪn'djʊə(r)] *vt (violence)* endurer; *(person, insult)* supporter • **endurance** *n* endurance *f*

enemy ['enəmɪ] **1** *(pl* **-ies)** *n* ennemi, -e *mf* **2** *adj (army, tank)* ennemi

energy ['enədʒɪ] *(pl* **-ies)** *n* énergie *f* • **energetic** [-'dʒetɪk] *adj* énergique

enforce [ɪn'fɔːs] *vt (law)* faire respecter; *(discipline)* imposer (**on** à)

engaged [ɪn'geɪdʒd] *adj* **(a)** *(occupied) (person, toilet, phone)* occupé **(b) e. (to be married)** fiancé; **to get e.** se fiancer • **engagement** *n (to marry)* fiançailles *fpl*; *(meeting)* rendez-vous *m inv*; **e. ring** bague *f* de fiançailles

engine ['endʒɪn] *n (of vehicle, aircraft)* moteur *m*; *(of train)* locomotive *f*

engineer [endʒɪ'nɪə(r)] *n* ingénieur *m*; *Br (repairer)* dépanneur *m*; **civil e.** ingénieur *m* des travaux publics • **engineering** *n* ingénierie *f*; **(civil) e.** génie *m* civil

England ['ɪŋglənd] *n* l'Angleterre

f • **English 1** *adj* anglais; **E. teacher** professeur *m* d'anglais; **the E. Channel** la Manche **2** *n* **(a)** *(language)* anglais *m* **(b) the E.** *(people)* les Anglais *mpl* • **Englishman** *(pl* **-men)** *n* Anglais *m* • **English-speaking** *adj* anglophone • **Englishwoman** *(pl* **-women)** *n* Anglaise *f*

engrossed [ɪn'grəʊst] *adj* **e. in one's work/book** absorbé par son travail/dans sa lecture

enhance [ɪn'hɑːns] *vt (beauty, prestige)* rehausser; *(value)* augmenter

enigma [ɪ'nɪgmə] *n* énigme *f*

enjoy [ɪn'dʒɔɪ] *vt (like)* aimer (**doing** faire); *(meal)* savourer; **to e. oneself** s'amuser • **enjoyable** *adj* agréable; *(meal)* excellent • **enjoyment** *n* plaisir *m*

enlarge [ɪn'lɑːdʒ] *vt* agrandir

enlighten [ɪn'laɪtən] *vt* éclairer (**sb on** *or* **about sth** qn sur qch)

enlist [ɪn'lɪst] **1** *vt (recruit)* engager; *(supporter)* recruter **2** *vi (in the army)* s'engager

enormous [ɪ'nɔːməs] *adj* énorme; *(gratitude, success)* immense • **enormously** *adv (very much)* énormément; *(very)* extrêmement

enough [ɪ'nʌf] **1** *adj* assez de; **e. time/cups** assez de temps/de tasses **2** *pron* assez; **to have e. to live on** avoir de quoi vivre; **to have had e. of sb/sth** en avoir assez de qn/qch; **that's e.** ça suffit **3** *adv (work, sleep)* assez; **big/good e.** assez grand/bon (**to** pour)

enquire [ɪn'kwaɪə(r)] *vti* = **inquire** • **enquiry** *n* = **inquiry**

enrich [ɪn'rɪtʃ] *vt* enrichir; *(soil)* fertiliser

enrol [ɪn'rəʊl] *(Am* **enroll)** *(pt &*

pp **-ll-) 1** *vt* inscrire **2** *vi* s'inscrire (**on** *or* **for** à)

ensure [ɪn'ʃʊə(r)] *vt* assurer; **to e. that...** s'assurer que...

entail [ɪn'teɪl] *vt* (*involve*) occasionner; **what does the job e.?** en quoi le travail consiste-t-il?

entangle [ɪn'tæŋgəl] *vt* **to get entangled in sth** (*of person, animal*) s'empêtrer dans qch

enter ['entə(r)] **1** *vt* (*room, army*) entrer dans; (*race, competition*) participer à; (*write down*) (*on list*) inscrire (**in** dans; **on** sur); *Comptr* (*data*) entrer; **it didn't e. my head** ça ne m'est pas venu à l'esprit (**that** que) **2** *vi* entrer; **to e. into** (*relations*) entrer en; (*agreement*) conclure; (*contract*) passer (**with** avec)

enterprise ['entəpraɪz] *n* (*undertaking, firm*) entreprise *f*; (*spirit, initiative*) initiative *f* • **enterprising** *adj* (*person*) entreprenant

entertain [entə'teɪn] **1** *vt* amuser, distraire; (*guest*) recevoir **2** *vi* (*receive guests*) recevoir • **entertainer** *n* (*comedian*) comique *mf*; (*singer, dancer*) artiste *mf* de music-hall • **entertainment** *n* amusement *m*; (*show*) spectacle *m*

enthusiasm [ɪn'θjuːzɪæzəm] *n* enthousiasme *m* • **enthusiast** *n* enthousiaste *mf*; **jazz e.** passionné, -e *mf* de jazz • **enthusiastic** [-'æstɪk] *adj* enthousiaste; (*golfer, photographer*) passionné; **to get e.** s'emballer (**about** pour)

enticing [ɪn'taɪsɪŋ] *adj* séduisant

entire [ɪn'taɪə(r)] *adj* entier, -ère • **entirely** *adv* entièrement

entitled [ɪn'taɪtəld] *adj* **to be e. to do sth** avoir le droit de faire qch; **to be e. to sth** avoir droit à qch

entrance ['entrəns] *n* entrée *f* (**to** de); (*to university, school*) admission *f* (**to** à); **e. fee** droit *m* d'entrée

entrée ['ɒntreɪ] *n Culin* (*course before main dish*) entrée *f*; *Am* (*main dish*) plat *m* principal

entrepreneur [ɒntrəprə'nɜː(r)] *n* entrepreneur *m*

entry ['entrɪ] *n* entrée *f*; (*to be judged in competition*) objet *m*/œuvre *f*/projet *m* soumis au jury; **e. form** feuille *f* d'inscription; **'no e.'** (*on door*) 'entrée interdite'; (*road sign*) 'sens interdit'

envelope ['envələʊp] *n* enveloppe *f*

envious ['envɪəs] *adj* envieux, -euse (**of** de); **to be e. of sb** envier qn

environment [ɪn'vaɪərənmənt] *n* (*social, moral*) milieu *m*; **the e.** (*natural*) l'environnement *m* • **environmental** [-'mentəl] *adj* (*policy*) de l'environnement; **e. disaster** catastrophe *f* écologique • **environmentally** *adv* **e. friendly product** produit *m* qui ne nuit pas à l'environnement

envy ['envɪ] (*pt & pp* **-ied**) *vt* envier; **to e. sb sth** envier qch à qn

epic ['epɪk] *n* (*poem, novel*) épopée *f*; (*film*) film *m* à grand spectacle

epidemic [epɪ'demɪk] *n* épidémie *f*

epileptic [epɪ'leptɪk] *adj & n* épileptique (*mf*)

episode ['epɪsəʊd] *n* (*part of story*) épisode *m*; (*incident*) incident *m*

equal ['iːkwəl] **1** *adj* égal (**to** à); **to be e. to sth** (*in quantity*) égaler qch; (*good enough*) être à

equation 84 **estimate**

la hauteur de qch **2** n (**a**) *(person)* égal, -e mf (**b**) **equal(s) sign** signe m d'égalité **3** (*Br* **-ll-**, *Am* **-l-**) *vt* égaler (**in** en) • **equality** [ɪ'kwɒlətɪ] n égalité f • **equally** *adv (to an equal degree, also)* également; *(divide)* en parts égales

equation [ɪ'kweɪʒən] n *Math* équation f

equator [ɪ'kweɪtə(r)] n équateur m; **at** or **on the e.** sous l'équateur

equip [ɪ'kwɪp] (*pt & pp* **-pp-**) *vt (provide with equipment)* équiper (**with** de); *(prepare)* préparer (**for** pour); **to be (well-)equipped to do sth** être compétent pour faire qch • **equipment** n équipement m; *(in factory)* matériel m

equivalent [ɪ'kwɪvələnt] *adj & n* équivalent (m)

era [*Br* 'ɪərə, *Am* 'erə] n époque f; *(historical, geological)* ère f

erase [*Br* ɪ'reɪz, *Am* ɪ'reɪs] *vt* effacer; *(with eraser)* gommer • **eraser** n gomme f

erect [ɪ'rekt] **1** *adj (upright)* droit **2** *vt (building)* construire; *(statue, monument)* ériger; *(scaffolding)* monter

erode [ɪ'rəʊd] *vt* éroder • **erosion** [-ʒən] n érosion f

erotic [ɪ'rɒtɪk] *adj* érotique

errand ['erənd] n commission f, course f; **to run errands for sb** faire des courses pour qn

erratic [ɪ'rætɪk] *adj (unpredictable) (behaviour)* imprévisible; *(service, machine)* fantaisiste; *(irregular) (performance, results)* irrégulier, -ère

error ['erə(r)] n *(mistake)* erreur f; **typing/printing e.** faute f de frappe/d'impression

erupt [ɪ'rʌpt] *vi (of volcano)* entrer

en éruption; *(of war, violence)* éclater

escalator ['eskəleɪtə(r)] n escalier m roulant

escape [ɪ'skeɪp] **1** n *(of gas, liquid)* fuite f; *(of person)* évasion f; **he had a lucky** or **narrow e.** il l'a échappé belle **2** *vt (death, punishment)* échapper à **3** *vi (of gas, animal)* s'échapper (**from** de); *(of prisoner)* s'évader (**from** de)

escort [ɪ'skɔːt] *vt* escorter; *(prisoner)* conduire sous escorte

Eskimo ['eskɪməʊ] (*pl* **-os**) n Esquimau, -aude mf

especially [ɪs'peʃəlɪ] *adv (in particular)* surtout; *(more than normally)* particulièrement; *(for a purpose)* (tout) spécialement; **e. as** d'autant plus que

espresso [e'spresəʊ] (*pl* **-os**) n express m, expresso m

essay ['eseɪ] n *(at school)* rédaction f; *(at university)* dissertation f (**on** sur)

essence ['esəns] n *(distinctive quality)* essence f; *Culin (extract)* extrait m; **the e. of sth** *(main point)* l'essentiel m de qch

essential [ɪ'senʃəl] **1** *adj (principal)* essentiel, -elle; *(necessary)* indispensable, essentiel, -elle; **it's e. that...** il est indispensable que... (*+ subjunctive*) **2** *npl* **the essentials** l'essentiel m (**of** de)

establish [ɪ'stæblɪʃ] *vt* établir; *(state, society, company)* fonder • **established** *adj* (**well-)e.** *(company)* solide; *(fact)* reconnu; *(reputation)* établi • **establishment** n *(institution, company)* établissement m

estate [ɪ'steɪt] n *(land)* terres fpl, propriété f; *Br* **e. agent** agent m immobilier; *Br* **e. car** break m

estimate 1 ['estɪmət] n évaluation

f; *Com* devis *m* **2** ['estɪmeɪt] *vt*
(value) estimer, évaluer; *(consider)*
estimer (**that** que)

etc [et'setərə] *(abbr* **et cetera)**
adv etc

eternal [ɪ'tɜːnəl] *adj* éternel, -elle
• **eternity** *n* éternité *f*

ethics ['eθɪks] *n* éthique *f*, morale
f; (of profession) déontologie *f* •
ethical *adj* moral, éthique

ethnic ['eθnɪk] *adj* ethnique

etiquette ['etɪket] *n* étiquette *f*

EU [iː'juː] *(abbr* **European Union)**
n UE *f*

euphemism ['juːfəmɪzəm] *n*
euphémisme *m*

euro ['jʊərəʊ] *(pl* **-os)** *n (currency)*
euro *m*

Euro- ['jʊərəʊ] *pref* euro-; **E.-MP**
député *m* européen

Europe ['jʊərəp] *n* l'Europe
f • **European** [-'piːən] **1** *adj*
européen, -enne; **E. Union** Union
f européenne **2** *n* Européen, -enne
mf

evacuate [ɪ'vækjʊeɪt] *vt* évacuer

evaluate [ɪ'væljʊeɪt] *vt* évaluer
(**at** à)

evaporate [ɪ'væpəreɪt] *vi (of
liquid)* s'évaporer; **evaporated
milk** lait *m* condensé

eve [iːv] *n* **on the e. of** à la veille
de

even ['iːvən] **1** *adj (equal, flat)* égal;
(smooth) uni; *(regular)* régulier,
-ère; *(temperature)* constant;
(number) pair; *Fig* **to get e. with
sb** prendre sa revanche sur qn; **to
break e.** *(financially)* s'y retrouver
2 *adv* même; **e. better/more**
encore mieux/plus; **e. if...** même
si...; **e. though...** bien que... (+
subjunctive); **e. so** quand même **3**
vt **to e. sth (out** *or* **up)** égaliser
qch • **evenly** *adv (equally)*

de manière égale; *(regularly)*
régulièrement

evening ['iːvnɪŋ] *n* soir *m*;
(referring to duration, event)
soirée *f*; **tomorrow/yesterday
e.** demain/hier soir; **in the e.,** *or
Am* **evenings** le soir; **at seven in
the e.** à sept heures du soir; **every
Tuesday e.** tous les mardis soir; **e.
meal/paper** repas *m*/journal *m*
du soir; **e. class** cours *m* du soir; **e.
dress** *(of man)* tenue *f* de soirée;
(of woman) robe *f* du soir

event [ɪ'vent] *n* événement *m; (in
sport)* épreuve *f* • **eventful** *adj
(day, journey, life)* mouvementé;
(occasion) mémorable

eventually [ɪ'ventʃʊəlɪ] *adv*
finalement; *(some day)* par la
suite

ever ['evə(r)] *adv* jamais; **have
you e. been to Spain?** es-
tu déjà allé en Espagne?; **the
first e.** le tout premier; **e. since
(1990)** depuis (1990); **for e.** pour
toujours; **e. so sorry** vraiment
désolé; **all she e. does is criticize**
elle ne fait que critiquer

every ['evrɪ] *adj* chaque; **e. time**
chaque fois (**that** que); **e. one**
chacun, -e; **e. second** *or* **other
day** tous les deux jours; **e. so
often, e. now and then** de
temps en temps • **everybody**
pron tout le monde • **everyday**
adj (happening, life) de tous les
jours; *(ordinary)* banal (*mpl* -
als); **in e. use** d'usage courant •
everyone *pron* = **everybody**
• **everything** *pron* tout; **e.
(that) I have** tout ce que j'ai •
everywhere *adv* partout; **e. she
goes** où qu'elle aille

evict [ɪ'vɪkt] *vt* expulser (**from**
de)

evidence ['evɪdəns] *n (proof)*

preuve(s) *f(pl)*; *(testimony)* témoignage *m*; **to give e.** témoigner (**against** contre) • **evident** *adj* évident (**that** que) • **evidently** *adv (clearly)* manifestement; *(apparently)* apparemment

evil ['i:vəl] **1** *adj (spell, influence, person)* malfaisant; *(deed, system)* mauvais **2** *n* mal *m*

evoke [ɪ'vəʊk] *vt (conjure up)* évoquer

evolve [ɪ'vɒlv] *vi (of society, idea)* évoluer; *(of plan)* se développer • **evolution** [i:və'lu:ʃən] *n* évolution *f*

ewe [ju:] *n* brebis *f*

ex [eks] *n Fam (former spouse)* ex *mf*

ex- [eks] *pref* ex-; **ex-minister** ancien ministre *m*

exact [ɪg'zækt] *adj* exact • **exactly** *adv* exactement

exaggerate [ɪg'zædʒəreɪt] *vti* exagérer

exam [ɪg'zæm] *(abbr* **examination)** *n* examen *m*

examine [ɪg'zæmɪn] *vt (evidence, patient, question)* examiner; *(accounts, luggage)* vérifier; *(passport)* contrôler; *(student)* interroger • **examination** *n* examen *m*; *(of accounts)* vérification *f*; *(of passport)* contrôle *m*

example [ɪg'zɑ:mpəl] *n* exemple *m*; **for e.** par exemple; **to set an e.** *or* **a good e.** donner l'exemple (**to** à); **to set a bad e.** donner le mauvais exemple (**to** à)

exasperate [ɪg'zɑ:spəreɪt] *vt* exaspérer

excavate ['ekskəveɪt] *vt (dig)* creuser; *(archaeological site)* faire des fouilles dans

exceed [ɪk'si:d] *vt* dépasser; *(one's powers)* excéder • **exceedingly** *adv* extrêmement

excel [ɪk'sel] *(pt & pp* **-ll-)** *vi* **to e. in** *or* **at sth** exceller en qch • **excellent** ['eksələnt] *adj* excellent

except [ɪk'sept] *prep* sauf, excepté; **e. for** à part; **e. that...** sauf que... • **exception** *n* exception *f*; **with the e. of...** l'exception de... • **exceptional** *adj* exceptionnel, -elle

excess ['ekses] *n* excès *m*; *(surplus)* excédent *m*; **a sum in e. of...** une somme qui dépasse...; **e. luggage** excédent *m* de bagages • **excessive** *adj* excessif, -ive

exchange [ɪks'tʃeɪndʒ] **1** *n* échange *m*; *Fin (of currency)* change *m*; **in e.** en échange (**for** de); **e. rate** taux *m* de change **2** *vt* échanger (**for** contre)

excited [ɪk'saɪtɪd] *adj (happy)* surexcité; *(nervous)* énervé; *(enthusiastic)* enthousiaste; **to get e. (about)** s'exciter (pour); *(angry)* s'énerver (contre) • **excitement** *n* agitation *f*; *(enthusiasm)* enthousiasme *m* • **exciting** *adj* *(book, adventure)* passionnant

exclaim [ɪk'skleɪm] *vti* s'écrier (**that** que) • **exclamation** [eksklə'meɪʃən] *n* exclamation *f*; *Br* **e. mark,** *Am* **e. point** point *m* d'exclamation

exclude [ɪk'sklu:d] *vt* exclure (**from** de); **excluding...** à l'exclusion de... • **exclusive** *adj (right, interview, design)* exclusif, -ive; *(club, group)* fermé

excruciating [ɪk'skru:ʃieɪtɪŋ] *adj* atroce

excursion [ɪk'skɜ:ʃən] *n* excursion *f*

excuse 1 [ɪk'skju:s] *n* excuse *f*; **to make an e., to make excuses** se trouver une excuse **2** [ɪk'skju:z] *vt (forgive, justify)* excuser; *(exempt)* dispenser (**from** de); **e. me!** excusez-moi!, pardon!

ex-directory [eksdaɪ'rektərɪ] *adj Br* **to be e.** être sur la liste rouge

execute ['eksɪkjuːt] *vt (prisoner, order)* exécuter; *(plan)* mettre à exécution • **execution** [-'kjuːʃən] *n* exécution *f*

executive [ɪg'zekjʊtɪv] **1** *adj (job)* de cadre; *(car)* de luxe **2** *n (person)* cadre *m*

exempt [ɪg'zempt] *adj (person)* dispensé (**from** de)

exercise ['eksəsaɪz] **1** *n* exercice *m*; **e. book** cahier *m* **2** *vi* faire de l'exercice

exert [ɪg'zɜːt] *vt* exercer; *(force)* employer; **to e. oneself** se donner du mal • **exertion** *n* effort *m*

exhale [eks'heɪl] *vi* expirer

exhaust [ɪg'zɔːst] **1** *n* **e. (fumes)** gaz *mpl* d'échappement; **e. (pipe)** tuyau *m* d'échappement **2** *vt (person, resources)* épuiser • **exhausted** *adj (person, resources)* épuisé • **exhausting** *adj* épuisant • **exhaustive** *adj (list)* exhaustif, -ive; *(analysis)* détaillé

exhibit [ɪg'zɪbɪt] **1** *n* objet *m* exposé; *(in court)* pièce *f* à conviction **2** *vt (put on display)* exposer • **exhibition** [eksɪ'bɪʃən] *n* exposition *f*

exhilarating [ɪg'zɪləreɪtɪŋ] *adj (experience)* exaltant, grisant

exile ['egzaɪl] *n (banishment)* exil *m*; *(person)* exilé, -e *mf*

exist [ɪg'zɪst] *vi* exister; *(live)* survivre (**on** avec) • **existence** *n* existence *f*

exit ['eksɪt, 'egzɪt] **1** *n* sortie *f* **2** *vi* sortir

exotic [ɪg'zɒtɪk] *adj* exotique

expand [ɪk'spænd] **1** *vt (production, influence)* accroître; *(knowledge)* étendre; *(trade, range, idea)* développer **2** *vi (of knowledge)* s'étendre; *(of trade)* se développer; *(of production)* augmenter; *(of gas)* se dilater; **to e. on** développer • **expanse** *n* étendue *f*

expatriate [*Br* eks'pætrɪət, *Am* eks'peɪtrɪət] *adj & n* expatrié, -e *(mf)*

expect [ɪk'spekt] *vt (anticipate)* s'attendre à; *(think)* penser (**that** que); *(await)* attendre; **to e. to do sth** compter faire qch; **to e. that...** *(anticipate)* s'attendre à ce que... (+ *subjunctive)*; **to be expecting a baby** attendre un enfant; **as expected** comme prévu • **expectation** [-'teɪʃən] *n* **to come up to expectations** se montrer à la hauteur

expedition [ekspɪ'dɪʃən] *n* expédition *f*

expel [ɪk'spel] *(pt & pp* **-ll-***) vt* expulser (**from** de); *(from school)* renvoyer

expense [ɪk'spens] *n* frais *mpl*, dépense *f*; *Com* **expenses** frais *mpl*; **at the e. of sb/sth** aux dépens de qn/qch • **expensive** *adj (goods, hotel, shop)* cher *(f* chère*)*

experience [ɪk'spɪərɪəns] **1** *n* expérience *f*; **from** *or* **by e.** par expérience **2** *vt (emotion)* ressentir; *(hunger, success)* connaître; *(difficulty)* éprouver • **experienced** *adj (person)* expérimenté; **to be e. in sth** s'y connaître en qch

experiment 1 [ɪk'sperɪmənt] *n* expérience *f* **2** [ɪk'sperɪment] *vi* expérimenter (**on** sur); **to e. with sth** *(technique, drugs)* essayer qch

expert ['eksp3ːt] **1** *n* expert *m* (**on** *or* **in** en) **2** *adj* expert (**in sth** en qch; **in** *or* **at doing** à faire) •

expertise [-tiːz] *n* compétence *f* (**in** en)

expiration [ekspə'reɪʃən] *n Am* = **expiry**

expire [ɪk'spaɪə(r)] *vi* expirer • **expired** *adj (ticket, passport)* périmé • **expiry** (*Am* • **expiration** [ekspə'reɪʃən]) *n* expiration *f*; **e. date** *(on ticket)* date *f* d'expiration; *(on product)* date *f* limite d'utilisation

explain [ɪk'spleɪn] *vt* expliquer (**to** à; **that** que); *(reasons)* exposer; *(mystery)* éclaircir • **explanation** [eksplə'neɪʃən] *n* explication *f*

explicit [ɪk'splɪsɪt] *adj* explicite

explode [ɪk'spləʊd] *vi (of bomb)* exploser

exploit 1 ['eksplɔɪt] *n* exploit *m* **2** [ɪk'splɔɪt] *vt (person, land)* exploiter • **exploitation** [eksplɔɪ'teɪʃən] *n* exploitation *f*

explore [ɪk'splɔː(r)] *vt* explorer; *(causes, possibilities)* examiner

explosion [ɪk'spləʊʒən] *n* explosion *f*

export [ɪk'spɔːt] *vt* exporter (**to** vers; **from** de)

expose [ɪk'spəʊz] *vt (to air, cold, danger)* exposer (**to** à); *(plot, scandal)* révéler; *(criminal)* démasquer • **exposure** *n* exposition *f* (**to** à); *(in the media)* couverture *f* médiatique

express¹ [ɪk'spres] *vt* exprimer; **to e. oneself** s'exprimer • **expression** *n* expression *f*

express² [ɪk'spres] **1** *adj (letter, delivery)* exprès *inv*; *(train)* rapide, express *inv* **2** *n (train)* rapide *m*, express *m inv* • **expressway** *n Am* autoroute *f*

exquisite [ɪk'skwɪzɪt] *adj* exquis

extend [ɪk'stend] **1** *vt (in space)* étendre; *(in time)* prolonger (**by** de); *(house)* agrandir **2** *vi (in*

space) s'étendre (**to** jusqu'à); *(in time)* se prolonger • **extension** *n (to building)* annexe *f*; *(for telephone)* poste *m*; *(for essay)* délai *m* supplémentaire • **extensive** *adj (powers, area)* vaste; *(repairs, damage)* important • **extensively** *adv (very much)* énormément • **extent** *n (scope)* étendue *f*; *(size)* importance *f*; **to a large** *or* **great e.** dans une large mesure; **to some e.** *or* **a certain e.** dans une certaine mesure

exterior [ɪk'stɪərɪə(r)] *adj & n* extérieur *(m)*

exterminate [ɪk'stɜːmɪneɪt] *vt* exterminer

external [ɪk'stɜːnəl] *adj (trade, event)* extérieur; *(wall)* externe

extinct [ɪk'stɪŋkt] *adj (volcano)* éteint; *(species, animal)* disparu

extinguish [ɪk'stɪŋgwɪʃ] *vt* éteindre • **extinguisher** *n* **(fire) e.** extincteur *m*

extortionate [ɪk'stɔːʃənət] *adj* exorbitant

extra ['ekstrə] **1** *adj (additional)* supplémentaire; **e. charge** supplément *m*; **e. time** *(in sport)* prolongation *f* **2** *adv (more than usual)* extrêmement; **to pay e.** payer un supplément; **wine costs** *or* **is £10 e.** il y a un supplément de 10 livres pour le vin **3** *n Cin* figurant, -e *mf*

extra- ['ekstrə] *pref* extra-

extract 1 ['ekstrækt] *n* extrait *m* **2** [ɪk'strækt] *vt* extraire (**from** de); *(information, money)* soutirer (**from** à)

extra-curricular [ekstrəkə'rɪk-jʊlə(r)] *adj Sch* extrascolaire

extraordinary [ɪk'strɔːdənərɪ] *adj* extraordinaire

extravagant [ɪk'strævəgənt] *adj (behaviour, idea)* extravagant;

(wasteful) dépensier, -ère; *(tastes)* dispendieux, -euse

extreme [ɪk'striːm] **1** *adj* extrême **2** *n* extrême *m*; **take sth to extremes** pousser qch à l'extrême • **extremely** *adv* extrêmement • **extremist** *adj & n* extrémiste *(mf)*

extrovert ['ekstrəvɜːt] *n* extraverti, -e *mf*

eye [aɪ] *n* œil *m* (*pl* yeux); **to have one's e. on sth** avoir qch en vue; **to keep an e. on sb/sth** surveiller qn/qch; *Am* **e. doctor** opticien, -enne *mf* • **eyebrow** *n* sourcil *m* • **eyelash** *n* cil *m* • **eyelid** *n* paupière *f* • **eyeliner** *n* eye-liner *m* • **eyeshadow** *n* fard *m* à paupières • **eyesight** *n* vue *f*

Ff

F, f [ef] *n (letter)* F, f *m inv*

fable ['feɪbəl] *n* fable *f*

fabric ['fæbrɪk] *n (cloth)* tissu *m*, étoffe *f*

fabulous ['fæbjʊləs] *adj (legendary, incredible)* fabuleux, -euse

face [feɪs] **1** *n (of person)* visage *m*, figure *f*; *(expression)* mine *f*; *(of clock)* cadran *m*; *(of building)* façade *f*; *(of cube)* face *f*; *(of cliff)* paroi *f*; **f. down(wards)** *(person)* face contre terre; *(thing)* à l'envers; **f. to f.** face à face; *Br* **f. cloth** gant *m* de toilette **2** *vt (danger, enemy, problem)* faire face à; **to f., to be facing** *(be opposite)* être en face de; *(of window, door, room)* donner sur; **faced with** *(prospect, problem)* confronté à; *(defeat)* menacé par **3** *vi* **to f. north** *(of building)* être orienté au nord; **to f. up to** *(danger, problem)* faire face à; *(fact)* accepter • **face-lift** *n (by surgeon)* lifting *m*; *(of building)* ravalement *m* • **facial** [-ʃəl] **1** *adj (expression)* du visage **2** *n* soin *m* du visage

facilities [fə'sɪlɪtɪz] *npl (for sports, cooking)* équipements *mpl*; *(toilets)* toilettes *fpl*

fact [fækt] *n* fait *m*; **as a matter of f., in f.** en fait

factor ['fæktə(r)] *n* facteur *m*

factory ['fæktərɪ] *(pl* **-ies***) n (large)* usine *f*; *(small)* fabrique *f*

faculty ['fækəltɪ] *(pl* **-ies***) n (of mind, in university)* faculté *f*

fade [feɪd] *vi (of flower, material, colour)* se faner; *(of light)* baisser; **to f. (away)** *(of memory, smile)* s'effacer; *(of sound)* s'affaiblir; *(of person)* dépérir

fag [fæg] *n Br Fam (cigarette)* clope *f*

fail [feɪl] **1** *n* **without f.** sans faute **2** *vt (exam)* échouer à; *(candidate)* recaler; **to f. to do** *(forget)* manquer de faire; *(not be able)* ne pas arriver à faire **3** *vi (of person, plan)* échouer; *(of business)* faire faillite; *(of health, sight)* baisser; *(of brakes)* lâcher • **failed** *adj (attempt, poet)* raté • **failure** *n* échec *m*; *(person)* raté, -e *mf*

faint [feɪnt] **1** (**-er, -est**) *adj (weak) (voice, trace, breeze, hope)* faible; *(colour)* pâle; **to feel f.** se sentir mal **2** *vi* s'évanouir (**with** *or* **from** de)

fair¹ [feə(r)] *n (trade fair)* foire *f*; *Br (funfair)* fête *f* foraine • **fairground** *n* parc *m* d'attractions

fair² [feə(r)] **1** (**-er, -est**) *adj* **(a)** *(just)* juste; *(game, fight)* loyal; **f. play** fair-play *m inv* **(b)** *(rather good)* assez bon *(f* bonne*)*; *(price)* raisonnable; **a f. amount (of)** *(a lot)* pas mal (de) **(c)** *(wind)* favorable; *(weather)* beau *(f* belle*)* **2** *adv (fight)* loyalement; **to play f.** jouer franc jeu • **fairly** *adv* **(a)** *(treat)* équitablement; *(act, fight, get)* loyalement **(b)** *(rather)* assez

fair³ [feə(r)] *adj (hair, person)* blond; *(complexion, skin)* clair • **fair-haired** *adj* blond

fairy ['feərɪ] (*pl* -**ies**) *n* fée *f* •
fairytale *n* conte *m* de fées
faith [feɪθ] *n* foi *f*; **to have f. in
sb** avoir foi en qn; **in good/bad
f.** *(act)* de bonne/mauvaise foi •
faithful *adj* fidèle • **faithfully**
adv fidèlement; *Br* **yours f.** *(in
letter)* veuillez agréer l'expression
de mes sentiments distingués
fake [feɪk] **1** *adj* faux *(f* fausse) **2** *n*
(object) faux *m*; *(person)* imposteur
m **3** *vt (signature)* contrefaire
fall [fɔːl] **1** *n (of person, snow, city)*
chute *f*; *(in price, demand)* baisse *f*;
Am (season) automne *m* **2** *(pt* **fell**,
pp **fallen**) *vi* tomber; *(of price,
temperature)* baisser; **to f. into**
(hole, trap) tomber dans; *(habit)*
prendre; **to f. off a bicycle/
ladder** tomber d'une bicyclette/
échelle; **to f. out of a window**
tomber d'une fenêtre; **to f. over
sth** tomber en butant contre qch;
to f. asleep s'endormir; **to f. ill**
tomber malade
▶**fall apart** *vi (of book, machine)*
tomber en morceaux; *(of person)*
s'effondrer
▶**fall down** *vi* tomber; *(of building)*
s'effondrer
▶**fall for** *vt insep (person)* tomber
amoureux, -euse de; *(trick)* se
laisser prendre à
▶**fall off** *vi (come off)* tomber
▶**fall out** *vi (quarrel)* se brouiller
(**with** avec)
▶**fall over** *vi* tomber; *(of table,
vase)* se renverser
false [fɔːls] *adj* faux *(f* fausse); **f.
teeth** dentier *m*
fame [feɪm] *n* renommée *f*
familiar [fə'mɪljə(r)] *adj (well-
known)* familier, -ère (**to** à); **to
be f. with sb/sth** bien connaître
qn/qch; **he looks f.** je l'ai déjà vu
(quelque part)

family ['fæmɪlɪ] **1** *(pl* -**ies**) *n* famille
f **2** *adj (name, doctor, jewels)*
de famille; *(planning, problems,
business)* familial; **f. man** homme
m attaché à sa famille
famine ['fæmɪn] *n* famine *f*
famished ['fæmɪʃt] *adj* affamé
famous ['feɪməs] *adj* célèbre (**for**
pour)
fan[1] [fæn] **1** *n (held in hand)*
éventail *m (pl* -**ails**); *(mechanical)*
ventilateur *m* **2** *(pt & pp* -**nn**-) *vt
(person)* éventer
fan[2] [fæn] *n (of person)* fan *mf*;
(of team) supporter *m*; **to be a
jazz/sports f.** être passionné de
jazz/de sport
fanatic [fə'nætɪk] *n* fanatique *mf*
fancy ['fænsɪ] **1** *n* **I took a f. to it,
it took my f.** j'en ai eu envie **2** *adj
(jewels, hat, button)* fantaisie *inv*;
(car) de luxe; *(house, restaurant)*
chic *inv*; *Br* **f. dress** déguisement
m; *Br* **f. dress party** soirée *f*
déguisée **3** *(pt & pp* -**ied**) *vt Br
Fam (want)* avoir envie de; **he
fancies her** elle lui plaît
fanfare ['fænfeə(r)] *n* fanfare *f*
fantastic [fæn'tæstɪk] *adj*
fantastique; *Fam (excellent)*
formidable
fantasy ['fæntəsɪ] *(pl* -**ies**) *n
(imagination)* fantaisie *f*; *(fanciful,
sexual)* fantasme *m*
far [fɑː(r)] **1** (**farther** or **further**,
farthest or **furthest**) *adj* **the f.
side/end** l'autre côté/bout; **the
F. East** l'Extrême-Orient *m*; *Pol*
the f. left/right l'extrême gauche
f/droite *f* **2** *adv* (**a**) *(in distance)*
loin (**from** de); **how f. is it to
Toulouse?** combien y a-t-il jusqu'à
Toulouse?; **is it f. to...?** sommes-
nous/suis-je/*etc* loin de...?; **how f.
has he got with his work?** où

en est-il dans son travail?; **as f. as** jusqu'à; **as f.** *or* **so f. as I know** autant que je sache; **as f.** *or* **so f. as I'm concerned** en ce qui me concerne; **f. from doing sth** loin de faire qch; **f. away** *or* **off** au loin; **to be f. away** être loin (**from** de) (**b**) *(in time)* **as f. back as 1820** dès 1820; **so f.** jusqu'ici (**c**) *(much)* **f. bigger/more expensive** beaucoup plus grand/ plus cher (*f* chère) (**than** que); **f. more/better** beaucoup plus/ mieux (**than** que); **by f.** de loin • **far-away** *adj (country)* lointain; *(look)* perdu dans le vague • **far-fetched** *adj* tiré par les cheveux

farce [fɑːs] *n* farce *f*

fare [feə(r)] *n (for journey) (in train, bus)* prix *m* du billet; *(in taxi)* prix *m* de la course

farewell [feə'wel] **1** *n & exclam* adieu *(m)* **2** *adj (party, speech)* d'adieu

farm [fɑːm] **1** *n* ferme *f* **2** *adj (worker, produce)* agricole • **farmer** *n* fermier, -ère *mf*, agriculteur, -trice *mf* • **farmhouse** *n* ferme *f* • **farming** *n* agriculture *f*; *(breeding)* élevage *m* • **farmyard** *n* cour *f* de ferme

fart [fɑːt] *Fam* **1** *n* pet *m* **2** *vi* péter

farther ['fɑːðə(r)] **1** *comparative of* **far 2** *adv* plus loin; **f. forward** plus avancé; **to get f. away** s'éloigner • **farthest 1** *superlative of* **far 2** *adj* le plus éloigné **3** *adv* le plus loin

fascinating ['fæsɪneɪtɪŋ] *adj* fascinant

fascist ['fæʃɪst] *adj & n* fasciste *(mf)*

fashion ['fæʃən] *n* (**a**) *(in clothes)* mode *f*; **in f.** à la mode; **out of** f. démodé; **f. show** défilé *m* de mode (**b**) *(manner)* façon *f* • **fashionable** *adj* à la mode • **fashionably** *adv (dressed)* à la mode

fast¹ [fɑːst] **1** (**-er, -est**) *adj* rapide; **to be f.** *(of clock)* avancer (**by** de); **f. food** restauration *f* rapide; **f. food restaurant** fast-food *m* **2** *adv* (**a**) *(quickly)* vite; **how f.?** à quelle vitesse? (**b**) **f. asleep** profondément endormi

fast² [fɑːst] *vi* jeûner

fasten ['fɑːsən] **1** *vt* attacher (**to** à); *(door, window)* fermer **2** *vi (of dress)* s'attacher; *(of door, window)* se fermer • **fastener, fastening** *n (clip)* attache *f*; *(hook)* agrafe *f*; *(press stud)* bouton-pression *m*; *(of bag)* fermoir *m*

fat [fæt] **1** (**fatter, fattest**) *adj* gras (*f* grasse); *(cheeks, salary, book)* gros (*f* grosse); **to get f.** grossir **2** *n* graisse *f*; *(on meat)* gras *m*

fatal ['feɪtəl] *adj* mortel, -elle • **fatally** *adv* **f. wounded** mortellement blessé

fate [feɪt] *n* destin *m*, sort *m*

father ['fɑːðə(r)] **1** *n* père *m*; **F. Christmas** le père Noël **2** *vt (child)* engendrer • **father-in-law** (*pl* **fathers-in-law**) *n* beau-père *m*

fattening ['fætənɪŋ] *adj (food)* qui fait grossir

faucet ['fɔːsɪt] *n Am (tap)* robinet *m*

fault [fɔːlt] *n (blame)* faute *f*; *(defect, failing)* défaut *m*; **it's your f.** c'est (de) ta faute • **faultless** *adj* irréprochable • **faulty** *adj* défectueux, -euse

favour ['feɪvə(r)] (*Am* **favor**) **1** *n (act of kindness)* service *m*; *(approval)* faveur *f*; **to do sb a f.** rendre service à qn; **to be in f. of sth** être partisan de qch **2** *vt* *(encourage)* favoriser; *(support)* être partisan de • **favourable** (*Am* **favorable**) *adj* favorable (**to** à) • **favourite** (*Am* **favorite**) **1** *adj* favori, -ite, préféré **2** *n* favori, -ite *mf*

fax [fæks] **1** *n (message)* télécopie *f*, fax *m*; **f. (machine)** télécopieur *m*, fax *m* **2** *vt (message)* faxer; **to f. sb** envoyer un fax à qn

fear [fɪə(r)] **1** *n* peur *f*; *(worry)* crainte *f*; **for f. of doing sth** de peur de faire qch; **for f. that...** de peur que... *(+ ne + subjunctive)* **2** *vt* craindre; **I f. that he might leave** je crains qu'il ne parte **3** *vi* **to f. for one's life** craindre pour sa vie • **fearful** *adj (person)* apeuré; *(noise, pain, consequence)* épouvantable • **fearless** *adj* intrépide

feasible ['fiːzəbəl] *adj* faisable

feast [fiːst] *n* festin *m*

feat [fiːt] *n* exploit *m*

feather ['feðə(r)] *n* plume *f*

feature ['fiːtʃə(r)] **1** *n (of face, person)* trait *m*; *(of thing, place, machine)* caractéristique *f*; **(article)** article *m* de fond; **f. (film)** long métrage *m* **2** *vt (of newspaper, exhibition, film) (present)* présenter; *(have, include)* comporter; **a film featuring Nicole Kidman** un film ayant pour vedette Nicole Kidman **3** *vi (appear)* figurer (**in** dans)

February ['februərɪ] *n* février *m*

fed [fed] **1** *pt & pp of* **feed 2** *adj Fam* **to be f. up** en avoir marre *ou* ras le bol (**with** de)

federal ['fedərəl] *adj* fédéral • **federation** [-'reɪʃən] *n* fédération *f*

fee [fiː] *n* **fee(s)** *(of doctor, lawyer)* honoraires *mpl*; *(for registration)* droits *mpl*; *(for membership)* cotisation *f*; **school** *or* **tuition fees** frais *mpl* d'inscription

feeble ['fiːbəl] (**-er, -est**) *adj* faible; *(excuse, smile)* pauvre; *(attempt)* peu convaincant

feed [fiːd] (*pt & pp* **fed**) *vt* donner à manger à; *(baby) (from breast)* donner la tétée à; *(from bottle)* donner son biberon à; **to f. sb sth** faire manger qch à qn

feedback ['fiːdbæk] *n (response)* réactions *fpl*

feel [fiːl] (*pt & pp* **felt**) **1** *vt (be aware of)* sentir; *(experience)* éprouver, ressentir; *(touch)* tâter; **to f. that...** penser que...; **to f. one's way** avancer à tâtons **2** *vi* **to f. (about)** *(grope)* tâtonner; *(in pocket)* fouiller (**for sth** pour trouver qch); **it feels hard** c'est dur au toucher; **to f. tired/old** se sentir fatigué/vieux (*f* vieille); **I f. hot/sleepy/hungry** j'ai chaud/sommeil/faim; **she feels better** elle va mieux; **to f. like sth** *(want)* avoir envie de qch; **it feels like cotton** on dirait du coton; **I f. bad about it** ça m'ennuie • **feeling** *n (emotion, impression)* sentiment *m*; *(physical)* sensation *f*

feet [fiːt] *pl of* **foot**

fell [fel] *pt of* **fall**

fellow ['feləʊ] *n* **(a)** *(man, boy)* gars *m* **(b)** *(companion)* **f. countryman/f. countrywoman** compatriote *mf*; **f. worker** collègue *mf*

felt¹ [felt] *pt & pp of* **feel**

felt² [felt] *n* feutre *m* • **felt-tip** *n* **f. (pen)** crayon-feutre *m*

female ['fiːmeɪl] **1** *adj (person, name, voice)* féminin; *(animal)* femelle **2** *n (woman)* femme *f*; *(girl)* fille *f*; *(animal, plant)* femelle *f*

feminine ['femɪnɪn] **1** *adj* féminin

2 *n (in grammar)* féminin *m* •
feminist *adj & n* féministe *(mf)*
fence [fens] **1** *n (barrier)* clôture
f; (more solid) barrière *f; (in race)*
obstacle *m* **2** *vt* **to f. (in)** *(land)*
clôturer • **fencing** *n (sport)*
escrime *f*
fend [fend] **1** *vi* **to f. for oneself**
se débrouiller **2** *vt* **to f. off** *(blow)*
parer
fender ['fendə(r)] *n Am (of car)*
aile *f*
ferocious [fə'rəʊʃəs] *adj* féroce
ferret ['ferɪt] *n (animal)* furet *m*
ferry ['ferɪ] *(pl* **-ies)** *n* ferry-boat
m; (small, for river) bac *m*
fertile [*Br* 'fɜːtaɪl, *Am* 'fɜːrtəl] *adj*
(land, imagination) fertile; *(person,*
animal) fécond • **fertilizer**
['fɜːtɪlaɪzə(r)] *n* engrais *m*
festival ['festɪvəl] *n (of music,*
film) festival *m (pl* -als); *(religious)*
fête *f*
festive ['festɪv] *adj* de fête;
(mood) festif, -ive; **the f. season**
les fêtes *fpl* de fin d'année •
festivities *npl* festivités *fpl*
fetch [fetʃ] *vt* aller chercher
fête [feɪt] *n Br* fête *f*
fetus ['fiːtəs] *n Am* = **foetus**
feud [fjuːd] *n* querelle *f*
fever ['fiːvə(r)] *n* fièvre *f*; **to**
have a f. *(temperature)* avoir de
la fièvre • **feverish** *adj (person,*
activity) fiévreux, -euse

few [fjuː] **1** *adj* **(a)** *(not many)*
peu de; **f. towns** peu de villes;
every f. days tous les trois ou
quatre jours; **one of the f. books**
l'un des rares livres; **f. and far**
between rarissime **(b)** *(some)*
a f. towns quelques villes; **a f.**
more books encore quelques
livres; **quite a f...., a good f....**
bon nombre de... **2** *pron* peu; **f.**

came peu sont venus; **f. of them**
un petit nombre d'entre eux; **a f.**
quelques-un(e)s **(of** de); **a f. of**
us quelques-un(e)s d'entre nous •
fewer 1 *adj* moins de; **f. houses**
moins de maisons **(than** que); **to**
be f. (than) être moins nombreux
(que) **2** *pron* moins

fiancé [fɪ'ɒnseɪ] *n* fiancé *m* •
fiancée *n* fiancée *f*
fiasco [fɪ'æskəʊ] *(pl* **-os,** *Am* **-oes)**
n fiasco *m*
fib [fɪb] *Fam* **1** *n* bobard *m* **2** *(pt &*
pp **-bb-)** *vi* raconter des bobards
fibre ['faɪbə(r)] *(Am* **fiber)** *n* fibre
f; (in diet) fibres *fpl*
fickle ['fɪkəl] *adj* inconstant
fiction ['fɪkʃən] *n (invention)*
fiction *f;* **(works of) f.** livres
mpl de fiction • **fictional** *adj*
(character) fictif, -ive
fiddle ['fɪdəl] **1** *n (violin)* violon
m **2** *vi* **to f. about** *(waste time)*
traînailler; **to f. (about) with sth**
tripoter qch • **fiddly** **(-ier, -iest)**
adj Fam (task) minutieux, -euse
fidget ['fɪdʒɪt] *vi* gigoter •
fidgety *adj* agité
field [fiːld] *n* champ *m; (for sports)*
terrain *m; (sphere)* domaine *m*
fierce [fɪəs] **(-er, -est)** *adj (animal,*
warrior, tone) féroce; *(attack,*
wind) violent
fifteen [fɪf'tiːn] *adj & n* quinze
(m) • **fifteenth** *adj & n* quinzième
(mf)
fifth [fɪfθ] *adj & n* cinquième *(mf);*
a f. *(fraction)* un cinquième
fifty ['fɪftɪ] *adj & n* cinquante *(m)*
• **fifty-fifty** *adj & adv* **a f. chance**
une chance sur deux; **to split the**
profits f. partager les bénéfices
moitié-moitié • **fiftieth** *adj & n*
cinquantième *(mf)*
fig [fɪg] *n* figue *f*

fight [faɪt] **1** n (between people) bagarre f; (between boxers, soldiers) combat m; (struggle) lutte f (**against/for** contre/pour); (quarrel) dispute f **2** (pt & pp **fought**) vt (person) se battre contre; (decision, enemy) combattre; (fire, temptation) lutter contre; **to f. a battle** livrer bataille; Pol **to f. an election** se présenter à une élection; **to f. off** (attacker, attack) repousser **3** vi se battre (**against** contre); (of soldiers) combattre; (struggle) lutter (**against/for** contre/pour); (quarrel) se disputer; **to f. back** (retaliate) se défendre; **to f. over sth** se disputer qch • **fighter** n (in brawl, battle) combattant, -e mf; (determined person) battant, -e mf • **fighting** n (brawling) bagarres fpl; Mil combat m

figure [Br 'fɪgə(r), Am 'fɪgjə(r)] **1** n (**a**) (numeral) chiffre m (**b**) (shape) forme f; (outline) silhouette f; **she has a nice f.** elle est bien faite; **f. skating** patinage m artistique (**c**) (expression, word) **a f. of speech** une figure de rhétorique **2** vt **to f. that...** (think) penser que...; (estimate) supposer que...; **to f. out** (person, motive) arriver à comprendre; (answer) trouver; (amount) calculer • **figurative** adj (meaning) figuré

file [faɪl] **1** n (folder) chemise f; (documents) dossier m (**on** sur); Comptr fichier m **2** vt (document) classer; (complaint, claim) déposer • **filing** adj **f. cabinet** classeur m (meuble)

fill [fɪl] **1** vt remplir (**with** de); (tooth) plomber; (time) occuper; **to f. in** or **out** (form) remplir; **to f. up** (container) remplir **2** vi **to f. (up)** se remplir (**with** de); **to**

f. up (with petrol) faire le plein • **filling 1** adj (meal) nourrissant **2** n (in tooth) plombage m; (in food) garniture f; **f. station** station-service f

fillet [Br 'fɪlɪt, Am fɪ'leɪ] n (of fish, meat) filet m

film [fɪlm] **1** n film m; (for camera, layer) pellicule f **2** adj (studio, technician, critic) de cinéma; **f. star** vedette f de cinéma **3** vt filmer **4** vi (of film maker, actor) tourner

filter ['fɪltə(r)] **1** n filtre m; **f. coffee** café m filtre **2** vt filtrer **3** vi **to f. through** filtrer

filthy ['fɪlθɪ] (**-ier, -iest**) adj (hands, shoes) sale; (language) obscène

fin [fɪn] n (of fish) nageoire f; (of shark) aileron m

final ['faɪnəl] **1** adj (last) dernier, -ère; (definite) définitif, -ive **2** n (in sport) finale f; Univ **finals** examens mpl de dernière année • **finalize** vt (plan) mettre au point; (date) fixer définitivement; (deal) conclure • **finally** adv (lastly) enfin; (eventually) finalement; (irrevocably) définitivement

finale [fɪ'nɑːlɪ] n (musical) finale m

finance ['faɪnæns] n finance f; **finances** (of person) finances fpl; (of company) situation f financière • **financial** [-'nænʃəl] adj financier, -ère

find [faɪnd] (pt & pp **found**) vt trouver; **I f. that...** je trouve que...
► **find out** vi (inquire) se renseigner (**about** sur); **to f. out about sth** (discover) apprendre qch

fine¹ [faɪn] **1** n (money) amende f; (for driving offence) contravention f **2** vt **to f. sb £100** infliger une amende de 100 livres à qn

fine² [faɪn] **1** (**-er, -est**) *adj* (**a**)
(thin, delicate) fin (**b**) *(very good)*
excellent; *(beautiful) (weather, statue)* beau (*f* belle); **it's f.** *(weather)*
il fait beau; **he's f.** *(healthy)* il va
bien **2** *adv (very well)* très bien •
finely *adv (dressed)* magnifique-
ment; *(embroidered, ground)* fine-
ment; **f. chopped** haché menu
finger ['fɪŋɡə(r)] *n* doigt *m*; **little
f.** petit doigt *m*, auriculaire *m* •
fingernail *n* ongle *m* • **fingertip**
n bout *m* du doigt
finish ['fɪnɪʃ] **1** *vt* **to f. sth (off** *or*
up) finir qch; **to f. doing sth** finir
de faire qch **2** *vi (of meeting, event)*
finir, se terminer; *(of person)* finir,
terminer; **to have finished with**
(object) ne plus avoir besoin de;
(activity, person) en avoir fini avec;
to f. off *(of person)* finir, terminer
• **finished** *adj (ended, complete,
ruined)* fini • **finishing** *adj* **f. line**
(of race) ligne *f* d'arrivée; **to put
the f. touches to sth** mettre la
dernière main à qch
Finland ['fɪnlənd] *n* la Finlande •
Finn *n* Finlandais, -e *mf*, Finnois,
-e *mf* • **Finnish 1** *adj* finlandais,
finnois **2** *n (language)* finnois *m*
fire ['faɪə(r)] **1** *n* feu *m*; *(accidental)*
incendie *m*; *Br (electric heater)*
radiateur *m*; **to light a f.** faire
du feu; **to set f. to sth** mettre
le feu à qch; **on f.** en feu; **f.!**
(alarm) au feu!; **f. alarm** sirène *f*
d'incendie; *Br* **f. brigade**, *Am* **f.
department** pompiers *mpl*; **f.
engine** voiture *f* des pompiers;
f. escape escalier *m* de secours;
f. station caserne *f* des pompiers
2 *vt* **to f. a gun** tirer un coup de
fusil/de pistolet; **to f. questions
at sb** bombarder qn de questions;
to f. sb *(dismiss)* renvoyer qn **3** *vi*
tirer (**at** sur); **f.!** feu! • **firearm** *n*

arme *f* à feu • **fireman** (*pl* **-men**)
n sapeur-pompier *m* • **fireplace** *n*
cheminée *f* • **fireproof** *adj (door)*
ignifugé • **firework** *n* fusée *f*;
(firecracker) pétard *m*; **fireworks**,
Br **f. display** feu *m* d'artifice
firm¹ [fɜːm] *n (company)* entreprise
f, firme *f*
firm² [fɜːm] (**-er, -est**) *adj (earth,
decision)* ferme; *(foundations)*
solide • **firmly** *adv (believe)*
fermement; *(shut)* bien
first [fɜːst] **1** *adj* premier, -ère; **f.
aid** premiers secours *mpl* **2** *adv*
d'abord; *(for the first time)* pour
la première fois; **f. of all** tout
d'abord; **at f.** d'abord; **to come f.**
(in race) arriver premier; *(in exam)*
être reçu premier **3** *n (person,
thing)* premier, -ère *mf*; **f. (gear)**
(of vehicle) première *f* • **first-
class 1** *adj* excellent; *(ticket)* de
première classe; *(mail)* ordinaire **2**
adv (travel) en première • **firstly**
adv premièrement
fish [fɪʃ] **1** (*pl inv or* **-es** [-ɪz]) *n*
poisson *m*; **f. bone** arête *f*; *Br* **f.
fingers**, *Am* **f. sticks** bâtonnets
mpl de poisson pané; **f. tank**
aquarium *m* **2** *vt* **to f. sth out**
(from water) repêcher qch **3** *vi*
pêcher • **fish-and-chip** *adj Br*
f. shop = magasin où l'on vend
du poisson frit et des frites •
fisherman [-əmən] (*pl* **-men**) *n*
pêcheur *m*• **fishing** *n* pêche *f*;
to go f. aller à la pêche; **f. boat**
bateau *m* de pêche; **f. net** filet *m*
(de pêche); **f. rod** canne *f* à pêche
• **fishmonger** [-mʌŋɡə(r)] *n*
poissonnier, -ère *mf* • **fishy** (**-ier,
-iest**) *adj (smell, taste)* de poisson;
Fig (suspicious) louche
fist [fɪst] *n* poing *m*
fit¹ [fɪt] **1** (**fitter, fittest**) *adj* (**a**)
(healthy) en forme; **to keep f.** se

maintenir en forme **(b)** *(suitable)* propre **(for** à; **to do** à faire); *(worthy)* digne **(for** de; **to do** de faire); *(able)* apte **(for** à; **to do** à faire) **2** *n* **a good f.** *(clothes)* à la bonne taille; **a tight f.** *(clothes)* ajusté **3** *(pt & pp* **-tt-)** *vt (be the right size for)* aller bien à; *(match)* correspondre à; *(put in)* poser; *(go in)* aller dans; *(go on)* aller sur; **to f. sth (on) to sth** *(put)* poser qch sur qch; *(adjust)* adapter qch à qch; *(fix)* fixer qch à qch; **to f. sth in** *(install)* poser qch; *(insert)* faire entrer qch **4** *vi (of clothes, lid, key, plug)* aller; **this shirt fits** *(fits me)* cette chemise me va; **to f. (in)** *(go in)* aller; *(of facts, plans)* cadrer **(with** avec); **he doesn't f. in** il n'est pas à sa place • **fitness** *n (health)* santé *f* • **fitted** *adj Br (cupboard)* encastré; *(garment)* ajusté; **f. carpet** moquette *f*; **f. kitchen** cuisine *f* intégrée

fit² [fɪt] *n (seizure)* attaque *f*; **a coughing f.** une quinte de toux

five [faɪv] *adj & n* cinq *(m)* • **fiver** *n Br Fam* billet *m* de cinq livres

fix [fɪks] *vt (make firm, decide)* fixer **(to** à); *(mend)* réparer; *(deal with)* arranger; *(prepare)* préparer; **to f. sth up** *(trip, meeting)* arranger qch • **fixed** *adj (price)* fixe; *(idea)* bien arrêté

fizzy ['fɪzɪ] **(-ier, -iest)** *adj* gazeux, -euse

flabby ['flæbɪ] **(-ier, -iest)** *adj (person)* bouffi; *(skin)* mou *(f* molle)

flag [flæg] *n* drapeau *m*
▸**flag down** *vt (taxi)* héler

flair [fleə(r)] *n (intuition)* don *m* **(for** pour); **to have a f. for business** avoir le sens des affaires

flake [fleɪk] **1** *n (of snow)* flocon *m*; *(of paint)* écaille *f*; *(of soap)* paillette *f* **2** *vi* **to f. (off)** *(of paint)* s'écailler • **flaky** *adj Br* **f. pastry** pâte *f* feuilletée

flamboyant [flæm'bɔɪənt] *adj (person)* extraverti

flame [fleɪm] *n* flamme *f*; **to go up in flames** prendre feu

flamingo [flə'mɪŋgəʊ] *(pl* **-os** or **-oes)** *n* flamant *m*

flammable ['flæməbəl] *adj* inflammable

flan [flæn] *n* tarte *f*

flannel ['flænəl] *n Br (face cloth)* gant *m* de toilette

flap [flæp] **1** *n (of pocket, envelope)* rabat *m*; *(of table)* abattant *m* **2** *(pt & pp* **-pp-)** *vt* **to f. its wings** *(of bird)* battre des ailes

▸**flare up** [fleə(r)] *vi (of fire)* s'embraser; *(of violence, trouble)* éclater • **flared** *adj (trousers)* (à) pattes d'éléphant; *(skirt)* évasé • **flares** *npl* **(pair of) flares** *(trousers)* pantalon *m* pattes d'éléphant

flash [flæʃ] **1** *n (of light)* éclair *m*; *(for camera)* flash *m*; **f. of lightning** éclair *m* **2** *vt (light)* projeter; *(aim)* diriger **(on** or **at** sur); *(show)* montrer rapidement; **to f. one's headlights** faire un appel de phares **3** *vi (shine)* briller; *(on and off)* clignoter; **to f. past** or **by** *(rush)* passer comme un éclair • **flashback** *n* retour *m* en arrière • **flashlight** *n Am (torch)* lampe *f* électrique; *(for camera)* flash *m* • **flashy** **(-ier, -iest)** *adj Fam (clothes, car)* tape-à-l'œil *inv*

flask [flɑːsk] *n (Thermos®)* Thermos® *f inv*; *(for alcohol)* flasque *f*

flat¹ [flæt] **1** **(flatter, flattest)** *adj* plat; *(tyre, battery)* à plat; *(drink)* éventé; *(refusal)* net *(f* nette); **f. rate** tarif *m* unique; **to put** or lay sth (down) f. mettre qch à plat 2 *adv* to fall f. on one's face tomber à plat ventre; to fall f. *(of joke, play)* tomber à plat; f. out *(work)* d'arrache-pied; *(run)* à toute vitesse • flatten *vt* aplatir

flat² [flæt] *n Br (in building)* appartement *m* • flatmate *n Br* colocataire *mf*

flatter ['flætə(r)] *vt* flatter • flattering *adj (remark, words)* flatteur, -euse

flaunt [flɔːnt] *vt (show off)* faire étalage de

flavour ['fleɪvə(r)] *(Am* flavor) 1 *n (taste)* goût *m; (of ice cream)* parfum *m* 2 *vt (food)* relever (with de); lemon-flavoured (parfumé) au citron • flavouring *(Am* flavoring) *n (seasoning)* assaisonnement *m; (in cake, ice cream)* parfum *m*

flaw [flɔː] *n* défaut *m* • flawed *adj* qui a un défaut/des défauts • flawless *adj* parfait

flea [fliː] *n* puce *f*; f. market marché *m* aux puces

flee [fliː] 1 *(pt & pp* fled) *vt (place)* s'enfuir de; *(danger)* fuir 2 *vi* s'enfuir, fuir

fleece [fliːs] *n (of sheep)* toison *f; (garment)* (fourrure *f*) polaire *f*

fleet [fliːt] *n (of ships)* flotte *f; (of taxis, buses)* parc *m*

Flemish ['flemɪʃ] 1 *adj* flamand 2 *n (language)* flamand *m*

flesh [fleʃ] *n* chair *f*; in the f. en chair et en os

flew [fluː] *pt of* fly²

flex [fleks] *vt (limb)* fléchir; *(muscle)* faire jouer • flexible *adj* flexible • flexitime *n* horaires *mpl* flexibles

flick [flɪk] 1 *vt (with finger)* donner une chiquenaude à; to f. sth off *(remove)* enlever

qch d'une chiquenaude; to f. a switch pousser un bouton 2 *vi* to f. through *(book, magazine)* feuilleter

flicker ['flɪkə(r)] *vi (of flame, light)* vaciller

flier ['flaɪə(r)] = flyer

flies [flaɪz] *npl (of trousers)* braguette *f*

flight [flaɪt] *n* (a) *(of bird, aircraft)* vol *m*; f. attendant *(man)* steward *m; (woman)* hôtesse *f* de l'air (b) *(floor)* étage *m*; f. of stairs escalier *m*

flimsy ['flɪmzɪ] (-ier, -iest) *adj (cloth, structure) (light)* (trop) léger, -ère; *(thin)* (trop) mince; *(excuse)* piètre

flinch [flɪntʃ] *vi (with pain)* tressaillir

fling [flɪŋ] 1 *n (affair)* aventure *f* 2 *(pt & pp* flung) *vt* jeter

flip [flɪp] 1 *(pt & pp* -pp-) *vt (with finger)* donner une chiquenaude à; to f. a coin jouer à pile ou face; to f. sth over retourner qch 2 *vi* to f. through a book feuilleter un livre

flip-flops ['flɪpflɒps] *npl* tongs *fpl*

flipper ['flɪpə(r)] *n (of swimmer)* palme *f; (of animal)* nageoire *f*

flirt [flɜːt] *vi* flirter (with avec)

float [fləʊt] *vi* flotter (on sur); to f. down the river descendre la rivière

flock [flɒk] *n (of sheep)* troupeau *m; (of birds)* volée *f*

flood [flʌd] 1 *n* inondation *f* 2 *vt (land, house, market)* inonder (with de) 3 *vi (of river)* déborder; to f. in *(of people, money)* affluer • flooding *n* inondation(s) *f(pl)* • floodlight *n* projecteur *m*

floor [flɔː(r)] *n (of room)* sol *m; (wooden)* plancher *m; (storey)* étage *m*; on the f. par terre; on

the first f. *Br* au premier étage; *Am (ground floor)* au rez-de-chaussée • **floorboard** *n* latte *f (de plancher)*

flop [flɒp] *Fam* **1** *n* fiasco *m; (play)* four *m* **2** *(pt & pp* **-pp-**) *vi (fail) (of business)* échouer; *(of play, film)* faire un four; **to f. down** s'effondrer • **floppy** (**-ier, -iest**) *adj (soft)* mou (*f* molle); *Comptr* **f. disk** disquette *f*

floral ['flɔːrəl] *adj (material, pattern)* à fleurs

florist ['flɒrɪst] *n* fleuriste *mf*

floss [flɒs] *n* (**dental**) **f.** fil *m* dentaire

flour ['flaʊə(r)] *n* farine *f*

flourish ['flʌrɪʃ] *vi (of person, plant)* prospérer; *(of arts, business)* être florissant

flow [fləʊ] **1** *n (of river)* courant *m; (of traffic, information, blood)* circulation *f; (of liquid)* écoulement *m* **2** *vi* couler; *(of electric current)* circuler; *(of hair, clothes)* flotter; *(of traffic)* s'écouler; **to f. in** *(of money)* affluer • **flowing** *adj (movement, style)* fluide; *(hair, beard)* flottant

flower ['flaʊə(r)] **1** *n* fleur *f;* **f. pot** pot *m* de fleurs; **f. shop** fleuriste *m* • **flowery** *adj (material)* à fleurs; *(style)* fleuri

flown [fləʊn] *pp of* **fly**²

flu [fluː] *n (influenza)* grippe *f*

fluent ['fluːənt] *adj* **he's f. in Russian, his Russian is f.** il parle couramment le russe; **to be a f. speaker** s'exprimer avec facilité • **fluently** *adv (write, express oneself)* avec facilité; *(speak language)* couramment

fluff [flʌf] *n* peluche *f* • **fluffy** (**-ier, -iest**) *adj (toy)* en peluche

fluid ['fluːɪd] **1** *adj* fluide; *(plans)* mal défini; **f. ounce** = 0,03 l **2** *n* fluide *m*, liquide *m*

fluke [fluːk] *n Fam* coup *m* de chance; **by a f.** par hasard

flung [flʌŋ] *pt & pp of* **fling**

flunk [flʌŋk] *vt Am Fam (exam)* être collé à; *(pupil)* coller

fluorescent [flʊə'resənt] *adj* fluorescent

fluoride ['flʊəraɪd] *n* fluorure *m*

flurry ['flʌrɪ] *(pl* **-ies**) *n (of snow)* bourrasque *f;* **a f. of activity** une soudaine activité

flush [flʌʃ] **1** *n (in toilet)* chasse *f* d'eau **2** *vt* **to f. sth (out)** *(clean)* nettoyer qch à grande eau; **to f. the toilet** tirer la chasse d'eau **3** *vi (blush)* rougir (**with** de)

fluster ['flʌstə(r)] *vt* démonter; **to get flustered** se démonter

flute [fluːt] *n* flûte *f*

flutter ['flʌtə(r)] *vi (of bird, butterfly)* voleter; *(of flag)* flotter

fly¹ [flaɪ] *(pl* **-ies**) *n (insect)* mouche *f*

fly² [flaɪ] **1** *(pt* **flew**, *pp* **flown**) *vt (aircraft)* piloter; *(passengers)* transporter; *(flag)* arborer; *(kite)* faire voler **2** *vi (of bird, aircraft)* voler; *(of passenger)* aller en avion; *(of time)* passer vite; *(of flag)* flotter; **to f. away** *or* **off** s'envoler; **to f. across** *or* **over** *(country, city)* survoler • **flyer** *n (leaflet)* prospectus *m* • **flying 1** *n (as passenger)* voyage *m* en avion **2** *adj* **to pass with f. colours** réussir haut la main; **to get off to a f. start** prendre un très bon départ; **f. saucer** soucoupe *f* volante; **f. visit** visite *f* éclair *inv* • **flyover** *n Br (bridge)* pont-route *m*

fly³ [flaɪ] *n Am (on trousers)* braguette *f*

foam [fəʊm] *n (on sea, mouth)*

écume *f*; *(on beer)* mousse *f*; **f. rubber** caoutchouc *m* Mousse®

focus ['fəʊkəs] **1** *(pl* **focuses** ['fəʊkəsəz] *or* **foci** ['fəʊkaɪ]) *n (of attention, interest)* centre *m*; **the photo is in f./out of f.** la photo est nette/floue **2** *vt (image, camera)* mettre au point; *(attention, efforts)* concentrer **(on** sur) **3** *vi* **to f. on sb/sth** *(with camera)* faire la mise au point sur qn/qch

foetus ['fiːtəs] *(Am* **fetus)** *n* fœtus *m*

fog [fɒg] *n* brouillard *m* • **foggy** (**-ier, -iest**) *adj* brumeux, -euse; **it's f.** il y a du brouillard; *Fam* **I haven't got the foggiest (idea)** je n'en ai pas la moindre idée • **foglamp, foglight** *n (on vehicle)* phare *m* anti-brouillard

foil [fɔɪl] *n (for cooking)* papier *m* alu

fold [fəʊld] **1** *n (in paper, cloth)* pli *m* **2** *vt* plier; **to f. up** *(chair, paper)* plier; **to f. over** *(blanket)* replier; **to f. one's arms** croiser les bras • **folding** *adj (chair, bed)* pliant

-fold [fəʊld] *suff* **1** *adj* **tenfold** par dix **2** *adv* **tenfold** dix fois

folder ['fəʊldə(r)] *n (file holder)* chemise *f*; *Comptr* répertoire *m*

folk [fəʊk] **1** *(Am* **folks)** *npl* gens *mpl*; *Fam* **my folks** *(parents)* mes parents *mpl* **2** *adj (dance, costume)* folklorique; **f. music** *(contemporary)* folk *m*

follow ['fɒləʊ] **1** *vt* suivre; *(career)* poursuivre; **to f. through** *(plan, idea)* mener à son terme; **to f. up** *(idea, story)* creuser; *(clue, case)* suivre; *(letter)* donner suite à **2** *vi (of person, event)* suivre; **to f. on** *(come after)* suivre • **follower** *n (of ideas, politician)* partisan *m* • **following** *adj* suivant

fond [fɒnd] (**-er, -est**) *adj (loving)* affectueux, -euse; *(memory, thought)* doux *(f* douce); **to be (very) f. of sb/sth** aimer beaucoup qn/qch • **fondly** *adv* tendrement

font [fɒnt] *n Typ & Comptr* police *f* de caractères

food [fuːd] *n* nourriture *f*; *(particular substance)* aliment *m*; *(for cats, dogs, pigs)* pâtée *f*; **f. poisoning** intoxication *f* alimentaire

fool [fuːl] **1** *n* imbécile *mf*; **to make a f. of sb** *(ridicule)* ridiculiser qn; *(trick)* rouler qn; **to make a f. of oneself** se couvrir de ridicule **2** *vt (trick)* duper **3** *vi* **to f. about** *or* **around** faire l'imbécile; *(waste time)* perdre son temps • **foolish** *adj* bête • **foolproof** *adj (scheme)* infaillible

foot [fʊt] *(pl* **feet)** *n* pied *m*; *(of animal)* patte *f*; *(unit of measurement)* = 30,48 cm, pied *m*; **at the f. of** *(page, stairs)* au bas de; **on f.** à pied • **football** *n (soccer)* football *m*; *(American game)* football *m* américain; *(ball)* ballon *m* • **footballer** *n Br* joueur, -euse *mf* de football • **footing** *n* **to lose one's f.** perdre l'équilibre; **to be on an equal f.** être sur un pied d'égalité • **footnote** *n* note *f* de bas de page • **footpath** *n* sentier *m* • **footstep** *n* pas *m*; **to follow in sb's footsteps** suivre les traces de qn

footage ['fʊtɪdʒ] *n Cin* séquences *fpl*

for [fɔː(r), *unstressed* fə(r)] **1** *prep* pour; *(for a distance or period of)* pendant; *(in spite of)* malgré; **what's it f.?** ça sert à quoi?; **I did it f. love/pleasure** je l'ai fait par amour/par plaisir; **to swim/rush f.**

(towards) nager/se précipiter vers; **a train f....** un train à destination de...; **the road f. London** la route de Londres; **it's time f. breakfast** c'est l'heure du petit déjeuner; **to come f. dinner** venir dîner; **to sell sth f. 7 dollars** vendre qch 7 dollars; **what's the French f. 'book'?** comment dit-on 'book' en français?; **she walked f. a kilometre** elle a marché pendant un kilomètre; **he was away f. a month** il a été absent pendant un mois; **he's been here f. a month** il est ici depuis un mois; **I haven't seen him f. ten years** ça fait dix ans que je ne l'ai pas vu, je ne l'ai pas vu depuis dix ans; **it's easy f. her to do it** il lui est facile de le faire; **f. that to be done** pour que ça soit fait **2** *conj (because)* car

forbid [fə'bɪd] *(pt* **forbade** [-bæd], *pp* **forbidden** [-'bɪdən], *pres p* **forbidding)** *vt* interdire, défendre **(sb to do** à qn de faire); **to f. sb sth** interdire qch à qn; **she is forbidden to leave** il lui est interdit de partir ● **forbidden 1** *pp of* **forbid 2** *adj (fruit, region)* défendu

force [fɔːs] **1** *n* force *f;* **the (armed) forces** les forces *fpl* armées; **by f.** de force; **in f.** *(rule)* en vigueur; *(in great numbers)* en force **2** *vt* forcer **(to do** à faire); *(impose)* imposer **(on** à); *(door, lock)* forcer; *(confession)* arracher **(from** à); **to f. sth into sth** faire entrer qch de force dans qch ● **forced** *adj* **f. to do** obligé *ou* forcé de faire; **a f. smile** un sourire forcé

forecast ['fɔːkɑːst] **1** *n (of weather)* prévisions *fpl;* (in racing)* pronostic *m* **2** *(pt & pp*

forecast(ed)) *vt* prévoir; *(in racing)* pronostiquer

forecourt ['fɔːkɔːt] *n (of hotel)* avant-cour *f; (of petrol station)* devant *m*

foreground ['fɔːɡraʊnd] *n* premier plan *m*

forehead ['fɒrɪd, 'fɔːhed] *n* front *m*

foreign ['fɒrɪn] *adj (language, person, country)* étranger, -ère; *(trade)* extérieur; *(travel, correspondent)* à l'étranger; **F. Minister,** *Br* **F. Secretary** ministre *m* des Affaires étrangères; *Br* **F. Office** ministère *m* des Affaires étrangères ● **foreigner** *n* étranger, -ère *mf*

foresee [fɔː'siː] *(pt* **-saw,** *pp* **-seen)** *vt* prévoir ● **foresight** [-saɪt] *n* prévoyance *f*

forest ['fɒrɪst] *n* forêt *f*

forever [fə'revə(r)] *adv (for always)* pour toujours; *(continually)* sans cesse

forfeit ['fɔːfɪt] **1** *n (in game)* gage *m* **2** *vt (lose)* perdre

forgave [fə'ɡeɪv] *pt of* **forgive**

forge [fɔːdʒ] *vt (signature, money)* contrefaire; **to f. a passport** faire un faux passeport ● **forged** *adj* faux *(f* fausse) ● **forgery** *(pl* **-ies)** *n* contrefaçon *f*

forget [fə'ɡet] **1** *(pt* **forgot,** *pp* **forgotten,** *pres p* **forgetting)** *vt* oublier **(to do** de faire); *Fam* **f. it!** laisse tomber! **2** *vi* oublier; **to f. about sb/sth** oublier qn/qch ● **forgetful** *adj* **to be f.** avoir une mauvaise mémoire

forgive [fə'ɡɪv] *(pt* **-gave,** *pp* **-given)** *vt* pardonner **(sb sth** qch à qn) ● **forgiveness** *n* pardon *m*

forgot [fə'ɡɒt] *pt of* **forget** ● **forgotten** *pp of* **forget**

fork [fɔːk] **1** *n (for eating)* fourchette *f; (for gardening, in* road) fourche f 2 vt Fam **to f. out** (money) allonger • **forklift** n f. **(truck)** chariot m élévateur

forlorn [fə'lɔːn] adj (forsaken) abandonné; (unhappy) triste

form [fɔːm] 1 n (shape, type, style) forme f; (document) formulaire m; Br Sch classe f; **in the f. of** sous forme de; **on f., in good** or **top f.** en (pleine) forme 2 vt (group, basis, character) former; (clay) façonner; (habit) contracter; (obstacle) constituer; **to f. part of sth** faire partie de qch

formal ['fɔːməl] adj (person, tone) cérémonieux, -euse; (announcement, dinner, invitation) officiel, -elle; (language) soutenu; **f. dress** tenue f de soirée • **formality** [-'mælɪtɪ] (pl -ies) n (procedure) formalité f • **formally** adv (declare) officiellement; **f. dressed** en tenue de soirée

format ['fɔːmæt] n format m

former ['fɔːmə(r)] 1 adj (previous) (president, teacher, job, house) ancien, -enne (before noun) 2 pron **the f.** celui-là, celle-là • **formerly** adv autrefois

formula ['fɔːmjʊlə] n (a) (pl -as or -ae [-iː]) (rule, symbols) formule f (b) (pl -as) (baby food) lait m en poudre

fort [fɔːt] n Mil fort m

forth [fɔːθ] adv en avant; **and so f.** et ainsi de suite • **forthcoming** [-'kʌmɪŋ] adj (a) (event) à venir (b) (informative) expansif, -ive (**about** sur)

fortieth ['fɔːtɪəθ] adj & n quarantième (mf)

fortify ['fɔːtɪfaɪ] (pt & pp -ied) vt fortifier

fortnight ['fɔːtnaɪt] n Br quinzaine f (de jours)

fortress ['fɔːtrɪs] n forteresse f

fortunate ['fɔːtʃənət] adj heureux, -euse; **to be f.** (of person) avoir de la chance; **it's f. (for her) that...** c'est heureux (pour elle) que... (+ subjunctive) • **fortunately** adv heureusement

fortune ['fɔːtʃuːn] n (wealth) fortune f; (luck) chance f • **fortune-teller** n diseur, -euse mf de bonne aventure

forty ['fɔːtɪ] adj & n quarante (m)

forum ['fɔːrəm] n forum m

forward ['fɔːwəd] 1 adj (position) avant inv; (movement) en avant; Fig (impudent) effronté 2 adv en avant; **to go f.** avancer 3 vt (letter) faire suivre; (goods) expédier • **forwards** adv = **forward**

fossil ['fɒsəl] n fossile m

foster ['fɒstə(r)] adj **f. child** = enfant placé dans une famille d'accueil; **f. parents** parents mpl nourriciers

fought [fɔːt] pt & pp of **fight**

foul [faʊl] 1 (-er, -est) adj (a) (smell, taste, weather, person) infect; (breath) fétide; (language) grossier, -ère; (place) immonde (b) **f. play** (in sport) jeu m irrégulier; (in law) acte m criminel 2 n (in sport) faute f

found¹ [faʊnd] pt & pp of **find**

found² [faʊnd] vt (town, party) fonder; (opinion, suspicions) fonder, baser (**on** sur) • **founder** n fondateur, -trice mf

foundation [faʊn'deɪʃən] n (basis) fondement m; **the foundations** (of building) les fondations fpl

fountain ['faʊntɪn] n fontaine f; **f. pen** stylo-plume m

four [fɔː(r)] adj & n quatre (m); **on all fours** à quatre pattes • **fourth** adj & n quatrième (mf)

fourteen [fɔː'tiːn] adj & n

quatorze *(m)* ● **fourteenth** *adj* & *n* quatorzième *(mf)*

fowl [faʊl] *n inv* volaille *f*

fox [fɒks] *n* renard *m*

foyer ['fɔɪeɪ] *n (in theatre)* foyer *m*; *(in hotel)* hall *m*

fraction ['frækʃən] *n* fraction *f*

fracture ['fræktʃə(r)] **1** *n* fracture *f* **2** *vt* fracturer; **to f. one's leg** se fracturer la jambe

fragile [*Br* 'frædʒaɪl, *Am* 'frædʒəl] *adj* fragile

fragment ['frægmənt] *n* fragment *m*

fragrance ['freɪgrəns] *n* parfum *m*

frail [freɪl] **(-er, -est)** *adj (person)* frêle; *(health)* fragile

frame [freɪm] **1** *n (of picture, bicycle)* cadre *m*; *(of door, window)* encadrement *m*; *(of spectacles)* monture *f*; **f. of mind** état *m* d'esprit **2** *vt (picture)* encadrer ● **framework** *n* structure *f*; **(with)in the f. of** *(context)* dans le cadre de

franc [fræŋk] *n* franc *m*

France [frɑːns] *n* la France

franchise ['fræntʃaɪz] *n (right to sell product)* franchise *f*

frank [fræŋk] **(-er, -est)** *adj (honest)* franc *(f* franche*)* ● **frankly** *adv* franchement

frantic ['fræntɪk] *adj (activity, shouts, pace)* frénétique; *(attempt, efforts)* désespéré ● **frantically** *adv* frénétiquement; *(run, search, work)* comme un fou/une folle

fraud [frɔːd] *n* fraude *f*

fraught [frɔːt] *adj (situation)* tendu; **f. with** plein de

frayed [freɪd] *adj (garment)* élimé

freak [friːk] *n (person)* monstre *m*; *Fam* **jazz f.** fana *mf* de jazz

▶**freak out** *Fam* **1** *vt sep (shock, scare)* faire flipper **2** *vi (panic)*

paniquer; *(get angry)* piquer une crise

freckle ['frekəl] *n* tache *f* de rousseur ● **freckled** *adj* couvert de taches de rousseur

free [friː] **1 (freer, freest)** *adj (at liberty, not occupied)* libre; *(without cost)* gratuit; **to be f. to do sth** être libre de faire qch; **f. of charge** gratuit; **f. kick** *(in football)* coup *m* franc **2** *adv* **f. (of charge)** gratuitement **3** *(pt & pp* **freed)** *vt (prisoner, country)* libérer; *(trapped person)* dégager ● **freedom** *n* liberté *f* ● **freelance 1** *adj* indépendant **2** *adv* **to work f.** travailler en indépendant ● **free-range** *adj Br* **f. egg** œuf *m* de ferme ● **freeway** *n Am* autoroute *f*

freeze [friːz] **1** *(pt* **froze,** *pp* **frozen)** *vt (food)* congeler; *(prices, wages)* bloquer; **frozen food** surgelés *mpl* **2** *vi* geler; **to f. to death** mourir de froid ● **freezer** *n* congélateur *m*; ● **freezing 1** *adj (weather)* glacial; *(hands, feet)* gelée; **it's f.** il gèle **2** *n* **it's five degrees below f.** il fait cinq degrés au-dessous de zéro **3** *adv* **f. cold** très froid

freight [freɪt] *n Com (goods)* cargaison *f*; **f. train** train *m* de marchandises

French [frentʃ] **1** *adj* français; *(teacher)* de français; *(embassy)* de France; **F. fries** frites *fpl* **2** *n* **(a)** *(language)* français *m* **(b)** **the F.** *(people)* les Français *mpl* ● **Frenchman** *(pl* **-men)** *n* Français *m* ● **French-speaking** *adj* francophone ● **Frenchwoman** *(pl* **-women)** *n* Française *f*

frenzy ['frenzɪ] *(pl* **-ies)** *n* frénésie *f* ● **frenzied** *adj (activity)* frénétique; *(attack)* violent

frequent ['friːkwənt] *adj* fréquent • **frequency** (*pl* **-ies**) *n* fréquence *f* • **frequently** *adv* fréquemment

fresh [freʃ] **1** (**-er, -est**) *adj* frais (*f* fraîche); *(new)* nouveau (*f* nouvelle); **to get some f. air** prendre l'air **2** *adv* **to be f. from** *(school, university)* sortir tout juste de • **freshly** *adv (arrived, picked)* fraîchement

►**freshen up** ['freʃən-] *(have a wash)* faire un brin de toilette

friction ['frɪkʃən] *n* friction *f*

Friday ['fraɪdeɪ] *n* vendredi *m*; **Good F.** le vendredi saint

fridge [frɪdʒ] *n* frigo *m*

fried [fraɪd] **1** *pt & pp of* **fry 2** *adj* frit; **f. egg** œuf *m* sur le plat

friend [frend] *n* ami, -e *mf* • **friendly** (**-ier, -iest**) *adj* amical • **friendship** *n* amitié *f*

fright [fraɪt] *n* peur *f*; **to give sb a f.** faire peur à qn • **frightened** *adj* effrayé; **to be f.** avoir peur (**of** de) • **frightening** *adj* effrayant

frill [frɪl] *n* volant *m*

fringe [frɪndʒ] *n* (**a**) *(of hair, on clothes)* frange *f* (**b**) *(margin)* **on the fringes of society** en marge de la société

frisky ['frɪskɪ] (**-ier, -iest**) *adj (lively)* vif (*f* vive)

fritter ['frɪtə(r)] **1** *n Culin* beignet *m* **2** *vt* **to f. away** gaspiller

frizzy ['frɪzɪ] *adj* crépu

fro [frəʊ] *adv* **to go to and f.** aller et venir

frock [frɒk] *n (dress)* robe *f*

frog [frɒg] *n* grenouille *f*

from [frɒm, *unstressed* frəm] *prep* (**a**) *(expressing origin)* de; **a letter f. sb** une lettre de qn; **to suffer f. sth** souffrir de qch; **where are you f.?** d'où êtes-vous?; **a train f. Paris** un train en provenance de

Paris; **to be 10 m (away) f. the house** être à 10 m de la maison (**b**) *(expressing time)* à partir de; **f. today (on), as f. today** à partir d'aujourd'hui; **f. the beginning** dès le début (**c**) *(expressing range)* **f.... to...** de... à...; **f. morning till night** du matin au soir; **they take children f. the age of five** ils acceptent les enfants à partir de cinq ans (**d**) *(expressing source)* de; **to take/borrow sth f. sb** prendre/emprunter qch à qn; **to drink f. a cup** boire dans une tasse (**e**) *(expressing removal)* de; **to take sth f. sb** prendre qch à qn; **to take sth f. a box/f. the table** prendre qch dans une boîte/sur la table (**f**) *(according to)* d'après; **f. what I saw...** d'après ce que j'ai vu... (**g**) *(on behalf of)* de la part de; **tell her f. me** dis-lui de ma part

front [frʌnt] **1** *n* devant *m*; *(of boat, car)* avant *m*; *(of building)* façade *f*; **in f. of sb/sth** devant qn/qch; **in f.** devant; *(further ahead)* en avant; *(in race)* en tête **2** *adj (tooth, garden)* de devant; *(car seat)* avant *inv*; *(row, page)* premier, -ère; **f. door** porte *f* d'entrée

frontier ['frʌntɪə(r)] *n* frontière *f*

frost [frɒst] *n* gel *m* • **frostbite** *n* gelure *f* • **frosty** (**-ier, -iest**) *adj (air, night)* glacé; **it's f.** il gèle

frosting ['frɒstɪŋ] *n Am (on cake)* glaçage *m*

froth [frɒθ] *n (on beer)* mousse *f*; *(on waves)* écume *f* • **frothy** (**-ier, -iest**) *adj (beer)* mousseux, -euse

frown [fraʊn] *vi* froncer les sourcils; *Fig* **to f. (up)on** désapprouver

froze [frəʊz] *pt of* **freeze** • **frozen** *pp of* **freeze**

fruit [fru:t] n fruit m; **some f.** *(one item)* un fruit; *(more than one)* des fruits; **f. juice** jus m de fruits; **f. salad** salade f de fruits; Br **f. machine** *(for gambling)* machine f à sous • **fruitcake** n cake m

frustrating [frʌ'streɪtɪŋ] adj frustrant • **frustration** n frustration f

fry [fraɪ] *(pt & pp **fried**)* **1** vt faire frire **2** vi frire • **frying** n **f. pan** poêle f (à frire)

ft *(abbr **foot, feet**)* pied(s) m(pl)

fudge [fʌdʒ] n *(sweet)* caramel m mou

fuel [fjʊəl] n combustible m; *(for engine)* carburant m; **f. tank** *(in vehicle)* réservoir m

fugitive ['fju:dʒɪtɪv] n fugitif, -ive mf

fulfil [fʊl'fɪl] *(Am **fulfill**) (pt & pp **-ll-**)* vt *(ambition, dream)* réaliser; *(condition, duty)* remplir; *(desire, need)* satisfaire • **fulfilling** adj satisfaisant

full [fʊl] **1** *(-er, -est)* adj plein *(of de)*, *(bus, theatre, hotel, examination)* complet, -ète; *(amount)* intégral; *(day, programme)* chargé; **to be f. (up)** *(of person)* n'avoir plus faim; *(of hotel)* être complet; **at f. speed** à toute vitesse; **f. name** nom et prénom; Br **f. stop** point m **2** n **in f.** en entier; *(write)* en toutes lettres • **full-length** adj *(portrait)* en pied; *(dress)* long (f longue); **f. film** long métrage m • **full-time** adj & adv *(work)* à plein temps • **fully** adv *(completely)* entièrement; *(understand)* parfaitement • **fully-grown** adj adulte

fumble ['fʌmbəl] vi **to f. (about)** *(grope)* tâtonner; *(search)* fouiller **(for** pour trouver)

fume [fju:m] vi **to be fuming** *(of person)* rager • **fumes** npl émanations fpl; *(from car)* gaz mpl d'échappement

fun [fʌn] n plaisir m; **for f., for the f. of it** pour le plaisir; **to be (good** or **great) f.** être (très) amusant; **to have (some) f.** s'amuser; **to make f. of sb/sth** se moquer de qn/qch

function ['fʌŋkʃən] **1** n *(role, duty)* & Comptr fonction f; *(party)* réception f **2** vi fonctionner; **to f. as** faire fonction de • **functional** adj fonctionnel, -elle

fund [fʌnd] **1** n *(of money)* fonds m; **funds** fonds mpl **2** vt financer

fundamental [fʌndə'mentəl] adj fondamental

funeral ['fju:nərəl] n enterrement m; *(grandiose)* funérailles fpl; **f. service** service m funèbre; Br **f. parlour,** Am **f. home** entreprise f de pompes funèbres

funfair ['fʌnfeə(r)] n Br fête f foraine

fungus ['fʌŋɡəs] *(pl **-gi** [-ɡaɪ])* n *(plant)* champignon m; *(on walls)* moisissure f

funnel ['fʌnəl] n entonnoir m

funny ['fʌnɪ] *(-ier, -iest)* adj *(amusing)* drôle; *(strange)* bizarre; **a f. idea** une drôle d'idée • **funnily** adv **f. enough, I was just about to...** bizarrement, j'étais sur le point de...

fur [fɜ:(r)] n *(of animal, for wearing)* fourrure f; *(of dog, cat)* poil m; **f. coat** manteau m de fourrure • **furry** adj *(animal)* à poil; *(toy)* en peluche

furious ['fjʊərɪəs] adj *(violent, angry)* furieux, -euse **(with** or **at** contre); *(efforts, struggle)* violent

furnish ['fɜ:nɪʃ] vt *(room, house)* meubler • **furniture** [-tʃə(r)] n meubles mpl; **a piece of f.** un meuble

further ['fɜːðə(r)] **1** *adv* & *adj* = **farther 2** *adj (additional)* supplémentaire; *Br* **f. education** = enseignement supérieur dispensé par un établissement autre qu'une université **3** *adv (more)* davantage • **furthest** *adj* & *adv* = **farthest**

fury ['fjʊərɪ] *n (violence, anger)* fureur *f*

fuse [fjuːz] **1** *n (wire)* fusible *m*; *(of bomb)* amorce *f* **2** *vt (join)* fusionner; *Br* **to f. the lights** faire sauter les plombs **3** *vi Br* **the lights have fused** les plombs ont sauté

fuss [fʌs] **1** *n* histoires *fpl*; **to kick up** *or* **make a f.** faire des histoires; **to make a f. of sb** être aux petits soins pour qn **2** *vi* faire des histoires; **to f. over sb** être aux petits soins pour qn • **fussy** **(-ier, -iest)** *adj* exigeant **(about** sur); **I'm not f.** *(I don't mind)* ça m'est égal

futile [*Br* 'fjuːtaɪl, *Am* 'fjuːtəl] *adj (remark)* futile; *(attempt)* vain

futon ['fuːtɒn] *n* futon *m*

future ['fjuːtʃə(r)] **1** *n* avenir *m*; *(in grammar)* futur *m*; **in (the) f.** à l'avenir **2** *adj* futur; **my f. wife** ma future épouse; **the f. tense** le futur

fuze [fjuːz] *n* & *vti Am* = **fuse**

Gg

G, g [dʒiː] *n (letter)* G, g *m inv*

gadget ['gædʒɪt] *n* gadget *m*

gag [gæg] **1** *n (on mouth)* bâillon *m* **2** *(pt & pp* **-gg-***) vt (person)* bâillonner; *Fig (press)* museler

gain [geɪn] **1** *n (increase)* augmentation *f* (**in** de); *(profit)* gain *m*; *Fig (advantage)* avantage *m* **2** *vt (obtain, win)* gagner; *(experience, reputation)* acquérir; **to g. speed/weight** prendre de la vitesse/du poids

galaxy ['gæləksɪ] *(pl* **-ies***) n* galaxie *f*

gale [geɪl] *n* grand vent *m*

gallery ['gælərɪ] *(pl* **-ies***) n (room)* galerie *f*; *(museum)* musée *m*; *(for public, press)* tribune *f*

gallon ['gælən] *n* gallon *m (Br =* 4,5 l, *Am =* 3,8 l*)*

gallop ['gæləp] *vi* galoper

gamble ['gæmbəl] **1** *n (risk)* coup *m* risqué **2** *vi* jouer (**on** sur; **with** avec); **to g. on sth** *(count on)* miser sur qch • **gambler** *n* joueur, -euse *mf* • **gambling** *n* jeu *m*

game [geɪm] *n (activity)* jeu *m*; *(of football, cricket)* match *m*; *(of tennis, chess, cards)* partie *f*; **to have a g. of football/tennis** faire un match de football/une partie de tennis; *Br* **games** *(in school)* le sport; **g. show** *(on television)* jeu *m* télévisé; *(on radio)* jeu *m* radiophonique

gang [gæŋ] **1** *n (of children, friends)* bande *f*; *(of criminals)* gang *m* **2** *vi* **to g. up on** *or* **against** se mettre

à plusieurs contre • **gangster** *n* gangster *m*

gangway ['gæŋweɪ] *n Br* passage *m*; *(in train, plane)* couloir *m*; *(on ship)* passerelle *f*; *(in bus, cinema, theatre)* allée *f*

gap [gæp] *n (space)* espace *m* (**between** entre); *(in wall, fence)* trou *m*; *(in time)* intervalle *m*; *(in knowledge)* lacune *f*

gape [geɪp] *vi (stare)* rester bouche bée; **to g. at sb/sth** regarder qn/qch bouche bée • **gaping** *adj* béant

garage [*Br* 'gærɑː(d)ʒ, 'gærɪdʒ, *Am* gə'rɑːʒ] *n* garage *m*

garbage ['gɑːbɪdʒ] *n Am* ordures *fpl*, **g. can** poubelle *f*; **g. man** *or* **collector** éboueur *m*

garden ['gɑːdən] **1** *n* jardin *m*; **gardens** *(park)* parc *m*; **g. centre** jardinerie *f* **2** *vi* faire du jardinage • **gardener** *n* jardinier, -ère *mf* • **gardening** *n* jardinage *m*

gargle ['gɑːgəl] *vi* se gargariser

garlic ['gɑːlɪk] *n* ail *m*; **g. bread** = pain chaud au beurre d'ail

garment ['gɑːmənt] *n* vêtement *m*

garnish ['gɑːnɪʃ] *vt* garnir (**with** de)

garter ['gɑːtə(r)] *n (round leg)* jarretière *f*; *Am (attached to belt)* jarretelle *f*

gas [gæs] *n* gaz *m inv*; *Am (gasoline)* essence *f*; *Br* **g. cooker** cuisinière *f* à gaz; *Br* **g. heater, g. fire** radiateur *m* à gaz; *Am* **g.**

station station-service *f*; **g. stove**
(large) cuisinière *f* à gaz; *(portable)*
réchaud *m* à gaz; *Am* **g. tank**
réservoir *m* à essence
gash [gæʃ] *n* entaille *f*
gasoline ['gæsəliːn] *n Am* essence
f
gasp [gɑːsp] **1** *n* halètement *m*;
(of surprise) sursaut *m* **2** *vi* avoir le
souffle coupé (**with** *or* **in** de); **to
g. for breath** haleter
gate [geɪt] *n (in garden, field)*
barrière *f*; *(made of metal)* grille *f*;
(of castle, at airport) porte *f*
gâteau ['gætəʊ] *(pl* -eaux [-əʊz])*
n Br (cake) gros gâteau *m* à la
crème
gatecrash ['geɪtkræʃ] *vt* **to g. a
party** s'inviter à une réception
gateway ['geɪtweɪ] *n* entrée *f*
gather ['gæðə(r)] **1** *vt* (a) *(people,
objects)* rassembler; *(pick up)*
ramasser; *(flowers, fruit)* cueillir;
(information) recueillir; **to g.
speed** prendre de la vitesse; **to
g. one's strength** rassembler
ses forces (**b**) *(understand)* **I g.
that...** je crois comprendre que...
2 *vi (of people)* se rassembler;
(of clouds) se former; *(of dust)*
s'accumuler; **to g. round** *(come
closer)* s'approcher; **to g. round
sb** entourer qn • **gathering** *n
(group)* rassemblement *m*
gauge [geɪdʒ] **1** *n (instrument)*
jauge *f* **2** *vt* évaluer
gaunt [gɔːnt] *adj* décharné
gauze [gɔːz] *n* gaze *f*
gave [geɪv] *pt of* **give**
gay [geɪ] (**-er, -est**) *adj* (**a**)
(homosexual) gay (**b**) *Old-
fashioned (cheerful)* gai
gaze [geɪz] **1** *n* regard *m* **2** *vi* **to
g. at sb/sth** regarder fixement
qn/qch

GB [dʒiːˈbiː] *(abbr* **Great Britain**)
n GB
GCSE [dʒiːsiːesˈiː] *(abbr* **General
Certificate of Secondary
Education**) *n Br* = diplôme de fin
de premier cycle de l'enseignement
secondaire, sanctionnant une
matière déterminée
gear [ɡɪə(r)] **1** *n* (**a**) *Fam
(equipment)* attirail *m*; *(belongings)*
affaires *fpl*; *(clothes)* fringues *fpl*
(**b**) *(on car, bicycle)* vitesse *f*; **in g.**
(vehicle) en prise; *Br* **g. lever,** *Am*
g. shift levier *m* de (changement
de) vitesse **2** *vt* **to g. sth to sth**
adapter qch à qch; **to be geared
up to do sth** être prêt à faire qch
• **gearbox** *n* boîte *f* de vitesses
geese [ɡiːs] *pl of* **goose**
gel [dʒel] *n* gel *m*
gelatin(e) [*Br* 'dʒelətiːn, *Am*
-tən] *n* gélatine *f*
gem [dʒem] *n* pierre *f* précieuse
gender ['dʒendə(r)] *n Gram* genre
m; *(of person)* sexe *m*
gene [dʒiːn] *n Biol* gène *m*
general ['dʒenərəl] **1** *adj* général;
in g. en général; **the g. public**
le grand public **2** *n Mil* général
m • **generalize** *vi* généraliser
• **generalization** [-'zeɪʃən] *n*
généralisation *f* • **generally** *adv*
généralement; **g. speaking** de
manière générale
generate ['dʒenəreɪt] *vt (fear,
hope, unemployment)* engendrer;
(heat, electricity) produire; *(interest, ideas)* faire naître; *(jobs)* créer
generation [dʒenə'reɪʃən] *n (of
people, products)* génération *f*; *(of
electricity)* production *f*; **g. gap**
conflit *m* des générations
generous ['dʒenərəs] *adj*
généreux, -euse • **generosity**
[-'rɒsɪtɪ] *n* générosité *f* •
generously *adv* généreusement

genetic [dʒɪ'netɪk] adj génétique; **g. engineering** génie m génétique • **genetically** adv g. **modified** génétiquement modifié • **genetics** n génétique f

Geneva [dʒɪ'niːvə] n Genève m ou f

genius ['dʒiːnɪəs] n (ability, person) génie m

gent [dʒent] n Br Fam monsieur m; **gents' shoes** chaussures fpl pour hommes; **the gents** (toilet) les toilettes fpl des hommes

gentle ['dʒentəl] (-er, -est) adj (person, sound, slope) doux (f douce); (hint) discret, -ète; (exercise, speed) modéré • **gentleman** (pl -men) n monsieur m; (well-bred) gentleman m • **gently** adv doucement; (land) en douceur

genuine ['dʒenjʊɪn] adj (leather, diamond) véritable; (signature, painting) authentique; (sincere) sincère • **genuinely** adv (sincerely) sincèrement

geography [dʒɪ'ɒgrəfɪ] n géographie f

geometry [dʒɪ'ɒmɪtrɪ] n géométrie f

germ [dʒɜːm] n (causing disease) microbe m

Germany ['dʒɜːmənɪ] n l'Allemagne f • **German 1** adj allemand; **G. teacher** professeur m d'allemand; **G. measles** rubéole f **2** n (person) Allemand, -e mf; (language) allemand m

gesture ['dʒestʃə(r)] n geste m

get [get] (pt & Br pp **got**, Am pp **gotten**, pres p **getting**) **1** vt (obtain) obtenir, avoir; (find) trouver; (buy) acheter; (receive) recevoir; (catch) attraper; (bus, train) prendre; (seize) prendre,

saisir; (fetch) aller chercher; (hit with fist, stick) atteindre; Fam (understand) piger; **to g. sb to do sth** faire faire qch à qn; **to g. sth done** faire faire qch; **to g. sth dirty** salir qch; **can I g. you anything?** je te rapporte quelque chose? **2** vi (go) aller (**to** à); (arrive) arriver (**to** à); (become) devenir; **to g. old** vieillir; **to g. caught/run over** se faire prendre/écraser; **to g. dressed/washed** s'habiller/se laver; **to g. paid** être payé; **where have you got or Am gotten to?** où en es-tu?; **you've got to stay** (must) tu dois rester; **to g. to do sth** (succeed in doing) parvenir à faire qch; **to g. going** (leave) se mettre en route; (start working) se mettre au travail • **getaway** n (escape) fuite f • **get-together** n Fam réunion f

▶**get across 1** vt sep (message) faire passer **2** vi (road, river) traverser; **to g. across to sb that** faire comprendre à qn que…

▶**get along** vi (be on good terms) s'entendre (**with** avec)

▶**get at** vt insep (reach) atteindre; **what is he getting at?** où veut-il en venir?

▶**get away** vi (leave) s'en aller; (escape) se sauver; **to g. away with a fine** s'en tirer avec une amende; **he got away with that crime** il n'a pas été inquiété pour ce crime

▶**get back 1** vt sep (recover) récupérer; **to g. one's own back on sb** se venger de qn **2** vi (return) revenir

▶**get by** vi (manage) se débrouiller

▶**get down 1** vi (go down) descendre (**from** de); **to g. down to** (work) se mettre à **2** vt sep (bring down) descendre (**from** de); *Fam* **to g. sb down** *(depress)* déprimer qn **3** *vt insep* **to g. down the stairs/a ladder** descendre l'escalier/d'une échelle

▶**get in** *vi (enter)* entrer; *(come home)* rentrer; *(enter vehicle or train)* monter; *(arrive)* arriver

▶**get into** *vt insep* entrer dans; *(vehicle, train)* monter dans; *(habit)* prendre

▶**get off 1** *vt insep* **to g. off a chair** se lever d'une chaise; **to g. off a bus** descendre d'un bus **2** *vi (leave)* partir; *(from vehicle or train)* descendre (**from** de); *(escape punishment)* s'en tirer

▶**get on 1** *vt insep (bus, train)* monter dans **2** *vi (enter bus or train)* monter; *(be on good terms)* s'entendre (**with** avec); **how are you getting on?** comment ça va?; **how did you g. on?** *(in exam)* comment ça s'est passé?; **to be getting on (in years)** se faire vieux (*f* vieille); **to g. on with** *(task)* continuer

▶**get out 1** *vt sep (remove)* enlever; *(bring out)* sortir **2** *vi* sortir; *(from vehicle or train)* descendre (**of** *or* **from** de); **to g. out of** *(obligation)* échapper à; *(danger)* se tirer de; *(habit)* perdre

▶**get over 1** *vt sep (ideas)* faire passer; **let's g. it over with** finissons-en **2** *vt insep (illness)* se remettre de; *(shock)* revenir de

▶**get round 1** *vt insep (obstacle)* contourner **2** *vi (visit)* passer; **to g. round to doing sth** trouver le temps de faire qch

▶**get through 1** *vt insep (hole)* passer par; *(task)* venir à bout de; *(exam, interview)* survivre à; *(food)* consommer **2** *vi (pass)* passer; *(pass exam)* être reçu; **to**

g. through to sb *(communicate with)* se faire comprendre de qn

▶**get together** *vi (of people)* se réunir

▶**get up 1** *vt sep* **to g. sb up** *(out of bed)* faire lever qn; **to g. sth up** *(bring up)* monter qch **2** *vt insep (ladder, stairs)* monter **3** *vi (rise, stand up)* se lever (**from** de); **to g. up to something** *or* **to mischief** faire des bêtises; **where have you got up to?** *(in book)* où en es-tu?

ghastly ['gɑːstlɪ] (**-ier, -iest**) *adj (horrible)* épouvantable

gherkin ['gɜːkɪn] *n* cornichon *m*

ghetto ['getəʊ] (*pl* **-oes** *or* **-os**) *n* ghetto *m*

ghost [gəʊst] *n* fantôme *m*; **g. story** histoire *f* de fantômes ● **ghostly** *adj* spectral

giant ['dʒaɪənt] **1** *adj (tree, packet)* géant **2** *n* géant *m*

giddy ['gɪdɪ] (**-ier, -iest**) *adj* **to be** *or* **feel g.** avoir le vertige; **to make sb g.** donner le vertige à qn

gift [gɪft] *n* cadeau *m*; *(talent, donation)* don *m*; *Br* **g. voucher** *or* **token** chèque-cadeau *m* ● **gifted** *adj* doué (**with** de; **for** pour) ● **gift-wrapped** *adj* sous paquet-cadeau

gig [gɪg] *n Fam (pop concert)* concert *m*

gigantic [dʒaɪˈgæntɪk] *adj* gigantesque

giggle ['gɪgəl] *vi* rire (bêtement)

gimmick ['gɪmɪk] *n (trick, object)* truc *m*

gin [dʒɪn] *n (drink)* gin *m*

ginger ['dʒɪndʒə(r)] **1** *adj (hair)* roux (*f* rousse) **2** *n (spice)* gingembre *m*; **g. beer** limonade *f* au gingembre ● **gingerbread** *n* pain *m* d'épice

gipsy ['dʒɪpsɪ] (*pl* **-ies**) *n*

bohémien, -enne *mf*; *(Eastern European)* tsigane *mf*; *(Spanish)* gitan, -e *mf*

giraffe [dʒɪˈræf, *Br* dʒɪˈrɑːf] *n* girafe *f*

girl [gɜːl] *n (child)* (petite) fille *f*, fillette *f*; *(young woman)* jeune fille *f*; **English g.** jeune Anglaise *f*; **G. Guide** éclaireuse *f* • **girlfriend** *n (platonic)* amie *f*; *(romantic)* petite amie *f*

give [gɪv] *(pt* **gave**, *pp* **given)** *vt* donner; *(as present)* offrir; *(support)* apporter; *(smile, gesture, pleasure)* faire; *(sigh)* pousser; *(look)* jeter; **to g. sth to sb, to g. sb sth** donner *ou* offrir qch à qn; **to g. way** *(of branch, person)* céder; *(of roof)* s'effondrer; *(in vehicle)* céder la priorité **(to** à); **given that...** étant donné que…

▶**give away** *vt sep (prize)* distribuer; *(money)* donner; *(betray)* trahir

▶**give back** *vt sep (return)* rendre

▶**give in** *vi (surrender)* céder **(to** à)

▶**give out** *vt sep* distribuer

▶**give up 1** *vt sep (possessions)* abandonner; *(activity)* renoncer à; **to g. up smoking** cesser de fumer **2** *vi* abandonner

glad [glæd] *adj (person)* content **(of/about** de; **that** que + *subjunctive)*

glamorous [ˈglæmərəs] *adj (person, dress)* élégant

glance [glɑːns] *vi* **to g. at sb/sth** jeter un coup d'œil à qn/qch

glare [gleə(r)] *vi* **to g. at sb** foudroyer qn (du regard)

glass [glɑːs] **1** *n* verre *m* **2** *adj (bottle)* de verre; **g. door** porte *f* vitrée • **glasses** *npl (spectacles)* lunettes *fpl*

glaze [gleɪz] *vt (window)* vitrer; *(pottery)* vernisser

gleam [gliːm] *vi* luire

glee [gliː] *n* joie *f*

glide [glaɪd] *vi* glisser; *(of aircraft, bird)* planer

glimpse [glɪmps] **1** *n* aperçu *m*; **to catch** *or* **get a g. of sth** entrevoir qch **2** *vt* entrevoir

glisten [ˈglɪsən] *vi (of wet surface)* briller; *(of water)* miroiter

glitter [ˈglɪtə(r)] *vi* scintiller

gloat [gləʊt] *vi* jubiler **(over** à l'idée de)

global [ˈgləʊbəl] *adj (universal)* mondial; *(comprehensive)* global; **g. warming** réchauffement *m* de la planète • **globalization** *n Econ* mondialisation *f*

globe [gləʊb] *n* globe *m*

gloomy [ˈgluːmɪ] **(-ier, -iest)** *adj (sad)* morose; *(dark, dismal)* sombre

glory [ˈglɔːrɪ] *n* gloire *f*; *(great beauty)* splendeur *f* • **glorious** *adj (splendid)* magnifique; *(full of glory)* glorieux, -euse

glossary [ˈglɒsərɪ] *(pl* **-ies)** *n* glossaire *m*

glossy [ˈglɒsɪ] **(-ier, -iest)** *adj* brillant; *(photo)* glacé; *(magazine)* de luxe

glove [glʌv] *n* gant *m*; **g. compartment** *(in car)* boîte *f* à gants

glow [gləʊ] **1** *n (light)* lueur *f* **2** *vi (of sky, fire)* rougeoyer; *Fig (of eyes, person)* rayonner **(with** de) • **glowing** *adj (account, terms, reference)* enthousiaste

glue [gluː] **1** *n* colle *f* **2** *vt* coller **(to/on** à)

gnaw [nɔː] *vti* **to g. (at) sth** ronger qch

gnome [nəʊm] *n* gnome *m*

go [gəʊ] **1** (*pl* **goes**) *n* (*turn*) tour *m*; (*energy*) dynamisme *m*; **to have a go at (doing) sth** essayer (de faire) qch; **at** *or* **in one go** d'un seul coup; **on the go** en mouvement **2** (*3rd person sing present tense* **goes**; *pt* **went**; *pp* **gone**; *pres p* **going**) *vt* (*make sound*) faire; **to go it alone** se lancer en solo **3** *vi* aller (**to** à; **from** de); (*depart*) partir, s'en aller; (*disappear*) disparaître; (*be sold*) se vendre; (*function*) marcher; (*progress*) aller; (*become*) devenir; (*of time*) passer; (*of hearing, strength*) baisser; **to go well/badly** (*of event*) se passer bien/mal; **she's going to do sth** (*is about to, intends to*) elle va faire qch; **it's going to rain** il va pleuvoir; **it's all gone** (*finished*) il n'y en a plus; **to go and get sb/sth** (*fetch*) aller chercher qn/qch; **to go and see** aller voir; **to go riding/on a trip** faire du cheval/un voyage; **to go to a doctor/lawyer** aller voir un médecin/un avocat; **two hours to go** encore deux heures

▶**go about** (*get on with*) s'occuper de; (*set about*) se mettre à; **how do you go about it?** comment est-ce qu'on procède?

▶**go after** *vt insep* (*chase*) poursuivre; (*job*) essayer d'obtenir

▶**go ahead** *vi* (*take place*) avoir lieu; (*go in front*) passer devant; **to go ahead with sth** entreprendre qch; **go ahead!** allez-y!

▶**go along** *vi* (*proceed*) se dérouler; **to go along with sb/sth** être d'accord avec qn/qch; **we'll see as we go along** nous verrons au fur et à mesure

▶**go around** *vi* = **go about**

▶**go away** *vi* partir, s'en aller

▶**go back** *vi* (*return*) revenir; (*step back, retreat*) reculer; **to go back to sleep** se rendormir; **to go back on one's promise** *or* **word** revenir sur sa promesse

▶**go by** *vi* passer

▶**go down 1** *vt insep* (*stairs, street*) descendre **2** *vi* descendre; (*fall down*) tomber; (*of sun*) se coucher; (*of temperature, price*) baisser; (*of tyre, balloon*) se dégonfler; **to go down well/badly** être bien/mal reçu

▶**go for** *vt insep* (*fetch*) aller chercher; (*attack*) attaquer; **the same goes for you** ça vaut aussi pour toi

▶**go in** *vi* (r)entrer; (*of sun*) se cacher; *Br* **to go in for sth** s'intéresser à qch

▶**go off 1** *vt insep* (*lose liking for*) se lasser de **2** *vi* (*leave*) partir; (*go bad*) se gâter; (*of alarm*) se déclencher; (*of bomb*) exploser

▶**go on** *vi* continuer (**doing** à faire); (*travel*) poursuivre sa route; (*happen*) se passer; (*last*) durer; **to go on to sth** passer à qch; *Fam* **to go on about sb/sth** parler sans cesse de qn/qch

▶**go out** *vi* sortir; (*of light, fire*) s'éteindre; (*date*) sortir ensemble; **to go out for a meal** aller au restaurant; **to go out with sb** sortir avec qn; **to go out to work** travailler (hors de chez soi)

▶**go over 1** *vt insep* (**a**) (*cross over*) traverser; **the ball went over the wall** la balle est passée par-dessus le mur (**b**) (*examine*) passer en revue; (*speech*) revoir **2** *vi* (*go*) aller (**to** à); **to go over to sb** aller vers qn; **to go over to sb's** (*visit*) faire un saut chez qn

▶**go round 1** *vt insep* **to go round a corner** tourner au coin; **to go**

round the world faire le tour du monde **2** vi *(turn)* tourner; *(make a detour)* faire le tour; *(of rumour)* circuler; **to go round to sb's** faire un saut chez qn; **there is enough to go round** il y en a assez pour tout le monde

▶**go through** vt insep *(suffer, undergo)* subir; *(examine)* passer en revue; *(search)* fouiller; *(wear out)* user; **to go through with sth** aller jusqu'au bout de qch

▶**go up 1** vt insep monter **2** vi monter; **to go up to sth** *(approach)* se diriger vers qch; *(reach)* aller jusqu'à qch

▶**go with** vt insep aller de pair avec; **the company car goes with the job** le poste donne droit à une voiture de fonction

▶**go without** vt insep se passer de

goal [gəʊl] n but m • **goalkeeper** n gardien m de but, goal m

goat [gəʊt] n chèvre f

gobble ['gɒbəl] vt **to g. (up** or **down)** *(food)* engloutir

god [gɒd] n dieu m; **G.** Dieu; *Fam* **oh G.!, my G.!** mon Dieu! • **goddaughter** n filleule f • **goddess** n déesse f • **godfather** n parrain m • **godmother** n marraine f • **godson** n filleul m

goes [gəʊz] *3rd person sing present tense & npl of* **go**

goggles ['gɒgəlz] npl lunettes fpl *(de protection, de plongée)*

going ['gəʊɪŋ] **1** n **it's hard** or **heavy g.** c'est difficile **2** adj **the g. rate** le tarif en vigueur

go-kart ['gəʊkɑːt] n *(for racing)* kart m

gold [gəʊld] **1** n or m **2** adj *(watch)* en or; *(coin, dust)* d'or; **g. medal** *(in sport)* médaille f d'or • **golden** adj *(of gold colour)* doré; **g. rule**

règle f d'or • **goldmine** n mine f d'or

goldfish ['gəʊldfɪʃ] n poisson m rouge

golf [gɒlf] n golf m; **g. club** *(stick, association)* club m de golf; **g. course** parcours m de golf • **golfer** n golfeur, -euse mf

gone [gɒn] pp of **go**

good [gʊd] **1** (**better, best**) adj bon *(f* bonne); *(kind)* gentil, -ille; *(well-behaved)* sage; **my g. friend** mon cher ami; **g.!** bon!, bien!; **that isn't g. enough** *(bad)* ça ne va pas; *(not sufficient)* ça ne suffit pas; **that's g. of you** c'est gentil de ta part; **to taste g.** avoir bon goût; **to feel g.** se sentir bien; **to have g. weather** avoir beau temps; **to be g. at French** être bon en français; **to be g. at swimming/telling jokes** savoir bien nager/raconter des blagues; **to be g. with children** savoir s'y prendre avec les enfants; **a g. many, a g. deal (of)** beaucoup (de); **as g. as** *(almost)* pratiquement; **g. afternoon, g. morning** bonjour; *(on leaving someone)* au revoir; **g. evening** bonsoir; **g. night** bonsoir; *(before going to bed)* bonne nuit **2** n *(advantage, virtue)* bien m; **for her (own) g.** pour son bien; **for the g. of your family/career** pour ta famille/carrière; **it will do you (some) g.** ça te fera du bien; **it's no g. crying/shouting** ça ne sert à rien de pleurer/crier; **that's no g.** *(worthless)* ça ne vaut rien; *(bad)* ça ne va pas; **for g.** *(leave, give up)* pour de bon • **goodbye** exclam au revoir • **good-for-nothing** n propre-à-rien mf • **good-looking** adj beau

(f belle) • **goodness** n bonté f;
my g.! mon Dieu! • **goodwill** n
bienvaillance f

goods [gʊdz] npl marchandises
fpl

goose [guːs] (pl **geese**) n oie f; **g.**
Br **pimples** or Am **bumps** chair f
de poule

gooseberry ['gʊzbərɪ] (pl **-ies**) n
groseille f à maquereau

gorge [gɔːdʒ] **1** n (ravine) gorge
f **2** vt **to g. oneself** se gaver (**on**
de)

gorgeous ['gɔːdʒəs] adj
magnifique

gorilla [gə'rɪlə] n gorille m

gory ['gɔːrɪ] (**-ier, -iest**) adj
(bloody) sanglant

gosh [gɒʃ] exclam Fam ça alors!

gossip ['gɒsɪp] **1** n (talk)
bavardages mpl; (malicious)
cancans mpl; (person) commère f;
g. column (in newspaper) échos
mpl **2** vi bavarder; (maliciously)
colporter des commérages

got [gɒt] pt & Br pp of **get** •
gotten Am pp of **get**

govern ['gʌvən] vt (rule)
gouverner; (city, province) ad-
ministrer; (influence) déterminer •
government 1 n gouvernement
m; **local g.** administration f
locale **2** adj (decision, policy)
gouvernemental

gown [gaʊn] n (of woman) robe f;
Br (of judge, lecturer) toge f

GP [dʒiː'piː] (abbr **general
practitioner**) n (médecin m)
généraliste mf

grab [græb] (pt & pp **-bb-**) vt **to g.
(hold of) sb/sth** saisir qn/qch; **to
g. sth from sb** arracher qch à qn

grace [greɪs] n (charm, goodwill,
mercy) grâce f; Rel **to say g.**
dire le bénédicité • **graceful** adj

(movement, person) gracieux,
-euse • **gracious** [-ʃəs] adj (kind)
aimable (**to** envers); Fam **good
g.!** bonté divine!

grade [greɪd] **1** n (a) (rank) grade
m; (in profession) échelon m;
(quality) qualité f; Am **g. crossing**
passage m à niveau (b) Am Sch
(mark) note f; (year) classe f;
g. school école f primaire **2** vt
(classify) classer; Am (exam) noter

gradient ['greɪdɪənt] n (slope)
dénivellation f

gradual ['grædʒʊəl] adj progressif,
-ive; (slope) doux (f douce) •
gradually adv progressivement

graduate 1 ['grædʒʊət] n Br
(from university) ≃ licencié, -e
mf; Am (from high school) ≃
bachelier, -ère mf **2** ['grædʒʊeɪt]
vi Br (from university) ≃ obtenir
sa licence; Am (from high school)
≃ obtenir son baccalauréat; **to g.
from sth to sth** passer de qch à
qch • **graduation** n Univ remise
f des diplômes

graffiti [grə'fiːtɪ] npl graffiti mpl

grain [greɪn] n (seed, particle)
grain m; (cereals) céréales fpl

gram [græm] n gramme m

grammar ['græmə(r)] n
grammaire f; Br **g. school** ≃ lycée
m • **grammatical** [grə'mætɪkəl]
adj grammatical

gramme [græm] n gramme m

grand [grænd] **1** (**-er, -est**)
adj (splendid) grandiose; Fam
(excellent) excellent; **g. piano**
piano m à queue; **g. total** somme
f totale **2** n inv Br Fam mille livres
fpl; Am Fam mille dollars mpl •
grandchild (pl **-children**) n petit-
fils m, petite-fille f; **grandchildren**
petits-enfants mpl • **grand(d)ad**
n Fam papi m • **granddaughter**
n petite-fille f • **grandfather** n

grand-père m • **grandma** n Fam mamie f • **grandmother** n grand-mère f • **grandpa** n Fam papi m • **grandparents** npl grands-parents mpl • **grandson** n petit-fils m

granny ['grænɪ] (pl **-ies**) n Fam mamie f

grant [grɑːnt] **1** n subvention f; (for student) bourse f **2** vt accorder (**to** à); (request) accéder à; (prayer, wish) exaucer; (admit) admettre (**that** que); **to take sth for granted** considérer qch comme allant de soi; **to take sb for granted** ne pas avoir d'égard pour qn

grape [greɪp] n grain m de raisin; **some grapes** du raisin; **g. juice** jus m de raisin

grapefruit ['greɪpfruːt] n pamplemousse m

graph [grɑːf] n graphique m

graphic ['græfɪk] adj (description) très détaillé; **g. artist** graphiste mf • **graphics** npl **(computer)** g. graphiques mpl

grasp [grɑːsp] vt (seize, understand) saisir

grass [grɑːs] n herbe f; (lawn) gazon m • **grasshopper** n sauterelle f

grate [greɪt] vt (cheese, carrot) râper • **grater** n râpe f • **grating** **1** adj (sound) grinçant **2** n (bars) grille f

grateful ['greɪtfəl] adj reconnaissant (**to** à; **for** de); (words, letter) de remerciement • **gratefully** adv avec reconnaissance • **gratitude** ['grætɪtjuːd] n gratitude f (**for** de)

grave[1] [greɪv] n tombe f • **gravestone** n pierre f tombale • **graveyard** n cimetière m

grave[2] [greɪv] (**-er**, **-est**) adj (serious) grave; (manner, voice) solennel, -elle

gravel ['grævəl] n gravier m

gravity ['grævɪtɪ] n (force) pesanteur f

gravy ['greɪvɪ] n = sauce à base de jus de viande

gray [greɪ] adj & n Am = **grey**

graze[1] [greɪz] vt (scrape) écorcher

graze[2] [greɪz] vi (of cattle) paître

grease [griːs] n graisse f • **greasy** (**-ier**, **-iest**) adj graisseux, -euse; (hair, skin, food) gras (f grasse)

great [greɪt] (**-er**, **-est**) adj grand; (effort, heat) gros (f grosse), grand; Fam (very good) génial; Fam **to be g. at tennis** être très doué pour le tennis; **a g. deal** or **number (of)**, **a g. many** beaucoup (de); **G. Britain** la Grande-Bretagne; **Greater London** le grand Londres • **great-grandfather** n arrière-grand-père m • **great-grandmother** n arrière-grand-mère f

Greece [griːs] n la Grèce

greed [griːd] n avidité f (**for** de); (for food) gourmandise f • **greedy** (**-ier**, **-iest**) adj avide (**for** de); (for food) gourmand

Greek [griːk] **1** adj grec (f grecque) **2** n (person) Grec m, Grecque f; (language) grec m

green [griːn] **1** (**-er**, **-est**) adj vert; Pol écologiste; **to turn** or **go g.** (of traffic lights) passer au vert; (of person, garden, tree) verdir; Am **g. card** ≃ permis m de travail **2** n (colour) vert m; (grassy area) pelouse f; **greens** (vegetables) légumes mpl verts; Pol **the Greens** les Verts mpl • **greenery** n verdure f • **greengrocer** n Br marchand, -e mf de fruits et légumes • **greenhouse** n serre f; **the g. effect** l'effet m de serre

greet [griːt] vt (say hello to) saluer; (welcome) accueillir • **greeting** n accueil *m*; **greetings** *(for birthday, festival)* vœux *mpl*

grenade [grə'neɪd] *n* *(bomb)* grenade *f*

grew [gruː] *pt of* **grow**

grey [greɪ] **1** *adj* (**-er, -est**) gris; **to be going g.** grisonner **2** *n* gris *m* • **grey-haired** *adj* aux cheveux gris

grid [grɪd] *n* *(bars)* grille *f*; *(on map)* quadrillage *m*

grieve [griːv] *vi* **to g. for sb/ over sth** pleurer qn/qch • **grief** *n* chagrin *m*

grill [grɪl] **1** *n* *(utensil)* gril *m*; *(dish)* grillade *f* **2** *vt* griller

grim [grɪm] (**grimmer, grimmest**) *adj* *(stern)* sinistre; *Fam (bad)* lamentable

grimace ['grɪməs] *vi* grimacer

grime [graɪm] *n* crasse *f* • **grimy** (**-ier, -iest**) *adj* crasseux, -euse

grin [grɪn] **1** *n* large sourire *m* **2** (*pt & pp* **-nn-**) *vi* avoir un large sourire

grind [graɪnd] **1** (*pt & pp* **ground**) *vt* *(coffee, pepper)* moudre; *Am (meat)* hacher **2** *vi* **to g. to a halt** s'immobiliser • **grinder** *n* **coffee g.** moulin *m* à café

grip [grɪp] **1** *n* *(hold)* prise *f*; *(handle)* poignée *f*; *Fig* **to get to grips with sth** s'attaquer à qch **2** (*pt & pp* **-pp-**) *vt* *(seize)* saisir; *(hold)* empoigner; **the audience was gripped by the play** la pièce a captivé les spectateurs • **gripping** *adj* passionnant

gristle ['grɪsəl] *n* *(in meat)* nerfs *mpl*

grit [grɪt] **1** *n* *(sand)* sable *m*; *(gravel)* gravillons *mpl* **2** (*pt & pp* **-tt-**) *vt* **to g. one's teeth** serrer les dents

groan [grəʊn] **1** *n* *(of pain)* gémissement *m*; *(of dissatisfaction)*

grognement *m* **2** *vi* *(with pain)* gémir; *(complain)* grogner

grocer ['grəʊsə(r)] *n* épicier, -ère *mf*; **g.'s (shop)** épicerie *f* • **groceries** *npl* *(food)* provisions *fpl* • **grocery** (*pl* **-ies**) *n Am (shop)* épicerie *f*

groin [grɔɪn] *n* aine *f*

groom [gruːm] **1** *n* (**a**) *(at wedding)* marié *m* (**b**) *(for horses)* lad *m* **2** *vt (horse)* panser; **to g. sb for sth** préparer qn pour qch

groove [gruːv] *n* *(in wood, metal)* rainure *f*; *(in record)* sillon *m*

grope [grəʊp] *vi* **to g. (about) for sth** chercher qch à tâtons

gross [grəʊs] *adj* (**a**) *(total) (weight, income, profit)* brut (**b**) (**-er, -est**) *(coarse)* grossier, -ère; *(injustice)* flagrant

grotesque [grəʊ'tesk] *adj* grotesque

grotty ['grɒtɪ] (**-ier, -iest**) *adj Br Fam* minable

ground¹ [graʊnd] *n* *(earth)* terre *f*, sol *m*; *(land)* terrain *m*; *(estate)* terres *fpl*; **grounds** *(gardens)* parc *m*; *Fig (reasons)* motifs *mpl*; **on the g.** *(lying, sitting)* par terre; *Br* **g. floor** rez-de-chaussée *m inv*

ground² [graʊnd] **1** *pt & pp of* **grind 2** *adj (coffee)* moulu; *Am* **g. meat** viande *f* hachée

group [gruːp] **1** *n* groupe *m* **2** *vt* **to g. (together)** grouper

grow [grəʊ] **1** (*pt* **grew,** *pp* **grown**) *vt (vegetables)* cultiver; **to g. a beard** se laisser pousser la barbe **2** *vi (of person)* grandir; *(of plant, hair)* pousser; *(of economy, feeling)* croître; *(of firm, town)* se développer; *(of gap, family)* s'agrandir; **to g. to like sth** finir par aimer qch; **when I g. up** quand je serai grand; **it'll g. on you** *(of music, book)* tu finiras par t'y intéresser • **growing** *adj (child)* en pleine croissance; *(number, discontent)* grandissant

growl [graʊl] **1** *n* grognement *m* **2** *vi* grogner (**at** contre)

grown [grəʊn] **1** *pp of* **grow** • **grown-up 1** *n* grande personne *f* **2** *adj (ideas, behaviour)* d'adulte

growth [grəʊθ] *n* croissance *f*; *(increase)* augmentation *f* (**in** de)

grub [grʌb] *n Fam (food)* bouffe *f*

grubby ['grʌbɪ] (**-ier, -iest**) *adj* sale

grudge [grʌdʒ] *n* rancune *f*; **to have a g. against sb** garder rancune à qn • **grudgingly** *adv* à contrecœur

gruelling ['grʊəlɪŋ] (*Am* **grueling**) *adj (journey, experience)* épuisant

gruesome ['gruːsəm] *adj* horrible

grumble ['grʌmbəl] *vi (complain)* grommeler; **to g. about sth** rouspéter contre qch

grumpy ['grʌmpɪ] (**-ier, -iest**) *adj* grincheux, -euse

grunt [grʌnt] **1** *n* grognement *m* **2** *vti* grogner

guarantee [gærən'tiː] **1** *n* garantie *f* **2** *vt* garantir (**against** contre); *(vouch for)* se porter garant de; **to g. sb that...** garantir à qn que...

guard [gɑːd] **1** *n (supervision)* garde *f*; *(sentry)* garde *m*; *(on train)* chef *m* de train; **under g.** sous surveillance; **on one's g.** sur ses gardes; **on g. (duty)** de garde; **to catch sb off (his/her) g.** prendre qn au dépourvu **2** *vt (protect)* garder

guardian ['gɑːdɪən] *n (of child)* tuteur, -trice *mf*; *(protector)* gardien, -enne *mf*

guess [ges] **1** *n (estimate)* estimation *f*; **to make** *or* **take a g.** deviner; **at a g.** à vue de nez **2** *vt* deviner (**that** que); *(suppose)* supposer, croire **3** *vi* deviner; **I g. (so)** je crois

guest [gest] *n* invité, -e *mf*; *(in hotel)* client, -e *mf*; *(at meal)* convive *mf*; **g. room** chambre *f* d'amis; **g. speaker** conférencier, -ère *mf* • **guesthouse** *n* pension *f* de famille

guide [gaɪd] **1** *n (person)* guide *m*; *(indication)* indication *f*; **g. (book)** guide *m*; *Br* **(Girl) G.** éclaireuse *f*; **g. dog** chien *m* d'aveugle **2** *vt (lead)* guider • **guidance** *n (advice)* conseils *mpl* • **guided** *adj* **g. tour** visite *f* guidée • **guidelines** *npl* directives *fpl*

guilt [gɪlt] *n* culpabilité *f* • **guilty** (**-ier, -iest**) *adj* coupable; **to find sb g./not g.** déclarer qn coupable/non coupable

guinea ['gɪnɪ] *n* **g. pig** *(animal)* & *Fig* cobaye *m*

guitar [gɪ'tɑː(r)] *n* guitare *f*

gulf [gʌlf] *n (in sea)* golfe *m*, *(chasm)* gouffre *m* (**between** entre)

gullible ['gʌlɪbəl] *adj* crédule

gulp [gʌlp] **1** *n (of drink)* gorgée *f*; **in** *or* **at one g.** d'un coup **2** *vt* **to g. (down)** engloutir **3** *vi (with surprise)* avoir la gorge serrée

gum¹ [gʌm] *n (in mouth)* gencive *f*

gum² [gʌm] *n (for chewing)* chewing-gum *m*

gun [gʌn] *n* pistolet *m*; *(rifle)* fusil *m* • **gunpowder** *n* poudre *f* à canon • **gunshot** *n* coup *m* de feu

gurgle ['gɜːgəl] *vi (of water)* gargouiller; *(of baby)* gazouiller

gush [gʌʃ] *vi* **to g. (out)** jaillir (**of** de)

gust [gʌst] *n (of wind)* rafale *f*

gut [gʌt] *n (inside body)* intestin

m; *Fam* **guts** *(insides)* entrailles *fpl*; *(courage)* cran *m*

gutter ['gʌtə(r)] *n (on roof)* gouttière *f*; *(in street)* caniveau *m*

guy [gaɪ] *n Fam (man)* type *m*

gym [dʒɪm] *n (room)* gymnase *m*; **g. shoes** chaussures *fpl* de gym ●

gymnastics *n* gymnastique *f*

gynaecologist [gaɪnɪ'kɒlədʒɪst] *(Am* **gynecologist***) n* gynécologue *mf*

gypsy ['dʒɪpsɪ] *n* = **gipsy**

Hh

H, h [eɪtʃ] *n (letter)* H, h *m inv*

habit ['hæbɪt] *n (custom, practice)* habitude *f*; **to be in/get into the h. of doing sth** avoir/prendre l'habitude de faire qch

habitat ['hæbɪtæt] *n (of animal, plant)* habitat *m*

hack [hæk] *vt (cut)* tailler • **hacker** *n Comptr* pirate *m* informatique

had [hæd] *pt & pp of* **have**

haemorrhage ['hemərɪdʒ] (*Am* **hemorrhage**) *n* hémorragie *f*

hag [hæg] *n Pej* **(old) h.** vieille taupe *f*

haggard ['hægəd] *adj* hâve

haggle ['hægəl] *vi* marchander; **to h. over the price of sth** chicaner sur le prix de qch

hail[1] [heɪl] **1** *n* grêle *f* **2** *vi* **it's hailing** il grêle

hail[2] [heɪl] *vt (greet)* saluer (**as** comme); *(taxi)* héler

hair [heə(r)] *n (on head)* cheveux *mpl*; *(on body, of animal)* poils *mpl*; **a h.** *(on head)* un cheveu; *(on body, of animal)* un poil • **hairbrush** *n* brosse *f* à cheveux • **haircut** *n* coupe *f* de cheveux; **to have a h.** se faire couper les cheveux • **hairdo** (*pl* **-dos**) *n Fam* coiffure *f* • **hairdresser** *n* coiffeur, -euse *mf* • **hairdryer** *n* sèche-cheveux *m inv* • **hairspray** *n* laque *f* • **hairstyle** *n* coiffure *f* • **hairy** (**-ier, -iest**) *adj (person, animal, body)* poilu

-haired [heəd] *suff* **long-/red-h.** aux cheveux longs/roux

half [hɑːf] **1** (*pl* **halves**) *n* moitié *f*; *(part of match)* mi-temps *f*; *Br (half fare)* demi-tarif *m*; *Br (beer)* demi *m*; **h. (of) the apple** la moitié de la pomme; **h. past one** une heure et demie; **ten and a h.** dix et demi; **h. a dozen** une demi-douzaine; **to cut in h.** couper en deux **2** *adj* demi; **h. board** demi-pension *f*; **h. fare** demi-tarif *m*; **at h. price** à moitié prix **3** *adv (dressed, full, asleep)* à moitié; **h. as much as** moitié moins que • **half-day** *n* demi-journée *f* • **half-hearted** *adj (person, manner)* peu enthousiaste • **half-hour** n demi-heure f • **half-open** adj entrouvert • **half-price** *adj & adv* à moitié prix • **half-term** *n Br Sch* petites vacances *fpl (de milieu de trimestre)* • **half-time** *n (in game)* mi-temps *f* • **halfway** *adv (between places)* à mi-chemin (**between** entre)

hall [hɔːl] *n (room)* salle *f*; *(entrance room)* entrée *f*; *(of hotel)* hall *m*; *Br Univ* **h. of residence** résidence *f* universitaire

Hallowe'en [hæləʊ'iːn] *n* Halloween *m*

hallucination [həluːsɪ'neɪʃən] *n* hallucination *f*

hallway ['hɔːlweɪ] *n* entrée *f*

halo ['heɪləʊ] (*pl* **-oes** *or* **-os**) *n* auréole *f*

halt [hɔːlt] **1** *n* halte *f*; **to come to a h.** s'arrêter **2** *vt* arrêter **3** *vi (of* *soldiers)* faire halte; *(of production)* s'arrêter

halve [hɑːv] *vt (reduce by half)* réduire de moitié; *(divide in two)* diviser en deux

ham [hæm] *n (meat)* jambon *m* • **hamburger** *n* hamburger *m*

hammer ['hæmə(r)] *n* marteau *m*

hammock ['hæmək] *n* hamac *m*

hamper ['hæmpə(r)] *n Br (for food)* panier *m*; *Am (laundry basket)* panier *m* à linge

hamster ['hæmstə(r)] *n* hamster *m*

hand [hænd] **1** *n (part of the body)* main *f*; *(of clock)* aiguille *f*; **to hold sth in one's h.** tenir qch à la main; **to hold hands** se tenir par la main; **by h.** *(make, sew)* à la main; **on the one h....** d'une part...; **on the other h....** d'autre part...; **to lend sb a (helping) h.** donner un coup de main à qn; **to get out of h.** *(of child)* devenir impossible; *(of situation)* devenir incontrôlable; **h. in h.** la main dans la main **2** *adj (luggage, grenade)* à main; *(cream, lotion)* pour les mains **3** *vt (give)* donner (**to** à); **to h. sth in** remettre qch; **to h. sth out** distribuer qch; **to h. sth over** remettre qch • **handbag** *n* sac *m* à main • **handbook** *n (manual)* manuel *m*; *(guide)* guide *m* • **handbrake** *n* frein *m* à main • **handful** *n (bunch, group)* poignée *f* • **handmade** *adj* fait à la main • **handwriting** *n* écriture *f* • **handwritten** *adj* écrit à la main

handicap ['hændɪkæp] **1** *n (disadvantage, in sport)* handicap *m* **2** *(pt & pp -pp-)* *vt* handicaper • **handicapped** *adj (disabled)* handicapé

handkerchief ['hæŋkətʃɪf] *(pl -chiefs)* *n* mouchoir *m*

handle ['hændəl] **1** *n (of door)* poignée *f*; *(of knife)* manche *m*; *(of cup)* anse *f*; *(of saucepan)* queue *f* **2** *vt (manipulate)* manier; *(touch)* toucher à; *(deal with)* s'occuper de; *(difficult person)* s'y prendre avec

handsome ['hænsəm] *adj (man)* beau; *(profit, sum)* considérable

handy ['hændɪ] *(-ier, -iest)* *adj (convenient)* commode; *(useful)* pratique; *(skilful)* habile (**at doing** à faire); **to come in h.** être utile; **the flat is h. for the shops** l'appartement est près des commerces

hang¹ [hæŋ] **1** *n Fam* **to get the h. of sth** piger qch **2** *(pt & pp hung)* *vt* suspendre (**on/from** à); *(on hook)* accrocher (**on/from** à) **3** *vi (dangle)* pendre • **hanging** *adj* suspendu (**from** à); **h. on the wall** accroché au mur • **hang-up** *n Fam* complexe *m*

▶**hang about, hang around** *vi (loiter)* traîner; *Fam (wait)* poireauter

▶**hang down** *vi (dangle)* pendre

▶**hang on** *vi (hold out)* tenir le coup; *Fam (wait)* patienter; **to h. on to sth** garder qch

▶**hang out 1** *vt sep (washing)* étendre **2** *vi Fam (spend time)* traîner

▶**hang up 1** *vt sep (picture)* accrocher **2** *vi (on phone)* raccrocher

hang² [hæŋ] *(pt & pp hanged)* *vt (criminal)* pendre (**for** pour)

hanger ['hæŋə(r)] *n* (**coat**) **h.** cintre *m*

hang-glider ['hæŋglaɪdə(r)] *n* Deltaplane *m*

hangover ['hæŋəʊvə(r)] *n Fam*
gueule *f* de bois
hankie, hanky ['hæŋkɪ] (*pl* -ies) *n*
Fam mouchoir *m*
haphazard [hæp'hæzəd] *adj*
(choice, decision) pris au hasard
happen ['hæpən] *vi* arriver, se
produire; **to h.** *to sb* arriver à qn;
do you h. *to have...?* est-ce que
par hasard vous avez...?
happy ['hæpɪ] (-ier, -iest) *adj*
heureux, -euse (**to do** de faire;
about de); **H. New Year!**
bonne année!; **H. Christmas!**
joyeux Noël!; **h. birthday!**
joyeux anniversaire! • **happily**
adv joyeusement; *(contentedly)*
tranquillement • **happiness** *n*
bonheur *m*
harass [*Br* 'hærəs, *Am* hə'ræs]
vt harceler • **harassment** *n*
harcèlement *m*
harbour ['hɑːbə(r)] (*Am* **harbor**)
n port *m*
hard [hɑːd] (-er, -est) **1** *adj (not
soft, severe)* dur; *(difficult)* difficile,
dur; *(water)* calcaire; **to be h. on**
sb être dur avec qn; **to be h. of**
hearing être dur d'oreille; *Fam* **h.**
up *(poor)* fauché; *Comptr* **h. disk**
disque *m* dur; **h. drugs** drogues *fpl*
dures; **h. shoulder** *(on motorway)*
bande *f* d'arrêt d'urgence **2** *adv*
(work) dur; *(pull, push, hit)* fort;
(study) assidûment; *(rain)* à verse;
to think h. réfléchir bien; **to try h.**
faire de son mieux; **h. at work** en
plein travail • **hardback** *n* livre *m*
cartonné • **hard-boiled** *adj (egg)*
dur • **harden** *vi (of substance,
attitude)* durcir • **hardware** *n inv*
quincaillerie *f*; *Comptr* matériel
m • **hard-wearing** *adj* résistant
• **hard-working** *adj* travailleur,
-euse
hardly ['hɑːdlɪ] *adv* à peine; I

had h. arrived when... j'étais à
peine arrivé que...; **h. anyone/**
anything presque personne/rien;
h. ever presque jamais
hare [heə(r)] *n* lièvre *m*
harm [hɑːm] **1** *n (hurt)* mal *m*;
(wrong) tort *m*; **to do sb h.** faire
du mal à qn **2** *vt (physically)* faire
du mal à; *(health, interests, cause)*
nuire à; *(object)* abîmer • **harmful**
adj (influence) néfaste; *(substance)*
nocif, -ive • **harmless** *adj*
(person) inoffensif, -ive; *(hobby,
joke)* innocent
harmonica [hɑː'mɒnɪkə] *n*
harmonica *m*
harmony ['hɑːmənɪ] (*pl* -ies) *n*
harmonie *f* • **harmonize 1** *vt*
harmoniser **2** *vi* s'harmoniser
harness ['hɑːnɪs] *n (for horse,
baby)* harnais *m*
harp [hɑːp] *n* harpe *f*
harrowing ['hærəʊɪŋ] *adj (story)*
poignant; *(experience)* très
éprouvant
harsh [hɑːʃ] (-er, -est) *adj (person,
treatment)* dur; *(winter, climate)*
rude; *(sound, voice)* strident; **to**
be h. with sb être dur envers qn
harvest ['hɑːvɪst] **1** *n* moisson *f*;
(of fruit) récolte *f* **2** *vt* moissonner;
(fruit) récolter
has [hæz] *see* **have**
hassle ['hæsəl] *n Fam* embête-
ments *mpl*
hasty ['heɪstɪ] (-ier, -iest) *adj*
(departure) précipité; *(visit)* rapide;
(decision) hâtif, -ive • **hastily** *adv*
(write, prepare) hâtivement; *(say)*
précipitamment
hat [hæt] *n* chapeau *m*; *(of child)*
bonnet *m*
hatch [hætʃ] **1** *vt* faire éclore; *Fig*
(plot) tramer **2** *vi (of chick, egg)*
éclore
hate [heɪt] *vt* haïr, détester; **to h.**

doing *or* **to do sth** détester faire qch • **hatred** ['heɪtrɪd] *n* haine *f*
haul [hɔːl] *vt (pull)* tirer
haunt [hɔːnt] *vt* hanter • **haunted** *adj (house)* hanté

have [hæv] **1** *(3rd person sing present tense* **has,** *pt & pp* **had,** *pres p* **having)** *vt* avoir; *(meal, bath, lesson)* prendre; **he has (got) a big house** il a une grande maison; **she doesn't h.** *or* **hasn't got a car** elle n'a pas de voiture; **to h. a drink** prendre un verre; **to h. a walk/dream** faire une promenade/un rêve; **to h. a wash** se laver; **to h. a nice holiday** passer d'agréables vacances; **to h. flu** avoir la grippe; **will you h. some tea?** est-ce que tu veux du thé?; **to let sb h. sth** donner qch à qn; *Fam* **you've had it!** tu es fichu!; *Fam* **I've been had** *(cheated)* je me suis fait avoir; **to h. gloves/a dress on** porter des gants/une robe; **to h. sb over** *or* **round** inviter qn chez soi **2** *v aux* avoir; *(with* **entrer, monter, sortir** *etc & pronominal verbs)* être; **to h. decided** avoir décidé; **to h. gone** être allé; **to h. cut oneself** s'être coupé; **she has been punished** elle a été punie, on l'a punie; **I've got to go, I h. to go** je dois partir, il faut que je parte; **I don't h. to go** je ne suis pas obligé de partir; **to h. sb do sth** faire faire qch à qn; **to h. one's hair cut** se faire couper les cheveux; **he's had his suitcase brought up** il a fait monter sa valise; **I've had my car stolen** on m'a volé mon auto; **I've been doing it for months** je le fais depuis des mois; **you h. told him, haven't you?** tu le lui as dit, n'est-ce pas?; **you've seen** this film before – no I haven't tu as déjà vu ce film – non; **you haven't done the dishes – yes I h.!** tu n'as pas fait la vaisselle – mais si, je l'ai faite!; **after he had eaten** *or* **after having eaten, he left** après avoir mangé, il est parti
►**have on** *vt sep* **(a)** *(be wearing)* porter **(b)** *(have arranged)* **to h. a lot on** avoir beaucoup à faire; **to h. nothing on** n'avoir rien de prévu

haven ['heɪvən] *n* refuge *m*
haven't ['hævənt] = **have not**
havoc ['hævək] *n* ravages *mpl*; **to wreak** *or* **cause h.** faire des ravages
hawk [hɔːk] *n* faucon *m*
hay [heɪ] *n* foin *m* • **hayfever** *n* rhume *m* des foins • **haystack** *n* meule *f* de foin
hazard ['hæzəd] **1** *n* risque *m*; *Br Aut* **h. (warning) lights** feux *mpl* de détresse **2** *vt (remark)* risquer • **hazardous** *adj* dangereux, -euse
hazelnut ['heɪzəlnʌt] *n* noisette *f*
hazy ['heɪzɪ] **(-ier, -iest)** *adj (weather)* brumeux, -euse; *(photo, idea)* flou

he [hiː] *pron* il; *(stressed)* lui; **he's a happy man** c'est un homme heureux; **he and I** lui et moi

head [hed] **1** *n (of person, hammer)* tête *f*; *(leader)* chef *m*; *Br (of school)* directeur, -trice *mf*; *(of bed)* chevet *m*, tête *f*; **h. first** la tête la première; **it didn't enter my h.** ça ne m'est pas venu à l'esprit **(that** que); **heads or tails?** pile ou face?; **per h., a h.** *(each)* par personne **2** *adj* **h. office** siège *m* social; **h. waiter** maître *m* d'hôtel **3** *vt (group, firm)* être à la tête de; *(list, poll)* être en tête de **4** *vi* **to h. for, to**

be heading for *(place)* se diriger vers • **headache** *n* mal *m* de tête; **to have a h.** avoir mal à la tête • **headed** *adj Br* h. **(note)paper** papier *m* à en-tête • **header** *n* *(in football)* (coup *m* de) tête *f* • **heading** *n (of chapter, page)* titre *m* • **headlamp, headlight** *n (of vehicle)* phare *m* • **headline** *n (of newspaper, TV news)* titre *m* • **headmaster** *n Br (of school)* directeur *m* • **headmistress** *n Br (of school)* directrice *f* • **headphones** *npl* écouteurs *mpl* • **headquarters** *npl (of company, political party)* siège *m* (social); *(of army, police)* quartier *m* général, QG *m* • **headscarf** *(pl* **-scarves)** *n* foulard *m*

heal [hiːl] **1** *vt (wound)* cicatriser; *(person)* guérir **2** *vi* **to h. (up)** *(of wound)* cicatriser

health [helθ] *n* santé *f*; **in good/ poor h.** en bonne/mauvaise santé; **h. food shop** *or Am* **store** magasin *m* de produits biologiques; *Br* **the (National) H. Service** ≃ la Sécurité sociale • **healthy** **(-ier, -iest)** *adj (person)* en bonne santé; *(food, attitude)* sain

heap [hiːp] *n* tas *m*; *Fam* **heaps of** *(money, people)* des tas de

hear [hɪə(r)] *(pt & pp* **heard** [hɜːd]) **1** *vt* entendre; *(listen to)* écouter; *(learn)* apprendre (**that** que); **I heard him come** *or* **coming** je l'ai entendu venir; **have you heard the news?** connais-tu la nouvelle?; **h., h.!** bravo! **2** *vi* entendre; **to h. from sb** avoir des nouvelles de qn; **I've heard of him** j'ai entendu parler de lui • **hearing** *n (sense)* ouïe *f*; **h. aid** audiophone *m*, appareil *m* auditif

heart [hɑːt] *n* cœur *m*; **hearts** *(in cards)* cœur *m*; **(off) by h.** *(know)* par cœur; **at h.** au fond; **h. attack** crise *f* cardiaque • **heartbeat** *n* battement *m* de cœur • **heartbreaking** *adj* navrant • **heartbroken** *adj* inconsolable

hearty ['hɑːtɪ] **(-ier, -iest)** *adj (appetite, meal)* gros *(f* grosse)

heat [hiːt] **1** *n* chaleur *f*; **h. wave** vague *f* de chaleur **2** *vti* **to h. (up)** chauffer • **heating** *n* chauffage *m* • **heater** *n* radiateur *m*

heave [hiːv] *vt (lift)* soulever avec effort; *(pull)* tirer fort

heaven ['hevən] *n* paradis *m*, ciel *m*; *Fam* **good heavens!** mon Dieu!

heavy ['hevɪ] **(-ier, -iest)** *adj* lourd; *(work, cold)* gros *(f* grosse); *(blow)* violent; *(rain)* fort; *(traffic)* dense; *(timetable, schedule)* chargé; **to be a h. drinker/smoker** boire/ fumer beaucoup • **heavily** *adv (breathe)* bruyamment; *(smoke, drink)* beaucoup; **to rain h.** pleuvoir à verse

Hebrew ['hiːbruː] *n (language)* hébreu *m*

heck [hek] *n Fam* zut!; **a h. of a lot** des masses (**of** de)

hectic ['hektɪk] *adj (busy)* agité; *(eventful)* mouvementé

he'd [hiːd] = **he had, he would**

hedge [hedʒ] *n (in garden, field)* haie *f*

hedgehog ['hedʒhɒg] *n* hérisson *m*

heel [hiːl] *n (of foot, shoe)* talon *m*

hefty ['heftɪ] **(-ier, -iest)** *adj (large, heavy)* gros *(f* grosse); *(person)* costaud

height [haɪt] *n* hauteur *f*; *(of person)* taille *f*; **at the h. of** *(summer, storm)* au cœur de

heir [eə(r)] *n* héritier *m*; **to be**

h. to sth être l'héritier de qch ● **heiress** n héritière f

held [held] pt & pp of **hold**

helicopter ['helɪkɒptə(r)] n hélicoptère m

hell [hel] n enfer m; Fam **a h. of a lot (of)** énormément (de); Fam **what the h. are you doing?** qu'est-ce que tu fous?

he'll [hiːl] = **he will**

hello [hə'ləʊ] exclam bonjour!; (answering phone) allô!

helmet ['helmɪt] n casque m

help [help] **1** n aide f; Br (cleaning woman) femme f de ménage; (office or shop workers) employés, -es mfpl; **with the h. of sth** à l'aide de qch; **h.!** au secours! **2** vt aider; **to h. sb do** or **to do sth** aider qn à faire qch; **to h. oneself (to sth)** se servir (de qch); **to h. sb out** aider qn; **I can't h. laughing** je ne peux pas m'empêcher de rire **3** vi aider ● **helpful** adj (person) serviable; (useful) utile ● **helping** n (serving) portion f ● **helpless** adj (powerless) impuissant

hem [hem] n ourlet m

hemisphere ['hemɪsfɪə(r)] n hémisphère m

hemorrhage ['hemərɪdʒ] n Am = **haemorrhage**

hen [hen] n poule f

hence [hens] adv (thus) d'où

her [hɜː(r)] **1** pron la, l'; (after prep, 'than', 'it is') elle; **(to) h.** (indirect) lui; **I saw h.** je l'ai vue; **I gave it (to) h.** je le lui ai donné **2** possessive adj son, sa, pl ses

herb [Br hɜːb, Am ɜːb] n herbe f aromatique ● **herbal** adj **h. tea** tisane f

herd [hɜːd] n troupeau m

here [hɪə(r)] **1** adv ici; **h. it/he is** le voici; **h. she comes!** la voilà!; **h. is a good example** voici un bon exemple; **I won't be h. tomorrow** je ne serai pas là demain; **h. and there** çà et là; **h. you are!** (take this) tenez! **2** exclam **h.!** (giving sb sth) tenez!

hero ['hɪərəʊ] (pl -oes) n héros m ● **heroic** [hɪ'rəʊɪk] adj héroïque ● **heroine** ['herəʊɪn] n héroïne f

heroin ['herəʊɪn] n (drug) héroïne f

herring ['herɪŋ] n hareng m

hers [hɜːz] possessive pron le sien, la sienne, pl les sien(ne)s; **this hat is h.** ce chapeau est à elle ou est le sien; **a friend of h.** un ami à elle

herself [hɜː'self] pron elle-même; (reflexive) se, s'; (after prep) elle; **she cut h.** elle s'est coupée

hesitate ['hezɪteɪt] **1** vt **to h. to do sth** hésiter à faire qch **2** vi hésiter (**over** or **about** sur) ● **hesitation** n hésitation f

heterosexual [hetərə'seksʃʊəl] adj & n hétérosexuel, -elle (mf)

hey [heɪ] exclam (calling sb) hé!; (expressing surprise, annoyance) ho!

hi [haɪ] exclam Fam salut!

hibernate ['haɪbəneɪt] vi hiberner

hiccup, hiccough ['hɪkʌp] **1** n hoquet m; **to have (the) hiccups** or **(the) hiccoughs** avoir le hoquet **2** vi hoqueter

hide [haɪd] (pt **hid** [hɪd], pp **hidden** ['hɪdən]) **1** vt cacher (**from** à) **2** vi **to h. (away** or **out)** se cacher (**from** de) ● **hide-and-seek** n **to play h.** jouer à cache-cache ● **hiding** n **to go into h.** se cacher; **h. place** cachette f

hideous ['hɪdɪəs] adj (ugly) hideux, -euse; (horrific) horrible

hierarchy ['haɪərɑːkɪ] (pl -ies) n hiérarchie f

hi-fi ['haɪfaɪ] n (system, equipment) chaîne f hi-fi

high [haɪ] **1** (**-er, -est**) adj haut; (speed) grand; (price, standards) élevé; (number, ideal) grand, élevé; (voice, tone) aigu (f aiguë); **to be five metres h.** avoir cinq mètres de haut; **it is h. time that you went** il est grand temps que tu y ailles; **h. jump** (sporting event) saut m en hauteur; **h. school** ≃ lycée m; Br **h. street** grand-rue f **2** adv **h.** (**up**) (fly, throw, aim) haut ● **highchair** n chaise f haute ● **higher 1** adj (number, speed, quality) supérieur (**than** à); **h. education** enseignement m supérieur **2** adv (fly, aim) plus haut (**than** que) ● **highlight 1** n (of visit, day) point m culminant; (in hair) reflet m **2** vt souligner; (with marker) surligner ● **highly** adv (very) très; (recommend) chaudement; **h. paid** très bien payé; **to speak h. of sb** dire beaucoup de bien de qn; Br **h. strung** hypersensible ● **high-rise** adj Br **h. building** tour f ● **high-speed** adj ultrarapide; **h. train** train m à grande vitesse ● **high-tech** adj (appliance) perfectionné; (industry) de pointe ● **highway** n Am (motorway) autoroute f; Br **H. Code** code m de la route

hijack ['haɪdʒæk] vt (plane) détourner ● **hijacker** n (of plane) pirate m de l'air

hike [haɪk] **1** n (walk) randonnée f **2** vi faire de la randonnée ● **hiker** n randonneur, -euse mf

hilarious [hɪ'leərɪəs] adj hilarant

hill [hɪl] n colline f; (slope) pente f ● **hillside** n **on the h.** à flanc de coteau ● **hilly** (**-ier, -iest**) adj vallonné

him [hɪm] pron le, l'; (after prep, 'than', 'it is') lui; (**to**) **h.** (indirect) lui; **I saw h.** je l'ai vu; **I gave it** (**to**) **h.** je le lui ai donné ● **himself** pron lui-même; (reflexive) se, s'; (after prep) lui; **he cut h.** il s'est coupé

hind [haɪnd] adj **h. legs** pattes fpl de derrière ● **hindsight** n **with h.** avec le recul

hinder ['hɪndə(r)] vt (obstruct) gêner; (delay) retarder ● **hindrance** n obstacle m

Hindu ['hɪnduː] **1** adj hindou **2** n Hindou, -e mf

hinge [hɪndʒ] n gond m, charnière f

hint [hɪnt] **1** n (insinuation) allusion f; (sign) signe m; (clue) indice m **2** vt laisser entendre (**that** que)

hip [hɪp] n hanche f

hippopotamus [hɪpə'pɒtəməs] n hippopotame m

hire ['haɪə(r)] **1** n location f; **for h.** à louer **2** vt (vehicle) louer; (worker) engager; **to h. sth out** louer qch

his [hɪz] **1** possessive pron le sien, la sienne, pl les sien(ne)s; **this hat is h.** ce chapeau est à lui ou est le sien; **a friend of h.** un ami à lui **2** possessive adj son, sa, pl ses

Hispanic [hɪ'spænɪk] Am **1** adj hispano-américain **2** n Hispano-Américain, -e mf

hiss [hɪs] vti siffler

history ['hɪstərɪ] (pl -ies) n (study, events) histoire f ● **historic(al)** [hɪ'stɒrɪk(əl)] adj historique

hit [hɪt] **1** n (success) succès m; **h.** (**song**) hit m **2** (pt & pp hit, pres p hitting) vt (beat) frapper; (bump into) heurter; (reach) atteindre; (affect) toucher; (problem, difficulty) rencontrer; Fam **to h. it off** s'entendre bien (**with sb** avec qn) **3** vi frapper; **to h. back** riposter (at à); **to h. out at sb** *(physically)* frapper qn; *(verbally)* s'en prendre à qn; **to h. (up)on sth** *(solution, idea)* trouver qch • **hit-and-run** *n* h. driver chauffard *m* (qui prend la fuite) • **hit-or-miss** *adj (chancy, random)* aléatoire

hitch [hɪtʃ] **1** *n (difficulty)* problème *m* **2** *vti* **to h. (a ride),** *Br* **to h. a lift** faire du stop (**to** jusqu'à) • **hitchhike** *vi* faire du stop (**to** jusqu'à) • **hitchhiker** *n* auto-stoppeur, -euse *mf* • **hitchhiking** *n* auto-stop *m*

HIV [eɪtʃaɪ'viː] *(abbr* **human immunodeficiency virus)** *n* VIH *m*; **HIV positive** séropositif, -ive

hive [haɪv] *n* ruche *f*

hoard [hɔːd] *n* réserve *f*; *(of money)* trésor *m*

hoarse [hɔːs] **(-er, -est)** *adj* enroué

hoax [həʊks] *n* canular *m*

hob [hɒb] *n (on stove)* plaque *f* chauffante

hobby ['hɒbɪ] *(pl* **-ies)** *n* passe-temps *m inv*

hockey ['hɒkɪ] *n* hockey *m*; *Br (field hockey)* hockey *m* sur gazon; *Am (ice hockey)* hockey *m* sur glace; **h. stick** crosse *f* de hockey

hog [hɒg] *(pt & pp* **-gg-)** *vt Fam* monopoliser

hoist [hɔɪst] *vt* hisser

hold [həʊld] **1** *n (grip)* prise *f*; *(of ship)* cale *f*; *(of plane)* soute *f*; **to get h. of** *(grab)* saisir; *(contact)* joindre; *(find)* trouver; **to be on h.** *(of project)* être en suspens; **to put sb on h.** *(on phone)* mettre qn en attente **2** *(pt & pp* **held)** *vt* tenir; *(heat, attention)* retenir; *(post)* occuper; *(record)* détenir; *(party, exhibition)* organiser; *(contain)* contenir; *(keep)* garder; **to h. sb**

prisoner retenir qn prisonnier; **to h. one's breath** retenir son souffle; **h. the line!** *(on phone)* ne quittez pas!; **to be held** *(of event)* avoir lieu • **holdall** *n Br* fourre-tout *m inv* • **holder** *n (container)* support *m* • **hold-up** *n (attack)* hold-up *m inv*; *Br (traffic jam)* ralentissement *m*; *(delay)* retard *m*

▶**hold back** *vt sep (restrain)* retenir; *(hide)* cacher (**from sb** à qn)

▶**hold down** *vt sep (person on ground)* maintenir au sol; **to h. down a job** *(keep)* garder un emploi; *(occupy)* avoir un emploi

▶**hold on** *vi (wait)* patienter; *(stand firm)* tenir bon; **h. on!** *(on phone)* ne quittez pas!; **h. on (tight)!** tenez bon!

▶**hold on to** *vt insep (cling to)* tenir bien; *(keep)* garder

▶**hold out** *vt sep (offer)* offrir; *(hand)* tendre

▶**hold up** *vt sep (raise)* lever; *(support)* soutenir; *(delay)* retarder; *(rob)* attaquer

hole [həʊl] *n* trou *m*

holiday ['hɒlɪdeɪ] **1** *n Br* **holiday(s)** *(from work, school)* vacances *fpl*; **a h.** *(day off)* un congé; **a (public** *or* **bank) h.,** *Am* **a legal h.** un jour férié; **to be/go on h.** être/partir en vacances **2** *adj (camp, clothes)* de vacances • **holidaymaker** *n Br* vacancier, -ère *mf*

Holland ['hɒlənd] *n* la Hollande

hollow ['hɒləʊ] **1** *adj* creux (*f* creuse) **2** *vt* **to h. sth out** évider qch

holy ['həʊlɪ] **(-ier, -iest)** *adj* saint; *(bread, water)* bénit

home [həʊm] **1** *n* maison *f*; *(country)* patrie *f*; **at h.** à la maison, chez soi; **to feel at h.**

se sentir chez soi; **make yourself at h.** faites comme chez vous **2** *adv* à la maison, chez soi; **to go** or **come (back) h.** rentrer chez soi **3** *adj (cooking)* familial; *(visit, match)* à domicile; **h. address** adresse *f* personnelle; *Br* **H. Office** ≃ ministère *m* de l'Intérieur; **h. owner** propriétaire *mf*; *Comptr* **h. page** page *f* d'accueil; *Br* **H. Secretary** ≃ ministre *m* de l'Intérieur; **h. town** ville *f* natale ● **homeless 1** *adj* sans abri **2** *npl* **the h.** les sans-abri *mpl* ● **homemade** *adj* (fait) maison *inv* ● **homesick** *adj* **to be h.** avoir le mal du pays ● **homework** *n Sch* devoirs *mpl*

homosexual [həʊmə'sekʃʊəl] *adj & n* homosexuel, -elle *(mf)*

honest ['ɒnɪst] *adj* honnête (**with** avec) ● **honestly** *adv* honnêtement ● **honesty** *n* honnêteté *f*

honey ['hʌnɪ] *n* miel *m* ● **honeymoon** *n* voyage *m* de noces

honk [hɒŋk] *vi (of driver)* klaxonner

honour ['ɒnə(r)] *(Am* **honor)** **1** *n* honneur *m*; **in h. of** en l'honneur de; *Br Univ* **honours degree** diplôme *m* universitaire **2** *vt* honorer (**with** de) ● **honourable** *(Am* **honorable)** *adj* honorable

hood [hʊd] *n (of coat)* capuche *f*; *(with eye-holes)* cagoule *f*; *Br (of car, pram)* capote *f*; *Am (car bonnet)* capot *m*

hoof [hu:f] *(pl* **hoofs** [hu:fs] *or* **hooves** [hu:vz]) *n* sabot *m*

hook [hʊk] **1** *n* crochet *m*; *(on clothes)* agrafe *f*; *(for fishing)* hameçon *m*; **off the h.** *(phone)* décroché **2** *vt* **to h. (on** or **up)** accrocher (**to** à) ● **hooked** *adj*

Fam **to be h. on sth** être accro à qch

hook(e)y ['hʊkɪ] *n Am Fam* **to play h.** sécher (les cours)

hooligan ['hu:lɪgən] *n* hooligan *m*

hoot [hu:t] *vi Br (of vehicle)* klaxonner; *(of owl)* hululer

hoover® ['hu:və(r)] *Br* **1** *n* aspirateur *m* **2** *vt (room)* passer l'aspirateur dans; *(carpet)* passer l'aspirateur sur; **to h. sth up** *(dust, crumbs)* enlever qch à l'aspirateur

hop [hɒp] *(pt & pp* **-pp-)** *vi (jump)* sautiller; *(on one leg)* sauter à cloche-pied

hope [həʊp] **1** *n* espoir *m* **2** *vt* **to h. to do sth** espérer faire qch; **to h. that...** espérer que... **3** *vi* espérer; **to h. for sth** espérer qch; **I h. so/not** j'espère que oui/non ● **hopeful** *adj (person)* optimiste; *(situation)* encourageant; **to be h. that...** avoir bon espoir que... ● **hopefully** *adv (with luck)* avec un peu de chance ● **hopeless** ['həʊplɪs] *adj* désespéré; *Fam (useless, bad)* nul *(f* nulle) ● **hopelessly** *adv (lost)* complètement; *(in love)* éperdument

horizon [hə'raɪzən] *n* horizon *m*; **on the h.** à l'horizon

horizontal [hɒrɪ'zɒntəl] *adj* horizontal

hormone ['hɔ:məʊn] *n* hormone *f*

horn [hɔ:n] *n (of animal)* corne *f*; *(on vehicle)* Klaxon® *m*; *(musical instrument)* cor *m*

hornet ['hɔ:nɪt] *n* frelon *m*

horoscope ['hɒrəskəʊp] *n* horoscope *m*

horrendous [hɒ'rendəs] *adj* horrible

horrible ['hɒrəbəl] *adj* horrible

horrid ['hɒrɪd] *adj (unpleasant)* affreux, -euse; *(unkind)* méchant

horrify ['hɒrɪfaɪ] *(pt & pp* **-ied)** *vt* horrifier ● **horrific** [hə'rɪfɪk] *adj* horrible

horror ['hɒrə(r)] *n* horreur *f*; **h. film** film *m* d'horreur; **h. story** histoire *f* épouvantable

horse [hɔːs] *n (animal)* cheval *m*; **to go h. riding** faire du cheval ● **horseback** *n* **on h.** à cheval; *Am* **to go h. riding** faire du cheval

hose [həʊz] **1** *n (pipe)* tuyau *m* **2** *vt* arroser (au jet d'eau); **to h. sth down** *(car)* laver qch au jet ● **hosepipe** *n Br* tuyau *m* d'arrosage

hospital ['hɒspɪtəl] *n* hôpital *m*; **in h.**, *Am* **in the h.** à l'hôpital; **h. bed** lit *m* d'hôpital

hospitality [hɒspɪ'tælɪtɪ] *n* hospitalité *f*

host [həʊst] **1** *n (of guests)* hôte *m*; *(on TV or radio show)* présentateur, -trice *mf* **2** *vt (programme)* présenter ● **hostess** *n (in house, nightclub)* hôtesse *f*; **(air) h.** hôtesse *f* (de l'air)

hostage ['hɒstɪdʒ] *n* otage *m*; **to take sb h.** prendre qn en otage

hostel ['hɒstəl] *n* foyer *m*; **(youth) h.** auberge *f* de jeunesse

hostile [*Br* 'hɒstaɪl, *Am* 'hɒstəl] *adj* hostile **(to** *or* **towards** à) ● **hostility** [hɒs'tɪlɪtɪ] *n* hostilité *f* **(to** *or* **towards** envers)

hot [hɒt] **(hotter, hottest)** *adj* chaud; *(spice)* fort; **to be** *or* **feel h.** avoir chaud; **it's h.** il fait chaud ● **hotdog** *n* hot dog *m* ● **hot-water bottle** *n* bouillotte *f*

hotel [həʊ'tel] *n* hôtel *m*; **h. room/bed** chambre *f*/lit *m* d'hôtel

hour ['aʊə(r)] *n* heure *f*; **half an h.** une demi-heure; **a quarter of an h.** un quart d'heure; **paid £10 an h.** payé 10 livres (de) l'heure; **10 miles an h.** 10 miles à l'heure; **h. hand** *(of watch, clock)* petite aiguille *f* ● **hourly 1** *adj (rate, pay)* horaire **2** *adv* toutes les heures

house 1 [haʊs] *(pl* **-ses** [-zɪz]**)** *n* maison *f*; *Pol* **the H. of Commons/Lords** la Chambre des communes/lords; **the Houses of Parliament** le Parlement; **the H. of Representatives** la Chambre des représentants; **at/to my h.** chez moi; **on the h.** *(free of charge)* aux frais de la maison; **h. prices** prix *mpl* de l'immobilier; **h. wine** vin *m* maison **2** [haʊz] *vt* loger; *(of building)* abriter ● **houseboat** *n* péniche *f* aménagée ● **household** *n* ménage *m*; **h. chores** tâches *fpl* ménagères ● **housing** ['haʊz-] *n* logement *m*; *(houses)* logements *mpl*; *Br* **h. estate** lotissement *m*; *(council-owned)* cité *f* ● **housekeeper** *n (employee)* gouvernante *f* ● **housetrained** *adj Br (dog)* propre ● **housewarming** *n & adj* **to have a h. (party)** pendre la crémaillère ● **housewife** *(pl* **-wives)** *n* ménagère *f* ● **housework** *n* ménage *m*

hovel ['hɒvəl] *n* taudis *m*

hover ['hɒvə(r)] *vi (of bird, aircraft)* planer; **to h. (around)** *(of person)* rôder ● **hovercraft** *n* aéroglisseur *m*

how [haʊ] *adv* comment; **h. kind!** comme c'est gentil!; **h. long/high is...?** quelle est la longueur/hauteur de...?; **h. much?, h. many?** combien?; **h. much time?** combien de temps?; **h. many apples?** combien de pommes?; **h. about some coffee?** (si on prenait) du café?; **h. do you do?** *(greeting)* enchanté; *Fam* **h.'s**

that?, **h. so?, h. come?** comment
ça? ● **however** [-ˈevə(r)] **1** *adv* h.
big he may be si grand soit-il; **h.
she may do it, h. she does it** de
quelque manière qu'elle le fasse;
h. did she find out? comment a-
t-elle bien pu l'apprendre? **2** *conj*
cependant

howl [haʊl] **1** *n* hurlement *m*; **h.
of laughter** éclat *m* de rire **2** *vi*
hurler; *(of wind)* mugir

hub [hʌb] *n* *Fig* centre *m*

huddle [ˈhʌdəl] *vi* **to h. (together)**
se blottir (les uns contre les autres)

huff [hʌf] *n* *Fam* **in a h.** *(offended)*
fâché

hug [hʌg] **1** *n* **to give sb a h.**
serrer qn (dans ses bras) **2** *(pt &
pp* **-gg-)** *vt (person)* serrer dans
ses bras

huge [hjuːdʒ] *adj* énorme

hum [hʌm] **1** *(pt & pp* **-mm-)** *vt
(tune)* fredonner **2** *vi (of person)*
fredonner; *(of engine)* ronronner

human [ˈhjuːmən] **1** *adj* humain;
h. being être *m* humain; **h. rights**
droits *mpl* de l'homme **2** *n* être *m*
humain ● **humane** [hjuːˈmeɪn]
adj (kind) humain ● **humanity**
[-ˈmænətɪ] *n (human beings,
kindness)* humanité *f*

humble [ˈhʌmbəl] *adj* humble

humid [ˈhjuːmɪd] *adj* humide ●
humidity *n* humidité *f*

humiliate [hjuːˈmɪlɪeɪt] *vt*
humilier ● **humiliation** [-ˈeɪʃən]
n humiliation *f*

humour [ˈhjuːmə(r)] *(Am* **humor)**
n humour *m* ● **humorous** *adj
(book, writer)* humoristique;
(person, situation) drôle

hunch [hʌntʃ] *vt* **to h. one's
shoulders** rentrer les épaules

hundred [ˈhʌndrəd] *adj & n*
cent *(m)*; **a h. pages** cent pages;
two h. pages deux cents pages;

hundreds of des centaines de ●
hundredth *adj & n* centième *(mf)*

hung [hʌŋ] *pt & pp of* **hang¹**

Hungary [ˈhʌŋgərɪ] *n* la Hongrie
● **Hungarian** [-ˈgeərɪən] **1** *adj*
hongrois **2** *n (person)* Hongrois, -e
mf; (language) hongrois *m*

hunger [ˈhʌŋgə(r)] *n* faim *f* ●
hungry (-ier, -iest) *adj* **to be h.**
avoir faim; **h. for sth** avide de
qch

hunt [hʌnt] **1** *n (search)* recherche
f **(for** de); *(for animals)* chasse *f*
2 *vt (animals)* chasser; *(pursue)*
poursuivre; **to h. down** *(animal,
fugitive)* traquer **3** *vi (kill animals)*
chasser; **to h. for sth** rechercher
qch ● **hunter** *n* chasseur *m* ●
hunting *n* chasse *f*

hurdle [ˈhɜːdəl] *n (fence in race)*
haie *f; Fig (problem)* obstacle *m*

hurl [hɜːl] *vt (throw)* jeter, lancer
(at à); **to h. insults** *or* **abuse at
sb** lancer des insultes à qn

hurray [hʊˈreɪ] *exclam* hourra!

hurricane [ˈhʌrɪkeɪn] *n* ouragan
m

hurry [ˈhʌrɪ] **1** *n* hâte *f;* **in a h.** à
la hâte; **to be in a h.** être pressé;
to be in a h. to do sth avoir hâte
de faire qch; **there's no h.** rien ne
presse **2** *(pt & pp* **-ied)** *vt* presser
3 *vi* se dépêcher, se presser **(to do**
de faire); **to h. up** se dépêcher; **to
h. out** sortir à la hâte

hurt [hɜːt] **1** *adj (wounded,
offended)* blessé **2** *(pt & pp*
hurt) *vt (physically)* faire du mal
à; *(causing a wound)* blesser;
(emotionally) faire de la peine à;
to h. sb's feelings blesser qn **3** *vi*
faire mal; **his arm hurts** son bras
lui fait mal

husband [ˈhʌzbənd] *n* mari *m*

hush [hʌʃ] *exclam* chut!

husky ['hʌskɪ] (**-ier, -iest**) *adj (voice)* rauque

hustle ['hʌsəl] *n* **h. and bustle** effervescence *f*

hut [hʌt] *n* cabane *f*; *(dwelling)* hutte *f*

hydrogen ['haɪdrədʒən] *n Chem* hydrogène *m*

hygiene ['haɪdʒiːn] *n* hygiène *f* • **hygienic** *adj* hygiénique

hymn [hɪm] *n* cantique *m*

hyper- ['haɪpə(r)] *pref* hyper- • **hypermarket** *n* hypermarché *m*

hyphen ['haɪfən] *n* trait *m* d'union

hypnotize ['hɪpnətaɪz] *vt* hypnotiser

hypocrite ['hɪpəkrɪt] *n* hypocrite *mf* • **hypocritical** [-'krɪtɪkəl] *adj* hypocrite

hypothesis [haɪ'pɒθɪsɪs] (*pl* **-theses** [-θɪsiːz]) *n* hypothèse *f*

hysterical [hɪs'terɪkəl] *adj (very upset)* qui fait une crise de nerfs; *Fam (funny)* tordant

I i

I¹, i [aɪ] *n (letter)* I, i *m inv*

I² [aɪ] *pron* je, j'; *(stressed)* moi

ice¹ [aɪs] *n* glace *f*; *(on road)* verglas *m*; **i. cream** glace *f*; **i. cube** glaçon *m*; **i. hockey** hockey *m* sur glace; **i. rink** patinoire *f* • **iceberg** *n* iceberg *m* • **iced** *adj (tea, coffee)* glacé • **ice-skating** *n* patinage *m* (sur glace) • **icicle** *n* glaçon *m (de gouttière etc)* • **icy** (**-ier, -iest**) *adj (road)* verglacé; *(water, hands)* glacé

ice² [aɪs] *vt Br (cake)* glacer • **icing** *n Br (on cake)* glaçage *m*

icon ['aɪkɒn] *n* icône *f*

ID [aɪ'diː] *n* pièce *f* d'identité

I'd [aɪd] = **I had, I would**

idea [aɪ'dɪə] *n* idée *f*

ideal [aɪ'dɪəl] *adj & n* idéal *(m)* • **ideally** *adv* idéalement; **i., we should stay** l'idéal, ce serait que nous restions

identical [aɪ'dentɪkəl] *adj* identique (**to** *or* **with** à)

identify [aɪ'dentɪfaɪ] *(pt & pp -ied) vt* identifier; **to i. (oneself) with** s'identifier avec • **identification** [-fɪ'keɪʃən] *n* identification *f*; **to have (some) i.** *(document)* avoir une pièce d'identité • **identity** (*pl* -**ies**) *n* identité *f*; **i. card** carte *f* d'identité

idiom ['ɪdɪəm] *n (phrase)* expression *f* idiomatique

idiot ['ɪdɪət] *n* idiot, -e *mf*

idle ['aɪdəl] *adj (unoccupied)* désœuvré; *(lazy)* oisif, -ive

idol ['aɪdəl] *n* idole *f*

idyllic [aɪ'dɪlɪk] *adj* idyllique

i.e. [aɪ'iː] *(abbr id est)* c'est-à-dire

if [ɪf] *conj* si; **if he comes** s'il vient; **if so** si c'est le cas; **if not** sinon; **as if** comme si; **if necessary** s'il le faut

ignore [ɪg'nɔː(r)] *vt* ignorer • **ignorant** ['ɪgnərənt] *adj* ignorant (**of** de)

I'll [aɪl] = **I will, I shall**

ill [ɪl] **1** *adj (sick)* malade; *(bad)* mauvais **2** *adv* mal • **ill-advised** *adj (person)* malavisé • **ill-informed** *adj* mal renseigné • **ill-mannered** *adj* mal élevé

illegal [ɪ'liːgəl] *adj* illégal

illegible [ɪ'ledʒəbəl] *adj* illisible

illicit [ɪ'lɪsɪt] *adj* illicite

illiterate [ɪ'lɪtərət] *adj & n* analphabète *(mf)*

illness ['ɪlnɪs] *n* maladie *f*

illogical [ɪ'lɒdʒɪkəl] *adj* illogique

illuminate [ɪ'luːmɪneɪt] *vt (monument)* illuminer; *(street, question)* éclairer

illusion [ɪ'luːʒən] *n* illusion *f* (**about** sur)

illustrate ['ɪləstreɪt] *vt (with pictures, examples)* illustrer (**with** de) • **illustration** *n* illustration *f*

image ['ɪmɪdʒ] *n* image *f*; **he's the (spitting) i. of his brother** c'est tout le portrait de son frère

imagine [ɪ'mædʒɪn] *vt* imaginer (**that** que) • **imaginary** *adj* imaginaire • **imagination** [-neɪʃən] *n* imagination *f* •

imaginative *adj (plan, novel)* original; *(person)* imaginatif, -ive

imitate ['ɪmɪteɪt] *vt* imiter ● **imitation** *n* imitation *f*; **i. diamonds** faux diamants *mpl*

immaculate [ɪ'mækjʊlət] *adj* impeccable

immature [ɪmə'tʃʊə(r)] *adj (person)* immature

immediate [ɪ'miːdɪət] *adj* immédiat ● **immediately** *adv (at once)* tout de suite, immédiatement; **it's i. above/below** c'est juste au-dessus/en dessous

immense [ɪ'mens] *adj* immense ● **immensely** *adv (rich)* immensément; **to enjoy oneself i.** s'amuser énormément

immerse [ɪ'mɜːs] *vt (in liquid)* plonger; *Fig* **to i. oneself in sth** se plonger dans qch

immigrant ['ɪmɪɡrənt] *adj & n* immigré, -e *(mf)* ● **immigration** *n* immigration *f*

imminent ['ɪmɪnənt] *adj* imminent

immoral [ɪ'mɒrəl] *adj* immoral

immortal [ɪ'mɔːtəl] *adj* immortel, -elle

immune [ɪ'mjuːn] *adj Med (to disease)* immunisé (**to** contre); *Fig* **i. to criticism** imperméable à la critique ● **immunize** ['ɪmjʊnaɪz] *vt* immuniser (**against** contre)

impact ['ɪmpækt] *n* impact *m*; **to have an i. on sb/sth** avoir un impact sur qn/qch

impartial [ɪm'pɑːʃəl] *adj* impartial

impatient [ɪm'peɪʃənt] *adj* impatient (**to do** de faire); **to get i. (with sb)** s'impatienter (contre qn)

impending [ɪm'pendɪŋ] *adj* imminent

imperative [ɪm'perətɪv] *n Gram* impératif *m*

imperfect [ɪm'pɜːfɪkt] *adj & n* **i. (tense)** *(in grammar)* imparfait *(m)* ● **imperfection** [-pə'fekʃən] *n* imperfection *f*

imperial [ɪm'pɪərɪəl] *adj* impérial; *Br* **i. measure** = système de mesure anglo-saxon utilisant les miles, les pints etc

impersonal [ɪm'pɜːsənəl] *adj* impersonnel, -elle

impersonate [ɪm'pɜːsəneɪt] *vt (pretend to be)* se faire passer pour; *(imitate)* imiter

impertinent [ɪm'pɜːtɪnənt] *adj* impertinent (**to** envers)

impetus ['ɪmpɪtəs] *n* impulsion *f*

impinge [ɪm'pɪndʒ] *vi* **to i. on sth** *(affect)* affecter qch; *(encroach on)* empiéter sur qch

implant *Med* **1** ['ɪmplɑːnt] *n* implant *m* **2** [ɪm'plɑːnt] *vt* implanter (**in** dans)

implement 1 ['ɪmplɪmənt] *n (tool)* instrument *m*; *(utensil)* ustensile *m* **2** ['ɪmplɪment] *vt (carry out)* mettre en œuvre

imply [ɪm'plaɪ] *(pt & pp -ied) vt (insinuate)* insinuer (**that** que); *(presuppose)* supposer (**that** que); *(involve)* impliquer (**that** que) ● **implication** [-plɪ'keɪʃən] *n (consequence)* conséquence *f*; *(innuendo)* insinuation *f*

impolite [ɪmpə'laɪt] *adj* impoli

import [ɪm'pɔːt] *vt* importer (**from** de)

importance [ɪm'pɔːtəns] *n* importance *f* ● **important** *adj* important (**to/for** pour); **it's i. that...** il est important que... (+ *subjunctive*)

impose [ɪm'pəʊz] **1** *vt (conditions, silence)* imposer (**on** à) **2** *vi (take advantage)* s'imposer; **to i. on sb**

abuser de la gentillesse de qn •
imposing *adj* imposant
impossible [ɪm'pɒsəbəl] *adj*
impossible (**to do** à faire); **it is
i. (for us) to do it** il (nous) est
impossible de le faire
impostor [ɪm'pɒstə(r)] *n* imposteur *m*
impotent ['ɪmpətənt] *adj* impuissant
impractical [ɪm'præktɪkəl] *adj*
peu réaliste
impregnate ['ɪmpregneɪt] *vt*
(soak) imprégner (**with** de)
impress [ɪm'pres] *vt (person)*
impressionner; **to be impressed
with** *or* **by sb/sth** être
impressionné par qn/qch •
impression [-ʃən] *n* impression
f; **to be under** *or* **have the i.
that...** avoir l'impression que...;
**to make a good/bad i. on
sb** faire une bonne/mauvaise
impression à qn • **impressive** *adj*
impressionnant

imprint ['ɪmprɪnt] *n* empreinte *f*
imprison [ɪm'prɪzən] *vt* emprisonner • **imprisonment** *n* emprisonnement *m*; **life i.** la prison à vie
improbable [ɪm'prɒbəbəl] *adj*
(unlikely) improbable; *(unbelievable)* invraisemblable
impromptu [ɪm'prɒmptjuː] *adj*
(speech, party) improvisé
improve [ɪm'pruːv] **1** *vt*
améliorer; *(technique, invention)*
perfectionner; **to i. one's English**
se perfectionner en anglais **2** *vi*
s'améliorer; *(of business)* reprendre
• **improvement** *n* amélioration *f*
(**in** de); *(progress)* progrès *mpl*; **to
be an i. on sth** *(be better than)*
être meilleur que qch
improvise ['ɪmprəvaɪz] *vti*
improviser
impulse ['ɪmpʌls] *n* impulsion *f* •

impulsive *adj (person)* impulsif,
-ive
impurity [ɪm'pjʊərətɪ] *(pl* -ies) *n*
impureté *f*

in [ɪn] **1** *prep* **(a)** dans; **in the
box/the school** dans la boîte/
l'école; **in an hour('s time)** dans
une heure; **in so far as** dans la
mesure où **(b)** à; **in school** à
l'école; **in Paris** à Paris; **in the
USA** aux USA; **in pencil** au
crayon; **in spring** au printemps;
the woman in the red dress la
femme à la robe rouge **(c)** en; **in
summer/French** en été/français;
in Spain en Espagne; **in May**
en mai; **in 2001** en 2001; **in an
hour** *(during an hour)* en une
heure; **in doing sth** en faisant
qch; **dressed in black** habillé
en noir **(d)** de; **in a soft voice**
d'une voix douce; **the best in the
class** le meilleur/la meilleure de la
classe; **an increase in salary** une
augmentation de salaire; **at six in
the evening** à six heures du soir
(e) chez; **in children/animals**
chez les enfants/les animaux; **in
Shakespeare** chez Shakespeare
(f) **in the morning** le matin; **he
hasn't done it in months** ça
fait des mois qu'il ne l'a pas fait;
one in ten un sur dix; **in tens** dix
par dix; **in here** ici; **in there** là-
dedans **2** *adv* **to be in** *(home)* être
là; *(in fashion)* être en vogue; **day
in, day out** jour après jour; **in on
a secret** au courant d'un secret;
we're in for some rain/trouble
on va avoir de la pluie/des ennuis
3 *npl* **the ins and outs of** les
moindres détails de

in- [ɪn] *pref* in-
inability [ɪnə'bɪlɪtɪ] *(pl* -ies) *n*
incapacité *f* (**to do** de faire)

inaccessible [ɪnək'sesəbəl] *adj* inaccessible

inaccurate [ɪn'ækjʊrət] *adj* inexact

inadequate [ɪn'ædɪkwət] *adj* (*quantity*) insuffisant; (*person*) pas à la hauteur; (*work*) médiocre

inadvertently [ɪnəd'vɜːtəntlɪ] *adv* par inadvertance

inadvisable [ɪnəd'vaɪzəbəl] *adj* **it is i. to go out alone** il est déconseillé de sortir seul

inappropriate [ɪnə'prəʊprɪət] *adj* (*unsuitable*) (*place, clothes*) peu approprié; (*remark, moment*) inopportun

inarticulate [ɪnɑː'tɪkjʊlət] *adj* (*person*) incapable de s'exprimer

inattentive [ɪnə'tentɪv] *adj* inattentif, -ive (**to** à)

inaudible [ɪn'ɔːdɪbəl] *adj* inaudible

incapable [ɪn'keɪpəbəl] *adj* incapable (**of doing** de faire)

incense ['ɪnsens] *n* encens *m*

incentive [ɪn'sentɪv] *n* motivation *f*; (*payment*) prime *f*; **to give sb an i. to work** encourager qn à travailler

incessant [ɪn'sesənt] *adj* incessant

inch [ɪntʃ] *n* pouce *m* (*2,54 cm*)

incident ['ɪnsɪdənt] *n* incident *m* • **incidentally** [ɪnsɪ'dentəlɪ]*adv* (*by the way*) au fait

incite [ɪn'saɪt] *vt* inciter (**to do** à faire)

incline [ɪn'klaɪn] *vt* (*bend, tilt*) incliner; **to be inclined to do sth** (*feel desire to*) avoir bien envie de faire qch; (*tend to*) avoir tendance à faire qch • **inclination** [-klɪ'neɪʃən] *n* (*liking*) inclination *f*; (*desire*) envie *f* (**to do** de faire)

include [ɪn'kluːd] *vt* (*contain*) comprendre, inclure; (*in letter*)

joindre; **to be included** être compris; (*on list*) être inclus • **including** *prep* y compris; **not i.** sans compter; **i. service** service compris • **inclusive** *adj* inclus; **from the fourth to the tenth of May i.** du quatre au dix mai inclus; **to be i. of** comprendre; **i. of tax** toutes taxes comprises

incoherent [ɪnkəʊ'hɪərənt] *adj* incohérent

income ['ɪŋkʌm] *n* revenu *m* (**from** de); **i. tax** impôt *m* sur le revenu

incompatible [ɪnkəm'pætəbəl] *adj* incompatible (**with** avec)

incompetent [ɪn'kɒmpɪtənt] *adj* incompétent

incomplete [ɪnkəm'pliːt] *adj* incomplet, -ète

incomprehensible [ɪnkɒmprɪ-'hensəbəl] *adj* incompréhensible

inconsiderate [ɪnkən'sɪdərət] *adj* (*action, remark*) inconsidéré; (*person*) sans égards pour les autres

inconsistent [ɪnkən'sɪstənt] *adj* (*person*) incohérent; (*uneven*) irrégulier, -ère

inconspicuous [ɪnkən'spɪkjʊəs] *adj* qui passe inaperçu

inconvenient [ɪnkən'viːnɪənt] *adj* (*moment*) mauvais; (*arrangement*) peu commode; **it's i. (for me) to...** ça me dérange de... • **inconvenience** *n* (*bother*) dérangement *m*; (*disadvantage*) inconvénient *m*

incorporate [ɪn'kɔːpəreɪt] *vt* (*contain*) contenir; (*introduce*) incorporer (**into** dans)

incorrect [ɪnkə'rekt] *adj* incorrect

increase 1 ['ɪnkriːs] *n* augmentation *f* (**in** or **of** de); **on the i.** en hausse **2** [ɪn'kriːs] *vti* augmenter; **to i. in price** augmenter • **in-**

creasing *adj* croissant ● **increasingly** *adv* de plus en plus

incredible [ɪn'kredəbəl] *adj* incroyable

incubator ['ɪŋkjʊbeɪtə(r)] *n (for baby)* couveuse *f*

incur [ɪn'kɜː(r)] *(pt & pp -rr-) vt (expenses)* encourir; *(debt)* contracter; *(criticism, anger)* s'attirer

incurable [ɪn'kjʊərəbəl] *adj* incurable

indebted [ɪn'detɪd] *adj* **i. to sb for sth/for doing sth** redevable à qn de qch/d'avoir fait qch

indecent [ɪn'diːsənt] *adj (obscene)* indécent

indecisive [ɪndɪ'saɪsɪv] *adj (person)* indécis

indeed [ɪn'diːd] *adv* en effet; **very good i.** vraiment très bon; **thank you very much i.!** merci infiniment!

indefinite [ɪn'defɪnət] *adj (duration, number)* indéterminé; *(plan)* mal défini ● **indefinitely** *adv* indéfiniment

independence [ɪndɪ'pendəns] *n* indépendance *f* ● **independent** *adj* indépendant **(of** de); *(opinions, reports)* de sources différentes ● **independently** *adv* de façon indépendante; **i. of** indépendamment de

index ['ɪndeks] *n (in book)* index *m*; *(number, sign)* indice *m*; **i. finger** index *m*

India ['ɪndɪə] *n* l'Inde *f* ● **Indian 1** *adj* indien, -enne **2** *n* Indien, -enne *mf*

indicate ['ɪndɪkeɪt] *vt* indiquer **(that** que); **I was indicating right** *(in vehicle)* j'avais mis mon clignotant à droite ● **indication** *n (sign)* signe *m*; *(information)* indication *f* ● **indicator** *n (sign)*

indication *f* **(of** de); *Br (in vehicle)* clignotant *m*

indifferent [ɪn'dɪfərənt] *adj* indifférent **(to** à); *(mediocre)* médiocre

indigestion [ɪndɪ'dʒestʃən] *n* troubles *mpl* digestifs; **(an attack of) i.** une indigestion

indignant [ɪn'dɪgnənt] *adj* indigné **(at** *or* **about** de)

indirect [ɪndaɪ'rekt] *adj* indirect

indiscreet [ɪndɪ'skriːt] *adj* indiscret, -ète

indiscriminately [ɪndɪ'skrɪmɪnətlɪ] *adv (at random)* au hasard; *(without discrimination)* sans discernement

indispensable [ɪndɪ'spensəbəl] *adj* indispensable **(to** à)

indistinct [ɪndɪ'stɪŋkt] *adj* indistinct

individual [ɪndɪ'vɪdʒʊəl] **1** *adj (separate, personal)* individuel, -elle; *(specific)* particulier, -ère **2** *n (person)* individu *m* ● **individually** *adv (separately)* individuellement

indoor ['ɪndɔː(r)] *adj (games, shoes)* d'intérieur; *(swimming pool)* couvert ● **indoors** *adv* à l'intérieur; **to go/come i.** rentrer

induce [ɪn'djuːs] *vt (persuade)* persuader **(to do** de faire); *(cause)* provoquer

indulge [ɪn'dʌldʒ] *vi* **to i. in sth** *(ice cream, cigar)* s'offrir qch; *(hobby, vice)* s'adonner à qch ● **indulgent** *adj* indulgent **(to** envers)

industry ['ɪndəstrɪ] *(pl* **-ies)** *n (economic sector)* industrie *f*; *(hard work)* application *f* ● **industrial** [ɪn'dʌstrɪəl] *adj* industriel, -elle; *Br* **to take i. action** se mettre en grève; *Br* **i. estate,** *Am* **i. park** zone *f* industrielle

inedible [ɪn'edəbəl] *adj* immangeable

ineffective [ɪnɪ'fektɪv] *adj (measure)* inefficace; *(person)* incapable

inefficient [ɪnɪ'fɪʃənt] *adj (person, measure)* inefficace; *(machine)* peu performant

ineligible [ɪn'elɪdʒəbəl] *adj (candidate)* inéligible; **to be i. for sth** *(scholarship)* ne pas avoir droit à qch

inept [ɪ'nept] *adj (incompetent)* incompétent; *(foolish)* inepte

inequality [ɪnɪ'kwɒlətɪ] *(pl -ies) n* inégalité *f*

inevitable [ɪn'evɪtəbəl] *adj* inévitable

inexpensive [ɪnɪk'spensɪv] *adj* bon marché *inv*

inexperienced [ɪnɪks'pɪərɪənst] *adj* inexpérimenté

inexplicable [ɪnɪk'splɪkəbəl] *adj* inexplicable

infallible [ɪn'fæləbəl] *adj* infaillible

infamous ['ɪnfəməs] *adj (well-known)* tristement célèbre; *(crime)* infâme

infant ['ɪnfənt] *n* bébé *m*; *Br* **i. school** = école primaire pour enfants de cinq à sept ans

infatuated [ɪn'fætʃʊeɪtɪd] *adj* entiché (**with** de)

infect [ɪn'fekt] *vt (wound, person)* infecter; *(water, food)* contaminer; **to get** *or* **become infected** s'infecter • **infection** *n* infection *f* • **infectious** [-ʃəs] *adj (disease)* infectieux, -euse

inferior [ɪn'fɪərɪə(r)] *adj* inférieur (**to** à); *(goods, work)* de qualité inférieure

infertile [*Br* ɪn'fɜːtaɪl, *Am* ɪn'fɜːrtəl] *adj (person, land)* stérile

infest [ɪn'fest] *vt* infester (**with** de)

infiltrate ['ɪnfɪltreɪt] *vt* infiltrer

infinite ['ɪnfɪnɪt] *adj* infini • **infinity** ['ɪnfɪnɪtɪ] *n Math* infini *m*

infinitive [ɪn'fɪnɪtɪv] *n Gram* infinitif *m*

infirmary [ɪn'fɜːmərɪ] *(pl -ies) n (hospital)* hôpital *m*

inflamed [ɪn'fleɪmd] *adj (throat, wound)* enflammé; **to become i.** s'enflammer

inflammable [ɪn'flæməbəl] *adj* inflammable

inflate [ɪn'fleɪt] *vt (balloon, prices)* gonfler • **inflatable** *adj* gonflable • **inflation** *n Econ* inflation *f*

inflict [ɪn'flɪkt] *vt (punishment, defeat)* infliger (**on** à); *(wound, damage)* occasionner (**on** à)

influence ['ɪnflʊəns] **1** *n* influence *f* (**on** sur) **2** *vt* influencer • **influential** [-'enʃəl] *adj* influent

info ['ɪnfəʊ] *n Fam* renseignements *mpl* (**on** sur)

inform [ɪn'fɔːm] *vt* informer (**of** *or* **about** de; **that** que) • **informed** *adj* **to keep sb i. of sth** tenir qn au courant de qch

informal [ɪn'fɔːməl] *adj (unaffected)* simple; *(casual)* décontracté; *(tone, language)* familier, -ère; *(unofficial)* officieux, -euse • **informally** *adv (unaffectedly)* avec simplicité; *(casually)* avec décontraction; *(meet, discuss)* officieusement

information [ɪnfə'meɪʃən] *n (facts, news)* renseignements *mpl* (**about** *or* **on** sur); **a piece of i.** un renseignement, une information; **to get some i.** se renseigner • **informative** [ɪn'fɔːmətɪv] *adj* instructif, -ive

infrequent [ɪn'friːkwənt] *adj* peu fréquent

infringe [ɪnˈfrɪndʒ] *vt insep* **to i.**
upon sth empiéter sur qch
infuriating [ɪnˈfjuːrɪeɪtɪŋ] *adj*
exaspérant
ingenious [ɪnˈdʒiːnɪəs] *adj*
ingénieux, -euse
ingredient [ɪnˈgriːdɪənt] *n*
ingrédient *m*
inhabit [ɪnˈhæbɪt] *vt* habiter ●
inhabitant *n* habitant, -e *mf*
inhale [ɪnˈheɪl] *vt (gas, fumes)*
inhaler
inherit [ɪnˈherɪt] *vt* hériter **(from**
de) ● **inheritance** *n (legacy)*
héritage *m*
inhibition [ɪnhɪˈbɪʃən] *n* inhibition *f*
inhospitable [ɪnhɒˈspɪtəbəl] *adj*
inhospitalier, -ère
inhuman [ɪnˈhjuːmən] *adj*
inhumain ● **inhumane** [-ˈmeɪn]
adj inhumain
initial [ɪˈnɪʃəl] **1** *adj* initial **2**
npl **initials** *(letters)* initiales *fpl*;
(signature) paraphe *m* ● **initially**
adv au début, initialement
initiative [ɪˈnɪʃətɪv] *n* initiative *f*
inject [ɪnˈdʒekt] *vt* injecter **(into**
dans); **to i. sth into sb, to i. sb**
with sth faire une piqûre de qch
à qn ● **injection** *n* injection *f*,
piqûre *f*; **to give sb an i.** faire une
piqûre à qn
injure [ˈɪndʒə(r)] *vt (physically)*
blesser; *(reputation)* nuire à; **to i.**
one's foot se blesser au pied ●
injured 1 *adj* blessé **2** *npl* **the i.**
les blessés *mpl* ● **injury** (*pl* **-ies**) *n*
(physical) blessure *f*
injustice [ɪnˈdʒʌstɪs] *n* injustice *f*
ink [ɪŋk] *n* encre *f*
inland 1 [ˈɪnlənd, ˈɪnlænd] *adj*
intérieur; *Br* **the I. Revenue** ≃
le fisc **2** [ɪnˈlænd] *adv (travel)* vers
l'intérieur
in-laws [ˈɪnlɔːz] *npl* belle-famille *f*

inmate [ˈɪnmeɪt] *n (of prison)*
détenu, -e *mf*; *(of asylum)* interné,
-e *mf*
inn [ɪn] *n* auberge *f*
innate [ɪˈneɪt] *adj* inné
inner [ˈɪnə(r)] *adj* intérieur;
(feelings) intime; **i. circle** *(of*
society) initiés *mpl*; **i. city** quartiers
mpl déshérités du centre-ville
innocent [ˈɪnəsənt] *adj* innocent
innovation [ɪnəˈveɪʃən] *n*
innovation *f*
inoffensive [ɪnəˈfensɪv] *adj*
inoffensif, -ive
input [ˈɪnpʊt] *n (contribution)*
contribution *f*
inquest [ˈɪnkwest] *n (legal*
investigation) enquête *f*
inquire [ɪnˈkwaɪə(r)] **1** *vt*
demander; **to i. how to get**
to... demander le chemin de...
2 *vi* se renseigner **(about** sur);
to i. after sb demander des
nouvelles de qn ● **inquiry** (*pl*
-ies) *n (request for information)*
demande *f* de renseignements;
(official investigation) enquête *f*;
to make inquiries demander
des renseignements; *(of police)*
enquêter
inquisitive [ɪnˈkwɪzɪtɪv] *adj*
curieux, -euse
insane [ɪnˈseɪn] *adj* dément, fou *(f*
folle); **to go i.** perdre la raison
inscription [ɪnˈskrɪpʃən] *n*
inscription *f*; *(in book)* dédicace *f*
insect [ˈɪnsekt] *n* insecte *m*; **i.**
repellent anti-moustiques *m inv*
insecure [ɪnsɪˈkjʊə(r)] *adj (unsafe)*
peu sûr; *(job, future)* précaire;
(person) angoissé
insensitive [ɪnˈsensɪtɪv] *adj*
(person) insensible **(to** à); *(remark)*
indélicat
inseparable [ɪnˈsepərəbəl] *adj*
inséparable **(from** de)

insert [ɪn'sɜːt] *vt* insérer (**in** *or* **into** dans)

inside 1 ['ɪnsaɪd] *adj* intérieur; *(information)* obtenu à la source; *Aut* **the i. lane** *Br* la voie de gauche, *Am* la voie de droite **2** ['ɪn'saɪd] *n* intérieur *m*; **on the i.** à l'intérieur (**of** de); **i. out** *(clothes)* à l'envers; *(know, study)* à fond **3** [ɪn'saɪd] *adv* à l'intérieur **4** [ɪn'saɪd] *prep* à l'intérieur de, dans; *(time)* en moins de ● **insider** [ɪn'saɪdə(r)] *n* initié, -e *mf*

insight ['ɪnsaɪt] *n* perspicacité *f*; *(into question)* aperçu *m*

insignificant [ɪnsɪg'nɪfɪkənt] *adj* insignifiant

insincere [ɪnsɪn'sɪə(r)] *adj* peu sincère

insinuate [ɪn'sɪnjʊeɪt] *vt (suggest)* insinuer (**that** que)

insist [ɪn'sɪst] **1** *vt (maintain)* soutenir (**that** que); **I i. that you come** *or* **on your coming** *(I demand it)* j'insiste pour que tu viennes **2** *vi* insister; **to i. on sth** *(demand)* exiger qch; *(assert)* affirmer qch; **to i. on doing sth** tenir à faire qch ● **insistence** *n* insistance *f* ● **insistent** *adj (person)* pressant; **to be i. (that)** insister (pour que + *subjunctive*)

insolent ['ɪnsələnt] *adj* insolent

insomnia [ɪn'sɒmnɪə] *n* insomnie *f*

inspect [ɪn'spekt] *vt* inspecter; *(tickets)* contrôler; *(troops)* passer en revue ● **inspector** *n* inspecteur, -trice *mf*; *(on train)* contrôleur, -euse *mf*

inspire [ɪn'spaɪə(r)] *vt* inspirer; **to i. sb to do sth** pousser qn à faire qch ● **inspiration** [-spə'reɪʃən] *n* inspiration *f*; *(person)* source *f* d'inspiration

install [ɪn'stɔːl] *(Am* **instal)** *vt* installer ● **instalment** *(Am* **installment)** *n (part payment)* versement *m*; *(of serial, story)* épisode *m*; **to pay by instalments** payer par versements échelonnés; *Am* **to buy on the i. plan** acheter à crédit

instance ['ɪnstəns] *n (example)* exemple *m*; *(case)* cas *m*; **for i.** par exemple; **in this i.** dans le cas présent

instant ['ɪnstənt] **1** *adj* immédiat; **i. coffee** café *m* instantané **2** *n (moment)* instant *m*; **this (very) i.** *(at once)* à l'instant; **the i. that I saw her** dès que je l'ai vue ● **instantly** *adv* immédiatement

instead [ɪn'sted] *adv (in place of sth)* à la place; *(in place of sb)* à ma/ta/*etc* place; **i. of sth** au lieu de qch; **i. of doing sth** au lieu de faire qch; **i. of him/her** à sa place

instinct ['ɪnstɪŋkt] *n* instinct *m*; **by i.** d'instinct ● **instinctive** [ɪn'stɪŋktɪv] *adj* instinctif, -ive

institute ['ɪnstɪtjuːt] *n* institut *m* ● **institution** [-'tjuːʃən] *n (organization, custom)* institution *f*; *(public, financial, religious, psychiatric)* établissement *m*

instruct [ɪn'strʌkt] *vt (teach)* enseigner (**sb in sth** qch à qn); **to i. sb about sth** *(inform)* instruire qn de qch; **to i. sb to do** *(order)* charger qn de faire ● **instruction** [-ʃən] *n (teaching, order)* instruction *f*; **instructions (for use)** mode *m* d'emploi ● **instructor** *n (for judo, dance)* professeur *m*; *(for skiing, swimming)* moniteur, -trice *mf*; **driving i.** moniteur, -trice *mf* d'auto-école

instrument ['ɪnstrəmənt] *n* instrument *m* ● **instrumental** [-'mentəl] *adj (music)* instrumental;

to be i. in sth/in doing sth
contribuer à qch/à faire qch
insufficient [ɪnsə'fɪʃənt] *adj*
insuffisant • **insufficiently** *adv*
insuffisamment
insulate ['ɪnsjʊleɪt] *vt (against cold)* & *El* isoler; *(against sound)*
insonoriser • **insulation** [-'leɪʃən]
n isolation *f*; *(against sound)* inso-
norisation *f*; *(material)* isolant *m*
insulin ['ɪnsjʊlɪn] *n* insuline *f*
insult 1 ['ɪnsʌlt] *n* insulte *f* (**to** à) **2**
[ɪn'sʌlt] *vt* insulter
insure [ɪn'ʃʊə(r)] *vt* (**a**) *(house, car, goods)* assurer (**against** contre)
(**b**) *Am* = **ensure** • **insurance**
n assurance *f*; **i. policy** police *f*
d'assurance
intact [ɪn'tækt] *adj* intact
integrate ['ɪntɪgreɪt] **1** *vt* intégrer
(**into** dans) **2** *vi* s'intégrer (**into**
dans) • **integration** [-'greɪʃən]
n intégration *f*; **(racial) i.**
déségrégation *f* raciale
intellectual [ɪntɪ'lektʃuːəl] *adj* &
n intellectuel, -elle *(mf)*
intelligence [ɪn'telɪdʒəns] *n*
intelligence *f* • **intelligent** *adj*
intelligent
intelligible [ɪn'telɪdʒəbəl] *adj*
intelligible
intend [ɪn'tend] *vt (gift, remark)*
destiner (**for** à); **to i. to do sth**
avoir l'intention de faire qch
intense [ɪn'tens] *adj* intense;
(interest) vif *(f* vive); *(person)*
passionné • **intensely** *adv*
(look at) intensément; *Fig (very)*
extrêmement • **intensify** *(pt & pp
-ied)* **1** *vt* intensifier **2** *vi* s'intensifier
• **intensive** *adj* intensif, -ive; **in i.
care** en réanimation
intent [ɪn'tent] *adj (look)* intense;
to be i. on doing être résolu à
faire
intention [ɪn'tenʃən] *n* intention *f*

(of doing de faire) • **intentional**
adj intentionnel, -elle; **it wasn't i.**
ce n'était pas fait exprès • **intentionally** *adv* intentionnellement,
exprès
inter- ['ɪntə(r)] *pref* inter-
interactive [ɪntə'ræktɪv] *adj*
interactif, -ive
intercept [ɪntə'sept] *vt*
intercepter
interchange ['ɪntətʃeɪndʒ] *n Br
(on road)* échangeur *m*
interchangeable [ɪntə'tʃeɪndʒə-
bəl] *adj* interchangeable
inter-city [ɪntə'sɪtɪ] *adj Br* **i. train**
train *m* de grandes lignes
intercom ['ɪntəkɒm] *n*
Interphone® *m*
intercourse ['ɪntəkɔːs] *n (sexual)*
rapports *mpl* sexuels
interest ['ɪntərest, 'ɪntrɪst] **1**
n intérêt *m*; *(hobby)* centre *m*
d'intérêt; *(money)* intérêts *mpl*; **to
take an i. in sb/sth** s'intéresser
à qn/qch; **to lose i. in sb/sth** se
désintéresser de qn/qch; **to be of
i. to sb** intéresser qn **2** *vt* intéresser
• **interested** *adj* intéressé; **to be
i. in sb/sth** s'intéresser à qn/qch;
are you i.? ça vous intéresse? •
interesting *adj* intéressant
interfere [ɪntə'fɪə(r)] *vi (meddle)*
se mêler (**in** de); **to i. with
sth** *(hinder)* gêner qch; *(touch)*
toucher à qch • **interference** *n*
ingérence *f*
interim ['ɪntərɪm] *n* **in the i.**
entre-temps
interior [ɪn'tɪərɪə(r)] *adj* & *n*
intérieur *(m)*
interlude ['ɪntəluːd] *n (on TV)*
interlude *m*; *(in theatre)* intermède
m; *(period of time)* intervalle *m*
intermediary [ɪntə'miːdɪərɪ] *(pl
-ies) n* intermédiaire *mf*
intermediate [ɪntə'miːdɪət] *adj*

intermédiaire; *(course, student)* de
niveau moyen

intermission [ɪntə'mɪʃən] *n*
entracte *m*

intermittent [ɪntə'mɪtənt] *adj*
intermittent

intern ['ɪntɜːn] *n Am (in office)*
stagiaire *mf*; *Med* interne *mf*

internal [ɪn'tɜːnəl] *adj* interne;
(flight, policy) intérieur; *Am* **the
I. Revenue Service** ≃ le fisc ●
internally *adv* intérieurement

international [ɪntə'næʃənəl] *adj*
international

Internet ['ɪntənet] *n Comptr* **the
I.** (l')Internet *m*; **I. access** accès *m*
(à l')Internet

interpret [ɪn'tɜːprɪt] **1** *vt*
interpréter **2** *vi* faire l'interprète
● **interpretation** [-'teɪʃən] *n*
interprétation *f* ● **interpreter** *n*
interprète *mf*

interrogate [ɪn'terəgeɪt] *vt* interroger ● **interrogation** [-'geɪʃən]
n interrogation *f*; *(by police)* interrogatoire *m*

interrupt [ɪntə'rʌpt] **1** *vt*
interrompre **2** *vi* **I'm sorry to i.** je
suis désolé de vous interrompre ●
interruption *n* interruption *f*

intersect [ɪntə'sekt] **1** *vt* couper
2 *vi* se couper ● **intersection** *n*
intersection *f*; *(of roads)* croisement
m

interval ['ɪntəvəl] *n* intervalle *m*;
Br (in theatre, cinema) entracte *m*;
at intervals *(in time)* de temps à
autre; *(in space)* par intervalles; **at
five-minute intervals** toutes les
cinq minutes

intervene [ɪntə'viːn] *vi (of
person)* intervenir (**in** dans); *(of
event)* survenir ● **intervention**
[-'venʃən] *n* intervention *f*

interview ['ɪntəvjuː] **1** *n*
entretien *m* (**with** avec); *TV &*

Journ interview *f* **2** *vt (for job)*
faire passer un entretien à; *TV &
Journ* interviewer ● **interviewer**
n TV intervieweur, -euse *mf*;
(for research, survey) enquêteur,
-euse *mf*

intestine [ɪn'testɪn] *n* intestin *m*

intimate ['ɪntɪmət] *adj* intime;
(friendship) profond; *(knowledge)*
approfondi ● **intimately** *adv*
intimement

intimidate [ɪn'tɪmɪdeɪt] *vt*
intimider

into ['ɪntuː, *unstressed* 'ɪntə] *prep*
(a) dans; **to put sth i. sth** mettre
qch dans qch; **to go i. a room**
entrer dans une pièce **(b)** en; **to
translate i. French** traduire en
français; **to change sb i. sth**
changer qn en qch; **to break sth
i. pieces** briser qch en morceaux;
to go i. town aller en ville **(c)** *Fam*
to be i. jazz être branché jazz

intolerant [ɪn'tɒlərənt] *adj*
intolérant

intoxicated [ɪn'tɒksɪkeɪtɪd] *adj*
ivre

intransitive [ɪn'trænsɪtɪv] *adj*
(verb) intransitif, -ive

intricate ['ɪntrɪkət] *adj*
compliqué

intrigue [ɪn'triːg] *vt (interest)*
intriguer ● **intriguing** *adj (news,
attitude)* curieux, -euse

introduce [ɪntrə'djuːs] *vt (bring
in, insert)* introduire (**into** dans);
(programme, subject) présenter;
to i. sb (to sb) présenter qn (à
qn) ● **introduction** [-'dʌkʃən]
n introduction *f*; *(of person to
person)* présentation *f*

introvert ['ɪntrəvɜːt] *n* introverti,
-e *mf*

intrude [ɪn'truːd] *vi (of person)*
déranger (**on sb** qn) ● **intruder** *n*
intrus, -e *mf* ● **intrusion** *n (bother)*

dérangement *m*; *(interference)* intrusion *f* (**into** dans);

intuition [ɪntjuːˈɪʃən] *n* intuition *f*

inundate [ˈɪnʌndeɪt] *vt* inonder (**with** de); **inundated with work/letters** submergé de travail/ lettres

invade [ɪnˈveɪd] *vt* envahir

invalid¹ [ˈɪnvəlɪd] *adj & n* malade *(mf)*; *(disabled person)* infirme *(mf)*

invalid² [ɪnˈvælɪd] *adj (ticket, passport)* non valable

invaluable [ɪnˈvæljʊəbəl] *adj* inestimable

invariably [ɪnˈveərɪəblɪ] *adv* invariablement

invasion [ɪnˈveɪʒən] *n* invasion *f*

invent [ɪnˈvent] *vt* inventer ● **invention** *n* invention *f* ● **inventor** *n* inventeur, -trice *mf*

inventory [ˈɪnvəntərɪ] *(pl* -**ies**) *n* inventaire *m*

inverted [ɪnˈvɜːtɪd] *vt Br* **i. commas** guillemets *mpl*

invest [ɪnˈvest] **1** *vt (money)* investir (**in** dans); *(time, effort)* consacrer (**in** à) **2** *vi* **to i. in** *(company)* investir dans; *Fig (car)* se payer ● **investment** *n* investissement *m*

investigate [ɪnˈvestɪgeɪt] *vt (examine)* examiner; *(crime)* enquêter sur ● **investigation** [-ˈgeɪʃən] *n* examen *m*, étude *f*; *(inquiry by journalist, police)* enquête *f* (**of** *or* **into** sur)

invigilator [ɪnˈvɪdʒɪleɪtə(r)] *n Br* surveillant, -e *mf* (à un examen)

invigorating [ɪnˈvɪgəreɪtɪŋ] *adj* vivifiant

invincible [ɪnˈvɪnsəbəl] *adj* invincible

invisible [ɪnˈvɪzəbəl] *adj* invisible

invite 1 [ɪnˈvaɪt] *vt* inviter (**to do** à faire) **2** [ˈɪnvaɪt] *n Fam* invit' *f* ● **invitation** [-vɪˈteɪʃən] *n* invitation *f*

invoice [ˈɪnvɔɪs] *n* facture *f*

involuntary [ɪnˈvɒləntərɪ] *adj* involontaire

involve [ɪnˈvɒlv] *vt (entail)* entraîner; **to i. sb in sth** impliquer qn dans qch; *(in project)* associer qn à qch; **the job involves going abroad** le poste nécessite des déplacements à l'étranger ● **involved** *adj* **fifty people were i. in the project** cinquante personnes ont pris part au projet; **to be i. with sb** *(emotionally)* avoir une liaison avec qn; **the person i.** *(concerned)* la personne en question

inward [ˈɪnwəd] **1** *adj & adv (movement, move)* vers l'intérieur **2** *adj (inner) (happiness)* intérieur; *(thoughts)* intime ● **inwardly** *adv (laugh, curse)* intérieurement ● **inwards** *adv* vers l'intérieur

IQ [aɪˈkjuː] *(abbr* **intelligence quotient)** *n* QI *m inv*

Iran [ɪˈrɑːn, ɪˈræn] *n* l'Iran *m* ● **Iranian** [ɪˈreɪnɪən, *Am* ɪˈrɑːnɪən] **1** *adj* iranien, -enne **2** *n* Iranien, -enne *mf*

Iraq [ɪˈrɑːk] *n* l'Irak *m* ● **Iraqi 1** *adj* irakien, -enne **2** *n* Irakien, -enne *mf*

irate [aɪˈreɪt] *adj* furieux, -euse

Ireland [ˈaɪələnd] *n* l'Irlande *f* ● **Irish** [ˈaɪrɪʃ] **1** *adj* irlandais **2** *n* (**a**) *(language)* irlandais *m* (**b**) **the I.** *(people)* les Irlandais *mpl* ● **Irishman** *(pl* -**men**) *n* Irlandais *m* ● **Irishwoman** *(pl* -**women**) *n* Irlandaise *f*

iris [ˈaɪərɪs] *n (plant, of eye)* iris *m*

iron [ˈaɪən] **1** *n* fer *m*; *(for clothes)* fer *m* à repasser **2** *vt (clothes)* repasser • **ironing** n repassage m; **i. board** planche f à repasser

irony ['aɪərənɪ] n ironie f • **ironic(al)** [aɪ'rɒnɪk(əl)] adj ironique

irrational [ɪ'ræʃənəl] adj irrationnel, -elle

irregular [ɪ'regjʊlə(r)] adj irrégulier, -ère • **irregularity** [-'lærɪtɪ] (pl -ies) n irrégularité f

irrelevant [ɪ'reləvənt] adj sans rapport (**to** avec); (remark) hors de propos; **that's i.** ça n'a rien à voir (avec la question)

irreparable [ɪ'repərəbəl] adj (harm, loss) irréparable

irreplaceable [ɪrɪ'pleɪsəbəl] adj irremplaçable

irresistible [ɪrɪ'zɪstəbəl] adj (person, charm) irrésistible

irresponsible [ɪrɪ'spɒnsəbəl] adj (act) irréfléchi; (person) irresponsable

irreversible [ɪrɪ'vɜːsəbəl] adj (process) irréversible; (decision) irrévocable

irritate ['ɪrɪteɪt] vt (annoy, inflame) irriter • **irritable** [-təbəl] adj (easily annoyed) irritable • **irritating** adj irritant

is [ɪz] see **be**

island ['aɪlənd] n île f

isle [aɪl] n île f

isn't ['ɪzənt] = **is not**

isolate ['aɪsəleɪt] vt isoler (**from** de) • **isolated** adj (remote, unique) isolé • **isolation** [-'leɪʃən] n isolement m; **in i.** isolément

Israel ['ɪzreɪəl] n Israël m • **Israeli** ['ɪzreɪəlɪ] **1** adj israélien, -enne **2** n Israélien, -enne mf

issue ['ɪʃuː] **1** n (of newspaper, magazine) numéro m; (matter) question f; **to make an i. of sth**

faire toute une affaire de qch **2** vt (tickets) distribuer; (passport) délivrer; (order) donner; (warning) lancer; **to i. a statement** faire une déclaration

it [ɪt] pron (**a**) (subject) il, elle; (object) le, la, l'; **(to) it** (indirect object) lui; **it bites** (dog) mord; **I've done it** je l'ai fait (**b**) (impersonal) il; **it's snowing** il neige; **it's hot** il fait chaud (**c**) (non-specific) ce, cela, ça; **it's good** c'est bon; **who is it?** qui est-ce?; **to consider it wise to do sth** juger prudent de faire qch; **it was Paul who...** c'est Paul qui... **to have it in for sb** en vouloir à qn (**d**) **of it, from it, about it** en; **in it, to it, at it** y; **on it** dessus; **under it** dessous

italics [ɪ'tælɪks] npl italique m; **in i.** en italique

Italy ['ɪtəlɪ] n l'Italie f • **Italian** [ɪ'tælɪən] **1** adj italien, -enne **2** n (person) Italien, -enne mf; (language) italien m

itch [ɪtʃ] vi (of person) avoir des démangeaisons; **his arm itches** son bras le ou lui démange; Fig **to be itching to do sth** brûler d'envie de faire qch

item ['aɪtəm] n (in collection, on list, in newspaper) article m; **i. of clothing** vêtement m; **news i.** information f

itinerary [aɪ'tɪnərərɪ] (pl -ies) n itinéraire m

its [ɪts] possessive adj son, sa, pl ses • **itself** pron lui-même, elle-même; (reflexive) se, s'; **by i.** tout seul

I've [aɪv] = **I have**

ivory ['aɪvərɪ] n ivoire m

J j

J, j [dʒeɪ] *n (letter)* J, j *m inv*

jab [dʒæb] **1** *n* coup *m*; *Br Fam (injection)* piqûre *f* **2** *(pt & pp* **-bb-**) *vt (knife, stick)* enfoncer (**into** dans); *(prick)* piquer (**with** du bout de)

jack [dʒæk] *n* (**a**) *(for vehicle)* cric *m* (**b**) *(in cards)* valet *m*

jacket ['dʒækɪt] *n (coat)* veste *f*; *(of book)* jaquette *f*; *Br* **j. potato** pomme *f* de terre en robe des champs

jackpot ['dʒækpɒt] *n* gros lot *m*

Jacuzzi® [dʒə'kuːzɪ] *n* Jacuzzi® *m*

jail [dʒeɪl] **1** *n* prison *f* **2** *vt* emprisonner (**for** pour)

jam¹ [dʒæm] *n (preserve)* confiture *f*; **strawberry j.** confiture *f* de fraises • **jamjar** *n* pot *m* à confiture

jam² [dʒæm] **1** *n* **(traffic) j.** embouteillage *m* **2** *(pt & pp* **-mm-**) *vt (squeeze, make stuck)* coincer; *(street, corridor)* encombrer; **to j. sth into sth** entasser qch dans qch; **to j. on the brakes** écraser la pédale de frein **3** *vi (get stuck)* se coincer • **jammed** *adj (machine)* coincé; *(street)* encombré • **jam-packed** *adj (hall, train)* bourré

Jamaica [dʒə'meɪkə] *n* la Jamaïque

jangle ['dʒæŋgəl] *vi* cliqueter

janitor ['dʒænɪtə(r)] *n Am & Scot (caretaker)* concierge *m*

January ['dʒænjʊərɪ] *n* janvier *m*

Japan [dʒə'pæn] *n* le Japon •

Japanese [dʒæpə'niːz] **1** *adj* japonais **2** *n (person)* Japonais, -e *mf*; *(language)* japonais *m*

jar¹ [dʒɑː(r)] *n (container)* pot *m*; *(large, glass)* bocal *m*

jar² [dʒɑː(r)] **1** *(pt & pp* **-rr-**) *vt (shake)* ébranler **2** *vi (of noise)* grincer; *(of colours, words)* jurer (**with** avec)

jargon ['dʒɑːgən] *n* jargon *m*

jaw [dʒɔː] *n Anat* mâchoire *f*

jazz [dʒæz] *n* jazz *m*

jealous ['dʒeləs] *adj* jaloux, -ouse (**of** de) • **jealousy** *n* jalousie *f*

jeans [dʒiːnz] *npl* **(pair of) j.** jean *m*

jeer [dʒɪə(r)] **1** *vt (boo)* huer; *(mock)* se moquer de **2** *vi* **to j. at sb/sth** *(boo)* huer qn/qch; *(mock)* se moquer de qn/qch • **jeering** *n (mocking)* railleries *fpl*; *(of crowd)* huées *fpl*

jello® ['dʒeləʊ] *n Am (dessert)* gelée *f*

jelly ['dʒelɪ] *(pl* **-ies**) *n (preserve, dessert)* gelée *f* • **jellyfish** *n* méduse *f*

jeopardy ['dʒepədɪ] *n* **in j.** en péril • **jeopardize** *vt* mettre en danger

jerk [dʒɜːk] **1** *n* secousse *f* **2** *vt (pull)* tirer brusquement

Jersey ['dʒɜːzɪ] *n* Jersey *m ou f*

jersey ['dʒɜːzɪ] *(pl* **-eys**) *n (garment)* tricot *m*; *(of footballer)* maillot *m*

Jesus ['dʒiːzəs] *n* Jésus *m*; **J. Christ** Jésus-Christ *m*

jet [dʒet] n (a) (plane) avion m
à réaction; **j. lag** fatigue f due
au décalage horaire (b) (steam,
liquid) jet m
jet-lagged ['dʒetlægd] adj qui
souffre du décalage horaire
jetty ['dʒetɪ] (pl -ies) n jetée f;
(landing place) embarcadère m
Jewish ['dʒuːɪʃ] adj juif (f juive)
jewel ['dʒuːəl] n bijou m (pl -oux);
(in watch) rubis m ● **jeweller** (Am
● **jeweler**) n bijoutier, -ère mf
● **jewellery** (Am ● **jewelry**) n
bijoux mpl
jig [dʒɪg] n (dance, music) gigue f
jigsaw ['dʒɪgsɔː] n **j. (puzzle)**
puzzle m
jingle ['dʒɪŋgəl] vi (of keys, bell)
tinter
job [dʒɒb] n (employment, post)
travail m, emploi m; (task) tâche f;
j. offer offre f d'emploi
jockey ['dʒɒkɪ] (pl -eys) n jockey
m
jog [dʒɒg] (pt & pp -gg-) **1** vt
(shake) secouer; (push) pousser;
Fig (memory) rafraîchir **2** vi (for
fitness) faire du jogging ● **jogging**
n (for fitness) jogging m; **to go
jogging** aller faire un jogging
join [dʒɔɪn] **1** vt (a) (put together)
joindre; (wires, pipes) raccorder;
(words, towns) relier; **to j. two
things together** relier une chose
à une autre; **to j. sb** (catch up
with, meet) rejoindre qn; (associate
oneself with, go with) se joindre
à qn (**in doing** pour faire) (b)
(become a member of) s'inscrire
à; (army, police, company) entrer
dans; **to j. the queue** or Am
line prendre la queue **3** vi (a)
(of roads, rivers) se rejoindre; **to
j. (together** or **up)** (of objects)
se joindre (**with** à); **to j. in sth**
prendre part à qch (b) (become

a member) devenir membre; Mil
to j. up s'engager ● **joint 1** n (a)
(in body) articulation f; Br (meat)
rôti m (b) Fam (cannabis cigarette)
joint m **2** adj (decision) commun; **j.
account** compte m joint ● **jointly**
adv conjointement
joke [dʒəʊk] **1** n plaisanterie
f; (trick) tour m **2** vi plaisanter
(**about** sur) ● **joker** n plaisantin
m; (card) joker m ● **jokingly** adv
(say) en plaisantant
jolly ['dʒɒlɪ] (-ier, -iest) adj
(happy) gai
jolt [dʒɒlt] **1** n secousse f **2** vt
(shake) secouer
jostle ['dʒɒsəl] vi (push each
other) se bousculer (**for sth** pour
obtenir qch)
jot [dʒɒt] (pt & pp -tt-) vt **to j. sth
down** noter qch
journal ['dʒɜːnəl] n (periodical)
revue f
journalist ['dʒɜːnəlɪst] n
journaliste mf
journey ['dʒɜːnɪ] (pl -eys) n (trip)
voyage m; (distance) trajet m; **to
go on a j.** partir en voyage
joy [dʒɔɪ] n joie f ● **joyful** adj
joyeux, -euse
joystick ['dʒɔɪstɪk] n (of aircraft,
computer) manche m à balai
jubilee ['dʒuːbɪliː] n **(golden) j.**
jubilé m
judge [dʒʌdʒ] **1** n juge m **2** vti
juger; **to j. sb by** or **on sth**
juger qn sur ou d'après qch;
judging by... à en juger par... ●
judg(e)ment n jugement m
judo ['dʒuːdəʊ] n judo m
jug [dʒʌg] n cruche f; (for milk)
pot m
juggle ['dʒʌgəl] **1** vt jongler avec
2 vi jongler (**with** avec) ● **juggler**
n jongleur, -euse mf
juice [dʒuːs] n jus m ● **juicy**

(**-ier**, **-iest**) *adj (fruit)* juteux, -euse; *(meat)* succulent; *Fig (story)* savoureux, -euse

jukebox ['dʒuːkbɒks] *n* juke-box *m*

July [dʒuː'laɪ] *n* juillet *m*

jumble ['dʒʌmbəl] **1** *n (disorder)* fouillis *m*; *Br (unwanted articles)* bric-à-brac *m inv*; *Br* **j. sale** vente *f* de charité *(articles d'occasion uniquement)* **2** *vt* **to j. (up)** *(objects, facts)* mélanger

jump [dʒʌmp] **1** *n (leap)* saut *m*; *(start)* sursaut *m*; *(increase)* hausse *f* soudaine; *Am* **j. rope** corde *f* à sauter **2** *vt (ditch)* sauter; *Br* **to j. the queue** passer avant son tour, resquiller **3** *vi* sauter (**at** sur); *(start)* sursauter; *(of price)* faire un bond; **to j. across sth** traverser qch d'un bond; **to j. in** *or* **on** *(train, vehicle, bus)* sauter dans; **to j. off** *or* **out** sauter; *(from bus)* descendre; **to j. off sth, to j. out of sth** sauter de qch; **to j. out of the window** sauter par la fenêtre, **to j. up** se lever d'un bond

jumper ['dʒʌmpə(r)] *n Br* pull(-over) *m*; *Am (dress)* robe *f* chasuble

junction ['dʒʌŋkʃən] *n (cross-roads)* carrefour *m*; *Br* **j. 23** *(on motorway) (exit)* la sortie 23; *(entrance)* l'entrée *f* 23

June [dʒuːn] *n* juin *m*

jungle ['dʒʌŋgəl] *n* jungle *f*

junior ['dʒuːnɪə(r)] *adj (younger)* plus jeune; *(in rank, status)* subalterne; *(teacher, doctor)* jeune; **to be sb's j.** être plus jeune que qn; *(in rank, status)* être au-

dessous de qn; *Br* **j. school** école *f* primaire *(entre 7 et 11 ans)*; *Am* **j. high school** ≃ collège *m* d'enseignement secondaire

junk [dʒʌŋk] *n (unwanted objects)* bric-à-brac *m inv*; *(inferior goods)* camelote *f*; **j. food** cochonneries *fpl*; **j. mail** prospectus *mpl*; **j. shop** boutique *f* de brocanteur

jury ['dʒʊərɪ] *(pl* **-ies)** *n (in competition, court)* jury *m*

just [dʒʌst] **1** *adv (exactly, slightly)* juste; *(only)* juste, seulement; *(simply)* (tout) simplement; **it's j. as I thought** c'est bien ce que je pensais; **she has/had j. left** elle vient/venait de partir; **he j. missed it** il l'a manqué de peu; **j. as big/light** tout aussi grand/ léger (**as** que); **j. a moment!** un instant!; **j. one** un(e) seul(e) (**of** de); **j. about** *(approximately)* à peu près; *(almost)* presque; **to be j. about to do sth** être sur le point do faire qch **2** *adj (fair)* juste (**to** envers)

justice ['dʒʌstɪs] *n* justice *f*; **it doesn't do you j.** *(hat, photo)* cela ne vous avantage pas

justify ['dʒʌstɪfaɪ] *(pt & pp* **-ied)** *vt* justifier; **to be justified in doing sth** avoir de bonnes raisons de faire qch • **justification** [-fɪ'keɪʃən] *n* justification *f*

jut [dʒʌt] *(pt & pp* **-tt-)** *vi* **to j. out** faire saillie

juvenile ['dʒuːvənaɪl, *Am* -ənəl] *adj (court)* pour enfants; *Pej (behaviour)* puéril; **j. delinquent** jeune délinquant, -e *mf*

Kk

K, k [keɪ] *n (letter)* K, k *m inv*

kangaroo [kæŋɡə'ruː] *n* kangourou *m*

karate [kə'rɑːtɪ] *n* karaté *m*

kebab [kə'bæb] *n* brochette *f*

keen [kiːn] *adj* (a) *Br (eager, enthusiastic)* plein d'enthousiasme; **to be k. on sth** *(music, sport)* être passionné de qch; **he is k. on her/the idea** elle/l'idée lui plaît beaucoup (b) *(edge, appetite)* aiguisé; *(interest)* vif *(f* vive)

keep [kiːp] **1** *(pt & pp* **kept**) *vt* garder; *(shop, car)* avoir; *(diary, promise)* tenir; *(family)* entretenir; *(rule)* respecter; *(delay, detain)* retenir; *(put)* mettre; **to k. doing sth** continuer à faire qch; **to k. sth clean** garder qch propre; **to k. sth from sb** dissimuler qch à qn; **to k. sb waiting/working** faire attendre/travailler qn; **2** *vi (remain)* rester; *(continue)* continuer; *(of food)* se conserver; **how is he keeping?** comment va-t-il?; **to k. still** rester immobile; **to k. going** continuer; **to k. at it** *(keep doing it)* persévérer • **keeper** *n (in park, in zoo, goal)* gardien, -enne *mf*

▶**keep away 1** *vt (person)* éloigner **(from** de) **2** *vi* ne pas s'approcher **(from** de)

▶**keep off 1** *vt sep (person)* éloigner; **k. your hands off!** n'y touche pas! **2** *vt insep* 'k. **off the grass**' 'défense de marcher sur les pelouses'

▶**keep on 1** *vt sep (hat, employee)* garder; **to k. on doing sth** continuer à faire qch **2** *vi* **to k. on at sb** harceler qn

▶**keep out 1** *vt sep* empêcher d'entrer **2** *vi* rester en dehors **(of** de)

▶**keep to** *vt insep (subject, path)* ne pas s'écarter de; *(room)* garder; **to k. to the left** tenir la gauche; **to k. to oneself** rester à l'écart

▶**keep up 1** *vt sep (continue, maintain)* continuer; *(keep awake)* empêcher de dormir; **to k. up appearances** sauver les apparences **2** *vi (continue)* continuer; *(follow)* suivre; **to k. up with sb** *(follow)* aller à la même allure que qn; *(in quality of work)* se maintenir à la hauteur de qn

kennel ['kenəl] *n Br* niche *f*

kept [kept] **1** *pt & pp of* **keep 2** *adj* **well k.** *(house)* bien tenu

kerb [kɜːb] *n Br* bord *m* du trottoir

ketchup ['ketʃəp] *n* ketchup *m*

kettle ['ketəl] *n* bouilloire *f*; **the k. is boiling** l'eau bout; **to put the k. on** mettre l'eau à chauffer

key [kiː] **1** *n* clef *f*, clé *f*; *(of piano, typewriter, computer)* touche *f* **2** *adj (industry, post)* clef, clé • **keyboard** *n (of piano, computer)* clavier *m* • **keyhole** *n* trou *m* de serrure • **keyring** *n* porte-clefs *m inv*, porte-clés *m inv*

khaki ['kɑːkɪ] *adj & n* kaki *(m) inv*

kick [kɪk] **1** *n* coup *m* de pied **2** *vt*

donner un coup de pied/des coups de pied à **3** *vi* donner des coups de pied • **kickoff** *n (in football)* coup *m* d'envoi

►**kick off** *vi (of footballer)* donner le coup d'envoi; *Fam (start)* démarrer

►**kick out** *vt sep Fam (throw out)* flanquer dehors

►**kick up** *vt sep Br Fam* **to k. up a fuss** faire des histoires

kid [kɪd] *Fam* **1** *n (child)* gosse *mf* **2** *(pt & pp* **-dd-**) *vt (tease)* faire marcher **3** *vi (joke)* **to be kidding** plaisanter; **no kidding!** sans blague!

kidnap ['kɪdnæp] *(pt & pp* **-pp-**) *vt* kidnapper • **kidnapper** *n* ravisseur, -euse *mf*

kidney ['kɪdnɪ] *(pl* **-eys**) *n* rein *m; (as food)* rognon *m;* **k. bean** haricot *m* rouge

kill [kɪl] **1** *vt (person, animal, plant)* tuer; **to k. oneself** se tuer; *Fam* **my feet are killing me** j'ai les pieds en compote; **to k. time** tuer le temps **2** *vi* tuer • **killer** *n* tueur, -euse *mf*

kilo ['ki:ləʊ] *(pl* **-os**) *n* kilo *m* • **kilogram(me)** ['kɪləgræm] *n* kilogramme *m* • **kilometre** [kɪ'lɒmɪtə(r)] *(Am* **kilometer**) *n* kilomètre *m*

kilt [kɪlt] *n* kilt *m*

kin [kɪn] *n* **one's next of k.** son plus proche parent

kind[1] [kaɪnd] *n (sort, type)* genre *m*, espèce *f* **(of** de); **what k. of drink is it?** qu'est-ce que c'est comme boisson?; *Fam* **k. of worried/sad** plutôt inquiet/triste

kind[2] [kaɪnd] *(-er, -est) adj (helpful, pleasant)* gentil, -ille **(to** avec); **that's k. of you** c'est gentil de votre part • **kindly** *adv* gentiment; **k. wait** ayez la bonté

d'attendre • **kindness** [-nɪs] *n* gentillesse *f*

kindergarten ['kɪndəgɑːtən] *n* jardin *m* d'enfants

king [kɪŋ] *n* roi *m* • **kingdom** *n* royaume *m*

kiosk ['kiːɒsk] *n* kiosque *m*

kipper ['kɪpə(r)] *n* hareng *m* salé et fumé

kiss [kɪs] **1** *n* baiser *m* **2** *vt (person)* embrasser **3** *vi* s'embrasser

kit [kɪt] *n* équipement *m*, matériel *m; (set of articles)* trousse *f; Br (belongings)* affaires *fpl; Br (sports clothes)* tenue *f;* **first-aid k.** trousse *f* de pharmacie

kitchen ['kɪtʃɪn] *n* cuisine *f;* **k. sink** évier *m*

kite [kaɪt] *n (toy)* cerf-volant *m*

kitten ['kɪtən] *n* chaton *m*

kiwi ['kiːwiː] *n (bird, fruit)* kiwi *m*

km *(abbr* **kilometre(s))** km

knack [næk] *n (skill)* talent *m;* **to have the k. of doing sth** avoir le don de faire qch

knead [niːd] *vt (dough)* pétrir

knee [niː] *n* genou *m;* **to go down on one's knees** s'agenouiller

kneel [niːl] *(pt & pp* **knelt** *or* **kneeled**) *vi* **to k. (down)** s'agenouiller **(before** devant); **to be kneeling (down)** être à genoux

knew [njuː] *pt of* **know**

knickers ['nɪkəz] *npl Br (underwear)* culotte *f*

knife [naɪf] *(pl* **knives**) *n* couteau *m; (penknife)* canif *m*

knight [naɪt] **1** *n* chevalier *m* **2** *vt Br* **to be knighted** être fait chevalier

knit [nɪt] *(pt & pp* **-tt-**) *vti* tricoter • **knitting** *n (activity, material)* tricot *m;* **k. needle** aiguille *f* à tricoter

knob [nɒb] *n (on door)* poignée *f; (on radio)* bouton *m*

knock [nɒk] **1** n (blow) coup m; **there's a k. at the door** on frappe à la porte **2** vt (strike) frapper; (collide with) heurter; **to k. one's head on sth** se cogner la tête contre qch **3** vi (strike) frapper; **to k. against** or **into sth** heurter qch ● **knocker** n (for door) marteau m ● **knockout** n (in boxing) knock-out m inv

▶**knock down** vt sep (object, pedestrian) renverser; (house, tree, wall) abattre; (price) baisser

▶**knock out** vt sep (make unconscious) assommer; (boxer) mettre K.-O.; (beat in competition) éliminer

▶**knock over** vt sep (pedestrian, object) renverser

knot [nɒt] **1** n (in rope) nœud m; Fig **to tie the k.** se marier **2** (pt & pp **-tt-**) vt nouer

know [nəʊ] **1** n Fam **to be in the k.** être au courant **2** (pt **knew**, pp **known**) vt (facts, language) savoir; (person, place) connaître; (recognize) reconnaître (**by** à); **to**

k. that... savoir que...; **to k. how to do sth** savoir faire qch; **for all I k.** que je sache; **I'll let you k.** je vous le ferai savoir; **to k. (a lot) about cars/sewing** s'y connaître en voitures/couture; **to get to k. sb** apprendre à connaître qn **3** vi savoir; **I k.** je (le) sais; **I wouldn't k., I k. nothing about it** je n'en sais rien; **to k. about sth** être au courant de qch; **do you k. of a good dentist?** connais-tu un bon dentiste? ● **know-all** n Fam Pej monsieur m/madame f je-sais-tout mf ● **know-how** n Fam savoir-faire m inv ● **knowingly** adv (consciously) sciemment ● **know-it-all** n = know-all ● **known** adj connu; **she is k. to be...** on sait qu'elle est...

knowledge ['nɒlɪdʒ] n (of fact) connaissance f; (learning) connaissances fpl, savoir m; **general k.** culture f générale

known [nəʊn] pp of **know**

knuckle ['nʌkəl] n articulation f (du doigt)

L

L, l [el] *n (letter)* L, l *m inv*

lab [læb] *n Fam* labo *m* •
laboratory [lə'bɒrətrɪ, *Am*
'læbrətɔːrɪ] *n* laboratoire *m*

label ['leɪbəl] **1** *n* étiquette *f; (of
record company)* label *m* **2** *(Br -ll-
, Am -l-) vt* étiqueter; *Fig* **to l. sb
(as) a liar** qualifier qn de menteur

labour ['leɪbə(r)] *(Am labor)* **1** *n
(work)* travail *m; (workers)* main-
d'œuvre *f; Br* **L.** *(political party)* le
parti travailliste; **in l.** *(woman)* en
train d'accoucher **2** *adj (market)*
du travail; **l. force** effectifs *mpl;
Am* **l. union** syndicat *m* **3** *vi (toil)*
peiner **(over** sur) • **laborious**
[lə'bɔːrɪəs] *adj* laborieux, -euse
• **labourer** *(Am laborer) n (on
roads)* manœuvre *m; (on farm)*
ouvrier *m* agricole

labyrinth ['læbərɪnθ] *n* labyrinthe
m

lace [leɪs] **1** *n* **(a)** *(cloth)* dentelle *f*
(b) *(of shoe)* lacet *m* **2** *vt* **to l. (up)**
(tie up) lacer

lack [læk] **1** *n* manque *m* **(of** de);
for l. of sth à défaut de qch **2** *vt*
manquer de **3** *vi* **to be lacking**
manquer **(in** de)

lad [læd] *n Fam (young man)* jeune
gars *m; (child)* garçon *m*

ladder ['lædə(r)] **1** *n* échelle *f; Br
(in tights)* maille *f* filée **2** *vti Br* filer

lady ['leɪdɪ] *(pl* **-ies)** *n* dame
f; **a young l.** une jeune fille;
(married) une jeune dame; **Ladies
and Gentlemen!** Mesdames,
Mesdemoiselles, Messieurs!; **the**
ladies' room, *Br* **the ladies** les
toilettes *fpl* pour dames

ladybird ['leɪdɪbɜːd] *(Am* **ladybug**
['leɪdɪbʌg]) *n* coccinelle *f*

lag [læg] *vi* **to l. behind** *(in
progress, work)* avoir du retard;
(dawdle) être à la traîne

lager ['lɑːgə(r)] *n Br* bière *f*
blonde

lagoon [lə'guːn] *n* lagune *f; (of
atoll)* lagon *m*

laid [leɪd] *pt & pp of* **lay²** • **laid-
back** *adj Fam* cool *inv*

lain [leɪn] *pp of* **lie²**

lake [leɪk] *n* lac *m*

lamb [læm] *n* agneau *m*

lame [leɪm] **(-er, -est)** *adj (person,
argument)* boiteux, -euse; *(excuse)*
piètre; **to be l.** *(of person)* boiter

laminated ['læmɪneɪtɪd] *adj
(wood)* stratifié; *(card)* plastifié

lamp [læmp] *n* lampe *f* • **lamppost**
n réverbère *m* • **lampshade** *n*
abat-jour *m inv*

land [lænd] **1** *n* terre *f; (country)*
pays *m; (for building on)* terrain *m*
2 *vi (of aircraft)* atterrir; *(of bomb)*
tomber • **landing** *n* **(a)** *(of aircraft)*
atterrissage *m* **(b)** *(of staircase)*
palier *m* • **landlady** *(pl* **-ies)** *n*
propriétaire *f; (of pub)* patronne
f • **landlord** *n* propriétaire *m;
(of pub)* patron *m* • **landmark** *n*
point *m* de repère • **landscape**
n paysage *m* • **landslide** *n*
glissement *m* de terrain

lane [leɪn] *n (in country)* chemin
m; (in town) ruelle *f; (division of*

road) voie f; (line of traffic) file f; (for swimming) couloir m

language ['læŋgwɪdʒ] **1** n (of a people) langue f; (faculty, style) langage m **2** adj (laboratory) de langues; (teacher, studies) de langue(s)

lanky ['læŋkɪ] (-ier, -iest) adj dégingandé

lantern ['læntən] n lanterne f

lap [læp] **1** n (a) (of person) genoux mpl (b) (in race) tour m de piste **2** (pt & pp -pp-) vt **to l. up** (drink) laper ● **laptop** adj & n **l. (computer)** ordinateur m portable

lapel [lə'pel] n revers m

lapse [læps] **1** n (in concentration, standards) baisse f; **a l. of memory** un trou de mémoire **2** vi (of concentration, standards) baisser

lard [lɑːd] n saindoux m

larder ['lɑːdə(r)] n garde-manger m inv

large [lɑːdʒ] (-er, -est) adj (big) grand; (fat, bulky) gros (f grosse); (quantity) grand, important; **to grow** or **get l.** s'agrandir; (of person) grossir; **at l.** (of prisoner, animal) en liberté; (as a whole) en général ● **largely** adv en grande partie

►**lark about** [lɑːk-] vi Br Fam faire le fou/la folle

lasagne, lasagna [lə'zænjə] n lasagnes fpl

laser ['leɪzə(r)] n laser m

lash [læʃ] n (eyelash) cil m

►**lash out** [læʃ-] vi **to l. out at sb** (hit) donner des coups à qn; (criticize) fustiger qn

last¹ [lɑːst] **1** adj dernier, -ère; **the l. ten lines** les dix dernières lignes; **l. night** (evening) hier soir; (night) la nuit dernière; **l. name** nom m

de famille **2** adv (lastly) en dernier lieu; (on the last occasion) (pour) la dernière fois; **to leave l.** sortir le dernier **3** n (person, object) dernier, -ère mf; **l. but one** avant-dernier m (f avant-dernière); **at (long) l.** enfin ● **last-minute** adj (decision) de dernière minute

last² [lɑːst] vi durer; **it lasted me ten years** ça m'a fait dix ans

latch [lætʃ] **1** n loquet m **2** vt insep Fam **to l. onto** (understand) piger; (adopt) adopter

late¹ [leɪt] **1** (-er, -est) adj (meal, season, hour) tardif, -ive; (stage) avancé; (edition) dernier, -ère; **to be l. (for sth)** être en retard (pour qch); **he's an hour l.** il a une heure de retard; **it's l.** il est tard; **in the l. nineties** à la fin des années 90; **to be in one's l. forties** approcher de la cinquantaine; **at a later date** à une date ultérieure; **at the latest** au plus tard **2** adv (in day, season) tard; (not on time) en retard; **it's getting l.** il se fait tard; **later (on)** plus tard; **of l.** récemment ● **lately** adv dernièrement

late² [leɪt] adj **the l. Mr Smith** feu Monsieur Smith

lather ['lɑːðə(r)] n mousse f

Latin ['lætɪn] **1** adj latin; **L. America** l'Amérique f latine **2** n (language) latin m ● **L. American 1** adj d'Amérique latine **2** n Latino-Américain, -e mf

latter ['lætə(r)] **1** adj (later, last-named) dernier, -ère; (second) deuxième **2** n **the l.** le dernier (f la dernière); (of two) le second (f la seconde)

laugh [lɑːf] **1** n rire m; **to have a good l.** bien rire **2** vt **to l. sth off** tourner qch en plaisanterie **3** vi rire (**at/about** de) ● **laughing** adj riant; **it's no l. matter** il n'y a pas

de quoi rire; **to be the l. stock of**
être la risée de • **laughter** n rire(s)
m(pl)
launch [lɔːntʃ] **1** vt (ship, rocket,
product) lancer **2** vi **to l. into**
(begin) se lancer dans
laundry ['lɔːndrɪ] n (place)
blanchisserie f; (clothes) linge
m; **to do the l.** faire la lessive •
launderette [lɔːndə'ret] (Am
Laundromat® ['lɔːndrəmæt]) n
laverie f automatique
lava ['lɑːvə] n lave f
lavatory ['lævətərɪ] (pl **-ies**) n
toilettes fpl
lavender ['lævɪndə(r)] n lavande
f
lavish ['lævɪʃ] adj prodigue (**with**
de); (meal, décor, gift) somptueux,
-euse; (expenditure) excessif, -ive
law [lɔː] n (rule, rules) loi f; (study,
profession, system) droit m;
against the l. illégal; **court of l.,**
l. court cour f de justice; **l. and**
order l'ordre m public • **lawful**
adj (action) légal; (claim) légitime
lawn [lɔːn] n pelouse f, gazon m; **l.**
mower tondeuse f à gazon
lawsuit ['lɔːsuːt] n procès m
lawyer ['lɔːjə(r)] n (in court)
avocat, -e mf; (for wills, sales)
notaire m; (legal expert) juriste mf
lay¹ [leɪ] pt of **lie²**
lay² [leɪ] (pt & pp **laid**) vt (put
down, place) poser; (blanket)
étendre (**over** sur); (egg) pondre;
Br **to l. the table** mettre la table •
lay-by (pl **-bys**) n Br (for vehicles)
aire f de stationnement • **layout**
n disposition f; (of text) mise f en
page
▶**lay down** vt sep (put down)
poser; (principle, condition)
établir; **to l. down the law** dicter
sa loi (**to** à)

▶**lay out** vt sep (house) concevoir;
(display) disposer
layer ['leɪə(r)] n couche f
laze [leɪz] vi **to l. (about** or
around) paresser • **lazy** (**-ier,**
-iest) adj (person) paresseux,
-euse
lb (abbr **libra**) **3lb** 3 livres (unité
de poids)
lead¹ [led] n (metal) plomb m; (of
pencil) mine f
lead² [liːd] **1** n (distance or time
ahead) avance f (**over** sur); Br
(for dog) laisse f; (electric wire)
fil m électrique; **to take the l.**
(in race) prendre la tête; **to be**
in the l. (in race) être en tête; (in
match) mener (à la marque) **2** (pt
& pp **led**) vt (guide, conduct, take)
mener, conduire (**to** à); (team,
government) diriger; (expedition,
attack) commander; (procession)
être en tête de; **to l. a happy**
life mener une vie heureuse; **to**
l. sb in/out faire entrer/sortir
qn; **to l. sb to do sth** (cause,
induce) amener qn à faire qch **3**
vi (of street, door) mener, conduire
(**to** à); (in race) être en tête; (in
match) mener (à la marque); (go
ahead) aller devant; **to l. to sth**
(result in) aboutir à qch; (cause)
mener à qch; **to l. up to** (precede)
précéder • **leading** adj (best, most
important) principal
▶**lead off** vt sep emmener
▶**lead on** vt sep (deceive) tromper,
duper
leader ['liːdə(r)] n (person) chef
m; (of country, party) dirigeant, -e
mf; (of strike, riot) meneur, -euse
mf; (guide) guide m • **leadership**
n direction f; (qualities) qualités
fpl de chef; (leaders) (of country,
party) dirigeants mpl

leaf [liːf] **1** (*pl* **leaves**) *n* feuille *f* **2** *vi* **to l. through** (*book*) feuilleter

leaflet ['liːflɪt] *n* prospectus *m*; (*containing instructions*) notice *f*

league [liːg] *n* ligue *f*; *Pej* **in l. with** de connivence avec

leak [liːk] **1** *n* (*in pipe, information*) fuite *f*; (*in boat*) voie *f* d'eau **2** *vt Fig* (*information*) divulguer; **the pipe was leaking gas** du gaz fuyait du tuyau **3** *vi* (*of liquid, pipe, tap*) fuir; (*of ship*) faire eau; *Fig* **to l. out** (*of information*) être divulgué

lean¹ [liːn] (**-er, -est**) *adj* (*meat*) maigre; (*person*) mince

lean² [liːn] (*pt & pp* **leaned** *or* **leant** [lent]) **1** *vt* **to l. sth on/against sth** appuyer qch sur/contre qch **2** *vi* (*of object*) pencher; (*of person*) se pencher; **to l. against/on sth** (*of person*) s'appuyer contre/sur qch; **to l. forward** (*of person*) se pencher (en avant); **to l. over** (*of person*) se pencher; (*of object*) pencher ● **leaning** *adj* penché; **l. against** (*resting*) appuyé contre

leap [liːp] **1** *n* (*jump*) bond *m*, saut *m*; *Fig* (*change, increase*) bond *m*; **l. year** année *f* bissextile **2** (*pt & pp* **leaped** *or* **leapt** [lept]) *vi* bondir, sauter; **to l. to one's feet, to l. up** se lever d'un bond

learn [lɜːn] (*pt & pp* **learned** *or* **learnt** [lɜːnt]) **1** *vt* apprendre (**that** que); **to l. (how) to do sth** apprendre à faire qch **2** *vi* apprendre; **to l. about sth** (*study*) étudier qch; (*hear about*) apprendre qch ● **learner** *n* (*beginner*) débutant, -e *mf*; (*student*) étudiant, -e *mf*

lease [liːs] *n* bail *m* (*pl* baux)

leash [liːʃ] *n* (*of dog*) laisse *f*; **on a l.** en laisse

least [liːst] **1** *adj* **the l.** (*smallest amount of*) le moins de; **he has (the) l. talent** c'est lui qui a le moins de talent (**of all** de tous); **the l. effort/noise** le moindre effort/bruit **2** *n* **the l.** le moins; **at l.** du moins; (*with quantity*) au moins; **not in the l.** pas du tout **3** *adv* (*work, eat*) le moins; **the l. difficult** le/la moins difficile; **l. of all** (*especially not*) surtout pas

leather ['leðə(r)] *n* cuir *m*

leave [liːv] **1** *n* (*holiday*) congé *m*; **to be on l.** être en congé **2** (*pt & pp* **left**) *vt* (*allow to remain, forget*) laisser; (*depart from*) quitter; **to l. sth with sb** (*entrust, give*) laisser qch à qn; **to be left (over)** rester; **there's no bread left** il ne reste plus de pain; **I'll l. it (up) to you** je m'en remets à toi **3** *vi* (*go away*) partir (**from** de; **for** pour)

▶**leave behind** *vt sep* **to l. sth behind** (*on purpose*) laisser qch; (*accidentally*) oublier qch; **to l. sb behind** (*not take*) partir sans qn; (*surpass*) dépasser qn; (*in race, at school*) distancer qn

▶**leave out** *vt sep* (*forget to put*) oublier de mettre; (*deliberately omit*) décider de ne pas inclure; (*when reading*) (*word, line*) sauter; (*exclude*) exclure

lecture ['lektʃə(r)] **1** *n* (*public speech*) conférence *f*; (*university class*) cours *m* magistral; (*scolding*) sermon *m*; **l. hall** amphithéâtre *m* **2** *vt Fam* (*scold*) faire la morale à **3** *vi* faire une conférence/un cours ● **lecturer** *n* conférencier, -ère *mf*; (*at university*) enseignant, -e *mf*

led [led] *pt & pp of* **lead**²

ledge [ledʒ] *n* (*on wall, window*) rebord *m*

leek [liːk] *n* poireau *m*

leer [lɪə(r)] *vi* **to l. at sb** (*lustfully*) regarder qn d'un air lubrique

left¹ [left] *pt* & *pp of* **leave** • **left-luggage** *n Br* **l. office** consigne *f* • **leftovers** *npl* restes *mpl*

left² [left] **1** *adj (side, hand)* gauche **2** *n* gauche *f*; **on** *or* **to the l.** à gauche **(of** de) **3** *adv* à gauche • **left-hand** *adj* de gauche; **on the l. side** à gauche **(of** de); **l. drive** conduite *f* à gauche • **left-handed** *adj (person)* gaucher, -ère • **left-wing** *adj (views, government)* de gauche

leg [leg] *n* jambe *f*; *(of dog, bird)* patte *f*; *(of table)* pied *m*; *(of journey)* étape *f*; **chicken l.** cuisse *f* de poulet; **to pull sb's l.** *(make fun of)* faire marcher qn

legacy ['legəsɪ] *(pl* **-ies)** *n (in a will)* & *Fig* legs *m*

legal ['liːgəl] *adj (lawful)* légal; *(affairs, adviser)* juridique • **legally** *adv* légalement

legend ['ledʒənd] *n (story, inscription)* légende *f* • **legendary** ... *adj* ... ...

leggings ['legɪŋz] *npl (of woman)* caleçon *m*

legible ['ledʒɪbəl] *adj* lisible

legislation [ledʒɪs'leɪʃən] *n* législation *f*

legitimate [lɪ'dʒɪtɪmət] *adj* légitime

leisure [*Br* 'leʒə(r), *Am* 'liːʒər] *n* **l. (time)** loisirs *mpl*; **l. centre** *or* **complex** centre *m* de loisirs; **at (one's) l.** à tête reposée • **leisurely** [*Br* 'leʒəlɪ, *Am* 'liːʒərlɪ] *adj (walk, occupation)* peu fatigant; *(meal, life)* tranquille; **at a l. pace, in a l. way** sans se presser

lemon ['lemən] *n* citron *m*; *Br* **l. squash** citronnade *f* • **lemonade** [-'neɪd] *n (still)* citronnade *f*; *Br (fizzy)* limonade *f*

lend [lend] *(pt* & *pp* **lent)** *vt* prêter

(to à) • **lender** *n* prêteur, -euse *mf*

length [leŋθ] *n (in space)* longueur *f*; *(duration)* durée *f*; **at (great) l.** *(in detail)* dans le détail; **to go to great lengths** se donner beaucoup de mal **(to do** pour faire) • **lengthwise** *adv* dans le sens de la longueur • **lengthy** (**-ier, -iest**) *adj* long *(f* longue)

lens [lenz] *(pl* **lenses** [-zəz]) *n* lentille *f*; *(in spectacles)* verre *m*; *(of camera)* objectif *m*

Lent [lent] *n Rel* carême *m*

lent [lent] *pt* & *pp of* **lend**

lentil ['lentəl] *n* lentille *f*

leopard ['lepəd] *n* léopard *m*

leotard ['liːətɑːd] *n* justaucorps *m*

lesbian ['lezbɪən] **1** *adj* lesbien, -enne **2** *n* lesbienne *f*

less [les] **1** *adj* & *pron* moins (de) **(than** que); **l. time** moins de temps; **she has l. (than you)** elle en a moins (que toi); **l. than a kilo** moins d'un kilo **2** *adv* moins **(than** que); **l. (often)** moins souvent; **one l.** un(e) de moins **3** *prep* moins

-less [ləs, lɪs] *suff* sans; **childless** sans enfants

lesson ['lesən] *n* leçon *f*; **an English l.** une leçon d'anglais; *Fig* **he has learnt his l.** ça lui a servi de leçon

let¹ [let] **1** *(pt* & *pp* **let,** *pres p* **letting)** *vt (allow)* **to l. sb do sth** laisser qn faire qch; **to l. sb have sth** donner qch à qn; **to l. go of sb/sth** lâcher qn/qch **2** *v aux* **l.'s eat/go** mangeons/partons; **l.'s go for a stroll** allons nous promener; **l. him come** qu'il vienne

▶ **let down** *vt sep (lower)* baisser; **to l. sb down** *(disappoint)*

décevoir qn; **don't l. me down** je compte sur toi

▶**let in** *vt sep (person, dog)* faire entrer; *(light)* laisser entrer; **to l. sb in on sth** mettre qn au courant de qch

▶**let off** *vt sep (firework)* tirer; *(bomb)* faire exploser; **to l. sb off** *(allow to leave)* laisser partir qn; *(not punish)* ne pas punir qn; **to be l. off with a fine** s'en tirer avec une amende; **to l. sb off doing sth** dispenser qn de faire qch

▶**let out** *vt sep (allow to leave)* laisser sortir; *(prisoner)* relâcher; *(secret)* laisser échapper

let² [let] *(pt & pp* **let**, *pres p* **letting)** *vt* **to l. (out)** *(house, room)* louer

lethal ['li:θəl] *adj (blow, dose)* mortel, -elle; *(weapon)* meurtrier, -ère

lethargic [lɪ'θɑ:dʒɪk] *adj* léthargique

letter ['letə(r)] *n (message, part of word)* lettre *f*; **l. opener** coupe-papier *m inv* • **letterbox** *n Br* boîte *f* aux lettres

lettuce ['letɪs] *n* laitue *f*

level ['levəl] **1** *n* niveau *m*; **at eye l.** à hauteur des yeux **2** *adj (surface)* plat; *(equal in score)* à égalité (**with** avec); *(in height)* à la même hauteur (**with** que); *Br* **l. crossing** *(for train)* passage *m* à niveau

lever [*Br* 'li:və(r), *Am* 'levər] *n* levier *m*

lewd [lu:d] **(-er, -est)** *adj* obscène

liable ['laɪəbəl] *adj* **l. to** *(dizziness)* sujet, -ette à; *(fine, tax)* passible de; **to be l. to do sth** risquer de faire qch; **l. for sth** *(responsible)* responsable de qch • **liability** [-'bɪlətɪ] *n (legal responsibility)* responsabilité *f* (**for** de); *(disadvantage)* handicap *m*

liaise [li:'eɪz] *vi* travailler en liaison (**with** avec)

liar ['laɪə(r)] *n* menteur, -euse *mf*

liberal ['lɪbərəl] *adj (open-minded) & Pol* libéral; *(generous)* généreux, -euse (**with** de)

liberate ['lɪbəreɪt] *vt* libérer • **liberation** *n* libération *f*

liberty ['lɪbətɪ] *(pl* **-ies)** *n* liberté *f*; **to be at l. to do sth** être libre de faire qch; **to take liberties with sb/sth** prendre des libertés avec qn/qch

library ['laɪbrərɪ] *(pl* **-ies)** *n* bibliothèque *f* • **librarian** [-'breərɪən] *n* bibliothécaire *mf*

lice [laɪs] *pl of* **louse**

licence ['laɪsəns] *(Am* **license)** *n (permit)* permis *m*; *(for trading)* licence *f*; **(TV) l.** redevance *f*; **l. plate/number** *(of vehicle)* plaque *f*/numéro *m* d'immatriculation • **license 1** *n Am =* **licence 2** *vt* accorder un permis/une licence à

lick [lɪk] *vt* lécher

licorice ['lɪkərɪʃ] *n* réglisse *f*

lid [lɪd] *n (of box, pan)* couvercle *m*

lie¹ [laɪ] **1** *n* mensonge *m* **2** *(pt & pp* **lied**, *pres p* **lying)** *vi (tell lies)* mentir

lie² [laɪ] *(pt* **lay**, *pp* **lain**, *pres p* **lying)** *vi* **(a)** *(of person, animal) (be in a flat position)* être allongé; *(get down)* s'allonger; **to be lying on the grass** être allongé sur l'herbe **(b)** *(of object)* être, se trouver • **lie-down** *n Br* **to have a l.** faire une sieste • **lie-in** *n Br* **to have a l.** faire la grasse matinée

▶**lie about, lie around** *vi (of objects, person)* traîner

▶**lie down** *vi* s'allonger; **to be lying down** être allongé

▶**lie in** *vi Br* faire la grasse matinée

life [laɪf] (*pl* **lives**) *n* vie *f*; *(of battery, machine)* durée *f* de vie; **to come to l.** *(of party, street)* s'animer; **to take one's (own) l.** se donner la mort; **l. insurance** assurance-vie *f*; **l. jacket** gilet *m* de sauvetage • **lifebelt** *n* ceinture *f* de sauvetage • **lifeboat** *n* canot *m* de sauvetage • **lifeguard** *n* maître nageur *m* • **lifelike** *adj* très ressemblant • **lifesize(d)** *adj* grandeur nature *inv* • **lifestyle** *n* style *m* de vie • **lifetime** *n* vie *f*; *Fig* éternité *f*

lift [lɪft] **1** *n Br (elevator)* ascenseur *m*; **to give sb a l.** emmener qn en voiture **(to** à**) 2** *vt* lever; *(heavy object)* soulever • **lift-off** *n (of spacecraft)* décollage *m*

▶**lift up** *vt sep (arm, object, eyes)* lever; *(heavy object)* soulever

light¹ [laɪt] **1** *n* lumière *f*; *(on vehicle)* feu *m*; *(vehicle headlight)* phare *m*; **to come to l.** être découvert; **do you have a l.?** *(for cigarette)* est-ce que vous avez du feu?; **to set l. to sth** mettre le feu à qch; **turn right at the lights** tournez à droite après les feux; **l. bulb** ampoule *f*; **l. switch** interrupteur *m* **2** *adj* **it will soon be l.** il fera bientôt jour **3** *(pt & pp* **lit** *or* **lighted***) vt (fire, candle, gas)* allumer; *(match)* allumer, gratter; **to l. (up)** *(room)* éclairer; *(cigarette)* allumer • **lighter** *n* briquet *m*

light² [laɪt] *adj (bright, not dark)* clair; **a l. green jacket** une veste vert clair

light³ [laɪt] *adj (in weight, quantity, strength)* léger, -ère; *(task)* facile; **l. rain** pluie *f* fine; **to travel l.**

voyager avec peu de bagages • **lighten** *vt (make less heavy)* alléger • **light-hearted** *adj* enjoué • **lighthouse** *n* phare *m* • **lightly** *adv* légèrement; **to get off l.** s'en tirer à bon compte • **lightweight** *adj (shoes, fabric)* léger, -ère

lightning ['laɪtnɪŋ] *n* éclairs *mpl*; **(flash of) l.** éclair *m*

like¹ [laɪk] **1** *prep* comme; **l. this** comme ça; **what's he l.?** comment est-il?; **to be** *or* **look l. sb/sth** ressembler à qn/qch; **what was the book l.?** comment as-tu trouvé le livre? **2** *adv* **nothing l. as big** loin d'être aussi grand **3** *conj Fam (as)* comme; **do l. I do** fais comme moi • **likewise** *adv (similarly)* de même

like² [laɪk] **1** *vt* aimer (bien) **(to do** *or* **doing** faire**); I l. him** je l'aime bien; **I'd l. to come** j'aimerais bien venir; **I'd l. a kilo of apples** je voudrais un kilo de pommes; **would you l. an apple?** voulez vous une pomme?; **if you l.** si vous voulez **2** *npl* **likes and dislikes** préférences *fpl* • **liking** *n* **a l. for** *(person)* de la sympathie pour; *(thing)* du goût pour; **to my l.** à mon goût

likely ['laɪklɪ] **1** **(-ier, -iest)** *adj (result, event)* probable; *(excuse)* vraisemblable; **it's l. (that) she'll come** il est probable qu'elle viendra **2** *adv* **very l.** très probablement

lilac ['laɪlək] **1** *n* lilas *m* **2** *adj (colour)* lilas *inv*

lily ['lɪlɪ] *(pl* **-ies***) n* lis *m*

limb [lɪm] *n (of body)* membre *m*

lime [laɪm] *n (fruit)* citron *m* vert

limelight ['laɪmlaɪt] *n* **to be in the l.** occuper le devant de la scène

limit ['lɪmɪt] **1** *n* limite *f*; *(restriction)*

limitation *f* (**on** de); **within limits** jusqu'à un certain point **2** *vt* limiter (**to** à); **to l.** oneself **to sth/doing sth** se borner à qch/faire qch ● **limitation** [-'teɪʃən] *n* limitation *f* ● **limited** *adj (restricted)* limité; *(edition)* à tirage limité

limousine [lɪmə'ziːn] *n (car)* limousine *f*

limp[1] [lɪmp] **1** *n* **to have a l.** boiter **2** *vi (of person)* boiter

limp[2] [lɪmp] (**-er, -est**) *adj (soft)* mou *(f* molle*); (flabby) (skin)* flasque; *(person, hat)* avachi

line[1] [laɪn] **1** *n* ligne *f; (stroke)* trait *m; (of poem)* vers *m; (wrinkle)* ride *f; (row)* rangée *f; (of vehicles, people)* file *f; (of goods)* ligne *f* (de produits); **to learn one's lines** *(of actor)* apprendre son texte; **to be on the l.** *(on the phone)* être au bout du fil; *Am* **to stand in l.** faire la queue; **in l. with sth** conforme à qch; **along the same lines** *(work, think, act)* de la même façon; *Fam* **to drop sb a l.** *(send a letter)* envoyer un mot à qn; **2** *vt* **to l. the street** *(of trees)* border la rue; *(of people)* s'aligner le long du trottoir; **to l. up** *(children, objects)* aligner; *(arrange)* organiser; **lined paper** papier *m* réglé **3** *vi* **to l. up** s'aligner; *Am (queue up)* faire la queue

line[2] [laɪn] *vt (clothes)* doubler ● **lining** *n (of clothes)* doublure *f*

linen ['lɪnɪn] *n (sheets)* linge *m; (material)* (toile *f* de) lin *m*

liner ['laɪnə(r)] *n* (**a**) (**ocean**) **l.** paquebot *m* (**b**) *Br* (**dust**)**bin l.**, *Am* **garbage can l.** sac-poubelle *m*

linger ['lɪŋgə(r)] *vi* **to l.** (**on**) *(of person)* s'attarder; *(of smell, memory)* persister; *(of doubt)* subsister

linguist ['lɪŋgwɪst] *n (specialist)* linguiste *mf* ● **linguistic** [-'gwɪstɪk] *adj* linguistique ● **linguistics** *n* linguistique *f*

link [lɪŋk] **1** *n (connection)* & *Comptr* lien *m; (of chain)* maillon *m; (by road, rail)* liaison *f* **2** *vt (connect)* relier (**to** à); *(relate, associate)* lier (**to** à); **to l. up** relier; *(computer)* connecter **3** *vi* **to l. up** *(of companies, countries)* s'associer; *(of roads)* se rejoindre

lino ['laɪnəʊ] (*pl* **-os**) *n Br* lino *m*

lion ['laɪən] *n* lion *m*; **l. cub** lionceau *m*

lip [lɪp] *n (of person)* lèvre *f; (of cup)* bord *m* ● **lip-read** [*pt* & *pp* **-read**] [-red] *vi* lire sur les lèvres ● **lipstick** *n* rouge *m* à lèvres

liqueur [*Br* lɪ'kjʊə(r), *Am* lɪ'kɜːr] *n* liqueur *f*

liquid ['lɪkwɪd] *n* & *adj* liquide *(m)* ● **liquidizer** [-daɪzə(r)] *n Br* mixeur *m*

liquor ['lɪkə(r)] *n Am* alcool *m*; **l. store** magasin *m* de vins et de spiritueux

liquorice ['lɪkərɪʃ] *n Br* réglisse *f*

lisp [lɪsp] **1** *n* **to have a l.** zézayer **2** *vi* zézayer

list [lɪst] **1** *n* liste *f* **2** *vt (things)* faire la liste de; *(name one by one)* énumérer

listen ['lɪsən] *vi* écouter; **to l. to sb/sth** écouter qn/qch; **to l. (out) for** *(telephone, person)* guetter ● **listener** *n (to radio)* auditeur, -trice *mf*

lit [lɪt] *pt* & *pp of* **light**[1]

liter ['liːtə(r)] *n Am* = **litre**

literally ['lɪtərəlɪ] *adv* littéralement; *(really)* réellement

literary ['lɪtərərɪ] *adj* littéraire

literate ['lɪtərət] *adj* qui sait lire et écrire

literature ['lɪtərətʃə(r)] n littérature f

litre ['liːtə(r)] (Am **liter**) n litre m

litter ['lɪtə(r)] n (a) (rubbish)
détritus mpl; (papers) papiers
mpl; Br l. **bin** boîte f à ordures
(b) (young animals) portée f; (for
cat) litière f

little ['lɪtəl] **1** n peu m; I've l.
left il m'en reste peu; she eats l.
elle mange peu; I have a l. j'en ai
un peu **2** adj (a) (small) petit; a l.
bit un (petit) peu (b) (not much)
peu de; l. **time/money** peu de
temps/d'argent; a l. **time/money**
un peu de temps/d'argent **3** adv
(somewhat, rather) peu; l. **by l.**
peu à peu; as l. as possible le
moins possible; a l. **heavy/better**
un peu lourd/mieux; to work a l.
travailler un peu

live¹ [laɪv] **1** adj (alive) vivant **2**
adj & adv (on radio, television)
en direct; a l. **broadcast** une
émission en direct • **lively** (-ier,
-iest) adj (person, style) plein de
vie; (story) vivant; (discussion,
conversation) animé

live² [lɪv] **1** vt (life) mener, vivre
2 vi vivre; where do you l.?
où habitez-vous?; to l. **in Paris**
habiter (à) Paris • **living 1** adj
(alive) vivant; the l. les vivants
mpl **2** n (livelihood) vie f; to make
or earn a or one's l. gagner sa vie;
l. **room** salle f de séjour

►**live off, live on** vt insep (eat)
vivre de; (sponge off) vivre aux
crochets de

►**live up to** vt insep (sb's
expectations) se montrer à la
hauteur de

liver ['lɪvə(r)] n foie m

lizard ['lɪzəd] n lézard m

load [ləʊd] **1** n (object carried,
burden) charge f; (freight)
chargement m; Fam a l. **of, loads**
of (people, money) un tas de **2**
vt (truck, gun) charger (with de)
• **loaded** adj (gun) chargé; Fam
(rich) plein aux as

loaf [ləʊf] (pl **loaves**) n pain m

loan [ləʊn] n (money lent) prêt m;
(money borrowed) emprunt m; on
l. **from** prêté par

loathe [ləʊð] vt détester (doing
faire)

lobby ['lɒbɪ] **1** (pl -ies) n (of hotel)
hall m; (of theatre) foyer m **2** (pt &
pp -ied) vt faire pression sur

lobster ['lɒbstə(r)] n homard m

local ['ləʊkəl] **1** adj local; (regional)
régional; (of the neighbourhood)
du quartier **2** n Br Fam (pub)
bistrot m du coin; the **locals**
(people) les gens mpl du coin •
locally adv dans le quartier

locate [ləʊ'keɪt] vt (find) repérer;
(pain, noise, leak) localiser;
(situate) situer; to be located in
Paris être situé à Paris • **location**
n (site) emplacement m; on l.
(shoot a film) en extérieur

lock [lɒk] **1** n (on door, chest)
serrure f **2** vti fermer à clé •
locker n (in school) casier m; (for
luggage) casier m de consigne
automatique; (for clothes) vestiaire
m (métallique); Am Sport l. **room**
vestiaire m • **locksmith** n serrurier
m

►**lock away** vt sep (prisoner)
enfermer; (jewels) mettre sous clé

►**lock in** vt sep (person) enfermer;
to l. **sb in sth** enfermer qn dans
qch

►**lock out** vt sep (person) enfermer
dehors

►**lock up** vt sep (house, car) fermer
à clé; (prisoner) enfermer; (jewels)
mettre sous clé

lodge [lɒdʒ] *n (house)* pavillon *m*; *(of porter)* loge *f* • **lodger** *n (room and meals)* pensionnaire *mf*; *(room only)* locataire *mf*

loft [lɒft] *n* grenier *m*

log [lɒg] **1** *n (tree trunk)* tronc *m* d'arbre; *(for fire)* bûche *f*; **l. cabin** hutte *f* en rondin; **l. fire** feu *m* de bois **2** *vi Comptr* **to l. in/out** entrer/sortir

logical ['lɒdʒɪkəl] *adj* logique • **logically** *adv* logiquement

logo ['ləʊgəʊ] *(pl -os)* *n* logo *m*

loiter ['lɔɪtə(r)] *vi* traîner

lollipop ['lɒlɪpɒp] *n* sucette *f*; *Br* **l. man/lady** = contractuel(elle) qui aide les écoliers à traverser la rue • **lolly** *(pl -ies)* *n Fam (lollipop)* sucette *f*; **(ice) l.** glace *f* à l'eau

London ['lʌndən] **1** *n* Londres *m* ou *f* **2** *adj* londonien, -enne

lone [ləʊn] *adj* solitaire • **lonely** **(-ier, -iest)** *adj (road, house, life)* solitaire; *(person)* seul

long[1] [lɒŋ] **1** (**-er, -est**) *adj* long *(f* longue); **to be 10 metres l.** avoir 10 mètres de long; **to be six weeks l.** durer six semaines; **how l. is...?** quelle est la longueur de...?; *(time)* quelle est la durée de...?; **a l. time** longtemps; **l. jump** *(sport)* saut *m* en longueur **2** *adv (a long time)* longtemps; **has he been here l.?** il y a longtemps qu'il est ici?; **how l.?** *(in time)* combien de temps?; **not l.** peu de temps; **before l.** sous peu; **no longer** ne... plus; **a bit longer** *(wait)* encore un peu; **I won't be l.** je n'en ai pas pour longtemps; **don't be l.** dépêche-toi; **all summer/winter l.** tout l'été/l'hiver; **l. live the queen!** vive la reine!; **as l. as, so l. as** *(provided that)* pourvu que (+ *subjunctive*);

as l. as I live tant que je vivrai • **long-distance** *adj (race)* de fond; *(phone call)* interurbain • **long-haired** *adj* aux cheveux longs • **long-life** *adj (battery)* longue durée *inv*; *(milk)* longue conservation *inv* • **longsighted** *adj (person)* presbyte • **long-term** *adj* à long terme • **long-winded** *adj (speech, speaker)* verbeux, -euse

long[2] [lɒŋ] *vi* **to l. for sth** avoir très envie de qch; **to l. to do sth** avoir très envie de faire qch • **longing** *n* désir *m*

loo [luː] *(pl loos)* *n Br Fam* **the l.** le petit coin

look [lʊk] **1** *n (glance)* regard *m*; *(appearance)* air *m*, allure *f*; **to have a l. (at sth)** jeter un coup d'œil (à qch); **to have a l. (for sth)** chercher (qch); **to have a l. (a)round** regarder; *(walk)* faire un tour; **let me have a l.** fais voir **2** *vt* **to l. sb in the eye** regarder qn dans les yeux **3** *vi* regarder; **to l. tired/happy** *(seem)* avoir l'air fatigué/heureux; **to l. pretty/ugly** être joli/laid; **you l. like** *or* **as if** *or* **as though you're tired** tu as l'air fatigué; **to l. like an apple** avoir l'air d'une pomme; **you l. like my brother** tu ressembles à mon frère; **it looks like rain** on dirait qu'il va pleuvoir; **what does he l. like?** comment est-il?; **to l. well** *or* **good** *(of person)* avoir bonne mine; **you l. good in that hat** ce chapeau te va très bien; **that looks bad** *(action)* ça fait mauvais effet • **lookout** *n* **to be on the l. for sb/sth** guetter qn/qch

▶ **look after** *vt insep (take care of)* s'occuper de; *(keep safely)* garder **(for sb** pour qn); **to l. after**

oneself *(keep healthy)* faire bien attention à soi; *(manage, cope)* se débrouiller
▶**look around 1** *vt insep (town, shops)* faire un tour dans **2** *vi (have a look)* regarder; *(walk round)* faire un tour
▶**look at** *vt insep* regarder; *(consider)* considérer
▶**look away** *vi* détourner les yeux
▶**look back** *vi* regarder derrière soi; *(in time)* regarder en arrière
▶**look down** *vi* baisser les yeux; *(from a height)* regarder en bas; **to l. down on** *(consider scornfully)* regarder de haut
▶**look for** *vt insep (seek)* chercher
▶**look forward to** *vt insep (event)* attendre avec impatience; **to l. forward to doing sth** avoir hâte de faire qch
▶**look into** *vt insep (examine)* examiner; *(find out about)* se renseigner sur
▶**look on** *vi (watch)* regarder; **to l. on to** *(of window, house)* donner sur
▶**look out** *vi (be careful)* faire attention; **to l. out for sb/sth** *(seek)* chercher qn/qch; *(watch)* guetter qn/qch; **to l. out on to** *(of window, house)* donner sur
▶**look round 1** *vt insep (visit)* visiter **2** *vi (have a look)* regarder; *(walk round)* faire un tour; *(look back)* se retourner; **to l. round for sb/sth** *(seek)* chercher qn/qch
▶**look through** *vt insep (inspect)* passer en revue
▶**look up 1** *vt sep (word)* chercher; **to l. sb up** *(visit)* passer voir qn **2** *vi (of person)* lever les yeux; *(into the air or sky)* regarder en l'air; *(improve) (of situation)* s'améliorer; *Fig* **to l. up to sb** respecter qn

-looking ['lʊkɪŋ] *suff* **pleasant-/tired-l.** à l'air agréable/fatigué
loom [luːm] **1** *n (weaving machine)* métier *m* à tisser **2** *vi (of event)* paraître imminent
loony ['luːnɪ] *(pl* **-ies)** *n & adj Fam* dingue *(mf)*
loop [luːp] *n* boucle *f*
loose [luːs] **1** *(-er, -est) adj (screw, belt, knot)* desserré; *(tooth, stone)* qui bouge; *(page)* détaché; *(clothes)* flottant; *(hair)* dénoué; *(translation)* vague; *(articles for sale)* en vrac; *Br (cheese, tea)* au poids; **there's an animal/prisoner l.** *(having escaped)* il y a un animal échappé/un prisonnier évadé; **l. change** petite monnaie *f*; **to come l.** *(of knot, screw)* se desserrer; *(of page)* se détacher; *(of tooth)* se mettre à bouger **2** *n* **on the l.** *(prisoner)* en cavale; *(animal)* en liberté • **loosely** *adv (hang)* lâchement; *(hold, tie)* sans serrer; *(translate)* de façon approximative • **loosen** *vt (knot, belt)* desserrer; **to l. one's grip** relâcher son étreinte
loot [luːt] **1** *n* butin *m*; *Fam (money)* fric *m* **2** *vt* piller
lop-sided [lɒpˈsaɪdɪd] *adj (crooked)* de travers
lord [lɔːd] *n* seigneur *m*; *(British title)* lord *m*; **the L.** *(God)* le Seigneur; *Fam* **good L.!** bon sang!
lorry ['lɒrɪ] *(pl* **-ies)** *n Br* camion *m*; *(heavy)* poids *m* lourd; **l. driver** camionneur *m*; **(long-distance) l. driver** routier *m*
lose [luːz] *(pt & pp* **lost)** **1** *vt* perdre; **to l. one's life** trouver la mort *(in dans)*; **to l. one's way, to get lost** *(of person)* se perdre; *Fam* **get lost!** fous le camp! **2** *vi* perdre • **loser** *n (in contest)*

perdant, -e *mf*; *Fam (failure in life)* minable *mf* • **losing** *adj (number, team, horse)* perdant • **loss** [lɒs] *n* perte *f* • **lost** [lɒst] *adj* perdu; *Br* **l. property,** *Am* **l. and found** objets *mpl* trouvés

lot¹ [lɒt] *n (destiny)* sort *m*; *(batch)* lot *m*; **to draw lots** tirer au sort

lot² [lɒt] *n* **the l.** *(everything)* (le) tout; **the l. of you** vous tous; **a l. of, lots of** beaucoup de; **a l.** beaucoup; **quite a l.** pas mal (**of** de)

lotion ['ləʊʃən] *n* lotion *f*

lottery ['lɒtərɪ] (*pl* -**ies**) *n* loterie *f*; **l. ticket** billet *m* de loterie

loud [laʊd] **1** (-**er, -est**) *adj (voice, music)* fort; *(noise, cry)* grand; *(laugh)* gros (*f* grosse); *(gaudy)* voyant **2** *adv (shout)* fort; **out l.** tout haut • **loudly** *adv (speak, laugh, shout)* fort • **loudspeaker** *n* haut-parleur *m*; *(for speaking to crowd)* porte-voix *m inv*; *(of stereo system)* enceinte *f*

lounge [laʊndʒ] **1** *n (in house, hotel)* salon *m*; **airport l.** salle *f* d'aéroport **2** *vi (loll in armchair)* se prélasser; **to l. about** *(idle)* paresser

louse [laʊs] (*pl* **lice**) *n (insect)* pou *m*

lousy ['laʊzɪ] (-**ier, -iest**) *adj Fam (bad)* nul (*f* nulle); *(food, weather)* dégueulasse; **to feel l.** être mal fichu

lout [laʊt] *n* voyou *m*

love [lʌv] **1** *n* **(a)** *(feeling)* amour *m*; **in l.** amoureux, -euse (**with** de); **they're in l.** ils s'aiment; **give him/her my l.** embrasse-le/-la pour moi *ou* de ma part; **l. affair** liaison *f* **(b)** *(in tennis)* rien *m*; **15 l.** 15 à rien **2** *vt (person)* aimer; *(thing, activity)* adorer (**to do** *or* **doing** faire) • **lover** *n (man)*

amant *m*; *(woman)* maîtresse *f*; **a l. of music/art** un amateur de musique/d'art • **loving** *adj* affectueux, -euse

lovely ['lʌvlɪ] (-**ier, -iest**) *adj (idea, smell)* très bon (*f* bonne); *(pretty)* joli; *(charming)* charmant; *(kind)* gentil, -ille; **the weather's l., it's l.** il fait beau; **(it's) l. to see you!** je suis ravi de te voir!

low [ləʊ] **1** (-**er, -est**) *adj* bas (*f* basse); *(speed, income, intelligence)* faible; *(opinion, quality)* mauvais; **to feel l.** *(depressed)* être déprimé; **lower** inférieur **2** *adv* bas; **to turn (down) l.** mettre plus bas; **to run l.** *(of supplies)* s'épuiser • **low-cut** *adj* décolleté • **lower** *vt* baisser; **to l. sb/sth** *(by rope)* descendre qn/qch; *Fig* **to l. oneself** s'abaisser • **low-fat** *adj (milk)* écrémé; *(cheese)* allégé • **low-paid** *adj* mal payé

loyal ['lɔɪəl] *adj* loyal (**to** envers) • **loyalty** *n* loyauté *f*

L-plate ['elpleɪt] *n Br* = plaque apposée sur une voiture pour signaler que le conducteur est en conduite accompagnée

Ltd (*abbr* **Limited**) *Br Com* ≃ SARL

luck [lʌk] *n (chance)* chance *f*; *(good fortune)* (bonne) chance *f*, bonheur *m*; **to be in l.** avoir de la chance; **to be out of l.** ne pas avoir de chance; **to wish sb l.** souhaiter bonne chance à qn; **bad l.** malchance *f*; **tough l.!** pas de chance! • **lucky** (-**ier, -iest**) *adj (person)* chanceux, -euse; **to be l.** *(of person)* avoir de la chance; **it's l. that...** c'est une chance que... (+ *subjunctive*); **l. number** chiffre *m* porte-bonheur • **luckily** *adv* heureusement

luggage ['lʌgɪdʒ] *n* bagages *mpl*; **a piece of l.** un bagage; **hand l.** bagages *mpl* à main; **l. compartment** compartiment *m* à bagages

lukewarm ['luːkwɔːm] *adj (water, soup)* tiède

lull [lʌl] *n* arrêt *m*; *(in storm)* accalmie *f* ● **lullaby** ['lʌləbaɪ] *(pl -ies) n* berceuse *f*

lumber ['lʌmbə(r)] *vt Br Fam* **to l. sb with sth** coller qn/qch à qn

luminous ['luːmɪnəs] *adj (colour, paper, ink)* fluorescent; *(dial, clock)* lumineux, -euse

lump [lʌmp] *n* morceau *m*; *(in soup)* grumeau *m*; *(bump)* bosse *f*; *(swelling)* grosseur *f*; **l. sum** somme *f* forfaitaire ● **lumpy** (-ier, -iest) *adj (soup)* grumeleux, -euse; *(surface)* bosselé

lunatic ['luːnətɪk] *n* fou *m*, folle *f*

lunch [lʌntʃ] *n* déjeuner *m*; **to have l.** déjeuner; **l. break, l. hour, l. time** heure *f* du déjeuner ● **lunchbox** *n* = boîte dans laquelle on transporte son déjeuner ●

luncheon *n* déjeuner *m*; *Br* **l. voucher** Chèque-Restaurant *m*

lung [lʌŋ] *n* poumon *m*

lunge [lʌndʒ] *vi* **to l. at sb** se ruer sur qn

lurch [lɜːtʃ] **1** *n Fam* **to leave sb in the l.** laisser qn dans le pétrin **2** *vi (of person)* tituber

lure [lʊə(r)] *vt* attirer (par la ruse) (**into** dans)

lurid ['lʊərɪd] *adj (story, description)* cru; *(gaudy)* voyant

lurk [lɜːk] *vi (hide)* être tapi (**in** dans); *(prowl)* rôder

lust [lʌst] *n (for person)* désir *m*; *(for object)* convoitise *f* (**for** de); *(for power, knowledge)* soif *f* (**for** de)

Luxembourg ['lʌksəmbɜːg] *n* le Luxembourg

luxury ['lʌkʃərɪ] **1** *n* luxe *m* **2** *adj (goods, car, home)* de luxe ● **luxurious** [lʌg'ʒʊərɪəs] *adj* luxueux, -euse

lyrics ['lɪrɪks] *npl (of song)* paroles *fpl*

Mm

M, m[1] [em] *n (letter)* M, m *m inv*
m[2] (**a**) (*abbr* **metre**) mètre *m* (**b**)
(*abbr* **mile**) mile *m*
MA (*abbr* **Master of Arts**) *n Univ*
to have an MA in French ≃
avoir une maîtrise de français
mac [mæk] *n Br Fam (raincoat)*
imper *m*
machine [məˈʃiːn] *n (apparatus,
car, system)* machine *f*; **m. gun**
mitrailleuse *f* • **machinery** *n
(machines)* machines *fpl*; *(works)*
mécanisme *m*
mackerel [ˈmækrəl] *n* maquereau
m
mad [mæd] (**madder, maddest**)
adj fou (*f* folle); **to be m. at sb** être
furieux, -euse contre qn • **madly**
adv (insanely, desperately) comme
un fou/une folle • **madman** (*pl*
-men) *n* fou *m* • **madness** *n*
folie *f*
madam [ˈmædəm] *n* **yes, m.** oui,
madame
made [meɪd] *pt & pp of* **make**
magazine [mægəˈziːn] *n*
magazine *m*
magic [ˈmædʒɪk] **1** *adj* magique **2**
n magie *f* • **magician** [məˈdʒɪʃən]
n magicien, -enne *mf*
magistrate [ˈmædʒɪstreɪt] *n*
magistrat *m*
magnet [ˈmægnɪt] *n* aimant
m • **magnetic** [-ˈnetɪk] *adj*
magnétique
magnificent [mægˈnɪfɪsənt] *adj*
magnifique
magnify [ˈmægnɪfaɪ] (*pt &*

pp **-ied**) *vt (image)* grossir;
magnifying glass loupe *f*
maid [meɪd] *n (servant)* bonne *f* •
maiden *adj* **m. name** nom *m* de
jeune fille
mail [meɪl] **1** *n (system)* poste *f*;
(letters) courrier *m*; *(e-mails)* e-mails
mpl, courrier *m* électronique **2** *adj
(bag, train)* postal; **m. order** vente
f par correspondance **3** *vt* poster •
mailbox *n Am & Comptr* boîte *f*
aux lettres
main [meɪn] **1** *adj* principal; **m.
course** plat *m* de résistance;
m. road grande route *f* **2** *n* **the
mains** *(electricity)* le secteur •
mainland *n* continent *m* • **mainly**
adv principalement; **they were
m. Spanish** la plupart étaient
espagnols
maintain [meɪnˈteɪn] *vt
(continue)* maintenir; *(machine,
road)* entretenir • **maintenance**
[ˈmeɪntənəns] *n (of vehicle, road)*
entretien *m*; *(alimony)* pension *f*
alimentaire
majesty [ˈmædʒəstɪ] *n* **Your M.**
Votre Majesté
major [ˈmeɪdʒə(r)] **1** *adj (main,
great) & Mus* majeur **2** *n* (**a**)
(officer) commandant *m* (**b**) *Am
Univ (subject)* dominante *f* **3** *vi Am
Univ* **to m. in** se spécialiser en
majority [məˈdʒɒrətɪ] (*pl* **-ies**)
n majorité *f* (**of** de); **the m. of
people** la plupart des gens
make [meɪk] **1** (*pt & pp* **made**)
vt faire; *(tool, vehicle)* fabriquer;

(money) gagner; **to m. a decision** prendre une décision; **to m. sb happy/sad** rendre qn heureux/ triste; **to m. sb do sth** faire faire qch à qn; *Fam* **to m. it** *(succeed)* réussir; **sorry I can't m. it to the meeting** désolé, je ne pourrai pas assister à la réunion; **what time do you m. it?** quelle heure avez-vous?; **what do you m. of it?** qu'en penses-tu?; **to be made of wood** être en bois; **made in France** fabriqué en France **2** *vi* **to m. do** *(manage)* se débrouiller **(with** avec); **to m. do with sb/ sth** *(be satisfied with)* se contenter de qn/qch; **to m. believe that one is...** faire semblant d'être... **3** *n (brand)* marque *f* • **make-up** *n (for face)* maquillage *m; (of team, group)* constitution *f*

►**make out** *vt sep (see, hear)* distinguer; *(understand)* comprendre; *(decipher)* déchiffrer; *(cheque, list)* faire; *Fam* **to m. out that...** *(claim)* prétendre que...

►**make up 1** *vt sep (story)* inventer; *(put together) (list, collection, bed)* faire; *(form)* former, composer; *(quantity)* compléter; *(quarrel)* régler **2** *vi (of friends)* se réconcilier; **to m. up for** *(loss, damage, fault)* compenser; *(lost time, mistake)* rattraper

malaria [məˈleərɪə] *n Med* paludisme *m*

male [meɪl] **1** *adj (child, animal)* mâle; *(sex)* masculin; **m. nurse** infirmier *m* **2** *n (person)* homme *m; (animal)* mâle *m*

malicious [məˈlɪʃəs] *adj* malveillant

mall [mɔːl] *n Am* **(shopping) m.** centre *m* commercial

malt [mɔːlt] *n* malt *m*

Malta [ˈmɔːltə] *n* Malte *f*

mammal [ˈmæməl] *n* mammifère *m*

man [mæn] *(pl* **men)** *n (adult male)* homme *m;* **M.** l'homme *m*

manage [ˈmænɪdʒ] **1** *vt (company, project)* diriger; *(shop, hotel)* être le gérant de; *(economy, money, time, situation)* gérer; **to m. to do sth** réussir *ou* arriver à faire qch **2** *vi (succeed)* y arriver; *(make do)* se débrouiller **(with** avec**)**; **to m. without sb/sth** se passer de qn/ qch; **managing director** directeur *m* général, directrice *f* générale • **management** *n (running, managers)* direction *f; (of property, economy)* gestion *f* • **manager** *n (of company)* directeur, -trice *mf; (of shop, café)* gérant, -e *mf; (of performer)* manager *m*

mane [meɪn] *n* crinière *f*

maneuver [məˈnuːvər] *n & vti Am* = **manoeuvre**

mangle [ˈmæŋgəl] *vt (body)* mutiler

mango [ˈmæŋgəʊ] *(pl* **-oes** *or* **-os)** *n* mangue *f*

maniac [ˈmeɪnɪæk] *n* fou *m*, folle *f*

manicure [ˈmænɪkjʊə(r)] *n* manucure *f*

manifesto [mænɪˈfestəʊ] *(pl* **-os** *or* **-oes)** *n Pol* manifeste *m*

manipulate [məˈnɪpjʊleɪt] *vt* manipuler

mankind [mænˈkaɪnd] *n* l'humanité *f*

man-made [ˈmænmeɪd] *adj (lake)* artificiel, -elle; *(fibre)* synthétique

manner [ˈmænə(r)] *n (way)* manière *f; (behaviour)* comportement *m;* **manners** *(social habits)* manières *fpl;* **in this m.** *(like this)* de cette manière; **to have good/ bad manners** être bien/mal élevé

mannerism ['mænərɪzəm] *n Pej* tic *m*

manoeuvre [mə'nuːvə(r)] *(Am* **maneuver)** 1 *n* manœuvre *f* 2 *vti* manœuvrer

mansion ['mænʃən] *n (in town)* hôtel *m* particulier; *(in country)* manoir *m*

mantelpiece ['mæntəlpiːs] *n* dessus *m* de cheminée; **on the m.** sur la cheminée

manual ['mænjʊəl] 1 *adj (work, worker)* manuel, -elle 2 *n (book)* manuel *m*

manufacture [mænjʊ'fæktʃə(r)] *vt* fabriquer; *(cars)* construire

manure [mə'njʊə(r)] *n* fumier *m*

manuscript ['mænjʊskrɪpt] *n* manuscrit *m*

many ['menɪ] 1 *adj* beaucoup de; **(a good** *or* **great) m. of** un (très) grand nombre de; **how m.?** combien (de)?; **too m.** trop de 2 *pron* beaucoup; **too m.** trop; **m. of them** beaucoup d'entre eux; **as m. as fifty** *(up to)* jusqu'à cinquante

map [mæp] *n* carte *f*; *(plan of town, underground)* plan *m*

maple ['meɪpəl] *n (tree, wood)* érable *m*; **m. syrup** sirop *m* d'érable

marathon ['mærəθən] *n* marathon *m*

marble ['mɑːbəl] *n (substance)* marbre *m*; *(toy)* bille *f*

March [mɑːtʃ] *n* mars *m*

march [mɑːtʃ] 1 *n* marche *f* 2 *vi* *(of soldiers, demonstrators)* défiler; *(walk in step)* marcher au pas

margarine [mɑːdʒə'riːn] *n* margarine *f*

margin ['mɑːdʒɪn] *n (on page)* marge *f*; **to win by a narrow m.** gagner de justesse

marijuana [mærɪ'wɑːnə] *n* marijuana *f*

marine [mə'riːn] 1 *adj (life, flora)* marin 2 *n (soldier)* fusilier *m* marin; *Am* marine *m*

marital ['mærɪtəl] *adj* **m. status** situation *f* de famille

mark [mɑːk] 1 *n (symbol)* marque *f*; *(stain, trace)* tache *f*, marque *f*; *(token, sign)* signe *m*; *(in test, exam)* note *f* 2 *vt* marquer; *(exam)* noter; **to m. sb out** distinguer qn ● **marked** *adj (noticeable)* marqué

market ['mɑːkɪt] *n* marché *m*; **on the black m.** au marché noir ● **marketing** *n* marketing *m*

marmalade ['mɑːməleɪd] *n* confiture *f* d'oranges

marooned [mə'ruːnd] *adj* abandonné

marriage ['mærɪdʒ] *n* mariage *m*; **m. certificate** extrait *m* d'acte de mariage

marry ['mærɪ] 1 *(pt & pp* **-ied)** *vt* épouser, se marier avec; *(of priest)* marier 2 *vi* se marier ● **married** *adj* marié; **m. life** vie *f* maritale; **m. name** nom *m* de femme mariée; **to get m.** se marier

marsh [mɑːʃ] *n* marais *m*, marécage *m*

martyr ['mɑːtə(r)] *n* martyr, -e *mf*

marvellous ['mɑːvələs] *(Am* **marvelous)** *adj* merveilleux, -euse

marzipan ['mɑːzɪpæn] *n* pâte *f* d'amandes

mascara [mæ'skɑːrə] *n* mascara *m*

masculine ['mæskjʊlɪn] *adj* masculin

mash [mæʃ] 1 *n Br (potatoes)* purée *f* (de pommes de terre) 2 *vt* **to m. (up)** *(vegetables)* écraser

(en purée); **mashed potatoes**
purée *f* de pommes de terre
mask [mɑːsk] *n* masque *m*
mass¹ [mæs] **1** *n* masse *f*; **a m.**
of *(many)* une multitude de;
the masses le peuple **2** *adj*
(demonstration, culture) de
masse; *(protests)* en masse;
(unemployment, destruction)
massif, -ive; **m. media** mass media
mpl; **m. production** production
f en série ● **mass-produce** *vt*
fabriquer en série
mass² [mæs] *n Rel* messe *f*
massacre ['mæsəkə(r)] **1** *n*
massacre *m* **2** *vt* massacrer
massage ['mæsɑːʒ] **1** *n* massage
m **2** *vt* masser
massive ['mæsɪv] *adj (increase,
dose, vote)* massif, -ive; *(amount,
building)* énorme
mast [mɑːst] *n (of ship)* mât *m*;
(for TV, radio) pylône *m*
master ['mɑːstə(r)] **1** *n* maître
m; *Br (teacher)* professeur *m*; **M.
of Arts/Science** *(qualification)*
≃ maîtrise *f* ès lettres/sciences;
(person) ≃ maître *mf* ès lettres/
sciences; **m. copy** original *m*;
m. plan plan *m* d'action **2** *vt*
maîtriser; *(subject, situation)*
dominer ● **masterpiece** *n* chef-
d'œuvre *m*
mat [mæt] *n* tapis *m*; *(at door)*
paillasson *m*; **(table) m.** *(for
plates)* set *m* de table; *(for dishes)*
dessous-de-plat *m inv*
match¹ [mætʃ] *n (for lighting fire,
cigarette)* allumette *f* ● **matchbox**
n boîte *f* d'allumettes ● **matchstick**
n allumette *f*
match² [mætʃ] **1** *n* **(a)** *(equal)* égal,
-e *mf*; *(marriage)* mariage *m*; **to
be a good m.** *(of colours, people)*
aller bien ensemble **(b)** *(in sport)*
match *m* **2** *vt (of clothes, colour)*

être assorti, -e à; *(coordinate)*
assortir; *(equal)* égaler; **to m. up**
(colours, clothes, plates) assortir **3**
vi (of colours, clothes) être assortis,
-es ● **matching** *adj* assorti
mate [meɪt] **1** *n (of animal) (male)*
mâle *m*; *(female)* femelle *f*; *Br Fam
(friend)* copain *m*, copine *f* **2** *vi (of
animals)* s'accoupler **(with** avec)
material [mə'tɪərɪəl] *n (substance)*
matière *f*; *(cloth)* tissu *m*; *(for
book)* matériaux *mpl*; **material(s)**
(equipment) matériel *m*
maternal [mə'tɜːnəl] *adj*
maternel, -elle
maternity [mə'tɜːnətɪ] *n* **m.
dress** robe *f* de grossesse; **m.
hospital, m. unit** maternité *f*; **m.
leave** congé *m* de maternité
mathematics [mæθə'mætɪks]
n (subject) mathématiques *fpl* ●
maths *(Am* **math)** *n Fam* maths
fpl
matinée ['mætɪneɪ] *n (of play,
film)* matinée *f*
matt [mæt] *adj (paint, paper)* mat
matter ['mætə(r)] **1** *n (substance)*
matière *f*; *(issue, affair)* question
f; **as a m. of fact** en fait; **no m.
what she does** quoi qu'elle
fasse; **no m. who you are** qui
que vous soyez; **what's the
m.?** qu'est-ce qu'il y a?; **there's
something the m. with my leg**
j'ai quelque chose à la jambe **2** *vi
(be important)* importer **(to** à); **it
doesn't m. if/when/who...** peu
importe si/quand/qui...; **it doesn't
m.** ça ne fait rien
mattress ['mætrəs] *n* matelas *m*
mature [mə'tʃʊə(r)] *adj (person)*
mûr; *(cheese)* fort
maximum ['mæksɪməm] **1**
(pl **-ima** [-ɪmə] *or* **-imums)** *n*
maximum *m* **2** *adj* maximal
May [meɪ] *n* mai *m*

may [meɪ] (*pt* **might** [maɪt])

May *et* **might** peuvent s'utiliser indifféremment ou presque dans les expressions de la catégorie **(a)**.

v aux **(a)** *(expressing possibility)* **he m. come** il se peut qu'il vienne; **I m.** *or* **might be wrong** je me trompe peut-être; **he m.** *or* **might have lost it** il se peut qu'il l'ait perdu; **we m.** *or* **might as well go** autant y aller; **she's afraid I m.** *or* **might get lost** elle a peur que je ne me perde **(b)** *Formal (for asking permission)* **m. I stay?** puis-je rester?; **you m. go** tu peux partir **(c)** *Formal (expressing wish)* **m. you be happy** sois heureux; **m. the best man win!** que le meilleur gagne!

maybe ['meɪbiː] *adv* peut-être
mayhem ['meɪhem] *n (chaos)* pagaille *f*
mayonnaise [meɪə'neɪz] *n* mayonnaise *f*
mayor [meə(r)] *n* maire *m*
maze [meɪz] *n* labyrinthe *m*
me [miː] *pron* me, m'; *(after prep, 'than', 'it is')* moi; **(to) me** *(indirect)* me, m'; **he helps me** il m'aide; **he gave it to me** il me l'a donné
meadow ['medəʊ] *n* pré *m*, prairie *f*
meagre ['miːgə(r)] *(Am* **meager)** *adj* maigre
meal [miːl] *n (food)* repas *m*
mean¹ [miːn] **(-er, -est)** *adj (miserly)* avare; *(nasty)* méchant
mean² [miːn] *(pt & pp* **meant)** *vt (of word, event)* signifier; *(of person)* vouloir dire; *(result in)* entraîner; *(represent)* représenter; **to m. to do sth** avoir l'intention de faire qch; **it means a lot to me** c'est très important pour moi;

I didn't m. to! je ne l'ai pas fait exprès! • **meaning** *n* sens *m*, signification *f* • **meaningless** *adj* vide de sens
means [miːnz] *n (method)* moyen *m* **(to do** *or* **of doing** de faire**); by m. of...** au moyen de...; **by no m.** nullement
meant [ment] *pt & pp of* **mean²**
meanwhile ['miːnwaɪl] *adv (at the same time)* pendant ce temps; *(between two events)* entre-temps
measles ['miːzəlz] *n Med* rougeole *f*
measure ['meʒə(r)] **1** *vt* mesurer; **to m. sth out** *(ingredient)* mesurer qch **2** *vi* **to m. up to** *(task)* être à la hauteur de • **measurement** *n* mesure *f*; **hip/waist measurement(s)** tour *m* de hanches/de taille
meat [miːt] *n* viande *f*
mechanic [mɪ'kænɪk] *n* mécanicien, -enne *mf* • **mechanical** *adj* mécanique • **mechanics** *n (science)* mécanique *f*; **the m.** *(working parts)* le mécanisme
mechanism ['mekənɪzəm] *n* mécanisme *m*
medal ['medəl] *n* médaille *f*
meddle ['medəl] *vi (interfere)* se mêler **(in** de**);** *(tamper)* toucher **(with** à**)**
media ['miːdɪə] *npl* **the m.** les médias *mpl*
medical ['medɪkəl] **1** *adj* médical; *(school, studies)* de médecine; *(student)* en médecine; **m. insurance** assurance *f* maladie **2** *n (in school, army)* visite *f* médicale; *(private)* examen *m* médical
medication [medɪ'keɪʃən] *n* médicaments *mpl*; **to be on m.** être sous traitement
medicine ['medəsən] *n (substance)*

médicament m; *(science)* médecine f; **m. cabinet, m. chest** (armoire f à) pharmacie f

medieval [medɪ'iːvəl] *adj* médiéval

mediocre [miːdɪ'əʊkə(r)] *adj* médiocre

meditate ['medɪteɪt] *vi* méditer (**on** sur) • **meditation** [-'teɪʃən] *n* méditation f

Mediterranean [medɪtə'reɪnɪən] *n* **the M.** la Méditerranée

medium ['miːdɪəm] *adj (average, middle)* moyen, -enne • **medium-sized** *adj* de taille moyenne

meet [miːt] **1** *vt* (*pt & pp* **met**) *(person, team)* rencontrer; *(by arrangement)* retrouver; *(pass in street, road)* croiser; *(debt, enemy, danger)* faire face à; *(need)* combler; **have you met my husband?** connaissez-vous mon mari? **2** *vi (of people, teams)* se rencontrer; *(by arrangement)* se retrouver; *(of club, society)* se réunir; *(of rivers)* se rejoindre • **meeting** *n (for business)* réunion f; *(large)* assemblée f; *(by accident)* rencontre f; *(by arrangement)* rendez-vous m *inv*; **to be in a m.** être en réunion

▸**meet up** *vi (by arrangement)* se retrouver; **to m. up with sb** retrouver qn

▸**meet with** *vt insep (problem, refusal)* se heurter à; *(accident)* avoir; *Am* **to m. with sb** rencontrer qn; *(as arranged)* retrouver qn

megaphone ['megəfəʊn] *n* porte-voix m *inv*

melodramatic [melədrə'mætɪk] *adj* mélodramatique

melody ['melədɪ] *(pl* -ies) *n* mélodie f

melon ['melən] *n* melon m

melt [melt] **1** *vt* faire fondre **2** *vi* fondre

member ['membə(r)] *n* membre m; *Br* **M. of Parliament,** *Am* **M. of Congress** ≃ député, -e *mf* • **membership** *n (state)* adhésion f (**of** à); *(members)* membres *mpl*; **m. card** carte f de membre; **m. fee** cotisation f

memento [mə'mentəʊ] *(pl* -**os** or -**oes**) *n* souvenir m

memo ['meməʊ] *(pl* -**os**) *n* note f de service

memoirs ['memwɑːz] *npl (autobiography)* mémoires *mpl*

memorial [mə'mɔːrɪəl] **1** *adj* **m. service** commémoration f **2** *n* mémorial m

memory ['memərɪ] *(pl* -**ies**) *n (faculty) & Comptr* mémoire f; *(recollection)* souvenir m; **in m. of...** à la mémoire de... • **memorable** *adj* mémorable • **memorize** *vt* mémoriser

men [men] *pl of* **man**; **the men's room** les toilettes *fpl* pour hommes

menace ['menɪs] *n (danger)* danger m; *(threat)* menace f

mend [mend] *vt (repair)* réparer; *(clothes)* raccommoder

menial ['miːnɪəl] *adj (work)* subalterne

meningitis [menɪn'dʒaɪtɪs] *n Med* méningite f

mental ['mentəl] *adj* mental; **m. block** blocage m • **mentally** *adv* mentalement; **she's m. ill** c'est une malade mentale

mention ['menʃən] **1** *n* mention f **2** *vt* mentionner; **not to m....** sans parler de...; **don't m. it!** il n'y a pas de quoi!

menu ['menjuː] *n (in restaurant) (for set meal)* menu m; *(list)* carte f

MEP [emiː'piː] (*abbr* **Member of the European Parliament**) *n* député, -e *mf* du Parlement européen

merchandise ['mɜːtʃəndaɪz] *n* marchandises *fpl*

mercy ['mɜːsɪ] (*pl* **-ies**) *n* pitié *f*; **at the m. of** à la merci de

mere [mɪə(r)] *adj* simple; **she's a m. child** ce n'est qu'une enfant ● **merely** *adv* simplement

merge [mɜːdʒ] **1** *vt* (*companies*) fusionner **2** *vi* (*blend*) se mêler (**with** à); (*of roads*) se rejoindre; (*of companies, banks*) fusionner

merit ['merɪt] **1** *n* mérite *m* **2** *vt* mériter

merry ['merɪ] (**-ier, -iest**) *adj* (*happy, drunk*) gai ● **merry-go-round** *n* manège *m*

mesh [meʃ] *n* (*of net, sieve*) mailles *fpl*

mess [mes] **1** *n* (*confusion*) désordre *m*; (*muddle*) gâchis *m*; (*dirt*) saletés *fpl*; **in a m.** en désordre; (*in trouble*) dans le pétrin; **to make a m. of sth** (*do badly, get dirty*) saloper qch **2** *vt Br Fam* **to m. sb about** (*bother, treat badly*) embêter qn; **to m. sth up** (*plans*) ficher qch en l'air; (*hair, room, papers*) mettre qch en désordre **3** *vi* **to m. about** *or* **around** (*waste time*) traîner; (*play the fool*) faire l'imbécile; **to m. about** *or* **around with sth** (*fiddle with*) tripoter qch ● **messy** (**-ier, -iest**) *adj* (*untidy*) en désordre; (*dirty*) sale; (*job*) salissant

message ['mesɪdʒ] *n* message *m* ● **messenger** [-ɪndʒə(r)] *n* messager, -ère *mf*; (*in office, hotel*) coursier, -ère *mf*

met [met] *pt & pp of* **meet**

metal ['metəl] *n* métal *m* ●

metallic [mɪ'tælɪk] *adj* (*sound*) métallique; (*paint*) métallisé

metaphor ['metəfə(r)] *n* métaphore *f*

meter ['miːtə(r)] *n* (**a**) (*device*) compteur *m*; (**parking**) **m.** parcmètre *m* (**b**) *Am* = **metre**

method ['meθəd] *n* méthode *f* ● **methodical** [mɪ'θɒdɪkəl] *adj* méthodique

metre ['miːtə(r)] (*Am* **meter**) *n* mètre *m* ● **metric** ['metrɪk] *adj* métrique

metropolitan [metrə'pɒlɪtən] *adj* métropolitain

Mexico ['meksɪkəʊ] *n* le Mexique ● **Mexican 1** *adj* mexicain **2** *n* Mexicain, -e *mf*

miaow [miː'aʊ] **1** *exclam* miaou! **2** *vi* miauler

mice [maɪs] *pl of* **mouse**

mickey ['mɪkɪ] *n Br Fam* **to take the m. out of sb** charrier qn

microphone ['maɪkrəfəʊn] *n* micro *m*

microscope ['maɪkrəskəʊp] *n* microscope *m*

microwave ['maɪkrəʊweɪv] *n* **m.** (**oven**) (four *m* à) micro-ondes *m inv*

mid [mɪd] *adj* (**in**) **m. June** (à) la mi-juin; **in m. air** en plein ciel; **to be in one's m.-twenties** avoir environ vingt-cinq ans

midday [mɪd'deɪ] **1** *n* **at m.** à midi **2** *adj* (*sun, meal*) de midi

middle ['mɪdəl] **1** *n* milieu *m*; *Fam* (*waist*) taille *f*; (**right**) **in the m. of sth** au (beau) milieu de qch **2** *adj* (*central*) du milieu; **the M. Ages** le Moyen Âge; **the M. East** le Moyen-Orient; **the m. class(es)** les classes moyennes; **m. name** deuxième prénom *m* ● **middle-aged** *adj* d'âge mûr ● **middle-class** *adj* bourgeois

midge [mɪdʒ] *n* moucheron *m*

midget ['mɪdʒɪt] *n (small person)* nain, -e *mf*

midnight ['mɪdnaɪt] *n* minuit *m*

midst [mɪdst] *n* **in the m. of** *(middle)* au milieu de

midweek [mɪd'wiːk] *adv* en milieu de semaine

midwife ['mɪdwaɪf] *(pl* **-wives)** *n* sage-femme *f*

might [maɪt] *v aux see* **may**

La forme **mightn't** s'écrit **might not** dans un style plus soutenu.

mighty ['maɪtɪ] **(-ier, -iest) 1** *adj* puissant; *Fam (very great)* sacré **2** *adv Am Fam (very)* rudement

migraine ['miːgreɪn, 'maɪgreɪn] *n* migraine *f*

migrate [maɪ'greɪt] *vi (of people)* émigrer; *(of birds)* migrer ● **migrant** ['maɪgrənt] *n* immigré, -e *mf*

mike [maɪk] *(abbr* **microphone)** *n Fam* micro *m*

mild [maɪld] **(-er, -est)** *adj* *(weather, cheese, soap, person)* doux *(f* douce); *(curry)* peu épicé

mile [maɪl] *n* mile *m*; **he lives miles away** il habite très loin d'ici ● **mileometer** *n Br* ≃ compteur *m* kilométrique ● **milestone** *n (in history, career)* étape *f* importante

military ['mɪlɪtərɪ] **1** *adj* militaire **2** *n* **the m.** les militaires *mpl*

milk [mɪlk] **1** *n* lait *m*; **m. chocolate** chocolat *m* au lait; **m. shake** milk-shake *m* **2** *vt (cow)* traire; *Fig (exploit)* exploiter

mill [mɪl] *n (for flour)* moulin *m*; *(textile factory)* filature *f*

millennium [mɪ'lenɪəm] *(pl* **-nia** [-nɪə]) *n* millénaire *m*

millimetre ['mɪlɪmiːtə(r)] *(Am* **millimeter)** *n* millimètre *m*

million ['mɪljən] *n* million *m*; **a m. men** un million d'hommes; **two m.** deux millions ● **millionaire** *n* millionnaire *mf*

mime [maɪm] **1** *n (art)* mime *m* **2** *vti* mimer; *(of singer)* chanter en play-back

mimic ['mɪmɪk] *(pt & pp* **-ck-)** *vt* imiter

mince [mɪns] **1** *n (meat)* viande *f* hachée; **m. pie** *(containing fruit)* = tartelette fourrée aux fruits secs et aux épices **2** *vt* hacher ● **mincemeat** *n (dried fruit)* = mélange de fruits secs et d'épices utilisé en pâtisserie

mind[1] [maɪnd] *n* esprit *m*; *(sanity)* raison *f*; **to change one's m.** changer d'avis; **to speak one's m.** dire ce que l'on pense; *Br* **to be in two minds** *(undecided)* hésiter; **to bear** *or* **keep sth in m.** garder qch à l'esprit; **to have sb/sth in m.** avoir qn/qch en vue; **to make up one's m.** se décider; *Fam* **to be out of one's m.** avoir perdu la tête; **it's on my m.** cela me préoccupe; *Br* **to have a good m. to do sth** avoir bien envie de faire qch

mind[2] [maɪnd] **1** *vt Br (pay attention to)* faire attention à; *(look after)* garder; *Br* **m. you don't fall** fais attention à ne pas tomber; **I don't m. the cold/noise** le froid/bruit ne me gêne pas; **if you don't m. my asking…** si je peux me permettre…; **never m. the car** peu importe la voiture; *Br* **m. you…** remarquez…; **m. your own business!** occupe-toi de tes affaires! **2** *vi* **I don't m.** ça m'est égal; **do you m. if I smoke?** ça vous gêne si je fume?; **never m.!** ça ne fait rien!, tant pis!; *Br* **m. (out)!** *(watch out)* attention!

mine¹ [maɪn] *possessive pron* le mien, la mienne, *pl* les mien(ne)s; **this hat is m.** ce chapeau est à moi *ou* est le mien; **a friend of m.** un ami à moi, un de mes amis

mine² [maɪn] **1** *n* (**a**) *(for coal, gold)* & *Fig* mine *f* (**b**) *(explosive)* mine *f* **2** *vt (coal, gold)* extraire ● **mining** *n* exploitation *f* minière

mineral ['mɪnərəl] *adj* & *n* minéral *(m)*; **m. water** eau *f* minérale

mingle ['mɪŋgəl] *vi (of things)* se mêler (**with** à); *(of people)* parler un peu à tout le monde

miniature ['mɪnɪtʃə(r)] *adj (train, model)* miniature *inv*

minicab ['mɪnɪkæb] *n Br* radio-taxi *m*

minimum ['mɪnɪməm] **1** *(pl* **-ima** [-ɪma] *or* **-imums)** *n* minimum *m* **2** *adj* minimal; **m. wage** salaire *m* minimum

miniskirt ['mɪnɪskɜːt] *n* minijupe *f*

minister ['mɪnɪstə(r)] *n Br (politician)* ministre *m*; *(of religion)* pasteur *m* ● **ministry** *(pl* **-ies)** *n Br Pol* ministère *m*

minor ['maɪnə(r)] **1** *adj (unimportant)* & *Mus* mineur; *(road)* secondaire **2** *n (in age)* mineur, -e *mf*

minority [maɪ'nɒrətɪ] *(pl* **-ies)** *n* minorité *f*; **to be in the** *or* **a m.** être minoritaire

mint [mɪnt] *n (herb)* menthe *f*; *(sweet)* bonbon *m* à la menthe

minus ['maɪnəs] **1** *adj* & *n* **m.** **(sign)** (signe *m*) moins *m* **2** *prep (with numbers)* moins; *Fam (without)* sans; **it's m. 10** **(degrees)** il fait moins 10

minute¹ ['mɪnɪt] *n (of time)* minute *f*; **this (very) m.** *(now)* tout de suite; **any m. (now)** d'une minute à l'autre ● **minutes** *npl (of meeting)* procès-verbal *m*

minute² [maɪ'njuːt] *adj (tiny)* minuscule

miracle ['mɪrəkəl] *n* miracle *m* ● **miraculous** [mɪ'rækjʊləs] *adj* miraculeux, -euse

mirror ['mɪrə(r)] *n* miroir *m*, glace *f*; **rearview m.** rétroviseur *m*

misbehave [mɪsbɪ'heɪv] *vi* se conduire mal

miscarriage [mɪs'kærɪdʒ] *n Med* **to have a m.** faire une fausse couche

miscellaneous [mɪsə'leɪnɪəs] *adj* divers

mischief ['mɪstʃɪf] *n* espièglerie *f*; **to get into m.** faire des bêtises ● **mischievous** *adj (naughty)* espiègle; *(malicious)* méchant

miser ['maɪzə(r)] *n* avare *mf*

misery ['mɪzərɪ] *(pl* **-ies)** *n (suffering)* malheur *m*; *(sadness)* détresse *f* ● **miserable** *adj (wretched)* misérable; *(unhappy)* malheureux, -euse

misfit ['mɪsfɪt] *n* inadapté, -e *mf*

misfortune [mɪs'fɔːtʃuːn] *n* malheur *m*

misgivings [mɪs'gɪvɪŋz] *npl (doubts)* doutes *mpl* (**about** sur); *(fears)* craintes *fpl* (**about** à propos de)

misguided [mɪs'gaɪdɪd] *adj (attempt)* malencontreux, -euse

mishap ['mɪshæp] *n* incident *m*

misinterpret [mɪsɪn'tɜːprɪt] *vt* mal interpréter

mislay [mɪs'leɪ] *(pt* & *pp* **-laid)** *vt* égarer

mislead [mɪs'liːd] *(pt* & *pp* **-led)** *vt* tromper ● **misleading** *adj* trompeur, -euse

misplace [mɪs'pleɪs] *vt (lose)* égarer

misprint ['mɪsprɪnt] *n* faute *f* d'impression, coquille *f*

mispronounce [mɪsprə'nauns] *vt* mal prononcer

Miss [mɪs] *n* Mademoiselle *f*

miss [mɪs] **1** *n* coup *m* raté; **that was a near m.** on l'a échappé belle; *Fam* **I'll give it a m.** *(not go)* je n'y irai pas **2** *vt (train, target, opportunity)* manquer, rater; *(not see)* ne pas voir; *(feel the lack of)* regretter; **to m. sth out** *(accidentally)* oublier qch; *(intentionally)* omettre qch **3** *vi* manquer *ou* rater son coup; **to m. out on sth** rater qch ● **missing** *adj (absent)* absent; *(in war, after disaster)* disparu; *(object)* manquant; **there are two cups/students m.** il manque deux tasses/étudiants; **to go m.** disparaître

missile [*Br* 'mɪsaɪl, *Am* 'mɪsəl] *n (rocket)* missile *m*; *(object thrown)* projectile *m*

mission ['mɪʃən] *n* mission *f*

misspell [mɪs'spel] *(pt & pp* **-ed** *or* **-spelt)** *vt* mal écrire

mist [mɪst] brume *f*

mistake [mɪ'steɪk] **1** *n* erreur *f*, faute *f*; **to make a m.** faire une erreur; **by m.** par erreur **2** *(pt* **-took,** *pp* **-taken)** *vt (meaning, intention)* se tromper sur; **to m. sb for** prendre qn pour ● **mistaken** *adj (belief, impression)* erroné; **to be m.** *(of person)* se tromper *(**about** sur)*

mistreat [mɪs'triːt] *vt* maltraiter

mistress ['mɪstrɪs] *n* maîtresse *f*

mistrust [mɪs'trʌst] *vt* se méfier de

misty ['mɪstɪ] *(**-ier, -iest**)* *adj (foggy)* brumeux, -euse

misunderstand [mɪsʌndə'stænd] *(pt & pp* **-stood)** *vti* mal comprendre ● **misunderstanding** *n (disagreement)* mésentente *f*; *(misconception)* malentendu *m*

misuse 1 [mɪs'juːs] *n (of equipment, resources)* mauvais emploi *m*; *(of power)* abus *m* **2** [mɪs'juːz] *vt (equipment, resources)* mal employer; *(power)* abuser de

mitt(en) [mɪt, 'mɪtən] *n (glove)* moufle *f*

mix [mɪks] **1** *n (mixture)* mélange *m* **2** *vt* mélanger; *(cement, drink, cake)* préparer; **to m. up** *(papers)* mélanger; *(mistake)* confondre *(**with** avec)*; **to be mixed up in sth** être mêlé à qch **3** *vi (blend)* se mélanger; **to m. with sb** *(socially)* fréquenter qn ● **mixed** *adj (school, marriage)* mixte; *(nuts, chocolates)* assortis; **to be (all) m. up** *(of person)* être désorienté; *(of facts, account)* être confus ● **mixer** *n (for cooking)* mixeur *m*

mixture ['mɪkstʃə(r)] *n* mélange *m*

mm *(abbr* **millimetre(s))** mm

moan [məun] **1** *n (sound)* gémissement *m* **2** *vi (make sound)* gémir; *(complain)* se plaindre *(**to** à; **about** de; **that** que)*

mob [mɒb] *n (crowd)* foule *f*

mobile [*Br* 'məubaɪl, *Am* 'məubəl] **1** *adj* mobile; **m. home** mobile home *m*; *Br* **m. phone** téléphone *m* portable **2** *n Br (phone)* portable *m*

mock [mɒk] **1** *adj (false)* simulé; *Br Sch* **m. exam** examen *m* blanc **2** *vt* se moquer de; *(mimic)* singer

mode [məud] *n* mode *m*

model ['mɒdəl] **1** *n (example, person)* modèle *m*; *(small version)* maquette *f*; *(in fashion show, magazine)* mannequin *m* **2** *adj (behaviour, student)* modèle; *(car,* *plane)* modèle réduit *inv* **3** *(Br* **-ll-,** *Am* **-l-)** *vt (clay)* modeler; *(hats, dresses)* présenter; **to m. sth on** modeler qch sur **4** *vi (for fashion)* être mannequin; *(pose for artist)* poser

modem ['məʊdəm] *n Comptr* modem *m*

moderate ['mɒdərət] *adj* modéré • **moderately** *adv (in moderation)* modérément; *(averagely)* moyennement • **moderation** [-'reɪʃən] *n* modération *f*; **in m.** avec modération

modern ['mɒdən] *adj* moderne; **m. languages** langues *fpl* vivantes • **modernize** *vt* moderniser

modest['mɒdɪst]*adj(unassuming, moderate)* modeste

modify ['mɒdɪfaɪ] *(pt & pp* **-ied)** *vt* modifier

moist [mɔɪst] **(-er, -est)** *adj* humide; *(skin, hand)* moite • **moisture** [-tʃə(r)] *n* humidité *f*; *(on glass)* buée *f* • **moisturizer** *n* crème *f* hydratante

mold [məʊld] *n & vt Am* = **mould**

mole [məʊl] *n* **(a)** *(on skin)* grain *m* de beauté **(b)** *(animal)* taupe *f*

molest [mə'lest] *vt (child, woman)* agresser (sexuellement)

mom [mɒm] *n Am Fam* maman *f*

moment ['məʊmənt] *n* moment *m*, instant *m*; **at the m.** en ce moment; **for the m.** pour le moment; **in a m.** dans un instant; **any m. (now)** d'un instant à l'autre

momentum [məʊ'mentəm] *n (speed)* élan *m*; **to gather** *or* **gain m.** *(of campaign)* prendre de l'ampleur

mommy ['mɒmɪ] *n Am Fam* maman *f*

monarchy ['mɒnəkɪ] *(pl* **-ies)** *n* monarchie *f*

monastery ['mɒnəstərɪ] *(pl* **-ies)** *n* monastère *m*

Monday ['mʌndeɪ] *n* lundi *m*

money ['mʌnɪ] *n* argent *m*; **to make m.** *(of person)* gagner de l'argent; *(of business)* rapporter de l'argent • **moneybox** *n* tirelire *f*

mongrel ['mʌŋgrəl] *n* bâtard *m*

monitor ['mɒnɪtə(r)] **1** *n Comptr, TV & Tech (screen, device)* moniteur *m* **2** *vt (check)* surveiller

monk [mʌŋk] *n* moine *m*

monkey ['mʌŋkɪ] *(pl* **-eys)** *n* singe *m*

monologue ['mɒnəlɒg] *n* monologue *m*

monopoly [mə'nɒpəlɪ] *n* monopole *m* • **monopolize** *vt* monopoliser

monotonous [mə'nɒtənəs] *adj* monotone

monster ['mɒnstə(r)] *n* monstre *m* • **monstrous** *adj* monstrueux, -euse

month [mʌnθ] *n* mois *m* • **monthly 1** *adj* mensuel, -elle **2** *adv* tous les mois

Montreal [mɒntrɪ'ɔːl] *n* Montréal *m ou f*

monument ['mɒnjʊmənt] *n* monument *m*

mood [muːd] *n* humeur *f*; **in a good/bad m.** de bonne/mauvaise humeur; **to be in the m. to do** *or* **for doing sth** être d'humeur à faire qch • **moody (-ier, -iest)** *adj (bad-tempered)* maussade; *(changeable)* lunatique

moon [muːn] *n* lune *f* • **moonlight** *n* **by m.** au clair de lune

moor [mʊə(r)] **1** *n (heath)* lande *f* **2** *vt (ship)* amarrer

mop [mɒp] **1** *n (for floor)* balai *m* à franges; *(with sponge)* balai-éponge *m* **2** (*pt & pp* **-pp-**) *vt* **to m. sth up** (*liquid*) éponger qch

mope [məʊp] *vi* **to m. about** broyer du noir

moped ['məʊped] *n* Mobylette® *f*

moral ['mɒrəl] **1** *adj* moral **2** *n* (*of story*) morale *f*; **morals** (*principles*) moralité *f* • **morale** [mɒ'rɑːl] *n* moral *m* • **morality** [mə'rælətɪ] *n* moralité *f*

morbid ['mɔːbɪd] *adj* morbide

more [mɔː(r)] **1** *adj* plus de; **m. cars** plus de voitures; **he has m. books than you** il a plus de livres que toi; **a few m. months** quelques mois de plus; **(some) m. tea** encore du thé; **(some) m. details** d'autres détails; **m. than a kilo/ten** plus d'un kilo/de dix **2** *adv* (*to form comparative of adjectives and adverbs*) plus (**than** que); **m. and m.** de plus en plus; **m. or less** plus ou moins **3** *pron* plus; **have some m.** reprenez-en; **she doesn't have any m.** elle n'en a plus; **the m. he shouts, the m. hoarse he gets** plus il crie, plus il s'enroue; **what's m.** qui plus est

morning ['mɔːnɪŋ] **1** *n* matin *m*; (*referring to duration*) matinée *f*; **in the m.** le matin; (*during the course of the morning*) pendant la matinée; (*tomorrow*) demain matin; **every Tuesday m.** tous les mardis matin **2** *adj* (*newspaper*) du matin

Morocco [mə'rɒkəʊ] *n* le Maroc • **Moroccan 1** *adj* marocain **2** *n* Marocain, -e *mf*

moron ['mɔːrɒn] *n* crétin, -e *mf*

mortal ['mɔːtəl] *adj & n* mortel, -elle (*mf*)

mortgage ['mɔːgɪdʒ] *n* (*money lent*) prêt *m* immobilier; (*money borrowed*) emprunt *m* immobilier

mosaic [məʊ'zeɪɪk] *n* mosaïque *f*

Moscow [*Br* 'mɒskəʊ, *Am* 'mɒskaʊ] *n* Moscou *m ou f*

mosque [mɒsk] *n* mosquée *f*

mosquito [mɒ'skiːtəʊ] (*pl* **-oes** *or* **-os**) *n* moustique *m*

moss [mɒs] *n* mousse *f*

most [məʊst] **1** *adj* (**a**) (*the majority of*) la plupart de; **m. women** la plupart des femmes (**b**) (*greatest amount of*) **the m.** le plus de; **I have the m. books** j'ai le plus de livres **2** *adv* (**a**) (*to form superlative of adjectives and adverbs*) plus; **the m. beautiful** le plus beau (*f* la plus belle) (**in/of** de); **to talk (the) m.** parler le plus; **m. of all** (*especially*) surtout (**b**) (*very*) extrêmement **3** *pron* (**a**) (*the majority*) la plupart; **m. of the people/the time** la plupart des gens/du temps; **m. of the cake** la plus grande partie du gâteau; **m. of them** la plupart d'entre eux (**b**) (*greatest amount*) le plus; **he earns the m.** c'est lui qui gagne le plus; **to make the m. of sth** (*situation, talent*) tirer le meilleur parti de qch; (*holiday*) profiter au maximum de qch; **at (the very) m.** tout au plus • **mostly** *adv* (*in the main*) surtout; (*most often*) le plus souvent

MOT [eməʊ'tiː] (*abbr* **Ministry of Transport**) *n Br* = contrôle obligatoire des véhicules de plus de trois ans

motel [məʊ'tel] *n* motel *m*

moth [mɒθ] *n* papillon *m* de nuit; (*in clothes*) mite *f*

mother ['mʌðə(r)] *n* mère *f*; **M.'s Day** la fête des Mères • **motherhood** *n* maternité *f* •

mother-in-law (*pl* **mothers-in-law**) *n* belle-mère *f* • **mother-to-be** (*pl* **mothers-to-be**) *n* future mère *f*

motion ['məʊʃən] *n* (*of arm*) mouvement *m*; **to set sth in m.** mettre qch en mouvement; **m. picture** film *m* • **motionless** *adj* immobile

motivate ['məʊtɪveɪt] *vt* (*person, decision*) motiver • **motivation** [-'veɪʃən] *n* motivation *f*

motive ['məʊtɪv] *n* motif *m* (**for** de)

motor ['məʊtə(r)] **1** *n* (*engine*) moteur *m* **2** *adj* (*industry, insurance*) automobile; **m. racing** courses *fpl* automobiles • **motorbike** *n* moto *f* • **motorboat** *n* canot *m* à moteur • **motorcycle** *n* moto *f*, motocyclette *f* • **motorist** *n* Br automobiliste *mf* • **motorway** *n* Br autoroute *f*

motto ['mɒtəʊ] (*pl* **-oes** *or* **-os**) *n* devise *f*

mould¹ [məʊld] (*Am* **mold**) **1** *n* (*shape*) moule *m* **2** *vt* (*clay, person's character*) modeler

mould² [məʊld] (*Am* **mold**) *n* (*fungus*) moisissure *f* • **mouldy** (*Am* **moldy**) (**-ier, -iest**) *adj* moisi; **to go m.** moisir

mound [maʊnd] *n* (*of earth*) tertre *m*; *Fig* (*untidy pile*) tas *m*

mount [maʊnt] *vi* (*increase, rise*) monter; **to m. up** (*add up*) monter, augmenter; (*accumulate*) (*of debts, bills*) s'accumuler

mountain ['maʊntɪn] *n* montagne *f*; **m. bike** vélo *m* tout-terrain, VTT *m* • **mountaineer** *n* alpiniste *mf* • **mountaineering** *n* alpinisme *m*

mourn [mɔːn] *vti* **to m. (for) sb** pleurer qn • **mourning** *n* deuil *m*; **in m.** en deuil

mouse [maʊs] (*pl* **mice** [maɪs]) *n* (*animal*) & *Comptr* souris *f*

mousse [muːs] *n* mousse *f*

moustache [*Br* mə'stɑːʃ, *Am* 'mʌstæʃ] *n* moustache *f*

mouth [maʊθ] (*pl* **-s** [maʊðz]) *n* (*of person, horse*) bouche *f*; (*of other animals*) gueule *f* • **mouthful** *n* (*of food*) bouchée *f*; (*of liquid*) gorgée *f* • **mouthwash** *n* bain *m* de bouche • **mouth-watering** *adj* appétissant

move [muːv] **1** *n* mouvement *m*; (*to new house*) déménagement *m*; **to make a m.** (*leave*) se préparer à partir; (*act*) passer à l'action; *Fam* **to get a m. on** se grouiller **2** *vt* déplacer; (*arm, leg*) remuer; **to m. house** déménager **3** *vi* bouger; (*change position*) se déplacer (**to** à); (*leave*) partir; (*to new house*) déménager; **to m. to Paris** aller habiter (à) Paris • **movement** *n* mouvement *m* • **moving** *adj* en mouvement; (*vehicle*) en marche; (*touching*) émouvant

▶**move about** *vi* se déplacer; (*fidget*) remuer

▶**move along** *vi* avancer

▶**move around** *vi* = **move about**

▶**move away** *vi* (*go away*) s'éloigner; (*move house*) déménager

▶**move forward** *vt sep & vi* avancer

▶**move in** *vi* (*into house*) emménager

▶**move out** *vi* (*out of house*) déménager

▶**move over, move up** *vi* (*make room*) se pousser

movie ['muːvɪ] *n* film *m*; **the movies** (*cinema*) le cinéma; **m. star** vedette *f* de cinéma; *Am* **m. theater** cinéma *m*

mow [məʊ] (*pp* **mown** [məʊn] *or* **mowed**) *vt* **to m. the lawn** tondre le gazon

MP [em'piː] (*abbr* **Member of Parliament**) *n* député, -e *mf*

mph [empiː'eɪtʃ] (*abbr* **miles per hour**) ≃ km/h

Mr ['mɪstə(r)] *n* **Mr Brown** M. Brown

Mrs ['mɪsɪz] *n* **Mrs Brown** Mme Brown

MS [em'es] (*abbr* **Master of Science**) *n Am Univ* **to have an MS in chemistry** avoir une maîtrise de chimie

Ms [mɪz] *n* **Ms Brown** ≃ Mme Brown (*ne renseigne pas sur le statut de famille*)

MSc [emes'siː] (*abbr* **Master of Science**) *n Univ* **to have an M. in chemistry** avoir une maîtrise de chimie

much [mʌtʃ] **1** *adj* beaucoup de; **not m. time/money** pas beaucoup de temps/d'argent; **how m. sugar do you want?** combien de sucre voulez-vous?; **twice as m. traffic** deux fois plus de circulation; **too m. work** trop de travail **2** *adv* beaucoup; **very m.** beaucoup; **m. better** bien meilleur; **I love him so m.** je l'aime tellement; **she doesn't say very m.** elle ne dit pas grand-chose **3** *pron* beaucoup; **there isn't m. left** il n'en reste pas beaucoup; **it's not m. of a garden** ce n'est pas terrible comme jardin; **twice as m.** deux fois plus; **as m. as you like** autant que tu veux; *Fam* **that's a bit m.!** c'est un peu fort!

muck [mʌk] *Br Fam* **1** *n* (*filth*) saleté *f* **2** *vt* **to m. sth up** (*task*) bâcler qch; (*plans*) chambouler qch **3** *vi* **to m. about** *or* **around** (*waste time*) traîner; (*play the fool*) faire l'imbécile ● **mucky** (**-ier, -iest**) *adj Fam* sale

mud [mʌd] *n* boue *f* ● **muddy** (**-ier, -iest**) *adj* (*water, road*) boueux, -euse; (*hands*) couvert de boue

muddle ['mʌdəl] **1** *n* confusion *f*; **to be in a m.** (*person*) ne plus s'y retrouver; (*of things*) être en désordre **2** *vt* (*facts*) mélanger; **to get muddled** (*of person*) s'embrouiller

muesli ['mjuːzlɪ, 'muːzlɪ] *n* muesli *m*

muffin ['mʌfɪn] *n* (*cake*) muffin *m*

muffled ['mʌfəld] *adj* (*noise*) sourd

mug¹ [mʌg] *n* (*for tea, coffee*) grande tasse *f*; (**beer**) **m.** chope *f*

mug² [mʌg] (*pt & pp* **-gg-**) *vt* (*attack in street*) agresser ● **mugger** *n* agresseur *m*

mule [mjuːl] *n* (*male*) mulet *m*; (*female*) mule *f*

multicoloured ['mʌltɪkʌləd] *adj* multicolore

multimedia [mʌltɪ'miːdɪə] *adj* multimédia

multiple ['mʌltɪpəl] *adj* multiple ● **multiple-choice** *adj* à choix multiple

multiply ['mʌltɪplaɪ] (*pt & pp* **-ied**) **1** *vt* multiplier **2** *vi* (*of animals, insects*) se multiplier ● **multiplication** [-plɪ'keɪʃən] *n* multiplication *f*

multistorey [mʌltɪ'stɔːrɪ] (*Am* **multistoried**) *adj* (*car park*) à plusieurs niveaux

mum [mʌm] *n Br Fam* maman *f*

mumble ['mʌmbəl] *vti* marmotter

mummy¹ ['mʌmɪ] (*pl* **-ies**) *n Br Fam* (*mother*) maman *f*

mummy² ['mʌmɪ] (*pl* **-ies**) *n* (*embalmed body*) momie *f*

munch [mʌntʃ] *vti (chew)* mâcher
municipal [mjuː'nɪsɪpəl] *adj* municipal
mural ['mjʊərəl] *n* peinture *f* murale
murder ['mɜːdə(r)] **1** *n* meurtre *m* **2** *vt (kill)* assassiner • **murderer** *n* meurtrier, -ère *mf*, assassin *m*
murmur ['mɜːmə(r)] *vti* murmurer
muscle ['mʌsəl] *n* muscle *m* • **muscular** ['mʌskjʊlə(r)] *adj (person, arm)* musclé
museum [mjuː'zɪəm] *n* musée *m*
mushroom ['mʌʃrʊm] *n* champignon *m*
mushy ['mʌʃɪ] (**-ier, -iest**) *adj (food)* en bouillie
music ['mjuːzɪk] *n* musique *f* • **musical 1** *adj* musical; **m. instrument** instrument *m* de musique **2** *n (film, play)* comédie *f* musicale • **musician** [-'zɪʃən] *n* musicien, -enne *mf*
Muslim ['mʊzlɪm] *adj & n* musulman, -e *(mf)*
mussel ['mʌsəl] *n* moule *f*
must [mʌst] **1** *n* **it's a m.** c'est indispensable; **this film is a m.** il faut absolument voir ce film **2** *v aux* (**a**) *(expressing necessity)* **you m. obey** tu dois obéir, il faut que tu obéisses (**b**) *(expressing probability)* **she m. be clever** elle doit être intelligente; **I m. have seen it** j'ai dû le voir

mustache ['mʌstæʃ] *n Am* = **moustache**
mustard ['mʌstəd] *n* moutarde *f*
mustn't ['mʌsənt] = **must not**
musty ['mʌstɪ] (**-ier, -iest**) *adj (smell, taste)* de moisi
mute [mjuːt] *adj (silent) & Ling* muet *(f* muette)
mutter ['mʌtə(r)] *vti* marmonner
mutton ['mʌtən] *n (meat)* mouton *m*
mutual ['mjuːtʃʊəl] *adj (help, love)* mutuel, -elle; *(friend)* commun • **mutually** *adv* mutuellement
muzzle ['mʌzəl] *n (device for dog)* muselière *f*; *(snout)* museau *m*
my [maɪ] *possessive adj* mon, ma, *pl* mes • **myself** *pron* moi-même; *(reflexive)* me, m'; *(after prep)* moi; **I wash m.** je me lave
mystery ['mɪstərɪ] (*pl* **-ies**) *n* mystère *m* • **mysterious** [mɪs'tɪərɪəs] *adj* mystérieux, -euse
mystify ['mɪstɪfaɪ] (*pt & pp* **-ied**) *vt (bewilder)* déconcerter
myth [mɪθ] *n* mythe *m* • **mythology** (*pl* **-ies**) *n* mythologie *f*

Nn

N, n [en] *n (letter)* N, n *m inv*

nab [næb] *(pt & pp* **-bb-***)* *vt Fam (catch, arrest)* coffrer

nag [næg] *(pt & pp* **-gg-***)* *vti* **to n. (at) sb** *(of person)* être sur le dos de qn

nail [neɪl] **1** *n* (a) *(of finger, toe)* ongle *m*; **n. file** lime *f* à ongles; **n. polish,** *Br* **n. varnish** vernis *m* à ongles (b) *(metal)* clou *m* **2** *vt* clouer; **to n. sth down** *(lid)* clouer qch

naïve [naɪ'iːv] *adj* naïf *(f* naïve)

naked ['neɪkɪd] *adj* nu

name [neɪm] **1** *n* nom *m*; *(reputation)* réputation *f*; **my n. is...** je m'appelle...; **in the n. of** au nom de, **first n.** prénom *m* **2** *vt* nommer; *(date, price)* fixer

nanny ['nænɪ] *(pl* **-ies***)* *n* nurse *f*

nap [næp] *n (sleep)* **to have** or **take a n.** faire un petit somme

napkin ['næpkɪn] *n (at table)* serviette *f*

nappy ['næpɪ] *(pl* **-ies***)* *n Br (for baby)* couche *f*

narrative ['nærətɪv] *n* récit *m* • **narrator** [nə'reɪtə(r)] *n* narrateur, -trice *mf*

narrow ['nærəʊ] **1** (**-er, -est***)* *adj* étroit **2** *vt* **to n. (down)** *(choice, meaning)* limiter • **narrowly** *adv (only just)* de peu; **he n. escaped being killed** il a bien failli être tué • **narrow-minded** *adj* borné

nasty ['nɑːstɪ] (**-ier, -iest***)* *adj (bad)* mauvais; *(spiteful)* méchant (**to** or **towards** avec)

nation ['neɪʃən] *n* nation *f*

national ['næʃənəl] *adj* national; **n. anthem** hymne *m* national; *Br* **N. Health Service** ≃ Sécurité *f* sociale; *Br* **n. insurance** contributions *fpl* sociales • **nationality** [-'nælətɪ] *(pl* **-ies***)* *n* nationalité *f*

native ['neɪtɪv] **1** *adj (country)* natal *(mpl* -als); *(tribe, plant)* indigène; **to be an English n. speaker** avoir l'anglais comme langue maternelle **2** *n (person)* indigène *mf*; **to be a n. of** être originaire de

NATO ['neɪtəʊ] *(abbr* **North Atlantic Treaty Organization***)* *n Mil* OTAN *f*

nature ['neɪtʃə(r)] *n (world, character)* nature *f*; **n. reserve** réserve *f* naturelle • **natural** ['nætʃərəl] *adj* naturel, -elle; *(talent)* inné • **naturally** *adv (unaffectedly, of course)* naturellement; *(by nature)* de nature

naughty ['nɔːtɪ] (**-ier, -iest***)* *adj (child)* vilain

nausea ['nɔːzɪə] *n* nausée *f* • **nauseous** ['nɔːʃəs] *adj Am* **to feel n.** *(sick)* avoir envie de vomir

navel ['neɪvəl] *n* nombril *m*

navigate ['nævɪgeɪt] **1** *vt (boat)* piloter; *(river)* naviguer sur **2** *vi* naviguer

navy ['neɪvɪ] **1** *(pl* **-ies***)* *n* marine *f* **2** *adj* **n. (blue)** bleu marine *inv*

near [nɪə(r)] **1** (**-er, -est***)* *prep* **n. (to)** près de; **n. (to) the end** vers la fin **2** *adv* près; **n. to sth** près de qch; **n. enough** *(more or less)* plus ou moins **3** *adj* proche; **in the n. future** dans un avenir proche; **to the nearest euro** *(calculate)* à un euro près; **4** *vt (approach)* approcher de • **nearby 1** [nɪə'baɪ] *adv* tout près **2** ['nɪəbaɪ] *adj* proche

nearly ['nɪəlɪ] *adv* presque; **she (very) n. fell** elle a failli tomber

neat [niːt] **(-er, -est)** *adj (clothes, work)* soigné; *(room)* bien rangé; *Am Fam (good)* super *inv* • **neatly** *adv (carefully)* avec soin; *(skilfully)* habilement

necessary ['nesɪsərɪ] *adj* nécessaire • **necessarily** [-'serəlɪ] *adv* **not n.** pas forcément • **necessity** [nɪ'sesətɪ] *(pl -ies)* *n (obligation, need)* nécessité *f*; **to be a n.** être indispensable

neck [nek] *n* cou *m*; *(of dress)* encolure *f*; *(of bottle)* goulot *m* • **necklace** [-lɪs] *n* collier *m* • **necktie** *n Am* cravate *f*

nectarine ['nektəriːn] *n (fruit)* nectarine *f*, brugnon *m*

need [niːd] **1** *n* besoin *m*; **to be in n. of sth** avoir besoin de qch; **there's no n. (for you) to do that** tu n'as pas besoin de faire cela **2** *vt* avoir besoin de; **you n. it** tu en as besoin; **her hair needs cutting** il faut qu'elle se fasse couper les cheveux **3** *v aux* **you needn't have rushed** ce n'était pas la peine de te presser; **you needn't worry** inutile de t'inquiéter • **needy (-ier, -iest)** *adj* nécessiteux, -euse

needle ['niːdəl] *n* aiguille *f*

negative ['negətɪv] **1** *adj* négatif, -ive **2** *n (of photo)* négatif *m*

neglect [nɪ'glekt] *vt (person, health, work)* négliger; *(garden,*

car) ne pas s'occuper de; *(duty)* manquer à; **to n. to do sth** négliger de faire qch • **neglected** *adj (appearance)* négligé; *(garden, house)* mal tenu; **to feel n.** se sentir abandonné

negotiate [nɪ'gəʊʃɪeɪt] *vti (discuss)* négocier • **negotiation** [-ʃɪ'eɪʃən] *n* négociation *f*

neighbour ['neɪbə(r)] *(Am* **neighbor)** *n* voisin, -e *mf* • **neighbourhood** *(Am* **neighborhood)** *n (district)* quartier *m*, voisinage *m*; *(neighbours)* voisinage *m*; **in the n. of $10/10 kilos** dans les 10 dollars/10 kilos • **neighbouring** *(Am* **neighboring)** *adj* voisin

neither ['naɪðə(r), 'niːðə(r)] **1** *conj* **n.... nor...** ni... ni...; **he n. sings nor dances** il ne chante ni ne danse **2** *adv* **n. do I/n. can I** (ni) moi non plus **3** *adj* **n. boy came** aucun des deux garçons n'est venu **4** *pron* **n. (of them)** aucun(e) (des deux)

neon ['niːɒn] *adj* **n. sign** enseigne *f* au néon

nephew ['nefjuː] *n* neveu *m*

nerve [nɜːv] *n* nerf *m*; *(courage)* courage *m*; *Fam (impudence)* culot *m*; *Fam* **he gets on my nerves** il me tape sur les nerfs • **nerve-racking** *adj* éprouvant

nervous ['nɜːvəs] *adj (apprehensive)* nerveux, -euse; **to be n. about sth/doing sth** être nerveux à l'idée de qch/de faire qch

nest [nest] *n* nid *m*

Net [net] *n Comptr* **the N.** le Net

net¹ [net] *n* filet *m*

net² [net] *adj (profit, weight)* net *(f* nette)

nettle ['netəl] *n* ortie *f*

network ['netwɜːk] *n* réseau *m*

neuter ['njuːtə(r)] **1** *adj & n Gram* neutre *(m)* **2** *vt (cat)* châtrer

neutral ['nju:trəl] **1** *adj* neutre **2** *n* in n. **(gear)** *(vehicle)* au point mort

never ['nevə(r)] *adv (not ever)* (ne...) jamais; **she n. lies** elle ne ment jamais; **n. again** plus jamais • **never-ending** *adj* interminable • **nevertheless** [-ðə'les] *adv* néanmoins

new [nju:] **(-er, -est)** *adj* **(a)** nouveau *(f* nouvelle*); (brand-new)* neuf *(f* neuve*);* **to be n. to** *(job)* être nouveau dans; *(city)* être un nouveau-venu *(f* une nouvelle-venue*)* dans **(b)** *(different)* **a n. glass/pen** un autre verre/stylo • **newborn** *adj* **a n. baby** un nouveau-né, une nouveau-née • **newcomer** [-kʌmə(r)] *n* nouveau-venu *m*, nouvelle-venue *f* **(to** dans*)* • **newly** *adv* nouvellement

news [nju:z] *n* nouvelles *fpl; (in the media)* informations *fpl;* **a piece of n.** une nouvelle; **sports n.** *(newspaper column)* rubrique *f* sportive • **newsagent** *(Am* **newsdealer**)*n* marchand, -e *mf* de journaux • **newsletter** *n (of club, group)* bulletin *m* • **newspaper** *n* journal *m* • **newsreader** *n Br* présentateur, -trice *mf* de journal

New Zealand [nju:'zi:lənd] *n* la Nouvelle-Zélande

next [nekst] **1** *adj* prochain; *(room, house)* d'à côté; *(following)* suivant; **n. month** *(in the future)* le mois prochain; **the n. day** le lendemain; **within the n. ten days** d'ici dix jours; **you're n.** c'est ton tour; **the n. size up** la taille au-dessus; **to live n. door** habiter à côté **(to** de*)* **2** *n (in series)* suivant, -e *mf* **3** *adv (afterwards)* ensuite, après; *(now)* maintenant; **when you come n.** la prochaine fois que tu viendras; **n. to** *(beside)* à côté de • **next-door** *adj* **n. neighbour/room** voisin *m*/pièce *f* d'à côté

NHS [eneɪtʃ'es] *(abbr* **National Health Service)** *n Br* ≃ Sécurité *f* sociale

nibble ['nɪbəl] *vti* grignoter

nice [naɪs] **(-er, -est)** *adj (pleasant)* agréable; *(tasty)* bon *(f* bonne*); (physically attractive)* beau *(f* belle*); (kind)* gentil, -ille **(to** avec*);* **n. and warm** bien chaud; **have a n. day!** bonne journée! • **nicely** *adv (well)* bien

niche [ni:ʃ, nɪtʃ] *n (recess)* niche *f*

nick [nɪk] **1** *n (on skin, wood)* entaille *f; (in blade, crockery)* brèche *f;* **in the n. of time** juste à temps **2** *vt Br Fam (steal)* piquer

nickel ['nɪkəl] *n Am (coin)* pièce *f* de cinq cents

nickname ['nɪkneɪm] **1** *n (informal)* surnom *m* **2** *vt* surnommer

niece [ni:s] *n* nièce *f*

night [naɪt] **1** *n* nuit *f; (evening)* soir *m;* **at n.** la nuit; **last n.** *(evening)* hier soir; *(night)* cette nuit; **to have an early/a late n.** se coucher tôt/tard **2** *adj (work, flight)* de nuit; **n. shift** *(job)* poste *m* de nuit; *(workers)* équipe *f* de nuit • **nightclub** *n* boîte *f* de nuit • **nightdress** ['naɪtdres], *Fam* **nightie** ['naɪtɪ] *n* chemise *f* de nuit • **nightlife** *n* vie *f* nocturne • **nightly 1** *adv* chaque nuit; *(every evening)* chaque soir **2** *adj* de chaque nuit/soir • **nightmare** *n* cauchemar *m* • **night-time** *n* nuit *f*

nil [nɪl] *n (nothing) & Br (score)* zéro *m;* **two n.** deux à zéro

nimble ['nɪmbəl] **(-er, -est)** *adj (person)* souple

nine [naɪn] *adj & n* neuf *(m)*

nineteen [naɪn'tiːn] *adj & n* dix-neuf *(m)*

ninety ['naɪntɪ] *adj & n* quatre-vingt-dix *(m)*

ninth ['naɪnθ] *adj & n* neuvième *(mf)*; **a n.** *(fraction)* un neuvième

nip [nɪp] **1** *(pt & pp* -pp-) *vt (pinch)* pincer **2** *vi Br Fam* **to n. round to sb's house** faire un saut chez qn; **to n. out** sortir un instant

nipple ['nɪpəl] *n* mamelon *m*; *Am (on baby's bottle)* tétine *f*

nitrogen ['naɪtrədʒən] *n* azote *m*

no [nəʊ] **1** *(pl* **noes** *or* **nos**) *n* non *m inv* **2** *adj (not any)* pas de; **there's no bread** il n'y a pas de pain; **I have no idea** je n'ai aucune idée; **of no importance** sans importance **3** *adv (interjection)* non; **no more time** plus de temps; **no more/fewer than ten** pas plus/moins de dix

noble ['nəʊbəl] (-er, -est) *adj* noble

nobody ['nəʊbɒdɪ] *pron* (ne...) personne; **n. came** personne n'est venu; **he knows n.** il ne connaît personne

nod [nɒd] **1** *(pt & pp* -dd-) *vti* **to n. (one's head)** faire un signe de tête **2** *vi Fam* **to n. off** s'assoupir

noise [nɔɪz] *n* bruit *m*; **to make a n.** faire du bruit • **noisy** (-ier, -iest) *adj (person, street)* bruyant

nominate ['nɒmɪneɪt] *vt (appoint)* nommer; *(propose)* proposer (**for** comme candidat à) • **nomination** [-'neɪʃən] *n (appointment)* nomination *f*; *(proposal)* candidature *f*

none [nʌn] **1** *pron* aucun, -e *mf*; *(in filling out a form)* néant; **n. of them** aucun d'eux; **she has n. (at all)** elle n'en a pas (du tout); **n. came** pas un(e) seul(e) n'est venu(e) **2** *adv* **he's n. the wiser (for it)** il n'est pas plus avancé • **nonetheless** *adv* néanmoins

nonexistent [nɒnɪg'zɪstənt] *adj* inexistant

non-fiction [nɒn'fɪkʃən] *n* ouvrages *mpl* généraux

nonsense ['nɒnsəns] *n* bêtises *fpl*; **that's n.** c'est absurde

non-smoker [nɒn'sməʊkə(r)] *n (person)* non-fumeur, -euse *mf*; *(compartment on train)* compartiment *m* non-fumeurs

non-stop [nɒn'stɒp] **1** *adj* sans arrêt; *(train, flight)* sans escale **2** *adv (work)* sans arrêt; *(fly)* sans escale

noodles ['nuːdəlz] *npl* nouilles *fpl*; *(in soup)* vermicelles *mpl*

noon [nuːn] *n* midi *m*

no-one ['nəʊwʌn] *pron* = **nobody**

noose [nuːs] *n* nœud *m* coulant

nor [nɔː(r)] *conj* ni; **neither you n. me** ni toi ni moi; **she neither drinks n. smokes** elle ne fume ni ne boit; **n. do I/can I/***etc* (ni) moi non plus

normal ['nɔːməl] **1** *adj* normal **2** *n* **above/below n.** au-dessus/au-dessous de la normale • **normally** *adv* normalement

north [nɔːθ] **1** *n* nord *m*; **(to the) n. of** au nord de **2** *adj (coast)* nord *inv*; *(wind)* du nord; **N. America/Africa** Amérique *f*/Afrique *f* du Nord; **N. American** *adj* nord-américain; *n* Nord-Américain, -e *mf* **3** *adv* au nord; *(travel)* vers le nord • **north-east** *n & adj* nord-est *(m)* • **northern** ['nɔːðən] *adj (coast)* nord *inv*; *(town)* du nord; **N. France** le nord de la France; **N. Ireland** l'Irlande *f* du Nord • **northerner** ['nɔːðənə(r)] *n* habitant, -e *mf* du Nord • **north-west** *n & adj* nord-ouest *(m)*

Norway ['nɔːweɪ] *n* la Norvège • **Norwegian** [nɔː'wiːdʒən] **1** *adj* norvégien, -enne **2** *n* *(person)* Norvégien, -enne *mf*; *(language)* norvégien *m*

nose [nəʊz] *n* nez *m*; **her n. is bleeding** elle saigne du nez • **nosebleed** *n* saignement *m* de nez • **nosey (-ier, -iest)** *adj Fam* indiscret, -ète

no-smoking [nəʊ'sməʊkɪŋ] *adj* *(carriage, area)* non-fumeurs

nostalgic [nɒs'tældʒɪk] *adj* nostalgique

nostril ['nɒstrəl] *n (of person)* narine *f*

nosy ['nəʊzɪ] *adj* = **nosey**

___

not [nɒt]

À l'oral, et à l'écrit dans un style familier, on utilise généralement **not** à la forme contractée lorsqu'il suit un modal ou un auxiliaire (don't go!, she wasn't there, he couldn't see me).

adv **(a)** (ne…) pas; **he's n. there, he isn't there** il n'est pas là; **n. yet** pas encore; **n. at all** pas du tout; *(after 'thank you')* je vous en prie **(b)** non; **I think/hope n.** je pense/j'espère que non; **n. guilty** non coupable; **isn't she?/don't you?/etc** non?

___

note [nəʊt] **1** *n (information, reminder) & Mus* note *f*; *Br (banknote)* billet *m*; *(letter)* mot *m*; **to take (a) n. of sth, to make a n. of sth** prendre note de qch **2** *vt (notice)* remarquer, noter; **to n. sth down** *(word, remark)* noter qch • **notable** *adj* notable • **notably** *adv (noticeably)* notablement; *(particularly)* notamment • **notebook** *n* carnet *m*; *(for school)*

cahier *m* • **notepad** *n* bloc-notes *m* • **notepaper** *n* papier *m* à lettres

nothing ['nʌθɪŋ] **1** *pron* (ne…) rien; **he knows n.** il ne sait rien; **n. at all** rien du tout; **n. much** pas grand-chose; **I've got n. to do with it** je n'y suis pour rien; **for n.** *(in vain, free of charge)* pour rien **2** *adv* **to look n. like sb** ne ressembler nullement à qn

notice ['nəʊtɪs] **1** *n (notification)* avis *m*; *(sign)* pancarte *f*, écriteau *m*; *(poster)* affiche *f*; **to give sb (advance) n.** *(inform)* avertir qn **(of** de); **n. (to quit), n. of dismissal** congé *m*; **to give in** or **hand in one's n.** *(resign)* donner sa démission; **to take n.** faire attention **(of** à); **until further n.** jusqu'à nouvel ordre; **at short n.** au dernier moment **2** *vt* remarquer **(that** que) • **noticeable** *adj* perceptible • **noticeboard** *n Br* tableau *m* d'affichage

notion ['nəʊʃən] *n* notion *f*

notorious [nəʊ'tɔːrɪəs] *adj* tristement célèbre; *(criminal)* notoire

nought [nɔːt] *n Br Math* zéro *m*

noun [naʊn] *n* nom *m*

nourish ['nʌrɪʃ] *vt* nourrir • **nourishment** *n* nourriture *f*

novel ['nɒvəl] **1** *n* roman *m* **2** *adj (new)* nouveau *(f* nouvelle), original • **novelist** *n* romancier, -ère *mf* • **novelty** *n* nouveauté *f*

November [nəʊ'vembə(r)] *n* novembre *m*

now [naʊ] **1** *adv* maintenant; **for n.** pour le moment; **from n. on** désormais; **until n., up to n.** jusqu'ici, jusqu'à maintenant; **n. and then** de temps à autre; **she ought to be here by n.** elle devrait déjà être ici **2** *conj*

n. (that)... maintenant que... •
nowadays *adv* de nos jours
nowhere ['nəʊweə(r)] *adv* nulle
part; **n. else** nulle part ailleurs; **n.
near enough** loin d'être assez
nozzle ['nɒzəl] *n* embout *m*; *(of
hose)* jet *m*
nuance ['njuːɑːns] *n* nuance *f*
nuclear ['njuːklɪə(r)] *adj* nucléaire
nucleus ['njuːklɪəs] *(pl* **-clei** [-
klɪaɪ]) *n* noyau *m (pl* -aux)
nude [njuːd] **1** *adj* nu **2** *n* nu *m*; **in
the n.** tout nu *(f* toute nue)
nudge [nʌdʒ] *vt* pousser du
coude
nuisance ['njuːsəns] *n* **to be a n.**
être embêtant
numb [nʌm] *adj (stiff) (hand)*
engourdi
number ['nʌmbə(r)] **1** *n* nombre
m; *(of page, house, telephone)*
numéro *m*; *(song)* chanson *f*;
a/any n. of un certain/grand
nombre de **2** *vt (assign number to)*
numéroter • **numberplate** *n Br*
plaque *f* d'immatriculation
numerous ['njuːmərəs] *adj*
nombreux, -euse

nun [nʌn] *n* religieuse *f*
nurse [nɜːs] **1** *n* infirmier, -ère *mf*;
(for children) nurse *f* **2** *vt (look
after)* soigner; *(suckle)* allaiter •
nursing *n (care)* soins *mpl*; *(job)*
profession *f* d'infirmière; *Br* **n.
home** *(for old people)* maison *f*
de retraite
nursery ['nɜːsərɪ] *(pl* **-ies)** *n*
(children's room) chambre *f*
d'enfants; *(childcare facility)*
garderie *f*; **n. rhyme** comptine *f*;
n. school école *f* maternelle
nut[1] [nʌt] *n (fruit)* = noix, noisette
ou autre fruit sec de cette nature;
Brazil n. noix *f* du Brésil • **nutcase**
n Fam cinglé, -e *mf* • **nutcrackers**
npl casse-noix *m inv* • **nutshell** *n*
Fig **in a n.** en un mot
nut[2] [nʌt] *n (for bolt)* écrou *m*
nutmeg ['nʌtmeg] *n* muscade *f*
nutritious [njuːˈtrɪʃəs] *adj*
nutritif, -ive • **nutrition** [-ʃən] *n*
nutrition *f*
nuts [nʌts] *adj Fam (crazy)* cinglé
nylon ['naɪlɒn] *n* Nylon® *m*; **n.
shirt** chemise *f* en Nylon®

Oo

O, o [əʊ] *n (letter)* O, o *m inv*
oak [əʊk] *n (tree, wood)* chêne *m*
oar [ɔː(r)] *n* aviron *m*, rame *f*
oath [əʊθ] *(pl* **-s** [əʊðz]) *n
(promise)* serment *m; (profanity)*
juron *m*
oats [əʊts] *npl* avoine *f;* **(porridge)**
o. flocons *mpl* d'avoine
obedient [əˈbiːdɪənt] *adj* obéissant
obese [əʊˈbiːs] *adj* obèse
obey [əˈbeɪ] **1** *vt* obéir à **2** *vi* obéir
obituary [əˈbɪtʃʊərɪ] *(pl* **-ies**) *n*
nécrologie *f*
object¹ [ˈɒbdʒɪkt] *n (thing)*
objet *m; (aim)* but *m*, objet; *(in
grammar)* complément *m* d'objet
object² [əbˈdʒekt] **1** *vt* **to o. that…**
objecter que… **2** *vi* émettre une
objection; **to o. to sth/to doing
sth** ne pas être d'accord avec
qch/pour faire qch ● **objection** *n*
objection *f*
objective [əbˈdʒektɪv] *adj
(impartial)* objectif, -ive
obligation [ɒblɪˈgeɪʃən] *n*
obligation *f;* **to be under an o.
to do sth** être dans l'obligation
de faire qch ● **obligatory**
[əˈblɪgətərɪ] *adj* obligatoire
oblige [əˈblaɪdʒ] *vt* **(a)** *(compel)*
to o. sb to do sth obliger qn à
faire qch **(b)** *(help)* rendre service
à; **to be obliged to sb** être
reconnaissant à qn **(for** de)
oblivious [əˈblɪvɪəs] *adj* inconscient **(to** *or* **of** de)

oblong [ˈɒblɒŋ] **1** *adj (rectangular)*
rectangulaire **2** *n* rectangle *m*
obnoxious [əbˈnɒkʃəs] *adj
(person, behaviour)* odieux, -euse
obscene [əbˈsiːn] *adj* obscène
obscure [əbˈskjʊə(r)] *adj* obscur
observe [əbˈzɜːv] *vt* observer;
to o. the speed limit respecter
la limitation de vitesse ●
observant *adj* observateur, -trice
● **observation** [ɒbzəˈveɪʃən] *n
(observing, remark)* observation *f*
obsession [əbˈseʃən] *n* obsession
f ● **obsessive** *adj (idea)* obsédant;
(person) obsessionnel, -elle; **to be
o. about sth** être obsédé par qch
obstacle [ˈɒbstəkəl] *n* obstacle *m*
obstinate [ˈɒbstɪnət] *adj* obstiné
obstruct [əbˈstrʌkt] *vt (block)
(road, pipe)* obstruer; *(view)*
cacher; *(hinder)* gêner ●
obstruction *n (action, in sport)*
obstruction *f; (obstacle)* obstacle
m; (in pipe) bouchon *m*
obtain [əbˈteɪn] *vt* obtenir
obvious [ˈɒbvɪəs] *adj* évident **(that**
que) ● **obviously** *adv (of course)*
évidemment; *(conspicuously)*
manifestement
occasion [əˈkeɪʒən] *n (time,
opportunity)* occasion *f; (event)*
événement *m;* **on several
occasions** à plusieurs reprises ●
occasional *adj* occasionnel, -elle;
she drinks the o. whisky elle
boit un whisky de temps en temps
● **occasionally** *adv* de temps en
temps

occupy ['ɒkjʊpaɪ] (pt & pp **-ied**) vt (space, time, attention) occuper; **to keep oneself occupied** s'occuper (**doing** à faire) • **occupation** [-'peɪʃən] n (**a**) (pastime) occupation f; (profession) métier m (**b**) (of house, land) occupation f • **occupier** n (of house) occupant, -e mf

occur [ə'kɜː(r)] (pt & pp **-rr-**) vi (happen) avoir lieu; (of opportunity) se présenter; (be found) se trouver; **it occurs to me that…** il me vient à l'esprit que…

ocean ['əʊʃən] n océan m

o'clock [ə'klɒk] adv (**it's**) **three o.** (il est) trois heures

October [ɒk'təʊbə(r)] n octobre m

octopus ['ɒktəpəs] n pieuvre f

odd [ɒd] adj (**a**) (strange) bizarre, curieux, -euse (**b**) (number) impair (**c**) (left over) **sixty o.** soixante et quelques; **an o. glove/sock** un gant/une chaussette dépareillé(e) (**d**) (occasional) **I smoke the o. cigarette** je fume une cigarette de temps en temps; **o. jobs** petits travaux mpl • **oddly** adv bizarrement; **o. enough, he was elected** chose curieuse, il a été élu • **odds** npl (**a**) (in betting) cote f; (chances) chances fpl (**b**) (expressions) **to be at o. (with sb)** être en désaccord (avec qn); Fam **o. and ends** des bricoles fpl

odour ['əʊdə(r)] (Am **odor**) n odeur f

of [əv, stressed ɒv] prep de, d'; **of the boy** du garçon; **of the boys** des garçons; **of wood/paper** de ou en bois/papier; **she has a lot of it/of them** elle en a beaucoup; **there are ten of us** nous sommes dix; **a friend of his** un ami à lui, un de ses amis; **that's nice of you** c'est gentil de ta part; **of no value/interest** sans valeur/intérêt; Br **the fifth of June** le cinq juin

off [ɒf] **1** adj (light, gas, radio) éteint; (tap) fermé; (switched off at mains) coupé; (cancelled) annulé; (milk, meat) tourné; **I'm o. today** je ne travaille pas aujourd'hui **2** adv **to be o.** (leave) partir; **a day o.** (holiday) un jour de congé; **five percent o.** une réduction de cinq pour cent; **on and o., o. and on** (sometimes) de temps à autre **3** prep (from) de; (distant) éloigné de; **to fall o. the wall/ladder** tomber du mur/de l'échelle; **to take sth o. the table** prendre qch sur la table; **she's o. her food** elle ne mange plus rien • **off-chance n on the o.** à tout hasard • **off-colour** (Am **off-color**) adj Br (ill) patraque; (indecent) d'un goût douteux • **offhand 1** adj désinvolte **2** adv (immediately) au pied levé • **off-licence** n Br ≃ magasin m de vins et de spiritueux • **off-peak** adj (rate, price) heures creuses inv • **offside** adj **to be o.** (of footballer) être hors jeu • **offspring** n progéniture f

offend [ə'fend] vt offenser; **to be offended** s'offenser (**at** de) • **offence** (Am **offense**) n (against the law) infraction f; (more serious) délit m; **to take o.** s'offenser (**at** de); **to give o.** offenser • **offensive 1** adj choquant **2** n offensive f; **to be on the o.** être passé à l'offensive

offer ['ɒfə(r)] **1** n offre f; **to make sb an o.** faire une offre à qn; **on (special) o.** en promotion **2** vt offrir; (explanation) donner; (apologies) présenter; **to o. sb**

sth, **to o. sth to sb** offrir qch à
qn; **to o. to do sth** proposer *ou*
offrir de faire qch

office ['ɒfɪs] *n* (a) *(room)* bureau
m; *Am (of doctor)* cabinet *m*; **o.
hours** heures *fpl* de bureau; **o.
worker** employé, -e *mf* de bureau
(b) *(position)* fonctions *fpl*; **to be
in o.** être au pouvoir

officer ['ɒfɪsə(r)] *n (in the army,
navy)* officier *m*; **(police) o.** agent
m de police

official [ə'fɪʃəl] **1** *adj* officiel, -elle
2 *n* responsable *mf*; *(civil servant)*
fonctionnaire *mf* • **officially** *adv*
officiellement

often ['ɒf(t)ən] *adv* souvent; **how
o.?** combien de fois?; **every so o.**
de temps en temps

oh [əʊ] *exclam* oh!, ah!; *(in pain)*
aïe!; **oh yes!** mais oui!

oil [ɔɪl] **1** *n (for machine, cooking)*
huile *f*; *(petroleum)* pétrole *m*;
(fuel) mazout *m* **2** *adj (industry)*
pétrolier, -ère; *(painting, paint)* à
l'huile; **o. lamp** lampe *f* à pétrole
3 *vt (machine)* huiler • **oily (-ier,
-iest)** *adj (hands, rag)* graisseux,
-euse; *(skin, hair)* gras *(f* grasse)

ointment ['ɔɪntmənt] *n*
pommade *f*

OK, okay ['əʊ'keɪ] *adj & adv =*
all right

old [əʊld] **(-er, -est)** *adj* vieux *(f*
vieille); *(former)* ancien, -enne;
how o. is he? quel âge a-t-il?;
he's ten years o. il a dix ans; **he's
older than me** il est plus âgé que
moi; **the oldest son** le fils aîné;
to get *or* **grow old(er)** vieillir; **o.
age** vieillesse *f*; **o. man** vieillard
m, vieil homme *m*; **o. people** les
personnes *fpl* âgées; **o. people's
home** maison *f* de retraite; *Fam*
any o. how n'importe comment
• **old-fashioned** [-'fæʃənd] *adj*

(out-of-date) démodé; *(person)*
vieux jeu *inv*; *(traditional)*
d'autrefois

olive ['ɒlɪv] *n (fruit)* olive *f*; **o. oil**
huile *f* d'olive

Olympic [ə'lɪmpɪk] *adj* **the O.
Games** les jeux *mpl* Olympiques

omelet(te) ['ɒmlɪt] *n* omelette *f*;
cheese o. omelette *f* au fromage

omen ['əʊmən] *n* augure *m*

ominous ['ɒmɪnəs] *adj* inquiétant;
(event) de mauvais augure

omit [əʊ'mɪt] *(pt & pp* **-tt-)**
vt omettre **(to do** de faire) •
omission *n* omission *f*

on [ɒn] **1** *prep* (a) *(expressing
position)* sur; **on page 4** à la
page 4; **on the right/left** à
droite/gauche (b) *(about)* sur (c)
(expressing manner or means)
on the train/plane dans le
train/l'avion; **to be on** *(a course)*
suivre; *(project)* travailler à; *(team,
committee)* faire partie de; *Fam* **it's
on me!** *(I'll pay)* c'est pour moi!
(d) *(with time)* **on Monday** lundi;
on Mondays le lundi; **on (the
evening of) May 3rd** le 3 mai
(au soir); **on my arrival** à mon
arrivée (e) *(+ present participle)*
en; **on learning that...** en
apprenant que... **2** *adv (ahead)* en
avant; *(in progress)* en cours; *(lid,
brake)* mis; *(light, radio)* allumé;
(gas, tap) ouvert; *(machine)* en
marche; **she has her hat on**
elle a mis son chapeau; **I've got
something on** *(I'm busy)* je suis
pris; **the strike is on** la grève aura
lieu; **what's on?** *(on TV)* qu'est-
ce qu'il y a à la télé?; *(in theatre,
cinema)* qu'est-ce qu'on joue?; **he
went on and on about it** il n'en
finissait pas; *Fam* **that's just not
on!** c'est inadmissible!

once [wʌns] **1** *adv* *(on one
occasion)* une fois; *(formerly)*
autrefois; **o. a month** une fois par
mois; **o. again, o. more** encore
une fois; **at o.** *(immediately)* tout
de suite; **all at o.** *(suddenly)* tout à
coup; *(at the same time)* à la fois **2**
conj une fois que

one [wʌn] **1** *adj* **(a)** un, une; **page
o.** la page un; **twenty-o.** vingt et
un **(b)** *(only)* seul **(c)** *(same)* le
même *(f* la même); **in the o. bus**
dans le même bus **2** *pron* **(a)** un,
une; **do you want o.?** en veux-
tu (un)?; **o. of them** l'un d'eux,
l'une d'elles; **a big/small o.** un
grand/petit; **this o.** celui-ci, celle-
ci; **that o.** celui-là, celle-là; **the o.
who/which…** celui/celle qui…;
another o. un(e) autre; **I for o.**
pour ma part **(b)** *(impersonal)* on;
o. knows on sait; **it helps o.** ça
vous aide; **o.'s family** sa famille
• **one-off, one-of-a-kind** *adj
Fam* unique • **oneself** *pron* soi-
même; *(reflexive)* se, s'; **to cut
o.** se couper • **one-to-one** *adj
(discussion)* en tête à tête • **one-
way** *adj (street)* à sens unique; **o.
ticket** billet *m* simple

onion [ˈʌnjən] *n* oignon *m*

online [ɒnˈlaɪn] *adj Comptr* en
ligne

only [ˈəʊnlɪ] **1** *adj* seul; **the o.
one** le seul, la seule; **an o. son** un
fils unique **2** *adv* seulement, ne…
que; **I o. have ten** je n'en ai que
dix, j'en ai seulement dix; **if o.** si
seulement; **I have o. just seen it**
je viens tout juste de le voir; **o. he
knows** lui seul le sait **3** *conj Fam
(but)* mais

onto [ˈɒntuː, *unstressed* ˈɒntə]
prep = **on to**

onward(s) [ˈɒnwəd(z)] *adv* en

avant; **from that day o.** à partir
de ce jour-là

opaque [əʊˈpeɪk] *adj* opaque

open [ˈəʊpən] **1** *adj* ouvert;
(view, road) dégagé; *(post, job)*
vacant; *(airline ticket)* open *inv*;
in the o. air au grand air; **o. to**
(criticism, attack) exposé à; *(ideas,
suggestions)* ouvert à; **to leave
sth o.** *(date)* ne pas préciser qch
2 *n* **(out) in the o.** *(outside)*
dehors; **to sleep (out) in the
o.** dormir à la belle étoile **3** *vt*
ouvrir; *(arms, legs)* écarter; **to o.
sth out** *(paper, map)* ouvrir qch;
to o. sth up *(bag, shop)* ouvrir
qch **4** *vi (of flower, door, eyes)*
s'ouvrir; *(of shop, office)* ouvrir;
(of play) débuter; **to o. on to
sth** *(of window)* donner sur qch;
to o. out *(widen)* s'élargir; **to o.
up** *(of flower, person)* s'ouvrir; *(of
shopkeeper)* ouvrir • **open-air** *adj
(pool)* en plein air • **opening 1** *n*
ouverture *f*; *(opportunity)* occasion
f favorable **2** *adj (time, hours,
speech)* d'ouverture; **o. night** *(of
play, musical)* première *f* • **openly**
adv ouvertement • **open-minded**
adj à l'esprit ouvert • **open-plan**
adj (office) paysager, -ère

opera [ˈɒprə] *n* opéra *m*

operate [ˈɒpəreɪt] **1** *vt (machine)*
faire fonctionner; *(service)* assurer
2 *vi* **(a) to o. on sb (for sth)**
(of surgeon) opérer qn (de qch)
(b) *(of machine)* fonctionner; *(of
company)* opérer • **operating**
adj Br **o. theatre,** *Am* **o. room**
salle *f* d'opération • **operation**
[-ˈreɪʃən] *n Med* opération *f*; *(of
machine)* fonctionnement *m*; **in
o.** *(machine)* en service; *(plan)* en
vigueur; **to have an o.** se faire
opérer

opinion [ə'pɪnjən] *n* opinion *f*; **in my o.** à mon avis

opponent [ə'pəʊnənt] *n* adversaire *mf*

opportunity [ɒpə'tjuːnətɪ] (*pl -ies*) *n* occasion *f* (**to do** *or* **of doing** de faire); **opportunities** (*prospects*) perspectives *fpl*; **to take the o. to do sth** profiter de l'occasion pour faire qch

opposed [ə'pəʊzd] *adj* opposé (**to** à); **as o. to...** par opposition à...

opposite ['ɒpəzɪt] **1** *adj* (*side*) opposé; (*house, page*) d'en face; **in the o. direction** en sens inverse **2** *adv* en face; **the house o.** la maison d'en face **3** *prep* **o. (to)** en face de **4** *n* **the o.** le contraire • **opposition** [-'zɪʃən] *n* opposition *f* (**to** à); **the o.** (*rival camp*) l'adversaire *m*; (*in business*) la concurrence

oppress [ə'pres] *vt* (*treat cruelly*) opprimer • **oppression** *n* oppression *f* • **oppressive** *adj* (*heat*) accablant, étouffant; (*ruler, regime*) oppressif, -ive

opt [ɒpt] *vi* **to o. for sth** opter pour qch; **to o. to do sth** choisir de faire qch; **to o. out** se désengager (**of** de)

optician [ɒp'tɪʃən] *n* (*dispensing*) opticien, -enne *mf*

optimistic [ɒptɪ'mɪstɪk] *adj* optimiste (**about** quant à)

option ['ɒpʃən] *n* (*choice*) choix *m*; (*school subject*) matière *f* à option; **she has no o.** elle n'a pas le choix • **optional** *adj* facultatif, -ive

or [ɔː(r)] *conj* ou; **he doesn't drink or smoke** il ne boit ni ne fume; **ten or so** environ dix

oral ['ɔːrəl] **1** *adj* oral **2** *n* (*exam*) oral *m*

orange ['ɒrɪndʒ] **1** *n* (*fruit*) orange *f*; **o. juice** jus *m* d'orange **2** *adj & n* (*colour*) orange (*m*) *inv*

orbit ['ɔːbɪt] **1** *n* (*of planet*) orbite *f* **2** *vt* être en orbite autour de

orchard ['ɔːtʃəd] *n* verger *m*

orchestra ['ɔːkɪstrə] *n* orchestre *m*; *Am* **the o.** (*in theatre*) l'orchestre *m*

orchid ['ɔːkɪd] *n* orchidée *f*

ordeal [ɔː'diːl] *n* épreuve *f*

order ['ɔːdə(r)] **1** *n* (*instruction, arrangement*) & *Rel* ordre *m*; (*purchase*) commande *f*; **in o.** (*passport*) en règle; **in o. of age** par ordre d'âge; **in o. to do sth** afin de faire qch; **in o. that...** afin que... (+ *subjunctive*); **out of o.** (*machine*) en panne; (*telephone*) en dérangement; **o. form** bon *m* de commande **2** *vt* (*meal, goods*) commander; (*taxi*) appeler; **to o. sb to do sth** ordonner à qn de faire qch **3** *vi* (*in café*) commander

ordinary ['ɔːdənrɪ] *adj* ordinaire; **it's out of the o.** ça sort de l'ordinaire; **she was just an o. tourist** c'était une touriste comme une autre

organ ['ɔːgən] *n* (**a**) (*part of body*) organe *m* (**b**) (*musical instrument*) orgue *m*

organic [ɔː'gænɪk] *adj* organique; (*vegetables, farming*) biologique

organize ['ɔːgənaɪz] *vt* organiser • **organization** [-'zeɪʃən] *n* organisation *f* • **organizer** *n* (*person*) organisateur, -trice *mf*; (**personal**) **o.** (*diary*) agenda *m*

oriental [ɔːrɪ'entəl] *adj* oriental

orientate ['ɔːrɪənteɪt] (*Am* **orient** ['ɔːrɪənt]) *vt* orienter

origin ['ɒrɪdʒɪn] *n* origine *f*

original [ə'rɪdʒɪnəl] **1** *adj* (*novel, innovative*) original; (*first*) d'origine **2** *n* (*document, painting*)

original *m* • **originally** *adv (at first)* à l'origine
ornament ['ɔːnəmənt] *n* ornement *m*
orphan ['ɔːfən] *n* orphelin, -e *mf*
orthodox ['ɔːθədɒks] *adj* orthodoxe
Oscar ['ɒskə(r)] *n Cin* oscar *m*
ostrich ['ɒstrɪtʃ] *n* autruche *f*
other ['ʌðə(r)] **1** *adj* autre; **o. doctors** d'autres médecins; **the o. one** l'autre *mf* **2** *pron* **the o.** l'autre *mf*; **(some) others** d'autres; **none o. than, no o. than** nul autre que **3** *adv* **o. than** autrement que • **otherwise** *adv & conj* autrement
ouch [aʊtʃ] *exclam* aïe!
ought [ɔːt]

La forme négative **ought not** s'écrit **oughtn't** en forme contractée.

v aux **(a)** *(expressing obligation, desirability)* **you o. to leave** tu devrais partir; **I o. to have done it** j'aurais dû le faire **(b)** *(expressing probability)* **it o. to be ready** ça devrait être prêt
ounce [aʊns] *n (unit of weight)* = 28,35 g, once *f*
our [aʊə(r)] *possessive adj* notre, *pl* nos • **ours** *possessive pron* le nôtre, la nôtre, *pl* les nôtres; **this book is o.** ce livre est à nous *ou* est le nôtre; **a friend of o.** un de nos amis • **ourselves** *pron* nous-mêmes; *(reflexive and after prep)* nous; **we wash o.** nous nous lavons

out [aʊt] **1** *adv (outside)* dehors; *(not at home)* sorti; *(light, fire)* éteint; *(book)* publié; **to have a day o.** sortir pour la journée; **the sun's o.** il fait soleil; **the tide's o.** la marée est basse; **you're o.** *(in game)* tu es éliminé (**of** de);

before the week is o. avant la fin de la semaine; **o. here** ici; **o. there** là-bas **2** *prep* **o. of** *(outside)* hors de; **she's o. of town** elle n'est pas en ville; **to look/jump o. of the window** regarder/sauter par la fenêtre; **to drink/take/copy sth o. of sth** boire/prendre/copier qch dans qch; **made o. of wood** fait en bois; **o. of pity/love** par pitié/amour; **four o. of five** quatre sur cinq • **out-of-date** *adj (expired)* périmé; *(old-fashioned)* démodé

outbreak ['aʊtbreɪk] *n (of war, epidemic)* début *m*; *(of violence)* flambée *f*
outburst ['aʊtbɜːst] *n (of anger, joy)* explosion *f*; *(of violence)* flambée *f*
outcast ['aʊtkɑːst] *n* **(social) o.** paria *m*
outcry ['aʊtkraɪ] *(pl* -ies) *n* tollé *m*
outdated [aʊt'deɪtɪd] *adj* démodé
outdo [aʊt'duː] *(pt* -did, *pp* -done) *vt* surpasser (**in** en)
outdoor ['aʊtdɔː(r)] *adj (pool, market)* découvert • **outdoors** *adv* dehors
outer ['aʊtə(r)] *adj* extérieur; **o. space** l'espace *m* intersidéral
outfit ['aʊtfɪt] *n (clothes)* ensemble *m*; **sports/ski o.** tenue *f* de sport/de ski
outgoing ['aʊtgəʊɪŋ] *adj (sociable)* liant
outgrow [aʊt'grəʊ] *(pt* -grew, *pp* -grown) *vt (habit)* passer l'âge de; **she's outgrown her jacket** sa veste est devenue trop petite pour elle
outing ['aʊtɪŋ] *n (excursion)* sortie *f*

outlaw ['autlɔː] **1** *n* hors-la-loi *m inv* **2** *vt (ban)* proscrire

outline ['autlaɪn] **1** *n (shape)* contour *m; (of play, novel)* résumé *m;* **rough o.** *(of article, plan)* esquisse *f* **2** *vt (plan, situation)* esquisser

outlook ['autluk] *n (for future)* perspectives *fpl; (point of view)* façon *f* de voir les choses; *(of weather)* prévisions *fpl*

outnumber [aut'nʌmbə(r)] *vt* l'emporter en nombre sur

output ['autput] *n (of goods)* production *f; (computer data)* données *fpl* de sortie

outrage ['autreɪdʒ] **1** *n (scandal)* scandale *m; (anger)* indignation *f* (**at** face à); *(crime)* atrocité *f* **2** *vt (make indignant)* scandaliser ● **outrageous** [-'reɪdʒəs] *adj (shocking)* scandaleux, -euse; *(atrocious)* atroce

outright 1 [aut'raɪt] *adv (refuse)* catégoriquement; *(be killed)* sur le coup **2** [ˈautraɪt] *adj (failure)* total; *(refusal)* catégorique; *(winner)* incontesté

outset ['autset] *n* **at the o.** au début; **from the o.** dès le départ

outside 1 [aut'saɪd] *adv* dehors, à l'extérieur; **to go o.** sortir **2** [aut'saɪd] *prep* à l'extérieur de, en dehors de; *(in front of)* devant; *(apart from)* en dehors de **3** [aut'saɪd] *n* extérieur *m* **4** ['autsaɪd] *adj* extérieur; **the o. lane** *(on road) Br* la voie de droite, *Am* la voie de gauche ● **outsider** [-'saɪdə(r)] *n (stranger)* étranger, -ère *mf; (horse in race)* outsider *m*

outskirts ['autskɜːts] *npl* banlieue *f*

outspoken [aut'spəukən] *adj (frank)* franc *(f* franche)

outstanding [aut'stændɪŋ] *adj*

exceptionnel, -elle; *(problem, business)* en suspens; *(debt)* impayé

outstay [aut'steɪ] *vt* **to o. one's welcome** abuser de l'hospitalité de son hôte

outward ['autwəd] *adj (sign, appearance)* extérieur; **o. journey** *or* **trip** aller *m* ● **outward(s)** *adv* vers l'extérieur

oval ['əuvəl] *adj & n* ovale *(m)*

ovation [əu'veɪʃən] *n* **to give sb a standing o.** se lever pour applaudir qn

oven ['ʌvən] *n* four *m*

over ['əuvə(r)] **1** *prep (on)* sur; *(above)* au-dessus de; *(on the other side of)* par-dessus; **the bridge o. the river** le pont qui traverse le fleuve; **to jump/look o. sth** sauter/regarder par-dessus qch; **o. it** *(on)* dessus; *(above)* au-dessus; **to fight o. sth** se battre pour qch; **o. the phone** au téléphone; **o. the holidays** pendant les vacances; **o. ten days** *(more than)* plus de dix jours; **men o. sixty** les hommes de plus de soixante ans; **he's o. his flu** il est remis de sa grippe **2** *adv (above)* par-dessus; **o. here** ici; **o. there** là-bas; **he's o. in Italy** il est en Italie; **she's o. from Paris** elle est venue de Paris; **to ask sb o.** inviter qn; **to be (all) o.** être terminé; **to start all o. (again)** recommencer à zéro; **a kilo or o.** *(more)* un kilo ou plus; **o. and o. (again)** *(often)* à plusieurs reprises; **children of five and o.** les enfants de cinq ans et plus

overall 1 ['əuvərɔːl] *adj (measurement, length)* total; *(result)* global **2** [əuvər'ɔːl] *adv* dans l'ensemble **3** ['əuvərɔːl] *n (protective coat)* blouse *f*; *Am (boiler suit)* bleu *m* de travail • **overalls** *npl Br (boiler suit)* bleu *m* de travail; *Am (dungarees)* salopette *f*

overboard ['əʊvəbɔːd] *adv* par-dessus bord

overcast [əʊvə'kɑːst] *adj* nuageux, -euse

overcharge [əʊvə'tʃɑːdʒ] *vt* **to o. sb for sth** faire payer qch trop cher à qn

overcoat ['əʊvəkəʊt] *n* pardessus *m*

overcome [əʊvə'kʌm] (*pt* **-came,** *pp* **-come**) *vt (problem, disgust)* surmonter; *(shyness, fear, enemy)* vaincre; **to be o. by grief** être accablé de chagrin

overcook [əʊvə'kʊk] *vt* faire cuire trop

overcrowded [əʊvə'kraʊdɪd] *adj (house, country)* surpeuplé; *(bus, train)* bondé

overdo [əʊvə'duː] (*pt* **-did,** *pp* **-done**) *vt* exagérer; *(overcook)* faire cuire trop; **to o. it** se surmener

overdose ['əʊvədəʊs] *n* overdose *f*

overdraft ['əʊvədrɑːft] *n Fin* découvert *m* • **overdrawn** [-'drɔːn] *adj Fin (account)* à découvert

overdue [əʊvə'djuː] *adj (train, bus)* en retard; *(bill)* impayé; *(book)* qui n'a pas été rendu

overestimate [əʊvər'estɪmeɪt] *vt* surestimer

overexcited [əʊvərɪk'saɪtɪd] *adj* surexcité

overflow [əʊvə'fləʊ] *vi (of river, bath)* déborder; **to be overflowing with sth** *(of town, shop, house)* regorger de qch

overgrown [əʊvə'grəʊn] *adj*

(garden, path) envahi par la végétation

overhaul [əʊvə'hɔːl] *vt (vehicle, schedule, text)* réviser

overhead 1 [əʊvə'hed] *adv* au-dessus **2** ['əʊvəhed] *adj (cable)* aérien, -enne

overhear [əʊvə'hɪə(r)] (*pt & pp* **-heard**) *vt (conversation)* surprendre; *(person)* entendre

overheat [əʊvə'hiːt] *vi (of engine)* chauffer

overjoyed [əʊvə'dʒɔɪd] *adj* fou (*f* folle) de joie

overlap [əʊvə'læp] *vi* se chevaucher

overleaf [əʊvə'liːf] *adv* au verso

overload [əʊvə'ləʊd] *vt* surchar-ger

overlook [əʊvə'lʊk] *vt* **(a)** *(not notice)* ne pas remarquer; *(forget)* oublier; *(disregard)* fermer les yeux sur **(b)** *(of window, house)* donner sur

overnight 1 [əʊvə'naɪt] *adv (during the night)* pendant la nuit; *Fig (suddenly)* du jour au lendemain; **to stay o.** passer la nuit **2** ['əʊvənaɪt] *adj (train, flight)* de nuit; *(stay)* d'une nuit; **o. bag** (petit) sac *m* de voyage

overpower [əʊvə'paʊə(r)] *vt* maîtriser • **overpowering** *adj (heat, smell)* suffocant

overpriced [əʊvə'praɪst] *adj* trop cher (*f* trop chère)

overrated [əʊvə'reɪtɪd] *adj* surfait

overreact [əʊvərɪ'ækt] *vi* réagir excessivement

override [əʊvə'raɪd] (*pt* **-rode,** *pp* **-ridden**) *vt (be more important than)* l'emporter sur; *(invalidate)* annuler; *(take no notice of)* passer outre à • **overriding** *adj* *(importance)* capital; *(factor)* prédominant

overrule [əʊvə'ruːl] *vt (decision)* annuler; *(objection)* rejeter

overrun [əʊvə'rʌn] *(pt* **-ran,** *pp* **-run,** *pres p* **-running)** *vt (invade)* envahir; *(go beyond)* dépasser

overseas 1 ['əʊvəsiːz] *adj* d'outre-mer; *(trade)* extérieur **2** [əʊvə'siːz] *adv* à l'étranger

oversight ['əʊvəsaɪt] *n* oubli *m*, omission *f*

oversleep [əʊvə'sliːp] *(pt & pp* **-slept)** *vi* ne pas se réveiller à temps

overstep [əʊvə'step] *(pt & pp* **-pp-)** *vt* outrepasser; *Fig* **to o. the mark** dépasser les bornes

overtake [əʊvə'teɪk] *(pt* **-took,** *pp* **-taken) 1** *vt* dépasser **2** *vi (in vehicle)* doubler, dépasser

overthrow [əʊvə'θrəʊ] *(pt* **-threw,** *pp* **-thrown)** *vt* renverser

overtime ['əʊvətaɪm] **1** *n* heures *fpl* supplémentaires **2** *adv* **to work o.** faire des heures supplémentaires

overturn [əʊvə'tɜːn] *vt (chair, table, car)* renverser; *(boat)* faire chavirer; *Fig (decision)* annuler

overweight [əʊvə'weɪt] *adj* trop gros *(f* trop grosse)

overwhelmed [əʊvə'welmd] *adj*

o. with *(work, offers)* submergé de; **o. by** *(kindness, gift)* vivement touché par ● **overwhelming** *adj (heat, grief)* accablant; *(majority, defeat)* écrasant; *(desire)* irrésistible

overworked [əʊvə'wɜːkt] *adj (person)* surchargé de travail

owe [əʊ] *vt* devoir; **to o. sb sth, to o. sth to sb** devoir qch à qn ● **owing** *prep* **o. to** à cause de

owl [aʊl] *n* hibou *m (pl* -oux)

own [əʊn] **1** *adj* propre **2** *pron* **my o.** le mien, la mienne; **a house of his o.** sa propre maison, sa maison à lui; **to do sth on one's o.** faire qch tout seul; **to be (all) on one's o.** être tout seul; **to get one's o. back (on sb)** se venger (de qn) **3** *vt (possess)* posséder; **who owns this ball?** à qui appartient cette balle? **4** *vi* **to o. up (to sth)** *(confess)* avouer (qch) ● **owner** *n* propriétaire *mf*

ox [ɒks] *(pl* **oxen** ['ɒksən]) *n* bœuf *m*

oxygen ['ɒksɪdʒən] *n* oxygène *m*; **o. mask** masque *m* à oxygène

oyster ['ɔɪstə(r)] *n* huître *f*

oz *(abbr* **ounce)** once *f*

ozone ['əʊzəʊn] *n Chem* ozone *m*; **o. layer** couche *f* d'ozone

Pp

P, p[1] [piː] *n (letter)* P, p *m inv*

p[2] [piː] *(abbr* **penny, pence)** *Br* penny *m*/pence *mpl*

pace [peɪs] **1** *n (speed)* allure *f*; *(step, measure)* pas *m*; **to keep p. with sb** *(follow)* suivre qn; *(in quality of work)* se maintenir à la hauteur de qn **2** *vi* **to p. up and down** faire les cent pas

Pacific [pəˈsɪfɪk] *adj* **the P. (Ocean)** le Pacifique, l'océan *m* Pacifique

pacify [ˈpæsɪfaɪ] *(pt & pp* -ied*) vt (crowd, person)* calmer • **pacifier** *n Am (of baby)* tétine *f* • **pacifist** *n* pacifiste *mf*

pack [pæk] **1** *n (of cigarettes, washing powder)* paquet *m*; *(of beer)* pack *m*; *(of cards)* jeu *m*; *(of hounds, wolves)* meute *f*; **a p. of lies** un tissu de mensonges **2** *vt (fill)* remplir (**with** de); *(object into box, suitcase)* mettre; *(make into package)* empaqueter; *(crush, compress)* tasser; **to p. one's bags** faire ses valises **3** *vi (fill one's bags)* faire sa valise/ses valises • **packed** *adj (bus, room)* bondé

▸**pack into 1** *vt sep (cram)* entasser dans; *(put)* mettre dans **2** *vt insep (crowd into)* s'entasser dans

▸**pack up 1** *vt sep (put into box)* emballer; *Fam (give up)* laisser tomber **2** *vi Fam (of machine, vehicle)* tomber en panne

package [ˈpækɪdʒ] **1** *n* paquet *m*; *Br* **p. deal** *or* **holiday** voyage *m* organisé **2** *vt* emballer •

packaging *n (material, action)* emballage *m*

packet [ˈpækɪt] *n* paquet *m*

pact [pækt] *n* pacte *m*

pad [pæd] **1** *n (of cotton wool)* tampon *m*; *(for writing)* bloc *m*; **ink p.** tampon encreur **2** *(pt & pp* -dd-*) vt* **to p. out** *(speech, essay)* étoffer • **padded** *adj (jacket)* matelassé • **padding** *n (material)* rembourrage *m*; *(in speech, essay)* remplissage *m*

paddle [ˈpædəl] **1** *n (for canoe)* pagaie *f*; **to have a p.** patauger **2** *vi (walk in water)* patauger • **paddling** *n Br* **p. pool** piscine *f* gonflable

padlock [ˈpædlɒk] *n* cadenas *m*

paediatrician [piːdɪəˈtrɪʃən] *(Am* **pediatrician)** *n* pédiatre *mf*

page[1] [peɪdʒ] *n (of book)* page *f*; **on p. 6** à la page 6

page[2] [peɪdʒ] **1** *n* **p. (boy)** *(at wedding)* page *m* **2** *vt* **to p. sb** faire appeler qn; *(by electronic device)* biper qn • **pager** *n* bip *m*

paid [peɪd] **1** *pt & pp of* **pay 2** *adj (person, work)* rémunéré

pain [peɪn] *n (physical)* douleur *f*; *(emotional)* peine *f*; **to have a p. in one's arm** avoir une douleur au bras; **to go to** *or* **take (great) pains to do sth** se donner du mal pour faire qch; *Fam* **to be a p. (in the neck)** être casse-pieds • **painful** *adj (physically)* douloureux, -euse; *(emotionally)*

pénible • **painkiller** n calmant m
• **painless** adj indolore
paint [peɪnt] **1** n peinture f **2** vt
peindre; **to p. sth blue** peindre qch
en bleu **3** vi peindre • **paintbrush**
n pinceau m • **painter** n peintre
m; Br **p. and decorator,** Am
(house) p. peintre-tapissier m •
painting n (activity) la peinture;
(picture) tableau m, peinture f
pair [peə(r)] n paire f; **a p. of
shorts/trousers** un short/
pantalon
pajamas [pə'dʒɑːməz] npl Am =
pyjamas
Pakistan [pɑːkɪ'stɑːn] n le
Pakistan • **Pakistani 1** adj
pakistanais **2** n Pakistanais, -e mf
pal [pæl] n Fam copain m, copine
f
palace ['pælɪs] n palais m
pale [peɪl] (**-er, -est**) adj pâle
Palestine ['pæləstaɪn] n la
Palestine • **Palestinian** [-'stɪnɪən]
1 adj palestinien, -enne **2** n
Palestinien, -enne mf
palm¹ [pɑːm] n (of hand) paume f
palm² [pɑːm] n **p. (tree)** palmier
m
pamper ['pæmpə(r)] vt dorloter
pamphlet ['pæmflɪt] n brochure f
pan [pæn] n (saucepan) casserole
f; (for frying) poêle f
pancake ['pænkeɪk] n crêpe f; **P.
Day** mardi m gras
panda ['pændə] n panda m
pander ['pændə(r)] vi **to p. to sb/
sth** flatter qn/qch
pane [peɪn] n vitre f
panel ['pænəl] n (**a**) (of door)
panneau m (**b**) (of judges) jury m;
(of experts) comité m; (of TV or
radio guests) invités mpl
panic ['pænɪk] **1** n panique f **2** (pt
& pp **-ck-**) vi paniquer

panorama [pænə'rɑːmə] n panorama m
pant [pænt] vi haleter
pantomime ['pæntəmaɪm] n Br
(show) = spectacle de Noël
pants [pænts] npl (underwear) slip
m; Am (trousers) pantalon m
pantyhose ['pæntɪhəʊz] n Am
(tights) collant m
paper ['peɪpə(r)] **1** n papier m;
(newspaper) journal m; (student's
exercise) copie f; (study, report)
article m; **a piece of p.** un bout
de papier; **papers** (documents)
papiers **2** adj (bag) en papier;
(cup, plate) en carton; Br **p.
shop** marchand m de journaux;
p. towel essuie-tout m inv •
paperback n livre m de poche
• **paperclip** n trombone m •
paperweight n presse-papiers
m inv • **paperwork** n (in office)
écritures fpl; Pej (red tape)
paperasserie f
par [pɑː(r)] n (in golf) par m; **on a
p.** au même niveau (**with** que)
paracetamol [pærə'siːtəmɒl] n
paracétamol m
parachute ['pærəʃuːt] n
parachute m
parade [pə'reɪd] **1** n (procession)
défilé m **2** vi **to p. about** se
pavaner
paradise ['pærədaɪs] n paradis m
paragraph ['pærəgrɑːf] n
paragraphe m
parallel ['pærəlel] adj Math
parallèle (**with** or **to** à); Fig
(comparable) semblable (**with** or
to à)
paralyse ['pærəlaɪz] (Am **paralyze**) vt paralyser
paramedic [pærə'medɪk] n
auxiliaire mf médical(e)
paranoid ['pærənɔɪd] adj para-
noïaque

paraphrase ['pærəfreɪz] *vt* paraphraser

parasite ['pærəsaɪt] *n (person, organism)* parasite *m*

parasol ['pærəsɒl] *n (over table, on beach)* parasol *m; (lady's)* ombrelle *f*

parcel ['pɑːsəl] *n* colis *m*, paquet *m*

pardon ['pɑːdən] *n (forgiveness)* pardon *m;* **I beg your p.** *(apologizing)* je vous prie de m'excuser; **I beg your p.?** *(not hearing)* pardon?

parent ['peərənt] *n (father)* père *m; (mother)* mère *f;* **parents** parents *mpl*

Paris ['pærɪs] *n* Paris *m ou f* • **Parisian** [pə'rɪzɪən, *Am* pə'riːʒən] **1** *adj* parisien, -enne **2** *n* Parisien, -enne *mf*

park¹ [pɑːk] *n (garden)* parc *m*

park² [pɑːk] **1** *vt (vehicle)* garer **2** *vi (of vehicle)* se garer; *(remain parked)* stationner • **parking** *n* stationnement *m;* **'no p.'** 'défense de stationner'; *Am* **p. lot** parking *m;* **p. meter** parcmètre *m;* **p. place** *or* **space** place *f* de parking; **p. ticket** contravention *f*

parliament ['pɑːləmənt] *n* parlement *m*

parody ['pærədɪ] *(pl* **-ies)** *n* parodie *f*

parole [pə'rəʊl] *n* **to be (out) on p.** être en liberté conditionnelle

parrot ['pærət] *n* perroquet *m*

parsley ['pɑːslɪ] *n* persil *m*

parsnip ['pɑːsnɪp] *n* panais *m*

part¹ [pɑːt] **1** *n* partie *f; (quantity in mixture)* mesure *f; (of machine)* pièce *f; (of serial)* épisode *m; (role in play, film)* rôle *m; Am (in hair)* raie *f;* **to take p.** participer **(in** à); **to be a p. of sth** faire partie de qch; **for the most p.** dans

l'ensemble; **on the p. of...** de la part de...; **for my p.** pour ma part **2** *adv (partly)* en partie; **p. silk, p. cotton** soie et coton • **part-time** *adj & adv* à temps partiel

part² [pɑːt] **1** *vt (separate)* séparer; **to p. one's hair** se faire une raie **2** *vi (of friends)* se quitter; *(of married couple)* se séparer; **to p. with sth** se défaire de qch

partial ['pɑːʃəl] *adj (not total)* partiel, -elle; *(biased)* partial **(towards** envers); **to be p. to sth** avoir un faible pour qch

participate [pɑː'tɪsɪpeɪt] *vi* participer **(in** à) • **participant** *n* participant, -e *mf* • **participation** [-'peɪʃən] *n* participation *f*

particular [pə'tɪkjʊlə(r)] **1** *adj (specific, special)* particulier, -ère; *(exacting)* méticuleux, -euse; **this p. book** ce livre en particulier; **to be p. about sth** faire très attention à qch **2** *n* **in p.** en particulier • **particularly** *adv* particulièrement

parting ['pɑːtɪŋ] *n Br (in hair)* raie *f*

partition [pɑː'tɪʃən] *n (of room)* cloison *f*

partly ['pɑːtlɪ] *adv* en partie

partner ['pɑːtnə(r)] *n (in game)* partenaire *mf; (in business)* associé, -e *mf; (in relationship)* compagnon *m*, compagne *f* • **partnership** *n* association *f;* **in p. with** en association avec

party ['pɑːtɪ] *(pl* **-ies)** *n* **(a)** *(gathering)* fête *f;* **to have** *or* **throw a p.** donner une fête **(b)** *Pol* parti *m*

pass [pɑːs] **1** *n (entry permit)* laissez-passer *m inv; (for travel)* carte *f* d'abonnement; **p. mark** *(in exam)* moyenne *f* **2** *vt (move, give)* passer **(to** à); *(go past)* passer devant; *(vehicle, runner)* dépasser;

(exam) être reçu à; *(law)* voter; **to p. sb** *(in street)* croiser qn; **to p. the time** passer le temps **3** *vi (go past, go away)* passer **(to à; through** par); *(in exam)* avoir la moyenne; *(of time)* passer

►**pass away** *vi* décéder

►**pass by** *vi* passer à côté

►**pass on** *vt sep (message, illness)* transmettre **(to à)**

►**pass out** *vi (faint)* s'évanouir

►**pass round** *vt sep (cakes, document)* faire passer; *(hand out)* distribuer

►**pass through** *vi* passer

passage ['pæsɪdʒ] *n* **(a)** *(way through)* passage *m*; *(corridor)* couloir *m*; **with the p. of time** avec le temps **(b)** *(of text)* passage *m*

passenger ['pæsɪndʒə(r)] *n* passager, -ère *mf*; *(on train)* voyageur, -euse *mf*

passer-by [pɑːsə'baɪ] *(pl* **passers-by)** *n* passant, -e *mf*

passion ['pæʃən] *n* passion *f*; **to have a p. for sth** adorer qch ● **passionate** *adj* passionné

passive ['pæsɪv] **1** *adj* passif, -ive **2** *n* Gram passif *m*; **in the p.** au passif

passport ['pɑːspɔːt] *n* passeport *m*; **p. photo** photo *f* d'identité

password ['pɑːswɜːd] *n* mot *m* de passe

past [pɑːst] **1** *n* passé *m*; **in the p.** autrefois **2** *adj (gone by)* passé; *(former)* ancien, -enne; **these p. months** ces derniers mois; **in the p. tense** au passé **3** *prep (in front of)* devant; *(after)* après; *(beyond)* au-delà de; **it's p. four o'clock** il est quatre heures passées **4** *adv* devant; **to go p.** passer

pasta ['pæstə] *n* pâtes *fpl*

paste [peɪst] *n* pâte *f*

pastel [*Br* 'pæstəl, *Am* pæ'stel] *n* pastel *m*

pastille [*Br* 'pæstɪl, *Am* pæ'stiːl] *n* pastille *f*

pastime ['pɑːstaɪm] *n* passe-temps *m inv*

pastry ['peɪstrɪ] *(pl* **-ies)** *n (dough)* pâte *f*; *(cake)* pâtisserie *f*

pat [pæt] *(pt & pp* **-tt-)** *vt (tap)* tapoter; *(animal)* caresser

patch [pætʃ] **1** *n (for clothes)* pièce *f*; *(over eye)* bandeau *m*; *(of colour)* tache *f*; *(of ice)* plaque *f*; *Fig* **to be going through a bad p.** traverser une mauvaise passe **2** *vt* **to p. (up)** *(clothing)* rapiécer; **to p. things up** *(after argument)* se raccommoder ● **patchwork** *n* patchwork *m*

patent ['peɪtənt, 'pætənt] **1** *n* brevet *m* d'invention **2** *vt* (faire) breveter

path [pɑːθ] *(pl* **-s** [pɑːðz]) *n* chemin *m*; *(narrow)* sentier *m*; *(in park)* allée *f* ● **pathway** *n* sentier *m*

pathetic [pə'θetɪk] *adj* pitoyable

patience ['peɪʃəns] *n* **(a)** *(quality)* patience *f*; **to lose p.** perdre patience **(with sb** avec qn) **(b)** *Br (card game)* **to play p.** faire une réussite ● **patient 1** *adj* patient **2** *n Med* patient, -e *mf* ● **patiently** *adv* patiemment

patio ['pætɪəʊ] *(pl* **-os)** *n* patio *m*

patriotic [pætrɪ'ɒtɪk, peɪtrɪ'ɒtɪk] *adj (views, speech)* patriotique; *(person)* patriote

patrol [pə'trəʊl] **1** *n* patrouille *f*; **to be on p.** être de patrouille; **p. car** voiture *f* de police **2** *(pt & pp* **-ll-)** *vt* patrouiller dans

patronize ['pætrənaɪz] *vt (be condescending towards)* traiter avec condescendance ● **patronizing** *adj* condescendant

pattern ['pætən] n (design) dessin m, motif m; (in sewing) patron m; (in knitting) & Fig (norm) modèle m; (tendency) tendance f

paunch [pɔːntʃ] n ventre m

pause [pɔːz] **1** n pause f; (in conversation) silence m **2** vi (stop) faire une pause; (hesitate) hésiter

pave [peɪv] vt (road) paver (**with** de); Fig **to p. the way for sth** ouvrir la voie à qch • **pavement** n Br (beside road) trottoir m; Am (roadway) chaussée f

paw [pɔː] n patte f

pawn¹ [pɔːn] n (chess piece) & Fig pion m

pawn² [pɔːn] vt mettre en gage • **pawnshop** n mont-de-piété m

pay [peɪ] **1** n paie f, salaire m; (of soldier) solde f; **p. rise** augmentation f de salaire; Br **p. slip,** Am **p. stub** fiche f de paie **2** (pt & pp **paid**) vt (person, money, bill) payer; (sum, deposit) verser; (yield) (of investment) rapporter; **I paid £5 for it** je l'ai payé 5 livres; **to p. sb to do sth** or **for doing sth** payer qn pour qu'il fasse qch; **to p. sb for sth** payer qch à qn **3** vi payer • **payment** n paiement m; (of deposit) versement m; **on p. of 20 euros** moyennant 20 euros • **payphone** n téléphone m public

▶**pay back** vt sep (person, loan) rembourser; Fig **I'll p. you back for this!** tu me le paieras!

▶**pay for** vt insep payer

▶**pay in** vt sep (cheque, money) verser sur un compte

▶**pay off 1** vt sep (debt) rembourser; (in instalments) rembourser par acomptes **2** vi (of work, effort) porter ses fruits

▶**pay up** vi payer

PC [piː'siː] **(a)** (abbr **personal computer**) PC m **(b)** (abbr **politically correct**) politiquement correct

PE [piː'iː] (abbr **physical education**) n EPS f

pea [piː] n pois m; **peas** petits pois mpl

peace [piːs] n paix f; **p. of mind** tranquillité f d'esprit; **at p.** en paix (**with** avec); **I'd like some p. and quiet** j'aimerais un peu de silence • **peaceful** adj (calm) paisible; (non-violent) pacifique

peach [piːtʃ] n (fruit) pêche f

peacock ['piːkɒk] n paon m

peak [piːk] **1** n (mountain top) sommet m; (mountain) pic m; (of cap) visière f; Fig (of fame, success) apogée m **2** adj (hours, period) de pointe

peanut ['piːnʌt] n cacah(o)uète f; **p. butter** beurre m de cacah(o)uètes

pear [peə(r)] n poire f

pearl [pɜːl] n perle f; **p. necklace** collier m de perles

peasant ['pezənt] n & adj paysan, -anne (mf)

pebble ['pebəl] n (stone) caillou m (pl -oux); (on beach) galet m

peculiar [pɪ'kjuːlɪə(r)] adj (strange) bizarre; (special, characteristic) particulier, -ère (**to** à)

pedal ['pedəl] **1** n pédale f **2** (Br -ll-, Am -l-) vi pédaler

pedantic [pɪ'dæntɪk] adj pédant

pedestrian [pə'destrɪən] n piéton m; Br **p. crossing** passage m pour piétons

pediatrician [piːdɪə'trɪʃən] n Am = **paediatrician**

pedigree ['pedɪgriː] adj (animal) de race

pee [piː] Fam **1** n **to go for a p.** faire pipi **2** vi faire pipi

peek [piːk] *vi* jeter un coup d'œil furtif (**at** à)

peel [piːl] **1** *n* *(of vegetable, fruit)* peau *f*; *(of orange, lemon)* écorce *f* **2** *vt* *(vegetable)* éplucher; *(fruit)* peler; **to p. sth off** *(label)* décoller qch **3** *vi* *(of skin, person)* peler; *(of paint)* s'écailler • **peeler** *n* **(potato) p.** épluche-légumes *m inv*

peep [piːp] *vi* jeter un coup d'œil furtif (**at** à); **to p. out** se montrer

peer [pɪə(r)] **1** *n* *(equal)* pair *m* **2** *vi* **to p. at sb/sth** scruter qn/qch du regard

peg [peg] *n* *(for coat, hat)* patère *f*; *(for drying clothes)* pince *f* à linge; *(for tent)* piquet *m*

pelican ['pelɪkən] *n* pélican *m*; *Br* **p. crossing** feux *mpl* à commande manuelle

pelvis ['pelvɪs] *n* *Anat* pelvis *m*

pen¹ [pen] *n* *(for writing)* stylo *m*; **p. friend** *or* **pal** correspondant, -e *mf*

pen² [pen] *n* *(for sheep, cattle)* parc *m*

penalize ['piːnəlaɪz] *vt* pénaliser

penalty ['penəltɪ] *(pl -ies)* *n* *(prison sentence)* peine *f*; *(fine)* amende *f*; *(in football)* penalty *m*; *(in rugby)* pénalité *f*

pence [pens] *pl of* **penny**

pencil ['pensəl] *n* crayon *m*; **in p.** au crayon; **p. sharpener** taille-crayon *m*

pendant ['pendənt] *n* *(around neck)* pendentif *m*

pendulum ['pendjʊləm] *n* pendule *m*

penetrate ['penɪtreɪt] *vt* *(substance)* pénétrer; *(mystery)* percer

penguin ['peŋgwɪn] *n* manchot *m*

penicillin [penɪ'sɪlɪn] *n* pénicilline *f*

peninsula [pə'nɪnsjʊlə] *n* presqu'île *f*; *(larger)* péninsule *f*

penknife ['pennaɪf] *(pl -knives)* *n* canif *m*

penny ['penɪ] *n* **(a)** *(pl -ies)* *Br* *(coin)* penny *m*; *Am & Can (cent)* cent *m*; *Fig* **I don't have a p.** je n'ai pas un sou **(b)** *(pl pence)* *Br (value, currency)* penny *m* • **penniless** *adj* sans le sou

pension ['penʃən] *n* pension *f*; **(retirement) p.** retraite *f* • **pensioner** *n* retraité, -e *mf*; *Br* **old age p.** retraité, -e *mf*

pent-up ['pent'ʌp] *adj* *(feelings)* refoulé

people ['piːpəl] **1** *n* *(nation)* peuple *m* **2** *npl* *(as group)* gens *mpl*; *(as individuals)* personnes *fpl*; **the p.** *(citizens)* le peuple; **two p.** deux personnes; **English p.** les Anglais *mpl*; **p. think that...** les gens pensent que...

pepper ['pepə(r)] *n* poivre *m*; *(vegetable)* poivron *m*; **p. mill** moulin *m* à poivre • **peppermint** *n* *(flavour)* menthe *f*

per [pɜː(r)] *prep* par; **p. annum** par an; **50 pence p. kilo** 50 pence le kilo; **40 km p. hour** 40 km à l'heure

percentage [pə'sentɪdʒ] *n* pourcentage *m* • **percent** *adv* pour cent

perception [pə'sepʃən] *n* perception *f* (**of** de) • **perceptive** *adj* *(person)* perspicace; *(study, remark)* pertinent

perch [pɜːtʃ] *vi* se percher

perfect 1 ['pɜːfɪkt] *adj* parfait; *Gram* **p. tense** parfait *m* **2** ['pɜːfɪkt] *n* *Gram* parfait *m* **3** [pə'fekt] *vt* parfaire; **to p. one's French** parfaire ses connaissances en français • **perfection**

[pə'fekʃən] n (quality) perfection f
• **perfectly** adv parfaitement
perform [pə'fɔ:m] 1 vt (task, miracle) accomplir; (duty, function) remplir; (play, piece of music) jouer 2 vi (act, play) jouer; (sing) chanter; (dance) danser; **to p. well/badly** (in job) bien/mal s'en tirer • **performance** n (a) (of play) représentation f (b) (of actor, musician) interprétation f; (of athlete) performance f • **performer** n (entertainer) artiste mf; (in play, of music) interprète mf (**of** de)
perfume ['pɜ:fju:m] n parfum m
perhaps [pə'hæps] adv peut-être; **p. not** peut-être que non; **p. she'll come** peut-être qu'elle viendra, elle viendra peut-être
period ['pɪərɪəd] n (a) (stretch of time) période f; (historical) époque f; (school lesson) heure f de cours; **(monthly) period(s)** (of woman) règles fpl (b) Am (full stop) point m; **I refuse, p.!** je refuse, un point c'est tout!
perish ['perɪʃ] vi (of person) périr • **perishable** adj (food) périssable
perjury ['pɜ:dʒərɪ] n faux témoignage m
perk [pɜ:k] 1 n Br Fam (in job) avantage m 2 vt **to p. sb up** (revive) ragaillardir qn; (cheer up) remonter le moral à qn 3 vi **to p. up** reprendre du poil de la bête
perm [pɜ:m] 1 n permanente f 2 vt **to have one's hair permed** se faire faire une permanente
permanent ['pɜ:mənənt] adj permanent; (address) fixe • **permanently** adv à titre permanent
permit 1 ['pɜ:mɪt] n permis m 2 [pə'mɪt] (pt & pp **-tt-**) vt permettre (**sb to do** à qn de faire) • **permission** [pə'mɪʃən]

n permission f, autorisation f (**to do** de faire); **to give sb p. (to do sth)** donner la permission à qn (de faire qch)
perpendicular [pɜ:pən'dɪkjʊlə(r)] adj & n perpendiculaire (f)
perpetual [pə'petʃʊəl] adj perpétuel, -elle
perplexed [pə'plekst] adj perplexe
persecute ['pɜ:sɪkju:t] vt persécuter • **persecution** [-'kju:ʃən] n persécution f
persevere [pɜ:sɪ'vɪə(r)] vi persévérer (**with** dans) • **perseverance** n persévérance f
persist [pə'sɪst] vi persister (**in doing** à faire; **in sth** dans qch) • **persistent** adj (person) tenace; (smell, rumours) persistant; (attempts) continuel, -elle
person ['pɜ:sən] n personne f; **in p.** en personne
personal ['pɜ:sənəl] adj personnel, -elle; (friend) intime; (life) privé; (indiscreet) indiscret, -ète; **p. computer** ordinateur m individuel; **p. organizer** agenda m électronique; **p. stereo** baladeur m • **personally** adv personnellement; (in person) en personne
personality [pɜ:sə'nælətɪ] (pl **-ies**) n (character, famous person) personnalité f
personnel [pɜ:sə'nel] n (staff) personnel m
perspective [pə'spektɪv] n perspective f; Fig **in p.** sous son vrai jour
perspire [pə'spaɪə(r)] vi transpirer
persuade [pə'sweɪd] vt persuader (**sb to do** qn de faire) • **persuasion** n persuasion f; (creed) religion f • **persuasive** adj (person, argument) persuasif, -ive

perturb [pə'tɜːb] *vt* troubler
perverse [pə'vɜːs] *adj (awkward)* contrariant
pervert 1 ['pɜːvɜːt] *n (sexual deviant)* pervers, -e *mf* **2** [pə'vɜːt] *vt* pervertir; *(mind)* corrompre ● **perversion** [-ʃən, *Am* -ʒən] *n (sexual)* perversion *f*
pessimistic [pesɪ'mɪstɪk] *adj* pessimiste (**about** quant à)
pest [pest] *n (animal)* animal *m* nuisible; *(insect)* insecte *m* nuisible; *Fam (person)* plaie *f*
pester ['pestə(r)] *vt* tourmenter; **to p. sb to do sth** harceler qn pour qu'il fasse qch
pesticide ['pestɪsaɪd] *n* pesticide *m*
pet [pet] **1** *n* animal *m* domestique; *(favourite person)* chouchou, -oute *mf* **2** *adj (dog, cat)* domestique; *(favourite)* favori, -ite; **p. shop** animalerie *f* **3** (*pt & pp* -tt-) *vt (fondle)* caresser
petal ['petəl] *n* pétale *m*
petition [pə'tɪʃən] *n* pétition *f*
petrol ['petrəl] *n Br* essence *f*; **p. station** station-service *f*; **p. tank** réservoir *m* d'essence
petticoat ['petɪkəʊt] *n* jupon *m*
petty ['petɪ] (**-ier, -iest**) *adj (trivial)* insignifiant; *(mean)* mesquin; **p. cash** petite caisse *f*
pew [pjuː] *n* banc *m* d'église
phantom ['fæntəm] *n* fantôme *m*
pharmacy ['fɑːməsɪ] (*pl* **-ies**) *n* pharmacie *f* ● **pharmacist** *n* pharmacien, -enne *mf*
phase [feɪz] *n* phase *f*
PhD [piːeɪtʃ'diː] (*abbr* **Doctor of Philosophy**) *n* doctorat *m* (**in** de)
phenomenon [fɪ'nɒmɪnən] (*pl* **-ena** [-ɪnə]) *n* phénomène *m* ● **phenomenal** *adj* phénoménal
philosophy [fɪ'lɒsəfɪ] (*pl* **-ies**) *n* philosophie *f* ● **philosophical**

[fɪlə'sɒfɪkəl] *adj* philosophique; *Fig (stoical, resigned)* philosophe
phlegm [flem] *n (in throat)* glaires *fpl*
phobia ['fəʊbɪə] *n* phobie *f*
phone [fəʊn] **1** *n* téléphone *m*; **to be on the p.** *(be talking)* être au téléphone; *(have a telephone)* avoir le téléphone; **p. call** coup *m* de téléphone; **to make a p. call** téléphoner (**to** à); **p. book** annuaire *m*; **p. box,** *Br* **p. booth** cabine *f* téléphonique; **p. number** numéro *m* de téléphone **2** *vt* téléphoner (**to** à); **to p. sb (up)** téléphoner à qn; **to p. sb back** rappeler qn **3** *vi* **to p. (up)** téléphoner; **to p. back** rappeler ● **phonecard** *n Br* carte *f* de téléphone
phonetic [fə'netɪk] *adj* phonétique
phoney ['fəʊnɪ] (**-ier, -iest**) *adj Fam (company, excuse)* bidon *inv*
photo ['fəʊtəʊ] (*pl* **-os**) *n* photo *f*; **to take sb's p.** prendre qn en photo; **to have one's p. taken** se faire prendre en photo; **p. album** album *m* de photos
photocopy ['fəʊtəʊkɒpɪ] **1** (*pl* **-ies**) *n* photocopie *f* **2** (*pt & pp* **-ied**) *vt* photocopier ● **photocopier** *n* photocopieuse *f*
photograph ['fəʊtəɡrɑːf] **1** *n* photographie *f* **2** *vt* photographier ● **photographer** [fə'tɒɡrəfə(r)] *n* photographe *mf* ● **photography** [fə'tɒɡrəfɪ] *n (activity)* photographie *f*
phrase [freɪz] **1** *n (saying)* expression *f*; *(idiom, in grammar)* locution *f*; **p. book** manuel *m* de conversation **2** *vt (verbally)* exprimer; *(in writing)* rédiger
physical ['fɪzɪkəl] *adj* physique; **p. education** éducation *f* physique

physics ['fızıks] *n (science)* physique *f*

physiotherapy [fızıəʊ'θerəpı] *n* kinésithérapie *f*

physique [fı'ziːk] *n* physique *m*

piano [pı'ænəʊ] (*pl* -os) *n* piano *m* • **pianist** ['pıənıst] *n* pianiste *mf*

pick [pık] *vt (choose)* choisir; *(flower, fruit)* cueillir; *(hole)* faire (**in** dans); *(lock)* crocheter; **to p. a fight** chercher la bagarre (**with** avec) ►**pick at** *vt insep* **to p. at one's food** picorer ►**pick on** *vt insep (nag, blame)* s'en prendre à ►**pick out** *vt sep (choose)* choisir; *(identify)* repérer ►**pick up 1** *vt sep (lift up)* ramasser; *(person into air, weight)* soulever; *(baby)* prendre dans ses bras; *(habit, accent, speed)* prendre; *(fetch, collect)* passer prendre; *(radio programme)* capter; *(learn)* apprendre; **to p. up the phone** décrocher le téléphone **2** *vi (improve)* s'améliorer; **let's p. up where we left off** reprenons (là où nous en étions restés)

pickaxe ['pıkæks] (*Am* **pickax**) *n* pioche *f*

picket ['pıkıt] *n (in strike)* **p. (line)** piquet *m* de grève

pickle ['pıkəl] **1** *n* **pickles** *(vegetables)* **Br** conserves *fpl* (au vinaigre); *Am* concombres *mpl*, cornichons *mpl*; *Fam* **to be in a p.** être dans le pétrin **2** *vt* conserver dans du vinaigre; **pickled onion** oignon *m* au vinaigre

pickpocket ['pıkpɒkıt] *n* pick-pocket *m*

pick-up ['pıkʌp] *n* **p. (truck)** pick-up *m inv (petite camionnette à plateau)*

picnic ['pıknık] *n* pique-nique *m*

picture ['pıktʃə(r)] **1** *n* image *f*; *(painting)* tableau *m*; *(drawing)* dessin *m*; *(photo)* photo *f*; *Br Fam* **the pictures** le cinéma; **p. frame** cadre *m* **2** *vt* **to p. sth (to oneself)** s'imaginer qch • **picturesque** [-'resk] *adj* pittoresque

pie [paı] *n (open)* tarte *f*; *(with pastry on top)* tourte *f*

piece [piːs] **1** *n* morceau *m*; *(smaller)* bout *m*; *(in chess, puzzle)* pièce *f*; **to take sth to pieces** démonter qch; **a p. of news/advice/luck** une nouvelle/un conseil/une chance; **in one p.** *(object)* intact **2** *vt* **to p. together** *(facts)* reconstituer

pier [pıə(r)] *n (for walking, with entertainments)* jetée *f*

pierce [pıəs] *vt* percer; *(of cold, bullet, sword)* transpercer; **to have one's ears pierced** se faire percer les oreilles • **piercing** *adj (voice, look)* perçant; *(wind)* vif (*f* vive)

pig [pıg] *n (animal)* cochon *m*, porc *m*; *Fam (greedy person)* goinfre *m* • **piggy** *n* **p. bank** tirelire *f* (en forme de cochon) • **piggyback** *n* **to give sb a p.** porter qn sur son dos • **pigtail** *n (hair)* natte *f*

pigeon ['pıdʒın] *n* pigeon *m* • **pigeonhole** *n* casier *m*

pile [paıl] **1** *n (heap)* tas *m*; *(neat stack)* pile *f*; *Fam* **to have piles of** *or* **a p. of things to do** avoir un tas de choses à faire **2** *vt* entasser; *(stack)* empiler ►**pile up 1** *vt sep* entasser; *(stack)* empiler **2** *vi (accumulate)* s'accumuler

pilgrim ['pılgrım] *n* pèlerin *m* • **pilgrimage** *n* pèlerinage *m*

pill [pıl] *n* pilule *f*; **to be on the p.** *(of woman)* prendre la pilule

pillar ['pılə(r)] *n* pilier *m*; *Br* **p. box** boîte *f* aux lettres

pillow ['pɪləʊ] *n* oreiller *m* • **pillowcase** *n* taie *f* d'oreiller

pilot ['paɪlət] **1** *n (of plane, ship)* pilote *m* **2** *adj* **p. light** veilleuse *f*; **p. scheme** projet *m* pilote

pimple ['pɪmpəl] *n* bouton *m*

PIN [pɪn] (*abbr* **personal identification number**) *n Br* **P. (number)** code *m* confidentiel

pin [pɪn] **1** *n* épingle *f*; *Br (drawing pin)* punaise *f* **2** (*pt & pp* **-nn-**) *vt (attach)* épingler (**to** à); *(to wall)* punaiser (**to** *or* **on** à); **to p. down** *(immobilize)* immobiliser; *(fix)* fixer; **to p. sth up** *(notice)* fixer qch au mur

pinball ['pɪnbɔːl] *n* flipper *m*; **p. machine** flipper *m*

pinch [pɪntʃ] **1** *n (of salt)* pincée *f* **2** *vt* pincer; *Br Fam (steal)* piquer (**from** à)

pine [paɪn] *n (tree, wood)* pin *m*; **p. forest** pinède *f*

pineapple ['paɪnæpəl] *n* ananas *m*

pink [pɪŋk] *adj & n (colour)* rose *(m)*

pint [paɪnt] *n* pinte *f* (*Br* = 0,57 l, *Am* = 0,47 l); **a p. of beer** ≃ un demi

pioneer [paɪə'nɪə(r)] *n* pionnier, -ère *mf*

pip [pɪp] *n Br (of fruit)* pépin *m*

pipe [paɪp] *n* tuyau *m*; *(for smoking)* pipe *f*; *(musical instrument)* pipeau *m*; **to smoke a p.** fumer la pipe • **pipeline** *n Fig* **in the p.** en préparation • **piping** *adv* **p. hot** très chaud

pirate ['paɪrət] *n* pirate *m* • **pirated** *adj (book, CD)* pirate

pistachio [pɪ'stæʃɪəʊ] (*pl* **-os**) *n (nut, flavour)* pistache *f*

pistol ['pɪstəl] *n* pistolet *m*

pit¹ [pɪt] *n (hole)* fosse *f*

pit² [pɪt] *n Am (stone of fruit)* noyau *m* (*pl* -aux); *(smaller)* pépin *m*

pitch [pɪtʃ] **1** *n* **(a)** *(for football)* terrain *m* **(b)** *(of voice)* hauteur *f*; *(musical)* ton *m* **2** *vt (tent)* dresser; *(ball)* lancer • **pitch-black, pitch-dark** *adj* noir comme dans un four

pitcher ['pɪtʃə(r)] *n* cruche *f*

pith [pɪθ] *n (of orange)* peau *f* blanche

pity ['pɪtɪ] **1** *n* pitié *f*; **to take** *or* **have p. on sb** avoir pitié de qn; **what a p.!** quel dommage!; **it's a p. that...** c'est dommage que... (+ *subjunctive*) **2** (*pt & pp* **-ied**) *vt* plaindre • **pitiful** *adj* pitoyable • **pitiless** *adj* impitoyable

pivot ['pɪvət] *vi* pivoter (**on** sur)

pizza ['piːtsə] *n* pizza *f*

placard ['plækɑːd] *n (on wall)* affiche *f*; *(hand-held)* pancarte *f*

place [pleɪs] **1** *n* endroit *m*, lieu *m*; *(seat, position, rank)* place *f*; *Fam* **my p.** chez moi; **to lose one's p.** *(in queue)* perdre sa place; *(in book)* perdre sa page; **to take the p. of sb/sth** remplacer qn/qch; **to take p.** *(happen)* avoir lieu; *Am* **some p.** *(somewhere)* quelque part; **all over the p.** un peu partout; **in the first p.** *(firstly)* en premier lieu; **in p. of** à la place de; **out of p.** *(remark)* déplacé; *(object)* pas à sa place **2** *vt (put, situate, invest, in sport)* placer; **to be placed third** se classer troisième; **to p. an order with sb** passer une commande à qn • **placement** *n (in company)* stage *m*

placid ['plæsɪd] *adj* placide

plague [pleɪg] **1** *n (disease)* peste *f* **2** *vt (of person)* harceler (**with** de)

plain [pleɪn] **1** (**-er, -est**) *adj (clear, obvious)* clair; *(simple)*

simple; *(without a pattern)* uni; *(not beautiful)* quelconque; **in p. clothes** en civil; **p. chocolate** chocolat *m* noir; **2** *adv Fam (utterly)* complètement • **plainly** *adv (clearly)* clairement; *(frankly)* franchement

plait [plæt] **1** *n* tresse *f*, natte *f* **2** *vt* tresser, natter

plan [plæn] **1** *n (proposal, intention)* projet *m*; *(of building, town, essay)* plan *m*; **to go according to p.** se passer comme prévu **2** *(pt & pp -nn-)* *vt (arrange)* projeter; *(crime)* comploter; *(building, town)* faire le plan de; **to p. to do** *or* **on doing sth** *(intend)* projeter de faire qch; **as planned** comme prévu **3** *vi* faire des projets • **planning** *n* conception *f*; **family p.** planning *m* familial

plane [pleɪn] *n (aircraft)* avion *m*

planet ['plænɪt] *n* planète *f*

plank [plæŋk] *n* planche *f*

plant [plɑːnt] **1** *n* **(a)** *(living thing)* plante *f* **(b)** *(factory)* usine *f* **2** *vt (tree, flower)* planter; *(crops, seeds)* semer; *Fig (bomb)* poser

plaque [plæk] *n (sign)* plaque *f*; *(on teeth)* plaque *f* dentaire

plaster ['plɑːstə(r)] **1** *n* **(a)** *(on wall)* plâtre *m*; **to put sb's leg in p.** mettre la jambe de qn dans le plâtre; **p. cast** *(for broken bone)* plâtre *m* **(b)** *Br* **(sticking) p.** pansement *m* adhésif **2** *vt (wall)* plâtrer; **to p. sth with** *(cover)* couvrir qch de

plastic ['plæstɪk] **1** *adj (object)* en plastique; **p. bag** sac *m* en plastique; **p. surgery** *(cosmetic)* chirurgie *f* esthétique **2** *n* plastique *m*

plate [pleɪt] *n (dish)* assiette *f*; *(metal sheet)* plaque *f*; *(book illustration)* gravure *f*

platform ['plætfɔːm] *n (raised surface)* plate-forme *f*; *(in train station)* quai *m*

platinum ['plætɪnəm] *n (metal)* platine *m*

plausible ['plɔːzəbəl] *adj (argument, excuse)* plausible

play [pleɪ] **1** *n (drama)* pièce *f* *(de théâtre)*; *(amusement)* jeu *m*; **a p. on words** un jeu de mots **2** *vt (part, tune, card)* jouer; *(game)* jouer à; *(instrument)* jouer de; *(match)* disputer **(with** avec**)**; *(team, opponent)* jouer contre; *(record, CD)* passer; *Fig* **to p. a part in doing/in sth** contribuer à faire/à qch **3** *vi* jouer **(with** avec; **at** à**)**; *(of CD player)* marcher; *Fam* **what are you playing at?** à quoi tu joues? • **playground** *n Br (in school)* cour *f* de récréation; *(in park)* terrain *m* de jeux • **player** *n (in game, of instrument)* joueur, -euse *mf* • **playful** *adj (mood, tone)* enjoué; *(child, animal)* joueur, -euse • **playgroup** *n* garderie *f* • **playing** *n* jeu *m*; **p. card** carte *f* à jouer; **p. field** terrain *m* de jeux • **playtime** *n (in school)* récréation *f* • **playwright** *n* dramaturge *mf*

▶**play around** *vi* jouer, s'amuser

▶**play up** *vi Fam (of child, machine)* faire des siennes

plea [pliː] *n (request)* appel *m*

plead [pliːd] **1** *vt (argue)* plaider; *(as excuse)* alléguer **2** *vi* **to p. with sb (to do sth)** implorer qn (de faire qch); **to p. guilty** plaider coupable

pleasant ['plezənt] *adj* agréable **(to** avec**)**

please [pliːz] **1** *adv* s'il te/vous plaît; **p. sit down** asseyez-vous, je vous prie; **p. do!** bien sûr!, je vous en prie! **2** *vt* **to p. sb** faire plaisir à qn; *(satisfy)* contenter qn **3** *vi* plaire; **do as you p.** fais comme tu veux • **pleased** *adj* content (**with** de); **p. to meet you!** enchanté!

pleasure ['pleʒə(r)] *n* plaisir *m*

pleated ['pliːtɪd] *adj* plissé

pledge [pledʒ] *vt* promettre (**to do** de faire)

plenty ['plentɪ] *n* **p. of** beaucoup de; **that's p.** *(of food)* merci, j'en ai assez

pliers ['plaɪəz] *npl* pince *f*

plimsolls ['plɪmsəʊlz] *npl* *Br* tennis *mpl*

plod [plɒd] *(pt & pp* **-dd-)** *vi* **to p. (along)** *(walk)* avancer laborieusement; *(work)* travailler laborieusement

plot [plɒt] **1** *n (conspiracy)* complot *m; (of novel, film)* intrigue *f;* **p. (of land)** parcelle *f* de terrain **2** *(pt & pp* **-tt-)** *vti* comploter (**to do** de faire) **3** *vt* **to p. (out)** *(route)* déterminer; *(graph)* tracer

plough [plaʊ] *(Am* **plow)** *n* charrue *f*

pluck [plʌk] *vt (hair, feathers)* arracher; *(bird)* plumer; *(eyebrows)* épiler; **to p. up the courage to do sth** trouver le courage de faire qch

plug [plʌg] *n* **(a)** *(of cotton wool, wood)* tampon *m; (for sink, bath)* bonde *f* **(b)** *(electrical) (on device)* fiche *f; (socket)* prise *f* (de courant) • **plughole** *n* trou *m* d'écoulement

▶**plug in** *(pt & pp* **-gg-)** *vt sep (appliance)* brancher

plum [plʌm] *n* prune *f*

plumber ['plʌmə(r)] *n* plombier *m*

plump [plʌmp] **(-er, -est)** *adj (person, arm)* potelé; *(chicken)* dodu; *(cheek)* rebondi

plunge [plʌndʒ] **1** *n (dive)*

plongeon *m; Fig (decrease)* chute *f; Fam* **to take the p.** *(take on difficult task)* se jeter à l'eau; *(get married)* se marier **2** *vt (thrust)* plonger (**into** dans) **3** *vi (dive)* plonger (**into** dans); *Fig (decrease)* chuter

plural ['plʊərəl] **1** *adj (noun)* au pluriel **2** *n* pluriel *m;* **in the p.** au pluriel

plus [plʌs] **1** *prep* plus; *(as well as)* en plus de **2** *adj* **twenty p.** plus de vingt **3** *(pl* **plusses** ['plʌsɪz]) *n* **p. (sign)** (signe *m*) plus *m;* **that's a p.** c'est un plus

p.m. [piː'em] *adv (afternoon)* de l'après-midi; *(evening)* du soir

pneumonia [njuː'məʊnɪə] *n* pneumonie *f*

poached [pəʊtʃt] *adj (egg)* poché

pocket ['pɒkɪt] **1** *n* poche *f;* **to be out of p.** en être de sa poche; **p. money** argent *m* de poche • **pocketbook** *n Am (handbag)* sac *m* à main

podium ['pəʊdɪəm] *n* podium *m*

poem ['pəʊɪm] *n* poème *m* • **poet** *n* poète *m* • **poetic** [pəʊ'etɪk] *adj* poétique • **poetry** *n* poésie *f*

point [pɔɪnt] **1** *n* **(a)** *(of knife, needle)* pointe *f* **(b)** *(dot, score, degree, argument)* point *m; (location)* endroit *m;* **to make a p. of doing sth** mettre un point d'honneur à faire qch; **you have a p.** tu as raison; **there's no p. (in) staying** ça ne sert à rien de rester; **to get to the p.** en arriver au fait; **to be on the p. of doing sth** être sur le point de faire qch; **his good points** ses qualités *fpl;* **p. of view** point *m* de vue **(c)** *Math* **three p. five** trois virgule cinq **2** *vt (aim)* diriger; *(camera, gun)* braquer (**at** sur); **to p. one's finger at sb** montrer qn du doigt; **to p. sth**

out *(show)* montrer qch; *(error, fact)* signaler qch **3** *vi* **to p. at** *or* **to sb/sth** *(with finger)* montrer qn/qch du doigt; **to p. north** *(of arrow, compass)* indiquer le nord • **pointed** *adj* pointu • **pointless** *adj* inutile

poison ['pɔɪzən] **1** *n* poison *m*; *(of snake)* venin *m* **2** *vt* empoisonner • **poisonous** *adj (fumes, substance)* toxique; *(snake)* venimeux, -euse; *(plant)* vénéneux, -euse

poke [pəʊk] *vt (person)* donner un coup à; *(object)* tâter; *(fire)* attiser; **to p. sth into sth** enfoncer qch dans qch; **to p. one's finger at sb** pointer son doigt vers qn; *Fig* **to p. one's nose into sth** mettre son nez dans qch • **poker¹** *n (for fire)* tisonnier *m*

poker² ['pəʊkə(r)] *n (card game)* poker *m*

Poland ['pəʊlənd] *n* la Pologne • **Pole** *n* Polonais, -e *mf* • **Polish** ['pəʊlɪʃ] **1** *adj* polonais **2** *n (language)* polonais *m*

polar ['pəʊlə(r)] *adj* polaire; **p. bear** ours *m* blanc

pole¹ [pəʊl] *n (rod)* perche *f*; *(fixed)* poteau *m*; **p. vault** *or* **vaulting** saut *m* à la perche

pole² [pəʊl] *n Geog* pôle *m*; **North/ South P.** pôle *m* Nord/Sud

police [pə'liːs] **1** *n* police *f* **2** *adj (inquiry, dog)* policier, -ère; **p. car** voiture *f* de police; **p. station** poste *m* de police • **policeman** *(pl* **-men)** *n* agent *m* de police • **policewoman** *(pl* **-women)** *n* agent *m* de police

policy ['pɒlɪsɪ] *(pl* **-ies)** *n* **(a)** *(of government, organization)* politique *f* **(b)** **(insurance) p.** police *f* (d'assurance)

polish ['pɒlɪʃ] **1** *n (for shoes)* cirage *m*; *(for floor, furniture)* cire *f*; *(for nails)* vernis *m*; *Fig* raffinement *m*; **to give sth a p.** faire briller qch **2** *vt (floor, table, shoes)* cirer; *(metal)* astiquer; *Fig (style)* polir; *Fam* **to p. off** *(food)* avaler; *(drink)* descendre

polite [pə'laɪt] *adj* poli **(to** *or* **with** avec) • **politely** *adv* poliment

political [pə'lɪtɪkəl] *adj* politique • **politically** *adv* **p. correct** politiquement correct • **politician** [pɒlɪ'tɪʃən] *n* homme *m*/femme *f* politique • **politics** ['pɒlɪtɪks] *n* politique *f*

poll [pəʊl] *(voting)* scrutin *m*; **(opinion) p.** sondage *m* (d'opinion) • **polling** *n Br* **p. station,** *Am* **p. place** bureau *m* de vote

pollen ['pɒlən] *n* pollen *m*

pollute [pə'luːt] *vt* polluer • **pollution** *n* pollution *f*

polo ['pəʊləʊ] *n (sport)* polo *m*; **p. neck** *(sweater, neckline)* col *m* roulé

polyester [pɒlɪ'estə(r)] *n* polyester *m*; **p. shirt** chemise *f* en polyester

pompous ['pɒmpəs] *adj* pompeux, -euse

pond [pɒnd] *n* étang *m*; *(smaller)* mare *f*

ponder ['pɒndə(r)] **1** *vt* réfléchir à **2** *vi* **to p. (over sth)** réfléchir (à qch)

pony ['pəʊnɪ] *(pl* **-ies)** *n* poney *m* • **ponytail** *n* queue *f* de cheval

poodle ['puːdəl] *n* caniche *m*

pool¹ [puːl] *n (of water)* flaque *f*; *(of blood)* mare *f*; *(for swimming)* piscine *f*

pool² [puːl] *n (game)* billard *m* américain

poor [pʊə(r)] **1** **(-er, -est)** *adj (not rich)* pauvre; *(bad)* mauvais; *(harvest, reward)* faible; **to be in**

p. health ne pas bien se porter **2** *npl* **the p.** les pauvres *mpl* ● **poorly 1** *adv* mal; *(clothed, furnished)* pauvrement **2** *adj Br Fam* malade

pop¹ [pɒp] **1** *exclam* pan! **2** *n (noise)* bruit *m* sec **3** *(pt & pp* **-pp-)** *vt* **(a)** *(balloon)* crever; *(cork)* faire sauter **(b)** *Fam (put)* mettre **4** *vi* **(a)** *(burst)* éclater; *(of cork)* sauter **(b)** *Br Fam* **to p. in** passer; **to p. out** sortir (un instant); **to p. up** surgir ● **popcorn** *n* pop-corn *m inv*

pop² [pɒp] **1** *n (music)* pop *f* **2** *adj (concert, singer, group)* pop *inv*

pope [pəʊp] *n* pape *m*

poppy ['pɒpɪ] *(pl* **-ies)** *n (red, wild)* coquelicot *m*; *(cultivated)* pavot *m*

Popsicle® ['pɒpsɪkəl] *n Am (ice lolly)* ≃ Esquimau® *m*

popular ['pɒpjʊlə(r)] *adj* populaire; *(fashionable)* à la mode; *(restaurant)* qui a beaucoup de succès ● **popularity** [-'lærɪtɪ] *n* popularité *f* **(with** auprès de)

population [pɒpjʊ'leɪʃən] *n* population *f*

porcelain ['pɔːsəlɪn] *n* porcelaine *f*

porch [pɔːtʃ] *n* porche *m*; *Am (veranda)* véranda *f*

pore [pɔː(r)] **1** *n (of skin)* pore *m* **2** *vi* **to p. over sth** *(book, question)* étudier qch de près

pork [pɔːk] *n (meat)* porc *m*; **p. pie** ≃ pâté *m* en croûte

pornography [pɔː'nɒgrəfɪ] *n* pornographie *f*

porridge ['pɒrɪdʒ] *n* porridge *m*

port¹ [pɔːt] *n (harbour)* port *m*; **p. of call** escale *f*

port² [pɔːt] *n (wine)* porto *m*

portable ['pɔːtəbəl] *adj* portable

porter ['pɔːtə(r)] *n (for luggage)* porteur *m*; *(door attendant)* chasseur *m*

portfolio [pɔːt'fəʊlɪəʊ] *(pl* **-os)** *n* porte-documents *m inv*

portion ['pɔːʃən] *n* partie *f*; *(share, helping)* portion *f*

portrait ['pɔːtreɪt] *n* portrait *m*

portray [pɔː'treɪ] *vt (describe)* dépeindre

Portugal ['pɔːtjʊgəl] *n* le Portugal ● **Portuguese** [-'giːz] **1** *adj* portugais **2** *n (person)* Portugais, -e *mf*; *(language)* portugais *m*; **the P.** *(people)* les Portugais

pose [pəʊz] **1** *n (position)* pose *f* **2** *vt (question)* poser; *(threat)* représenter **3** *vi* poser **(for** pour); **to p. as a lawyer** se faire passer pour un avocat

posh [pɒʃ] *adj Fam (smart)* chic *inv*

position [pə'zɪʃən] *n (place, posture, opinion)* position *f*; *(of building, town)* emplacement *m*; *(job, circumstances)* situation *f*; **in a p. to do sth** en mesure de faire qch; **in p.** en place

positive ['pɒzɪtɪv] *adj (person, answer, test)* positif, -ive; *(progress, change)* réel *(f* réelle); *(certain)* sûr, certain **(of** de; **that** que) ● **positively** *adv (identify)* formellement; *(think, react)* de façon positive; *(for emphasis)* véritablement

possess [pə'zes] *vt* posséder ● **possession** *n (ownership)* possession *f*; *(thing possessed)* bien *m*; **to be in p. of sth** être en possession de qch ● **possessive** *adj & n Gram* possessif *(m)*

possible ['pɒsəbəl] *adj* possible; **it is p. (for us) to do it** il (nous) est possible de le faire; **it is p. that...** il est possible que... *(+ subjunctive)*; **as soon as p.** dès que possible ●

possibility [-'bɪlətɪ] (*pl* **-ies**) *n* possibilité *f* ● **possibly** *adv* **(a)** *(perhaps)* peut-être **(b)** *(for emphasis)* **to do all one p. can** faire tout son possible **(to do** pour faire); **he can't p. stay** il ne peut absolument pas rester

post- [pəʊst] *pref* post-; **post-1800** après 1800

post¹ [pəʊst] **1** *n Br (postal system)* poste *f*; *(letters)* courrier *m*; **by p.** par la poste; **p. office** (bureau *m* de) poste *f* **2** *vt (letter)* poster; **to keep sb posted** tenir qn au courant ● **postage** *n* affranchissement *m* **(to** pour); **p. stamp** timbre-poste *m*● **postbox** *n Br* boîte *f* aux lettres ● **postcard** *n* carte *f* postale ● **postcode** *n Br* code *m* postal ● **postman** (*pl* **-men**) *n Br* facteur *m* ● **postmark** *n* cachet *m* de la poste

post² [pəʊst] *n* **(a)** *(pole)* poteau *m*; **finishing p.** *(in race)* poteau *m* d'arrivée **(b)** *(job, place)* poste *m*

poster ['pəʊstə(r)] *n* affiche *f*; *(for decoration)* poster *m*

postgraduate [pəʊst'grædjʊət] **1** *adj* de troisième cycle **2** *n* étudiant, -e *mf* de troisième cycle

postpone [pəʊs'pəʊn] *vt* reporter

posture ['pɒstʃə(r)] *n (of body)* posture *f*; *Fig* attitude *f*

pot [pɒt] *n* pot *m*; *(for cooking)* casserole *f*

potato [pə'teɪtəʊ] (*pl* **-oes**) *n* pomme *f* de terre; *Br* **p. crisps,** *Am* **p. chips** chips *fpl*

potential [pə'tenʃəl] **1** *adj* potentiel, -elle **2** *n* potentiel *m*; **to have p.** avoir du potentiel

pothole ['pɒthəʊl] *n (in road)* nid-de-poule *m*; *(cave)* caverne *f*

potion ['pəʊʃən] *n* potion *f*

pottery ['pɒtərɪ] *n (art)* poterie *f*; *(objects)* poteries *fpl*; **a piece of p.** une poterie

potty ['pɒtɪ] *n (for baby)* pot *m*

pouch [paʊtʃ] *n* bourse *f*

poultry ['pəʊltrɪ] *n* volaille *f*

pounce [paʊns] *vi (of animal)* bondir **(on** sur); *(of person)* se précipiter **(on** sur)

pound¹ [paʊnd] *n* **(a)** *(weight)* livre *f* (= 453,6 g) **(b)** **p. (sterling)** livre *f* (sterling)

pound² [paʊnd] *vi (of heart)* battre à tout rompre

pour [pɔː(r)] **1** *vt* verser; **to p. sb a drink** verser à boire à qn **2** *vi* **it's pouring** il pleut à verse

▸**pour down** *vi* **it's pouring down** il pleut à verse

▸**pour in 1** *vt sep (liquid)* verser **2** *vi (of water, sunshine)* entrer à flots; *Fig (of people, money)* affluer

▸**pour out 1** *vt sep (liquid)* verser; *Fig (anger, grief)* déverser **2** *vi (of liquid)* se déverser; *Fig (of people)* sortir en masse **(from** de)

pout [paʊt] *vi* faire la moue

poverty ['pɒvətɪ] *n* pauvreté *f*

powder ['paʊdə(r)] *n* poudre *f*; **p. puff** houppette *f*; **p. room** toilettes *fpl* pour dames ● **powdered** *adj (milk, eggs)* en poudre

power ['paʊə(r)] *n (ability, authority)* pouvoir *m*; *(strength)* puissance *f*; *(electric current)* courant *m*; **to be in p.** être au pouvoir; **to have sb in one's p.** tenir qn à sa merci; *Br* **p. failure** *or* **cut** coupure *f* de courant; *Br* **p. station,** *Am* **p. plant** centrale *f* électrique ● **powerful** *adj* puissant

practical ['præktɪkəl] *adj (tool, knowledge, solution)* pratique; **to be p.** *(of person)* avoir l'esprit pratique; **p. joke** farce *f* • **practically** *adv (almost)* pratiquement

practice ['præktɪs] **1** *n (action, exercise, custom)* pratique *f*; *(in sport)* entraînement *m*; *(surgery)* centre *m* médical; **in p.** *(in reality)* dans la *ou* en pratique; **to put sth into p.** mettre qch en pratique; **to be out of p.** avoir perdu l'habitude **2** *vti Am* = **practise** • **practise** *(Am* **practice)** **1** *vt (sport, language, art, religion)* pratiquer; *(medicine, law)* exercer; *(musical instrument)* travailler **2** *vi (of musician)* s'exercer; *(of sportsperson)* s'entraîner; *(of doctor, lawyer)* exercer • **practising** *adj (doctor, lawyer)* en exercice; *Rel* pratiquant

praise [preɪz] **1** *n* éloges *mpl* **2** *vt* faire l'éloge de; *(God)* louer; **to p. sb for doing** *or* **having done sth** louer qn d'avoir fait qch

pram [præm] *n Br* landau *m (pl -aus)*

prank [præŋk] *n* farce *f*

prawn [prɔːn] *n* crevette *f* rose

pray [preɪ] **1** *vt* **to p. that...** prier pour que... *(+ subjunctive)* **2** *vi* prier; *Fig* **to p. for good weather** prier pour qu'il fasse beau

prayer [preə(r)] *n* prière *f*

pre- [priː] *pref* **pre-1800** avant 1800

preach [priːtʃ] *vti* prêcher; **to p. to sb** prêcher qn; *Fig* faire la morale à qn

precarious [prɪ'keərɪəs] *adj* précaire

precaution [prɪ'kɔːʃən] *n* précaution *f*; **as a p.** par précaution

precede [prɪ'siːd] *vti* précéder • **precedence** ['presɪdəns] *n* **to take p. over sb** avoir la préséance sur qn; **to take p. over**

sth passer avant qch • **precedent** ['presɪdənt] *n* précédent *m*

precinct ['priːsɪŋkt] *n Br (for shopping)* zone *f* commerçante piétonnière; *Am (electoral district)* circonscription *f*; *Am (police district)* secteur *m*

precious ['preʃəs] **1** *adj* précieux, -euse **2** *adv* **p. little** très peu (de)

precipice ['presɪpɪs] *n* précipice *m*

precise [prɪ'saɪs] *adj (exact)* précis; *(meticulous)* méticuleux, -euse • **precisely** *adv* précisément; **at three o'clock p.** à trois heures précises • **precision** [-'sɪʒən] *n* précision *f*

precocious [prɪ'kəʊʃəs] *adj* précoce

predator ['predətə(r)] *n* prédateur *m*

predecessor ['priːdɪsesə(r)] *n* prédécesseur *m*

predicament [prɪ'dɪkəmənt] *n* situation *f* difficile

predict [prɪ'dɪkt] *vt* prédire • **predictable** *adj* prévisible • **prediction** *n* prédiction *f*

preface ['prefɪs] *n (of book)* préface *f*

prefect ['priːfekt] *n Br Sch* = élève chargé de la surveillance

prefer [prɪ'fɜː(r)] *(pt & pp* **-rr-)** *vt* préférer **(to** à); **to p. to do sth** préférer faire qch • **preferable** ['prefərəbəl] *adj* préférable **(to** à) • **preference** ['prefərəns] *n* préférence *f* **(for** pour)

prefix ['priːfɪks] *n (before word)* préfixe *m*

pregnant ['pregnənt] *adj* enceinte; **five months p.** enceinte de cinq mois • **pregnancy** *(pl -ies)* *n* grossesse *f*; **p. test** test *m* de grossesse

prehistoric [priːhɪˈstɒrɪk] *adj* préhistorique

prejudice [ˈpredʒədɪs] *n (bias)* préjugé *m* • **prejudiced** *adj* **to be p.** avoir des préjugés (**against/in favour of** contre/en faveur de)

preliminary [prɪˈlɪmɪnərɪ] *adj* préliminaire

premature [*Br* ˈpremətʃʊə(r), *Am* priːməˈtʃʊər] *adj* prématuré

première [*Br* ˈpremɪeə(r), *Am* prɪˈmɪər] *n (of play, film)* première *f*

premises [ˈpremɪsɪz] *npl* locaux *mpl*; **on the p.** sur place

premium [ˈpriːmɪəm] *n Fin (for insurance)* prime *f*; *(additional sum)* supplément *m*

premonition [*Br* preməˈnɪʃən, *Am* priːməˈnɪʃən] *n* prémonition *f*

preoccupied [priːˈɒkjʊpaɪd] *adj* préoccupé (**with** par) • **preoccupation** [-ˈpeɪʃən] *n* préoccupation *f* (**with** pour)

prepaid [priːˈpeɪd] *adj* prépayé

prepare [prɪˈpeə(r)] **1** *vt* préparer (**sth for** qch pour; **sb for** qn à) **2** *vi* se préparer pour; **to p. to do sth** se préparer à faire qch • **preparation** [prepəˈreɪʃən] *n* préparation *f*; **preparations** préparatifs *mpl* (**for** de) • **prepared** *adj (ready)* prêt (**to do** à faire); **to be p. for sth** s'attendre à qch

preposition [prepəˈzɪʃən] *n* préposition *f*

prerequisite [priːˈrekwɪzɪt] *n (condition f)* préalable *m*

preschool [ˈpriːskuːl] *adj* préscolaire

prescribe [prɪˈskraɪb] *vt (of doctor)* prescrire • **prescription** *n (for medicine)* ordonnance *f*; **on p.** sur ordonnance

presence [ˈprezəns] *n* présence *f*; **in the p. of** en présence de; **p. of mind** présence *f* d'esprit

present¹ [ˈprezənt] **1** *adj* **(a)** *(in attendance)* présent (**at** à; **in** dans) **(b)** *(current)* actuel, -elle; **the p. tense** le présent **2** *n* **the p.** *(time, tense)* le présent; **for the p.** pour l'instant; **at p.** en ce moment • **presently** *adv (soon)* bientôt; *Am (now)* actuellement

present² **1** [ˈprezənt] *n (gift)* cadeau *m* **2** [prɪˈzent] *vt (show, introduce)* présenter (**to** à); *(concert, film)* donner; **to p. sb with** *(gift)* offrir à qn; *(prize)* remettre à qn • **presentable** [prɪˈzentəbəl] *adj (person, appearance)* présentable • **presentation** [prezənˈteɪʃən] *n* présentation *f* • **presenter** [prɪˈzentə(r)] *n* présentateur, -trice *mf*

preserve [prɪˈzɜːv] *vt (keep, maintain)* conserver; *(fruit)* mettre en conserve • **preservation** [prezəˈveɪʃən] *n (of building)* conservation *f*; *(of species)* protection *f*

president [ˈprezɪdənt] *n (of country)* président, -e *mf*

press¹ [pres] *n* **the p.** *(newspapers)* la presse; **p. conference** conférence *f* de presse

press² [pres] **1** *vt (button, doorbell)* appuyer sur **2** *vi* appuyer (**on** sur) • **pressed** *adj* **to be p. for time** être pressé par le temps • **press-up** *n (exercise)* pompe *f*

▶**press down** *vt insep (button)* appuyer sur

▶**press on** *vi (carry on)* continuer

pressure [ˈpreʃə(r)] **1** *n* pression *f*; **to be under p.** être stressé; **to put p. on sb (to do sth)** faire pression sur qn (pour qu'il fasse qch) **2** *vt* **to p. sb to do sth** *or* **into doing sth** faire pression sur qn pour qu'il

fasse qch • **pressurize** *vt* **to p. sb (into doing sth)** faire pression sur qn (pour qu'il fasse qch)
prestigious [pres'tɪdʒəs, pre'stiːdʒəs] *adj* prestigieux, -euse
presume [prɪ'zjuːm] *vt (suppose)* présumer (**that** que) • **presumably** *adv* sans doute
pretend [prɪ'tend] **1** *vt (make believe)* faire semblant (**to do** de faire); *(claim, maintain)* prétendre (**to do** faire; **that** que) **2** *vi* faire semblant • **pretentious** *adj* prétentieux, -euse
pretext ['priːtekst] *n* prétexte *m*; **on the p. of/that** sous prétexte de/que
pretty ['prɪtɪ] **1** (**-ier, -iest**) *adj* joli **2** *adv Fam (rather, quite)* assez; **p. well, p. much** *(almost)* pratiquement
prevail [prɪ'veɪl] *vi (predominate)* prédominer; *(be successful)* l'emporter (**over** sur); **to p. (up)on sb to do sth** persuader qn de faire qch • **prevailing** *adj* prédominant; *(wind)* dominant
prevent [prɪ'vent] *vt* empêcher (**from doing** de faire) • **prevention** *n* prévention *f*
preview ['priːvjuː] *n (of film, play)* avant-première *f*
previous ['priːvɪəs] **1** *adj* précédent; **to have p. experience** avoir une expérience préalable **2** *adv* **p. to** avant • **previously** *adv* auparavant
prey [preɪ] **1** *n* proie *f* **2** *vi* **to p. on** *(person)* prendre pour cible; *(fears, doubts)* exploiter; **to p. on sb's mind** tourmenter qn
price [praɪs] **1** *n* prix *m*; **he wouldn't do it at any p.** il ne le ferait à aucun prix **2** *adj (control, rise)* des prix; **p. list** tarif *m* **3** *vt* **it's priced at £5** ça coûte 5 livres •

priceless *adj (invaluable)* qui n'a pas de prix • **pricey** (**-ier, -iest**) *adj Fam* cher (*f* chère)
prick [prɪk] *vt* piquer (**with** avec) • **prickly** (**-ier, -iest**) *adj (plant)* à épines; *(animal)* couvert de piquants; *(beard)* piquant
pride [praɪd] **1** *n (satisfaction)* fierté *f*; *(self-esteem)* amour-propre *m*; *Pej (vanity)* orgueil *m*; **to take p. in sth** mettre toute sa fierté dans qch **2** *vt* **to p. oneself on sth/on doing sth** s'enorgueillir de qch/de faire qch
priest [priːst] *n* prêtre *m*
primary ['praɪmərɪ] *adj (main)* principal; *Br* **p. school** école *f* primaire • **primarily** [praɪ'merəlɪ] *adv* essentiellement
prime [praɪm] **1** *adj (principal)* principal; *(importance)* capital; *(excellent)* excellent; **P. Minister** Premier ministre *m* **2** *n* **in the p. of life** dans la fleur de l'âge
primitive ['prɪmɪtɪv] *adj (original)* primitif, -ive; *(basic)* de base
prince [prɪns] *n* prince *m* • **princess** *n* princesse *f*
principal ['prɪnsɪpəl] **1** *adj (main)* principal **2** *n (of school)* proviseur *m*; *(of university)* ≃ président, -e *mf*
principle ['prɪnsɪpəl] *n* principe *m*; **in p.** en principe; **on p.** par principe
print [prɪnt] **1** *n (of finger, foot)* empreinte *f*; *(letters)* caractères *mpl*; *(photo)* épreuve *f*; **out of p.** *(book)* épuisé **2** *vt (book, newspaper)* imprimer; *(photo)* tirer; *(write)* écrire en script; *Comptr* **to p. out** imprimer • **printer** *n (machine)* imprimante *f* • **printing** *n (technique, industry)* imprimerie *f*; *(action)* tirage *m*; **p. error** faute *f*

d'impression • **printout** n Comptr sortie f papier

prior ['praɪə(r)] **1** adj antérieur; (experience) préalable **2** adv **p. to sth** avant qch

priority [praɪ'ɒrətɪ] (pl -ies) n priorité f (**over** sur)

prison ['prɪzən] **1** n prison f; **in p.** en prison **2** adj (life, system) pénitentiaire; (camp) de prisonniers; **p. officer** gardien, -enne mf de prison • **prisoner** n prisonnier, -ère mf; **to take sb p.** faire qn prisonnier; **p. of war** prisonnier m de guerre

private ['praɪvɪt] **1** adj privé; (lesson) particulier, -ère; (letter) confidentiel, -elle; (personal) personnel, -elle; (dinner, wedding) intime; **p. detective, p. investigator,** Fam **p. eye** détective m privé **2** n **in p.** (not publicly) en privé; (have dinner, get married) dans l'intimité • **privacy** ['praɪvəsɪ, Br 'prɪvəsɪ] n intimité f • **privately** adv (in private) en privé; (in one's heart of hearts) en son for intérieur; (personally) à titre personnel; **p. owned** (company) privé • **privatize** vt privatiser

privilege ['prɪvɪlɪdʒ] n privilège m • **privileged** adj privilégié; **to be p. to do sth** avoir le privilège de faire qch

prize [praɪz] n prix m; (in lottery) lot m

pro [prəʊ] (pl **pros**) n Fam (professional) pro mf

probable ['prɒbəbəl] adj probable (**that** que) • **probably** adv probablement

probation [prə'beɪʃən] n **on p.** (criminal) en liberté surveillée; (in job) en période d'essai

probe [prəʊb] **1** vt (inquire into)

enquêter sur **2** vi **to p. into sth** (past, private life) fouiller dans qch

problem ['prɒbləm] n problème m; Fam **no p.!** pas de problème! • **problematic** [-'mætɪk] adj problématique

procedure [prə'siːdʒə(r)] n procédure f

proceed [prə'siːd] vi (go on) se poursuivre; **to p. with sth** poursuivre qch; **to p. to do sth** se mettre à faire qch • **proceedings** npl (events) opérations fpl; **to take (legal) p.** intenter un procès (**against** contre)

proceeds ['prəʊsiːdz] npl recette f

process ['prəʊses] **1** n processus m; (method) procédé m; **in the p. of doing sth** en train de faire qch **2** vt (food, data) traiter; (film) développer; **processed food** aliments mpl conditionnés • **processor** n **food p.** robot m de cuisine

procession [prə'seʃən] n défilé m

proclaim [prə'kleɪm] vt proclamer (**that** que)

prod [prɒd] (pt & pp **-dd-**) vt (poke) donner un petit coup dans

prodigy ['prɒdɪdʒɪ] (pl -ies) n prodige m; **child p.** enfant mf prodige

produce 1 [prə'djuːs] vt (create) produire; (machine) fabriquer; (passport, ticket) présenter; (documents) fournir; (from bag, pocket) sortir; (film, play, programme) produire **2** ['prɒdjuːs] n (products) produits mpl • **producer** [prə'djuːsə(r)] n producteur, -trice mf

product ['prɒdʌkt] n produit m • **production** [prə'dʌkʃən] n production f; (of play) mise f en scène • **productive** [prə'dʌktɪv] adj productif, -ive

profession [prəˈfeʃən] n profession f • **professional 1** adj professionnel, -elle; (man, woman) qui exerce une profession libérale; (army) de métier; (piece of work) de professionnel **2** n professionnel, -elle mf

professor [prəˈfesə(r)] n Br ≃ professeur m d'université; Am = enseignant d'université

profile [ˈprəʊfaɪl] n (of person, object) profil m; (description) portrait m; **in p.** de profil; Fig **to keep a low p.** garder un profil bas

profit [ˈprɒfɪt] **1** n profit m, bénéfice m **2** vi **to p. by** or **from sth** tirer profit de qch • **profitable** adj (commercially) rentable; Fig (worthwhile) profitable

profound [prəˈfaʊnd] adj profond • **profoundly** adv profondément

profusely [prəˈfjuːslɪ] adv (bleed) abondamment; (thank) avec effusion; **to apologize p.** se confondre en excuses

programme [ˈprəʊɡræm] (Am **program**) **1** n (for play, political party, computer) programme m; (on TV, radio) émission f **2** (pt & pp **-mm-**) vt (machine) programmer • **programmer** n (computer) **p.** programmeur, -euse mf • **programming** n (computer) p. programmation f

progress 1 [ˈprəʊɡres] n progrès m; **to make (good) p.** faire des progrès; **in p.** en cours **2** [prəˈɡres] vi (advance, improve) progresser; (of story, meeting) se dérouler

prohibit [prəˈhɪbɪt] vt interdire (**sb from doing** à qn de faire)

project 1 [ˈprɒdʒekt] n (plan, undertaking) projet m; (at school) dossier m; Am **(housing) p.** cité f HLM **2** [prəˈdʒekt] vi

(protrude) dépasser • **projector** [prəˈdʒektə(r)] n projecteur m

prologue [ˈprəʊlɒɡ] n prologue m (**to** de)

prolong [prəˈlɒŋ] vt prolonger

prom [prɒm] (abbr **promenade**) n (**a**) Br (at seaside) front m de mer (**b**) Am (dance) bal m d'étudiants

promenade [prɒməˈnɑːd] n Br (at seaside) front m de mer

prominent [ˈprɒmɪnənt] adj (important) important; (nose, chin) proéminent • **prominently** adv bien en vue

promise [ˈprɒmɪs] **1** n promesse f; **to show p.** promettre **2** vt promettre (**to do** de faire); **to p. sth to sb, to p. sb sth** promettre qch à qn **3** vi **I p.!** je te le promets! • **promising** adj prometteur, -euse

promote [prəˈməʊt] vt (raise in rank, encourage) promouvoir; (advertise) faire la promotion de • **promotion** n promotion f

prompt [prɒmpt] **1** adj (speedy) rapide; (punctual) ponctuel, -elle **2** vt (cause) provoquer; **to p. sb to do sth** pousser qn à faire qch • **promptly** adv (rapidly) rapidement; (punctually) ponctuellement; (immediately) immédiatement

prone [prəʊn] adj **to be p. to sth** être sujet, -ette à qch; **to be p. to do sth** avoir tendance à faire qch

pronoun [ˈprəʊnaʊn] n pronom m

pronounce [prəˈnaʊns] vt (say, articulate) prononcer • **pronunciation** [-nʌnsɪˈeɪʃən] n prononciation f

proof [pruːf] n (evidence) preuve f; **p. of identity** pièce f d'identité • **proofreader** n correcteur, -trice mf

prop [prɒp] **1** n (physical support) support m; (in a play) accessoire m **2** (pt & pp **-pp-**) vt **to p. sth (up) against sth** appuyer qch contre qch; **to p. sth up** étayer qch

propaganda [prɒpə'gændə] n propagande f

propel [prə'pel] (pt & pp **-ll-**) vt propulser • **propeller** n hélice f

proper ['prɒpə(r)] adj (a) (correct) vrai; (word) correct (b) (appropriate) bon (f bonne); (behaviour) convenable • **properly** adv (suitably) convenablement; (correctly) correctement

property ['prɒpətɪ] **1** (pl **-ies**) n (a) (land, house) propriété f; (possessions) biens mpl (b) (quality) propriété f **2** adj (market) immobilier, -ère; **p. developer** promoteur m immobilier

prophet ['prɒfɪt] n prophète m

proportion [prə'pɔːʃən] n (ratio, part) proportion f; **proportions** (size) proportions fpl; **in p.** proportionné (**to** avec); **out of p.** disproportionné (**to** par rapport à) • **proportional** adj proportionnel, -elle (**to** à)

propose [prə'pəʊz] **1** vt proposer; **to p. to do sth, to p. doing sth** (suggest) proposer de faire qch; (intend) se proposer de faire qch **2** vi **to p. to sb** demander qn en mariage • **proposal** n proposition f; (plan) projet m; (for marriage) demande f en mariage

pros [prəʊz] npl **the p. and cons** le pour et le contre

prose [prəʊz] n prose f; Br (translation) thème m

prosecute ['prɒsɪkjuːt] vt (in law court) poursuivre (en justice) • **prosecution** [-'kjuːʃən]n (in law court) poursuites fpl judiciaires;

the p. (lawyers) ≃ le ministère public

prospect ['prɒspekt] n (expectation, thought) perspective f; (chance, likelihood) perspectives fpl; **(future) prospects** perspectives fpl d'avenir • **prospective** [prə'spektɪv] adj (potential) potentiel, -elle; (future) futur

prospectus [prə'spektəs] n (publicity leaflet) prospectus m; Br (for university) guide m (de l'étudiant)

prosperous ['prɒspərəs] adj prospère

prostitute ['prɒstɪtjuːt] n prostituée f • **prostitution** [-'tjuːʃən] n prostitution f

protect [prə'tekt] vt protéger (**from** or **against** de) • **protection** n protection f • **protective** adj (clothes, screen) de protection; (person, attitude) protecteur, -trice (**to** or **towards** envers)

protein ['prəʊtiːn] n protéine f

protest 1 ['prəʊtest] n protestation f (**against** contre); **in p.** en signe de protestation (**at** contre) **2** [prə'test] vt protester contre; (one's innocence) protester de; **to p. that...** protester en disant que... **3** [prə'test] vi protester (**against** contre) • **protester** [prə'testə(r)] n contestataire mf

Protestant ['prɒtɪstənt] adj & n protestant, -e (mf)

protrude [prə'truːd] vi dépasser (**from** de); (of tooth) avancer • **protruding** adj (chin, veins, eyes) saillant

proud [praʊd] (**-er**, **-est**) adj (person) fier (f fière) (**of** de) • **proudly** adv fièrement

prove [pruːv] **1** vt prouver (**that** que); **to p. sb wrong** prouver que qn a tort **2** *vi* **to p. (to be) difficult** s'avérer difficile ● **proven** *adj (method)* éprouvé

proverb ['prɒvɜːb] *n* proverbe *m*

provide [prə'vaɪd] **1** *vt (supply)* fournir; *(service)* offrir (**to** à); **to p. sb with sth** fournir qch à qn **2** *vi* **to p. for sb** *(sb's needs)* pourvoir aux besoins de qn; *(sb's future)* assurer l'avenir de qn; **to p. for sth** *(make allowance for)* prévoir qch ● **provided, providing** *conj* **p. (that)...** pourvu que... (+ subjunctive)

province ['prɒvɪns] *n* province *f*; **in the provinces** en province

provision [prə'vɪʒən] *n (clause)* disposition *f*; **provisions** *(supplies)* provisions *fpl* ● **provisional** *adj* provisoire

provoke [prə'vəuk] *vt* provoquer; **to p. sb into doing sth** pousser qn à faire qch ● **provocation** [prɒvə'keɪʃən] *n* provocation *f* ● **provocative** [prə'vɒkətɪv] *adj* provocateur, -trice

prowl [praul] *vi* **to p. (around)** rôder

proxy ['prɒksɪ] *(pl* **-ies)** *n* **by p.** par procuration

prune [pruːn] *n (dried plum)* pruneau *m*

pry [praɪ] *(pt & pp* **pried)** *vi* être indiscret, -ète; **to p. into sth** *(meddle)* mettre son nez dans qch; *(sb's reasons)* chercher à découvrir qch

PS [piːˈes] *(abbr* **postscript)** *n* PS *m*

psalm [sɑːm] *n* psaume *m*

pseudonym ['sjuːdənɪm] *n* pseudonyme *m*

psychiatrist [saɪ'kaɪətrɪst] *n* psychiatre *mf*

psychic ['saɪkɪk] *adj (paranormal)*

parapsychique; **to be p.** avoir un sixième sens

psycho- ['saɪkəu] *pref* psycho- ● **psychoanalyst** *n* psychanalyste *mf*

psychology [saɪ'kɒlədʒɪ] *n* psychologie *f* ● **psychological** [-kə'lɒdʒɪkəl] *adj* psychologique ● **psychologist** *n* psychologue *mf*

psychopath ['saɪkəupæθ] *n* psychopathe *mf*

PTO *(abbr* **please turn over)** TSVP

pub [pʌb] *n Br* pub *m*

public ['pʌblɪk] **1** *adj* public, -ique; *(library, swimming pool)* municipal; **p. holiday** jour *m* férié; **p. school** *Br* école *f* privée; *Am* école *f* publique; **p. transport** transports *mpl* en commun **2** *n* public *m*; **in p.** en public ● **publicly** *adv* publiquement

publication [pʌblɪ'keɪʃən] *n* publication *f*

publicize ['pʌblɪsaɪz] *vt* faire connaître au public ● **publicity** [-'lɪsɪtɪ] *n* publicité *f*

publish ['pʌblɪʃ] *vt* publier ● **publisher** *n (person)* éditeur, -trice *mf*; *(company)* maison *f* d'édition

pudding ['pudɪŋ] *n (dish)* pudding *m*; *Br (dessert)* dessert *m*

puddle ['pʌdəl] *n* flaque *f* (d'eau)

puff [pʌf] **1** *n (of smoke)* bouffée *f*; *(of wind, air)* souffle *m*; **p. pastry** pâte *f* feuilletée **2** *vt* **to p. sth out** *(cheeks, chest)* gonfler qch **3** *vi (of person)* souffler; **to p. at a cigar** tirer sur un cigare

puke [pjuːk] *vi Fam* dégueuler

pull [pul] **1** *vt (draw, tug)* tirer; *(trigger)* appuyer sur; *(muscle)* se froisser; *Fig* **to p. sth apart** *or* **to**

bits *or* **to pieces** démolir qch **2** *vi*
(tug) tirer (**on** sur)
▶**pull away 1** *vt sep (move)*
éloigner; *(snatch)* arracher (**from**
à) **2** *vi (in vehicle)* démarrer
▶**pull back 1** *vt sep* retirer;
(curtains) ouvrir **2** *vi (withdraw)*
se retirer
▶**pull down** *vt sep (lower)* baisser;
(knock down) faire tomber;
(demolish) démolir
▶**pull in 1** *vt sep* faire entrer
(de force) **2** *vi (stop in vehicle)*
s'arrêter
▶**pull off** *vt sep (remove)* enlever;
Fig (plan, deal) réaliser
▶**pull on** *vt sep (boots, clothes)*
mettre
▶**pull out 1** *vt sep (tooth, hair)*
arracher; *(cork, pin)* enlever (**from**
de); *(from pocket, bag)* sortir
(**from** de) **2** *vi (of car)* déboîter;
(withdraw) se retirer (**of** de)
▶**pull over 1** *vt sep (drag)* traîner
(**to** jusqu'à) **2** *vi (in vehicle)*
s'arrêter
▶**pull through** *vi (recover)* s'en
tirer
▶**pull together** *vt sep* **to p.**
oneself together se ressaisir
▶**pull up 1** *vt sep (socks, blinds)*
remonter; *(haul up)* hisser; *(plant,*
tree) arracher; *(stop)* arrêter **2** *vi*
(of car) s'arrêter

pullover ['pʊləʊvə(r)] *n* pull-over
m
pulp [pʌlp] *n (of fruit)* pulpe *f*
pulse [pʌls] *n Med* pouls *m*
pump¹ [pʌmp] **1** *n (machine)*
pompe *f*; *Br* **petrol p.**, *Am* **gas p.**
pompe *f* à essence **2** *vt* pomper; **to**
p. sth up *(mattress)* gonfler qch
pump² [pʌmp] *n (flat shoe)*
escarpin *m*; *(for sports)* tennis *f*
pumpkin ['pʌmpkɪn] *n* potiron *m*

pun [pʌn] *n* jeu *m* de mots
punch¹ [pʌntʃ] **1** *n (blow)* coup *m*
de poing; **p. line** *(of joke, story)*
chute *f* **2** *vt (person)* donner un
coup de poing à; *(sb's nose)*
donner un coup de poing sur
punch² [pʌntʃ] *vt (ticket)*
poinçonner; *(with date)* composter;
(paper, card) perforer; **to p. a hole**
in sth faire un trou dans qch
punch³ [pʌntʃ] *n (drink)* punch *m*
punctual ['pʌŋktʃʊəl] *adj*
ponctuel, -elle • **punctually** *adv*
à l'heure
punctuation [pʌŋktjʊ'eɪʃən] *n*
ponctuation *f*; **p. mark** signe *m* de
ponctuation
puncture ['pʌŋktʃə(r)] **1** *n (in*
tyre) crevaison *f*; **to have a p.**
crever **2** *vt (tyre)* crever
pungent ['pʌndʒənt] *adj* âcre
punish ['pʌnɪʃ] *vt* punir (**for** de);
to p. sb for doing sth punir qn
pour avoir fait qch • **punishment**
n punition *f*; *(in law)* peine *f*
punk [pʌŋk] *n* punk *mf*; **p. (rock)**
le punk
puny ['pjuːnɪ] (**-ier, -iest**) *adj*
chétif, -ive
pupil¹ ['pjuːpəl] *n (student)* élève
mf
pupil² ['pjuːpəl] *n (of eye)* pupille
f
puppet ['pʌpɪt] *n* marionnette
f; **p. show** spectacle *m* de
marionnettes
puppy ['pʌpɪ] (*pl* **-ies**) *n (dog)*
chiot *m*
purchase ['pɜːtʃɪs] **1** *n (action,*
thing bought) achat *m* **2** *vt* acheter
(**from** à)
pure [pjʊə(r)] (**-er, -est**) *adj* pur •
purely *adv* purement
purée ['pjʊəreɪ] *n* purée *f*
purify ['pjʊərɪfaɪ] (*pt & pp* **-ied**)
vt purifier

purple ['pɜːpəl] **1** adj violet, -ette **2** n violet m

purpose ['pɜːpəs] n (a) (aim) but m; **on p.** exprès; **for the purposes of** pour les besoins de (b) (determination) résolution f

purr [pɜː(r)] vi ronronner

purse [pɜːs] **1** n (for coins) porte-monnaie m inv; Am (handbag) sac m à main **2** vt **to p. one's lips** pincer les lèvres

pursue [pə'sjuː] vt poursuivre; (fame, pleasure) rechercher • **pursuit** n (of person) poursuite f; (of pleasure, glory) quête f; (activity) occupation f

pull [pʊl] **1** n (act of pushing, attack) poussée f; **to give sb/sth a p.** pousser qn/qch; **at a p.** à la rigueur **2** vt pousser (**to** or **as far as** jusqu'à); (button) appuyer sur; (lever) abaisser; (product) faire la promotion de; **to p. sth into/ between** enfoncer qch dans/ entre, Fig **to p. sb into doing sth** pousser qn à faire qch; **to p. sth off the table** faire tomber qch de la table (en le poussant) **3** vi pousser; (on button) appuyer (**on** sur) • **pushchair** n Br poussette f • **pushed** adj **to be p. for time** être très pressé • **push-up** n Am (exercise) pompe f • **pushy** (-**ier,** -**iest**) adj Fam batailleur, -euse

▶**push around** vt sep Fam **to p. sb around** faire de qn ce que l'on veut

▶**push in** vi Br (in queue) resquiller

▶**push on** vi (go on) continuer; **to p. on with sth** continuer qch

▶**push over** vt sep faire tomber

▶**push up** vt sep (lever, collar) relever; (sleeves) remonter; (increase) augmenter

put [pʊt] (pt & pp **put,** pres p **putting**) vt mettre; (on flat surface) poser; (question) poser (**to** à); **to p. a lot of work into sth** beaucoup travailler à qch; **to p. it bluntly** pour parler franc

▶**put away** vt sep (tidy away) ranger

▶**put back** vt sep (replace, postpone) remettre; (clock) retarder

▶**put down** vt sep (on floor, table) poser; (write down) inscrire; (attribute) attribuer (**to** à); **to p. oneself down** se rabaisser

▶**put forward** vt sep (clock, meeting, argument) avancer; (candidate) proposer (**for** à)

▶**put in** vt sep (into box) mettre dedans; (insert) introduire; (add) ajouter; (install) installer

▶**put off** vt sep (postpone) remettre (à plus tard); (dismay) déconcerter; **to p. off doing sth** retarder le moment de faire qch; **to p. sb off sth** dégoûter qn de qch

▶**put on** vt sep (clothes, shoe, record) mettre; (accent) prendre; (play, show) monter; (gas, radio) allumer; **to p. on weight** prendre du poids; **p. me on to him!** (on phone) passez-le-moi!

▶**put out** vt sep (take outside) sortir; (arm, leg, hand) tendre; (gas, light) éteindre; (inconvenience) déranger; (upset) vexer

▶**put through** vt sep **to p. sb through (to sb)** (on phone) passer qn (à qn)

▶**put together** vt sep (assemble) assembler; (file, report) préparer; (collection) rassembler

▶**put up** vt sep (lift) lever; (tent, fence) monter; (statue, ladder) dresser; (building) construire; (umbrella) ouvrir; (picture, poster) mettre; (price) augmenter; (guest)

loger; **to p. sth up for sale** mettre
qch en vente
▶**put up with** *vt insep* supporter

puzzle ['pʌzəl] **1** *n* *(jigsaw)*
puzzle *m*; *(game)* casse-tête *m*
inv; *(mystery)* mystère *m* **2** *vt*
laisser perplexe **3** *vi* **to p. over**

sth essayer de comprendre qch ●
puzzled *adj* perplexe
PVC [piːviːˈsiː] *n* PVC *m*
pyjamas [pəˈdʒɑːməz] *npl Br*
pyjama *m*; **a pair of p.** un pyjama
pylon ['paɪlən] *n* pylône *m*
pyramid ['pɪrəmɪd] *n* pyramide *f*

Qq

Q, q [kjuː] *n (letter)* Q, q *m inv*

quaint [kweɪnt] **(-er, -est)** *adj (picturesque)* pittoresque; *(old-fashioned)* vieillot, -otte

quake [kweɪk] *vi* trembler (**with** de)

qualify ['kwɒlɪfaɪ] *(pt & pp* **-ied)** *vi (of sportsperson)* se qualifier (**for** pour); **to q. as a doctor** obtenir son diplôme de médecin; **to q. for sth** *(be eligible)* avoir droit à qch • **qualification** [-fɪ'keɪʃən] *n (diploma)* diplôme *m* • **qualified** *adj (having diploma)* diplômé; *(competent)* compétent

quality ['kwɒlətɪ] *(pl* **-ies)** *n* qualité *f*

quantity ['kwɒntɪtɪ] *(pl* **-ies)** *n* quantité *f*

quarantine ['kwɒrəntiːn] *n* quarantaine *f*

quarrel ['kwɒrəl] **1** *n* dispute *f*, querelle *f* **2** *(Br* **-ll-,** *Am* **-l-)** *vi* se disputer (**with** avec); **to q. with sth** ne pas être d'accord avec qch

quart [kwɔːt] *n (liquid measurement) Br* = 1,14 l, *Am* = 0,95 l

quarter ['kwɔːtə(r)] *n* **(a)** *(fraction)* quart *m*; *(of fruit, moon)* quartier *m*; *(division of year)* trimestre *m*; *Am & Can (money)* pièce *f* de 25 cents; *Br* **a q. past nine,** *Am* **a q. after nine** neuf heures et quart; **a q. to nine** neuf heures moins le quart **(b)** *(district)* quartier *m* • **quarterly 1** *adj (magazine, payment)* trimestriel, -elle **2** *adv* tous les trimestres

quay [kiː] *n* quai *m*

queasy ['kwiːzɪ] **(-ier, -iest)** *adj* **to feel** *or* **be q.** avoir mal au cœur

Quebec [kwɪ'bek] *n* le Québec

queen [kwiːn] *n* reine *f*

queer ['kwɪə(r)] **(-er, -est)** *adj (strange)* bizarre

quench [kwentʃ] *vt (thirst)* étancher

query ['kwɪərɪ] **1** *(pl* **-ies)** *n* question *f* **2** *(pt & pp* **-ied)** *vt* mettre en question

quest [kwest] *n* quête *f* (**for** de)

question ['kwestʃən] **1** *n* question *f*; **there's no q. of it, it's out of the q.** c'est hors de question; **the matter/person in q.** l'affaire/la personne en question; **q. mark** point *m* d'interrogation **2** *vt* interroger (**about** sur); *(doubt)* mettre en question • **questionnaire** [-'neə(r)] *n* questionnaire *m*

queue [kjuː] *Br* **1** *n (of people)* queue *f*; *(of cars)* file *f*; **to form a q., to stand in a q.** faire la queue **2** *vi* **to q. (up)** faire la queue

quiche [kiːʃ] *n* quiche *f*

quick [kwɪk] **(-er, -est)** *adj* rapide; **be q.!** fais vite!; **to have a q. shower/meal** se doucher/manger en vitesse • **quickly** *adv* vite

quid [kwɪd] *n inv Br Fam (pound)* livre *f*

quiet ['kwaɪət] **(-er, -est)** *adj (silent, still, peaceful)* tranquille, calme; *(machine, vehicle)* silencieux, -euse; *(person, voice, mu-*

sic) doux *(f* douce); **to be** *or* **keep q.** *(say nothing)* se taire; *(make no noise)* ne pas faire de bruit; **to keep q. about sth, to keep sth q.** ne rien dire au sujet de qch; **q.!** silence! ● **quietly** *adv* tranquillement; *(gently, not loudly)* doucement; *(silently)* silencieusement; *(discreetly)* discrètement

quilt [kwɪlt] *n* édredon *m*

quirky ['kwɜːkɪ] **(-ier, -iest)** *adj* bizarre

quit [kwɪt] *(pt & pp* **quit,** *pres p* **quitting) 1** *vt (leave)* quitter; **to q. doing sth** arrêter de faire qch **2** *vi (give up)* abandonner; *(resign)* démissionner

quite [kwaɪt] *adv (entirely)* tout à fait; *(really)* vraiment; *(fairly)* assez; **q. good** *(not bad)* pas mal

du tout; **q. (so)!** exactement!; **q. a lot** pas mal **(of** de)

quits [kwɪts] *adj* quitte **(with** envers); **to call it q.** en rester là

quiver ['kwɪvə(r)] *vi (of voice)* trembler

quiz [kwɪz] *(pl* **-zz-)** *n (on radio)* jeu *m* radiophonique; *(on TV)* jeu *m* télévisé; *(in magazine)* questionnaire *m*

quota ['kwəʊtə] *n* quota *m*

quotation [kwəʊ'teɪʃən] *n (from author)* citation *f; (estimate)* devis *m;* **in q. marks** entre guillemets

quote [kwəʊt] **1** *n (from author)* citation *f; (estimate)* devis *m;* **in quotes** entre guillemets **2** *vt (author, passage)* citer; *(reference number)* rappeler; *(price)* indiquer **3** *vi* **to q. from** *(author, book)* citer

Rr

R, r [ɑː(r)] *n (lettre)* R, r *m inv*
rabbi ['ræbaɪ] *n* rabbin *m*
rabbit ['ræbɪt] *n* lapin *m*
rabies ['reɪbiːz] *n* rage *f*
raccoon [rə'kuːn] *n* raton *m* laveur
race¹ [reɪs] **1** *n (contest)* course *f* **2** *vt* **to r. (against** *or* **with) sb** faire une course avec qn **3** *vi (run)* courir • **racecourse** *n* champ *m* de courses • **racehorse** *n* cheval *m* de course • **racetrack** *n Am (for horses)* champ *m* de courses; *Br (for cars, bicycles)* piste *f* • **racing** *n* courses *fpl;* **r. car** voiture *f* de course; **r. driver** coureur *m* automobile
race² [reɪs] *n (group)* race *f* • **racial** ['reɪʃəl] *adj* racial • **racism** *n* racisme *m* • **racist** *adj & n* raciste *(mf)*
rack [ræk] **1** *n (for bottles, letters, CDs)* casier *m; (for plates)* égouttoir *m;* **(roof) r.** *(of car)* galerie *f* **2** *vt* **to r. one's brains** se creuser la cervelle
racket¹ ['rækɪt] *n (for tennis)* raquette *f*
racket² ['rækɪt] *n Fam (noise)* vacarme *m*
radar ['reɪdɑː(r)] *n* radar *m*
radiant ['reɪdɪənt] *adj (person, face)* resplendissant **(with** de)
radiation [reɪdɪ'eɪʃən] *n (radioactivity)* radiation *f*
radiator ['reɪdɪeɪtə(r)] *n (heater)* radiateur *m*

radical ['rædɪkəl] *adj & n* radical, -e *(mf)*
radio ['reɪdɪəʊ] *(pl* **-os)** *n* radio *f;* **on the r.** à la radio
radioactive [reɪdɪəʊ'æktɪv] *adj* radioactif, -ive
radish ['rædɪʃ] *n* radis *m*
radius ['reɪdɪəs] *(pl* **-dii)** *n* rayon *m;* **within a r. of 10 km** dans un rayon de 10 km
RAF [ɑːreɪ'ef] *(abbr* **Royal Air Force)** *n* = armée de l'air britannique
raffle ['ræfəl] *n* tombola *f*
raft [rɑːft] *n* radeau *m*
rag [ræg] *n (piece of old clothing)* chiffon *m;* **in rags** *(person)* en haillons • **ragged** [-ɪd] *adj (clothes)* en loques; *(person)* en haillons
rage [reɪdʒ] **1** *n (of person)* rage *f;* **to fly into a r.** entrer dans une rage folle; *Fam* **to be all the r.** *(of fashion)* faire fureur **2** *vi (of storm, battle)* faire rage • **raging** *adj (storm, fever, fire)* violent
raid [reɪd] **1** *n (military)* raid *m; (by police)* descente *f;* **air r.** raid *m* aérien **2** *vt* faire un raid/une descente/un hold-up dans
rail [reɪl] **1** *n* **(a)** *(for train)* rail *m;* **by r.** par le train **(b)** *(rod on balcony)* balustrade *f; (on stairs)* rampe *f; (curtain rod)* tringle *f* **2** *adj (ticket)* de chemin de fer; *(strike)* des cheminots • **railcard** *n* carte *f* d'abonnement de train • **railings** *npl* grille *f* • **railway** *(Am*

railroad) 1 *n (system)* chemin *m* de fer; *(track)* voie *f* ferrée **2** *adj (ticket)* de chemin de fer; *(network, company)* ferroviaire; **r. line** ligne *f* de chemin de fer; **r. station** gare *f*

rain [reɪn] **1** *n* pluie *f*; **in the r.** sous la pluie **2** *vi* pleuvoir; **it's raining** il pleut • **rainbow** *n* arc-en-ciel *m* • **raincoat** *n* imperméable *m* • **rainforest** *n* forêt *f* tropicale humide • **rainwater** *n* eau *f* de pluie • **rainy** **(-ier, -iest)** *adj* pluvieux, -euse; *(day)* de pluie; **the r. season** la saison des pluies

raise [reɪz] **1** *vt (lift)* lever; *(child, family, voice)* élever; *(salary, price)* augmenter; *(temperature)* faire monter; *(question, protest)* soulever; **to r. money** réunir des fonds **2** *n Am (pay rise)* augmentation *f* (de salaire)

raisin ['reɪzən] *n* raisin *m* sec

rake [reɪk] **1** *n* râteau *m* **2** *vt (soil)* ratisser

rally ['rælɪ] **1** *(pl -ies)* *n (political)* rassemblement *m*; *(car race)* rallye *m* **2** *vi* **to r. round sb** venir en aide à qn

ram [ræm] **1** *n (animal)* bélier *m* **2** *(pt & pp -mm-)* *vt (vehicle)* emboutir; *(ship)* aborder; **to r. sth into sth** enfoncer qch dans qch

ramble ['ræmbəl] *vi (hike)* faire une randonnée; **to r. on** *(talk)* divaguer • **rambler** *n* randonneur, -euse *mf* • **rambling** *adj* **(a)** *(house)* plein de coins et de recoins; *(spread out)* vaste **(b)** *(speech)* décousu

ramp [ræmp] *n (slope)* rampe *f*; *(for wheelchair)* rampe d'accès

ran [ræn] *pt of* **run**

ranch [rɑːntʃ] *n* ranch *m*

rancid ['rænsɪd] *adj* rance

random ['rændəm] **1** *n* **at r.** au hasard **2** *adj (choice)* (fait)

au hasard; *(sample)* prélevé au hasard

rang [ræŋ] *pt of* **ring²**

range [reɪndʒ] **1** *n* **(a)** *(of gun, voice)* portée *f*; *(of colours, prices, products)* gamme *f*; *(of sizes)* choix *m* **(b)** *(of mountains)* chaîne *f* **2** *vi (vary)* varier **(from** de; **to** à); *(extend)* s'étendre

rank [ræŋk] **1** *n (position, class)* rang *m*; *(military grade)* grade *m*; *(row)* rangée *f*; *(for taxis)* station *f* **2** *vt* placer **(among** parmi) **3** *vi* compter **(among** parmi)

ransack ['rænsæk] *vt (house)* mettre sens dessus dessous; *(shop, town)* piller

ransom ['rænsəm] *n* rançon *f*; **to hold sb to r.** rançonner qn

rant [rænt] *vi Fam* **to r. and rave** tempêter **(at** contre)

rap [ræp] *n* **(a)** *(blow)* coup *m* sec **(b) r. (music)** rap *m*

rape [reɪp] **1** *n* viol *m* **2** *vt* violer • **rapist** *n* violeur *m*

rapid ['ræpɪd] *adj* rapide • **rapidly** *adv* rapidement

rare [reə(r)] *adj* **(a)** **(-er, -est)** *(uncommon)* rare **(b)** *(meat)* saignant • **rarely** *adv* rarement • **rarity** *(pl -ies)* *n (quality, object)* rareté *f*

rash¹ [ræʃ] *n (on skin)* rougeurs *fpl*; *(spots)* éruption *f*

rash² [ræʃ] **(-er, -est)** *adj (imprudent)* irréfléchi

raspberry ['rɑːzbərɪ] *(pl -ies)* *n (fruit)* framboise *f*

rat [ræt] *n* rat *m*

rate [reɪt] **1** *n (level, percentage)* taux *m*; *(speed)* rythme *m*; *(price)* tarif *m*; **interest r.** taux *m* d'intérêt; **at the r. of** au rythme de; *(amount)* à raison de; **at this r.** *(slow speed)* à ce train-là; **at any r.** en tout cas **2** *vt (regard)* considérer (**as** comme); (deserve) mériter; **to r. sb/sth highly** tenir qn/qch en haute estime

rather ['rɑːðə(r)] adv (preferably, quite) plutôt; **I'd r. stay** j'aimerais mieux rester (**than** que); **I r. liked it** j'ai bien aimé

ratio ['reɪʃɪəʊ] (pl **-os**) n rapport m

ration ['ræʃən] **1** n ration f; **rations** (food) vivres mpl **2** vt rationner

rational ['ræʃənəl] adj (sensible) raisonnable; (sane) rationnel, -elle • **rationally** adv (behave) raisonnablement

rattle ['rætəl] **1** vt (window) faire vibrer; (keys, chains) faire cliqueter **2** vi (of window) vibrer

rave [reɪv] **1** n (party) rave f **2** vi (talk nonsense) délirer; **to r. about sb/sth** (enthuse) ne pas tarir d'éloges sur qn/qch

raven ['reɪvən] n corbeau m

ravioli [rævɪ'əʊlɪ] n ravioli(s) mpl

raw [rɔː] (**-er**, **-est**) adj (vegetable) cru; (data) brut; **r. material** matière f première

ray [reɪ] n (of light, sun) rayon m; Fig (of hope) lueur f

razor ['reɪzə(r)] n rasoir m; **r. blade** lame f de rasoir

Rd (abbr **road**) rue

re [riː] prep Com en référence à; **re your letter** suite à votre lettre

reach [riːtʃ] **1** n portée f; **within r. of** à portée de; (near) à proximité de; **within (easy) r.** (object) à portée de main; (shops) tout proche **2** vt (place, aim, distant object) atteindre, arriver à; (decision) prendre; (agreement) aboutir à; (contact) joindre; **to r. a conclusion** arriver à une conclusion; **to r. out one's arm** tendre le bras **3** vi (extend)

s'étendre (**to** jusqu'à); **to r. (out) for sth** tendre le bras pour prendre qch

react [rɪ'ækt] vi réagir (**against** contre; **to** à) • **reaction** n réaction f

read [riːd] **1** (pt & pp **read** [red]) vt lire; (meter) relever; (of instrument) indiquer; Br Univ (study) étudier **2** vi (of person) lire (**about** sur); **to r. to sb** faire la lecture à qn **3** n **to be a good r.** être agréable à lire • **readable** adj (handwriting) lisible; (book) facile à lire • **reader** n lecteur, -trice mf; (book) livre m de lecture • **reading** n lecture f; **r. glasses** lunettes fpl de lecture

▶**read out** vt sep lire (à haute voix)

▶**read through** vt sep (skim) parcourir

ready ['redɪ] (**-ier**, **-iest**) adj prêt (**to do** à faire; **for sth** pour qch); **to get sb/sth r.** préparer qn/qch; **to get r.** se préparer (**for sth** pour qch; **to do** à faire) • **ready-made** adj (food) tout prêt (f toute prête)

real [rɪəl] adj vrai; (leather) véritable; (world, danger) réel (f réelle); **in r. life** dans la réalité; Am **r. estate** immobilier m • **realistic** [-'lɪstɪk] adj réaliste • **reality** [rɪ'ælətɪ] n réalité f; **in r.** en réalité • **really** adv vraiment

realize ['rɪəlaɪz] vt (a) (become aware of) se rendre compte de; **to r. that...** se rendre compte que... (b) (carry out) réaliser

reappear [riːə'pɪə(r)] vi réapparaître

rear¹ [rɪə(r)] **1** n (back part) arrière m; **in** or **at the r.** à l'arrière (**of** de) **2** adj (entrance, legs) de derrière; (lights, window) arrière inv

rear² [rɪə(r)] **1** vt (child, animals)

élever **2** *vi* **to r. (up)** *(of horse)* se cabrer

rearrange [riːəˈreɪndʒ] *vt (hair, room)* réarranger; *(plans)* changer

rearview [ˈrɪəvjuː] *n* **r. mirror** rétroviseur *m*

reason [ˈriːzən] **1** *n (cause, sense)* raison *f*; **the r. for/why** la raison de/pour laquelle; **for no r.** sans raison; **it stands to r.** cela va de soi; **within r.** dans des limites raisonnables **2** *vi* raisonner **(about** sur); **to r. with sb** raisonner qn • **reasoning** *n* raisonnement *m*

reasonable [ˈriːzənəbəl] *adj (fair)* raisonnable; *(quite good)* passable • **reasonably** *adv (behave, act)* raisonnablement; *(quite)* plutôt

reassure [riːəˈʃʊə(r)] *vt* rassurer • **reassuring** *adj* rassurant

rebel 1 [ˈrebəl] *n* rebelle *mf* **2** [ˈrebəl] *adj (camp, chief, attack)* des rebelles **3** [rɪˈbel] *(pt & pp -ll-) vi* se rebeller **(against** contre) • **rebellion** [rɪˈbeljən] *n* rébellion *f*

rebuild [riːˈbɪld] *(pt & pp -built) vt* reconstruire

recall [rɪˈkɔːl] *vt (remember)* se rappeler **(that** que; **doing** avoir fait); *(call back)* rappeler; **to r. sth to sb** rappeler qch à qn

recap [ˈriːkæp] **1** *n* récapitulation *f* **2** *(pt & pp -pp-) vi* récapituler

recede [rɪˈsiːd] *vi (into the distance)* s'éloigner; *(of floods)* baisser

receipt [rɪˈsiːt] *n (for payment, object)* reçu *m* **(for** de); *(for letter, parcel)* récépissé *m*; **on r. of sth** dès réception de qch

receive [rɪˈsiːv] *vt* recevoir • **receiver** *n (of phone)* combiné *m*; **to lift the r.** décrocher

recent [ˈriːsənt] *adj* récent; *(development)* dernier, -ère; **in**

r. months au cours des derniers mois • **recently** *adv* récemment

reception [rɪˈsepʃən] *n (party, of radio)* réception *f*; *(welcome)* accueil *m*; **r. (desk)** réception *f* • **receptionist** *n* réceptionniste *mf*

recess [*Br* rɪˈses, *Am* ˈriːses] *n* **(a)** *(in wall)* renfoncement *m*; *(smaller)* recoin *m* **(b)** *Am (at school)* récréation *f*

recharge [riːˈtʃɑːdʒ] *vt (battery, mobile phone)* recharger • **rechargeable** *adj (battery)* rechargeable

recipe [ˈresɪpɪ] *n (for food)* & *Fig* recette *f* **(for sth** de qch)

recipient [rɪˈsɪpɪənt] *n (of gift, letter)* destinataire *mf*; *(of award)* lauréat, -e *mf*

reciprocate [rɪˈsɪprəkeɪt] *vi* rendre la pareille

recite [rɪˈsaɪt] *vt (poem)* réciter; *(list)* énumérer • **recital** *n (of music)* récital *m (pl* -als)

reckless [ˈreklɪs] *adj (rash)* imprudent

reckon [ˈrekən] **1** *vt (calculate)* calculer; *(consider)* considérer; *Fam (think)* penser **(that** que) **2** *vi* calculer, compter; **to r. with** *(take into account)* compter avec; *(deal with)* avoir affaire à; **to r. on sb/ sth** *(rely on)* compter sur qn/qch

reclaim [rɪˈkleɪm] *vt (lost property, luggage)* récupérer; *(expenses)* se faire rembourser

recline [rɪˈklaɪn] *vi (be stretched out)* être allongé • **reclining** *adj* **r. seat** siège *m* à dossier inclinable

recluse [rɪˈkluːs] *n* reclus, -e *mf*

recognize [ˈrekəgnaɪz] *vt* reconnaître • **recognition** [rekəgˈnɪʃən] *n* reconnaissance *f*; **to gain r.** être reconnu

recollect [rekəˈlekt] *vt* se souvenir de

recommend [rekə'mend] *vt* (*praise, support, advise*) recommander (**to** à; **for** pour); **to r. sb to do sth** recommander à qn de faire qch • **recommendation** [-'deɪʃən] *n* recommandation *f*

reconcile ['rekənsaɪl] *vt* (*person*) réconcilier (**with** *or* **to** avec); (*opinions, facts*) concilier; **to r. oneself to sth** se résigner à qch

reconsider [riːkən'sɪdə(r)] **1** *vt* réexaminer **2** *vi* réfléchir

reconstruct [riːkən'strʌkt] *vt* (*crime*) reconstituer

record 1 ['rekɔːd] *n* (**a**) (*disc*) disque *m*; **r. player** tourne-disques *m inv* (**b**) (*best performance*) record *m* (**c**) (*report*) rapport *m*; (*background*) antécédents *mpl*; (*file*) dossier *m*; **to make** *or* **keep a r. of sth** garder une trace écrite de qch; **on r.** (*fact, event*) attesté; **(public) records** archives *fpl* **2** ['rekɔːd] *adj* record *inv*; **to be at a r. high/low** être à son taux le plus haut/bas **3** [rɪ'kɔːd] *vt* (*on tape, in register*) enregistrer; (*in diary*) noter **4** [rɪ'kɔːd] *vi* (*on tape*) enregistrer • **recorded** [rɪ'kɔːdɪd] *adj* enregistré; (*fact*) attesté; *Br* **to send sth (by) r. delivery** ≃ envoyer qch en recommandé avec accusé de réception • **recording** [rɪ'kɔːdɪŋ] *n* enregistrement *m*

recorder [rɪ'kɔːdə(r)] *n* (*musical instrument*) flûte *f* à bec

recover [rɪ'kʌvə(r)] **1** *vt* (*get back*) récupérer; (*one's appetite, balance*) retrouver **2** *vi* (*from illness, shock, surprise*) se remettre (**from** de); (*of economy, country*) se redresser; (*of sales*) reprendre • **recovery** (*pl* **-ies**) *n* (*from illness*) rétablissement *m*; (*of economy*) redressement *m*

re-create [riːkrɪ'eɪt] *vt* recréer

recruit [rɪ'kruːt] **1** *n* recrue *f* **2** *vt* recruter

rectangle ['rektæŋɡəl] *n* rectangle *m* • **rectangular** [rɪ'tæŋɡələ] *adj* rectangulaire

recuperate [rɪ'kuːpəreɪt] *vi* (*from illness*) récupérer

recur [rɪ'kɜː(r)] (*pt & pp* **-rr-**) *vi* (*of event, problem*) se reproduire; (*of illness*) réapparaître; (*of theme*) revenir

recycle [riː'saɪkəl] *vt* recycler

red [red] **1** (**redder, reddest**) *adj* rouge; (*hair*) roux (*f* rousse); **to turn** *or* **go r.** rougir; **the R. Cross** la Croix-Rouge; **r. light** (*traffic light*) feu *m* rouge; *Fig* **r. tape** paperasserie *f* **2** *n* (*colour*) rouge *m*; **in the r.** (*in debt*) dans le rouge • **red-handed** *adv* **to be caught r.** être pris la main dans le sac • **redhead** *n* roux *m*, rousse *f* • **red-hot** *adj* brûlant

redcurrant [red'kʌrənt] *n* groseille *f*

redecorate [riː'dekəreɪt] *vt* (*repaint*) refaire la peinture de

redeem [rɪ'diːm] *vt* (*restore to favour, buy back, free*) racheter; (*gift token, coupon*) échanger; **his one redeeming feature is...** la seule chose qui le rachète, c'est...

redo [riː'duː] (*pt* **-did**, *pp* **-done**) *vt* refaire

reduce [rɪ'djuːs] *vt* réduire (**to** à; **by** de); (*temperature, price*) baisser; **at a reduced price** à prix réduit; **to be reduced to doing sth** en être réduit à faire qch • **reduction** [-'dʌkʃən] *n* (*of temperature, price*) baisse *f*; (*discount*) réduction *f* (**in/on** de/sur)

redundant [rɪ'dʌndənt] *adj* (*not needed*) superflu; *Br* **to make sb r.** licencier qn

reef [riːf] *n* récif *m*

reel [riːl] **1** n (of thread, film) bobine f **2** vt sep **to r. off** (names, statistics) débiter

ref [ref] (abbr **referee**) n Fam arbitre m

refer [rɪˈfɜː(r)] (pt & pp -rr-) **1** vt **to r. sth to sb** (submit) soumettre qch à qn; **to r. sb to a specialist** envoyer qn voir un spécialiste **2** vt insep **to r. to** (allude to) faire allusion à; (mention) parler de; (apply to) s'appliquer à; (consult) consulter

referee [refəˈriː] **1** n (in sport) arbitre m; **to give the names of two referees** (for job) fournir deux références **2** vti arbitrer

reference [ˈrefərəns] n (source, consultation) référence f; (allusion) allusion f (**to** à); (mention) mention f (**to** de); (for employer) lettre f de référence; **with** or **in r. to** concernant; **r. book** ouvrage m de référence

referendum [refəˈrendəm] n référendum m

refill 1 [ˈriːfɪl] n (for pen) cartouche f; (for lighter) recharge f; **would you like a r.?** (of drink) je te ressers? **2** [riːˈfɪl] vt (glass) remplir à nouveau; (lighter, pen) recharger

refine [rɪˈfaɪn] vt (oil, sugar, manners) raffiner; (technique, machine) perfectionner • **refined** adj (person, manners) raffiné

reflect [rɪˈflekt] **1** vt (a) (light, image) refléter, réfléchir; Fig (portray) refléter; **to be reflected (in)** (of light) se refléter (dans) (b) **to r. that...** se dire que... **2** vi (a) **to r. on sb** (of prestige, honour) rejaillir sur qn; **to r. badly on sb** faire du tort à qn (b) (think) réfléchir (**on** à) • **reflection** n (a) (image) & Fig reflet m (b) (thought, criticism) réflexion (**on** sur); **on r.** tout bien réfléchi

reflex [ˈriːfleks] n & adj réflexe (m) • **reflexive** [rɪˈfleksɪv] adj (verb) réfléchi

reform [rɪˈfɔːm] **1** n réforme f **2** vt réformer; (person, conduct) corriger **3** vi (of person) se réformer

refrain [rɪˈfreɪn] **1** n (of song) & Fig refrain m **2** vi s'abstenir (**from sth** de qch; **from doing** de faire)

refresh [rɪˈfreʃ] vt (of drink) rafraîchir; (of bath) revigorer; (of sleep, rest) reposer; **to r. one's memory** se rafraîchir la mémoire • **refreshing** adj (drink) rafraîchissant; (bath) revigorant; (original) nouveau (f nouvelle) • **refreshments** npl rafraîchissements mpl

refrigerate [rɪˈfrɪdʒəreɪt] vt réfrigérer • **refrigerator** n réfrigérateur m

refuel [riːˈfjʊəl] **1** (Br **-ll-**, Am **-l-**) vt (aircraft) ravitailler en carburant **2** vi (of aircraft) se ravitailler en carburant

refuge [ˈrefjuːdʒ] n refuge m; **to take r.** se réfugier (**in** dans) • **refugee** [refjʊˈdʒiː] n réfugié, -e mf

refund 1 [ˈriːfʌnd] n remboursement m **2** [rɪˈfʌnd] vt rembourser

refurbish [riːˈfɜːbɪʃ] vt rénover

refuse¹ [rɪˈfjuːz] **1** vt refuser; **to r. to do sth** refuser de faire qch; **to r. sb sth** refuser qch à qn **2** vi refuser • **refusal** n refus m

refuse² [ˈrefjuːs] n Br (rubbish) ordures fpl

regain [rɪˈgeɪn] vt (lost ground, favour) regagner; (health, sight) retrouver; **to r. consciousness** reprendre connaissance

regard [rɪˈgɑːd] **1** n (admiration)

respect *m*; *(consideration)* égard *m*; **with r. to** en ce qui concerne; **to give** *or* **send one's regards to sb** transmettre son meilleur souvenir à qn **2** *vt (admire, respect)* estimer; **to r. sb/sth as…** considérer qn/ qch comme… ● **regarding** *prep* en ce qui concerne ● **regardless 1** *adj* **r. of…** *(without considering)* sans tenir compte de… **2** *adv (all the same)* quand même

reggae ['regeɪ] *n (music)* reggae *m*

régime [reɪ'ʒiːm] *n* régime *m*

regiment ['redʒɪmənt] *n* régiment *m*

region ['riːdʒən] *n* région *f*; *Fig* **in the r. of** *(about)* environ ● **regional** *adj* régional

register ['redʒɪstə(r)] **1** *n* registre *m*; *(in school)* cahier *m* d'appel; **electoral r.** liste *f* électorale; **to take the r.** *(of teacher)* faire l'appel **2** *vt (birth, death)* déclarer; *(record, note)* enregistrer; *(complaint)* déposer **3** *vi (enrol)* s'inscrire **(for** à); *(at hotel)* signer le registre; *(of voter)* s'inscrire sur les listes électorales ● **registered** *adj (member)* inscrit; *(letter, package)* recommandé; **to send sth by r. post** *or Am* **mail** envoyer qch en recommandé ● **registration** [-'streɪʃən] *n (enrolment)* inscription *f*; *Br* **r. (number)** *(of vehicle)* numéro *m* d'immatriculation; *Br* **r. document** *(of vehicle)* ≃ carte *f* grise ● **registry** *adj* & *n Br* **r. (office)** bureau *m* de l'état civil; **to get married in a r. office** se marier à la mairie

regret [rɪ'gret] **1** *n* regret *m* **2** *(pt & pp* **-tt-)** *vt* regretter **(to do** de faire; **that** que + *subjunctive)*; **to r. doing sth** regretter d'avoir fait qch

regular ['regjʊlə(r)] *adj (steady, even, in grammar)* régulier, -ère; *(usual)* habituel, -elle; *(price)* normal; *(size)* moyen, -enne; *(listener, reader)* fidèle ● **regularly** *adv* régulièrement

regulate ['regjʊleɪt] *vt (adjust)* régler; *(control)* réglementer ● **regulations** [-'leɪʃənz] *npl (rules)* règlement *m*

rehearse [rɪ'hɜːs] *vti* répéter ● **rehearsal** *n* répétition *f*

reign [reɪn] **1** *n* règne *m*; **in** *or* **during the r. of** sous le règne de **2** *vi* régner **(over** sur)

reimburse [riːɪm'bɜːs] *vt* rembourser **(for** de)

reindeer ['reɪndɪə(r)] *n inv* renne *m*

reinforce [riːɪn'fɔːs] *vt* renforcer **(with** de) ● **reinforcements** *npl (troops)* renforts *mpl*

reject [rɪ'dʒekt] *vt* rejeter; *(candidate, goods, offer)* refuser ● **rejection** *n* rejet *m*; *(of candidate, goods, offer)* refus *m*

rejoice [rɪ'dʒɔɪs] *vi* se réjouir **(over** *or* **at** de)

relate [rɪ'leɪt] **1** *vt (connect)* mettre en rapport **(to** avec) **2** *vi* **to r. to** *(apply to)* avoir rapport à; *(person)* avoir des affinités avec ● **related** *adj (linked)* lié **(to** à); *(languages, styles)* apparenté; **to be r. to sb** *(by family)* être parent de qn

relation [rɪ'leɪʃən] *n* **(a)** *(relative)* parent, -e *mf* **(b)** *(relationship)* rapport *m*; **international relations** relations *fpl* internationales ● **relationship** *n (within family)* lien *m* de parenté; *(between people)* relation *f*; *(between countries)* relations *fpl*; *(connection)* rapport *m*

relative ['relətɪv] **1** *n* parent, -e *mf* **2** *adj (comparative)* relatif, -ive; *(respective)* respectif, -ive; **r.**

to *(compared to)* relativement à • **relatively** *adv* relativement

relax [rɪ'læks] **1** *vt (person, mind)* détendre; *(grip, pressure)* relâcher; *(law, control)* assouplir **2** *vi (of person)* se détendre; **r.!** *(calm down)* du calme! • **relaxation** [riːlæk'seɪʃən] *n (of person)* détente *f* • **relaxed** *adj (person, atmosphere)* détendu • **relaxing** *adj* délassant

relay ['riːleɪ] *n* **r. (race)** *(course f de)* relais *m*

release [rɪ'liːs] **1** *n (of prisoner)* libération *f*; *(of film)* sortie *f* (**of** de); *(film)* nouveau film *m*; *(record)* nouveau disque *m* **2** *vt (person)* libérer (**from** de); *(brake)* desserrer; *(film, record)* sortir; *(news)* communiquer; **to r. sb's hand** lâcher la main de qn

relent [rɪ'lent] *vi (of person)* céder • **relentless** *adj* implacable

relevant ['reləvənt] *adj* (a) *(apt)* pertinent; **to be r. to sth** avoir rapport à qch; **that's not r.** ça n'a rien à voir (b) *(appropriate) (chapter)* correspondant; *(authorities)* compétent

reliable [rɪ'laɪəbəl] *adj (person, machine)* fiable; *(information)* sûr

relieve [rɪ'liːv] *vt (alleviate)* soulager; *(boredom)* tromper; **to r. sb of sth** débarrasser qn de qch; *Hum* **to r. oneself** se soulager • **relief** [rɪ'liːf] *n* soulagement *m*

religion [rɪ'lɪdʒən] *n* religion *f* • **religious** *adj* religieux, -euse

relish ['relɪʃ] **1** *n (pickle)* condiments *mpl*; *(pleasure)* goût *m* (**for** pour); **to do sth with r.** faire qch avec délectation **2** *vt* savourer

reluctant [rɪ'lʌktənt] *adj (greeting, promise)* accordé à contrecœur; **to be r. (to do sth)** être réticent (à faire qch) • **reluctantly** *adv* à contrecœur

rely [rɪ'laɪ] *(pt & pp -ied)* *vi* **to r. (up)on** *(count on)* compter sur; *(be dependent on)* dépendre de

remain [rɪ'meɪn] *vi (stay behind, continue to be)* rester; *(be left)* subsister • **remainder** *n* reste *m* • **remaining** *adj* restant • **remains** *npl* restes *mpl*

remark [rɪ'mɑːk] **1** *n* remarque *f* **2** *vt* faire remarquer • **remarkable** *adj* remarquable • **remarkably** *adv* remarquablement

remarry [riː'mærɪ] *(pt & pp -ied)* *vi* se remarier

remedy ['remɪdɪ] *(pl -ies)* *n* remède *m*

remember [rɪ'membə(r)] **1** *vt* se souvenir de, se rappeler; *(commemorate)* commémorer; **to r. that/doing** se rappeler que/d'avoir fait; **to r. to do sth** penser à faire qch; **to r. sb to sb** rappeler qn au bon souvenir de qn **2** *vi* se souvenir, se rappeler

remind [rɪ'maɪnd] *vt* **to r. sb of sth** rappeler qch à qn; **to r. sb to do sth** rappeler à qn de faire qch • **reminder** *n (letter, of event)* rappel *m*

reminisce [remɪ'nɪs] *vi* évoquer des souvenirs; **to r. about sth** évoquer qch

remorse [rɪ'mɔːs] *n* remords *m*; **to feel r.** avoir du *ou* des remords • **remorseless** *adj* impitoyable

remote [rɪ'məʊt] *(-er, -est)* *adj* (a) *(far-off)* éloigné (**from** de); **r. control** télécommande *f* (b) *(slight)* vague • **remotely** *adv (slightly)* vaguement

remove [rɪ'muːv] *vt (clothes, stain, object)* enlever (**from sb** à qn; **from sth** de qch); *(obstacle, word)* supprimer • **removal** *n* (a) *(of obstacle, word)* suppression *f* **(b)** *Br* **r. van** camion *m* de déménagement • **remover** *n (for nail polish)* dissolvant *m*

rendezvous ['rɒndɪvuː, *pl* -vuːz] *n inv* rendez-vous *m inv*

renew [rɪ'njuː] *vt* renouveler; *(resume)* reprendre; *(library book)* renouveler le prêt de • **renewed** *adj (efforts)* renouvelé; *(attempt)* nouveau *(f* nouvelle*)*

renovate ['renəveɪt] *vt (house)* rénover; *(painting)* restaurer

renowned [rɪ'naʊnd] *adj* renommé **(for** pour)

rent [rent] **1** *n (for house, flat)* loyer *m* **2** *vt* louer; **to r. out** louer; **rented car** voiture *f* de location • **rental** *n (of television, car)* location *f; (of telephone)* abonnement *m*

reopen [riː'əʊpən] *vti* rouvrir

reorganize [riː'ɔːɡənaɪz] *vt* réorganiser

rep [rep] *(abbr* **representative)** *n Fam* VRP *m*

repair [rɪ'peə(r)] *vt* réparer

repay [riː'peɪ] *(pt & pp* **-paid)** *vt (pay back)* rembourser; *(reward)* remercier **(for** de) • **repayment** *n* remboursement *m*

repeat [rɪ'piːt] **1** *n (of event)* répétition *f; (on TV, radio)* rediffusion *f* **2** *vt* répéter **(that** que); *(promise, threat)* réitérer; *(class)* redoubler; *(TV programme)* rediffuser; **to r. oneself** se répéter • **repeated** *adj (attempts)* répété; *(efforts)* renouvelé • **repeatedly** *adv* à maintes reprises

repellent [rɪ'pelənt] *n* **insect r.** anti-moustiques *m inv*

repetition [repɪ'tɪʃən] *n* répétition *f* • **repetitive** [rɪ'petɪtɪv] *adj* répétitif, -ive

rephrase [riː'freɪz] *vt* reformuler

replace [rɪ'pleɪs] *vt (take the place*

of) remplacer **(by** *or* **with** par); *(put back)* remettre (à sa place) • **replacement** *n (substitution)* remplacement *m* **(of** de); *(person)* remplaçant, -e *mf; (machine part)* pièce *f* de rechange

replay ['riːpleɪ] *n (match)* nouvelle rencontre *f;* **(instant** *or* **action) r.** *(on TV)* = répétition d'une séquence précédente

replica ['replɪkə] *n* réplique *f*

reply [rɪ'plaɪ] **1** *(pl* **-ies)** *n* réponse *f;* **in r.** en réponse **(to** à) **2** *(pt & pp* **-ied)** *vti* répondre **(to** à; **that** que)

report [rɪ'pɔːt] **1** *n (analysis)* rapport *m; (account)* compte rendu *m; (in media)* reportage *m; Br* **(school) r.,** *Am* **r. card** bulletin *m* scolaire **2** *vt (information)* rapporter; *(accident, theft)* signaler **(to** à); **to r. sb to the police** dénoncer qn à la police **3** *vi (give account)* faire un rapport **(on** sur); *(of journalist)* faire un reportage **(on** sur); *(go)* se présenter **(to** à) • **reported** *adj* **r. speech** *(in grammar)* discours *m* indirect; **it is r. that...** on dit que...; **to be r. missing** être porté disparu • **reporter** *n* reporter *m*

represent [reprɪ'zent] *vt* représenter • **representation** [-'teɪʃən] *n* représentation *f* • **representative** *n* représentant, -e *mf; Am Pol* ≃ député, -e *mf*

reprimand ['reprɪmɑːnd] *vt* réprimander

reprint 1 ['riːprɪnt] *n* réimpression *f* **2** [riː'prɪnt] *vt* réimprimer

reproach [rɪ'prəʊtʃ] **1** *n (blame)* reproche *m* **2** *vt* faire des reproches à; **to r. sb with sth** reprocher qch à qn

reproduce [riːprə'djuːs] **1** *vt* reproduire **2** *vi* se reproduire

- **reproduction** [-'dʌkʃən] *n* reproduction *f*

reptile ['reptaɪl] *n* reptile *m*

republic [rɪ'pʌblɪk] *n* république *f* • **republican** *adj & n* républicain, -e *(mf)*

repulsive [rɪ'pʌlsɪv] *adj* repoussant

reputable ['repjʊtəbəl] *adj* de bonne réputation

reputation [repjʊ'teɪʃən] *n* réputation *f*

request [rɪ'kwest] **1** *n* demande *f* (**for** de); **on r.** sur demande; **at sb's r.** à la demande de qn; *Br* **r. stop** *(for bus)* arrêt *m* facultatif **2** *vt* demander; **to r. sb to do sth** prier qn de faire qch

require [rɪ'kwaɪə(r)] *vt (of task, problem, situation)* requérir; *(of person)* avoir besoin de; **to be required to do sth** être tenu de faire qch; **the required qualities** les qualités *fpl* requises • **requirement** *n (need)* exigence *f*; *(condition)* condition *f* (requise)

reschedule [*Br* riː'ʃedjuːl, *Am* riː'skedʒʊəl] *vt* changer la date/l'heure de

rescue ['reskjuː] **1** *n (action)* sauvetage *m* (**of** de); **to go/come to sb's r.** aller/venir au secours de qn **2** *adj (team, operation, attempt)* de sauvetage **3** *vt (save)* sauver; *(set free)* délivrer (**from** de)

research [rɪ'sɜːtʃ] **1** *n* recherches *fpl* (**on** *or* **into** sur) **2** *vi* faire des recherches (**on** *or* **into** sur) • **researcher** *n* chercheur, -euse *mf*

resemble [rɪ'zembəl] *vt* ressembler à • **resemblance** *n* ressemblance *f* (**to** avec)

resent [rɪ'zent] *vt* ne pas aimer • **resentment** *n* ressentiment *m*

reserve [rɪ'zɜːv] **1** *n (stock, land)* réserve *f*; **in r.** en réserve **2** *vt (room, decision)* réserver; *(right)* se réserver • **reservation** [rezə'veɪʃən] *n (for table, room)* réservation *f*; **to make a r.** réserver • **reserved** *adj (person, table, room)* réservé

reservoir ['rezəvwɑː(r)] *n (of water)* réservoir *m*

reset [riː'set] *vt (counter)* remettre à zéro

resident ['rezɪdənt] *n (of country, street)* habitant, -e *mf*; *(of hotel)* pensionnaire *mf*; *(foreigner)* résident, -e *mf* • **residential** [-'denʃəl] *adj (neighbourhood)* résidentiel, -elle

resign [rɪ'zaɪn] **1** *vt (job)* démissionner de; **to r. oneself to sth/to doing sth** se résigner à qch/à faire qch **2** *vi* démissionner (**from** de) • **resignation** [rezɪg'neɪʃən] *n (from job)* démission *f*; *(attitude)* résignation *f* • **resigned** *adj* résigné

resilient [rɪ'zɪlɪənt] *adj* élastique; *Fig (person)* résistant

resist [rɪ'zɪst] **1** *vt* résister à; **to r. doing sth** s'empêcher de faire qch **2** *vi* résister • **resistance** *n* résistance *f* (**to** à) • **resistant** *adj* résistant (**to** à)

resit [riː'sɪt] *(pt & pp* **-sat,** *pres p* **-sitting)** *vt Br (exam)* repasser

resolve [rɪ'zɒlv] *vt (problem)* résoudre; **to r. to do sth** *(of person)* se résoudre à faire qch • **resolution** [rezə'luːʃən] *n* résolution *f*

resort [rɪ'zɔːt] **1** *n* **(a)** *(holiday place)* lieu *m* de villégiature; *Br* **seaside r.,** *Am* **beach r.** station *f* balnéaire **(b)** *(recourse)* **as a last r.** en dernier ressort **2** *vi* **to r. to sth** avoir recours à qch; **to r. to doing sth** finir par faire qch

resounding [rɪ'zaʊndɪŋ] *adj*

(failure) retentissant; *(success)* éclatant

resource [rɪ'sɔːs, rɪ'zɔːs] *n* ressource *f* • **resourceful** *adj* ingénieux, -euse

respect [rɪ'spekt] **1** *n* respect *m* (**for** pour); *(aspect)* égard *m*; **in many respects** à bien des égards; **with r. to, in r. of** en ce qui concerne **2** *vt* respecter • **respectable** *adj (decent)* respectable; *(fairly good)* honorable

respective [rɪ'spektɪv] *adj* respectif, -ive • **respectively** *adv* respectivement

respond [rɪ'spɒnd] *vi (answer)* répondre (**to** à); *(react)* réagir (**to** à); **to r. to treatment** bien réagir (au traitement) • **response** *n (answer)* réponse *f*; *(reaction)* réaction *f*; **in r. to** en réponse à

responsible [rɪ'spɒnsəbəl] *adj* responsable (**for** de); *(job)* à responsabilités • **responsibility** [-'bɪlɪtɪ] *(pl -ies)* n responsabilité *f* (**for** de) • **responsibly** *adv* de façon responsable

rest¹ [rest] **1** *n (relaxation)* repos *m*; *(support)* support *m*; **to have** or **take a r.** se reposer; **to set** or **put sb's mind at r.** tranquilliser qn; *Am* **r. room** toilettes *fpl* **2** *vt (lean)* poser (**on** sur); *(horse)* laisser reposer **3** *vi (relax)* se reposer; *(lean)* être posé (**on** sur); **to r. on** *(of argument, roof)* reposer sur • **restless** *adj* agité

rest² [rest] *n (remainder)* reste *m* (**of** de); **the r.** *(others)* les autres *mfpl*

restaurant ['restərɒnt] *n* restaurant *m*; *Br* **r. car** *(on train)* wagon-restaurant *m*

restore [rɪ'stɔː(r)] *vt (give back)* rendre (**to** à); *(order, peace,*

rights) rétablir; *(building, painting, monarchy)* restaurer

restrain [rɪ'streɪn] *vt (person, dog)* maîtriser; *(crowd, anger)* contenir; **to r. sb from doing sth** retenir qn pour qu'il ne fasse pas qch • **restrained** *adj (manner)* réservé • **restraint** *n (moderation)* mesure *f*; *(restriction)* restriction *f*

restrict [rɪ'strɪkt] *vt* restreindre; **to r. oneself to sth/doing sth** se limiter à qch/à faire qch • **restricted** *adj* restreint • **restriction** *n* restriction *f* (**on** à)

result [rɪ'zʌlt] **1** *n (outcome, success)* résultat *m*; **as a r.** en conséquence; **as a r. of** à la suite de **2** *vi* résulter (**from** de); **to r. in sth** aboutir à qch

resume [rɪ'zjuːm] *vti* reprendre; **to r. doing sth** se remettre à faire qch

résumé ['rezjʊmeɪ] *n (summary)* résumé *m*; *Am (CV)* curriculum vitae *m inv*

resurrect [rezə'rekt] *vt* *Fig (fashion)* remettre au goût du jour • **resurrection** *n* *Rel* résurrection *f*

resuscitate [rɪ'sʌsɪteɪt] *vt* *Med* ranimer

retail ['riːteɪl] *n* (vente *f* au) détail *m*

retain [rɪ'teɪn] *vt (keep)* conserver; *(hold in place)* retenir

retaliate [rɪ'tælɪeɪt] *vi* riposter • **retaliation** [-lɪ'eɪʃən] *n* représailles *fpl*; **in r. for** en représailles à

retch [retʃ] *vi* avoir des haut-le-cœur

rethink [riː'θɪŋk] *(pt & pp* **-thought)** *vt* repenser

retire [rɪ'taɪə(r)] *vi (from work)* prendre sa retraite • **retired** *adj*

(no longer working) retraité •
retirement *n* retraite *f*
retrace [riː'treɪs] *vt* **to r. one's
steps** revenir sur ses pas
retract [rɪ'trækt] *vt* **(a)** *(statement)*
revenir sur **(b)** *(claws)* rentrer
retrain [riː'treɪn] *vi* se recycler
retreat [rɪ'triːt] *vi* se réfugier; *(of
troops)* battre en retraite
retrieve [rɪ'triːv] *vt* *(recover)*
récupérer
retrospect ['retrəspekt] *n* **in r.**
rétrospectivement
return [rɪ'tɜːn] **1** *n* retour *m*; *Br* **r.
(ticket)** (billet *m*) aller (et) retour
m; **many happy returns!** bon
anniversaire!; **in r.** en échange (**for**
de) **2** *adj (trip, flight)* (de) retour **3**
vt (give back) rendre; *(put back)*
remettre; *(bring back)* rapporter;
(send back) renvoyer; **to r. sb's
call** *(on phone)* rappeler qn **4** *vi
(come back)* revenir; *(go back)*
retourner; *(go back home)* rentrer;
to r. to *(subject)* revenir à
reunion [riː'juːnjən] *n* réunion *f* •
reunite [riːjʊ'naɪt] *vt* réconcilier;
to be reunited with sb retrouver
qn
reuse [riː'juːz] *vt* réutiliser
reveal [rɪ'viːl] *vt (make known)*
révéler (**that** que); *(make visible)*
laisser voir • **revealing** *adj (sign,
comment)* révélateur, -trice
revelation [revə'leɪʃən] *n*
révélation *f*
revenge [rɪ'vendʒ] *n* vengeance
f; **to have** *or* **get one's r. (on
sb)** se venger (de qn); **in r.** pour
se venger
revenue ['revənjuː] *n (income)*
revenu *m*; *(from sales)* recettes *fpl*
reverse [rɪ'vɜːs] **1** *adj (opposite)*
contraire; *(image)* inverse; **in r.
order** dans l'ordre inverse **2** *n*
contraire *m*; *(of coin)* revers *m*; *(of*

fabric) envers *m*; *(of paper)* verso
m; **in r. (gear)** *(when driving)*
en marche arrière **3** *vt (situation)*
renverser; *(order, policy)* inverser;
(decision) revenir sur; **to r. the
car** faire marche arrière; *Br* **to
r. the charges** *(when phoning)*
téléphoner en PCV **4** *vi Br (in
car)* faire marche arrière; **to r.
in/out** rentrer/sortir en marche
arrière • **reversal** *n (of situation,
roles)* renversement *m*; *(of policy,
opinion)* revirement *m*
review [rɪ'vjuː] **1** *n (of book, film)*
critique *f* **2** *vt (book, film)* faire la
critique de; *(situation)* faire le point
sur • **reviewer** *n* critique *m*
revise [rɪ'vaɪz] **1** *vt (opinion,
notes, text)* réviser **2** *vi (for exam)*
réviser (**for** pour) • **revision**
[-'vɪʒən] *n* révision *f*
revive [rɪ'vaɪv] *vt (person)*
ranimer; *(custom, industry)* faire
renaître; *(fashion)* relancer •
revival *n (of custom, business)*
reprise *f*; *(of fashion)* renouveau *m*
revolt [rɪ'vəʊlt] **1** *n* révolte *f* **2**
vt (disgust) révolter **3** *vi (rebel)*
se révolter (**against** contre) •
revolting *adj* dégoûtant
revolution [revə'luːʃən] *n*
révolution *f* • **revolutionary** *(pl
-ies)* *adj & n* révolutionnaire *(mf)*
revolve [rɪ'vɒlv] *vi* tourner
(**around** autour de) • **revolving**
adj **r. door(s)** porte *f* à tambour
revolver [rɪ'vɒlvə(r)] *n* revolver
m
reward [rɪ'wɔːd] **1** *n* récompense
f (**for** de) **2** *vt* récompenser (**for**
de *ou* pour) • **rewarding** *adj*
intéressant
rewind [riː'waɪnd] *(pt &
pp* **-wound***)* *vt (tape, film)*
rembobiner

rewrite [riːˈraɪt] (*pt* **-wrote**, *pp* **-written**) *vt* réécrire

rhinoceros [raɪˈnɒsərəs] *n* rhinocéros *m*

rhubarb [ˈruːbɑːb] *n* rhubarbe *f*

rhyme [raɪm] **1** *n* rime *f*; *(poem)* vers *mpl* **2** *vi* rimer (**with** avec)

rhythm [ˈrɪðəm] *n* rythme *m*

rib [rɪb] *n (bone)* côte *f*

ribbon [ˈrɪbən] *n* ruban *m*

rice [raɪs] *n* riz *m*; **r. pudding** riz *m* au lait

rich [rɪtʃ] **1** (**-er**, **-est**) *adj (person, food)* riche; **to be r. in sth** être riche en qch **2** *npl* **the r.** les riches *mpl* • **riches** *npl* richesses *fpl*

rid [rɪd] (*pt & pp* **rid**, *pres p* **ridding**) *vt* débarrasser (**of** de); **to get r. of, to r. oneself of** se débarrasser de

ridden [ˈrɪdən] *pp of* **ride**

riddle [ˈrɪdəl] *n (puzzle)* devinette *f*; *(mystery)* énigme *f*

ride [raɪd] **1** *n (on horse)* promenade *f*; *(on bicycle, in car)* tour *m*; *(in taxi)* course *f*; **to go for a r.** aller faire un tour; **to give sb a r.** *(in car)* emmener qn en voiture **2** (*pt* **rode**, *pp* **ridden**) *vt (horse, bicycle)* monter à; *(a particular horse)* monter; **to know how to r. a bicycle** savoir faire du vélo **3** *vi (on horse)* faire du cheval; *(on bicycle)* faire du vélo; **to go riding** *(on horse)* faire du cheval; **I ride to work** *(on bicycle)* je vais travailler à vélo • **rider** *n (on horse)* cavalier, -ère *mf*; *(cyclist)* cycliste *mf* • **riding** *n* (**horse**) **r.** équitation *f*

ridiculous [rɪˈdɪkjʊləs] *adj* ridicule

rifle [ˈraɪfəl] *n* fusil *m*

rig [rɪɡ] **1** *n* (**oil**) **r.** derrick *m*; *(at sea)* plate-forme *f* pétrolière **2** (*pt & pp* **-gg-**) *vt Fam (result, election)* truquer; **to r. up** *(equipment)* installer

right¹ [raɪt] **1** *adj* **(a)** *(correct)* bon (*f* bonne), exact; *(word)* juste; **to be r.** *(of person)* avoir raison (**to do** de faire); **it's the r. time** c'est l'heure exacte; **that's r.** c'est ça; **r.!** bon! **(b)** *(appropriate)* bon (*f* bonne); **he's the r. man** c'est l'homme qu'il faut **(c)** *(morally good)* bien *inv*; **to do the r. thing** faire ce qu'il faut **(d)** *Math* **r. angle** angle *m* droit **2** *adv (straight)* (tout) droit; *(completely)* tout à fait; *(correctly)* correctement; **to put sth r.** *(rectify)* corriger qch; *(fix)* arranger qch; **to put sb r.** détromper qn; **r. round** tout autour (**sth** de qch); **r. behind** juste derrière; **r. here** ici même; **r. away, r. now** tout de suite **3** *n* **to be in the r.** avoir raison; **r. and wrong** le bien et le mal • **rightly** *adv (correctly)* bien; *(justifiably)* à juste titre

right² [raɪt] **1** *adj (not left) (hand, side)* droit **2** *adv* à droite **3** *n* droite *f*; **on** *or* **to the r.** à droite (**of** de) • **right-hand** *adj* de droite; **on the r. side** à droite (**of** de) • **right-handed** *adj (person)* droitier, -ère • **right-wing** *adj Pol* de droite

right³ [raɪt] *n (entitlement)* droit *m* (**to do** de faire); **to have a r. to sth** avoir droit à qch; **to have (the) r. of way** *(on road)* avoir la priorité

rigid [ˈrɪdʒɪd] *adj* rigide

rigorous [ˈrɪɡərəs] *adj* rigoureux, -euse

rim [rɪm] *n* bord *m*

rind [raɪnd] *n (of cheese)* croûte *f*; *(of bacon)* couenne *f*

ring¹ [rɪŋ] *n (for finger, curtain)* anneau *m*; *(for finger, with stone)* bague *f*; *(of people, chairs)* cercle m; *(at circus)* piste *f; (for boxing)* ring *m;* **to have rings under one's eyes** avoir les yeux cernés; *Br* **r. road** périphérique *m*

ring² [rɪŋ] **1** *n Fam* **to give sb a r.** passer un coup de fil à qn **2** *(pt* **rang,** *pp* **rung)** *vt (bell)* sonner; *(alarm)* déclencher; **to r. sb** *(on phone)* téléphoner à qn; **to r. the doorbell** sonner à la porte; *Fam* **that rings a bell** ça me dit quelque chose **3** *vi (of bell, phone, person)* sonner; *(of sound, words)* retentir; *(make a phone call)* téléphoner

▸**ring back 1** *vt sep* **to r. sb back** rappeler qn **2** *vi* rappeler

▸**ring up 1** *vt sep* **to r. sb up** téléphoner à qn **2** *vi* téléphoner

rinse [rɪns] **1** *n* rinçage *m;* **to give sth a r.** rincer qch **2** *vt* rincer; **to r. one's hands** se rincer les mains; **to r. out** rincer

riot ['raɪət] **1** *n (uprising)* émeute *f;* **to run r.** se déchaîner **2** *vi (rise up)* faire une émeute; *(of prisoners)* se mutiner • **rioter** *n* émeutier, -ère *mf; (vandal)* casseur *m*

rip [rɪp] **1** *n* déchirure *f* **2** *(pt & pp* **-pp-)** *vt* déchirer; **to r. sth off** arracher qch **(from** de); *Fam* **to r. sb off** *(deceive)* rouler qn; **to r. sth up** déchirer qch **3** *vi (of fabric)* se déchirer • **rip-off** *n Fam* arnaque *f*

ripe [raɪp] **(-er, -est)** *adj (fruit)* mûr; *(cheese)* fait • **ripen** *vti* mûrir

rise [raɪz] **1** *n (in price, pressure)* hausse *f* **(in** de); *(of leader, party)* ascension *f; Br* **(pay) r.** augmentation *f* (de salaire); **to give r. to sth** donner lieu à qch **2** *(pt* **rose,** *pp* **risen** ['rɪzən]) *vi (of temperature, balloon, price)* monter; *(of sun)* se lever; *(of dough)* lever; *(get up from chair*

or bed) se lever • **rising** *adj (sun)* levant; *(number)* croissant; *(prices)* en hausse

risk [rɪsk] **1** *n* risque *m;* **at r.** *(person)* en danger; *(job)* menacé; **to run the r. of doing sth** courir le risque de faire qch **2** *vt (life, reputation)* risquer; **I can't r. going** je ne peux pas prendre le risque d'y aller • **risky (-ier, -iest)** *adj* risqué

ritual ['rɪtjuəl] *n* rituel *m*

rival ['raɪvəl] **1** *n* rival, -e *mf* **2** *adj* rival **3** *(Br* **-ll-,** *Am* **-l-)** *vt (equal)* égaler **(in** en) • **rivalry** *(pl* **-ies)** *n* rivalité *f* **(between** entre)

river ['rɪvə(r)] *n (small)* rivière *f; (flowing into sea)* fleuve *m*

Riviera [rɪvɪ'eərə] *n* **the (French) R.** la Côte d'Azur

road [rəʊd] **1** *n* route *f; (small)* chemin *m; (in town)* rue *f; (roadway)* chaussée *f;* **the Paris r.** la route de Paris; **by r.** par la route; **to live across** *or* **over the r.** habiter en face **2** *adj (map, safety)* routier, -ère; *(accident)* de la route; **r. sign** panneau *m* de signalisation; *Br* **r. works,** *Am* **r. work** travaux *mpl* de voirie • **roadside** *n* bord *m* de la route

roam [rəʊm] **1** *vt* parcourir; **to r. the streets** traîner dans les rues **2** *vi* errer

roar [rɔː(r)] *vi (of lion, wind, engine)* rugir; *(of person, crowd)* hurler; **to r. with laughter** hurler de rire • **roaring** *adj* **a r. fire** une belle flambée; **to do a r. trade** faire des affaires en or

roast [rəʊst] **1** *n (meat)* rôti *m* **2** *adj* rôti; **r. beef** rosbif *m* **3** *vt (meat, potatoes)* faire rôtir **4** *vi (of meat)* rôtir

rob [rɒb] *(pt & pp* **-bb-)** *vt (person)* voler; *(shop, bank)* dévaliser;

to r. sb of sth voler qch à qn; *Fig (deprive)* priver qn de qch • **robber** *n* voleur, -euse *mf* • **robbery** (*pl* **-ies**) *n* vol *m*; **it's daylight r.!** c'est du vol pur et simple!

robe [rəʊb] *n (of priest, judge)* robe *f*

robin ['rɒbɪn] *n (bird)* rouge-gorge *m*

robot ['rəʊbɒt] *n* robot *m*

rock¹ [rɒk] **1** *n (music)* rock *m* **2** *vt (boat)* balancer; *(building)* secouer **3** *vi (sway)* se balancer; *(of building, ground)* trembler • **rocking** *adj* **r. chair** fauteuil *m* à bascule

rock² [rɒk] **1** *n (substance)* roche *f*; *(boulder, rock face)* rocher *m*; *Am (stone)* pierre *f*; **r. climbing** varappe *f* • **rocky** (**-ier, -iest**) *adj (road)* rocailleux, -euse; *Fig (relationship)* instable

rocket ['rɒkɪt] **1** *n* fusée *f* **2** *vi (of prices, unemployment)* monter en flèche

rod [rɒd] *n (wooden)* baguette *f*; *(metal)* tige *f*; *(for fishing)* canne *f* à pêche

rode [rəʊd] *pt of* **ride**

rodent ['rəʊdənt] *n* rongeur *m*

rogue [rəʊg] *n (dishonest)* crapule *f*; *(mischievous)* coquin, -e *mf*

role [rəʊl] *n* rôle *m*; **r. model** modèle *m*

roll [rəʊl] **1** *n (of paper)* rouleau *m*; *(of drum, thunder)* roulement *m*; *(bread)* petit pain *m*; *(list)* liste *f*; **r. of film** pellicule *f* **2** *vt (cigarette)* rouler; *(ball)* faire rouler **3** *vi (of ball)* rouler; *(of camera)* tourner • **rolling** *adj (hills)* ondulant; **r. pin** rouleau *m* à pâtisserie

▶**roll down** *vt sep (car window)* baisser; *(sleeves)* redescendre

▶**roll on** *vi Fam* **r. on tonight!** vivement ce soir!

▶**roll out** *vt sep (dough)* étaler

▶**roll over 1** *vt sep* retourner **2** *vi (many times)* se rouler; *(once)* se retourner

▶**roll up** *vt sep (map, cloth)* rouler; *(sleeve)* retrousser

roller ['rəʊlə(r)] *n (for hair, painting)* rouleau *m*; **r. coaster** montagnes *fpl* russes; **r. skate** patin *m* à roulettes • **roller-skate** *vi* faire du patin à roulettes

rollerblades ['rəʊləbleɪdz] *npl* patins *mpl* en ligne

Roman ['rəʊmən] **1** *adj* romain **2** *n* Romain, -e *mf* **3** *adj & n* **R. Catholic** catholique *(mf)*

romance [rəʊ'mæns] *n (love)* amour *m*; *(affair)* aventure *f* amoureuse; *(story)* histoire *f* d'amour • **romantic** *adj (of love, tenderness)* romantique; *(fanciful, imaginary)* romanesque

romp [rɒmp] *vi* s'ébattre

rompers ['rɒmpəz] *npl (for baby)* barboteuse *f*

roof [ru:f] *n* toit *m*; **r. rack** *(of car)* galerie *f* • **rooftop** *n* toit *m*

room [ru:m, rʊm] *n* **(a)** *(in house)* pièce *f*; *(bedroom)* chambre *f*; *(large, public)* salle *f* **(b)** *(space)* place *f*; **to make r.** faire de la place (**for** pour) • **roommate** *n* camarade *mf* de chambre

root [ru:t] **1** *n (of plant, tooth, hair)* & *Math* racine *f*; *Fig (origin)* origine *f*; *(cause)* cause *f*; **to take r.** *(of plant, person)* prendre racine **2** *vt* **to r. sth out** supprimer qch

rope [rəʊp] *n (of love)* corde *f*; *(on ship)* cordage *m*; *Fam* **to know the ropes** connaître son affaire

rose¹ [rəʊz] *n (flower)* rose *f*

rose² [rəʊz] *pt of* **rise**

rosette [rəʊ'zet] *n* rosette *f*

rosy ['rəʊzɪ] (**-ier, -iest**) *adj (pink)* rose; *Fig (future)* prometteur, -euse

rot [rɒt] (*pt & pp* **-tt-**) *vti* pourrir

rota ['rəʊtə] *n* roulement *m*

rotary ['rəʊtərɪ] (*pl* **-ies**) *n Am (for traffic)* rond-point *m*

rotate [rəʊ'teɪt] **1** *vt* faire tourner **2** *vi* tourner ● **rotation** *n* **in r.** à tour de rôle

rotten ['rɒtən] *adj (fruit, egg, wood)* pourri; *Fam (bad)* nul (*f* nulle); *Fam* **to feel r.** *(ill)* être mal fichu

rough¹ [rʌf] **1** (**-er, -est**) *adj (surface)* rugueux, -euse; *(ground)* accidenté; *(life)* rude; *(neighbourhood)* dur; *(sea)* agité; *(brutal)* brutal **2** *adv Br* **to sleep/live r.** coucher/vivre à la dure **3** *vt Fam* **to r. it** vivre à la dure ● **roughly¹** *adv (brutally)* brutalement

rough² [rʌf] (**-er, -est**) *adj (approximate)* approximatif, -ive; **r. guess, r. estimate** approximation *f*; **r. copy, r. draft** brouillon *m*; **r. paper** papier *m* brouillon ● **roughly²** *adv (approximately)* à peu près

round [raʊnd] **1** (**-er, -est**) *adj* rond; *Am* **r. trip** aller (et) retour *m* **2** *adv* autour; **all r., right r.** tout autour; **all year r.** toute l'année; **the wrong way r.** à l'envers **3** *prep* autour de; **r. here** par ici; **about** *(approximately)* environ **4** *n (in competition)* manche *f*; *(of golf)* partie *f*; *(in boxing)* round *m*; *(of drinks)* tournée *f* **5** *vt* **to r. up** *(gather)* rassembler; *(price)* arrondir au chiffre supérieur ● **roundabout** *n Br (at funfair)* manège *m*; *(road junction)* rond-point *m*

rouse [raʊz] *vt (awaken)* éveiller

route [ruːt] *n* itinéraire *m*; *(of aircraft, ship)* route *f*; **bus r.** ligne *f* d'autobus

routine [ruː'tiːn] **1** *n (habit)* routine *f*; **the daily r.** le train-train quotidien **2** *adj (inquiry, work)* de routine

row¹ [rəʊ] *n (line)* rangée *f*; **two days in a r.** deux jours d'affilée

row² [rəʊ] **1** *n Am* **r. boat** bateau *m* à rames **2** *vt (boat)* faire avancer à la rame; *(person)* transporter en canot **3** *vi (in boat)* ramer ● **rowing** *n (as sport)* aviron *m*; *Br* **r. boat** bateau *m* à rames

row³ [raʊ] **1** *n (noise)* vacarme *m*; *(quarrel)* dispute *f* **2** *vi* se disputer (**with** avec)

rowdy ['raʊdɪ] (**-ier, -iest**) *adj* chahuteur, -euse

royal ['rɔɪəl] *adj* royal ● **royalty 1** *n* royauté *f* **2** *npl* **royalties** *(from book)* droits *mpl* d'auteur

rub [rʌb] (*pt & pp* **-bb-**) *vti* frotter
► **rub in** *vt sep (cream)* faire pénétrer (en massant); *Fam* **to r. it in** retourner le couteau dans la plaie
► **rub off** *vt sep (mark)* effacer
► **rub out** *vt sep (mark, writing)* effacer

rubber ['rʌbə(r)] *n (substance)* caoutchouc *m*; *Br (eraser)* gomme *f*; **r. band** élastique *m*; **r. stamp** tampon *m*

rubbish ['rʌbɪʃ] *n Br (waste)* ordures *fpl*; *Fig (nonsense)* idioties *fpl*; *Fam* **that's r.** *(absurd)* c'est absurde; *(worthless)* ça ne vaut rien; **r. bin** poubelle *f*

rubble ['rʌbəl] *n* décombres *mpl*

ruby ['ruːbɪ] (*pl* **-ies**) *n (gem)* rubis *m*

rucksack ['rʌksæk] *n* sac *m* à dos

rude [ruːd] (**-er, -est**) *adj (impolite)*

impoli (**to** envers); *(indecent)* obscène

rug [rʌg] *n* tapis *m*; *(over knees)* plaid *m*

rugby [ˈrʌgbɪ] *n* rugby *m*

rugged [ˈrʌgɪd] *adj (terrain, coast)* accidenté; *(features)* rude

ruin [ˈruːɪn] **1** *n (destruction, rubble, building)* ruine *f*; **in ruins** *(building)* en ruine **2** *vt (health, country, person)* ruiner; *(clothes)* abîmer; *(effect, meal, party)* gâcher • **ruined** *adj (person, country)* ruiné; *(building)* en ruine

rule [ruːl] **1** *n (principle)* règle *f*; *(regulation)* règlement *m*; *(government)* autorité *f*; *Br* **against the rules** or *Am* **r.** contraire au règlement; **as a r.** en règle générale **2** *vt (country)* gouverner; *(decide) (of judge, referee)* décider (**that** que); **to r. sth out** *(exclude)* exclure qch • **ruler** *n* (a) *(for measuring)* règle *f* (b) *(king, queen)* souverain, -e *mf*; *(political leader)* dirigeant, -e *mf* • **ruling** *adj Pol* **the r. party** le parti au pouvoir

rum [rʌm] *n* rhum *m*

rumble [ˈrʌmbəl] *vi (of train, thunder)* gronder; *(of stomach)* gargouiller

rummage [ˈrʌmɪdʒ] *vi* **to r. (about)** farfouiller; *Am* **r. sale** vente *f* de charité *(articles d'occasion uniquement)*

rumour [ˈruːmə(r)] *(Am* **rumor***)* *n* rumeur *f* • **rumoured** *(Am* **rumored***) adj* **it is r. that...** on dit que...

run [rʌn] **1** *n (series)* série *f*; *(running)* course *f*; *(in cricket, baseball)* point *m*; *(in stocking)* maille *f* filée; **to go for a r.** aller courir; **on the r.** *(prisoner)* en

fuite; **in the long r.** à long terme **2** *(pt* **ran,** *pp* **run,** *pres p* **running***) vt (distance, race)* courir; *(machine)* faire fonctionner; *(business, country)* diriger; *(courses, events)* organiser; *(bath)* faire couler; **to r. one's hand over** passer la main sur **3** *vi* courir; *(of river, nose, tap)* couler; *(of colour in washing)* déteindre; *(of machine)* marcher; **to r. down/in/out** descendre/ entrer/sortir en courant; **to go running** faire du jogging; **to r. for president** être candidat à la présidence; **it runs in the family** c'est de famille • **runaway** *n* fugitif, -ive *mf* • **run-down** *adj (weak, tired)* fatigué; *(district)* délabré • **runner** *n (athlete)* coureur *m*; *Br* **r. bean** haricot *m* d'Espagne • **runner-up** *n (in race)* second, -e *mf* • **running** *adj* **six days r.** six jours de suite; **r. water** eau *f* courante; • **runway** *n (for aircraft)* piste *f* (d'envol) • **runny** *(-ier, -iest) adj (cream, sauce)* liquide; *(nose)* qui coule

▶**run about, run around** *vi* courir çà et là

▶**run away** *vi (flee)* s'enfuir (**from** de)

▶**run down** *vt sep (knock down)* renverser; *(kill)* écraser

▶**run into** *vt insep (meet)* tomber sur; *(crash into) (of vehicle)* percuter

▶**run off** *vi (flee)* s'enfuir (**with** avec)

▶**run out** *vi (of stocks)* s'épuiser; *(of lease)* expirer; *(of time)* manquer; **to r. out of time/ money** manquer de temps/ d'argent; **we've r. out of coffee** on n'a plus de café; **I ran out of petrol** *or Am* **gas** je suis tombé en panne d'essence

►**run over** *vt sep* = **run down**
►**run through** *vt insep (recap)* revoir
►**run up** *vt sep (debts, bill)* laisser s'accumuler

rung[1] [rʌŋ] *n (of ladder)* barreau *m*
rung[2] [rʌŋ] *pp of* **ring**[2]
rural ['rʊərəl] *adj* rural
rush [rʌʃ] **1** *n (demand)* ruée *f* (**for** vers; **on** sur); *(confusion)* bousculade *f*; **to be in a r.** être pressé (**to do** de faire); **r. hour** heures *fpl* de pointe **2** *vt* **to r. sb** *(hurry)* bousculer qn; **to r. sb to hospital** *or Am* **the hospital** transporter qn d'urgence à

l'hôpital; **to r. sth** *(job)* faire qch en vitesse; *(decision)* prendre qch à la hâte **3** *vi (move fast, throw oneself)* se ruer (**at** sur; **towards** vers); *(hurry)* se dépêcher (**to do** de faire); *(of vehicle)* foncer; **to r. out** sortir précipitamment
Russia ['rʌʃə] *n* la Russie ●
Russian 1 *adj* russe **2** *n (person)* Russe *mf*; *(language)* russe *m*
rust [rʌst] **1** *n* rouille *f* **2** *vi* rouiller ● **rusty** (**-ier, -iest**) *adj* rouillé
rustle ['rʌsəl] *vi (of leaves)* bruire
rut [rʌt] *n* ornière *f*; *Fig* **to be in a r.** être encroûté
ruthless ['ruːθlɪs] *adj* impitoyable

Ss

S, s [es] *n (letter)* S, s *m inv*
sabotage ['sæbətɑːʒ] *vt* saboter
sachet ['sæʃeɪ] *n* sachet *m*
sack [sæk] **1** *n (bag)* sac *m*; *Fam* **to get the s.** se faire virer **2** *vt Fam (dismiss)* virer
sacred ['seɪkrɪd] *adj* sacré
sacrifice ['sækrɪfaɪs] **1** *n* sacrifice *m* **2** *vt* sacrifier (**to** à)
sad [sæd] (**sadder, saddest**) *adj* triste • **sadly** *adv (unhappily)* tristement; *(unfortunately)* malheureusement • **sadness** *n* tristesse *f*
saddle ['sædəl] *n* selle *f*
safari [sə'fɑːrɪ] *n* safari *m*
safe [seɪf] **1** (**-er, -est**) *adj (person)* en sécurité; *(equipment, animal)* sans danger; *(place, method)* sûr; **s. (and sound)** sain et sauf (*f* saine et sauve) **2** *n (for money)* coffre-fort *m* • **safely** *adv (without risk)* en toute sécurité; *(drive)* prudemment; *(with certainty)* avec certitude • **safety 1** *n* sécurité *f* **2** *adj (belt, device, margin)* de sécurité; *(pin, chain, valve)* de sûreté
sag [sæg] (*pt & pp* **-gg-**) *vi (of roof, bed)* s'affaisser
said [sed] *pt & pp of* **say**
sail [seɪl] **1** *n (on boat)* voile *f*; **to set s.** prendre la mer **2** *vt (boat)* commander **3** *vi (of person, ship)* naviguer; *(leave)* prendre la mer • **sailing** *n (sport)* voile *f*; **to go s.** faire de la voile; *Br* **s. boat** voilier *m* • **sailboat** *n Am* voilier *m* • **sailor** *n* marin *m*

saint [seɪnt] *n* saint, -e *mf*
sake [seɪk] *n* **for my/your/his s.** pour moi/toi/lui; **for heaven's** *or* **God's s.!** pour l'amour de Dieu!; **(just) for the s. of eating** simplement pour manger
salad ['sæləd] *n* salade *f*; *Br* **s. cream** = sorte de mayonnaise; **s. dressing** = sauce pour salade
salami [sə'lɑːmɪ] *n* salami *m*
salary ['sælərɪ] (*pl* **-ies**) *n* salaire *m*
sale [seɪl] *n (action, event)* vente *f*; *(at reduced price)* solde *m*; **on s.** en vente; **in the sales** en solde; **(up) for s.** à vendre; *Am* **sales check** *or* **clip reçu m • salesman** (*pl* **-men**) *n (in shop)* vendeur *m*; *(for company)* représentant *m* • **saleswoman** (*pl* **-women**) *n (in shop)* vendeuse *f*; *(for company)* représentante *f*
salmon ['sæmən] *n inv* saumon *m*
salon ['sælɒn] *n* **beauty s.** institut *m* de beauté; **hairdressing s.** salon *m* de coiffure
saloon [sə'luːn] *n Am (bar)* bar *m*; *Br* **s. car** berline *f*
salt [sɔːlt] *n* sel *m* • **salt-cellar** *Br* (*Am* **salt-shaker**) *n* salière *f* • **salty** (**-ier, -iest**) *adj* salé
salute [sə'luːt] *vt* saluer
same [seɪm] **1** *adj* même; **the (very) s. house as...** (exactement) la même maison que... **2** *pron* **the s.** le même, la même, *pl* les mêmes; **I would have done the**

s. j'aurais fait la même chose; **it's all the s. to me** ça m'est égal **3** *adv* **to look the s.** *(of two things)* sembler pareils; **all the s.** *(nevertheless)* tout de même

sample ['sɑːmpəl] **1** *n* échantillon *m*; *(of blood)* prélèvement *m* **2** *vt* *(wine, cheese)* goûter

sanctuary [*Br* 'sæŋktʃʊərɪ, *Am* -erɪ] *(pl* **-ies)** *n (for fugitive, refugee)* refuge *m*; *(for wildlife)* réserve *f*

sand [sænd] *n* sable *m*; **s. castle** château *m* de sable ● **sandy (-ier, -iest)** *adj* **(a)** *(beach)* de sable; *(ground)* sablonneux, -euse **(b)** *(hair)* blond roux *inv*

sandal ['sændəl] *n* sandale *f*

sandwich ['sænwɪdʒ] *n* sandwich *m*; **cheese s.** sandwich *m* au fromage

sane [seɪn] **(-er, -est)** *adj (person)* sain d'esprit

sang [sæŋ] *pt of* **sing**

sanitary [*Br* 'sænɪtərɪ, *Am* -erɪ] *adj (fittings)* sanitaire; *Br* **s. towel,** *Am* **s. napkin** serviette *f* hygiénique

sanity ['sænətɪ] *n* santé *f* mentale

sank [sæŋk] *pt of* **sink²**

Santa Claus ['sæntəklɔːz] *n* le Père Noël

sap [sæp] *n (of tree, plant)* sève *f*

sapphire ['sæfaɪə(r)] *n* saphir *m*

sarcastic [sɑːˈkæstɪk] *adj* sarcastique

sardine [sɑːˈdiːn] *n* sardine *f*

sat [sæt] *pt & pp of* **sit**

satchel ['sætʃəl] *n* cartable *m*

satellite ['sætəlaɪt] *n* satellite *m*; **s. dish** antenne *f* parabolique; **s. television** télévision *f* par satellite

satin ['sætɪn] *n* satin *m*

satire ['sætaɪə(r)] *n* satire *f* **(on** contre) ● **satirical** *adj* satirique

satisfaction [sætɪsˈfækʃən] *n* satisfaction *f* ● **satisfactory** *adj* satisfaisant

satisfy ['sætɪsfaɪ] *(pt & pp* **-ied)** *vt* satisfaire; *(convince)* persuader **(that** que); *(condition)* remplir; **to be satisfied (with)** être satisfait (de) ● **satisfying** *adj* satisfaisant; *(meal, food)* substantiel, -elle

satsuma [sætˈsuːmə] *n Br* mandarine *f*

saturate ['sætʃəreɪt] *vt* saturer **(with** de)

Saturday ['sætədeɪ] *n* samedi *m*

sauce [sɔːs] *n* sauce *f*; **mint s.** sauce à la menthe ● **saucepan** [-pən] *n* casserole *f*

saucer ['sɔːsə(r)] *n* soucoupe *f*

sauna ['sɔːnə] *n* sauna *m*

sausage ['sɒsɪdʒ] *n* saucisse *f*; *Br* **s. roll** feuilleté *m* à la viande

savage ['sævɪdʒ] **1** *adj (animal, person)* féroce; *(attack, criticism)* violent **2** *vt (physically)* attaquer

save [seɪv] **1** *vt (rescue)* sauver **(from** de); *(keep)* garder; *(money)* économiser; *(time)* gagner; *Comptr* sauvegarder; **to s. sb's life** sauver la vie de qn; **to s. sb from doing sth** empêcher qn de faire qch **2** *vi* **to s. (up)** faire des économies **(for/on** pour/sur) ● **savings** *n (money saved)* économies *fpl*; **savings account** compte *m* d'épargne

saviour ['seɪvjə(r)] *(Am* **savior)** *n* sauveur *m*

savoury ['seɪvərɪ] *(Am* **savory)** *adj (not sweet)* salé

saw¹ [sɔː] **1** *n* scie *f* **2** *(pt* **sawed,** *pp* **sawn** *or* **sawed)** *vt* scier; **to s. sth off** scier qch ● **sawdust** *n* sciure *f*

saw² [sɔː] *pt of* **see**

saxophone ['sæksəfəʊn] *n* saxophone *m*

say [seɪ] **1** (*pt & pp* **said**) *vt* dire
(**to** à; **that** que); (*of dial, watch*)
indiquer; **to s. again** répéter;
that is to s. c'est-à-dire **2** *vi* dire;
Am Fam **s.!** dis donc!; **that goes
without saying** ça va sans dire **3**
n **to have one's s.** avoir son mot
à dire; **to have no s.** ne pas avoir
voix au chapitre (**in** concernant) ●
saying *n* maxime *f*

scab [skæb] *n* (*of wound*) croûte *f*

scaffolding ['skæfəldɪŋ] *n*
échafaudage *m*

scald [skɔːld] *vt* ébouillanter

scale¹ [skeɪl] **1** *n* (*of instrument,
map*) échelle *f*; (*of salaries*) barème
m; *Fig* (*of problem*) étendue *f*; **on
a small/large s.** sur une petite/
grande échelle **2** *vt* **to s. sth
down** revoir qch à la baisse

scale² [skeɪl] *n* (*on fish*) écaille *f*

scales [skeɪlz] *npl* (*for weighing*)
balance *f*; (**bathroom**) **s.** pèse-
personne *m*

scalp [skælp] *n* cuir *m* chevelu

scampi ['skæmpɪ] *n* scampi *mpl*

scan [skæn] (*pt & pp* **-nn-**) *vt* (*look
at briefly*) parcourir; (*scrutinize*)
scruter; *Comptr* passer au scanner

scandal ['skændəl] *n* (*outrage*)
scandale *m*; (*gossip*) ragots *mpl* ●
scandalous *adj* scandaleux, -euse

Scandinavia [skændɪ'neɪvɪə] *n*
la Scandinavie ● **Scandinavian 1**
adj scandinave **2** *n* Scandinave *mf*

scanner ['skænə(r)] *n* *Med &
Comptr* scanner *m*

scar [skɑː(r)] **1** *n* cicatrice *f* **2** (*pt &
pp* **-rr-**) *vt* marquer d'une cicatrice;
Fig (*of experience*) marquer

scarce [skeəs] (**-er, -est**) *adj* rare ●
scarcely *adv* à peine; **s. anything**
presque rien

scare [skeə(r)] *vt* faire peur à; **to
s. sb off** faire fuir qn ● **scared** *adj*
effrayé; **to be s. of sb/sth** avoir

peur de qn/qch ● **scary** (**-ier,
-iest**) *adj* *Fam* effrayant

scarf [skɑːf] (*pl* **scarves**) *n* (*long*)
écharpe *f*; (*square*) foulard *m*

scatter ['skætə(r)] *vt*
(*demonstrators*) disperser; (*corn,
seed*) jeter à la volée; (*papers*)
laisser traîner

scavenge ['skævɪndʒ] *vi* **to s. for
sth** fouiller pour trouver qch

scenario [sɪ'nɑːrɪəʊ] (*pl* **-os**) *n* (*of
film*) scénario *m*

scene [siːn] *n* (*in book, film, play*)
scène *f*; (*of event, crime, accident*)
lieu *m*; *also Fig* **behind the scenes**
dans les coulisses; **on the s.** sur
les lieux; **to make a s.** faire un
scandale ● **scenery** *n* (*landscape*)
paysage *m*; (*in play, film*) décors
mpl ● **scenic** *adj* pittoresque; **s.
route** route *f* touristique

scent [sent] *n* (*smell*) odeur *f*;
(*perfume*) parfum *m*

sceptical ['skeptɪkəl] (*Am*
skeptical) *adj* sceptique

schedule [*Br* 'ʃedjuːl, *Am*
'skedjʊl] **1** *n* (*plan*) planning *m*;
(*for trains, buses*) horaire *m*; (*list*)
liste *f*; **according to s.** comme
prévu **2** *vt* prévoir; (*event*) fixer
la date/l'heure de ● **scheduled**
[*Br* 'ʃedjuːld, *Am* 'skedjuːld] *adj*
(*planned*) prévu; (*service, flight,
train*) régulier, -ère

scheme [skiːm] **1** *n* (*plan*) plan *m*
(**to do** pour faire); (*plot*) complot
m; (*arrangement*) arrangement *m*
2 *vi* *Pej* comploter

scholarship ['skɒləʃɪp] *n*
(*learning*) érudition *f*; (*grant*)
bourse *f* d'études

school [skuːl] **1** *n* école *f*; (*within
university*) département *m*;
Am Fam (*college*) université *f*;
Br **secondary s.**, *Am* **high s.**
établissement *m* d'enseignement

secondaire **2** *adj (year, book, equipment)* scolaire; **s. bag** cartable *m*; **s. fees** frais *mpl* de scolarité; *Am* **s. yard** cour *f* de récréation • **schoolboy** *n* écolier *m* • **schoolchildren** *npl* écoliers *mpl* • **schoolgirl** *n* écolière *f* • **schoolteacher** *n (primary)* instituteur, -trice *mf*; *(secondary)* professeur *m*

science ['saɪəns] *n* science *f*; **to study s.** étudier les sciences; **s. fiction** science-fiction *f* • **scientific** [-'tɪfɪk] *adj* scientifique • **scientist** *n* scientifique *mf*

scissors ['sɪzəz] *npl* ciseaux *mpl*

scoff [skɒf] **1** *vt* **to s. at sb/sth** se moquer de qn/qch **2** *vti Br Fam (eat)* bouffer

scold [skəʊld] *vt* gronder (**for doing** pour avoir fait)

scone [skəʊn, skɒn] *n Br* scone *m*

scoop [skuːp] **1** *n (for flour, sugar)* pelle *f*; *(for ice cream)* cuillère *f*; *(amount) (of ice cream)* boule *f* **2** *vt* **to s. sth out** *(hollow out)* évider qch; **to s. sth up** ramasser qch

scooter ['skuːtə(r)] *n (for child)* trottinette *f*; *(motorbike)* scooter *m*

scope [skəʊp] *n (range)* étendue *f*; *(of action)* possibilité *f*

scorch [skɔːtʃ] *vt* roussir • **scorching** *adj (day)* torride; *(sun, sand)* brûlant

score [skɔː(r)] **1** *n (in sport)* score *m*; *(in music)* partition *f* **2** *vti (in game, match)* marquer

scorn [skɔːn] *n* mépris *m* • **scornful** *adj* méprisant

scorpion ['skɔːpɪən] *n* scorpion *m*

Scot [skɒt] *n* Écossais, -e *mf* • **Scotland** *n* l'Écosse *f* • **Scotsman** (*pl* -**men**) *n* Écossais *m* • **Scotswoman** (*pl* -**women**) *n* Écossaise *f* • **Scottish** *adj* écossais

Scotch [skɒtʃ] **1** *n (whisky)* scotch *m* **2** *adj Am* **S. tape®** Scotch® *m*

scout [skaʊt] *n* **(boy) s.** scout *m*, éclaireur *m*; *Am* **(girl) s.** éclaireuse *f*

scowl [skaʊl] *vi* lancer des regards noirs (**at** à)

scramble ['skræmbəl] **1** *vt* **scrambled eggs** œufs *mpl* brouillés **2** *vi* **to s. up a hill** gravir une colline en s'aidant des mains

scrap [skræp] **1** *n (piece)* bout *m* (**of** de); *(of information)* bribe *f*; **scraps** *(food)* restes *mpl*; **s. paper** papier *m* brouillon **2** (*pt & pp* -**pp**-) *vt (get rid of)* se débarrasser de; *Fig (plan, idea)* abandonner • **scrapbook** *n* album *m (de coupures de presse etc)*

scrape [skreɪp] *vt* gratter; *(skin)* érafler

► **scrape away, scrape off** *vt sep* racler

► **scrape through** *vt insep & vi* **to s. through (an exam)** passer de justesse (à un examen)

scratch [skrætʃ] **1** *n (mark, injury)* éraflure *f*; *(on glass, wood)* rayure *f*; *Fam* **to start from s.** repartir de zéro; **it isn't up to s.** ce n'est pas au niveau **2** *vt (to relieve itching)* gratter; *(by accident)* érafler; *(glass)* rayer; *(with claw)* griffer **3** *vi (of person)* se gratter; *(of pen, new clothes)* gratter • **scratchcard** *n (lottery card)* carte *f* à gratter

scrawl [skrɔːl] *vt* gribouiller

scream [skriːm] **1** *n* hurlement *m* **2** *vti* hurler **to s. at sb** crier après qn

screech [skriːtʃ] *vti* hurler

screen [skriːn] **1** *n (of TV set, computer, cinema)* écran *m*; *Comptr* **s. saver** économiseur *m* d'écran **2** *vt (hide)* cacher (**from sb** à qn); *(protect)* protéger (**from**

de); *(film)* projeter; *(visitors, calls)* filtrer; *(for disease)* faire subir un test de dépistage à

screw [skru:] **1** *n* vis *f* **2** *vt* visser (**to** à); **to s. sth on** visser qch; **to s. sth up** *(paper)* chiffonner qch ● **screwdriver** *n* tournevis *m*

scribble ['skrɪbəl] *vti* griffonner

script [skrɪpt] *n (of film)* script *m*; *(of play)* texte *m*

scroll [skrəʊl] **1** *n* rouleau *m*; *(manuscript)* manuscrit *m* **2** *vi* Comptr défiler; **to s. down/up** défiler vers le bas/haut

scrounge [skraʊndʒ] *vt Fam (meal)* se faire payer (**off** or **from sb** par qn); *(steal)* taper (**off** or **from sb** à qn); **to s. money off** or **from sb** taper qn

scrub [skrʌb] **1** *n* **to give sth a s.** bien frotter qch; *Am* **s. brush** brosse *f* dure **2** *(pt & pp* -bb-*)* *vt (surface)* frotter; *(pan)* récurer; **to s. sth off** *(remove)* enlever qch (à la brosse ou en frottant) ● **scrubbing** *n* **s. brush** brosse *f* dure

scruffy ['skrʌfɪ] *(-ier, -iest)* *adj (person)* peu soigné

scrum [skrʌm] *n (in rugby)* mêlée *f*

scrupulous ['skru:pjʊləs] *adj* scrupuleux, -euse

scuba ['sku:bə] *n* **s. diving** la plongée sous-marine

sculpt [skʌlpt] *vti* sculpter ● **sculptor** *n* sculpteur *m* ● **sculpture** *n (art, object)* sculpture *f*

scum [skʌm] *n* écume *f*

sea [si:] **1** *n* mer *f*; **(out) at s.** en mer; **by** or **beside the s.** au bord de la mer **2** *adj (level, breeze)* de la mer; *(water, fish, salt)* de mer; *(air)* marin; **s. bed, s. floor** fond *m* de la mer ● **seafood** *n* fruits

mpl de mer ● **seafront** *n Br* front *m* de mer ● **seagull** *n* mouette *f* ● **seashell** *n* coquillage *m* ● **seashore** *n* rivage *m* ● **seasick** *adj* **to be s.** avoir le mal de mer ● **seaside** *n Br* bord *m* de la mer; **s. resort** station *f* balnéaire ● **seaweed** *n* algues *fpl*

seal¹ [si:l] *n (animal)* phoque *m*

seal² [si:l] **1** *n (stamp)* sceau *m* **2** *vt (document, container)* sceller; *(stick down)* cacheter; *(make airtight)* fermer hermétiquement; **to s. off an area** boucler un quartier

seam [si:m] *n (in cloth)* couture *f*

search [sɜ:tʃ] **1** *n* recherches *fpl* (**for** de); *(of place)* fouille *f*; **in s. of** à la recherche de; *Comptr* **to do a s. for sth** rechercher qch; *Comptr* **s. engine** moteur *m* de recherche **2** *vt (person, place)* fouiller (**for** pour trouver) **3** *vi* chercher; **to s. for sth** chercher qch

season¹ ['si:zən] *n* saison *f*; *(of films)* cycle *m*; **peak** or **high s.** haute saison; **low** or **off s.** basse saison; **s. ticket** abonnement *m* ● **seasonal** *adj (work, change)* saisonnier, -ère

season² ['si:zən] *vt (food)* assaisonner ● **seasoning** *n Culin* assaisonnement *m*

secluded [sɪ'klu:dɪd] *adj (remote)* isolé

second¹ ['sekənd] **1** *adj* deuxième, second; **every s. week** une semaine sur deux **2** *adv (say)* deuxièmement; **to come s.** *(in competition)* se classer deuxième; **the s. biggest** le deuxième en ordre de grandeur **3** *n (in series)* deuxième *mf*, second, -e *mf*; *(of month)* deux *m*; **Louis the S.** Louis Deux ● **second-class** *adj (ticket on train)* de seconde (classe);

(mail) non urgent; *(product)* de qualité inférieure • **second-hand** *adj & adv (not new)* d'occasion • **secondly** *adv* deuxièmement

second² ['sekənd] *n (part of minute)* seconde *f*

secondary ['sekəndərɪ] *adj* secondaire; *Br* **s. school** établissement *m* secondaire

secret ['siːkrɪt] **1** *adj* secret, -ète **2** *n* secret *m*; **in s.** en secret • **secretive** *adj (person)* secret, -ète; **to be s. about sth** faire des cachotteries à propos de qch • **secretly** *adv* secrètement

secretary [*Br* 'sekrətərɪ, *Am* -erɪ] *(pl* **-ies)** *n* secrétaire *mf*; *Br* **Foreign S.,** *Am* **S. of State** ≃ ministre *m* des Affaires étrangères • **secretarial** [-'teərɪəl] *adj (work)* administratif, -ive; *(job, course)* de secrétariat

sect [sekt] *n* secte *f*

section ['sekʃən] *n* partie *f*; *(of road)* tronçon *m*; *(of machine)* élément *m*; *(of organization)* département *m*; **the sports s.** *(of newspaper)* la page des sports

sector ['sektə(r)] *n* secteur *m*

secure [sɪ'kjʊə(r)] **1** *adj (person)* en sécurité; *(investment, place)* sûr; *(door, window)* bien fermé **2** *vt (fasten)* attacher; *(window, door)* bien fermer; *(position, future)* assurer; **to s. sth (for oneself)** se procurer qch • **securely** *adv (firmly)* solidement; *(safely)* en sûreté • **security** sécurité *f*

sedan [sɪ'dæn] *n Am (saloon)* berline *f*

sedate [sɪ'deɪt] *adj* calme • **sedative** ['sedətɪv] *n* calmant *m*

seduce [sɪ'djuːs] *vt* séduire • **seductive** [-'dʌktɪv] *adj (person, offer)* séduisant

see [siː] *(pt* **saw,** *pp* **seen)** *vti* voir; **we'll s.** on verra; **I can s. a hill** je vois une colline; **I saw him run(ning)** je l'ai vu courir; **to s. reason** entendre raison; **s. you (later)!** à tout à l'heure!; **to s. that...** *(make sure that)* faire en sorte que... *(+ subjunctive)*; *(check)* s'assurer que... *(+ indicative)*; **to s. sb to the door** accompagner qn jusqu'à la porte

▶**see about** *vt insep (deal with)* s'occuper de; *(consider)* songer à

▶**see off** *vt sep (say goodbye to)* dire au revoir à

▶**see through** *vt insep* **to s. through sb** percer qn à jour

▶**see to** *vt insep (deal with)* s'occuper de; *(mend)* réparer; **to s. to it that...** *(make sure that)* faire en sorte que... *(+ subjunctive)*; *(check)* s'assurer que... *(+ indicative)*

seed [siːd] *n* graine *f*; *(of fruit)* pépin *m*

seedy ['siːdɪ] *(-ier, -iest)* *adj* miteux, -euse

seek [siːk] *(pt & pp* **sought)** *vt* chercher *(to do à faire); (ask for)* demander *(from à);* **to s. sb out** dénicher qn

seem [siːm] *vi* sembler **(to do** faire); **it seems that...** *(impression)* il semble que... *(+ subjunctive);* **it seems to me that...** il me semble que... *(+ indicative)*

seen [siːn] *pp of* **see**

seesaw ['siːsɔː] *n* balançoire *f* à bascule

see-through ['siːθruː] *adj* transparent

segment ['segmənt] *n* segment *m*; *(of orange)* quartier *m*

segregation [segrɪ'geɪʃən] *n* ségrégation *f*

seize [siːz] *vt* saisir; *(power, land)* s'emparer de

seizure ['siːʒə(r)] *n Med* crise *f*

seldom ['seldəm] *adv* rarement

select [sɪ'lekt] *vt* sélectionner • **selection** *n* sélection *f*

self [self] (*pl* **selves** [selvz]) *n* **he's back to his old s.** il est redevenu comme avant • **self-assured** *adj* sûr de soi • **self-catering** *adj Br* *(holiday)* en appartement meublé; *(accommodation)* meublé • **self-centred** (*Am* **-centered**) *adj* égocentrique • **self-confident** *adj* sûr de soi • **self-conscious** *adj* gêné • **self-control** *n* maîtrise *f* de soi • **self-defence** (*Am* **-defense**) *n* *(in law)* légitime défense *f*; **in s.** en état de légitime défense • **selfish** *adj* égoïste • **self-portrait** *n* autoportrait *m* • **self-respect** *n* amour-propre *m* • **self-righteous** *adj* suffisant • **self-service** *n* & *adj* libre-service *(m inv)* • **self-sufficient** *adj* indépendant

sell [sel] **1** (*pt* & *pp* **sold**) *vt* vendre; **to s. sb sth, to s. sth to sb** vendre qch à qn; **she sold it to me for £20** elle me l'a vendu 20 livres **2** *vi* *(of product)* se vendre; *(of person)* vendre • **sell-by** *adj* **s. date** date *f* limite de vente • **seller** *n* vendeur, -euse *mf*

▶**sell out** *vt insep* **to have** *or* **be sold out of sth** n'avoir plus de qch; **to be sold out** *(of book, item)* être épuisé; *(of show, concert)* afficher complet

Sellotape® ['seləteɪp] *n Br* Scotch® *m*

semester [sɪ'mestə(r)] *n* semestre *m*

semi- ['semɪ] *pref* semi-, demi- • **semi-circle** *n* demi-cercle *m* • **semicolon** *n* point-virgule *m* • **semi-detached** *adj Br* **s. house** maison *f* jumelée • **semi-final** *n* demi-finale *f* • **semi-skimmed** *adj* *(milk)* demi-écrémé

seminar ['semɪnɑː(r)] *n* séminaire *m*

senate ['senɪt] *n* **the S.** le Sénat • **senator** [-nətə(r)] *n* sénateur *m*

send [send] (*pt* & *pp* **sent**) *vt* envoyer (**to** à); **to s. sth to sb, to s. sb sth** envoyer qch à qn; **to s. sb home** renvoyer qn chez soi • **sender** *n* expéditeur, -trice *mf*

▶**send away 1** *vt sep (person)* renvoyer **2** *vi* **to s. away for sth** se faire envoyer qch

▶**send back** *vt sep* renvoyer

▶**send for** *vt insep* envoyer chercher; *(doctor)* faire venir; *(send away for)* se faire envoyer

▶**send in** *vt sep (form, invoice, troops)* envoyer; *(person)* faire entrer

▶**send off 1** *vt sep (letter)* envoyer (**to** à); *(player)* expulser **2** *vi* **to s. off for sth** se faire envoyer qch

▶**send out** *vt sep* envoyer

senile ['siːnaɪl] *adj* sénile

senior ['siːnɪə(r)] **1** *adj (in age)* aîné; *(in position, rank)* supérieur; **to be sb's s., to be s. to sb** être l'aîné de qn; *(in rank, status)* être le supérieur de qn; **s. citizen** personne *f* âgée; *Am* **s. year** *(in school, college)* dernière année *f* **2** *n* aîné, -e *mf*; *Am (in last year of school or college)* étudiant, -e *mf* de dernière année; *(in sport)* senior *mf*

sensation [sen'seɪʃən] *n* sensation *f* • **sensational** *adj* sensationnel, -elle

sense [sens] **1** *n (faculty, awareness, meaning)* sens *m*; **s. of smell** odorat *m*; **a s. of shame** un sentiment de honte; **s. of direction** sens de l'orientation;

to have a s. of humour avoir le sens de l'humour; **to have the s. to do sth** avoir l'intelligence de faire qch; **to bring sb to his/her senses** ramener qn à la raison; **to make s.** être logique; **to make s. of sth** comprendre qch **2** *vt* sentir (**that** que)

sensible ['sensəbəl] *adj* *(wise)* sensé; *(clothes, shoes)* pratique

sensitive ['sensɪtɪv] *adj* *(person)* sensible (**to** à); *(skin, question)* délicat; *(information)* confidentiel, -elle ● **sensitivity** *n* sensibilité *f*; *(touchiness)* susceptibilité *f*

sent [sent] *pt & pp of* **send**

sentence ['sentəns] **1** *n* **(a)** *(words)* phrase *f* **(b)** *(in prison)* peine *f* **2** *vt* *(criminal)* condamner; **to s. sb to three years (in prison)/to death** condamner qn à trois ans de prison/à mort

sentimental ['sentɪməntəl] *adj* sentimental

separate 1 ['sepərət] *adj* *(distinct)* séparé; *(organization)* indépendant; *(occasion, entrance)* différent; *(room)* à part **2** ['sepəreɪt] *vt* séparer (**from** de) **3** ['sepəreɪt] *vi* se séparer (**from** de) ● **separately** *adv* séparément ● **separation** [-'reɪʃən] *n* séparation *f*

September [sep'tembə(r)] *n* septembre *m*

septic ['septɪk] *adj* *(wound)* infecté; **to go** *or* **turn s.** s'infecter

sequel ['siːkwəl] *n* *(book, film)* suite *f*

sequence ['siːkwəns] *n* *(order)* ordre *m*; *(series)* succession *f*; *(in film)* & *Comptr, Mus & Cards* séquence *f*; **in s.** dans l'ordre

sequin ['siːkwɪn] *n* paillette *f*

serene [sə'riːn] *adj* serein

sergeant ['saːdʒənt] *n* *Mil* sergent *m*; *(in police)* brigadier *m*

serial ['sɪərɪəl] *n* *(story, film)* feuilleton *m*; **s. killer** tueur *m* en série; **s. number** numéro *m* de série

series ['sɪəriːz] *n inv* série *f*

serious ['sɪərɪəs] *adj* *(person)* sérieux, -euse; *(illness, mistake, tone)* grave; *(damage)* important; **to be s. about doing sth** envisager sérieusement de faire qch ● **seriously** *adv* sérieusement; *(ill, damaged)* gravement; **to take sb/sth s.** prendre qn/qch au sérieux

sermon ['sɜːmən] *n* sermon *m*

servant ['sɜːvənt] *n* domestique *mf*

serve [sɜːv] **1** *vt* *(country, cause, meal, customer)* servir; *(prison sentence)* purger; *Fam* **(it) serves you right!** ça t'apprendra! **2** *vi* servir (**as** de) ● **service** ['sɜːvɪs] *n* *(with army, firm, in restaurant)* & *Rel* service *m*; **to be at sb's s.** être au service de qn; *Comptr* **s. provider** fournisseur *m* d'accès Internet; **s. station** station-service *f*

serviette [sɜːvɪ'et] *n* *Br* serviette *f* de table

session ['seʃən] *n* séance *f*

set [set] **1** *n* *(of keys, tools)* jeu *m*; *(of stamps, numbers)* série *f*; *(of people)* groupe *m*; *(of books)* collection *f*; *(of dishes)* service *m*; *(in theatre)* décor *m*; *(for film)* plateau *m*; *(in tennis)* set *m*; **chess s.** jeu *m* d'échecs; **tea s.** service *m* à thé; **television s., TV s.** téléviseur *m* **2** *adj* *(time, price)* fixe; *(lunch)* à prix fixe; *(school book)* au programme; *(ideas, purpose)* déterminé; **to be s. on doing sth** être résolu à faire qch; **to be all s.** être prêt (**to do**

pour faire); **s. menu** menu *m*; **s. phrase** expression *f* figée **3** (*pt & pp* **set,** *pres p* **setting**) *vt* (*put*) mettre, poser; (*date, limit, task*) fixer; (*homework*) donner (**for sb** à qn); (*watch*) régler; (*alarm clock*) mettre (**for** pour); (*trap*) tendre (**for** à); **to s. a record** établir un record; **to s. a precedent** créer un précédent; **to s. sb free** libérer qn **4** *vi* (*of sun*) se coucher; (*of jelly, jam*) prendre ● **setback** *n* revers *m*

▶**set about** *vt insep* (*begin*) se mettre à; **to s. about doing sth** se mettre à faire qch

▶**set back** *vt sep* (*in time*) retarder; *Fam* (*cost*) coûter à

▶**set down** *vt sep* (*object*) poser

▶**set off** *vi* (*leave*) partir

▶**set out 1** *vt sep* (*display, explain*) exposer; (*arrange*) disposer **2** *vi* **to s. out to do sth** avoir l'intention de faire qch

▶**set up 1** *vt sep* (*tent, statue*) dresser; (*company*) créer; (*meeting*) organiser **2** *vi* **to s. up in business** s'installer (**as** comme)

settee [se'ti:] *n* canapé *m*

setting ['setɪŋ] *n* (*surroundings*) cadre *m*; (*of sun*) coucher *m*; (*on machine*) réglage *m*

settle ['setəl] **1** *vt* (*put in place*) installer; (*decide, arrange, pay*) régler; (*nerves*) calmer; **that settles it!** c'est décidé! **2** *vi* (*of person, family*) s'installer; (*of dust*) se déposer ● **settled** *adj* (*weather, period*) stable; (*life*) rangé

▶**settle down** *vi* (*in chair, house*) s'installer; (*become quieter*) s'assagir; (*of situation*) se calmer; **to s. down with sb** mener une vie stable avec qn; **to s. down to work** se mettre au travail

▶**settle in** *vi* (*in new home*) s'installer

seven ['sevən] *adj & n* sept (*m*) ● **seventh** *adj & n* septième (*mf*)

seventeen [sevən'ti:n] *adj & n* dix-sept (*m*) ● **seventeenth** *adj & n* dix-septième (*mf*)

seventy ['sevəntɪ] *adj & n* soixante-dix (*m*); **s.-one** soixante et onze ● **seventieth** *adj & n* soixante-dixième (*mf*)

several ['sevərəl] *adj & pron* plusieurs (**of** d'entre)

severe [sə'vɪə(r)] *adj* (*person, punishment, tone*) sévère; (*winter*) rigoureux, -euse; (*illness, injury*) grave; (*cold, frost*) intense ● **severely** *adv* (*criticize, punish*) sévèrement; (*damaged, wounded*) gravement

sew [səʊ] (*pt* **sewed**, *pp* **sewn** or **sewed**) *vt* coudre; **to s. a button on a shirt** coudre un bouton à une chemise; **to s. sth up** recoudre qch ● **sewing** *n* couture *f*; **s. machine** machine *f* à coudre

sewage ['su:ɪdʒ] *n* eaux *fpl* d'égout ● **sewer** *n* égout *m*

sewn [səʊn] *pp of* sew

sex [seks] **1** *n* sexe *m*; **to have s. with sb** coucher avec qn **2** *adj* (*education, life, act*) sexuel, -elle ● **sexist** *adj & n* sexiste (*mf*) ● **sexual** ['sekʃʊəl] *adj* sexuel, -elle ● **sexy** (**-ier, -iest**) *adj Fam* sexy *inv*

sh [ʃ] *exclam* chut!

shabby ['ʃæbɪ] (**-ier, -iest**) *adj* miteux, -euse

shack [ʃæk] *n* cabane *f*

shade [ʃeɪd] **1** *n* ombre *f*; (*of colour, meaning, opinion*) nuance *f*; (*for lamp*) abat-jour *m inv*; **in the s.** à l'ombre **2** *vt* (*of tree*) ombrager ● **shady** (**-ier, -iest**) *adj* (*place*) ombragé; *Fig* (*person, business*) louche

shadow ['ʃædəʊ] **1** n ombre f **2** adj Br Pol **s. cabinet** cabinet m fantôme

shaggy ['ʃægɪ] (**-ier**, **-iest**) adj (hairy) hirsute

shake [ʃeɪk] **1** n secousse f; **to give sth a s.** secouer qch **2** (pt **shook**, pp **shaken**) vt (move up and down) secouer; (bottle, fist) agiter; (building) faire trembler; **to s. one's head** faire non de la tête; **to s. hands with sb** serrer la main à qn; **to s. off** (dust) secouer; Fig (illness, pursuer) se débarrasser de; **to s. up** (reorganize) réorganiser de fond en comble **3** vi (of person, windows, voice) trembler (**with** de) • **shaky** (**-ier**, **-iest**) adj (voice) tremblant; (table, chair) branlant; (handwriting) tremblé

shall [ʃæl, unstressed ʃəl]

On trouve généralement **I/you/ he/**etc **shall** sous leur forme contractée **I'll/you'll/he'll/**etc. La forme négative correspondante est **shan't**, que l'on écrira **shall not** dans des contextes formels.

v aux (**a**) (expressing future tense) **I s. come, I'll come** je viendrai; **we s. not come, we shan't come** nous ne viendrons pas (**b**) (making suggestion) **s. I leave?** veux-tu que je parte?; **let's go in, s. we?** entrons, tu veux bien?

shallow ['ʃæləʊ] (**-er**, **-est**) adj (water, river) peu profond; Fig & Pej (argument, person) superficiel, -elle

shambles ['ʃæmbəlz] n pagaille f

shame [ʃeɪm] **1** n (guilt, disgrace) honte f; **it's a s.** c'est dommage (**to do** de faire); **it's a s. (that)…** c'est dommage que… (+ subjunctive); **what a s.!** quel dommage! **2** vt

(make ashamed) faire honte à • **shameful** adj honteux, -euse

shampoo [ʃæm'puː] n shampooing m

shandy ['ʃændɪ] n Br panaché m

shan't [ʃɑːnt] = **shall not**

shape [ʃeɪp] **1** n forme f; **what s. is it?** quelle forme cela a-t-il?; **to be in good/bad s.** (of person) être en bonne/mauvaise forme; (of business) marcher bien/mal; **to keep in s.** garder la forme **2** vt (clay) modeler (**into** en); Fig (events, future) influencer **3** vi **to s. up** (of person) progresser; (of teams, plans) prendre forme • **-shaped** suff **pear-s.** en forme de poire • **shapeless** adj informe

share [ʃeə(r)] **1** n part f (**of** or **in** de); Fin (in company) action f; **to do one's (fair) s.** mettre la main à la pâte **2** vt partager; (characteristic) avoir en commun; **to s. sth out** partager qch **3** vi **to s. in sth** avoir sa part de qch

shark [ʃɑːk] n requin m

sharp [ʃɑːp] **1** (**-er**, **-est**) adj (knife) bien aiguisé; (pencil) bien taillé; (point) aigu (f aiguë); (claws) acéré; (rise, fall) brusque; (focus) net (f nette); (eyesight) perçant; (taste) acide; (intelligent) vif (f vive) **2** adv **five o'clock s.** cinq heures pile; **to turn s. right/left** tourner tout de suite à droite/à gauche • **sharpen** vt (knife) aiguiser; (pencil) tailler • **sharply** adv (rise, fall) brusquement

shatter ['ʃætə(r)] **1** vt (glass) faire voler en éclats; (health, hopes) briser **2** vi (of glass) voler en éclats • **shattered** adj Fam (exhausted) crevé

shave [ʃeɪv] **1** n **to have a s.** se raser **2** vt (person, head) raser **3**

vi se raser • **shaver** *n* rasoir *m* électrique • **shaving** *n (strip of wood)* copeau *m*; **s. cream, s. foam** mousse *f* à raser

shawl [ʃɔːl] *n* châle *m*

she [ʃiː] *pron* elle; **she's a happy woman** c'est une femme heureuse

shears [ʃɪəz] *npl* cisaille *f*

shed[1] [ʃed] *n (in garden)* abri *m*

shed[2] [ʃed] *(pt & pp* **shed,** *pres p* **shedding)** *vt (leaves)* perdre; *(tears, blood)* verser; *Fig* **to s. light on sth** éclairer qch

she'd [ʃiːd] = **she had, she would**

sheep [ʃiːp] *n inv* mouton *m* • **sheepdog** *n* chien *m* de berger

sheer [ʃɪə(r)] *adj (pure)* pur; *(stockings)* très fin; *(cliff)* à pic; **by s. chance** tout à fait par hasard

sheet [ʃiːt] *n (on bed)* drap *m*; *(of paper)* feuille *f*; *(of glass, ice)* plaque *f*

shelf [ʃelf] *(pl* **shelves** [ʃelvz]) *n* étagère *f*; *(in shop)* rayon *m*

shell [ʃel] *n (of egg, snail, nut)* coquille *f*; *(of tortoise, lobster)* carapace *f*; *(on beach)* coquillage *m*; *(of peas)* cosse *f* • **shellfish** *npl* fruits *mpl* de mer

she'll [ʃiːl] = **she will, she shall**

shelter ['ʃeltə(r)] **1** *n (place, protection)* abri *m*; **to take s.** se mettre à l'abri **(from** de) **2** *vt* abriter **(from** de); *(criminal)* accueillir **3** *vi* s'abriter **(from** de) • **sheltered** *adj (place)* abrité

shepherd ['ʃepəd] *n* berger *m*; *Br* **s.'s pie** ≈ hachis *m* Parmentier

sherbet ['ʃɜːbət] *n Br (powder)* poudre *f* acidulée; *Am (sorbet)* sorbet *m*

sheriff ['ʃerɪf] *n Am* shérif *m*

sherry ['ʃerɪ] *n* sherry *m*, xérès *m*

shield [ʃiːld] **1** *n (of warrior)* bouclier *m* **2** *vt* protéger **(from** de)

shift [ʃɪft] **1** *n (change)* changement *m* **(of** *or* **in** de); *(period of work)* poste *m*; *(workers)* équipe *f*; **s. key** *(on computer, typewriter)* touche *f* des majuscules **2** *vt (move)* déplacer; *Am* **to s. gear(s)** *(in vehicle)* changer de vitesse **3** *vi (move)* bouger

shimmer ['ʃɪmə(r)] *vi (of silk)* chatoyer; *(of water)* miroiter

shin [ʃɪn] *n* tibia *m*; **s. pad** *(of footballer)* jambière *f*

shine [ʃaɪn] **1** *n* brillant *m*; *(on metal)* éclat *m* **2** *(pt & pp* **shone)** *vt (light, torch)* braquer **3** *vi* briller • **shiny (-ier, -iest)** *adj* brillant

ship [ʃɪp] *n* navire *m* • **shipwreck** *n* naufrage *m* • **shipwrecked** *adj* naufragé; **to be s.** faire naufrage

shirt [ʃɜːt] *n* chemise *f*; *(of woman)* chemisier *m*; *(of sportsman)* maillot *m*

shiver ['ʃɪvə(r)] *vi* frissonner **(with** de)

shock [ʃɒk] **1** *n (impact, emotional blow)* choc *m*; **(electric) s.** décharge *f* (électrique) **2** *vt (offend)* choquer; *(surprise)* stupéfier • **shocking** *adj (outrageous)* choquant; *(very bad)* atroce

shoe [ʃuː] *n* chaussure *f*; *(for horse)* fer *m* à cheval; **s. polish** cirage *m*; **s. shop** magasin *m* de chaussures • **shoelace** *n* lacet *m*

shone [*Br* ʃɒn, *Am* ʃəʊn] *pt & pp of* **shine**

shook [ʃʊk] *pt of* **shake**

shoot [ʃuːt] **1** *n (of plant)* pousse *f* **2** *(pt & pp* **shot)** *vt (bullet)* tirer; *(arrow)* lancer; *(film, scene)* tourner; **to s. sb** *(kill)* tuer qn par balle; *(wound)* blesser qn par balle **3** *vi (with gun)* tirer **(at** sur) • **shooting** *n (shots)* coups *mpl* de

feu; *(incident)* fusillade *f*; *(of film, scene)* tournage *m*
►**shoot off** *vi (leave quickly)* filer
►**shoot up** *vi (of price)* monter en flèche; *(of plant)* pousser vite; *(of child)* grandir
shop [ʃɒp] **1** *n* magasin *m*; *(small)* boutique *f*; *(workshop)* atelier *m*; **at the baker's s.** à la boulangerie, chez le boulanger; *Br* **s. assistant** vendeur, -euse *mf*; **s. window** vitrine *f* **2** *(pt & pp -pp-)* *vi* faire ses courses (**at** chez); **to s. around** comparer les prix • **shopkeeper** *n* commerçant, -e *mf* • **shoplifter** *n* voleur, -euse *mf* à l'étalage • **shopper** *n (customer)* client, -e *mf* • **shopping 1** *n (goods)* achats *mpl*; **to go s.** faire des courses; **to do one's s.** faire ses courses **2** *adj (street, district)* commerçant; **s. bag** sac *m* à provisions; **s. centre** centre *m* commercial; **s. list** liste *f* de courses
shore [ʃɔː(r)] *n (of sea)* rivage *m*; *(of lake)* bord *m*
short [ʃɔːt] **1** (**-er, -est**) *adj* court; *(person, distance)* petit; *(impatient, curt)* brusque; **to be s. of sth** être à court de qch; **money/time is s.** l'argent/le temps manque; **a s. time** *or* **while ago** il y a peu de temps; **Tony is s. for Anthony** Tony est le diminutif d'Anthony; **in s.** bref; **s. cut** raccourci *m*; **s. story** nouvelle *f* **2** *adv* **to cut s.** *(hair)* couper court; *(visit)* abréger; *(person)* couper la parole à; **to stop s. of doing sth** se retenir tout juste de faire qch; **to be running s. of sth** n'avoir presque plus de qch • **shortage** *n* pénurie *f* • **shortbread** *n* sablé *m* • **short-circuit 1** *n* court-circuit *m* **2** *vt* court-circuiter • **shorten** *vt* raccourcir • **short-lived** *adj*

de courte durée • **shortly** *adv (soon)* bientôt; **s. before/after** peu avant/après • **short-sighted** *adj* myope • **short-sleeved** *adj* à manches courtes • **short-term** *adj* à court terme
shorts [ʃɔːts] *npl* **(pair of) s.** short *m*; **boxer s.** caleçon *m*
shot [ʃɒt] **1** *pt & pp of* **shoot 2** *n (from gun)* coup *m*; *(with camera)* prise *f* de vue; *(in football)* coup *m* de pied; *Fam (injection)* piqûre *f*; **to fire a s.** tirer; **to be a good s.** *(of person)* être bon tireur; **to have a s. at sth/doing sth** essayer qch/de faire qch • **shotgun** *n* fusil *m* de chasse

should [ʃʊd, *unstressed* ʃəd]
La forme négative **should not** s'écrit **shouldn't** en forme contractée.

v aux **(a)** *(expressing obligation)* **you s. do it** vous devriez le faire; **I s. have stayed** j'aurais dû rester **(b)** *(expressing possibility)* **the weather s. improve** le temps devrait s'améliorer; **she s. have arrived by now** elle devrait être arrivée à l'heure qu'il est **(c)** *(expressing preferences)* **I s. like to stay** j'aimerais bien rester; **I s. like to** j'aimerais bien; **I s. hope so** j'espère bien **(d)** *(in subordinate clauses)* **it's strange (that) she s. say no** il est étrange qu'elle dise non; **he insisted that she s. meet her parents** il a insisté pour qu'elle rencontre ses parents **(e)** *(in conditional clauses)* **if he s. come, s. he come** s'il vient **(f)** *(in rhetorical questions)* **why s. you suspect me?** pourquoi me soupçonnez-vous?; **who s. I meet but Martin!** et qui a-t-il fallu que je rencontre? Martin!

shoulder ['ʃəʊldə(r)] *n* épaule *f*; **s. bag** sac *m* besace; **s. pad** épaulette *f*

shout [ʃaʊt] **1** *n* cri *m* **2** *vt* **to s. sth (out)** crier qch **3** *vi* **to s. (out)** crier; **to s. to sb to do sth** crier à qn de faire qch; **to s. at sb** crier après qn • **shouting** *n (shouts)* cris *mpl*

shove [ʃʌv] **1** *n* poussée *f*; **to give sb/sth a s.** pousser qn/qch **2** *vt* pousser; *Fam* **to s. sth into sth** fourrer qch dans qch

shovel ['ʃʌvəl] **1** *n* pelle *f* **2** *(Br* **-ll-**, *Am* **-l-***) vt* pelleter; **to s. leaves up** ramasser des feuilles à la pelle

show [ʃəʊ] **1** *n (concert, play)* spectacle *m*; *(on TV)* émission *f*; *(exhibition)* exposition *f*; **to be on s.** être exposé; **to put sth on s.** exposer qch; **s. business** le monde du spectacle; **s. jumping** jumping *m* **2** *(pt* **showed**, *pp* **shown***) vt* montrer **(to** à; **that** que); *(in exhibition)* exposer; *(film)* passer; *(indicate)* indiquer; **to s. sb sth, to s. sth to sb** montrer qch à qn; **to s. sb to the door** reconduire qn à la porte **3** *vi (be visible)* se voir; *(of film)* passer • **show-off** *n Pej* crâneur, -euse *mf* • **showroom** *n* magasin *m* d'exposition

▶**show around** *vt sep* **to s. sb around the town/the house** faire visiter la ville/la maison à qn

▶**show off 1** *vt sep Pej (display)* étaler; *(highlight)* faire valoir **2** *vi Pej* crâner

▶**show round** *vt sep* = **show around**

▶**show up** *vi (stand out)* ressortir **(against** contre); *Fam (of person)* se présenter

shower ['ʃaʊə(r)] **1** *n (bathing, device)* douche *f*; *(of rain)* averse *f*; **to have** or **take a s.** prendre une douche; **s. gel** gel *m* de douche **2** *vt* **to s. sb with** *(gifts, abuse)* couvrir qn de

shown [ʃəʊn] *pp of* **show**

shrank [ʃræŋk] *pt of* **shrink**

shred [ʃred] **1** *n* lambeau *m*; **to tear sth to shreds** mettre qch en lambeaux **2** *(pt & pp* **-dd-***) vt* mettre en lambeaux; *(documents)* déchiqueter

shrewd [ʃruːd] **(-er, -est)** *adj (person, plan)* astucieux, -euse

shriek [ʃriːk] **1** *n* cri *m* strident **2** *vi* pousser un cri strident; **to s. with pain/laughter** hurler de douleur/de rire

shrill [ʃrɪl] **(-er, -est)** *adj* aigu *(f* aiguë)

shrimp [ʃrɪmp] *n* crevette *f*

shrine [ʃraɪn] *n (place of worship)* lieu *m* saint; *(tomb)* tombeau *m*

shrink [ʃrɪŋk] **1** *(pt* **shrank** *or Am* **shrunk**, *pp* **shrunk** *or* **shrunken***) vt (of clothes)* faire rétrécir **2** *vi* rétrécir

shrivel ['ʃrɪvəl] *(Br* **-ll-**, *Am* **-l-***)* **1** *vt* **to s. (up)** dessécher **2** *vi* **to s. (up)** se dessécher

shrub [ʃrʌb] *n* arbuste *m*

shrug [ʃrʌg] **1** *n* haussement *m* d'épaules **2** *(pt & pp* **-gg-***) vt* **to s. one's shoulders** hausser les épaules; **to s. sth off** dédaigner qch

shrunk(en) ['ʃrʌŋk(ən)] *pp of* **shrink**

shudder ['ʃʌdə(r)] *vi (of person)* frémir **(with** de); *(of machine)* vibrer

shuffle ['ʃʌfəl] **1** *vt (cards)* battre **2** *vti* **to s. (one's feet)** traîner les pieds

shun [ʃʌn] *(pt & pp* **-nn-***) vt* fuir, éviter

shush [ʃʊʃ] *exclam* chut!

shut [ʃʌt] **1** *(pt & pp* **shut**, *pres p*

shutting) *vt* fermer **2** *vi (of door)* se fermer; *(of shop, museum)* fermer
▶**shut away** *vt sep (lock away)* enfermer
▶**shut down 1** *vt sep* fermer (définitivement) **2** *vi* fermer (définitivement)
▶**shut in** *vt sep (lock in)* enfermer
▶**shut out** *vt sep (keep outside)* empêcher d'entrer; *(exclude)* exclure (**of** *or* **from** de); **to s. sb out** enfermer qn dehors
▶**shut up 1** *vt sep (close)* fermer; *(confine)* enfermer; *Fam (silence)* faire taire **2** *vi Fam (be quiet)* se taire

shutter ['ʃʌtə(r)] *n (on window)* volet *m*; *(of shop)* store *m*; *(of camera)* obturateur *m*

shuttle ['ʃʌtəl] *n (bus, train, plane)* navette *f*

shy [ʃaɪ] **(-er, -est)** *adj* timide

sibling ['sɪblɪŋ] *n (brother)* frère *m*; *(sister)* sœur *f*

sick [sɪk] **1 (-er, -est)** *adj (ill)* malade; **to be s.** *(be ill)* être malade; *(vomit)* vomir; **to feel s.** avoir mal au cœur; **to be off s., to be on s. leave** être en congé (de) maladie; **to be s. of sb/sth** en avoir assez de qn/qch; *Fig* **he makes me s.** il m'écœure **2** *npl* **the s.** *(sick people)* les malades *mpl* • **sickening** *adj* écœurant • **sickly (-ier, -iest)** *adj* maladif, -ive; *(taste)* écœurant • **sickness** *n (illness)* maladie *f*

side [saɪd] **1** *n* côté *m*; *(of hill, animal)* flanc *m*; *(of road, river)* bord *m*; *(of character)* aspect *m*; *(team)* équipe *f*; **at** *or* **by the s. of** *(nearby)* à côté de; **at** *or* **by my s.** à côté de moi, à mes côtés; **s. by s.** l'un à côté de l'autre; **to move to one s.** s'écarter; **on this**

s. de ce côté; **to take sides with sb** se ranger du côté de qn; **she's on our s.** elle est de notre côté **2** *adj (lateral)* latéral; *(view, glance)* de côté; *(street)* transversal; *(effect, issue)* secondaire **3** *vi* **to s. with sb** se ranger du côté de qn • **sideboard** *n* buffet *m* • **sideburns** *npl (hair)* pattes *fpl* • **-sided** *suff* **ten-sided** à dix côtés • **sidestep** *(pt & pp* **-pp-)** *vt* éviter • **sidetrack** *vt* distraire; **to get sidetracked** s'écarter du sujet • **sidewalk** *n Am* trottoir *m* • **sideways** *adv (look, walk)* de côté

siege [siːdʒ] *n (by soldiers, police)* siège *m*; **under s.** assiégé

siesta [sɪ'estə] *n* sieste *f*; **to take** *or* **have a s.** faire la sieste

sieve [sɪv] *n* tamis *m*; *(for liquids)* passoire *f*

sift [sɪft] **1** *vt (flour)* tamiser **2** *vi* **to s. through** *(papers)* examiner (à la loupe)

sigh [saɪ] **1** *n* soupir *m* **2** *vti* soupirer

sight [saɪt] *n (faculty)* vue *f*; *(thing seen)* spectacle *m*; *(on gun)* viseur *m*; **to lose s. of sb/sth** perdre qn/qch de vue; **to catch s. of sb/sth** apercevoir qn/qch; **at first s.** à première vue; **by s.** de vue; **in s.** *(target, end, date)* en vue; **out of s.** *(hidden)* caché; *(no longer visible)* disparu; **he hates the s. of me** il ne peut pas me voir; **the (tourist) sights** les attractions *fpl* touristiques; **to set one's sights on** *(job)* viser • **sightseeing** *n* **to go s., to do some s.** faire du tourisme

sign [saɪn] **1** *n* signe *m*; *(notice)* panneau *m*; *(over shop, pub)* enseigne *f*; **no s. of** aucune trace de **2** *vt (put signature to)* signer; **to**

s. up (worker, soldier) engager 3 vi signer; **to s. for** (letter) signer le reçu de; Br **to s. on** (on the dole) s'inscrire au chômage; **to s. up** (of soldier, worker) s'engager; (for course) s'inscrire

signal ['sɪgnəl] 1 n signal m 2 (Br **-ll-**, Am **-l-**) vt (be a sign of) indiquer; (make gesture to) faire signe à 3 vi (make gesture) faire signe (**to** à); (of driver) mettre son clignotant; **to s. (to) sb to do sth** faire signe à qn de faire qch

signature ['sɪgnətʃə(r)] n signature f

significant [sɪg'nɪfɪkənt] adj (important, large) important; (meaningful) significatif, -ive • **significantly** adv (appreciably) sensiblement

signpost ['saɪnpəʊst] n poteau m indicateur

silence ['saɪləns] n silence m; **in s.** en silence • **silent** adj silencieux, -euse; (film, anger) muet (f muette); to keep or be s. garder le silence (**about** sur) • **silently** adv silencieusement

silhouette [sɪluː'et] n silhouette f

silk [sɪlk] n soie f

silly ['sɪlɪ] (**-ier, -iest**) adj bête, idiot; **to do something s.** faire une bêtise; **to look s.** avoir l'air ridicule

silver ['sɪlvə(r)] 1 n argent m 2 adj (spoon) en argent, d'argent; (colour) argenté; **s. jubilee** vingt-cinquième anniversaire m • **silver-plated** adj plaqué argent

similar ['sɪmɪlə(r)] adj semblable (**to** à) • **similarity** [-'lærətɪ] (pl **-ies**) n ressemblance f (**between** entre; **to** avec)

simile ['sɪmɪlɪ] n comparaison f

simmer ['sɪmə(r)] 1 vt (vegetables) mijoter 2 vi (of vegetables) mijoter; (of water) frémir; Fig (of revolt, hatred) couver

simple ['sɪmpəl] (**-er, -est**) adj (easy) simple • **simplify** (pt & pp **-ied**) vt simplifier • **simply** adv (plainly, merely) simplement; (absolutely) absolument

simultaneous [Br sɪməl'teɪnɪəs, Am saɪməl'teɪnɪəs] adj simultané • **simultaneously** [Br sɪməl'teɪnɪəslɪ, Am saɪməl'teɪnɪəslɪ] adv simultanément

sin [sɪn] n péché m

since [sɪns] 1 prep (in time) depuis; **s. then** depuis 2 conj (in time) depuis que; (because) puisque; **it's a year s. I saw him** ça fait un an que je ne l'ai pas vu 3 adv (ever) **s.** depuis

sincere [sɪn'sɪə(r)] adj sincère • **sincerely** adv sincèrement; Br **yours s.,** Am **s.** (in letter) veuillez agréer, Madame/Monsieur, mes salutations distinguées

sing [sɪŋ] (pt **sang**, pp **sung**) vti chanter • **singer** n chanteur, -euse mf • **singing** n (activity) chant m; **s. lesson/teacher** leçon f/professeur m de chant

single ['sɪŋgəl] 1 adj (only one) seul; (room, bed) pour une personne; (unmarried) célibataire; **not a s. book** pas un seul livre; **every s. day** tous les jours sans exception; Br **s. ticket** aller m simple; **s. parent** père m/mère f célibataire 2 n Br (ticket) aller m simple; (record) single m; **singles** (in tennis) simples mpl 3 vt **to s. sb out** sélectionner qn • **single-handedly** adv tout seul (f toute seule) • **single-minded** adj (person) résolu; (determination) farouche

singular ['sɪŋgjʊlə(r)] Gram 1 adj singulier, -ère 2 n singulier m; **in the s.** au singulier

sinister ['sɪnɪstə(r)] *adj* sinistre

sink¹ [sɪŋk] *n (in kitchen)* évier *m*; *(in bathroom)* lavabo *m*

sink² [sɪŋk] *(pt* **sank***, pp* **sunk) 1** *vt (ship)* couler **2** *vi (of ship, person)* couler; *(of water level, sun, price)* baisser; *(collapse)* s'affaisser; **my heart sank** j'ai eu un pincement de cœur; **to s. (down) into** *(mud)* s'enfoncer dans; *(armchair)* s'affaler dans; *Fam* **it hasn't sunk in yet** je n'ai/il n'a/*etc* pas encore digéré la nouvelle

sip [sɪp] **1** *n* petite gorgée *f* **2** *(pt & pp* **-pp-)** *vt* siroter

sir [sɜː(r)] *n* monsieur *m*; **S. Walter Raleigh** *(title)* sir Walter Raleigh

siren ['saɪərən] *n* sirène *f*

sister ['sɪstə(r)] *n* sœur *f*; *(nurse)* infirmière-chef *f* ● **sister-in-law** *(pl* **sisters-in-law)** *n* belle-sœur *f*

sit [sɪt] *(pt & pp* **sat***, pres p* **sitting) 1** *vt (child on chair)* asseoir; *Br (exam)* se présenter à **2** *vi (of person)* s'asseoir; *(for artist)* poser **(for** pour); **to be sitting** *(of person, cat)* être assis; **she was sitting reading, she sat reading** elle était assise à lire ● **sitting** *n (in restaurant)* service *m*; **s. room** salon *m*

▶**sit around** *vi* rester assis à ne rien faire

▶**sit back** *vi (in chair)* se caler; *(rest)* se détendre; *(do nothing)* ne rien faire

▶**sit down 1** *vt* **to s. sb down** asseoir qn **2** *vi* s'asseoir; **to be sitting down** être assis

▶**sit through** *vt insep (film)* rester jusqu'au bout de

▶**sit up** *vi* **to s. up (straight)** s'asseoir (bien droit); **to s. up waiting for sb** veiller jusqu'au retour de qn

sitcom ['sɪtkɒm] *n* sitcom *m*

site [saɪt] *n (position)* emplacement *m*; *(archaeological, on Internet)* site *m*; **(building) s.** chantier *m* (de construction)

situate ['sɪtjʊeɪt] *vt* situer; **to be situated** être situé ● **situation** [-'eɪʃən] *n* situation *f*

six [sɪks] *adj & n* six *(m)* ● **sixth** *adj & n* sixième *(mf)*; **a s.** *(fraction)* un sixième; *Br Sch* **(lower) s. form** ≃ classe *f* de première; *Br Sch* **(upper) s. form** ≃ classe *f* terminale

sixteen [sɪk'stiːn] *adj & n* seize *(m)* ● **sixteenth** *adj & n* seizième *(mf)*

sixty ['sɪkstɪ] *adj & n* soixante *(m)* ● **sixtieth** *adj & n* soixantième *(mf)*

size [saɪz] *n (of person, animal, clothes)* taille *f*; *(of shoes, gloves)* pointure *f*; *(measurements)* dimensions *fpl*; *(of packet)* grosseur *f*; *(of town, damage, problem)* étendue *f*; **hip/chest s.** tour *m* de hanches/de poitrine

sizzle ['sɪzəl] *vi* grésiller

skate [skeɪt] **1** *n* patin *m* **2** *vi (on ice-skates)* faire du patin à glace; *(on roller-skates)* faire du roller ● **skateboard** *n* skateboard *m* ● **skating** *n* patinage *m*; **to go s.** faire du patinage

skeleton ['skelɪtən] *n* squelette *m*

skeptical ['skeptɪkəl] *adj Am* sceptique

sketch [sketʃ] **1** *n (drawing)* croquis *m*; *(comic play)* sketch *m* **2** *vt* **to s. (out)** *(idea, view)* exposer brièvement **3** *vi* faire un/ des croquis

skewer ['skjuːə(r)] *n (for meat)* broche *f*; *(for kebab)* brochette *f*

ski [skiː] **1** *(pl* **skis)** *n* ski *m*; **s. boot** chaussure *f* de ski; **s. lift** remonte-pente *m*; **s. pants** fuseau *m*; **s. resort** station *f* de ski; **s. slope** piste *f* de ski **2** (*pt* **skied** [skiːd], *pres p* **skiing**) *vi* skier, faire du ski ● **skier** *n* skieur, -euse *mf* ● **skiing 1** *n* (*sport*) ski *m* **2** *adj* (*clothes*) de ski

skid [skɪd] (*pt* & *pp* **-dd-**) *vi* déraper

skill [skɪl] *n* (*ability*) qualités *fpl*; (*technique*) compétence *f* ● **skilful** (*Am* **skillful**) *adj* habile (**at doing** à faire; **at sth** en qch) ● **skilled** *adj* habile (**at doing** à faire; **at sth** en qch); (*worker*) qualifié; (*work*) de spécialiste

skim [skɪm] (*pt* & *pp* **-mm-**) **1** *vt* **to s. over sth** (*surface*) effleurer qch **2** *vt insep* **to s. through** (*book*) parcourir ● **skimmed** *adj* **s. milk** lait *m* écrémé

skin [skɪn] **1** *n* peau *f* **2** (*pt* & *pp* **-nn-**) *vt* (*animal*) écorcher ● **skinhead** *n Br* skinhead *mf* ● **skin-tight** *adj* moulant

skinny ['skɪnɪ] (**-ier, -iest**) *adj* maigre

skint [skɪnt] *adj Br Fam* (*penniless*) fauché

skip¹ [skɪp] **1** (*pt* & *pp* **-pp-**) *vt* (*miss, omit*) sauter; **to s. classes** sécher les cours **2** *vi* (*hop about*) sautiller; *Br* (*with rope*) sauter à la corde; *Br* **skipping rope** corde *f* à sauter

skip² [skɪp] *n Br* (*for rubbish*) benne *f*

skirt [skɜːt] *n* jupe *f*

skittle ['skɪtəl] *n Br* quille *f*; **to play skittles** jouer aux quilles

skull [skʌl] *n* crâne *m*

skunk [skʌŋk] *n* (*animal*) moufette *f*

sky [skaɪ] *n* ciel *m* ● **skylight** *n* lucarne *f* ● **skyscraper** *n* gratte-ciel *m inv*

slack [slæk] (**-er, -est**) *adj* (*not tight*) mou (*f* molle); (*careless*)

négligent; **to be s.** (*of rope*) avoir du mou; **business is s.** les affaires vont mal ● **slacken 1** *vt* **to s. (off)** (*rope*) relâcher; (*pace, effort*) ralentir **2** *vi* **to s. (off)** (*in effort*) se relâcher; (*of production, speed*) diminuer

slam [slæm] **1** (*pt* & *pp* **-mm-**) *vt* (*door, lid*) claquer; (*hit*) frapper violemment; **to s. sth (down)** (*put down*) poser qch violemment; **to s. on the brakes** écraser la pédale de frein **2** *vi* (*of door*) claquer

slang [slæŋ] **1** *n* argot *m* **2** *adj* (*word*) d'argot, argotique

slant [slɑːnt] **1** *n* pente *f*; *Fig* (*point of view*) perspective *f*; *Fig* (*bias*) parti *m* pris **2** *vi* (*of roof, handwriting*) être incliné ● **slanted, slanting** *adj* penché; (*roof*) en pente

slap [slæp] **1** *n* (*with hand*) claque *f*; **a s. in the face** une gifle **2** (*pt* & *pp* **-pp-**) *vt* (*person*) donner une claque à; **to s. sb's face** gifler qn; **to s. sb's bottom** donner une fessée à qn

slapstick ['slæpstɪk] *adj* & *n* **s. (comedy)** grosse farce *f*

slash [slæʃ] **1** *n* entaille *f* **2** *vt* (*cut*) taillader; (*reduce*) réduire considérablement

slate [sleɪt] *n* ardoise *f*

slaughter ['slɔːtə(r)] **1** *n* (*of people*) massacre *m*; (*of animal*) abattage *m* **2** *vt* (*people*) massacrer; (*animal*) abattre

slave [sleɪv] **1** *n* esclave *mf* **2** *vi* **to s. (away)** trimer ● **slavery** *n* esclavage *m*

sleazy ['sliːzɪ] (**-ier, -iest**) *adj Fam* sordide

sledge [sledʒ] (*Am* **sled** [sled]) *n Br* luge *f*

sledgehammer ['sledʒhæmə(r)] *n* masse *f*

sleek [sliːk] (**-er, -est**) *adj* lisse et brillant

sleep [sliːp] **1** *n* sommeil *m*; **to have a s., to get some s.** dormir; **to go to s.** *(of person)* s'endormir; **to put an animal to s.** *(kill)* faire piquer un animal **2** *(pt & pp* **slept)** *vi* dormir; *Euph* **to s. with sb** coucher avec qn **3** *vt* **this flat sleeps six** on peut dormir à six dans cet appartement • **sleeper** *n* **(a) to be a light/heavy s.** avoir le sommeil léger/lourd **(b)** *Br Rail (on track)* traverse *f*; *(train)* train-couchettes *m* • **sleeping** *adj (asleep)* endormi; **s. bag** sac *m* de couchage; **s. pill** somnifère *m* • **sleepless** *adj (night)* d'insomnie • **sleepy** (**-ier, -iest**) *adj* **to be s.** *(of person)* avoir sommeil

sleet [sliːt] **1** *n* neige *f* fondue **2** *vi* **it's sleeting** il tombe de la neige fondue

sleeve [sliːv] *n (of shirt, jacket)* manche *f*; *(of record)* pochette *f*; **long-/short-sleeved** à manches longues/courtes

sleigh [sleɪ] *n* traîneau *m*

slender ['slendə(r)] *adj (person)* svelte; *(neck, hand, waist)* fin

slept [slept] *pt & pp of* **sleep**

slice [slaɪs] **1** *n* tranche *f* **2** *vt* **to s. sth (up)** couper qch en tranches; **to s. sth off** couper qch

slick [slɪk] (**-er, -est**) *adj (campaign)* bien mené; *(reply, person)* habile

slide [slaɪd] **1** *n (in playground)* toboggan *m*; *(for hair)* barrette *f*; *Phot* diapositive *f* **2** *(pt & pp* **slid** [slɪd]) *vt* glisser (**into** dans); *(table, chair)* faire glisser **3** *vi* glisser

slight [slaɪt] (**-er, -est**) *adj (small, unimportant)* léger, -ère; *(chance)* faible; **the slightest thing** la moindre chose; **not in the slightest** pas le moins du monde

• **slightly** *adv* légèrement

slim [slɪm] (**slimmer, slimmest**) *adj* mince

slime [slaɪm] *n* vase *f*; *(of snail)* bave *f* • **slimy** (**-ier, -iest**) *adj (muddy)* boueux (*f* boueuse); *Fig (sticky, smarmy)* visqueux, -euse

sling [slɪŋ] *n (for injured arm)* écharpe *f*; **in a s.** en écharpe

slip [slɪp] **1** *n (mistake)* erreur *f*; *(garment)* combinaison *f*; *(fall)* chute *f*; **a s. of paper** un bout de papier; *(printed)* un bordereau; **a s. of the tongue** un lapsus **2** *(pt & pp* **-pp-**) *vt (slide)* glisser (**to** à; **into** dans); **it slipped my mind** ça m'est sorti de l'esprit **3** *vi* glisser; *Fam (of popularity, ratings)* baisser; **to let sth s.** *(chance, secret)* laisser échapper qch

▶**slip away** *vi (escape)* s'éclipser

▶**slip on** *vt sep (coat)* mettre

▶**slip out** *vi (leave)* sortir furtivement; *(for a moment)* sortir (un instant); *(of secret)* s'éventer

▶**slip up** *vi Fam* se planter

slipper ['slɪpə(r)] *n* pantoufle *f*

slippery ['slɪpərɪ] *adj* glissant

slit [slɪt] **1** *n* fente *f* **2** *(pt & pp* **slit,** *pres p* **slitting)** *vt (cut)* couper; **to s. open** *(sack)* éventrer

slob [slɒb] *n Fam (lazy person)* flemmard, -e *mf*; *(dirty person)* porc *m*

slobber ['slɒbə(r)] *vi (of dog, baby)* baver

slogan ['sləʊgən] *n* slogan *m*

slope [sləʊp] **1** *n* pente *f*; *(of mountain)* versant *m*; *(for skiing)* piste *f* **2** *vi (of ground, roof)* être en pente • **sloping** *adj (roof)* en pente

sloppy ['slɒpɪ] (**-ier, -iest**) *adj (work, appearance)* négligé; *(person)* négligent; *(sentimental)* sentimental

slot [slɒt] **1** n *(slit)* fente f; **s. machine** *(for vending)* distributeur m automatique; *(for gambling)* machine f à sous **2** *(pt & pp* -**tt**-) vt *(insert)* insérer (**into** dans) **3** vi s'insérer (**into** dans)

slouch [slaʊtʃ] vi ne pas se tenir droit; *(in chair)* être avachi

slow [sləʊ] **1** (-**er**, -**est**) *adj* lent; **in s. motion** au ralenti; **to be s.** *(of clock, watch)* retarder; **business is s.** les affaires tournent au ralenti **2** adv lentement • **slowly** adv lentement; *(bit by bit)* peu à peu
▶**slow down 1** vt ralentir; *(delay)* retarder **2** vi ralentir

slug [slʌg] n limace f

sluggish ['slʌgɪʃ] adj *(person)* amorphe; **business is s.** les affaires ne marchent pas très bien

slum [slʌm] n *(house)* taudis m; **the slums** les quartiers mpl délabrés

slump [slʌmp] **1** n baisse f soudaine (**in** de); *(economic depression)* crise f **2** vi *(of person, prices)* s'effondrer

slur [slɜː(r)] *(pt & pp* -**rr**-) vt mal articuler • **slurred** adj *(speech)* indistinct

slush [slʌʃ] n *(snow)* neige f fondue

sly [slaɪ] (-**er**, -**est**) adj *(deceitful)* sournois; *(cunning, crafty)* rusé

smack [smæk] **1** n *(blow)* claque f; *(on bottom)* fessée f **2** vt *(person)* donner une claque à; **to s. sb's face** gifler qn; **to s. sb('s bottom)** donner une fessée à qn

small [smɔːl] **1** (-**er**, -**est**) adj petit; **s. change** petite monnaie f; **s. talk** banalités fpl **2** adv *(cut, chop)* menu; *(write)* petit • **small-scale** adj *(model)* réduit; *(research)* à petite échelle

smart [smɑːt] (-**er**, -**est**) adj *(in*

appearance) élégant; *(clever)* intelligent; *(astute)* astucieux, -euse; *(quick)* rapide; **s. card** carte f à puce • **smartly** adv *(dressed)* avec élégance
▶**smarten up** ['smɑːtən-] vt sep **to s. sth up** égayer qch; **to s. oneself up** se faire beau *(f* belle)

smash [smæʃ] **1** vt *(break)* briser; *(shatter)* fracasser **2** vi **to s. into sth** *(of vehicle)* entrer dans qch; **to s. into pieces** éclater en mille morceaux • **smashing** adj Br Fam *(excellent)* génial
▶**smash up** vt sep *(vehicle)* esquinter

smear [smɪə(r)] **1** n *(mark)* trace f **2** vt *(coat)* enduire (**with** de); *(smudge)* faire une trace sur

smell [smel] **1** n odeur f; **(sense of) s.** odorat m **2** *(pt & pp* **smelled** or **smelt**) vt sentir; *(of animal)* flairer **3** vi *(stink)* sentir mauvais; *(have a smell)* sentir; **to s. of smoke** sentir la fumée • **smelly** (-**ier**, -**iest**) adj **to be s.** sentir mauvais

smile [smaɪl] **1** n sourire m **2** vi sourire (**at sb** à qn; **at sth** de qch)

smirk [smɜːk] n *(smug)* sourire m suffisant; *(scornful)* sourire m goguenard

smog [smɒg] n smog m

smoke [sməʊk] **1** n fumée f; **to have a s.** fumer; **s. detector** or **alarm** détecteur m de fumée **2** vt *(cigarette)* fumer; **smoked salmon** saumon m fumé **3** vi fumer; **'no smoking'** 'défense de fumer' • **smoker** n fumeur, -euse mf • **smoky** (-**ier**, -**iest**) adj *(room, air)* enfumé

smooth [smuːð] **1** (-**er**, -**est**) adj *(surface, skin)* lisse; *(cream, sauce)* onctueux, -euse; *(sea, flight)* calme; Pej *(person, manners)* doucereux,

-euse; **the s. running of** *(machine, service, business)* la bonne marche de **2** *vt* **to s. sth down** *(hair, sheet, paper)* lisser qch; **to s. sth out** *(paper, sheet, dress)* lisser qch; *(crease)* faire disparaître qch ● **smoothly** *adv (without problems)* sans problèmes

smother ['smʌðə(r)] *vt (stifle)* étouffer; **to s. sth in sth** recouvrir qch de qch

smoulder ['sməʊldə(r)] *(Am* **smolder)** *vi (of fire, passion)* couver

smudge [smʌdʒ] **1** *n* tache *f* **2** *vt (paper)* faire des taches sur; *(ink)* étaler

smug [smʌg] *(smugger, smuggest) adj (person)* content de soi

smuggle ['smʌgəl] *vt* passer en fraude; **smuggled goods** contrebande *f* ● **smuggler** *n* contrebandier, -ère *mf*; *(of drugs)* trafiquant, -e *mf*

snack [snæk] *n (meal)* casse-croûte *m inv*; **s. bar** snack-bar *m*

snag [snæg] *n (hitch)* problème *m*

snail [sneɪl] *n* escargot *m*

snake [sneɪk] *n* serpent *m*

snap [snæp] **1** *n Fam (photo)* photo *f* **2** *(pt & pp -pp-) vt (break)* casser net; *(fingers)* faire claquer; **to s. up a bargain** sauter sur une occasion **3** *vi* se casser net; *Fig (of person)* parler sèchement (**at** à); **to s. off** se casser net

snarl [snɑːl] *vi* grogner (en montrant les dents)

snatch [snætʃ] *vt (grab)* saisir; *(steal)* arracher; **to s. sth from sb** arracher qch à qn

sneak [sniːk] *(pt & pp* **sneaked** *or Am* **snuck)** *vi Br Fam (tell tales)* rapporter; **to s. in/out** entrer/sortir furtivement; **to s. off** s'esquiver

sneaker ['sniːkə(r)] *n Am (shoe)* chaussure *f* de sport

sneer [snɪə(r)] *vi* ricaner; **to s. at sb/sth** se moquer de qn/qch

sneeze [sniːz] *vi* éternuer

sniff [snɪf] *vti* renifler

snigger ['snɪgə(r)] *vi* ricaner

snip [snɪp] *(pt & pp -pp-) vt* **to s. sth (off)** couper qch

snob [snɒb] *n* snob *mf* ● **snobbish** *adj* snob *inv*

snooker ['snuːkə(r)] *n (game)* snooker *m*

snoop [snuːp] *vi* fouiner; **to s. on sb** espionner qn

snooze [snuːz] **1** *n* petit somme *m*; **to have a s.** faire un petit somme **2** *vi* faire un petit somme

snore [snɔː(r)] *vi* ronfler ● **snoring** *n* ronflements *mpl*

snorkel ['snɔːkəl] **1** *n* tuba *m* **2** *(Br -ll-, Am -l-) vi* nager sous l'eau avec un tuba

snort [snɔːt] *vi (of person)* grogner; *(of horse)* s'ébrouer

snot [snɒt] *n Fam* morve *f*

snout [snaʊt] *n* museau *m*

snow [snəʊ] **1** *n* neige *f* **2** *vi* **it's snowing** il neige **3** *vt* **to be snowed in** être bloqué par la neige; *Fig* **to be snowed under with work** être submergé de travail ● **snowball 1** *n* boule *f* de neige **2** *vi (increase)* faire boule de neige ● **snowflake** *n* flocon *m* de neige ● **snowman** *(pl* **-men)** *n* bonhomme *m* de neige ● **snowplough** *(Am* **snowplow)** *n* chasse-neige *m inv* ● **snow-storm** *n* tempête *f* de neige

snub [snʌb] *(pt & pp -bb-) vt (offer)* rejeter; **to s. sb** snober qn

snuck [snʌk] *Am pt & pp of* **sneak**

snuff [snʌf] *vt* **to s. (out)** *(candle)* moucher

snug [snʌg] (**snugger, snuggest**) *adj (house)* douillet, -ette; *(garment)* bien ajusté

snuggle ['snʌgəl] *vi* **to s. up to sb** se blottir contre qn

so [səʊ] **1** *adv (to such a degree)* si, tellement (**that** que); *(thus)* ainsi, comme ça; **to work/drink so much that…** travailler/boire tellement que…; **so much courage** tellement de courage (**that** que); **so many books** tant de livres (**that** que); **and so on** et ainsi de suite; **I think so** je crois que oui; **is that so?** c'est vrai?; **so am I** moi aussi; **I told you so** je vous l'avais bien dit; *Fam* **so long!** au revoir! **2** *conj (therefore)* donc; *(in that case)* alors; **so what?** et alors?; **so that…** pour que… *(+ subjunctive)*; **so as to do sth** pour faire qch ● **So-and-so** *n* **Mr S.** Monsieur Untel ● **so-called** *adj* soi-disant *inv*

soak [səʊk] **1** *vt (drench)* tremper; *(washing, food)* faire tremper; **to be soaked (through** *or* **to the skin)** être trempé (jusqu'aux os); **to s. sth up** absorber qch **2** *vi (of washing)* tremper ● **soaking** *adj & adv* **s. (wet)** trempé

soap [səʊp] *n* savon *m*; **s. opera** feuilleton *m* populaire; **s. powder** lessive *f*

soar [sɔː(r)] *vi (of bird)* s'élever; *(of price)* monter en flèche

sob [sɒb] **1** *n* sanglot *m* **2** *(pt & pp* **-bb-)** *vi* sangloter

sober ['səʊbə(r)] **1** *adj (sensible)* sobre; **he's s.** *(not drunk)* il n'est pas ivre **2** *vti* **to s. up** dessoûler

soccer ['sɒkə(r)] *n* football *m*

sociable ['səʊʃəbəl] *adj (person)* sociable; *(evening)* amical

social ['səʊʃəl] *adj* social; **to have a good s. life** sortir beaucoup; **S.**

Security ≃ la Sécurité sociale; **s. security** *(aid)* aide *f* sociale; *Am (retirement pension)* pension *f* de retraite; **the s. services** les services *mpl* sociaux; **s. worker** assistant, -e *mf* social(e) ● **socialize** *vi* fréquenter des gens; **to s. with sb** fréquenter qn

socialist ['səʊʃəlɪst] *adj & n* socialiste *(mf)*

society [sə'saɪətɪ] *(pl* **-ies)** *n (community, club, companionship)* société *f*; *(school/university club)* club *m*

sociology [səʊsɪ'ɒlədʒɪ] *n* sociologie *f*

sock [sɒk] *n* chaussette *f*

socket ['sɒkɪt] *n Br (of electric plug)* prise *f* de courant; *Br (of lamp)* douille *f*

soda ['səʊdə] *n Am* **s. (pop)** boisson *f* gazeuse; **s. (water)** eau *f* de Seltz

sofa ['səʊfə] *n* canapé *m*; **s. bed** canapé-lit *m*

soft [sɒft] **(-er, -est)** *adj (gentle, not stiff)* doux *(f* douce); *(butter, ground, paste, snow)* mou *(f* molle); *(wood, heart, colour)* tendre; **s. drink** boisson *f* non alcoolisée; **s. toy** peluche *f* ● **soft-boiled** *adj (egg)* à la coque ● **soften** ['sɒfən] *vti (object)* ramollir ● **softly** *adv* doucement ● **software** *n inv Comptr* logiciel *m*

soggy ['sɒgɪ] **(-ier, -iest)** *adj* trempé

soil [sɔɪl] *n (earth)* terre *f*

sold [səʊld] *pt & pp of* **sell**

soldier ['səʊldʒə(r)] *n* soldat *m*

sole¹ [səʊl] *n (of shoe)* semelle *f*; *(of foot)* plante *f*

sole² [səʊl] *adj (only)* unique; *(rights, representative, responsibility)* exclusif, -ive ● **solely** *adv* uniquement

solemn ['sɒləm] *adj* solennel, -elle

solicitor [sə'lɪsɪtə(r)] *n Br (for wills)* notaire *m*

solid ['sɒlɪd] **1** *adj (not liquid)* solide; *(not hollow)* plein; *(gold, silver)* massif, -ive **2** *adv* **frozen s.** complètement gelé; **ten days s.** dix jours d'affilée ● **solidly** *adv (built)* solidement; *(work)* sans interruption

solidarity [sɒlɪ'dærətɪ] *n* solidarité *f* (**with** avec)

solitary ['sɒlɪtərɪ] *adj (lonely, alone)* solitaire; *(only)* seul ● **solitude** *n* solitude *f*

solo ['səʊləʊ] (*pl* **-os**) *n Mus* solo *m*

solution [sə'luːʃən] *n* (a) *(to problem)* solution *f* (**to** de) (b) *(liquid)* solution *f*

solve [sɒlv] *vt (problem)* résoudre

sombre ['sɒmbə(r)] (*Am* **somber**) *adj* sombre

some [sʌm] **1** *adj* (a) *(a quantity of)* du, de la, des; **s. wine** du vin; **s. water** de l'eau; **s. dogs** des chiens; **s. pretty flowers** de jolies fleurs (b) *(unspecified)* un, une; **s. man (or other)** un homme (quelconque); **for s. reason or other** pour une raison ou pour une autre; **I have been waiting s. time** ça fait un moment que j'attends (c) *(a few)* quelques; *(in contrast to others)* certains; **s. days ago** il y a quelques jours; **s. people think that...** certains pensent que... **2** *pron* (a) *(a certain quantity)* en; **I want s.** j'en veux; **s. of my wine** un peu de mon vin; **s. of the time** une partie du temps (b) *(as opposed to others)* certain(e)s; **some say...** certains disent...; **s. of the guests** certains invités **3** *adv*

(about) environ; **s. ten years** environ dix ans ● **somebody** *pron* quelqu'un; **s. small** quelqu'un de petit ● **someday** *adv* un jour ● **somehow** *adv (in some way)* d'une manière ou d'une autre; *(for some reason)* on ne sait pourquoi ● **someone** *pron* quelqu'un; **s. small** quelqu'un de petit ● **someplace** *adv Am* quelque part ● **something 1** *pron* quelque chose; **s. awful** quelque chose d'affreux **2** *adv* **she plays s. like...** elle joue un peu comme... ● **sometime** *adv* un jour; **s. in May** au mois de mai ● **sometimes** *adv* quelquefois, parfois ● **somewhat** *adv* quelque peu, assez ● **somewhere** *adv* quelque part; **s. about fifteen** *(approximately)* environ quinze

somersault ['sʌməsɔːlt] *n (on ground)* roulade *f*; *(in air)* saut *m* périlleux

son [sʌn] *n* fils *m* ● **son-in-law** (*pl* **sons-in-law**) *n* gendre *m*

song [sɒŋ] *n* chanson *f*; *(of bird)* chant *m*

soon [suːn] (**-er**, **-est**) *adv (in a short time)* bientôt; *(quickly)* vite; *(early)* tôt; **s. after** peu après; **as s. as...** aussitôt que...; **no sooner had he spoken than...** à peine avait-il parlé que...; **sooner or later** tôt ou tard

soothe [suːð] *vt* calmer

sophisticated [sə'fɪstɪkeɪtɪd] *adj (person, taste)* raffiné; *(machine, method)* sophistiqué

sophomore ['sɒfəmɔː(r)] *n Am* étudiant, -e *mf* de deuxième année

sopping ['sɒpɪŋ] *adj & adv* **s. (wet)** trempé

soppy ['sɒpɪ] (**-ier**, **-iest**) *adj Br Fam (sentimental)* sentimental

sordid ['sɔːdɪd] *adj* sordide
sore [sɔː(r)] (**-er, -est**) *adj* douloureux, -euse; **to have a s. throat** avoir mal à la gorge
sorrow ['sɒrəʊ] *n* chagrin *m*
sorry ['sɒrɪ] (**-ier, -iest**) *adj (sight, state)* triste; **to be s. (about sth)** *(regret)* être désolé (de qch); **to feel** *or* **be s. for sb** plaindre qn; **I'm s. she can't come** je regrette qu'elle ne puisse pas venir; **s.!** pardon!; **to say s.** demander pardon (**to** à)
sort¹ [sɔːt] *n* sorte *f*; **a s. of** une sorte de; **all sorts of** toutes sortes de; **what s. of drink is it?** qu'est-ce que c'est comme boisson?; **s. of sad** *(somewhat)* plutôt triste
sort² [sɔːt] **1** *vt (papers)* trier; **to s. out** *(classify, select)* trier; *(separate)* séparer (**from** de); *(organize)* ranger; *(problem)* régler **2** *vi* **to s. through letters/magazines** trier des lettres/magazines
sought [sɔːt] *pt & pp of* **seek**
soul [səʊl] *n* âme *f*
sound¹ [saʊnd] **1** *n* son *m*; *(noise)* bruit *m* **2** *vt (bell, alarm)* sonner; **to s. one's horn** *(in vehicle)* klaxonner **3** *vi (seem)* sembler; **to s. like** sembler être; *(resemble)* ressembler à; **it sounds like** *or* **as if…** il semble que… (+ *subjunctive or indicative*) • **soundproof** *adj* insonorisé • **soundtrack** *n (of film)* bande *f* sonore
sound² [saʊnd] **1** (**-er, -est**) *adj (healthy)* sain; *(in good condition)* en bon état; *(basis)* solide; *(advice)* bon (*f* bonne) **2** *adv* **s. asleep** profondément endormi • **soundly** *adv (asleep, sleep)* profondément
soup [suːp] *n* soupe *f*
sour ['saʊə(r)] (**-er, -est**) *adj* aigre; *(milk)* tourné; **to turn s.** *(of milk)* tourner

source [sɔːs] *n (origin)* source *f*
south [saʊθ] **1** *n* sud *m*; (**to the) s. of** au sud de **2** *adj (coast)* sud *inv*; *(wind)* du sud; **S. America/Africa** l'Amérique *f*/l'Afrique *f* du Sud; **S. American** *adj* sud-américain; *n* Sud-Américain, -e *mf*; **S. African** *adj* sudafricain; *n* Sud-Africain, -e *mf* **3** *adv* au sud; *(travel)* vers le sud • **south-east** *n & adj* sud-est *(m)* • **southern** ['sʌðən] *adj (town)* du sud; *(coast)* sud *inv*; **S. Italy** le sud de l'Italie • **southerner** ['sʌðənə(r)] *n* habitant, -e *mf* du sud • **south-west** *n & adj* sud-ouest *(m)*
souvenir [suːvə'nɪə(r)] *n* souvenir *m*
sow [səʊ] (*pt* **sowed**, *pp* **sowed** *or* **sown** [səʊn]) *vt (seeds, doubt)* semer
soya ['sɔɪə] *n Br* soja *m*; **s. bean** graine *f* de soja • **soybean** *n Am* graine *f* de soja
spa [spɑː] *n (town)* station *f* thermale
space [speɪs] **1** *n (gap, emptiness, atmosphere)* espace *m*; *(for parking)* place *f*; **to take up s.** prendre de la place; **s. bar** *(on keyboard)* barre *f* d'espacement **2** *adj (voyage, capsule)* spatial **3** *vt* **to s. out** espacer • **spaceship** *n* vaisseau *m* spatial
spacious ['speɪʃəs] *adj* spacieux, -euse
spade [speɪd] *n* (**a**) *(for garden)* bêche *f* (**b**) **spades** *(in cards)* pique *m*
spaghetti [spə'getɪ] *n* spaghettis *mpl*
Spain [speɪn] *n* l'Espagne *f*
span [spæn] (*pt & pp* **-nn-**) *vt (of bridge)* enjamber; *Fig (in time)* couvrir
Spaniard ['spænjəd] *n* Espagnol,

-e *mf* • **Spanish 1** *adj* espagnol **2** *n (language)* espagnol *m*

spank [spæŋk] *vt* donner une tape sur les fesses à • **spanking** *n* fessée *f*

spanner ['spænə(r)] *n Br (tool)* clef *f*

spare [speə(r)] **1** *adj (extra, surplus)* de *ou* en trop; *(reserve)* de rechange; *(wheel)* de secours; *(available)* disponible; **s. room** chambre *f* d'ami; **s. time** loisirs *mpl* **2** *vt (do without)* se passer de; *(efforts, sb's feelings)* ménager; **to s. sb sth** *(grief, details)* épargner qch à qn; **I can't s. the time** je n'ai pas le temps; **with five minutes to s.** avec cinq minutes d'avance

spark [spɑːk] *n* étincelle *f*

sparkle ['spɑːkəl] *vi* briller; *(of diamond, star)* scintiller • **sparkling** *adj (wine, water)* pétillant

sparrow ['spærəʊ] *n* moineau *m*

sparse [spɑːs] *adj* clairsemé • **sparsely** *adv (populated)* peu; **s. furnished** à peine meublé

spat [spæt] *pt & pp of* **spit**¹

speak [spiːk] **1** *(pt* **spoke,** *pp* **spoken)** *vt (language)* parler; *(say)* dire; **to s. one's mind** dire ce que l'on pense **2** *vi* parler **(about** *or* **of** de); *(formally, in assembly)* prendre la parole; **so to s.** pour ainsi dire; **that speaks for itself** c'est évident; **Jayne speaking!** *(on the telephone)* Jayne à l'appareil!; **to s. out** *or* **up** *(boldly)* parler (franchement); **to s. up** *(more loudly)* parler plus fort

speaker ['spiːkə(r)] *n (for stereo)* enceinte *f*

spear [spɪə(r)] *n* lance *f*

special ['speʃəl] **1** *adj* spécial; *(care, attention)* particulier, -ère;

Br **by s. delivery** en exprès; **s. effects** effets *mpl* spéciaux **2** *n* **today's s.** *(in restaurant)* le plat du jour • **specialist** *n* spécialiste *mf* **(in** de) • **speciality** [-ʃɪ'ælɪtɪ] *(pl* **-ies)** *n Br* spécialité *f* • **specialize** *vi* se spécialiser **(in** dans) • **specially** *adv (specifically)* spécialement; *(particularly)* particulièrement • **specialty** *(pl* **-ies)** *n Am* = **speciality**

species ['spiːʃiːz] *n inv* espèce *f*

specific [spə'sɪfɪk] *adj* précis • **specifically** *adv (explicitly)* expressément; *(exactly)* précisément; *(specially)* spécialement

specimen ['spesɪmɪn] *n (individual example)* spécimen *m*; *(of urine, blood)* échantillon *m*

speck [spek] *n (stain)* petite tache *f*; *(of dust)* grain *m*; *(dot)* point *m*

spectacle ['spektəkəl] *n (sight)* spectacle *m* • **spectacles,** *Fam* **specs** *npl (glasses)* lunettes *fpl*

spectacular [spek'tækjʊlə(r)] *adj* spectaculaire

spectator [spek'teɪtə(r)] *n* spectateur, -trice *mf*

spectrum ['spektrəm] *(pl* **-tra** [-trə]) *n* spectre *m*; *Fig (range)* gamme *f*

speculate ['spekjʊleɪt] *vt* **to s. that...** *(guess)* conjecturer que... • **speculation** [-'leɪʃən] *n* suppositions *fpl*

sped [sped] *pt & pp of* **speed**

speech [spiːtʃ] *n (talk, lecture)* discours *m* **(on** *or* **about** sur); *(faculty)* parole *f*; *(diction)* élocution *f*; **to make a s.** faire un discours • **speechless** *adj* muet *(f* muette) **(with** de)

speed [spiːd] **1** *n (rapidity, gear)* vitesse *f*; **at top** *or* **full s.** à toute vitesse; **s. limit** *(on road)* limitation *f* de vitesse **2** (*pt & pp* **sped**) *vt* **to s. sth up** accélérer qch **3** *vi* (**a**) **to s. up** (*of person*) aller plus vite; **to s. past sth** passer à toute vitesse devant qch (**b**) (*pt & pp* **speeded**) (*exceed speed limit*) faire un excès de vitesse • **speedboat** *n* vedette *f* • **speeding** *n* (*in vehicle*) excès *m* de vitesse • **speedometer** [spi:'dɒmɪtə(r)d] *n Br* (*in vehicle*) compteur *m* de vitesse • **speedy** (**-ier, -iest**) *adj* rapide

spell¹ [spel] *n* (*magic words*) formule *f* magique; **to cast a s. on sb** jeter un sort à qn

spell² [spel] *n* (*period*) période *f*; **cold s.** vague *f* de froid

spell³ [spel] (*pt & pp* **spelled** or **spelt** [spelt]) *vt* (*write*) écrire; (*say aloud*) épeler; (*of letters*) former; **how do you s. it?** comment ça s'écrit?; **to s. sth out** (*word*) épeler qch; *Fig* (*explain*) expliquer clairement qch • **spelling** *n* orthographe *f*; **s. mistake** faute *f* d'orthographe

spend [spend] (*pt & pp* **spent** [spent]) *vt* (*money*) dépenser (**on** pour/en); (*time*) passer (**on sth** sur qch; **doing** à faire); (*energy*) consacrer (**on sth** à qch; **doing** à faire)

sphere [sfɪə(r)] *n* sphère *f*

spice [spaɪs] **1** *n* épice *f* **2** *vt* (*food*) épicer; **to s. sth (up)** (*add interest to*) ajouter du piquant à qch • **spicy** (**-ier, -iest**) *adj* épicé

spider ['spaɪdə(r)] *n* araignée *f*

spike [spaɪk] *n* (*of metal*) pointe *f* • **spiky** (**-ier, -iest**) *adj* (*hair*) tout hérissé

spill [spɪl] (*pt & pp* **spilled** or **spilt** [spɪlt]) **1** *vt* (*liquid*) renverser **2** *vi* se répandre
► **spill out** *vt sep* (*empty*) vider
► **spill over** *vi* (*of liquid*) déborder

spin [spɪn] **1** (*pt & pp* **spun**, *pres p* **spinning**) *vt* faire tourner **2** *vi* tourner; **to s. round** (*of dancer, wheel, top, planet*) tourner; **my head's spinning** j'ai la tête qui tourne

spinach ['spɪnɪdʒ] *n* épinards *mpl*

spin-dry ['spɪndraɪ] *vt* essorer • **spin-dryer** *n* essoreuse *f*

spine [spaɪn] *n* (*backbone*) colonne *f* vertébrale; (*of book*) dos *m*

spinster ['spɪnstə(r)] *n* vieille fille *f*

spiral ['spaɪərəl] **1** *n* spirale *f* **2** *adj* en spirale; (*staircase*) en colimaçon

spire ['spaɪə(r)] *n* (*of church*) flèche *f*

spirit ['spɪrɪt] *n* (*soul, ghost, mood*) esprit *m*; **spirits** (*drink*) spiritueux *mpl*; **in good spirits** de bonne humeur • **spiritual** *adj* spirituel, -elle

spit¹ [spɪt] **1** *n* (*on ground*) crachat *m*; (*in mouth*) salive *f* **2** (*pt & pp* **spat** or **spit**, *pres p* **spitting**) *vt* cracher; **to s. sth out** cracher qch; **to be the spitting image of sb** être le portrait (tout craché) de qn **3** *vi* cracher

spit² [spɪt] *n* (*for meat*) broche *f*

spite [spaɪt] **1** *n* (*dislike*) dépit *m*; **in s. of sb/sth** malgré qn/qch; **in s. of the fact that...** bien que... (+ *subjunctive*) **2** *vt* vexer • **spiteful** *adj* vexant

splash [splæʃ] **1** *n* (*of liquid*) éclaboussure *f*; *Fig* (*of colour*) tache *f* **2** *vt* éclabousser (**with** de) **3** *vi* (*of mud*) faire des éclaboussures; (*of waves*) clapoter; **to s. about** (*in river, mud*) patauger; (*in bath*) barboter; *Fam* **to s. out** (*spend money*) claquer des ronds

splinter ['splɪntə(r)] *n* (*of wood, glass*) éclat *m*; (*in finger*) écharde *f*

split [splɪt] **1** n fente f **2** adj **in a s. second** en une fraction de seconde **3** (pt & pp **split,** pres p **splitting**) vt (break apart) fendre; (tear) déchirer; **to s. (up)** (group) diviser; (money, work) partager (**between** entre) **4** vi se fendre; (tear) se déchirer; **to s. (up)** (of group) se diviser (**into** en); **to s. up** (because of disagreement) (of couple, friends) se séparer; (of crowd) se disperser; **to s. up with sb** rompre avec qn

spoil [spɔɪl] (pt & pp **spoilt** [spɔɪlt] or **spoiled**) vt (ruin) gâcher; (indulge) gâter • **spoilsport** n rabat-joie mf inv

spoke [spəʊk] pt of **speak** • **spoken 1** pp of **speak 2** adj (language) parlé • **spokesman** (pl **-men**), **spokesperson, spokeswoman** (pl **-women**) n porte-parole mf inv (**for** or **of** de)

sponge [spʌndʒ] **1** n éponge f; Br **s. bag** trousse f de toilette; **s. cake** génoise f **2** vt **to s. sth down/off** laver/enlever qch avec une éponge

sponsor ['spɒnsə(r)] **1** n sponsor m **2** vt sponsoriser • **sponsorship** n sponsoring m

spontaneous [spɒn'teɪnɪəs] adj spontané

spooky ['spuːkɪ] (**-ier, -iest**) adj Fam qui donne le frisson

spoon [spuːn] n cuillère f • **spoonful** n cuillerée f

sport [spɔːt] n sport m; **to play** Br **s.** or Am **sports** faire du sport; **sports club** club m de sport; **sports car/ground** voiture f/terrain m de sport • **sportsman** (pl **-men**) n sportif m • **sportswoman** (pl **-women**) n sportive f • **sporty** (**-ier, -iest**) adj sportif, -ive

spot [spɒt] **1** n (stain, mark) tache f; (dot) point m; (polka dot) pois m; (pimple) bouton m; (place) endroit m; **on the s.** sur place **2** (pt & pp **-tt-**) vt (notice) apercevoir • **spotless** adj (clean) impeccable • **spotlight** n projecteur m • **spotty** (**-ier, -iest**) adj (face, person) boutonneux, -euse

spouse [spaʊs, spaʊz] n époux m, épouse f

spout [spaʊt] n (of teapot, jug) bec m

sprain [spreɪn] vt **to s. one's ankle/wrist** se fouler la cheville/le poignet

sprang [spræŋ] pt of **spring**[1]

spray [spreɪ] **1** n (can, device) vaporisateur m; (water drops) gouttelettes fpl **2** vt (liquid, surface) vaporiser; (plant, crops) pulvériser

spread [spred] **1** n (of idea, religion, language) diffusion f; (of disease) propagation f; **chocolate s.** chocolat m à tartiner **2** (pt & pp **spread**) vt (stretch, open out) étendre; (legs, fingers) écarter; (paint) étaler; (news, fear) répandre; (disease) propager; **to s. out** (map, payments, visits) étaler; (fingers) écarter **3** vi (of fog) s'étendre; (of fire, epidemic) se propager; (of news, fear) se répandre; **to s. out** (of people) se disperser • **spreadsheet** n Comptr tableur m

spring[1] [sprɪŋ] **1** n (device) ressort m **2** (pt **sprang**, pp **sprung**) vi (leap) bondir; **to s. to mind** venir à l'esprit; **to s. from** (stem from) provenir de; **to s. up** (appear) surgir

spring[2] [sprɪŋ] n (season) printemps m; **in (the) s.** au printemps; Br **s. onion** petit oignon m • **spring-cleaning**

n nettoyage *m* de printemps •
springtime *n* printemps *m*
spring³ [sprɪŋ] *n* (of water) source
f; **s. water** eau *f* de source
sprinkle ['sprɪŋkəl] *vt* (sand)
répandre (**on** *or* **over** sur); **to s.
sth with water, to s. water on
sth** arroser qch; **to s. sth with
sth** (sugar, salt, flour) saupoudrer
qch de qch
sprint [sprɪnt] *vi* piquer un sprint
sprout [spraʊt] **1** *n* (**Brussels**) **s.**
chou *m* de Bruxelles **2** *vt* (leaves)
faire **3** *vi* (of seed, bulb) pousser
sprung [sprʌŋ] *pp of* **spring¹**
spun [spʌn] *pt & pp of* **spin**
spur [spɜː(r)] **1** *n* (of horse rider)
éperon *m*; Fig (stimulus) aiguillon
m; **to do sth on the s. of the
moment** faire qch sur un coup de
tête **2** (*pt & pp* **-rr-**) *vt* **to s. sb on**
(urge on) aiguillonner qn
spurt [spɜːt] *vi* **to s. (out)** (of
liquid) gicler
spy [spaɪ] **1** (*pl* **-ies**) *n* espion,
-onne *mf* **2** *adj* (story, film)
d'espionnage **3** (*pt & pp* **-ied**) *vt*
(notice) repérer **4** *vi* espionner; **to
s. on sb** espionner qn
squabble ['skwɒbəl] *vi* se
quereller (**over** à propos de)
squad [skwɒd] *n* (team) équipe *f*;
(of soldiers) section *f*; (of police)
brigade *f*
squalid ['skwɒlɪd] *adj* sordide •
squalor *n* (poverty) misère *f*
square ['skweə(r)] **1** *n* carré *m*;
(on map) case *f*; (in town) place
f **2** *adj* carré; Math **s. root** racine
f carrée
squash [skwɒʃ] **1** *n* (game)
squash *m*; (vegetable) courge *f*; Br
lemon/orange s. ≃ sirop *m* de
citron/d'orange **2** *vt* écraser
squat [skwɒt] (*pt & pp* **-tt-**) *vi*
squatter; **to s. (down)** s'accroupir;

to be squatting (down) être
accroupi
squeak [skwiːk] *vi* (of person)
pousser un cri aigu; (of door)
grincer
squeal [skwiːl] *vi* pousser un cri
perçant
squeamish ['skwiːmɪʃ] *adj* de
nature délicate
squeeze [skwiːz] **1** *n* **to give
sth a s.** presser qch; **to give sb's
hand/arm a s.** serrer la main/le
bras à qn **2** *vt* (press) presser; **to
s. sb's hand** serrer la main à qn;
to s. sth into sth faire rentrer qch
dans qch; **to s. the juice (out)**
faire sortir le jus (**of** de) **3** *vi* **to s.
through/into sth** (force oneself)
se glisser par/dans qch; **to s. in**
trouver de la place; **to s. up** se
serrer (**against** contre)
squelch [skweltʃ] *vi* patauger
squid [skwɪd] *n inv* calmar *m*
squint [skwɪnt] **1** *n* **to have a
s,** loucher **2** *vi* loucher; (in the
sunlight) plisser les yeux
squirm [skwɜːm] *vi* (wriggle) se
tortiller
squirrel [Br 'skwɪrəl, Am
'skwɜːrəl] *n* écureuil *m*
squirt [skwɜːt] **1** *vt* (liquid) faire
gicler **2** *vi* (of liquid) gicler
St (a) (abbr **Street**) rue (b) (abbr
Saint) St, Ste
stab [stæb] (*pt & pp* **-bb-**) *vt* (with
knife) poignarder
stabilize ['steɪbəlaɪz] **1** *vt*
stabiliser **2** *vi* se stabiliser •
stability [stə'bɪlətɪ] *n* stabilité *f* •
stable¹ (**-er, -est**) *adj* stable
stable² ['steɪbəl] *n* écurie *f*
stack [stæk] **1** *n* (heap) tas *m* **2** *vt*
to s. (up) entasser
stadium ['steɪdɪəm] *n* stade *m*
staff [stɑːf] *n* personnel *m*; (of
school, university) professeurs

mpl; *Br* **s. room** *(in school)* salle *f* des professeurs

stag [stæg] *n* cerf *m*; **s. night** *or* **party** enterrement *m* de la vie de garçon

stage¹ [steɪdʒ] *n (platform)* scène *f*; **on s.** sur scène

stage² [steɪdʒ] *n (phase)* stade *m*

stagger ['stægə(r)] **1** *vt (holidays)* échelonner; *(astound)* stupéfier **2** *vi (reel)* chanceler • **staggering** *adj* stupéfiant

stagnant ['stægnənt] *adj* stagnant

stain [steɪn] **1** *n (mark)* tache *f* **2** *vt (mark)* tacher (**with** de); *(dye)* teinter • **stained-glass** *adj* **s. window** vitrail *m (pl* -aux) • **stainless** *n* **s. steel** acier *m* inoxydable, Inox® *m*

stair [steə(r)] *n* **a s.** *(step)* une marche; **the stairs** *(staircase)* l'escalier *m* • **staircase, stairway** *n* escalier *m*

stake [steɪk] *n* **(a)** *(post)* pieu *m* **(b) at s.** en jeu

stale [steɪl] (**-er, -est**) *adj (bread)* rassis; *(air)* vicié

stalk [stɔːk] **1** *n (of plant)* tige *f*; *(of fruit)* queue *f* **2** *vt (animal, criminal)* traquer; *(celebrity)* harceler **3** *vi* **to s. out** *(walk angrily)* sortir d'un air furieux mais digne

stall [stɔːl] **1** *n (in market)* étal *m*; *Br (for newspapers, flowers)* kiosque *m*; *Br* **the stalls** *(in cinema, theatre)* l'orchestre *m* **2** *vt (engine, car)* caler **3** *vi (of car)* caler; **to s. (for time)** chercher à gagner du temps

stamina ['stæmɪnə] *n* résistance *f* physique

stammer ['stæmə(r)] **1** *n* **to have a s.** être bègue **2** *vi* bégayer

stamp [stæmp] **1** *n (for letter)* timbre *m*; *(mark)* cachet *m*; *(device)*

tampon *m*; **s. collector** philatéliste *mf* **2** *vt (document)* tamponner; *(letter)* timbrer; *(metal)* estamper; **to s. one's foot** taper du pied; *Br* **stamped addressed envelope,** *Am* **stamped self-addressed envelope** enveloppe *f* timbrée libellée à son nom et adresse **3** *vi* **to s. on sth** écraser qch

stampede [stæm'piːd] *n* débandade *f*

stand [stænd] **1** *n (stall)* étal *m*; *(at exhibition)* stand *m* **2** *(pt & pp* **stood)** *vt (bear)* supporter; *(put straight)* mettre debout; **to s. a chance** avoir des chances; **I can't s. him** je ne peux pas le supporter **3** *vi (be upright)* se tenir debout; *(get up)* se mettre debout; *(remain)* rester debout; *(of building)* se trouver; *(of object)* être • **stand-by** *n* **on s.** *(troops, emergency services)* prêt à intervenir • **standing** *adj (upright)* debout; *(permanent)* permanent; *Br* **s. order** virement *m* automatique

▸**stand about, stand around** *vi (in street)* traîner

▸**stand aside** *vi* s'écarter

▸**stand back** *vi* reculer

▸**stand by 1** *vt insep (opinion)* s'en tenir à; *(person)* soutenir **2** *vi (do nothing)* rester sans rien faire; *(be ready)* être prêt

▸**stand for** *vt insep (mean)* signifier; *(represent)* représenter; *Br (be candidate for)* être candidat à; *(tolerate)* supporter

▸**stand out** *vi (be visible)* ressortir (**against** sur)

▸**stand up 1** *vt sep* mettre debout; *Fam* **to s. sb up** poser un lapin à qn **2** *vi (get up)* se lever

▸**stand up for** *vt insep (defend)* défendre

▶**stand up to** *vt insep (resist)* résister à; *(defend oneself against)* tenir tête à

standard ['stændəd] **1** *n (norm)* norme *f; (level)* niveau *m*; **standards** *(principles)* principes *mpl* moraux; **s. of living** niveau *m* de vie **2** *adj (average)* ordinaire; *(model, size)* standard *inv*

stank [stæŋk] *pt of* **stink**

staple[1] ['steɪpəl] *adj (basic)* de base; **s. food** *or* **diet** nourriture *f* de base

staple[2] ['steɪpəl] **1** *n (for paper)* agrafe *f* **2** *vt* agrafer • **stapler** *n (for paper)* agrafeuse *f*

star [stɑː(r)] **1** *n* étoile *f; (celebrity)* star *f* **2** *(pt & pp* **-rr-***) vt (of film)* avoir pour vedette **3** *vi (of actor, actress)* être la vedette (**in** de)

starch [stɑːtʃ] *n* amidon *m*

stare [steə(r)] **1** *n* regard *m* fixe **2** *vi* **to s. at sb/sth** fixer qn/qch (du regard)

stark [stɑːk] **1** *(-er, -est) adj (fact, reality)* brutal; **to be in s. contrast to** contraster nettement avec **2** *adv* **s. naked** complètement nu

start[1] [stɑːt] **1** *n* début *m; (of race)* départ *m*; **for a s.** pour commencer; **from the s.** dès le début; **to make a s.** commencer **2** *vt* commencer; *(packet, conversation)* entamer; *(fashion, campaign, offensive)* lancer; *(engine, vehicle)* mettre en marche; *(business, family)* fonder; **to s. doing** *or* **to do sth** commencer à faire qch **3** *vi* commencer (**with sth** par qch; **by doing** par faire); *(of vehicle)* démarrer; *(leave)* partir (**for** pour); *(in job)* débuter; **to s. with** *(firstly)* pour commencer; **starting from now/10 euros** à partir de maintenant/10 euros • **starter**

n (in meal) entrée *f; Fam* **for starters** *(firstly)* pour commencer • **starting** *adj (point, line, salary)* de départ; **s. post** *(in race)* ligne *f* de départ

▶**start off** *vi (leave)* partir (**for** pour); *(in job)* débuter

▶**start up 1** *vt sep (engine, vehicle)* mettre en marche; *(business)* fonder **2** *vi (of engine, vehicle)* démarrer

start[2] [stɑːt] **1** *n (movement)* sursaut *m* **2** *vi* sursauter

startle ['stɑːtəl] *vt* faire sursauter

starve [stɑːv] **1** *vt (make suffer)* faire souffrir de la faim; *Fig (deprive)* priver (**of** de) **2** *vi (suffer)* souffrir de la faim; **to s. to death** mourir de faim; *Fam* **I'm starving!** je meurs de faim! • **starvation** [-'veɪʃən] *n* faim *f*

state[1] [steɪt] **1** *n* **(a)** *(condition)* état *m; (situation)* situation *f*; **not in a (fit) s. to…, in no (fit) s. to…** hors d'état de… **(b) S.** *(nation)* État *m; Fam* **the States** les États-Unis *mpl* **2** *adj (secret)* d'État; *Br (school, education)* public, -ique; **s. visit** voyage *m* officiel

state[2] [steɪt] *vt* déclarer (**that** que); *(opinion)* formuler • **statement** *n* déclaration *f; (in court)* déposition *f*; **(bank) s.** relevé *m* de compte

station ['steɪʃən] *n (for trains)* gare *f; (underground)* station *f; (social)* rang *m*; **bus s.** gare *f* routière; **radio s.** station *f* de radio; *Am* **s. wagon** break *m*

stationary ['steɪʃənərɪ] *adj (vehicle)* à l'arrêt

stationer ['steɪʃənə(r)] *n* papetier, -ère *mf*; **s.'s (shop)** papeterie *f* • **stationery** *n (articles)* articles *mpl* de bureau; *(paper)* papier *m*

statistic [stə'tɪstɪk] *n (fact)* statistique *f*; **statistics** *(science)* la statistique

statue ['stætʃuː] n statue f

status ['steɪtəs] n (position) situation f; (legal, official) statut m; (prestige) prestige m; **s. symbol** marque f de prestige

stay [steɪ] **1** n (visit) séjour m **2** vi (remain) rester; (reside) loger; (visit) séjourner; **to s. put** ne pas bouger

►**stay away** vi ne pas s'approcher (**from** de)

►**stay behind** vi rester

►**stay in** vi (at home) rester à la maison; (of nail, screw, tooth) tenir

►**stay out** vi (outside) rester dehors; (not come home) ne pas rentrer; **to s. out of sth** (not interfere in) ne pas se mêler de qch; (avoid) éviter qch

►**stay up** vi (at night) ne pas se coucher; (of fence) tenir; **to s. up late** se coucher tard

steady ['stedɪ] **1** (**-ier, -iest**) adj (firm, stable) stable; (hand, voice) assuré; (progress, speed, demand) constant; **to be s. on one's feet** être solide sur ses jambes **2** vt faire tenir; **to s. one's nerves** se calmer; **to s. oneself** retrouver son équilibre ● **steadily** adv (gradually) progressivement; (regularly) régulièrement; (continuously) sans arrêt; (walk) d'un pas assuré

steak [steɪk] n (beef) steak m

steal [stiːl] (pt **stole**, pp **stolen**) vti voler (**from sb** à qn)

stealthy ['stelθɪ] (**-ier, -iest**) adj furtif, -ive

steam [stiːm] **1** n vapeur f; (on glass) buée f; Fam **to let off s.** se défouler; **s. engine** locomotive f à vapeur **2** vt (food) cuire à la vapeur **3** vi **to s. up** (of glass) s'embuer

steel [stiːl] n acier m

steep [stiːp] (**-er, -est**) adj (stairs, slope) raide; (hill, path) escarpé; Fig (price) excessif, -ive

steeple ['stiːpəl] n clocher m

steer [stɪə(r)] **1** vt diriger **2** vi (of person) conduire; (of ship) se diriger (**for** vers); **to s. clear of sb/sth** éviter qn/qch ● **steering** n (in vehicle) direction f; **s. wheel** volant m

stem [stem] **1** n (of plant) tige f **2** vi **to s. from sth** provenir de qch

stench [stentʃ] n puanteur f

step [step] **1** n (movement, sound) pas m; (of stairs) marche f; (doorstep) pas de la porte; Fig (action) mesure f; (**flight of**) **steps** (indoors) escalier m; (outdoors) perron m; **s. by s.** pas à pas **2** (pt & pp **-pp-**) vi (walk) marcher (**on** sur) ● **stepdaughter** n belle-fille f ● **stepfather** n beau-père m ● **stepladder** n escabeau m ● **stepmother** n belle-mère f ● **stepson** n beau-fils m

►**step aside** vi s'écarter

►**step back** vi reculer

►**step forward** vi faire un pas en avant

►**step in** vi (intervene) intervenir

►**step over** vt insep (obstacle) enjamber

stereo ['sterɪəʊ] (pl **-os**) n chaîne f stéréo

stereotype ['sterɪətaɪp] n stéréotype m

sterilize ['sterəlaɪz] vt stériliser ● **sterile** [Br 'steraɪl, Am 'sterəl] adj stérile

sterling ['stɜːlɪŋ] n Br (currency) livre f sterling

stern [stɜːn] (**-er, -est**) adj sévère

stethoscope ['steθəskəʊp] n stéthoscope m

stew [stjuː] **1** n ragoût m **2** vt (meat) faire cuire en ragoût; (fruit) faire de la compote de; **stewed fruit** compote f

steward ['stjuːəd] *n (on plane, ship)* steward *m* • **stewardess** *n (on plane)* hôtesse *f*

stick¹ [stɪk] *n (piece of wood, chalk, dynamite)* bâton *m; (for walking)* canne *f*

stick² [stɪk] **1** *(pt & pp* **stuck**) *vt (glue)* coller; *Fam (put)* fourrer; **to s. sth into sth** fourrer qch dans qch **2** *vi* coller (**to** à); *(of food in pan)* attacher (**to** dans); *(of drawer)* se coincer • **sticker** *n* autocollant *m* • **sticky** (**-ier, -iest**) *adj* collant; *(label)* adhésif, -ive

▶**stick by** *vt insep* rester fidèle à

▶**stick on** *vt sep (stamp, label)* coller

▶**stick out 1** *vt sep (tongue)* tirer; *Fam (head or arm from window)* sortir **2** *vi (of shirt)* dépasser; *(of tooth)* avancer

▶**stick up for** *vt insep* défendre

stiff [stɪf] (**-er, -est**) *adj* raide; *(joint)* ankylosé; *(brush, paste)* dur; **to have a s. neck** avoir un torticolis, *Fam* **to be bored s.** s'ennuyer à mourir

stifle ['staɪfəl] **1** *vt (feeling, person)* étouffer **2** *vi* **it's stifling** on étouffe

stigma ['stɪgmə] *n (moral stain)* flétrissure *f*

stiletto [stɪ'letəʊ] *adj Br* **s. heels** talons *mpl* aiguille

still¹ [stɪl] *adv* encore, toujours; *(even)* encore; *(nevertheless)* tout de même; **better s.** encore mieux

still² [stɪl] (**-er, -est**) *adj (not moving)* immobile; *(calm)* calme; *Br (drink)* non gazeux, -euse; **to stand s.** rester immobile; **s. life** nature *f* morte

stimulate ['stɪmjʊleɪt] *vt* stimuler

sting [stɪŋ] **1** *n* piqûre *f* **2** *(pt & pp* **stung**) *vt (of insect, ointment, wind)* piquer **3** *vi* piquer

stingy ['stɪndʒɪ] (**-ier, -iest**) *adj* avare

stink [stɪŋk] **1** *n* puanteur *f* **2** *(pt & pp* **stank** *or* **stunk,** *pp* **stunk**) *vi* puer

stir [stɜː(r)] **1** *n* **to give sth a s.** remuer qch; *Fig* **to cause a s.** faire du bruit **2** *(pt & pp* **-rr-**) *vt (coffee)* remuer; *Fig (excite)* exciter; **to s. up trouble** semer la zizanie; **to s. things up** envenimer les choses **3** *vi (move)* remuer, bouger

stitch [stɪtʃ] **1** *n* point *m; (in knitting)* maille *f; (in wound)* point *m* de suture; *(sharp pain)* point *m* de côté **2** *vt* **to s. (up)** *(sew up)* coudre; *Med* recoudre

stock [stɒk] **1** *n (supply)* provisions *fpl; Com* stock *m; (soup)* bouillon *m; Fin* **stocks and shares** valeurs *fpl* mobilières; **in s.** *(goods)* en stock; **out of s.** *(goods)* épuisé; (**of** de); **the S. Exchange** *or* **Market** la Bourse **2** *vt (sell)* vendre; *(keep in store)* stocker; **to s. (up)** *(shop)* approvisionner; *(fridge, cupboard)* remplir **3** *vi* **to s. up** s'approvisionner (**with** en)

stole [stəʊl] *pt of* **steal** • **stolen** *pp of* **steal**

stomach ['stʌmək] *n* ventre *m; (organ)* estomac *m* • **stomachache** *n* mal *m* de ventre; **to have (a) s.** avoir mal au ventre

stone [stəʊn] *n* pierre *f; (pebble)* caillou *m; (in fruit)* noyau *m; Br (unit of weight)* = 6,348 kg

stood [stʊd] *pt & pp of* **stand**

stool [stuːl] *n* tabouret *m*

stoop [stuːp] *vi* se baisser; *Fig* **to s. to doing sth** s'abaisser à faire qch

stop [stɒp] **1** *n (place, halt)* arrêt *m; (for plane, ship)* escale *f;* **to put a s. to sth** mettre fin à qch; **to come to a s.** s'arrêter; **s. sign**

(on road) stop **2** *(pt & pp* **-pp-***)* *vt* arrêter; *(end)* mettre fin à; *(cheque)* faire opposition à; **to s. sb/sth from doing sth** empêcher qn/qch de faire qch **3** *vi* s'arrêter; *(of pain, bleeding)* cesser; *(stay)* rester; **to s. snowing** cesser de neiger ● **stopover** *n* arrêt *m*; *(in plane journey)* escale *f* ● **stopwatch** *n* chronomètre *m*

▶**stop off, stop over** *vi (on journey)* s'arrêter

stopper ['stɒpə(r)] *n* bouchon *m*

store [stɔː(r)] **1** *n (supply)* provision *f*; *(shop)* Br grand magasin *m*, Am magasin *m*; **to have sth in s. for sb** réserver qch à qn **2** *vt (furniture)* entreposer; *(food)* ranger ● **storage** *n* emmagasinage *m*; **s. space** espace *m* de rangement ● **storeroom** *n (in house)* débarras *m*; *(in office, shop)* réserve *f*

storey ['stɔːrɪ] *(pl* **-eys***) n Br (of building)* étage *m*

stork [stɔːk] *n* cigogne *f*

storm [stɔːm] **1** *n (bad weather)* tempête *f*; *(thunderstorm)* orage *m* **2** *vi* **to s. out** *(angrily)* sortir comme une furie ● **stormy** *(***-ier, -iest***) adj (weather, meeting)* orageux, -euse

story[1] ['stɔːrɪ] *(pl* **-ies***) n* histoire *f*

story[2] ['stɔːrɪ] *(pl* **-ies***) n Am =* **storey**

stout [staʊt] *(***-er, -est***) adj (person)* corpulent; *(shoes)* solide

stove [stəʊv] *n (for cooking)* cuisinière *f*; *(for heating)* poêle *m*

straddle ['strædəl] *vt (chair, fence)* se mettre à califourchon sur; *(step over, span)* enjamber

straight [streɪt] **1** *(***-er, -est***) adj* droit; *(hair)* raide; *(honest)* honnête; *(answer)* clair; *Fam (heterosexual)* hétéro **2** *adv (in*

straight line) droit; *(directly)* directement; *(immediately)* tout de suite; *Br* **s. ahead** *or* **on** *(walk)* tout droit; **to look s. ahead** regarder droit devant soi ● **straightaway** [-ə'weɪ] *adv* tout de suite ● **straighten** *vt* redresser ● **straightforward** [-'fɔːwed] *adj (easy, clear)* simple; *(frank)* franc *(f* franche)

strain [streɪn] **1** *n* tension *f*; *(mental stress)* stress *m* **2** *vt* **(a)** *(rope, wire)* tendre excessivement; *(muscle)* se froisser; *(ankle, wrist)* se fouler; *(eyes)* fatiguer; *Fig (patience, friendship)* mettre à l'épreuve; **to s. oneself** *(hurt oneself)* se faire mal; *(tire oneself)* se fatiguer **(b)** *(soup)* passer; *(vegetables)* égoutter **3** *vi* faire un effort **(to do** pour faire)

strand [strænd] *n (of hair)* mèche *f*

stranded ['strændɪd] *adj (person, vehicle)* en rade

strange [streɪndʒ] *(***-er, -est***) adj (odd)* bizarre; *(unknown)* inconnu ● **strangely** *adv* étrangement; **s. (enough), she...** chose étrange, elle... ● **stranger** *n (unknown)* inconnu, -e *mf*; *(outsider)* étranger, -ère *mf*

strangle ['stræŋgəl] *vt* étrangler

strap [stræp] **1** *n* sangle *f*; *(on dress)* bretelle *f*; *(on watch)* bracelet *m*; *(on sandal)* lanière *f* **2** *(pt & pp* **-pp-***) vt* **to s. (down** *or* **in)** attacher *(avec une sangle)*; **to s. sb in** attacher qn avec une ceinture de sécurité

strategy ['strætədʒɪ] *(pl* **-ies***)* stratégie *f*

straw [strɔː] *n (from wheat, for drinking)* paille *f*

strawberry ['strɔːbərɪ] **1** *(pl* **-ies***) n* fraise *f* **2** *adj (flavour, ice cream)* à la fraise; *(jam)* de fraises; *(tart)* aux fraises

stray [streɪ] **1** *adj (animal, bullet)* perdu; **a few s. cars** quelques rares voitures **2** *n (dog)* chien *m* errant; *(cat)* chat *m* égaré **3** *vi* s'égarer; **to s. from** *(subject, path)* s'écarter de

streak [striːk] *n (of paint, dirt)* traînée *f*; *(in hair)* mèche *f*

stream [striːm] **1** *n (brook)* ruisseau *m*; *(of light, blood)* jet *m*; *(of people)* flot *m* **2** *vi* ruisseler (**with** de); **to s. in** *(of sunlight, people)* entrer à flots

street [striːt] *n* rue *f*; **s. lamp, s. light** lampadaire *m*; **s. map** plan *m* des rues ● **streetcar** *n Am (tram)* tramway *m*

strength [streŋθ] *n* force *f*; *(of wood, fabric)* solidité *f* ● **strengthen** *vt (building, position)* renforcer; *(body, limb)* fortifier

strenuous ['strenjʊəs] *adj (effort)* vigoureux, -euse; *(work)* fatigant

stress [stres] **1** *n (physical)* tension *f*; *(mental)* stress *m*; *(emphasis, in grammar)* accent *m*; **under s.** *(person)* stressé, sous pression; *(relationship)* tendu **2** *vt* insister sur; *(word)* accentuer; **to s. that...** souligner que... ● **stressful** *adj* stressant

stretch [stretʃ] **1** *n (area)* étendue *f*; *(period of time)* période *f*; *(of road)* tronçon *m* **2** *vt (rope, neck)* tendre; *(shoe, rubber)* étirer; *Fig (income, supplies)* faire durer; **to s. (out)** *(arm, leg)* tendre; *Fig* **to s. one's legs** se dégourdir les jambes **3** *vi (of person, elastic)* s'étirer; *(of influence)* s'étendre; **to s. (out)** *(of rope, plain)* s'étendre

stretcher ['stretʃə(r)] *n* brancard *m*

strict [strɪkt] **(-er, -est)** *adj*

(severe, absolute) strict ● **strictly** *adv* strictement; **s. forbidden** formellement interdit

stride [straɪd] **1** *n* pas *m* **2** *(pt* **strode,** *pp* **stridden** ['strɪdən]) *vi* **to s. across** *or* **over** *(fields)* traverser à grandes enjambées; **to s. along/out** avancer/sortir à grands pas

strike [straɪk] **1** *n (of workers)* grève *f*; **to go on s.** se mettre en grève **2** *(pt & pp* **struck)** *vt (hit, impress)* frapper; *(match)* craquer; **it strikes me that...** il me semble que... *(+ indicative)* **3** *vi (of workers)* faire grève; *(attack)* attaquer ● **striking** *adj (impressive)* frappant

▶**strike back** *vi (retaliate)* riposter

▶**strike down** *vt sep (of illness)* terrasser

▶**strike off** *vt sep (from list)* rayer (**from** de); **to be struck off** *(of doctor)* être radié

▶**strike up** *vt sep* **to s. up a friendship** se lier amitié (**with sb** avec qn)

string [strɪŋ] *n* ficelle *f*; *(of violin, racket)* corde *f*; *(of questions)* série *f*; *Fig* **to pull strings** faire jouer ses relations

strip [strɪp] **1** *n (piece)* bande *f*; *(of metal)* lame *f*; *(of sports team)* tenue *f*; **s. cartoon** bande *f* dessinée **2** *(pt & pp* **-pp-)** *vt (undress)* déshabiller; *(deprive)* dépouiller (**of** de); **to s. off** *(remove)* enlever **3** *vi* **to s. (off)** *(get undressed)* se déshabiller ● **stripper** *n (woman)* strip-teaseuse *f*; **paint s.** *(substance)* décapant *m*

stripe [straɪp] *n* rayure *f* ● **striped** *adj* rayé (**with** de)

strode [strəud] *pt of* **stride**

stroke [strəuk] **1** *n (movement)* coup *m*; *(of brush)* touche *f*;

(caress) caresse *f*; *Med (illness)* attaque *f*; **s. of luck** coup *m* de chance **2** *vt (caress)* caresser

stroll [strəʊl] **1** *n* promenade *f* **2** *vi* se promener; **to s. in** entrer sans se presser ● **stroller** *n Am (for baby)* poussette *f*

strong [strɒŋ] **1** (**-er, -est**) *adj* fort; *(shoes, chair, nerves)* solide; *(interest)* vif (*f* vive); *(supporter)* ardent **2** *adv* **to be going s.** aller toujours bien ● **strongly** *adv (protest, defend)* énergiquement; *(advise, remind, desire)* fortement

struck [strʌk] *pt & pp of* **strike**

structure ['strʌktʃə(r)] *n* structure *f*; *(building)* édifice *m*

struggle ['strʌgəl] **1** *n (fight)* lutte *f* (**to do** pour faire); **to have a s. doing** *or* **to do sth** avoir du mal à faire qch **2** *vi (fight)* lutter (**with** avec); **to be struggling** *(financially)* avoir du mal; **to s. to do sth** s'efforcer de faire qch

strut [strʌt] *(pt & pp* **-tt-**) *vi* **to s.** **(about** *or* **around)** se pavaner

stub [stʌb] **1** *n (of pencil, cigarette)* bout *m*; *(of cheque)* talon *m* **2** (*pt & pp* **-bb-**) *vt* **to s. one's toe** se cogner l'orteil (**on** *or* **against** contre); **to s. out** *(cigarette)* écraser

stubble ['stʌbəl] *n (on face)* barbe *f* de plusieurs jours

stubborn ['stʌbən] *adj (person)* têtu

stuck [stʌk] **1** *pt & pp of* **stick²** **2** *adj (caught, jammed)* coincé; **s. in bed/indoors** cloué au lit/chez soi; **to get s.** être coincé; **to be s. with sb/sth** se farcir qn/qch ● **stuck-up** *adj Fam* snob

stud [stʌd] *n (on football boot)* crampon *m*; *(earring)* clou *m* d'oreille

student ['stjuːdənt] **1** *n (at*

university) étudiant, -e *mf*; *(at school)* élève *mf*; **music s.** étudiant, -e *mf* en musique **2** *adj (life, protest)* étudiant; *(residence, grant)* universitaire

studio ['stjuːdɪəʊ] *(pl* **-os**) *n* studio *m*; *(of artist)* atelier *m*; *Br* **s. flat,** *Am* **s. apartment** studio *m*

study ['stʌdɪ] **1** *(pl* **-ies**) *n* étude *f*; *(office)* bureau *m* **2** *(pp & pp* **-ied**) *vt (learn, observe)* étudier **3** *vi* étudier; **to s. to be a doctor** faire des études de médecine; **to s. for an exam** préparer un examen ● **studious** ['stjuːdɪəs] *adj (person)* studieux, -euse

stuff [stʌf] **1** *n (possessions)* affaires *fpl*; *Fam* **some s.** *(substance)* un truc; *(things)* des trucs; *Fam* **this s.'s good, it's good s.** c'est bien **2** *vt (pocket)* remplir (**with** de); *(animal)* empailler; *(chicken, tomatoes)* farcir; **to s. sth into sth** fourrer qch dans qch ● **stuffing** *n (for chicken, tomatoes)* farce *f*

stuffy ['stʌfɪ] (**-ier, -iest**) *adj (room)* qui sent le renfermé; *(person)* vieux jeu *inv*

stumble ['stʌmbəl] *vi* trébucher; **to s. across** *or* **on** *(find)* tomber sur

stump [stʌmp] *n (of tree)* souche *f*; *(of limb)* moignon *m*

stun [stʌn] *(pt & pp* **-nn-**) *vt (make unconscious)* assommer; *Fig (amaze)* stupéfier ● **stunned** *adj (amazed)* stupéfait (**by** par) ● **stunning** *adj Fam (excellent)* excellent; *Fam (beautiful)* superbe

stung [stʌŋ] *pt & pp of* **sting**

stunk [stʌŋk] *pt & pp of* **stink**

stunt [stʌnt] *n (in film)* cascade *f*; **s. man** cascadeur *m*

stupid ['stjuːpɪd] *adj* stupide; **to do/say a s. thing** faire/dire une stupidité ● **stupidity** [-'pɪdɪtɪ] *n* stupidité *f*

sturdy ['stɜːdɪ] (**-ier, -iest**) *adj* *(person, shoe)* robuste

stutter ['stʌtə(r)] **1** *n* **to have a s.** être bègue **2** *vti* bégayer

style [staɪl] *n* style *m* • **stylish** *adj* chic *inv*

sub- [sʌb] *pref* sous-, sub-

subconscious [sʌb'kɒnʃəs] *adj & n* subconscient *(m)* • **subconsciously** *adv* inconsciemment

subdued [səb'djuːd] *adj* *(light)* tamisé; *(voice, tone)* bas (*f* basse); *(person)* inhabituellement calme

subject¹ ['sʌbdʒɪkt] *n* *(topic, in grammar)* sujet *m*; *(at school, university)* matière *f*

subject² **1** ['sʌbdʒekt] *adj* **s. to my agreement** sous réserve de mon accord **2** [səb'dʒekt] *vt* soumettre (**to** à)

subjective [səb'dʒektɪv] *adj* subjectif, -ive

subjunctive [səb'dʒʌŋktɪv] *n* subjonctif *m*

submarine ['sʌbməriːn] *n* sous-marin *m*

submerge [səb'mɜːdʒ] *vt* *(flood, overwhelm)* submerger; *(immerse)* immerger (**in** dans)

submit [səb'mɪt] **1** (*pt & pp* **-tt-**) *vt* soumettre (**to** à) **2** *vi* se soumettre (**to** à)

subordinate [sə'bɔːdɪnət] **1** *adj* subalterne; **s. to** subordonné à **2** *n* subordonné, -e *mf*

subscribe [səb'skraɪb] *vi* *(pay money)* cotiser (**to** à); **to s. to a newspaper** s'abonner à un journal • **subscriber** *n* *(to newspaper, telephone)* abonné, -e *mf* • **subscription** [sʌb'skrɪpʃən] *n* *(to newspaper)* abonnement *m*; *(to club)* cotisation *f*

subsequent ['sʌbsɪkwənt] *adj* ultérieur (**to** à); **our s. problems** les problèmes que nous avons eus

par la suite • **subsequently** *adv* par la suite

subside [səb'saɪd] *vi* *(of ground, building)* s'affaisser; *(of wind, flood, fever)* baisser

subsidiary [*Br* səb'sɪdɪərɪ, *Am* -dɪerɪ] *adj* subsidiaire

subsidize ['sʌbsɪdaɪz] *vt* subventionner • **subsidy** (*pl* **-ies**) *n* subvention *f*

substance ['sʌbstəns] *n* substance *f*; *(solidity, worth)* fondement *m*

substantial [səb'stænʃəl] *adj* important; *(meal)* substantiel, -elle • **substantially** *adv* considérablement

substitute ['sʌbstɪtjuːt] **1** *n* *(thing)* produit *m* de remplacement; *(person)* remplaçant, -e *mf* (**for** de) **2** *vt* **to s. sb/sth for** substituer qn/qch à **3** *vi* **to s. for sb** remplacer qn • **substitution** [-'tjuːʃən] *n* substitution *f*

subtitle ['sʌbtaɪtəl] **1** *n* *(of film)* sous-titre *m* **2** *vt* *(film)* sous-titrer

subtle ['sʌtəl] (**-er, -est**) *adj* subtil

subtract [səb'trækt] *vt* soustraire (**from** de) • **subtraction** *n* soustraction *f*

suburb ['sʌbɜːb] *n* banlieue *f*; **the suburbs** la banlieue • **suburban** [sə'bɜːbən] *adj* *(train, house)* de banlieue

subway ['sʌbweɪ] *n* *Br* *(under road)* passage *m* souterrain; *Am* *(railroad)* métro *m*

succeed [sək'siːd] **1** *vt* **to s. sb** succéder à qn **2** *vi* réussir (**in doing** à faire; **in sth** dans qch)

success [sək'ses] *n* succès *m*, réussite *f*; **he was a s.** il a eu du succès; **it was a s.** c'était réussi • **successful** *adj* *(effort, venture)* couronné de succès; *(company, businessman)* prospère; *(candidate in exam)* admis, reçu; *(candidate* *in election)* élu; *(writer, film)* à succès; **to be s.** réussir (**in doing** à faire) ● **successfully** *adv* avec succès

succession [sək'seʃən] *n* succession *f*; **ten days in s.** dix jours consécutifs

succumb [sə'kʌm] *vi* succomber (**to** à)

such [sʌtʃ] **1** *adj (of this or that kind)* tel (*f* telle); **s. a car** une telle voiture; **s. happiness/noise** tant de bonheur/bruit; **there's no s. thing** ça n'existe pas; **s. as** comme, tel que **2** *adv (so very)* si; *(in comparisons)* aussi; **s. long trips** de si longs voyages **3** *pron* **happiness as s.** le bonheur en tant que tel ● **suchlike** *pron & adj* **...and s.** ...et autres

suck [sʌk] *vt* sucer; *(of baby)* téter; **to s. (up)** *(with straw, pump)* aspirer; **to s. up** *or* **in** *(absorb)* absorber

sudden ['sʌdən] *adj* soudain; **all of a s.** tout à coup ● **suddenly** *adv* tout à coup, soudain; *(die)* subitement

sue [suː] **1** *vt* poursuivre (en justice) **2** *vi* engager des poursuites judiciaires

suede [sweɪd] *n* daim *m*

suffer ['sʌfə(r)] **1** *vt (loss, damage, defeat)* subir; *(pain)* ressentir **2** *vi* souffrir (**from** de); **your work will s.** ton travail s'en ressentira ● **sufferer** *n (from misfortune)* victime *f*; **AIDS s.** malade *mf* du SIDA ● **suffering** *n* souffrance *f*

sufficient [sə'fɪʃənt] *adj* suffisant; **s. money** *(enough)* suffisamment d'argent; **to be s.** suffire ● **sufficiently** *adv* suffisamment

suffix ['sʌfɪks] *n* suffixe *m*

suffocate ['sʌfəkeɪt] **1** *vt* étouffer **2** *vi* suffoquer

sugar ['ʃʊɡə(r)] *n* sucre *m*; **s. bowl** sucrier *m*; **s. lump** morceau *m* de sucre

suggest [sə'dʒest] *vt (propose)* suggérer; *(imply)* indiquer ● **suggestion** *n* suggestion *f* ● **suggestive** *adj* suggestif, -ive; **to be s. of** évoquer

suicide ['suːɪsaɪd] *n* suicide *m*; **to commit s.** se suicider

suit[1] [suːt] *n* **(a)** *(man's)* costume *m*; *(woman's)* tailleur *m*; **diving/ ski s.** combinaison *f* de plongée/ ski **(b)** *(in card games)* couleur *f*; *Fig* **to follow s.** faire de même

suit[2] [suːt] *vt (please, be acceptable to)* convenir à; *(of dress, colour)* aller (bien) à; *(adapt)* adapter (**to** à); **suited to** *(job, activity)* fait pour; *(appropriate to)* qui convient à; **to be well suited** *(of couple)* être bien assorti ● **suitable** *adj* convenable (**for** à); *(candidate, date)* adéquat; *(example)* approprié; **this film is not s. for children** ce film n'est pas pour les enfants

suitcase ['suːtkeɪs] *n* valise *f*

suite [swiːt] *n (rooms)* suite *f*

sulk [sʌlk] *vi* bouder

sullen ['sʌlən] *adj* maussade

sultana [sʌl'tɑːnə] *n (raisin)* raisin *m* de Smyrne

sum [sʌm] **1** *n (amount of money)* somme *f*; *(mathematical problem)* problème *m* **2** *(pt & pp* **-mm-***) vti* **to s. up** *(summarize)* résumer

summarize ['sʌməraɪz] *vt* résumer ● **summary** *(pl* **-ies***) n* résumé *m*

summer ['sʌmə(r)] **1** *n* été *m*; **in (the) s.** en été **2** *adj* d'été; *Am* **s. camp** colonie *f* de vacances; *Br* **s. holidays,** *Am* **s. vacation** grandes vacances *fpl* ● **summertime** *n* été *m*; **in (the) s.** en été

summit [ˈsʌmɪt] *n* sommet *m*

summon [ˈsʌmən] *vt (call)* appeler; *(meeting, person)* convoquer (**to** à); **to s. up one's courage/ strength** rassembler son courage/ ses forces

sun [sʌn] *n* soleil *m*; **in the s.** au soleil; **the s. is shining** il fait soleil • **sunbathe** *vi* prendre un bain de soleil • **sunbed** *n* lit *m* à ultraviolets • **sunblock** *n (cream)* écran *m* total • **sunburnt** *adj* brûlé par le soleil • **sunflower** *n* tournesol *m* • **sunglasses** *npl* lunettes *fpl* de soleil • **sunhat** *n* chapeau *m* de soleil • **sunlight** *n* lumière *f* du soleil • **sunrise** *n* lever *m* du soleil • **sunroof** *n (in car)* toit *m* ouvrant • **sunset** *n* coucher *m* du soleil • **sunshade** *n (on table)* parasol *m*; *(portable)* ombrelle *f* • **sunshine** *n* soleil *m* • **suntan** *n* bronzage *m*; **s. lotion/ oil** crème *f*/huile *f* solaire • **sunny** (**-ier, -iest**) *adj (day)* ensoleillé; **it's s.** il fait soleil

Sunday [ˈsʌndeɪ] *n* dimanche *m*; **S. school** ≃ catéchisme *m*

sung [sʌŋ] *pp of* **sing**

sunk [sʌŋk] *pp of* **sink²**

super [ˈsuːpə(r)] *adj Fam* super *inv*

super- [ˈsuːpə(r)] *pref* super-

superb [suːˈpɜːb] *adj* superbe

superficial [suːpəˈfɪʃəl] *adj* superficiel, -elle

superglue [ˈsuːpəgluː] *n* colle *f* extra-forte

superior [suːˈpɪərɪə(r)] **1** *adj* supérieur (**to** à) **2** *n (person)* supérieur, -eure *mf* • **superiority** [-rɪˈɒrətɪ] *n* supériorité *f*

superlative [suːˈpɜːlətɪv] *adj & n Gram* superlatif *(m)*

supermarket [ˈsuːpəmɑːkɪt] *n* supermarché *m*

supernatural [suːpəˈnætʃərəl] *adj & n* surnaturel, -elle *(m)*

superstition [suːpəˈstɪʃən] *n* superstition *f* • **superstitious** *adj* superstitieux, -euse

supervise [ˈsuːpəvaɪz] *vt (person, work)* surveiller; *(research)* superviser • **supervisor** *n* surveillant, -e *mf*; *(in office)* chef *m* de service

supper [ˈsʌpə(r)] *n (meal)* dîner *m*; *(snack)* = casse-croûte pris avant d'aller se coucher

supple [ˈsʌpəl] *adj* souple

supplement 1 [ˈsʌplɪmənt] *n* supplément *m* (**to** à) **2** [ˈsʌplɪment] *vt* compléter; **to s. one's income** arrondir ses fins de mois • **supplementary** [-ˈmentərɪ] *adj* supplémentaire

supply [səˈplaɪ] **1** (*pl* **-ies**) *n (stock)* provision *f*; **s. and demand** l'offre *f* et la demande; *Br* **s. teacher** suppléant, -e *mf* **2** (*pt & pp* **-ied**) *vt (provide)* fournir; *(equip)* équiper (**with** de); **to s. sb with sth, to s. sth to sb** fournir qch à qn

support [səˈpɔːt] **1** *n (backing, person supporting)* soutien *m*; *(thing supporting)* support *m* **2** *vt (bear weight of)* supporter; *(help, encourage)* soutenir; *(theory, idea)* appuyer; *(family)* subvenir aux besoins de • **supporter** *n* partisan *m*; *(of sports team)* supporter *m* • **supportive** *adj* **to be s. of sb** être d'un grand soutien à qn

suppose [səˈpəʊz] *vti* supposer (**that** que); **I'm supposed to be working** je suis censé travailler; **he's supposed to be rich** on le dit riche; **I s. (so)** je pense; **s. or supposing (that) you're right** supposons que tu aies raison

suppress [səˈpres] *vt (revolt, feelings, smile)* réprimer; *(fact, evidence)* faire disparaître

supreme [suːˈpriːm] *adj* suprême

sure [ʃʊə(r)] (**-er, -est**) *adj* sûr (**of** de; **that** que); **she's s. to accept** c'est sûr qu'elle acceptera; **to make s. of sth** s'assurer de qch; **for s.** à coup sûr; *Fam* **s.!, s. thing!** bien sûr! • **surely** *adv* (*certainly*) sûrement; **s. he didn't refuse?** il n'a quand même pas refusé?

surf [sɜːf] **1** *n* (*waves*) ressac *m* **2** *vt Comptr* **to s. the Net** naviguer sur Internet • **surfboard** *n* planche *f* de surf • **surfing** *n* (*sport*) surf *m*; **to go s.** faire du surf

surface [ˈsɜːfɪs] *n* surface *f*; **s. area** superficie *f*; **on the s.** (*of water*) à la surface; *Fig* (*to all appearances*) en apparence

surge [ˈsɜːdʒ] *n* (*of enthusiasm*) vague *f*; (*of anger, pride*) bouffée *f*

surgeon [ˈsɜːdʒən] *n* chirurgien *m* • **surgery** [ˈsɜːdʒərɪ] *n Br* (*doctor's office*) cabinet *m*; (*science*) chirurgie *f*; **to have heart s.** se faire opérer du cœur

surname [ˈsɜːneɪm] *n* nom *m* de famille

surplus [ˈsɜːpləs] **1** *n* surplus *m* **2** *adj* (*goods*) en surplus

surprise [səˈpraɪz] **1** *n* surprise *f*; **to give sb a s.** faire une surprise à qn; **s. visit/result** visite *f*/résultat *m* inattendu(e) **2** *vt* étonner, surprendre • **surprised** *adj* surpris (**that** que + *subjunctive*; **at sth** de qch; **at seeing** de voir) • **surprising** *adj* surprenant

surrender [səˈrendə(r)] *vi* (*give oneself up*) se rendre (**to** à)

surrogate [ˈsʌrəgət] *n* substitut *m*; **s. mother** mère *f* porteuse

surround [səˈraʊnd] *vt* entourer (**with** de); (*of army, police*) cerner; **surrounded by** entouré de • **surrounding** *adj* environnant • **surroundings** *npl* (*of town*) environs *mpl*; (*setting*) cadre *m*

survey 1 [ˈsɜːveɪ] *n* (*investigation*) enquête *f*; (*of opinion*) sondage *m*; (*of house*) inspection *f* **2** [səˈveɪ] *vt* (*look at*) regarder; (*review*) passer en revue; (*house*) inspecter; (*land*) faire un relevé de • **surveyor** [səˈveɪə(r)] *n* (*of land*) géomètre *m*; (*of house*) expert *m*

survive [səˈvaɪv] **1** *vt* survivre à **2** *vi* survivre • **survival** *n* (*act*) survie *f*; (*relic*) vestige *m* • **survivor** *n* survivant, -e *mf*

susceptible [səˈseptəbəl] *adj* (*sensitive*) sensible (**to** à)

suspect 1 [ˈsʌspekt] *n & adj* suspect, -e (*mf*) **2** [səˈspekt] *vt* soupçonner (**sb of sth** qn de qch; **sb of doing** qn d'avoir fait); (*have intuition of*) se douter de

suspend [səˈspend] *vt* (**a**) (*hang*) suspendre (**from** à) (**b**) (*service, employee, player*) suspendre; (*pupil*) renvoyer temporairement • **suspense** *n* suspense *m*; **to keep sb in s.** tenir qn en haleine

suspicion [səˈspɪʃən] *n* soupçon *m*; **to be under s.** être soupçonné • **suspicious** *adj* (*person*) soupçonneux, -euse; (*behaviour*) suspect; **to be s. of** *or* **about sth** se méfier de qch

sustain [səˈsteɪn] *vt* (*effort, theory*) soutenir; (*damage, loss, attack*) subir; **to s. an injury** être blessé

swagger [ˈswægə(r)] *vi* (*walk*) se pavaner

swallow [ˈswɒləʊ] *vt* avaler; **to s. sth down** avaler qch

swam [swæm] *pt of* **swim**

swamp [swɒmp] **1** *n* marais *m* **2** *vt* (*flood, overwhelm*) submerger (**with** de)

swan [swɒn] *n* cygne *m*

swap [swɒp] **1** n échange m **2** (pt & pp **-pp-**) vt échanger (**for** contre); **to s. seats** or **places** changer de place **3** vi échanger

swarm [swɔːm] n (of bees, people) essaim m

swat [swɒt] (pt & pp **-tt-**) vt écraser

sway [sweɪ] **1** vt balancer; Fig (person, public opinion) influencer **2** vi se balancer

swear [sweə(r)] **1** (pt **swore**, pp **sworn**) vt (promise) jurer (**to do** de faire; **that** que); **to s. an oath** prêter serment **2** vi (take an oath) jurer (**to sth** de qch); **to s. at sb** injurier qn • **swearword** n juron m

sweat [swet] **1** n sueur f **2** vi suer • **sweatshirt** n sweat-shirt m • **sweaty** (**-ier**, **-iest**) adj (shirt) plein de sueur; (hand) moite; (person) en sueur

sweater ['swetə(r)] n pull m

Swede [swiːd] n Suédois, -e mf • **Sweden** n la Suède • **Swedish 1** adj suédois **2** n (language) suédois m

sweep [swiːp] **1** (pt & pp **swept**) vt (with broom) balayer; (chimney) ramoner **2** vi balayer
►**sweep aside** vt sep (opposition, criticism) écarter
►**sweep up** vt sep & vi balayer

sweet [swiːt] **1** (**-er**, **-est**) adj doux (f douce); (tea, coffee, cake) sucré; (pretty, kind) adorable; **to have a s. tooth** aimer les sucreries **2** n Br (piece of confectionery) bonbon m; Br (dessert) dessert m; Br **s. shop** confiserie f • **sweetcorn** n Br maïs m • **sweetheart** [-hɑːt] n chéri, -e mf

swell [swel] (pt **swelled**, pp **swollen** or **swelled**) vi (of hand, leg) enfler; (of river) grossir; **to s. up** (of body part) enfler •

swelling n (on body) enflure f

sweltering ['sweltərɪŋ] adj étouffant; **it's s.** on étouffe

swept [swept] pt & pp of **sweep**

swerve [swɜːv] vi (of vehicle) faire une embardée; (of player) faire un écart

swift [swɪft] (**-er**, **-est**) adj rapide • **swiftly** adv rapidement

swim [swɪm] **1** n **to go for a s.** aller nager **2** (pt **swam**, pp **swum**, pres p **swimming**) vt (river) traverser à la nage; (length, crawl) nager **3** vi nager; (as sport) faire de la natation; **to go swimming** aller nager; **to s. away** s'éloigner à la nage • **swimmer** n nageur, -euse mf • **swimming** n natation f; **s. cap** bonnet m de bain; Br **s. costume** maillot m de bain; Br **s. pool** piscine f; **s. trunks** slip m de bain

swindle ['swɪndəl] vt escroquer

swing [swɪŋ] **1** n (in playground) balançoire f; (movement) balance-ment m **2** (pt & pp **swung**) vt (arms, legs) balancer **3** vi (sway) se balancer; (turn) virer; **to s. round** (turn suddenly) se retourner

swipe [swaɪp] vt (card) passer dans un lecteur de cartes; Fam **to s. sth** (steal) faucher qch (**from sb** à qn)

swirl [swɜːl] vi tourbillonner

Swiss [swɪs] **1** adj suisse; Br **S. roll** roulé m **2** n inv Suisse m, Suissesse f; **the S.** les Suisses mpl

switch [swɪtʃ] **1** n (electrical) interrupteur m; (change) change-ment m (**in** de); (reversal) re-virement m (**in** de) **2** vt (support, affection) reporter (**to** sur) **3** vi **to s. to** (change to) passer à • **switchboard** n Tel standard m
►**switch off 1** vt sep (lamp, gas, radio) éteindre; (engine) arrêter;

(electricity) couper **2** *vi (of appliance)* s'éteindre

▶**switch on 1** *vt sep (lamp, gas, radio)* allumer; *(engine)* mettre en marche **2** *vi (of appliance)* s'allumer

▶**switch over** *vi (change TV channels)* changer de chaîne; **to s. over to** *(change to)* passer à

Switzerland ['swɪtsələnd] *n* la Suisse

swivel ['swɪvəl] **1** (*Br* **-ll-,** *Am* **-l-**) *vi* **to s. (round)** *(of chair)* pivoter **2** *adj* **s. chair** chaise *f* pivotante

swollen ['swəʊlən] **1** *pp of* **swell 2** *adj (leg)* enflé; *(stomach)* gonflé

swoop [swuːp] *vi* faire une descente **(on** dans); **to s. (down) on** *(of bird)* fondre sur

swop [swɒp] *n & vti* = **swap**

sword [sɔːd] *n* épée *f*

swore [swɔː(r)] *pt of* **swear** • **sworn** *pp of* **swear**

swot [swɒt] *Br Fam Pej* **1** *n* bûcheur, -euse *mf* **2** (*pt & pp* **-tt-**) *vti* **to s. (up)** bûcher; **to s. up on sth** bûcher qch

swum [swʌm] *pp of* **swim**

swung [swʌŋ] *pt & pp of* **swing**

syllable ['sɪləbəl] *n* syllabe *f*

syllabus ['sɪləbəs] *n* programme *m*

symbol ['sɪmbəl] *n* symbole *m* • **symbolic** [-'bɒlɪk] *adj* symbolique • **symbolize** *vt* symboliser

symmetrical [sɪ'metrɪkəl] *adj* symétrique

sympathetic [sɪmpə'θetɪk] *adj (showing pity)* compatissant;

(understanding) compréhensif, -ive; **s. to sb/sth** *(favourable)* bien disposé à l'égard de qn/qch • **sympathize** ['sɪmpəθaɪz] *vi* **I s. with you** *(pity)* je suis désolé (pour vous); *(understanding)* je vous comprends • **sympathy** ['sɪmpəθɪ] *n (pity)* compassion *f*; *(understanding)* compréhension *f*; **to have s. for sb** éprouver de la compassion pour qn

symphony ['sɪmfənɪ] (*pl* **-ies**) *n* symphonie *f*

symptom ['sɪmptəm] *n Med & Fig* symptôme *m*

synagogue ['sɪnəgɒg] *n* synagogue *f*

synchronize ['sɪŋkrənaɪz] *vt* synchroniser

syndicate ['sɪndɪkət] *n* syndicat *m*

syndrome ['sɪndrəʊm] *n Med & Fig* syndrome *m*

synonym ['sɪnənɪm] *n* synonyme *m*

synopsis [sɪ'nɒpsɪs] (*pl* **-opses** [-ɒpsiːz]) *n* résumé *m*; *(of film)* synopsis *m*

synthetic [sɪn'θetɪk] *adj* synthétique

syringe [sə'rɪndʒ] *n* seringue *f*

syrup ['sɪrəp] *n* sirop *m*; *Br* **(golden) s.** mélasse *f* raffinée

system ['sɪstəm] *n (structure) & Comptr* système *m*; *(method)* méthode *f*; **the digestive s.** l'appareil *m* digestif • **systematic** [-'mætɪk] *adj* systématique

Tt

T, t [tiː] *n (letter)* T, t *m inv*

tab [tæb] *n* **(a)** *(label)* étiquette *f*
(b) *Am Fam (bill)* addition *f*

table ['teɪbəl] *n* **(a)** *(furniture)*
table *f*; *Br* **to set** *or* **lay/clear
the t.** mettre/débarrasser la table;
(sitting) at the t. à table; **t.
tennis** tennis *m* de table **(b)** *(list)*
table *f*; **t. of contents** table *f* des
matières • **tablecloth** *n* nappe
f • **tablespoon** *n* ≃ cuillère *f* à
soupe

tablet ['tæblɪt] *n (pill)* comprimé
m

tabloid ['tæblɔɪd] *n (newspaper)*
tabloïd *m*

taboo [tə'buː] *(pl* **-oos)** *adj & n*
tabou *(m)*

tackle ['tækəl] **1** *n (in rugby)*
placage *m*; *(in football)* tacle *m*
2 *vt (task, problem)* s'attaquer à;
(rugby player) plaquer; *(football
player)* tacler

tacky ['tækɪ] **(-ier, -iest)** *adj Fam*
minable; *(jewellery, decor)* kitch
inv

tact [tækt] *n* tact *m* • **tactful** *adj*
(remark) diplomatique; **to be t.**
(of person) avoir du tact • **tactless**
adj (person, remark) qui manque
de tact

tactic ['tæktɪk] *n* **a t.** une tactique;
tactics la tactique

tag [tæg] **1** *n (label)* étiquette *f*
2 *vi* **to t. along with sb** venir
avec qn

tail [teɪl] **1** *n (of animal)* queue *f*;

the t. end la fin **(of** de) **2** *vi* **to t.
off** *(lessen)* diminuer

tailor ['teɪlə(r)] **1** *n (person)*
tailleur *m* **2** *vt Fig (adjust)* adapter
(to à)

tainted ['teɪntɪd] *adj (air)* pollué;
(food) gâté; *Fig (reputation,
system)* souillé

take [teɪk] *(pt* **took,** *pp* **taken)**
vt prendre; *(bring)* amener **(to** à);
(by car) conduire **(to** à); *(escort)*
accompagner **(to** à); *(lead away)*
emmener **(to** à); *(exam)* passer;
(credit card) accepter; *(tolerate)*
supporter; **to t. sth to sb** apporter
qch à qn; **to t. sth with one**
emporter qch; **it takes courage** il
faut du courage **(to do** pour faire);
I took an hour to do it j'ai mis
une heure à le faire; **I t. it that...**
je présume que... • **takeaway**
Br **1** *adj (meal)* à emporter **2** *n*
(shop) restaurant *m* qui fait des
plats à emporter; *(meal)* plat *m* à
emporter • **taken** *adj (seat)* pris;
(impressed) impressionné **(with**
or **by** par); **to be t. ill** tomber
malade • **takeoff** *n (of plane)*
décollage *m* • **take-out** *adj & n*
Am = **takeaway** • **takeover** *n*
(of company) rachat *m*

▶**take after** *vt insep* **to t. after sb**
ressembler à qn

▶**take apart** *vt sep (machine)*
démonter

▶**take away** *vt sep (thing)*
emporter; *(person)* emmener;

(remove) enlever (**from** à); *Math (subtract)* soustraire (**from** de)

▶**take back** *vt sep* reprendre; *(return)* rapporter; *(statement)* retirer; *(accompany)* ramener (**to** à)

▶**take down** *vt sep (object)* descendre; *(notes)* prendre

▶**take in** *vt sep (chair, car)* rentrer; *(understand)* saisir; *Fam (deceive)* rouler

▶**take off** **1** *vt sep (remove)* enlever; *(lead away)* emmener **2** *vi (of aircraft)* décoller

▶**take on** *vt sep (work, staff, passenger, shape)* prendre

▶**take out** *vt sep (from pocket)* sortir; *(tooth)* arracher; *(insurance policy)* prendre; *Fam* **to t. it out on sb** passer sa colère sur qn

▶**take over** **1** *vt sep (become responsible for)* reprendre; *(buy out)* racheter; *(overrun)* envahir; **to t. over sb's job** remplacer qn **2** *vi (relieve)* prendre la relève (**from** de); *(succeed)* prendre la succession (**from** de)

▶**take up** *vt sep (carry up)* monter; *(continue)* reprendre; *(space, time)* prendre; *(offer)* accepter; *(hobby)* se mettre à

tale [teɪl] *n (story)* histoire *f*; **to tell tales** rapporter (**on sb** sur qn)

talent ['tælənt] *n* talent *m* • **talented** *adj* talentueux, -euse

talk [tɔːk] **1** *n (conversation)* conversation *f* (**about** à propos de); *(lecture)* exposé *m* (**on** sur); **to have a t. with sb** parler avec qn **2** *vt (nonsense)* dire; **to t. politics** parler politique; **to t. sb into doing/out of doing sth** persuader qn de faire/de ne pas faire qch; **to t. sth over** discuter (de) qch **3** *vi* parler (**to/about**

à/de); *(gossip)* jaser • **talkative** *adj* bavard

tall [tɔːl] (**-er, -est**) *adj (person)* grand; *(tree, house)* haut

tambourine [tæmbə'riːn] *n* tambourin *m*

tame [teɪm] **1** (**-er, -est**) *adj (animal)* apprivoisé; *Fig (book, play)* fade **2** *vt (animal)* apprivoiser

tamper ['tæmpə(r)] *vt insep* **to t. with** *(lock, car)* essayer de forcer; *(machine)* toucher à; *(documents)* trafiquer

tampon ['tæmpɒn] *n* tampon *m* (hygiénique)

tan [tæn] *n (suntan)* bronzage *m*

tangerine [tændʒə'riːn] *n* mandarine *f*

tangle ['tæŋgəl] *n* **to get into a t.** *(of rope)* s'enchevêtrer; *(of hair)* s'emmêler; *Fig (of person)* s'embrouiller • **tangled** *adj* enchevêtré; *(hair)* emmêlé

tango ['tæŋgəʊ] (*pl* **-os**) *n* tango *m*

tangy ['tæŋɪ] (**-ier, -iest**) *adj* acidulé

tank [tæŋk] *n (container)* réservoir *m*; *(military vehicle)* tank *m*; (**fish**) **t.** aquarium *m*

tantrum ['tæntrəm] *n* caprice *m*

tap¹ [tæp] *n Br (for water)* robinet *m*; **t. water** eau *f* du robinet

tap² [tæp] **1** *n (blow)* petit coup *m*; **t. dancing** claquettes *fpl* **2** (*pt & pp* **-pp-**) *vt (hit)* tapoter

tape [teɪp] **1** *n* (**a**) *(ribbon)* ruban *m*; (**sticky** *or* **adhesive**) **t.** ruban *m* adhésif; **t. measure** mètre *m* (à) ruban (**b**) *(for recording)* bande *f*; *(cassette)* cassette *f*; **t. recorder** magnétophone *m* **2** *vt* (**a**) *(stick)* scotcher (**b**) *(record)* enregistrer

tapestry ['tæpəstrɪ] *n* tapisserie *f*

tar [tɑː(r)] *n* goudron *m*

target ['tɑːgɪt] *n* cible *f*; *(objective)* objectif *m*

tariff ['tærɪf] *n Br (price list)* tarif *m*

tarmac ['tɑːmæk] *n Br (on road)* macadam *m*; *(runway)* piste *f*

tart [tɑːt] *n (pie) (large)* tarte *f*; *(small)* tartelette *f*

tartan ['tɑːtən] **1** *n* tartan *m* **2** *adj (skirt, tie)* écossais

task [tɑːsk] *n* tâche *f*

tassel ['tæsəl] *n* gland *m*

taste [teɪst] **1** *n* goût *m*; **in good/bad t.** de bon/mauvais goût; **to have a t. of sth** goûter à qch **2** *vt (detect flavour of)* sentir; *(sample)* goûter **3** *vi* **to t. of** *or* **like sth** avoir un goût de qch; **to t. good** être bon (*f* bonne) • **tasteful** *adj* de bon goût • **tasteless** *adj (food)* insipide; *Fig (joke)* de mauvais goût • **tasty** (**-ier, -iest**) *adj* savoureux, -euse

tattoo [tæ'tuː] **1** (*pl* **-oos**) *n (design)* tatouage *m* **2** (*pt & pp* **-ooed**) *vt* tatouer

taught [tɔːt] *pt & pp of* **teach**

taunt [tɔːnt] *vt* railler

taut [tɔːt] *adj* tendu

tax [tæks] **1** *n (on goods)* taxe *f*, impôt *m*; *(on income)* impôts *mpl*; *Br* **road t.** ≃ vignette *f* automobile **2** *adj* fiscal; **t. collector** percepteur *m*; *Br* **(road) t. disc** ≃ vignette *f* automobile • **tax-free** *adj* exempt d'impôts • **taxpayer** *n* contribuable *mf*

taxi ['tæksɪ] *n* taxi *m*; *Br* **t. rank,** *Am* **t. stand** station *f* de taxis

tea [tiː] *n (plant, drink)* thé *m*; *Br (snack)* goûter *m*; *Br* **t. break** ≃ pause-café *f*; **t. leaves** feuilles *fpl* de thé; **t. set** service *m* à thé; *Br* **t. towel** torchon *m* • **teabag** *n* sachet *m* de thé • **teacup** *n* tasse *f* à thé • **teapot** *n* théière

f • **teaspoon** *n* petite cuillère *f*

• **teatime** *n (in the afternoon)* l'heure *f* du thé; *(in the evening)* l'heure *f* du dîner

teach [tiːtʃ] **1** (*pt & pp* **taught**) *vt* apprendre (**sb sth** qch à qn; **that** que); *(in school, at university)* enseigner (**sb sth** qch à qn); **to t. sb (how) to do sth** apprendre à qn à faire qch **2** *vi* enseigner • **teacher** *n* professeur *m*; *(in primary school)* instituteur, -trice *mf* • **teaching** *n* enseignement *m*

team [tiːm] *n* équipe *f*; **t. mate** coéquipier, -ère *mf*

tear¹ [teə(r)] **1** *n* déchirure *f* **2** (*pt* **tore**, *pp* **torn**) *vt (rip)* déchirer; *(snatch)* arracher (**from** à); **to t. off** *or* **out** arracher; **to t. up** déchirer **3** *vi* **to t. along/past** aller/passer à toute vitesse

tear² [tɪə(r)] *n* larme *f*; **in tears** en larmes

tease [tiːz] *vt* taquiner

technical ['teknɪkəl] *adj* technique

technique [tek'niːk] *n* technique *f*

technology [tek'nɒlədʒɪ] (*pl* **-ies**) *n* technologie *f*

tedious ['tiːdɪəs] *adj* fastidieux, -euse

teenage ['tiːneɪdʒ] *adj (boy, girl, behaviour)* adolescent; *(fashion, magazine)* pour adolescents • **teenager** *n* adolescent, -e *mf* • **teens** *npl* **to be in one's t.** être adolescent

tee-shirt ['tiːʃɜːt] *n* tee-shirt *m*

teeth [tiːθ] *pl of* **tooth**

teetotaller [tiː'təʊtələ(r)] (*Am* **teetotaler**) *n* = personne qui ne boit jamais d'alcool

telephone ['telɪfəʊn] **1** *n* téléphone *m*; **to be on the t.** être au téléphone **2** *adj (call, line,* *message)* téléphonique; *Br* **t. booth, t. box** cabine *f* téléphonique; **t. directory** annuaire *m* du téléphone; **t. number** numéro *m* de téléphone **3** *vt (message)* téléphoner (**to** à); **to t. sb** téléphoner à qn **4** *vi* téléphoner

telescope ['telɪskəʊp] *n* télescope *m*

television [telɪ'vɪʒən] **1** *n* télévision *f*; **on (the) t.** à la télévision **2** *adj (programme, screen)* de télévision; *(interview, report)* télévisé

tell [tel] **1** (*pt & pp* **told**) *vt* dire (**sb sth** qch à qn; **that** que); *(story)* raconter; *(distinguish)* distinguer (**from** de); **to t. sb to do sth** dire à qn de faire qch; **to t. the difference** voir la différence (**between** entre); **I could t. she was lying** je savais qu'elle mentait; *Fam* **to t. sb off** disputer qn **2** *vi* dire; *(have an effect)* se faire sentir; **to t. of** *or* **about sb/sth** parler de qn/qch; **you can never t.** on ne sait jamais; *Fam* **to t. on sb** dénoncer qn

telly ['telɪ] *n Br Fam* télé *f*; **on the t.** à la télé

temp [temp] *Br Fam* **1** *n* intérimaire *mf* **2** *vi* faire de l'intérim

temper ['tempə(r)] *n (mood, nature)* humeur *f*; *(bad mood)* mauvaise humeur *f*; **in a bad t.** de mauvaise humeur; **to lose one's t.** se mettre en colère

temperamental [tempərə'mentəl] *adj (person, machine)* capricieux, -euse

temperature ['tempərətʃə(r)] *n* température *f*

temple ['tempəl] *n (religious building)* temple *m*

temporary [*Br* 'tempərərɪ, *Am* -erɪ] *adj* temporaire; *(secretary)*

intérimaire • **temporarily** [*Br* tempə'reərəlɪ, *Am* tempə'reərəlɪ] *adv* temporairement

tempt [tempt] *vt* tenter; **tempted to do sth** tenté de faire qch • **temptation** [-'teɪʃən] *n* tentation *f* • **tempting** *adj* tentant

ten [ten] *adj & n* dix *(m)*

tenant ['tenənt] *n* locataire *mf*

tend¹ [tend] *vi* **to t. to do sth** avoir tendance à faire qch; **to t. towards** incliner vers • **tendency** *(pl* **-ies)** *n* tendance *f* (**to do** à faire)

tend² [tend] *vt (look after)* s'occuper de

tender ['tendə(r)] *adj (soft, delicate, loving)* tendre; *(painful)* sensible

tenner ['tenə(r)] *n Br Fam* billet *m* de 10 livres

tennis ['tenɪs] *n* tennis *m*; **t. court** court *m* de tennis

tenpin ['tenpɪn] *adj Br* **t. bowling** bowling *m*

tense¹ [tens] **1** (**-er, -est**) *adj (person, muscle, situation)* tendu **2** *vt* tendre; *(muscle)* contracter • **tension** [-ʃən] *n* tension *f*

tense² [tens] *n Gram* temps *m*

tent [tent] *n* tente *f*; *Br* **t. peg** piquet *m* de tente; *Br* **t. pole,** *Am* **t. stake** mât *m* de tente

tenth [tenθ] *adj & n* dixième *(mf)*; **a t.** *(fraction)* un dixième

tepid ['tepɪd] *adj* tiède

term [tɜːm] *n (word)* terme *m*; *(period)* période *f*; *Br (of school or university year)* trimestre *m*; *Am (semester)* semestre *m*; **terms** *(conditions)* conditions *fpl*; *(of contract)* termes *mpl*; **to be on good/bad terms** être en bons/ mauvais termes (**with sb** avec qn); **in terms of** *(speaking of)* sur le plan de; **to come to terms**

with sth se résigner à qch; **in the long/short/medium t.** à long/court/moyen terme

terminal ['tɜːmɪnəl] **1** n (air) t. aérogare f **2** adj (patient, illness) en phase terminale

terminate ['tɜːmɪneɪt] **1** vt mettre fin à; (contract) résilier; (pregnancy) interrompre **2** vi se terminer

terminus ['tɜːmɪnəs] n terminus m

terrace ['terɪs] n (next to house, on hill) terrasse f; Br (houses) = rangée de maisons attenantes; Br **the terraces** (at football ground) les gradins mpl • **terraced** n Br **t. house** = maison située dans une rangée d'habitations attenantes

terrain [tə'reɪn] n terrain m

terrible ['terəbəl] adj terrible • **terribly** adv Fam (extremely) terriblement; (badly) affreusement mal

torrific [tə'rɪfɪk] adj Fam (excellent) super inv

terrify ['terɪfaɪ] (pt & pp -ied) vt terrifier; **to be terrified of sb/sth** avoir une peur bleue de qn/qch • **terrifying** adj terrifiant

territory ['terɪtərɪ] (pl -ies) n territoire m

terror ['terə(r)] n terreur f • **terrorism** n terrorisme m • **terrorist** n & adj terroriste (mf) • **terrorize** vt terroriser

test [test] **1** n (trial) essai m; (of product) test m; Sch & Univ interrogation f; (by doctor) examen m; (of blood) analyse f **2** adj **t. drive** essai m sur route; **t. tube** éprouvette f **3** vt (try) essayer; (product, machine) tester; (pupil) interroger; (of doctor) examiner; (blood) analyser; Fig (try out) mettre à l'épreuve; **to t.**

sb for AIDS faire subir à qn un test de dépistage du SIDA **4** vi **to t. positive** (for drugs) être positif, -ive

testament ['testəmənt] n (will) testament m; (tribute) preuve f; Rel **the Old/New T.** l'Ancien/le Nouveau Testament

testify ['testɪfaɪ] (pt & pp -ied) vi (in law) témoigner (**against** contre); **to t. to sth** (be proof of) témoigner de qch • **testimony** ['testɪmənɪ] (pl -ies) n témoignage m

text [tekst] n texte m; **t. message** message m texte, mini-message m • **textbook** n manuel m

textile ['tekstaɪl] n textile m

texture ['tekstʃə(r)] n (of fabric, cake) texture f; (of paper, wood) grain m

Thames [temz] n **the (River) T.** la Tamise

than [ðən, stressed ðæn] conj que; happier t. me plus heureux que moi; **he has more/less t. you** il en a plus/moins que toi; **more t. six** plus de six

thank [θæŋk] vt remercier (**for sth** de qch; **for doing** d'avoir fait); **t. you** merci; **no, t. you** (non) merci; **t. God!, t. heavens!, t. goodness!** Dieu merci! • **thankful** adj reconnaissant (**for** de); **to be t. that...** être heureux, -euse que... (+ subjunctive) • **thanks** npl remerciements mpl; **(many) t.!** merci (beaucoup)!; **t. to** (because of) grâce à • **Thanksgiving** n Am **T. (Day)** = quatrième jeudi de novembre, commémorant la première action de grâce des colons anglais

that [ðæt] **1** conj [unstressed ðət] (conjonction souvent omise) que;

she said t. she **would come** elle a dit qu'elle viendrait **2** *relative pron* [*unstressed* ðət]

On peut omettre le pronom relatif **that** sauf s'il est en position sujet.

(subject) qui; *(object)* que; *(with preposition)* lequel, laquelle, *pl* lesquel(le)s; **the boy t. left** le garçon qui est parti; **the book t. I read** le livre que j'ai lu; **the house t. she told me about** la maison dont elle m'a parlé; **the day/morning t. she arrived** le jour/matin où elle est arrivée **3** (*pl* **those**) *demonstrative adj* ce, cet *(before vowel or mute h)*, cette; *(opposed to 'this')* ce…-là (*f* cette…-là); **t. woman** cette femme(-là); **t. day** ce jour-là; **t. one** celui-là *m*, celle-là *f* **4** (*pl* **those**) *demonstrative pron* cela, *Fam* ça; **give me t.** donne-moi ça; **t.'s right** c'est exact; **who's t.?** qui est-ce?; **t.'s the house** voilà la maison; **what do you mean by t.?** qu'entends-tu par là?; **t. is (to say)…** c'est-à-dire… **5** *adv Fam (so)* si; **not t. good** pas si bon que ça; **it cost t. much** ça a coûté tant que ça

thatched [θætʃt] *adj (roof)* de chaume

thaw [θɔː] **1** *vt (snow, ice)* faire fondre; **to t. (out)** *(food)* se décongeler **2** *vi* dégeler; *(of snow, ice)* fondre; *(of food)* décongeler

the [ðə, *before vowel* ðɪ, *stressed* ðiː] *definite article* le, l', la, *pl* les; **of t., from t.** du, de l', de la, *pl* des; **to t., at t.** au, à l', à la, *pl* aux; **Elizabeth t. Second** Élisabeth Deux

theatre [ˈθɪətə(r)] *(Am* **theater)** *n (place, art)* théâtre *m*; *Br*

(operating) t. *(in hospital)* salle *f* d'opération • **theatrical** [θɪˈætrɪkəl] *adj also Fig* théâtral

theft [θeft] *n* vol *m*

their [ðeə(r)] *possessive adj* leur, *pl* leurs • **theirs** *possessive pron* le leur, la leur, *pl* les leurs; **this book is t.** ce livre est à eux *ou* est le leur; **a friend of t.** un ami à eux

them [ðəm, *stressed* ðem] *pron* les; *(after prep, 'than', 'it is')* eux *mpl*, elles *fpl*; **(to) t.** *(indirect)* leur; **I see t.** je les vois; **I gave it (to) t.** je le leur ai donné; **ten of t.** dix d'entre eux/elles; **all of t. came** tous/toutes sont venu(e)s; **I like all of t.** je les aime tous/toutes • **themselves** *pron* eux-mêmes *mpl*, elles-mêmes *fpl*; *(reflexive)* se, s'; *(after prep)* eux *mpl*, elles *fpl*; **they cut t.** ils/elles se sont coupé(e)s

theme [θiːm] *n* thème *m*; **t. tune** *(of TV, radio programme)* indicatif *m*; **t. park** parc *m* à thème

then [ðen] *adv (at that time)* à cette époque-là, alors; *(just a moment ago)* à ce moment-là; *(next)* ensuite, puis; *(therefore)* donc, alors; **from t. on** dès lors; **before t.** avant cela; **until t.** jusque-là, jusqu'alors

theory [ˈθɪərɪ] (*pl* **-ies**) *n* théorie *f*; **in t.** en théorie • **theoretical** *adj* théorique

therapy [ˈθerəpɪ] (*pl* **-ies**) *n* thérapie *f*

there [ðeə(r)] *adv* là; **(down/ over) t.** là-bas; **on t.** là-dessus; **she'll be t.** elle y sera; **t. is, t. are** il y a; *(pointing)* voilà; **t. he is** voilà; **that man t.** cet homme-là; **t. (you are)!** *(take this)* tenez! • **therefore** *adv* donc

thermometer [θəˈmɒmɪtə(r)] *n* thermomètre *m*

these [ði:z] (*sing* **this**) **1**
demonstrative adj ces; *(opposed
to 'those')* ces...-ci; **t. men** ces
hommes(-ci); **t. ones** ceux-ci *mpl*,
celles-ci *fpl* **2** *demonstrative pron*
ceux-ci *mpl*, celles-ci *fpl*; **t. are my
friends** ce sont mes amis
thesis ['θi:sɪs] (*pl* **theses** ['θi:si:z])
n thèse *f*
they [ðeɪ] *pron* (a) *(subject)* ils
mpl, elles *fpl*; *(stressed)* eux *mpl*,
elles *fpl*; **t. are doctors** ce sont des
médecins (b) *(people in general)*
on • **they'd** = **they had, they
would** • **they'll** = **they will**
thick [θɪk] **1** (**-er, -est**) *adj* épais
(*f* épaisse); *Fam (stupid)* bête **2**
adv (spread) en couche épaisse
• **thicken 1** *vt* épaissir **2** *vi (of
fog)* s'épaissir; *(of cream, sauce)*
épaissir • **thickly** *adv (spread)*
en couche épaisse • **thickness** *n*
épaisseur *f*
thief [θi:f] (*pl* **thieves**) *n* voleur,
-euse *mf*
thigh [θaɪ] *n* cuisse *f*
thimble ['θɪmbəl] *n* dé *m* à
coudre
thin [θɪn] **1** (**thinner, thinnest**)
adj (person, slice, paper) mince;
(soup) peu épais (*f* peu épaisse);
(crowd, hair) clairsemé **2** *adv
(spread)* en couche mince; *(cut)* en
tranches minces **3** (*pt & pp* **-nn-**)
vt **to t. (down)** *(paint)* diluer **4** *vi*
to t. out *(of crowd, mist)* s'éclaircir
• **thinly** *adv (spread)* en couche
mince; *(cut)* en tranches minces
thing [θɪŋ] *n* chose *f*; **things**
(belongings, clothes) affaires *fpl*;
poor little t.! pauvre petit!; **how
are things?,** *Fam* **how's things?**
comment ça va?; **for one t....
and for another t....** d'abord...
et ensuite...
think [θɪŋk] **1** (*pt & pp* **thought**) *vt*

penser (**that** que); **I t. so** je pense
ou crois que oui; **what do you
t. of him?** que penses-tu de lui?;
to t. out *(plan, method)* élaborer;
(reply) réfléchir sérieusement à;
to t. sth over réfléchir à qch; **to
t. sth up** *(invent)* inventer qch
2 *vi* penser (**about/of** à); **to t.
(carefully)** réfléchir (**about/of** à);
to t. of doing sth penser à faire
qch; **to t. highly of sb** penser
beaucoup de bien de qn **3** *n Fam*
to have a t. réfléchir (**about** à)
third [θɜːd] **1** *adj* troisième; **the
T. World** le tiers-monde **2** *n*
troisième *mf*; **a t.** *(fraction)* un
tiers **3** *adv* **to come t.** *(in race)* se
classer troisième
thirst [θɜːst] *n* soif *f* (**for** de) •
thirsty (**-ier, -iest**) *adj* **to be** *or*
feel t. avoir soif; **to make sb t.**
donner soif à qn
thirteen [θɜːˈti:n] *adj & n* treize
(m) • **thirteenth** *adj & n* treizième
(mf)
thirty ['θɜːtɪ] *adj & n* trente *(m)* •
thirtieth *adj & n* trentième *(mf)*
this [ðɪs] **1** (*pl* **these**) *demonstrative
adj* ce, cet *(before vowel or mute
h)*, cette; *(opposed to 'that')* ce...-
ci; **t. man** cet homme(-ci); **t. one**
celui-ci *m*, celle-ci *f* **2** (*pl* **these**)
demonstrative pron (subject) ce,
ceci; *(object)* ceci; **I prefer t.** je
préfère celui-ci/celle-ci; **who's t.?**
qui est-ce?; **t. is Paul** c'est Paul;
(pointing) voici Paul **3** *adv (so)* **t.
high** *(pointing)* haut comme ceci;
t. far *(until now)* jusqu'ici
thistle ['θɪsəl] *n* chardon *m*
thorn [θɔːn] *n* épine *f*
thorough ['θʌrə] *adj (search,
cleaning, preparation)* minutieux,
-euse; *(knowledge, examination)*
approfondi • **thoroughly** *adv
(completely)* tout à fait; *(carefully)*

avec minutie; *(know, clean, wash)* à fond

those [ðəʊz] *(sing* **that)** **1** *demonstrative adj* ces; *(opposed to 'these')* ces...-là; **t. men** ces hommes(-là); **t. ones** ceux-là *mpl*, celles-là *fpl* **2** *demonstrative pron* ceux-là *mpl*, celles-là *fpl*; **t. are my friends** ce sont mes amis

though [ðəʊ] **1** *conj* bien que *(+ subjunctive)*; **(even) t.** même si; **as t.** comme si; **strange t. it may seem** si étrange que cela puisse paraître **2** *adv (however)* pourtant

thought [θɔːt] **1** *pt & pp of* **think** **2** *n* pensée *f*; **(careful) t.** réflexion *f*; **to have second thoughts** changer d'avis; *Br* **on second thoughts,** *Am* **on second t.** à la réflexion ● **thoughtful** *adj (considerate, kind)* attentionné; *(pensive)* pensif, -ive

thousand ['θaʊzənd] *adj & n* mille *(m) inv*; **a t. pages** mille pages; **two t. pages** deux mille pages; **thousands of** des milliers de

thrash [θræʃ] *vt* **to t. sb** donner une correction à qn; *(defeat)* écraser qn

thread [θred] **1** *n (yarn) &* Fig fil *m* **2** *vt (needle, beads)* enfiler

threat [θret] *n* menace *f* ● **threaten** *vti* menacer **(to do** de faire; **with sth** de qch) ● **threatening** *adj* menaçant

three [θriː] *adj & n* trois *(m)* ● **three-dimensional** *adj* à trois dimensions ● **three-quarters** *n* **t. (of)** les trois quarts *mpl* (de)

threshold ['θreʃhəʊld] *n* seuil *m*

threw [θruː] *pt of* **throw**

thrilled [θrɪld] *adj* ravi **(with sth** de qch; **to do** de faire) ● **thriller** *n* thriller *m*

thrive [θraɪv] *vi (of business, person, plant)* prospérer; **to**

t. on sth avoir besoin de qch pour s'épanouir ● **thriving** *adj (business)* prospère

throat [θrəʊt] *n* gorge *f*

throb [θrɒb] *(pt & pp* **-bb-)** *vi (of heart)* palpiter; **my head is throbbing** j'ai une douleur lancinante dans la tête

throne [θrəʊn] *n* trône *m*

through [θruː] **1** *prep (place)* à travers; *(by means of)* par; *(because of)* à cause de; **t. the window/door** par la fenêtre/porte; **t. ignorance** par ignorance; *Am* **Tuesday t. Saturday** de mardi à samedi **2** *adv* à travers; **to go t.** *(of bullet, nail)* traverser; **to let sb t.** laisser passer qn; **to be t. with sb/sth** *(finished)* en avoir fini avec qn/qch; **t. to** *or* **till** jusqu'à; **I'll put you t. (to him)** *(on telephone)* je vous le passe ● **throughout** [θruː'aʊt] **1** *prep* **t. the neighbourhood** dans tout le quartier; **t. the day** pendant toute la journée **2** *adv (everywhere)* partout; *(all the time)* tout le temps

throw [θrəʊ] **1** *n (in sport)* lancer *m*; *(of dice)* coup *m* **2** *(pt* **threw,** *pp* **thrown)** *vt* jeter **(to/at** à); *(javelin, discus)* lancer; *(party)* donner; *Fam (baffle)* déconcerter

▶**throw away** *vt sep (discard)* jeter; *Fig (life, chance)* gâcher

▶**throw out** *vt sep (unwanted object)* jeter; *(suggestion)* repousser; *(expel)* mettre à la porte

▶**throw up** *vi Fam (vomit)* vomir

thrust [θrʌst] *(pt & pp* **thrust)** *vt* **to t. sth into sth** enfoncer qch dans qch

thud [θʌd] *n* bruit *m* sourd

thug [θʌg] *n* voyou *m (pl* -ous)

thumb [θʌm] *n* pouce *m*

thump [θʌmp] **1** *n (blow)* coup *m*; *(noise)* bruit *m* sourd **2** *vt (hit)* frapper; **to t. one's head** se cogner la tête (**on** contre) **3** *vi* frapper, cogner (**on** sur); *(of heart)* battre la chamade

thunder ['θʌndə(r)] **1** *n* tonnerre *m* **2** *vi* tonner; **to t. past** *(of train, truck)* passer dans un bruit de tonnerre • **thunderstorm** *n* orage *m*

Thursday ['θɜːzdeɪ] *n* jeudi *m*

thus [ðʌs] *adv* ainsi

thyme [taɪm] *n* thym *m*

tick [tɪk] **1** *n (of clock)* tic-tac *m inv*; *(mark)* ≃ croix *f*; *Fam (moment)* instant *m* **2** *vt* **to t. sth (off)** *(on list)* cocher qch **3** *vi* faire tic-tac

ticket ['tɪkɪt] *n* billet *m*; *(for bus, metro)* ticket *m*; *Fam (for parking, speeding)* contravention *f*; **t. collector** contrôleur, -euse *mf*; **t. office** guichet *m*

tickle ['tɪkəl] *vt* chatouiller • **ticklish** *adj (person)* chatouilleux, -euse

tide [taɪd] **1** *n* marée *f* **2** *vt* **to t. sb over** dépanner qn

tidy ['taɪdɪ] **1** (-ier, -iest) *adj (place, toys)* bien rangé; *(clothes, hair)* soigné; *(person) (methodical)* ordonné; *(in appearance)* soigné **2** *vt* **to t. sth (up** or **away)** ranger qch; **to t. oneself up** s'arranger **3** *vi* **to t. up** ranger

tie [taɪ] **1** *n (garment)* cravate *f*; *(link)* lien *m*; *(draw)* égalité *f*; *(drawn match)* match *m* nul **2** *vt (fasten)* attacher (**to** à); *(knot)* faire (**in** à); *(shoe)* lacer **3** *vi (draw)* être à égalité; *(in match)* faire match nul; *(in race)* être ex aequo

▶**tie down** *vt sep* attacher

▶**tie up** *vt sep (animal)* attacher; *(parcel)* ficeler; *Fig* **to be tied up** *(busy)* être occupé

tier [tɪə(r)] *n (of seats)* gradin *m*; *(of cake)* étage *m*

tiger ['taɪɡə(r)] *n* tigre *m*

tight [taɪt] **1** (-er, -est) *adj (clothes, knot, race, bend)* serré; *(control)* strict; *Fam (mean)* radin **2** *adv (hold, shut)* bien; *(squeeze)* fort • **tighten** *vt* **to t. (up)** *(bolt)* serrer; *(rope)* tendre; *Fig (security)* renforcer • **tight-fitting** *adj (garment)* ajusté • **tightly** *adv (hold)* bien; *(squeeze)* fort • **tightrope** *n* corde *f* raide

tights [taɪts] *npl Br (garment)* collant *m*

tile [taɪl] *n (on roof)* tuile *f*; *(on wall, floor)* carreau *m* • **tiled** *adj (roof)* de tuiles; *(wall, floor)* carrelé

till[1] [tɪl] *prep & conj* = **until**

till[2] [tɪl] *n Br (for money)* caisse *f* enregistreuse

tilt [tɪlt] *vti* pencher

timber ['tɪmbə(r)] *n Br (wood)* bois *m* (de construction)

time [taɪm] **1** *n* temps *m*; *(period, moment)* moment *m*; *(age)* époque *f*; *(on clock)* heure *f*; *(occasion)* fois *f*; **in t., with t.** avec le temps; **it's t. to do sth** il est temps de faire qch; **some of the t.** *(not always)* une partie du temps; **most of the t.** la plupart du temps; **all (of) the t.** tout le temps; **in a year's t.** dans un an; **a long t.** longtemps; **a short t.** peu de temps; **to have a good** or **a nice t.** s'amuser (bien); **to have t. off** avoir du temps libre; **in no t. (at all)** en un rien de temps; **(just) in t.** *(arrive)* à temps (**for sth** pour qch; **to do** pour faire); **from t. to t.** de temps en temps; **what t. is it?** quelle heure est-il?; **on t.** à l'heure; **at the same t.** en même temps (**as** que); *(simultaneously)* à la fois; **for the t. being** pour le moment; **at the** or that t. à ce moment-là; **at times** parfois; **(the) next t. you come** la prochaine fois que tu viendras; **(the) last t.** la dernière fois; **one at a t.** un à un; **ten times ten** dix fois dix; **t. limit** délai *m*; **t. zone** fuseau *m* horaire **2** *vt (sportsman, worker)* chronométrer; *(activity, programme)* minuter ● **time-consuming** *adj* qui prend du temps ● **timer** *n (device)* minuteur *m*; *(sand-filled)* sablier *m* ● **timetable** *n* horaire *m*; *(in school)* emploi *m* du temps

timid ['tɪmɪd] *adj* timide

tin [tɪn] *n (metal)* étain *m*; *Br (can)* boîte *f*; **cake t.** moule *m* à gâteaux; **t. opener** ouvre-boîtes *m inv* ● **tinfoil** *n* papier *m* aluminium ● **tinned** *adj Br* **t. pears/salmon** poires *fpl*/saumon *m* en boîte; **t. food** conserves *fpl*

tingle ['tɪŋgəl] *vi* picoter

tinsel ['tɪnsəl] *n* guirlandes *fpl* de Noël

tinted ['tɪntɪd] *adj (glass)* teinté

tiny ['taɪnɪ] (**-ier**, **-iest**) *adj* minuscule

tip¹ [tɪp] *n (end)* bout *m*; *(pointed)* pointe *f*

tip² [tɪp] **1** *n Br (rubbish dump)* décharge *f* **2** *(pt & pp* **-pp-***) vt (pour)* déverser; **to t. sth up** *or* **over** renverser qch; **to t. sth out** *(liquid, load)* déverser qch **(into** dans) **3** *vi* **to t. (up** *or* **over)** *(tilt)* se renverser; *(overturn)* basculer

tip³ [tɪp] **1** *n (money)* pourboire *m*; *(advice)* conseil *m*; *(information)* tuyau *m* **2** *(pt & pp* **-pp-***) vt (waiter)* donner un pourboire à; **to t. off** *(police)* prévenir

tiptoe ['tɪptəʊ] **1** *n* **on t.** sur la pointe des pieds **2** *vi* marcher sur la pointe des pieds; **to t. into/out of a room** entrer dans une pièce/

sortir d'une pièce sur la pointe des pieds

tire¹ ['taɪə(r)] **1** *vt* fatiguer; **to t. sb out** épuiser qn **2** *vi* se fatiguer ● **tired** *adj* fatigué; **to be t. of sth/ doing sth** en avoir assez de qch/ de faire qch ● **tiring** *adj* fatigant

tire² ['taɪə(r)] *n Am* pneu *m* (*pl* pneus)

tissue ['tɪʃuː] *n (handkerchief)* mouchoir *m* en papier; **t. paper** papier *m* de soie

title ['taɪtəl] **1** *n* titre *m* **2** *vt* intituler

to [tə, *stressed* tuː] **1** *prep* **(a)** *(towards)* à; *(until)* jusqu'à; **give it to him/her** donne-le-lui; **to go to town** aller en ville; **to go to France/Portugal** aller en France/au Portugal; **to go to the butcher's** aller chez le boucher; **the road to London** la route de Londres; **the train to Paris** le train pour Paris; **kind/cruel to sb** gentil/cruel envers qn; **to my surprise** à ma grande surprise; **it's ten (minutes) to one** il est une heure moins dix; **ten to one** *(proportion)* dix contre un; **one person to a room** une personne par chambre **(b)** *(with infinitive)* **to say/jump** dire/sauter; **(in order) to do sth** pour faire qch; **she tried to** elle a essayé **(c)** *(with adjective)* **I'd be happy to do it** je serais heureux de le faire; **it's easy to do** c'est facile à faire **2** *adv* **to push the door to** fermer la porte; **to go** *or* **walk to and fro** aller et venir

toad [təʊd] *n* crapaud *m*

toadstool ['təʊdstuːl] *n* champignon *m* vénéneux

toast¹ [təʊst] **1** *n (bread)* pain *m*

grillé **2** *vt* *(bread)* faire griller •
toaster *n* grille-pain *m inv*
toast² [təʊst] **1** *n* *(drink)* toast *m*
2 *vt* *(person)* porter un toast à;
(success, event) arroser
tobacco [təˈbækəʊ] *(pl* **-os)** *n*
tabac *m*; *Am* **t. store** (bureau *m*
de) tabac
toboggan [təˈbɒgən] *n* luge *f*
today [təˈdeɪ] *adv* aujourd'hui
toddler [ˈtɒdlə(r)] *n* enfant *mf* (en
bas âge)
toe [təʊ] *n* orteil *m*
toffee [ˈtɒfɪ] *n Br* caramel *m* (dur);
t. apple pomme *f* d'amour
together [təˈgeðə(r)] *adv* ensemble; *(at the same time)* en même
temps
toilet [ˈtɔɪlɪt] *n Br (room)* toilettes
fpl; *(bowl, seat)* cuvette *f* des
toilettes; *Br* **to go to the t.** aller
aux toilettes; **t. paper** papier *m*
hygiénique; **t. roll** rouleau *m* de
papier hygiénique; *(paper)* papier
m hygiénique • **toiletries** *npl*
articles *mpl* de toilette
token [ˈtəʊkən] **1** *n (for vending
machine)* jeton *m*; *(symbol)* signe
m; *Br* **book t.** chèque-livre *m* **2**
adj symbolique
told [təʊld] *pt & pp of* **tell**
tolerate [ˈtɒləreɪt] *vt* tolérer •
tolerant [-rənt] *adj* tolérant *(of*
à l'égard de)
toll [təʊl] **1** *n* **(a)** *(fee)* péage *m*;
t. road/bridge route *f*/pont *m* à
péage **(b) the death t.** le nombre
de morts; *Fig* **to take its t.** faire
des dégâts **2** *vi (of bell)* sonner •
toll-free *Am adj* **t. number** ≈
numéro *m* vert
tomato [*Br* təˈmɑːtəʊ, *Am*
təˈmeɪtəʊ] *(pl* **-oes)** *n* tomate *f*; **t.
sauce** sauce *f* tomate
tomb [tuːm] *n* tombeau *m* •
tombstone *n* pierre *f* tombale

tomorrow [təˈmɒrəʊ] *adv & n*
demain *(m)*; **t. morning/evening**
demain matin/soir; **the day after
t.** après-demain
ton [tʌn] *n* tonne *f*; *Fam* **tons of**
(lots of) des tonnes de
tone [təʊn] **1** *n* ton *m*; *(of
telephone, radio)* tonalité *f*; *(of
answering machine)* signal *m*
sonore; *Br* **the engaged t.** *(on
telephone)* la sonnerie 'occupé' **2**
vt **to t. sth down** atténuer qch; **to
t. up** *(muscles, skin)* tonifier
tongs [tɒŋz] *npl* pinces *fpl*; **curling
t.** fer *m* à friser
tongue [tʌŋ] *n* *(in mouth,
language)* langue *f*
tonic [ˈtɒnɪk] *n (medicine)* fortifiant
m; **gin and t.** gin-tonic *m*
tonight [təˈnaɪt] *adv & n (this
evening)* ce soir *(m)*; *(during the
night)* cette nuit *(f)*
tonne [tʌn] *n (metric)* tonne *f*
tonsil [ˈtɒnsəl] *n* amygdale *f* •
tonsillitis [-ˈlaɪtɪs] *n* **to have t.**
avoir une angine
too [tuː] *adv* **(a)** *(excessively)* trop;
t. tired to play trop fatigué pour
jouer; **t. much, t. many** trop; **t.
much salt** trop de sel; **t. many
people** trop de gens; **one t.
many** un de trop **(b)** *(also)* aussi;
(moreover) en plus
took [tʊk] *pt of* **take**
tool [tuːl] *n* outil *m*; **t. kit** trousse
f à outils
tooth [tuːθ] *(pl* **teeth)** *n* dent *f*
• **toothache** *n* mal *m* de dents;
to have t. avoir mal aux dents •
toothbrush *n* brosse *f* à dents •
toothpaste *n* dentifrice *m*
top¹ [tɒp] **1** *n (of mountain, tower,
tree)* sommet *m*; *(of wall, ladder,
page)* haut *m*; *(of table, box,
surface)* dessus *m*; *(of list)* tête
f; *(of bottle, tube)* bouchon *m*;

(of pen) capuchon *m*; *(garment)* haut *m*; **(at the) t. of the class** le premier/la première de la classe; **on t.** dessus; **on t. of** sur; *Fig (in addition to)* en plus de; **from t. to bottom** de fond en comble; *Fam* **over the t.** *(excessive)* exagéré **2** *adj (drawer, shelf)* du haut; *(step, layer)* dernier, -ère; *(upper)* supérieur; *(in rank, exam)* premier, -ère; *(chief)* principal; *(best)* meilleur; **on the t. floor** au dernier étage; **at t. speed** à toute vitesse • **top-secret** *adj* top secret *inv*

top² [tɒp] *(pt & pp -pp-) vt (exceed)* dépasser; *Br* **to t. up** *(glass)* remplir (de nouveau); **topped with cream** nappé de crème • **topping** *n (of pizza)* garniture *f*

topic ['tɒpɪk] *n* sujet *m* • **topical** *adj* d'actualité

topple ['tɒpəl] *vi* **to t. (over)** tomber

torch [tɔːtʃ] *n Br (electric)* lampe *f* de poche; *(flame)* torche *f*

tore [tɔː(r)] *pt of* **tear¹**

torment 1 ['tɔːment] *n* supplice *m* **2** [tɔː'ment] *vt* tourmenter

torn [tɔːn] *pp of* **tear¹**

tornado [tɔː'neɪdəʊ] *(pl -oes) n* tornade *f*

torrential [tə'renʃəl] *adj* **t. rain** pluie *f* torrentielle

tortoise ['tɔːtəs] *n* tortue *f*

torture ['tɔːtʃə(r)] **1** *n* torture *f* **2** *vt* torturer

Tory ['tɔːrɪ] *Pol* **1** *n* tory *m* **2** *adj* tory *inv*

toss [tɒs] **1** *vt (throw)* lancer (**to** à); *(pancake)* faire sauter; **to t. a coin** jouer à pile ou face **2** *vi* **to t. (about), to t. and turn** *(in bed)* se tourner et se retourner; **let's t. for it** jouons-le à pile ou face

total ['təʊtəl] **1** *adj* total; **the t.**

sales le total des ventes **2** *n* total *m*; **in t.** au total • **totally** *adv* totalement

touch [tʌtʃ] **1** *n (contact)* contact *m*; *(sense)* toucher *m*; **a t. of** *(small amount)* une pointe de; **to have a t. of flu** être un peu grippé; **to be/ get in t. with sb** être/se mettre en contact avec qn **2** *vt* toucher; *(interfere with, eat)* toucher à **3** *vi (of lines, hands, ends)* se toucher • **touched** *adj (emotionally)* touché (**by** de) • **touching** *adj (moving)* touchant • **touchy** (**-ier, -iest**) *adj (sensitive)* susceptible (**about** à propos de)

▶**touch down** *vi (of plane)* atterrir

▶**touch up** *vt sep (photo)* retoucher

tough [tʌf] (**-er, -est**) *adj (strict, hard)* dur; *(sturdy)* solide • **toughen** *vt (body, person)* endurcir

tour [tʊə(r)] **1** *n (journey)* voyage *m*; *(visit)* visite *f*; *(by artiste, team)* tournée *f*; *(on bicycle, on foot)* randonnée *f*; **to go on t.** *(of artiste, team)* être en tournée; **(package) t.** voyage *m* organisé; **t. guide** guide *mf* **2** *vt* visiter; *(of artiste, team)* être en tournée en/ dans • **tourist 1** *n* touriste *mf* **2** *adj (region)* touristique; **t. office** office *m* du tourisme

tournament ['tʊənəmənt] *n* tournoi *m*

tout [taʊt] *n* racoleur, -euse *mf*

tow [təʊ] *vt* remorquer; **to t. a car away** *(of police)* mettre une voiture à la fourrière

toward(s) [tə'wɔːd(z)] *prep* vers; *(of feelings)* envers; **cruel t. sb** cruel envers qn

towel ['taʊəl] *n* serviette *f* (de toilette); **(kitchen) t.** *(paper)* essuie-tout *m inv*

tower ['taʊə(r)] **1** *n* tour *f*; *Br* **t. block** tour **2** *vi* **to t. over sb/sth** dominer qn/qch

town [taʊn] *n* ville *f*; **to go into t.** aller en ville; **t. centre** centre-ville *m*; *Br* **t. hall** mairie *f*

toxic ['tɒksɪk] *adj* toxique

toy [tɔɪ] **1** *n* jouet *m*; **t. shop** magasin *m* de jouets **2** *adj* (*gun*) d'enfant; (*car, train*) miniature

trace [treɪs] **1** *n* trace *f*; **without t.** sans laisser de traces **2** *vt* (*diagram, picture*) tracer

track [træk] **1** *n* (*mark*) trace *f*; (*trail*) piste *f*; (*path*) chemin *m*, piste *f*; (*for trains*) voie *f*; (*of record, CD*) morceau *m*; **to keep t. of sth** surveiller qch; **to lose t. of** (*friend*) perdre de vue; **to be on the right t.** être sur la bonne voie; *Fig* **t. record** passé *m* **2** *vt* **to t. (down)** (*find*) retrouver ● **tracksuit** *n* survêtement *m*

tractor ['træktə(r)] *n* tracteur *m*

trade [treɪd] **1** *n* commerce *m*; (*job*) métier *m*; (*exchange*) échange *m*; *Br* **t. union** syndicat *m* **2** *vt* (*exchange*) échanger (**for** contre); **to t. sth in** (*old article*) faire reprendre qch **3** *vi* faire du commerce (**with** avec) ● **trademark** *n* marque *f* de fabrique

tradition [trə'dɪʃən] *n* tradition *f* ● **traditional** *adj* traditionnel, -elle

traffic ['træfɪk] **1** *n* (*on road*) circulation *f*; (*air, sea, rail*) trafic *m*; *Am* **t. circle** rond-point *m*; **t. jam** embouteillage *m*; **t. lights** feux *mpl* (de signalisation); **t. warden** contractuel, -elle *mf* **2** (*pt & pp* **-ck-**) *vi* trafiquer (**in** de)

tragedy ['trædʒədɪ] (*pl* **-ies**) *n* tragédie *f* ● **tragic** *adj* tragique

trail [treɪl] **1** *n* (*of smoke, blood, powder*) traînée *f*; (*path*) piste *f*, sentier *m* **2** *vt* (*drag*) traîner; (*follow*) suivre **3** *vi* (*drag*) traîner; (*move slowly*) se traîner ● **trailer** *n* (**a**) (*for car*) remorque *f*; *Am* (*caravan*) caravane *f*; *Am* (*camper*) camping-car *m* (**b**) (*advertisement for film*) bande-annonce *f*

train [treɪn] **1** *n* (**a**) (*engine, transport*) train *m*; (*underground*) rame *f*; **t. set** (*toy*) petit train *m* (**b**) (*of events*) suite *f*; (*of dress*) traîne *f*; **my t. of thought** le fil de ma pensée **2** *vt* (*person*) former (**to do** à faire); (*athlete*) entraîner; (*animal*) dresser (**to do** à faire); **to t. oneself to do sth** s'entraîner à faire qch; **to t. sth on sb/sth** (*aim*) braquer qch sur qn/qch **3** *vi* (*of athlete*) s'entraîner; **to t. as a nurse** faire une formation d'infirmière ● **trained** *adj* (*skilled*) qualifié; (*nurse, engineer*) diplômé ● **trainee** *n & adj* stagiaire (*mf*) ● **trainer** *n* (*of athlete*) entraîneur *m*; (*of animals*) dresseur *m*; *Br* **trainers** (*shoes*) baskets *mpl* ● **training** *n* formation *f*; (*in sport*) entraînement *m*; (*of animal*) dressage *m*; **to be in t.** (*of sportsman*) s'entraîner

traitor ['treɪtə(r)] *n* traître, -esse *mf*

tram [træm] *n* tram(way) *m*

tramp [træmp] *n* *Br* (*vagrant*) clochard, -e *mf*

trample ['træmpəl] *vti* **to t. sth (underfoot), to t. on sth** piétiner qch

trampoline [træmpə'liːn] *n* trampoline *m*

trance [trɑːns] *n* **to be in a t.** être en transe

transaction [træn'zækʃən] *n* opération *f*, transaction *f*

transatlantic [trænzət'læntɪk] *adj* transatlantique

transfer 1 ['trænsfɜː(r)] *n* transfert *m* (**to** à); *(of money)* virement *m*; *Br (picture, design)* décalcomanie *f* **2** [træns'fɜː(r)] *(pt & pp* **-rr-**) *vt* transférer (**to** à)

transform [træns'fɔːm] *vt* transformer (**into** en) • **transformation** [-fə'meɪʃən] *n* transformation *f*

transfusion [træns'fjuːʒən] *n* (**blood**) **t.** transfusion *f* (sanguine)

transition [træn'zɪʃən] *n* transition *f*

transitive ['trænsɪtɪv] *adj (verb)* transitif

translate [trænz'leɪt] *vt* traduire (**from** de; **into** en) • **translation** *n* traduction *f* • **translator** *n* traducteur, -trice *mf*

transmit [trænz'mɪt] **1** *(pt & pp* **-tt-**) *vt* transmettre **2** *vti (broadcast)* émettre • **transmission** *n* transmission *f*; *(broadcast)* émission *f*

transparent [træn'spærənt] *adj* transparent

transplant 1 ['trænsplɑːnt] *n (surgical)* greffe *f*, transplantation *f* **2** [træns'plɑːnt] *vt* transplanter

transport 1 ['trænspɔːt] *n* transport *m* (**of** de) **2** [træn'spɔːt] *vt* transporter

trap [træp] **1** *n* piège *m* **2** *(pt & pp* **-pp-**) *vt* prendre au piège; **to t. one's finger** se coincer le doigt (**in** dans) • **trapdoor** *n* trappe *f*

trash [træʃ] *n (nonsense)* bêtises *fpl*; *(junk)* bric-à-brac *m inv*; *Am (waste)* ordures *fpl*; *Am* **t. can** poubelle *f*

trauma ['trɔːmə] *n* traumatisme *m* • **traumatic** [-'mætɪk] *adj* traumatisant • **traumatize** *vt* traumatiser

travel ['trævəl] **1** *n* voyage *m*; **t. agent** agent *m* de voyages; **t. insurance** assurance *f* voyage **2** *(Br* **-ll-**, *Am* **-l-**) *vi (of person)* voyager; *(of vehicle, light, sound)* se déplacer • **traveller** (*Am* **traveler**) *n* voyageur, -euse *mf*; **t.'s cheque** chèque *m* de voyage • **travelling** (*Am* **traveling**) **1** *n* voyages *mpl* **2** *adj (bag, clothes)* de voyage; *(expenses)* de déplacement; *(musician, circus)* ambulant

tray [treɪ] *n* plateau *m*; **baking t.** plaque *f* de four

treacherous ['tretʃərəs] *adj (road, conditions)* très dangereux, -euse; *(person, action)* traître

treacle ['triːkəl] *n Br* mélasse *f*

tread [tred] *(pt* **trod**, *pp* **trodden**) *vi (walk)* marcher (**on** sur)

treason ['triːzən] *n* trahison *f*

treasure ['treʒə(r)] **1** *n* trésor *m*; **t. hunt** chasse *f* au trésor **2** *vt (value)* tenir beaucoup à • **treasurer** *n* trésorier, -ère *mf*

treat [triːt] **1** *n (pleasure)* plaisir *m*; *(gift)* cadeau *m* **2** *vt (person, illness, product)* traiter; **to t. sb to sth** offrir qch à qn • **treatment** *n* traitement *m*

treaty ['triːtɪ] *(pl* **-ies**) *n (international)* traité *m*

treble ['trebəl] **1** *adj* triple **2** *n* le triple; **it's t. the price** c'est le triple du prix **3** *vti* tripler

tree [triː] *n* arbre *m*; **t. trunk** tronc *m* d'arbre

trek [trek] **1** *n (long walk)* randonnée *f* **2** *(pt & pp* **-kk-**) *vi* faire de la randonnée

tremble ['trembəl] *vi* trembler (**with** de)

tremendous [trə'mendəs] *adj (huge)* énorme; *(dreadful)* terrible; *(wonderful)* formidable

trench [trentʃ] *n* tranchée *f*

trend [trend] *n* tendance *f* (**towards** à); *(fashion)* mode *f* • **trendy** (**-ier, -iest**) *adj Br Fam* branché

trespass ['trespəs] *vi* = s'introduire illégalement dans une propriété privée; **'no trespassing'** 'entrée interdite'

trial ['traɪəl] **1** *n (in law)* procès *m*; *(test)* essai *m*; *(ordeal)* épreuve *f*; **to go** *or* **be on t., to stand t.** passer en jugement; **by t. and error** par tâtonnements **2** *adj (period, flight, offer)* d'essai

triangle ['traɪæŋgəl] *n* triangle *m* • **triangular** [-'æŋgjʊlə(r)] *adj* triangulaire

tribe [traɪb] *n* tribu *f*

tribunal [traɪ'bjuːnəl] *n* tribunal *m*

tribute ['trɪbjuːt] *n* hommage *m*; **to pay t. to** rendre hommage à

trick [trɪk] **1** *n (joke, deception, of conjurer)* tour *m*; *(clever method)* astuce *f*; *(in card game)* pli *m*; **to play a t. on sb** jouer un tour à qn **2** *vt (deceive)* duper; **to t. sb into doing sth** amener qn à faire qch par la ruse

trickle ['trɪkəl] *vi (of liquid)* couler goutte à goutte

tricky ['trɪkɪ] (**-ier, -iest**) *adj* difficile

tricycle ['traɪsɪkəl] *n* tricycle *m*

trifle ['traɪfəl] **1** *n (insignificant thing)* bagatelle *f*; *Br (dessert)* = dessert où alternent génoise, fruits en gelée et crème anglaise **2** *vi* **to t. with** plaisanter avec

trigger ['trɪgə(r)] **1** *n (of gun)* détente *f* **2** *vt* **to t. sth (off)** déclencher qch

trim [trɪm] **1** *n* **to give sb's hair a t.** faire une coupe d'entretien à qn **2** (*pt & pp* **-mm-**) *vt* couper (un peu)

trip [trɪp] **1** *n (journey)* voyage *m*; *(outing)* excursion *f* **2** (*pt & pp* **-pp-**) *vt* **to t. sb up** faire trébucher qn **3** *vi* **to t. (over** *or* **up)** trébucher; **to t. over sth** trébucher sur qch

triple ['trɪpəl] **1** *adj* triple **2** *vti* tripler • **triplets** *npl (children)* triplés, -es *mfpl*

triumph ['traɪəmf] **1** *n* triomphe *m* (**over** sur) **2** *vi* triompher (**over** de) • **triumphant** [traɪ'ʌmfənt] *adj* triomphant; *(success, welcome, return)* triomphal

trivial ['trɪvɪəl] *adj (unimportant)* insignifiant; *(trite)* banal (*mpl* -als)

trod [trɒd] *pt of* **tread** • **trodden** *pp of* **tread**

trolley ['trɒlɪ] (*pl* **-eys**) *n Br* chariot *m*; *Am* **t. (car)** tramway *m*

trombone [trɒm'bəʊn] *n* trombone *m*

troop [truːp] **1** *n* bande *f*; *(of soldiers)* troupe *f*; **the troops** *(soldiers)* les troupes *fpl* **2** *vi* **to t. in/out** entrer/sortir en groupe

trophy ['trəʊfɪ] (*pl* **-ies**) *n* trophée *m*

tropical ['trɒpɪkəl] *adj* tropical

trot [trɒt] **1** *n* trot *m*; *Fam* **on the t.** *(consecutively)* de suite **2** (*pt & pp* **-tt-**) *vi (of horse)* trotter

trouble ['trʌbəl] *n (difficulty)* ennui *m*; *(inconvenience)* problème *m*; *(social unrest, illness)* trouble *m*; **to be in t.** avoir des ennuis; **to get into t.** s'attirer des ennuis; **to have t. doing sth** avoir du mal à faire qch; **to go to the t. of doing sth** se donner la peine de faire qch; **it's no t.** pas de problème • **troublemaker** *n (in school)* élément *m* perturbateur;

(political) fauteur *m* de troubles ●
troublesome *adj* pénible
trough [trɒf] *n (for drinking)*
abreuvoir *m*; *(for feeding)* auge *f*
trousers ['trauzəz] *npl Br*
pantalon *m*; **a pair of t., some t.**
un pantalon
trout [traut] *n inv* truite *f*
trowel ['trauəl] *n (for cement
or plaster)* truelle *f*; *(for plants)*
déplantoir *m*
truant ['tru:ənt] *n* **to play t.** faire
l'école buissonnière
truck [trʌk] *n (lorry)* camion *m*; **t.
driver** camionneur *m*; *Am* **t. stop**
(restaurant) routier *m* ● **trucker** *n*
Am camionneur *m*
true [tru:] **(-er, -est)** *adj* vrai;
(genuine) véritable; *(accurate)*
exact; *(faithful)* fidèle **(to** à) ●
truly *adv* vraiment; **well and t.**
bel et bien
trumpet ['trʌmpɪt] *n* trompette *f*
truncheon ['trʌntʃən] *n Br*
matraque *f*
trunk [trʌŋk] *n (of tree, body)*
tronc *m*; *(of elephant)* trompe *f*;
(case) malle *f*; *Am (of vehicle)*
coffre *m*; **trunks** *(for swimming)*
slip *m* de bain
trust [trʌst] **1** *n (faith)* confiance
f **(in** en) **2** *vt (believe in)* faire
confiance à; **to t. sb with sth,
to t. sth to sb** confier qch à
qn; **I t. that...** j'espère que...
● **trustworthy** *adj* digne de
confiance
truth [tru:θ] *(pl* **-s** [tru:ðz]) *n*
vérité *f*; **there's some t. in...** il
y a du vrai dans... ● **truthful** *adj*
(story) véridique; *(person)* sincère
try [traɪ] **1** *(pl* **-ies)** *n* essai *m*;
it's worth a t. ça vaut la peine
d'essayer **2** *(pt & pp* **-ied)** *vt*
(attempt, sample) essayer; *(food,
drink)* goûter à; *(in law court)*

juger **(for** pour); **to t. doing** *or*
to do sth essayer de faire qch **3**
vi essayer
►**try on** *vt sep (clothes, shoes)*
essayer
►**try out** *vt sep (car, method,
recipe)* essayer; *(person)* mettre à
l'essai
T-shirt ['ti:ʃɜːt] *n* tee-shirt *m*
tub [tʌb] *n (basin)* baquet *m*; *(bath)*
baignoire *f*; *Br (for ice cream)* pot
m; *Br (for flower, bush)* bac *m*
tube [tju:b] *n* tube *m*; *Br Fam* **the
t.** *(underground railway)* le métro
tuck [tʌk] **1** *vt (put)* mettre; **to t.
sth away** *(put)* ranger qch; *(hide)*
cacher qch; **to t. in** *(shirt, blanket)*
rentrer; *(child)* border **2** *vi Br Fam*
to t. in *(start eating)* attaquer
Tuesday ['tju:zdeɪ] *n* mardi *m*
tuft [tʌft] *n* touffe *f*
tug [tʌg] **1** *(pt & pp* **-gg-)** *vt (pull)*
tirer sur **2** *vi* tirer **(at** *or* **on** sur)
tulip ['tju:lɪp] *n* tulipe *f*
tumble ['tʌmbəl] **1** *n (fall)* chute *f*;
Br **t. dryer** *or* **drier** sèche-linge *m*
inv **2** *vi* faire une chute
tumbler ['tʌmblə(r)] *n (glass)*
verre *m* droit
tummy ['tʌmɪ] *n Fam* ventre *m*
tumour ['tju:mə(r)] *(Am* **tumor)**
n tumeur *f*
tuna ['tju:nə] *n* **t. (fish)** thon *m*
tune [tju:n] **1** *n (melody)* air *m*; **in
t.** *(instrument)* accordé; **out of t.**
(instrument) désaccordé; **to be** *or*
sing in t./out of t. chanter juste/
faux **2** *vt (instrument)* accorder **3**
vi **to t. in** brancher son poste **(to**
sur)
tunic ['tju:nɪk] *n* tunique *f*
tunnel ['tʌnəl] *n* tunnel *m*
turban ['tɜːbən] *n* turban *m*
turbulence ['tɜːbjuləns] *n*
turbulence *f*
Turkey ['tɜːkɪ] *n* la Turquie ● **Turk**

n Turc *m*, Turque *f* • **Turkish 1**
adj turc (*f* turque); **T. delight** des
loukoums *mpl* **2** *n* (*language*)
turc *m*
turkey ['tɜːkɪ] (*pl* **-eys**) *n* (*bird*)
dinde *f*
turmoil ['tɜːmɔɪl] *n* **to be in t.** (*of*
person) être dans tous ses états; (*of*
country) être en ébullition

turn [tɜːn] **1** *n* (*of wheel, in game,*
queue) tour *m*; (*in road*) tournant
m; **to take turns** se relayer; **in t.** à
tour de rôle; **it's your t. (to play)**
c'est à toi (de jouer); **the t. of the**
century le tournant du siècle; **t.**
of phrase tournure de phrase **2**
vt tourner; (*mechanically*) faire
tourner; (*mattress, pancake*)
retourner; **to t. sb/sth into sb/**
sth changer qn/qch en qn/qch;
to t. sth red/black rougir/noircir
qch; **to t. sth on sb** (*aim*) braquer
qch sur qn; **she has turned**
twenty elle a vingt ans passés **3**
vi (*of wheel, driver*) tourner; (*of*
person) se retourner; **to t. red/**
black rougir/noircir; **to t. nasty**
(*of person*) devenir méchant;
(*of situation*) mal tourner; **to t.**
to sb se tourner vers qn; **to t.**
into sb/sth devenir qn/qch; **to**
t. against sb se retourner contre
qn • **turning** *n* (*bend in road*) &
Fig tournant *m* • **turn-off** *n* (*on*
road) sortie *f* • **turn-up** *n Br* (*on*
trousers) revers *m*
▶**turn around** *vi* (*of person*) se
retourner
▶**turn away 1** *vt sep* (*eyes*)
détourner (**from** de); (*person*)
refuser **2** *vi* se détourner
▶**turn back 1** *vt sep* (*sheets*)
rabattre; (*clock*) retarder **2** *vi*
(*return*) faire demi-tour
▶**turn down** *vt sep* (*gas, radio*)

baisser; (*fold down*) rabattre;
(*refuse*) rejeter
▶**turn off 1** *vt sep* (*light, radio*)
éteindre; (*tap*) fermer; (*machine*)
arrêter **2** *vi* (*leave road*) sortir
▶**turn on 1** *vt sep* (*light, radio*)
allumer; (*tap*) ouvrir; (*machine*)
mettre en marche; *Fam* **to t. sb**
on (*sexually*) exciter qn **2** *vi* **to t.**
on sb (*attack*) attaquer qn
▶**turn out 1** *vt sep* (*light*) éteindre
2 *vi* (*appear, attend*) se déplacer; **it**
turns out that... il s'avère que...;
she turned out to be... elle s'est
révélée être...
▶**turn over 1** *vt sep* (*page*) tourner
2 *vi* (*of person*) se retourner; (*of*
car) faire un tonneau
▶**turn round 1** *vt sep* (*head*)
tourner; (*object*) retourner;
(*situation*) renverser **2** *vi* (*of*
person) se retourner; (*in vehicle*)
faire demi-tour
▶**turn up 1** *vt sep* (*radio, heat*)
mettre plus fort; (*collar*) remonter
2 *vi* (*arrive*) arriver; (*be found*) être
retrouvé

turnip ['tɜːnɪp] *n* navet *m*
turquoise ['tɜːkwɔɪz] *adj*
turquoise *inv*
turtle ['tɜːtəl] *n Br* tortue *f* de mer;
Am tortue *f*
tusk [tʌsk] *n* défense *f* (*dent*)
tutor ['tjuːtə(r)] *n* professeur *m*
particulier; (*in British university*)
directeur, -trice *mf* d'études •
tutorial [-'tɔːrɪəl] *n Univ* ≃
travaux *mpl* dirigés
tuxedo [tʌk'siːdəʊ] (*pl* **-os**) *n Am*
smoking *m*
TV [tiː'viː] *n* télé *f*; **on TV** à la télé
tweed [twiːd] *n* tweed *m*; **t.**
jacket veste *f* en tweed
tweezers ['twiːzəz] *npl* pince *f*
à épiler

twelve *adj & n* douze *(m)*
• **twelfth** [twelfθ] *adj & n* douzième *(mf)*
twenty ['twentɪ] *adj & n* vingt *(m)*
• **twentieth** *adj & n* vingtième *(mf)*
twice [twaɪs] *adv* deux fois; **t. as heavy (as)** deux fois plus lourd (que); **t. a month, t. monthly** deux fois par mois
twig [twɪg] *n (of branch)* brindille *f*
twilight ['twaɪlaɪt] *n* crépuscule *m*
twin [twɪn] *n* jumeau *m*, jumelle *f*; **t. brother** frère *m* jumeau; **t. sister** sœur *f* jumelle; **t. beds** lits *mpl* jumeaux
twinkle ['twɪŋkəl] *vi (of star)* scintiller; *(of eye)* pétiller
twirl [twɜːl] **1** *vt* faire tournoyer **2** *vi* tournoyer
twist [twɪst] **1** *n (action)* tour *m*; *(bend)* tortillement *m*; *Fig (in story)* tour *m* inattendu **2** *vt (wire, arm)* tordre; *(roll)* enrouler **(round** autour de); **to t. one's ankle** se tordre la cheville; *Fig* **to t. sb's arm** forcer la main à qn; **to t. sth off** *(lid)* dévisser qch **3** *vi (wind)*

s'entortiller **(round sth** autour de qch); *(of road, river)* serpenter • **twisted** *adj (person, mind, logic)* tordu
twitch [twɪtʃ] *vi (of person)* avoir un tic; *(of muscle)* se contracter nerveusement
twitter ['twɪtə(r)] *vi (of bird)* pépier
two [tuː] *adj & n* deux *(m)* • **two-dimensional** *adj* à deux dimensions • **two-faced** *adj Fig* hypocrite • **two-piece** *adj (suit, swimsuit)* deux-pièces
type¹ [taɪp] *n (sort)* genre *m*, type *m*
type² [taɪp] **1** *vti (write)* taper (à la machine) **2** *vt* **to t. sth in** *(on computer)* entrer qch au clavier; **to t. sth out** *(letter)* taper qch • **typewriter** *n* machine *f* à écrire • **typing** *n* dactylographie *f*; **t. error** faute *f* de frappe • **typist** *n* dactylo *mf*
typhoon [taɪ'fuːn] *n* typhon *m*
typical ['tɪpɪkəl] *adj* typique **(of** de)
tyrant ['taɪrənt] *n* tyran *m*
tyre ['taɪə(r)] *n Br* pneu *m* *(pl* pneus)

Uu

U, u [ju:] *n (letter)* U, u *m inv*
ugly ['ʌglɪ] (**-ier, -iest**) *adj* laid
UK [ju:'keɪ] (*abbr* **United Kingdom**) *n* **the UK** le Royaume-Uni
ulcer ['ʌlsə(r)] *n* ulcère *m*
ultimate ['ʌltɪmət] *adj (last)* final; *(supreme, best)* absolu
  ● **ultimately** *adv (finally)* finalement; *(basically)* en fin de compte
ultimatum [ʌltɪ'meɪtəm] *n* ultimatum *m*
ultra- ['ʌltrə] *pref* ultra-
ultraviolet [ʌltrə'vaɪələt] *adj* ultraviolet, -ette
umbrella [ʌm'brelə] *n* parapluie *m*
umpire ['ʌmpaɪə(r)] *n* arbitre *m*
UN [ju:'en] (*abbr* **United Nations**) *n* **the UN** les Nations *fpl* unies
unable [ʌn'eɪbəl] *adj* **to be u. to do sth** être incapable de faire qch
unabridged [ʌnə'brɪdʒd] *adj* intégral
unacceptable [ʌnək'septəbəl] *adj* inacceptable
unaccustomed [ʌnə'kʌstəmd] *adj* inaccoutumé; **to be u. to sth/to doing sth** ne pas être habitué à qch/à faire qch
unanimous [ju:'nænɪməs] *adj* unanime
unappetizing [ʌn'æpɪtaɪzɪŋ] *adj* peu appétissant
unattached [ʌnə'tætʃt] *adj (without partner)* sans attaches
unattended [ʌnə'tendɪd] *adj* **to leave sb/sth u.** laisser qn/qch sans surveillance
unattractive [ʌnə'træktɪv] *adj* peu attrayant
unauthorized [ʌn'ɔ:θəraɪzd] *adj* non autorisé
unavailable [ʌnə'veɪləbəl] *adj* **to be u.** ne pas être disponible
unavoidable [ʌnə'vɔɪdəbəl] *adj* inévitable
unaware [ʌnə'weə(r)] *adj* **to be u. of sth** ignorer qch; **to be u. that...** ignorer que...
unbalanced [ʌn'bælənst] *adj (mind, person)* instable
unbearable [ʌn'beərəbəl] *adj* insupportable
unbeatable [ʌn'bi:təbəl] *adj* imbattable
unbelievable [ʌnbɪ'li:vəbəl] *adj* incroyable
unblock [ʌn'blɒk] *vt (sink, pipe)* déboucher
unborn [ʌn'bɔ:n] *adj* **u. child** enfant *mf* à naître
unbreakable [ʌn'breɪkəbəl] *adj* incassable
unbutton [ʌn'bʌtən] *vt* déboutonner
uncalled-for [ʌn'kɔ:ldfɔ:(r)] *adj* déplacé
uncanny [ʌn'kænɪ] (**-ier, -iest**) *adj* étrange
uncertain [ʌn's3:tən] *adj* incertain; **to be u. about sth** ne pas être certain de qch; **it's u. whether** *or* **that...** il n'est pas certain que... *(+ subjunctive)*

unchanged [ʌn'tʃeɪndʒd] *adj* inchangé

uncle ['ʌŋkəl] *n* oncle *m*

unclear [ʌn'klɪə(r)] *adj* vague; *(result)* incertain; **it's u. whether...** on ne sait pas très bien si...

uncomfortable [ʌn'kʌmftəbəl] *adj* inconfortable; *(heat, experience)* désagréable; **to feel u.** *(physically)* ne pas être à l'aise; *(ill at ease)* être mal à l'aise

uncommon [ʌn'kɒmən] *adj* peu commun

unconditional [ʌnkən'dɪʃənəl] *adj* sans condition

unconfirmed [ʌnkən'fɜːmd] *adj* non confirmé

unconnected [ʌnkə'nektɪd] *adj* sans lien

unconscious [ʌn'kɒnʃəs] **1** *adj (person)* sans connaissance; *(desire)* inconscient; **to be u. of sth** ne pas avoir conscience de qch **2** *n* **the u.** l'inconscient *m* • **unconsciously** *adv* inconsciemment

uncontrollable [ʌnkən'trəʊləbəl] *adj* incontrôlable

unconventional [ʌnkən'venʃənəl] *adj* non conformiste

unconvincing [ʌnkən'vɪnsɪŋ] *adj* peu convaincant

uncooked [ʌn'kʊkt] *adj* cru

uncooperative [ʌnkəʊ'ɒpərətɪv] *adj* peu coopératif, -ive

uncover [ʌn'kʌvə(r)] *vt* découvrir

under ['ʌndə(r)] **1** *prep* sous; *(less than)* moins de; **children u. nine** les enfants de moins de neuf ans; **u. it** dessous; **u. (the command of) sb** sous les ordres de qn; **u. the circumstances** dans ces circonstances; **to be u. discussion/repair** être en discussion/réparation; **to be u.**

way *(in progress)* être en cours; *(on the way)* être en route; **to get u. way** *(of campaign)* démarrer **2** *adv* au-dessous

undercharge [ʌndə'tʃɑːdʒ] *vt* **I undercharged him (for it)** je ne (le) lui ai pas fait payer assez

undercooked [ʌndə'kʊkt] *adj* pas assez cuit

undercover ['ʌndəkʌvə(r)] *adj* secret, -ète

underestimate [ʌndər'estɪmeɪt] *vt* sous-estimer

underfoot [ʌndə'fʊt] *adv* sous les pieds

undergo [ʌndə'gəʊ] *(pt* **-went,** *pp* **-gone)** *vt* subir; **to u. surgery** être opéré

undergraduate [ʌndə'grædʒʊət] *n* étudiant, -e *mf* de licence

underground 1 ['ʌndəgraʊnd] *adj (subterranean)* souterrain **2** ['ʌndəgraʊnd] *n Br (railway)* métro *m* **3** [ʌndə'graʊnd] *adv* sous terre

underline [ʌndə'laɪn] *vt* souligner

underneath [ʌndə'niːθ] **1** *prep* sous **2** *adv* (en) dessous; **the book u.** le livre d'en dessous **3** *n* **the u. (of)** le dessous (de)

underpaid [ʌndə'peɪd] *adj* sous-payé

underpants ['ʌndəpænts] *npl (male underwear)* slip *m*

underpass ['ʌndəpɑːs] *n (for pedestrians)* passage *m* souterrain; *(for vehicles)* passage *m* inférieur

underprivileged [ʌndə'prɪvɪlɪdʒd] *adj* défavorisé

understaffed [ʌndə'stɑːft] *adj* **to be u.** manquer de personnel

understand [ʌndə'stænd] *(pt & pp* **-stood)** *vti* comprendre; **I u. that...** je crois comprendre que... • **understandable** *adj* compréhensible • **understanding**

1 n (act, faculty) compréhension f; (agreement) accord m, entente f; (sympathy) entente f; **on the u. that…** à condition que… (+ subjunctive) **2** adj (person) compréhensif, -ive ● **understood** adj (agreed) entendu; (implied) sous-entendu

understatement [ˈʌndəsteɪtmənt] n euphémisme m

undertake [ʌndəˈteɪk] (pt **-took**, pp **-taken**) vt (task) entreprendre; **to u. to do sth** entreprendre de faire qch

undertaker [ˈʌndəteɪkə(r)] n entrepreneur m de pompes funèbres

underwater [ʌndəˈwɔːtə(r)] adv sous l'eau

underwear [ˈʌndəweə(r)] n sous-vêtements mpl

undesirable [ʌndɪˈzaɪərəbəl] adj & n indésirable (mf)

undignified [ʌnˈdɪɡnɪfaɪd] adj indigne

undisciplined [ʌnˈdɪsɪplɪnd] adj indiscipliné

undiscovered [ʌndɪˈskʌvəd] adj **to remain u.** (of crime, body) ne pas être découvert

undo [ʌnˈduː] (pt **-did**, pp **-done**) vt (knot) défaire; (mistake, damage) réparer; Comptr (command) annuler ● **undone** adj **to come u.** (of knot) se défaire; **to leave sth u.** (work) ne pas faire qch

undoubtedly [ʌnˈdaʊtɪdlɪ] adv indubitablement

undress [ʌnˈdres] **1** vt déshabiller; **to get undressed** se déshabiller **2** vi se déshabiller

undue [ʌnˈdjuː] adj excessif, -ive

uneasy [ʌnˈiːzɪ] adj (person) mal à l'aise; (silence) gêné

uneducated [ʌnˈedjʊkeɪtɪd] adj (person) sans éducation

unemployed [ʌnɪmˈplɔɪd] **1**

adj au chômage **2** npl **the u.** les chômeurs mpl ● **unemployment** n chômage m; Br **u. benefit** allocation f chômage

unenthusiastic [ʌnɪnθjuːzɪˈæstɪk] adj peu enthousiaste

unequal [ʌnˈiːkwəl] adj inégal

uneven [ʌnˈiːvən] adj inégal

uneventful [ʌnɪˈventfəl] adj sans histoires

unexpected [ʌnɪkˈspektɪd] adj inattendu ● **unexpectedly** adv (arrive) à l'improviste; (fail, succeed) contre toute attente

unfailing [ʌnˈfeɪlɪŋ] adj (optimism, courage) à toute épreuve

unfair [ʌnˈfeə(r)] adj injuste (**to sb** envers qn); (competition) déloyal ● **unfairly** adv injustement

unfaithful [ʌnˈfeɪθfəl] adj infidèle (**to** à)

unfamiliar [ʌnfəˈmɪlɪə(r)] adj inconnu; **to be u. with sth** ne pas connaître qch

unfashionable [ʌnˈfæʃənəbəl] adj démodé

unfasten [ʌnˈfɑːsən] vt défaire

unfavourable [ʌnˈfeɪvərəbəl] (Am **unfavorable**) adj défavorable

unfinished [ʌnˈfɪnɪʃt] adj inachevé

unfit [ʌnˈfɪt] adj (unsuitable) inapte; (in bad shape) pas en forme; **to be u. to do sth** être incapable de faire qch

unflattering [ʌnˈflætərɪŋ] adj peu flatteur, -euse

unfold [ʌnˈfəʊld] **1** vt déplier; (wings) déployer **2** vi (of story) se dérouler

unforeseen [ʌnfɔːˈsiːn] adj imprévu

unforgettable [ʌnfəˈɡetəbəl] adj inoubliable

unforgivable [ʌnfə'gɪvəbəl] *adj* impardonnable

unfortunate [ʌn'fɔːtʃənət] *adj* malchanceux, -euse; *(event)* fâcheux, -euse • **unfortunately** *adv* malheureusement

unfounded [ʌn'faʊndɪd] *adj (rumour)* sans fondement

unfriendly [ʌn'frendlɪ] *adj* peu aimable (**to** avec)

unfurnished [ʌn'fɜːnɪʃt] *adj* non meublé

ungrateful [ʌn'greɪtfəl] *adj* ingrat

unhappy [ʌn'hæpɪ] (**-ier, -iest**) *adj (sad, unfortunate)* malheureux, -euse; *(not pleased)* mécontent; **to be u. about doing sth** ne pas vouloir faire qch

unharmed [ʌn'hɑːmd] *adj* indemne

unhealthy [ʌn'helθɪ] (**-ier, -iest**) *adj (person)* maladif, -ive; *(climate, place, job)* malsain

unheard-of [ʌn'hɜːdɒv] *adj (unprecedented)* inouï

unhelpful [ʌn'helpfəl] *adj (person)* peu serviable; *(advice)* peu utile

unhurt [ʌn'hɜːt] *adj* indemne

unhygienic [ʌnhaɪ'dʒiːnɪk] *adj* contraire à l'hygiène

uniform ['juːnɪfɔːm] *n* uniforme *m*

unimaginable [ʌnɪ'mædʒɪnəbəl] *adj* inimaginable • **unimaginative** *adj (person, plan)* qui manque d'imagination

unimportant [ʌnɪm'pɔːtənt] *adj* sans importance

uninhabited [ʌnɪn'hæbɪtɪd] *adj* inhabité

uninspiring [ʌnɪn'spaɪərɪŋ] *adj (subject)* pas très inspirant

unintentional [ʌnɪn'tenʃənəl] *adj* involontaire

uninterested [ʌn'ɪntrɪstɪd] *adj* indifférent (**in** à) • **uninteresting** *adj* inintéressant

uninvited [ʌnɪn'vaɪtɪd] *adv (arrive)* sans invitation • **uninviting** *adj* peu attrayant

union ['juːnɪən] *n* union *f*; *(trade union)* syndicat *m*; **the U. Jack** = le drapeau britannique

unique [juː'niːk] *adj* unique

unisex ['juːnɪseks] *adj (clothes)* unisexe

unison ['juːnɪsən] *n* **in u.** à l'unisson (**with** de)

unit ['juːnɪt] *n* unité *f*; *(of furniture)* élément *m*; *(system)* bloc *m*; *(group, team)* groupe *m*; **psychiatric/heart u.** *(of hospital)* service *m* de psychiatrie/ cardiologie

unite [juː'naɪt] **1** *vt* unir; *(country, party)* unifier; **the United Kingdom** le Royaume-Uni; **the United Nations** les Nations *fpl* unies; **the United States (of America)** les États-Unis *mpl* (d'Amérique) **2** *vi* s'unir

universe ['juːnɪvɜːs] *n* univers *m* • **universal** [-'vɜːsəl] *adj* universel, -elle

university [juːnɪ'vɜːsətɪ] **1** (*pl* **-ies**) *n* université *f*; **to go to u.** aller à l'université; *Br* **at u.** à l'université **2** *adj (teaching, town, restaurant)* universitaire; *(student, teacher)* d'université

unjust [ʌn'dʒʌst] *adj* injuste

unjustified [ʌn'dʒʌstɪfaɪd] *adj* injustifié

unkind [ʌn'kaɪnd] *adj* pas gentil (*f* pas gentille) (**to sb** avec qn)

unknown [ʌn'nəʊn] *adj* inconnu

unleaded [ʌn'ledɪd] *adj* sans plomb

unless [ʌn'les] *conj* à moins que (+ *subjunctive*); **u. she comes**

à moins qu'elle ne vienne; **u. you work harder, you'll fail** à moins de travailler plus dur, vous échouerez

unlike [ʌn'laɪk] *prep* **to be u. sb/ sth** ne pas être comme qn/qch; **u. her brother, she...** à la différence de son frère, elle...; **it's very u. him to...** ça ne lui ressemble pas du tout de...

unlikely [ʌn'laɪklɪ] *adj* improbable; *(unbelievable)* invraisemblable; **she's u. to win** il est peu probable qu'elle gagne

unlimited [ʌn'lɪmɪtɪd] *adj* illimité

unlisted [ʌn'lɪstɪd] *adj Am (phone number)* sur liste rouge

unload [ʌn'ləʊd] *vti* décharger

unlock [ʌn'lɒk] *vt* ouvrir

unlucky [ʌn'lʌkɪ] **(-ier, -iest)** *adj (person)* malchanceux, -euse; *(number, colour)* qui porte malheur • **unluckily** *adv* malheureusement

unmarried [ʌn'mærɪd] *adj* non marié

unmistakable [ʌnmɪ'steɪkəbəl] *adj (obvious)* indubitable; *(face, voice)* caractéristique

unnatural [ʌn'nætʃərəl] *adj (abnormal)* anormal; *(affected)* affecté

unnecessary [ʌn'nesəsərɪ] *adj* inutile; *(superfluous)* superflu

unnerve [ʌn'nɜːv] *vt* troubler

unnoticed [ʌn'nəʊtɪst] *adv* **to go u.** passer inaperçu

unoccupied [ʌn'ɒkjʊpaɪd] *adj (house)* inoccupé; *(seat)* libre

unofficial [ʌnə'fɪʃəl] *adj* officieux, -euse; *(visit)* privé; *(strike)* sauvage

unorthodox [ʌn'ɔːθədɒks] *adj* peu orthodoxe

unpack [ʌn'pæk] **1** *vt (suitcase)* défaire; *(contents)* déballer **2** *vi* défaire sa valise

unpaid [ʌn'peɪd] *adj (bill, sum)* impayé; *(work, worker)* bénévole; *(leave)* non payé

unplanned [ʌn'plænd] *adj* imprévu

unpleasant [ʌn'plezənt] *adj* désagréable (**to sb** avec qn)

unplug [ʌn'plʌg] *(pt & pp* **-gg-)** *vt (appliance)* débrancher

unpopular [ʌn'pɒpjʊlə(r)] *adj* impopulaire; **to be u. with sb** ne pas plaire à qn

unpredictable [ʌnprɪ'dɪktəbəl] *adj* imprévisible; *(weather)* indécis

unprepared [ʌnprɪ'peəd] *adj* **to be u. for sth** *(not expect)* ne pas s'attendre à qch

unprofessional [ʌnprə'feʃənəl] *adj (person, behaviour)* pas très professionnel, -elle

unprovoked [ʌnprə'vəʊkt] *adj* gratuit

unqualified [ʌn'kwɒlɪfaɪd] *adj (teacher)* non diplômé; *(support)* sans réserve; *(success)* parfait; **to be u. to do sth** ne pas être qualifié pour faire qch

unravel [ʌn'rævəl] *(Br* **-ll-,** *Am* **-l-)** *vt (threads)* démêler; *Fig (mystery)* éclaircir

unreal [ʌn'rɪəl] *adj* irréel, -elle • **unrealistic** [-'lɪstɪk] *adj* irréaliste

unreasonable [ʌn'riːzənəbəl] *adj (person, attitude)* déraisonnable

unrecognizable [ʌn'rekəgnaɪz-əbəl] *adj* méconnaissable

unreliable [ʌnrɪ'laɪəbəl] *adj* peu fiable

unrest [ʌn'rest] *n* agitation *f*, troubles *mpl*

unrivalled [ʌn'raɪvəld] *(Am* **unrivaled)** *adj* hors pair *inv*

unroll [ʌn'rəʊl] **1** *vt* dérouler **2** *vi* se dérouler

unruly [ʌn'ruːlɪ] **(-ier, -iest)** *adj* indiscipliné

unsafe [ʌnˈseɪf] *adj (place, machine)* dangereux, -euse
unsaid [ʌnˈsed] *adj* **to leave sth u.** passer qch sous silence
unsatisfactory [ʌnsætɪsˈfæktərɪ] *adj* peu satisfaisant • **unsatisfied** *adj* insatisfait; **u. with sb/sth** peu satisfait de qn/qch
unscrew [ʌnˈskruː] *vt* dévisser
unscrupulous [ʌnˈskruːpjʊləs] *adj (person)* peu scrupuleux, -euse
unsettled [ʌnˈsetəld] *adj (weather, situation)* instable
unshaven [ʌnˈʃeɪvən] *adj* pas rasé
unsightly [ʌnˈsaɪtlɪ] *adj* laid
unskilled [ʌnˈskɪld] *adj* non qualifié
unsociable [ʌnˈsəʊʃəbəl] *adj* peu sociable
unsolved [ʌnˈsɒlvd] *adj (mystery)* inexpliqué; *(crime)* dont l'auteur n'est pas connu
unsophisticated [ʌnsəˈfɪstɪkeɪtɪd] *adj* simple
unsound [ʌnˈsaʊnd] *adj (construction)* peu solide; *(method)* peu sûr; *(decision)* peu judicieux, -euse
unspeakable [ʌnˈspiːkəbəl] *adj* indescriptible
unstable [ʌnˈsteɪbəl] *adj* instable
unsteady [ʌnˈstedɪ] *adj (hand, voice, step)* mal assuré; *(table, ladder)* bancal *(mpl -als)* • **unsteadily** *adv (walk)* d'un pas mal assuré
unsuccessful [ʌnsəkˈsesfəl] *adj (attempt)* infructueux, -euse; *(outcome, candidate)* malheureux, -euse; *(application)* non retenu; **to be u.** ne pas réussir **(in doing** à faire); *(of book, film, artist)* ne pas avoir de succès • **unsuccessfully** *adv* en vain, sans succès

unsuitable [ʌnˈsuːtəbəl] *adj* qui ne convient pas **(for** à); *(manners, clothes)* peu convenable; **to be u. for sth** ne pas convenir à qch
unsure [ʌnˈʃʊə(r)] *adj* incertain **(of** *or* **about** de)
unsympathetic [ʌnsɪmpəˈθetɪk] *adj* peu compatissant **(to** à); **u. to a cause/request** insensible à une cause/requête
untangle [ʌnˈtæŋgəl] *vt (rope, hair)* démêler
unthinkable [ʌnˈθɪŋkəbəl] *adj* impensable, inconcevable
untidy [ʌnˈtaɪdɪ] **(-ier, -iest)** *adj (clothes, hair)* peu soigné; *(room)* en désordre; *(person)* désordonné
untie [ʌnˈtaɪ] *vt (person, hands)* détacher; *(knot, parcel)* défaire
until [ʌnˈtɪl] **1** *prep* jusqu'à; **u. now** jusqu'à présent; **u. then** jusque-là; **not u. tomorrow** pas avant demain; **I didn't see her u. Monday** c'est seulement lundi que je l'ai vue **2** *conj* jusqu'à ce que **(+** *subjunctive)*; **u. she comes** jusqu'à ce qu'elle vienne; **do nothing u. I come** ne fais rien avant que j'arrive
untrue [ʌnˈtruː] *adj* faux *(f* fausse)
unused[1] [ʌnˈjuːzd] *adj (new)* neuf *(f* neuve); *(not in use)* inutilisé
unused[2] [ʌnˈjuːst] *adj* **u. to sth/ to doing sth** peu habitué à qch/à faire qch
unusual [ʌnˈjuːʒʊəl] *adj (not common)* inhabituel, -elle; *(strange)* étrange • **unusually** *adv* exceptionnellement
unveil [ʌnˈveɪl] *vt* dévoiler
unwanted [ʌnˈwɒntɪd] *adj* non désiré
unwelcome [ʌnˈwelkəm] *adj (news)* fâcheux, -euse; *(gift, visit)* inopportun; *(person)* importun

unwell [ʌn'wel] *adj* souffrant
unwieldy [ʌn'wiːldɪ] *adj (package)* encombrant; *(system)* lourd
unwilling [ʌn'wɪlɪŋ] *adj* **to be u. to do sth** être réticent à faire qch • **unwillingly** *adv* à contrecœur
unwind [ʌn'waɪnd] *(pt & pp -wound)* **1** *vt (thread)* dérouler **2** *vi* se dérouler; *Fam (relax)* décompresser
unwise [ʌn'waɪz] *adj* imprudent
unwittingly [ʌn'wɪtɪŋlɪ] *adv* involontairement
unworthy [ʌn'wɜːðɪ] *adj* indigne **(of** de)
unwrap [ʌn'ræp] *(pt & pp -pp-) vt* déballer
unwritten [ʌn'rɪtən] *adj (agreement)* verbal
unzip [ʌn'zɪp] *(pt & pp -pp-) vt* ouvrir (la fermeture Éclair® de)

up [ʌp] **1** *adv* en haut; **to come/ go up** monter; **to walk up and down** marcher de long en large; **up there** là-haut; **up above** au-dessus; **further** *or* **higher up** plus haut; **up to** *(as far as)* jusqu'à; **to be up to doing sth** *(capable of)* être de taille à faire qch; **to feel up to doing sth** *(well enough)* être assez bien pour faire qch; **it's up to you to do it** c'est à toi de le faire; **it's up to you** *(you decide)* c'est à toi de décider; *Fam* **what are you up to?** qu'est-ce que tu fais? **2** *prep* **up a hill** en haut d'une colline; **up a tree** dans un arbre; **up a ladder** sur une échelle; **to live up the street** habiter plus loin dans la rue **3** *adj (out of bed)* levé; **we were up all night** nous sommes restés debout toute la nuit; **the two weeks were up** les deux semaines étaient terminées; *Fam* **what's up?** qu'est-ce qu'il

y a? **4** *npl* **ups and downs** des hauts et des bas *mpl* • **up-and-coming** *adj* qui monte • **upbeat** *adj Fam* optimiste • **upbringing** *n* éducation *f* • **update** *vt* mettre à jour • **uphill 1** [ʌp'hɪl] *adv* **to go u.** monter **2** ['ʌphɪl] *adj Fig (struggle, task)* pénible • **upkeep** *n* entretien *m* • **up-market** *adj Br (car, product)* haut de gamme *inv*; *(area, place)* chic *inv* • **upright 1** *adv (straight)* droit **2** *adj (vertical, honest)* droit • **upside** *adv* **u. down** à l'envers; **to turn sth u. down** retourner qch; *Fig* mettre qch sens dessus dessous • **upstairs 1** [ʌp'steəz] *adv* en haut; **to go u.** monter **2** ['ʌpsteəz] *adj (people, room)* du dessus • **uptight** *adj Fam (tense)* crispé; *(inhibited)* coincé • **up-to-date** *adj* moderne; *(information)* à jour; *(well-informed)* au courant (**on** de) • **upward** *adj (movement)* ascendant; *(path)* qui monte; *(trend)* à la hausse • **upwards** *adv* vers le haut; **from five euros u.** à partir de cinq euros; **u. of fifty** cinquante et plus

upheaval [ʌp'hiːvəl] *n* bouleversement *m*
upon [ə'pɒn] *prep* sur
upper ['ʌpə(r)] *adj* supérieur; **u. class** aristocratie *f*; **to have/ get the u. hand** avoir/prendre le dessus • **upper-class** *adj* aristocratique
uproar ['ʌprɔː(r)] *n* tumulte *m*
upset 1 [ʌp'set] *(pt & pp -set, pres p -setting) vt (knock over, spill)* renverser; *(person, plans, schedule)* bouleverser **2** [ʌp'set] *adj (unhappy)* bouleversé (**about** par); **to have an u. stomach** avoir l'estomac dérangé **3** ['ʌpset]

n **to have a stomach u.** avoir l'estomac dérangé • **upsetting** *adj* bouleversant

urban ['ɜːbən] *adj* urbain

urge [ɜːdʒ] **1** *n* forte envie *f*; **to have an u. to do sth** avoir très envie de faire qch **2** *vt* **to u. sb to do sth** presser qn de faire qch • **urgent** *adj* urgent • **urgently** *adv* d'urgence

urine ['jʊərɪn] *n* urine *f* • **urinate** *vi* uriner

US [juː'es] (*abbr* **United States**) *n* **the US** les USA *mpl*

us [əs, *stressed* ʌs] *pron* nous; **(to) us** (*indirect*) nous; **she saw us** elle nous a vus; **he gave it (to) us** il nous l'a donné

USA [juːes'eɪ] (*abbr* **United States of America**) *n* **the U.** les USA *mpl*

use 1 [juːs] *n* (*utilization*) emploi *m*, usage *m*; (*ability, permission to use*) emploi *m*; **to make (good) u. of sth** faire (bon) usage de qch; **to be of u. to sb** être utile à qn; **in u.** en usage; **not in u.,** **out of u.** hors d'usage; **it's no u. crying** ça ne sert à rien de pleurer; **what's the u. of worrying?** à quoi bon s'inquiéter? **2** [juːz] *vt* (*utilize*) utiliser, se servir de; (*force, diplomacy*) avoir recours à; (*electricity*) consommer; **it's used to do** *or* **for doing sth** ça sert à faire qch; **it's used as...**

ça sert de...; **to u. sth up** (*food, fuel*) finir; (*money*) dépenser • **used 1** *adj* (**a**) [juːzd] (*secondhand*) d'occasion (**b**) [juːst] **to be u. to sth/to doing sth** être habitué à qch/à faire qch; **to get u. to sb/sth** s'habituer à qn/qch **2** [juːst] *v aux* **I u. to sing** avant, je chantais; **she u. to jog every Sunday** elle faisait du jogging tous les dimanches • **useful** ['juːs-] *adj* utile (**to** à); **to come in u.** être utile • **useless** ['juːs-] *adj* inutile; (*person*) nul (*f* nulle) (**at** en) • **user-friendly** ['juːzə-] *adj* convivial

usher ['ʌʃə(r)] **1** *n* (*in church, theatre*) ouvreur *m* **2** *vt* **to u. sb in** faire entrer qn

usual ['juːʒʊəl] *adj* habituel, -elle; **as u.** comme d'habitude • **usually** *adv* d'habitude

utensil [juː'tensəl] *n* ustensile *m*

utmost ['ʌtməʊst] *adj* **it is of the u. importance that...** il est de la plus haute importance que... (+ *subjunctive*)

utter¹ ['ʌtə(r)] *adj* total; **it's u. nonsense** c'est complètement absurde • **utterly** *adv* complètement

utter² ['ʌtə(r)] *vt* (*cry, sigh*) pousser; (*word*) prononcer

U-turn ['juːtɜːn] *n* (*in vehicle*) demi-tour *m*; *Fig* (*change of policy*) virage *m* à 180°

Vv

V, v [viː] *n (letter)* V, v *m inv*

vacant ['veɪkənt] *adj (room, seat)* libre; *(post)* vacant ● **vacancy** *(pl -ies) n (post)* poste *m* vacant; *(room)* chambre *f* libre

vacation [veɪ'keɪʃən] *n Am* vacances *fpl*; **to take a v.** prendre des vacances

vaccinate ['væksɪneɪt] *vt* vacciner ● **vaccination** [-'neɪʃən] *n* vaccination *f* ● **vaccine** [-'siːn] *n* vaccin *m*

vacuum ['vækjuəm] **1** *n* vide *m*; **v. cleaner** aspirateur *m*; *Br* **v. flask** Thermos® *f* **2** *vt (room)* passer l'aspirateur dans; *(carpet)* passer l'aspirateur sur

vague [veɪg] **(-er, -est)** *adj* vague; *(outline)* flou; **he was v. (about it)** il est resté vague ● **vaguely** *adv* vaguement

vain [veɪn] **(-er, -est)** *adj* **(a)** *(attempt, hope)* vain; **in v.** en vain; **her efforts were in v.** ses efforts ont été inutiles **(b)** *(conceited)* vaniteux, -euse

valentine ['væləntaɪn] *n (card)* carte *f* de la Saint-Valentin; **V.'s Day** la Saint-Valentin

valid ['vælɪd] *adj* valable ● **validate** *vt* valider

valley ['vælɪ] *(pl -eys) n* vallée *f*

valuable ['væljuəbəl] **1** *adj (object)* de valeur; *Fig (help, time)* précieux, -euse **2** *npl* **valuables** objets *mpl* de valeur

value ['væljuː] **1** *n* valeur *f*; **to be good v. (for money)** être d'un bon rapport qualité-prix **2** *vt (appreciate)* apprécier; *(assess)* évaluer

valve [vælv] *n (of machine, car)* soupape *f*; *(of pipe, tube)* valve *f*

van [væn] *n (vehicle)* camionnette *f*, fourgonnette *f*

vandal ['vændəl] *n* vandale *mf* ● **vandalism** *n* vandalisme *m* ● **vandalize** *vt* saccager

vanilla [və'nɪlə] **1** *n* vanille *f* **2** *adj (ice cream)* à la vanille

vanish ['vænɪʃ] *vi* disparaître

variety [və'raɪətɪ] *n* variété *f*; **a v. of** toutes sortes de ● **variation** [veərɪ'eɪʃən] *n* variation *f* ● **varied** ['veərɪd] *adj* varié ● **various** ['veərɪəs] *adj* divers ● **vary** ['veərɪ] *(pt & pp -ied) vti* varier **(in/with** en/selon)

varnish ['vɑːnɪʃ] **1** *n* vernis *m* **2** *vt* vernir

vase [*Br* vɑːz, *Am* veɪs] *n* vase *m*

vast [vɑːst] *adj* immense

VAT [viːeɪ'tiː, væt] *(abbr* **value added tax)** *n Br* TVA *f*

vat [væt] *n* cuve *f*

Vatican ['vætɪkən] *n* **the V.** le Vatican

vault[1] [vɔːlt] *n (cellar)* cave *f*; *(in bank)* salle *f* des coffres

vault[2] [vɔːlt] *vti (jump)* sauter

VCR [viːsiː'ɑː(r)] *(abbr* **video cassette recorder)** *n* magnéto-scope *m*

veal [viːl] *n* veau *m*

veer [vɪə(r)] *vi (of car)* virer; **to v. off the road** quitter la route

vegetable ['vedʒtəbəl] n légume m • **vegetarian** [vedʒɪ'teərɪən] adj & n végétarien, -enne (mf)

vehicle ['viːɪkəl] n véhicule m

veil [veɪl] n voile m

vein [veɪn] n (in body) veine f

Velcro® ['velkrəʊ] n Velcro® m

velvet ['velvɪt] 1 n velours m 2 adj de velours

vending ['vendɪŋ] n v. machine distributeur m automatique

vengeance ['vendʒəns] n vengeance f; Fig with a v. de plus belle

ventilation [ventɪ'leɪʃən] n ventilation f, aération f

venture ['ventʃə(r)] vi s'aventurer (into dans)

venue ['venjuː] n (for meeting, concert) salle f; (for football match) stade m

veranda(h) [və'rændə] n véranda f

verb [vɜːb] n verbe m

verdict ['vɜːdɪkt] n verdict m

verge [vɜːdʒ] 1 n Br (of road) bord m; on the v. of ruin/tears au bord de la ruine/des larmes; to be on the v. of doing sth être sur le point de faire qch 2 vi to v. on friser; (of colour) tirer sur

verify ['verɪfaɪ] (pt & pp -ied) vt vérifier

vermin ['vɜːmɪn] n (animals) animaux mpl nuisibles; (insects) vermine f

versatile [Br 'vɜːsətaɪl, Am 'vɜːrsətəl] adj polyvalent

verse [vɜːs] n (poetry) vers mpl; (stanza) strophe f

version [Br 'vɜːʃən, Am 'vɜːrʒən] n version f

versus ['vɜːsəs] prep (in sport, law) contre; (compared to) comparé à

vertical ['vɜːtɪkəl] adj vertical

very ['verɪ] 1 adv très; v. much beaucoup; the v. first le tout premier (f la toute première); the v. next day le lendemain même; at the v. least/most tout au moins/plus; at the v. latest au plus tard 2 adj (emphatic use) this v. house cette maison même; at the v. end tout à la fin

vest [vest] n maillot m de corps; Am (waistcoat) gilet m

vet [vet] n vétérinaire mf

veteran ['vetərən] n Mil ancien combattant m; Fig vétéran m

veto ['viːtəʊ] (pt & pp -oed) vt mettre son veto à

via ['vaɪə, 'vɪə] prep via, par

vibrate [vaɪ'breɪt] vi vibrer • **vibration** n vibration f

vicar ['vɪkə(r)] n (in Church of England) pasteur m

vice [vaɪs] n (depravity, fault) vice m; Br (tool) étau m

vice- [vaɪs] pref vice-

vice versa [vaɪs(ɪ)'vɜːsə] adv vice versa

vicious ['vɪʃəs] adj (malicious) méchant; (violent) brutal; v. circle cercle m vicieux

victim ['vɪktɪm] n victime f; to be the v. of être victime de

Victorian [vɪk'tɔːrɪən] 1 adj victorien, -enne 2 n Victorien, -enne mf

victory ['vɪktərɪ] (pl -ies) n victoire f

video ['vɪdɪəʊ] 1 (pl -os) n (medium) vidéo f; (cassette) cassette f vidéo; (recorder) magnétoscope m; on v. sur cassette vidéo 2 adj (camera, cassette, game) vidéo inv; v. recorder magnétoscope m 3 (pt & pp -oed) vt (on camcorder) filmer en vidéo; (on video recorder) enregistrer (sur magnétoscope)

vie [vaɪ] (*pres p* **vying**) *vi* **to v. with sb (for sth/to do sth)** rivaliser avec qn (pour qch/pour faire qch)

view [vju:] **1** *n* vue *f*; *(opinion)* opinion *f*; **in my v.** *(opinion)* à mon avis; **on v.** *(exhibit)* exposé; **with a v. to doing sth** dans l'intention de faire qch **2** *vt (regard)* considérer; *(look at)* voir; *(house)* visiter ● **viewer** *n TV* téléspectateur, -trice *mf* ● **viewpoint** *n* point *m* de vue

vigilant ['vɪdʒɪlənt] *adj* vigilant

vigorous ['vɪgərəs] *adj* vigoureux, -euse

vile [vaɪl] **(-er, -est)** *adj (unpleasant)* abominable; *(food, drink)* infect

villa ['vɪlə] *n* villa *f*

village ['vɪlɪdʒ] *n* village *m*

villain ['vɪlən] *n (scoundrel)* scélérat *m*; *(in story, play)* méchant *m*

vindictive [vɪn'dɪktɪv] *adj* vindicatif, -ive

vine [vaɪn] *n* vigne *f* ● **vineyard** ['vɪnjəd] *n* vigne *f*

vinegar ['vɪnɪgə(r)] *n* vinaigre *m*

vintage ['vɪntɪdʒ] *adj (wine)* de cru; *(car)* de collection *(datant généralement des années 1920)*

vinyl ['vaɪnəl] *n* vinyle *m*

violate ['vaɪəleɪt] *vt (agreement)* violer

violence ['vaɪələns] *n* violence *f* ● **violent** *adj* violent ● **violently** *adv* violemment

violet ['vaɪələt] **1** *adj (colour)* violet, -ette **2** *n (colour)* violet *m*; *(plant)* violette *f*

violin [vaɪə'lɪn] *n* violon *m*

VIP [vi:aɪ'pi:] *(abbr* **very important person)** *n* VIP *mf*

virgin ['vɜ:dʒɪn] *n* vierge *f*

virtual ['vɜ:tʃʊəl] *adj* quasi; *Comptr* virtuel, -elle ● **virtually** *adv (almost)* quasiment

virtue ['vɜ:tʃu:] *n (goodness, chastity)* vertu *f*; *(advantage)* mérite *m* ● **virtuous** [-tjʊəs] *adj* vertueux, -euse

virus ['vaɪərəs] *n Med & Comptr* virus *m*

visa ['vi:zə] *n* visa *m*

visible ['vɪzəbəl] *adj* visible ● **visibility** [-'bɪlɪtɪ] *n* visibilité *f*

vision ['vɪʒən] *n (eyesight)* vue *f*; *(foresight)* clairvoyance *f*; *(apparition)* vision *f*

visit ['vɪzɪt] **1** *n* visite *f*; **to pay sb a v.** rendre visite à qn **2** *vt (place)* visiter; *(person)* rendre visite à **3** *vi* **to be visiting** être de passage; *Br* **v. hours/card** heures *fpl*/carte *f* de visite ● **visitor** *n* visiteur, -euse *mf*; *(guest)* invité, -e *mf*

visual ['vɪʒʊəl] *adj* visuel, -elle; **v. arts** arts *mpl* plastiques

vital ['vaɪtəl] *adj* vital; **it's v. that...** il est vital que... *(+ subjunctive)*

vitamin [*Br* 'vɪtəmɪn, *Am* 'vaɪtəmɪn] *n* vitamine *f*

vivid ['vɪvɪd] *adj* vif *(f* vive); *(description)* vivant; *(memory)* clair

V-neck ['vi:nek] *adj* à col en V

vocabulary [*Br* və'kæbjʊlərɪ, *Am* -erɪ] *n* vocabulaire *m*

vocal ['vəʊkəl] *adj (cords, music)* vocal; *(noisy, critical)* qui se fait entendre

vocation [vəʊ'keɪʃən] *n* vocation *f* ● **vocational** *adj* professionnel, -elle

vodka ['vɒdkə] *n* vodka *f*

vogue [vəʊg] *n* vogue *f*; **in v.** en vogue

voice [vɔɪs] *n* voix *f*; **at the top of one's v.** à tue-tête

volcano [vɒl'keɪnəʊ] (pl -oes) n volcan m

volleyball ['vɒlɪbɔːl] n volley(-ball) m

voltage ['vəʊltɪdʒ] n voltage m

volume ['vɒljuːm] n (book, capacity, loudness) volume m

volunteer [vɒlən'tɪə(r)] **1** n volontaire mf; (for charity) bénévole mf **2** vi se porter volontaire (**for sth** pour qch; **to do** pour faire) ● **voluntary** [Br 'vɒləntərɪ, Am -erɪ] adj volontaire; (unpaid) bénévole

vomit ['vɒmɪt] vti vomir

vote [vəʊt] **1** n (choice) vote m; (election) scrutin m; (paper) voix f; **to take a v. on sth** voter sur qch; **to have the v.** avoir le droit de vote **2** vi voter; **to v. Labour** travailliste ● **voter** n (elector) électeur, -trice mf

vouch [vaʊtʃ] vi **to v. for sb/sth** répondre de qn/qch

voucher ['vaʊtʃə(r)] n coupon m, bon m; (**gift-)v.** chèque-cadeau m

vow [vaʊ] **1** n vœu m **2** vt jurer (**to** à); **to v. to do sth** jurer de faire qch

vowel ['vaʊəl] n voyelle f

voyage ['vɔɪɪdʒ] n voyage m

vulgar ['vʌlgə(r)] adj vulgaire

vulnerable ['vʌlnərəbəl] adj vulnérable

vulture ['vʌltʃə(r)] n vautour m

Ww

W, w [ˈdʌbəljuː] n (letter) W, w
m inv

wad [wɒd] n (of papers,
banknotes) liasse f; (of cotton
wool) morceau m

waddle [ˈwɒdəl] vi Fig (of duck,
person) se dandiner

wade [weɪd] vi **to w. through**
(mud, water) patauger dans; Fig
(book) venir péniblement à bout
de

wafer [ˈweɪfə(r)] n (biscuit)
gaufrette f; Rel hostie f

waffle [ˈwɒfəl] n (cake) gaufre f

waft [wɒft] vi (of smell, sound)
parvenir

wag [wæg] (pt & pp -gg-) vt
remuer, agiter; **to w. one's finger
at sb** menacer qn du doigt

wage [weɪdʒ] n **wage(s)** salaire
m, paie f; Br **w. packet** (money)
paie

wag(g)on [ˈwægən] n Br (of train)
wagon m (découvert); (horse-
drawn) charrette f

wail [weɪl] vi (of person) gémir; (of
siren) hurler

waist [weɪst] n taille f • **waistcoat**
n Br gilet m

wait [weɪt] 1 n attente f; **to lie in
w. for sb** guetter qn 2 vt **to w.
one's turn** attendre son tour 3
vi (a) attendre; **to w. for sb/sth**
attendre qn/qch; **to keep sb
waiting** faire attendre qn; **w. till
or until I've gone, w. for me to
go** attends que je sois parti; **I can't
w. to see her** j'ai vraiment hâte

de la voir (b) **to w. on sb** servir
qn • **waiting 1** n attente f **2** adj **w.
list/room** liste f/salle f d'attente
▶**wait around** vi attendre
▶**wait up** vi veiller; **to w. up for
sb** attendre le retour de qn pour
aller se coucher

waiter [ˈweɪtə(r)] n serveur m •
waitress n serveuse f

wake¹ [weɪk] (pt **woke**, pp
woken) **1** vt **to w. sb (up)**
réveiller qn **2** vi **to w. (up)** se
réveiller

wake² [weɪk] n (of ship) sillage
m; Fig **in the w. of sth** à la suite
de qch

Wales [weɪlz] n le pays de Galles

walk [wɔːk] **1** n (short) promenade
f; (long) marche f; (gait) démarche
f; (path) avenue f; **to go for a w.,
to take a w.** aller se promener; **to
take the dog for a w.** promener
le chien; **five minutes' w.
(away)** à cinq minutes à pied **2** vt
to w. the dog promener le chien;
to w. sb home raccompagner
qn; **I walked 3 miles** ≃ j'ai fait
presque 5 km à pied **3** vi marcher;
(as opposed to cycling, driving)
aller à pied; (for exercise, pleasure)
se promener; **to w. home** rentrer
à pied • **walking** n marche f (à
pied); **w. stick** canne f
▶**walk away** vi s'en aller (**from**
de)
▶**walk in** vi entrer
▶**walk off** vi s'en aller

▶**walk out** *vi* sortir; **to w. out on sb** quitter qn

▶**walk over** *vi* **to w. over to** *(go up to)* s'approcher de

wall [wɔːl] *n* mur *m*; *(of cabin, tunnel)* paroi *f* • **wallpaper** *n* papier *m* peint

wallet ['wɒlɪt] *n* portefeuille *m*

walnut ['wɔːlnʌt] *n* noix *f*

walrus ['wɔːlrəs] *(pl* **-ruses** [-rəsəz]) *n* morse *m*

waltz [*Br* wɔːls, *Am* wɒlts] **1** *n* valse *f* **2** *vi* valser

wand [wɒnd] *n* **(magic) w.** baguette *f* magique

wander ['wɒndə(r)] **1** *vt* **to w. the streets** errer dans les rues **2** *vi (of thoughts)* vagabonder; *(of person)* errer, vagabonder

▶**wander about, wander around** *vi (roam)* errer, vagabonder; *(stroll)* flâner

▶**wander off** *vi (go away)* s'éloigner

want [wɒnt] *vt* vouloir (**to do** faire); **I w. him to go** je veux qu'il parte; **the lawn wants cutting** la pelouse a besoin d'être tondue; **you're wanted on the phone** on vous demande au téléphone • **wanted** *adj (criminal)* recherché par la police

war [wɔː(r)] **1** *n* guerre *f*; **at w.** en guerre (**with** avec); **to declare w.** déclarer la guerre (**on** à) **2** *adj (wound, crime)* de guerre; **w. memorial** monument *m* aux morts

ward [wɔːd] *n (in hospital)* salle *f*

warden ['wɔːdən] *n (of institution, hostel)* directeur, -trice *mf*

wardrobe ['wɔːdrəʊb] *n (cupboard)* penderie *f*; *(clothes)* garde-robe *f*

warehouse ['weəhaʊs] *(pl* **-ses** [-zɪz]) *n* entrepôt *m*

warm [wɔːm] **1** (**-er, -est**) *adj* chaud; *Fig (welcome)* chaleureux, -euse; **to be** *or* **feel w.** avoir chaud; **to get w.** *(of person, room)* se réchauffer; **it's w.** *(of weather)* il fait chaud • **warmly** *adv (dress)* chaudement; *Fig (welcome, thank)* chaleureusement • **warmth** *n* chaleur *f*

▶**warm up 1** *vt (person, food)* réchauffer **2** *vi (of person, room)* se réchauffer; *(of athlete)* s'échauffer

warn [wɔːn] *vt* avertir, prévenir (**that** que); **to w. sb against** *or* **of sth** mettre qn en garde contre qch • **warning** *n (caution)* avertissement *m*; *(advance notice)* avis *m*; **without w.** sans prévenir; **w. light** *(on appliance)* voyant *m* lumineux; *Br* **(hazard) w. lights** feux *mpl* de détresse

warrant ['wɒrənt] *n (in law)* mandat *m* • **warranty** *(pl* **-ies**) *n Com* garantie *f*

warrior ['wɒrɪə(r)] *n* guerrier, -ère *mf*

wart [wɔːt] *n* verrue *f*

wary ['weərɪ] (**-ier, -iest**) *adj* prudent; **to be w. of sb/sth** se méfier de qn/qch; **to be w. of doing sth** hésiter beaucoup à faire qch

was [wəz, *stressed* wɒz] *pt of* **be**

wash [wɒʃ] **1** *n* **to have a w.** se laver; **to give sth a w.** laver qch **2** *vt* laver; **to w. one's hands** se laver les mains (**of sth** de qch) **3** *vi (have a wash)* se laver • **washbasin** *n Br* lavabo *m* • **washcloth** *n Am* gant *m* de toilette • **washing** *n (action)* lavage *m*; *(clothes)* linge *m*; **to do the w.** faire la lessive; **w. machine** machine *f* à laver; *Br* **w. powder** lessive *f* • **washing-up** *n Br* vaisselle *f*; **to do the w.**

faire la vaisselle; **w. liquid** liquide *m* vaisselle

▶**wash off 1** *vt sep* enlever **2** *vi* partir

▶**wash out** *vt sep (bowl, cup)* rincer; *(stain)* faire partir (en lavant)

▶**wash up** *vi Br (do the dishes)* faire la vaisselle; *Am (have a wash)* se débarbouiller

wasp [wɒsp] *n* guêpe *f*

waste [weɪst] **1** *n* gaspillage *m*; *(of time)* perte *f*; *(rubbish)* déchets *mpl*; **w. material** *or* **products** déchets *mpl*; **w. land** *(uncultivated)* terres *fpl* incultes; *(in town)* terrain *m* vague **2** *vt (money, food)* gaspiller; *(time)* perdre; *(opportunity)* gâcher; **to w. no time doing sth** ne pas perdre de temps pour faire qch **3** *vi* **to w. away** dépérir ● **wastebin** *n (in kitchen)* poubelle *f* ● **wasted** *adj (effort)* inutile ● **wasteful** *adj (person)* gaspilleur, *-euse; (process)* peu économique

watch [wɒtʃ] **1** *n (timepiece)* montre *f* **2** *vt* regarder; *(observe)* observer; *(suspect, baby, luggage)* surveiller; *(be careful of)* faire attention à; **w. it!** attention! **3** *vi* regarder; **to w. out for sb/sth** guetter qn/qch; **to w. out** *(take care)* faire attention **(for** à); **w. out!** attention!; **to w. over** surveiller

water [ˈwɔːtə(r)] **1** *n* eau *f*; **under w.** *(road, field)* inondé; *(swim)* sous l'eau; **w. pistol** pistolet *m* à eau; **w. skiing** ski *m* nautique **2** *vt (plant)* arroser; **to w. sth down** diluer qch **3** *vi (of eyes)* larmoyer; **it makes my mouth w.** ça me met l'eau à la bouche ● **watercolour** *(Am* **-color)** *n* aquarelle *f* ● **watercress** *n* cresson *m* (de fontaine) ● **waterfall** *n* cascade

f ● **watering** *n* **w. can** arrosoir *m* ● **watermelon** *n* pastèque *f* ● **waterproof** *adj* imperméable; *(watch)* étanche ● **watertight** *adj (container)* étanche

watt [wɒt] *n* watt *m*

wave [weɪv] **1** *n (of water, crime)* vague *f* **2** *vt (arm, flag)* agiter; *(stick)* brandir **3** *vi (of person)* faire signe (de la main); **to w. to sb** *(signal)* faire signe de la main à qn; *(greet)* saluer qn de la main ● **wavelength** *n* longueur *f* d'onde; *Fig* **on the same w.** sur la même longueur d'onde ● **wavy** (**-ier, -iest**) *adj (hair)* ondulé

wax [wæks] **1** *n* cire *f* **2** *adj (candle, doll)* de cire; **3** *vt* cirer; *(legs)* épiler (à la cire)

way [weɪ] **1** *n* **(a)** *(path, road)* chemin *m* **(to** de); *(direction)* sens *m*, direction *f*; **the w. in** l'entrée *f*; **the w. out** la sortie; **the w. to the station** le chemin pour aller à la gare; **to ask sb the w.** demander son chemin à qn; **to show sb the w.** montrer le chemin à qn; **to lose one's w.** se perdre; **I'm on my w.** j'arrive; **to make w. for sb** faire de la place à qn; **out of the w.** *(isolated)* isolé; **to get out of the w.** s'écarter; **to go all the w.** aller jusqu'au bout; **to give w.** céder; *Br (in vehicle)* céder le passage **(to** à); **it's a long w. away** *or* **off** c'est très loin; **it's the wrong w. up** c'est dans le mauvais sens; **this w.** par ici; **that w.** par là; **which w.?** par où? **(b)** *(manner)* manière *f*; **in this w.** de cette manière; *Fig* **by the w.** à propos; *Fam* **no w.!** *(certainly not)* pas question!; **w. of life** mode *m* de vie **2** *adv Fam* **w. behind** très en arrière; **w. ahead** très en avance **(of** sur)

WC [dʌbəlju:'si:] n W.-C. mpl

we [wi:] pron nous; (indefinite) on; **we teachers** nous autres professeurs; **we all make mistakes** tout le monde peut se tromper

weak [wi:k] (-er, -est) adj faible; (tea, coffee) léger, -ère; **to have a w. heart** avoir le cœur fragile • **weaken 1** vt affaiblir **2** vi s'affaiblir • **weakness** n faiblesse f; (fault) point m faible; **to have a w. for sb/sth** avoir un faible pour qn/qch

wealth [welθ] n richesse f; Fig **a w. of sth** une abondance de qch • **wealthy 1** (-ier, -iest) adj riche **2** npl **the w.** les riches mpl

weapon ['wepən] n arme f

wear [weə(r)] **1** n **w. and tear** usure f naturelle **2** (pt **wore**, pp **worn**) vt (garment, glasses) porter; **to w. black** porter du noir **3** vi **to w. thin** (of clothing) s'user; **to w. well** (of clothing) bien vieillir

▶**wear down 1** vt sep user; **to w. sb down** avoir qn à l'usure **2** vi s'user

▶**wear off** vi (of colour, pain) disparaître

▶**wear out 1** vt sep (clothes) user; **to w. sb out** épuiser qn **2** vi (of clothes) s'user; Fig (of patience) s'épuiser

weary ['wɪərɪ] (-ier, -iest) adj las (f lasse) (**of doing** de faire)

weather ['weðə(r)] **1** n temps m; **what's the w. like?** quel temps fait-il?; **in hot w.** par temps chaud; **under the w.** (ill) patraque **2** adj **w. forecast** prévisions fpl météorologiques; **w. report** (bulletin m) météo f • **weatherman** (pl **-men**) n (on TV, radio) présentateur m météo

weave [wi:v] **1** (pt **wove**, pp

woven) vt (cloth, plot) tisser; (basket, garland) tresser **2** vi tisser; Fig **to w. in and out of** (crowd, cars) se faufiler entre

web [web] n (of spider) toile f; Fig (of lies) tissu m; Comptr **the W.** le Web; **w. page** page f Web; **w. site** site m Web

we'd [wi:d] = **we had, we would**

wedding ['wedɪŋ] **1** n mariage m; **golden/silver w.** noces fpl d'or/d'argent **2** adj (anniversary, present, cake) de mariage; (dress) de mariée; Br **w. ring**, Am **w. band** alliance f

wedge [wedʒ] vt (wheel, table) caler; (push) enfoncer (**into** dans); **to w. a door open** maintenir une porte ouverte avec une cale; **wedged (in) between** coincé entre

Wednesday ['wenzdeɪ] n mercredi m

wee[1] [wi:] adj Scot Fam (tiny) tout petit (f toute petite)

wee[2] [wi:] vi Br Fam faire pipi

weed [wi:d] **1** n (plant) mauvaise herbe f **2** vti désherber • **weedy** (-ier, -iest) adj Fam (person) malingre

week [wi:k] n semaine f; **a w. tomorrow** demain en huit • **weekday** n jour m de semaine • **weekend** n week-end m; **at** or **on** or **over the w.** ce week-end; (every weekend) le week-end • **weekly 1** adj & n hebdomadaire (m) **2** adv toutes les semaines

weep [wi:p] (pt & pp **wept**) vi pleurer

weigh [weɪ] **1** vt peser; **to w. sb/sth down** (with load) surcharger qn/qch (**with** de); **to w. up** (chances) peser **2** vi peser; **it's weighing on my mind** ça me

tracasse • **weight** n poids m;
to put on w. grossir; **to lose
w.** maigrir • **weightlifting** n
haltérophilie f

weird [wɪəd] (**-er, -est**) adj bizarre

welcome ['welkəm] **1** adj (person,
news, change) bienvenu; **to make
sb w.** faire un bon accueil à qn;
w.! bienvenue!; **you're w.!** (after
'thank you') il n'y a pas de quoi!;
you're w. to use my bike mon
vélo est à ta disposition **2** n accueil
m; **to give sb a warm w.** faire
un accueil chaleureux à qn **3** vt
(person) souhaiter la bienvenue
à; (news, change) accueillir
favorablement • **welcoming** adj
accueillant; (speech, words) de
bienvenue

welfare ['welfeə(r)] n (wellbeing)
bien-être m; Am Fam **to be on w.**
recevoir l'aide sociale

well¹ [wel] n (for water, oil) puits
m

well² [wel] **1** (**better, best**) adj
bien; **to be w.** aller bien; **to get
w.** se remettre; **it's just as w....**
heureusement que... **2** adv bien;
you'd do w. to refuse tu ferais
bien de refuser; **she might (just)
as w. have stayed at home** elle
aurait mieux fait de rester chez
elle; **as w.** (also) aussi; **as w. as**
aussi bien que; **as w. as two cats,
he has...** en plus de deux chats,
il a... **3** exclam eh bien!; **w., w.!**
(surprise) tiens, tiens!; **huge, w.
quite big** énorme, enfin, assez
grand • **well-behaved** adj sage •
well-built adj (person, car) solide
• **well-dressed** adj bien habillé •
well-known adj (bien) connu •
well-off adj riche • **well-paid** adj
bien payé • **well-to-do** adj aisé
we'll [wiːl] = **we will, we shall**
wellington ['welɪŋtən] (Fam

welly [welɪ], pl **-ies**) n Br **w.
(boot)** botte f de caoutchouc

Welsh [welʃ] **1** adj gallois **2**
n (language) gallois m; **the
W.** (people) les Gallois mpl •
Welshman (pl **-men**) n Gallois m
• **Welshwoman** (pl **-women**) n
Galloise f

went [went] pt of **go**

wept [wept] pt & pp of **weep**

were [wə(r), stressed wɜː(r)] pt
of **be**

we're [wɪə(r)] = **we are**

west [west] **1** n ouest m; (**to the)
w. of** à l'ouest de; Pol **the W.**
l'Occident m **2** adj (coast) ouest
inv; (wind) d'ouest; **W. Africa**
l'Afrique f occidentale; **W. Indian**
adj antillais; n Antillais, -e mf;
the W. Indies les Antilles fpl **3**
adv à l'ouest; (travel) vers l'ouest
• **western 1** adj (coast) ouest
inv; Pol (culture) occidental; **W.
Europe** l'Europe f de l'Ouest **2** n
(film) western m • **westerner** n
Pol occidental, -e mf

wet [wet] **1** (**wetter, wettest**)
adj mouillé; (weather) pluvieux,
-euse; (day) de pluie; **to get w.** se
mouiller; **to be w. through** être
trempé; **it's w.** (raining) il pleut;
'w. paint' 'peinture fraîche'; **w.
suit** combinaison f de plongée **2**
(pt & pp **-tt-**) vt mouiller

we've [wiːv] = **we have**

whack [wæk] vt Fam donner un
grand coup à

whale [weɪl] n baleine f

what [wɒt] **1** adj quel, quelle, pl
quel(le)s; **w. book?** quel livre?;
w. a fool! quel idiot! **2** pron (**a**)
(in questions) (subject) qu'est-ce
qui; (object) (qu'est-ce) que; (after
prep) quoi; **w.'s happening?**
qu'est-ce qui se passe?; **w. does**

he do? qu'est-ce qu'il fait?, que fait-il?; **w. is it?** qu'est-ce que c'est?; **w.'s that book?** c'est quoi, ce livre?; **w.!** *(surprise)* quoi!, comment!; **w.'s it called?** comment ça s'appelle?; **w. for?** pourquoi?; **w. about going out for lunch?** si on allait déjeuner? **(b)** *(in relative construction) (subject)* ce qui; *(object)* ce que; **I know w. will happen/w. she'll do** je sais ce qui arrivera/ce qu'elle fera; **w. I need...** ce dont j'ai besoin... • **whatever** [-'evə(r)] **1** *adj* **w. (the) mistake** quelle que soit l'erreur; **of w. size** de n'importe quelle taille; **nothing w.** rien du tout **2** *pron (no matter what)* quoi que *(+ subjunctive)*; **w. you do** quoi que tu fasses; **do w. you want** fais tout ce que tu veux • **whatsoever** [-səʊ'evə(r)] *adj* **for no reason w.** sans aucune raison; **none w.** aucun

wheat [wiːt] *n* blé *m*

wheel [wiːl] **1** *n* roue *f* **2** *vt (push)* pousser • **wheelbarrow** *n* brouette *f* • **wheelchair** *n* fauteuil *m* roulant • **wheelclamp** *n* sabot *m* de Denver

wheeze [wiːz] *vi* respirer bruyamment

when [wen] **1** *adv* quand **2** *conj (with time)* quand, lorsque; **w. I finish, w. I've finished** quand j'aurai fini; **the day/moment w.** le jour/moment où • **whenever** [-'evə(r)] *conj (at whatever time)* quand; *(each time that)* chaque fois que

where [weə(r)] **1** *adv* où; **w. are you from?** d'où êtes-vous? **2** *conj* où; **I found it w. she'd left it** je l'ai trouvé là où elle l'avait laissé; **the place/house w. I live**

l'endroit/la maison où j'habite; • **whereabouts 1** [weərə'baʊts] *adv* où **2** ['weərəbaʊts] *n* **his w.** l'endroit *m* où il est • **whereas** [-'æz] *conj* alors que • **wherever** [-'evə(r)] *conj* **w. you go** *(everywhere)* partout où tu iras, où que tu ailles; **I'll go w. you like** j'irai (là) où vous voudrez

whether ['weðə(r)] *conj* si; **I don't know w. to leave** je ne sais pas si je dois partir; **w. she does it or not** qu'elle le fasse ou non; **it's doubtful w....** il est douteux que... *(+ subjunctive)*

which [wɪtʃ] **1** *adj (in questions)* quel, quelle, *pl* quel(le)s; **w. book?** quel livre?; **w. one?** lequel/laquelle?; **in w. case** auquel cas **2** *relative pron (subject)* qui; *(object)* que; *(after prep)* lequel, laquelle, *pl* lesquel(le)s; *(referring to a whole clause) (subject)* ce qui; *(object)* ce que; **the house, w. is old...** la maison, qui est vieille...; **the book w. I like...** le livre que j'aime...; **the table w. I put it on...** la table sur laquelle je l'ai mis...; **the film of w. she was speaking** le film dont *ou* duquel elle parlait; **she's ill, w. is sad** elle est malade, ce qui est triste; **he lies, w. I don't like** il ment, ce que je n'aime pas; **after w.** *(whereupon)* après quoi **3** *interrogative pron (in questions)* lequel, laquelle, *pl* lesquel(le)s; **w. of us?** lequel/laquelle d'entre nous?; **w. are the best of the books?** quels sont les meilleurs de ces livres? **4** *pron* **w. (one)** *(the one that) (subject)* celui qui, celle qui, *pl* ceux qui, celles qui; *(object)* celui que, celle que, *pl* ceux que, celles que; **I know w. (ones) you want** je sais ceux/celles que vous

désirez • **whichever** [-'evə(r)]
1 *adj (no matter which)* **take w.
books interest you** prenez les
livres qui vous intéressent; **take
w. one you like** prends celui/celle
que tu veux **2** *pron (no matter
which)* quel que soit celui qui (*f*
quelle que soit celle qui); **w. you
choose...** quel/quelle que soit
celui/celle que tu choisiras...; **take
w. you want** prends celui/celle
que tu veux

while [waɪl] **1** *conj (when)*
pendant que; *(although)* bien que
(+ *subjunctive)*; *(as long as)* tant
que; *(whereas)* tandis que; **w.
eating** en mangeant **2** *n* **a w.** un
moment; **all the w.** tout le temps
• **whilst** *conj Br* = **while**
whimper ['wɪmpə(r)] *vi* gémir
whine [waɪn] *vi* gémir
whip [wɪp] **1** *n* fouet *m* **2** *(pt & pp
-pp-) vt* fouetter; **whipped cream**
crème *f* fouettée
►**whip up** *vt sep (interest)* susciter;
Fam (meal) préparer rapidement
whirl [wɜ:l] **1** *vt* **to w. sb/sth
(round)** faire tourbillonner qn/qch
2 *vi* **to w. (round)** tourbillonner
• **whirlpool** *n* tourbillon *m* •
whirlwind *n* tourbillon *m*
whirr [wɜ:(r)] *vi* ronfler
whisk [wɪsk] **1** *n (for eggs)* fouet
m **2** *vt* battre; **to w. away** *or*
off *(object)* enlever rapidement;
(person) emmener rapidement
whiskers ['wɪskəz] *npl (of cat)*
moustaches *fpl*
whisky ['wɪskɪ] *(Am* **whiskey***) n*
whisky *m*
whisper ['wɪspə(r)] **1** *n* chuchote-
ment *m* **2** *vti* chuchoter; **to w. sth
to sb** chuchoter qch à l'oreille de
qn

whistle ['wɪsəl] **1** *n* sifflement *m*;
(object) sifflet *m* **2** *vti* siffler
white [waɪt] **1** *(-er, -est) adj* blanc
(*f* blanche); **to go** *or* **turn w.**
blanchir; *Br* **w. coffee** café *m* au
lait; **w. man** Blanc *m*; **w. woman**
Blanche *f* **2** *n (colour, of egg, eye)*
blanc *m*
whizz [wɪz] *vi (rush)* aller à toute
vitesse; **to w. past** *or* **by** passer à
toute vitesse
who [hu:] *pron* qui; **w. did it?** qui
(est-ce qui) a fait ça?; **the woman
w. came** la femme qui est venue;
w. were you talking to? à qui
est-ce que tu parlais? • **whoever**
[-'evə(r)] *pron (no matter who)
(subject)* qui que ce soit qui;
(object) qui que ce soit que; **w.
has seen this** *(anyone who)*
quiconque a vu cela; **w. you are**
qui que vous soyez; **this man, w.
he is** cet homme, quel qu'il soit
whole [həʊl] **1** *adj* entier, -ère;
the w. time tout le temps; **the w.
apple** toute la pomme, la pomme
tout entière; **the w. world** le
monde entier **2** *n* totalité *f*; **the w.
of the village** le village tout entier,
tout le village; **on the w., as a w.**
dans l'ensemble • **wholemeal**
(Am **wholewheat***) adj (bread)*
complet, -ète • **wholesome** *adj
(food, climate)* sain
whom [hu:m] *pron Formal (object)*
que; *(in questions and after prep)*
qui; **w. did she see?** qui a-t-elle
vu?; **the man of w. we were
speaking** l'homme dont nous
parlions
whoops [wʊps] *exclam* houp-là!
whose [hu:z] *possessive pron
& adj* à qui, de qui; **w. book is
this?, w. is this book?** à qui est
ce livre?; **w. daughter are you?**
de qui es-tu la fille?; **the woman**

w. book I have la femme dont j'ai le livre; **the man w. mother I spoke to** l'homme à la mère de qui j'ai parlé

why [waɪ] **1** *adv* pourquoi; **w. not?** pourquoi pas? **2** *conj* **the reason w. they...** la raison pour laquelle ils...

wicked ['wɪkɪd] *adj* *(evil)* méchant

wicker ['wɪkə(r)] *n* osier *m*

wide [waɪd] **1** (**-er, -est**) *adj* large; *(choice, variety, knowledge)* grand; **to be three metres w.** avoir trois mètres de large **2** *adv* *(fall, shoot)* loin du but; **w. open** *(eyes, mouth, door)* grand ouvert; **w. awake** complètement réveillé • **widely** *adv* *(travel)* beaucoup; *(spread)* largement; **it's w. thought that...** on pense généralement que... • **widen** *vi* s'élargir • **widespread** *adj* répandu

widow ['wɪdəʊ] *n* veuve *f* • **widower** *n* veuf *m*

width [wɪdθ] *n* largeur *f*

wife [waɪf] (*pl* **wives**) *n* femme *f*, épouse *f*

wig [wɪg] *n* perruque *f*

wiggle ['wɪgəl] **1** *vt* remuer **2** *vi* *(of worm)* se tortiller; *(of tail)* remuer

wild [waɪld] **1** (**-er, -est**) *adj* *(animal, flower, region)* sauvage; *(idea)* fou (*f* folle); **w. with joy/anger** fou de joie/colère; **to be w.** *(of person)* mener une vie agitée; *Fam* **I'm not w. about it** ça ne m'emballe pas; **the W. West** le Far West **2** *adv* **to run w.** *(of animals)* courir en liberté; *(of crowd)* se déchaîner **3** *n* **in the w.** à l'état sauvage; **in the wilds** en pleine brousse • **wildlife** *n* nature *f* • **wildly** *adv* *(cheer)* frénétiquement; *(guess)* au hasard

wilderness ['wɪldənɪs] *n* région *f* sauvage

will¹ [wɪl]

On trouve généralement **I/you/he/**etc **will** sous leur forme contractée **I'll/you'll/he'll/**etc. La forme négative correspondante est **won't**, que l'on écrira **will not** dans des contextes formels.

v aux (expressing future tense) **he w. come, he'll come** il viendra; **you w. not come, you won't come** tu ne viendras pas; **w. you have some tea?** veux-tu du thé?; **w. you be quiet!** veux-tu te taire!; **it won't open** ça ne s'ouvre pas

will² [wɪl] *n* *(resolve, determination)* volonté *f*; *(legal document)* testament *m*; **free w.** libre arbitre *m*; **against one's w.** à contrecœur; **at w.** à volonté; *(cry)* à la demande • **willing** *adj* *(helper, worker)* plein de bonne volonté; **to be w. to do sth** bien vouloir faire qch • **willingly** *adv* *(with pleasure)* volontiers; *(voluntarily)* de son plein gré • **willpower** *n* volonté *f*

wilt [wɪlt] *vi* *(of plant)* dépérir

wimp [wɪmp] *n* *Fam* *(weakling)* mauviette *f*

win [wɪn] (*pt & pp* **won,** *pres p* **winning**) *vti* gagner • **winning 1** *adj* *(number, horse)* gagnant; *(team)* victorieux, -euse; *(goal)* décisif, -ive **2** *npl* **winnings** gains *mpl*

wind¹ [wɪnd] *n* vent *m*; *(breath)* souffle *m*; **to have w.** *(in stomach)* avoir des gaz • **windcheater** (*Am* **windbreaker**) *n* coupe-vent *m inv* • **windfall** *n* *(unexpected money)* aubaine *f* • **windmill** *n* moulin *m* à vent • **windscreen**

(*Am* **windshield**) *n* (*of vehicle*) pare-brise *m inv*; **w. wiper** essuie-glace *m* • **windsurfing** *n* **to go w.** faire de la planche à voile • **windy** (**-ier, -iest**) *adj* **it's w.** (*of weather*) il y a du vent; **w. day** jour *m* de grand vent

wind² [waɪnd] **1** (*pt & pp* **wound**) *vt* (*roll*) enrouler (**round** autour de); (*clock*) remonter; **to w. a tape back** rembobiner une cassette **2** *vi* (*of river, road*) serpenter • **winding** *adj* (*road*) sinueux, -euse

▶**wind down 1** *vt sep* (*car window*) baisser **2** *vi Fam* (*relax*) se détendre

▶**wind up 1** *vt sep* (*clock*) remonter; (*meeting, speech*) terminer; *Br Fam* **to w. sb up** faire marcher qn **2** *vi* (*end up*) finir (**doing sth** par faire qch); **to w. up with sb/sth** se retrouver avec qn/qch

window ['wɪndəʊ] *n* fenêtre *f*; (*pane*) vitre *f*; (*of shop*) vitrine *f*; (*counter*) guichet *m*; *Br* **French w.** porte-fenêtre *f*; **w. box** jardinière *f*; *Br* **w. cleaner,** *Am* **w. washer** laveur, -euse *mf* de vitres • **windowpane** *n* vitre *f*, carreau *m* • **window-shopping** *n* **to go w.** faire du lèche-vitrines • **windowsill** *n* rebord *m* de fenêtre

wine [waɪn] *n* vin *m*; **w. bar/ bottle** bar *m*/bouteille *f* à vin; **w. cellar** cave *f* à vin; **w. list** carte *f* des vins; **w. tasting** dégustation *f* • **wineglass** *n* verre *m* à vin

wing [wɪŋ] *n* aile *f*; **the wings** (*in theatre*) les coulisses *fpl*

wink [wɪŋk] *vi* faire un clin d'œil (**at** à)

winner ['wɪnə(r)] *n* gagnant, -e *mf*

winter ['wɪntə(r)] **1** *n* hiver *m*; **in (the) w.** en hiver **2** *adj* d'hiver • **wintertime** *n* hiver *m*

wipe [waɪp] **1** *n* **to give sth a w.** essuyer qch **2** *vt* essuyer; **to w. one's feet/hands** s'essuyer les pieds/les mains; **to w. sth away** *or* **off** *or* **up** (*liquid*) essuyer qch; *Fig* **to w. sb out** anéantir qn

wire ['waɪə(r)] *n* fil *m* qn

wise [waɪz] (**-er, -est**) *adj* (*in knowledge*) sage; (*advisable*) prudent; **to be none the wiser** ne pas être plus avancé • **wisdom** ['wɪzdəm] *n* sagesse *f* • **wisely** *adv* sagement

-wise [waɪz] *suff* (*with regard to*) **money-w.** question argent

wish [wɪʃ] **1** *n* (*specific*) souhait *m*, vœu *m*; (*general*) désir *m*; **to do sth against sb's wishes** faire qch contre le souhait de qn; **best wishes, all good wishes** (*in letter*) amitiés *fpl*; **send him my best wishes** fais-lui mes amitiés **2** *vt* souhaiter (**to do faire**); **I w. (that) you could help me** je voudrais que vous m'aidiez; **I w. she could come** j'aurais bien aimé qu'elle vienne; **I w. you (a) happy birthday/(good) luck** je vous souhaite bon anniversaire/ bonne chance; **I w. I could** si seulement je pouvais **3** *vi* **to w. for sth** souhaiter qch; **as you w.** comme vous voudrez

wisp [wɪsp] *n* (*of smoke*) traînée *f*; (*of hair*) mèche *f*

wistful ['wɪstfəl] *adj* nostalgique

wit [wɪt] *n* (*humour*) esprit *m*; **wits** (*intelligence*) intelligence *f*; **to be at one's wits'** *or* **w.'s end** ne plus savoir que faire

witch [wɪtʃ] *n* sorcière *f*

with [wɪð] *prep* (**a**) (*expressing accompaniment*) avec; **come w.**

me viens avec moi; **w. no hat/ gloves** sans chapeau/gants; **I'll be right w. you** je suis à vous dans une seconde; *Fam* **I'm w. you** *(I understand)* je te suis (b) *(at the house, flat of)* chez; **she's staying w.** me elle loge chez moi (c) *(expressing cause)* de; **to tremble w. fear** trembler de peur; **to be ill w. measles** être malade de la rougeole (d) *(expressing instrument, means)* **to write w. a pen** écrire avec un stylo; **to fill w. sth** remplir de qch; **satisfied w. sb/sth** satisfait de qn/qch; **w. my own eyes** de mes propres yeux (e) *(in description)* à; **a woman w. blue eyes** une femme aux yeux bleus (f) *(despite)* malgré; **w. all his faults** malgré tous ses défauts

withdraw [wɪð'drɔː] 1 *(pt* **-drew,** *pp* **-drawn)** *vt* retirer **(from** de) 2 *vi* se retirer **(from** de) • **withdrawal** *n* retrait *m* • **withdrawn** *adj (person)* renfermé

within [wɪð'ɪn] 1 *prep (inside)* à l'intérieur de; **w. 10 km (of)** *(less than)* à moins de 10 km (de); *(inside an area of)* dans un rayon de 10 km (de); **w. a month** *(return)* avant un mois; *(finish)* en moins d'un mois; **w. sight** en vue 2 *adv* à l'intérieur

without [wɪð'aʊt] 1 *prep* sans; **w. a tie** sans cravate; **w. doing sth** sans faire qch; **to do w. sb/sth** se passer de qn/qch 2 *adv* **to do w.** se priver

witness ['wɪtnɪs] 1 *n (person)* témoin *m* 2 *vt (accident)* être témoin de; *(document)* signer (pour attester l'authenticité de)

witty ['wɪtɪ] **(-ier, -iest)** *adj* spirituel, -elle

wives [waɪvz] *pl of* **wife**

wizard ['wɪzəd] *n* magicien *m*

wobble ['wɒbəl] *vi (of chair)* branler; *(of jelly, leg)* trembler; *(of person)* chanceler • **wobbly** *adj (table, chair)* branlant

woe [wəʊ] *n* malheur *m*

woke [wəʊk] *pt of* **wake¹** • **woken** *pp of* **wake¹**

wolf [wʊlf] 1 *(pl* **wolves)** *n* loup *m* 2 *vt* **to w. (down)** *(food)* engloutir

woman ['wʊmən] *(pl* **women)** *n* femme *f*; **women's** *(clothes, attitudes, magazine)* féminin; **women's rights** droits *mpl* des femmes

womb [wuːm] *n Anat* utérus *m*

women ['wɪmɪn] *pl of* **woman**

won [wʌn] *pt & pp of* **win**

wonder ['wʌndə(r)] 1 *n (marvel)* merveille *f*; *(feeling)* émerveillement *m*; **it's no w.** ce n'est pas étonnant **(that** que + *subjunctive)* 2 *vt (ask oneself)* se demander **(if** si; **why** pourquoi) 3 *vi (ask oneself questions)* s'interroger **(about** au sujet de *ou* sur); **I was just wondering** je réfléchissais • **wonderful** *adj* merveilleux, -euse

wonky ['wɒŋkɪ] **(-ier, -iest)** *adj Br Fam (table)* déglingué; *(hat, picture)* de travers

won't [wəʊnt] = **will not**

wood [wʊd] *n (material, forest)* bois *m* • **wooden** *adj* en bois • **woodland** *n* région *f* boisée • **woodwork** *n (school subject)* menuiserie *f*

wool [wʊl] *n* laine *f* • **woollen** *(Am* **woolen)** *adj (dress)* en laine • **woolly** *(Am* **wooly) (-ier, -iest)** *adj* en laine

word [wɜːd] *n* mot *m*; *(promise)* parole *f*; **words** *(of song)* paroles *fpl*; **to have a w. with sb** parler à qn; **to keep one's w.** tenir sa promesse; **in other words** autrement dit; **w. for w.** *(report)* mot pour mot; *(translate)* mot à mot;

wore [wɔː(r)] *pt of* **wear**

work [wɜːk] **1** *n* travail *m*; *(literary, artistic)* œuvre *f*; **to be at w.** travailler; **it's hard w. (doing that)** ça demande beaucoup de travail (de faire ça); **to be out of w.** être sans travail; **a day off w.** un jour de congé; **w. permit** permis *m* de travail; **w. of art** œuvre *f* d'art **2** *vt (person)* faire travailler; *(machine)* faire marcher **3** *vi (of person)* travailler; *(of machine)* marcher, fonctionner; *(of drug)* agir • **worker** *n* travailleur, -euse *mf*; *(manual)* ouvrier, -ère *mf*; **(office) w.** employé, -e *mf* (de bureau) • **working** *adj (day, clothes)* de travail; **w. class** classe *f* ouvrière; **w. conditions** conditions *fpl* de travail • **working-class** *adj* ouvrier, -ère • **workload** *n* charge *f* de travail • **workman** *(pl -men)* *n* ouvrier *m* • **workmate** *n* *Br* camarade *mf* de travail • **workout** *n* *(sports training)* séance *f* d'entraînement • **workshop** *n* *(place, study course)* atelier *m*

▶**work on** *vt insep (book, problem)* travailler à; *(French)* travailler

▶**work out 1** *vt sep (calculate)* calculer; *(problem)* résoudre; *(plan)* préparer; *(understand)* comprendre **2** *vi (succeed)* marcher; *(exercise)* s'entraîner; **it works out at 50 euros** ça fait 50 euros

▶**work up** *vt sep* **I worked up an appetite** ça m'a ouvert l'appétit; **to get worked up** s'énerver

world [wɜːld] **1** *n* monde *m*; **all over the w.** dans le monde entier **2** *adj (war, production)* mondial; *(champion, record)* du monde; **the W. Cup** *(in football)* la Coupe du Monde • **worldwide 1** *adj* mondial **2** *adv* dans le monde entier

worm [wɜːm] **1** *n* ver *m* **2** *vt* **to w. one's way into** s'insinuer dans

worn [wɔːn] **1** *pp of* **wear 2** *adj (clothes, tyre)* usé • **worn-out** *adj (object)* complètement usé; *(person)* épuisé

worry ['wʌrɪ] **1** *(pl -ies)* *n* souci *m*; **it's a w.** ça me cause du souci **2** *(pt & pp -ied)* *vt* inquiéter **3** *vi* s'inquiéter **(about sth** de qch; **about sb** pour qn) • **worried** *adj* inquiet, -ète **(about** au sujet de) • **worrying** *adj* inquiétant

worse [wɜːs] **1** *adj* pire **(than** que); **to get w.** se détériorer; **he's getting w.** *(in health)* il va de plus en plus mal; *(in behaviour)* il se conduit de plus en plus mal **2** *adv* plus mal **(than** que); **I could do w.** j'aurais pu tomber plus mal; **she's w. off (than before)** sa situation est pire (qu'avant); *(financially)* elle est encore plus pauvre (qu'avant) **3** *n* **there's w. to come** le pire reste à venir; **a change for the w.** une détérioration • **worst 1** *adj* pire; **the w. book I've ever read** le plus mauvais livre que j'aie jamais lu **2** *adv* **(the) w.** le plus mal **3** *n* **the w. (one)** *(object, person)* le/la pire, le/la plus mauvais(e); **the w. (thing) is that...** le pire, c'est que...; **at (the) w.** au pire

worship ['wɜːʃɪp] *(pt & pp -pp-)* *vt (person, god)* adorer

worth [wɜːθ] **1** *adj* **to be w. sth** valoir qch; **how much** *or* **what is it w.?** ça vaut combien?; **the film's (well) w. seeing** le film vaut la peine d'être vu **2** *n* valeur *f*; **to buy 50 pence w. of sweets** acheter pour 50 pence de bonbons; **to get one's money's w.** en avoir pour son argent • **worthless** *adj* qui ne vaut rien • **worthwhile** *adj* (*activity*) qui vaut la peine; (*plan, contribution*) valable; (*cause*) louable; (*satisfying*) qui donne des satisfactions • **worthy** ['wɜːðɪ] (-**ier, -iest**) *adj* (*person*) digne; (*cause, act*) louable; **to be w. of sb/sth** être digne de qn/qch

would [wʊd, *unstressed* wəd]

On trouve généralement **I/you/ he** etc **would** sous leur forme contractée **I'd/you'd/he'd** etc. La forme négative correspondante est **wouldn't**, que l'on écrira **would not** dans des contextes formels.

v aux (**a**) (*expressing conditional tense*) **I w. stay if I could** je resterais si je le pouvais; **he w. have done it** il l'aurait fait; **I said she'd come** j'ai dit qu'elle viendrait (**b**) (*willingness, ability*) **w. you help me, please?** veux-tu bien m'aider?; **she wouldn't help me** elle n'a pas voulu m'aider; **w. you like some tea?** prendrez-vous du thé?; **the car wouldn't start** la voiture ne démarrait pas (**c**) (*expressing past habit*) **I w. see her every day** je la voyais chaque jour

wound¹ [wuːnd] **1** *n* blessure *f* **2** *vt* (*hurt*) blesser
wound² [waʊnd] *pt* & *pp of* **wind²**
wove [wəʊv] *pt of* **weave** • **woven** *pp of* **weave**
wow [waʊ] *exclam Fam* oh là là!
wrap [ræp] **1** (*pt* & *pp* **-pp-**) *vt* **to w. (up)** envelopper; (*parcel*) emballer; *Fig* **wrapped up in** (*engrossed*) absorbé par **2** *vti* **to w. up** (*dress warmly*) s'emmitoufler • **wrapper** *n* (*of sweet*) papier *m* • **wrapping** *n* (*action, material*) emballage *m*; **w. paper** papier *m* d'emballage
wreath [riːθ] (*pl* **-s** [riːðz]) *n* couronne *f*
wreck [rek] **1** *n* (*ship*) épave *f*; (*train*) train *m* accidenté; (*person*) épave *f* (humaine); **to be a nervous w.** être à bout de nerfs **2** *vt* (*break, destroy*) détruire; *Fig* (*spoil*) gâcher; (*career, hopes*) briser • **wreckage** [-ɪdʒ] *n* (*of plane, train*) débris *mpl*
wrench [rentʃ] **1** *n Am* (*tool*) clef *f* (à écrous) **2** *vt* **to w. sth from sb** arracher qch à qn
wrestle ['resəl] *vi* lutter (**with sb** avec qn); *Fig* **to w. with a problem** se débattre avec un problème • **wrestler** *n* lutteur, -euse *mf*; (*in all-in wrestling*) catcheur, -euse *mf* • **wrestling** *n* lutte *f*; (**all-in**) **w.** (*with relaxed rules*) catch *m*
wretched ['retʃɪd] *adj* (*poor, pitiful*) misérable; (*dreadful*) affreux, -euse; *Fam* (*annoying*) maudit
wriggle ['rɪgəl] **1** *vt* (*toes, fingers*) tortiller **2** *vi* **to w. (about)** se tortiller; (*of fish*) frétiller; **to w. out of sth** couper à qch
wring [rɪŋ] (*pt* & *pp* **wrung**) *vt* **to w. (out)** (*clothes*) essorer; **to w. one's hands** se tordre les mains
wrinkle ['rɪŋkəl] *n* (*on skin*) ride *f*; (*in cloth, paper*) pli *m* • **wrinkled** *adj* (*skin*) ridé; (*cloth*) froissé
wrist [rɪst] *n* poignet *m*
write [raɪt] (*pt* **wrote,** *pp* **written**) *vti* écrire; **to w. to sb** écrire à qn • **writer** *n* auteur *m* (**of** de);

(literary) écrivain *m* • **writing** *n* *(handwriting, action, profession)* écriture *f*; **to put sth (down) in w.** mettre qch par écrit; **w. paper** papier *m* à lettres
►**write back** *vi* répondre
►**write down** *vt sep* noter
►**write in** *vi (send letter)* écrire
►**write out** *vt sep (list, recipe)* noter; *(cheque)* faire
►**write up** *vt sep (notes)* rédiger
wrong [rɒŋ] **1** *adj (sum, idea)* faux (*f* fausse); *(direction, time)* mauvais; *(unfair)* injuste; **to be w.** *(of person)* avoir tort (**to do** de faire); **it's the w. road** ce n'est pas la bonne route; **the clock's w.** la pendule n'est pas à l'heure; **to get the w. number** *(on phone)* se tromper de numéro;

something's w. with the phone le téléphone ne marche pas bien; **something's w. with her leg** elle a quelque chose à la jambe; **what's w. with you?** qu'est-ce que tu as?; **the w. way round** *or* **up** à l'envers **2** *adv* mal; **to go w.** *(of plan)* mal tourner; *(of vehicle, machine)* tomber en panne **3** *n* *(injustice)* injustice *f*; **to be in the w.** être dans son tort; **right and w.** le bien et le mal **4** *vt* faire du tort à • **wrongly** *adv (inform, translate)* mal; *(accuse, condemn, claim)* à tort
wrote [rəʊt] *pt of* **write**
wrung [rʌŋ] *pt & pp of* **wring**
wry [raɪ] (**wryer, wryest**) *adj* ironique

X, x [eks] *n (letter)* X, x *m inv*
Xmas ['krɪsməs] *n Fam* Noël *m*
X-ray ['eksreɪ] **1** *n (picture)* radio *f*; **to have an X.** passer une radio **2** *vt* radiographier

Yy

Y, y [waɪ] n (letter) Y, y m inv
yacht [jɒt] n (sailing boat) voilier m; (large private boat) yacht m
yard¹ [jɑːd] n (of house, farm, school, prison) cour f; (for working) chantier m; (for storage) dépôt m de marchandises; Am (garden) jardin m
yard² [jɑːd] n (measure) yard m (= 91,44 cm)
yarn [jɑːn] n (thread) fil m; Fam (tale) histoire f à dormir debout
yawn [jɔːn] vi bâiller
year [jɪə(r)] n an m, année f; (of wine) année f; **school y.** année f scolaire; **in the y.** 2004 en (l'an) 2004; **he's ten years old** il a dix ans; **New Y.** Nouvel An m; **New Y.'s Day** le jour de l'An; **New Y.'s Eve** la Saint-Sylvestre • **yearly 1** adj annuel, -elle **2** adv annuellement; **twice y.** deux fois par an
yeast [jiːst] n levure f
yell [jel] vti **to y. (out)** hurler; **to y. at sb** (scold) crier après qn
yellow ['jeləʊ] **1** adj (in colour) jaune; **y. card** (in football) carton m jaune **2** n jaune m
yes [jes] **1** adv oui; (after negative question) si **2** n oui m inv
yesterday ['jestədeɪ] **1** adv hier **2** n hier m; **y. morning/evening** hier matin/soir; **the day before y.** avant-hier
yet [jet] **1** adv (a) (still) encore; (already) déjà; **she hasn't arrived (as) y.** elle n'est pas encore arrivée;

the best y. le meilleur jusqu'ici; **y. another mistake** encore une erreur; **not (just) y.** pas pour l'instant **(b)** (in questions) **has he come y.?** est-il arrivé? **2** conj (nevertheless) pourtant
yield [jiːld] **1** vt (result) donner; (territory, right) céder; **to y. a profit** rapporter **2** vi (surrender) se rendre; Am **'y.'** (road sign) 'cédez le passage'
yob [jɒb] n Br Fam loubard m
yoga ['jəʊgə] n yoga m
yog(h)urt [Br 'jɒgət, Am 'jəʊgərt] n yaourt m
yolk [jəʊk] n jaune m (d'œuf)
you [juː] pron **(a)** (subject) (pl, polite form sing) vous; (familiar form sing) tu; (object) vous, te, t', pl vous; (after prep, 'than', 'it is') vous, toi, pl vous; **(to) y.** (indirect) vous, te, t', pl vous; **I gave it (to) y.** je vous/te l'ai donné; **y. teachers** vous autres professeurs; **y. idiot!** espèce d'imbécile! **(b)** (indefinite) on; (object) vous, te, t', pl vous; **y. never know** on ne sait jamais • **you'd = you had, you would** • **you'll = you will**
young [jʌŋ] **1** (-er, -est) adj jeune; **she's two years younger than me** elle a deux ans de moins que moi; **my young(er) brother** mon (frère) cadet; **my youngest sister** la cadette de mes sœurs; **y. people** les jeunes mpl **2** n **the y.** (people) les jeunes mpl • **youngster** n jeune mf

your [jɔː(r)] *possessive adj (polite form sing, polite and familiar form pl)* votre, *pl* vos; *(familiar form sing)* ton, ta, *pl* tes; *(one's)* son, sa, *pl* ses • **yours** *possessive pron* le vôtre, la vôtre, *pl* les vôtres; *(familiar form sing)* le tien, la tienne, *pl* les tien(ne)s; **this book is y.** ce livre est à vous *ou* est le vôtre/ce livre est à toi *ou* est le tien; **a friend of y.** un ami à vous/toi • **yourself** *pron (polite form)* vous-même; *(familiar form)* toi-même; *(reflexive)* vous, te, t'; *(after prep)* vous, toi; **you wash y.** vous vous lavez/tu te laves • **yourselves** *pron pl* vous-mêmes; *(reflexive and after prep)* vous; **did you cut y.?** est-ce que vous vous êtes coupés?

youth [juːθ] *(pl* **-s** [juːðz]*) n (age)* jeunesse *f*; *(young man)* jeune *m*; **y. club** centre *m* de loisirs pour les jeunes; **y. hostel** auberge *f* de jeunesse • **youthful** *adj (person)* jeune • **you've** [juːv] = **you have**

yo-yo [ˈjəʊjəʊ] *(pl* **yo-yos**) *n* Yo-Yo® *m inv*

Zz

Z, z [*Br* zed, *Am* ziː] *n (letter)* Z,
z *m inv*

zap [zæp] (*pt & pp* **-pp-**) *vt Fam*
Comptr effacer

zebra [ˈziːbrə, *Br* ˈzebrə] *n* zèbre
m; *Br* **z. crossing** passage *m* pour
piétons

zero [ˈzɪərəʊ] (*pl* **-os**) *n* zéro *m*

zest [zest] *n (enthusiasm)*
enthousiasme *m*; *(of lemon,*
orange) zeste *m*

zigzag [ˈzɪgzæg] *n* zigzag *m*

zinc [zɪŋk] *n* zinc *m*

zip [zɪp] **1** *n Br* fermeture *f* Éclair®

2 *adj Am* **z. code** code *m* postal
3 (*pt & pp* **-pp-**) *vt* **to z. sth (up)**
remonter la fermeture Éclair® de
qch • **zipper** *n Am* fermeture *f*
Éclair®

zodiac [ˈzəʊdɪæk] *n* zodiaque *m*

zone [zəʊn] *n* zone *f*

zoo [zuː] (*pl* **zoos**) *n* zoo *m*

zoom [zuːm] **1** *n* **z. lens** zoom *m*
2 *vi* **to z. in** *(of camera)* faire un
zoom avant (**on** sur); *Fam* **to z.**
past passer comme une flèche

zucchini [zuːˈkiːnɪ] (*pl* **-ni** *or* **-nis**)
n Am courgette *f*

French Verb Conjugations

Regular Verbs

	-ER verbs	**-IR verbs**	**-RE verbs**
Infinitive	*donn/er*	*fin/ir*	*vend/re*
1 Present	je donne	je finis	je vends
	tu donnes	tu finis	tu vends
	il donne	il finit	il vend
	nous donnons	nous finissons	nous vendons
	vous donnez	vous finissez	vous vendez
	ils donnent	ils finissent	ils vendent
2 Imperfect	je donnais	je finissais	je vendais
	tu donnais	tu finissais	tu vendais
	il donnait	il finissait	il vendait
	nous donnions	nous finissions	nous vendions
	vous donniez	vous finissiez	vous vendiez
	ils donnaient	ils finissaient	ils vendaient
3 Past historic	je donnai	je finis	je vendis
	tu donnas	tu finis	tu vendis
	il donna	il finit	il vendit
	nous donnâmes	nous finîmes	nous vendîmes
	vous donnâtes	vous finîtes	vous vendîtes
	ils donnèrent	ils finirent	ils vendirent
4 Future	je donnerai	je finirai	je vendrai
	tu donneras	tu finiras	tu vendras
	il donnera	il finira	il vendra
	nous donnerons	nous finirons	nous vendrons
	vous donnerez	vous finirez	vous vendrez
	ils donneront	ils finiront	ils vendront
5 Subjunctive	je donne	je finisse	je vende
	tu donnes	tu finisses	tu vendes
	il donne	il finisse	il vende
	nous donnions	nous finissions	nous vendions
	vous donniez	vous finissiez	vous vendiez
	ils donnent	ils finissent	ils vendent
6 Imperative	donne	finis	vends
	donnons	finissons	vendons
	donnez	finissez	vendez
7 Present participle	donnant	finissant	vendant
8 Past participle	donné	fini	vendu

Note The conditional is formed by adding the following endings to the infinitive: **-ais**, **-ais**, **-ait**, **-ions**, **-iez**, **-aient**. The final **e** is dropped in infinitives ending **-re**.

Irregular French Verbs

Listed below are those verbs considered to be the most useful. Forms and tenses not given are fully derivable, such as the third person singular of the **present tense** which is normally formed by substituting 't' for the final 's' of the first person singular, eg 'crois' becomes 'croit', 'dis' becomes 'dit'. Note that the endings of the **past historic** fall into three categories, the 'a' and 'i' categories shown at donner, and at finir and vendre, and the 'u' category which has the following endings: -us, -ut, -ûmes, -ûtes, -urent. Most of the verbs listed below form their past historic with 'u'.

The **imperfect** may usually be formed by adding -ais, -ait, -ions, -iez, -aient to the stem of the first person plural of the present tense, eg 'je buvais' etc may be derived from 'nous buvons' (stem 'buv-' and ending '-ons'); similarly, the **present participle** may generally be formed by substituting -ant for -ons (eg buvant). The **future** may usually be formed by adding -ai, -as, -a, -ons, -ez, -ont to the infinitive or to an infinitive without final 'e' where the ending is -re (eg conduire). The **imperative** usually has the same forms as the second persons singular and plural and first person plural of the present tense.

1 = Present	2 = Imperfect	3 = Past historic	4 = Future
5 = Subjunctive	6 = Imperative	7 = Present participle	8 = Past participle
n = nous	v = vous	*verbs conjugated with **être** only	

abattre	*like*	**battre**
absoudre	1 j'absous, n absolvons 2 j'absolvais	
	3 j'absolus *(rarely used)* 5 j'absolve 7 absolvant	
	8 absous, absoute	
s'abstenir	*like*	**tenir**
abstraire	1 j'abstrais, n abstrayons 2 j'abstrayais 3 *none* 5 j'abstraie	
	7 abstrayant 8 abstrait	
accourir	*like*	**courir**
accroître	*like*	**croître** *except* 8 accru
accueillir	*like*	**cueillir**
acquérir	1 j'acquiers, n acquérons 2 j'acquérais 3 j'acquis	
	4 j'acquerrai 5 j'acquière 7 acquérant 8 acquis	
adjoindre	*like*	**joindre**
admettre	*like*	**mettre**
advenir	*like*	**venir** *(third person only)*
***aller**	1 je vais, tu vas, il va, n allons, v allez, ils vont 4 j'irai	
	5 j'aille, n allions, ils aillent 6 va, allons, allez *(but note* vas-y)	
apercevoir	*like*	**recevoir**
apparaître	*like*	**connaître**
appartenir	*like*	**tenir**

(2)

apprendre	*like*	**prendre**
asseoir	1 j'assieds, il assied, n asseyons, ils asseyent 2 j'asseyais	
	3 j'assis 4 j'assiérai 5 j'asseye 7 asseyant 8 assis	
astreindre	*like*	**atteindre**
atteindre	1 j'atteins, n atteignons, ils atteignent 2 j'atteignais	
	3 j'atteignis 4 j'atteindrai 5 j'atteigne 7 atteignant 8 atteint	
avoir	1 j'ai, tu as, il a, n avons, v avez, ils ont 2 j'avais 3 j'eus	
	4 j'aurai 5 j'aie, il ait, n ayons, ils aient 6 aie, ayons, ayez	
	7 ayant 8 eu	
battre	1 je bats, il bat, n battons 5 je batte	
boire	1 je bois, n buvons, ils boivent 2 je buvais 3 je bus	
	5 je boive, n buvions 7 buvant 8 bu	
bouillir	1 je bous, n bouillons, ils bouillent 2 je bouillais	
	3 je bouillis 5 je bouille 7 bouillant	
braire	*(defective)* 1 il brait, ils braient 4 il braira, ils brairont	
circonscrire	*like*	**écrire**
circonvenir	*like*	**tenir**
clore	*like*	**éclore**
combattre	*like*	**battre**
commettre	*like*	**mettre**
comparaître	*like*	**connaître**
complaire	*like*	**plaire**
comprendre	*like*	**prendre**
compromettre	*like*	**mettre**
concevoir	*like*	**recevoir**
conclure	1 je conclus, n concluons, ils concluent 5 je conclue	
concourir	*like*	**courir**
conduire	1 je conduis, n conduisons 3 je conduisis 5 je conduise	
	8 conduit	
confire	*like*	**suffire**
connaître	1 je connais, il connaît, n connaissons 3 je connus	
	5 je connaisse 7 connaissant 8 connu	
conquérir	*like*	**acquérir**
consentir	*like*	**mentir**
construire	*like*	**conduire**
contenir	*like*	**tenir**
contraindre	*like*	**craindre**
contredire	*like*	**dire** *except* 1 v contredisez
convaincre	*like*	**vaincre**
convenir	*like*	**tenir**
corrompre	*like*	**rompre**
coudre	1 je couds, il coud, n cousons, ils cousent 3 je cousis	
	5 je couse 7 cousant 8 cousu	
courir	1 je cours, n courons 3 je courus 4 je courrai 5 je coure	
	8 couru	
couvrir	1 je couvre, n couvrons 2 je couvrais 5 je couvre 8 couvert	
craindre	1 je crains, n craignons, ils craignent 2 je craignais	

	3 je craignis 4 je craindrai 5 je craigne 7 craignant
	8 craint
croire	1 je crois, n croyons, ils croient 2 je croyais 3 je crus
	5 je croie, n croyions 7 croyant 8 cru
croître	1 je crois, il croît, n croissons 2 je croissais 3 je crûs
	5 je croisse 7 croissant 8 crû, crue
cueillir	1 je cueille, n cueillons 2 je cueillais 4 je cueillerai
	5 je cueille 7 cueillant
cuire	1 je cuis, n cuisons 2 je cuisais 3 je cuisis 5 je cuise
	7 cuisant 8 cuit
débattre	*like*	**battre**
décevoir	*like*	**recevoir**
déchoir	(*defective*) 1 je déchois 2 *none* 3 je déchus 4 je déchoirai
	6 *none* 7 *none* 8 déchu
découdre	*like*	**coudre**
découvrir	*like*	**couvrir**
décrire	*like*	**écrire**
décroître	*like*	**croître** *except* 8 décru
se dédire	*like*	**dire**
déduire	*like*	**conduire**
défaillir	1 je défaille, n défaillons 2 je défaillais 3 je défaillis
	5 je défaille 7 défaillant 8 défailli
défaire	*like*	**faire**
démentir	*like*	**mentir**
démettre	*like*	**mettre**
se départir	*like*	**mentir**
dépeindre	*like*	**atteindre**
déplaire	*like*	**plaire**
déteindre	*like*	**atteindre**
détenir	*like*	**tenir**
détruire	*like*	**conduire**
*devenir	*like*	**tenir**
se dévêtir	*like*	**vêtir**
devoir	1 je dois, n devons, ils doivent 2 je devais 3 je dus
	4 je devrai 5 je doive, n devions 6 *not used* 7 devant
	8 dû, due, *pl* dus, dues
dire	1 je dis, n disons, v dites 2 je disais 3 je dis 5 je dise
	7 disant 8 dit
disconvenir	*like*	**tenir**
disjoindre	*like*	**joindre**
disparaître	*like*	**connaître**
dissoudre	*like*	**absoudre**
distraire	*like*	**abstraire**
dormir	*like*	**mentir**
échoir	(*defective*) 1 il échoit 2 *none* 3 il échut, ils échurent
	4 il échoira 6 *none* 7 échéant 8 échu
éclore	1 il éclôt, ils éclosent 8 éclos

éconduire	*like*	**conduire**
écrire	1 j'écris, n écrivons 2 j'écrivais 3 j'écrivis 5 j'écrive 7 écrivant 8 écrit	
élire	*like*	**lire**
émettre	*like*	**mettre**
émouvoir	*like*	**mouvoir** *except* 8 ému
enclore	*like*	**éclore**
encourir	*like*	**courir**
endormir	*like*	**mentir**
enduire	*like*	**conduire**
enfreindre	*like*	**atteindre**
*s'enfuir	*like*	**fuir**
enjoindre	*like*	**joindre**
s'enquérir	*like*	**acquérir**
s'ensuivre	*like*	**suivre** (*third person only*)
entreprendre	*like*	**prendre**
entretenir	*like*	**tenir**
entrevoir	*like*	**voir**
entrouvrir	*like*	**couvrir**
envoyer	4 j'enverrai	
*s'éprendre	*like*	**prendre**
équivaloir	*like*	**valoir**
éteindre	*like*	**atteindre**
être	1 je suis, tu es, il est, n sommes, v êtes, ils sont 2 j'étais 3 je fus 4 je serai 5 je sois, n soyons, ils soient 6 sois, soyons, soyez 7 étant 8 été	
étreindre	*like*	**atteindre**
exclure	*like*	**conclure**
extraire	*like*	**abstraire**
faillir	(*defective*) 3 je faillis 4 je faillirai 8 failli	
faire	1 je fais, n faisons, v faites, ils font 2 je faisais 3 je fis 4 je ferai 5 je fasse 7 faisant 8 fait	
falloir	(*impersonal*) 1 il faut 2 il fallait 3 il fallut 4 il faudra 5 il faille 6 *none* 7 *none* 8 fallu	
feindre	*like*	**atteindre**
foutre	1 je fous, n foutons 2 je foutais 3 *none* 5 je foute 7 foutant 8 foutu	
frire	(*defective*) 1 je fris, tu fris, il frit 4 je frirai 6 fris 8 frit (*for other persons and tenses use* faire frire)	
fuir	1 je fuis, n fuyons, ils fuient 2 je fuyais 3 je fuis 5 je fuie 7 fuyant 8 fui	
geindre	*like*	**atteindre**
haïr	1 je hais, il hait, n haïssons	
inclure	*like*	**conclure**
induire	*like*	**conduire**
inscrire	*like*	**écrire**
instruire	*like*	**conduire**

(5)

interdire	*like*	**dire** *except* 1 v interdisez
interrompre	*like*	**rompre**
intervenir	*like*	**tenir**
introduire	*like*	**conduire**
joindre		1 je joins, n joignons, ils joignent 2 je joignais 3 je joignis 4 je joindrai 5 je joigne 7 joignant 8 joint
lire		1 je lis, n lisons 2 je lisais 3 je lus 5 je lise 7 lisant 8 lu
luire	*like*	**nuire**
maintenir	*like*	**tenir**
maudire		1 je maudis, n maudissons 2 je maudissais 3 je maudis 4 je maudirai 5 je maudisse 7 maudissant 8 maudit
méconnaître	*like*	**connaître**
médire	*like*	**dire** *except* 1 v médisez
mentir		1 je mens, n mentons 2 je mentais 5 je mente 7 mentant
mettre		1 je mets, n mettons 2 je mettais 3 je mis 5 je mette 7 mettant 8 mis
moudre		1 je mouds, il moud, n moulons 2 je moulais 3 je moulus 5 je moule 7 moulant 8 moulu
*mourir		1 je meurs, n mourons, ils meurent 2 je mourais 3 je mourus 4 je mourrai 5 je meure, n mourions 7 mourant 8 mort
mouvoir		1 je meus, n mouvons, ils meuvent 2 je mouvais 3 je mus 4 je mouvrai 5 je meuve, n mouvions 8 mû, mue, *pl* mus, mues
*naître		1 je nais, il naît, n naissons 2 je naissais 3 je naquis 4 je naîtrai 5 je naisse 7 naissant 8 né
nuire		1 je nuis, n nuisons 2 je nuisais 3 je nuisis 5 je nuise 7 nuisant 8 nui
obtenir	*like*	**tenir**
offrir	*like*	**couvrir**
omettre	*like*	**mettre**
ouvrir	*like*	**couvrir**
paître		(*defective*) 1 il paît 2 ils paissait 3 *none* 4 il paîtra 5 il paisse 7 paissant 8 *none*
paraître	*like*	**connaître**
parcourir	*like*	**courir**
parfaire	*like*	**faire** (*present tense, infinitive and past participle only*)
*partir	*like*	**mentir**
*parvenir	*like*	**tenir**
peindre	*like*	**atteindre**
percevoir	*like*	**recevoir**
permettre	*like*	**mettre**
plaindre	*like*	**craindre**
plaire		1 je plais, il plaît, n plaisons 2 je plaisais 3 je plus 5 je plaise 7 plaisant 8 plu
pleuvoir		(*impersonal*) 1 il pleut 2 il pleuvait 3 il plut 4 il pleuvra 5 il pleuve 6 *none* 7 pleuvant 8 plu

(6)

poindre	(*defective*) 1 il point 4 il poindra 8 point	
poursuivre	*like*	**suivre**
pourvoir	*like*	**voir** *except* 3 je pourvus *and* 4 je pourvoirai
pouvoir	1 je peux *or* je puis, tu peux, il peut, n pouvons, ils peuvent 2 je pouvais 3 je pus 4 je pourrai 5 je puisse 6 *not used* 7 pouvant 8 pu	
prédire	*like*	**dire** *except* v prédisez
prendre	1 je prends, il prend, n prenons, ils prennent 2 je prenais 3 je pris 5 je prenne 7 prenant 8 pris	
prescrire	*like*	**écrire**
pressentir	*like*	**mentir**
prévaloir	*like*	**valoir** *except* 5 je prévale
prévenir	*like*	**tenir**
prévoir	*like*	**voir** *except* 4 je prévoirai
produire	*like*	**conduire**
promettre	*like*	**mettre**
promouvoir	*like*	**mouvoir** *except* 8 promu
proscrire	*like*	**écrire**
*provenir	*like*	**tenir**
rabattre	*like*	**battre**
rasseoir	*like*	**asseoir**
réapparaître	*like*	**connaître**
recevoir	1 je reçois, n recevons, ils reçoivent 2 je recevais 3 je reçus 4 je recevrai 5 je reçoive, n recevions, ils reçoivent 7 recevant 8 reçu	
reconduire	*like*	**conduire**
reconnaître	*like*	**connaître**
reconquérir	*like*	**acquérir**
reconstruire	*like*	**conduire**
recoudre	*like*	**coudre**
recourir	*like*	**courir**
recouvrir	*like*	**couvrir**
récrire	*like*	**écrire**
recueillir	*like*	**cueillir**
redevenir	*like*	**tenir**
redire	*like*	**dire**
réduire	*like*	**conduire**
réécrire	*like*	**écrire**
réélire	*like*	**lire**
refaire	*like*	**faire**
rejoindre	*like*	**joindre**
relire	*like*	**lire**
reluire	*like*	**nuire**
remettre	*like*	**mettre**
*renaître	*like*	**naître**
rendormir	*like*	**mentir**

renvoyer	*like*	**envoyer**
se repaître	*like*	**paître**
reparaître	*like*	**connaître**
*repartir	*like*	**mentir**
repeindre	*like*	**atteindre**
repentir	*like*	**mentir**
reprendre	*like*	**prendre**
reproduire	*like*	**conduire**
résoudre	1 je résous, n résolvons 2 je résolvais 3 je résolus 5 je résolve 7 résolvant 8 résolu	
ressentir	*like*	**mentir**
resservir	*like*	**mentir**
ressortir	*like*	**mentir**
restreindre	*like*	**atteindre**
retenir	*like*	**tenir**
retransmettre	*like*	**mettre**
*revenir	*like*	**tenir**
revêtir	*like*	**vêtir**
revivre	*like*	**vivre**
revoir	*like*	**voir**
rire	1 je ris, n rions 2 je riais 3 je ris 5 je rie, n riions 7 riant 8 ri	
rompre	*regular except* 1 il rompt	
rouvrir	*like*	**couvrir**
satisfaire	*like*	**faire**
savoir	1 je sais, n savons, il savent 2 je savais 3 je sus 4 je saurai 5 je sache 6 sache, sachons, sachez 7 sachant 8 su	
séduire	*like*	**conduire**
sentir	*like*	**mentir**
servir	*like*	**mentir**
sortir	*like*	**mentir**
souffrir	*like*	**couvrir**
soumettre	*like*	**mettre**
sourire	*like*	**rire**
souscrire	*like*	**écrire**
soustraire	*like*	**abstraire**
soutenir	*like*	**tenir**
*se souvenir	*like*	**tenir**
subvenir	*like*	**tenir**
suffire	1 je suffis, n suffisons 2 je suffisais 3 je suffis 5 je suffise 7 suffisant 8 suffi	
suivre	1 je suis, n suivons 2 je suivais 3 je suivis 5 je suive 7 suivant 8 suivi	
surprendre	*like*	**prendre**
*survenir	*like*	**tenir**
survivre	*like*	**vivre**
taire	1 je tais, n taisons 2 je taisais 3 je tus 5 je taise 7 taisant 8 tu	

teindre	*like*	**atteindre**
tenir		1 je tiens, ne tenons, ils tiennent 2 je tenais
		3 je tins, tu tins, il tint, n tînmes, v tîntes, ils tinrent
		4 je tiendrai 5 je tienne 7 tenant 8 tenu
traduire	*like*	**conduire**
traire	*like*	**abstraire**
transcrire	*like*	**écrire**
transmettre	*like*	**mettre**
transparaître	*like*	**connaître**
tressaillir	*like*	**défaillir**
vaincre		1 je vaincs, il vainc, n vainquons 2 je vainquais 3 je vainquis
		5 je vainque 7 vainquant 8 vaincu
valoir		1 je vaux, il vaut, n valons 2 je valais 3 je valus 4 je vaudrai
		5 je vaille 6 *not used* 7 valant 8 valu
*venir	*like*	**tenir**
vêtir		1 je vêts, n vêtons 2 je vêtais 5 je vête 7 vêtant 8 vêtu
vivre		1 je vis, n vivons 2 je vivais 3 je vécus 5 je vive 7 vivant
		8 vécu
voir		1 je vois, n voyons 2 je voyais 3 je vis 4 je verrai
		5 je voie, n voyions 7 voyant 8 vu
vouloir		1 je veux, il veut, n voulons, ils veulent 2 je voulais
		3 je voulus 4 je voudrai 5 je veuille
		6 veuille, veuillons, veuillez 7 voulant 8 voulu

Verbes anglais irréguliers

Infinitif	Prétérit	Participe passé
arise	arose	arisen
awake	awoke	awoken
awaken	awoke, awakened	awakened, awoken
be	were/was	been
bear	bore	borne
beat	beat	beaten
become	became	become
begin	began	begun
bend	bent	bent
beseech	besought, beseeched	besought, beseeched
bet	bet, betted	bet, betted
bid	bade, bid	bidden, bid
bind	bound	bound
bite	bit	bitten
bleed	bled	bled
blow	blew	blown
break	broke	broken
breed	bred	bred
bring	brought	brought
build	built	built
burn	burnt, burned	burnt, burned
burst	burst	burst
bust	bust, busted	bust, busted
buy	bought	bought
cast	cast	cast
catch	caught	caught
chide	chided, chid	chided, chidden
choose	chose	chosen
cleave	cleaved, cleft, clove	cleaved, cleft, cloven
cling	clung	clung
clothe	clad, clothed	clad, clothed
come	came	come
cost	cost	cost
creep	crept	crept
crow	crowed, crew	crowed
cut	cut	cut
deal	dealt	dealt
dig	dug	dug
dive	dived, *Am* dove	dived
do	did	done
draw	drew	drawn
dream	dreamt, dreamed	dreamt, dreamed
drink	drank	drunk
drive	drove	driven
dwell	dwelt	dwelt
eat	ate	eaten

Infinitif	Prétérit	Participe passé
fall	fell	fallen
feed	fed	fed
feel	felt	felt
fight	fought	fought
find	found	found
flee	fled	fled
fling	flung	flung
fly	flew	flown
forget	forgot	forgotten
forgive	forgave	forgiven
forsake	forsook	forsaken
freeze	froze	frozen
get	got	got, *Am* gotten
gild	gilded, gilt	gilded, gilt
gird	girded, girt	girded, girt
give	gave	given
go	went	gone
grind	ground	ground
grow	grew	grown
hang	hung/hanged	hung/hanged
have	had	had
hear	heard	heard
hew	hewed	hewn, hewed
hide	hid	hidden
hit	hit	hit
hold	held	held
hurt	hurt	hurt
keep	kept	kept
kneel	knelt	knelt
knit	knitted, knit	knitted, knit
know	knew	known
lay	laid	laid
lead	led	led
lean	leant, leaned	leant, leaned
leap	leapt, leaped	leapt, leaped
learn	learnt, learned	learnt, learned
leave	left	left
lend	lent	lent
let	let	let
lie	lay	lain
light	lit	lit
lose	lost	lost
make	made	made
mean	meant	meant
meet	met	met
mow	mowed	mown
pay	paid	paid
plead	pleaded, *Am* pled	pleaded, *Am* pled
prove	proved	proved, proven
put	put	put
quit	quit	quit
read	read	read

(12)

Infinitif	Prétérit	Participe passé
rend	rent	rent
rid	rid	rid
ride	rode	ridden
ring	rang	rung
rise	rose	risen
run	ran	run
saw	sawed	sawn, sawed
say	said	said
see	saw	seen
seek	sought	sought
sell	sold	sold
send	sent	sent
set	set	set
sew	sewed	sewn
shake	shook	shaken
shear	sheared	shorn, sheared
shed	shed	shed
shine	shone	shone
shoe	shod	shod
shoot	shot	shot
show	showed	shown
shrink	shrank	shrunk
shut	shut	shut
sing	sang	sung
sink	sank	sunk
sit	sat	sat
slay	slew	slain
sleep	slept	slept
slide	slid	slid
sling	slung	slung
slink	slunk	slunk
slit	slit	slit
smell	smelled, smelt	smelled, smelt
smite	smote	smitten
sow	sowed	sown, sowed
speak	spoke	spoken
speed	sped, speeded	sped, speeded
spell	spelt, spelled	spelt, spelled
spend	spent	spent
spill	spilt, spilled	spilt, spilled
spin	span	spun
spit	spat, *Am* spit	spat, *Am* spit
split	split	split
spoil	spoilt, spoiled	spoilt, spoiled
spread	spread	spread
spring	sprang	sprung
stand	stood	stood
stave in	staved in, stove in	staved in, stove in
steal	stole	stolen
stick	stuck	stuck
sting	stung	stung
stink	stank, stunk	stunk

Infinitif	Prétérit	Participe passé
strew	strewed	strewed, strewn
stride	strode	stridden
strike	struck	struck
string	strung	strung
strive	strove	striven
swear	swore	sworn
sweep	swept	swept
swell	swelled	swollen, swelled
swim	swam	swum
swing	swung	swung
take	took	taken
teach	taught	taught
tear	tore	torn
tell	told	told
think	thought	thought
thrive	thrived, throve	thrived
throw	threw	thrown
thrust	thrust	thrust
tread	trod	trodden
wake	woke	woken
wear	wore	worn
weave	wove, weaved	woven, weaved
weep	wept	wept
wet	wet, wetted	wet, wetted
win	won	won
wind	wound	wound
wring	wrung	wrung
write	wrote	written

Français-Anglais

French-English

Aa

A, a [ɑ] *nm inv* A, a; **A1** *(auto-route) Br* ≃ M1, *Am* ≃ I1
a [a] *voir* **avoir**

à [a]

à + le = au [o], à + les = aux [o]

prép **(a)** *(indique la direction)* to; **aller à Paris** to go to Paris; **partir au Venezuela** to leave for Venezuela; **de Paris à Lyon** from Paris to Lyons **(b)** *(indique la position)* at; **être au bureau/à la ferme/à Paris** to be at *or* in the office/on *or* at the farm/in Paris; **à la maison** at home **(c)** *(dans l'expression du temps)* **à 8 heures** at 8 o'clock; **du lundi au vendredi** from Monday to Friday, *Am* Monday through Friday; **au vingt-et-unième siècle** in the twenty-first century; **à mon arrivée** on (my) arrival; **à lundi!** see you (on) Monday! **(d)** *(dans les descriptions)* **l'homme à la barbe** the man with the beard; **verre à vin** wine glass **(e)** *(introduit le complément d'objet indirect)* **donner qch à qn** to give sth to sb, to give sb sth; **penser à qn/qch** to think about *or* of sb/sth **(f)** *(devant un infinitif)* **apprendre à lire** to learn to read; **avoir du travail à faire** to have work to do; **maison à vendre** house for sale; **prêt à partir** ready to leave **(g)** *(indique l'appartenance)* **un ami à moi** a friend of mine; **c'est à lui** it's his; **c'est à vous de...** *(il vous incombe de)* it's up to you to...;

(c'est votre tour) it's your turn to... **(h)** *(indique le moyen, la manière)* **à bicyclette** by bicycle; **à pied** on foot; **à la main** by hand; **au crayon** in pencil; **deux à deux** two by two **(i)** *(prix)* **pain à 1 euro** loaf for 1 euro **(j)** *(poids)* **vendre au kilo** to sell by the kilo **(k)** *(vitesse)* **100 km à l'heure** 100 km an *or* per hour **(l)** *(pour appeler)* **au voleur!** (stop) thief!; **au feu!** (there's a) fire!

abaisser [abese] *vt* to lower
abandonner [abɑ̃dɔne] **1** *vt* *(personne, animal, lieu)* to desert, to abandon; *(pouvoir, combat)* to give up; *(projet)* to abandon; **a ses études** to drop out (of school) **2** *vi (renoncer)* to give up
abat-jour [abaʒur] *nm inv* lampshade
abats [aba] *nmpl* offal
abattoir [abatwar] *nm* abattoir
abattre* [abatr] *vt (arbre)* to cut down; *(personne)* to kill; *(animal)* to slaughter
abbaye [abei] *nf* abbey
abcès [apsɛ] *nm* abscess
abeille [abɛj] *nf* bee
abîme [abim] *nm* abyss
abîmer [abime] **1** *vt* to spoil, to damage **2 s'abîmer** *vpr (object)* to get spoilt; *(fruit)* to go bad
abolir [abɔlir] *vt* to abolish
abominable [abɔminabl] *adj* appalling
abondant, -e [abɔ̃dɑ̃, -ɑ̃t] *adj* plentiful, abundant

abonné, -e [abɔne] *nmf (d'un journal, du téléphone)* subscriber; *(du gaz)* consumer ● **abonnement** *nm (de journal)* subscription; *(de téléphone)* line rental ● **s'abonner** *vpr (à un journal)* to subscribe (**à** to)

abord [abɔr] **(tout) d'a.** *adv (pour commencer)* at first, to begin with; *(premièrement)* first of all

abordable [abɔrdabl] *adj (prix, marchandises)* affordable

aborder [abɔrde] *vt (personne)* to approach; *(problème)* to tackle

aboutir [abutir] *vi (réussir)* to be successful; **a. à qch** *(avoir pour résultat)* to result in sth

aboyer [abwaje] *vi* to bark

abrégé [abreʒe] *nm* summary

abréviation [abrevjasjɔ̃] *nf* abbreviation

abri [abri] *nm* shelter; **mettre qn/qch à l'a.** to shelter sb/sth; **se mettre à l'a.** to take shelter; **être à l'a. de qch** to be sheltered from sth; **sans a.** homeless ● **abriter 1** *vt (protéger)* to shelter (**de** from); *(loger)* to house **2 s'abriter** *vpr* to (take) shelter (**de** from)

abricot [abriko] *nm* apricot

absence [apsɑ̃s] *nf (d'une personne)* absence; *(manque)* lack ● **absent, -e 1** *adj (personne)* absent (**de** from); *(chose)* missing **2** *nmf* absentee ● **s'absenter** *vpr* to go away

absolu, -e [apsɔly] *adj* absolute ● **absolument** *adv* absolutely

absorber [apsɔrbe] *vt* to absorb

abstenir* [apstənir] **s'abstenir** *vpr (ne pas voter)* to abstain; **s'a. de qch/de faire qch** to refrain from sth/from doing sth

abstrait, -e [apstrɛ, -ɛt] *adj* abstract

absurde [apsyrd] *adj* absurd

abus [aby] *nm (excès)* overindulgence (**de** in); *(pratique)* abuse (**de** of); **a. d'alcool** alcohol abuse ● **abuser 1** *vi* to go too far; **a. de** *(situation, personne)* to take advantage of; *(nourriture)* to overindulge in **2 s'abuser** *vpr* **si je ne m'abuse** if I am not mistaken

académie [akademi] *nf* academy; **l'A. française** = learned society responsible for promoting the French language and imposing standards

accabler [akɑble] *vt* to overwhelm (**de** with) ● **accablant, -e** *adj (chaleur)* oppressive; *(témoignage)* damning

accéder [aksede] *vi* **a. à** *(lieu)* to reach

accélérer [akselere] *vi (en voiture)* to accelerate ● **accélérateur** *nm Aut* accelerator

accent [aksɑ̃] *nm (prononciation)* accent; *(sur une syllabe)* stress; *Fig* **mettre l'a. sur qch** to stress sth; **a. aigu/circonflexe/grave** acute/circumflex/grave (accent) ● **accentuer** *vt (syllabe)* to stress; *(lettre)* to put an accent on; *Fig (renforcer)* to emphasize

accepter [aksepte] *vt* to accept; **a. de faire qch** to agree to do sth ● **acceptable** *adj (recevable)* acceptable

accès [aksɛ] *nm* **(a)** access (**à** to); **avoir a. à qch** to have access to sth; **'a. interdit'** 'no entry' **(b)** *(de folie, de colère)* fit; *(de fièvre)* bout ● **accessible** *adj (lieu, livre)* accessible

accessoires [akseswar] *nmpl (de mode)* accessories; **a. de toilette** toiletries

accident [aksidɑ̃] *nm* accident; **a. de chemin de fer** train crash; **a. de la route** road accident;

par a. by accident, by chance • **accidentel, -elle** *adj* accidental
acclimater [aklimate] **s'acclimater** *vpr* to become *Br* acclimatized or *Am* acclimated (**à** to)
accommoder [akɔmɔde] **1** *vt* (*nourriture*) to prepare **2 s'accommoder** *vpr* **s'a. de qch** to put up with sth • **accommodant, -e** *adj* accommodating
accompagner [akɔ̃paɲe] *vt* (*personne*) to accompany; **a. qn à la gare** (*en voiture*) to take sb to the station • **accompagnement** *nm* (*de musique*) accompaniment
accomplir [akɔ̃plir] *vt* (*tâche*) to carry out • **accompli, -e** *adj* (*parfait*) accomplished
accord [akɔr] *nm* (*traité, entente*) & *Gram* agreement; (*autorisation*) consent; (*musical*) chord; **être d'a.** to agree (**avec** with); **d'a.!** all right! • **accorder 1** *vt* (*instrument*) to tune; **a. qch à qn** (*faveur*) to grant sb sth; (*prêt*) to authorize sth to sb **2 s'accorder** *vpr* (*se mettre d'accord*) to agree (**avec/sur** with/on); *Gram* (*mots*) to agree (**avec** with); **s'a. qch** to allow oneself sth
accordéon [akɔrdeɔ̃] *nm* accordion
accoucher [akuʃe] *vi* to give birth (**de** to)
accouder [akude] **s'accouder** *vpr* **s'a. à** *ou* **sur qch** to lean one's elbows on sth
accoutumer [akutyme] **s'accoutumer** *vpr* to get accustomed (**à** to)
accroc [akro] *nm* (*déchirure*) tear; (*difficulté*) hitch; **sans a.** without a hitch
accrocher [akrɔʃe] **1** *vt* (*déchirer*) to catch; (*fixer*) to hook (**à** onto); (*suspendre*) to hang up (**à** on) **2 s'accrocher** *vpr* (*se fixer*) to fasten; *Fam* (*persévérer*) to stick

at it; **s'a. à qn/qch** (*s'agripper*) to cling to sb/sth • **accrocheur, -euse** *adj* (*slogan*) catchy
accroître* [akrwatr] **1** *vt* to increase **2 s'accroître** *vpr* to increase • **accroissement** *nm* increase (**de** in)
accroupir [akrupir] **s'accroupir** *vpr* to squat (down)
accueil [akœj] *nm* (*bureau*) reception; (*manière*) welcome • **accueillant, -e** *adj* welcoming • **accueillir*** *vt* (*personne*) to greet; (*sujet: hôtel*) to accommodate
accumuler [akymyle] *vt*, **s'accumuler** *vpr* to accumulate
accuser [akyze] *vt* (*dénoncer*) to accuse; **a. qn de qch/de faire qch** to accuse sb of sth/of doing sth • **accusation** *nf* accusation • **accusé, -e** *nmf* **l'a.** the accused
achalandé, -e [aʃalɑ̃de] *adj* **bien a.** (*magasin*) well-stocked
acharner [aʃarne] **s'acharner** *vpr* **s'a. sur** *ou* **contre qn** (*persécuter*) to persecute sb; **s'a. à faire qch** to try very hard to do sth • **acharné, -e** *adj* (*effort, travail*) relentless; (*combat*) fierce
achat [aʃa] *nm* purchase; **achats** (*paquets*) shopping
acheter [aʃəte] **1** *vt* to buy; **a. qch à qn** (*faire une transaction*) to buy sth from sb; (*faire un cadeau*) to buy sth for sb **2 s'acheter** *vpr* **je vais m'acheter une glace** I'm going to buy (myself) an ice cream • **acheteur, -euse** *nmf* buyer
achever [aʃəve] *vt* (**a**) (*finir*) to end; (*travail*) to complete; **a. de faire qch** to finish doing sth (**b**) (*tuer*) (*animal malade*) to put out of its misery; **a. qn** to finish sb off • **achèvement** *nm* completion
acide [asid] **1** *adj* acid(ic); (*au goût*) sour **2** *nm* acid

acier [asje] *nm* steel

acné [akne] *nf* acne

acompte [akɔ̃t] *nm* deposit; **verser un a.** to pay a deposit

à-coup [aku] *(pl* **à-coups)** *nm* jolt; **sans à-coups** smoothly; **par à-coups** *(avancer)* in fits and starts

acquérir* [akerir] *vt (acheter)* to purchase; *(obtenir)* to acquire; **tenir qch pour acquis** to take sth for granted • **acquis** *nm (expérience)* experience

acquitter [akite] *vt (accusé)* to acquit; *(dette)* to pay

acrobate [akrɔbat] *nmf* acrobat • **acrobatie** *nf* acrobatics *(sing)*

acrylique [akrilik] *nm* acrylic

acte [akt] *nm (action)* & *Théât* act; **prendre a. de qch** to take note of sth; **a. de naissance** birth certificate

acteur [aktœr] *nm* actor

actif, -ive [aktif, -iv] *adj* active

action [aksjɔ̃] *nf (acte)* action; **passer à l'a.** to take action

activer [aktive] **s'activer** *vpr (être actif)* to be busy

activité [aktivite] *nf* activity

actrice [aktris] *nf* actress

actualité [aktɥalite] *nf* **l'a.** current affairs; **les actualités** *(à la radio, à la télévision)* the news

actuel, -elle [aktɥɛl] *adj (présent)* present; *(d'actualité)* topical • **actuellement** *adv* at present

adapter [adapte] **1** *vt* to adapt (**à** to) **2 s'adapter** *vpr (s'acclimater)* to adapt (**à** to); **s'a. à qn/qch** to get used to sb/sth • **adaptateur** *nm* adapter • **adaptation** *nf* adaptation

addition [adisjɔ̃] *nf* addition (**à** to); *(de restaurant)* Br bill, Am check • **additionner** *vt* to add (up) (**à** to)

adepte [adept] *nmf* follower

adéquat, -e [adekwa, -at] *adj* appropriate; *(quantité)* adequate

adhérer [adere] *vi* **a. à qch** *(coller)* to stick to sth; *(s'inscrire)* to join sth • **adhérent, -e** *nmf* member

adhésif, -ive [adezif, -iv] *adj* adhesive

adieu, -x [adjø] *nm* & *exclam* farewell

adjacent, -e [adʒasɑ̃, -ɑ̃t] *adj* adjacent (**à** to)

adjectif [adʒɛktif] *nm* adjective

adjoint, -e [adʒwɛ̃, -ɛ̃t] *nmf* assistant

admettre* [admɛtr] *vt (accueillir, reconnaître)* to admit; *(autoriser)* to allow; **être admis à un examen** to pass an exam

administration [administrasjɔ̃] *nf* administration; **l'A.** *(service public)* ≃ the Civil Service; *(fonctionnaires)* civil servants

admirer [admire] *vt* to admire • **admirateur, -trice** *nmf* admirer • **admiration** *nf* admiration

admissible [admisibl] *adj (tolérable)* acceptable, admissible • **admission** *nf* admission (**à/dans** to)

adolescent, -e [adɔlesɑ̃, -ɑ̃t] *nmf* adolescent, teenager • **adolescence** *nf* adolescence

adonner [adɔne] **s'adonner** *vpr* **s'a. à qch** to devote oneself to sth; **s'a. à la boisson** to be an alcoholic

adopter [adɔpte] *vt* to adopt • **adoption** *nf* adoption

adorer [adɔre] **1** *vt* to adore; **a. faire qch** to adore doing sth **2 s'adorer** *vpr* **ils s'adorent** they adore each other • **adorable** *adj* adorable

adosser [adose] **s'adosser** *vpr* **s'a. à qch** to lean (back) against sth

adoucir [adusir] *vt* to soften

adresse [adrɛs] *nf* **(a)** *(domicile)*

address; **a. électronique** e-mail address (**b**) *(habileté)* skill • **adresser 1** *vt (lettre, remarque)* to address (**à** to); **a. qch à qn** *(lettre)* to send sb sth; **a. la parole à qn** to speak to sb **2 s'adresser** *vpr* **s'a. à qn** *(parler)* to speak to sb; *(aller trouver)* to go and see sb; *(être destiné à)* to be aimed at sb

adroit, -e [adrwa, -at] *adj (habile)* skilful

adulte [adylt] *adj & nmf* adult

adverbe [adverb] *nm* adverb

adversaire [adverser] *nmf* opponent

aérer [aere] *vt (pièce, lit)* to air

aéro- [aero] *préf* aero- • **aérobic** *nm* aerobics *(sing)* • **aérogare** *nf* air terminal • **aéroglisseur** *nm* hovercraft • **aéroport** *nm* airport • **aérosol** *nm* aerosol

affaiblir [afeblir] *vt,* **s'affaiblir** *vpr* to weaken • **affaiblissement** *nm* weakening

affaire [afer] *nf (question)* matter, affair; *(marché)* deal; *(scandale)* affair; *(procès)* case; **affaires** *(commerce)* business *(sing)*; *(effets personnels)* belongings; **avoir a. à qn/qch** to have to deal with sb/sth; **faire une bonne a.** to get a bargain; **c'est mon a.** that's my business; **ça fera l'a.** that will do nicely; **a. de cœur** love affair

affaler [afale] **s'affaler** *vpr* to collapse; **affalé dans un fauteuil** slumped in an armchair

affamé, -e [afame] *adj* starving

affecté, -e [afɛkte] *adj Péj (manières, personne)* affected

affection [afɛksjɔ̃] *nf (attache-ment)* affection; *(maladie)* ailment; **avoir de l'a. pour qn** to be fond of sb • **affectueux, -euse** *adj* affectionate

affiche [afiʃ] *nf* notice; *(publicitaire)* poster; **être à l'a.** *(spectacle)* to be on • **afficher** *vt (avis)* to put up; *(prix, horaire, résultat)* to display

affinité [afinite] *nf* affinity

affirmer [afirme] **1** *vt (manifester)* to assert; *(soutenir)* to maintain **2 s'affirmer** *vpr (personne)* to assert oneself

affoler [afɔle] **s'affoler** *vpr* to panic • **affolant, -e** *adj* terrifying

affranchir [afrɑ̃ʃir] *vt (timbrer)* to put a stamp on; *(émanciper)* to free • **affranchissement** *nm (tarif)* postage

affreux, -euse [afrø, -øz] *adj (laid)* hideous; *(atroce)* dreadful

affront [afrɔ̃] *nm* insult; **faire un a. à qn** to insult sb

affronter [afrɔ̃te] **1** *vt* to face **2 s'affronter** *vpr (ennemis, équipes)* to clash

afin [afɛ̃] **1** *prép* **a. de faire qch** in order to do sth **2** *conj* **a. que...** *(+ subjunctive)* so that...

Afrique [afrik] *nf* **l'A.** Africa • **africain, -e 1** *adj* African **2** *nmf* **A., Africaine** African

agacer [agase] *vt (personne)* to irritate • **agaçant, -e** *adj* irritating

âge [aʒ] *nm* age; **quel â. as-tu?** how old are you?; **d'un certain â.** middle-aged • **âgé, -e** *adj* old; **être â. de six ans** to be six years old; **un enfant â. de six ans** a six-year-old child

agence [aʒɑ̃s] *nf* agency; *(de banque)* branch; **a. de voyage** travel agent's; **a. immobilière** *Br* estate agent's, *Am* real estate office

agenda [aʒɛ̃da] *nm Br* diary, *Am* datebook

agenouiller [aʒənuje] **s'age-nouiller** *vpr* to kneel (down)

agent [aʒɑ̃] *nm (employé, espion)*

agent; **a. de police** police officer; **a. immobilier** *Br* estate agent, *Am* real estate agent; **a. secret** secret agent

agglomération [aglɔmerasjɔ̃] *nf (ville)* built-up area, town; **l'a. parisienne** Paris and its suburbs

aggraver [agrave] **1** *vt (situation, maladie)* to make worse; *(difficultés)* to increase **2 s'aggraver** *vpr (situation, maladie)* to get worse; *(état de santé)* to deteriorate; *(difficultés)* to increase

agile [aʒil] *adj* agile ● **agilité** *nf* agility

agir [aʒir] **1** *vi* to act **2 s'agir** *v impersonnel* **de quoi s'agit-il?** what is it about?; **il s'agit de se dépêcher** we have to hurry

agitation [aʒitasjɔ̃] *nf (fébrilité)* restlessness; *(troubles)* unrest

agiter [aʒite] *vt (remuer)* to stir; *(secouer)* to shake; *(troubler)* to agitate ● **agité, -e** *adj (mer)* rough; *(personne)* restless; *(period)* unsettled

agneau, -x [aɲo] *nm* lamb

agonie [agɔni] *nf* death throes; **être à l'a.** to be at death's door

agrafe [agraf] *nf (pour vêtement)* hook; *(pour papiers)* staple ● **agrafer** *vt (vêtement)* to fasten; *(papiers)* to staple ● **agrafeuse** *nf* stapler

agrandir [agrɑ̃dir] **1** *vt (rendre plus grand)* to enlarge; *(grossir)* to magnify **2 s'agrandir** *vpr (entreprise)* to expand; *(ville)* to grow ● **agrandissement** *nm (d'entreprise)* expansion; *(de ville)* growth; *(de photo)* enlargement

agréable [agreabl] *adj* pleasant

agréer [agree] *vt (fournisseur)* to approve; **veuillez a. l'expression de mes salutations distinguées** *(dans une lettre)* *(à quelqu'un*

dont on ne connaît pas le nom) B* yours faithfully, *Am* sincerely; *(* *quelqu'un dont on connaît le nom* *Br* yours sincerely, *Am* sincerely ● **agréé, -e** *adj (fournisseur, centre* approved

agresser [agrese] *vt* to attack; **s** **faire a.** to be attacked; *(pour son argent)* to be mugged ● **agresseu** *nm* attacker; *(dans un conflit* aggressor ● **agression** *nf* attack *(pour de l'argent)* mugging; *(d'un* *État)* aggression; **être victim** **d'une a.** to be attacked; *(pour son* argent)* to be mugged

agressif, -ive [agresif, -iv] *ad* aggressive

agricole [agrikɔl] *adj* agricultural

agriculture [agrikyltyr] *n* farming

agrume [agrym] *nm* citrus fruit

aguets [age] **aux aguets** *adv* o the lookout

aguichant, -e [agiʃɑ̃, -ɑ̃t] *ac* seductive

ai [ɛ] *voir* **avoir**

aide [ɛd] *nf* help, assistance; **l'a. de qch** with the aid of sth **appeler à l'a.** to call for help **a. humanitaire** aid ● **aide** **mémoire** *nm inv* notes

aider [ede] **1** *vt* to help; **a. qn faire qch** to help sb to do sth **s'aider** *vpr* **s'a. de qch** to use sth

aïe [aj] *exclam* ouch!

aie(s), aient [ɛ] *voir* **avoir**

aigle [ɛgl] *nm* eagle

aigre [ɛgr] *adj* sour

aigu, -ë [egy] *adj (douleur, crise* accent)* acute; *(son)* high-pitched

aiguille [egɥij] *nf (à coudre* needle; *(de montre)* hand; *(d* balance)* pointer

aiguiser [egize] *vt (outil)* t sharpen

ail [aj] *nm* garlic

aile [εl] *nf* wing

aille(s), aillent [aj] *voir* **aller¹**

ailleurs [ajœr] *adv* somewhere else, elsewhere; **d'a.** *(du reste)* besides, anyway; **par a.** *(en outre)* moreover

aimable [εmabl] *adj (gentil)* kind

aimant¹ [εmã] *nm* magnet

aimant², -e [εmã, -ãt] *adj* loving

aimer [eme] **1** *vt* to love; **a. bien qn/qch** to like sb/sth; **a. faire qch** to like doing sth; **j'aimerais qu'il vienne** I would like him to come; **a. mieux qch** to prefer sth **2 s'aimer** *vpr* **ils s'aiment** they're in love

aine [εn] *nf* groin

aîné, -e [ene] *nmf (de deux enfants)* elder; *(de plus de deux)* eldest

ainsi [ẽsi] *adv (de cette façon)* in this way; *(alors)* so; **a. que...** as well as...; **et a. de suite** and so on; **pour a. dire** so to speak

air [εr] *nm* **(a)** *(gaz)* air; **prendre l'a.** to get some fresh air; **au grand a.** in the fresh air; **en plein a.** outside; **en l'a.** *(jeter)* (up) in the air **(b)** *(expression)* look, appearance; **avoir l'a. content** to look happy; **avoir l'a. de s'ennuyer** to look bored **(c)** *(mélodie)* tune

aire [εr] *nf* area; **a. de jeux** (children's) play area; **a. de repos** *(sur autoroute)* rest area; **a. de stationnement** lay-by

aise [εz] *nf* **à l'a.** comfortable; **mal à l'a.** uncomfortable, ill at ease • **aisé, -e** *adj (fortuné)* comfortably off; *(facile)* easy

aisselle [εsεl] *nf* armpit

ait [ε] *voir* **avoir**

ajouter [aʒute] *vti* to add **(à** to)

ajuster [aʒyste] *vt (appareil, outil)* to adjust; *(vêtement)* to alter

alarme [alarm] *nf* alarm; **donner l'a.** to raise the alarm; **a. antivol/d'incendie** burglar/fire alarm • **alarmer 1** *vt* to alarm **2 s'alarmer** *vpr* **s'a. de qch** to become alarmed at sth

album [albɔm] *nm* album; **a. de photos** photo album

alcool [alkɔl] *nm* alcohol; **a. à 90°** *Br* surgical spirit, *Am* rubbing alcohol • **alcoolique** *adj* & *nmf* alcoholic • **alcoolisée** *adj* f **boisson a.** alcoholic drink; **boisson non a.** soft drink

alcôve [alkov] *nf* alcove

aléatoire [aleatwar] *adj (résultat)* uncertain; *(nombre)* random

alentours [alãtur] *nmpl* surroundings; **aux a. de la ville** in the vicinity of the town

alerte [alεrt] **1** *adj (leste)* sprightly; *(éveillé)* alert **2** *nf* alarm; **en état d'a.** on the alert; **donner l'a.** to give the alarm; **a. à la bombe** bomb scare; **fausse a.** false alarm

algèbre [alʒεbr] *nf* algebra

Algérie [alʒeri] *nf* **l'A.** Algeria • **algérien, -enne 1** *adj* Algerian **2** *nmf* **A., Algérienne** Algerian

algues [alg] *nfpl* seaweed

alibi [alibi] *nm* alibi

aliment [alimã] *nm* food • **alimentaire** *adj (ration, industrie)* food; **produits alimentaires** foods • **alimentation** *nf (action)* feeding; *(en eau, en électricité)* supply(ing); *(nourriture)* food; **magasin d'a.** grocer's, grocery store

allaiter [alete] *vt* to breastfeed

allécher [aleʃe] *vt* to tempt

allée [ale] *nf (de parc)* path; *(de ville)* avenue; *(de cinéma, de supermarché)* aisle; **allées et venues** comings and goings

allégation [alegasjɔ̃] *nf* allegation

allégé, -e [aleʒe] *adj (aliment)* low-fat

Allemagne [almaɲ] *nf* **l'A.** Germany • **allemand, -e 1** *adj* German **2** *nmf* **A.**, **Allemande** German **3** *nm (langue)* German

aller*¹ [ale] **1** *(aux être) vi* to go; **a. à Paris** to go to Paris; **a. à la pêche** to go fishing; **a. faire qch** to go and do sth; **a. à qn** *(convenir à)* to suit sb; **a. avec** *(vêtement)* to go with; **a. bien/mieux** *(personne)* to be well/better; **comment vas-tu?**, **(comment) ça va?** how are you?; **ça va!** all right!, fine!; **allez-y** go ahead **2** *v aux (futur proche)* **a. faire qch** to be going to do sth; **il va venir** he'll come; **il va partir** he's about to leave **3** **s'en aller** [sɑ̃nale] *vpr (personne)* to go away; *(tache)* to come out

aller² [ale] *nm* outward journey; **a. (simple)** *Br* single (ticket), *Am* one-way (ticket); **a. (et) retour** *Br* return (ticket), *Am* round-trip (ticket)

allergie [alɛrʒi] *nf* allergy • **allergique** *adj* allergic (**à** to)

alliance [aljɑ̃s] *nf (anneau)* wedding ring; *(mariage)* marriage; *(de pays)* alliance

allier [alje] **1** *vt (associer)* to combine (**à** with); *(pays)* to ally (**à** with); *(famille)* to unite by marriage **2** **s'allier** *vpr (couleurs)* to combine; *(pays)* to become allied (**à** with); **s'a. contre qn/qch** to unite against sb/sth • **allié, -e** *nmf* ally

allô [alo] *exclam* hello!

allocation [alɔkasjɔ̃] *nf (somme)* allowance; **a. (de) chômage/ (de) logement** unemployment/ housing benefit; **allocations familiales** child benefit

allonger [alɔ̃ʒe] **1** *vt (bras)* to stretch out **2** **s'allonger** *vpr (jours)* to get longer; *(personne)* to lie down • **allongé, -e** *adj (étiré)* elongated; **être a.** *(personne)* to be lying down

allumer [alyme] **1** *vt (feu, pipe)* to light; *(électricité, radio)* to switch on; *(incendie)* to start **2** **s'allumer** *vpr (lumière, lampe)* to come on

allumette [alymɛt] *nf* match

allure [alyr] *nf (vitesse)* speed; *(démarche)* gait, walk; *(maintien)* bearing; **à toute a.** at top speed; **avoir de l'a.** to look stylish

allusion [alyzjɔ̃] *nf (référence)* allusion (**à** to); *(voilée)* hint; **faire a. à qch** to allude to sth; *(en termes voilés)* to hint at sth

alors [alɔr] *adv (donc)* so; *(à ce moment-là)* then; *(dans ce cas)* in that case; **a. que...** *(lorsque)* when...; *(tandis que)* whereas...; **et a.?** so what?

alouette [alwɛt] *nf* lark

Alpes [alp] *nfpl* **les A.** the Alps

alphabet [alfabɛ] *nm* alphabet • **alphabétique** *adj* alphabetical

alpinisme [alpinism] *nm* mountaineering; **faire de l'a.** to go mountaineering • **alpiniste** *nmf* mountaineer

altérer [altere] *vt (changer)* to affect

alternatif, -ive [altɛrnatif, -iv] *adj & nf* alternative • **alternativement** *adv* alternately

alterner [altɛrne] *vi (se succéder)* to alternate (**avec** with) • **alternance** *nf* alternation; **en a.** alternately

altitude [altityd] *nf* altitude

aluminium [alyminjɔm] *nm Br* aluminium, *Am* aluminum; **papier (d')a.** tinfoil

amande [amɑ̃d] *nf* almond

amant [amɑ̃] *nm* lover

amateur [amatœr] **1** *nm (non professionnel)* amateur; **a. de tennis** tennis enthusiast; **faire de la photo en a.** to be an amateur photographer **2** *adj* **une équipe a.** an amateur team

ambassade [ãbasad] *nf* embassy • **ambassadeur, -drice** *nmf* ambassador

ambiance [ãbjãs] *nf* atmosphere • **ambiant, -e** *adj* **température a.** room temperature

ambigu, -ë [ãbigy] *adj* ambiguous

ambitieux, -euse [ãbisjø, -øz] *adj* ambitious • **ambition** *nf* ambition

ambulance [ãbylãs] *nf* ambulance

âme [ɑm] *nf* soul; **rendre l'â.** to give up the ghost; **â. sœur** soul mate

améliorer [ameljɔre] *vt*, **s'améliorer** *vpr* to improve • **amélioration** *nf* improvement

amen [amɛn] *adv* amen

aménager [amenaʒe] *vt (changer)* to adjust, *(maison)* to convert (**en** into) • **aménagement** *nm (changement)* adjustment; *(de pièce)* conversion (**en** into)

amende [amãd] *nf* fine

amener [amne] *vt (apporter)* to bring; *(causer)* to bring about; **a. qn à faire qch** *(sujet: personne)* to get sb to do sth; **ce qui nous amène à parler de...** which brings us to the issue of...

amer, -ère [amɛr] *adj* bitter

Amérique [amerik] *nf* **l'A.** America; **l'A. du Nord/du Sud** North/South America; **l'A. latine** Latin America • **américain, -e 1** *adj* American **2** *nmf* **A., Américaine** American

amertume [amɛrtym] *nf* bitterness

ami, -e [ami] **1** *nmf* friend; **petit a.** boyfriend; **petite amie** girlfriend **2** *adj* friendly; **être a. avec qn** to be friends with sb

amical, -e, -aux, -ales [amikal, -o] *adj* friendly

amincir [amɛ̃sir] *vt* to make thin or thinner; **cette robe t'amincit** that dress makes you look thinner

amitié [amitje] *nf* friendship; **mes amitiés à votre mère** give my best wishes to your mother

amont [namɔ̃] **en amont** *adv* upstream (**de** from)

amorcer [amɔrse] **1** *vt (commencer)* to start; *Ordinat* to boot up **2 s'amorcer** *vpr* to start

amortir [amɔrtir] *vt (coup)* to absorb; *(bruit)* to deaden; *(chute)* to break; *(achat)* to recoup the costs of

amour [amur] *nm (sentiment, liaison)* love; **faire l'a. avec qn** to make love with *or* to sb; **pour l'a. du ciel!** for heaven's sake!; **mon a.** my darling, my love • **amoureux, -euse 1** *adj* **être a. de qn** to be in love with sb; **tomber a. de qn** to fall in love with sb **2** *nmpl* **un couple d'a.** a pair of lovers

amphithéâtre [ãfiteatr] *nm (romain)* amphitheatre; *(à l'université)* lecture hall

ample [ãpl] *adj (vêtement)* full; **de plus amples renseignements** more detailed information • **ampleur** *nf (importance)* scale, extent; **prendre de l'a.** to grow in size

amplifier [ãplifje] **1** *vt (son)* to amplify **2 s'amplifier** *vpr (son)* to increase • **amplificateur** *nm* amplifier

ampoule [ãpul] *nf (électrique)* (light) bulb; *(sur la peau)* blister

amputer [ãpyte] *vt (membre)* to

amputate; **a. qn de la jambe** to amputate sb's leg

amuser [amyze] **1** *vt* to amuse **2 s'amuser** *vpr* to amuse oneself; **s'a. avec qn/qch** to play with sb/sth; **s'a. à faire qch** to amuse oneself doing sth; **bien s'a.** to have a good time • **amusant, -e** *adj* amusing

amygdales [amidal] *nfpl* tonsils

an [ã] *nm* year; **il a dix ans** he's ten (years old); **par a.** per year; **en l'an 2008** in the year 2008; **bon a., mal a.** on average over the years

anagramme [anagram] *nf* anagram

analogue [analɔg] *adj* similar (**à** to)

analphabète [analfabɛt] *adj* & *nmf* illiterate

analyse [analiz] *nf* analysis; **a. de sang/d'urine** blood/urine test • **analyser** *vt* to analyse

ananas [anana(s)] *nm* pineapple

anarchie [anarʃi] *nf* anarchy • **anarchiste** *nmf* anarchist

anatomie [anatɔmi] *nf* anatomy

ancêtre [ãsɛtr] *nm* ancestor

anchois [ãʃwa] *nm* anchovy

ancien, -enne [ãsjɛ̃, -ɛn] *adj (vieux)* old; *(meuble)* antique; *(qui n'est plus)* former, old; **a. combattant** *Br* ex-serviceman, *Am* veteran • **anciennement** *adv* formerly

ancre [ãkr] *nf* anchor

andouille [ãduj] *nf* **(a)** *(charcuterie)* = sausage made from pigs' intestines **(b)** *Fam (idiot)* twit

âne [ɑn] *nm (animal)* donkey

anéantir [aneãtir] *vt (ville)* to destroy; *(espoirs)* to shatter • **anéanti, -e** *adj (épuisé)* exhausted; *(accablé)* overwhelmed

anecdote [anɛkdɔt] *nf* anecdote

anémie [anemi] *nf* an(a)emia • **anémique** *adj* an(a)emic

anesthésie [anɛstezi] *nf* an(a)esthesia; **être sous a.** to be under ana(e)sthetic; **a. générale/locale** general/local an(a)esthetic

ange [ãʒ] *nm* angel

angine [ãʒin] *nf* sore throat; **a. de poitrine** angina (pectoris)

anglais, -e [ãglɛ, -ɛz] **1** *adj* English **2** *nmf* **A., Anglaise** Englishman, *f* Englishwoman; **les A.** the English **3** *nm (langue)* English

angle [ãgl] *nm (point de vue)* & *Math* angle; *(coin de rue)* corner; **la maison qui fait l'a.** the house on the corner

Angleterre [ãglətɛr] *nf* **l'A.** England

anglo-normand, -e [ãglonɔrmã, -ãd] *adj* **les îles anglo-normandes** the Channel Islands

anglophone [ãglofɔn] **1** *adj* English-speaking **2** *nmf* English speaker

anglo-saxon, -onne [ãglosaksɔ̃, -ɔn] *(mpl* **anglo-saxons**, *fpl* **anglo-saxonnes**) *adj* & *nmf* Anglo-Saxon

angoisse [ãgwas] *nf* anguish • **angoissant, -e** *adj (nouvelle)* distressing; *(attente)* agonizing; *(livre)* frightening • **s'angoisser** *vpr* to get anxious

anguille [ãgij] *nf* eel

anicroche [anikrɔʃ] *nf* hitch, snag

animal, -aux [animal, -o] *nm* animal; **a. domestique** pet

animateur, -trice [animatœr, -tris] *nmf (de télévision, de radio)* presenter; *(de club)* leader

animer [anime] **s'animer** *vpr (rue)* to come to life; *(visage)* to light up; *(conversation)* to get more lively • **animation** *nf (vie)* life; *(divertissement)* event; *Cin* animation; **mettre de l'a. dans une soirée** to liven up a party •

animé, -e *adj (personne, conversation)* lively; *(rue, quartier)* busy

anis [ani(s)] *nm* aniseed

ankylosé, -e [ākiloze] *adj* stiff

anneau, -x [ano] *nm* ring

année [ane] *nf* year; **les années 90** the nineties

annexe [anɛks] *nf (bâtiment)* annexe; *(de lettre)* enclosure; *(de livre)* appendix; **document en a.** enclosed document

anniversaire [anivɛrsɛr] *nm (d'événement)* anniversary; *(de naissance)* birthday

annonce [anɔ̃s] *nf (déclaration)* announcement; *(publicitaire)* advertisement; *(indice)* sign; **passer une a. dans un journal** to put an ad(vertisement) in a newspaper; **petites annonces** classified advertisements, *Br* small ads • **annoncer 1** *vt (déclarer)* to announce; *(soldes, exposition)* to advertise; **a. qn** *(visiteur)* to show sb in **2 s'annoncer** *vpr* **ça s'annonce bien/mal** things aren't looking too bad/good

annuaire [anɥɛr] *nm (liste d'adresses)* directory; **a. téléphonique** telephone directory

annuel, -elle [anɥɛl] *adj* annual

annulaire [anɥlɛr] *nm* ring finger

annuler [anɥle] *vt* to cancel • **annulation** *nf* cancellation

anodin, -e [anɔdɛ̃, -in] *adj (remarque)* harmless; *(personne)* insignificant

anonyme [anɔnim] *adj* anonymous

anorak [anɔrak] *nm* anorak

anorexie [anɔrɛksi] *nf* anorexia • **anorexique** *adj & nmf* anorexic

anormal, -e, -aux, -ales [anɔrmal, -o] *adj* abnormal

Antarctique [ātarktik] *nm* **l'A.** the Antarctic, Antarctica

antenne [ātɛn] *nf (de radio, de satellite)* aerial, antenna; *(d'insecte)* antenna, feeler; *(société)* branch; **être à l'a.** to be on air; **a. parabolique** satellite dish

antérieur, -e [āterjœr] *adj (période)* former; *(année)* previous; *(date)* earlier; *(placé devant)* front; **a. à qch** prior to sth

anthologie [ātɔlɔʒi] *nf* anthology

antibiotique [ātibjɔtik] *nm* antibiotic

antibrouillard [ātibrujar] *adj & nm* **(phare) a.** fog lamp

anticipation [ātisipasjɔ̃] *nf* anticipation; **d'a.** *(roman, film)* futuristic • **anticipé, -e** *adj (retraite, retour)* early; *(paiement)* advance

antidépresseur [ātidepresœr] *nm* antidepressant

antidote [ātidɔt] *nm* antidote

antigel [ātiʒɛl] *nm* antifreeze

antihistaminique [ātiistaminik] *adj Méd* antihistamine

Antilles [ātij] *nfpl* **les A.** the West Indies • **antillais, -e 1** *adj* West Indian **2** *nmf* **A., Antillaise** West Indian

antilope [ātilɔp] *nf* antelope

antipathique [ātipatik] *adj* unpleasant; **elle m'est a.** I find her unpleasant

antipodes [ātipɔd] *nmpl* **être aux a. de** to be on the other side of the world from; *Fig* to be the exact opposite of

antique [ātik] *adj (de l'Antiquité)* ancient • **antiquité** *nf (objet ancien)* antique; **l'a. grecque/romaine** ancient Greece/Rome

antiseptique [ātisɛptik] *adj & nm* antiseptic

antisocial, -e, -aux, -ales [ɑtisɔsjal, -o] *adj* antisocial

antitabac [ātitaba] *adj inv* **lutte a.** anti-smoking campaign

antivol [ɑ̃tivɔl] *nm* anti-theft device

anxieux, -eux [ɑ̃ksjø, -øz] *adj* anxious

août [u(t)] *nm* August

apaiser [apeze] *vt* *(personne)* to calm (down); *(douleur)* to soothe; *(craintes)* to allay

apathique [apatik] *adj* apathetic

apercevoir* [apɛrsəvwar] **1** *vt* to see; *(brièvement)* to catch a glimpse of **2 s'apercevoir** *vpr* **s'a. de qch** to realize sth; **s'a. que...** to realize that...

apéritif [aperitif] *nm* aperitif; **prendre un a.** to have a drink before dinner

aphte [aft] *nm* mouth ulcer

apitoyer [apitwaje] **s'apitoyer** *vpr* **s'a. sur qn** to feel sorry for sb; **s'a. sur son sort** to feel sorry for oneself

aplatir [aplatir] **1** *vt* to flatten **2 s'aplatir** *vpr* *(être plat)* to be flat; *(devenir plat)* to go flat; **s'a. contre qch** to flatten oneself against sth ● **aplati, -e** *adj* flat

aplomb [aplɔ̃] *nm* *(assurance)* self-confidence

apogée [apɔʒe] *nm* apogée, peak; **être à l'a. de sa carrière** to be at the height of one's career

apostrophe [apɔstrɔf] *nf* *(signe)* apostrophe

apparaître* [aparɛtr] *(aux être)* *vi* *(se montrer, sembler)* to appear

appareil [aparɛj] *nm* *(instrument, machine)* apparatus; *(téléphone)* telephone; **qui est à l'a.?** *(au téléphone)* who's speaking?; **a. (dentaire)** *(correctif)* brace; **a. photo** camera; **appareils ménagers** household appliances

apparence [aparɑ̃s] *nf* appearance ● **apparemment** *adv* apparently ● **apparent, -e** *adj* apparent ●

apparition *nf* *(manifestation, appearance; (fantôme)* apparition **faire son a.** *(personne)* to make one's appearance

appartement [apartəmɑ̃] *nm* *B* flat, *Am* apartment

appartenir* [apartənir] *vi* t belong (**à** to)

appauvrir [apovrir] **s'appauvri** *vpr* to become impoverished

appel [apɛl] *nm* *(cri, attrait)* call *(invitation)* & *Jur* appeal; **fair l'a.** *(à l'école)* to take the register **faire a. à qn** to appeal to sb *(plombier, médecin)* to send fo sb; **a. au secours** call for help **a. téléphonique** telephone cal ● **appeler 1** *vt* *(personne, nom* to call; *(en criant)* to call out to **a. qn à l'aide** to call to sb fo help; **a. qn au téléphone** to cal sb **2 s'appeler** *vpr* to be called **comment vous appelez-vous** what's your name?; **je m'appell David** my name is David

appellation *nf* **a. contrôlée** *(d vin)* guaranteed vintage

appendice [apɛ̃dis] *nm* *(du corp de livre)* appendix ● **appendicit** *nf* appendicitis

appétit [apeti] *nm* appetite (**d** for); **bon a.!** enjoy your meal! **appétissant, -e** *adj* appetizing

applaudir [aplodir] *vti* to applau ● **applaudissements** *nm* applause

applicable [aplikabl] *adj* applicabl (**à** to) ● **application** *nf* *(action, soir* application; *(de loi)* enforcemen **entrer en a.** to come into force

appliquer [aplike] **1** *vt* to appl (**à/sur** to); *(loi, décision)* to enforc **2 s'appliquer** *vpr* *(se concentrer* to apply oneself (**à** to); **s'a. faire qch** to take pains to do sth **cette décision s'applique à...**

(concerne) this decision applies to… • **appliqué, -e** *adj (personne)* hard-working; *(écriture)* careful; *(sciences)* applied

apporter [apɔrte] *vt* to bring (**à** to); *(preuve)* to provide; *(modification)* to bring about • **apport** *nm* contribution (**à** to)

apprécier [apresje] *vt (aimer, percevoir)* to appreciate; *(évaluer)* to estimate

appréhender [apreɑ̃de] *vt (craindre)* to dread (**de faire qch** doing sth); *(arrêter)* to arrest; *(comprendre)* to grasp • **appréhension** *nf (crainte)* apprehension (**de** about)

apprendre* [aprɑ̃dr] *vti (étudier)* to learn; *(nouvelle)* to hear; **a. à faire qch** to learn to do sth; **a. qch à qn** *(enseigner)* to teach sb sth; *(informer)* to tell sb sth; **a. à qn à faire qch** to teach sb to do sth

apprenti, -e [aprɑ̃ti] *nmf* apprentice • **apprentissage** *nm (professionnel)* training; *(chez un artisan)* apprenticeship; *(d'une langue)* learning (**de** of)

apprivoiser [aprivwaze] *vt* to tame

approbation [aprɔbasjɔ̃] *nf* approval

approche [aprɔʃ] *nf* approach; **approches** *(de ville)* outskirts

approcher [aprɔʃe] **1** *vt (objet)* to bring up; *(personne)* to approach, to get close to; **a. qch de qn** to bring sth near (to) sb **2** *vi* to approach, to get closer **3** **s'approcher** *vpr* to approach, to get closer; **s'a. de qn/qch** to approach sb/sth; **il s'est approché de moi** he came up to me

approfondi, -e [aprɔfɔ̃di] *adj (étude, examen)* thorough

approprié, -e [aprɔprije] *adj* appropriate (**à** for)

approuver [apruve] *vt (facture, contrat)* to approve; *(décision)* to approve of

approvisionner [aprɔvizjɔne] *vt (ville, armée)* to supply (**en** with); *(magasin)* to stock (**en** with)

approximatif, -ive [aprɔksimatif, -iv] *adj* approximate • **approximation** *nf* approximation

appui [apɥi] *nm* support; **prendre a. sur qch** to lean on sth; **à l'a. de qch** in support of sth; **a. de fenêtre** window sill • **appui-tête** *(pl* **appuis-tête)** *nm* headrest

appuyer [apɥije] **1** *vt (poser)* to lean, to rest; **a. qch sur qch** *(poser)* to rest sth on sth; *(presser)* to press sth on sth **2** *vi (presser)* to press; **a. sur un bouton** to press a button **3** **s'appuyer** *vpr* **s'a. sur qch** to lean on sth; *Fig (être basé sur)* to be based on sth

après [aprɛ] **1** *prép (dans le temps)* after; *(dans l'espace)* beyond; **a. tout** after all; **a. avoir mangé** after eating; **a. qu'il t'a vu** after he saw you; **d'a.** *(selon)* according to **2** *adv* after(wards); **l'année d'a.** the following year; **et a.?** *(et ensuite)* and then what? • **après-demain** *adv* the day after tomorrow • **après-midi** *nm ou f inv* afternoon; **trois heures de l'a.** three o'clock in the afternoon • **après-rasage** *(pl* **après-rasages)** *nm* aftershave • **après-shampooing** *nm inv* conditioner • **après-ski** *(pl* **après-skis)** *nm* snowboot • **après-vente** *adj inv Com* **service a.** after-sales service

à-propos [aprɔpo] *nm* aptness; **avoir l'esprit d'a.** to have presence of mind

apte [apt] *adj* **a. à qch/à faire qch** fit for sth/for doing sth • **aptitude** *nf* aptitude (**à** *ou* **pour** for); **avoir**

des aptitudes pour qch to have an aptitude for sth

aquarelle [akwarɛl] *nf* water-colour

aquarium [akwarjɔm] *nm* aquarium

arabe 1 *adj (peuple, littérature)* Arab; *(langue)* Arabic **2** *nmf* **A.** Arab **3** *nm (langue)* Arabic

araignée [areɲe] *nf* spider

arbitre [arbitr] *nm (de football)* referee; *(de tennis)* umpire

arbre [arbr] *nm (végétal)* tree; **a. fruitier** fruit tree; **a. généalogique** family tree ● **arbuste** *nm* shrub

arc [ark] *nm (arme)* bow; *(voûte)* arch; *(de cercle)* arc ● **arcade** *nf* archway; **arcades** *(de place)* arcade

arc-en-ciel [arkɑ̃sjɛl] *(pl* **arcs-en-ciel***) nm* rainbow

arche [arʃ] *nf (voûte)* arch

archéologie [arkeɔlɔʒi] *nf* archaeology ● **archéologue** *nmf* archaeologist

architecte [arʃitɛkt] *nm* architect ● **architecture** *nf* architecture

archives [arʃiv] *nfpl* archives, records

arctique [arktik] **1** *adj* arctic **2** *nm* **l'A.** the Arctic

ardent, -e [ardɑ̃, -ɑ̃t] *adj (désir)* burning; *(soleil)* scorching

ardoise [ardwaz] *nf* slate

arène [arɛn] *nf (pour taureaux)* bullring; *(romaine)* arena; **arènes** bullring; *(romaines)* amphitheatre

arête [arɛt] *nf (de poisson)* bone; *(de cube)* edge

argent [arʒɑ̃] **1** *nm (métal)* silver; *(monnaie)* money; **a. liquide** cash; **a. de poche** pocket money **2** *adj (couleur)* silver ● **argenté, -e** *adj (plaqué)* silver-plated; *(couleur)* silvery

argile [arʒil] *nf* clay

argot [argo] *nm* slang ● **argotique** *adj (terme)* slang

argument [argymɑ̃] *nm* argument ● **argumenter** *vi* to argue

aride [arid] *adj* arid, dry

aristocrate [aristɔkrat] *nmf* aristocrat ● **aristocratique** *adj* aristocratic

arithmétique [aritmetik] *nf* arithmetic

armature [armatyr] *nf (charpente)* framework; *(de lunettes)* frame

arme [arm] *nf* weapon; **a. à feu** firearm

armée [arme] *nf* army; **a. de l'air** air force; **a. de terre** army

armer [arme] **s'armer** *vpr* to arm oneself **(de** with)

armoire [armwar] *nf (penderie)* Br wardrobe, Am closet; **a. à pharmacie** medicine cabinet

armure [armyr] *nf* armour

aromatique [arɔmatik] *adj* aromatic

arôme [arom] *nm (goût)* flavour; *(odeur)* aroma

arpenter [arpɑ̃te] *vt (parcourir)* to pace up and down

arrache-pied [araʃpje] **d'arrache-pied** *adv* relentlessly

arracher [araʃe] *vt (plante)* to uproot; *(clou, dent, mauvaise herbe)* to pull out; *(page)* to tear out; **a. qch à qn** *(objet)* to snatch sth from sb; *(promesse)* to force sth out of sb; **se faire a. une dent** to have a tooth out

arrangement [arɑ̃ʒmɑ̃] *nm (disposition)* arrangement; *(accord)* agreement

arranger [arɑ̃ʒe] **1** *vt (fleurs)* to arrange; *(col)* to straighten; *(réparer)* to repair; **ça m'arrange** that suits me (fine) **2** **s'arranger** *vpr (se mettre d'accord)* to come to an agreement; *(finir bien)* to turn out fine; *(s'organiser)* to manage

arrestation [arɛstasjɔ̃] *nf* arrest

arrêt [arɛ] *nm (halte, endroit)* stop; *(action)* stopping; **temps d'a.** pause; **sans a.** continuously; **a. du cœur** cardiac arrest; *Sport* **a. de jeu** stoppage

arrêté [arete] *nm (décret)* decree

arrêter [arete] **1** *vt (personne, animal, véhicule)* to stop; *(criminel)* to arrest; *(études)* to give up **2** *vi* to stop; **a. de faire qch** to stop doing sth **3 s'arrêter** *vpr* to stop

arrière [arjɛr] **1** *nm (de maison)* back, rear; **à l'a.** in/at the back **2** *adj inv (siège)* back, rear; **feu a.** rear light **3** *adv* **en a.** *(marcher, tomber)* backwards; *(rester)* behind; *(regarder)* back, behind; **en a. de qn/qch** behind sb/sth • **arrière-plan** *nm* background; **à l'a.** in the background

arriver [arive] **1** *(aux être) vi (venir)* to arrive; **a. à** *(lieu)* to reach; *(résultat)* to achieve; **a. à faire qch** to manage to do sth **2** *v impersonnel (survenir)* to happen; **a. à qn** to happen to sb; **qu'est-ce qu'il t'arrive?** what's wrong with you? • **arrivée** *nf* arrival; *(ligne, poteau)* winning post

arrogant, -e [arɔgɑ̃, -ɑ̃t] *adj* arrogant

arrondir [arɔ̃dir] *vt (chiffre, angle)* to round off; **a. qch** to make sth round; **a. à l'euro supérieur/ inférieur** to round up/down to the nearest euro; *Fam* **a. ses fins de mois** to supplement one's income

arrondissement [arɔ̃dismɑ̃] *nm* = administrative subdivision of Paris, Lyons and Marseilles

arroser [aroze] *vt (plante)* to water; *Fam (succès)* to drink to • **arrosoir** *nm* watering can

art [ar] *nm* art; **arts martiaux** martial arts; **arts plastiques** fine arts

artère [artɛr] *nf (veine)* artery; *(rue)* main road

artichaut [artiʃo] *nm* artichoke

article [artikl] *nm (de presse, de contrat)* & *Gram* article; *Com* item; **articles de toilette** toiletries

articuler [artikyle] *vt (mot)* to articulate • **articulation** *nf (de membre)* joint; *(prononciation)* articulation

artifice [artifis] *nm* trick

artificiel, -elle [artifisjɛl] *adj* artificial

artisan [artizɑ̃] *nm* craftsman, artisan • **artisanal, -e, -aux, -ales** *adj* **objet a.** handmade object

artiste [artist] *nmf* artist; *(acteur, musicien)* performer, artiste • **artistique** *adj* artistic

as [ɑs] *nm (carte, champion)* ace

ascendant [asɑ̃dɑ̃] *adj* ascending; *(mouvement)* upward

ascenseur [asɑ̃sœr] *nm Br* lift, *Am* elevator

ascension [asɑ̃sjɔ̃] *nf (escalade)* ascent; *Rel* **l'A.** Ascension Day

Asie [azi] *nf* **l'A.** Asia • **asiatique 1** *adj* Asian **2** *nmf* **A.** Asian

asile [azil] *nm (abri)* refuge, shelter; *(pour vieillards)* home; *Péj* **a. (d'aliénés)** (lunatic) asylum; **a. politique** (political) asylum

aspect [aspɛ] *nm (air)* appearance; *(perspective)* aspect

asperger [aspɛrʒe] **1** *vt (par jeu ou accident)* to splash **(de** with) **2 s'asperger** *vpr* **s'a. de parfum** to splash oneself with perfume

asperges [aspɛrʒ] *nfpl* asparagus

asphalte [asfalt] *nm* asphalt

asphyxier [asfiksje] *vt,* **s'asphyxier** *vpr* to suffocate

aspirateur [aspiratœr] *nm*

vacuum cleaner, *Br* Hoover®; **passer l'a. dans la maison** to vacuum the house
aspirer [aspire] **1** *vt (liquide)* to suck up; *(air)* to breathe in, to inhale **2** *vi* **a. à qch** *(bonheur, gloire)* to aspire to sth ● **aspiration** *nf (inhalation)* inhalation; *(ambition)* aspiration (**à** for)
aspirine [aspirin] *nf* aspirin
assaillir [asajir] *vt* to attack ● **assaillant, -e** *nmf* attacker, assailant
assainir [asenir] *vt* to clean up
assaisonner [asezɔne] *vt* to season ● **assaisonnement** *nm* seasoning
assassin [asasɛ̃] *nm* murderer; *(de politicien)* assassin ● **assassiner** *vt* to murder; *(politicien)* to assassinate
assaut [aso] *nm* attack, assault
assemblée [asɑ̃ble] *nf (personnes réunies)* gathering; *(réunion)* meeting; **l'A. nationale** *Br* ≃ the House of Commons, *Am* ≃ the House of Representatives
assembler [asɑ̃ble] **1** *vt* to put together, to assemble **2** **s'assembler** *vpr* to gather
asseoir* [aswar] **s'asseoir** *vpr* to sit (down)
assez [ase] *adv* **(a)** *(suffisament)* enough; **a. de pain/de gens** enough bread/people; **j'en ai a. (de)** I've had enough (of); **a. grand/intelligent (pour faire qch)** big/clever enough (to do sth) **(b)** *(plutôt)* quite, rather
assidu, -e [asidy] *adj (toujours présent)* regular; *(appliqué)* diligent; **a. auprès de qn** attentive to sb
assiette [asjɛt] *nf (récipient)* plate; *Culin* **a. anglaise** *Br* (assorted) cold meats, *Am* cold cuts
assimiler [asimile] *vt (aliments, savoir, immigrés)* to assimilate

assis, -e [asi, -iz] *(pp de* **asseoir***) adj* sitting (down), seated; **rester a.** to remain seated; **place assise** seat
assistance [asistɑ̃s] *nf* **(a)** *(public)* audience **(b)** *(aide)* assistance
assister [asiste] **1** *vt (aider)* to assist **2** *vi* **a. à** *(réunion, cours)* to attend; *(accident)* to witness ● **assistant, -e** *nmf* assistant; **assistante sociale** social worker
association [asɔsjasjɔ̃] *nf* association; **a. sportive** sports club
associer [asɔsje] **1** *vt* to associate (**à** with) **2** **s'associer** *vpr* to join forces (**à** *ou* **avec** with) ● **associé, -e** *nmf* associate
assoiffé, -e [aswafe] *adj* thirsty (**de** for)
assommer [asɔme] *vt* **a. qn** to knock sb unconscious; *Fig (ennuyer)* to bore sb to death ● **assommant, -e** *adj* very boring
assorti, -e [asɔrti] *adj (objet semblable)* matching; *(bonbons)* assorted; **a. de** accompanied by ● **assortiment** *nm* assortment
assoupir [asupir] **s'assoupir** *vpr* to doze off
assujettir [asyʒetir] *vt (soumettre)* to subject (**à** to)
assumer [asyme] *vt (tâche, rôle)* to take on; *(risque)* to take
assurance [asyrɑ̃s] *nf (confiance)* (self-)assurance; *(contrat)* insurance; **prendre une a.** to take out insurance; **a. maladie/vie** health/life insurance
assurer [asyre] **1** *vt (garantir) Br* to ensure, *Am* to insure; *(par contrat)* to insure; **a. qn de qch, a. qch à qn** to assure sb of sth; **un service régulier est assuré** there is a regular service **2** **s'assurer** *vpr (par contrat)* to insure oneself; **s'a. de qch/que...** to make sure of sth/

that... • **assuré, -e** *adj (succès)* guaranteed; *(personne)* confident

asthme [asm] *nm* asthma • **asthmatique** *adj* asthmatic

astrologie [astrɔlɔʒi] *nf* astrology • **astrologue** *nm* astrologer

astronaute [astrɔnot] *nmf* astronaut

astronomie [astrɔnɔmi] *nf* astronomy • **astronome** *nmf* astronomer

astuce [astys] *nf (truc)* trick • **astucieux, -euse** *adj* clever

atelier [atəlje] *nm (d'ouvrier)* workshop; *(de peintre)* studio

Athènes [atɛn] *nm ou f* Athens

athlète [atlɛt] *nmf* athlete • **athlétique** *adj* athletic • **athlétisme** *nm* athletics *(sing)*

Atlantique [atlɑ̃tik] *nm* **l'A.** the Atlantic

atlas [atlɑs] *nm* atlas

atmosphère [atmɔsfɛr] *nf* atmosphere • **atmosphérique** *adj* atmospheric

atomiser [atɔmize] *vt (liquide)* to spray • **atomiseur** *nm* spray

atout [atu] *nm* trump; *Fig (avantage)* asset

atroce [atrɔs] *adj* atrocious; *(douleur)* excruciating • **atrocité** *nf* **les atrocités de la guerre** the atrocities committed in wartime

attache [ataʃ] *nf (lien)* fastener

attaché, -e [ataʃe] *adj (fixé)* fastened; *(chien)* chained up; **être a. à qn** to be attached to sb

attacher [ataʃe] **1** *vt* **a. qch à qch** to fasten sth to sth; *(avec de la ficelle)* to tie sth to sth; *(avec une chaîne)* to chain sth to sth; **a. de l'importance à qch** to attach great importance to sth **2 s'attacher** *vpr (se fixer)* to be fastened; **s'a. à qn** to get attached to sb

attaque [atak] *nf* attack •

attaquer 1 *vt (physiquement, verbalement)* to attack **2 s'attaquer** *vpr* **s'a. à** *(adversaire)* to attack; *(problème)* to tackle • **attaquant, -e** *nmf* attacker

attarder [atarde] **s'attarder** *vpr* to linger

atteindre* [atɛ̃dr] *vt (parvenir à)* to reach; **être atteint d'une maladie** to be suffering from an illness

atteinte [atɛ̃t] *nf* attack (**à** on); **hors d'a.** *(objet, personne)* out of reach

attendre [atɑ̃dr] **1** *vt (personne, train)* to wait for; **a. son tour** to wait one's turn; **elle attend un bébé** she's expecting a baby; **a. que qn fasse qch** to wait for sb to do sth; **a. qch de qn** to expect sth from sb **2** *vi* to wait; **faire a. qn** to keep sb waiting; **en attendant** meanwhile; **en attendant que...** *(+ subjunctive)* until... **3 s'attendre** *vpr* **s'a. à qch** to expect sth; **s'a. à ce que qn fasse qch** to expect sb to do sth • **attendu, -e** *adj (prévu)* expected

attentat [atɑ̃ta] *nm* attack; **a. à la bombe** bombing

attente [atɑ̃t] *nf (fait d'attendre)* waiting; *(période)* wait; **en a.** *(au téléphone)* on hold; **contre toute a.** against all expectations

attentif, -ive [atɑ̃tif, -iv] *adj* attentive

attention [atɑ̃sjɔ̃] *nf (soin, amabilité)* attention; **faire a. à qch** to pay attention to sth; **faire a. (à ce) que...** *(+ subjunctive)* to be careful that...; **a.!** watch out!; **a. à la voiture!** watch out for the car!; **à l'a. de qn** *(sur lettre)* for the attention of sb

atterrir [aterir] *vi* to land •

atterrissage *nm* landing

attester [ateste] *vt* to testify to; **a. que...** to testify that... ● **attestation** *nf (document)* certificate

attirer [atire] *vt (sujet: aimant, personne)* to attract; *(sujet: matière, pays)* to appeal to; **a. l'attention de qn** to catch sb's attention ● **attirant, -e** *adj* attractive

attitude [atityd] *nf* attitude

attraction [atraksjɔ̃] *nf* attraction

attraper [atrape] *vt (ballon, maladie, voleur)* to catch; **a. froid** to catch cold

attrayant, -e [atrɛjɑ̃, -ɑ̃t] *adj* attractive

attribuer [atribɥe] *vt (allouer)* to assign (**à** to); *(prix, bourse)* to award (**à** to); *(œuvre)* to attribute (**à** to); **a. de l'importance à qch** to attach importance to sth

attribut [atriby] *nm* attribute

au [o] *voir* **à**

aube [ob] *nf* dawn; **dès l'a.** at the crack of dawn

auberge [obɛrʒ] *nf* inn; **a. de jeunesse** youth hostel

aubergine [obɛrʒin] *nf Br* aubergine, *Am* eggplant

aucun, -e [okœ̃, -yn] **1** *adj* no, not any; **il n'a a. talent** he has no talent; **a. professeur n'est venu** no teacher came **2** *pron* none; **il n'en a a. a.** he has none (at all); **a. d'entre nous** none of us; **a. des deux** neither of the two

audacieux, -euse [odasjø, -øz] *adj (courageux)* daring, bold

au-dehors [odəɔr] *adv* outside

au-delà [odəla] **1** *adv* beyond; **100 euros mais pas a.** 100 euros but no more **2** *prép* **a. de** beyond **3** *nm* **l'a.** the next world

au-dessous [odəsu] **1** *adv (à l'étage inférieur)* downstairs; *(moins, dessous)* below, under **2** *prép* **a. de** *(dans l'espace)* below, under, beneath; *(âge, prix)* under; *(température)* below

au-dessus [odəsy] **1** *adv* above; *(à l'étage supérieur)* upstairs **2** *prép* **a. de** above; *(âge, température, prix)* over; *(posé sur)* on top of

audible [odibl] *adj* audible

audience [odjɑ̃s] *nf* audience

audiovisuel, -elle [odjɔvizɥɛl] *adj* audiovisual

auditeur, -trice [oditœr, -tris] *nmf (de radio)* listener ● **audition** *nf (d'acteurs)* audition; **passe une a.** to have an audition

auditorium *nm* concert hall

augmenter [ɔgmɑ̃te] **1** *vt* to increase (**de** by); **a. qn** to give sb a *Br* rise *or Am* raise **2** *vi* to increase (**de** by); *(prix, population)* to rise ● **augmentation** *nf* increase (**de** in, of); **a. de salaire** *Br* (pay) rise *Am* raise

aujourd'hui [oʒurdɥi] *adv* today; *(de nos jours)* nowadays, today; **a. en quinze** two weeks from today

auparavant [oparavɑ̃] *adv (avant)* before(-hand); *(d'abord)* first

auprès [oprɛ] **auprès de** *prép (près de)* by, next to; **se renseigner a. de qn** to ask sb

auquel [okɛl] *voir* **lequel**

aura, aurait [ora, orɛ] *voir* **avoir**

auréole [oreɔl] *nf (de saint)* halo

auriculaire [orikylɛr] *nm* little finger

aurore [orɔr] *nf* dawn, daybreak

aussi [osi] *adv* **(a)** *(comparaison)* as; **a. lourd que...** as heavy as... **(b)** *(également)* too, as well; **mo a.** so do/can/am/etc I; **a. bier que...** as well as... **(c)** *(tellement* so; **un repas a. délicieux** such a delicious meal **(d)** *(quelque,* **a. bizarre que cela paraisse** however odd this may seem

aussitôt [osito] *adv* immediately, straight away; **a. que...** as soon as...; **a. dit, a. fait** no sooner said than done

austère [ɔstɛr] *adj (vie, style)* austere; *(vêtement)* severe

Australie [ostrali] *nf* l'A. Australia • **australien, -enne 1** *adj* Australian **2** *nmf* A., **Australienne** Australian

autant [otɑ̃] *adv* (a) **a. de... que** *(quantité)* as much... as; *(nombre)* as many... as; **il a a. d'argent/de pommes que vous** he has as much money/as many apples as you (b) **a. de** *(tant de)* so much; *(nombre)* so many; **je n'ai jamais vu a. d'argent/de pommes** I've never seen so much money/so many apples; **pourquoi manges-tu a.?** why are you eating so much? (c) **a. que** *(quantité)* as much as; *(nombre)* as many as; **il lit a. que vous/que possible** he reads as much as you/as possible; **il n'a jamais souffert a.** he's never suffered as *or* so much (d) *(expressions)* **d'a. (plus) que...** all the more (so) since...; **en faire a.** to do the same; **j'aimerais a. aller au musée** I'd just as soon go to the museum

autel [otɛl] *nm* altar

auteur [otœr] *nm* author, writer

authentique [otɑ̃tik] *adj* genuine, authentic

autiste [otist] *adj* autistic

auto [oto] *nf* car; **autos tamponneuses** bumper cars, Dodgems®

autobiographie [otobjɔgrafi] *nf* autobiography • **autobiographique** *adj* autobiographical

autobus [otobys] *nm* bus

autocar [otokar] *nm* bus, *Br* coach

autocollant, -e [otokɔlɑ̃, -ɑ̃t] *nm* sticker

auto-école [otoekɔl] *(pl* **auto-écoles)** *nf* driving school

autographe [otograf] *nm* autograph

automatique [ɔtɔmatik] *adj* automatic • **automatiquement** *adv* automatically

automne [otɔn] *nm* autumn, *Am* fall

automobile [otɔmɔbil] *nf* car • **automobiliste** *nmf* driver

autonome [otonɔm] *adj (région)* autonomous; *(personne)* self-sufficient • **autonomie** *nf (de région)* autonomy; *(de personne)* self-sufficiency

autoradio [otoradjo] *nm* car radio

autoriser [otorize] *vt* **a. qn à faire qch** to authorize *or* permit sb to do sth • **autorisation** *nf (permission)* permission, authorization; **demander à qn l'a. de faire qch** to ask sb permission to do sth; **donner à qn l'a. de faire qch** to give sb permission to do sth • **autorisé, -e** *adj (qualifié)* authoritative; *(permis)* permitted, allowed

autorité [otorite] *nf* authority • **autoritaire** *adj* authoritarian

autoroute [otorut] *nf Br* motorway, *Am* freeway; **a. à péage** *Br* toll motorway, *Am* turnpike (road)

auto-stop [otostɔp] *nm* hitchhiking; **faire de l'a.** to hitchhike • **auto-stoppeur, -euse** *nmf* hitchhiker

autour [otur] **1** *adv* around; **tout a.** all around **2** *prép* **a. de** around, round; *(environ)* around, round about

autre [otr] *adj & pron* other;

un a. livre another book; **un a.** another (one); **d'autres** others; **d'autres livres** other books; **quelqu'un d'a.** somebody else; **personne/rien d'a.** no-one/nothing else; **a. chose/part** something/somewhere else; **qui/quoi d'a.?** who/what else?; **l'un ou l'a.** either (of them); **ni l'un ni l'a.** neither (of them)

autrefois [otrəfwa] *adv* in the past, once

autrement [otrəmɑ̃] *adv (différemment)* differently; *(sinon)* otherwise (**que** than)

Autriche [otriʃ] *nf* **l'A.** Austria • **autrichien, -enne 1** *adj* Austrian **2** *nmf* **A., Autrichienne** Austrian

autruche [otryʃ] *nf* ostrich

autrui [otrɥi] *pron* others, other people

aux [o] *voir* **à**

auxiliaire [ɔksiljɛr] **1** *nm (verbe)* auxiliary **2** *nmf (aide)* assistant; *(d'hôpital)* auxiliary

auxquels, -elles [okɛl] *voir* **lequel**

av. *(abrév* **avenue)** Ave

avait [avɛ] *voir* **avoir**

aval [aval] **en aval** *adv* downstream (**de** from)

avalanche [avalɑ̃ʃ] *nf* avalanche

avaler [avale] *vti* to swallow

avance [avɑ̃s] *nf (progression, acompte)* advance; *(avantage)* lead; **faire une a. à qn** *(donner de l'argent)* to give sb an advance; **avoir de l'a. sur qn** to be ahead of sb; **à l'a., d'a., par a.** in advance; **en a.** early; **avoir une heure d'a.** to be an hour early • **avancé, -e** *adj* advanced

avancer [avɑ̃se] **1** *vt (dans le temps)* to bring forward; *(dans l'espace)* to move forward; *(mon-*

tre) to put forward **2** *vi (aller de l'avant)* to move forward; *(armée)* to advance; *(faire des progrès)* to progress

avant [avɑ̃] **1** *prép* before; **a. de faire qch** before doing sth; **je vous verrai a. de partir/que vous (ne) partiez** I'll see you before I/you leave; **a. tout** above all **2** *adv (auparavant)* before; *(d'abord)* beforehand; **a. j'avais les cheveux longs** I used to have long hair; **en a.** *(mouvement)* forward; *(en tête)* ahead; **en a. de** in front of; **la nuit d'a.** the night before **3** *nm (de navire, de voiture)* front; *(joueur de football)* forward; **à l'a.** in (the) front; **aller de l'a.** to get on with it **4** *adj inv (pneu, roue)* front • **avant-dernier, -ère** *(mpl* **avant-derniers,** *fpl* **avant-dernières)** *adj & nmf* second last • **avant-hier** *adv* the day before yesterday • **avant-première** *(pl* **avant-premières)** *nf* preview

avantage [avɑ̃taʒ] *nm* advantage; **à l'a. de qn** to sb's advantage • **avantageux, -euse** *adj (offre)* attractive; *(prix)* reasonable

avare [avar] **1** *adj* miserly **2** *nmf* miser

avec [avɛk] *prép* with; **méchant/aimable a. qn** nasty/kind to sb; **a. enthousiasme** with enthusiasm, enthusiastically; *Fam* **et a. ça?** *(dans un magasin)* anything else?

avenir [avnir] *nm* future; **à l'a.** *(désormais)* in future; **d'a.** *(métier)* with good prospects

aventure [avɑ̃tyr] *nf* adventure; *(en amour)* affair; **dire la bonne a. à qn** to tell sb's fortune

avenue [avny] *nf* avenue

avérer [avere] **s'avérer** *vpr (se révéler)* to prove to be; **il s'avère**

que... it turns out that...

averse [avɛrs] *nf* shower

avertir [avɛrtir] *vt* **a. qn de qch** *(informer)* to inform sb of sth; *(danger)* to warn sb of sth • **avertissement** *nm* warning; *(de livre)* foreword

aveu, -x [avø] *nm* confession

aveugle [avœgl] **1** *adj* blind; **devenir a.** to go blind **2** *nmf* blind man, *f* blind woman; **les aveugles** the blind • **aveugler** *vt (éblouir)* & *Fig* to blind; **aveuglé par la colère** blind with rage

aveuglette [avœglɛt] **à l'aveuglette** *adv* blindly; **chercher qch à l'a.** to grope for sth

avide [avid] *adj (cupide)* greedy; *(passionné)* eager **(de** for)

avion [avjɔ̃] *nm* plane, *Br* aeroplane, *Am* airplane; **par a.** *(sur lettre)* airmail; **en a., par a.** *(voyager)* by plane

aviron [avirɔ̃] *nm* oar; **l'a.** *(sport)* rowing; **faire de l'a.** to row

avis [avi] *nm* opinion; *(communiqué)* notice; *(conseil)* advice; **à mon a.** in my opinion **être de l'a. de qn** to be of the same opinion as sb; **changer d'a.** to change one's mind; **sauf a. contraire** unless I/you/*etc* hear to the contrary

avocat¹, -e [avɔka, -at] *nmf Jur* lawyer; *Fig* advocate

avocat² [avɔka] *nm (fruit)* avocado

avoine [avwan] *nf* oats

avoir* [avwar] **1** *v aux* to have; **je l'ai vu** I have *or* I've seen him **2** *vt (posséder)* to have; *(obtenir)* to get; *(porter)* to wear; *Fam (tromper)* to take for a ride; **qu'est-ce que tu as?** what's the matter with you?; **j'ai à faire** I have things to do; **il n'a qu'à essayer** he only has to try; **a. faim/chaud** to be *or* feel hungry/hot; **a. cinq ans** to be five (years old) **3** *v impersonnel* **il y a** there is, *pl* there are; **il y a six ans** six years ago; **il n'y a pas de quoi!** *(en réponse à 'merci')* don't mention it!; **qu'est-ce qu'il y a?** what's the matter?

avorter [avɔrte] *vi* **se faire a.** to have an abortion • **avortement** *nm* abortion

avouer [avwe] *vt (crime)* to confess to; **il faut a. que...** it must be admitted that...

avril [avril] *nm* April

axe [aks] *nm (géométrique)* axis; *(essieu)* axle; **les grands axes** *(routes)* the main roads

ayant [ɛjɑ̃], **ayez** [ɛje], **ayons** [ɛjɔ̃] *voir* **avoir**

Bb

B, b [be] *nm inv* B, b

baby-foot [babifut] *nm inv* table football

baby-sitting [babisitiŋ] *nm* baby-sitting • **baby-sitter** (*pl* **baby-sitters**) *nmf* baby-sitter

bac¹ [bak] *nm* (*bateau*) ferry(boat); (*cuve*) tank

baccalauréat [bakalɔrea] *Fam*

bac² [bak] *nm* = secondary school examination qualifying for entry to university, *Br* ≃ A-levels, *Am* ≃ high school diploma

bâche [baʃ] *nf* tarpaulin

bachelier, -ère [baʃəlje, -ɛr] *nmf* = student who has passed the "baccalauréat"

bâcler [bakle] *vt Fam* to botch

bactérie [bakteri] *nf* bacterium

badge [badʒ] *nm Br* badge, *Am* button

badiner [badine] to jest

bafouiller [bafuje] *vti* to stammer

bagages [bagaʒ] *nmpl* (*valises*) luggage, baggage; **faire ses b.** to pack (one's bags)

bagarre [bagar] *nf* fight, brawl • **se bagarrer** to fight

bague [bag] *nf* ring

baguette [bagɛt] *nf* (*canne*) stick; (*de chef d'orchestre*) baton; (*pain*) baguette; **baguettes** (*de tambour*) drumsticks; (*pour manger*) chopsticks

baie¹ [bɛ] *nf Géog* bay

baie² [bɛ] *nf* (*fruit*) berry

baignade [bɛɲad] *nf* (*activité*) swimming, *Br* bathing; '**b.**

interdite' 'no swimming'

baigner [beɲe] **1** *vt* (*pied, blessure*) to bathe; (*enfant*) *Br* to bath, *Am* to bathe; (*sujet: mer*) to wash **2 se baigner** *vpr* (*nager*) to have a swim • **baignoire** *nf* bath (tub)

bail [baj] (*pl* **baux** [bo]) *nm* lease; *Fam* **ça fait un b. que je ne l'ai pas vu** I haven't seen him for ages

bâiller [baje] *vi* to yawn

bâillon [bajɔ̃] *nm* gag; **mettre un b. à qn** to gag sb

bain [bɛ̃] *nm* bath; **prendre un b.** to have *or* take a bath; **prendre un b. de soleil** to sunbathe

baiser [beze] *nm* kiss

baisse [bɛs] *nf* fall, drop (**de** in)

baisser [bese] **1** *vt* (*rideau, prix*) to lower; (*radio, chauffage*) to turn down; **b. la tête** to lower one's head; **b. les yeux** to look down **2** *vi* (*prix, température*) to fall; (*popularité, qualité*) to decline **3 se baisser** *vpr* to bend down

bal [bal] (*pl* **bals**) *nm* (*élégant*) ball; (*populaire*) dance; **b. costumé, b. masqué** fancy dress ball

balade [balad] *nf Fam* (*à pied*) walk; (*en voiture*) drive; **faire une b.** (*à pied*) to go for a walk; (*en voiture*) to go for a drive • **baladeur** *nm* personal stereo

balafre [balafr] *nf* (*cicatrice*) scar; (*coupure*) gash

balai [balɛ] *nm* broom; **donner un coup de b.** to give the floor a sweep

balance [balãs] *nf (instrument)* (pair of) scales; **la B.** *(signe)* Libra

balancer [balãse] *vt (bras, jambe)* to swing

balançoire [balãswar] *nf (suspendue)* swing; *(bascule)* see-saw

balayer [baleje] *vt (pièce)* to sweep; *(feuilles, saletés)* to sweep up • **balayage** *nm (nettoyage)* sweeping; *(coiffure)* highlighting

balbutier [balbysje] *vti* to stammer

balcon [balkɔ̃] *nm* balcony; *(de théâtre)* circle, *Am* mezzanine

baleine [balɛn] *nf* whale

balle [bal] *nf (pour jouer)* ball; *(d'arme)* bullet; **b. de tennis** tennis ball

ballet [balɛ] *nm* ballet • **ballerine** *nf (danseuse)* ballerina; *(chaussure)* pump

ballon [balɔ̃] *nm (balle, dirigeable)* balloon; **jouer au b.** to play with a ball; **b. de football** *Br* football, *Am* soccer ball

balnéaire [balneɛr] *adj* **station b.** *Br* seaside resort, *Am* beach resort

balustrade [balystrad] *nf (de pont)* railing; *(de balcon)* balustrade

bambou [bãbu] *nm* bamboo

banal, -e, -als, -ales [banal] *adj (objet, gens)* ordinary; *(idée)* banal; **pas b.** unusual

banane [banan] *nf (fruit)* banana

banc [bã] *nm (siège)* bench; **b. des accusés** dock

bancal, -e, -als, -ales [bãkal] *adj (meuble)* wobbly

bandage [bãdaʒ] *nm (pansement)* bandage

bande [bãd] *nf* **(a)** *(de tissu, de papier, de terre)* strip; *(pansement)* bandage; *(pellicule)* film; *Aut* **b. d'arrêt d'urgence** *Br* hard shoulder, *Am* shoulder; **b. dessinée** comic strip; **b. sonore** soundtrack **(b)** *(de personnes)* band, group; *(de voleurs)* gang • **bande-annonce** *(pl* **bandes-annonces)** *nf* trailer **(de** for) • **bande-son** *(pl* **bandes-son)** *nf* soundtrack

bandeau, -x [bãdo] *nm (pour cheveux)* headband; *(sur les yeux)* blindfold

bander [bãde] *vt (blessure, main)* to bandage; *(arc)* to bend; **b. les yeux à qn** to blindfold sb

banderole [bãdrɔl] *nf* banner

bandit [bãdi] *nm (escroc)* crook

banlieue [bãljø] *nf* suburbs; **la b. parisienne** the suburbs of Paris; **de b.** *(maison, magasin)* suburban; **train de b.** commuter train

bannière [banjɛr] *nf* banner

bannir [banir] *vt (personne, idée)* to banish **(de** from)

banque [bãk] *nf (établissement)* bank; **la b.** *(activité)* banking; **employé de b.** bank clerk

banqueroute [bãkrut] *nf* bankruptcy; **faire b.** to go bankrupt

banquet [bãkɛ] *nm* banquet

banquette [bãkɛt] *nf (siège)* (bench) seat

baptême [batɛm] *nm* christening, baptism • **baptiser** *vt* to christen, to baptize

bar [bar] *nm (café, comptoir)* bar

baraque [barak] *nf (cabane)* hut, shack; *(de foire)* stall

baratin [baratɛ̃] *nm* *Fam (verbiage)* waffle; *(de séducteur)* sweet talk; *(de vendeur)* sales talk

barbare [barbar] **1** *adj (cruel, sauvage)* barbaric **2** *nmf* barbarian

barbe [barb] *nf* beard; **b. à papa** *Br* candyfloss, *Am* cotton candy

barbecue [barbəkju] *nm* barbecue

barbelés [barbəle] *nmpl* barbed wire

barbiche [barbiʃ] *nf* goatee
barboter [barbɔte] *vi* to splash about ● **barboteuse** *nf* rompers
barbouiller [barbuje] *vt (salir)* to smear (**de** with)
barbu, -e [barby] *adj* bearded
barème [barɛm] *nm (de notes, de salaires, de prix)* scale
baril [baril] *nm* barrel
barman [barman] (*pl* **-men** [-mɛn] *ou* **-mans**) *nm Br* barman, *Am* bartender
baromètre [barɔmɛtr] *nm* barometer
baron [barɔ̃] *nm* baron ● **baronne** *nf* baroness
barque [bark] *nf* (small) boat ● **barquette** *nf (de fruit)* punnet
barrage [baraʒ] *nm (sur l'eau)* dam; **b. routier** roadblock
barre [bar] *nf (de fer, de bois)* bar; *(trait)* line, stroke; **b. chocolatée** chocolate bar; *Jur* **b. des témoins** *Br* witness box, *Am* witness stand
barreau, -x [baro] *nm (de fenêtre, de cage)* bar; **être derrière les barreaux** *(en prison)* to be behind bars
barrer [bare] **1** *vt (voie)* to block off; *(porte)* to bar; *(chèque)* to cross; *(mot)* to cross out; **'route barrée'** 'road closed' **2 se barrer** *vpr Fam* to beat it
barrette [barɛt] *nf (pour cheveux) Br* (hair)slide, *Am* barrette
barricade [barikad] *nf* barricade ● **barricader 1** *vt (rue, porte)* to barricade **2 se barricader** *vpr* to barricade oneself (**dans** in)
barrière [barjɛr] *nf* barrier
bas¹, basse¹ [bɑ, bɑs] **1** *adj (dans l'espace, en quantité, en intensité) & Mus* low; **à b. prix** cheaply **2** *adv (dans l'espace)* low (down); *(dans une hiérarchie)* low;

(parler) quietly; **plus b.** further or lower down; **voir plus b.** *(sur document)* see below; **en b.** at the bottom; **en b. de** at the bottom of **3** *nm (partie inférieure)* bottom; **l'étagère du b.** the bottom shelf; **au b. de** at the bottom of; **de b. en haut** upwards
bas² [bɑ] *nm (chaussette)* stocking
bascule [baskyl] *nf (balançoire)* seesaw; *(balance)* weighing machine; **fauteuil à b.** rocking chair ● **basculer** *vi (tomber)* to topple over; **faire b.** *(personne)* to knock over; *(chargement)* to tip over
base [bɑz] *nf (partie inférieure) & Chim, Math & Mil* base; *(principe)* basis; **avoir de bonnes bases en anglais** to have a good grounding in English; **de b.** basic; *Ordinat* **b. de données** database ● **baser** *vt* to base (**sur** on)
basilic [bazilik] *nm (plante)* basil
basket-ball [baskɛtbol], **basket** [baskɛt] *nm* basketball
baskets [baskɛt] *nmpl ou nfpl (chaussures) Br* trainers, *Am* sneakers
basque [bask] **1** *adj* Basque **2** *nm,* **B.** Basque
basse² [bɑs] **1** *voir* **bas¹ 2** *n, Mus (contrebasse)* (double) bass; *(guitare)* bass (guitar)
basse-cour [bɑskur] (*pl* **basses-cours**) *nf Br* farmyard, *Am* barnyard
bassin [basɛ̃] *nm* (**a**) *(pièce d'eau)* ornamental lake; *(récipient)* bowl, basin (**b**) *(du corps)* pelvis
bat [ba] *voir* **battre**
bataille [bataj] *nf* battle
bateau, -x [bato] *nm (embarcation)* boat; *(grand)* ship; **b. à voiles** *Br* sailing boat, *Am* sailboat ● **bateau-mouche** *(p*

bateaux-mouches) *nm* river boat *(on the Seine)*

bâtiment [bɑtimɑ̃] *nm* building

bâtir [bɑtir] *vt* to build

bâton [bɑtɔ̃] *nm (canne)* stick; *(de maréchal)* baton; *(d'agent de police) Br* truncheon, *Am* nightstick; **donner des coups de b. à qn** to beat sb (with a stick); **bâtons de ski** ski sticks

batterie [batri] *nf (d'orchestre)* drums; **être à la b.** *(sujet: musicien)* to be on drums; **élevage en b.** battery farming

battre* [batr] **1** *vt (frapper, vaincre)* to beat; *(œufs)* to whisk; *(record)* to break; *(cartes)* to shuffle **2** *vi (cœur)* to beat; **b. des mains** to clap one's hands; **b. des ailes** to flap its wings **3 se battre** *vpr* to fight (**avec** with) • **battu, -e** *adj (femme, enfant)* battered

baux [bo] *voir* **bail**

bavard, -e [bavar, -ard] **1** *adj (qui parle beaucoup)* chatty **2** *nmf (qui parle beaucoup)* chatterbox • **bavardage** *nm* chatting • **bavarder** *vi* to chat

baver [bave] *vi (personne)* to dribble; *(chien)* to slaver

bavette [bavεt] *nf* bib

baveux, -euse [bavø, -øz] *adj (omelette)* runny

bavoir [bavwar] *nm* bib

bazar [bazar] *nm (marché)* bazaar; *(magasin)* general store; *Fam (désordre)* shambles *(sing)*; *Fam (affaires)* gear; *Fam* **mettre du b. dans qch** to make a mess

BD [bede] *(abrév* **bande dessinée)** *nf* comic strip

bd *(abrév* **boulevard)** Blvd

béat, -e [bea, -at] *adj Hum (heureux)* blissful; **b. d'admiration** open-mouthed in admiration

beau, belle [bo, bεl] *(pl* **beaux, belles)**

bel is used before masculine singular nouns beginning with a vowel or mute h.

1 *adj* **(a)** *(femme, enfant, fleur, histoire)* beautiful; *(homme)* handsome, good-looking; *(spectacle, discours)* fine; *(maison, voyage, temps)* lovely; **une belle somme** a tidy sum; **se faire b.** to smarten oneself up; **c'est trop b. pour être vrai** it's too good to be true; **c'est le plus b. jour de ma vie!** it's the best day of my life! **(b)** *(expressions)* **au b. milieu de** right in the middle of; **bel et bien** *(complètement)* well and truly **2** *adv* **il fait b.** the weather's nice; **j'ai b. crier...** it's no use (my) shouting... • **beau-fils** *(pl* **beaux-fils)** *nm (gendre)* son-in-law; *(après remariage)* stepson • **beau-frère** *(pl* **beaux-frères)** *nm* brother-in-law • **beau-père** *(pl* **beaux-pères)** *nm (père du conjoint)* father-in-law; *(après remariage)* stepfather • **beaux-arts** *nmpl* fine arts; **école des b., les B.** art school • **beaux-parents** *nmpl* parents-in-law

beaucoup [boku] *adv (intensément, en grande quantité)* a lot; **aimer b. qch** to like sth very much; **s'intéresser b. à qch** to be very interested in sth; **b. d'entre nous** many of us; **b. de** *(quantité)* a lot of; *(nombre)* many, a lot of; **pas b. d'argent** not much money; **pas b. de gens** not many people; **j'en ai b.** *(quantité)* I have a lot; *(nombre)* I have lots; **b. plus/moins (que)** *(quantité)* much more/less (than), a lot more/ less (than); *(nombre)* many *or* a lot more/a lot fewer (than)

beauté [bote] *nf (qualité, femme)* beauty

bébé [bebe] *nm* baby

bec [bɛk] *nm (d'oiseau)* beak; *(de pot)* lip; *(de flûte)* mouthpiece

bêche [bɛʃ] *nf* spade • **bêcher** *vt* to dig

bée [be] *adj f* **j'en suis resté bouche b.** I was speechless

bégayer [begeje] *vi* to stutter, to stammer

bègue [bɛg] *adj* **être b.** to stutter, to stammer

beige [bɛʒ] *adj & nm* beige

beignet [beɲe] *nm* fritter; *(au sucre, à la confiture)* doughnut

bel [bɛl] *voir* **beau**

Belgique [bɛlʒik] *nf* **la B.** Belgium • **belge 1** *adj* Belgian **2** *nmf* **B.** Belgian

bélier [belje] *nm (animal, machine)* ram; **le B.** *(signe)* Aries

belle [bɛl] *voir* **beau** • **belle-famille** *(pl* **belles-familles)** *nf* in-laws • **belle-fille** *(pl* **belles-filles)** *nf (épouse du fils)* daughter-in-law; *(après remariage)* stepdaughter • **belle-mère** *(pl* **belles-mères)** *nf (mère du conjoint)* mother-in-law; *(après remariage)* stepmother • **belle-sœur** *(pl* **belles-sœurs)** *nf* sister-in-law

bénéfice [benefis] *nm (financier)* profit; *(avantage)* benefit; **accorder le b. du doute à qn** to give sb the benefit of the doubt

bénéficiaire [benefisjɛr] *nmf (de chèque)* payee; *Jur* beneficiary

bénéficier [benefisje] *vi* **b. de qch** *(profiter de)* to benefit from sth; *(avoir)* to have sth

bénévolat [benevɔla] *nm* voluntary work

bénévole [benevɔl] **1** *adj* voluntary **2** *nmf* volunteer

bénir [benir] *vt* to bless; **que**

Dieu te bénisse! God bless you! • **bénit, -e** *adj* **eau bénite** holy water

benne [bɛn] *nf* **b. à ordures** bin lorry

BEP [beape] *(abrév* **brevet d'études professionnelles)** *nm Scol=* vocational diploma taken at 18

béquille [bekij] *nf (canne)* crutch

berceau, -x [bɛrso] *nm* cradle

bercer [bɛrse] *vt (bébé)* to rock • **berceuse** *nf* lullaby

béret [berɛ] *nm* beret

berger [bɛrʒe] *nm* shepherd

berline [bɛrlin] *nf (voiture) Br* (four-door) saloon, *Am* sedan

bermuda [bɛrmyda] *nm* Bermuda shorts

besogne [bəzɔɲ] *nf* job, task

besoin [bəzwɛ̃] *nm* need; **avoir b. de qn/qch** to need sb/sth; **avoir b. de faire qch** to need to do sth; **au b., si b. est** if necessary, if need be

bestiole [bɛstjɔl] *nf (insecte) Br* creepy-crawly, *Am* creepy-crawler

bétail [betaj] *nm* livestock

bête¹ [bɛt] *adj* stupid, silly • **bêtement** *adv* stupidly; **tout b.** quite simply • **bêtise** *nf (manque d'intelligence)* stupidity; *(action, parole)* stupid thing; **faire une b.** to do something stupid; **dire des bêtises** to talk nonsense

bête² [bɛt] *nf* animal; *(insecte)* bug

béton [betɔ̃] *nm* concrete

betterave [betrav] *nf Br* beetroot, *Am* beet

beur [bœr] *nmf =* North African born in France of immigrant parents

beurre [bœr] *nm* butter • **beurrer** *vt* to butter

biais [bjɛ] *nm (de mur)* slant; *(moyen)* way; **par le b. de**

through
bibelot [biblo] *nm* trinket
biberon [bibrɔ̃] *nm* (feeding)
bottle; **nourrir un bébé au b.** to
bottle-feed a baby
Bible [bibl] *nf* **la B.** the Bible
bibliothèque [biblijɔtɛk] *nf*
(*lieu*) library; (*meuble*) bookcase;
b. municipale public library •
bibliothécaire *nmf* librarian
Bic® [bik] *nm* ballpoint, *Br* biro®
bicarbonate [bikarbɔnat] *nm* **b.
de soude** bicarbonate of soda
biceps [bisɛps] *nm* biceps
bicyclette [bisiklɛt] *nf* bicycle;
faire de la b. to go cycling
bidet [bidɛ] *nm* (*cuvette*) bidet
bidon [bidɔ̃] **1** *nm* (*d'essence*) can
2 *adj inv Fam* (*simulé*) phoney,
fake
bidonville [bidɔ̃vil] *nm* shanty-
town
bidule [bidyl] *nm Fam* (*chose*)
whatsit; **B.** (*personne*) what's-his-
name, *f* what's-her-name

bien [bjɛ̃] **1** *adv* (a)
(*convenablement*) well; **il joue b.** he
plays well; **je vais b.** I'm fine *or* well;
écoutez-moi b.! listen carefully! (b)
(*moralement*) right; **b. se conduire**
to behave (well); **vous avez b. fait**
you did the right thing; **tu ferais b.
de te méfier** you would be wise to
behave (c) (*très*) very (d) (*beaucoup*)
a lot, a great deal; **b. plus/moins**
much more/less; **b. des fois** many
times; **tu as b. de la chance** you're
really lucky; **merci b.!** thanks very
much! (e) (*en intensif*) **regarder
qn b. en face** to look sb right in the
face; **je sais b.** I'm well aware of it; **je
vous l'avais b. dit!** I told you so!;
nous verrons b.! we'll see!; **c'est b.
fait pour lui** it serves him right; **c'est
b. ce que je pensais** that's what I

thought (f) (*locutions*) **b. que...** (+
subjunctive) although, though; **b.
entendu, b. sûr** of course; **b. sûr
que non!** of course, not!; **b. sûr que
je viendrai!** of course I'll come! **2**
adj inv (*satisfaisant*) good; (*à l'aise*)
comfortable; (*en forme*) well; (*moral*)
decent; (*beau*) attractive; **on est b.
ici** it's nice here; **ce n'est pas b. de
mentir** it's not nice to lie **3** *exclam*
fine!, right!; **eh b.!** well! **4** *nm Phil
& Rel* good; *Jur* **biens** property; **le
b. et le mal** good and evil; **ça te
fera du b.** it will do you good; **dire
du b. de qn** to speak well of sb •
bien-aimé, -e (*mpl* **bien-aimés,** *fpl*
bien-aimées) *adj & nmf* beloved •
bien-être *nm* well-being

bienfaisance [bjɛ̃fəzɑ̃s] *nf*
œuvre de b. charity
bienheureux, -euse [bjɛ̃nœrø,
-øz] *adj* blissful
bientôt [bjɛ̃to] *adv* soon; **à b.!**
see you soon!
bienvenu, -e [bjɛ̃vny] **1** *adj*
(*repos, explication*) welcome **2**
nmf **soyez le b.!** welcome! **3** *nf*
bienvenue welcome; **souhaiter
la bienvenue à qn** to welcome sb
bière [bjɛr] *nf* (*boisson*) beer; **b.
blonde** lager; **b. brune** *Br* brown
ale, *Am* dark beer; **b. pression** *Br*
draught beer, *Am* draft beer
biffer [bife] *vt* to cross out
bifteck [biftɛk] *nm* steak; **b.
haché** *Br* mince, *Am* mincemeat
bifurcation [bifyrkasjɔ̃] *nf* (*de
route*) fork
bigoudi [bigudi] *nm* curler, roller
bijou, -x [biʒu] *nm* jewel •
bijouterie *nf Br* jeweller's shop,
Am jewelry store
bilan [bilɑ̃] *nm* (*de situation*)
assessment; (*résultats*) results;
(*d'un accident*) toll

bilingue [bilɛ̃g] *adj* bilingual

billard [bijar] *nm (jeu)* billiards; *(table)* billiard table; **b. américain** pool

bille [bij] *nf (de verre)* marble; *(de billard)* billiard ball

billet [bijɛ] *nm* ticket; **b. (de banque)** *Br* (bank)note, *Am* bill; **b. d'avion/de train** plane/train ticket; **b. de première/seconde** first-class/second-class ticket; **b. simple** single ticket, *Am* one-way ticket; **b. aller retour** return ticket, *Am* round trip ticket

billetterie [bijɛtri] *nf (lieu)* ticket office; **b. automatique** *(de billet de transport)* ticket machine

billion [biljɔ̃] *nm* trillion

bimensuel, -elle [bimɑ̃sɥɛl] *adj* bimonthly, *Br* fortnightly

biochimie [bjɔʃimi] *nf* biochemistry

biodégradable [bjɔdegradabl] *adj* biodegradable

biographie [bjɔgrafi] *nf* biography • **biographique** *adj* biographical

biologie [bjɔlɔʒi] *nf* biology • **biologique** *adj* biological; *(sans engrais chimiques)* organic • **biologiste** *nmf* biologist

bip [bip] *nm (son)* beep; *(appareil)* beeper

bis [bis] *adv (au théâtre)* encore; **4 bis** *(adresse)* ≃ 4A

biscotte [biskɔt] *nf* rusk

biscuit [biskɥi] *nm Br* biscuit, *Am* cookie

bise [biz] *nf Fam (baiser)* kiss; **faire la b. à qn** to kiss sb on both cheeks

bisexuel, -elle [bisɛksɥɛl] *adj* bisexual

bisou [bizu] *nm Fam* kiss

bissextile [bisɛkstil] *adj f* **année b.** leap year

bistro(t) [bistro] *nm Fam* bar

bitume [bitym] *nm (revêtement)* asphalt

bizarre [bizar] *adj* odd

blafard, -e [blafar, -ard] *adj* pale

blague [blag] *nf (plaisanterie)* joke; **faire une b. à qn** to play a joke on sb

blaireau, -x [blɛro] *nm (animal)* badger; *(brosse)* shaving brush

blâmer [blame] *vt (désapprouver)* to blame; *(sanctionner)* to reprimand

blanc, blanche [blɑ̃, blɑ̃ʃ] **1** *adj* white; *(peau)* pale; *(page)* blank **2** *nm (couleur)* white; *(espace)* blank; *(vin)* white wine; **en b.** *(chèque)* blank; **b. d'œuf** egg white; **b. de poulet** chicken breast **2** *nmf* **B.** *(personne)* White man, *f* White woman; **les B.** the Whites • **blancheur** *nf* whiteness

blanchir [blɑ̃ʃir] **1** *vt* to whiten; *(linge)* & *Fig (argent)* to launder **2** *vi* to turn white • **blanchiment** *nm (d'argent)* laundering • **blanchisserie** *nf (lieu)* laundry

blasé, -e [blaze] *adj* blasé

bld *(abrév* **boulevard)** Blvd

blé [ble] *nm* wheat, *Br* corn

blême [blɛm] *adj* sickly pale • **blêmir** *vi* to turn pale

blesser [blese] **1** *vt (dans un accident)* to injure, to hurt; *(par arme)* to wound; *(offenser)* to hurt **2 se blesser** *vpr (par accident)* to hurt or injure oneself; *(avec une arme)* to wound oneself; **se b. au bras** to hurt one's arm • **blessé, -e** *nmf (victime d'accident)* injured person; *(victime d'aggression)* wounded person; **les blessés** the injured/wounded • **blessure** *nf (dans un accident)* injury; *(par arme)* wound

bleu, -e [blø] *(mpl* **-s)** **1** *adj* blue; *(steak)* very rare **2** *nm (couleur)* blue; *(ecchymose)* bruise; *(fromage)* blue cheese; **b. de travail** *Br* overalls, *Am* overall

blindé, -e [blɛ̃de] *adj Mil* armoured; *(voiture)* bulletproof

bloc [blɔk] *nm (de pierre, de bois)* block; *(de papier)* pad; **en b.** *(démissionner)* all together • **bloc-notes** *(pl* **blocs-notes***) nm* notepad

blond, -e [blɔ̃, -ɔ̃d] **1** *adj (cheveux, personne)* blond **2** *nmf* blond man, *f* blonde (woman)

bloquer [blɔke] *vt (route, compte)* to block; *(porte, mécanisme)* to jam; *(roue)* to lock; **b. le passage à qn** to block sb's way

blottir [blɔtir] **se blottir** *vpr* to snuggle up; **se b. contre qn** to snuggle up to sb

blouse [bluz] *nf (tablier)* overall; *(corsage)* blouse; **b. blanche** *(de médecin, de biologiste)* white coat • **blouson** *nm short jacket*; **b. en cuir** leather jacket

boa [bɔa] *nm (serpent, tour de cou)* boa

bobine [bɔbin] *nf (de ruban, de fil)* reel; *(de machine à coudre)* bobbin; *(de film, de papier)* roll

bocal, -aux [bɔkal, -o] *nm* jar

bœuf [bœf] *(pl* **bœufs** [bø]*) nm (animal)* bullock; *(viande)* beef

bohème [bɔɛm] *adj & nmf* bohemian • **bohémien, -enne** *adj & nmf* gypsy

boire* [bwar] *vti* to drink; *Fam* **b. un coup** to have a drink

bois [bwa] *nm (matériau, forêt)* wood; **en** *ou* **de b.** wooden

boisson [bwasɔ̃] *nf* drink

boit [bwa] *voir* **boire**

boîte [bwat] *nf* **(a)** *(récipient)* box; *(de conserve)* can, *Br* tin; **b. d'allumettes** *(pleine)* box of matches; *(vide)* matchbox; **des**

haricots en b. canned *or Br* tinned beans; **b. à gants** glove compartment; **b. à** *ou* **aux lettres** *Br* postbox, *Am* mailbox; *Aut* **b. de vitesses** gearbox; **b. vocale** voice mail **(b)** *Fam (entreprise)* firm; **b. de nuit** nightclub

boiter [bwate] *vi* to limp • **boiteux, -euse** *adj (personne)* lame

boive [bwav] *voir* **boire**

bol [bɔl] *nm (récipient, contenu)* bowl

bombarder [bɔ̃barde] *vt (avec des bombes)* to bomb; **b. qn de questions** to bombard sb with questions • **bombardement** *nm* bombing

bombe [bɔ̃b] *nf* **(a)** *(explosif)* bomb **(b)** *(atomiseur)* spray (can)

bon¹, bonne¹ [bɔ̃, bɔn] **1** *adj* **(a)** *(satisfaisant)* good; **c'est b.** *(d'accord)* that's fine **(b)** *(agréable)* nice, good; **passer une bonne soirée** to spend a pleasant evening; **b. anniversaire!** happy birthday!; **bonne année!** Happy New Year! **(c)** *(charitable)* kind, good **(avec qn** to sb) **(d)** *(correct)* right **(e)** *(apte)* fit; **b. à manger** fit to eat; **elle n'est bonne à rien** she's useless **(f)** *(prudent)* wise, good; **juger b. de partir** to think it wise to leave **(g)** *(compétent)* good; **b. en français** good at French **(h)** *(profitable)* *(investissement, conseil, idée)* good; **c'est b. à savoir** it's worth knowing **(i)** *(valable)* valid **(j)** *(en intensif)* **un b. rhume** a bad cold; **dix bonnes minutes** a good ten minutes; **un b. moment** quite a while **(k)** *(locutions)* **à quoi b.?** what's the point?; **quand b. vous semble** whenever you like; **pour de b.** *(partir, revenir)* for good **2** *nm* **un b. à rien** a good-for-nothing; **les**

bons et les méchants the goodies and the baddies **3** *adv* **sentir b.** to smell good; **il fait b.** it's nice and warm **4** *exclam* **b.! on y va?** right, shall we go?; **ah b.?** really?

bon² [bɔ̃] *nm (papier)* coupon, *Br* voucher; **b. d'achat** gift voucher

bonbon [bɔ̃bɔ̃] *nm Br* sweet, *Am* candy

bond [bɔ̃] *nm* leap, jump; **faire un b.** to leap up; **se lever d'un b.** *(du lit)* to jump out of bed; *(d'une chaise)* to leap up; **faire faux b. à qn** to leave sb in the lurch

bondé, -e [bɔ̃de] *adj* packed

bondir [bɔ̃dir] *vi* to leap, to jump

bonheur [bɔnœr] *nm (bien-être)* happiness; *(chance)* good fortune; **porter b. à qn** to bring sb luck; **par b.** luckily

bonhomme [bɔnɔm] (*pl* **bonshommes** [bɔ̃zɔm]) *nm* chap, guy; **b. de neige** snowman

bonjour [bɔ̃ʒur] *nm & exclam (le matin)* hello, good morning; *(l'après-midi)* hello, good afternoon

bonne [bɔn] **1** *voir* **bon¹ 2** *nf (domestique)* maid

bonnet [bɔnɛ] *nm (coiffure)* hat; *(de soutien-gorge)* cup; **b. de bain** bathing cap

bonsoir [bɔ̃swar] *nm & exclam (en rencontrant quelqu'un)* hello, good evening; *(en partant)* goodbye

bonté [bɔ̃te] *nf* kindness

bonus [bɔnys] *nm* bonus

bord [bɔr] *nm (limite)* edge; *(de verre)* rim; **le b. du trottoir** *Br* the kerb, *Am* the curb; **au b. de la route** at the side of the road; **au b. de la rivière** beside the river; **au b. de la mer** at the seaside; **au b. des larmes** on the verge of tears; **à b. d'un bateau/d'un avion** on board a boat/a plane; **monter à b.** to go

on board; **par-dessus b.** overboard

bordeaux [bɔrdo] **1** *nm (vin)* Bordeaux (wine); *(rouge)* claret **2** *adj inv* burgundy

border [bɔrde] *vt (lit)* to tuck in; *(sujet: arbres)* to line

bordure [bɔrdyr] *nf (bord)* edge; **en b. de route** by the roadside

borne [bɔrn] *nf (limite)* boundary marker; *Fig* **sans bornes** boundless; *Fig* **dépasser les bornes** to go too far

borné, -e [bɔrne] *adj (personne)* narrow-minded; *(esprit)* narrow

borner [bɔrne] **se borner** *vpr* **se b. à qch/à faire qch** *(personne)* to restrict oneself to sth/to doing sth; **se b. à qch** *(chose)* to be limited to sth

bosse [bɔs] *nf (de chameau)* hump; *(enflure)* bump, lump; *(de terrain)* bump

bosser [bɔse] *vi Fam* to work

botanique [bɔtanik] *adj* botanical

botte [bɔt] *nf (chaussure)* boot; *(de fleurs, de radis)* bunch; **bottes en caoutchouc** rubber boots

bouc [buk] *nm (animal)* billy goat; **b. émissaire** scapegoat

bouche [buʃ] *nf* mouth; **de b. à oreille** by word of mouth; **b. d'égout** manhole; **b. d'incendie** *Br* fire hydrant, *Am* fireplug

bouche-à-bouche *nm* mouth-to-mouth resuscitation • **bouchée** *nf* mouthful

boucher¹ [buʃe] *vt (fente, trou)* to fill in; *(vue, rue, artère)* to block; *(bouteille)* to cork • **bouché, -e** *adj (conduite)* blocked; **j'ai le nez b.** I have a blocked-up nose

boucher², -ère [buʃe, -ɛr] *nm* butcher • **boucherie** *nf* butcher's (shop)

bouchon [buʃɔ̃] *nm* **(a)** *(à vis*

cap, top; *(de liège)* cork **(b)** *(embouteillage)* traffic jam

boucle [bukl] *nf (de ceinture)* buckle; *(de cheveu)* curl; **b. d'oreille** earring ● **bouclé, -e** *adj (cheveux)* curly

boucler [bukle] *vt (ceinture, valise)* to buckle

bouclier [buklije] *nm* shield

bouddhiste [budist] *adj & nmf* Buddhist

bouder [bude] *vi* to sulk

boudin [budɛ̃] *nm* **b. noir** *Br* black pudding, *Am* blood sausage

boue [bu] *nf* mud ● **boueux, -euse** *adj* muddy

bouée [bwe] *nf Naut* buoy; **b. (gonflable)** *(d'enfant)* (inflatable) rubber ring; **b. de sauvetage** lifebelt

bouffe [buf] *nf Fam (nourriture)* grub

bouffée [bufe] *nf (de fumée)* puff; *(de parfum)* whiff

bouffer [bufe] *vti Fam (manger)* to eat

bouffi, -e [bufi] *adj (yeux, visage)* puffy

bouger [buʒe] **1** *vti* to move; **rester sans b.** to keep still **2 se bouger** *vpr Fam (se déplacer)* to move; *(s'activer)* to get a move on

bougie [buʒi] *nf* candle

bouillabaisse [bujabɛs] *nf* bouillabaisse, = Provençal fish soup

bouilli, -e [buji] **1** *adj* boiled **2** *nf* **bouillie** baby food

bouillir* [bujir] *vi* to boil; **faire b. qch** to boil sth; **b. de colère** to be seething (with anger) ● **bouillant, -e** *adj (qui bout)* boiling; *(très chaud)* boiling hot

bouilloire [bujwar] *nf* kettle

bouillon [bujɔ̃] *nm* stock

bouillotte [bujɔt] *nf* hot-water bottle

boulanger, -ère [bulɑ̃ʒe, -ɛr] *nmf* baker ● **boulangerie** *nf* bakery

boule [bul] *nf (sphère)* ball; **boules** *(jeu)* bowls; **b. de neige** snowball; **boules Quiès®** earplugs

boulette [bulɛt] *nf (de papier)* ball; *(de viande)* meatball

boulevard [bulvar] *nm* boulevard

bouleverser [bulvɛrse] *vt (perturber)* to distress; *(vie)* to turn upside down ● **bouleversant, -e** *adj* distressing

boulon [bulɔ̃] *nm* bolt

boulot [bulo] *nm Fam (emploi)* job; *(travail)* work

bouquet [bukɛ] *nm* bunch of flowers; *Fig* **c'est le b.!** that takes the *Br* biscuit *or Am* cake!

bouquin [bukɛ̃] *nm Fam* book

bourdon [burdɔ̃] *nm (insecte)* bumblebee ● **bourdonner** *vi* to buzz

bourgeois, -e [burʒwa, -waz] *adj* middle class ● **bourgeoisie** *nf* middle class

bourgeon [burʒɔ̃] *nm* bud

bourrer [bure] *vt (coussin)* to stuff **(de** with); *(sac)* to cram **(de** with); **b. qn de qch** *(gaver)* to fill sb up with sth ● **bourré, -e** *adj* **(a)** *(plein)* **b. à craquer** full to bursting **(b)** *Fam (ivre)* plastered

bourrique [burik] *nf Fam* **faire tourner qn en b.** to drive sb crazy

bourse [burs] *nf (sac)* purse; *Scol & Univ* **b. (d'étude)** grant; **la B.** the Stock Exchange

bous [bu] *voir* **bouillir**

bousculer [buskyle] **1** *vt (pousser)* to jostle; *(presser)* to rush; *Fig (habitudes)* to disrupt **2 se bousculer** *(foule)* to push and shove

bousiller [buzije] *vt Fam* to wreck

boussole [busɔl] *nf* compass

bout¹ [bu] *voir* **bouillir**

bout² [bu] *nm (extrémité)* end; *(de langue, de doigt)* tip; *(morceau)* bit; **d'un b. à l'autre** from one end to the other; **au b. de la rue** at the end of the street; **au b. d'un moment** after a while; **jusqu'au b.** *(lire, rester)* (right) to the end; **à b. de forces** exhausted; **à b. de souffle** out of breath

bouteille [butɛj] *nf* bottle

boutique [butik] *nf Br* shop, *Am* store; *(de couturier)* boutique

bouton [butɔ̃] *nm (au visage)* spot; *(de vêtement)* button; *(de porte, de télévision)* knob • **boutonnière** *nf* buttonhole

bowling [boliŋ] *nm (jeu) Br* tenpin bowling, *Am* tenpins; *(lieu)* bowling alley

box [bɔks] *(pl* **boxes)** *nm (d'écurie)* stall; *(de dortoir)* cubicle

boxe [bɔks] *nf* boxing • **boxeur** *nm* boxer

boycotter [bɔjkɔte] *vt* to boycott

bracelet [braslɛ] *nm (bijou)* bracelet; *(rigide)* bangle; *(de montre) Br* strap, *Am* band

braderie [bradri] *nf* clearance sale

braguette [bragɛt] *nf (de pantalon)* fly, *Br* flies

braille [braj] *nm* Braille; **en b.** in Braille

brailler [braje] *vti* to yell

brancard [brɑ̃kar] *nm* stretcher

branche [brɑ̃ʃ] *nf (d'arbre, de science)* branch; *(de lunettes)* side piece

brancher [brɑ̃ʃe] *vt (à une prise)* to plug in; *(à un réseau)* to connect

branlant, -e [brɑ̃lɑ̃, ɑ̃t] *adj (chaise, escalier)* rickety

braquer [brake] *vt (diriger)* to point (**sur** at); *(regard)* to fix (**sur** on); *Fam (banque)* to hold up; **b. qn contre qn/qch** to turn sb against sb/sth

bras [bra] *nm* arm; **b. dessus b. dessous** arm in arm; **les b. croisés** with one's arms folded

brasse [bras] *nf (nage)* breaststroke; **b. papillon** butterfly stroke

brasserie [brasri] *nf (usine)* brewery; *(café)* brasserie

brassière [brasjɛr] *nf (de bébé) Br* vest, *Am* undershirt

brave [brav] *adj (courageux)* brave; *(bon)* good

bravo [bravo] *exclam* bravo!

bravoure [bravur] *nf* bravery

break [brɛk] *nm (voiture) Br* estate car, *Am* station wagon

brebis [brəbi] *nf* ewe

brèche [brɛʃ] *nf* gap

bredouiller [brəduje] *vti* to mumble

bref, brève [bref, brɛv] **1** *adj* brief, short **2** *adv* in short; **enfin b....** in a word...

Bretagne [brətaɲ] *nf* **la B.** Brittany • **breton, -onne 1** *adj* Breton **2** *nmf* **B., Bretonne** Breton

bretelle [brətɛl] *nf* strap; **bretelles** *(de pantalon) Br* braces, *Am* suspenders

brève [brɛv] *voir* **bref**

brevet [brəvɛ] *nm (certificat)* certificate; *(diplôme)* diploma; **b. de technicien supérieur** = advanced vocational training certificate; **b. (d'invention)** patent

bric-à-brac [brikabrak] *nm inv (vieux objets)* odds and ends

bricoler [brikɔle] **1** *vt (construire)* to put together; *(réparer)* to fix **2** *vi* to do some DIY • **bricolage** *nm (travail)* DIY, do-it-yourself; **faire du b.** to do some DIY • **bricoleur, -euse** *nmf* handyman, *f* handywoman

bride [brid] *nf (de cheval)* bridle

● **bridé, -e** *adj* **avoir les yeux bridés** to have slanting *eyes*

bridge [bridʒ] *nm (jeu)* bridge

brièvement [brijɛvmã] *adv* briefly

brigade [brigad] *nf (de gendarmerie)* squad; *Mil* brigade

brillant, -e [brijã, -ãt] **1** *adj (luisant)* shining; *(couleur)* bright; *(cheveux, cuir)* shiny; *Fig (remarquable)* brilliant **2** *nm (éclat)* shine; **b. à lèvres** lip gloss ● **brillamment** [-amã] *adv* brilliantly

briller [brije] *vi* to shine; **faire b. qch** to polish sth

brimer [brime] *vt* to bully ● **brimades** *nfpl (vexations)* bullying

brin [brɛ̃] *nm (d'herbe)* blade; *(de fil)* strand; *Fig* **un b. de qch** a bit of sth; **faire un b. de toilette** to have a quick wash

brioche [brijɔʃ] *nf* brioche

brique [brik] *nf (de construction)* brick

briquet [brikɛ] *nm* lighter

brise [briz] *nf* breeze

briser [brize] **1** *vt* to break **2 se briser** *vpr* to break

britannique [britanik] **1** *adj* British **2** *nmf* **B.** Briton; **les Britanniques** the British

brocante [brɔkãt] *nf (commerce)* second-hand trade

broche [brɔʃ] *nf (pour rôtir)* spit; *(bijou)* brooch; **faire cuire qch à la b.** to spit-roast sth ● **brochette** *nf (tige)* skewer; *(plat)* kebab

broché, -e [brɔʃe] *adj* **livre b.** paperback

brochure [brɔʃyr] *nf* brochure

brocolis [brɔkɔli] *nmpl* broccoli

broder [brɔde] *vt* to embroider (**de** with) ● **broderie** *nf (activité)* embroidery

bronchite [brɔ̃ʃit] *nf* bronchitis; **avoir une b.** to have bronchitis

bronze [brɔ̃z] *nm* bronze

bronzer [brɔ̃ze] *vi* to tan ● **bronzage** *nm* (sun)tan

brosse [brɔs] *nf* brush; **b. à dents** toothbrush ● **brosser 1** *vt (tapis, cheveux)* to brush **2 se brosser** *vpr* **se b. les dents/les cheveux** to brush one's teeth/one's hair

brouette [bruɛt] *nf* wheelbarrow

brouillard [brujar] *nm* fog; **il y a du b.** it's foggy

brouiller [bruje] **1** *vt (idées)* to muddle up; *(vue)* to blur **2 se brouiller** *vpr (vue)* to get blurred; *(se disputer)* to fall out (**avec** with)

brouillon [brujɔ̃] *nm* rough draft; **(papier) b.** *Br* scrap paper, *Am* scratch paper

brousse [brus] *nf* **la b.** the bush

broyer [brwaje] *vt* to grind

bru [bry] *nf* daughter-in-law

bruine [bruin] *nf* drizzle ● **bruiner** *v impersonnel* to drizzle; **il bruine** it's drizzling

bruit [brui] *nm* noise, sound; *(nouvelle)* rumour; **faire du b.** to make a noise

brûlant, -e [brylã, -ãt] *adj (objet, soupe, soleil)* boiling (hot)

brûlé [bryle] *nm* **odeur de b.** burnt smell; **sentir le b.** to smell burnt

brûler [bryle] **1** *vt (sujet: flamme, acide)* to burn; *Fig* **b. un feu rouge** to go through a red light **2** *vi* to burn **3 se brûler** *vpr* to burn oneself; **se b. la langue** to burn one's tongue ● **brûlure** *nf* burn

brume [brym] *nf* mist, haze ● **brumeux, -euse** *adj* misty, hazy

brun, -e [brœ̃, bryn] **1** *adj (cheveux)* dark, brown; *(personne)* dark-haired **2** *nm (couleur)* brown **3** *nmf* dark-haired man, *f* dark-haired woman ● **brunette** *nf* brunette

brushing® [brœʃiŋ] *nm* blow-dry; **faire un b. à qn** to blow-dry sb's hair

brusque [brysk] *adj* abrupt
● **brusquement** [-əmã] *adv* abruptly

brut, -e [bryt] *adj (pétrole)* crude; *(poids, salaire)* gross; *(champagne)* extra-dry

brutal, -e, -aux, -ales [brytal, -o] *adj (personne, manières)* brutal; *(franchise, réponse)* crude, blunt; *(changement)* abrupt; **être b. avec qn** to be rough with sb ● **brutalité** *nf* brutality

Bruxelles [brysɛl] *nm ou f* Brussels

bruyant, -e [brɥijã, -ãt] *adj* noisy

BTS [beteɛs] *(abrév* **brevet de technicien supérieur)** *nm Scol* = advanced vocational training certificate

bu, -e [by] *pp de* **boire**

buanderie [bɥãdri] *nf (lieu)* laundry

bûche [byʃ] *nf* log; **b. de Noël** Yule log

bûcheur, -euse [byʃœr, -øz] *nmf Br* swot, *Am* grind

budget [bydʒɛ] *nm* budget

buée [bɥe] *nf* condensation

buffet [byfɛ] *nm (meuble)* sideboard; *(repas)* buffet

buisson [bɥisɔ̃] *nm* bush

buissonnière [bɥisɔnjɛr] *adj f* **faire l'école b.** *Br* to play truant, *Am* to play hookey

bulldozer [byldozœr] *nm* bulldozer

bulle [byl] *nf* bubble; **faire des bulles** to blow bubbles

bulletin [byltɛ̃] *nm (communiqué, revue)* bulletin; **b. d'informations** news bulletin; **b. météo(rologique)** weather report; **b. scolaire** *Br* school report, *Am* report card; **b. de vote** ballot paper

bureau, -x [byro] *nm (table)* desk; *(lieu)* office; *(comité)* committee; **b. de change** bureau de change; **b. de poste** post office; **b. de tabac** *Br* tobacconist's (shop), *Am* tobacco store

bureaucratie [byrokrasi] *nf* bureaucracy

bus¹ [bys] *nm* bus

bus² [by] *pt de* **boire**

buste [byst] *nm (torse)* chest; *(sculpture)* bust

but¹ [by(t)] *nm aussi Sport* goal

but² [by] *pt de* **boire**

buter [byte] *vi* **b. contre qch** *(cogner)* to bump into sth; *(trébucher)* to stumble over sth ● **buté, -e** *adj* obstinate

butin [bytɛ̃] *nm* loot

butoir [bytwar] *nm (pour train)* buffer; *(de porte)* stopper, *Br* stop

buvette [byvɛt] *nf* snack bar

buveur, -euse [byvœr, -øz] *nmf* drinker; **un grand b.** a heavy drinker

buviez [byvje] *voir* **boire**

Cc

C, c [se] *nm inv* C, c

c' [s] *voir* **ce²**

ça [sa] *pron démonstratif (pour désigner)* that; *(plus près)* this; *(sujet indéfini)* it, that; **où/quand ça?** where?/when?; **ça dépend** it depends; **ça va?** how are things?; **ça va!** fine!, OK!; **c'est ça** that's right

çà [sa] **çà et là** *adv* here and there

cabane [kaban] *nf (baraque)* hut; *(en rondin)* cabin; *(de jardin)* shed

cabillaud [kabijo] *nm* cod

cabine [kabin] *nf (de bateau)* cabin; **c. d'essayage** fitting room; **c. téléphonique** phone box

cabinet [kabinɛ] *nm (de médecin) Br* surgery, *Am* office; *(d'avocat)* firm; *(de ministre)* departmental staff; **c. de toilette** (small) bathroom; *Fam* **les cabinets** *Br* the loo, *Am* the john

câble [kabl] *nm* cable; *TV* **le c.** cable

cabriolet [kabriɔlɛ] *nm (auto)* convertible

cacah(o)uète [kakawɛt] *nf* peanut

cacao [kakao] *nm (poudre)* cocoa

cache-cache [kaʃkaʃ] *nm inv* **jouer à c.** to play hide and seek

cachemire [kaʃmir] *nm* cashmere

cache-nez [kaʃne] *nm inv* scarf

cacher [kaʃe] **1** *vt* to hide (**à** from) **2 se cacher** *upr* to hide

cachet [kaʃɛ] *nm (marque)* stamp; *(comprimé)* tablet

cachette [kaʃɛt] *nf* hiding place; **en c.** in secret

cactus [kaktys] *nm* cactus

cadavre [kadavr] *nm* corpse

caddie® [kadi] *nm Br* trolley, *Am* cart

cadeau, -x [kado] *nm* present, gift; **faire un c. à qn** to give sb a present

cadenas [kadna] *nm* padlock

cadet, -ette [kade, -ɛt] *nmf (de deux)* younger (one); *(de plus de deux)* youngest (one)

cadran [kadrã] *nm (de téléphone)* dial; *(de montre)* face

cadre [kadr] *nm* (**a**) *(de photo, de vélo)* frame; **dans le c. de** within the framework of (**b**) *(d'entreprise)* executive; **les cadres** management

cafard [kafar] *nm* cockroach

café [kafe] *nm (produit, boisson)* coffee; *(bar)* café; **c. au lait, c. crème** *Br* white coffee, *Am* coffee with milk; **c. noir** black coffee; **c. soluble** *ou* **instantané** instant coffee • **caféine** *nf* caffeine • **cafétéria** *nf* cafeteria • **cafetière** *nf (récipient)* coffeepot; *(électrique)* coffee machine

cage [kaʒ] *nf* cage

cageot [kaʒo] *nm* crate

cagoule [kagul] *nf (de bandit)* hood; *(d'enfant) Br* balaclava, *Am* ski mask

cahier [kaje] *nm* notebook; *(d'écolier)* exercise book

caillou, -x [kaju] *nm* stone; *(sur la plage)* pebble

caisse [kɛs] *nf* (**a**) *(boîte)* case; *(d'outils)* box; *(cageot)* crate (**b**) *(de* *magasin)* cash desk; *(de supermarché)* checkout; **c. enregistreuse** cash register; **c. d'épargne** savings bank • **caissier, -ère** *nmf* cashier

cajou [kaʒu] *nm* **noix de c.** cashew nut

calcium [kalsjɔm] *nm* calcium

calcul [kalkyl] *nm* calculation; *Scol* **le c.** arithmetic; **faire un c.** to make a calculation

calculatrice [kalkylatris] *nf* **c. (de poche)** (pocket) calculator

calculer [kalkyle] *vt* to calculate

cale [kal] *nf (de meuble, de porte)* wedge

caleçon [kalsɔ̃] *nm* boxer shorts

calembour [kalɑ̃bur] *nm* pun

calendrier [kalɑ̃drije] *nm (mois et jours)* calendar; *(programme)* timetable

calepin [kalpɛ̃] *nm* notebook

caler [kale] **1** *vt (meuble, porte)* to wedge **2** *vi (moteur)* to stall **3 se caler** *vpr (dans un fauteuil)* to settle oneself comfortably

calibre [kalibr] *nm* calibre

califourchon [kalifurʃɔ̃] **à califourchon** *adv* astride; **se mettre à c. sur qch** to sit astride sth

câlin [kɑlɛ̃] *nm* cuddle; **faire un c. à qn** to give sb a cuddle

calmant [kalmɑ̃] *nm* sedative

calmar [kalmar] *nm* squid

calme [kalm] **1** *adj (flegmatique)* calm; *(tranquille)* quiet; *(mer)* calm **2** *nm* calm; **garder/perdre son c.** to keep/lose one's calm; **du c.!** *(taisez-vous)* keep quiet!; *(pas de panique)* keep calm!

calmer [kalme] **1** *vt (douleur)* to soothe; *(inquiétude)* to calm; **c. qn** to calm sb down **2 se calmer** *vpr (personne)* to calm down; *(vent)* to die down; *(mer)* to become calm; *(douleur)* to subside

calorie [kalɔri] *nf* calorie

camarade [kamarad] *nmf* friend• **c. de classe** classmate

cambrer [kɑ̃bre] **se cambrer** *vp* to arch one's back

cambrioler [kɑ̃brijɔle] *vt* B to burgle, *Am* to burglarize • **cambriolage** *nm* burglary • **cambrioleur, -euse** *nmf* burglar

camelote [kamlɔt] *nf (pacotille* junk; *(marchandise)* stuff

camembert [kamɑ̃bɛr] *nm (fromage)* Camembert (cheese)

caméra [kamera] *nf* (TV/film camera • **cameraman** (*pl* **-man** *ou* **-men** [-mɛn]) *nm* cameraman

Caméscope® [kameskɔp] *nm* camcorder

camion [kamjɔ̃] *nm Br* lorry, *Am* truck; **c. de déménagement** B removal van, *Am* moving van • **camionnette** *nf* van

camomille [kamɔmij] *nf (plante* camomile; *(tisane)* camomile tea

camouflage [kamuflaʒ] *nm M* camouflage

camp [kɑ̃] *nm (campement)* camp *(de parti)* side; **c. de concen tration** concentration camp

campagne [kɑ̃paɲ] *nf* (**a**) *(pa opposition à la ville)* country, *(paysage)* countryside; **à la c. i** the country (**b**) *Mil, Com & Pc* campaign

camper [kɑ̃pe] *vi* to camp • **campeur, -euse** *nmf* camper

camping [kɑ̃piŋ] *nm (activité* camping; *(terrain)* camp(ing) site **faire du c.** to go camping; **c sauvage** unauthorized camping • **camping-car** (*pl* **camping-cars** *nm* camper

campus [kɑ̃pys] *nm* campus

Canada [kanada] *nm* **le C** Canada • **canadien, -enne 1** *ac* Canadian **2** *nmf* **C., Canadienn** Canadian

canal, -aux [kanal, -o] *nm* canal; *Fig* channel

canapé [kanape] *nm* (a) *(siège)* sofa, couch (b) *(pour l'apéritif)* canapé • **canapé-lit** *(pl* **canapés-lits)** *nm* sofa bed

canard [kanar] *nm* duck

canari [kanari] *nm* canary

cancans [kɑ̃kɑ̃] *nmpl* gossip

cancer [kɑ̃sɛr] *nm* *(maladie)* cancer; **avoir un c.** to have cancer; **le C.** *(signe)* Cancer

candidat, -e [kɑ̃dida, -at] *nmf* *(d'examen, d'élection)* candidate (à for); *(de poste)* applicant (à for); **être c. aux élections** to stand for election • **candidature** *nf (à un poste)* application (à for); *(aux élections)* candidature (à for); **poser sa c.** to apply (à for); **c. spontanée** unsolicited application

candide [kɑ̃did] *adj* guileless

canette [kanɛt] *nf (boîte)* can

canevas [kanva] *nm* canvas

caniche [kaniʃ] *nm* poodle

canicule [kanikyl] *nf* heatwave

canif [kanif] *nm* penknife

caniveau, -x [kanivo] *nm* gutter

canne [kan] *nf (tige)* cane; *(pour marcher)* (walking) stick; **c. à pêche** fishing rod

cannelle [kanɛl] *nf* cinnamon

cannette [kanɛt] *nf* = **canette**

cannibale [kanibal] *nmf* cannibal

canoë-kayak [kanɔekajak] *nm* canoeing

canon [kanɔ̃] *nm* gun; *(ancien, à boulets)* cannon

canot [kano] *nm* boat; **c. de sauvetage** lifeboat; **c. pneumatique** rubber dinghy

cantine [kɑ̃tin] *nf* canteen

canton [kɑ̃tɔ̃] *nm (en France)* canton *(division of a department)*; *(en Suisse)* canton *(semi-autonomous region)*

canular [kanylar] *nm Fam* hoax

caoutchouc [kautʃu] *nm* rubber

CAP [seape] *(abrév* **certificat d'aptitude professionnelle)** *nm Scol* = vocational training certificate

cap [kap] *nm Géog* cape

capable [kapabl] *adj* capable, able; **c. de qch** capable of sth; **c. de faire qch** able to do sth, capable of doing sth • **capacité** *nf* capacity; *(aptitude)* ability

CAPES [kapɛs] *(abrév* **certificat d'aptitude professionnelle à l'enseignement secondaire)** *nm* = postgraduate teaching certificate

capitaine [kapitɛn] *nm* captain

capital, -e, -aux, -ales [kapital, -o] *adj f* **lettre capitale** capital letter • **capitale** *nf (lettre, ville)* capital

capitalisme [kapitalism] *nm* capitalism

capituler [kapityle] *vi* to surrender

capot [kapo] *nm Aut Br* bonnet, *Am* hood

caprice [kapris] *nm* whim; **faire un c.** to throw a tantrum • **capricieux, -euse** *adj (personne)* capricious

Capricorne [kaprikɔrn] *nm* **le C.** *(signe)* Capricorn

capsule [kapsyl] *nf (spatiale)* capsule; *(de bouteille)* cap

capter [kapte] *vt (signal, radio)* to pick up; *(attention)* to capture

captif, -ive [kaptif, -iv] *adj & nmf* captive • **captivité** *nf* captivity; **en c.** in captivity

captiver [kaptive] *vt* to captivate

capture [kaptyr] *nf* capture • **capturer** *vt* to capture

capuche [kapyʃ] *nf* hood • **capuchon** *nm (de manteau)* hood; *(de stylo, de tube)* cap, top

car[1] [kar] *conj* because, for

car[2] [kar] *nm* bus, *Br* coach

caractère¹ [karaktɛr] *nm* *(lettre)* character; **caractères d'imprimerie** block letters

caractère² [karaktɛr] *nm* *(tempérament, nature)* character, nature; **avoir bon c.** to be good-natured; **avoir mauvais c.** to be bad-tempered

caractériser [karakterize] **se caractériser** *vpr* **se c. par** to be characterized by

caractéristique [karakteristik] *adj & nf* characteristic

carafe [karaf] *nf* carafe, pitcher

caramel [karamɛl] *nm* caramel

carapace [karapas] *nf* *(de tortue) & Fig* shell

caravane [karavan] *nf* *Br* caravan, *Am* trailer • **caravaning** *nm* caravanning; **faire du c.** to go caravanning

carbone [karbɔn] *nm* carbon

carburant [karbyrɑ̃] *nm* fuel

carcasse [karkas] *nf* carcass

cardigan [kardigɑ̃] *nm* cardigan

cardinal, -e, -aux, -ales [kardinal, -o] **1** *adj (nombre, point, vertu)* cardinal **2** *nm Rel* cardinal

carême [karɛm] *nm Rel* **le c.** Lent

caresse [karɛs] *nf* caress; **faire des caresses à qn** to caress sb • **caresser** *vt (personne)* to caress; *(animal)* to stroke

cargaison [kargɛzɔ̃] *nf* cargo

caricature [karikatyr] *nf* caricature

carie [kari] *nf* **c. (dentaire)** tooth decay; **avoir une c.** to have a cavity

carnaval, -als [karnaval] *nm* carnival

carnet [karnɛ] *nm* notebook; *(de tickets)* = book of tickets; **c. d'adresses** address book; **c. de chèques** cheque book; **c. de notes** *Br* school report, *Am* report card

carotte [karɔt] *nf* carrot

carpette [karpɛt] *nf* rug

carré, -e [kare] **1** *adj* square; *(épaules)* square, broad; **mètre c.** square metre **2** *nm* square

carreau, -x [karo] *nm (motif)* square; *(sur tissu)* check; *(de céramique)* tile; *Cartes* diamonds

carrefour [karfur] *nm* crossroads *(sing)*

carrelage [karlaʒ] *nm* tiles

carrément [karemɑ̃] *adv Fam (franchement)* straight out; *(très)* really

carrière [karjɛr] *nf (métier)* career

cartable [kartabl] *nm* school bag

carte [kart] *nf* **(a)** *(carton, document officiel, informatisé)* card; *(géographique)* map; *Fig* **avoir c. blanche** to have a free hand; **c. (à jouer)** (playing) card; **jouer aux cartes** to play cards; **c. de crédit** credit card; **c. d'identité** identity card; **c. de séjour** residence permit; **c. de téléphone** phonecard; **c. de visite** *Br* visiting card, *Am* calling card; *(professionnelle)* business card; **c. de vœux** greetings card; **c. postale** postcard; **c. routière** road map **(b)** *(de restaurant)* menu; **manger à la c.** to eat à la carte; **c. des vins** wine list

carton [kartɔ̃] *nm (matière)* cardboard; *(boîte)* cardboard box; **c. jaune/rouge** *(au football)* yellow/red card • **cartonné, -e** *adj* **livre c.** hardback

cartouche [kartuʃ] *nf* cartridge; *(de cigarettes)* carton

cas [kɑ] *nm* case; **en tout c.** in any case; **en c. de besoin** if need be; **en c. d'accident** in the event of an accident; **en c. d'urgence** in an emergency; **au c. où elle tomberait** if she should fall

cascade [kaskad] *nf* (**a**) *(d'eau)* waterfall (**b**) *(de cinéma)* stunt • **cascadeur, -euse** *nmf* stunt man, *f* stunt woman

case [kɑz] *nf* *(de tiroir)* compartment; *(de formulaire)* box

caser [kaze] **se caser** *vpr Fam (se marier)* to get married and settle down

caserne [kazɛrn] *nf* barracks

casier [kɑzje] *nm* compartment; *(pour courrier)* pigeonhole; *(pour vêtements)* locker

casino [kazino] *nm* casino

casque [kask] *nm* helmet; **c. (à écouteurs)** headphones

casquette [kaskɛt] *nf* cap

casser [kase] **1** *vt (briser)* to break; *(noix)* to crack; *(voix)* to strain; *Fam* **c. les pieds à qn** to get on sb's nerves **2** *vi* to break **3** **se casser** *vpr* to break; **se c. la jambe** to break one's leg; *Fam* **se c. la figure** *(tomber)* to fall flat on one's face • **casse-croûte** *nm inv Fam* snack • **casse-pieds** *nmf inv Fam (personne)* pain (in the neck) • **casse-tête** *nm inv (problème)* headache; *(jeu)* puzzle

casserole [kasrɔl] *nf* (sauce)pan

cassette [kasɛt] *nf (magnétique)* cassette, tape; **enregistrer qch sur c.** to tape sth; **c. video** video cassette

cassis [kasis] *nm (fruit)* blackcurrant; *(boisson)* blackcurrant liqueur

cassoulet [kasule] *nm* cassoulet, = stew of beans, pork and goose

castor [kastɔr] *nm* beaver

catalogue [katalɔg] *nm Br* catalogue, *Am* catalog

catapulte [katapylt] *nf* catapult

catastrophe [katastrɔf] *nf* disaster, catastrophe

catch [katʃ] *nm* wrestling

catégorie [kategɔri] *nf* category

catégorique [kategɔrik] *adj* categorical; **c'est lui, je suis c.** I'm positive it's him

cathédrale [katedral] *nf* cathedral

catholique [katɔlik] *adj & nmf* (Roman) Catholic

cauchemar [koʃmar] *nm aussi Fig* nightmare; **faire un c.** to have a nightmare

cause [koz] *nf (origine)* cause; *(procès, parti)* case; **à c. de qn/ qch** because of sb/sth

causer¹ [koze] *vt (provoquer)* to cause

causer² [koze] *vi (bavarder)* to chat (**de** about)

caution [kosjɔ̃] *nf (d'appartement)* deposit; *Jur* bail; *(personne)* guarantor; *Jur* **sous c.** on bail

cavalier, -ère [kavalje, -ɛr] *nmf (à cheval)* rider; *(de bal)* partner

cave [kav] *nf* cellar

caverne [kavɛrn] *nf* cave; **homme des cavernes** caveman

caviar [kavjar] *nm* caviar

cavité [kavite] *nf* hollow, cavity

CD [sede] *(abrév* **compact disc***) nm* CD

CD-Rom [sederɔm] *nm inv Ordinat* CD-Rom

CE [seə] **1** *(abrév* **cours élémentaire***) nm Scol* **CE1** = second year of primary school; **CE2** = third year of primary school **2** *(abrév* **Communauté européenne***) nf* EC

ce¹, cette, ces [sə, sɛt, se]

cet is used before a masculine singular adjective beginning with a vowel or mute h.

adj démonstratif this, that, *pl* these, those; **cet homme** this/that man; **cet homme-ci** this man; **cet homme-là** that man

ce² [sə]

ce becomes **c'** before a vowel.

pron démonstratif (a) *(pour désigner, pour qualifier)* it, that; **c'est facile** it's easy; **c'est exact** that's right; **c'est mon père** that's my father; *(au téléphone)* it's my father; **ce sont eux qui...** they are the people who...; **qui est-ce?** *(en général)* who is it?; *(en désignant)* who is that?; **ce faisant** in so doing; **sur ce** thereupon (b) *(après une proposition)* **ce que..., ce qui...** what...; **je sais ce qui est bon/ce que tu veux** I know what is good/what you want; **ce que c'est beau!** it's so beautiful!

ceci [səsi] *pron démonstratif* this; **c. étant dit** having said this

céder [sede] **1** *vt (donner)* to give up (**à** to); **'cédez le passage'** *Br* 'give way', *Am* 'yield' **2** *vi (personne)* to give in (**à/devant** to); *(branche, chaise)* to give way

cédérom [sederɔm] *nm* = **CD-Rom**

ceinture [sɛ̃tyr] *nf (accessoire)* belt; *(taille)* waist; **c. de sécurité** *(de véhicule)* seatbelt

cela [s(ə)la] *pron démonstratif (pour désigner)* that; *(sujet indéfini)* it, that; **quand/comment c.?** when?/how?

célèbre [selɛbr] *adj* famous • **célébrité** *nf* fame; *(personne)* celebrity

célébrer [selebre] *vt* to celebrate • **célébration** *nf* celebration (**de** of)

céleri [sɛlri] *nm* celery

célibataire [selibatɛr] **1** *adj (non marié)* single, unmarried **2** *nmf* bachelor, *f* single woman

celle *voir* **celui**

Cellophane® [selɔfan] *nf* cellophane®

cellule [selyl] *nf (de prison)* & *Biol* cell

celui, celle, ceux, celles [səlɥi, sɛl, sø, sɛl] *pron démonstratif* the one, *pl* those, the ones; **c. de Jean** Jean's (one); **ceux de Jean** Jean's (ones), those of Jean; **c. qui appartient à Jean** the one that belongs to Jean; **c.-ci** this one; *(le dernier)* the latter; **c.-là** that one; *(le premier)* the former

cendre [sɑ̃dr] *nf* ash • **cendrier** *nm* ashtray

censé, -e [sɑ̃se] *adj* **être c. faire qch** to be supposed to do sth

censeur [sɑ̃sœr] *nm* censor • **censure** *nf* censorship • **censurer** *vt (film)* to censor

cent [sɑ̃] *adj & nm* a hundred; **c. pages** a *or* one hundred pages; **deux cents pages** two hundred pages; **cinq pour c.** five per cent • **centaine** *nf* **une c. (de)** about a hundred; **des centaines de** hundreds of • **centenaire 1** *nmf* centenarian **2** *nm (anniversaire)* centenary • **centième** *adj & nmf* hundredth

centigrade [sɑ̃tigrad] *adj* centigrade

centimètre [sɑ̃timɛtr] *nm* centimetre

central, -e, -aux, -ales [sɑ̃tral, -o] *adj* central • **centrale** *nf* **c. électrique** *Br* power station, *Am* power plant; **c. nucléaire** nuclear *Br* power station *or Am* power plant

centre [sɑ̃tr] *nm* centre; **c. aéré** outdoor activity centre; **c. commercial** shopping centre • **centre-ville** *(pl* **centres-villes)** *nm* town centre; *(de grande ville) Br* city centre, *Am* downtown

cependant [səpɑ̃dɑ̃] *conj* however

céramique [seramik] *nf (matière)*

ceramic; *(art)* ceramics *(sing)*; **de**
ou **en c.** ceramic

cercle [sɛrkl] *nm (forme, groupe)*
circle; **c. vicieux** vicious circle

cercueil [sɛrkœj] *nm* coffin

céréale [sereal] *nf* cereal

cérémonie [seremɔni] *nf*
ceremony

cerf [sɛr] *nm* stag ● **cerf-volant**
(pl **cerfs-volants)** *nm (jeu)* kite

cerise [sǝriz] *nf* cherry

cerner [sɛrne] *vt* to surround;
avoir les yeux cernés to have
rings under one's eyes

certain, -e [sɛrtɛ̃, -ɛn] **1** *adj (sûr)*
certain; **je suis c. de réussir** I'm
certain I'll be successful *or* of being
successful; **être c. de qch** to be
certain of sth **2** *adj indéfini (avant
nom)* certain; **un c. temps** a while
3 *pron indéfini* **certains pensent
que...** some people think that...;
certains d'entre nous some of us ●
certainement *adv* most probably

certificat [sɛrtifika] *nm* certificate

certifier [sɛrtifje] *vt* to certify; **je
te certifie que...** I assure you
that...

certitude [sɛrtityd] *nf* certainty;
avoir la c. que... to be certain
that...

cerveau, -x [sɛrvo] *nm (organe)*
brain; *(intelligence)* mind, brain(s)

cervelle [sɛrvɛl] *nf (substance)*
brain; *(plat)* brains

ces *voir* ce[1]

esse [sɛs] *nf* **sans c.** constantly

cesser [sese] *vti* to stop; **faire c.
qch** to put a stop to sth; **c. de faire
qch** to stop doing sth

c'est-à-dire [sɛtadir] *conj* that is
(to say)

cet, cette *voir* ce[1]

ceux *voir* celui

chacun, -e [ʃakœ̃, -yn] *pron
indéfini* each (one), every one;

(tout le monde) everyone; **(à) c.
son tour!** wait your turn!

chagrin [ʃagrɛ̃] *nm* grief, sorrow

chahut [ʃay] *nm Fam* racket

chaîne [ʃɛn] *nf (attache, décoration, série)* chain; *(de montagnes)*
range; *Aut* **chaînes** (snow) chains;
c. de télévision television channel;
c. (hi-fi) hi-fi (system)

chair [ʃɛr] *nf* flesh; **en c. et en os**
in the flesh; **avoir la c. de poule**
to have goose bumps

chaise [ʃɛz] *nf* chair; **c. longue**
deckchair

châle [ʃɑl] *nm* shawl

chalet [ʃalɛ] *nm* chalet

chaleur [ʃalœr] *nf* heat; *(de
personne, de couleur)* warmth ●
chaleureux, -euse *adj* warm

chambre [ʃɑ̃br] *nf* bedroom; *(de
tribunal)* division; **c. (d'hôtel)** (hotel)
room; **c. à coucher** bedroom; **c.
d'amis** spare room; **c. d'hôte** ≃
guest house; **C. de commerce**
Chamber of Commerce; *Pol* **C.
des députés** = lower chamber of
Parliament

chameau, -x [ʃamo] *nm* camel

champ [ʃɑ̃] *nm* field; **c. de
bataille** battlefield; **c. de courses**
Br racecourse, *Am* racetrack

champagne [ʃɑ̃paɲ] *nm* champagne

champignon [ʃɑ̃piɲɔ̃] *nm* mushroom

champion, -onne [ʃɑ̃pjɔ̃, -ɔn]
nmf champion ● **championnat**
nm championship

chance [ʃɑ̃s] *nf (sort favorable)*
luck; *(possibilité)* chance; **avoir de
la c.** to be lucky; **ne pas avoir de
c.** to be unlucky; **par c.** luckily ●
chanceux, -euse *adj* lucky

chanceler [ʃɑ̃sle] *vi* to stagger

chancelier [ʃɑ̃sǝlje] *nm Pol*
chancellor

chandail [ʃɑ̃daj] *nm* sweater
chandelier [ʃɑ̃dəlje] *nm (à une branche)* candlestick; *(à plusieurs branches)* candelabra
chandelle [ʃɑ̃dɛl] *nf* candle
change [ʃɑ̃ʒ] *nm* Fin exchange
changer [ʃɑ̃ʒe] **1** *vt (modifier, remplacer, convertir)* to change; **c. qch de place** to move sth **2** *vi* to change; **c. d'adresse** to change one's address; **c. de vitesse/de couleur** to change gear/colour **3 se changer** *vpr* to change (one's clothes); **se c. en qch** to change into sth ● **changement** *nm* change; *Aut* **c. de vitesse** *(levier)* *Br* gear lever, *Am* gear shift
chanson [ʃɑ̃sɔ̃] *nf* song ● **chant** *nm (art)* singing; *(chanson)* song
chanter [ʃɑ̃te] **1** *vt (chanson)* to sing **2** *vi (personne, oiseau)* to sing; **faire c. qn** to blackmail sb ● **chantage** *nm* blackmail ● **chanteur, -euse** *nmf* singer
chantier [ʃɑ̃tje] *nm* (building) site; *(sur route)* roadworks
chantilly [ʃɑ̃tiji] *nf* whipped cream
chantonner [ʃɑ̃tɔne] *vti* to hum
chaos [kao] *nm* chaos ● **chaotique** *adj* chaotic
chapeau, -x [ʃapo] *nm* hat; **c. de paille** straw hat
chapelle [ʃapɛl] *nf* chapel
chapelure [ʃaplyr] *nf* breadcrumbs
chapiteau, -x [ʃapito] *nm (de cirque)* big top; *(pour expositions)* tent, *Br* marquee
chapitre [ʃapitr] *nm* chapter
chaque [ʃak] *adj* each, every
char [ʃar] *nm* Mil tank
charbon [ʃarbɔ̃] *nm* coal
charcuterie [ʃarkytri] *nf* cooked (pork) meats
charge [ʃarʒ] *nf (poids)* load; *(responsabilité)* responsibility; *(d'une*

arme) & *Él, Mil* charge; *(fonction* office; **être en c. de qch** to be i charge of sth; **prendre qn/qch en c.** to take charge of sb/sth; **être à la c. de qn** *(personne* to be dependent on sb; *(frais* to be payable by sb; **charge sociales** *Br* national insurance contributions, *Am* Social Security contributions
charger [ʃarʒe] **1** *vt (véhicule marchandises, arme)* & *Ordina* to load; *(batterie)* & *Mil* to charge **c. qn de qch** to entrust sb wit sth; **c. qn de faire qch** to give s the responsibility of doing sth **2** *v Ordinat* to load up; *Mil* to charg **3 se charger** *vpr (s'encombrer* to weigh oneself down; **se c. de qn/qch** to take care of sb/sth; **s c. de faire qch** to undertake t do sth ● **chargé, -e** *adj (véhicule* loaded *(de* with); *(arme)* loaded *(journée, programme)* busy; **êtr c. de faire qch** to be responsibl for doing sth
chariot [ʃarjo] *nm (de super marché)* *Br* trolley, *Am* cart
charité [ʃarite] *nf (vertu)* charit **faire la c.** to give to charity
charme [ʃarm] *nm (attrait)* charm *(magie)* spell ● **charmant, -e** *a* charming
charpentier [ʃarpɑ̃tje] *n* carpenter
charrette [ʃarɛt] *nf* cart
charrue [ʃary] *nf* *Br* plough, *A* plow
chasse¹ [ʃas] *nf (activité)* huntin *(événement)* hunt; *(poursuite* chase; **aller à la c.** to go huntin **c. au trésor** treasure hunt
chasse² [ʃas] *nf* **c. d'eau** flus **tirer la c.** to flush the toilet
chassé-croisé [ʃasekrwaze] *(p chassés-croisés)* *nm (de pe*

sonnes) comings and goings

chasser [ʃase] **1** *vt (animal)* to hunt; **c. qn** *(expulser)* to chase sb away **2** *vi* to hunt • **chasse-neige** *nm inv Br* snowplough, *Am* snowplow • **chasseur, -euse** *nmf* hunter

chat [ʃa] *nm* cat

châtain [ʃatɛ] *adj (cheveux)* (chestnut) brown; *(personne)* brown-haired

château, -x [ʃato] *nm (forteresse)* castle; *(manoir)* mansion

châtiment [ʃatimɑ̃] *nm* punishment

chaton [ʃatɔ̃] *nm (chat)* kitten

chatouiller [ʃatuje] *vt* to tickle • **chatouilleux, -euse** *adj* ticklish

chatoyer [ʃatwaje] *vi* to sparkle

chaud, -e [ʃo, ʃod] **1** *adj (modérément)* warm; *(intensément)* hot; *Fig (couleur)* warm **2** *nm* **avoir c.** to be hot; **il fait c.** it's hot

chaudière [ʃodjɛr] *nf* boiler

chauffage [ʃofaʒ] *nm* heating

chauffard [ʃofar] *nm* reckless driver

chauffer [ʃofe] **1** *vt* to heat (up) **2** *vi* to heat up; **faire c. qch** to heat sth up

chauffeur [ʃofœr] *nm (de véhicule)* driver; *(employé)* chauffeur; **c. de taxi** taxi driver

chaussée [ʃose] *nf* road(way)

chausser [ʃose] *vt (chaussures, skis)* to put on; **c. qn** to put shoes on sb; **c. du 40** to take a size 40

chaussette [ʃosɛt] *nf* sock

chausson [ʃosɔ̃] *nm (pantoufle)* slipper; *Culin* **c. aux pommes** apple turnover

chaussure [ʃosyr] *nf* shoe

chauve [ʃov] *adj* bald

chauve-souris [ʃovsuri] *(pl* **chauves-souris)** *nf* bat

chavirer [ʃavire] *vti (bateau)* to capsize

chef [ʃɛf] *nm* **(a)** *(de parti, de bande)* leader; *(de tribu)* chief; **rédacteur en c.** editor in chief; **c. d'État** head of state; **c. d'orchestre** conductor **(b)** *(cuisinier)* chef

chef-d'œuvre [ʃedœvr] *(pl* **chefs-d'œuvre)** *nm* masterpiece

chef-lieu [ʃɛfljø] *(pl* **chefs-lieux)** *nm* = administrative centre of a 'département'

chemin [ʃəmɛ̃] *nm (route étroite)* path, track; *(itinéraire)* way (**de** to); **à mi-c.** half-way • **chemin de fer** *(pl* **chemins de fer)** *nm Br* railway, *Am* railroad

cheminée [ʃəmine] *nf (âtre)* fireplace; *(encadrement)* mantelpiece; *(sur le toit)* chimney

chemise [ʃəmiz] *nf (vêtement)* shirt; **c. de nuit** *(de femme)* nightdress • **chemisier** *nm (corsage)* blouse

chêne [ʃɛn] *nm (arbre, bois)* oak

chenil [ʃəni(l)] *nm Br* kennels, *Am* kennel

chenille [ʃənij] *nf (insecte)* caterpillar; *(de char)* caterpillar track

chèque [ʃɛk] *nm Br* cheque, *Am* check; **faire un c. à qn** to write sb a cheque; **payer qch par c.** to pay sth by cheque; **c. de voyage** *Br* traveller's cheque, *Am* traveler's check • **chèque-repas** *(pl* **chèques-repas)**, **chèque-restaurant** *(pl* **chèques-restaurants)** *nm Br* luncheon voucher, *Am* meal ticket • **chéquier** *nm Br* cheque book, *Am* checkbook

cher, chère [ʃɛr] **1** *adj* **(a)** *(aimé)* dear (**à** to); **C. Monsieur** *(dans une lettre)* Dear Mr X; *(officiel)* Dear Sir **(b)** *(coûteux)* expensive, dear **2** *adv* **coûter c.** to be expensive **3** *nmf* **mon c., ma chère** my dear

chercher [ʃɛrʃe] *vt* to look for;

(dans un dictionnaire) to look up; **aller c.** qn/qch to (go and) fetch sb/sth; **c. à faire qch** to try to do sth • **chercheur, -euse** *nmf (scientifique)* researcher

chéri, -e [ʃeri] *adj & nmf* darling

cheval, -aux [ʃəval, -o] *nm* horse; **à c.** on horseback; **faire du c.** *Br* to go horse riding, *Am* to go horseback riding; **c. de course** racehorse

chevalier [ʃəvalje] *nm* knight

chevelure [ʃəvlyr] *nf* hair

chevet [ʃəvɛ] *nm* bedhead; **rester au c. de qn** to stay at sb's bedside

cheveu, -x [ʃəvø] *nm* **un c.** a hair; **cheveux** hair; **avoir les cheveux noirs** to have black hair

cheville [ʃəvij] *nf* ankle

chèvre [ʃɛvr] **1** *nf* goat **2** *nm (fromage)* goat's cheese

chez [ʃe] *prép* **c. qn** at sb's house; **il n'est pas c. lui** he isn't at home; **elle est rentrée c. elle** she's gone home; **c. Mme Dupont** *(adresse)* c/o Mme Dupont • **chez-soi** *nm inv* **son petit c.** one's own little home

chic [ʃik] *adj inv* smart, stylish; *Fam (gentil)* decent

chien, chienne [ʃjɛ̃, ʃjɛn] *nmf* dog; **c. d'aveugle** guide dog; **c. de garde** guard dog; **c. policier** police dog

chiffon [ʃifɔ̃] *nm* rag, cloth

chiffonner [ʃifɔne] *vt* to crumple; *Fam (ennuyer)* to bother

chiffre [ʃifr] *nm (nombre)* figure, number; **chiffres romains/arabes** Roman/Arabic numerals

chignon [ʃiɲɔ̃] *nm* bun, chignon

chimie [ʃimi] *nf* chemistry • **chimique** *adj* chemical • **chimiste** *nmf* (research) chemist

chimpanzé [ʃɛ̃pɑ̃ze] *nm* chimpanzee

Chine [ʃin] *nf* **la C.** China • **chinois, -e 1** *adj* Chinese **2** *nmf* **C., Chinoise** Chinese; **les C.** the Chinese **3** *nm (langue)* Chinese

chiot [ʃjo] *nm* puppy

chipoter [ʃipɔte] *vi (contester)* to quibble (**sur** about)

chips [ʃips] *nf Br* (potato) crisp, *Am* (potato) chip

chirurgie [ʃiryrʒi] *nf* surgery; **c. esthétique** plastic surgery • **chirurgien, -enne** *nmf* surgeon

chlore [klɔr] *nm* chlorine

choc [ʃɔk] **1** *nm (coup)* impact; *(forte émotion)* shock; **faire un c. à qn** to give sb a shock **2** *adj* **'prix-chocs'** 'prices slashed'

chocolat [ʃɔkɔla] *nm* chocolate; **gâteau au c.** chocolate cake; **c. au lait** milk chocolate

chœur [kœr] *nm* choir

choisir [ʃwazir] *vt* to choose; **c. de faire qch** to choose to do sth

choix [ʃwa] *nm* choice; *(assortiment)* selection; **avoir le c.** to have a choice

chômer [ʃome] *vi* **vous n'avez pas chômé!** you've not been idle!; **jour chômé** (public) holiday • **chômage** *nm* unemployment; **être au c.** to be unemployed • **chômeur, -euse** *nmf* unemployed person; **les chômeurs** the unemployed

choquer [ʃɔke] *vt (scandaliser)* to shock • **choquant, -e** *adj* shocking

chorale [kɔral] *nf* choir

chose [ʃoz] *nf* thing

chou, -x [ʃu] *nm* cabbage; **choux de Bruxelles** Brussels sprouts • **chou-fleur** *(pl* **choux-fleurs**) *nm* cauliflower

choucroute [ʃukrut] *nf* sauerkraut

chouette [ʃwɛt] **1** *nf (oiseau)* owl **2** *adj Fam (chic)* great

chrétien, -enne [kretjɛ̃, -ɛn] *adj & nmf* Christian • **Christ** [krist] *nm* **le C.** Christ

chronique¹ [krɔnik] *adj (malade, chômage)* chronic

chronique² [krɔnik] *nf (de journal)* column; *(annales)* chronicle

chronologie [krɔnɔlɔʒi] *nf* chronology • **chronologique** *adj* chronological

chronomètre [krɔnɔmɛtr] *nm* stopwatch • **chronométrer** *vt* to time

chrysanthème [krizɑ̃tɛm] *nm* chrysanthemum

chuchoter [ʃyʃɔte] *vti* to whisper

chut [ʃyt] *exclam* sh!, shush!

chute [ʃyt] *nf* fall; **c. de neige** snowfall • **chuter** *vi (diminuer)* to fall, to drop; *Fam (tomber)* to fall

Chypre [ʃipr] *nm ou f* Cyprus • **chypriote 1** *adj* Cypriot **2** *nmf* **C.** Cypriot

ci [si] *pron démonstratif* **comme çi comme ça** so so

-ci [si] *adv* **(a) par-ci, par-là** here and there **(b)** *voir* **ce¹, celui** • **ci-après** *adv* below • **ci-contre** *adv* opposite • **ci-dessous** *adv* below • **ci-dessus** *adv* above • **ci-joint, -e** *(mpl* **ci-joints,** *fpl* **ci-jointes) 1** *adj* **le document c.** the enclosed document **2** *adv* **vous trouverez c. copie de...** please find enclosed a copy of...

cible [sibl] *nf* target

ciboulette [sibulet] *nf* chives

cicatrice [sikatris] *nf* scar

cidre [sidr] *nm* cider

Cie *(abrév* **compagnie)** Co

ciel [sjɛl] *nm* **(a)** *(pl* **ciels)** sky **(b)** *(pl* **cieux** [sjø]) *(paradis)* heaven

cierge [sjɛrʒ] *nm Rel* candle

cigare [sigar] *nm* cigar • **cigarette** *nf* cigarette

cigogne [sigɔɲ] *nf* stork

cil [sil] *nm* eyelash

ciment [simɑ̃] *nm* cement

cimetière [simtjɛr] *nm* cemetery

cinéma [sinema] *nm (art, industrie)* Br cinema, Am movies; *(salle)* Br cinema, Am movie theater; **faire du c.** to be a film actor/actress; **aller au c.** to go to the Br cinema or Am movies • **cinéphile** *nmf* Br film *or* Am movie enthusiast

cinglant, -e [sɛ̃glɑ̃, -ɑ̃t] *adj (pluie)* lashing; *(remarque)* cutting

cinglé, -e [sɛ̃gle] *adj Fam* crazy

cinq [sɛ̃k] *adj inv & nm inv* five • **cinquième** *adj & nmf* fifth; **un c.** a fifth

cinquante [sɛ̃kɑ̃t] *adj inv & nm inv* fifty • **cinquantaine** *nf* **une c. (de)** about fifty; **avoir la c.** to be about fifty • **cinquantième** *adj & nmf* fiftieth

cintre [sɛ̃tr] *nm* coathanger

circonscription [sirkɔ̃skripsjɔ̃] *nf* division, district; **c. (électorale)** Br constituency, Am district

circonstance [sirkɔ̃stɑ̃s] *nf* circumstance

circuit [sirkɥi] *nm* circuit; **c. automobile** racing circuit

circulaire [sirkylɛr] *adj* circular

circulation [sirkylasjɔ̃] *nf (du sang, de l'information, de billets)* circulation; *(d'autos)* traffic • **circuler** *vi (sang, air, information)* to circulate; *(train, bus)* to run

cire [sir] *nf* wax; *(pour meubles)* polish • **cirer** *vt* to polish

cirque [sirk] *nm (spectacle)* circus

ciseaux [sizo] *nmpl* **(une paire de) c.** (a pair of) scissors

citation [sitasjɔ̃] *nf* quotation

cité [site] *nf (ville)* city; *(immeubles)* Br housing estate, Am housing development; **c. universitaire** Br halls of residence, Am dormitory

citerne [sitɛrn] *nf* tank

citoyen, -enne [sitwajɛ̃, -ɛn] *nmf* citizen

citron [sitrɔ̃] *nm* lemon; **c. pressé** = fresh lemonade; **c. vert** lime • **citronnade** *nf Br* lemon squash, *Am* lemonade

citrouille [sitruj] *nf* pumpkin

civière [sivjɛr] *nf* stretcher

civil, -e [sivil] **1** *adj (guerre, mariage, droits)* civil; *(non militaire)* civilian; *(courtois)* civil **2** *nm* civilian; **en c.** *(policier)* in plain clothes

civilisation [sivilizasjɔ̃] *nf* civilization • **civilisé, -e** *adj* civilized

clair, -e [klɛr] **1** *adj (net, limpide, évident)* clear; *(éclairé, pâle)* light; **bleu/vert c.** light blue/green **2** *adv (voir)* clearly; **il fait c.** it's light **3** *nm* **c. de lune** moonlight

clairsemé, -e [klɛrsəme] *adj* sparse

clairvoyant, -e [klɛrvwajã, -ãt] *adj* perceptive

clan [klã] *nm* clan

clandestin, -e [klãdɛstɛ̃, -in] *adj (rencontre)* clandestine; *(mouvement)* underground; *(travailleur)* illegal

clapier [klapje] *nm* (rabbit) hutch

claque [klak] *nf Fam* slap

claquer [klake] **1** *vt (porte)* to slam **2** *vi (porte)* to slam; **elle claque des dents** her teeth are chattering

claquettes [klakɛt] *nfpl* tap dancing; **faire des c.** to do tap dancing

clarifier [klarifje] *vt* to clarify • **clarification** *nf* clarification

clarinette [klarinɛt] *nf* clarinet

clarté [klarte] *nf (lumière)* light; *aussi Fig* clarity; **avec c.** clearly

classe [klas] *nf (catégorie, leçon, élèves)* class; **en c. de sixième** *Br* in the first year, *Am* in fifth grade; **aller en c.** to go to school; **avoir de la c.** *(personne)* to have class; **(salle de) c.** classroom; **de première c.** *(billet, compartiment)* first-class; **c. ouvrière/moyenne** working/middle class; **c. sociale** social class

classer [klase] *vt (objets)* to classify; *(papiers)* to file • **classement** *nm* classification; *(de papiers)* filing; *(rang)* place • **classeur** *nm (meuble)* filing cabinet; *(portefeuille)* ring binder

classique [klasik] **1** *adj (période)* classical; *(typique, conventionnel)* classic **2** *nm (œuvre)* classic

claustrophobe [klostrɔfɔb] *adj* claustrophobic

clavier [klavje] *nm* keyboard

clé, clef [kle] **1** *nf (de porte)* key; *(outil) Br* spanner, *Am* wrench; **fermer qch à c.** to lock sth; **c. de contact** ignition key **2** *adj* key; **mot c.** key word

clémentine [klemãtin] *nf* clementine

clergé [klɛrʒe] *nm* clergy

cliché [kliʃe] *nm (photo)* photo; *(négatif)* negative; *(idée)* cliché

client, -e [klijã, -ãt] *nmf (de magasin)* customer; *(d'avocat)* client • **clientèle** *nf* customers

clignoter [kliɲɔte] *vi (lumière, voyant)* to flash • **clignotant** *nm (de voiture) Br* indicator, *Am* flasher; **mettre son c.** to indicate

climat [klima] *nm* climate

climatisation [klimatizasjɔ̃] *nf* air-conditioning • **climatisé, -e** *adj* air-conditioned

clin d'œil [klɛ̃dœj] *(pl* clins d'œil) *nm* wink; **faire un c. à qn** to wink at sb; **en un c.** in a flash

clinique [klinik] *nf (hôpital)* clinic

clip [klip] *nm* (music) video

cliquer [klike] *vi Ordinat* to click

clochard, -e [klɔʃar, -ard] *nmf* tramp

cloche [klɔʃ] *nf (d'église)* bell •

clocher 1 nm (d'église) bell tower, steeple **2** vi Fam **il y a quelque chose qui cloche** there's something wrong somewhere

cloche-pied [klɔʃpje] **à cloche-pied** adv **sauter à c.** to hop

clone [klon] nm Biol clone

cloque [klɔk] nf (au pied) blister

clore* [klɔr] vt (réunion) to conclude; Ordinat **c. une session** to log off

clos, -e [klo, kloz] adj (porte, volets) closed; **l'incident est c.** the matter is closed

clôture [klotyr] nf (barrière) fence; (de réunion) conclusion

clou [klu] nm nail • **clouer** vt (au mur) to nail up; (ensemble) to nail together; **cloué au lit** confined to (one's) bed

clown [klun] nm clown; **faire le c.** to clown around

club [klœb] nm club

cm (abrév **centimètre**) cm

coalition [kɔalisjɔ̃] nf coalition

cobaye [kɔbaj] nm (animal) & Fig guinea pig

cocaïne [kɔkain] nf cocaine

coccinelle [kɔksinɛl] nf (insecte) Br ladybird, Am ladybug

cocher [kɔʃe] vt Br to tick, Am to check

cochon [kɔʃɔ̃] nm (animal) pig; (viande) pork; **c. d'Inde** guinea pig • **cochonnerie** nf (chose sans valeur) trash, Br rubbish; (obscénité) smutty remark; **manger des cochonneries** to eat junk food

cocktail [kɔktɛl] nm (boisson) cocktail; (réunion) cocktail party; **c. de fruits** fruit cocktail

coco [koko] nm **noix de c.** coconut

code [kɔd] nm (symboles, lois) & Ordinat code; **codes** (phares) Br dipped headlights, Am low beams; **le C. de la route** Br the Highway Code, Am the traffic regulations; **c. confidentiel** (de carte bancaire) PIN; **c. postal** Br postcode, Am zip code • **code-barres** (pl **codes-barres**) nm bar code

cœur [kœr] nm heart; Cartes hearts; **avoir mal au c.** to feel sick; **par c.** (off) by heart

coffre [kɔfr] nm (meuble) chest; (pour objets de valeur) safe; (de voiture) Br boot, Am trunk • **coffre-fort** (pl **coffres-forts**) nm safe • **coffret** nm box

cogner [kɔɲe] **1** vt (heurter) to knock **2** vi (buter) to bang (**sur/contre** on) **3 se cogner** vpr to bang oneself; **se c. la tête contre qch** to bang one's head on sth; **se c. à qch** to bang into sth

cohabiter [kɔabite] vi to live together; **c. avec qn** to live with sb

cohérent, -e [kɔerɑ̃, -ɑ̃t] adj (discours) coherent; (attitude) consistent

coiffer [kwafe] **1** vt **c. qn de qch** to put sth on sb's head; **elle est bien coiffée** her hair is lovely **2 se coiffer** vpr to do one's hair; **se c. de qch** to put sth on

coiffeur, -euse [kwafœr, -øz] nmf hairdresser • **coiffeuse** nf (meuble) dressing table • **coiffure** nf hairstyle

coin [kwɛ̃] nm (angle) corner; (endroit) spot; **dans le c.** in the area; Fam **le petit c.** (toilettes) the smallest room in the house

coincer [kwɛ̃se] **1** vi (mécanisme, tiroir) to jam **2 se coincer** vpr (mécanisme) to jam; **se c. le doigt dans la porte** to catch one's finger in the door • **coincé, -e** adj (mécanisme, tiroir) stuck, jammed

coïncider [kɔɛ̃side] vi to coincide (**avec** with) • **coïncidence** nf coincidence

col [kɔl] *nm (de chemise)* collar; **c. en V** V-neck; **c. roulé** *Br* polo neck, *Am* turtleneck

colère [kɔlɛr] *nf* anger; **être en c. (contre qn)** to be angry (with sb); **se mettre en c.** to get angry (**contre** with)

colis [kɔli] *nm* parcel

collaborer [kɔlabɔre] *vi* collaborate (**avec** with); **c. à qch** *(projet)* to take part in sth • **collaborateur, -trice** *nmf (aide)* assistant

collage [kɔlaʒ] *nm* collage

collant, -e [kɔlɑ̃, -ɑ̃t] **1** *adj* sticky **2** *nm Br* tights, *Am* pantihose

colle [kɔl] *nf* glue; *Fam (question)* poser

collection [kɔlɛksjɔ̃] *nf (ensemble)* collection; **faire la c. de qch** to collect sth • **collectionner** *vt* to collect

collège [kɔlɛʒ] *nm (école)* school • **collégien, -enne** *nmf* schoolboy, *f* schoolgirl

collègue [kɔlɛg] *nmf* colleague

coller [kɔle] *vt (timbre)* to stick; *(à la colle)* to glue; *(enveloppe)* to stick (down); *(deux objets)* to stick together; *(affiche)* to stick up

collier [kɔlje] *nm (bijou)* necklace; *(de chien)* collar

colline [kɔlin] *nf* hill

collision [kɔlizjɔ̃] *nf (de véhicules)* collision

colombe [kɔlɔ̃b] *nf* dove

colonel [kɔlɔnɛl] *nm (d'infanterie)* colonel

colonie [kɔlɔni] *nf* colony; **c. de vacances** *Br* (children's) holiday camp, *Am* summer camp

coloniser [kɔlɔnize] *vt* to colonize

colonne [kɔlɔn] *nf* column; *Anat* **c. vertébrale** spine

colorer [kɔlɔre] *vt* to colour; **c. qch en vert** to colour sth green •

colorier *vt (dessin)* to colour (in)

coma [kɔma] *nm* coma; **être dans le c.** to be in a coma

combat [kɔ̃ba] *nm* fight

combattre* [kɔ̃batr] **1** *vt (personne, incendie)* to fight (against); *(maladie)* to fight **2** *vi* to fight

combien [kɔ̃bjɛ̃] **1** *adv* **(a)** *(quantité)* how much; *(nombre)* how many; **c. d'argent** how much money; **c. de temps** how long; **c. de gens** how many people; **c. y a-t-il d'ici à…?** how far is it to…? **(b)** *(comme)* how; **tu verras c. il est bête** you'll see how silly he is **2** *nm inv Fam* **le c. sommes-nous?** what's the date?

combinaison [kɔ̃binɛzɔ̃] *nf (assemblage)* combination; *(vêtement de travail) Br* boiler suit, *Am* coveralls; **c. de ski** ski suit

combiner [kɔ̃bine] *vt (unir)* to combine • **combiné** *nm (de téléphone)* receiver

comble [kɔ̃bl] **1** *adj (salle, bus)* packed; *Théât* **faire salle c.** to have a full house **2** *nm* **le c. du bonheur** the height of happiness; **c'est le c.!** that's the last straw!

combler [kɔ̃ble] *vt (trou)* to fill in; *(désir)* to satisfy

combustible [kɔ̃bystibl] *nm* fuel

comédie [kɔmedi] *nf* comedy; **jouer la c.** to act; **c. musicale** musical • **comédien, -enne** *nm* actor, *f* actress

comète [kɔmɛt] *nf* comet

comique [kɔmik] **1** *adj (amusant,* funny; *(acteur, rôle)* comedy **2** *nm (genre)* comedy; *(acteur,* comedian

comité [kɔmite] *nm* committee

commande [kɔmɑ̃d] *nf (achat,* order; **sur c.** to order; **passer une c.** to place an order

commander [kɔmɑ̃de] **1** *v*

(diriger, exiger) to command; *(marchandises)* to order (**à** from) **2** *vi* **c. à qn de faire qch** to command sb to do sth

---

comme [kɔm] **1** *adv* **(a)** *(devant nom, pronom)* like; **c. moi/elle** like me/her; **c. cela** like that; **qu'as-tu c. diplômes?** what do you have in the way of certificates?; **les femmes c. les hommes** men and women alike; **P c. pomme** p as in 'pomme' **(b)** *(devant proposition)* as; **c. si** as if; **c. pour faire qch** as if to do sth **2** *adv (exclamatif)* **regarde c. il pleut!** look how it's raining!; **c. c'est petit!** isn't it small! **3** *conj* **(a)** *(cause)* as, since; **c. tu es mon ami…** as *or* since you're my friend… **(b)** *(alors que)* **c. elle entrait** (just) as she was coming in

---

commémorer [kɔmemɔre] *vt* to commemorate • **commémoration** *nf* commemoration

commencer [kɔmɑ̃se] *vti* to begin, to start (**à faire** to do, doing; **par qch** with sth; **par faire** by doing); **pour c.** to begin with

comment [kɔmɑ̃] *adv* how; **c. le sais-tu?** how do you know?; **c. t'appelles-tu?** what's your name?; **c. est-il?** what is he like?; **c. va-t-il?** how is he?; **c.?** *(pour faire répéter)* pardon?

commentaire [kɔmɑ̃tɛr] *nm (remarque)* comment; *(de radio, de télévision)* commentary • **commentateur, -trice** *nmf* commentator • **commenter** *vt* to comment on

commérages [kɔmeraʒ] *nmpl* gossip

commerçant, -e [kɔmɛrsɑ̃, -ɑ̃t] *nmf* trader; *(de magasin)* shopkeeper

commerce [kɔmɛrs] *nm (activité,*

secteur) trade; *(affaires, magasin)* business • **commercial, -e, -aux, -ales** *adj* commercial

commère [kɔmɛr] *nf* gossip

commettre* [kɔmɛtr] *vt (meurtre)* to commit; *(erreur)* to make

commissariat [kɔmisarja] *nm* **c. (de police)** (central) police station

commission [kɔmisjɔ̃] *nf (course)* errand; *(comité)* commission; *Com (pourcentage)* commission; **faire les commissions** to go shopping

commode [kɔmɔd] **1** *adj (pratique)* handy; **pas c.** *(pas aimable)* awkward; *(difficile)* tricky **2** *nf Br* chest of drawers, *Am* dresser

commun, -e [kɔmœ̃, -yn] **1** *adj* common; **peu c.** uncommon; **en c.** in common **2** *nm* **hors du c.** out of the ordinary

communauté [kɔmynote] *nf (collectivité)* community **la C. (économique) européenne** the European (Economic) Community

commune [kɔmyn] *nf (municipalité)* commune

communication [kɔmynikasjɔ̃] *nf* communication; **c. téléphonique** telephone call; **je vous passe la c.** I'll put you through

communion [kɔmynjɔ̃] *nf* communion; *Rel* (Holy) Communion

communiquer [kɔmynike] **1** *vt* to communicate (**à** to); *(maladie)* to pass on (**à** to) **2** *vi (personne, pièces)* to communicate (**avec** with) • **communiqué** *nm* **c. de presse** press release

communiste [kɔmynist] *adj & nmf* communist

commutateur [kɔmytatœr] *nm (bouton)* switch

compact, -e [kɔ̃pakt] *adj (foule, amas)* dense; *(appareil)* compact

compagne [kɔ̃paɲ] *nf (camarade)*

companion; *(concubine)* partner

compagnie [kɔ̃paɲi] *nf (présence, société, soldats)* company; **tenir c. à qn** to keep sb company

compagnon [kɔ̃paɲɔ̃] *nm* companion; *(concubin)* partner

comparer [kɔ̃pare] *vt* to compare (**à** to, with) • **comparable** *adj* comparable (**à** to, with) • **comparaison** *nf* comparison (**avec** with); **en c. de...** in comparison with...

compartiment [kɔ̃partimɑ̃] *nm* compartment; **c. à bagages** *(de car)* luggage compartment; **c. fumeurs** smoking compartment

compas [kɔ̃pa] *nm Math Br* (pair of) compasses, *Am* compass; *Naut* compass

compassion [kɔ̃pasjɔ̃] *nf* compassion

compatible [kɔ̃patibl] *adj* compatible (**avec** with)

compenser [kɔ̃pɑ̃se] *vt (perte, défaut)* to make up for, to compensate for • **compensation** *nf (de perte)* compensation; **en c.** in compensation (**de** for)

compétent, -e [kɔ̃petɑ̃, -ɑ̃t] *adj* competent • **compétence** *nf* competence; **compétences** *(connaissances)* skills, abilities

compétition [kɔ̃petisjɔ̃] *nf (rivalité)* competition; **être en c. avec qn** to compete with sb; **sport de c.** competitive sport • **compétitif, -ive** *adj* competitive

complément [kɔ̃plemɑ̃] *nm (reste)* rest; *Gram* complement; **un c. d'information** additional information; **c. d'objet direct/indirect** direct/indirect object • **complémentaire** *adj* complementary; *(détails)* additional

complet, -ète [kɔ̃ple, -ɛt] **1** *adj (entier, absolu)* complete; *(train, hôtel, théâtre)* full; *(pain)* wholemeal **2** *nm (costume)* suit

compléter [kɔ̃plete] *vt (collection)* to complete; *(formulaire)* to fill in

complexe [kɔ̃plɛks] **1** *adj* complex **2** *nm (sentiment, construction)* complex

complication [kɔ̃plikasjɔ̃] *nf* complication

complice [kɔ̃plis] *nmf* accomplice

compliment [kɔ̃plimɑ̃] *nm* compliment; **faire des compliments à qn** to pay sb compliments

compliquer [kɔ̃plike] **1** *vt* to complicate **2 se compliquer** *vpr (situation)* to get complicated; **se c. la vie** to make life complicated for oneself • **compliqué, -e** *adj* complicated

complot [kɔ̃plo] *nm* conspiracy (**contre** against)

comporter [kɔ̃pɔrte] **1** *vt (contenir)* to contain; *(être constitué de)* to consist of **2 se comporter** *vpr (personne)* to behave • **comportement** *nm* behaviour

composer [kɔ̃poze] **1** *vt (faire partie de)* to make up; *(musique, poème)* to compose; *(numéro de téléphone)* to dial; **être composé de** to be made up *or* composed of **2 se composer** *vpr* **se c. de qch** to be made up *or* composed of sth

compositeur, -trice [kɔ̃pozitœr, -tris] *nmf* composer

composition [kɔ̃pozisjɔ̃] *nf (de musique, de poème)* composition; *(examen)* test

composter [kɔ̃pɔste] *vt (billet)* to punch

compote [kɔ̃pɔt] *nf Br* stewed fruit, *Am* sauce; **c. de pommes** *Br* stewed apples, *Am* applesauce

compréhensible [kɔ̃preɑ̃sibl] *adj*

(justifié) understandable; *(clair)* comprehensible ● **compréhensif, -ive** *adj* understanding ● **compréhension** *nf* understanding

comprendre* [kɔ̃prɑ̃dr] **1** *vt* *(par l'esprit, par les sentiments)* to understand; *(comporter)* to include; **mal c. qch** to misunderstand sth; **je n'y comprends rien** I can't make head or tail of it **2 se comprendre** *vpr* **ça se comprend** that's understandable

comprimer [kɔ̃prime] *vt (gaz, artère)* to compress ● **comprimé** *nm* tablet

compris, -e [kɔ̃pri, -iz] **1** *pp de* **comprendre 2** *adj (inclus)* included **(dans** in); **y c.** including

compromettre* [kɔ̃prɔmɛtr] *vt* to compromise ● **compromis** *nm* compromise

comptabilité [kɔ̃tabilite] *nf (science)* accounting; *(service)* accounts department ● **comptable** *nmf* accountant

compte [kɔ̃t] *nm* **(a)** *(bancaire)* account; **avoir un c. en banque** to have a bank account; **faire ses comptes** to do one's accounts; **c. courant** *Br* current account, *Am* checking account; **c. à rebours** countdown **(b)** *(expressions)* **en fin de c.** all things considered; **tenir c. de qch** to take sth into account; **c. tenu de qch** considering sth; **se rendre c. de qch** to realize sth; **travailler à son c.** to be self-employed

compter [kɔ̃te] **1** *vt (calculer)* to count; *(prévoir)* to allow; *(include)* to include; **c. faire qch** *(espérer)* to expect to do sth; *(avoir l'intention de)* to intend to do sth; **c. qch à qn** *(facturer)* to charge sb for sth; **sans c....** *(sans parler de)*

not to mention... **2** *vi (calculer, être important)* to count; **c. sur qn/qch** to count or rely on sb/sth; **à c. de demain** as from tomorrow ● **compteur** *nm* meter; **c. de gaz** gas meter; *Aut* **c. kilométrique** *Br* milometer, *Am* odometer; *Aut* **c. de vitesse** speedometer

compte rendu [kɔ̃trɑ̃dy] *(pl* **comptes rendus)** *nm* report; *(de livre, de film)* review

comptoir [kɔ̃twar] *nm (de magasin)* counter; *(de café)* bar

comte [kɔ̃t] *nm (noble)* count ● **comtesse** *nf* countess

concentrer [kɔ̃sɑ̃tre] **1** *vt* to concentrate **2 se concentrer** *vpr (réfléchir)* to concentrate ● **concentration** *nf* concentration ● **concentré, -e** *adj (lait)* condensed; *(attentif)* concentrating (hard)

concept [kɔ̃sɛpt] *nm* concept ● **conception** *nf (d'idée)* conception; *(création)* design

concerner [kɔ̃sɛrne] *vt* to concern; **en ce qui me concerne** as far as I'm concerned ● **concernant** *prép* concerning

concert [kɔ̃sɛr] *nm* concert

concession [kɔ̃sesjɔ̃] *nf (compromis)* concession **(à** to) ● **concessionnaire** *nmf* dealer

concevoir* [kɔ̃səvwar] *vt (enfant, plan)* to conceive; *(produit)* to design; *(comprendre)* to understand

concierge [kɔ̃sjɛrʒ] *nmf* caretaker, *Am* janitor

concis, -e [kɔ̃si, -iz] *adj* concise

conclure* [kɔ̃klyr] *vt (terminer)* to conclude; *(accord)* to finalize ● **conclusion** *nf* conclusion; **tirer une c. de qch** to draw a conclusion from sth

concombre [kɔ̃kɔ̃br] *nm* cucumber

concorder [kɔ̃kɔrde] *vi (preuves, dates)* to tally **(avec** with)

concourir* [kɔ̃kurir] *vi* to compete (**pour** for)

concours [kɔ̃kur] *nm (examen)* competitive examination; *(jeu)* competition, contest; *(aide)* assistance

concret, -ète [kɔ̃kre, -ɛt] *adj* concrete

conçu, -e [kɔ̃sy] **1** *pp de* **concevoir 2** *adj* **c. pour faire qch** designed to do sth

concubin, -e [kɔ̃kybɛ̃, -in] *nmf* partner; *Jur* cohabitant

concurrent, -e [kɔ̃kyrɑ̃, -ɑ̃t] *nmf* competitor • **concurrence** *nf* competition; **faire c. à** to compete with

condamnation [kɔ̃danasjɔ̃] *nf (critique)* condemnation; *Jur (jugement)* conviction (**pour** for); *(peine)* sentence (**à** to); **c. à mort** death sentence

condamner [kɔ̃dane] *vt (blâmer)* to condemn; *Jur* to sentence (**à** to) • **condamné, -e** *nmf (prisonnier)* convicted person

condensation [kɔ̃dɑ̃sasjɔ̃] *nf* condensation

condescendant, -e [kɔ̃dɛsɑ̃dɑ̃, -ɑ̃t] *adj* condescending

condition [kɔ̃disjɔ̃] *nf (état, stipulation)* condition; *(classe sociale)* station; **conditions** *(circonstances)* conditions; *(de contrat)* terms; **à c. de faire qch, à c. que l'on fasse qch** providing *or* provided (that) one does sth • **conditionnel** *nm Gram* conditional

condoléances [kɔ̃dɔleɑ̃s] *nfpl* condolences

conducteur, -trice [kɔ̃dyktœr, -tris] *nmf (de véhicule)* driver

conduire* [kɔ̃dɥir] **1** *vt (voiture)* to drive; *(moto)* to ride; **c. qn à** *(accompagner)* to take sb to **2** *vi (en voiture)* to drive; **c. à** *(lieu)* to lead to **3 se conduire** *vpr (se*

comporter) to behave

conduite [kɔ̃dɥit] *nf (de véhicule)* driving (**de** of); *(tuyau)* pipe; *(comportement)* conduct, behaviour

cône [kon] *nm* cone

conférence [kɔ̃ferɑ̃s] *nf (réunion)* conference; *(exposé)* lecture; **c. de presse** press conference

confession [kɔ̃fesjɔ̃] *nf* confession

confettis [kɔ̃feti] *nmpl* confetti

confiance [kɔ̃fjɑ̃s] *nf* confidence; **faire c. à qn, avoir c. en qn** to trust sb; **de c.** *(mission)* of trust; *(personne)* trustworthy; **c. en soi** self-confidence; **avoir c. en soi** to be self-confident

confidence [kɔ̃fidɑ̃s] *nf* confidence; **faire une c. à qn** to confide in sb • **confident, -e** *nmf* confidant, *f* confidante • **confidentiel, -elle** *adj* confidential

confier [kɔ̃fje] **1** *vt* **c. qch à qn** *(laisser)* to entrust sb with sth; *(dire)* to confide sth to sb **2 se confier** *vpr* **se c. à qn** to confide in sb

confiner [kɔ̃fine] *vt* to confine

confirmation [kɔ̃firmasjɔ̃] *nf* confirmation

confirmer [kɔ̃firme] *vt* to confirm (**que** that)

confiserie [kɔ̃fizri] *nf (magasin)* Br sweetshop, Am candy store; **confiseries** *(bonbons)* Br sweets, Am candy

confisquer [kɔ̃fiske] *vt* to confiscate (**à qn** from sb)

confit [kɔ̃fi] *nm* **c. d'oie** potted goose

confiture [kɔ̃fityr] *nf* jam; **c. de fraises** strawberry jam

conflit [kɔ̃fli] *nm* conflict

confondre [kɔ̃fɔ̃dr] *vt (choses, personnes)* to mix up, to confuse; *(consterner)* to astound; **c. qn/qch**

avec **qn/qch** to mistake sb/sth for sb/sth

conforme [kɔ̃fɔrm] *adj* **c. à** in accordance with; *(modèle)* true to • **se conformer** *upr* to conform (**à** to)

confort [kɔ̃fɔr] *nm* comfort • **confortable** *adj* comfortable

confronter [kɔ̃frɔ̃te] *ut (personnes)* to confront; *(expériences, résultats)* to compare; **confronté à** *(difficulté)* confronted with • **confrontation** *nf (face-à-face)* confrontation; *(comparaison)* comparison

confus, -e [kɔ̃fy, -yz] *adj (esprit, situation, explication)* confused; *(gêné)* embarrassed • **confusion** *nf (désordre, méprise)* confusion; *(gêne)* embarrassment

congé [kɔ̃ʒe] *nm (vacances) Br* holiday, *Am* vacation; *(arrêt de travail)* leave; *(avis de renvoi)* notice; **donner son c. à qn** *(employé, locataire)* to give notice to sb; **c. de maladie** sick leave; **c. de maternité/paternité** maternity/paternity leave; **congés payés** *Br* paid holidays, *Am* paid vacation

congeler [kɔ̃ʒle] *ut* to freeze • **congélateur** *nm* freezer

congrès [kɔ̃grɛ] *nm* conference

conjoint, -e [kɔ̃ʒwɛ̃, -wɛ̃t] **1** *adj* joint **2** *nmf* spouse

conjugal, -e, -aux, -ales [kɔ̃ʒygal, -o] *adj (bonheur)* marital; *(vie)* married

conjuguer [kɔ̃ʒyge] *Gram* **1** *ut* to conjugate **2 se conjuguer** *upr (verbe)* to be conjugated • **conjugaison** *nf Gram* conjugation

connaissance [kɔnɛsɑ̃s] *nf (savoir)* knowledge; *(personne)* acquaintance; **à ma c.** to my

knowledge; **avoir c. de qch** to be aware of sth; **faire c. avec qn** to get to know sb; **perdre/reprendre c.** to lose/regain consciousness; **sans c.** unconscious • **connaisseur, -euse** *nmf* connoisseur

connaître* [kɔnɛtr] **1** *ut (personne, endroit, faits)* to know; *(rencontrer)* to meet; *(famine, guerre)* to experience **2 se connaître** *upr* **nous nous connaissons déjà** we've met before; **s'y c. en qch** to know all about sth

connecter [kɔnɛkte] *ut (appareil électrique)* to connect; *Ordinat* **connecté** on line • **connexion** *nf* connection

connu, -e [kɔny] **1** *pp de* **connaître 2** *adj (célèbre)* well-known

conquérir* [kɔ̃kerir] *ut* to conquer

consacrer [kɔ̃sakre] **1** *ut (temps)* to devote (**à** to) **2 se consacrer** *upr* **se c. à** to devote oneself to

conscience [kɔ̃sjɑ̃s] *nf* (a) *(esprit)* consciousness; **avoir/prendre c. de qch** to be/become aware of sth; **perdre c.** to lose consciousness (b) *(morale)* conscience; **avoir bonne/mauvaise c.** to have a clear/guilty conscience • **consciencieux, -euse** *adj* conscientious

conscient, -e [kɔ̃sjɑ̃, -ɑ̃t] *adj (lucide)* conscious; **c. de qch** aware *or* conscious of sth

consécutif, -ive [kɔ̃sekytif, -iv] *adj* consecutive

conseil [kɔ̃sɛj] *nm* (a) **un c.** *(recommandation)* a piece of advice; **des conseils** advice (b) *(assemblée)* council, committee

conseiller¹ [kɔ̃seje] *ut (guider)* to advise; **c. qch à qn** to recommend sth to sb; **c. à qn de faire qch** to advise sb to do sth

conseiller², -ère [kɔ̃seje, -ɛr] *nmf*
(expert) consultant, adviser

consentir* [kɔ̃sɑ̃tir] *vi* **c. à qch/à
faire qch** to consent to sth/to do
sth • **consentement** *nm* consent

conséquence [kɔ̃sekɑ̃s] *nf*
consequence; **sans c.** *(sans
importance)* of no importance

conservateur, -trice [kɔ̃servatœr,
-tris] *adj & nmf Pol* Conservative

conservatoire [kɔ̃sɛrvatwar] *nm*
school, academy

conserve [kɔ̃sɛrv] *nf* **conserves**
canned *or Br* tinned food; **en c.**
canned, *Br* tinned

conserver [kɔ̃sɛrve] **1** *vt* to keep
2 se conserver *vpr (aliment)* to
keep

considérable [kɔ̃siderabl] *adj*
considerable

considérer [kɔ̃sidere] *vt* to
consider (**que** that); **tout bien
considéré** all things considered •
considération *nf (respect)* regard,
esteem; **prendre qch en c.** to take
sth into consideration

consigne [kɔ̃siɲ] *nf (instructions)*
orders; *(de bouteille)* deposit; **c. (à
bagages)** *Br* left-luggage office,
Am checkroom; **c. automatique**
lockers

consistant, -e [kɔ̃sistɑ̃, -ɑ̃t] *adj*
(sauce) thick; *(repas)* substantial

consister [kɔ̃siste] *vi* **c. en qch**
to consist of sth; **c. à faire qch** to
consist in doing sth

console [kɔ̃sɔl] *nf* console

consoler [kɔ̃sɔle] *vt* to console •
consolation *nf* consolation

consommateur, -trice [kɔ̃sɔma-
tœr, -tris] *nmf* consumer •
consommation *nf (de nourriture, d'électricité)* consumption;
(boisson) drink

consommer [kɔ̃sɔme] *vt* to
consume

consonne [kɔ̃sɔn] *nf* consonant

conspirer [kɔ̃spire] *vi (comploter)*
to conspire (**contre** against); **c. à
faire qch** *(concourir)* to conspire
to do sth • **conspirateur, -trice**
nmf conspirator • **conspiration**
nf conspiracy

constant, -e [kɔ̃stɑ̃, -ɑ̃t] *adj*
constant • **constamment** [-amɑ̃]
adv constantly

constater [kɔ̃state] *vt (observer)*
to note (**que** that)

constellation [kɔ̃stɛlasjɔ̃] *nf*
constellation

consterner [kɔ̃stɛrne] *vt* to
dismay

constipation [kɔ̃stipasjɔ̃] *nf*
constipation

constituer [kɔ̃stitɥe] *vt (composer)* to make up; *(équivaloir à)* to
constitute; **constitué de** made
up of

constitution [kɔ̃stitysjɔ̃] *nf*
(santé, lois) constitution

construction [kɔ̃stryksjɔ̃] *nf*
(de pont, de maison) building,
construction (**de** of); *(édifice)*
building; **en c.** under construction

construire* [kɔ̃strɥir] *vt (maison,
route)* to build

consulat [kɔ̃syla] *nm* consulate

consulter [kɔ̃sylte] *vt* to consult •
consultation *nf* consultation

contact [kɔ̃takt] *nm* contact; **être
en c. avec qn** to be in contact
with sb; **prendre c.** to get in touch
(**avec** with); *Aut* **mettre/couper
le c.** to switch the ignition on/off •
contacter *vt* to contact

contagieux, -euse [kɔ̃taʒjø, -øz]
adj (maladie, personne) contagious

contaminer [kɔ̃tamine] *vt* to
contaminate

conte [kɔ̃t] *nm* tale; **c. de fées**
fairy tale

contempler [kɔ̃tɑ̃ple] *vt* to gaze at, to contemplate

contemporain, -e [kɔ̃tɑ̃pɔrɛ̃, -ɛn] *adj & nmf* contemporary

contenir* [kɔ̃tnir] *vt (renfermer, contrôler)* to contain • **conteneur** *nm* container

content, -e [kɔ̃tɑ̃, -ɑ̃t] *adj* pleased, happy (**de** with; **de faire** to do); **être c. de soi** to be pleased with oneself

contenter [kɔ̃tɑ̃te] **1** *vt (satisfaire)* to satisfy; *(faire plaisir à)* to please **2 se contenter** *vpr* **se c. de qch** to content oneself with sth

contenu [kɔ̃tny] *nm (de paquet, de bouteille)* contents; *(de lettre, de film)* content

contester [kɔ̃tɛste] *vt* to dispute

contexte [kɔ̃tɛkst] *nm* context

contigu, -ë [kɔ̃tigy] *adj (maisons)* adjoining; **c. à qch** adjoining sth

continent [kɔ̃tinɑ̃] *nm* continent; *(opposé à une île)* mainland

continu, -e [kɔ̃tiny] *adj* continuous • **continuel, -elle** *adj (ininterrompu)* continuous; *(qui se répète)* continual • **continuellement** *adv (de façon ininterrompue)* continuously; *(de façon répétitive)* continually

continuer [kɔ̃tinɥe] **1** *vt (études, efforts, politique)* to continue, to carry on with; **c. à** *ou* **de faire qch** to continue *or* carry on doing sth **2** *vi* to continue, to go on

contour [kɔ̃tur] *nm* outline

contourner [kɔ̃turne] *vt* to go round

contraceptif, -ive [kɔ̃trasɛptif, -iv] *adj & nm* contraceptive

contracter [kɔ̃trakte] **1** *vt (muscle, habitude)* to contract **2 se contracter** *vpr (muscle)* to contract; *(personne)* to tense up • **contraction** *nf* contraction

contractuel, -elle [kɔ̃traktɥɛl] *nmf Br* ≃ traffic warden, *Am* ≃ traffic policeman, *f* traffic policewoman

contradiction [kɔ̃tradiksjɔ̃] *nf* contradiction

contraindre* [kɔ̃trɛ̃dr] *vt* to compel, to force (**à faire** to do) • **contrainte** *nf* constraint

contraire [kɔ̃trɛr] **1** *adj (opposé)* conflicting; **c. à qch** contrary to sth; **en sens c.** in the opposite direction **2** *nm* opposite; **(bien) au c.** on the contrary • **contrairement** *adv* **c. à** contrary to; **c. à qn** unlike sb

contrarier [kɔ̃trarje] *vt (action)* to thwart; *(personne)* to annoy • **contrariant, -e** *adj (situation)* annoying; *(personne)* contrary

contraste [kɔ̃trast] *nm* contrast • **contraster** *vi* to contrast (**avec** with)

contrat [kɔ̃tra] *nm* contract

contravention [kɔ̃travɑ̃sjɔ̃] *nf (amende)* fine; *(pour stationnement interdit)* (parking) ticket

contre [kɔ̃tr] *prép* against; *(en échange de)* (in exchange) for; **échanger qch c. qch** to exchange sth for sth; **fâché c. qn** angry with sb; **six voix c. deux** six votes to two; **Nîmes c. Arras** *(match)* Nîmes versus *or* against Arras; *Fam* **par c.** on the other hand

contrebande [kɔ̃trəbɑ̃d] *nf (activité)* smuggling; *(marchandises)* contraband; **faire de la c.** to smuggle goods • **contrebandier, -ère** *nmf* smuggler

contrebasse [kɔ̃trəbas] *nf (instrument)* double-bass

contrecœur [kɔ̃trəkœr] **à contrecœur** *adv* reluctantly

contredire* [kɔ̃trədir] **1** *vt* to contradict **2 se contredire** *vpr (soi-même)* to contradict oneself;

(l'un l'autre) to contradict each other

contrefaçon [kɔ̃trəfasɔ̃] *nf (pratique)* counterfeiting; *(produit)* fake • **contrefaire*** *vt (écriture)* to disguise; *(argent)* to counterfeit; *(signature)* to forge

contresens [kɔ̃trəsɑ̃s] *nm* misinterpretation; *(en traduisant)* mistranslation; **prendre une rue à c.** to go down/up a street the wrong way

contretemps [kɔ̃trətɑ̃] *nm* hitch, mishap

contribuable [kɔ̃tribɥabl] *nmf* taxpayer

contribuer [kɔ̃tribɥe] *vi* to contribute (**à** to); **c. à faire qch** to help (to) do sth

contribution [kɔ̃tribysjɔ̃] *nf* contribution (**à** to); *(impôt)* tax

contrôle [kɔ̃trol] *nm (vérification)* checking (**de** of); *(surveillance)* monitoring; *(maîtrise)* control; *Scol* test; **avoir le c. de qch** to have control of sth; **le c. des naissances** birth control; **c. de soi** self-control

contrôler [kɔ̃trole] **1** *vt (vérifier)* to check; *(surveiller)* to monitor; *(maîtriser)* to control **2 se contrôler** *vpr* to control oneself • **contrôleur, -euse** *nmf (de train, de bus) Br* (ticket) inspector, *Am* conductor

controversé [kɔ̃trɔvɛrse] *adj* controversial

contusion [kɔ̃tyzjɔ̃] *nf* bruise

convaincre* [kɔ̃vɛ̃kr] *vt* to convince (**de** of); **c. qn de faire qch** to persuade sb to do sth • **convaincant, -e** *adj* convincing • **convaincu, -e** *adj* convinced (**de** of; **que** that)

convalescence [kɔ̃valɛsɑ̃s] *nf* convalescence

convenable [kɔ̃vnabl] *adj (appro-*

prié) suitable; *(décent)* decent

convenir* [kɔ̃vnir] **1** *vi* **c. à** *(être fait pour)* to be suitable for; *(plaire à, aller à)* to suit; **c. de qch** *(lieu, prix)* to agree upon sth; **c. de faire qch** to agree to do sth; **c. que...** to admit that... **2** *v impersonnel* **il convient de...** it is advisable to...; **il fut convenu que...** *(décidé)* it was agreed that...

convention [kɔ̃vɑ̃sjɔ̃] *nf (accord)* agreement; *(règle)* convention • **conventionnel, -elle** *adj* conventional

conversation [kɔ̃vɛrsasjɔ̃] *nf* conversation

conversion [kɔ̃vɛrsjɔ̃] *nf* conversion (**en** into; **à** to • **convertir 1** *vt* to convert (**en** into; **à** to **2 se convertir** *vpr (à une doctrine)* to be converted (**à** to)

conviction [kɔ̃viksjɔ̃] *nf (certitude, croyance)* conviction; **avoir la c. que...** to be convinced that...

convivial, -e, -aux, -ales [kɔ̃vivjal, -jo] *adj* convivial; *Ordinat* user-friendly

convoi [kɔ̃vwa] *nm (véhicules, personnes)* convoy; *(train)* train; **c. funèbre** funeral procession

convoquer [kɔ̃vɔke] *vt (employé, postulant)* to call in; **c. qn à un examen** to notify sb of an examination • **convocation** *nf (lettre)* notice to attend; **c. à un examen** notification of an examination

coopérer [kɔɔpere] *vi* to cooperate (**à** in, **avec** with) • **coopération** *nf* cooperation (**entre** between)

coordonner [kɔɔrdɔne] *vt* to coordinate (**à** *ou* **avec** with) • **coordination** *nf* coordination • **coordonnées** *nfpl (adresse, téléphone)* address and phone number

copain [kɔpɛ̃] *nm Fam (camarade)* pal; *(petit ami)* boyfriend

copie [kɔpi] *nf (manuscrit, double)* copy; *Scol (devoir, examen)* paper

copier [kɔpje] *vt (texte, musique, document) & Scol (à un examen)* to copy (**sur** from)

copieux, -euse [kɔpjø, -øz] *adj (repas)* copious; *(portion)* generous

copine [kɔpin] *nf Fam (camarade)* pal; *(petite amie)* girlfriend

coq [kɔk] *nm* cock, *Am* rooster

coque [kɔk] *nf (de noix)* shell; *(fruit de mer)* cockle

coquelicot [kɔkliko] *nm* poppy

coquet, -ette [kɔkɛ, -ɛt] *adj (intérieur)* charming

coquille [kɔkij] *nf* shell; *(faute d'imprimerie)* misprint; *Culin* **c. Saint-Jacques** scallop • **coquillage** *nm (mollusque)* shellfish *inv; (coquille)* shell

coquin, -e [kɔkɛ̃, -in] *adj* mischievous

cor [kɔr] *nm (instrument)* horn; *(durillon)* corn

corail, -aux [kɔraj, -o] *nm* coral

corbeau, -x [kɔrbo] *nm (oiseau)* crow

corbeille [kɔrbɛj] *nf (panier)* basket; **c. à papier** wastepaper basket

corde [kɔrd] *nf (lien)* rope; *(de raquette, de violon)* string; **c. à linge** washing *or* clothes line; **c. à sauter** *Br* skipping rope, *Am* jump-rope; **cordes vocales** vocal cords

cordial, -e, -aux, -ales [kɔrdjal, -o] **1** *adj (accueil, personne)* cordial **2** *nm (remontant)* tonic

cordon [kɔrdɔ̃] *nm (de tablier, de sac)* string; *(de rideau)* cord • **cordon-bleu** (*pl* **cordons-bleus**) *nm Fam* gourmet cook

cordonnier [kɔrdɔnje] *nm* shoe repairer • **cordonnerie** *nf (boutique)* shoe repairer's shop

corne [kɔrn] *nf (d'animal, instrument)* horn

corner [kɔrnɛr] *nm (au football)* corner; **tirer un c.** to take a corner

cornet [kɔrnɛ] *nm (glace)* cone

cornichon [kɔrniʃɔ̃] *nm* gherkin

corporel, -elle [kɔrpɔrɛl] *adj (besoin)* bodily; *(hygiène)* personal

corps [kɔr] *nm (organisme, cadavre)* body; *(partie principale)* main part; **c. et âme** body and soul; **c. diplomatique** diplomatic corps

corpulent, -e [kɔrpylɑ̃, -ɑ̃t] *adj* stout, corpulent

correct, -e [kɔrɛkt] *adj (exact, courtois)* correct; *Fam (acceptable)* reasonable • **correctement** *adv (sans faire de fautes, décemment)* correctly; *Fam (de façon acceptable)* reasonably

correcteur, -trice [kɔrɛktœr, -tris] *nmf (d'examen)* examiner; *(en typographie)* proofreader

correction [kɔrɛksjɔ̃] *nf (rectification)* correction; *(punition)* beating; *Scol (de devoirs, d'examens)* marking

correspondance [kɔrɛspɔ̃dɑ̃s] *nf (relation, lettres)* correspondence; *(de train, d'autocar) Br* connection, *Am* transfer

correspondre [kɔrɛspɔ̃dr] *vi* **c. à qch** to correspond to sth; **c. avec qn** *(par lettres)* to correspond with sb • **correspondant, -e 1** *adj* corresponding (**à** to) **2** *nmf (reporter)* correspondent; *(par lettres)* pen friend, pen pal; *(au téléphone)* caller

corrida [kɔrida] *nf* bullfight

corriger [kɔriʒe] *vt (texte, erreur, myopie, injustice)* to correct;

(exercice, devoir) to mark; **c. qn** *(pour punir)* to give sb a beating; **c. qn de qch** to cure sb of sth • **corrigé** *nm (d'exercice)* correct answers (**de** to)

corrompre* [kɔrɔ̃pr] *vt (personne, goût)* to corrupt • **corrompu, -e** *adj* corrupt • **corruption** *nf* corruption

corsage [kɔrsaʒ] *nm* blouse

Corse [kɔrs] *nf* **la C.** Corsica • **corse 1** *adj* Corsican **2** *nmf* **C.** Corsican

corsé, -e [kɔrse] *adj (café)* full-flavoured; *Fig (histoire)* spicy

corset [kɔrsɛ] *nm* corset

cortège [kɔrtɛʒ] *nm (défilé)* procession

cosmétique [kɔsmetik] *adj & nm* cosmetic

cosmopolite [kɔsmɔpɔlit] *adj* cosmopolitan

costaud [kɔsto] *adj* sturdy

costume [kɔstym] *nm (habit)* costume; *(complet)* suit

côte [kot] *nf* (**a**) *(os)* rib; **à côtes** *(étoffe)* ribbed; **c. à c.** side by side; **c. d'agneau/de porc** lamb/pork chop (**b**) *(de montagne)* slope (**c**) *(littoral)* coast; **la C. d'Azur** the French Riviera

côté [kote] *nm* side; **de l'autre c.** on the other side (**de** of); *(partir)* the other way; **de ce c.** *(passer)* this way; **du c. de** *(près de)* near; **à c.** close by, nearby; *(pièce)* in the other room; *(maison)* next door; **la maison d'à c.** the house next door; **à c. de qn/ qch** next to sb/sth; *(en comparaison de)* compared to sb/sth; **passer à c.** *(balle)* to fall wide (**de** of); **mettre qch de c.** to put sth aside

côtelé, -e [kotle] *adj* **velours c.** corduroy

côtelette [kotlɛt] *nf (d'agneau, de porc)* chop

cotisation [kɔtizasjɔ̃] *nf (de club)* dues, subscription; *(de retraite, de chômage)* contribution

coton [kɔtɔ̃] *nm* cotton; **c. hydrophile** *Br* cotton wool, *Am* absorbent cotton

côtoyer [kotwaje] *vt (personnes)* to mix with

cou [ku] *nm* neck

couchage [kuʃaʒ] *nm* **sac de c.** sleeping bag

couchant [kuʃɑ̃] *adj m* **soleil c.** setting sun

couche [kuʃ] *nf* (**a**) *(épaisseur)* layer; *(de peinture)* coat; **la c. d'ozone** the ozone layer (**b**) *(linge de bébé) Br* nappy, *Am* diaper • **couche-culotte** *(pl* **couches-culottes**) *nf Br* disposable nappy, *Am* disposable diaper

coucher [kuʃe] **1** *nm (moment)* bedtime; **l'heure du c.** bedtime; **c. de soleil** sunset **2** *vt (allonger)* to lay down; **c. qn** to put sb to bed **3** *vi* to sleep (**avec** with) **4 se coucher** *vpr (personne)* to go to bed; *(s'allonger)* to lie down; *(soleil)* to set, to go down; **aller se c.** to go to bed • **couché, -e** *adj* **être c.** to be in bed; *(étendu)* to be lying (down)

couchette [kuʃɛt] *nf (de train)* couchette; *(de bateau)* bunk

coude [kud] *nm* elbow; **donner un coup de c. à qn** to nudge sb

coudre* [kudr] *vti* to sew

couette¹ [kwɛt] *nf (édredon)* duvet

couette² [kwɛt] *nf (coiffure)* bunch

couffin [kufɛ̃] *nm (de bébé) Br* Moses basket, *Am* bassinet

couler [kule] *vi* (**a**) *(eau, rivière)* to flow; *(nez, sueur)* to run; *(robinet)* to leak (**b**) *(bateau, nageur)* to sink

couleur [kulœr] *nf (teinte) Br*

colour, *Am* color; *(colorant)* paint; *(pour cheveux)* dye; **de quelle c. est…?** what colour is…?

coulisse [kulis] *nf* **porte à c.** sliding door; *Théât* **les coulisses** the wings

couloir [kulwar] *nm* corridor

coup [ku] *nm* (**a**) *(choc)* blow; *(essai)* attempt, go; **donner un c. à qn** to hit sb; **se donner un c. contre qch** to knock against sth; **donner un c. de couteau à qn** to knife sb; **c. de pied** kick; **donner un c. de pied à qn** to kick sb; **c. de poing** punch; **donner un c. de poing à qn** to punch sb; **c. de tête** header (**b**) *(action soudaine, événement soudain)* **c. de vent** gust of wind; **prendre un c. de soleil** to get sunburned; *Fig* **ça a été le c. de foudre** it was love at first sight; **c. d'État** coup (**c**) *(bruit)* **c. de feu** shot; **c. de tonnerre** clap of thunder; (**d**) *(expressions)* **après c.** after the event; **sur le c.** *(alors)* at the time; **tué sur le c.** killed outright; **tout à c., tout d'un c.** suddenly; **d'un seul c.** *(avaler)* in one go; *(soudain)* all of a sudden; **du premier c.** at the first attempt; **tenir le c.** to hold out; **c. d'envoi** *(au football, au rugby)* kickoff; **c. franc** *(au football)* free kick

coupable [kupabl] **1** *adj* guilty (**de** of); **se sentir c.** to feel guilty **2** *nmf* culprit

coupe[1] [kup] *nf (trophée)* cup; *(récipient)* bowl; **la C. du monde** the World Cup; **c. à champagne** champagne glass

coupe[2] [kup] *nf (de vêtement)* cut; *(plan)* section; **c. de cheveux** haircut • **coupe-vent** *nm inv (blouson) Br* windcheater, *Am* Windbreaker®

couper [kupe] **1** *vt (trancher, supprimer)* to cut; *(arbre)* to cut down; **c. la parole à qn** to interrupt sb; **nous avons été coupés** *(au téléphone)* we were cut off **2** *vi (être tranchant)* to be sharp **3 se couper** *upr (routes)* to intersect; **se c. au doigt** to cut one's finger; **se c. les cheveux** to cut one's hair • **coupé** *nm (voiture)* coupé

couple [kupl] *nm* couple

coupole [kupɔl] *nf* dome

coupon [kupɔ̃] *nm (tissu)* scrap; **c. de réduction** money-off coupon

coupure [kupyr] *nf (blessure)* cut; **5 000 euros en petites coupures** 5,000 euros in small notes; **c. d'électricité** *ou* **de courant** blackout, *Br* power cut

cour [kur] *nf* (**a**) *(de maison, de ferme)* yard; **c. de récréation** *Br* playground, *Am* schoolyard (**b**) *(de roi, tribunal)* court; **c. d'appel** court of appeal

courage [kuraʒ] *nm* courage; **bon c.!** good luck! • **courageux, -euse** *adj (brave)* courageous; *(énergique)* spirited

couramment [kuramɑ̃] *adv (parler)* fluently; *(généralement)* commonly

courant, -e [kurɑ̃, -ɑ̃t] **1** *adj (common)* common; *(en cours)* current **2** *nm (de rivière, électrique)* current; **être au c. de qch** to know about sth; **mettre qn au c. de qch** to tell sb about sth; **c. d'air** *Br* draught, *Am* draft

courbature [kurbatyr] *nf* ache; **avoir des courbatures** to be aching (all over)

courbe [kurb] *nf* curve • **courber 1** *vt* to bend **2 se courber** *upr (personne)* to bend down; **se c. en deux** to bend double

courgette [kurʒɛt] *nf Br* courgette, *Am* zucchini

courir* [kurir] **1** *vi* to run; *(à une course automobile)* to race; **c. après qn/qch** to run after sb/sth; **descendre une colline en courant** to run down a hill; **le bruit court que...** rumour has it that... **2** *vt* **c. un risque** to run a risk; **c. le 100 mètres** to run the 100 metres • **coureur, -euse** *nmf (sportif)* runner; *(cycliste)* cyclist

couronne [kurɔn] *nf (de roi)* crown; *(pour enterrement)* wreath

courrier [kurje] *nm (lettres)* mail, *Br* post; *Journ* **c. du cœur** problem page; **c. électronique** e-mail

cours [kur] *nm* **(a)** *(de rivière, d'astre)* course; *(de monnaie)* currency; **suivre son c.** to run its course; **avoir c.** *(monnaie)* to be legal tender; *(pratique)* to be current; **en c.** *(travail)* in progress; *(année)* current; **au c. de qch** in the course of sth **(b)** *(leçon)* class; *(série de leçons)* course; *(conférence)* lecture; **suivre un c.** to take a course; **c. particulier** private lesson

course¹ [kurs] *nf (action de courir)* running; *(épreuve)* race; *(trajet en taxi)* journey; **les courses de chevaux** the races; **faire la c. avec qn** to race sb; **c. automobile** motor race; **c. cycliste** cycle race

course² [kurs] *nf (commission)* errand; **courses** *(achats)* shopping; **faire une c.** to run an errand; **faire les courses** to do the shopping

coursier, -ère [kursje, -ɛr] *nmf* messenger

court, -e [kur, kurt] **1** *adj* short **2** *adv* short; **à c. d'argent** short of money **3** *nm* **c. (de tennis)** tennis court • **court-circuit** *(pl* **courts-circuits)** *nm* short-circuit

courtois, -e [kurtwa, -az] *adj* courteous • **courtoisie** *nf* courtesy

cousin, -e [kuzɛ̃, -in] **1** *nmf* cousin **2** *nm (insecte)* mosquito

coussin [kusɛ̃] *nm* cushion

coût [ku] *nm* cost; **le c. de la vie** the cost of living • **coûter** *vti* to cost; **ça coûte combien?** how much does it cost?

couteau, -x [kuto] *nm* knife

coutume [kutym] *nf (habitude, tradition)* custom

couture [kutyr] *nf (activité)* sewing • **couturier** *nm* fashion designer • **couturière** *nf* dressmaker

couvent [kuvã] *nm (de religieuses)* convent; *(de moines)* monastery; *(pensionnat)* convent school

couver [kuve] *vt (œufs)* to sit on; *(maladie)* to be coming down with

couvercle [kuvɛrkl] *nm* lid; *(vissé)* cap

couvert¹ [kuvɛr] *nm* **(a)** **mettre le c.** to set *or Br* lay the table; **table de cinq couverts** table set *or Br* laid for five; **couverts** *(ustensiles)* cutlery **(b)** **sous le c. de** *(sous l'apparence de)* under cover of; **se mettre à c.** to take cover

couvert², -e [kuvɛr, -ɛrt] **1** *pp de* **couvrir 2** *adj* covered *(de* with *or* in); *(ciel)* overcast; **être bien c.** *(personne)* to be wrapped up

couverture [kuvɛrtyr] *nf (de lit)* blanket; *(de livre)* cover

couvrir* [kuvrir] **1** *vt* to cover *(de* with); *(bruit)* to drown **2** **se couvrir** *vpr (s'habiller)* to wrap up; *(ciel)* to cloud over • **couvre-feu** *(pl* **couvre-feux)** *nm* curfew

cow-boy [kɔbɔj] *(pl* **cow-boys)** *nm* cowboy

crabe [krab] *nm* crab

cracher [kraʃe] **1** *vt* to spit out *vi* to spit

craie [krɛ] *nf (matière)* chalk; *(bâton)* stick of chalk

craindre* [krɛ̃dr] *vt (redouter)* to be afraid of, to fear; *(chaleur, froid)* to be sensitive to; **c. de faire qch** to be afraid of doing sth; **je crains qu'elle ne soit partie** I'm afraid she's left

crainte [krɛ̃t] *nf* fear; **de c. de faire qch** for fear of doing sth

crampe [krɑ̃p] *nf* cramp

crâne [krɑn] *nm* skull

crapaud [krapo] *nm* toad

craquer [krake] *vi (branche)* to crack; *(escalier)* to creak; *(se casser)* to snap

crasse [kras] *nf* filth ● **crasseux, -euse** *adj* filthy

cravate [kravat] *nf* tie

crayon [krɛjɔ̃] *nm (en bois)* pencil; *(en cire)* crayon

créateur, -trice [kreatœr, -tris] *nmf* creator ● **création** *nf* creation; **1000 créations d'emplois** 1,000 new jobs

créature [kreatyr] *nf* creature

crèche [krɛʃ] *nf (de Noël)* manger, *Br* crib; *(garderie)* (day) nursery, *Br* crèche

crédit [kredi] *nm (prêt, influence)* credit; **à c.** on credit ● **créditer** *vt (compte)* to credit (**de** with); *Fig* **c. qn de qch** to give sb credit for sth

créer [kree] *vt* to create

crémaillère [kremajɛr] *nf* **pendre la c.** to have a housewarming (party)

crématorium [krematɔrjɔm] *nm Br* crematorium, *Am* crematory

crème [krɛm] *nf (de lait, dessert, cosmétique)* cream; **c. Chantilly** whipped cream; **c. glacée** ice cream; **c. pâtissière** confectioner's custard; **c. à raser** shaving cream ● **crémeux, -euse** *adj* creamy

crêpe [krɛp] *nf* pancake, crêpe ● **crêperie** *nf* pancake restaurant

crépiter [krepite] *vi (feu)* to crackle

crépu, -e [krepy] *adj* frizzy

crépuscule [krepyskyl] *nm* twilight

cresson [kresɔ̃] *nm* watercress

creuser [krøze] **1** *vt (trou, puits)* to dig; *(évider)* to hollow (out) **2** *vi* to dig

creux, -euse [krø, -øz] **1** *adj (tube, joues, arbre, paroles)* hollow; *(sans activité)* slack **2** *nm* hollow

crevaison [krəvɛzɔ̃] *nf (de pneu)* flat, *Br* puncture

crevasse [krəvas] *nf (trou)* crack; *(de glacier)* crevasse

crever [krəve] *vti (bulle, ballon, pneu)* to burst ● **crevé, -e** *adj (ballon, pneu)* burst; *Fam (épuisé)* worn out

crevette [krəvɛt] *nf (grise)* shrimp; *(rose)* prawn

cri [kri] *nm* cry, shout; *(perçant)* scream ● **criard, -e** *adj (son)* shrill; *(couleur)* loud

crier [krije] **1** *vt (injure, ordre)* to shout (**à** to) **2** *vi (personne)* to shout, to cry out; *(fort)* to scream; *(parler très fort)* to shout; **c. au secours** to shout for help

crime [krim] *nm* crime; *(assassinat)* murder ● **criminel, -elle 1** *adj* criminal **2** *nmf* criminal; *(assassin)* murderer

crinière [krinjɛr] *nf* mane

crise [kriz] *nf* crisis; *(de maladie)* attack; **c. de nerfs** fit of hysteria

crisper [krispe] **1** *vt (poing)* to clench; *(muscle)* to tense **2 se crisper** *upr (visage)* to tense; *(personne)* to get tense ● **crispé, -e** *adj (personne)* tense

crisser [krise] *vi (pneu, roue)* to squeal; *(neige)* to crunch

cristal, -aux [kristal, -o] *nm* crystal

critère [kritɛr] *nm* criterion

critique [kritik] **1** *adj (situation, phase)* critical **2** *nf (reproche)* criticism; *(de film, de livre)* review; **faire la c. de** *(film)* to review **3** *nm* critic • **critiquer** *vt* to criticize

croc [kro] *nm (crochet)* hook; *(dent)* fang

croche-pied [krɔʃpje] *nm* trip; **faire un c. à qn** to trip sb up

crochet [krɔʃɛ] *nm (pour accrocher)* hook; *(aiguille)* crochet hook; **faire du c.** to crochet; **faire un c.** *(détour)* to make a detour; *(route)* to make a sudden turn

crocodile [krɔkɔdil] *nm* crocodile

croire* [krwar] **1** *vt* to believe; *(penser)* to think (**que** that); **j'ai cru la voir** I thought I saw her; **je crois que oui** I think *or* believe so **2** *vi* to believe (**à** *ou* **en** in) **3** **se croire** *vpr* **il se croit malin** he thinks he's smart

croisade [krwazad] *nf* crusade

croiser [krwaze] **1** *vt (passer)* to pass; *(ligne)* to cross; **c. les jambes** to cross one's legs; **c. les bras** to fold one's arms; *Fig* **c. les doigts** to keep one's fingers crossed **2** **se croiser** *vpr (voitures)* to pass each other; *(lignes, routes, lettres)* to cross

croisière [krwazjɛr] *nf* cruise

croître* [krwatr] *vi (plante)* to grow; *(augmenter)* to grow, to increase (**de** by) • **croissance** *nf* growth • **croissant, -e 1** *adj (nombre)* growing **2** *nm* crescent; *(pâtisserie)* croissant

croix [krwa] *nf* cross; **la C.-Rouge** the Red Cross

croquant, -e [krɔkɑ̃, -ɑ̃t] *adj* crunchy • **croque-monsieur** *nm inv* = toasted cheese and ham sandwich

croquis [krɔki] *nm* sketch

crotte [krɔt] *nf (d'animal)* droppings; **c. de chien** dog dirt

crouler [krule] *vi (édifice)* to crumble; **c. sous le travail** to be snowed under with work

croustillant, -e [krustijɑ̃, -ɑ̃t] *adj* crunchy; *(pain)* crusty

croûte [krut] *nf (de pain)* crust; *(de fromage)* rind; *(de plaie)* scab • **croûton** *nm (de pain)* end; **croûtons** croûtons

croyance [krwajɑ̃s] *nf* belief (**en** in) • **croyant, -e 1** *adj* **être c.** to be a believer **2** *nmf* believer

CRS [seɛrɛs] *(abrév* **compagnie républicaine de sécurité)** *nm* = French riot policeman

cru¹, -e [kry] *pp de* **croire**

cru², -e [kry] **1** *adj (aliment)* raw; *(propos)* crude **2** *nm* **un grand c.** *(vin)* a vintage wine

cruauté [kryote] *nf* cruelty (**envers** to)

cruche [kryʃ] *nf* pitcher, jug

crucifix [krysifiks] *nm* crucifix

crudités [krydite] *nfpl (légumes)* assorted raw vegetables

cruel, -elle [kryɛl] *adj* cruel (**envers** *ou* **avec** to)

crustacés [krystase] *nmpl Culin* shellfish *inv*

crypte [kript] *nf* crypt

crypté, -e [kripte] *adj (message)* & *TV* coded

cube [kyb] **1** *nm* cube; *(de jeu)* building block **2** *adj* **mètre c.** cubic metre • **cubique** *adj* cubic

cueillir* [kœjir] *vt* to pick

cuiller, cuillère [kɥijɛr] *nf* spoon; *(mesure)* spoonful; **c. à café, petite c.** teaspoon; **c. à soupe** tablespoon • **cuillerée** *nf* spoonful

cuir [kɥir] *nm* leather; **pantalon en c.** leather trousers; **c. chevelu** scalp

cuire* [kɥir] **1** *vt (aliment, plat)* to cook; **c. qch à l'eau** to boil sth; **c. qch au four** to bake sth; *(viande)* to roast sth **2** *vi (aliment)* to cook; **faire c. qch** to cook sth

cuisine [kɥizin] *nf (pièce)* kitchen; *(art)* cookery, cooking; **faire la c.** to do the cooking • **cuisiner** *vti* to cook

cuisinier, -ère¹ [kɥizinje, -ɛr] *nmf* cook

cuisinière² [kɥizinjɛr] *nf (appareil)* stove, *Br* cooker

cuisse [kɥis] *nf* thigh; **c. de poulet** chicken leg; **cuisses de grenouilles** frogs' legs

cuisson [kɥisɔ̃] *nf* cooking

cuit, -e [kɥi, kɥit] **1** *pp de* **cuire 2** *adj* cooked; **bien c.** well done

cuivre [kɥivr] *nm (rouge)* copper; *(jaune)* brass

cul-de-sac [kydsak] *(pl* **culs-de-sac***) nm* dead end, *Br* cul-de-sac

culot [kylo] *nm Fam (audace)* nerve, *Br* cheek

culotte [kylɔt] *nf (de femme)* knickers, *Am* panties; *(d'enfant)* pants

culte [kylt] **1** *nm (de dieu)* worship; *(religion)* religion **2** *adj* **film c.** cult film

cultiver [kyltive] *vt (terre, amitié)* to cultivate; *(plantes)* to grow • **cultivé, -e** *adj (terre)* cultivated; *(personne)* cultured, cultivated

culture [kyltyr] *nf* **(a)** *(action)* farming, cultivation; *(de plantes)* growing; **cultures** crops **(b)** *(éducation, civilisation)* culture; **c. générale** general knowledge • **culturel, -elle** *adj* cultural

cure [kyr] *nf (traitement)* (course of) treatment

curé [kyre] *nm* parish priest

curer [kyre] **se curer** *vpr* **se c. les dents** to clean one's teeth • **cure-dents** *nm inv* toothpick

curieux, -euse [kyrjø, -øz] **1** *adj (bizarre)* curious; *(indiscret)* inquisitive, curious (**de** about) **2** *nmf* inquisitive person; *(badaud)* onlooker • **curiosité** *nf* curiosity

curriculum vitae [kyrikylɔmvite] *nm inv Br* curriculum vitae, *Am* résumé

cuve [kyv] *nf* tank; *(de fermentation)* vat • **cuvée** *nf (récolte)* vintage • **cuvette** *nf (récipient)* basin; *(des cabinets)* bowl

CV [seve] *(abrév* **curriculum vitae***) nm Br* CV, *Am* résumé

cybercafé [siberkafe] *nm* cybercafé

cycle [sikl] *nm* **(a)** *(série, mouvement)* cycle **(b)** **premier/second c.** *Scol* = lower/upper classes in secondary school; *Univ* = first/last two years of a degree course

cycliste [siklist] *nmf* cyclist

cyclone [siklon] *nm* cyclone

cygne [siɲ] *nm* swan

cylindre [silɛ̃dr] *nm* cylinder

cymbale [sɛ̃bal] *nf* cymbal

cynique [sinik] **1** *adj* cynical **2** *nmf* cynic

Dd

D, d [de] **1** *nm inv* D, d **2** *(abrév* **route départementale)** = designation of a secondary road

dactylo [daktilo] *nmf (personne)* typist

daim [dɛ̃] *nm (cuir)* suede

dalle [dal] *nf (de pierre)* paving stone; *(de marbre)* slab

dame [dam] *nf (femme)* lady; *Cartes* queen; **dames** *(jeu) Br* draughts, *Am* checkers

Danemark [danmark] *nm* **le D.** Denmark • **danois, -e 1** *adj* Danish **2** *nmf* **D., Danoise** Dane **3** *nm (langue)* Danish

danger [dɑ̃ʒe] *nm* danger; **en d.** in danger • **dangereux, -euse** *adj* dangerous (**pour** to)

dans [dɑ̃] *prép* (a) in; *(changement de lieu)* into; *(à l'intérieur de)* inside (b) *(provenance)* from, out of; **boire d. un verre** to drink out of a glass (c) *(exprime la temporalité)* in; **d. deux jours** in two days' time

danse [dɑ̃s] *nf* dance; **d. classique** ballet • **danser** *vti* to dance • **danseur, -euse** *nmf* dancer

date [dat] *nf* date; **d. de naissance** date of birth; **d. limite** deadline

datte [dat] *nf* date

dauphin [dofɛ̃] *nm* dolphin

davantage [davɑ̃taʒ] *adv* more; **d. de temps/d'argent** more time/money

---

de¹ [də]

de becomes **d'** before vowel and mute h; **de + le = du** [dy], **de + les = des** [dɛ].

prép (a) *(complément de nom)* of; **le livre de Paul** Paul's book; **un livre de Flaubert** a book by Flaubert; **le train de Londres** the London train; **une augmentation de salaire** an increase in salary (b) *(complément d'adjectif)* **digne de qn** worthy of sb; **content de qn/qch** pleased with sb/sth; **heureux de partir** happy to leave (c) *(complément de verbe)* **parler de qn/qch** to speak of sb/sth; **se souvenir de qn/qch** to remember sb/sth; **décider de faire qch** to decide to do sth; **empêcher qn de faire qch** to stop sb from doing sth (d) *(indique la provenance)* from; **venir de…** to come from…; **sortir de qch** to come out of sth; **le train de Londres** the train from London (e) *(introduit l'agent)* **accompagné de qn** accompanied by sb; **entouré de qch** surrounded by *or* with sth (f) *(introduit le moyen)* **armé de qch** armed with sth (g) *(introduit la manière)* **d'une voix douce** in a gentle voice (h) *(introduit la cause)* **mourir de faim** to die of hunger (i) *(introduit le temps)* **travailler de nuit** to work by night; **six heures du matin** six o'clock in the morning (j) *(mesure)* **avoir six** mètres de haut, être haut de six mètres to be six metres high; homme de trente ans thirty-year-old man

de² [də] *article partitif* some; **elle boit du vin** she drinks (some) wine; **il ne boit pas de vin** he doesn't drink (any) wine; **est-ce que vous buvez du vin?** do you drink (any) wine?

de³ [də] *article indéfini* de, des some; **des fleurs** (some) flowers; **de jolies fleurs** (some) pretty flowers; **d'agréables soirées** (some) pleasant evenings

dé [de] *nm (à jouer)* dice; *(à coudre)* thimble

débardeur [debardœr] *nm (vêtement)* vest

débarquer [debarke] *vi (passagers)* to disembark

débarrasser [debarase] **1** *vt (table)* to clear (de of), d. qn de qch to relieve sb of sth **2 se débarrasser** *vpr* **se d. de qn/qch** to get rid of sb/sth

débat [deba] *nm* debate

débattre* [debatr] *vt* to discuss, to debate; **d. de qch** to discuss sth

débit [debi] *nm Fin* debit; **d. de tabac** *Br* tobacconist's (shop), *Am* tobacco store

débiter [debite] *vt (compte)* to debit

débloquer [debloke] *vt (mécanisme)* to unjam

déborder [deborde] **1** *vi (fleuve, liquide)* to overflow **2** *vt (dépasser)* to stick out from; **débordé de travail** snowed under with work

déboucher [debuʃe] **1** *vt (bouteille)* to uncork; *(bouchon vissé)* to uncap; *(lavabo, tuyau)*

to unblock **2** *vi (surgir)* to emerge (de from); **d. sur** *(rue)* to lead out onto/into

debout [dəbu] *adv (personne)* standing; *(objet)* upright; **se mettre d.** to stand up; **rester d.** to stand; **être d.** *(hors du lit)* to be up

déboutonner [debutɔne] *vt* to unbutton

débrancher [debrãʃe] *vt* to unplug

débris [debri] *nmpl (de voiture, d'avion)* debris

débrouiller [debruje] **se débrouiller** *vpr Fam* to manage (**pour faire** to do)

début [deby] *nm* beginning, start; **au d. (de)** at the beginning (of); **dès le d.** (right) from the start *or* beginning • **débutant, -e** *nmf* beginner

décaféiné, -e [dekafeine] *adj* decaffeinated

décaler [dekale] **1** *vt (dans le temps)* to change the time of; *(dans l'espace)* to shift, to move **2 se décaler** *vpr* to move, to shift • **décalage** *nm (écart)* gap (**entre** between); **d. horaire** time difference; **souffrir du d. horaire** to have jet lag

décapotable [dekapɔtabl] *adj & nf* convertible

décapsuleur [dekapsylœr] *nm* bottle opener

décédé, -e [desede] *adj* deceased

décembre [desãbr] *nm* December

décennie [deseni] *nf* decade

décent, -e [desã, -ãt] *adj (comportement)* proper; *(vêtements)* decent

déception [desɛpsjɔ̃] *nf* disappointment

décerner [desɛrne] *vt (prix)* to award (**à** to)

décès [desɛ] *nm* death

décevant, -e [desəvɑ̃, -ɑ̃t] *adj* disappointing

décevoir* [desəvwar] *vt* to disappoint

déchaîner [deʃene] **1** *vt* (colère, violence) to unleash **2 se déchaîner** *vpr* (tempête) to rage; (personne) to fly into a rage (**contre** with)

décharge [deʃarʒ] *nf* **d. (électrique)** (electric) shock; **d. (publique)** *Br* (rubbish) dump, *Am* (garbage) dump

décharger [deʃarʒe] *vt* (camion, navire, cargaison) to unload

déchets [deʃɛ] *nmpl* scraps; **d. radioactifs** radioactive waste

déchiffrer [deʃifre] *vt* (message, écriture) to decipher

déchiqueté, -e [deʃikte] *adj* (tissu) torn to shreds

déchirer [deʃire] *vt* (accidentellement) to tear; (volontairement) to tear up

décidé, -e [deside] *adj* (personne, air) determined; (fixé) settled; **être d. à faire qch** to be determined to do sth

décidément [desidemɑ̃] *adv* really

décider [deside] **1** *vt* **d. quand/que...** to decide when/that... **2** *vi* **d. de qch** to decide on sth; **d. de faire qch** to decide to do sth **3 se décider** *vpr* **se d. (à faire qch)** to make up one's mind (to do sth)

décisif, -ive [desizif, -iv] *adj* (bataille) decisive; (moment) critical • **décision** *nf* decision (**de faire** to do); **prendre une d.** to make a decision

déclaration [deklarasjɔ̃] *nf* (annonce) statement; (de naissance, de décès) registration; (à la police) report

déclarer [deklare] *vt* (annoncer)

to declare (**que** that); (naissance, décès) to register; **d. qn coupable** to find sb guilty (**de** of); **d. la guerre** to declare war (**à** on); **rien à d.** (en douane) nothing to declare

déclencher [deklɑ̃ʃe] *vt* (appareil) to start; (mécanisme) to activate (révolte) to trigger

déclic [deklik] *nm* (bruit) click

déclin [deklɛ̃] *nm* decline; **être er d.** to be in decline

décliner [dekline] **1** *vi* (forces) tc decline; (jour) to draw to a close **2** *vt* (refuser) to decline

décoder [dekɔde] *vt* to decode

décoiffer [dekwafe] *vt* **d. qn** tc mess up sb's hair

décollage [dekɔlaʒ] *nm* (d'avion takeoff

décoller [dekɔle] **1** *vt* (enlever) tc peel off **2** *vi* (avion) to take off

décolleté, -e [dekɔlte] **1** *ad* (robe) low-cut **2** *nm* (de robe) lov neckline

décolorer [dekɔlɔre] **1** *v* (cheveux) to bleach **2 se décolorer** *vpr* (tissu) to fade; **se d les cheveux** to bleach one's hair

décomposer [dekɔ̃poze] **s décomposer** *vpr* (pourrir) tc decompose

décompte [dekɔ̃t] *nm* (soustrac tion) deduction; (détail) breakdowr

déconcentrer [dekɔ̃sɑ̃tre] **s déconcentrer** *vpr* to los concentration

déconcerter [dekɔ̃sɛrte] *vt* tc disconcert

décongeler [dekɔ̃ʒle] *vt* to thaw to defrost

déconnecter [dekɔnɛkte] *u* (appareil, fil) to disconnect

déconseiller [dekɔ̃seje] *vt* **d. qcl à qn** to advise sb against sth; **d à qn de faire qch** to advise s against doing sth

décontracter [dekɔ̃trakte] **1** *vt* *(muscle)* to relax **2 se décontracter** *vpr* to relax • **décontracté, -e** *adj* *(ambiance, personne)* relaxed; *(vêtement)* casual

décor [dekɔr] *nm* *(de maison)* decor; *(paysage)* surroundings

décorer [dekɔre] *vt* *(maison, soldat)* to decorate (**de** with) • **décorateur, -trice** *nmf* (interior) decorator • **décoration** *nf* *(action, ornement, médaille)* decoration

décortiquer [dekɔrtike] *vt* *(riz)* to hull; *(crevette, noisette)* to shell

découper [dekupe] *vt* to cut up

décourager [dekuraʒe] **1** *vt* *(dissuader, démoraliser)* to discourage (**de faire** from doing) **2 se décourager** *vpr* to get discouraged

découvert, -e[1] [dekuvɛr, -ɛrt] **1** *adj* *(terrain)* open; *(tête, épaule)* bare **2** *nm* *(de compte)* overdraft

découverte[2] [dekuvɛrt] *nf* discovery, **faire une d.** to make a discovery

découvrir* [dekuvrir] *vt* *(trouver, apprendre à connaître)* to discover; *(secret)* to uncover; **faire d. qch à qn** to introduce sb to sth

décrire* [dekrir] *vt* to describe

décrocher [dekrɔʃe] *vt* *(détacher)* to unhook; **d. (le téléphone)** *(pour répondre)* to pick up the phone; *(pour ne pas être dérangé)* to take the phone off the hook

décrypter [dekripte] *vt* to decipher

déçu, -e [desy] **1** *pp de* **décevoir 2** *adj* disappointed

dédaigner [dedɛɲe] *vt* *(offre, richesses)* to scorn • **dédaigneux, -euse** *adj* scornful, disdainful (**de** of)

dedans [dədɑ̃] *adv* inside; **en d.** on the inside

dédicace [dedikas] *nf* dedication

dédier [dedje] *vt* to dedicate (**à** to)

dédommager [dedɔmaʒe] *vt* to compensate (**de** for) • **dédommagement** *nm* compensation

déduire* [dedɥir] *vt* *(retirer)* to deduct (**de** from); *(conclure)* to deduce (**de** from) • **déduction** *nf* *(raisonnement, décompte)* deduction

déesse [deɛs] *nf* goddess

défaire* [defɛr] *vt* *(nœud)* to undo; *(valises)* to unpack

défaite [defɛt] *nf* defeat

défaut [defo] *nm* *(de personne)* fault; *(de machine)* defect; **à d. de qch** for lack of sth; **ou, à d....** or, failing that…

défavorable [defavɔrabl] *adj* unfavourable (**à** to) • **défavorisé, -e** *adj* *(milieu)* underprivileged

défectueux, -euse [defɛktɥø, -øz] *adj* faulty, defective

défendre [defɑ̃dr] **1** *vt* *(protéger, soutenir)* to defend (**contre** against); **d. à qn de faire qch** to forbid sb to do sth; **d. qch à qn** to forbid sb sth **2 se défendre** *vpr* to defend oneself

défense [defɑ̃s] *nf* *(protection)* *Br* defence, *Am* defense; **sans d.** *Br* defenceless, *Am* defenseless; **'d. de fumer'** 'no smoking' • **défenseur** *nm* defender • **défensif, -ive 1** *adj* defensive **2** *nf* **sur la défensive** on the defensive

défi [defi] *nm* challenge (**à** to); **lancer un d. à qn** to challenge sb

déficit [defisit] *nm* deficit • **déficitaire** *adj* *(budget)* in deficit; *(compte)* in debit

défier [defje] *vt* *(provoquer)* to challenge; *(danger)* to defy; **d. qn de faire qch** to defy sb to do sth

défiguré, -e [defigyre] *adj (personne)* disfigured

défilé [defile] *nm (cortège)* procession; *(de manifestants)* march; **d. de mode** fashion show

définir [definir] *vt* to define • **défini, -e** *adj* definite • **définition** *nf* definition; *(de mots croisés)* clue

définitif, -ive [definitif, -iv] *adj (version)* final; *(fermeture)* permanent • **définitivement** *adv (partir, exclure)* for good

défoncer [defɔ̃se] *vt (porte, mur)* to smash in • **défoncé, -e** *adj (route)* bumpy

déformer [defɔrme] *vt (membre)* to deform; *(vêtement, chaussures)* to put out of shape; *(image)* to distort; *(propos)* to twist • **déformé, -e** *adj (objet)* misshapen; *(corps)* deformed

défroisser [defrwase] *vt* to smooth out

défunt, -e [defœ̃, -œ̃t] *nmf* **le d., la défunte** the deceased

dégager [degaʒe] *vt (passage, voie)* to clear **(de** of); *(odeur, chaleur)* to emit • **dégagé, -e** *adj (ciel)* clear; *(vue)* open

dégâts [dega] *nmpl* damage

dégeler [deʒle] **1** *vt* to thaw; *(surgelé)* to defrost **2** *vi* to thaw; **faire d. qch** *(surgelé)* to defrost sth

dégonfler [degɔ̃fle] **1** *vt (pneu)* to let the air out of **2 se dégonfler** *vpr (pneu)* to go flat • **dégonflé, -e** *adj (pneu)* flat

dégourdi, -e [degurdi] *adj (malin)* smart

dégoût [degu] *nm* disgust

dégoûter [degute] *vt* to disgust; **d. qn de qch** to put sb off sth • **dégoutant, -e** *adj* disgusting • **dégouté, -e** *adj* disgusted; **être d. de qch** to be sick of sth

dégrader [degrade] **se dégrader** *vpr (situation)* to deteriorate • **dégradant, -e** *adj* degrading

degré [dəgre] *nm (d'angle, de température)* degree; *(d'alcool)* proof; **au plus haut d.** in the extreme

déguiser [degize] **1** *vt (pour tromper)* to disguise; **d. qn en qch** *(costumer)* to dress sb up as sth **2 se déguiser** *vpr (pour s'amuser)* to dress oneself up **(en** as) • **déguisement** *nm* disguise; *(de bal costumé)* fancy dress

déguster [degyste] *vt (savourer)* to savour • **dégustation** *nf* tasting

dehors [dəɔr] **1** *adv* outside; *(pas chez soi)* out; *(en plein air)* outdoors; **en d. de la ville** out of town; *Fig* **en d. de** *(excepté)* apart from **2** *nm (extérieur)* outside; **au d.** on the outside; *(se pencher)* out

déjà [deʒa] *adv* already; **est-il d. parti?** has he left yet *or* already?; **elle l'a d. vu** she's seen it before, she's already seen it

déjeuner [deʒœne] **1** *nm* lunch; **petit d.** breakfast **2** *vi (à midi)* to have lunch; *(le matin)* to have breakfast

délai [delɛ] *nm (laps de temps)* time allowed; **dans les plus brefs délais** as soon as possible; **dernier d.** final date

délaisser [delese] *vt* to neglect

délavé, -e [delave] *adj (tissu, jean)* faded

délayer [deleje] *vt (poudre)* to add water to; *(liquide)* to dilute

déléguer [delege] *vt* to delegate **(à** to) • **délégué, -e** *nmf* delegate

délibéré, -e [delibere] *adj (intentionnel)* deliberate

délicat, -e [delika, -at] *adj (santé, question)* delicate; *(peau)* sensitive • **délicatesse** *nf (tact)* tact

délice [delis] *nm* delight •

délicieux, -euse *adj* delicious

délier [delje] *vt* to untie

délimiter [delimite] *vt (terrain)* to mark off; *(sujet)* to define

délinquant, -e [delɛ̃kɑ̃, -ɑ̃t] *nmf* delinquent

délire [delir] *nm Méd* delirium; *(exaltation)* frenzy

délit [deli] *nm Br* offence, *Am* offense

délivrer [delivre] *vt* **(a)** *(captif)* to rescue; **d. qn de qch** to rid sb of sth **(b)** *(marchandises)* to deliver; *(passeport)* to issue **(à** to)

deltaplane [deltaplan] *nm* hang-glider; **faire du d.** to go hang-gliding

déluge [delyʒ] *nm* downpour

demain [dəmɛ̃] *adv* tomorrow; **d. soir** tomorrow evening; **à d.!** see you tomorrow!

demande [dəmɑ̃d] *nf (requête)* request (**de** for); *Écon* demand; **faire une d. de qch** *(prêt, permis)* to apply for sth; **demandes d'emploi** *(dans le journal)* jobs wanted, *Br* situations wanted

demander [dəmɑ̃de] **1** *vt (conseil)* to ask for; *(prix, raison)* to ask; *(nécessiter)* to require; **d. son chemin/l'heure** to ask the way/the time; **d. qch à qn** to ask sb for sth; **d. à qn de faire qch** to ask sb to do sth; **d. qn en mariage** to propose (marriage) to sb **2 se demander** *vpr* to wonder, to ask oneself (**pourquoi** why; **si** if) • **demandeur, -euse** *nmf* **d. d'emploi** job seeker

démanger [demɑ̃ʒe] *vti* to itch • **démangeaisons** *nfpl* **avoir des d.** to be itching

démaquiller [demakije] **se démaquiller** *vpr* to remove one's make-up • **démaquillant** *nm* cleanser

démarche [demarʃ] *nf (allure)* walk, gait; *(requête)* step; **faire les démarches nécessaires pour…** to take the necessary steps to…

démarrer [demare] *vi (moteur)* to start; *(voiture)* to move off;

démêler [demele] *vt* to untangle

déménager [demenaʒe] *vi* to move • **déménagement** *nm* move • **déménageur** *nm Br* removal man, *Am* (furniture) mover

démesuré, -e [deməzyre] *adj* excessive

demi, -e [dəmi] **1** *adj* half; **une heure et demie** *(90 minutes)* an hour and a half; *(à l'horloge)* half past one, one-thirty **2** *adv* **(à) d. plein** half-full; **à d. nu** half-naked **3** *nmf (moitié)* half **4** *nm* **un d.** *(bière)* a beer, *Br* a half(-pint) **5** *nf* **à la demie** *(à l'horloge)* at half-past • **demi-cercle** *(pl* **demi-cercles)** *nm* semicircle • **demi-douzaine** *(pl* **demi-douzaines)** *nf* **une d. (de)** half a dozen • **demi-écrémé** *adj* semi-skimmed • **demi-finale** *(pl* **demi-finales)** *nf Sport* semi-final • **demi-frère** *(pl* **demi-frères)** *nm* half brother • **demi-heure** *(pl* **demi-heures)** *nf* **une d.** half an hour • **demi-journée** *(pl* **demi-journées)** *nf* half-day • **demi-pension** *nf Br* half-board, *Am* breakfast and one meal • **demi-sœur** *(pl* **demi-sœurs)** *nf* half sister • **demi-tarif** *(pl* **demi-tarifs)** *nm* half-price • **demi-tour** *(pl* **demi-tours)** *nm Br* about turn, *Am* about face; *(en voiture)* U-turn; **faire d.** *(à pied)* to turn back; *(en voiture)* to do a U-turn

démission [demisjɔ̃] *nf* resignation; **donner sa d.** to hand in one's resignation • **démissionner** *vi* to resign

démocrate [demɔkrat] **1** *adj* democratic **2** *nmf* democrat • **démocratie** [-asi] *nf* democracy • **démocratique** *adj* democratic

démodé, -e [demɔde] *adj* old-fashioned

demoiselle [dəmwazɛl] *nf (jeune fille)* young lady; **d. d'honneur** bridesmaid

démolir [demɔlir] *vt (bâtiment)* to demolish • **démolition** *nf* demolition

démon [demɔ̃] *nm* demon

démonstratif, -ive [demɔ̃stratif, -iv] *adj* demonstrative

démonstration [demɔ̃strasjɔ̃] *nf* demonstration

démonter [demɔ̃te] *vt (mécanisme, tente)* to dismantle

démontrer [demɔ̃tre] *vt* to demonstrate

démoraliser [demɔralize] **1** *vt* to demoralize **2 se démoraliser** *vpr* to become demoralized

dénier [denje] *vt (responsabilité)* to deny; **d. qch à qn** to deny sb sth

dénombrer [denɔ̃bre] *vt* to count

dénommer [denɔme] *vt* to name

dénoncer [denɔ̃se] *vt (injustice, abus, malfaiteur)* to denounce (**à** to); *(élève)* to tell on (**à** to)

dénoter [denɔte] *vt* to denote

dénouement [denumɑ̃] *nm (de livre)* ending; *(d'affaire)* outcome

dénouer [denwe] *vt (nœud, corde)* to undo, to untie; *(cheveux)* to let down, to undo

denrée [dɑ̃re] *nf* foodstuff; **denrées périssables** perishable goods

dense [dɑ̃s] *adj* dense

dent [dɑ̃] *nf* tooth (*pl* teeth); **d. de lait/sagesse** milk/wisdom tooth; **faire ses dents** *(enfant)* to be teething • **dentaire** *adj* dental

dentelle [dɑ̃tɛl] *nf* lace

dentier [dɑ̃tje] *nm* (set of) false teeth, dentures

dentifrice [dɑ̃tifris] *nm* toothpaste

dentiste [dɑ̃tist] *nmf* dentist

déodorant [deɔdɔrɑ̃] *nm* deodorant

dépanner [depane] *vt (machine)* to repair • **dépannage** *nm* (emergency) repairs; **voiture/service de d.** breakdown vehicle/service • **dépanneur** *nm (de télévision)* repairman; *(de voiture)* breakdown mechanic • **dépanneuse** *nf (voiture) Br* breakdown lorry, *Am* wrecker

dépareillé, -e [depareje] *adj (chaussure)* odd

départ [depar] *nm* departure; *(de course)* start; **point/ligne de d.** starting point/post; **au d.** at the outset, at the start; **au d. de Paris** *(excursion)* leaving from Paris

département [departəmɑ̃] *nm* department *(division of local government)* • **départemental, -e, -aux, -ales** *adj* departmental; **route départementale** secondary road, *Br* ≃ B road

dépasser [depase] *vt (véhicule) Br* to overtake, *Am* to pass; *(endroit)* to go past; *(vitesse)* to exceed; **d. qn** *(en hauteur)* to be taller than sb • **dépassé, -e** *adj (démodé)* outdated; *(incapable)* unable to cope

dépayser [depeize] *vt Br* to disorientate, *Am* to disorient

dépêcher [depɛʃe] **se dépêcher** *vpr* to hurry (up); **se d. de faire qch** to hurry to do sth

dépendant, -e [depɑ̃dɑ̃, -ɑ̃t] dependent (**de** on)

dépendre [depɑ̃dr] *vi* to depend (**de** on *or* upon); **d. de** *(appartenir à)* to belong to; *(être soumis à)* to be dependent on

dépens [depɑ̃] *nmpl* **apprendre qch à ses d.** to learn sth to one's cost

dépense [depɑ̃s] *nf (frais)* expense, expenditure; **faire des dépenses** to spend money • **dépenser** *vt (argent)* to spend; *(forces)* to exert • **dépensier, -ère** *adj* extravagant

dépilatoire [depilatwar] *nm* hair-remover

dépit [depi] *nm* spite; **en d. de qn/qch** in spite of sb/sth

déplacement [deplasmɑ̃] *nm (voyage)* trip; **être en d.** *(homme d'affaires)* to be on a business trip

déplacer [deplase] **1** *vt (objet)* to move **2 se déplacer** *vpr (personne, animal)* to move; *(voyager)* to travel • **deplacé, -e** *adj (mal à propos)* out of place; **personne déplacée** *(réfugié)* displaced person

déplaire* [depler] **1** *vi* **d. à qn** to displease sb; **ça me déplaît** I don't like it **2 se déplaire** *vpr* **il se déplaît à Paris** he doesn't like it in Paris • **déplaisant, -e** *adj* unpleasant

dépliant [deplijɑ] *nm (prospectus)* leaflet

déplorer [deplɔre] *vt (regretter)* to deplore; **d. que...** *(+ subjunctive)* to deplore the fact that...; **d. la mort de qn** to mourn sb's death

déposer [depoze] *vt (poser)* to put down; **d. qn** *(en voiture)* to drop sb off; **d. de l'argent sur un compte** to deposit money in an account; **d. une plainte contre qn** to lodge a complaint against sb

dépôt [depo] *nm (de vin)* deposit, sediment; *(entrepôt)* depot

dépouiller [depuje] **1** *vt (analyser)* to go through; **d. un** scrutin to count the votes **2 se dépouiller** *vpr* **se d. de qch** to rid oneself of sth

dépourvu, -e [depurvy] *adj* **d. de qch** devoid of sth; **prendre qn au d.** to catch sb off guard

dépression [depresjɔ̃] *nf (creux, maladie)* depression; **d. nerveuse** nervous breakdown; **faire de la d.** to be suffering from depression • **déprimé, -e** *adj* depressed

depuis [dəpɥi] **1** *prép* since; **d. lundi/2001** since Monday/2001; **j'habite ici d. un mois** I've been living here for a month; **d. quand êtes-vous là?, d. combien de temps êtes-vous là?** how long have you been here?; **d. peu/longtemps** for a short/long time **2** *adv* since (then), ever since **3** *conj* **d. que** since

député, -e [depyte] *nmf* Pol deputy, Br ≃ MP, Am ≃ representative; **d. du Parlement européen** Member of the European Parliament

déraciner [derasine] *vt (arbre, personne)* to uproot

dérailler [deraje] *vi (train)* to leave the rails; **faire d. un train** to derail a train

déranger [derɑ̃ʒe] **1** *vt (affaires)* to disturb; **je viendrai si ça ne te dérange pas** I'll come if that's all right with you; **ça vous dérange si je fume?** do you mind if I smoke? **2 se déranger** *vpr* to put oneself to a lot of trouble (**pour faire** to do); *(se déplacer)* to move; **ne te dérange pas!** don't bother! • **dérangement** *nm (gêne)* trouble; **en d.** *(téléphone)* out of order

déraper [derape] *vi (véhicule)* to skid; *(personne)* to slip

dérive [deriv] *nf Naut* drift; **à la d.**
adrift • **dériver** *vi* to drift

dermatologue [dermatɔlɔg] *nmf*
dermatologist

dernier, -ère [dernje, -ɛr] **1** *adj*
(ultime) last; *(marquant la fin)* final;
(nouvelles, mode) latest; *(étage)*
top; *(degré)* highest; **le d. rang**
the back *or* last row; **ces derniers
mois** these past few months; **les
dix dernières minutes** the last
ten minutes; **en d.** last **2** *nmf* last;
ce d. *(de deux)* the latter; *(de
plusieurs)* the last-mentioned

dérouler [derule] *vt (tapis)* to
unroll; *(fil)* to unwind

derrière [derjɛr] **1** *prép & adv*
behind; **d. moi** behind me; **assis
d.** *(dans une voiture)* sitting in
the back; **par d.** *(attaquer)* from
behind, from the rear **2** *nm (de
maison)* back, rear; *(fesses)* behind;
roue de d. back *or* rear wheel

des [dɛ] *voir* **de, un**

dès [dɛ] *prép* from; **d. le
début** (right) from the start; **d.
maintenant** from now on; **d. lors**
(dans le temps) from then on; **d.
le VIe siècle** as early as *or* as far
back as the sixth century; **d. leur
arrivée** as soon as they arrive/
arrived; **d. qu'elle viendra** as
soon as she comes

désabusé, -e [dezabyze] *adj*
disillusioned

désaccord [dezakɔr] *nm*
disagreement; **être en d. avec qn**
to disagree with sb

désagréable [dezagreabl] *adj*
unpleasant

désaltérer [dezaltere] **se désaltérer** *upr* to quench one's thirst

désapprouver [dezapruve] **1** *vt*
to disapprove of **2** *vi* to disapprove
• **désapprobation** *nf* disapproval

désarmer [dezarme] *vt (soldat,*

nation) to disarm • **désarmemen**
nm (de nation) disarmament

désarroi [dezarwa] *nm* confusion

désastre [dezastr] *nm* disaster •
désastreux, -euse *adj* disastrous

désavantage [dezavãtaʒ] *nm*
disadvantage

descendant, -e [desãdã, -ãt] *nmj*
descendant

descendre [desãdr] **1** *(aux* **être**
vi to come/go down (**de** from)
(d'un train) to get off (**de** from)
(d'un arbre) to climb down (**de**
from); **d. de** *(être issu de)* to be
descended from **2** *(aux* **avoir***) vi*
(escalier) to come/go down; *(objet)*
to bring/take down

descente [desãt] *nf (d'avion)*
descent; *(pente)* slope; *(de police)*
raid (**dans** upon)

description [deskripsjɔ] *nf* description

désemparé, -e [dezãpare] *ad*
(personne) at a loss

désenchanté, -e [dezãʃãte] *adj*
disillusioned

déséquilibre [dezekilibr] *nm*
imbalance; **en d.** unsteady •
déséquilibré, -e *adj* unbalanced
• **déséquilibrer** *vt* to throw off
balance

désert, -e [dezɛr, -ɛrt] **1** *adj (lieu)*
deserted; *(région)* uninhabited; **île
déserte** desert island **2** *nm* desert

déserter [dezɛrte] *vti* to desert

désespérer [dezɛspere] *vi* to
despair (**de** of) • **désespéré, -e**
adj (personne) in despair; *(cas,
situation, efforts)* desperate

désespoir [dezɛspwar] *nm*
despair

déshabiller [dezabije] *vt,* **se
déshabiller** *upr* to undress

déshonneur [dezɔnœr] *nm*
dishonour

déshonorer [dezɔnɔre] *vt* to disgrace

déshydrater [dezidrate] **se déshydrater** *vpr* to become dehydrated

désigner [deziɲe] *vt (montrer)* to point to; *(choisir)* to choose; **d. qn par son nom** to refer to sb by name

désinfecter [dezɛ̃fɛkte] *vt* to disinfect • **désinfectant** *nm* disinfectant

désintégrer [dezɛ̃tegre] **se désintégrer** *vpr* to disintegrate

désintéressé, -e [dezɛ̃terese] *adj (altruiste)* disinterested

désinvolte [dezɛ̃vɔlt] *adj (dégagé)* casual; *(insolent)* offhand

désir [dezir] *nm* desire • **désirable** *adj* desirable • **désirer** *vt* to wish; *(convoiter)* to desire

désobéir [dezɔbeir] *vi* to disobey; **d. à qn** to disobey sb • **désobéissant, -e** *adj* disobedient

désolé, -e [dezɔle] *adj (région) désolate, (affligé)* upset; **être d. que...** *(+ subjunctive)* to be sorry that...; **je suis d. de vous déranger** I'm sorry to disturb you

désordonné, -e [dezɔrdɔne] *adj (personne, chambre)* untidy

désordre [dezɔrdr] *nm (manque d'ordre)* mess; *(manque d'organisation)* disorder; **en d.** untidy, messy

désorganisation [dezɔrganizasjɔ̃] *nf* disorganization • **désorganisé, -e** *adj* disorganized

désormais [dezɔrmɛ] *adv* from now on, in future

desquels, desquelles [dekɛl] *voir* **lequel**

dessécher [deseʃe] **se dessécher** *vpr (peau)* to dry up; *(végétation)* to wither

desserrer [desere] *vt (ceinture)* to loosen; *(poing)* to unclench; *(frein)* to release

dessert [desɛr] *nm* dessert

desservir [desɛrvir] *vt (table)* to clear (away); **le car dessert ce village** the bus stops at this village; **ce quartier est bien desservi** this district is well served by public transport

dessin [desɛ̃] *nm* drawing; *(rapide)* sketch; *(motif)* design, pattern; **d. animé** cartoon

dessiner [desine] *vt* to draw; *(rapidement)* to sketch; *(meuble, robe)* to design; **d. (bien) la taille** *(vêtement)* to show off the figure

dessous [dəsu] **1** *adv* underneath; **en d.** underneath; **en d. de** below **2** *nm* underside; **des d.** *(sous-vêtements)* underwear • **dessous-de-plat** *nm inv* table mat

dessus [dəsy] **1** *adv (marcher, écrire)* on it/them; *(monter)* on top (of it/them), on it/them; *(passer)* over it/them; **de d. la table** off or from the table **2** *nm* top; **avoir le d.** to have the upper hand; **reprendre le d.** *(se remettre)* to get over it

destin [dɛstɛ̃] *nm* fate, destiny

destinataire [dɛstinatɛr] *nmf* addressee

destination [dɛstinasjɔ̃] *nf (lieu)* destination; **trains à d. de...** trains to...; **arriver à d.** to reach one's destination

destiner [dɛstine] *vt* **d. qch à qn** to intend sth for sb; **d. qn à** *(carrière, fonction)* to intend *or* destine sb for

destruction [dɛstryksjɔ̃] *nf* destruction

désuet, -ète [desɥe, -ɛt] *adj* obsolete

détacher [detaʃe] **1** *vt (ceinture, vêtement)* to undo; *(mains)* to untie; *(mots)* to pronounce clearly; **d. qn** *(libérer)* to untie sb **2 se**

détacher *vpr (chien, prisonnier)* to break loose; *(se dénouer)* to come undone; *(fragment)* to come off (**de qch** sth); **se d. de qn** to break away from sb; **se d. sur qch** *(ressortir)* to stand out against sth ● **détaché, -e** *adj (air, ton)* detached

détail [detaj] *nm* detail; **en d.** in detail; **entrer dans les détails** to go into detail ● **détaillé, -e** *adj (récit, description)* detailed; *(facture)* itemized

détective [detɛktiv] *nm* **d. (privé)** (private) detective

déteindre* [detɛ̃dr] *vi (couleur, tissu)* to run

détendre [detɑ̃dr] **se détendre** *vpr (corde)* to slacken; *(atmosphère)* to become less tense; *(personne)* to relax ● **détendu, -e** *adj (visage, atmosphère)* relaxed; *(corde)* slack

détenir* [detənir] *vt (record, pouvoir, titre, prisonnier)* to hold; *(secret, objet volé)* to be in possession of ● **détenu, -e** *nmf* prisoner

détente [detɑ̃t] *nf (repos)* relaxation; *(entre deux pays)* détente

détergent [detɛrʒɑ̃] *nm* detergent

détériorer [deterjɔre] **se détériorer** *vpr* to deteriorate ● **détérioration** *nf* damage (**de** to); *(de situation)* deterioration (**de** in)

détermination [detɛrminasjɔ̃] *nf (fermeté)* determination

déterminer [detɛrmine] *vt (préciser)* to determine; *(causer)* to bring about ● **déterminé, -e** *adj (précis)* specific; *(résolu)* determined

déterrer [detere] *vt* to dig up

détester [detɛste] *vt* to hate, to detest; **d. faire qch** to hate doing *or* to do sth

détour [detur] *nm (crochet)* detour; *(de route)* bend, curve

détourner [deturne] **1** *vt (dévier)* to divert; *(avion)* to hijack; *(conversation, sens)* to change; *(fonds)* to embezzle; **d. la tête** to turn one's head away; **d. les yeux** to look away; **d. qn de** *(son devoir)* to take sb away from; *(sa route)* to lead sb away from **2 se détourner** *vpr* to turn away ● **détournement** [-əmɑ̃] *nm (de cours d'eau)* diversion; **d. d'avion** hijack(ing); **d. de fonds** embezzlement

détresse [detrɛs] *nf* distress; **en d.** *(navire)* in distress

détritus [detritys] *nmpl Br* rubbish, *Am* garbage

détroit [detrwa] *nm* strait

détruire* [detrɥir] *vt* to destroy

dette [dɛt] *nf* debt; **avoir des dettes** to be in debt; **faire des dettes** to run into debt

DEUG [døg] *(abrév* **diplôme d'études universitaires générales)** *nm* = degree gained after two years' study at university

deuil [dœj] *nm* mourning; **être en d.** to be in mourning

deux [dø] *adj inv & nm inv* two; **d. fois** twice; **mes d. sœurs** both my sisters, my two sisters; **tous (les) d.** both ● **deuxième** *adj & nmf* second ● **deux-pièces** *nm inv (maillot de bain)* bikini; *(appartement)* two-roomed *Br* flat *or Am* apartment

devant [dəvɑ̃] **1** *prép & adv* in front (of); **passer d. une église** to go past a church; **marcher d. qn** to walk in front of sb; **assis d.** *(dans une voiture)* sitting in the front **2** *nm* front; **roue/porte de d.** front wheel/door; **prendre les devants** *(action)* to take the initiative

développer [devlɔpe] *vt*, **se développer** *vpr* to develop • **développement** *nm* development; *(de photo)* developing; **en plein d.** *(entreprise, pays)* growing fast

devenir* [dəvnir] *(aux* **être***) vi* to become; **d. médecin** to become a doctor; **d. vieux** to get *or* grow old; **d. tout rouge** to go all red; **qu'est-elle devenue?** what has become of her?

déviation [devjasjɔ] *nf (itinéraire)* *Br* diversion, *Am* detour

deviner [dəvine] *vt* to guess (**que** that) • **devinette** *nf* riddle

devis [dəvi] *nm* estimate

dévisager [devizaʒe] *vt* **d. qn** to stare at sb

devise [dəviz] *nf (légende)* motto; *(monnaie)* currency; **devises étrangères** foreign currency

dévisser [devise] **1** *vt* to unscrew **2 se dévisser** *vpr (bouchon)* to unscrew; *(par accident)* to come unscrewed

dévoiler [devwale] *vt (statue)* to unveil; *Fig (secret)* to disclose

devoir*¹ [dəvwar] *v aux* (**a**) *(indique la nécessité)* **je dois refuser** I must refuse, I have (got) to refuse; **j'ai dû refuser** I had to refuse (**b**) *(indique une forte probabilité)* **il doit être tard** it must be late; **elle a dû oublier** she must have forgotten; **cela devait arriver** it had to happen (**c**) *(indique l'obligation)* **tu dois apprendre tes leçons** you must learn your lessons; **vous devriez rester** you should stay, you ought to stay; **il aurait dû venir** he should have come, he ought to have come (**d**) *(indique l'intention)* **elle doit venir** she's supposed to be coming, she's due to come; **le**

train devait arriver à midi the train was due (to arrive) at noon; **je devais le voir** I was (due) to see him

devoir*² [dəvwar] **1** *vt* to owe; **d. qch à qn** to owe sb sth, to owe sth to sb **2** *nm (obligation)* duty; **présenter ses devoirs à qn** to pay one's respects to sb; *Scol* **devoirs** homework; **faire ses devoirs** to do one's homework

dévorer [devɔre] *vt (manger)* to devour

dévotion [devosjɔ] *nf (adoration)* devotion

dévouer [devwe] **se dévouer** *vpr (se sacrifier)* to volunteer; *(se consacrer)* to devote oneself (**à** to) • **dévoué, -e** *adj (ami, femme)* devoted (**à** to)

diabète [djabɛt] *nm Méd* diabetes • **diabétique** *adj & nmf* diabetic

diable [djabl] *nm* devil; **le d.** the Devil

diagnostic [djagnɔstik] *nm* diagnosis

diagonal, -e, -aux, -ales [djagɔnal, -o] *adj* diagonal • **en diagonale** *adv* diagonally

dialecte [djalɛkt] *nm* dialect

dialogue [djalɔg] *nm Br* dialogue, *Am* dialog

diamant [djamã] *nm* diamond

diapositive [djapozitiv] *nf* slide

diarrhée [djare] *nf* diarrhoea

dictateur [diktatœr] *nm* dictator

dicter [dikte] *vt* to dictate (**à** to) • **dictée** *nf* dictation

dictionnaire [diksjɔnɛr] *nm* dictionary

diesel [djezɛl] *adj & nm* (**moteur**) **d.** diesel (engine)

diète [djɛt] *nf (partielle)* diet; *(totale)* fast; **être à la d.** to be on a diet/to be fasting

diététicien, -enne [djetetisjɛ̃, -ɛn] *nmf* dietician ● **diététique** *adj* **aliment d.** health food; **magasin d.** health-food shop

dieu, -x [djø] *nm* god; **D.** God; **le bon D.** God

différence [diferɑ̃s] *nf* difference (**de** in); **à la d. de qn/qch** unlike sb/sth; **faire la d. entre** to make a distinction between

différencier [diferɑ̃sje] **1** *vt* to differentiate (**de** from) **2 se différencier** *vpr* to differ (**de** from)

différent, -e [diferɑ̃, -ɑ̃t] *adj* different; **différents** *(divers)* different, various; **d. de** different from ● **différemment** [-amɑ̃] *adv* differently (**de** from)

différer [difere] *vi* to differ (**de** from)

difficile [difisil] *adj* difficult; **c'est d. à faire** it's hard *or* difficult to do ● **difficilement** *adv* with difficulty

difficulté [difikylte] *nf* difficulty (**à faire** in doing); **avoir de la d. à faire qch** to have difficulty (in) doing sth

diffus, -e [dify, -yz] *adj (lumière)* diffuse; *(impression)* vague

diffuser [difyze] *vt (émission)* to broadcast; *(nouvelle)* to spread; *(lumière, chaleur)* to diffuse ● **diffusion** *nf (d'émission)* broadcasting; *(de lumière, de chaleur)* diffusion

digérer [diʒere] *vt* to digest

digestif, -ive [diʒɛstif, -iv] *nmf* after-dinner liqueur

digestion [diʒɛstjɔ̃] *nf* digestion

digne [diɲ] *adj* dignified; **d. de qn/qch** worthy of sb/sth

dignité [diɲite] *nf* dignity

digue [dig] *nf* dike, dyke; *(en bord de mer)* sea wall

dilemme [dilɛm] *nm* dilemma

diluer [dilɥe] *vt (liquide, substance)* to dilute (**dans** in)

dimanche [dimɑ̃ʃ] *nm* Sunday

dimension [dimɑ̃sjɔ̃] *nf (mesure, aspect)* dimension; *(taille)* size; **à deux dimensions** two-dimensional; **prendre les dimensions de qch** to measure sth up

diminuer [diminɥe] **1** *vt (réduire)* to reduce, to decrease; *(affaiblir)* to affect **2** *vi (réserves, nombre)* to decrease, to diminish; *(prix, profits)* to decrease, to drop ● **diminution** *nf* reduction, decrease (**de** in)

dinde [dɛ̃d] *nf* turkey

dîner [dine] **1** *nm (repas du soir)* dinner; *(repas de midi)* lunch; *(soirée)* dinner party **2** *vi* to have dinner; *Belg & Can* to have lunch

dinosaure [dinozɔr] *nm* dinosaur

diplomate [diplomat] **1** *adj* diplomatic **2** *nmf* diplomat ● **diplomatie** [-asi] *nf (tact)* diplomacy ● **diplomatique** *adj* diplomatic

diplôme [diplom] *nm* diploma; *(d'université)* degree ● **diplômé, -e 1** *adj* qualified **2** *nmf* holder of a diploma; *Univ* graduate

dire* [dir] **1** *vt (mot)* to say; *(vérité, secret)* to tell; **d. des bêtises** to talk nonsense; **d. qch à qn** to tell sb sth, to say sth to sb; **d. à qn que...** to tell sb that..., to say to sb that...; **d. à qn de faire qch** to tell sb to do sth; **d. du mal/du bien de qn** to speak ill/well of sb; **on dirait un château** it looks like a castle; **on dirait du cabillaud** it tastes like cod; **autrement dit** in other words; **à vrai d.** to tell the truth **2 se dire** *vpr* **il se dit malade** he says he's ill; **comment ça se dit en anglais?** how do you say that in English?

direct, -e [dirɛkt] **1** *adj* direct **2** *nm*

Radio & TV live broadcasting; **en d. (de)** live (from) • **directement** [-əmã] *adv (sans intermédiaire)* directly; *(sans détour)* straight

directeur, -trice [dirɛktœr, -tris] *nmf* director; *(de magasin, de service)* manager; *(d'école) Br* headmaster, *f* headmistress, *Am* principal

direction [dirɛksjõ] *nf* **(a)** *(sens)* direction; **train en d. de Lille** train to Lille **(b)** *(de société, de club)* running, management; *(de parti)* leadership; **poste de d.** management post

dirigeant, -e [diriʒã, -ãt] **1** *adj (classe)* ruling **2** *nm (de pays)* leader; *(d'entreprise)* manager

diriger [diriʒe] **1** *vt (entreprise)* to run, to manage; *(pays, parti)* to lead; *(orchestre)* to conduct; *(acteur)* to direct; *(orienter)* to turn (**vers** to) **2 se diriger** *vpr* **se d. vers** *(lieu, objet)* to head for; *(personne)* to go up to

dis, disant [di, dizã] *voir* **dire**

discerner [disɛrne] *vt (voir)* to make out; *(différencier)* to distinguish (**de** from)

disciple [disipl] *nmf* disciple

discipline [disiplin] *nf (règle, matière)* discipline • **discipliné, -e** disciplined

discothèque [diskɔtɛk] *nf (organisme)* record library; *(club)* disco

discours [diskur] *nm* speech; **faire un d.** to make a speech

discréditer [diskredite] *vt* to discredit

discret, -ète [diskrɛ, -ɛt] *adj (personne, manière)* discreet; *(vêtement)* simple • **discrètement** *adv (avec retenue)* discreetly; *(sobrement)* simply • **discrétion** *nf* discretion; **laisser qch à la d. de qn** to leave sth to sb's discretion

discrimination [diskriminasjõ] *nf* discrimination

discussion [diskysjõ] *nf* discussion; **avoir une d.** to have a discussion (**sur** about)

discuter [diskyte] **1** *vt* to discuss; *(contester)* to question **2** *vi* **d. de qch avec qn** to discuss sth with sb

dise, disent [diz] *voir* **dire**

disloquer [dislɔke] **se disloquer** *vpr* **se d. le bras** to dislocate one's arm

disons [dizõ] *voir* **dire**

disparaître* [disparɛtr] *vi* to disappear; *(être porté manquant)* to go missing; *(mourir)* to die; **faire d. qch** to get rid of sth • **disparu, -e 1** *adj (personne)* missing; **être porté d.** to be reported missing **2** *nmf (absent)* missing person; *(mort)* departed

dispenser [dispãse] *vt (soins, bienfaits)* to dispense; **d. qn de qch** to exempt sb from sth; **d. qn de faire qch** to exempt sb from doing sth

disperser [dispɛrse] **1** *vt (papiers, foule)* to scatter; *(brouillard)* to disperse; *(collection)* to break up **2 se disperser** *vpr (foule)* to scatter, to disperse

disponible [dispɔnibl] *adj (article, place, personne)* available • **disponibilité** *nf* availability

disposé, -e [dispoze] *adj* **bien/mal d.** in a good/bad mood; **d. à faire qch** disposed to do sth

disposer [dispoze] **1** *vt (objets)* to arrange; **d. qn à (faire) qch** to dispose sb to (do) sth **2** *vi* **d. de qch** to have sth at one's disposal **3 se disposer** *vpr* **se d. à faire qch** to prepare to do sth

dispositif [dispozitif] *nm (mécanisme)* device

disposition [dispozisjɔ̃] *nf* arrangement; *(tendance)* tendency (à to); *(de maison, de page)* layout; **être** *ou* **rester à la d. de qn** to be *or* remain at sb's disposal

dispute [dispyt] *nf* quarrel ● **disputer 1** *vt (match)* to play; *(combat de boxe)* to fight; *(droit)* to contest; **d. qch à qn** *(prix, première place)* to fight with sb for *or* over sth **2 se disputer** *vpr* to quarrel (**avec** with); *(match)* to take place; **se d. qch** to fight over sth

disqualifier [diskalifje] *vt (équipe, athlète)* to disqualify

disque [disk] *nm (de musique)* record; *(cercle)* Br disc, Am disk; Ordinat disk; **d. compact** compact Br disc *or* Am disk; **d. dur** hard disk ● **disquette** *nf* Ordinat floppy (disk), diskette

disséquer [diseke] *vt* to dissect

dissertation [disɛrtasjɔ̃] *nf* essay

dissimuler [disimyle] **1** *vt (cacher)* to conceal (à from) **2 se dissimuler** *vpr* to be hidden

dissiper [disipe] **1** *vt (nuages)* to disperse; *(brouillard)* to clear; **d. qn** to lead sb astray **2 se dissiper** *vpr (nuage)* to disperse; *(brume)* to clear; *(élève)* to misbehave

dissocier [disɔsje] *vt* to dissociate (**de** from)

dissolvant [disɔlvã] *nm* solvent; *(pour vernis à ongles)* nail polish remover

dissoudre* [disudr] *vt,* **se dissoudre** *vpr* to dissolve

dissuader [disɥade] *vt* to dissuade (**de qch** from sth; **de faire** from doing)

distance [distãs] *nf* distance; **à deux mètres de d.** two metres apart; **à d.** at *or* from a distance; **garder ses distances** to keep one's distance (**vis-à-vis de** from)

distant, -e [distã, -ãt] *adj* distant; *(personne)* aloof, distant; **d. de dix kilomètres** *(éloigné)* ten kilometres away

distinct, -e [distɛ̃, -ɛ̃kt] *adj (différent)* distinct, separate (**de** from); *(net)* clear, distinct ● **distinction** *nf (différence, raffinement)* distinction

distinguer [distɛ̃ge] **1** *vt (différencier)* to distinguish; *(voir)* to make out; **d. le bien du mal** to tell good from evil **2 se distinguer** *vpr* **se d. de qn/qch (par)** to be distinguishable from sb/sth (by) ● **distingué, -e** *adj (bien élevé, éminent)* distinguished

distraction [distraksjɔ̃] *nf (étourderie)* absent-mindedness ● **distraire* 1** *vt (divertir)* to entertain; **d. qn** to distract sb (**de** from) **2 se distraire** *vpr* to amuse oneself ● **distrait, -e** *adj* absent-minded ● **distrayant, -e** *adj* entertaining

distribuer [distribɥe] *vt (donner)* & Com to distribute; *(courrier)* to deliver; *(cartes)* to deal

distributeur [distribytœr] *nm* Com distributor; **d. automatique** vending machine; **d. de billets** *(de train)* ticket machine; *(de billets de banque)* cash machine

distribution [distribysjɔ̃] *nf* distribution; *(du courrier)* delivery

district [distrikt] *nm* district

dit¹, -e [di, dit] **1** *pp de* **dire 2** *adj (convenu)* agreed; *(surnommé)* called

dit², dites [di, dit] *voir* **dire**

divan [divã] *nm* divan, couch

divers, -e [divɛr, -ɛrs] *adj (varié)* varied; **divers(es)** *(plusieurs)* various

diversion [divɛrsjɔ̃] *nf* diversion; **faire d.** to create a diversion

diversité [divɛrsite] *nf* diversity

divertir [divɛrtir] **1** *vt* to entertain **2 se divertir** *vpr* to enjoy oneself ● **divertissement** *nm* entertainment, amusement

divin, -e [divɛ̃, -in] *adj* divine

diviser [divize] *vt*, **se diviser** *vpr* to divide (**en** into) ● **division** *nf* division

divorce [divɔrs] *nm* divorce ● **divorcer** *vi* to get divorced; **d. d'avec qn** to divorce sb ● **divorcé, -e 1** *adj* divorced (**d'avec** from) **2** *nmf* divorcee

divulguer [divylge] *vt* to divulge

dix [dis] ([di] *before consonant*, [diz] *before vowel*) *adj & nm* ten ● **dix-huit** *adj & nm* eighteen ● **dixième** [dizjɛm] *adj & nmf* tenth; **un d.** a tenth ● **dix-neuf** *adj & nm* nineteen ● **dix-sept** *adj & nm* seventeen

dizaine [dizɛn] *nf* **une d. (de)** about ten

docile [dɔsil] *adj* docile

docteur [dɔktœr] *nm* (*en médecine, d'université*) doctor (**ès, en** of) ● **doctorat** *nm* doctorate, ≃ PhD (**ès/en** in)

doctrine [dɔktrin] *nf* doctrine

document [dɔkymɑ̃] *nm* document ● **documentaire** *adj & nm* documentary

documentation [dɔkymɑ̃tasjɔ̃] *nf* documentation

dodu, -e [dɔdy] *adj* plump

doigt [dwa] *nm* finger; **d. de pied** toe; **petit d.** little finger, *Am & Scot* pinkie; **montrer qn du d.** to point at sb

dois, doit [dwa] *voir* **devoir**

dollar [dɔlar] *nm* dollar

domaine [dɔmɛn] *nm* (*terres*) estate, domain; (*matière*) field; **être du d. public** to be in the public domain

dôme [dom] *nm* dome

domestique [dɔmɛstik] *adj* domestic

domicile [dɔmisil] *nm* home; (*demeure légale*) abode; **sans d. fixe** of no fixed abode

dominer [dɔmine] **1** *vt* to dominate; (*situation, sentiment*) to master **2** *vi* (*être le plus fort*) to be dominant ● **dominant, -e** *adj* dominant

dommage [dɔmaʒ] *nm* (*tort*) harm; **dommages** (*dégâts*) damage; **quel d.!** what a pity! what a shame!; **c'est (bien) d. qu'elle ne soit pas venue** it's a (great) pity *or* shame she didn't come; **dommages-intérêts** damages

dompter [dɔ̃(p)te] *vt* (*animal*) to tame

DOM-TOM [dɔmtɔm] (*abrév* **départements et territoires d'outre-mer**) *nmpl* = French overseas departments and territories

don [dɔ̃] *nm* (*cadeau, aptitude*) gift; (*d'argent*) donation; **d. du sang** blood donation

donation [dɔnasjɔ̃] *nf* donation

donc [dɔ̃(k)] *conj* so, then; (*par conséquent*) so, therefore; **asseyez-vous d.!** (*intensif*) do sit down!

donjon [dɔ̃ʒɔ̃] *nm* keep

données [dɔne] *nfpl Ordinat* data

donner [dɔne] **1** *vt* to give; (*récolte, résultat*) to produce; (*cartes*) to deal; (*pièce, film*) to put on; **pourriez-vous me d. l'heure?** could you tell me the time?; **d. un coup à qn** to hit sb; **d. à manger à qn** (*animal, enfant*) to feed sb; **elle m'a donné de ses nouvelles** she told me how she was doing; **ça donne soif/faim** it makes you thirsty/hungry; **étant**

donné... considering..., in view of...; **étant donné que...** seeing (that)…, considering (that)…; **à un moment donné** at some stage **2** *vi* **d. sur** *(fenêtre)* to overlook, to look out onto; *(porte)* to open onto **3 se donner** *vpr (se consacrer)* to devote oneself (**à** to); **se d. du mal** to go to a lot of trouble (**pour faire** to do)

donneur, -euse [dɔnœr, -øz] *nmf (de sang, d'organe)* donor

dont [dɔ̃] (= **de qui, duquel, de quoi**) *pron relatif (exprime la partie d'un tout) (personne)* of whom; *(chose)* of which; *(exprime l'appartenance) (personne)* whose, of whom; *(chose)* of which, whose; **une mère d. le fils est malade** a mother whose son is ill; **la fille d. il est fier** the daughter he is proud of *or* of whom he is proud; **les outils d. j'ai besoin** the tools I need; **la façon d. elle joue** the way (in which) she plays; **cinq enfants d. deux filles** five children two of whom are daughters, five children including two daughters; **voici ce d. il s'agit** here's what it's about

doper [dɔpe] **se doper** *vpr* to take drugs

dorénavant [dɔrenavɑ̃] *adv* from now on

dorer [dɔre] **1** *vt (objet)* to gild **2** *vi (à la cuisson)* to brown **3 se dorer** *vpr* **se d. au soleil** to sunbathe ● **doré, -e** *adj (objet)* gilt, gold; *(couleur)* golden

dormir* [dɔrmir] *vi* to sleep; *(être endormi)* to be asleep

dortoir [dɔrtwar] *nm* dormitory

dos [do] *nm (de personne, d'animal)* back; *(de livre)* spine; **'voir au d.'** *(verso)* 'see over'

dose [doz] *nf* dose; *(dans un mélange)* proportion ● **doser** *vt (médicament, ingrédients)* to measure out

dossier [dosje] *nm (de siège)* back; *(documents)* file

doter [dɔte] *vt (équiper)* to equip (**de** with); **doté d'une grande intelligence** endowed with great intelligence

douane [dwan] *nf* customs; **passer la d.** to go through customs ● **douanier, -ère** *nmf* customs officer

double [dubl] **1** *adj* double; **en d. exemplaire** in duplicate **2** *adv* double **3** *nm (de personne)* double; *(copie)* copy, duplicate; **le d. (de)** *(quantité)* twice as much (as); **je l'ai en d.** I have two of them

doubler [duble] **1** *vt (augmenter)* to double; *(vêtement)* to line; *(film)* to dub **2** *vi (augmenter)* to double **3** *vti (en voiture)* *Br* to overtake, *Am* to pass

doublure [dublyr] *nf (étoffe)* lining; *(au théâtre)* understudy

douce [dus] *voir* **doux** ● **doucement** *adv (délicatement)* gently; *(bas)* softly; *(lentement)* slowly; *(sans bruit)* quietly ● **douceur** *nf (de miel)* sweetness; *(de peau)* softness; *(de temps)* mildness; *(de personne)* gentleness

douche [duʃ] *nf* shower; **prendre une d.** to have *or* take a shower ● **se doucher** *vpr* to have *or* take a shower

doué, -e [dwe] *adj* gifted, talented (**en** at); **être d. pour qch** to have a gift for sth

douillet, -ette [duje, -ɛt] *adj (lit) Br* cosy, *Am* cozy

douleur [dulœr] *nf (mal)* pain; *(chagrin)* sorrow, grief ● **douloureux, -euse** *adj* painful

doute [dut] *nm* doubt; **sans d.** no doubt, probably; **sans aucun d.** without (any) doubt; **mettre qch en d.** to cast doubt on sth

douter [dute] **1** *vi* to doubt; **d. de qn/qch** to doubt sb/sth **2** *vt* **je doute qu'il soit assez fort** I doubt whether he's strong enough **3 se douter** *upr* **se d. de quelque chose** to suspect something

douteux, -euse [dutø, -øz] *adj (peu certain)* doubtful; *(louche, médiocre)* dubious

doux, douce [du, dus] *adj (miel, son)* sweet; *(peau, lumière)* soft; *(temps, climat)* mild; *(personne, pente)* gentle

douze [duz] *adj & nm* twelve • **douzaine** *nf (douze)* dozen; *(environ)* about twelve; **une d. d'œufs** a dozen eggs

dragée [draʒe] *nf* sugared almond

dragon [dragɔ̃] *nm* dragon

drainer [drene] *vt* to drain

drame [dram] *nm (genre littéraire)* drama; *(catastrophe)* tragedy • **dramatique** *adj* dramatic

drap [dra] *nm (de lit)* sheet; **d.-housse** fitted sheet; **d. de bain** bath towel

drapeau, -x [drapo] *nm* flag

dresser [drese] *vt (échelle, statue)* to put up, to erect; *(liste)* to draw up; *(animal)* to train; **d. les oreilles** to prick up one's ears • **dressage** *nm* training • **dresseur, -euse** *nmf* trainer

drogue [drɔg] *nf* drug; **d. dure/douce** hard/soft drug • **drogué, -e** *nmf* drug addict • **se droguer** *upr* to take drugs

droguerie [drɔgri] *nf* hardware *Br* shop *or Am* store

droit¹ [drwa] *nm (privilège)* right; *(d'inscription)* fee(s); **le d.** *(science juridique)* law; **avoir d. à qch** to be entitled to sth; **avoir le d. de faire qch** to be entitled to do sth, to have the right to do sth; **droits de l'homme** human rights

droit², droite¹ [drwa, drwat] **1** *adj (route, ligne)* straight; *(angle)* right **2** *adv* straight; **tout d.** straight *or* right ahead; **aller d. au but** to go straight to the point

droit³, droite² [drwa, drwat] *adj (côté, bras)* right

droite³ [drwat] *nf* **la d.** *(côté)* the right (side); *Pol* the right (wing); **à d.** *(tourner)* (to the) right; *(rouler, se tenir)* on the right, on the right(-hand) side; **de d.** *(fenêtre)* right-hand; *(candidat)* right-wing; **à d. de** on *or* to the right of

droitier, -ère [drwatje, -ɛr] *adj* right-handed

drôle [drol] *adj* funny

du [dy] *voir* **de¹,²**

dû, due [dy] *adj* **d. à** due to

duc [dyk] *nm* duke • **duchesse** *nf* duchess

dune [dyn] *nf* (sand) dune

duo [dɥo] *nm Mus* duet

duper [dype] *vt* to fool, to dupe

duplex [dypleks] *nm Br* maisonette, *Am* duplex

duquel [dykɛl] *voir* **lequel**

dur, -e [dyr] **1** *adj (substance)* hard; *(difficile)* hard, tough; *(hiver, ton)* harsh; *(personne)* hard, harsh; **d. d'oreille** hard of hearing **2** *adv (travailler)* hard • **durement** *adv* harshly

durant [dyrɑ̃] *prép* during; **d. l'hiver** during the winter; **des heures d.** for hours and hours

durée [dyre] *nf (de film, d'événement)* length; *(période)* duration; **de longue d.** *(bonheur)* lasting; **de courte d.** *(attente)* short; *(bonheur)* short-lived

durer [dyʀe] *vi* to last

duvet [dyvɛ] *nm (d'oiseau)* down; *(sac)* sleeping bag

dynamique [dinamik] *adj* dynamic

dynamite [dinamit] *nf* dynamite

dynamo [dinamo] *nf* dynamo

dyslexique [dislɛksik] *adj* dyslexic

Ee

E, e [ə] nm inv E, e

eau, -x [o] nf water; e. de toilette eau de toilette; e. du robinet tap water; e. douce fresh water • eau-de-vie (pl eaux-de-vie) nf brandy

éblouir [ebluir] vt to dazzle

éboueur [ebwœr] nm Br dustman, Am garbage collector

ébouillanter [ebujɑ̃te] 1 vt to scald 2 s'ébouillanter vpr to scald oneself

ébouriffé, -e [eburife] adj dishevelled

ébranler [ebrɑ̃le] vt (mur, confiance, personne) to shake

ébrécher [ebreʃe] vt (assiette) to chip; (lame) to nick

ébullition [ebylisjɔ̃] nf boiling; porter qch à é. to bring sth to the boil

écaille [ekaj] nf (de poisson) scale • s'écailler vpr (peinture) to peel (off)

écarquiller [ekarkije] vt é. les yeux to open one's eyes wide

écart [ekar] nm (intervalle) gap, distance; (différence) difference (de in; entre between); faire le grand é. to do the splits; à l'é. out of the way; à l'é. de qch away from sth

écarter [ekarte] 1 vt (objets, personnes) to move apart; (jambes, doigts) to spread; (idée) to brush aside; é. qch de qch to move sth away from sth 2 s'écarter vpr (a) (se séparer) (personnes) to move apart (de from); (foule) to part (b) (piéton) to move away (de from); s'é. du sujet to wander from the subject • écarté, -e adj les jambes écartées with one's legs (wide) apart

écervelé, -e [esɛrvəle] adj scatterbrained

échafaudage [eʃafodaʒ] nm scaffolding; des échafaudages scaffolding

échalote [eʃalɔt] nf shallot

échancré, -e [eʃɑ̃kre] adj low-cut

échange [eʃɑ̃ʒ] nm exchange; en é. in exchange (de for) • échanger vt to exchange (contre for)

échantillon [eʃɑ̃tijɔ̃] nm sample

échapper [eʃape] 1 vi é. à qn to escape from sb; son nom m'échappe his/her name escapes me; ça lui a échappé des mains it slipped out of his/her hands 2 s'échapper vpr (personne, gaz, eau) to escape (de from)

écharde [eʃard] nf splinter

écharpe [eʃarp] nf scarf; avoir le bras en é. to have one's arm in a sling

échauffer [eʃofe] s'échauffer vpr (sportif) to warm up

échéant [eʃeɑ̃] le cas échéant adv if need be

échec [eʃɛk] nm failure; les échecs (jeu) chess

échelle [eʃɛl] nf (a) (marches) ladder (b) (de carte) scale; à l'é. nationale on a national scale

échelon [eʃlɔ̃] *nm (d'échelle)* rung; *(d'employé)* grade

échiquier [eʃikje] *nm* chessboard

écho [eko] *nm (de son)* echo

échouer [eʃwe] *vi* to fail; **é. à** *(examen)* to fail

éclabousser [eklabuse] *vt* to splash, to spatter (**avec** with)

éclair [eklɛr] *nm* (**a**) *(lumière)* flash; *(d'orage)* flash of lightning (**b**) *(gâteau)* éclair

éclaircie [eklɛrsi] *nf* sunny spell

éclaircir [eklɛrsir] **1** *vt (couleur)* to lighten; *(mystère)* to clear up **2 s'éclaircir** *vpr (ciel)* to clear; *(mystère)* to be cleared up; **s'é. la voix** to clear one's throat ● **éclaircissement** *nm (explication)* explanation

éclairer [eklere] **1** *vt (pièce)* to light (up); **é. qn** *(avec une lampe)* to give sb some light; *(informer)* to enlighten sb (**sur** about) **2 s'éclairer** *vpr (visage)* to light up; **s'é. à la bougie** to use candlelight

éclaireur, -euse [eklɛrœr, -øz] *nmf* (boy) scout, (girl) guide

éclat [ekla] *nm* (**a**) *(de lumière)* brightness; *(de diamant)* flash (**b**) **é. de rire** burst of laughter

éclater [eklate] *vi (pneu)* to burst; *(bombe)* to go off, to explode; *(guerre)* to break out; **é. de rire** to burst out laughing; **é. en sanglots** to burst into tears

éclipse [eklips] *nf* eclipse

éclore* [eklɔr] *vi (œuf)* to hatch; *(fleur)* to open (out), to blossom

écœurer [ekœre] *vt* **é. qn** *(aliment)* to make sb feel sick; *(moralement)* to sicken sb ● **écœurant, -e** *adj* disgusting, sickening

école [ekɔl] *nf* school; **à l'é.** at school; **les grandes écoles** = university-level colleges specializing in

professional training; **é. privée** private school, *Br* public school, **é. publique** *Br* state school, *Am* public school ● **écolier, -ère** *nm* schoolboy, *f* schoolgirl

écologique [ekɔlɔʒik] *adj* ecological ● **écologiste** *adj & nm* environmentalist

économe [ekɔnɔm] *adj* thrifty

économie [ekɔnɔmi] *nf* economy; **économies** *(argent)* savings; **faire des économies** to save (up) ● **économique** *adj* (**a**) *(relatif à l'économie)* economic (**b**) *(avantageux)* economical

économiser [ekɔnɔmize] *vt* to save

écoper [ekɔpe] *vi Fam* **é. de qch** *(punition, amende)* to get sth

écorce [ekɔrs] *nf (d'arbre)* bark; *(de fruit)* peel

écorcher [ekɔrʃe] **1** *vt (érafler)* to graze **2 s'écorcher** *vpr* **s'é. le genou** to graze one's knee

Écosse [ekɔs] *nf* **l'É.** Scotland ● **écossais, -e 1** *adj* Scottish; *(tissu)* tartan **2** *nmf* **É., Écossaise** Scot

écouler [ekule] **s'écouler** *vpr (eau)* to flow out, to run out; *(temps)* to pass

écoute [ekut] *nf* listening; **être à l'é.** to be listening in (**de** to)

écouter [ekute] *vt* to listen to; **faire é. qch à qn** *(disque)* to play sb sth ● **écouteurs** *nmpl (casque)* headphones

écran [ekrɑ̃] *nm* screen; **à l'é.** on screen

écraser [ekraze] **1** *vt (broyer)* to crush; *(fruit, insecte)* to squash; *(piéton)* to run over; **se faire é. par une voiture** to get run over by a car **2 s'écraser** *vpr (avion)* to crash (**contre** into)

écrire* [ekrir] **1** *vt* to write; *(noter)* to write down **2** *vi* to write **3 s'écrire**

vpr (mot) to be spelt; **comment ça s'écrit?** how do you spell it? • **écrit** *nm* **par é.** in writing

écriteau, -x [ekrito] *nm* sign

écriture [ekrityr] *nf (système)* writing; *(calligraphie)* (hand)writing

écrivain [ekrivɛ̃] *nm* writer

écrou [ekru] *nm (de boulon)* nut

écrouler [ekrule] **s'écrouler** *vpr (édifice, personne)* to collapse

écru, -e [ekry] *adj (beige)* écru

écume [ekym] *nf (de mer)* foam

écureuil [ekyrœj] *nm* squirrel

écurie [ekyri] *nf* stable

édifice [edifis] *nm* edifice

Édimbourg [edɛ̃bur] *nm ou f* Edinburgh

éditer [edite] *vt (publier)* to publish; *Ordinat* to edit • **éditeur, -trice** *nmf (dans l'édition)* publisher • **édition** *nf (livre, journal)* edition; *(métier, diffusion)* publishing

éditorial, -aux [editɔrjal, -o] *nm (article)* editorial, *Br* leader

éducatif, -ive [edykatif, -iv] *adj* educational

éducation [edyk²sjɔ̃] *nf (enseignement)* education; *(des parents)* upbringing; **avoir de l'é.** to have good manners; **l'É. nationale** ≃ the Department of Education; **é. physique** physical education *or* training • **éduquer** *vt (à l'école)* to educate; *(à la maison)* to bring up

effacer [efase] *vt (avec une gomme)* to rub out, to erase; *(avec un chiffon)* to wipe away

effectif, -ive [efɛktif, -iv] **1** *adj (réel)* effective **2** *nm (employés)* staff • **effectivement** *adv (en effet)* actually

effectuer [efɛktɥe] *vt (expérience, geste difficile)* to carry out, to perform; *(paiement, trajet)* to make

effervescent, -e [efɛrvesã, -ãt] *adj (médicament)* effervescent

effet [efɛ] *nm (résultat)* effect; *(impression)* impression **(sur** on); **en e.** indeed, in fact; *Cin* **e. sonore** sound effect; *Cin* **effets spéciaux** special effects

efficace [efikas] *adj (mesure)* effective; *(personne)* efficient • **efficacité** *nf (de mesure)* effectiveness; *(de personne)* efficiency

effleurer [eflœre] *vt (frôler)* to brush against

effondrer [efɔ̃dre] **s'effondrer** *vpr (tomber, chuter)* to collapse; *Fig (perdre ses forces)* to go to pieces; **s'e. en larmes** to break down and cry

efforcer [efɔrse] **s'efforcer** *vpr* **s'e. de faire qch** to try hard to do sth

effort [efɔr] *nm* effort; **faire des efforts** to make an effort

effrayer [efreje] **1** *vt* to frighten, to scare **2 s'effrayer** *vpr* to be frightened *or* scared • **effrayant, -e** *adj* frightening, scary

effronté, -e [efrɔ̃te] *adj* rude

égal, -e, -aux, -ales [egal, -o] **1** *adj* equal **(à** to); *(régulier)* even; **ça m'est é.** it's all the same to me **2** *nmf (personne)* equal • **également** *adv (au même degré)* equally; *(aussi)* also, as well • **égaler** *vt* to equal, to match **(en** in); **3 plus 4 égale(nt) 7** 3 plus 4 equals 7 • **égalité** *nf* equality; *(régularité)* evenness; *(au tennis)* deuce; *Sport* **à é.** even, equal • **égalitaire** *adj* egalitarian

égard [egar] *nm* **à l'é. de** *(envers)* towards; **à cet é.** in this respect

égarer [egare] **1** *vt (objet)* to mislay; *(personne)* to mislead **2 s'égarer** *vpr (personne, lettre)* to get lost; *(objet)* to go astray

église [egliz] *nf* church

égoïste [egɔist] *adj* selfish

égout [egu] *nm* sewer

égoutter [egute] *vt* to drain

égratigner [egratiɲe] **1** *vt* to scratch **2 s'égratigner** *vpr* to scratch oneself

Égypte [eʒipt] *nf* **l'É.** Egypt ● **égyptien, -enne 1** *adj* Egyptian **2** *nmf* **É., Égyptienne** Egyptian

éjecter [eʒɛkte] *vt* to eject

élaborer [elabɔre] *vt (plan, idée)* to develop ● **élaboration** *nf (de plan, d'idée)* development

élan [elɑ̃] *nm (vitesse)* momentum; *(course)* run-up; **prendre son é.** to take a run-up

élargir [elarʒir] **1** *vt* to widen **2 s'élargir** *vpr* to widen (out)

élastique [elastik] **1** *adj (tissu)* elastic **2** *nm (lien)* rubber band, *Br* elastic band; *(pour la couture)* elastic

élection [elɛksjɔ̃] *nf* election ● **électoral, -e, -aux, -ales** *adj* **campagne électorale** election campaign; **liste électorale** electoral roll ● **électorat** *nm (électeurs)* electorate

électricien, -enne [elɛktrisjɛ̃, -ɛn] *nmf* electrician ● **électricité** *nf* electricity ● **électrique** *adj* electric

électrocuter [elɛktrɔkyte] *vt* to electrocute

électroménager [elɛktrɔmenaʒe] *adj m* **appareil é.** household electrical appliance

électronique [elɛktrɔnik] **1** *adj* electronic **2** *nf* electronics *(sing)*

élégant, -e [elegɑ̃, -ɑ̃t] *adj (bien habillé)* smart, elegant

élément [elemɑ̃] *nm* element

élémentaire [elemɑ̃tɛr] *adj* basic

éléphant [elefɑ̃] *nm* elephant

élevage [elvaʒ] *nm (production)* breeding (**de** of)

élevé, -e [elve] *adj (haut)* high; *(noble)* noble; **bien/mal é.** well-/bad-mannered

élève [elɛv] *nmf (à l'école)* pupil

élever [elve] **1** *vt (objection)* to raise; *(enfant)* to bring up; *(animal)* to breed **2 s'élever** *vpr (montagne)* to rise; *(monument)* to stand; **s'é. à** *(prix)* to amount to; **s'é. contre** to rise up against ● **éleveur, -euse** *nmf* breeder

éliminer [elimine] *vt* to eliminate ● **éliminatoire** *adj* **épreuve é.** *Sport* qualifying round, heat

élire* [elir] *vt* to elect (**à** to)

élite [elit] *nf* elite (**de** of)

elle [ɛl] *pron personnel* **(a)** *(sujet)* she; *(chose, animal)* it; **elles** they **(b)** *(complément)* her; *(chose, animal)* it; **elles** them ● **elle-même** *pron (personne)* herself; *(chose, animal)* itself; **elles-mêmes** themselves

éloge [elɔʒ] *nm* praise

éloigné, -e [elwaɲe] *adj (lieu)* far away, remote; **é. de** *(village, maison)* far (away) from; *(très différent)* far removed from

éloigner [elwaɲe] **1** *vt (chose, personne)* to move away (**de** from); **é. qn de qch** *(sujet, but)* to take sb away from sth **2 s'éloigner** *vpr (partir)* to move away (**de** from); **s'é. de qch** *(sujet, but)* to wander from sth

éloquent, -e [elɔkɑ̃, -ɑ̃t] *adj* eloquent

élu, -e [ely] **1** *pp de* **élire 2** *nmf Pol* elected member *or* representative

Élysée [elize] *nm* **(le palais de) l'É.** French President's residence

e-mail [imɛl] *nm* e-mail; **envoyer un e.** to send an e-mail (**à** to)

émail, -aux [emaj, -o] *nm* enamel

emballer [ɑ̃bale] *vt (dans une*

boîte) to pack; *(dans du papier)* to wrap (up) ● **emballage** *nm (action)* packing; *(dans du papier)* wrapping; *(boîte)* packaging; **papier d'e.** wrapping paper

embarquer [ɑ̃barke] **1** *vt (passagers)* to take on board; *(marchandises)* to load **2** *vi* to (go on) board ● **embarquement** *nm (de passagers)* boarding

embarras [ɑ̃bara] *nm (gêne)* embarrassment; **dans l'e.** in an awkward situation; *(financièrement)* in financial difficulties

embarrasser [ɑ̃barase] **1** *vt (encombrer)* to clutter up; *(mettre mal à l'aise)* to embarrass **2** **s'embarrasser** *vpr* **s'e. de qch** to burden oneself with sth ● **embarrassant, -e** *adj (paquet)* cumbersome; *(question)* embarrassing

embaucher [ɑ̃boʃe] *vt (ouvrier)* to hire, to take on

embellir [ɑ̃belir] *vt (pièce, personne)* to make more attractive

embêter [ɑ̃bete] *Fam* **1** *vt (agacer)* to annoy; *(ennuyer)* to bore **2** **s'embêter** *vpr (s'ennuyer)* to get bored ● **embêtant, -e** *adj Fam* annoying

emblème [ɑ̃blɛm] *nm* emblem

embouteillage [ɑ̃butɛjaʒ] *nm* traffic jam

embrasser [ɑ̃brase] **1** *vt* **e. qn** *(donner un baiser à)* to kiss sb; *(serrer)* to hug sb **2** **s'embrasser** *vpr* to kiss (each other)

embrayage [ɑ̃brejaʒ] *nm Aut (mécanisme, pédale)* clutch

embrouiller [ɑ̃bruje] **1** *vt (fils)* to tangle (up); **e. qn** to confuse sb, to get sb muddled **2** **s'embrouiller** *vpr* to get confused *or* muddled (**dans** in *or* with)

embuscade [ɑ̃byskad] *nf* ambush

émeraude [emrod] *nf & adj inv* emerald

émerger [emɛrʒe] *vi* to emerge (**de** from)

émerveiller [emɛrveje] **1** *vt* to amaze, to fill with wonder **2** **s'émerveiller** *vpr* to marvel, to be filled with wonder (**de** at)

émettre* [emɛtr] *vt (lumière, son)* to emit; *(message radio)* to broadcast; *(monnaie)* to issue

émeute [emøt] *nf* riot

émigrer [emigre] *vi (personne)* to emigrate ● **émigrant, -e** *nmf* emigrant ● **émigration** *nf* emigration ● **émigré, -e** *nmf* exile

éminent, -e [eminɑ̃, -ɑ̃t] *adj* eminent

émission [emisjɔ̃] *nf (de radio)* programme; *(de lumière, de son)* emission (**de** of)

emmêler [ɑ̃mele] **1** *vt (fil, cheveux)* to tangle (up) **2** **s'emmêler** *vpr* to get tangled

emménager [ɑ̃menaʒe] *vi* to move in; **e. dans** to move into

emmener [ɑ̃mne] *vt* to take (**à** to); *(prisonnier)* to take away; **e. qn faire une promenade** to take sb for a walk; **e. qn en voiture** to give sb a *Br* lift *or Am* ride

emmitoufler [ɑ̃mitufle] **s'emmitoufler** *vpr* to wrap (oneself) up (**dans** in)

émotion [emosjɔ̃] *nf* emotion

émoussé, -e [emuse] *adj (pointe)* blunt

émouvoir* [emuvwar] **1** *vt (affecter)* to move, to touch **2** **s'émouvoir** *vpr* to be moved *or* touched ● **émouvant, -e** *adj* moving, touching

emparer [ɑ̃pare] **s'emparer** *vpr* **s'e. de** *(personne, objet)* to seize; *(sujet: émotion)* to take hold of

empêcher [ɑ̃peʃe] *vt* to prevent, to stop; **e. qn de faire qch** to prevent *or* stop sb from doing sth • **empêchement** [-ɛʃmɑ̃] *nm* hitch; **il a/j'ai eu un e.** something came up

empereur [ɑ̃prœr] *nm* emperor

empester [ɑ̃pɛste] **1** *vt (tabac)* to stink of; *(pièce)* to stink out **2** *vi* to stink

empire [ɑ̃pir] *nm* empire

emplacement [ɑ̃plasmɑ̃] *nm (de construction)* site, location; *(de stationnement)* place

emploi [ɑ̃plwa] *nm* **(a)** *(usage)* use; **e. du temps** timetable **(b)** *(travail)* job; **sans e.** unemployed

employer [ɑ̃plwaje] **1** *vt (utiliser)* to use; *(personne)* to employ **2** **s'employer** *vpr (expression)* to be used • **employé, -e** *nmf* employee; **e. de banque** bank clerk; **e. de bureau** office worker • **employeur, -euse** *nmf* employer

empoisonner [ɑ̃pwazɔne] **1** *vt (personne, aliment)* to poison **2** **s'empoisonner** *vpr (par accident)* to be poisoned; *(volontairement)* to poison oneself

emporter [ɑ̃pɔrte] **1** *vt (prendre)* to take (**avec soi** with one); *(transporter)* to take away; *(entraîner)* to carry along *or* away; *(par le vent)* to blow off *or* away; **pizza à e.** takeaway pizza; **l'e. sur qn** to get the upper hand over sb **2** **s'emporter** *vpr* to lose one's temper (**contre** with)

empreinte [ɑ̃prɛ̃t] *nf* mark; **e. digitale** fingerprint

empresser [ɑ̃prese] **s'empresser** *vpr* **s'e. de faire qch** to hasten to do sth

emprise [ɑ̃priz] *nf* hold (**sur** over)

emprisonner [ɑ̃prizɔne] *vt* to imprison • **emprisonnement** *nm* imprisonment

emprunt [ɑ̃prœ̃] *nm (argent)* loan; **faire un e.** *(auprès d'une banque)* to take out a loan • **emprunter** *vt (argent, objet)* to borrow (**à qn** from sb); *(route)* to take

ému, -e [emy] **1** *pp de* **émouvoir** **2** *adj (attendri)* moved; *(attristé)* upset; **une voix émue** a voice charged with emotion

en[1] [ɑ̃] *prép* **(a)** *(indique le lieu)* in; *(indique la direction)* to **(b)** *(indique le temps)* in **(c)** *(indique le moyen)* by; *(indique l'état)* in; **en avion** by plane; **en fleur** in flower; **en congé** on leave **(d)** *(indique la matière)* in; **en bois** made of wood, wooden; **chemise en Nylon®** nylon shirt; **c'est en or** it's (made of) gold **(e)** *(domaine)* **étudiant en anglais** English student; **docteur en médecine** doctor of medicine **(f)** *(comme)* **en cadeau** as a present; **en ami** as a friend **(g)** *(+ participe présent)* **en souriant** smiling, with a smile; **en chantant** while singing; **en apprenant que...** on hearing that...; **sortir en courant** to run out **(h)** *(transformation)* into; **traduire en français** to translate into French

en[2] [ɑ̃] *pron* **(a)** *(indique la provenance)* from there; **j'en viens** I've just come from there **(b)** *(remplace les compléments introduits par 'de')* **en parler** to talk about it; **il en est content** he's pleased with it/them; **il s'en souviendra** he'll remember it **(c)** *(partitif)* some; **j'en ai** I have some; **en veux-tu?** do you want some?; **donne-m'en** give some to me

ENA [ena] (*abrév* **École natio-nale d'administration**) *nf* = university-level college preparing students for senior positions in law and economics

encadrer [ãkadre] *vt* (*tableau*) to frame; (*mot*) to circle; (*personnel*) to manage

encaisser [ãkese] *vt* (*argent*) to collect; (*chèque*) to cash

enceinte¹ [ãsɛ̃t] *adj f* (*femme*) pregnant

enceinte² [ãsɛ̃t] *nf* (*muraille*) (surrounding) wall; (*espace*) enclosure; **dans l'e. de** within, inside; **e. (acoustique)** speaker

encercler [ãsɛrkle] *vt* (*lieu, ennemi*) to surround, to encircle; (*mot*) to circle

enchaîner [ãʃene] *vt* (*animal, prisonnier*) to chain up; (*idées*) to link (up) • **enchaînement** *nm* (*succession*) chain, series; (*liaison*) link(ing) (*de between or of*)

enchanter [ãʃãte] *vt* (*ravir*) to delight, to enchant • **enchanté, -e** *adj* (*ravi*) delighted (**de** with); (*magique*) enchanted; **e. de faire votre connaissance!** pleased to meet you!

enchère [ãʃɛr] *nf* (*offre*) bid; **vente aux enchères** auction

enchevêtrer [ãʃəvetre] **s'enche-vêtrer** *vpr* to get entangled (**dans** in)

enclos [ãklo] *nm* enclosure

encolure [ãkɔlyr] *nf* (*de vêtement*) neck

encombre [ãkɔ̃br] **sans encombre** *adv* without a hitch

encombrer [ãkɔ̃bre] **1** *vt* (*pièce, couloir*) to clutter up (**de** with); (*rue, passage*) to block; **e. qn** to hamper sb **2 s'encombrer** *vpr* **s'e. de qch** to load oneself down with sth • **encombrant, -e** *adj* (*paquet*)

bulky, cumbersome • **encombré, -e** *adj* (*lignes téléphoniques, route*) jammed

encontre [ãkɔ̃tr] **à l'encontre de** *prép* against

encore [ãkɔr] *adv* (a) (*toujours*) still (b) (*avec négation*) **pas e.** not yet; **je ne suis pas e. prêt** I'm not ready yet (c) (*de nouveau*) again (d) (*de plus, en plus*) **e. un café** another coffee; **e. une fois** (once) again, once more; **e. un** another (one), one more; **e. du pain** (some) more bread; **quoi e.?** what else? (e) (*avec comparatif*) even, still; **e. mieux** even better, better still (f) (*aussi*) **mais e.** but also (g) **et e.** (*à peine*) if that, only just (h) **e. que...** (+ *subjunctive*) although...

encourager [ãkuraʒe] *vt* to encourage (**à faire** to do) • **encourageant, -e** *adj* encouraging • **encouragement** *nm* encouragement

encre [ãkr] *nf* ink

encyclopédie [ãsiklɔpedi] *nf* encyclopedia

endetter [ãdete] **s'endetter** *vpr* to get into debt • **endettement** *nm* debt

endive [ãdiv] *nf* chicory, endive

endormir* [ãdɔrmir] **1** *vt* (*enfant*) to put to sleep; (*ennuyer*) to send to sleep **2 s'endormir** *vpr* to fall asleep, to go to sleep • **endormi, -e** *adj* asleep, sleeping

endroit [ãdrwa] *nm* (*lieu*) place

enduire* [ãdɥir] *vt* to smear, to coat (**de** with)

endurance [ãdyrãs] *nf* stamina • **endurer** *vt* to endure, to bear

énergie [enɛrʒi] *nf* energy • **énergique** *adj* (*personne*) ener-getic; (*mesure, ton*) forceful

énerver [enɛrve] **1** *vt* **é. qn** *(irriter)* to get on sb's nerves; *(rendre nerveux)* to make sb nervous **2 s'énerver** *vpr* to get worked up • **énervé, -e** *adj (agacé)* irritated; *(excité)* on edge, agitated

enfance [ãfãs] *nf* childhood • **enfantin, -e** *adj (voix, joie)* childlike; *(simple)* easy

enfant [ãfã] *nmf* child *(pl* children); **attendre un e.** to be expecting a baby

enfer [ãfɛr] *nm* hell

enfermer [ãfɛrme] **1** *vt (personne, chose)* to shut up; **e. qn/qch à clé** to lock sb/sth up **2 s'enfermer** *vpr* **s'e. dans** *(chambre)* to shut oneself (up) in; **s'e. à clé** to lock oneself in

enfiler [ãfile] *vt (aiguille, perles)* to thread; *Fam (vêtement)* to slip on

enfin [ãfɛ̃] *adv (à la fin)* finally, at last; *(en dernier lieu)* lastly; *(en somme)* in a word; *(de résignation)* well; *Fam* **e. bref...** *(en somme)* in a word...; **(mais) e.!** for heaven's sake!

enfler [ãfle] *vi* to swell (up)

enfoncer [ãfɔ̃se] *vt (clou)* to bang in; *(porte)* to smash in; **e. dans qch** *(couteau, mains)* to plunge into sth

enfuir* [ãfɥir] **s'enfuir** *vpr* to run away **(de** from)

engager [ãgaʒe] **1** *vt (discussion, combat)* to start; *(clé)* to insert **(dans** into); **e. qn** *(embaucher)* to hire sb **2 s'engager** *vpr (dans l'armée)* to enlist; *(prendre position)* to commit oneself; *(partie)* to start; **s'e. à faire qch** to undertake to do sth; **s'e. dans** *(voie)* to enter; *(affaire)* to get involved in • **engagé, -e** *adj (écrivain)* committed • **engagement** *nm (promesse)* commitment; **prendre l'e. de faire qch** to undertake to do sth

engin [ãʒɛ̃] *nm (machine)* machine; *(outil)* device; **e. spatial** spacecraft

englober [ãglɔbe] *vt* to include

engloutir [ãglutir] *vt (nourriture)* to wolf down

engorger [ãgɔrʒe] *vt* to block up, to clog

engouement [ãgumã] *nm* craze **(pour** for)

engouffrer [ãgufre] **s'engouffrer** *vpr* **s'e. dans** to rush into

engourdir [ãgurdir] **s'engourdir** *vpr (membre)* to go numb

engrais [ãgrɛ] *nm* fertilizer

engraisser [ãgrese] *vt (animal, personne)* to fatten up

engrenage [ãgrənaʒ] *nm Tech* gears; *Fig* **pris dans l'e.** caught in a trap

énigme [enigm] *nf (devinette)* riddle; *(mystère)* enigma • **énigmatique** *adj* enigmatic

enjeu, -x [ãʒø] *nm (mise)* stake; *Fig (de pari, de guerre)* stakes

enjoliver [ãʒɔlive] *vt* to embellish

enlacer [ãlase] *vt (mêler)* to entwine; *(embrasser)* to clasp

enlever [ãl(ə)ve] **1** *vt* to remove; *(meubles)* to take away, to remove; *(vêtement, couvercle)* to take off, to remove; *(enfant)* to kidnap, to abduct; *(ordures)* to collect **2 s'enlever** *vpr (tache)* to come out; *(vernis)* to come off • **enlèvement** [-ɛvmã] *nm (d'enfant)* kidnapping, abduction *(d'objet)* removal

enliser [ãlize] **s'enliser** *vpr* to get bogged down **(dans** in)

ennemi, -e [enmi] *nmf* enemy

ennui [ãnɥi] *nm (lassitude)* boredom; *(souci)* problem; **avoir des ennuis** *(soucis)* to be worried *(problèmes)* to have problems

ennuyer [ãnɥije] **1** *vt (agacer)* to annoy; *(préoccuper)* to bother; *(lasser)* to bore **2 s'ennuyer** *vpr* to get bored • **ennuyé, -e** *adj (air)* bored • **ennuyeux, -euse** *adj (contrariant)* annoying; *(lassant)* boring

énoncer [enɔ̃se] *vt* to state

énorme [enɔrm] *adj* enormous, huge • **énormément** *adv (travailler, pleurer)* an awful lot; **je le regrette é.** I'm awfully sorry about it; **il n'a pas é. d'argent** he hasn't got a huge amount of money

enquête [ãkɛt] *nf (de policiers, de journalistes)* investigation; *(judiciaire, administrative)* inquiry; *(sondage)* survey • **enquêter** *vi (policier, journaliste)* to investigate; **e. sur qch** to investigate sth

enrager [ãraʒe] *vi* to be furious **(de faire** about doing); **faire e. qn** to get on sb's nerves

enregistrer [ãrəʒistre] *vt (par écrit, sur bande)* to record; *(afficher)* to register; **faire e. ses bagages** *(à l'aéroport)* to check in, to check one's baggage in • **enregistrement** *nm (sur bande)* recording; **l'e. des bagages** *(à l'aéroport)* **se présenter à l'e.** to check in

enrhumer [ãryme] **s'enrhumer** *vpr* to catch a cold; **être enrhumé** to have a cold

enrichir [ãriʃir] **1** *vt* to enrich **(de** with) **2 s'enrichir** *vpr (personne)* to get rich

enrober [ãrɔbe] *vt* to coat **(de** in)

enrouler [ãrule] **1** *vt (fil)* to wind **2 s'enrouler** *vpr* **s'e. dans qch** *(couvertures)* to wrap oneself up in sth; **s'e. sur** *ou* **autour de qch** to wind round sth

enseignant, -e [ãsɛɲã, -ãt] *nmf*

teacher

enseigne [ãsɛɲ] *nf* sign

enseigner [ãseɲe] **1** *vt* to teach; **e. qch à qn** to teach sb sth **2** *vi* to teach • **enseignement** [-ɛɲmã] *nm* education; *(action, métier)* teaching; **e. privé** private education; **e. public** *Br* state *or* *Am* public education

ensemble [ãsãbl] **1** *adv* together; **aller (bien) e.** *(couleurs)* to go (well) together; *(personnes)* to be well-matched **2** *nm (d'objets)* group, set; *(vêtement)* outfit; **l'e. du personnel** *(totalité)* the whole staff; **dans l'e.** on the whole

ensoleillé, -e [ãsɔleje] *adj* sunny

ensorceler [ãsɔrsəle] *vt* to bewitch

ensuite [ãsɥit] *adv (puis)* next, then; *(plus tard)* afterwards

entailler [ãtaje] *vt (fendre)* to notch; *(blesser)* to gash, to slash

entamer [ãtame] *vt (pain)* to cut into; *(bouteille, boîte)* to open; *(négociations)* to enter into

entasser [ãtase] *vt*, **s'entasser** *vpr (objets)* to pile up, to heap up

entendre [ãtãdr] **1** *vt* to hear; *(comprendre)* to understand; **e. parler de qn/qch** to hear of sb/sth; **e. dire que...** to hear (it said) that... **2 s'entendre** *vpr (être entendu)* to be heard; *(être compris)* to be understood; **s'e.** *(être d'accord)* to agree **(sur** on); **(bien) s'e. avec qn** to get along *or Br* on with sb

entendu, -e [ãtãdy] *adj (convenu)* agreed; *(sourire, air)* knowing; **e.!** all right!; **bien e.** of course

entente [ãtãt] *nf* agreement

enterrer [ãtere] *vt (défunt)* to bury • **enterrement** [-ɛrmã] *nm (ensevelissement)* burial; *(funérailles)* funeral

en-tête [ãtɛt] (*pl* **en-têtes**) *nm* (*de papier*) heading; **papier à e.** headed paper, letterhead

entêté, -e [ãtete] *adj* stubborn

enthousiasme [ãtuzjasm] *nm* enthusiasm • **enthousiaste** *adj* enthusiastic

enticher [ãtiʃe] **s'enticher** *vpr* **s'e. de qn/qch** to become infatuated with sb/sth

entier, -ère [ãtje, -ɛr] **1** *adj* (*total*) whole, entire; (*intact*) intact; **le pays tout e.** the whole *or* entire country **2** *nm* **en e.** in its entirety, completely

entonnoir [ãtɔnwar] *nm* funnel

entorse [ãtɔrs] *nf Méd* sprain; **se faire une e. à la cheville** to sprain one's ankle

entourage [ãturaʒ] *nm* (*proches*) circle of family and friends

entourer [ãture] **1** *vt* to surround (**de** with); (*envelopper*) to wrap (**de** in); **entouré de** surrounded by **2 s'entourer** *vpr* **s'e. de** to surround oneself with

entracte [ãtrakt] *nm Br* interval, *Am* intermission

entraider [ãtrede] **s'entraider** *vpr* to help each other

entraîner [ãtrene] **1** *vt* (**a**) (*charrier*) to carry away; (*causer*) to bring about; (*dépenses*) to entail; **e. qn** (*emmener*) to lead sb away; (*de force*) to drag sb away; (*attirer*) to lure sb; **se laisser e.** to allow oneself to be led astray (**b**) (*athlète, cheval*) to train (**à** for) **2 s'entraîner** *vpr* to train oneself (**à faire qch** to do sth); *Sport* to train • **entraînement** *nm Sport* training • **entraîneur** *nm* (*d'athlète*) coach; (*de cheval*) trainer

entre [ãtr] *prép* between; (*parmi*) among(st); **l'un d'e. vous** one of you

entrecôte [ãtrəkot] *nf* rib steak

entrée [ãtre] *nf* (*action*) entry, entrance; (*porte*) entrance; (*vestibule*) entrance hall; (*accès*) admission, entry (**de** to); (*plat*) starter; **'e. interdite'** 'no entry', 'no admittance'; **'e. libre'** 'admission free'

entrepôt [ãtrəpo] *nm* warehouse

entreprendre* [ãtrəprãdr] *vt* (*travail, voyage*) to undertake; **e. de faire qch** to undertake to do sth

entrepreneur [ãtrəprənœr] *nm* (*en bâtiment*) contractor; (*chef d'entreprise*) entrepreneur

entreprise [ãtrəpriz] *nf* (*firme*) company, firm

entrer [ãtre] *vi* (*aux* **être**) (*aller*) to go in, to enter; (*venir*) to come in, to enter; **e. dans** to go into; (*pièce*) to come/go into, to enter; **e. à l'université** to start university; **e. dans les détails** to go into detail; **entrez!** come in!

entre-temps [ãtrətã] *adv* meanwhile

entretenir* [ãtrətnir] *vt* (*voiture, maison, famille*) to maintain; (*relations*) to keep; **e. qn de qch** to talk to sb about sth • **entretenu, -e** *adj* **bien/mal e.** (*maison*) well-kept/badly kept

entretien [ãtrətjɛ̃] *nm* (*de route, de maison*) maintenance, upkeep; (*entrevue*) interview

entrevoir* [ãtrəvwar] *vt* (*rapidement*) to catch a glimpse of

entrevue [ãtrəvy] *nf* interview

entrouvert, -e [ãtruvɛr, -ɛrt] *adj* (*porte, fenêtre*) half-open

énumérer [enymere] *vt* to list

envahir [ãvair] *vt* (*pays*) to invade; *Fig* **e. qn** (*doute, peur*) to overcome sb • **envahisseur** *nm* invader

enveloppe [ãvlɔp] *nf (pour lettre)* envelope

envelopper [ãvlɔpe] **1** *vt* to wrap (up) (**dans** in) **2 s'envelopper** *vpr* to wrap oneself (up) (**dans** in)

envers [ãvɛr] **1** *prép Br* towards, *Am* toward(s), to **2** *nm (de tissu)* wrong side; **à l'e.** *(chaussette)* inside out; *(pantalon)* back to front; *(la tête en bas)* upside down

envie [ãvi] *nf (jalousie)* envy; *(désir)* desire; **avoir e. de qch** to want sth; **avoir e. de faire qch** to feel like doing sth ● **envier** *vt* to envy (**qch à qn** sb sth) ● **envieux, -euse** *adj* envious

environ [ãvirɔ̃] *adv (à peu près)* about ● **environs** *nmpl* outskirts, surroundings; **aux e. de qch** around sth, in the vicinity of sth

environnement [ãvirɔnmã] *nm* environment

envisager [ãvizaʒe] *vt (considérer)* to consider; *(projeter) Br* to envisage, *Am* to envision; **e. de faire qch** to consider doing sth

envoi [ãvwa] *nm (action)* sending

envoler [ãvɔle] **s'envoler** *vpr (oiseau)* to fly away; *(avion)* to take off; *(chapeau, papier)* to blow away; *Fig (espoir)* to vanish

envoûter [ãvute] *vt* to bewitch

envoyer* [ãvwaje] *vt* to send; **e. chercher qn** to send for sb

épais, -aisse [epɛ, -ɛs] *adj* thick ● **épaisseur** *nf* thickness; **avoir une mètre d'é.** to be one metre thick

épanouir [epanwir] **s'épanouir** *vpr (fleur)* to bloom; *Fig (personne)* to blossom; *(visage)* to beam ● **épanoui, -e** *adj (fleur, personne)* in full bloom; *(visage)* beaming ● **épanouissement** *nm (de fleur)* full bloom; *(de personne)* blossoming

épargne [eparɲ] *nf (action)* saving; *(sommes)* savings ● **épargner** *vt (argent, provisions)* to save; *(ennemi)* to spare; **e. qch à qn** *(ennuis, chagrin)* to spare sb sth

éparpiller [eparpije] *vt,* **s'éparpiller** *vpr* to scatter;

épaule [epol] *nf* shoulder ● **épaulette** *nf (de veste)* shoulder pad

épave [epav] *nf (bateau, personne)* wreck

épée [epe] *nf* sword

épeler [eple] *vt* to spell

épi [epi] *nm (de blé)* ear

épice [epis] *nf* spice ● **épicé, -e** *adj (plat, récit)* spicy

épicier, -ère [episje, -ɛr] *nmf* grocer ● **épicerie** *nf (magasin) Br* grocer's (shop), *Am* grocery (store)

épidémie [epidemi] *nf* epidemic

épier [epje] *vt (observer)* to watch closely; *(occasion)* to watch out for; **é. qn** to spy on sb

épiler [epile] **s'épiler** *vpr* to remove unwanted hair; **s'é. les jambes à la cire** to wax one's legs

épilogue [epilɔg] *nm* epilogue

épinards [epinar] *nmpl* spinach

épineux, -euse [epinø, -øz] *adj (tige, question)* thorny

épingle [epɛ̃gl] *nf* pin; **é. à nourrice** safety pin; **é. à linge** *Br* clothes peg, *Am* clothes pin

épisode [epizɔd] *nm* episode

éplucher [eplyʃe] *vt (carotte, pomme)* to peel

éponge [epɔ̃ʒ] *nf* sponge; *Fig* **jeter l'é.** to throw in the towel ● **éponger** *vt (liquide)* to mop up

époque [epɔk] *nf (date)* time, period; *(historique)* age; **à l'é.** at the *or* that time

épouse [epuz] *nf* wife

épouser [epuze] *vt* to marry

épousseter [epuste] *vt* to dust

épouvantable [epuvɑ̃tabl] *adj* appalling

époux [epu] *nm* husband; **les é.** the husband and wife

épreuve [eprœv] *nf* (*essai, examen*) test; (*sportive*) event; (*malheur*) ordeal, trial; (*photo*) print; **mettre à l'é.** to put to the test

éprouver [epruve] *vt* (*méthode, personne*) to test; (*sentiment*) to feel; (*difficultés*) to meet with

éprouvette [epruvɛt] *nf* test tube

épuiser [epɥize] **1** *vt* (*personne, provisions, sujet*) to exhaust **2** **s'épuiser** *vpr* (*réserves, patience*) to run out; **s'é. à faire qch** to exhaust oneself doing sth • **épuisant, -e** *adj* exhausting • **épuisé, -e** *adj* exhausted; (*marchandise*) sold out

équateur [ekwatœr] *nm* equator; **sous l'é.** at the equator

équation [ekwasjɔ̃] *nf* Math equation

équerre [ekɛr] *nf* **é. (à dessin)** *Br* set square, *Am* triangle

équilibre [ekilibr] *nm* balance; **garder/perdre l'é.** to keep/lose one's balance

équilibrer [ekilibre] *vt* (*charge, budget*) to balance

équipage [ekipaʒ] *nm* (*de navire, d'avion*) crew

équipe [ekip] *nf* team

équiper [ekipe] **1** *vt* to equip (**de** with) **2** **s'équiper** *vpr* to equip oneself (**de** with) • **équipement** *nm* equipment

équitable [ekitabl] *adj* fair

équitation [ekitasjɔ̃] *nf Br* (horse) riding, *Am* (horseback) riding; **faire de l'é.** to go riding

équivalent, -e [ekivalɑ̃, -ɑ̃t] *adj* & *nm* equivalent • **équivaloir*** *vi* **é. à qch** to be equivalent to sth

équivoque [ekivɔk] *adj* (*ambigu*) equivocal; (*douteux*) dubious

érable [erabl] *nm* maple

érafler [erafle] *vt* to graze, to scratch • **éraflure** *nf* graze, scratch

ère [ɛr] *nf* era; **avant notre è.** BC; **en l'an 800 de notre è.** in the year 800 AD

érosion [erozjɔ̃] *nf* erosion • **éroder** *vt* to erode

errer [ɛre] *vi* to wander • **errant, -e** *adj* **chien/chat e.** stray dog/cat

erreur [ɛrœr] *nf* (*faute*) mistake, error; **par e.** by mistake

éruption [erypsjɔ̃] *nf* (*de volcan*) eruption; (*de boutons*) rash

es [ɛ] *voir* **être**

ès [ɛs] *prép* of; **licencié ès lettres** ≃ BA; **docteur ès lettres** ≃ PhD

escabeau, -x [ɛskabo] *nm* (*marchepied*) stepladder

escalade [ɛskalad] *nf* climbing

escale [ɛskal] *nf* **faire e. à** (*avion*) to stop (over) at; (*navire*) to put in at

escalier [ɛskalje] *nm* (*marches*) stairs; (*cage*) staircase; **l'é., les escaliers** the stairs; **e. mécanique** *ou* **roulant** escalator; **e. de secours** fire escape

escalope [ɛskalɔp] *nf* escalope

escargot [ɛskargo] *nm* snail

escarpé, -e [ɛskarpe] *adj* steep • **escarpement** [-əmɑ̃] *nm* (*côte*) steep slope

escarpin [ɛskarpɛ̃] *nm* (*soulier*) pump, *Br* court shoe

esclave [ɛsklav] *nmf* slave • **esclavage** *nm* slavery

escorte [ɛskɔrt] *nf* escort • **escorter** *vt* to escort

escrime [ɛskrim] *nf* fencing; **faire de l'e.** to fence

escroc [ɛskro] *nm* crook, swindler • **escroquer** *vt* e. qn to swindle sb; **e. qch à qn** to swindle sb out of sth • **escroquerie** *nf (action)* swindling; *(résultat)* swindle

espace [ɛspas] *nm* space; **e. vert** garden, park

espacer [ɛspase] *vt* to space out

espadrille [ɛspadrij] *nf* = rope-soled sandal

Espagne [ɛspaɲ] *nf* l'E. Spain • **espagnol, -e 1** *adj* Spanish **2** *nmf* E., **Espagnole** Spaniard **3** *nm (langue)* Spanish

espèce [ɛspɛs] *nf (race)* species; *(genre)* kind, sort • **espèces** *nfpl (argent)* cash; **en e.** in cash

espérance [ɛsperɑ̃s] *nf* hope; **e. de vie** life expectancy

espérer [ɛspere] **1** *vt* to hope for; **e. que...** to hope that...; **e. faire qch** to hope to do sth **2** *vi* to hope; **j'espère (bien)!** I hope so!

espiègle [ɛspjɛgl] *adj* mischievous

espion, -onne [ɛspjɔ̃, -ɔn] *nmf* spy • **espionnage** *nm* spying, espionage • **espionner 1** *vt* to spy on **2** *vi* to spy

espoir [ɛspwar] *nm* hope

esprit [ɛspri] *nm (attitude, fantôme)* spirit; *(intellect)* mind; *(humour)* wit; **venir à l'e. de qn** to cross sb's mind; **avoir de l'e.** to be witty; **avoir l'e. large/étroit** to be broad-/narrow-minded

esquimau, -aude, -aux, -audes [ɛskimo, -od] **1** *adj* Eskimo, *Am* Inuit **2** *nmf* E., **Esquimaude** Eskimo, *Am* Inuit

esquisse [ɛskis] *nf (croquis, plan)* sketch • **esquisser** *vt* to sketch

esquiver [ɛskive] **1** *vt (coup, problème)* to dodge **2** s'**esquiver** *vpr* to slip away

essai [ɛsɛ] *nm (test)* test, trial; *(tentative)* try; *(ouvrage)* essay

essayer [eseje] *vt* to try (**de faire** to do); *(vêtement)* to try on; *(méthode)* to try out

essence [esɑ̃s] *nf (carburant) Br* petrol, *Am* gas; *(extrait) & Phil* essence; **e. sans plomb** unleaded

essentiel, -elle [esɑ̃sjɛl] **1** *adj* essential (**à/pour** for) **2** *nm* l'e. *(le plus important)* the main thing; *(le minimum)* the essentials

essor [esɔr] *nm (de pays, d'entreprise)* rapid growth; **en plein e.** booming

essorer [esɔre] *vt* to spin-dry

essuyer [esɥije] *vt (objet, surface)* to wipe; *(liquide)* to wipe up; *(larmes)* to wipe away; *(refus)* to meet with; **e. la vaisselle** to dry the dishes • **essuie-glace** *(pl* **essuie-glaces)** *nm Br* windscreen wiper, *Am* windshield wiper

est¹ [ɛ] *voir* être

est² [ɛst] **1** *nm* east; **à l'e.** in the east; *(direction)* (to the) east (**de** of); **d'e.** *(vent)* east(erly); **de l'e.** eastern **2** *adj inv (côte)* east(ern)

esthéticienne [ɛstetisjɛn] *nf* beautician

estimer [ɛstime] *vt (tableau)* to value (**à** at); *(prix, distance, poids)* to estimate; *(dommages, besoins)* to assess; *(juger)* to consider (**que** that); **e. qn** to esteem sb • **estimation** *nf (de mobilier)* valuation; *(de prix, de distance, de poids)* estimation; *(de dommages, de besoins)* assessment

estomac [ɛstɔma] *nm* stomach

estomper [ɛstɔ̃pe] **1** *vt (rendre flou)* to blur **2** s'**estomper** *vpr* to become blurred

et [e] *conj* and; **vingt et un** twenty-one; **et moi?** what about me?

établir [etablir] **1** *vt (relations, principe)* to establish; *(liste)* to draw up; *(démontrer)* to establish, to prove **2 s'établir** *vpr (pour habiter)* to settle; *(pour exercer un métier)* to set up in business ● **établissement** *nm (de relations, de principe)* establishment; *(entreprise)* business, firm; **é. scolaire** school

étage [etaʒ] *nm (d'immeuble)* floor, *Br* storey, *Am* story; **à l'é.** upstairs; **au premier é.** on the *Br* first *or Am* second floor

étagère [etaʒɛr] *nf* shelf

étais, était [etɛ] *voir* **être**

étal [etal] *(pl* **étals)** *nm (au marché)* stall

étalage [etalaʒ] *nm* display

étaler [etale] **1** *vt (disposer)* to lay out; *(en vitrine)* to display; *(beurre)* to spread; *(vacances, paiements)* to stagger **2 s'étaler** *vpr* **s'é. sur** *(congés, paiements)* to be spread over

étanche [etɑ̃ʃ] *adj* watertight; *(montre)* waterproof

étang [etɑ̃] *nm* pond

étant [etɑ̃] *voir* **être**

étape [etap] *nf (de voyage)* stage; **par étapes** in stages

état [eta] *nm* **(a)** *(condition, manière d'être)* state; **à l'é. neuf** as new; **en bon é.** in good condition; **é. d'esprit** state *or* frame of mind; **é. civil** register office **(b)** *(autorité centrale)* **É.** *(nation)* State

États-Unis [etazyni] *nmpl* **les É. les É. (d'Amérique)** the United States (of America)

été¹ [ete] *nm* summer

été² [ete] *pp de* **être**

éteindre* [etɛ̃dr] **1** *vt (feu, cigarette)* to put out; *(lampe)* to switch off **2** *vi* to switch off **3 s'éteindre** *vpr (feu)* to go out; *(personne)* to pass away ● **éteint, -e** *adj (feu, bougie)* out; *(lampe, lumière)* off

étendre [etɑ̃dr] **1** *vt (linge)* to hang out; *(agrandir)* to extend; **é. le bras** to stretch out one's arm **2 s'étendre** *vpr (personne)* to lie down; *(plaine)* to stretch

étendu, -e 1 [etɑ̃dy] *adj (forêt, vocabulaire)* extensive; *(personne)* lying **2 étendue** *nf (importance)* extent; *(surface)* area

éternel, -elle [etɛrnɛl] *adj* eternal ● **éternité** *nf* eternity

éternuer [etɛrnɥe] *vi* to sneeze

êtes [ɛt] *voir* **être**

ethnique [ɛtnik] *adj* ethnic

étinceler [etɛ̃sle] *vi* to sparkle

étiquette [etikɛt] *nf (marque)* label; *(protocole)* etiquette

étirer [etire] **1** *vt* to stretch **s'étirer** *vpr* to stretch (oneself)

étoffe [etɔf] *nf* material, fabric

étoffer [etɔfe] *vt* to fill out; *(texte)* to make more meaty

étoile [etwal] *nf* star; **à la belle é.** in the open; **é. filante** shooting star

étonner [etɔne] **1** *vt* to surprise **2 s'étonner** *vpr* to be surprised **(de qch** at sth) ● **étonnant, -e** *adj (ahurissant)* surprising; *(remarquable)* amazing

étouffant, -e [etufɑ̃, -ɑ̃t] *adj (air)* stifling

étouffer [etufe] **1** *vt (tuer)* to suffocate; *Fig (révolte)* to stifle; *(scandale)* to hush up **2** *vi* to suffocate **3 s'étouffer** *vpr (en mangeant)* to choke **(avec** on); *(mourir)* to suffocate

étourdi, -e [eturdi] *adj* scatterbrained

étourdissement [eturdismɑ̃] *nm (malaise)* dizzy spell

étrange [etrɑ̃ʒ] *adj* strange, odd ● **étranger, -ère 1** *adj (d'un autre pays)* foreign; *(non familier)* strange **(à** to) **2** *nmf (d'un autre* *pays)* foreigner; *(inconnu)* stranger; **à l'é.** abroad

étrangler [etrãgle] **1** *vt* **é. qn** *(tuer)* to strangle sb **2 s'étrangler** *vpr (en mangeant)* to choke

être* [ɛtr] **1** *vi* to be; **il est professeur** he's a teacher; **est-ce qu'elle vient?** is she coming?; **il vient, n'est-ce pas?** he's coming, isn't he?; **est-ce qu'il aime le thé?** does he like tea?; **nous sommes dix** there are ten of us; **nous sommes le dix** today is the tenth; **il a été à Paris** *(il y est allé)* he has been to Paris; **elle est de Paris** she's from Paris; **il est cinq heures** it's five (o'clock); **c'est à lui** it's his **2** *v aux (avec 'venir', 'partir' etc)* to have/to be; **elle est arrivée** she has arrived; **elle est née en 1999** she was born in 1999 **3** *nm (personne)* being; **les êtres chers** the loved ones; **ê. humain** human being, **ê. vivant** living being

étroit, -e [etrwa, -at] *adj* narrow; *(vêtement)* tight; *(lien)* close

étude [etyd] *nf (action, ouvrage)* study; *(de notaire)* office; **faire des études de français** to study French

étudiant, -e [etydjã, -ãt] *nmf* student

étudier [etydje] *vti* to study

étui [etɥi] *nm (à lunettes, à cigarettes)* case

eu, eue [y] *pp de* **avoir**

eurent [yr] *voir* **avoir**

euro [əro] *nm (monnaie)* Euro

euro- [øro] *préf* Euro-

eurodéputé, -e [ørodepyte] *nmf* Euro MP

Europe [ørɔp] *nf* **l'E.** Europe ● **européen, -enne 1** *adj* European **2** *nmf* **E., Européenne** European

eut [y] *voir* **avoir**

eux [ø] *pron personnel (sujet)* they; *(complément)* them; *(réfléchi, emphase)* themselves ● **eux-mêmes** *pron* themselves

évacuer [evakɥe] *vt (bâtiment)* to evacuate; *(liquide)* to drain off ● **évacuation** *nf* evacuation

évader [evade] **s'évader** *vpr* to escape (**de** from) ● **évadé, -e** *nmf* escaped prisoner

évaluer [evalɥe] *vt (fortune)* to estimate; *(bien)* to value ● **évaluation** *nf* estimation; *(de bien)* valuation

évanouir [evanwir] **s'évanouir** *vpr* to faint

évaporer [evapɔre] **s'évaporer** *vpr* to evaporate; *Fig (disparaître)* to vanish into thin air

évasé, -e [evaze] *adj (jupe)* flared

évasif, -ive [evazif, -iv] *adj* evasive ● **évasion** *nf* escape (**de** from); **é. fiscale** tax evasion

éveil [evɛj] *nm* awakening; **être en é.** to be alert

éveiller [eveje] **1** *vt (susciter)* to arouse **2 s'éveiller** *vpr* to awaken (**à** to) ● **éveillé, -e** *adj* awake; *(vif)* alert

événement [evɛnmã] *nm* event

éventail [evãtaj] *nm (instrument)* fan; *(choix)* range

éventuel, -elle [evãtɥɛl] *adj* possible ● **éventualité** *nf* possibility ● **éventuellement** *adv* possibly

évêque [evɛk] *nm* bishop

éviction [eviksjɔ̃] *nf* eviction

évident, -e [evidã, -ãt] *adj* obvious (**que** that) ● **évidemment** [-amã] *adv* obviously ● **évidence** *nf* obviousness; **une é.** an obvious fact; **en é.** in a prominent position

évier [evje] *nm* (kitchen) sink

éviter [evite] *vt* to avoid (**de faire**

doing); **é. qch à qn** to spare *or* save sb sth

évoluer [evɔlɥe] *vi (changer)* to develop; *(société, situation)* to evolve • **évolution** *nf (changement)* development; *Biol* evolution

évoquer [evɔke] *vt* to evoke

exact, -e [ɛgzakt] *adj (quantité, poids, nombre)* exact, precise; *(rapport, description)* exact, accurate; *(mot)* right, correct • **exactement** [-əmɑ̃] *adv* exactly

exagérer [ɛgzaʒere] **1** *vt* to exaggerate **2** *vi (parler)* to exaggerate; *(agir)* to go too far • **exagération** *nf* exaggeration • **exagéré, -e** *adj* excessive

examen [ɛgzamɛ̃] *nm* examination • **examinateur, -trice** *nmf* examiner • **examiner** *vt (considérer, regarder)* to examine

exaspérer [ɛgzaspere] *vt (personne)* to exasperate

excavation [ɛkskavasjɔ̃] *nf (trou, action)* excavation

excéder [ɛksede] *vt (dépasser)* to exceed • **excédent** *nm* surplus, excess

excellent, -e [ɛkselɑ̃, -ɑ̃t] *adj* excellent

excentrique [ɛksɑ̃trik] *adj & nmf* eccentric

excepté¹ [ɛksɛpte] *prép* except

excepté², -e [ɛksɛpte] *adj* **les femmes exceptées** except for *or* apart from women

exception [ɛksɛpsjɔ̃] *nf* exception; **à l'e. de** except (for), with the exception of • **exceptionnel, -elle** *adj* exceptional

excès [ɛksɛ] *nm* excess; **e. de vitesse** speeding • **excessif, -ive** *adj* excessive

exciter [ɛksite] **1** *vt (faire naître)* to arouse; **e. qn** *(énerver)* to excite

sb **2 s'exciter** *vpr* to get excited • **excité, -e** *adj* excited

exclamer [ɛksklame] **s'exclamer** *vpr* to exclaim • **exclamation** *nf* exclamation

exclure* [ɛksklyr] *vt (écarter)* to exclude (**de** from) • **exclu, -e** *adj (solution)* out of the question; *(avec une date)* exclusive

exclusif, -ive [ɛksklyzif, -iv] *adj (droit, modèle)* exclusive • **exclusivité** *nf (dans la presse)* scoop; **en e.** *(film)* having an exclusive showing

exclusion [ɛksklyzjɔ̃] *nf* exclusion; **à l'e. de** with the exception of

excursion [ɛkskyrsjɔ̃] *nf* trip, excursion; *(de plusieurs jours)* tour; **faire une e.** to go on a trip/tour

excuse [ɛkskyz] *nf (prétexte)* excuse; **excuses** *(regrets)* apology; **faire des excuses** to apologize (**à** to) • **excuser 1** *vt (justifier, pardonner)* to excuse (**qn d'avoir fait/qn de faire** sb for doing) **2 s'excuser** *vpr* to apologize (**de** for; **auprès de** to); **excusez-moi!, je m'excuse!** excuse me!

exécuter [ɛgzekyte] *vt (tâche)* to carry out; **e. qn** to execute sb • **exécution** *nf (de tâche)* carrying out; *(de condamné)* execution

exécutif [ɛgzekytif] *nm* **l'e.** the executive

exemplaire [ɛgzɑ̃plɛr] **1** *adj* exemplary **2** *nm (livre)* copy

exemple [ɛgzɑ̃pl] *nm* example; **par e.** for example, for instance; **donner l'e.** to set an example (**à** to)

exempt, -e [ɛgzɑ̃, -ɑ̃t] *adj* **e. de** *(dispensé de)* exempt from; *(sans)* free from

exercer [ɛgzɛrse] **1** *vt (voix, droits)* to exercise; *(autorité, influence)* to exert (**sur** on); *(profession)* to practise; **e. qn à qch** to train sb in sth **2 s'exercer** *vpr (s'entraîner)* to train; **s'e. à qch** to practise sth; **s'e. à faire qch** to practise doing sth

exercice [εgzεrsis] *nm (physique) & Scol* exercise; **prendre** *ou* **faire de l'e.** to exercise

exhiber [εgzibe] *vt (documents, passeport)* to produce; *Péj (savoir, richesses)* to show off, to flaunt

exiger [εgziʒe] *vt (demander)* to demand (**de** from); *(nécessiter)* to require • **exigeant, -e** *adj* demanding, exacting • **exigence** *nf (condition)* demand

exil [εgzil] *nm* exile • **exilé, -e** *nmf (personne)* exile

existence [εgzistɑ̃s] *nf* existence • **exister** *vi* to exist

exorbitant, -e [εgzɔrbitɑ̃, -ɑ̃t] *adj* exorbitant

exotique [εgzɔtik] *adj* exotic

expansion [εkspɑ̃sjɔ̃] *nf (de commerce, de pays, de gaz)* expansion; **en (pleine) e.** (fast *or* rapidly) expanding

expédier [εkspedje] *vt (envoyer)* to send, to dispatch; *(affaires, client)* to deal promptly with • **expéditeur, -trice** *nmf* sender • **expédition** *nf (envoi)* dispatch; *(voyage)* expedition

expérience [εksperjɑ̃s] *nf (connaissance)* experience; *(scientifique)* experiment; **faire l'e. de qch** to experience sth; **avoir de l'e.** to have experience • **expérimental, -e, -aux, -ales** *adj* experimental

expérimenter [εksperimɑ̃te] *vt (remède, vaccin)* to try out (**sur** on) • **expérimenté, -e** *adj* experienced

expert, -e [εkspεr, -εrt] **1** *adj* expert, skilled (**en** in) **2** *nm* expert

(**en** on *or* in) • **expert-comptable** (*pl* **experts-comptables**) *nm Br* ≃ chartered accountant, *Am* ≃ certified public accountant • **expertise** *nf* expertise

expirer [εkspire] **1** *vti (respirer)* to breathe out **2** *vi (mourir)* to pass away; *(finir, cesser)* to expire • **expiration** *nf (respiration)* breathing out; *(échéance) Br* expiry, *Am* expiration

explication [εksplikasjɔ̃] *nf* explanation; *(mise au point)* discussion

explicite [εksplisit] *adj* explicit

expliquer [εksplike] **1** *vt* to explain (**à** to; **que** that) **2 s'expliquer** *vpr* to explain oneself; **s'e. qch** *(comprendre)* to understand sth

exploit [εksplwa] *nm* feat

exploiter [εksplwate] *vt (champs)* to farm; *Fig & Péj (personne, situation)* to exploit • **exploitation** *nf (de champs)* farming; *Péj* exploitation

explorer [εksplɔre] *vt* to explore • **explorateur, -trice** *nmf* explorer

exploser [εksploze] *vi (gaz, bombe)* to explode; **faire e. qch** to explode sth • **explosif, -ive** *adj & nm* explosive • **explosion** *nf* explosion; *(de colère)* outburst

exporter [εkspɔrte] *vt* to export (**vers** to; **de** from) • **exportation** *nf* export(ation)

exposer [εkspoze] **1** *vt (tableau)* to exhibit; *(marchandises)* to display; *(théorie)* to set out **2 s'exposer** *vpr* **s'e. au danger** to put oneself in danger; **s'e. à la critique** to lay oneself open to criticism • **exposé** *nm (compte rendu)* account (**de** of); *(présentation)* talk; *Scol* paper

exposition [εkspozisjɔ̃] *nf (d'objets d'art)* exhibition; *(de marchandises)* display

exprès [εksprε] **1** *adv* deliberately;

(spécialement) specially **2** *adj inv*
lettre e. special delivery letter
express [εksprεs] *adj & nm inv*
(train) express; *(café)* espresso
expression [εkspresjɔ] *nf*
expression
exprimer [εksprime] **1** *vt* to
express **2 s'exprimer** *vpr* to
express oneself
expulser [εkspylse] *vt* to expel
(de from); *(joueur)* to send off
● **expulsion** *nf* expulsion; *(de
joueur)* sending off
exquis, -e [εkski, -iz] *adj*
(nourriture) exquisite
extase [εkstɑz] *nf* ecstasy ●
s'extasier *vpr* to be in raptures
(sur over *or* about)
extension [εkstɑsjɔ] *nf (de
muscle)* stretching; *(de durée, de
contrat)* extension
extérieur, -e [εksterjœr] **1** *adj*
(monde) outside; *(surface)* outer,
external; *(signe)* outward, external
2 *nm* outside, exterior; **à l'e. (de)**
outside

exterminer [εkstεrmine] *vt* to
exterminate
externe [εkstεrn] *adj* external
extincteur [εkstε̃ktœr] *nm* fire
extinguisher ● **extinction** *nf (de feu)*
extinguishing; *(de race)* extinction
extorquer [εkstɔrke] *vt* to extort
(à from) ● **extorsion** *nf* extortion
extraire* [εkstrεr] *vt* to extract
(de from) ● **extrait** *nm* extract; **e.
de naissance** birth certificate
extraordinaire [εkstraɔrdinεr]
adj extraordinary
extraterrestre [εkstraterεstr]
adj & nmf extraterrestrial
extravagant, -e [εkstravagɑ,
-ɑt] *adj* extravagant
extraverti, -e [εkstravεrti] *nmf*
extrovert
extrême [εkstrεm] **1** *adj* extreme;
Pol **l'e. droite/gauche** the far *or*
extreme right/left **2** *nm* extreme
● **Extrême-Orient** *nm* **l'E.** the
Far East ● **extrémiste** *adj & nmf*
extremist

Ff

F, f [ɛf] *nm inv* F, f

fabricant, -e [fabrikɑ̃, -ɑ̃t] *nmf* manufacturer • **fabrication** *nf* manufacture

fabrique [fabrik] *nf* factory

fabriquer [fabrike] *vt (objet)* to make; *(en usine)* to manufacture

fabuleux, -euse [fabylø, -øz] *adj (légendaire, incroyable)* fabulous

façade [fasad] *nf* façade

face [fas] *nf (visage)* face; *(de cube, de montagne)* side; *(de pièce de monnaie)* head; **en f.** opposite; **en f. de** opposite, facing; *(en présence de)* in front of; **f. à** *(vis-à-vis)* facing; **f. à f.** face to face; **faire f. à qch** *(situation, difficultés)* to face up to sth

fâcher [faʃe] **se fâcher** *vpr* to get angry (**contre** with); **se f. avec qn** to fall out with sb • **fâché, -e** *adj* angry (**contre** with)

facile [fasil] *adj* easy; **f. à vivre** easy to get along with

façon [fasɔ̃] *nf (manière)* way; **la f. dont elle parle** the way (in which) she talks; **de quelle f.?** how?; **de toute f.** anyway, anyhow; **de f. à** so as to; **de f. générale** generally speaking; **d'une f. ou d'une autre** one way or another; **à ma f.** my way, (in) my own way

facteur [faktœr] *nm (a) (employé)* Br postman, Am mailman **(b)** *(élément)* factor

facture [faktyr] *nf Com* bill

facultatif, -ive [fakyltatif, -iv] *adj (travail)* optional

faculté [fakylte] *nf (a) (aptitude)* faculty **(b)** *(d'université)* faculty; **à la f.** Br at university, Am at school

fade [fad] *adj* insipid

faible [fɛbl] *adj* weak, feeble; *(voix)* faint; *(chances)* slight; *(revenus)* small • **faiblesse** *nf* weakness

faiblir [fɛblir] *vi* to weaken; to fail

faïence [fajɑ̃s] *nf (matière)* earthenware; **faïences** *(objets)* earthenware

faille [faj] *voir* **falloir**

faillir* [fajir] *vi* **il a failli tomber** he almost *or* nearly fell

faillite [fajit] *nf Com* bankruptcy; **faire f.** to go bankrupt

faim [fɛ̃] *nf* hunger; **avoir f.** to be hungry

fainéant, -e [feneɑ̃, -ɑ̃t] *adj* idle

faire* [fɛr] **1** *vt (faute, gâteau, voyage, repas)* to make; *(devoir, ménage)* to do; *(rêve, chute)* to have; *(sourire)* to give; *(promenade, sieste)* to have, to take; **ça fait 10 mètres de large** it's 10 metres wide; **ça fait 10 euros** it's *or* that's 10 euros; **2 et 2 font 4** 2 and 2 are 4; **que f.?** what's to be done?; **f. du tennis/ du piano** to play tennis/the piano; **f. du bien à qn** to do sb good; **f. du mal à qn** to hurt *or* harm sb; **ça ne fait rien** that doesn't matter; **comment as-tu fait pour...?** how did you manage to...?; **'oui', fit-elle** 'yes,' she said **2** *vi (agir)* to do; *(paraître)* to look; **f. comme chez soi** to make oneself at home; **elle ferait bien de partir** she'd do well to leave **3** *v impersonnel* **il fait beau/froid** it's fine/cold; **quel temps fait-il?** what's the weather like?; **ça fait deux ans que je ne l'ai pas vu** I haven't seen him for two years, it's (been) two years since I saw him **4** *v aux (suivi d'un infinitif)* **f. construire une maison** to have a house built (**à qn** for sb; **par qn** by sb); **f. souffrir qn** to make sb suffer **5 se faire** *vpr (fabrication)* to be made; *(activité)* to be done; **se f. couper les cheveux** to have one's hair cut; **se f. renverser** to get knocked down; **se f. des amis** to make friends; **il se fait tard** it's getting late; **comment se fait-il que...?** how is it that...?; **ça se fait beaucoup** people do that a lot; **se f. à qch** to get used to sth; **ne t'en fais pas!** don't worry!

fais, fait[1] [fɛ] *voir* **faire**
faisable [fəzabl] *adj* feasible
fait, -e[2] [fɛ, fɛt] **1** *pp de* **faire 2** *adj* ready-made **3** *nm (événement)* event; *(donnée, réalité)* fact; **du f. de** on account of; **au f.** *(à propos)* by the way; **en f.** in fact; *Journ* **faits divers** ≃ news in brief
faites [fɛt] *voir* **faire**
falaise [falɛz] *nf* cliff

falloir* [falwar] *v impersonnel* **il faut qn/qch** you/we/etc need sb/sth; **il te faut un stylo** you need a pen; **il faut partir** you/we/etc have to go; **il faut que je parte** I have to go; **il faudrait qu'elle reste** she ought to stay; **il faut un jour** it takes a day (**pour faire** to do); **comme il faut** *(adjectif)* proper; *(adverbe)* properly; **s'il le faut** if need be

famé, -e [fame] *adj* **mal f.** disreputable
fameux, -euse [famø, -øz] *adj* *(célèbre)* famous
familial, -e, -aux, -ales [familjal, -o] *adj* family
familier, -ère [familje, -ɛr] *adj* *(connu)* familiar (**à** to); *(locution)* colloquial
famille [famij] *nf* family
famine [famin] *nf* famine
fanatique [fanatik] **1** *adj* fanatical **2** *nmf* fanatic
faner [fane] **se faner** *vpr (fleur, beauté)* to fade • **fané, -e** *adj* faded
fantaisie [fɑ̃tezi] *nf (imagination)* imagination; **bijoux f.** costume jewellery
fantastique [fɑ̃tastik] *adj* fantastic
fantôme [fɑ̃tom] **1** *nm* ghost, phantom **2** *adj* **ville f.** ghost town
farce [fars] *nf (tour)* practical joke, prank; **faire une f. à qn** to play a practical joke *or* a prank on sb
farci, -e [farsi] *adj Culin (poulet, poivron)* stuffed
fardeau, -x [fardo] *nm* burden
farder [farde] **se farder** *vpr (se maquiller)* to put on one's make-up; **se f. les yeux** to put eyeshadow on
farine [farin] *nf (de blé)* flour
farouche [faruʃ] *adj (personne)* shy; *(animal)* timid; *(haine)* fierce
fasciner [fasine] *vt* to fascinate • **fascination** *nf* fascination
fasciste [faʃist] *adj & nmf* fascist
fasse(s), fassent [fas] *voir* **faire**
fastidieux, -euse [fastidjø, -øz] *adj* tedious
fatal, -e, -als, -ales [fatal] *adj (mortel)* fatal; *(inévitable)* inevitable; *(moment)* fateful • **fatalité** *nf (destin)* fate

fatigant, -e [fatigɑ̃, -ɑ̃t] *adj (épuisant)* tiring; *(ennuyeux)* tiresome

fatigue [fatig] *nf* tiredness

fatiguer [fatige] **1** *vt (épuiser)* to tire; *(yeux)* to strain; *(ennuyer)* to bore **2 se fatiguer** *vpr (s'épuiser, se lasser)* to get tired (**de** of); **se f. à faire qch** to tire oneself out doing sth

faucon [fokɔ̃] *nm* hawk, falcon

faudra, faudrait [fodra, fodrɛ] *voir* **falloir**

faufiler [fofile] **se faufiler** *vpr* to work one's way (**dans** through *or* into; **entre** between)

fausse [fos] *voir* **faux**[1]

faut [fo] *voir* **falloir**

faute [fot] *nf (erreur)* mistake; *(responsabilité)* & *(au tennis)* fault; *(au football)* foul; **c'est de ta f.** it's your fault; **f. de mieux** for want of anything better; **faire une f.** to make a mistake

fauteuil [fotœj] *nm* armchair; **f. roulant** wheelchair

faux, fausse [fo, fos] **1** *adj (pas vrai)* false, untrue; *(inexact)* wrong; *(inauthentique)* false; *(monnaie)* forged; *(tableau)* fake; **faire une fausse couche** to have a miscarriage **2** *adv (chanter)* out of tune **3** *nm (tableau)* fake; *(document)* forgery ● **faux-filet** *(pl* **faux-filets)** *nm* sirloin

faveur [favœr] *nf* favour; **en f. de** *(au profit de)* in aid of; **être en f. de qch** to be in favour of sth ● **favorable** *adj* favourable (**à** to) ● **favori, -e** *adj* & *nmf* favourite

fax [faks] *nm (appareil, message)* fax ● **faxer** *vt (message)* to fax

fécondité [fekɔ̃dite] *nf* fertility

fédéral, -e, -aux, -ales [federal, -o] *adj* federal ● **fédération** *nf* federation

fée [fe] *nf* fairy

feint, -e [fɛ̃, ɛt] *adj* feigned

fêler [fele] *vt*, **se fêler** *vpr* to crack

féliciter [felisite] *vt* to congratulate (**de** *ou* **sur** on) ● **félicitations** *nfpl* congratulations (**pour** on)

femelle [fəmɛl] *adj* & *nf* female

féminin, -e [feminɛ̃, -in] *adj (prénom, hormone)* female; *(trait, pronom)* feminine; *(mode)* women's ● **féministe** *adj* & *nmf* feminist ● **féminité** *nf* femininity

femme [fam] *nf* woman *(pl* women); *(épouse)* wife; **f. de ménage** cleaning lady, maid; **f. au foyer** housewife

fendre [fɑ̃dr] **1** *vt (bois, lèvre)* to split; *Fig (cœur)* to break **2 se fendre** *vpr (se fissurer)* to crack

fenêtre [fənɛtr] *nf* window

fenouil [fənuj] *nm* fennel

fente [fɑ̃t] *nf (de tirelire, de palissade)* slit; *(de rocher)* split, crack

fer [fɛr] *nm* iron; **barre de** *ou* **en f.** iron bar; **f. à cheval** horseshoe; **f. à repasser** iron

fera, ferait *etc* [fəra, fərɛ] *voir* **faire**

férié [ferje] *adj m* **jour f.** (public) holiday

ferme[1] [fɛrm] *nf* farm

ferme[2] [fɛrm] *adj (fruit, beurre)* firm; *(autoritaire)* firm (**avec** with)

fermer [fɛrme] **1** *vt* to close, to shut; *(gaz, radio)* to turn *or* switch off; *(passage)* to block; **f. qch à clé** to lock sth; **f. un magasin** *(définitivement)* to close *or* shut (down) a shop **2** *vi*, **se fermer** *vpr* to close, to shut ● **fermé, -e** *adj (porte, magasin)* closed, shut; *(route, circuit)* closed; *(gaz)* off

fermeture [fɛrmətyr] *nf* closing, closure; *(heure)* closing time; *(mécanisme)* catch; **f. Éclair®** *Br* zip, *Am* zipper

fermier, -ère [fɛrmje, -ɛr] *nmf* farmer

féroce [ferɔs] *adj* ferocious

feront [fərɔ̃] *voir* **faire**

ferroviaire [ferɔvjɛr] *adj* **compagnie f.** *Br* railway company, *Am* railroad company

ferry [feri] (*pl* **ferrys** *ou* **ferries**) *nm* ferry

fertile [fɛrtil] *adj* (*terre, imagination*) fertile • **fertiliser** *vt* to fertilize • **fertilité** *nf* fertility

fesse [fɛs] *nf* buttock; **fesses** *Br* bottom, *Am* butt • **fessée** *nf* spanking

festin [fɛstɛ̃] *nm* feast

festival, -als [fɛstival] *nm* festival

fête [fɛt] *nf* (*civile*) holiday; (*religieuse*) festival, feast; (*entre amis*) party; **jour de f.** (public) holiday; **les fêtes (de Noël et du nouvel an)** the Christmas holidays; **faire la f.** to party; **c'est sa f.** it's his/her saint's day; **la f. des Mères** Mother's Day; **la f. du Travail** Labour Day • **fêter** *vt* (*événement*) to celebrate

feu, -x [fø] *nm* fire; *Aut* (*lumière*) light; **en f.** on fire, ablaze; **faire du f.** to light *or* make a fire; **mettre le f. à qch** to set fire to sth; **prendre f.** to catch fire; **donner du f. à qn** to give sb a light; **avez-vous du f.?** have you got a light?; **au f.!** fire!; *Aut* **f. rouge** (*lumière*) red light; (*objet*) traffic lights

feuille [fœj] *nf* leaf; (*de papier*) sheet

feuilleter [fœjte] *vt* (*livre*) to flip through

feuilleton [fœjtɔ̃] *nm* serial; **f. (télévisé)** (television) serial

feutre [føtr] *nm* felt; **(crayon) f.** felt-tip(ped) pen

fève [fɛv] *nf* (broad) bean

février [fevrije] *nm* February

fiable [fjabl] *adj* reliable

fiancer [fijɑ̃se] **se fiancer** *vpr* to get engaged (**avec** to) • **fiançailles** *nfpl* engagement • **fiancé, -é** *nmf* fiancé, *f* fiancée

fibre [fibr] *nf* fibre

ficelle [fisɛl] *nf* (*de corde*) string; (*pain*) = long thin loaf • **ficeler** *vt* to tie up

fiche [fiʃ] *nf* (*papier*) form • **fichier** *nm Ordinat* file

fiction [fiksjɔ̃] *nf* fiction

fidèle [fidɛl] **1** *adj* faithful (**à** to) **2** *nmf* **les fidèles** the faithful • **fidélité** *nf* fidelity, faithfulness

fier¹ [fje] **se fier** *vpr* **se f. à qn/qch** to trust sb/sth

fier², fière [fjɛr] *adj* proud (**de** of) • **fierté** *nf* pride

fièvre [fjɛvr] *nf* (*maladie*) fever; **avoir de la f.** to have a temperature *or* a fever • **fiévreux, -euse** *adj* feverish

figue [fig] *nf* fig

figurant, -e [figyrɑ̃, -ɑ̃t] *nmf* (*de film*) extra

figure [figyr] *nf* (*visage*) face; (*personnage*) figure

figurer [figyre] **1** *vt* to represent **2 se figurer** *vpr* to imagine; **figure-toi que...** would you believe that...?

fil [fil] *nm* (a) (*de coton, de pensée*) thread; (*lin*) linen; **f. dentaire** dental floss (b) (*métallique*) wire

file [fil] *nf* line; **f. d'attente** *Br* queue, *Am* line

filer [file] *vi* (*partir*) to rush off; (*aller vite*) to speed along; (*collant*) to run, *Br* to ladder

filet [filɛ] *nm* (a) (*en maille*) net (b) (*de poisson, de viande*) fillet

filiale [filjal] *nf* subsidiary

filière [filjɛr] *nf* (*voie obligée*) channels; (*domaine d'études*) field of study; **suivre la f. normale** to go through the official channels

fille [fij] *nf (enfant)* girl; *(descendante)* daughter; **petite f.** (little *or* young) girl; **jeune f.** girl, young lady • **fillette** *nf* little girl

film [film] *nm (œuvre)* film, movie; *(pour photo)* film; **f. muet** silent film; **f. policier** thriller • **filmer** *vt (personne, scène)* to film

fils [fis] *nm* son

filtre [filtr] *nm* filter • **filtrer 1** *vt (liquide, lumière)* to filter; *(nouvelles)* to screen **2** *vi (liquide)* to filter (through); *(nouvelle)* to leak out

fin¹ [fɛ̃] *nf (conclusion)* end; **mettre f. à qch** to put an end to sth; **à la f.** in the end; **f. mai** at the end of May

fin², fine [fɛ̃, fin] **1** *adj (pointe, tissu)* fine; *(couche)* thin; *(visage, mets)* delicate **2** *adv (couper, moudre)* finely

final, -e, -aux *ou* **-als, -ales** [final, -o] *adj* final • **finale** *nf* Sport final

finance [finãs] *nf* finance • **financer** *vt* to finance • **financier, -ère** *adj* financial

finesse [fines] *nf (de pointe)* fineness; *(de taille)* thinness; *(de visage)* delicacy

finir [finir] **1** *vt* to finish; *(discours, vie)* to end, to finish **2** *vi* to finish, to end; **f. de faire qch** to finish doing sth; **f. par faire qch** to end up doing sth; **f. par qch** to finish (up) *or* end (up) with sth • **fini, -e** *adj* finished

Finlande [fɛ̃lɑ̃d] *nf* **la F.** Finland • **finlandais, -e 1** *adj* Finnish **2** *nmf* **F., Finlandaise** Finn

fisc [fisk] *nm Br* ≃ Inland Revenue, *Am* ≃ Internal Revenue • **fiscal, -e, -aux, -ales** *adj* **fraude fiscale** tax fraud *or* evasion

fissure [fisyr] *nf* crack • **se fissurer** *vpr* to crack

fixation [fiksasjɔ̃] *nf (action)* fixing; *(dispositif)* fastening, binding; *(idée fixe)* fixation; **faire une f. sur qn/qch** to be fixated on sb/sth

fixe [fiks] *adj* fixed • **fixement** [-əmɑ̃] *adv* **regarder qn/qch f.** to stare at sb/sth

fixer [fikse] **1** *vt (attacher)* to fix (à to); *(date, règle)* to decide, to fix; **f. qn/qch du regard** to stare at sb/sth; **être fixé** *(décidé)* to be decided **2 se fixer** *vpr (regard)* to become fixed; *(s'établir)* to settle

flacon [flakɔ̃] *nm* small bottle

flagrant, -e [flagrɑ̃, -ɑ̃t] *adj (injustice)* blatant; **pris en f. délit** caught in the act *or* red-handed

flairer [flɛre] *vt* to smell, to sniff at

flamand, -e [flamɑ̃, -ɑ̃d] **1** *adj* Flemish **2** *nmf* **F., Flamande** Fleming **3** *nm (langue)* Flemish

flamant [flamɑ̃] *nm* **f. rose** flamingo

flambeau, -x [flɑ̃bo] *nm* torch

flamme [flam] *nf* flame; **en flammes** on fire

flan [flɑ̃] *nm* baked custard

flanc [flɑ̃] *nm* side

flâner [flɑne] *vi* to stroll

flaque [flak] *nf (d'eau)* puddle

flash [flaʃ] *(pl* **flashes***) nm Phot* flashlight

flatteur, -euse [flatœr, -øz] *adj* flattering

flèche [flɛʃ] *nf (projectile)* arrow; **monter en f.** *(prix)* to shoot up • **fléchette** *nf* dart; **fléchettes** *(jeu)* darts

fléchir [fleʃir] *vi (ployer)* to bend; *(faiblir)* to give way

fleur [flœr] *nf* flower; *(d'arbre, d'arbuste)* blossom; **en fleur(s)** in flower, in bloom; *(arbre)* in blossom • **fleuri, -e** *adj (fleur, jardin)* in bloom; *(tissu)* floral • **fleuriste** *nmf* florist

fleuve [flœv] *nm* river

flexible [flɛksibl] *adj* flexible

flocon [flɔkɔ̃] *nm* flake; **f. de neige** snowflake

floral, -e, -aux, -ales [flɔral, -ō] *adj* floral

flot [flo] *nm (de larmes)* flood; *Fig* **couler à flots** *(argent, vin)* to flow freely

flotte [flɔt] *nf (de bateaux, d'avions)* fleet

flotter [flɔte] *vi* to float

flou, -e [flu] *adj (image)* fuzzy, blurred; *(idée)* vague

fluide [flµid] *adj & nm* fluid

fluorescent, -e [flyɔresɑ̃, -āt] *adj* fluorescent

flûte [flyt] *nf (instrument)* flute; *(verre)* champagne glass

foi [fwa] *nf* faith; **être de bonne/ mauvaise f.** to be sincere/insincere

foie [fwa] *nm* liver; **f. gras** foie gras; **crise de f.** bout of indigestion

foin [fwɛ̃] *nm* hay

foire [fwar] *nf* fair

fois [fwa] *nf* time; **une f.** once; **deux f.** twice; **trois f.** three times; **deux f. trois** two times three; **chaque f. que…** whenever…, each time (that)…; **une f. qu'il sera arrivé** once he has arrived; **à la f.** at the same time, at once; **il était une f. …** once upon a time there was…

fol [fɔl] *voir* **fou**

folie [fɔli] *nf* madness

folklorique [fɔlklɔrik] *adj (costume)* traditional; *(musique, danse)* folk

folle [fɔl] *voir* **fou**

foncé, -e [fɔ̃se] *adj* dark

foncer [fɔ̃se] *vi (aller vite)* to tear

or charge along; **f. sur qn/qch** to swoop on sb/sth

fonction [fɔ̃ksjɔ̃] *nf* function; *(emploi)* office; **en f. de** according to; **faire f. de** *(personne)* to act as; *(objet)* to serve *or* act as; **prendre ses fonctions** to take up one's duties; **la f. publique** the civil service • **fonctionnaire** *nmf* civil servant

fonctionner [fɔ̃ksjɔne] *vi (machine)* to work, to function; **faire f. qch** to operate sth • **fonctionnement** *nm (de machine)* working; **en état de f.** in working order

fond [fɔ̃] *nm (de boîte, de jardin, de vallée)* bottom; *(de salle, d'armoire)* back; *(arrière-plan)* background; **au f. de** *(boîte, jardin)* at the bottom of; *(salle)* at the back of; *Fig* **au f., dans le f.** basically; **à f.** *(connaître)* thoroughly; **ski de f.** cross-country skiing; **bruits de f.** background noise

fondamental, -e, -aux, -ales [fɔ̃damātal, -o] *adj* fundamental

fonder [fɔ̃de] **1** *vt (ville)* to found; *(commerce)* to set up; *(famille)* to start; **f. qch sur qch** to base sth on sth **2** **se fonder** *vpr* **se f. sur qch** *(sujet: théorie)* to be based on sth • **fondateur, -trice** *nmf* founder • **fondation** *nf (création, œuvre)* foundation (**de** of); **fondations** *(de bâtiment)* foundations

fondre [fɔ̃dr] **1** *vt (métal)* to melt down; *(neige)* to melt; **faites f. le chocolat** melt the chocolate **2** *vi (se liquéfier)* to melt; **f. en larmes** to burst into tears; **f. sur qch** to swoop on sth **3** **se fondre** *vpr* **se f. dans qch** *(disparaître)* to merge into sth • **fondant, -e** *adj (aliment)* which melts in the mouth

fonds [fɔ̃] **1** *nm (organisme)* fund;

2 *nmpl (argent)* funds

font [fɔ̃] *voir* **faire**

fontaine [fɔ̃tɛn] *nf (construction)* fountain; *(source)* spring

football [futbol] *nm Br* football, *Am* soccer • **footballeur, -euse** *nmf Br* footballer, *Am* soccer player

force [fɔrs] *nf (violence) & Phys* force; *(vigueur)* strength; **de toutes ses forces** with all one's strength; **de f.** by force, forcibly; **à f. de faire qch** through doing sth; **les forces armées** the armed forces • **forcément** *adv* inevitably; **pas f.** not necessarily

forcer [fɔrse] **1** *vt (obliger)* to force; *(porte)* to force open; **f. qn à faire qch** to force sb to do sth **2 se forcer** *vpr* to force oneself (**à faire** to do)

forêt [fɔrɛ] *nf* forest

forfait [fɔrfɛ] *nm (prix)* all-in price; *(de ski)* pass

forger [fɔrʒe] *vt (métal, liens)* to forge; *Fig (caractère)* to form • **forgeron** [-ərɔ̃] *nm* blacksmith

formalité [fɔrmalite] *nf* formality

format [fɔrma] *nm* format

formation [fɔrmasjɔ̃] *nf (de roche, de mot)* formation; *(éducation)* education

forme [fɔrm] *nf (contour)* shape, form; *(manière, bonne santé)* form; **en f. de qch** in the shape of sth; **en f. de poire** pear-shaped; **sous f. de qch** in the form of sth; **en (pleine) f.** *(en bonne santé)* on (top) form

formel, -elle [fɔrmɛl] *adj (structure)* formal; *(personne, preuve)* positive; *(interdiction)* strict

former [fɔrme] **1** *vt (groupe, caractère)* to form; *(apprenti)* to train **2 se former** *vpr (apparaître)* to form; *(association, liens)* to be formed

formidable [fɔrmidabl] *adj (excellent)* great; *(gigantesque)* tremendous

formulaire [fɔrmylɛr] *nm* form

formule [fɔrmyl] *nf Math* formula; *(phrase)* expression; **f. magique** magic formula • **formuler** *vt* to formulate

fort¹, -e [fɔr, fɔrt] **1** *adj (vigoureux)* strong; *(gros, important)* large; *(pluie, chute de neige)* heavy; *(voix)* loud; **être f. en qch** *(doué)* to be good at sth **2** *adv (frapper, pleuvoir)* hard; *(parler)* loud(ly); *(serrer)* tight; **sentir f.** to have a strong smell; **respirer f.** to breathe heavily

fort² [fɔr] *nm Hist & Mil* fort • **forteresse** *nf* fortress

fortifier [fɔrtifje] *vt (mur, ville)* to fortify; *(corps)* to strengthen • **fortifiant** *nm* tonic • **fortifié, -e** *adj (ville, camp)* fortified

fortune [fɔrtyn] *nf (richesse, hasard)* fortune; **faire f.** to make one's fortune

fosse [fos] *nf (trou)* pit

fossé [fose] *nm* ditch

fossette [fosɛt] *nf* dimple

fou, folle [fu, fɔl]

fol is used before masculine singular nouns beginning with a vowel or mute h.

1 *adj (personne, projet)* mad, insane; *(succès, temps)* tremendous; *(espoir)* foolish; **f. de qch** *(musique, personne)* mad about sth; **f. de joie** beside oneself with joy **2** *nmf* madman, *f* madwoman

foudre [fudr] *nf* **la f.** lightning • **foudroyant, -e** *adj (succès, vitesse)* staggering • **foudroyer** *vt* to strike; **f. qn du regard** to give sb a withering look

fouet [fwɛ] *nm* whip; *Culin* whisk;

coup de f. lash (with a whip) • **fouetter** *vt* to whip; *(sujet: pluie)* to lash (against); **crème fouettée** whipped cream

fouille [fuj] **1** *nf (de personne, de bagages)* search **2** *nfpl* **fouilles archéologiques** excavations, dig • **fouiller 1** *vt (personne, maison)* to search **2** *vi* **f. dans qch** *(tiroir)* to search through sth

fouillis [fuji] *nm* jumble

foulard [fular] *nm* (head)scarf

foule [ful] *nf* crowd

fouler [fule] **se fouler** *vpr* **se f. la cheville** to sprain one's ankle

four [fur] *nm* oven; **petit f.** *(gâteau)* (small) fancy cake

fourche [furʃ] *nf (outil, embranchement)* fork; **faire une f.** to fork • **fourchette** *nf (pour manger)* fork; *(de salaires)* bracket

fourgon [furgɔ̃] *nm (camion)* van

fourmi [furmi] *nf (insecte)* ant; **avoir des fourmis dans les jambes** to have pins and needles in one's legs • **fourmiller** *vi* to teem, to swarm (**de** with)

fourneau, -x [furno] *nm* stove

fournir [furnir] *vt (approvisionner)* to supply (**en** with); *(preuve, document)* to provide; *(effort)* to make; **f. qch à qn** to provide sb with sth; **pièces à f.** required documents • **fournisseur** *nm (commerçant)* supplier • **fournitures** *nfpl* stationery; **f. de bureau** office supplies

fourré, -e [fure] *adj (vêtement)* fur-lined; *(gâteau)* jam-/cream-filled • **fourrer** *vt (vêtement)* to fur-line; *(gâteau)* to fill • **fourre-tout** *nm inv (sac) Br* holdall, *Am* carryall

fourrure [furyr] *nf* fur

foyer [fwaje] *nm (maison)* home; *(d'étudiants)* residence; *(de*

travailleurs) hostel; *(de théâtre)* foyer; *(famille)* family

fracas [fraka] *nm* crash • **fracasser** *vt*, **se fracasser** *vpr* to smash

fraction [fraksjɔ̃] *nf* fraction; *(partie)* part

fracture [fraktyr] *nf* fracture • **fracturer 1** *vt (os)* to fracture **2 se fracturer** *vpr* **se f. la jambe** to fracture one's leg

fragile [fraʒil] *adj (objet, matériau)* fragile; *(santé, équilibre)* delicate *(personne)* frail

fragment [fragmɑ̃] *nm* fragment

fraîcheur [freʃœr] *nf (d'aliments)* freshness; *(de température)* coolness

frais¹, fraîche [frɛ, frɛʃ] **1** *adj (aliment, fleurs)* fresh; *(vent, air)* cool, fresh; *(peinture)* wet **2** *adv* **servir f.** *(vin)* to serve chilled **3** *nm* **mettre qch au f.** to put sth in a cool place; *(au réfrigérateur)* to refrigerate sth; **il fait f.** it's cool

frais² [frɛ] *nmpl* expenses; **à mes f.** at my (own) expense; **f. de scolarité** school fees

fraise [frɛz] *nf (fruit)* strawberry; *(de dentiste)* drill

framboise [frɑ̃bwaz] *nf* raspberry

franc¹, franche [frɑ̃, frɑ̃ʃ] *adj (sincère)* frank; *(visage)* open • **franchement** *adv (sincèrement)* frankly; *(vraiment)* really; *(sans ambiguïté)* clearly

franc² [frɑ̃] *nm (monnaie)* franc

France *nf* **la F.** France • **français, -e 1** *adj* French **2** *nmf* **F., Française** Frenchman, *f* Frenchwoman; **les F.** the French **3** *nm (langue)* French

franchir [frɑ̃ʃir] *vt (obstacle)* to get over; *(frontière, ligne d'arrivée)* to cross; *(porte)* to go through

franchise [frãʃiz] *nf (sincérité)* frankness; *Com* franchise

francophone [frãkɔfɔn] **1** *adj* French-speaking **2** *nmf* French speaker

frange [frãʒ] *nf (de cheveux) Br* fringe, *Am* bangs; *(de vêtement)* fringe

frapper [frape] **1** *vt (battre)* to strike, to hit; *(monnaie)* to mint; **f. qn** *(impressionner)* to strike sb; *(impôt, mesure)* to hit sb **2** *vi (donner un coup)* to strike, to hit; **f. du pied** to stamp (one's foot); **f. du poing sur la table** to bang (on) the table; **f. à une porte** to knock on a door • **frappant, -e** *adj* striking • **frappé, -e** *adj (boisson)* chilled

fraude [frod] *nf* fraud; **passer qch en f.** to smuggle sth in; **f. fiscale** tax evasion • **frauder** *vt* **f. le fisc** to evade tax • **frauduleux, -euse** *adj* fraudulent

frayer [frɛje] **se frayer** *vpr* **se f. un chemin** to clear a way (à travers/dans through)

fredonner [frədɔne] *vti* to hum

frein [frɛ̃] *nm* brake; **donner un coup de f.** to put on the brakes; **f. à main** handbrake • **freiner** *vi* to brake

frémir [fremir] *vi (personne)* to tremble (**de** with); *(feuilles)* to rustle; *(eau chaude)* to simmer • **frémissement** *nm (de peur)* shudder; *(de plaisir)* thrill; *(de colère)* quiver; *(de feuilles)* rustle

frénétique [frenetik] *adj* frenzied

fréquent, -e [frekã, -ãt] *adj* frequent • **fréquence** *nf* frequency

fréquenter [frekãte] **1** *vt (lieu)* to frequent; **f. qn** to see sb regularly **2 se fréquenter** *vpr (se voir régulièrement)* to see each other socially

frère [frɛr] *nm* brother

friand, -e [frijã, -ãd] *adj* **f. de** fond of • **friandise** *nf Br* titbit, *Am* tidbit

frileux, -euse [frilø, -øz] *adj* **être f.** to feel the cold

fripé, -e [fripe] *adj* crumpled

frire* [frir] **1** *vt* to fry **2** *vi* to fry; **faire f. qch** to fry sth

friser [frize] *vt (cheveux)* to curl; *(effleurer)* to skim; **f. la catastrophe** to come within an inch of disaster • **frisé, -e** *adj (cheveux)* curly

frisson [frisɔ̃] *nm (de froid, de peur)* shiver; *(de plaisir)* thrill • **frissonner** *vi (de froid, de peur)* to shiver

frit, -e [fri, -it] **1** *pp de* **frire 2** *adj* fried • **frites** *nfpl Br* chips, *Am* French fries • **friture** *nf (cuisson)* frying; *(aliment)* fried food

frivole [frivɔl] *adj* frivolous

froid, -e [frwa, frwad] **1** *adj* cold **2** *nm* cold; **avoir f.** to be cold; **il fait f.** it's cold

froisser [frwase] **1** *vt (tissu)* to crumple, to crease **2 se froisser** *vpr (tissu)* to crease, to crumple; **se f. un muscle** to strain a muscle

frôler [frole] *vt (effleurer)* to brush against; *Fig (catastrophe)* to come close to

fromage [frɔmaʒ] *nm* cheese; **f. de chèvre** goat's cheese; **f. blanc** soft cheese; **f. frais** fromage frais

froment [frɔmã] *nm* wheat

froncer [frɔ̃se] *vt (tissu)* to gather; **f. les sourcils** to frown

front [frɔ̃] *nm (du visage)* forehead; *(avant)*, *Mil & Pol* front; **faire f. à qn/qch** to face up to sb/sth; **f. de mer** sea front

frontière [frɔ̃tjɛr] *nf (de pays)* border

frotter [frɔte] **1** *vt* to rub;

(plancher) to scrub **2 se frotter** *vpr* to rub oneself; **se f. le dos** to scrub one's back

frugal, -e, -aux, -ales [frygal, -o] *adj* frugal

fruit [frɥi] *nm* fruit; **des fruits** fruit; **un f.** a piece of fruit; **fruits de mer** seafood; **fruits secs** dried fruit ● **fruité, -e** *adj* fruity

frustration [frystrasjɔ̃] *nf* frustration ● **frustré, -e** *adj* frustrated

fuel [fjul] *nm* fuel oil

fugitif, -ive [fyʒitif, -iv] *nmf* runaway, fugitive

fugue [fyg] *nf* **faire une f.** *(enfant)* to run away

fuir* [fɥir] **1** *vt (pays)* to flee; *(personne)* to run away from **2** *vi (s'échapper)* to run away (**devant** from); *(gaz, robinet, stylo)* to leak ● **fuite** *nf (évasion)* flight (**devant** from); *(de gaz)* leak; **en f.** on the run; **prendre la f.** to take flight

fumer [fyme] **1** *vt (cigarette, poisson)* to smoke; **f. la pipe** to smoke a pipe **2** *vi (fumeur,* *moteur)* to smoke; *(liquide brûlant)* to steam ● **fumé, -e** *adj (poisson, verre)* smoked ● **fumée** *nf* smoke; *(vapeur)* steam ● **fumeur, -euse** *nmf* smoker

fumier [fymje] *nm (engrais)* manure, dung

funérailles [fyneraj] *nfpl* funeral

fur [fyr] **au fur et à mesure** *adv* as one goes along, progressively; **au f. et à mesure que...** as...

furent [fyr] *voir* **être**

furie [fyri] *nf (colère)* fury ● **furieux, -euse** *adj (en colère)* furious (**contre** with)

fuseau, -x [fyzo] *nm (pantalon)* ski pants; **f. horaire** time zone

fusée [fyze] *nf* rocket

fusible [fyzibl] *nm* fuse

fusil [fyzi] *nm* rifle, gun

fusion [fyzjɔ̃] *nf* **(a)** *(de métal)* melting **(b)** *Com* merger

fut [fy] *voir* **être**

futur, -e [fytyr] **1** *adj* future; **future mère** mother-to-be **2** *nm (avenir)* future

Gg

G, g [ʒe] *nm inv* G, g

gâcher [gɑʃe] *vt (gâter)* to spoil; *(gaspiller)* to waste • **gâchis** *nm* waste

gâchette [gɑʃɛt] *nf* trigger

gadget [gadʒɛt] *nm* gadget

gage [gaʒ] *nm (garantie)* guarantee; *(au jeu)* forfeit

gagnant, -e [gaɲɑ̃, -ɑ̃t] **1** *adj* winning **2** *nmf* winner

gagner [gaɲe] **1** *vt (par le travail)* to earn; *(par le jeu)* to win; *(obtenir)* to gain; **g. sa vie** to earn one's living; **g. du temps** to save time **2** *vi* to win

gai, -e [gɛ] *adj* cheerful

gain [gɛ̃] *nm (profit)* gain, profit; *(succès)* winning

gala [gala] *nm* gala

galant, -e [galɑ̃, -ɑ̃t] *adj (homme)* gallant; *(rendez-vous)* romantic

galaxie [galaksi] *nf* galaxy

galerie [galri] *nf (passage, salle)* gallery; **g. d'art** art gallery; **g. marchande** (shopping) mall

galet [galɛ] *nm* pebble

galette [galɛt] *nf (gâteau)* butter biscuit; *(crêpe)* buckwheat pancake; **g. des Rois** = Twelfth Night cake

Galles [gal] *nm* **le pays de G.** Wales • **gallois, -e 1** *adj* Welsh **2** *nmf* **G., Galloise** Welshman, *f* Welshwoman **3** *nm (langue)* Welsh

galop [galo] *nm* gallop; **aller au g.** to gallop • **galoper** *vi (cheval)* to gallop

gambader [gɑ̃bade] *vi* to leap *or* frisk about

gamelle [gamɛl] *nf (de chien)* bowl

gamin, -e [gamɛ̃, -in] *nmf (enfant)* kid

gamme [gam] *nf Mus* scale; *(éventail)* range; **haut/bas de g.** top-/bottom-of-the-range

gang [gɑ̃g] *nm* gang

gant [gɑ̃] *nm* glove; **g. de toilette** ≃ facecloth

garage [garaʒ] *nm (de voitures)* garage • **garagiste** *nmf (mécanicien)* garage mechanic; *(propriétaire)* garage owner

garantie [garɑ̃ti] *nf* guarantee; *Fig (précaution)* safeguard; **sous g.** under guarantee • **garantir** *vt* to guarantee; *(emprunt)* to secure; **g. à qn que...** to guarantee sb that...

garçon [garsɔ̃] *nm* boy; *(jeune homme)* young man; *(serveur)* waiter; **g. d'honneur** best man

garde [gard] **1** *nm (gardien)* guard; **g. du corps** bodyguard **2** *nf (d'enfants, de bagages)* care, custody (**de** of); **avoir la g. de** to be in charge of; **être de g.** to be on duty; **médecin de g.** duty doctor • **garde-robe** (*pl* **garde-robes**) *nf* wardrobe

garder [garde] **1** *vt (conserver)* to keep; *(vêtement)* to keep on; *(surveiller)* to look after **2** **se garder** *vpr (aliment)* to keep • **garderie** *nf Br* (day) nursery, *Am* daycare center

gardien, -enne [gardjɛ̃, -ɛn] *nmf* *(d'immeuble, d'hôtel)* caretaker, *Am* janitor; *(de prison)* (prison) guard; **g. de but** *(au football)* goalkeeper; **gardienne d'enfants** child minder, baby-sitter

gare [gar] *nf (pour trains)* station; **g. routière** bus *or Br* coach station

garer [gare] **1** *vt (voiture)* to park **2 se garer** *vpr* to park

gargariser [gargarize] **se gargariser** *vpr* to gargle

garnir [garnir] *vt (décorer)* to trim (**de** with); *(équiper)* to fit out (**de** with); *(couvrir)* to cover ● **garniture** *nf Culin* garnish

gaspiller [gaspije] *vt* to waste ● **gaspillage** *nm* waste

gâté, -e [gate] *adj (dent, fruit)* bad; *(enfant)* spoilt

gâteau, -x [gato] *nm* cake; **g. sec** *Br* biscuit, *Am* cookie

gâter [gate] **1** *vt* to spoil **2 se gâter** *vpr (aliment, dent)* to go bad; *(temps)* to change for the worst

gauche¹ [goʃ] **1** *adj (côté, main)* left **2** *nf* **la g.** *(côté)* the left (side); *Pol* the left (wing); **à g.** *(tourner)* (to the) left; *(marcher)* on the left, on the left(-hand) side; **de g.** *(fenêtre, colonne)* left-hand; *(parti, politique)* left-wing; **à g. de** on *or* to the left of ● **gaucher, -ère** *adj* left-handed

gauche² [goʃ] *adj (maladroit)* awkward

gaufre [gofr] *nf* waffle

gaver [gave] **se gaver** *vpr* to stuff oneself (**de** with)

gaz [gaz] *nm inv* gas; ● **gazeux, -euse** *adj (boisson)* fizzy; *(eau)* sparkling

gazole [gazɔl] *nm* diesel oil

gazon [gazɔ̃] *nm (herbe)* grass; *(surface)* lawn

géant, -e [ʒeɑ̃, -ɑ̃t] *adj & nmf* giant

gel [ʒɛl] *nm* **(a)** *(temps, glace)* frost **(b)** *(pour cheveux)* gel ● **gelé, -e** *adj* frozen ● **gelée** *nf* **(a)** frost **(b)** *(de fruits, de viande)* jelly ● **geler 1** *vt* to freeze **2** *vi* to freeze; **on gèle ici** it's freezing here

Gémeaux [ʒemo] *nmpl* **les G.** *(signe)* Gemini

gémir [ʒemir] *vi* to groan, to moan ● **gémissement** *nm* groan, moan

gênant, -e [ʒɛnɑ̃, -ɑ̃t] *adj (objet)* cumbersome; *(situation)* awkward; *(bruit, personne)* annoying

gencive [ʒɑ̃siv] *nf* gum

gendarme [ʒɑ̃darm] *nm* gendarme, policeman ● **gendarmerie** *nf (local)* police headquarters

gendre [ʒɑ̃dr] *nm* son-in-law

gène [ʒɛn] *nm Biol* gene

gêne [ʒɛn] *nf (trouble physique)* discomfort; *(confusion)* embarrassment; *(dérangement)* inconvenience

gêner [ʒene] *vt (déranger, irriter)* to bother; *(troubler)* to embarrass; *(mouvement)* to hamper; **ça ne me gêne pas** I don't mind (**si** if) ● **gêné, -e** *adj (intimidé)* embarrassed; *(silence, sourire)* awkward

général, -e, -aux, -ales [ʒeneral, -o] *adj* general; **en g.** in general ● **généraliste** *nmf (médecin)* general practitioner, GP

génération [ʒenerasjɔ̃] *nf* generation

générer [ʒenere] *vt* to generate

généreux, -euse [ʒenerø, -øz] *adj* generous (**de** with)

générique [ʒenerik] *nm (de film)* credits

génétique [ʒenetik] *adj* genetic ● **génétiquement** *adv* **g. modifié** genetically modified

Genève [ʒənɛv] *nm ou f* Geneva

génial, -e, -aux, -ales [ʒenjal, -jo] *adj* brilliant

génie [ʒeni] *nm* **(a)** *(aptitude, personne)* genius **(b) g. civil** civil engineering; **g. génétique** genetic engineering **(c)** *(esprit)* genie

genou, -x [ʒ(ə)nu] *nm* knee; **se mettre à genoux** to kneel (down)

genre [ʒɑ̃r] *nm (espèce)* kind, sort; *(attitude)* manner; *Beaux-Arts* genre; *Gram* gender

gens [ʒɑ̃] *nmpl* people

gentil, -ille [ʒɑ̃ti, -ij] *adj (aimable)* nice **(avec** to); *(sage)* good • **gentillesse** *nf* kindness • **gentiment** *adv (aimablement)* kindly; *(sagement)* nicely

géographie [ʒeɔgrafi] *nf* geography • **géographique** *adj* geographical

géologie [ʒeɔlɔʒi] *nf* geology • **géologique** *adj* geological

géométrie [ʒeɔmetri] *nf* geometry • **géométrique** *adj* geometric(al)

gérant, -e [ʒerɑ̃, -ɑ̃t] *nmf* manager

gerbe [ʒɛrb] *nf (de blé)* sheaf; *(de fleurs)* bunch; *(d'eau)* spray

gercer [ʒɛrse] *vi*, **se gercer** *vpr (peau, lèvres)* to chap

gérer [ʒere] *vt* to manage

germe [ʒɛrm] *nm (microbe)* germ; *(de plante)* shoot

geste [ʒɛst] *nm* gesture; **faire un g.** *(bouger, agir)* to make a gesture; **ne pas faire un g.** *(ne pas bouger)* not to make a move

gestion [ʒɛstjɔ̃] *nf (action)* management

gibier [ʒibje] *nm* game

gicler [ʒikle] *vi (liquide)* to spurt out; *(boue)* to splash up

gifle [ʒifl] *nf* slap in the face • **gifler** *vt* to slap

gigantesque [ʒigɑ̃tɛsk] *adj* gigantic

gigot [ʒigo] *nm* leg of/lamb

gilet [ʒilɛ] *nm (cardigan)* cardigan; *(de costume) Br* waistcoat, *Am* vest; **g. de sauvetage** life jacket

gingembre [ʒɛ̃ʒɑ̃br] *nm* ginger

girafe [ʒiraf] *nf* giraffe

giratoire [ʒiratwar] *adj Aut* **sens g.** *Br* roundabout, *Am* traffic circle

girofle [ʒirɔfl] *nm* **clou de g.** clove

gitan, -e [ʒitɑ̃, -an] *nmf* gipsy

gîte [ʒit] *nm* **g. (rural)** gîte, = self-catering holiday cottage

givre [ʒivr] *nm* frost • **givré, -e** *adj* frost-covered

glace [glas] *nf* **(a)** *(eau gelée)* ice; *(crème glacée)* ice cream **(b)** *(vitre)* window; *(miroir)* mirror • **glacé, -e** *adj (eau, pièce)* ice-cold, icy; *(vent)* freezing, icy; *(thé, café)* iced

glacial, -e, -aux, -ales [glasjal, -o] *adj* icy

glacier [glasje] *nm Géol* glacier

glaçon [glasɔ̃] *nm* ice cube

glisse [glis] *nf* **sports de g.** = sports involving sliding motion, *eg* skiing, surfing *etc*

glisser [glise] **1** *vt (introduire)* to slip **(dans** into) **2** *vi (involontairement)* to slip; *(volontairement)* to slide; **ça glisse** it's slippery **3 se glisser** *vpr* **se g. dans/sous qch** to slip into/under sth

global, -e, -aux, -ales [glɔbal, -o] *adj* total, global • **globalement** *adv* overall

globe [glɔb] *nm* globe

gloire [glwar] *nf* glory • **glorieux, -euse** *adj* glorious

glousser [gluse] *vi (poule)* to cluck; *(personne)* to chuckle

glouton, -onne [glutɔ̃, -ɔn] **1** *adj* greedy, gluttonous **2** *nmf* glutton

gluant, -e [glyɑ̃, -ɑ̃t] *adj* sticky

goal [gol] *nm (au football)* goalkeeper

gobelet [gɔblɛ] *nm* tumbler; *(de plastique, de papier)* cup

golf [gɔlf] *nm* golf; *(terrain)* golf course • **golfeur, -euse** *nmf* golfer

golfe [gɔlf] *nm* gulf, bay

gomme [gɔm] *nf (pour effacer)* eraser, *Br* rubber • **gommer** *vt (effacer)* to rub out, to erase

gonflable [gɔ̃flabl] *adj* inflatable

gonfler [gɔ̃fle] **1** *vt* to swell; *(pneu)* to inflate **2** *vi* to swell • **gonflé, -e** *adj* swollen

gorge [gɔrʒ] *nf* throat; *Géog* gorge; **avoir la g. serrée** to have a lump in one's throat

gorgée [gɔrʒe] *nf* mouthful; **petite g.** sip

gorille [gɔrij] *nm* gorilla

goudron [gudrɔ̃] *nm* tar

goulot [gulo] *nm (de bouteille)* neck; **boire au g.** to drink from the bottle

gourde [gurd] *nf* water bottle

gourmand, -e [gurmɑ̃, -ɑ̃d] *nmf* hearty eater • **gourmandise** *nf* fondness for food; **gourmandises** *(mets)* delicacies

gourmet [gurmɛ] *nm* gourmet

gousse [gus] *nf* **g. d'ail** clove of garlic

goût [gu] *nm* taste; **de bon g.** in good taste; **avoir du g.** *(personne)* to have (good) taste; **avoir un g. de noisette** to taste of hazelnut

goûter [gute] **1** *vt (aliment)* to taste; **g. à qch** to taste (a little of) sth **2** *vi* to have an afternoon snack **3** *nm* afternoon snack

goutte [gut] *nf (de liquide)* drop;

gouttière [gutjɛr] *nf (du toit)* gutter; *(du mur)* drainpipe

gouvernement [guvɛrnəmɑ̃] *nm* government

gouverner [guvɛrne] *vti Pol & Fig* to govern, to rule • **gouverneu** *nm* governor

grâce [grɑs] **1** *nf (charme)* grace *(acquittement)* pardon; **de bonne mauvaise g.** with good/bad grace **2** *prép* **g. à** thanks to

gracieux, -euse [grasjø, -øz] *adj (élégant)* graceful; *(aimable* gratuitous • **gracieusemen** *adv (avec élégance)* gracefully *(aimablement)* graciously

grade [grad] *nm (militaire)* rank

gradins [gradɛ̃] *nmpl (d'amphi théâtre)* rows of seats; *(de stade) B* terraces, *Am* bleachers

graduel, -elle [graduɛl] *ad* gradual

graffiti [grafiti] *nmpl* graffiti

grain [grɛ̃] *nm (de blé) & Fi* grain; *(de poussière)* speck; **g de beauté** mole; *(sur le visage* beauty spot; **g. de raisin** grape

graine [grɛn] *nf* seed

graisse [grɛs] *nf* fat; *(lubrifiant* grease • **graisseux, -euse** *ad* greasy, oily

grammaire [gramɛr] *nf* gramma • **grammatical, -e, -aux, -ale** *adj* grammatical

gramme [gram] *nm* gram(me)

grand, -e [grɑ̃, grɑ̃d] **1** *adj* big large; *(en hauteur)* tall; *(chaleu* découverte, âge, mérite, ami great; *(bruit)* loud; *(différence* big, great; *(adulte)* grown-up, big *(illustre)* great; **g. frère** *(plus âgé* big brother; **le g. air** the open air **il est g. temps que je parte** it' high time that I left; **il n'y avai pas g. monde** there were no many people **2** *adv* **g. ouver** *(yeux, fenêtre)* wide open; **ouvri g.** to open wide; **en g.** on a gran or large scale **3** *nmf (enfant)* senio *(adulte)* grown-up • **grand-mère** *(pl* **grands-mères)** *nf* grandmother • **grand-père** *(pl* **grands-pères)** *nm* grandfather • **grands-parents** *nmpl* grandparents

grand-chose [grãʃoz] *pron* **pas g.** not much

Grande-Bretagne [grãdbrətaɲ] *nf* **la G.** Great Britain

grandeur [grãdœr] *nf (gloire)* greatness; *(dimension)* size; *(splendeur)* grandeur; **g. nature** life-size

grandir [grãdir] *vi (en taille)* to grow; *(en âge)* to grow up; **g. de 2 cm** to grow 2 cm

grange [grãʒ] *nf* barn

graphique [grafik] *nm* graph; *Ordinat* graphic

grappe [grap] *nf* **g. de raisin** bunch of grapes

gras, grasse [gra, gras] **1** *adj (personne, ventre)* fat; *(aliment)* fatty; *(graisseux)* greasy, oily; **faire la grasse matinée** to have a lie-in **2** *nm (de viande)* fat

gratin [gratɛ̃] *nm (plat)* = baked dish with a cheese topping; **chou-fleur au g.** cauliflower cheese

gratitude [gratityd] *nf* gratitude

gratte-ciel [gratsjɛl] *nm inv* skyscraper

gratter [grate] **1** *vt (avec un outil)* to scrape; *(avec les ongles, les griffes)* to scratch; *Fam* **ça me gratte** it's itchy **2** *vi (tissu)* to be scratchy **3** **se gratter** *vpr* to scratch oneself

gratuit, -e [gratɥi, -it] *adj (billet, entrée)* free • **gratuitement** *adv (sans payer)* free (of charge)

grave [grav] *adj (maladie, faute)* serious; *(visage)* grave; *(voix)* deep, low; **ce n'est pas g.!** it's not important! • **gravement** *adv* seriously

graver [grave] *vt (sur métal)* to engrave; *(sur bois)* to carve

gravier [gravje] *nm* gravel

gravité [gravite] *nf (de situation)* seriousness; *Phys* gravity

gravure [gravyr] *nf (image)* print; *(action, art)* engraving

gré [gre] *nm* **de son plein g.** of one's own free will; **de bon g.** willingly; **contre le g. de qn** against sb's will; **bon g. mal g.** whether we/you/*etc* like it or not

Grèce [grɛs] *nf* **la G.** Greece • **grec, grecque 1** *adj* Greek **2** *nmf* **G., Grecque** Greek **3** *nm (langue)* Greek

greffier [grɛfje] *nf (de peau, d'arbre)* graft; *(d'organe)* transplant *nm Jur* clerk (of the court)

grêle [grɛl] *nf* hail • **grêler** *v impersonnel* to hail; **il grêle** it's hailing • **grêlon** *nm* hailstone

grenade [grənad] *nf (fruit)* pomegranate; *(projectile)* grenade

grenier [grənje] *nm* attic

grenouille [grənuj] *nf* frog

grève [grɛv] *nf (arrêt du travail)* strike; **faire g.** to be on strike; **g. de la faim** hunger strike

gribouiller [gribuje] *vti* to scribble

grief [grijɛf] *nm (plainte)* grievance

grièvement [grijɛvmã] *adv* seriously, badly

griffe [grif] *nf (ongle)* claw • **griffer** *vt* to scratch

grignoter [griɲote] *vti* to nibble

gril [gril] *nm (ustensile) Br* grill, *Am* broiler • **grillade** *nf (viande) Br* grilled meat, *Am* broiled meat • **grille-pain** *nm inv* toaster • **griller 1** *vt (viande) Br* to grill, *Am* to broil; *(pain)* to toast; *(ampoule électrique)* to blow; *Fam* **g. un feu rouge** to jump the lights **2** *vi* *(viande)* to grill; *(pain)* to toast

grille [grij] *nf (clôture)* railings; *(porte)* gate; *Fig (de salaires)* scale

grimace [grimas] *nf (pour faire rire)* (funny) face; *(de douleur)* grimace; **faire la g.** to pull a face

grimper [grɛ̃pe] **1** *vi* to climb (**à qch** up sth) **2** *vt (escalier)* to climb

grincer [grɛ̃se] *vi* to creak; **g. des dents** to grind one's teeth

grincheux, -euse [grɛ̃ʃø, -øz] *adj* grumpy

grippe [grip] *nf (maladie)* flu

gris, -e [gri, griz] **1** *adj Br* grey, *Am* gray; *(temps)* dull, grey **2** *nm Br* grey, *Am* gray

grogner [grɔɲe] *vi (personne)* to grumble (**contre** at) • **grognon, -onne** *adj* grumpy

gronder [grɔ̃de] **1** *vt (réprimander)* to scold, to tell off **2** *vi (chien)* to growl; *(tonnerre)* to rumble

gros, grosse [gro, gros] **1** *adj (corpulent, important)* big; *(gras)* fat; *(épais)* thick; *(effort, progrès)* great; *(somme, fortune)* large; **g. mot** swearword **2** *adv* **écrire g.** to write big; **en g.** *(globalement)* roughly; *(écrire)* in big letters **3** *nmf (personne)* fat person

groseille [grozɛj] *nf* redcurrant

grossesse [grosɛs] *nf* pregnancy

grosseur [grosœr] *nf (volume)* size; *(tumeur)* lump

grossier, -ère [grosje, -ɛr] *adj (tissu, traits)* rough, coarse; *(personne, manières)* rude, coarse; *(ruse, instrument)* crude

grossir [grosir] **1** *vt (sujet: verre, loupe)* to magnify **2** *vi (personne)* to put on weight; *(bosse, foule)* to get bigger

grotesque [grotɛsk] *adj* ludicrous

grotte [grɔt] *nf* cave

grouiller [gruje] *vi (se presser)*

to swarm around; **g. de qch** to swarm with sth

groupe [grup] *nm* group; **g. sanguin** blood group • **grouper 1** *vt* to group (together) **2 se grouper** *vpr (en association)* to form a group

grue [gry] *nf* crane

grumeau, -x [grymo] *nm (dans une sauce)* lump

Guadeloupe [gwadlup] *nf* **la G.** Guadeloupe

guépard [gepar] *nm* cheetah

guêpe [gɛp] *nf* wasp

guère [gɛr] *adv* **(ne...) g.** *(pas beaucoup)* not much; *(pas longtemps)* hardly, scarcely; **il n'a g. d'amis** he hasn't got many friends

guérilla [gerija] *nf* guerrilla warfare

guérir [gerir] **1** *vt (personne, maladie)* to cure (**de** of); *(blessure)* to heal **2** *vi (personne)* to get better, to recover; *(blessure)* to heal

Guernesey [gɛrnzɛ] *nf* Guernsey

guerre [gɛr] *nf* war; *(technique)* warfare; **en g.** at war (**avec** with); **faire la g.** to wage war (**à** on *or* against); *(soldat)* to fight; **crime de g.** war crime • **guerrier, -ère** *nmf* warrior

guetter [gɛte] *vt (occasion)* to watch out for; *(gibier)* to lie in wait for

gueule [gœl] *nf (d'animal)* & *Fam* mouth

guichet [giʃɛ] *nm (de gare, de banque)* window • **guichetier, -ère** *nmf (de banque) Br* counter clerk, *Am* teller; *(de gare)* ticket clerk

guide [gid] *nm (personne, livre)* guide; **g. touristique** tourist guide • **guider** *vt* to guide

guidon [gidɔ̃] *nm* handlebars

guillemets [gijmɛ] *nmpl Typ*

inverted commas, quotation marks; **entre g.** in inverted commas, in quotation marks

guillotine [gijɔtin] *nf* guillotine

guimauve [gimov] *nf (confiserie)* marshmallow

guirlande [girlɑ̃d] *nf (de fleurs)* garland; **guilandes de Noël** tinsel

guitare [gitar] *nf* guitar

gymnaste [ʒimnast] *nmf* gymnast
• **gymnastique** *nf* gymnastics *(sing)*

gynécologue [ʒinekɔlɔg] *nmf Br* gynaecologist, *Am* gynecologist

Hh

H, h [aʃ] *nm inv* H, h

habile [abil] *adj* skilful, *Am* skillful (**à qch** at sth); **h. de ses mains** good with one's hands

habillé, -e [abije] *adj* dressed (**de** in; **en** as); *(costume, robe)* smart

habiller [abije] **1** *vt* to dress (**de** in) **2 s'habiller** *vpr* to dress, to get dressed; *(avec élégance)* to dress up

habit [abi] *nm (de soirée)* evening dress; **habits** *(vêtements)* clothes

habitable [abitabl] *adj* (in)habitable; *(maison)* fit to live in

habitat [abita] *nm* habitat

habitation [abitasjɔ̃] *nf (lieu)* dwelling

habiter [abite] **1** *vt (maison, région)* to live in **2** *vi* to live (**à/en** in) • **habitant, -e** *nmf (de pays)* inhabitant

habitude [abityd] *nf* habit; **avoir l'h. de qch** to be used to sth; **avoir l'h. de faire qch** to be used to doing sth; **prendre l'h. de faire qch** to get into the habit of doing sth; **d'h.** usually; **comme d'h.** as usual

habituel, -elle [abityɛl] *adj* usual

habituer [abitye] **1** *vt* **h. qn à qch** to accustom sb to sth; **être habitué à qch/à faire qch** to be used to sth/to doing sth **2 s'habituer** *vpr* **s'h. à qn/qch** to get used to sb/sth • **habitué, -e** *nmf* regular

hache [ˈaʃ] *nf* axe, *Am* ax

hacher [ˈaʃe] *vt (au couteau)* to chop up; *(avec un appareil) Br* to mince, *Am* to grind • **haché, -e** *adj (viande) Br* minced, *Am* ground • **hachis** *nm* **h. Parmentier** ≃ cottage pie

haie [ˈɛ] *nf (clôture)* hedge; *(en équitation)* fence; **400 mètres haies** *(épreuve d'athlétisme)* 400-metre hurdles

haine [ˈɛn] *nf* hatred, hate

haïr* [ˈair] *vt* to hate

hâlé, -e [ˈale] *adj* suntanned

haleine [alɛn] *nf* breath; **reprendre h.** to get one's breath back

haleter [ˈalte] *vi* to pant, to gasp • **haletant, -e** *adj* panting, gasping

hall [ˈol] *nm (de maison)* entrance hall; *(d'hôtel)* lobby

halle [ˈal] *nf* (covered) market; **les halles** the central food market

hallucination [alysinasjɔ̃] *nf* hallucination • **hallucinant, -e** *adj* extraordinary

halte [ˈalt] *nf* stop

haltère [altɛr] *nm* dumbbell • **haltérophile** *nmf* weightlifter

hamac [ˈamak] *nm* hammock

hamburger [ˈãbœrgœr] *nm* burger

hameau, -x [ˈamo] *nm* hamlet

hamster [ˈamstɛr] *nm* hamster

hanche [ˈãʃ] *nf* hip

handball [ˈãdbal] *nm Sport* handball

handicap [ˈãdikap] *nm (physique, mental)* disability; *Fig* handicap •

handicapé, -e 1 *adj* disabled **2** *nmf* disabled person; **h. physique/mental** physically/mentally handicapped person

hanter ['āte] *vt* to haunt ● **hantise** *nf* **avoir la h. de qch** to really dread sth

harceler ['arsəle] *vt* (*importuner*) to harass ● **harcèlement** *nm* harassment

hardi, -e ['ardi] *adj* bold

hargneux, -euse ['arɲø, -øz] *adj* bad-tempered

haricot ['ariko] *nm* bean; **h. rouge** kidney bean; **h. vert** green bean, *Br* French bean

harmonica [armɔnika] *nm* harmonica, mouthorgan

harmonie [armɔni] *nf* harmony ● **harmoniser** *vt*, **s'harmoniser** *vpr* to harmonize

harnais ['arnɛ] *nm* harness

harpe ['arp] *nf* harp

harpon ['arpɔ̃] *nm* harpoon

hasard ['azar] *nm* **le h.** chance; **un h.** a coincidence; **par h.** by chance; **au h.** (*choisir, répondre*) at random; (*marcher*) aimlessly ● **hasardeux, -euse** *adj* risky, hazardous

hâte ['at] *nf* haste; **à la h.** hastily; **en (toute) h.** hurriedly; **avoir h. de faire qch** to be eager to do sth ● **hâter 1** *vt* (*pas, départ*) to hasten **2 se hâter** *vpr* to hurry (**de faire** to do)

hausse ['os] *nf* rise (**de** in); **en h.** rising ● **hausser** *vt* (*prix, voix*) to raise; (*épaules*) to shrug

haut, -e ['o, 'ot] **1** *adj* high; (*en taille*) tall; **h. de cinq mètres** five metres high *or* tall; **à haute voix, à voix haute** aloud; **un renseignement de la plus haute importance** news of the utmost

importance **2** *adv* (*dans l'espace*) & *Mus* high; (*dans une hiérarchie*) highly; (*parler*) loud, loudly; **tout h.** (*lire, penser*) out loud; **h. placé** (*personne*) in a high position; **plus h.** (*dans un texte*) above **3** *nm* (*partie haute*) top; **en h. de** at the top of; **en h.** (*loger*) upstairs; (*regarder*) up; (*mettre*) on (the) top; **d'en h.** (*de la partie haute, du ciel*) from high up, from up above; **avoir cinq mètres de h.** to be five metres high *or* tall; *Fig* **des hauts et des bas** ups and downs ● **haut-parleur** (*pl* **haut-parleurs**) *nm* loudspeaker

hauteur ['otœr] *nf* height; **à la h. de** (*objet*) level with; (*rue*) opposite; **arriver à la h. de qch** (*mesurer*) to reach sth; **il n'est pas à la h.** he isn't up to it

hebdomadaire [ɛbdɔmadɛr] *adj* & *nm* weekly

héberger [eberʒe] *vt* to put up

hébreu, -x [ebrø] **1** *adj m* Hebrew **2** *nm* (*langue*) Hebrew

hectare [ɛktar] *nm* hectare (= 2.47 acres)

hélas ['elas] *exclam* unfortunately

héler ['ele] *vt* (*taxi*) to hail

hélice [elis] *nf* propeller

hélicoptère [elikɔptɛr] *nm* helicopter

hémisphère [emisfɛr] *nm* hemisphere

hémorragie [emɔraʒi] *nf Méd* haemorrhage

herbe [ɛrb] *nf* grass; **mauvaise h.** weed; *Culin* **fines herbes** herbs

hérissé, -e ['erise] *adj* (*cheveux*) bristly

hérisson ['erisɔ̃] *nm* hedgehog

hériter [erite] **1** *vt* to inherit (**qch de qn** sth from sb) **2** *vi* **h. de qch** to inherit sth ● **héritage** *nm* *(biens)* inheritance; *Fig (culturel)* heritage • **héritier, -ère** *nmf* heir, *f* heiress (**de** to)

héros ['ero] *nm* hero • **héroïne** *nf (femme)* heroine; *(drogue)* heroin • **héroïque** *adj* heroic

hésiter [ezite] *vi* to hesitate (**sur** over *or* about; **entre** between; **à faire** to do) • **hésitant, -e** *adj* hesitant • **hésitation** *nf* hesitation; **avec h.** hesitatingly

heure [œr] *nf (mesure)* hour; *(moment)* time; **quelle h. est-il?** what time is it?; **il est six heures** it's six (o'clock); **six heures moins cinq** five to six; **six heures cinq** *Br* five past six, *Am* five after six; **à l'h.** *(arriver)* on time; *(être payé)* by the hour; **100 km à l'h.** 100 km an hour; **de bonne h.** early; **tout à l'h.** *(futur)* in a few moments, later; *(passé)* a moment ago; **à tout à l'h.!** *(au revoir)* see you soon!; **à toute h.** *(continuellement)* at all hours; **24 heures sur 24** 24 hours a day; **faire des heures supplémentaires** to work *or* do overtime; **heures de pointe** *(circulation)* rush hour; *(dans les magasins)* peak period; **heures creuses** off-peak *or* slack periods; **h. d'été** *Br* summer time, *Am* daylight-saving time

heureux, -euse [œrø, -øz] **1** *adj* happy (**de** with); *(chanceux)* lucky, fortunate **2** *adv (vivre, mourir)* happily • **heureusement** *adv (par chance)* fortunately, luckily (**pour** for); *(avec succès)* successfully

heurter ['œrte] **1** *vt (cogner)* to hit (**contre** against); *(entrer en collision avec)* to collide with **2 se heurter** *vpr* to collide (**à** *ou* **contre** against); *Fig* **se h. à qch** to meet with sth

hexagone [ɛgzagɔn] *nm* hexagon; *Fig* **l'H.** France

hiberner [ibɛrne] *vi* to hibernate

hibou, -x ['ibu] *nm* owl

hier [(i)jɛr] *adv* yesterday; **h. soi** yesterday evening

hiérarchie ['jerarʃi] *nf* hierarchy

hi-fi ['ifi] *adj inv & nf inv* hi-fi

hilarant, -e [ilarɑ̃, -ɑ̃t] *ad* hilarious

hindou, -e [ɛ̃du] *adj & nm* Hindu

hippodrome [ipɔdrom] *nm* B racecourse, *Am* racetrack

hippopotame [ipɔpɔtam] *nm* hippopotamus

histoire [istwar] *nf (science événements)* history; *(récit)* story

historique [istɔrik] *ad* *(concernant l'histoire)* historical *(important)* historic

hiver [ivɛr] *nm* winter

HLM ['aʃɛlɛm] *(abrév* **habitation à loyer modéré)** *nm ou f B* ≃ council flats, *Am* ≃ low-ren apartment building

hocher ['ɔʃe] *vt* **h. la tête** *(pou dire oui)* to nod; *(pour dire non)* to shake one's head

hockey ['ɔkɛ] *nm Br* hockey, *Ar* field hockey; **h. sur glace** ic hockey

Hollande ['ɔlɑ̃d] *nf* **la H.** Hollan • **hollandais, -e 1** *adj* Dutch *nmf* **H., Hollandaise** Dutchman, Dutchwoman; **les H.** the Dutch *nm (langue)* Dutch

homard ['ɔmar] *nm* lobster

hommage [ɔmaʒ] *nm* homag (**à** to); **rendre h. à qn** to pa homage to sb

homme [ɔm] *nm* man *(pl* men' **l'h.** *(genre humain)* man(kind); **de vêtements d'h.** men's clothe **h. d'affaires** businessman; **h politique** politician

homosexuel, -elle [ɔmɔsɛksɥɛl] *adj & nmf* homosexual

Hongrie ['ɔ̃gri] *nf* **la H.** Hungary • **hongrois, -e 1** *adj* Hungarian **2** *nmf* **H., Hongroise** Hungarian **3** *nm (langue)* Hungarian

honnête [ɔnɛt] *adj (intègre)* honest; *(vie, gens)* decent; *(prix)* fair • **honnêtement** *adv (avec intégrité)* honestly; *(raisonnablement)* decently • **honnêteté** *nf (intégrité)* honesty

honneur [ɔnœr] *nm* honour; **en l'h. de qn** in honour of sb; **invité d'h.** guest of honour

honorable [ɔnɔrabl] *adj* honourable

honoraires [ɔnɔrɛr] *nmpl* fees

honorer [ɔnɔre] *vt* to honour (**de** with)

honte ['ɔ̃t] *nf* shame; **avoir h.** to be *or* feel ashamed (**de qch/ de faire qch** of sth/to do *or* of doing sth); **faire h. à qn** to put sb to shame • **honteux, -euse** *adj (personne)* ashamed (**de** of); *(conduite, acte)* shameful

hôpital, -aux [ɔpital, -o] *nm* hospital; **à l'h.** *Br* in hospital, *Am* in the hospital

hoquet ['ɔkɛ] *nm* hiccup; **avoir le h.** to have the hiccups

horaire [ɔrɛr] **1** *adj (salaire)* hourly; *(vitesse)* per hour **2** *nm* timetable, schedule; **horaires de travail** working hours

horizon [ɔrizɔ̃] *nm* horizon; **à l'h.** on the horizon • **horizontal, -e, -aux, -ales** *adj* horizontal

horloge [ɔrlɔʒ] *nf* clock

hormone [ɔrmɔn] *nf* hormone

horoscope [ɔrɔskɔp] *nm* horoscope

horreur [ɔrœr] *nf* horror; **avoir h. de qch** to hate *or* loathe sth; **quelle h.!** how horrible!

horrible [ɔribl] *adj* horrible • **horriblement** [-əmɑ̃] *adv (défiguré)* horribly

horrifié, -e [ɔrifje] *adj* horrified

hors ['ɔr] *prép* **h. de** *(maison, boîte)* outside; *Fig (danger, haleine)* out of; *(au football)* **être h. jeu** to be offside • **hors-d'œuvre** *nm inv (plat)* hors-d'œuvre, starter • **hors-jeu** *nm inv (au football)* offside • **hors service** *adj inv (appareil)* out of order • **hors taxe** *adj inv (magasin, objet)* duty-free

hospitalier, -ère [ɔspitalje, -ɛr] *adj* **centre h.** hospital (complex)

hospitalité [ɔspitalite] *nf* hospitality

hostile [ɔstil] *adj* hostile (**à** to *or* towards) • **hostilité** *nf* hostility (**envers** to *or* towards)

hôte [ot] **1** *nm (qui reçoit)* host **2** *nmf (invité)* guest • **hôtesse** *nf* hostess; **h. de l'air** air hostess

hôtel [otɛl] *nm* hotel; **h. de ville** *Br* town hall, *Am* city hall

housse ['us] *nf (protective)* cover

huer ['ɥe] *vt* to boo • **huées** *nfpl* boos

huile [ɥil] *nf* oil; **h. d'olive** olive oil

huissier [ɥisje] *nm (portier)* usher; *Jur* bailiff

huit ['ɥit] (['ɥi] *before consonant*) *adj & nm inv* eight; **h. jours** a week • **huitième** *adj & nmf* eighth; **un h.** an eighth

huître [ɥitr] *nf* oyster

humain, -e [ymɛ̃, -ɛn] **1** *adj (relatif à l'homme)* human; *(compatissant)* humane **2** *nmpl* **les humains** humans • **humanitaire** *adj* humanitarian • **humanité** *nf (genre humain, sentiment)* humanity

humble [œ̃bl] *adj* humble

humecter [ymɛkte] *vt* to moisten

humeur [ymœr] *nf (disposition)* mood; **être de bonne/mauvaise h.** to be in a good/bad mood

humide [ymid] *adj (linge)* damp, wet; *(climat, temps)* humid • **humidité** *nf (de maison)* dampness; *(de climat)* humidity

humilier [ymilje] *vt* to humiliate • **humiliant, -e** *adj* humiliating • **humiliation** *nf* humiliation

humour [ymur] *nm* humour; **avoir le sens de l'h.** to have a sense of humour • **humoristique** *adj (récit, ton)* humorous

hurler ['yrle] **1** *vt (slogans, injures)* to yell **2** *vi (loup, vent)* to howl; *(personne)* to scream

hydrater [idrate] *vt (peau)* to moisturize

hydrophile [idrɔfil] *adj* **coton h.** *Br* cotton wool, *Am* (absorbent) cotton

hyène [jɛn] *nf* hyena

hygiène [iʒjɛn] *nf* hygiene • **hygiénique** *adj* hygienic; *(serviette, conditions)* sanitary

hymne [imn] *nm* hymn; **h. national** national anthem

hypermarché [ipɛrmarʃe] *nm* hypermarket

hypermétrope [ipɛrmetrɔp] *adj* longsighted

hypnotiser [ipnotize] *vt* to hypnotize

hypocrisie [ipɔkrizi] *nf* hypocrisy • **hypocrite**

hypothèque [ipɔtɛk] *nf* mortgage

hypothèse [ipɔtɛz] *nf* hypothesis

I, i [i] *nm inv* I, i
iceberg [ajsbɛrg] *nm* iceberg
ici [isi] *adv* here; **par i.** *(passer)*
this way; *(habiter)* around here;
jusqu'i. *(temps)* up to now; *(lieu)*
as far as this *or* here; **d'i. à mardi**
by Tuesday
icône [ikon] *nf Rel & Ordinat* icon
idéal, -e, -aux *ou* **-als, -ales**
[ideal, -o] **1** *adj* ideal **2** *nm* ideal;
l'i. serait de/que... the ideal *or*
best solution would be to/if...
idée [ide] *nf* idea (**de** of; **que** that)
identifier [idɑ̃tifje] *vt,* **s'identifier** *vpr* to identify (**à** with) ●
identification *nf* identification
identique [idɑ̃tik] *adj* identical
(**à** to)
identité [idɑ̃tite] *nf* identity
idiot, -e [idjo, -ɔt] **1** *adj* silly,
idiotic **2** *nmf* idiot
idole [idɔl] *nf* idol
idyllique [idilik] *adj* idyllic
ignorant, -e [iɲɔrɑ̃, -ɑ̃t] *adj*
ignorant (**de** of)
ignorer [iɲɔre] *vt* not to know;
j'ignore si... I don't know if...; **je
n'ignore pas les difficultés** I am
not unaware of the difficulties; **i.
qn** *(mépriser)* to ignore sb
il [il] *pron personnel (personne)* he;
(chose, animal, impersonnel) it; **il
est** he/it is; **il pleut** it's raining; **il est
vrai que...** it's true that...; **il y a...**
there is/are...; **il y a six ans** six years
ago; **qu'est-ce qu'il y a?** what's the
matter?, what's wrong?; **il n'y a pas
de quoi!** don't mention it!

île [il] *nf* island; **les îles Anglo-
Normandes** the Channel Islands;
les îles Britanniques the British
Isles
illégal, -e, -aux, -ales [il(l)egal,
-o] *adj* illegal
illimité, -e [il(l)imite] *adj*
unlimited
illisible [il(l)izibl] *adj* illegible
illogique [il(l)ɔʒik] *adj* illogical
illuminer [il(l)ymine] **1** *vt* to light
up **2 s'illuminer** *vpr (visage, ciel)*
to light up ● **illumination** *nf*
(action, lumière) illumination
illusion [il(l)yzjɔ̃] *nf* illusion (**sur**
about); **se faire des illusions**
to delude oneself (**sur** about); **i.
d'optique** optical illusion
illustrer [il(l)ystre] *vt (livre, récit)*
to illustrate (**de** with) ● **illustration**
nf illustration ● **illustré, -e** *adj*
(livre, magazine) illustrated
îlot [ilo] *nm (île)* small island;
(maisons) block
ils [il] *pron personnel mpl* they; **i.
sont ici** they are here
image [imaʒ] *nf* picture;
(ressemblance, symbole) image
imaginaire [imaʒinɛr] *adj*
imaginary ● **imaginatif, -ive** *adj*
imaginative
imagination [imaʒinasjɔ̃] *nf*
imagination
imaginer [imaʒine] **1** *vt (se
figurer)* to imagine; *(inventer)*
to devise **2 s'imaginer** *vpr (se
figurer)* to imagine (**que** that); *(se
voir)* to picture oneself

imbécile [ɛ̃besil] *nmf* idiot
imbuvable [ɛ̃byvabl] *adj* undrinkable
imiter [imite] *vt* to imitate; *(signature)* to forge; **i. qn** *(pour rire)* to mimic sb; *(faire comme)* to do the same as sb; *(imitateur professionnel)* to impersonate sb • **imitateur, -trice** *nmf* imitator; *(professionnel)* impersonator • **imitation** *nf* imitation
immaculé, -e [imakyle] *adj* immaculate
immangeable [ɛ̃mɑ̃ʒabl] *adj* inedible
immatriculer [imatrikyle] *vt* to register; **se faire i.** to register • **immatriculation** *nf* registration
immédiat, -e [imedja, -jat] **1** *adj* immediate **2** *nm* **dans l'i.** for the time being • **immédiatement** *adv* immediately
immense [imɑ̃s] *adj* immense
immerger [imɛrʒe] *vt* to immerse
immeuble [imœbl] *nm* building; *(appartements)* Br block of flats, Am apartment block
immigrant, -e [imigrɑ̃, -ɑ̃t] *nmf* immigrant • **immigration** *nf* immigration • **immigré, -e** *adj & nmf* immigrant
imminent, -e [iminɑ̃, -ɑ̃t] *adj* imminent
immobile [imɔbil] *adj* still, motionless
immobilier, -ère [imɔbilje, -ɛr] **1** *adj* **marché i.** property market **2** *nm* **l'i.** Br property, Am real estate
immoral, -e, -aux, -ales [i(m)mɔral, -o] *adj* immoral
immortel, -elle [i(m)mɔrtɛl] *adj* immortal • **immortalité** *nf* immortality
immuniser [i(m)mynize] *vt* to immunize **(contre** against) • **immunité** *nf* immunity

impact [ɛ̃pakt] *nm* impact **(sur** on)
impair, -e [ɛ̃pɛr] *adj (nombre)* odd, uneven
impardonnable [ɛ̃pardɔnabl] *adj* unforgivable
imparfait, -e [ɛ̃parfɛ, -ɛt] *adj (connaissance)* imperfect
impartial, -e, -aux, -ales [ɛ̃parsjal, -o] *adj* impartial, unbiased
impasse [ɛ̃pɑs] *nf (rue)* dead end; *Fig (situation)*
impatient, -e [ɛ̃pasjɑ̃, -ɑ̃t] *adj* impatient; **i. de faire qch** impatient to do sth • **impatience** *nf* impatience • **s'impatienter** *vpr* to get impatient
impeccable [ɛ̃pekabl] *adj* impeccable
impératif, -ive [ɛ̃peratif, -iv] *adj (consigne, besoin)* imperative
imperfection [ɛ̃pɛrfɛksjɔ̃] *nf* imperfection
imperméable [ɛ̃pɛrmeabl] **1** *adj* waterproof **2** *nm* raincoat
impersonnel, -elle [ɛ̃pɛrsɔnɛl] *adj* impersonal
impertinent, -e [ɛ̃pɛrtinɑ̃, -ɑ̃t] *adj* impertinent **(envers** to)
impitoyable [ɛ̃pitwajabl] *adj* merciless
implacable [ɛ̃plakabl] *adj (personne, vengeance)* implacable; *(avancée)* relentless
implanter [ɛ̃plɑ̃te] *vt (installer)* to establish; *Méd* to implant
implicite [ɛ̃plisit] *adj* implicit
impliquer [ɛ̃plike] *vt (entraîner)* to imply; **i. que...** to imply that...; **i. qn** to implicate sb **(dans** in) • **implication** *nf* implication
implorer [ɛ̃plɔre] *vt* to implore **(qn de faire** sb to do)
impoli, -e [ɛ̃pɔli] *adj* rude
import [ɛ̃pɔr] *nm* import
important, -e [ɛ̃pɔrtɑ̃, -ɑ̃t] **1**

adj (personnage, événement) important; *(quantité, somme, ville)* large; *(dégâts, retard)* considerable **2** *nm* **l'i., c'est de...** the important thing is to... • **importance** *nf* importance; *(taille)* size; *(de dégâts)* extent; **ça n'a pas d'i.** it doesn't matter

importer¹ [ɛ̃pɔrte] **1** *vi* to matter (**à** to) **2** *v impersonnel* **peu importe, n'importe** it doesn't matter; **n'importe qui/quoi/où/quand/ comment** anyone/anything/anywhere/any time/anyhow

importer² [ɛ̃pɔrte] *vt (marchandises)* to import (**de** from) • **importation** *nf* importation

imposer [ɛ̃poze] **1** *vt (condition)* to impose; **i. qch à qn** to impose sth on sb **2 s'imposer** *vpr (faire reconnaître sa valeur)* to assert oneself; *(gagner)* to win; *(être nécessaire)* to be essential; *Péj (chez quelqu'un)* to impose • **imposant, -e** *adj* imposing

impossible [ɛ̃pɔsibl] **1** *adj* impossible (**à faire** to do); **il est i. que...** (+ *subjunctive*) it is impossible that... **2** *nm* **tenter l'i.** to attempt the impossible

imposteur [ɛ̃pɔstœr] *nm* impostor

impôt [ɛ̃po] *nm* tax; **(service des) impôts** tax authorities; **impôts locaux** local taxes; **i. sur le revenu** income tax

imprécis, -e [ɛ̃presi, -iz] *adj* imprecise

imprenable [ɛ̃prənabl] *(vue)* unobstructed

impression [ɛ̃presjɔ̃] *nf* impression; **avoir l'i. que...** to have the impression that...; **faire bonne i. à qn** to make a good impression on sb • **impressionnant, -e** *adj* impressive

imprévisible [ɛ̃previzibl] *adj (temps, personne)* unpredictable; *(événement)* unforeseeable • **imprévu, -e** *adj* unexpected, unforeseen

imprimer [ɛ̃prime] *vt (livre, tissu)* to print; *Ordinat* to print (out) • **imprimante** *nf* printer • **imprimerie** *nf (lieu) Br* printing works, *Am* print shop

improbable [ɛ̃prɔbabl] *adj* improbable, unlikely

impropre [ɛ̃prɔpr] *adj* inappropriate; **i. à qch** unfit for sth; **i. à la consommation** unfit for human consumption

improviser [ɛ̃prɔvize] *vti* to improvise

improviste [ɛ̃prɔvist] **à l'improviste** *adv* unexpectedly

imprudent, -e [ɛ̃prydɑ̃, -ɑ̃t] *adj (personne, action)* rash; **il est i. de...** it is unwise to...

impuissant, -e [ɛ̃pɥisɑ̃, -ɑ̃t] *adj* powerless; *Méd* impotent

impulsif, -ive [ɛ̃pylsif, -iv] *adj* impulsive • **impulsion** *nf* impulse

impuni, -e [ɛ̃pyni] *adj* unpunished

impur, -e [ɛ̃pyr] *adj* impure • **impureté** *nf* impurity

inabordable [inabɔrdabl] *adj (prix)* prohibitive; *(lieu)* inaccessible; *(personne)* unapproachable

inacceptable [inaksɛptabl] *adj* unacceptable

inaccessible [inaksɛsibl] *adj (lieu)* inaccessible; *(personne)* unapproachable

inactif, -ive [inaktif, -iv] *adj (personne)* inactive; *(remède)* ineffective

inadapté, -e [inadapte] *adj (socialement)* maladjusted; *(handicapé)* disabled; *(matériel)* unsuitable (**à** for)

inadmissible [inadmisibl] *adj* inadmissible

inanimé, -e [inanime] *adj (mort)* lifeless; *(évanoui)* unconscious; *(matière)* inanimate

inaperçu, -e [inapɛrsy] *adj* **passer i.** to go unnoticed

inapte [inapt] *adj (intellectuelle-ment)* unsuited (**à** for); *(médi-calement)* unfit (**à** for)

inattendu, -e [inatɑ̃dy] *adj* unexpected

inattention [inatɑ̃sjɔ̃] *nf* lack of attention

inaudible [inodibl] *adj* inaudible

incapable [ɛ̃kapabl] *adj* incapable; **i. de faire qch** incapable of doing sth ● **incapacité** *nf (impossibilité)* inability (**de faire** to do); *(invalidité)* disability; **être dans l'i. de faire qch** to be unable to do sth

incarcérer [ɛ̃karsere] *vt* to incarcerate ● **incarcération** *nf* incarceration

incarnation [ɛ̃karnasjɔ̃] *nf* incar-nation ● **incarner** *vt* to embody

incassable [ɛ̃kasabl] *adj* unbreakable

incendie [ɛ̃sɑ̃di] *nm* fire; **i. de forêt** forest fire

incertain, -e [ɛ̃sɛrtɛ̃, -ɛn] *adj (résultat)* uncertain; *(personne)* indecisive ● **incertitude** *nf* uncertainty

incident [ɛ̃sidɑ̃] *nm* incident

incinérer [ɛ̃sinere] *vt (ordures)* to incinerate; *(cadavre)* to cremate

inciter [ɛ̃site] *vt* to encourage (**à faire** to do)

incliner [ɛ̃kline] **1** *vt (pencher)* to tilt; **i. la tête** *(approuver)* to nod; *(saluer)* to bow one's head **2 s'incliner** *vpr (se pencher)* to lean forward; *(pour saluer)* to bow ● **inclinaison** *nf* incline,

slope ● **inclination** *nf (tendance)* inclination

inclure* [ɛ̃klyr] *vt* to include; *(dans un courrier)* to enclose (**dans** with) ● **inclus, -e** *adj* **du 4 au 10 i.** from the 4th to the 10th inclusive; **jusqu'à lundi i.** *Br* to and including Monday, *Am* through Monday ● **inclusion** *nf* inclusion

incohérent, -e [ɛ̃kɔerɑ̃, -ɑ̃t] *adj (propos)* incoherent; *(histoire)* inconsistent

incomber [ɛ̃kɔ̃be] *vi* **i. à qn** *(devoir)* to fall to sb; **il lui incombe de faire qch** it falls to him/her to do sth

incomparable [ɛ̃kɔ̃parabl] *adj* matchless

incompatible [ɛ̃kɔ̃patibl] *adj* incompatible (**avec** with)

incompétent, -e [ɛ̃kɔ̃petɑ̃, -ɑ̃t] *adj* incompetent ● **incompétence** *nf* incompetence

incomplet, -ète [ɛ̃kɔ̃plɛ, -ɛt] *adj* incomplete

incompréhensible [ɛ̃kɔ̃preɑ̃sibl] *adj* incomprehensible ● **incom-préhension** *nf* incomprehension

inconcevable [ɛ̃kɔ̃səvabl] *adj* inconceivable

inconfortable [ɛ̃kɔ̃fɔrtabl] *adj* uncomfortable

inconnu, -e [ɛ̃kɔny] **1** *adj* unknown (**de** to) **2** *nmf (étranger)* stranger; *(auteur)* unknown

inconscient, -e [ɛ̃kɔ̃sjɑ̃, -ɑ̃t] *adj (sans connaissance)* unconscious; *(imprudent)* reckless; **i. de qch** unaware of sth ● **inconsciemment** [-amɑ̃] *adv* subconsciously ● **inconscience** *nf (perte de connaissance)* unconsciousness; *(irréflexion)* recklessness

inconsidéré, -e [ɛ̃kɔ̃sidere] *adj* thoughtless

inconsistant, -e [ɛ̃kɔ̃sistɑ̃, -ɑ̃t] *adj (personne)* weak; *(sauce)* thin

inconsolable [ɛ̃kɔ̃sɔlabl] *adj* inconsolable

inconstant, -e [ɛ̃kɔ̃stɑ̃, -ɑ̃t] *adj* fickle

incontestable [ɛ̃kɔ̃tɛstabl] *adj* indisputable

incontournable [ɛ̃kɔ̃turnabl] *adj Fig (film)* unmissable

inconvénient [ɛ̃kɔ̃venjɑ̃] *nm (désavantage)* drawback

incorporer [ɛ̃kɔrpɔre] *vt (insérer)* to insert (**à** in); **i. qch à qch** to blend sth into sth • **incorporation** *nf (mélange)* blending (**de qch dans qch** of sth into sth)

incorrect, -e [ɛ̃kɔrɛkt] *adj (inexact)* incorrect; *(grossier)* impolite; *(inconvenant)* improper

incorrigible [ɛ̃kɔriʒibl] *adj* incorrigible

incrédule [ɛ̃kredyl] *adj* incredulous

incroyable [ɛ̃krwajabl] *adj* incredible

incrusté, -e [ɛ̃kryste] *adj* **i. de** *(orné)* inlaid with

incubation [ɛ̃kybasjɔ̃] *nf* incubation

inculper [ɛ̃kylpe] *vt (accuser)* to charge (**de** with) • **inculpé, -e** *nmf* **l'i.** the accused

inculte [ɛ̃kylt] *adj (terre, personne)* uncultivated

incurable [ɛ̃kyrabl] *adj* incurable

Inde [ɛ̃d] *nf* **l'I.** India

indécent, -e [ɛ̃desɑ̃, -ɑ̃t] *adj* indecent

indéchiffrable [ɛ̃deʃifrabl] *adj (illisible)* undecipherable

indécis, -e [ɛ̃desi, -iz] *adj (personne) (de caractère)* indecisive; *(ponctuellement)* undecided

indéfini, -e [ɛ̃defini] *adj (illimité)* indefinite; *(imprécis)* undefined •

indéfiniment *adv* indefinitely

indélébile [ɛ̃delebil] *adj* indelible

indélicat, -e [ɛ̃delika, -at] *adj (grossier)* insensitive; *(malhonnête)* unscrupulous

indemne [ɛ̃dɛmn] *adj* unhurt

indemniser [ɛ̃dɛmnize] *vt* to compensate (**de** for) • **indemnité** *nf (dédommagement)* compensation; *(allocation)* allowance

indépendant, -e [ɛ̃depɑ̃dɑ̃, -ɑ̃t] *adj* independent (**de** of); *(travailleur)* self-employed • **indépendance** *nf* independence

indestructible [ɛ̃dɛstryktibl] *adj* indestructible

indéterminé, -e [ɛ̃detɛrmine] *adj (date, heure)* unspecified; *(raison)* unknown

index [ɛ̃dɛks] *nm (doigt)* index finger; *(liste) & Ordinat* index

indicatif, -ive [ɛ̃dikatif, -iv] **1** *adj* indicative (**de** of) **2** *nm Radio* theme tune; **i. téléphonique** *Br* dialling code, *Am* area code

indication [ɛ̃dikasjɔ̃] *nf* indication (**de** of); *(renseignement)* (piece of) information; *(directive)* instruction; **indications...** *(de médicament)* suitable for...

indice [ɛ̃dis] *nm (signe)* sign; *(d'enquête)* clue

indien, -enne [ɛ̃djɛ̃, -ɛn] **1** *adj* Indian **2** *nmf* **I., Indienne** Indian

indifférent, -e [ɛ̃diferɑ̃, -ɑ̃t] *adj* indifferent (**à** to) • **indifférence** *nf* indifference (**à** to)

indigène [ɛ̃diʒɛn] *adj & nmf* native

indigestion [ɛ̃diʒɛstjɔ̃] *nf* **avoir une i.** to have a stomach upset

indigne [ɛ̃diɲ] *adj (personne)* unworthy; *(conduite)* shameful; **i. de qn/qch** unworthy of sb/sth

indigné, -e [ɛ̃diɲe] *adj* indignant

indiquer [ɛ̃dike] *vt (sujet:*

personne) to point out; *(sujet: panneau)* to show, to indicate; *(donner) (date, adresse)* to give; **i. le chemin à qn** to tell sb the way ● **indiqué, -e** *adj* **à l'heure indiquée** at the appointed time
indirect, -e [ɛ̃dirɛkt] *adj* indirect
indiscipliné, -e [ɛ̃disipline] *adj* unruly
indiscret, -ète [ɛ̃diskrɛ, -ɛt] *adj* *Péj (curieux)* inquisitive; *(qui parle trop)* indiscreet ● **indiscrétion** *nf* indiscretion
indispensable [ɛ̃dispɑ̃sabl] *adj* essential, indispensable (**à qch** for sth); **i. à qn** indispensable to sb
indisponible [ɛ̃dispɔnibl] *adj* unavailable
indisposé, -e [ɛ̃dispoze] *adj* *(malade)* indisposed, unwell
individu [ɛ̃dividy] *nm* individual; *Péj* individual, character
individuel, -elle [ɛ̃dividɥɛl] *adj* individual; *(maison)* detached
indulgent, -e [ɛ̃dylʒɑ̃, -ɑ̃t] *adj* indulgent
industrie [ɛ̃dystri] *nf* industry ● **industriel, -elle** *adj* industrial
inédit, -e [inedi, -it] *adj (texte)* unpublished
inefficace [inefikas] *adj (mesure)* ineffective; *(personne)* inefficient
inégal, -e, -aux, -ales [inegal, -o] *adj (parts, lutte)* unequal; *(sol, humeur)* uneven; *Fig (travail)* inconsistent ● **inégalité** *nf (injustice)* inequality; *(de sol)* unevenness
inepte [inɛpt] *adj (remarque, histoire)* inane; *(personne)* inept
inépuisable [inepɥizabl] *adj* inexhaustible
inestimable [inɛstimabl] *adj (objet d'art)* priceless
inévitable [inevitabl] *adj* inevitable, unavoidable

inexact, -e [inɛgzakt] *adj (erroné)* inaccurate; *(calcul)* wrong
inexcusable [inɛkskyzabl] *adj* inexcusable
inexistant, -e [inɛgzistɑ̃, -ɑ̃t] *adj* non-existent
inexplicable [inɛksplikabl] *adj* inexplicable
infaillible [ɛ̃fajibl] *adj* infallible
infâme [ɛ̃fam] *adj (personne)* despicable; *(acte)* unspeakable; *(aliment)* revolting
infantile [ɛ̃fɑ̃til] *adj (maladie)* childhood; *Péj (comportement, personne)* infantile
infarctus [ɛ̃farktys] *nm Méd* heart attack
infect, -e [ɛ̃fɛkt] *adj* foul
infecter [ɛ̃fɛkte] **1** *vt (atmosphère)* to contaminate; *Méd* to infect **2** **s'infecter** *vpr* to become infected ● **infection** *nf Méd* infection
inférieur, -e [ɛ̃ferjœr] *adj (étagère, niveau)* bottom; *(étage, lèvre, membre)* lower; *(qualité, marchandises)* inferior; **i. à la moyenne** below average; **à l'étage i.** on the floor below ● **infériorité** *nf* inferiority
infernal, -e, -aux, -ales [ɛ̃fɛrnal, -o] *adj (chaleur, bruit)* infernal
infidèle [ɛ̃fidɛl] *adj* unfaithful (**à** to)
infiltrer [ɛ̃filtre] **1** *vt (party)* to infiltrate **2** **s'infiltrer** *vpr (liquide)* to seep (**dans** into); *Fig* **s'i. dans** *(groupe, esprit)* to infiltrate
infime [ɛ̃fim] *adj* tiny
infini, -e [ɛ̃fini] **1** *adj* infinite **2** *nm Math* infinity; **à l'i.** *(discuter)* ad infinitum ● **infiniment** *adv* infinitely; **je regrette i.** I'm very sorry
infirme [ɛ̃firm] *adj* disabled
infirmerie [ɛ̃firməri] *nf (d'école, de bateau)* sick room; *(de caserne,*

de prison) infirmary • **infirmier, -ère** *nmf* nurse

inflammable [ɛ̃flamabl] *adj* (in)flammable

inflammation [ɛ̃flamasjɔ̃] *nf Méd* inflammation

inflation [ɛ̃flasjɔ̃] *nf Écon* inflation

inflexion [ɛ̃flɛksjɔ̃] *nf (de courbe, de voix)* inflection

infliger [ɛ̃fliʒe] *vt* to inflict (**à** on); *(amende)* to impose (**à** on)

influence [ɛ̃flyɑ̃s] *nf* influence • **influencer** *vt* to influence

informaticien, -enne [ɛ̃fɔrmatisjɛ̃, -ɛn] *nmf* computer scientist

information [ɛ̃fɔrmasjɔ̃] *nf* information; *(nouvelle)* piece of news; *Ordinat* data, information; *Radio & TV* **les informations** the news *(sing)*

informatique [ɛ̃fɔrmatik] **1** *nf* IT **2** *adj* **programme i.** computer program • **informatisé, -e** *adj* computerized

informer [ɛ̃fɔrme] **1** *vt* to inform (**de** of *or* about; **que** that) **2 s'informer** *vpr (se renseigner)* to inquire (**de** about; **si** if *or* whether)

infraction [ɛ̃fraksjɔ̃] *nf (à un règlement)* infringement; *(délit) Br* offence, *Am* offense

infranchissable [ɛ̃frɑ̃ʃisabl] *adj (mur, fleuve)* impassable; *Fig (difficulté)* insurmountable

infrarouge [ɛ̃fraruʒ] *adj* infrared

infusion [ɛ̃fyzjɔ̃] *nf (tisane)* herbal tea

ingénieur [ɛ̃ʒenjœr] *nm* engineer • **ingénierie** [-iri] *nf* engineering

ingénieux, -euse [ɛ̃ʒenjø, -øz] *adj* ingenious

ingrat, -e [ɛ̃gra, -at] *adj (personne)* ungrateful (**envers** to); *(tâche)* thankless; *(visage)* unattractive • **ingratitude** *nf* ingratitude

ingrédient [ɛ̃gredjɑ̃] *nm* ingredient

inhabité, -e [inabite] *adj* uninhabited

inhabituel, -elle [inabitɥɛl] *adj* unusual

inhibition [inibisjɔ̃] *nf* inhibition

inhumain, -e [inymɛ̃, -ɛn] *adj (cruel, terrible)* inhuman

inimaginable [inimaʒinabl] *adj* unimaginable

inimitable [inimitabl] *adj* inimitable

ininflammable [inɛ̃flamabl] *adj* nonflammable

initial, -e, -aux, -ales [inisjal, -o] *adj* initial • **initiale** *nf* initial

initiation [inisjasjɔ̃] *nf* initiation

initiative [inisjativ] *nf* initiative; **de ma propre i.** on my own initiative

initier [inisje] *vt (former)* to introduce (**à** to); *(rituellement)* to initiate (**à** into)

injecter [ɛ̃ʒɛkte] *vt* to inject (**dans** into) • **injection** *nf* injection

injurier [ɛ̃ʒyrje] *vt* to insult, to abuse • **injurieux, -euse** *adj* abusive, insulting (**pour** to)

injuste [ɛ̃ʒyst] *adj (contraire à la justice)* unjust; *(non équitable)* unfair • **injustice** *nf* injustice

injustifié, -e [ɛ̃ʒystifje] *adj* unjustified

innocent, -e [inɔsɑ̃, -ɑ̃t] **1** *adj* innocent (**de** of) **2** *nmf* innocent person • **innocence** *nf* innocence

innombrable [inɔ̃brabl] *adj* countless, innumerable; *(foule)* huge

innovation [inɔvasjɔ̃] *nf* innovation

inoculer [inɔkyle] *vt* **i. qch à qn** to inoculate sb with sth; **i. qn contre qch** to inoculate sb against sth

inoffensif, -ive [inɔfɑ̃sif, -iv] *adj* harmless

inonder [inɔ̃de] *vt* to flood •
inondation *nf* flood; *(action)*
flooding
inoubliable   [inublijabl]   *adj*
unforgettable
inouï, -e [inwi] *adj* incredible
Inox® [inɔks] *nm* stainless steel;
couteau en I. stainless-steel knife
inquiet, -ète [ɛ̃kjɛ, -ɛt] *adj*
worried, anxious (**de** about)
inquiéter [ɛ̃kjete] **1** *vt* *(préoccuper)* to worry **2 s'inquiéter**
vpr to worry (**de** about); **s'i.
pour qn** to worry about sb •
inquiétant, -e *adj* worrying •
inquiétude *nf* anxiety, worry
insatisfait, -e [ɛ̃satisfɛ, -ɛt] *adj*
(personne) dissatisfied
inscription [ɛ̃skripsjɔ̃] *nf* *(action)*
entering; *(immatriculation)* registration; *(sur écriteau, tombe)* inscription
inscrire* [ɛ̃skrir] **1** *vt* *(renseignements, date)* to write down;
(graver) to inscribe; **i. qn à un
club** to *Br* enrol *or Am* enroll sb
in a club **2 s'inscrire** *vpr* to put
one's name down; *(à une activité)*
Br to enrol, *Am* to enroll (**à** at); *(à
l'université)* to register (**à** at); **s'i. à
un club** to join a club
insecte [ɛ̃sɛkt] *nm* insect
insécurité [ɛ̃sekyrite] *nf* inse-
curity
insensible [ɛ̃sɑ̃sibl] *adj* *(indifférent)* insensitive (**à** to)
inséparable [ɛ̃separabl] *adj*
inseparable (**de** from)
insérer [ɛ̃sere] *vt* to insert (**dans**
in) • **insertion** [ɛ̃sɛrsjɔ̃] *nf*
insertion
insigne [ɛ̃siɲ] *nm* badge
insignifiant, -e [ɛ̃siɲifjɑ̃, -ɑ̃t] *adj*
insignificant
insinuer [ɛ̃sinɥe] **1** *vt* *Péj* to
insinuate (**que** that) **2 s'insinuer**
vpr *(froid)* to creep (**dans** into);

(personne) to worm one's way
(**dans** into)
insipide [ɛ̃sipid] *adj* insipid
insister [ɛ̃siste] *vi* to insist (**pour
faire** on doing); **i. sur qch** to stress
sth; **i. pour que...** *(+ subjunctive)*
to insist that... • **insistance** *nf*
insistence
insolent, -e [ɛ̃sɔlɑ̃, -ɑ̃t] *adj*
insolent
insolite [ɛ̃sɔlit] *adj* unusual
insoluble [ɛ̃sɔlybl] *adj* insoluble
insomnie [ɛ̃sɔmni] *nf* insomnia •
insomniaque *nmf* insomniac
insouciant, -e [ɛ̃susjɑ̃, -ɑ̃t] *adj*
carefree • **insouciance** *nf* carefree
attitude
inspecter [ɛ̃spɛkte] *vt* to inspect •
inspecteur, -trice *nmf* inspector •
inspection *nf* inspection
inspirer [ɛ̃spire] **1** *vt* to inspire; **i.
qch à qn** to inspire sb with sth **2** *vi*
to breathe in **3 s'inspirer** *vpr* **s'i.
de qn/qch** to take one's inspiration
from sb/sth • **inspiration** *nf* *(idée)*
inspiration; *(respiration)* breathing
in • **inspiré, -e** *adj* inspired
instable [ɛ̃stabl] *adj* unstable;
(temps) changeable
installer [ɛ̃stale] **1** *vt* *(appareil,
meuble)* to install, to put in; **i.
qn** *(dans une fonction, dans un
logement)* to install sb (**dans** in) **2
s'installer** *vpr* *(s'asseoir)* to settle
down; *(dans un bureau)* to install
oneself; **s'i. à la campagne** to
settle in the country • **installation**
nf installation
instant [ɛ̃stɑ̃] *nm* moment,
instant; **à l'i.** a moment ago; **à
l'i. où...** just as...; **pour l'i.** for
the moment • **instantané, -e 1**
adj instantaneous **2** *nm* *(photo)*
snapshot
instinct [ɛ̃stɛ̃] *nm* instinct •
instinctif, -ive *adj* instinctive

institut [ɛ̃stity] *nm* institute; **i. de beauté** beauty salon

instituteur, -trice [ɛ̃stitytœr, -tris] *nmf Br* primary *or Am* elementary school teacher

institution [ɛ̃stitysjɔ̃] *nf (création)* establishment; *(coutume)* institution; *(école)* private school ● **institutionnel, -elle** *adj* institutional

instruction [ɛ̃stryksjɔ̃] *nf (éducation)* education; **instructions** *(ordres)* instructions ● **instructeur** *nm* instructor

instruire* [ɛ̃strɥir] *vt* to teach, to educate; **i. qn de qch** to inform sb of sth ● **instruit, -e** *adj* educated

instrument [ɛ̃strymɑ̃] *nm* instrument

insu [ɛ̃sy] **à l'insu de** *prép* without the knowledge of; **à son i.** without his/her being aware of it

insuffisant, -e [ɛ̃syfizɑ̃, -ɑ̃t] *adj (en quantité)* insufficient; *(en qualité)* inadequate ● **insuffisance** *nf (manque)* insufficiency; *(de moyens)* inadequacy

insulte [ɛ̃sylt] *nf* insult (**à** to) ● **insulter** *vt* to insult

insupportable [ɛ̃syportabl] *adj* unbearable

insurrection [ɛ̃syrɛksjɔ̃] *nf* uprising

intact, -e [ɛ̃takt] *adj* intact

intégral, -e, -aux, -ales [ɛ̃tegral, -o] *adj (paiement)* full; *(édition)* unabridged; *(film)* uncut

intégrer [ɛ̃tegre] **1** *vt* to integrate (**dans** in); *(école)* to get into **2 s'intégrer** *vpr* to become integrated ● **intégration** *nf (au sein d'un groupe)* integration

intégrité [ɛ̃tegrite] *nf* integrity

intellectuel, -elle [ɛ̃telɛktɥɛl] *adj & nmf* intellectual

intelligent, -e [ɛ̃teliʒɑ̃, -ɑ̃t] *adj* intelligent, clever ● **intelligence** *nf (faculté)* intelligence; *Ordinat* **i. artificielle** artificial intelligence

intempéries [ɛ̃tɑ̃peri] *nfpl* **les i.** the bad weather

intense [ɛ̃tɑ̃s] *adj* intense ● **intensif, -ive** *adj* intensive

intention [ɛ̃tɑ̃sjɔ̃] *nf* intention; **avoir l'i. de faire qch** to intend to do sth ● **intentionnel, -elle** *adj* intentional

interactif, -ive [ɛ̃tɛraktif, -iv] *adj* interactive

interchangeable [ɛ̃tɛrʃɑ̃ʒabl] *adj* interchangeable

interdire* [ɛ̃tɛrdir] *vt* to forbid (**qch à qn** sb sth); *(film, manifestation)* to ban; **i. à qn de faire qch** *(personne)* to forbid sb to do sth ● **interdiction** *nf* ban (**de** on); **'i. de fumer'** 'no smoking' ● **interdit, -e** *adj* forbidden; **'stationnement i.'** 'no parking'

intéresser [ɛ̃terese] **1** *vt (captiver)* to interest; *(concerner)* to concern **2 s'intéresser** *vpr* **s'i. à qn/ qch** to be interested in sb/sth ● **intéressant, -e** *adj (captivant)* interesting; *(prix)* attractive ● **intéressé, -e 1** *adj (motif)* selfish; *(concerné)* concerned **2** *nmf* **l'i.** the person concerned

intérêt [ɛ̃terɛ] *nm* interest; *Fin* **intérêts** interest; **tu as i. à le faire** you'd better do it; **sans i.** *(personne, film)* uninteresting

intérieur, -e [ɛ̃terjœr] **1** *adj (escalier, paroi)* interior; *(cour, vie)* inner; *(partie)* internal **2** *nm (de boîte, de maison)* inside (**de** of); *(de pays)* interior; *(maison)* home; **à l'i. (de)** inside; **d'i.** *(vêtement, jeux)* indoor

intérim [ɛ̃terim] *nm (travail temporaire)* temporary work ● **intérimaire 1** *adj (fonction,* *employé)* temporary **2** *nmf (travailleur)* temporary worker; *(secrétaire)* temp

interlocuteur, -trice [ɛ̃tɛrlɔkytœr, -tris] *nmf (de conversation)* speaker; **mon i.** the person I am/was speaking to

intermédiaire [ɛ̃tɛrmedjɛr] **1** *adj* intermediate **2** *nmf* intermediary; **par l'i. de** through

interminable [ɛ̃tɛrminabl] *adj* interminable

intermittent, -e [ɛ̃tɛrmitɑ̃, -ɑ̃t] *adj* intermittent

internat [ɛ̃tɛrna] *nm* boarding school • **interne 1** *adj (douleur)* internal; *(oreille)* inner **2** *nmf (élève)* boarder; **i. des hôpitaux** *Br* house doctor, *Am* intern

international, -e, -aux, -ales [ɛ̃tɛrnasjɔnal, -o] *adj* international

Internet [ɛ̃tɛrnɛt] *nm* Internet; **sur (l')I.** on the Internet • **internaute** *nmf* Internet surfer

interpeller [ɛ̃tɛrpəle] *vt (appeler)* to call out to; *(dans une réunion)* to question; **i. qn** *(police)* to take sb in for questioning

interprète [ɛ̃tɛrprɛt] *nmf (traducteur)* interpreter; *(chanteur)* singer; *(musicien, acteur)* performer • **interprétariat** *nm* interpreting • **interprétation** *nf (de texte, de rôle, de rêve)* interpretation; *(traduction)* interpreting • **interpréter** *vt (texte, rôle, musique)* to interpret; *(chanter)* to sing

interroger [ɛ̃tɛrɔʒe] *vt* to question; *(élève)* to test • **interrogation** *nf (question)* question; *(de prisonnier)* questioning; *Scol* **i. écrite/orale** written/oral test • **interrogatoire** *nm* interrogation

interrompre* [ɛ̃tɛrɔ̃pr] *vt* to interrupt • **interrupteur** *nm* switch • **interruption** *nf* interruption; *(de négociations)* breaking off; **sans i.** continuously; *Méd* **i. volontaire de grossesse** abortion

intersection [ɛ̃tɛrsɛksjɔ̃] *nf* intersection

intervalle [ɛ̃tɛrval] *nm (dans l'espace)* space; *(dans le temps)* interval; **dans l'i.** *(entretemps)* in the meantime; **par intervalles** (every) now and then, at intervals

intervenir* [ɛ̃tɛrvənir] *vi (agir, prendre la parole)* to intervene; *(survenir)* to occur • **intervention** *nf* intervention; *(discours)* speech; **i. chirurgicale** operation

interview [ɛ̃tɛrvju] *nf* interview • **interviewer** [-vjuve] *vt* to interview

intestin [ɛ̃tɛstɛ̃] *nm* intestine

intime [ɛ̃tim] *adj* intimate; *(ami)* close; *(cérémonie)* quiet • **intimité** *nf (familiarité)* intimacy; *(vie privée)* privacy; **dans l'i.** in private

intimider [ɛ̃timide] *vt* to intimidate

intituler [ɛ̃tityle] **1** *vt* to give a title to **2** **s'intituler** *vpr* to be entitled

intolérable [ɛ̃tɔlerabl] *adj* intolerable • **intolérance** *nf* intolerance • **intolérant, -e** *adj* intolerant

intoxication [ɛ̃tɔksikasjɔ] *n* poisoning; **i. alimentaire** food poisoning

intrigue [ɛ̃trig] *nf (de film, roman)* plot

introduire* [ɛ̃trɔdɥiɔ̃] **1** *v (insérer)* to insert (**dans** into) *(réforme, mode)* to introduce **2** **s'introduire** *vpr* **s'i. dans une maison** to get into a house • **introduction** *nf (texte, action* introduction

introuvable [ɛ̃truvabl] *ad* nowhere to be found

introverti, -e [ɛ̃trɔvɛrti] *nmf* introvert

intrus, -e [ɛ̃try, -yz] *nmf* intruder • **intrusion** *nf* intrusion (**dans** into)

intuition [ɛ̃tɥisjɔ̃] *nf* intuition

inutile [inytil] *adj (qui ne sert à rien)* useless; *(précaution, bagage)* unnecessary; **c'est i.** de crier it's pointless shouting

inutilisé [inytilize] *adj* unused

invalide [ɛ̃valid] **1** *adj* disabled **2** *nmf* disabled person

invariable [ɛ̃varjabl] *adj* invariable

invasion [ɛ̃vazjɔ̃] *nf* invasion

inventaire [ɛ̃vɑ̃tɛr] *nm Com (liste)* inventory; **faire l'i.** to do the stocktaking (**de** of)

inventer [ɛ̃vate] *vt (créer)* to invent; *(concept)* to think up; *(histoire, excuse)* to make up • **inventeur, -trice** *nmf* inventor • **invention** *nf* invention

inverse [ɛ̃vɛrs] **1** *adj (sens)* opposite; *(ordre)* reverse **2** *nm* **l'i.** the reverse, the opposite • **inverser** *vt (ordre)* to reverse

investigation [ɛ̃vɛstigasjɔ̃] *nf* investigation

investir [ɛ̃vɛstir] **1** *vt (capitaux)* to invest (**dans** in) **2** *vi* to invest (**dans** in) • **investissement** *nm Fin* investment

invincible [ɛ̃vɛ̃sibl] *adj* invincible

invisible [ɛ̃vizibl] *adj* invisible

inviter [ɛ̃vite] *vt* to invite; **i. qn à faire qch** *(prier)* to request sb to do sth; *(inciter)* to urge sb to do sth; **i. qn à dîner** to invite sb to dinner • **invitation** *nf* invitation • **invité, -e** *nmf* guest

involontaire [ɛ̃vɔlɔ̃tɛr] *adj* involuntary

invraisemblable [ɛ̃vrɛsɑ̃blabl] *adj (extraordinaire)* incredible; *(alibi)* implausible

ira, irait *etc* [ira, irɛ] *voir* **aller**[1]

Irak [irak] *nm* **l'I.** Iraq • **irakien, -enne 1** *adj* Iraqi **2** *nmf* **I., Irakienne** Iraqi

Iran [irɑ̃] *nm* **l'I.** Iran • **iranien, -enne 1** *adj* Iranian **2** *nmf* **I., Iranienne** Iranian

iris [iris] *nm (plante) & Anat* iris

Irlande [irlɑ̃d] *nf* **l'I.** Ireland; **l'I. du Nord** Northern Ireland • **irlandais, -e 1** *adj* Irish **2** *nmf* **I., Irlandaise** Irishman, *f* Irishwoman; **les I.** the Irish **3** *nm (langue)* Irish

ironie [irɔni] *nf* irony • **ironique** *adj* ironic(al)

iront [irɔ̃] *voir* **aller**[1]

irrationnel, -elle [irasjɔnɛl] *adj* irrational

irréaliste [irealist] *adj* unrealistic

irréel, -elle [ireɛl] *adj* unreal

irrégulier, -ère [iregylje, -ɛr] *adj (rythme, verbe)* irregular; *(sol, résultats)* uneven • **irrégularité** *nf* irregularity; *(de sol)* unevenness

irremplaçable [irɑ̃plasabl] *adj* irreplaceable

irréparable [ireparabl] *adj (véhicule)* beyond repair; *(tort, perte)* irreparable

irrépressible [irepresibl] *adj* irrepressible

irréprochable [ireprɔʃabl] *adj* irreproachable

irrésistible [irezistibl] *adj (personne, charme)* irresistible

irresponsable [irɛspɔ̃sabl] *adj (personne)* irresponsible

irriter [irite] **1** *vt* to irritate **2 s'irriter** *vpr (s'énerver)* to get irritated (**de** with; **contre** at); *(s'enflammer)* to become irritated • **irritable** *adj* irritable • **irritation** *nf (colère) & Méd* irritation

irruption [irypsjɔ̃] *nf* **faire i. dans** to burst into

islamique [islamik] *adj* Islamic

isoler [izɔle] *vt* to isolate (**de** from); *(du froid) & Él* to insulate • **isolation** *nf* insulation • **isolé, -e** *adj (personne, endroit, maison)* isolated; *(du froid)* insulated; **i. de** cut off *or* isolated from

Israël [israel] *nm* Israel • **israélien, -enne 1** *adj* Israeli **2** *nmf* **I., Israélienne** Israeli

issu, -e[1] [isy] *adj* **être i. de** to come from

issue[2] [isy] *nf (sortie)* exit; *Fig (solution)* way out; *(résultat)* outcome; **à l'i. de** at the end of; **i. de secours** emergency exit

Italie [itali] *nf* **l'I.** Italy • **italien, -enne 1** *adj* Italian **2** *nmf* **I., Italienne** Italian **3** *nm (langue)* Italian

italique [italik] **1** *adj (lettre)* italic **2** *nm* italics; **en i.** in italics

itinéraire [itinerɛr] *nm* itinerary

IUT [iyte] *(abrév* **institut universitaire de technologie)** *nm* = vocational higher education college

IVG [iveʒe] *(abrév* **interruption volontaire de grossesse)** *nf Med* abortion

ivoire [ivwar] *nm* ivory; **statuette en i.** *ou* **d'i.** ivory statuette

ivre [ivr] *adj* drunk (**de** with); *Fig* **i. de joie** wild with joy • **ivresse** *nf* drunkenness; **en état d'i.** drunk • **ivrogne** *nmf* drunk(ard)

J j

J, j [ʒi] *nm inv* J, j; **le jour J.** D-day

j' [ʒ] *voir* **je**

jaillir [ʒajir] *vi (liquide)* to gush out; *(étincelles)* to shoot out

jaloux, -ouse [ʒalu, -uz] *adj* jealous (**de** of) ● **jalousie** *nf* jealousy

Jamaïque [ʒamaik] *nf* **la J.** Jamaica

jamais [ʒamɛ] *adv* (**a**) *(négatif)* never; **elle ne sort j.** she never goes out; **sans j. sortir** without ever going out (**b**) *(positif)* ever; **si j.** if ever; **le film le plus drôle que j'aie j. vu** the funniest film I have ever seen

jambe [ʒɑ̃b] *nf* leg

jambon [ʒɑ̃bɔ̃] *nm* ham

janvier [ʒɑ̃vje] *nm* January

Japon [ʒapɔ̃] *nm* **le J.** Japan ● **japonais, -e 1** *adj* Japanese **2** *nmf* **J., Japonaise** Japanese *inv*; **les J.** the Japanese **3** *nm (langue)* Japanese

jardin [ʒardɛ̃] *nm* garden; **j. d'enfants** kindergarten; **j. des plantes** botanical gardens; **j. public** gardens ● **jardinage** *nm* gardening ● **jardinier** *nm* gardener

jargon [ʒargɔ̃] *nm* jargon

jasmin [ʒasmɛ̃] *nm* jasmine

jaune [ʒon] **1** *adj* yellow **2** *nm (couleur)* yellow; **j. d'œuf** (egg) yolk

Javel [ʒavɛl] **eau de J.** *nf* bleach

jazz [dʒaz] *nm* jazz

je [ʒə]

j' is used before a word beginning with a vowel or mute h.

pron personnel I; **je suis ici** I'm here

jean [dʒin] *nm* (pair of) jeans; **veste en j.** denim jacket

Jersey [ʒɛrzɛ] *nf* Jersey

jet [ʒɛ] *nm (de pierre)* throwing; *(de vapeur, de liquide)* jet; **j. d'eau** fountain

jetable [ʒətabl] *adj* disposable

jeter [ʒəte] **1** *vt* to throw (**à** to; **dans** into); *(à la poubelle)* to throw away; **j. un coup d'œil à qn/qch** to have a quick look at sb/sth **2 se jeter** *vpr (personne)* to throw oneself; **se j. sur qn** to throw oneself at sb; **se j. sur qch** *(occasion)* to jump at sth

jeton [ʒətɔ̃] *nm (pièce)* token; *(au jeu)* chip

jeu, -x [ʒø] *nm* (**a**) *(activité, au tennis)* game; **le j.** *(au casino)* gambling; **en j.** at stake; **j.-concours** competition; **j. électronique** computer game; **j. de mots** play on words, pun; **jeux de société** board games; **j. télévisé** television game show; **j. vidéo** video game (**b**) *(série complète)* set; *(de cartes)* deck, *Br* pack; **j. d'échecs** *(boîte, pièces)* chess set

jeudi [ʒødi] *nm* Thursday

jeun [ʒœ̃] **à jeun 1** *adv* on an empty stomach **2** *adj* **être à j.** to have eaten no food

jeune [ʒœn] **1** *adj* young **2** *nmf*

young person; **les jeunes** young people • **jeunesse** *nf* youth; **la j.** *(les jeunes)* the young

joaillier, -ère [ʒɔaje, -ɛr] *nmf Br* jeweller, *Am* jeweler • **joaillerie** *nf (bijoux) Br* jewellery, *Am* jewelry; *(magasin) Br* jewellery shop, *Am* jewelry store

jockey [ʒɔkɛ] *nm* jockey

jogging [dʒɔgiŋ] *nm Sport* jogging; *(survêtement)* tracksuit

joie [ʒwa] *nf* joy, delight; **avec j.** with pleasure, gladly

joindre* [ʒwɛ̃dr] **1** *vt (réunir)* to join; *(ajouter)* to add (**à** to); *(dans une enveloppe)* to enclose (**à** with); **j. qn** *(contacter)* to get in touch with sb **2 se joindre** *vpr* **se j. à qn** to join sb • **joint, -e** *adj* **à pieds joints** with feet together; **pièces jointes** *(de lettre)* enclosures

joker [ʒɔkɛr] *nm Cartes* joker

joli, -e [ʒɔli] *adj* pretty

jonction [ʒɔ̃ksjɔ̃] *nf* junction

jongler [ʒɔ̃gle] *vi* to juggle (**avec** with)

joue [ʒu] *nf (du visage)* cheek

jouer [ʒwe] **1** *vt (musique, carte, rôle)* to play; *(pièce de théâtre)* to perform; *(film)* to show **2** *vi* to play; *(acteur)* to act; *(être important)* to count; **j. au tennis/aux cartes** to play tennis/cards; **j. du piano/du violon** to play the piano/violin; **à toi de j.!** it's your turn (to play)!

jouet [ʒwɛ] *nm* toy

joueur, -euse [ʒwœr, -øz] *nmf* player

jour [ʒur] *nm (journée, date)* day; *(clarté)* (day)light; **il fait j.** it's (day)light; **du j. au lendemain** overnight; **en plein j., au grand j.** in broad daylight; **de nos jours** nowadays, these days; **mettre qch à j.** to bring sth up to date; **quel j. sommes-nous?** what day

is it?; **le j. de l'an** New Year's Day

journal, -aux [ʒurnal, -o] *nm* (news)paper; *(spécialisé)* journal; *(intime)* diary; **j. télévisé** (TV) news *(sing)* • **journaliste** *nmf* journalist

journalier, -ère [ʒurnalje, -ɛr] *adj* daily

journée [ʒurne] *nf* day; **pendant la j.** during the day(time); **toute la j.** all day (long)

joyeux, -euse [ʒwajø, -øz] *adj* joyful; **j. anniversaire!** happy birthday!; **j. Noël!** merry *or Br* happy Christmas!

judo [ʒydo] *nm* judo

juge [ʒyʒ] *nm* judge

jugement [ʒyʒmɑ̃] *nm (opinion, discernement)* judgement; *(verdict)* sentence; **porter un j. sur qch** to pass judgement on sth

juger [ʒyʒe] *vt (personne, question)* to judge; *(au tribunal)* to try; *(estimer)* to consider (**que** that)

juif, juive [ʒɥif, ʒɥiv] **1** *adj* Jewish **2** *nmf* **J.** Jew

juillet [ʒɥijɛ] *nm* July

juin [ʒɥɛ̃] *nm* June

jumeau, -elle, -x, -elles [ʒymo, -ɛl] **1** *adj* **frère j.** twin brother; **sœur jumelle** twin sister; **lits jumeaux** twin beds **2** *nmf* twin • **jumelles** *nfpl (pour regarder)* binoculars

jungle [ʒœ̃gl] *nf* jungle

jupe [ʒyp] *nf* skirt

jurer [ʒyre] **1** *vt (promettre)* to swear (**que** that; **de faire** to do) **2** *vi (dire un gros mot)* to swear (**contre** at); **j. de qch** to swear to sth • **juré, -e** *nm Jur* juror

juron [ʒyrɔ̃] *nm* swearword

jury [ʒyri] *nm Jur* jury

jus [ʒy] *nm (de fruits)* juice; *(de viande)* gravy; **j. d'orange** orange juice

usque [ʒysk] **1** *prép* **jusqu'à** *(espace)* as far as, (right) up to; *(temps)* until, (up) till, to; *(même)* even; **jusqu'en mai** until May; **jusqu'ici** as far as this; *(temps)* up till now; **j. chez moi** as far as my place **2** *conj* **jusqu'à ce qu'il vienne** until he comes

uste [ʒyst] **1** *adj (équitable)* fair, just; *(exact)* right, correct; *(étroit)* tight; **un peu j.** *(quantité, qualité)* barely enough **2** *adv (deviner, compter)* correctly, right; *(chanter)* in tune; *(précisément, à peine)* just; **un peu j.** *(mesurer, compter)* a bit on the short side • **justement** [-əmɑ̃] *adv (précisément)* exactly; **j. j'allais t'appeler** I was just going to ring you

justesse [ʒystɛs] *nf (exactitude)* accuracy; **de j.** *(éviter, gagner)* just

justice [ʒystis] *nf (équité)* justice; **la j.** *(autorité)* the law; **rendre j. à qn** to do justice to sb

justifier [ʒystifje] *vt* to justify • **justification** *nf (explication)* justification; *(preuve)* proof

juteux, -euse [ʒytø, -øz] *adj* juicy

Kk

K, k [kɑ] *nm inv* K, k

kangourou [kãguru] *nm* kangaroo

karaté [karate] *nm* karate

kayak [kajak] *nm* canoe

kidnapper [kidnape] *vt* to kidnap • **kidnappeur, -euse** *nmf* kidnapper

kilo [kilo] *nm* kilo • **kilogramme** *nm* kilogram(me)

kilomètre [kilɔmɛtr] *nm* kilometre

kinésithérapeute [kineziterapøt] *nmf* physiotherapist

kiosque [kjɔsk] *nm (à fleurs)* kiosk Br stall; **k. à journaux** news-stand

kit [kit] *nm (self-assembly)* kit; **e**▸ **k.** in kit form

kiwi [kiwi] *nm (oiseau, fruit)* kiwi

Klaxon® [klaksɔn] *nm* horn • **klaxonner** *vi* to sound one's horn

km (*abrév* **kilomètre**) km • **km/I** (*abrév* **kilomètre-heure**) kph, ≈ mph

L

L, l [ɛl] *nm inv* L, l

l', la [l, la] *voir* **le**

là [la] **1** *adv (là-bas)* there; *(ici)* here; **c'est là que...** *(lieu)* that's where...; **à cinq mètres de là** five metres away **2** *exclam* **oh là là!** oh dear! **3** *voir* **ce¹, celui** • **là-bas** *adv* over there

laboratoire [labɔratwar] *nm* laboratory

lac [lak] *nm* lake

lacet [lasɛ] *nm (de chaussure)* lace; **faire ses lacets** to tie one's laces

lâche [laʃ] **1** *adj (nœud)* loose, slack; *Péj (personne, acte)* cowardly **2** *nmf* coward

lâcher [laʃe] *vt (ne plus tenir)* to let go of; *(bombe)* to drop

là-dedans [ladədɑ̃] *adv (lieu)* in there, inside

là-dessous [ladəsu] *adv* underneath

là-dessus [ladəsy] *adv* on there; *(monter)* on top

là-haut [lao] *adv* up there; *(à l'étage)* upstairs

laid, -e [lɛ, lɛd] *adj* ugly • **laideur** *nf* ugliness

laine [lɛn] *nf* wool; **de l., en l.** *Br* woollen, *Am* woolen

laisse [lɛs] *nf* lead, leash

laisser [lese] **1** *vt* to leave; **l. qn partir** *(permettre)* to let sb go **2 se laisser** *vpr* **se l. aller** to let oneself go; **se l. faire** to be pushed around

lait [lɛ] *nm* milk; **l. entier/ demi-écrémé/écrémé** whole/ semi-skimmed/skimmed milk • **laitier** *adj m* **produit l.** dairy product

laitue [lɛty] *nf* lettuce

lame [lam] *nf* blade

lamentable [lamɑ̃tabl] *adj (mauvais)* terrible; *(personne)* pathetic

lampadaire [lɑ̃padɛr] *nm* floor lamp; *(de rue)* street lamp

lampe [lɑ̃p] *nf* lamp; **l. de poche** *Br* torch, *Am* flashlight

lancer [lɑ̃se] **1** *vt (jeter)* to throw (**à** to); *(fusée, produit)* to launch **2 se lancer** *vpr (se précipiter)* to rush; **se l. dans** *(aventure)* to launch into **3** *nm Sport* throw

landau, -s [lɑ̃do] *nm Br* pram, *Am* baby carriage

langage [lɑ̃gaʒ] *nm* language

langue [lɑ̃g] *nf Anat* tongue; *Ling* language; **de l. anglaise/fran-çaise** English-/French-speaking; **l. maternelle** mother tongue; **langues vivantes** modern languages

lanière [lanjɛr] *nf* strap; *(d'étoffe)* strip

lapin [lapɛ̃] *nm* rabbit

laque [lak] *nf (pour cheveux)* hair spray

laquelle [lakɛl] *voir* **lequel**

lard [lar] *nm (viande)* bacon • **lardon** *nm Culin* cube of bacon

large [larʒ] **1** *adj (route, porte, chaussure)* wide; *(considérable)* **l. de six mètres** six metres wide **2** *nm* **avoir six mètres de l.** to be six metres wide • **largement**

[-əmɑ̃] *adv (répandu, critiqué)* widely; *(payer, servir)* generously; **avoir l. le temps** to have plenty of time ● **largeur** *nf (dimension)* width, breadth

larme [larm] *nf* tear; **en larmes** in tears

las, lasse [lɑ, lɑs] *adj* weary (**de** of) ● **lassant, -e** *adj* tiresome ● **se lasser** *vpr* **se l. de qch/de faire qch** to get tired of sth/of doing sth

laser [lazɛr] *nm* laser

latin, -e [latɛ̃, -in] *adj & nm* Latin *nm (langue)* Latin

lavabo [lavabo] *nm* washbasin; **lavabos** *(toilettes) Br* toilet(s), *Am* washroom

lavande [lavɑ̃d] *nf* lavender

laver [lave] **1** *vt* to wash; **l. qch à l'eau froide** to wash sth in cold water **2** **se laver** *vpr* to wash (oneself); **se l. les mains** to wash one's hands ● **lave-linge** *nm inv* washing machine ● **laverie** *nf (automatique) Br* launderette, *Am* Laundromat® ● **lave-vaisselle** *nm inv* dishwasher

le, la, les [lə, la, le]

l' is used instead of **le** or **la** before a word beginning with a vowel or h mute.

1 *article défini* (**a**) *(pour définir le nom)* the; **le garçon** the boy; **la fille** the girl; **les petits** the little ones (**b**) *(avec les notions)* **la vie** life; **la France** France; **les Français** the French; **les hommes** men; **aimer le café** to like coffee (**c**) *(avec les parties du corps)* **il ouvrit la bouche** he opened his mouth; **se blesser au pied** to hurt one's foot; **avoir les cheveux blonds** to have blond hair (**d**) *(distributif)* **dix euros le kilo** ten euros a kilo (**e**) *(dans les*

compléments de temps) **elle vient le lundi** she comes on Mondays; **l'an prochain** next year **2** *pron* *(homme)* him; *(femme)* her; *(chose, animal)* it; **les** them; **je la vois** I see her/it; **je le vois** I see him/it; **je les vois** I see them

lécher [leʃe] *vt* to lick

leçon [ləsɔ̃] *nf* lesson

lecteur, -trice [lɛktœr, -tris] *nmf* reader; *Univ* foreign language assistant; **l. de CD/de DVD** CD/DVD player ● **lecture** *nf* reading

légal, -e, -aux, -ales [legal, -o] *adj* legal

légende [leʒɑ̃d] *nf* *(histoire)* legend; *(de carte)* key; *(de photo)* caption

léger, -ère [leʒe, -ɛr] *adj* light; *(blessure, odeur)* slight; *(café, thé)* weak ● **légèrement** *adv* *(inconsidérément)* lightly; *(un peu)* slightly ● **légèreté** *nf (poids)* lightness; *(de blessure)* slightness

légitime [leʒitim] *adj (action, enfant)* legitimate; *(colère)* justified

légume [legym] *nm* vegetable

lendemain [lɑ̃dmɛ̃] *nm* **le l.** the next day; **le l. de** the day after; **le l. matin** the next morning

lent, -e [lɑ̃, lɑ̃t] *adj* slow

lentille [lɑ̃tij] *nf (plante, graine)* lentil; *(verre)* lens; **lentilles de contact** contact lenses

lequel, laquelle [ləkɛl, lakɛl] *(mpl* **lesquels**, *fpl* **lesquelles** [lekɛl]*)*

lequel and **lesquel(le)s** contract with **à** to form **auquel** and **auxquel(le)s**, and with **de** to form **duquel** and **desquel(le)s**.

1 *pron relatif (chose, animal)* which; *(personne)* who; *(indirect)* whom; **dans l.** in which; **parmi lesquels** *(choses, animaux)* among which; *(personnes)* among whom **2** *pron interrogatif* which (one); **l. préférez-vous?** which (one) do you prefer?

les [le] *voir* **le**

lessive [lɛsiv] *nf (produit)* washing powder; *(liquide)* liquid detergent; *(linge)* washing; **faire la l.** to do the washing

lettre [lɛtr] *nf (missive, caractère)* letter; **les lettres** *(discipline)* arts, humanities

leur [lœr] **1** *adj possessif* their; **l. chat** their cat; **leurs voitures** their cars **2** *pron possessif* **le l., la l., les leurs** theirs **3** *pron personnel (indirect)* to them; **donne-l. ta carte** give them your card

lever [ləve] **1** *vt* to lift, to raise **2** **se lever** *upr* to get up; *(soleil)* to rise; *(jour)* to break **3** *nm* **le l. du soleil** sunrise ● **levé, -e** *adj* **être l.** *(debout)* to be up

levier [ləvje] *nm* lever; *Aut* **l. de vitesse** *Br* gear lever, *Am* gearshift

lèvre [lɛvr] *nf* lip

levure [ləvyr] *nf* yeast

lézard [lezar] *nm* lizard

liaison [ljɛzɔ̃] *nf (rapport)* connection; *(entre mots)* liaison; **l. aérienne/ferroviaire** air/rail link; **l. amoureuse** love affair

libeller [libele] *vt (chèque)* to make out

libéral, -e, -aux, -ales [liberal, -o] *adj & nmf* liberal

libérer [libere] **1** *vt (prisonnier)* to free, to release; *(pays)* to liberate **(de** from); *(chambre)* to vacate **2** **se libérer** *upr* to free oneself **(de** from); **je n'ai pas pu me l.** I couldn't get away ● **libération** *nf (de prisonnier)* release; *(de pays)* liberation

liberté [libɛrte] *nf* freedom, liberty;

mettre qn en l. to set sb free

librairie [libreri] *nf* bookshop

libre [libr] *adj (personne, siège)* free **(de qch** from sth; **de faire** to do); *(voie)* clear ● **libre-service** *(pl* **libres-services)** *nm (système, magasin)* self-service

licence [lisɑ̃s] *nf Br* licence, *Am* license; *Univ* (bachelor's) degree

licencier [lisɑ̃sje] *vt (employé)* to lay off, *Br* to make redundant ● **licenciement** *nm* lay-off, *Br* redundancy

lien [ljɛ̃] *nm (rapport)* link, connection; *(attache)* bond

lier [lje] *vt (attacher)* to tie up; *(personnes)* to bind together; *(paragraphes)* to link; **l. qn** *(unir, engager)* to bind sb; **être très lié avec qn** to be very close to sb

lieu, -x [ljø] *nm* place; **avoir l.** to take place; **au l. de qch/de faire qch** instead of sth/of doing sth; **en dernier l.** lastly; **l. de naissance** place of birth

lièvre [ljɛvr] *nm* hare

ligne [liɲ] *nf (trait, rangée)* line; *(silhouette)* figure; **l. d'autobus** bus service; *(parcours)* bus route; **l. de chemin de fer** *Br* railway *or Am* railroad line

ligoter [ligɔte] *vt* to tie up **(à** to)

limace [limas] *nf* slug

lime [lim] *nf (outil)* file; **l. à ongles** nail file

limitation [limitasjɔ̃] *nf* limitation; **l. de vitesse** speed limit

limite [limit] **1** *nf* limit **(à** to); **sans l.** unlimited, limitless **2** *adj (vitesse, âge)* maximum

limiter [limite] **1** *vt (restreindre)* to limit, to restrict **(à** to); *(territoire)* to bound **2** **se limiter** *upr* **se l. à qch/à faire qch** to limit *or* restrict oneself to sth/to doing sth

limonade [limɔnad] *nf* lemonade

lin [lɛ̃] *nm (tissu)* linen

linge [lɛ̃ʒ] *nm (vêtements)* linen; *(à laver)* washing • **lingerie** *nf (de femmes)* underwear

lion [ljɔ̃] *nm* lion; **le L.** *(signe)* Leo

liqueur [likœr] *nf* liqueur

liquidation [likidasjɔ̃] *nf (de stock)* clearance

liquide [likid] **1** *adj* liquid **2** *nm* liquid; *(argent)* cash; **payer en l.** to pay cash **lire*** [lir] **1** *vt* to read; **l. qch à qn** to read sth to sb **2** *vi* to read

lis, lisant, lise(nt) *etc* [li, lizã, liz] *voir* **lire**

lisible [lizibl] *adj (écriture)* legible

lisse [lis] *adj* smooth

liste [list] *nf* list; **l. d'attente** waiting list; **l. électorale** electoral roll

lit¹ [li] *nm* bed; **aller au l.** to go to bed; **l. de camp** *Br* camp bed, *Am* cot; **l. d'enfant** *Br* cot, *Am* crib; **lits superposés** bunk beds

lit² [li] *voir* **lire**

litre [litr] *nm Br* litre, *Am* liter

littérature [literatyr] *nf* literature

littoral [litɔral] *nm* coast(line)

livraison [livrɛzɔ̃] *nf* delivery

livre [livr] **1** *nm* book; **l. de poche** paperback (book) **2** *nf (monnaie, poids)* pound

livrer [livre] **1** *vt (marchandises)* to deliver (**à** to); **l. qn à la police** to hand sb over to the police **2 se livrer** *upr (se rendre)* to give oneself up (**à** to) • **livreur, -euse** *nmf* delivery man, *f* delivery woman

livret [livrɛ] *nm (livre)* booklet; **l. d'épargne** bankbook, *Br* passbook; **l. scolaire** school report book

local, -e, -aux, -ales [lɔkal, -o] *adj* local

locataire [lɔkatɛr] *nmf* tenant

location [lɔkɑsjɔ̃] *nf (de maison)* *(par le locataire)* renting; *(par le propriétaire)* renting out, *Br* letting; *(de voiture)* renting, *Br* hiring; *(logement)* rented *Br* accommodation *or Am* accommodations; *(loyer)* rent; *(pour spectacle)* booking; **bureau de l.** booking office; **en l.** on hire; **voiture de l.** rented *or Br* hired car

locomotive [lɔkɔmotiv] *nf (de train)* engine

loge [lɔʒ] *nf* lodge; *(d'acteur)* dressing-room; *Théât (de spectateur)* box

loger [lɔʒe] **1** *vt (recevoir, mettre)* to accommodate; *(héberger)* to put up; **être logé et nourri** to have board and lodging **2** *vi (temporairement)* to stay; *(en permanence)* to live **3 se loger** *upr* **trouver à se l.** to find somewhere to live; *(temporairement)* to find somewhere to stay • **logement** *nm (habitation)* lodging, *Br* accommodation, *Am* accommodations; **le l.** housing

logiciel [lɔʒisjɛl] *nm Ordinat* software *inv*

logique [lɔʒik] *adj* logical

loi [lwa] *nf* law

loin [lwɛ̃] *adv* far (away) (**de** from); **Nice est l. de Paris** Nice is a long way from Paris; **plus l.** further, farther; **au l.** in the distance, far away; **de l.** from a distance • **lointain, -e** *adj* distant, far-off

loisirs [lwazir] *nmpl (temps libre)* spare time; *(distractions)* leisure activities

Londres [lɔ̃dr] *nm ou f* London

long, longue [lɔ̃, lɔ̃g] **1** *adj* long; **l. de deux mètres** two metres long **2** *nm* **avoir deux mètres de l.** to be two metres long; **le l. de qch** along sth; **de l. en large** *(marcher)* up and down

longer [lɔ̃ʒe] *vt (sujet: personne, voiture)* to go along; *(sujet: sentier, canal)* to run alongside

longtemps [lɔ̃tɑ̃] *adv* (for) a long time; **trop l.** too long; **aussi l. que** as long as

longue [lɔ̃g] *voir* **long** • **longueur** *nf* length; *Radio* **l. d'onde** wavelength

lors [lɔr] *adv* **l. de** at the time of; **dès l.** from then on

lorsque [lɔrsk(ə)] *conj* when

lot [lo] *nm (de marchandises)* batch; *(de loterie)* prize; **gros l.** jackpot

loterie [lɔtri] *nf* lottery

lotion [losjɔ̃] *nf* lotion

lotissement [lɔtismɑ̃] *nm* housing *Br* estate *or Am* development

loto [lɔto] *nm (jeu)* lotto; *(jeu national)* national lottery

louange [lwɑ̃ʒ] *nf* praise

louche¹ [luʃ] *nf (cuillère)* ladle

louche² [luʃ] *adj (suspect)* dodgy

loucher [luʃe] *vi* to squint

louer [lwe] *vt (prendre en location) (maison, appartement)* to rent; *(voiture)* to rent, *Br* to hire; *(donner en location) (logement)* to rent out, *Br* to let; *(voiture)* to rent out, *Br* to hire out; *(réserver)* to book; **maison/chambre à l.** house/room to rent *or Br* to let

loup [lu] *nm* wolf

loupe [lup] *nf* magnifying glass

lourd, -e [lur, lurd] **1** *adj* heavy **(de** with); *(temps)* close **2** *adv* **peser l.** *(personne, objet)* to be heavy • **lourdeur** *nf* heaviness; **avoir des lourdeurs d'estomac** to feel bloated

loyal, -e, -aux, -ales [lwajal, -o] *adj (honnête)* fair **(envers** to); *(dévoué)* loyal **(envers** to) • **loyauté** *nf (honnêteté)* fairness; *(dévouement)* loyalty **(envers** to)

loyer [lwaje] *nm* rent

lu [ly] *pp de* **lire**

luge [lyʒ] *nf Br* sledge, *Am* sled

lui [lɥi] *pron personnel* **(a)** *(objet indirect)* (to) him; *(femme)* (to) her; *(chose, animal)* (to) it; **je le l. ai montré** I showed it to him/her **(b)** *(complément direct)* him; **elle n'aime que l.** she only loves him **(c)** *(après une préposition)* him; **pour/avec l.** for/with him; **elle pense à l.** she thinks of him; **ce livre est à l.** this book is his **(d)** *(dans les comparaisons)* **elle est plus grande que l.** she's taller than he is *or* than him **(e)** *(sujet)* **l., il ne viendra pas** *(emphatique)* HE won't come; **c'est l. qui me l'a dit** he is the one who told me • **lui-même** *pron* himself; *(chose, animal)* itself

luisant, -ante [lɥizɑ̃, -ɑ̃t] *adj (métal)* shiny

lumière [lymjɛr] *nf* light

lumineux, -euse [lyminø, -øz] *adj (idée, ciel)* bright; *(cadran)* luminous

lundi [lœ̃di] *nm* Monday

lune [lyn] *nf* moon; **l. de miel** honeymoon

lunettes [lynɛt] *nfpl (de vue)* glasses; *(de protection, de plongée)* goggles; **lunettes de soleil** sunglasses

lutte [lyt] *nf* fight, struggle; *Sport* wrestling • **lutter** *vi* to fight, to struggle; *Sport* to wrestle

luxe [lyks] *nm* luxury; **modèle de l. de luxe** model • **luxueux, -euse** *adj* luxurious

Luxembourg [lyksɑ̃bur] *nm* **le L.** Luxembourg

lycée [lise] *nm Br* ≃ secondary school, *Am* ≃ high school • **lycéen, -enne** *nmf* pupil *(at a lycée)*

Mm

M¹, m¹ [ɛm] *nm inv* M, m
M² (*abrév* **Monsieur**) Mr
m² (*abrév* **mètre(s)**) m
m' [m] *voir* **me**
ma [ma] *voir* **mon**
mâcher [mɑʃe] *vt* to chew
machine [maʃin] *nf (appareil)* machine; **m. à écrire** typewriter; **m. à laver** washing machine; **m. à laver la vaisselle** dishwasher
mâchoire [mɑʃwar] *nf* jaw
maçon [masɔ̃] *nm (de briques)* bricklayer; *(de pierres)* mason
madame [madam] *(pl* **mesdames**) *nf (en apostrophe)* madam; **bonjour mesdames** good morning(, ladies); **M. Legras** Mrs Legras; **M.** *(dans une lettre)* Dear Madam
madeleine [madlɛn] *nf* (small) sponge cake
mademoiselle [madmwazɛl] *(pl* **mesdemoiselles**) *nf (avant nom)* Miss; **M. Legras** Miss Legras; **M.** *(dans une lettre)* Dear Madam
magasin [magazɛ̃] *nm Br* shop, *Am* store; **grand m.** department store
magazine [magazin] *nm* magazine
magie [maʒi] *nf* magic • **magicien, -enne** *nmf* magician • **magique** *adj (surnaturel)* magic; *(enchanteur)* magical
magistrat [maʒistra] *nm* magistrate
magnétique [maɲetik] *adj* magnetic

magnétophone [maɲetɔfɔn] *nm* tape recorder
magnétoscope [maɲetɔskɔp] *nm Br* video (recorder), *Am* VCR
magnifique [maɲifik] *adj* magnificent
mai [mɛ] *nm* May
maigre [mɛgr] *adj (personne)* thin; *(viande)* lean; *(fromage)* low-fat • **maigrir** *vi* to get thinner
maillot [majo] *nm (de sportif)* jersey, shirt; **m. de bain** *(de femme)* swimsuit; *(d'homme)* (swimming) trunks; **m. jaune** *(du Tour de France)* yellow jersey
main [mɛ̃] **1** *nf* hand; **à la m.** *(faire, écrire)* by hand; **tenir qch à la m.** to hold sth in one's hand; **donner la m. à qn** to hold sb's hand; **haut les mains!** hands up! **2** *adj* **fait m.** hand-made
maintenant [mɛ̃tnã] *adv* now; *(de nos jours)* nowadays; **m. que...** now that...; **dès m.** from now on
maintenir* [mɛ̃tnir] *vt (conserver)* to keep, to maintain; *(retenir)* to hold in position; *(affirmer)* to maintain (**que** that)
maire [mɛr] *nm* mayor • **mairie** *nf Br* town hall, *Am* city hall; *(administration) Br* town council, *Am* city hall
mais [mɛ] *conj* but; **m. oui, m. si** of course; **m. non** definitely not
maïs [mais] *nm Br* maize, *Am* corn
maison [mɛzɔ̃] **1** *nf (bâtiment*

famille) house; *(foyer)* home; *(entreprise)* company; **à la m.** at home; **rentrer à la m.** to go/come (back) home; **m. de retraite** old people's home **2** *adj inv (artisanal)* home-made

maître [mɛtr] *nm* master; **m. d'école** teacher; **m. d'hôtel** *(de restaurant)* head waiter; **m. chanteur** blackmailer

maîtresse [mɛtrɛs] *nf* mistress; **m. d'école** teacher

maîtrise [mɛtriz] *nf (diplôme)* ≃ master's degree **(de** in) • **maîtriser** *vt (incendie, passion)* to control; *(peur)* to overcome; *(sujet)* to master; **m. qn** to overpower sb

Majesté [maʒɛste] *nf* **Votre M.** *(titre)* Your Majesty

majeur, -e [maʒœr] **1** *adj (important)* & *Mus* major; *Jur* **être m.** to be of age **2** *nm (doigt)* middle finger

majoritaire [maʒɔritɛr] *adj* majority; **être m.** to be in the majority

majorité [maʒɔrite] *nf* majority **(de** of); **en m.** *(pour la plupart)* in the main

majuscule [maʒyskyl] **1** *adj (lettre)* capital **2** *nf* capital letter

mal, maux [mal, mo] **1** *nm (douleur)* pain; *(préjudice)* harm; *(maladie)* illness; *(malheur)* misfortune; *Phil* **le m.** evil; **avoir m. à la tête/à la gorge** to have a headache/sore throat; **ça me fait m., j'ai m.** it hurts (me); **faire du m. à qn** to harm sb; **avoir du m. à faire qch** to have trouble doing sth; **avoir le m. de mer** to be seasick; **avoir le m. du pays** to be homesick; **m. de gorge** sore throat; **m. de tête** headache **2** *adv (avec médiocrité)* badly; *(incorrectement)* wrongly;

aller m. *(personne)* to be ill; **m. comprendre** to misunderstand; *Fam* **pas m.** *(beaucoup)* quite a lot **(de** of)

malade [malad] **1** *adj* ill, sick **2** *nmf* sick person; **les malades** the sick • **maladie** *nf* illness, disease

maladroit, -e [maladrwa, -at] *adj (malhabile)* clumsy; *(indélicat)* tactless

malaise [malɛz] *nm (angoisse)* uneasiness, malaise; *(indisposition)* sick feeling; *(étourdissement)* dizzy spell; **avoir un m.** to feel faint

malchance [malʃɑ̃s] *nf* bad luck • **malchanceux, -euse** *adj* unlucky

mâle [mal] **1** *adj (du sexe masculin)* male; *(viril)* manly **2** *nm* male

malédiction [malediksjɔ̃] *nf* curse

maléfique [malefik] *adj* evil

malentendu [malɑ̃tɑ̃dy] *nm* misunderstanding

malfaiteur [malfɛtœr] *nm* criminal

malgré [malgre] *prép* in spite of; **m. tout** for all that, after all

malheur [malœr] *nm (drame)* misfortune; *(malchance)* bad luck; **par m.** unfortunately; **porter m. à qn** to bring sb bad luck • **malheureusement** *adv* unfortunately • **malheureux, -euse 1** *adj (triste)* unhappy, miserable; *(malchanceux)* unlucky **2** *nmf* poor wretch

malhonnête [malɔnɛt] *adj* dishonest • **malhonnêteté** *nf* dishonesty

malicieux, -euse [malisjø, -øz] *adj* mischievous

malin, -igne [malɛ̃, -iɲ] *adj (astucieux)* clever, smart

malle [mal] *nf (coffre)* trunk; *(de véhicule)* *Br* boot, *Am* trunk

mallette [malɛt] *nf* briefcase

malpoli, -e [malpɔli] *adj Fam* rude

malsain, -e [malsɛ̃, -ɛn] *adj* unhealthy

Malte [malt] *nf* Malta ● **maltais, -e 1** *adj* Maltese **2** *nmf* **M., Maltaise** Maltese

maltraiter [maltrɛte] *vt* to ill-treat

maman [mamɑ̃] *nf Br* mum, *Am* mom

mamie [mami] *nf* grandma

mammifère [mamifɛr] *nm* mammal

Manche [mɑ̃ʃ] *nf* **la M.** the Channel

manche¹ [mɑ̃ʃ] *nf (de vêtement)* sleeve; *Sport & Cartes* round

manche² [mɑ̃ʃ] *nm (d'outil)* handle

mandarine [mɑ̃darin] *nf (fruit)* mandarin (orange)

mandat [mɑ̃da] *nm (de député)* mandate; *(de président)* term of office

manège [manɛʒ] *nm (de foire)* merry-go-round, *Br* roundabout; *Équitation* riding school

manette [manɛt] *nf* lever

manger [mɑ̃ʒe] **1** *vt* to eat **2** *vi* to eat; **donner à m. à qn** to give sb sth to eat ● **mangeable** *adj (médiocre)* eatable

mangue [mɑ̃g] *nf* mango

maniaque [manjak] *adj* fussy

manie [mani] *nf (habitude)* odd habit; *(idée fixe)* mania (**de** for)

manier [manje] *vt* to handle

manière [manjɛr] *nf* way, manner; **la m. dont elle parle** the way (in which) she talks; **manières** *(politesse)* manners; **de toute m.** anyway, anyhow; **de cette m.** (in) this way; **à la m. de** in the style of; **d'une m. générale** generally speaking

manifeste [manifɛst] *nm Pol* manifesto

manifester [manifɛste] **1** *vt (ex-*

primer) to show **2** *vi (protester)* to demonstrate ● **manifestant, -e** *nmf* demonstrator ● **manifestation** *nf (défilé)* demonstration

manipuler [manipyle] *vt (appareils, produits)* to handle ● **manipulation** *nf (d'appareils, de produits)* handling; **manipulations génétiques** genetic engineering

mannequin [mankɛ̃] *nm (personne)* model; *(statue)* dummy

manœuvre [manœvr] *nf Br* manoeuvre, *Am* maneuver ● **manœuvrer** *vt (véhicule, personne) Br* to manoeuvre, *Am* to maneuver

manoir [manwar] *nm* manor house

manque [mɑ̃k] *nm (insuffisance)* lack (**de** of)

manquer [mɑ̃ke] **1** *vt (cible, train, chance)* to miss; *(échouer)* to fail **2** *vi (faire défaut)* to be lacking; *(être absent)* to be missing; *(échouer)* to fail; **m. de** *(pain, argent)* to be short of; *(attention, cohérence)* to lack; **tu me manques** I miss you; **ne m. de rien** to have all one needs **3** *v impersonnel* **il manque/il nous manque dix tasses** there are/we are ten cups short; **il manque quelques pages** there are a few pages missing ● **manquant, -e** *adj* missing ● **manqué, -e** *adj (occasion)* missed; *(tentative)* unsuccessful

manteau, -x [mɑ̃to] *nm* coat

manuel, -elle [manɥɛl] **1** *adj (travail)* manual **2** *nm (livre)* handbook, manual; **m. scolaire** textbook

manuscrit [manyskri] *nm* manuscript

maquereau, -x [makro] *nm (poisson)* mackerel

maquiller [makije] **1** *vt (personne, visage)* to make up **2** *se maquiller*

vpr to put one's make-up on ●
maquillage *nm (fard)* make-up
marais [marɛ] *nm* marsh
marathon [maratɔ̃] *nm* marathon
marbre [marbr] *nm* marble
marchand, -e [marʃɑ̃, -ɑ̃d] *nmf*
Br shopkeeper, Am storekeeper;
(de voitures, de meubles) dealer;
m. de journaux *(dans la rue)*
newsvendor; *(dans un magasin)*
Br newsagent, Am newsdealer
marchander [marʃɑ̃de] *vi* to
haggle
marchandises [marʃɑ̃diz] *nfpl*
goods, merchandise
marche [marʃ] *nf* **(a)** *(d'escalier)*
step, stair **(b)** *(action)* walking;
un train en m. a moving train;
mettre qch en m. to start sth
(up); **faire m. arrière** *(en voiture)*
Br to reverse, Am to back up;
Fig to backtrack; **m. à suivre**
procedure
marché [marʃe] **1** *nm (lieu)* &
Écon market; *(contrat)* deal,
vendre qch au m. noir to sell
sth on the black market; **le m. du
travail** the labour market **2** *adj inv*
être bon m. to be cheap; **c'est
meilleur m.** it's cheaper
marcher [marʃe] *vi (personne)* to
walk; *(machine)* to run; *(plans)* to
work; **faire m. qch** to operate sth
mardi [mardi] *nm* Tuesday; **M.
gras** Shrove Tuesday
mare [mar] *nf (étang)* pond
marécage [mareka3] *nm* marsh
marée [mare] *nf* tide; **m. haute/
basse** high/low tide; **m. noire** oil
slick
margarine [margarin] *nf*
margarine
marge [mar3] *nf (de page)* margin;
en m. de *(en dehors de)* on the
fringes of ● **marginal, -e, -aux,
-ales** *nmf* dropout

marguerite [margərit] *nf (fleur)*
daisy
mari [mari] *nm* husband
mariage [marja3] *nm (union)*
marriage; *(cérémonie)* wedding
marier [marje] **1** *vt (couleurs)*
to blend; **m. qn** *(sujet: prêtre,
maire)* to marry sb; *(sujet: père)*
to marry sb off **2 se marier** *vpr*
to get married; **se m. avec qn**
to get married to sb, to marry sb
● **marié, -e 1** *adj* married **2** *nm*
(bride)groom; **les mariés** the bride
and groom **3** *nf* **mariée** bride
marin, -e [marɛ̃, -in] **1** *adj (flore)*
marine; **air m.** sea air **2** *nm* sailor
● **marine** *nf* **m. de guerre** navy;
m. marchande merchant navy
marionnette [marjɔnɛt] *nf*
puppet; *(à fils)* marionette
maritime [maritim] *adj (droit,
climat)* maritime
marmite [marmit] *nf (cooking)*
pot
Maroc [marɔk] *nm* **le M.** Morocco
● **marocain, -e 1** *adj* Moroccan **2**
nmf **M., Marocaine** Moroccan
maroquinerie [marɔkinri] *nf*
(magasin) leather goods shop
marque [mark] *nf (trace)* mark;
(de produit) brand; *(de voiture)*
make; **m. déposée** (registered)
trademark
marquer [marke] **1** *vt (par une
marque)* to mark; *(écrire)* to note
down; *(indiquer)* to show; Sport
(point, but) to score **2** *vi (laisser
une trace)* to leave a mark; Sport
to score ● **marqueur** *nm (stylo)*
marker
marraine [marɛn] *nf* godmother
marre [mar] *adv* Fam **en avoir m.**
to be fed up **(de** with)
marron [marɔ̃] **1** *nm (fruit)* chestnut; *(couleur)* (chestnut) brown **2**
adj inv (couleur) (chestnut) brown

mars [mars] *nm* March

marteau, -x [marto] *nm* hammer

Martinique [martinik] *nf* **la M.** Martinique ● **martiniquais, -e 1** *adj* Martinican **2** *nmf* **M., Martiniquaise** Martinican

masculin, -e [maskylɛ̃, -in] **1** *adj (sexe, mode)* male; *(caractère, femme, nom)* masculine **2** *nm (en grammaire)* masculine

masque [mask] *nm* mask; **m. à gaz** gas mask

massacre [masakr] *nm (tuerie)* massacre

massage [masaʒ] *nm* massage

masse [mas] *nf (volume)* mass; *(gros morceau, majorité)* bulk (**de** of); **de m.** *(culture, communication)* mass; **en m.** en masse

masser [mase] **1** *vt (rassembler)* to assemble; *(pétrir)* to massage **2 se masser** *vpr (foule)* to form ● **masseur, -euse** *nmf* masseur, *f* masseuse

massif, -ive [masif, -iv] *adj* massive; *(or, chêne)* solid

mastiquer [mastike] *vt (mâcher)* to chew

mat, -e [mat] *adj (papier, couleur)* matt

mât [mɑ] *nm (de navire)* mast; *(poteau)* pole

match [matʃ] *nm Sport Br* match, *Am* game; **m. nul** draw; **faire m. nul** to draw

matelas [matla] *nm* mattress

matelot [matlo] *nm* sailor

matériau, -x [materjo] *nm* material; **matériaux** *(de construction)* building material(s)

matériel [materjɛl] *nm (de camping)* equipment; *Ordinat* **m. informatique** computer hardware

maternel, -elle [maternɛl] **1** *adj (amour, femme)* maternal; *(langue)* native **2** *adj & nf* **(école)**

maternelle *Br* nursery school, *Am* kindergarten ● **maternité** *nf (hôpital)* maternity hospital

mathématiques [matematik] *nfpl* mathematics *(sing)* ● **maths** *nfpl Fam Br* maths, *Am* math

matière [matjɛr] *nf Scol* subject; *(de livre)* subject matter; *(substance)* material; **m. première** raw material; **matières grasses** fat

Matignon [matiɲɔ̃] *nm* **(l'hôtel) M.** = the French Prime Minister's offices

matin [matɛ̃] *nm* morning; **le m.** *(chaque matin)* in the morning(s); **le mardi matin** every Tuesday morning; **tous les matins** every morning; **le 8 au m.** on the morning of the 8th; **à sept heures du m.** at seven in the morning; **au petit m.** very early (in the morning)

matinée [matine] *nf* morning; *Théât & Cin* matinée; **dans la m.** in the course of the morning

matraque [matrak] *nf (de policier) Br* truncheon, *Am* nightstick

maudit, -e [modi, -it] *adj (damné)* cursed

maussade [mosad] *adj (personne)* sullen; *(temps)* gloomy

mauvais, -e [move, -ɛz] **1** *adj* bad; *(santé, vue)* poor; *(méchant)* nasty; *(mal choisi)* wrong; **plus m. que...** worse than...; **le plus m.** the worst; **être m. en anglais** to be bad at English; **être en mauvaise santé** to be in bad *or* ill *or* poor health **2** *adv* **il fait m.** the weather's bad; **ça sent m.** it smells bad **3** *nm* **le bon et le m.** the good and the bad

mauve [mov] *adj & nm (couleur)* mauve

maux [mo] *pl de* mal

maximum [maksimɔm] *(pl*

maxima *ou* **maximums**) **1** *nm* maximum; **faire le m.** to do one's very best; **au m.** at the most **2** *adj* maximum

mayonnaise [majɔnɛz] *nf* mayonnaise

mazout [mazut] *nm* (fuel) oil

me [mə]

m' is used before a vowel or mute h.

pron personnel **(a)** *(complément direct)* me; **il me voit** he sees me **(b)** *(complément indirect)* (to) me; **elle me parle** she speaks to me; **tu me l'as dit** you told me **(c)** *(réfléchi)* myself; **je me lave** I wash myself **(d)** *(avec les pronominaux)* **je me suis trompé** I made a mistake

mécanicien [mekanisjɛ̃] *nm* mechanic; *(de train) Br* train driver, *Am* engineer

mécanique [mekanik] **1** *adj* mechanical **2** *nf (science)* mechanics *(sing)*; *(mécanisme)* mechanism ● **mécanisme** *nm* mechanism

méchant, -e [meʃɑ̃, -ɑ̃t] *adj (personne, remarque)* nasty; *(enfant)* naughty; *(chien)* vicious; **'attention! chien m.'** 'beware of the dog' ● **méchanceté** *nf* nastiness; **une m.** *(parole)* a nasty remark; *(acte)* a nasty action

mèche [mɛʃ] *nf (de cheveux)* lock; *(de bougie)* wick

méconnaissable [mekɔnɛsabl] *adj* unrecognizable

mécontent, -e [mekɔ̃tɑ̃, -ɑ̃t] *adj (insatisfait)* displeased **(de** with); *(contrarié)* annoyed

médaille [medaj] *nf* medal

médecin [medsɛ̃] *nm* doctor, physician; **m. généraliste** general practitioner, GP ● **médecine** *nf* medicine; **étudiant en m.** medical

student ● **médical, -e, -aux, -ales** *adj* medical ● **médicament** *nm* medicine

médias [medja] *nmpl* **les m.** the media

médiéval, -e, -aux, -ales [medjeval, -o] *adj* medieval

médiocre [medjɔkr] *adj* mediocre

médisances [medizɑ̃s] *nfpl (propos)* gossip

méditer [medite] *vi* to meditate **(sur** on) ● **méditation** *nf* meditation

Méditerranée [mediterane] *nf* **la M.** the Mediterranean ● **méditerranéen, -enne** *adj* Mediterranean

méduse [medyz] *nf* jellyfish

méfiance [mefjɑ̃s] *nf* distrust

méfier [mefje] **se méfier** *vpr* to be careful; **se m. de qn** not to trust sb; **se m. de qch** to watch out for sth; **méfie-toi!** watch out! ● **méfiant, -e** *adj* suspicious

mégaoctet [megaɔktɛ] *nm* *Ordinat* megabyte

mégot [mego] *nm* cigarette end

meilleur, -e [mejœr] **1** *adj* better **(que** than); **le m. résultat/ moment** the best result/moment **2** *nmf* **le m., la meilleure** the best (one) **3** *adv* **il fait m.** it's warmer

mélancolique [melɑ̃kɔlik] *adj* melancholy

mélange [melɑ̃ʒ] *nm (résultat)* mixture; *(opération)* mixing ● **mélanger 1** *vt (mêler)* to mix; *(brouiller)* to mix up **2 se mélanger** *vpr (s'incorporer)* to mix; *(idées)* to get mixed up

mêler [mele] **1** *vt* to mix **(à** with); *(odeurs, thèmes)* to combine; **m. qn à qch** *(affaire, conversation)* to involve sb in sth **2 se mêler** *vpr* to combine **(à** with); **se m. à qch** *(foule)* to mingle with sth; *(conversation)* to join in sth; **se**

m. de qch to get involved in sth; **mêle-toi de tes affaires!** mind your own business!

mélodie [melɔdi] *nf* melody

mélodramatique [melɔdramatik] *adj* melodramatic

melon [məlɔ̃] *nm (fruit)* melon; **(chapeau) m.** *Br* bowler (hat), *Am* derby

membre [mãbr] *nm (bras, jambe)* limb; *(de groupe)* member

même [mɛm] **1** *adj (identique)* same; **en m. temps** at the same time **(que** as); **le m. jour** the same day; **le jour m.** *(exact)* the very day; **lui-m./vous-m.** himself/yourself **2** *pron* **le/la m.** the same (one); **j'ai les mêmes** I have the same (ones) **3** *adv (y compris, aussi)* even; **m. si…** even if…; **ici m.** in this very place; **tout de m.,** *Fam* **quand m.** all the same; **de m.** likewise

mémoire [memwar] **1** *nf* memory; **de m.** from memory; **à la m. de** in memory of **2** *nm Univ* dissertation; **Mémoires** *(chronique)* memoirs ● **mémorable** *adj* memorable

mémorial, -aux [memɔrjal, -o] *nm (monument)* memorial

menaçant, -e [mənasã, -ãt] *adj* threatening

menace [mənas] *nf* threat ● **menacer** *vt* to threaten **(de faire** to do)

ménage [menaʒ] *nm (entretien)* housekeeping; *(couple)* couple, household; **faire le m.** to do the housework

mendier [mãdje] **1** *vt* to beg for **2** *vi* to beg ● **mendiant, -e** *nmf* beggar

mener [məne] **1** *vt (personne)* to take **(à** to); *(course, vie)* to lead; *(enquête)* to carry out **2** *vi* **m. à** to lead to

méningite [menɛ̃ʒit] *nf* meningitis

menottes [mənɔt] *nfpl* handcuffs

mensonge [mãsɔ̃ʒ] *nm* lie ● **mensonger, -ère** *adj* untrue

mensuel, -elle [mãsɥɛl] *adj* monthly

mensurations [mãsyrasjɔ̃] *nfpl* measurements

mental, -e, -aux, -ales [mãtal -o] *adj* mental

menthe [mãt] *nf* mint

mention [mãsjɔ̃] *nf (fait de citer)* mention; *(à un examen)* ≃ distinction; *Scol* **m. assez bien/ bien/très bien** ≃ C/B/A; **faire m. de qch** to mention sth; **'rayez les mentions inutiles'** 'delete as appropriate' ● **mentionner** *vt* to mention

mentir* [mãtir] *vi* to lie **(à** to) ● **menteur, -euse** *nmf* liar

menton [mãtɔ̃] *nm* chin

menu¹ [məny] *nm (de restaurant)* set menu; *Ordinat* menu

menu², -e [məny] *adj (petit)* tiny; *(mince)* slim

menuisier [mənɥizje] *nm* carpenter, joiner ● **menuiserie** *nf* woodwork

mépris [mepri] *nm* contempt **(pour** for), scorn **(pour** for); **au m. de qch** without regard to sth ● **méprisant, -e** *adj* contemptuous, scornful ● **mépriser** *vt* to despise

méprise [mepriz] *nf* mistake

mer [mɛr] *nf* sea; **en (haute) mer** at sea; **aller à la m.** to go to the seaside

mercerie [mɛrsəri] *nf (magasin) Br* haberdasher's, *Am* notion store

merci [mɛrsi] **1** *exclam* thank you, thanks **(de** *ou* **pour** for); **non m.** no thank you; **m. bien** thanks very much **2** *nf* **à la m. de** at the mercy of; **sans m.** merciless

mercredi [mɛrkrədi] *nm* Wednesday

mère [mɛr] *nf* mother

mériter [merite] *vt* *(être digne de)* to deserve; *(demander)* to be worth; **m. réflexion** to be worth thinking about; **ce livre mérite d'être lu** this book is worth reading

merveille [mɛrvɛj] *nf* wonder, marvel; **à m.** wonderfully (well) • **merveilleux, -euse** *adj* wonderful, *Br* marvellous, *Am* marvelous

mes [me] *voir* **mon**

mesdames [medam] *pl de* **madame**

mesdemoiselles [medmwazɛl] *pl de* **mademoiselle**

mesquin, -e [meskɛ̃, -in] *adj* mean, petty

message [mesaʒ] *nm* message; **m. publicitaire** advertisement • **messagerie** *nf* courier company; **m. électronique** electronic mail service; **m. vocale** voice mail

messe [mɛs] *nf* *(office, musique)* mass; **aller à la m.** to go to mass

messeigneurs [mesɛɲœr] *pl de* **monseigneur**

messieurs [mesjø] *pl de* **monsieur**

mesure [məzyr] *nf* *(dimension)* measurement; *(moyen)* measure; **sur m.** *(vêtement)* made to measure; **être en m. de faire qch** to be in a position to do sth; **prendre des mesures** to take measures; **à m. que...** as...; **dans la m. où...** in so far as...; **dans la m. du possible** as far as possible

mesurer [məzyre] **1** *vt* to measure **2** *vi* **m. 1 mètre 83** *(personne)* ≃ to be 6 feet tall; *(objet)* ≃ to measure 6 feet

met [mɛ] *voir* **mettre**

métal, -aux [me... • **métallique** a...

météo [meteo] *nf* ... weather forecast

méthode [metɔd] *nf* *(manu... soin)* method; *(livre)* course • **méthodique** *adj* methodical

métier [metje] *nm* *(manuel, commercial)* trade; *(intellectuel)* profession; *(savoir-faire)* experience; **être du m.** to be in the business

métrage [metraʒ] *nm* Cin **long/ court m.** feature/short film

mètre [mɛtr] *nm* *(mesure)* Br metre, *Am* meter; **m. carré/cube** square/cubic metre

métro [metro] *nm Br* underground, *Am* subway

métropole [metrɔpɔl] *nf* *(ville)* metropolis • **métropolitain, -e** *adj* metropolitan

mets [mɛ] *nm* *(aliment)* dish

metteur [metœr] *nm* **m. en scène** director

mettre* [mɛtr] **1** *vt* to put; *(vêtement, lunettes)* to put on; *(chauffage, radio)* to switch on; *(réveil)* to set (à for); **j'ai mis une heure** it took me an hour; **m. qn en colère** to make sb angry; **m. qn à l'aise** to put sb at ease; **m. de la musique** to put some music on; **mettons que...** *(+ subjunctive)* let's suppose that... **2 se mettre** *vpr* *(se placer)* to put oneself; *(debout)* to stand; *(assis)* to sit; *(objet)* to go; **se m. en pyjama** to get into one's pyjamas; **se m. à table** to sit (down) at the table; **se m. à l'aise** to make oneself comfortable; **se m. au travail** to start work; **se m. à faire qch** to start doing sth

meuble [mœbl] *nm* piece of furniture; **meubles** furniture •

…eublé *nm* furnished *Br* flat *or Am* apartment • **meubler** *vt* to furnish

meurt [mœr] *voir* **mourir**

meurtre [mœrtr] *nm* murder • **meurtrier, -ère 1** *nmf* murderer **2** *adj* murderous; *(épidémie)* deadly

mi- [mi] *préf* **la mi-mars** mid March; **cheveux mi-longs** shoulder-length hair; **à mi-chemin** halfway

miauler [mjole] *vi (chat)* to miaow

micro [mikro] *nm (microphone)* mike • **microphone** *nm* microphone

microbe [mikrɔb] *nm* germ

micro-ondes [mikrɔɔ̃d] *nm inv* **(four) à m.** microwave (oven)

microscope [mikrɔskɔp] *nm* microscope • **microscopique** *adj* microscopic

midi [midi] *nm* **(a)** *(heure)* midday; *(heure du déjeuner)* lunchtime; **entre m. et deux heures** at lunchtime **(b) le M.** the South of France

miel [mjɛl] *nm* honey

mien, mienne [mjɛ̃, mjɛn] **1** *pron possessif* **le m., la mienne** mine, *Br* my one; **les miens, les miennes** mine, *Br* my ones; **les deux miens** my two **2** *nmpl* **les miens** *(ma famille)* my family

miette [mjɛt] *nf (de pain)* crumb

mieux [mjø] **1** *adv* better **(que** than); **aller m.** to be (feeling) better; **de m. en m.** better and better; **le/la/les m.** *(de plusieurs)* the best; *(de deux)* the better; **le m. serait de…** the best thing would be to…; **le plus tôt sera le m.** the sooner the better **2** *adj inv* better; **si tu n'as rien de m. à faire** if you've got nothing better to do **3** *nm* **faire de son m.** to do one's best

mignon, -onne [miɲɔ̃, -ɔn] *adj (charmant)* cute

migraine [migrɛn] *nf* headache; *Méd* migraine

migration [migrasjɔ̃] *nf* migration

mijoter [miʒɔte] **1** *vt (avec soin)* to cook (lovingly); *(lentement)* to simmer **2** *vi* to simmer

mil [mil] *adj inv* **l'an deux m.** the year two thousand

milieu, -x [miljø] *nm (centre)* middle; *(cadre, groupe social)* environment; **au m. de** in the middle of

militaire [militɛr] **1** *adj* military **2** *nm* soldier

mille [mil] **1** *adj inv & nm inv* thousand; **m. hommes** a *or* one thousand men; **deux m.** two thousand **2** *nm (de cible)* bull's eye • **mille-feuille** *(pl* **mille-feuilles)** *nm Br* ≃ vanilla slice, *Am* ≃ napoleon • **millième** *adj & nmf* thousandth; **un m.** a thousandth • **millier** *nm* thousand; **un m. (de)** a thousand or so

millénaire [milenɛr] *nm* millennium

milliard [miljar] *nm* billion • **milliardaire** *adj & nmf* billionaire

millimètre [milimɛtr] *nm* millimetre

million [miljɔ̃] *nm* million; **un m. d'euros** a million euros; **deux millions** two million • **millionnaire** *adj & nmf* millionaire

mime [mim] *nm* mime • **mimer** *vti (exprimer)* to mime

minable [minabl] *adj (lieu, personne)* shabby

mince [mɛ̃s] *adj* thin; *(élancé)* slim • **minceur** *nf* thinness; *(sveltesse)* slimness • **mincir** *vi* to get slimmer

mine [min] *nf* **(a)** *(physionomie)* look; **avoir bonne/mauvaise m.** to look well/ill **(b)** *(gisement)* & *Fig*

mine; **m. de charbon** coalmine
(**c**) *(de crayon)* lead (**d**) *(engin explosif)* mine

minéral, -e, -aux, -ales [mineral, -o] *adj & nm* mineral

mineur, -e [minœr] **1** *nm (ouvrier)* miner **2** *adj (secondaire) & Mus* minor **3** *nmf Jur* minor

miniature [minjatyr] *adj & nf* miniature

minigolf [minigɔlf] *nm* crazy golf

minijupe [miniʒyp] *nf* miniskirt

minimum [minimɔm] *(pl* **minima** *ou* **minimums**) **1** *nm* minimum; **le m. de** *(force)* the minimum (amount of); **faire le m.** to do the bare minimum; **au m.** at the very least **2** *adj* minimum

ministère [ministɛr] *nm (département)* ministry; *(gouvernement)* government, cabinet; **m. des Affaires étrangères** *Br* ≃ Foreign Office, *Am* ≃ State Department

ministre [ministr] *nm Pol* secretary, *Br* minister; **m. des Affaires étrangères** *Br* ≃ Foreign Secretary, *Am* ≃ Secretary of State

Minitel® [minitɛl] *nm* = consumer information network accessible via home computer terminal

minorité [minɔrite] *nf* minority • **minoritaire** *adj* **être m.** to be in the minority

minuit [minɥi] *nm* midnight

minuscule [minyskyl] **1** *adj (petit)* tiny, minute **2** *adj & nf* (**lettre**) **m.** small letter

minute [minyt] *nf* minute; **d'une m. à l'autre** any minute (now)

minutieux, -eux [minysjø, -øz] *adj* meticulous

mirabelle [mirabɛl] *nf* mirabelle plum

miracle [mirakl] *nm* miracle; **par**

m. miraculously • **miraculeux, -euse** *adj* miraculous

miroir [mirwar] *nm* mirror

mis, -e¹ [mi, miz] *pp de* **mettre**

mise² [miz] *nf* (**a**) *(placement)* putting; **m. au point** perfecting; **m. en scène** *Théât* production; *Cin* direction (**b**) *(argent)* stake

miser [mize] *vt (argent)* to stake (**sur** on); **m. sur qn/qch** *(parier)* to bet on sb/sth; *(compter sur)* to count on sb/sth

misère [mizɛr] *nf* extreme poverty; **être dans la m.** to be poverty-stricken • **misérable** *(pitoyable)* miserable; *(pauvre)* destitute; *(vie)* wretched; *(logement)* seedy

missile [misil] *nm* missile

mission [misjɔ̃] *nf (tâche, organisation)* mission; *(d'employé)* task; **partir en m.** *(cadre)* to go away on business

mistral [mistral] *nm* **le m.** the mistral

mite [mit] *nf* moth

mi-temps [mitɑ̃] **1** *nf inv Sport (pause)* half-time **2** *nm inv* **travailler à m.** to work part-time

mixer¹ [mikse] *vt (à la main)* to mix; *(au mixer)* to blend

mixer², mixeur [miksœr] *nm (pour mélanger)* (food) mixer; *(pour rendre liquide)* liquidizer

mixte [mikst] *adj* mixed; *(école)* co-educational, *Br* mixed

mixture [mikstyr] *nf* mixture

Mlle *(abrév* **Mademoiselle**) Miss

mm *(abrév* **millimètre(s)**) mm

Mme *(abrév* **Madame**) Mrs

mobile [mɔbil] **1** *adj (panneau)* movable; *(personne)* mobile **2** *nm (décoration)* mobile; *(motif)* motive (**de** for)

mobilier [mɔbilje] *nm* furniture

Mobylette® [mɔbilɛt] *nf* moped

mode¹ [mɔd] *nf (tendance)* fashion;

à la m. fashionable; **à la m. de** in the manner of

mode² [mɔd] *nm (manière)* mode; **m. d'emploi** instructions; **m. de vie** way of life

modèle [mɔdɛl] **1** *nm (exemple, personne)* model **2** *adj* **élève m.** model pupil • **modeler 1** *vt* to model (**sur** on) **2 se modeler** *vpr* **se m. sur qn** to model oneself on sb

modem [mɔdɛm] *nm Ordinat* modem

modération [mɔderasjɔ] *nf* moderation; **avec m.** in moderation • **modéré, -e** *adj* moderate

moderne [mɔdɛrn] *adj* modern • **moderniser** *vt,* to modernize

modeste [mɔdɛst] *adj* modest • **modestie** *nf* modesty

modifier [mɔdifje] *vt* to alter, to modify • **modification** *nf* alteration, modification; **apporter une m. à qch** to make an alteration to sth

moelleux, -euse [mwalø, -øz] *adj (lit, tissu)* soft

mœurs [mœr(s)] *nfpl (morale)* morals; *(habitudes)* customs; **entrer dans les m.** to become part of everyday life

moi [mwa] *pron personnel* (a) *(après une préposition)* me; **pour/avec m.** for/with me; *Fam* **un ami à m.** a friend of mine (b) *(complément direct)* me; **laissez-m.** leave me (c) *(complément indirect)* (to) me; **montrez-le-m.** show it to me, show me it (d) *(sujet)* I; **c'est m. qui vous le dis!** I'm telling you!; **il est plus grand que m.** he's taller than I am *or* than me • **moi-même** *pron* myself

moindre [mwɛ̃dr] *adj (comparatif)* lesser; *(prix)* lower; *(quantité)*

smaller; **le/la m.** *(superlatif)* the least; **la m. erreur** the slightest mistake; **dans les moindres détails** in the smallest detail; **c'est la m. des choses** it's the least I/we/*etc* can do

moineau, -x [mwano] *nm* sparrow

moins [mwɛ̃] ([mwɛ̃z] *before vowel*) **1** *adv (comparatif)* less (**que** than); **m. de** *(temps, travail)* less (**que** than); *(gens, livres)* fewer (**que** than); **le/la/les m.** *(superlatif)* the least; **le m. grand, la m. grande, les m. grand(e)s** the smallest; **au m., du m.** at least; **qch de m., qch en m.** *(qui manque)* sth missing; **dix ans de m.** ten years less; **en m.** *(personne, objet)* less; *(personnes, objets)* fewer; **les m. de dix-huit ans** under-eighteens; **à m. que...** (+ *subjunctive*) unless... **2** *prép Math* minus; **deux heures m. cinq** five to two; **il fait m. 10 (degrés)** it's minus 10 (degrees)

mois [mwa] *nm* month; **au m. de juin** in (the month of) June

moisir [mwazir] *vi* to go *Br* mouldy *or Am* moldy • **moisi, -e 1** *adj Br* mouldy, *Am* moldy **2** *nm Br* mould, *Am* mold; **sentir le m.** to smell musty

moisson [mwasɔ̃] *nf* harvest; **faire la m.** to harvest

moite [mwat] *adj* sticky

moitié [mwatje] *nf* half; **la m. de la pomme** half (of) the apple; **à m. plein/vide** half-full/-empty; **à m. prix** (at) half-price

mol [mɔl] *voir* **mou**

molaire [mɔlɛr] *nf* molar

molécule [mɔlekyl] *nf* molecule

molester [mɔlɛste] *vt* to manhandle

molle [mɔl] *voir* **mou**

mollet¹ [mɔlɛ] *nm (de jambe)* calf

mollet² [mɔlɛ] *adj* **œuf m.** soft-boiled egg

moment [mɔmɑ̃] *nm (instant, durée)* moment; **un petit m.** a little while; **en ce m.** at the moment; **pour le m.** for the moment, for the time being; **à ce m.-là** *(à ce moment précis)* at that (very) moment, at that time; *(dans ce cas)* then; **à un m. donné** at one point; **d'un m. à l'autre** any moment; **au m. de partir** when just about to leave; **au m. où...** just as...; **jusqu'au m. où...** until...

mon, ma, mes [mɔ̃, ma, me]

> ma becomes **mon** [mɔ̃n] before a vowel or mute h.

adj possessif my; **m. père** my father; **ma mère** my mother; **m. ami(e)** my friend; **mes parents** my parents

Monaco [mɔnako] *nm* Monaco

monarchie [mɔnarʃi] *nf* monarchy

monastère [mɔnastɛr] *nm* monastery

monde [mɔ̃d] *nm* world; *(gens)* people; **dans le m. entier** worldwide, all over the world; **tout le m.** everybody; **il y a du m.** there are a lot of people • **mondial, -e, -aux, -ales** *adj (crise, renommée)* worldwide; **guerre mondiale** world war • **mondialisation** *nf* globalization

moniteur, -trice [mɔnitœr, -tris] **1** *nmf* instructor; *(de colonie) Br* assistant, *Am* camp counselor **2** *nm Ordinat (écran)* monitor

monnaie [mɔnɛ] *nf (argent)* money; *(d'un pays)* currency; *(pièces)* change; **faire de la m.** to get change; **avoir la m. de 100 euros** to have change for 100 euros; **m. unique** single currency

monopole [mɔnɔpɔl] *nm* monopoly; **avoir le m. de qch** to have a monopoly on sth • **monopoliser** *vt* to monopolize

monotone [mɔnɔtɔn] *adj* monotonous

monseigneur [mɔ̃sɛɲœr] *(pl* **messeigneurs)** *nm (évêque)* His/Your Lordship; *(prince)* His/Your Highness

monsieur [məsjø] *(pl* **messieurs)** *nm (homme quelconque)* gentleman; **M. Legras** Mr Legras; **bonsoir, messieurs-dames!** good evening!; **M.** *(dans une lettre)* Dear Sir

monstre [mɔ̃str] *nm* monster • **monstrueux, -euse** *adj (affreux)* monstrous; *(énorme)* huge

mont [mɔ̃] *nm* mount

montage [mɔ̃taʒ] *nm* Tech assembly; *Cin* editing; *(image truquée)* montage

montagne [mɔ̃taɲ] *nf* mountain; **la m.** *(zone)* the mountains; **à la m.** in the mountains; **montagnes russes** *(attraction foraine)* rollercoaster • **montagneux, -euse** *adj* mountainous

montant [mɔ̃tɑ̃] *nm (somme)* amount

montée [mɔ̃te] *nf (ascension)* climb, ascent; *(des prix, des eaux)* rise

monter [mɔ̃te] **1** *(aux* **avoir)** *vt (côte)* to climb (up); *(objet)* to bring/take up; *(son)* to turn up; *(tente)* to put up; *(machine)* to assemble; **m. l'escalier** to go/come upstairs *or* up the stairs **2** *(aux* **être)** *vi (personne)* to go/come up; *(prix)* to rise; **m. dans un véhicule** to get in(to) a vehicle; **m. sur qch** to climb onto sth; **m. sur** *ou* **à une échelle** to climb up a ladder; **m. en courant** to run up; *Sport* **m. à cheval** to ride (a horse)

montre [mɔ̃tr] *nf (instrument)* (wrist-)watch; *Sport & Fig* **contre la m.** against the clock

Montréal [mɔ̃real] *nm ou f* Montreal

montrer [mɔ̃tre] **1** *vt* to show (**à** to); **m. qn/qch du doigt** to point at sb/sth; **m. le chemin à qn** to show sb the way **2 se montrer** *vpr* to show oneself; **se m. courageux** to be courageous

monture [mɔ̃tyr] *nf (de lunettes)* frame

monument [mɔnymɑ̃] *nm* monument

moquer [mɔke] **se moquer** *vpr* **se m. de qn** to make fun of sb; **se m. de qch** *(rire de)* to make fun of sth; *(ne pas se soucier)* not to care about sth

moquette [mɔkɛt] *nf Br* fitted carpet, *Am* wall-to-wall carpeting

moral, -e, -aux, -ales [mɔral, -o] **1** *adj* moral **2** *nm* **avoir le m.** to be in good spirits • **morale** *nf (d'histoire)* moral; *(principes)* morals; **faire la m. à qn** to lecture sb

morceau, -x [mɔrso] *nm* piece, bit; *(de sucre)* lump; **tomber en morceaux** to fall to pieces

mordre [mɔrdr] *vti* to bite; **m. qn au bras** to bite sb's arm

mordu, -e [mɔrdy] *pp de* **mordre**

morne [mɔrn] *adj (temps)* dismal; *(personne)* glum

morose [mɔroz] *adj* morose

morsure [mɔrsyr] *nf* bite

mort¹ [mɔr] *nf* death; **se donner la m.** to take one's own life • **mortel, -elle 1** *adj (hommes, ennemi, danger)* mortal; *(accident)* fatal **2**

nmf mortal • **mortellement** *ad* *(blessé)* fatally

mort², -e [mɔr, mɔrt] **1** *ad* *(personne, plante, ville)* dead **m. de fatigue** dead tired; **m. de froid** numb with cold; **m. de peu** frightened to death; **m. ou vi** dead or alive **2** *nmf* dead man, dead woman; **les morts** the dead **la fête des Morts** All Souls' Day

morue [mɔry] *nf* cod

Moscou [mɔsku] *nm ou* Moscow

mot [mo] *nm* word; **envoyer u m. à qn** to drop sb a line; **m. à m** word for word; **avoir le dernie m.** to have the last word; **mot croisés** crossword (puzzle); **m. d passe** password

moteur [mɔtœr] *nm (de véhicule* engine; *(électrique)* motor

motif [mɔtif] *nm (raison)* reaso *(de* for); *(dessin)* pattern

motiver [mɔtive] *vt* to motivat • **motivation** *nf* motivation **motivé, -e** *adj* motivated

moto [mɔto] *nf* motorbike **motocycliste** *nmf* motorcyclist

mou, molle [mu, mɔl]

mol is used before masculine singular nouns beginning with a vowel or mute h.

adj soft; *(sans énergie)* feeble

mouche [muʃ] *nf (insecte)* fly **moucheron** *nm* midge

moucher [muʃe] **se moucher** *vp* to blow one's nose

mouchoir [muʃwar] *nn* handkerchief; **m. en papier** tissu

moudre* [mudr] *vt* to grind

mouette [mwɛt] *nf* (sea)gull

moufle [mufl] *nf* mitten, mitt

mouiller [muje] **1** *vt* to wet **2 s mouiller** *vpr* to get wet • **mouillé -e** *adj* wet (**de** with)

moule¹ [mul] *nm Br* mould, *Am* mold; **m. à gâteaux** cake tin • **moulant, -e** *adj (vêtement)* tight-fitting • **mouler** *vt Br* to mould, *Am* to mold; *(statue)* to cast

moule² [mul] *nf (mollusque)* mussel

moulin [mulɛ̃] *nm* mill; **m. à café** coffee grinder; **m. à vent** windmill

moulu, -e [muly] **1** *pp de* **moudre 2** *adj (café)* ground

mourir* [murir] *(aux* **être)** *vi* to die (**de** of *or* from); **m. de froid** to die of exposure; *Fig* **m. de peur** to be frightened to death; *Fig* **je meurs de faim!** I'm starving!

mousse [mus] *nf (plante)* moss; *(écume)* foam, froth; **m. à raser** shaving foam; *Culin* **m. au chocolat** chocolate mousse • **mousseux, -euse 1** *adj (vin)* sparkling **2** *nm* sparkling wine

moustache [mustaʃ] *nf (d'homme) Br* moustache, *Am* mustache; *(de chat)* whiskers

moustique [mustik] *nm* mosquito

moutarde [mutard] *nf* mustard

mouton [mutɔ̃] *nm* sheep *inv*; *(viande)* mutton

mouvement [muvmɑ̃] *nm* movement; **en m.** moving • **mouvementé, -e** *adj (vie, voyage)* eventful

mouvoir* [muvwar] *vi* to move

moyen¹, -enne [mwajɛ̃, -ɛn] **1** *adj* average; *(format, entreprise)* medium(-sized) **2** *nf* **moyenne** average; **en moyenne** on average; **avoir la moyenne** *(à un examen) Br* to get a pass mark, *Am* to get a pass; *(à un devoir)* to get 50 percent, *Br* to get half marks; **le M. Âge** the Middle Ages

moyen² [mwajɛ̃] *nm (procédé, façon)* means, way **(de faire** of doing *or* to do); **moyens** *(argent, ressources)* means; **je n'ai pas les moyens** *(argent)* I can't afford it; **au m. de qch** by means of sth

muer [mɥe] **1** *vi (animal) Br* to moult, *Am* to molt; *(voix)* to break **2 se muer** *vpr* **se m. en qch** to change into sth

muet, muette [mɥe, mɥɛt] *adj (infirme)* dumb; *(de surprise)* speechless; *(film)* silent

muguet [mɥgɛ] *nm* lily of the valley

mule [myl] *nf (pantoufle, animal)* mule

multicolore [myltikɔlɔr] *adj Br* multicoloured, *Am* multicolored

multiple [myltipl] *adj (nombreux)* numerous; *(varié)* multiple • **multiplication** *nf (calcul)* multiplication; *(augmentation)* increase • **multiplier 1** *vt* to multiply **2 se multiplier** *vpr* to increase; *(se reproduire)* to multiply

municipal, -e, -aux, -ales [mynisipal, -o] *adj* municipal • **municipalité** *nf (dirigeants)* local council; *(commune)* municipality

munir [mynir] **se munir** *vpr* **se m. de qch** to take sth

mur [myr] *nm* wall

mûr, -e¹ [myr] *adj (fruit)* ripe; *(personne)* mature • **mûrir** *vti (fruit)* to ripen; *(personne)* to mature

mûre² [myr] *nf (baie)* blackberry

murmure [myrmyr] *nm* murmur • **murmurer** *vti* to murmur

muscle [myskl] *nm* muscle • **musclé, -e** *adj (bras)* muscular

musée [myze] *nm* museum

musique [myzik] *nf* music • **musical, -e, -aux, -ales** *adj* musical • **musicien, -enne** *nmf* musician

musulman, -e [myzylmɑ̃, -an]
adj & nmf Muslim

mutiler [mytile] *vt* to mutilate, to
maim; **être mutilé** to be disabled

mutuel, -elle [mytɥɛl] **1** *adj*
(réciproque) mutual **2** *nf* **mutuelle**
mutual insurance company •
mutuellement *adv* each other

myope [mjɔp] *adj* shortsighted

myrtille [mirtij] *nf (baie)* bilberry

mystère [mistɛr] *nm* mystery
• **mystérieux, -euse** *adj*
mysterious

mythe [mit] *nm* myth • **mythique**
adj mythical • **mythologie** *nf*
mythology

Nn

N¹, n [ɛn] *nm inv* N, n
N² (*abrév* **route nationale**) *Br* ≃ A
road, *Am* ≃ highway
n' [n] *voir* **ne**
nacre [nakr] *nf* mother-of-pearl
nage [naʒ] *nf* (swimming) stroke;
traverser une rivière à la n.
to swim across a river; **n. libre**
freestyle
nager [naʒe] *vti* to swim • **nageur,
-euse** *nmf* swimmer
naïf, naïve [naif, naiv] *adj* naïve
nain, -e [nɛ̃, nɛn] *adj & nmf*
dwarf
naissance [nɛsɑ̃s] *nf* (*de
personne, d'animal*) birth; **donner
n. à** (*enfant*) to give birth to; **de
n.** from birth
naître* [nɛtr] *vi* to be born;
(*sentiment, difficulté*) to arise (**de**
from)
naïveté [naivte] *nf* naïvety
nanti, -e [nɑ̃ti] **1** *adj* well-to-do
2 *nmpl Péj* **les nantis** the well-
to-do
nappe [nap] *nf* (*de table*)
tablecloth; **n. de pétrole** layer of
oil; (*de marée noire*) oil slick
napper [nape] *vt* to coat (**de** with)
narine [narin] *nf* nostril
natal, -e, -als, -ales [natal] *adj*
native
natation [natasjɔ̃] *nf* swimming
natif, -ive [natif, -iv] *adj & nmf*
native; **être n. de** to be a native
of
nation [nasjɔ̃] *nf* nation; **les
Nations unies** the United Nations

• **national, -e, -aux, -ales** *adj*
national • **nationale** *nf* (*route*)
Br ≃ A road, *Am* ≃ highway •
nationaliste 1 *adj* nationalistic **2**
nmf nationalist • **nationalité** *nf*
nationality
natte [nat] *nf* (*de cheveux*) *Br*
plait, *Am* braid
naturaliser [natyralize] *vt* to
naturalize
nature [natyr] **1** *nf* (*univers,
caractère*) nature; (*campagne*)
country; **en pleine n.** in the
middle of the country; **n. morte**
still life **2** *adj inv* (*omelette, yaourt*)
plain; (*thé*) without milk
naturel, -elle [natyrɛl] *adj* natural
• **naturellement** *adv* naturally
naufrage [nofraʒ] *nm* (ship)wreck;
faire n. (*bateau*) to be wrecked;
(*marin*) to be shipwrecked
nausée [noze] *nf* nausea, sickness;
avoir la n. to feel sick
navet [navɛ] *nm* (*légume*) turnip
navette [navɛt] *nf* (*véhicule*)
shuttle; **faire la n.** (*véhicule,
personne*) to shuttle back and
forth (**entre** between); **n. spatiale**
space shuttle
navigation [navigasjɔ̃] *nf*
navigation
naviguer [navige] *vi* (*bateau*) to
sail; **n. sur Internet** to surf the
Net
navire [navir] *nm* ship
navré, -e [navre] *adj* **je suis n.** I'm
terribly sorry
ne [nə]

n' before vowel or mute h; used to form negative verb with **pas, jamais, personne, rien** etc.

adv **ne... pas** not; **il ne boit pas** he does not *or* doesn't drink; **elle n'ose (pas)** she doesn't dare; **ne... que** only; **je crains qu'il ne parte** I'm afraid he'll leave

né, -e [ne] **1** *pp de* **naître** born; **il est né en 2001** he was born in 2001; **née Dupont** née Dupont **2** *adj* born

néanmoins [neãmwɛ̃] *adv* nevertheless

nécessaire [nesesɛr] **1** *adj* necessary **2** *nm* **le n.** the necessities; **faire le n.** to do what's necessary; **n. de toilette** toilet bag

nécessité [nesesite] *nf* necessity • **nécessiter** *vt* to require, to necessitate

nectarine [nektarin] *nf* nectarine

néerlandais, -e [neɛrlãdɛ, -ɛz] **1** *adj* Dutch **2** *nmf* **N., Néerlandaise** Dutchman, *f* Dutchwoman **3** *nm* *(langue)* Dutch

négatif, -ive [negatif, -iv] **1** *adj* negative **2** *nm* *(de photo)* negative

négligent, -e [negliʒã, -ãt] *adj* careless, negligent • **négligence** *nf* *(défaut)* carelessness, negligence

négliger [negliʒe] *vt* *(personne, travail, conseil)* to neglect; **n. de faire qch** to neglect to do sth

négocier [negɔsje] *vti* to negotiate • **négociant, -e** *nmf* merchant, dealer • **négociation** *nf* negotiation

neige [nɛʒ] *nf* snow • **neiger** *v impersonnel* to snow; **il neige** it's snowing

néon [neɔ̃] *nm* *(gaz)* neon; *(enseigne)* neon sign

néo-zélandais, -e [neɔzelãdɛ, -ɛz] *(mpl* **néo-zélandais,** *fpl* **néo-zélandaises)** **1** *adj* New Zealand **2** *nmf* **N., Néo-Zélandaise** New Zealander

nerf [nɛr] *nm* nerve • **nerveux, -euse** *adj* nervous

n'est-ce pas [nɛspa] *adv* isn't he?/don't you?/won't they?/*etc*; **tu viendras, n.?** you'll come, won't you?; **il fait beau, n.?** the weather's nice, isn't it?

Net [nɛt] *nm* **le N.** the Net

net, nette [nɛt] **1** *adj (propre)* clean; *(image, refus)* clear; *(prix, salaire)* net **2** *adv (casser, couper)* clean; *(refuser)* flatly; **s'arrêter n.** to stop dead • **nettement** *adv (avec précision)* clearly; *(incontestablement)* definitely; **n. mieux** much better

nettoyer [netwaje] **1** *vt* to clean **2** **se nettoyer** *vpr* **se n. les oreilles** to clean one's ears • **nettoyage** *nm* cleaning; **n. à sec** dry-cleaning

neuf¹, neuve [nœf, nœv] **1** *adj* new; **quoi de n.?** what's new? **2** *nm* **remettre qch à n.** to make sth as good as new

neuf² [nœf] *([nœv] before vowel or mute h) adj & nm* nine • **neuvième** *adj & nmf* ninth

neutre [nøtr] *adj (pays, personne)* neutral

neveu, -x [nəvø] *nm* nephew

nez [ne] *nm* nose; **n. à n.** face to face (**avec** with); **rire au n. de qn** to laugh in sb's face; **parler du n.** to speak through one's nose

ni [ni] *conj* **ni... ni...** neither... nor...; **ni Pierre ni Paul ne sont venus** neither Pierre nor Paul came; **il n'a ni faim ni soif** he's neither hungry nor thirsty; **sans manger ni boire** without eating or drinking; **ni l'un(e) ni l'autre** neither (of them)

niche [niʃ] *nf (de chien) Br* kennel, *Am* doghouse; *(cavité)* niche, recess

nicotine [nikɔtin] *nf* nicotine

nid [ni] *nm* nest

nièce [njɛs] *nf* niece

nier [nje] *vt* to deny (**que** that)

n'importe [nɛ̃pɔrt] *voir* **importer¹**

niveau, -x [nivo] *nm (hauteur, étage, degré)* level; **au n. de la mer** at sea level; **n. de vie** standard of living

noble [nɔbl] **1** *adj* noble **2** *nmf* nobleman, *f* noblewoman

noce [nɔs] *nf* wedding; **noces d'or** golden wedding

nocif, -ive [nɔsif, -iv] *adj* harmful

nocturne [nɔktyrn] *adj (animal)* nocturnal

Noël [nɔɛl] *nm* Christmas; **arbre de N.** Christmas tree; **le père N.** Father Christmas, Santa Claus

nœud [nø] *nm (entrecroisement)* knot; *(ruban)* bow; **n. papillon** bow tie

noir, -e [nwar] **1** *adj* black; *(sombre)* dark; **il fait n.** it's dark; **film n.** film noir **2** *nm (couleur)* black; *(obscurité)* dark; **N. (homme)** Black (man) **3** *nf* **Noire (femme)** Black (woman)

noisette [nwazɛt] *nf* hazelnut

noix [nwa] *nf (du noyer)* walnut

nom [nɔ̃] *nm* name; *Gram* noun; **au n. de qn** on sb's behalf; **n. de famille** surname; **n. de jeune fille** maiden name

nombre [nɔ̃br] *nm* number; **être au** *ou* **du n. de** to be among; **ils sont au n. de dix** there are ten of them; **le plus grand n. de** the majority of

nombreux, -euse [nɔ̃brø, -øz]

adj (amis, livres) numerous, many; *(famille, collection)* large; **peu n.** few; **venir n.** to come in large numbers

nombril [nɔ̃bri(l)] *nm* navel

nomination [nɔminasjɔ̃] *nf (à un poste)* appointment; *(pour récompense)* nomination

nommer [nɔme] *vt (appeler)* to name; **n. qn** *(désigner)* to appoint sb (**à un poste** to a post); **n. qn président** to appoint sb chairman

non [nɔ̃] *adv* no; **tu viens ou n.?** are you coming or not?; **n. seulement** not only; **n. (pas) que...** *(+ subjunctive)* not that...; **n. loin** not far; **je crois que n.** I don't think so; **(ni) moi n. plus** neither do/am/can/*etc* I

nonante [nɔnɑ̃t] *adj & nm inv (en Belgique, en Suisse)* ninety

non-fumeur, -euse [nɔ̃fymœr, -øz] **1** *adj* non-smoking **2** *nmf* non-smoker

non-voyants [nɔ̃vwajɑ̃] *nmpl* **les n.** the unsighted

nord [nɔr] **1** *nm* north; **au n.** in the north; *(direction)* (to the) north (**de** of); **du n.** *(vent, direction)* northerly; *(ville)* northern; *(gens)* from/in the north; **l'Afrique du N.** North Africa; **l'Europe du N.** Northern Europe; **le grand N.** the Frozen North **2** *adj inv (côte)* north; *(régions)* northern ● **nord-africain, -e** *(mpl* **nord-africains,** *fpl* **nord-africaines) 1** *adj* North African **2** *nmf* **N., Nord-Africaine** North African ● **nord-américain, -e** *(mpl* **nord-américains,** *fpl* **nord-américaines) 1** *adj* North American **2** *nmf* **N., Nord-Américaine** North American ● **nord-est** *nm & adj inv* northeast ● **nord-ouest** *nm & adj inv* northwest

normal, -e, -aux, -ales [nɔrmal, -o] *adj* normal • **normale** *nf* norm; **au-dessus/au-dessous de la n.** above/below average • **normalement** *adv* normally

normand, -e [nɔrmã, -ãd] **1** *adj* Norman **2** *nmf* **N., Normande** Norman • **Normandie** *nf* **la N.** Normandy

Norvège [nɔrvɛʒ] *nf* **la N.** Norway • **norvégien, -enne 1** *adj* Norwegian **2** *nmf* **N., Norvégienne** Norwegian **3** *nm* *(langue)* Norwegian

nos [no] *voir* **notre**

nostalgie [nɔstalʒi] *nf* nostalgia • **nostalgique** *adj* nostalgic

notaire [nɔtɛr] *nm* lawyer, *Br* notary (public)

notamment [nɔtamã] *adv* notably

note [nɔt] *nf* *(annotation, communication)* & *Mus* note; *Scol Br* mark, *Am* grade; *(facture) Br* bill, *Am* check; **prendre n. de qch** to make a note of sth; **prendre des notes** to take notes

noter [nɔte] *vt (remarquer)* to note; *(écrire)* to note down; *(devoir) Br* to mark, *Am* to grade

notice [nɔtis] *nf (mode d'emploi)* instructions; *(de médicament)* directions

notion [nosjɔ̃] *nf* notion; **avoir des notions de qch** to know the basics of sth

notoriété [nɔtɔrjete] *nf (renom)* fame; **il est de n. publique que...** it's common knowledge that...

notre, nos [nɔtr, no] *adj possessif* our

nôtre [notr] **1** *pron possessif* **le/la n., les nôtres** ours **2** *nmpl* **les nôtres** *(parents)* our family

nouer [nwe] *vt (lacets)* to tie; *(cravate)* to knot

nougat [nuga] *nm* nougat

nouilles [nuj] *nfpl* noodles

nourrice [nuris] *nf* (children's) nurse, *Br* childminder

nourrir [nurir] **1** *vt (alimenter)* to feed **2 se nourrir** *vpr* to eat; **se n. de qch** to feed on sth

nourrisson [nurisɔ̃] *nm* infant

nourriture [nurityr] *nf* food

nous [nu] *pron personnel* **(a)** *(sujet)* we; **n. sommes ici** we are here **(b)** *(complément direct)* us; **il n. connaît** he knows us **(c)** *(complément indirect)* (to) us; **il n. l'a donné** he gave it to us, he gave us it **(d)** *(réfléchi)* ourselves; **n. n. lavons** we wash ourselves; **n. n. habillons** we get dressed **(e)** *(réciproque)* each other; **n. n. détestons** we hate each other • **nous-mêmes** *pron* ourselves

nouveau, -elle¹, -x, -elles [nuvo, -ɛl]

nouvel is used before masculine singular nouns beginning with a vowel or mute h.

1 *adj* new; *(mode)* latest; **on craint de nouvelles inondations** *(d'autres)* further flooding is feared **2** *nmf (à l'école)* new boy, *f* new girl **3** *nm* **du n.** something new • *adv* **de n., à n.** again • **nouveau-né, -e** *(mpl* **nouveau-nés,** *fpl* **nouveau-nées) 1** *adj* newborn **2** *nmf* newborn baby

nouveauté [nuvote] *nf* novelty; **nouveautés** *(livres)* new books; *(disques)* new releases

nouvelle² [nuvɛl] *nf* **(a)** **une n.** *(annonce)* a piece of news; **la n. de sa mort** the news of his/her death; **les nouvelles** the news *(sing)*; **avoir des nouvelles de qn** *(directement)* to have heard from sb **(b)** *(récit)* short story

Nouvelle-Calédonie [nuvɛl-kaledɔni] *nf* **la N.** New Caledonia

Nouvelle-Zélande [nuvɛlzelɑ̃d] *nf* **la N.** New Zealand

novembre [nɔvɑ̃br] *nm* November

noyau, -x [nwajo] *nm (de fruit)* stone, *Am* pit; *(d'atome, de cellule)* nucleus

noyer [nwaje] **1** *vt* to drown **2 se noyer** *vpr* to drown; *Fig* **se n. dans les détails** to get bogged down in details

nu, -e [ny] **1** *adj (personne, vérité)* naked; *(mains, chambre)* bare; **tout nu** (stark) naked, (in the) nude; **tête nue, nu-tête** bareheaded; **aller pieds nus** to go barefoot **2** *nm* nude; **mettre qch à nu** to expose sth

nuage [nɥaʒ] *nm* cloud; *Fig* **être dans les nuages** to have one's head in the clouds • **nuageux, -euse** *adj (ciel)* cloudy

nuance [nɥɑ̃s] *nf (de couleur)* shade; *(de sens)* nuance

nucléaire [nykleɛr] **1** *adj* nuclear **2** *nm* nuclear energy

nudiste [nydist] *nmf* nudist

nuire* [nɥir] *vi* **n. à qn/qch** to harm sb/sth • **nuisible** *adj* harmful (**à** to)

nuit [nɥi] *nf* night; *(obscurité)* dark(ness); **la n.** *(se promener)* at night; **cette n.** *(hier)* last night; *(aujourd'hui)* tonight; **il fait n.** it's dark; **bonne n.!** good night!

nul, nulle [nyl] *adj (médiocre)* hopeless, useless; *Jur (non valable)* null (and void); **être n. en qch** to be hopeless at sth • **nulle part** *adv* nowhere; **n. ailleurs** nowhere else

numérique [nymerik] *adj* numerical; *(montre, appareil photo)* digital

numéro [nymero] *nm (chiffre)* number; *(de journal)* issue; *Tél* **n. vert** *Br* ≃ Freefone® number, *Am* ≃ toll-free number; **n. de téléphone** telephone number • **numéroter** *vt (pages, sièges)* to number

nuque [nyk] *nf* back of the neck

nutrition [nytrisjɔ̃] *nf* nutrition

Nylon® [nilɔ̃] *nm (fibre)* nylon

Oo

O, o [o] *nm inv* O, o

obéir [ɔbeir] *vi* to obey; **o. à qn/ qch** to obey sb/sth ● **obéissant, -e** *adj* obedient

obèse [ɔbɛz] *adj* obese

objection [ɔbʒɛksjɔ̃] *nf* objection

objectif, -ive [ɔbʒɛktif, -iv] **1** *adj* objective **2** *nm (but)* objective; *(d'appareil photo)* lens

objet [ɔbʒɛ] *nm (chose, sujet, but)* object; **objets trouvés** *(bureau) Br* lost property, *Am* lost and found

obligatoire [ɔbligatwar] *adj* compulsory

obliger [ɔbliʒe] *vt (contraindre)* to force (**à faire** to do); **être obligé de faire qch** to be obliged to do sth ● **obligé, -e** *adj (obligatoire)* necessary

obscène [ɔpsɛn] *adj* obscene

obscur, -e [ɔpskyr] *adj (sombre)* dark; *(confus, inconnu)* obscure ● **obscurité** *nf (noirceur)* darkness; **dans l'o.** in the dark

obséder [ɔpsede] *vt* to obsess

obsèques [ɔpsɛk] *nfpl* funeral

observateur, -trice [ɔpsɛrvatœr, -tris] *nmf* observer

observation [ɔpsɛrvasjɔ̃] *nf (étude, remarque)* observation; *(reproche)* remark; *(respect)* observance

observer [ɔpsɛrve] *vt (regarder, respecter)* to observe; *(remarquer)* to notice; **faire o. qch à qn** to point sth out to sb

obsession [ɔpsesjɔ̃] *nf* obsession

obstacle [ɔpstakl] *nm* obstacle; **faire o. à qch** to stand in the way of sth

obstiné, -e [ɔpstine] *adj* stubborn, obstinate

obstruction [ɔpstryksjɔ̃] *nf* obstruction

obtenir* [ɔptənir] *vt* to get, to obtain

occasion [ɔkazjɔ̃] *nf* **(a)** *(chance)* chance, opportunity (**de faire** to do); *(moment)* occasion; **à l'o.** when the occasion arises; **à l'o. de qch** on the occasion of sth **(b)** *(affaire)* bargain; *(objet non neuf)* second-hand item; **d'o.** second-hand

occident [ɔksidɑ̃] *nm* **l'O.** the West ● **occidental, -e, -aux, -ales 1** *adj Géog & Pol* western **2** *nmpl Pol* **les Occidentaux** Westerners

occupant, -e [ɔkypɑ̃, -ɑ̃t] *nmf* occupant

occupation [ɔkypasjɔ̃] *nf* occupation

occupé, -e [ɔkype] *adj* busy (**à faire** doing); *(place, maison)* occupied; *(ligne téléphonique) Br* engaged, *Am* busy

occuper [ɔkype] **1** *vt (bâtiment, pays)* to occupy; *(place)* to take up, to occupy; **o. qn** *(jeu, travail)* to keep sb busy *or* occupied **2 s'occuper** *vpr* to keep oneself busy (**à faire** doing); **s'o. de** *(affaire, problème)* to deal with; **s'o. de qn** *(malade)* to take care of sb; *(client)* to see to sb

océan [ɔseã] *nm* ocean; **l'o. Atlantique/Pacifique** the Atlantic/Pacific Ocean

octante [ɔktãt] *adj & nm inv (en Belgique, en Suisse)* eighty

octobre [ɔktɔbr] *nm* October

odeur [ɔdœr] *nf* smell

œil [œj] *(pl* **yeux** [jø]) *nm* eye; **avoir les yeux verts** to have green eyes; **avoir de grands yeux** to have big eyes; **lever/baisser les yeux** to look up/down; **coup d'o.** *(regard)* look, glance; **jeter un coup d'o. sur qch** to have a look at sth; **regarder qn dans les yeux** to look sb in the eye

œuf [œf] *(pl* **œufs** [ø]) *nm* egg; **œufs** *(de poissons)* (hard) roe; **o. à la coque** boiled egg; **o. sur le plat** fried egg; **o. dur** hard-boiled egg; **œufs brouillés** scrambled eggs; **o. de Pâques** Easter egg

œuvre [œvr] *nf (travail, livre)* work; **o. d'art** work of art; **o. de charité** *(organisation)* charity

offenser [ɔfãse] **1** *vt* to offend **2 s'offenser** *vpr* **s'o. de qch** to take *Br* offence *or Am* offense at sth • **offensif, -ive 1** *adj* offensive **2** *nf* **offensive** offensive; **passer à l'offensive** to go on the offensive

offert, -e [ɔfɛr, -ɛrt] *pp de* **offrir**

office [ɔfis] *nm (établissement)* office, bureau; **o. du tourisme** tourist information centre; **faire o. de qch** to serve as sth

officiel, -elle [ɔfisjɛl] *adj & nm* official

officieux, -euse [ɔfisjø, -øz] *adj* unofficial

offre [ɔfr] *nf* offer; *Écon* **l'o. et la demande** supply and demand; **offres d'emploi** *(de journal)* job vacancies, *Br* situations vacant

offrir* [ɔfrir] **1** *vt (donner)* to give; *(proposer)* to offer; **o. qch à qn** *(donner)* to give sb sth, to give sth to sb; *(proposer)* to offer sb sth, to offer sth to sb; **o. de faire qch** to offer to do sth **2 s'offrir** *vpr (cadeau)* to treat oneself to; *(se proposer)* to offer oneself (**comme** as)

oie [wa] *nf* goose *(pl* geese)

oignon [ɔɲõ] *nm (légume)* onion

oiseau, -x [wazo] *nm* bird

oisif, -ive [wazif, -iv] *adj* idle

olive [ɔliv] *nf* olive

olympique [ɔlɛpik] *adj* Olympic; **les jeux Olympiques** the Olympic games

ombre [õbr] *nf (forme)* shadow; *(zone sombre)* shade; **30° à l'o.** 30° in the shade; **sans l'o. d'un doute** without the shadow of a doubt

ombrelle [õbrɛl] *nf* sunshade, parasol

omelette [ɔmlɛt] *nf* omelette

omettre* [ɔmɛtr] *vt* to omit *(de faire* to do) • **omission** *nf* omission

omnibus [ɔmnibys] *adj & nm* **(train) o.** slow train *(stopping at all stations)*

on [õ] *(sometimes* **l'on** [lõ]) *pron indéfini (les gens)* they, people; *(nous)* we, one; *(vous)* you, one; **on m'a dit que...** I was told that...; **on me l'a donné** somebody gave it to me

oncle [õkl] *nm* uncle

onctueux, -euse [õktɥø, -øz] *adj* smooth

ondulé, -e [õdyle] *adj (cheveux)* wavy

ongle [õgl] *nm* (finger)nail

ont [õ] *voir* **avoir**

ONU [ɔny] *(abrév* **Organisation des Nations unies)** *nf* UN

onze [õz] *adj inv & nm inv* eleven • **onzième** *adj & nmf* eleventh

opéra [ɔpera] *nm (musique)* opera; *(édifice)* opera house

opérateur, -trice [ɔperatœr, -tris] *nmf (personne)* operator

opération [ɔperasjɔ̃] *nf* operation

opérer [ɔpere] **1** *vt (exécuter)* to carry out; *(patient)* to operate on (**de** for); **se faire o.** to have an operation **2** *vi (agir)* to work; *(procéder)* to proceed; *(chirurgien)* to operate

opinion [ɔpinjɔ̃] *nf* opinion (**sur** about *or* on); **o. publique** public opinion

opportun, -e [ɔpɔrtœ̃, -yn] *adj* opportune, timely • **opportunité** *nf* timeliness

opposant, -e [ɔpozɑ̃, -ɑ̃t] *nmf* opponent (**à** of)

opposé, -e [ɔpoze] **1** *adj (direction)* opposite; *(intérêts)* conflicting; *(armées, équipe)* opposing; **être o. à qch** to be opposed to sth **2** *nm* **l'o.** the opposite (**de** of); **à l'o.** *(côté)* on the opposite side (**de** to); **à l'o. de** *(contrairement à)* contrary to

opposer [ɔpoze] **1** *vt (résistance, argument)* to put up (**à** against); **match qui oppose...** match between... **2 s'opposer** *vpr (équipes)* to confront each other; **s'o. à qch** to be opposed to sth; **je m'y oppose** I'm opposed to it

opposition [ɔpozisjɔ̃] *nf* opposition (**à** to); **faire o. à** to oppose; *(chèque)* to stop; **par o. à** as opposed to

oppressant, -e [ɔpresɑ̃, -ɑ̃t] *adj* oppressive • **oppression** *nf* oppression • **opprimer** *vt (peuple, nation)* to oppress

opter [ɔpte] *vi* **o. pour qch** to opt for sth

opticien, -enne [ɔptisjɛ̃, -ɛn] *nmf* optician

optimiste [ɔptimist] **1** *adj* optimistic **2** *nmf* optimist

option [ɔpsjɔ̃] *nf (choix)* option; *(chose)* optional extra; *Scol Br* optional subject, *Am* elective (subject)

or¹ [ɔr] *nm* gold; **montre en or** gold watch; **mine d'or** gold mine

or² [ɔr] *conj (cependant)* now, well

orage [ɔraʒ] *nm* (thunder)storm • **orageux, -euse** *adj* stormy

oral, -e, -aux, -ales [ɔral, -o] **1** *adj* oral **2** *nm Scol & Univ* oral

orange [ɔrɑ̃ʒ] **1** *nf* orange; **o. pressée** (fresh) orange juice **2** *adj inv & nm inv (couleur)* orange

orbite [ɔrbit] *nf (d'astre)* orbit; *(d'œil)* socket; **mettre qch sur o.** *(fusée)* to put sth into orbit

orchestre [ɔrkɛstr] *nm (classique)* orchestra; *(de jazz)* band; *Théât (places) Br* stalls, *Am* orchestra

ordinaire [ɔrdinɛr] *adj* ordinary; **d'o., à l'o.** usually; **comme d'o., comme à l'o.** as usual

ordinateur [ɔrdinatœr] *nm* computer; **o. portable** laptop

ordonnance [ɔrdɔnɑ̃s] *nf (de médecin)* prescription

ordonner [ɔrdɔne] *vt* **(a)** *(commander)* to order (**que** + *subjunctive* that); **o. à qn de faire qch** to order sb to do sth **(b)** *(ranger)* to organize • **ordonné, -e** *adj (personne, maison)* tidy

ordre [ɔrdr] *nm (organisation, discipline, catégorie, commandement)* order; *(absence de désordre)* tidiness; **en o.** *(chambre)* tidy; **mettre de l'o. dans qch** to tidy sth up; **rentrer dans l'o.** to return to normal; **de l'o. de** *(environ)* of the order of; **du même o.** of the same order; **par o. d'âge** in order of age

ordures [ɔrdyr] *nfpl (déchets) Br* rubbish, *Am* garbage

oreille [ɔrɛj] *nf* ear

oreiller [ɔrɛje] *nm* pillow

oreillons [ɔrɛjɔ̃] *nmpl (maladie)* mumps

organe [ɔrgan] *nm Anat & Fig* organ • **organisme** *nm (corps)* body; *Biol* organism

organisateur, -trice [ɔrganiza-tœr, -tris] *nmf* organizer

organisation [ɔrganizasjɔ̃] *nf (arrangement, association)* organization

organiser [ɔrganize] **1** *vt* to organize **2 s'organiser** *vpr* to get organized • **organisé, -e** *adj* organized

orgue [ɔrg] **1** *nm* organ **2** *nfpl* **orgues** organ

orgueil [ɔrgœj] *nm* pride • **orgueilleux, -euse** *adj* proud

orient [ɔrjɑ̃] *nm* l'O. the Orient, the East; **en O.** in the East • **oriental, -e, -aux, -ales 1** *adj (côte, région)* eastern; *(langue)* oriental **2** *nmf* O., **Orientale** Oriental

orientation [ɔrjɑ̃tasjɔ̃] *nf (de position)* orientation; *(de maison)* aspect; **avoir le sens de l'o.** to have a good sense of direction

orienter [ɔrjɑ̃te] **1** *vt (bâtiment)* to orientate; *(canon, télescope)* to point (**vers** at); **o. ses recherches sur** to direct one's research on **2 s'orienter** *vpr* to get one's bearings • **orienté, -e** *adj* **o. à l'ouest** *(maison)* facing west

originaire [ɔriʒinɛr] *adj* **être o. de** *(natif)* to be a native of

original, -e, -aux, -ales [ɔriʒinal, -o] **1** *adj (idée, artiste, version)* original **2** *nm (texte, tableau)* original • **originalité** *nf* originality

origine [ɔriʒin] *nf* origin; **à l'o.** originally; **être à l'o. de qch** to be at the origin of sth; **être d'o. française** to be of French origin • **originel, -elle** *adj* original

ornement [ɔrnəmɑ̃] *nm* ornament • **ornemental, -e, -aux, -ales** *adj* ornamental

orner [ɔrne] *vt* to decorate (**de** with)

orphelin, -e [ɔrfəlɛ̃, -in] *nmf* orphan • **orphelinat** *nm* orphanage

orteil [ɔrtɛj] *nm* toe

orthodoxe [ɔrtɔdɔks] *adj* orthodox

orthographe [ɔrtɔgraf] *nf* spelling • **orthographier** *vt* to spell; **mal o. qch** to misspell sth

os [ɔs, *pl* o *ou* ɔs] *nm* bone

oscar [ɔskar] *nm (récompense)* Oscar

oser [oze] *vt* to dare; **o. faire qch** to dare (to) do sth • **osé, -e** *adj* daring

otage [ɔtaʒ] *nm* hostage; **prendre qn en o.** to take sb hostage

OTAN [ɔtɑ̃] *(abrév* **Organisation du traité de l'Atlantique Nord)** *nf* NATO

ôter [ote] *vt* to take away, to remove (**à qn** from sb); *(vêtement)* to take off; *(déduire)* to take (away)

ou [u] *conj* or; **ou elle ou moi** either her or me

où [u] *adv & pron relatif* where; **le jour où...** the day when...; **la table où...** the table on which...; **le pays d'où je viens** the country from which I come

ouate [wat] *nf (pour pansement) Br* cotton wool, *Am* absorbent cotton

oubli [ubli] *nm (trou de mémoire)* oversight; *(lacune)* omission

oublier [ublije] *vt* to forget (**de faire** to do); *(omettre)* to leave out

oubliettes [ublijɛt] *nfpl (de château)* dungeons

ouest [west] **1** *nm* west; **à l'o.** in the west; *(direction)* (to the) west (**de** of); **d'o.** *(vent)* west(erly); **de l'o.** western **2** *adj inv (côte)* west; *(région)* western

oui [wi] *adv* yes; **ah, ça o.!** oh yes (indeed)!; **je crois que o.** I think so

ouragan [uragã] *nm* hurricane

ourlet [urlɛ] *nm* hem

ours [urs] *nm* bear; **o. blanc** polar bear; **o. en peluche** teddy bear

outil [uti] *nm* tool

outrage [utraʒ] *nm* insult (**à** to)

outre [utr] **1** *prép* besides; **o. mesure** unduly **2** *adv* **en o.** besides; **passer o.** to take no notice (**à** of) ● **outre-Manche** *adv* across the Channel ● **outre-mer** *adv* overseas; **d'o.** *(marché)* overseas; **territoires d'o.** overseas territories

outré, -e [utre] *adj (révolté)* outraged; *(excessif)* exaggerated

ouvert, -e [uvɛr, -ɛrt] **1** *pp d*◌ **ouvrir 2** *adj* open; *(robinet, gaz* on ● **ouverture** *nf* opening; *(trou* hole

ouvrable [uvrabl] *adj* **jour o** working *or Am* work day

ouvrage [uvraʒ] *nm (travail, livre objet)* work; **un o.** *(travail)* a piec◌ of work

ouvreuse [uvrøz] *nf* usherette

ouvrier, -ère [uvrije, -ɛr] **1** *nm* worker; **o. qualifié/spécialis◌** skilled/semi-skilled worker; **o** **agricole** farm worker **2** *ad*◌ *(quartier)* working-class

ouvrir* [uvrir] **1** *vt* to open; *(gaz radio)* to turn on **2** *vi* to open ◌ **s'ouvrir** *vpr (porte, boîte, fleur* to open ● **ouvre-boîtes** *nm in*◌ *Br* tin opener, *Am* can opener ◌ **ouvre-bouteilles** *nm inv* bottl◌ opener

ovale [ɔval] *adj & nm* oval

ovni [ɔvni] *(abrév* **objet volan** **non identifié)** *nm* UFO

oxygène [ɔksiʒɛn] *nm* oxygen◌ **masque à o.** oxygen mask

ozone [ozɔn] *nm Chim* ozone

Pp

P, p [pe] *nm inv* P, p
Pacifique [pasifik] *nm* **le P.** the
Pacific
pacifiste [pasifist] *nmf* pacifist
pacte [pakt] *nm* pact
pagaie [page] *nf* paddle
pagaïe, pagaille [pagaj] *nf Fam
(désordre)* mess; **semer la p.** to
cause chaos
page [paʒ] *nf (de livre)* page;
Ordinat **p. d'accueil** home page;
les Pages Jaunes® *(de l'annuaire)*
the Yellow Pages®; *Radio* **p. de
publicité** commercial break
paie [pɛ] *nf* pay, wages
paiement [pemã] *nm* payment
paillasson [pajasɔ̃] *nm (door)mat*
paille [paj] *nf* straw; *(pour boire)*
(drinking) straw
paillette [pajɛt] *nf* sequin;
paillettes *(de savon, lessive)*
flakes; *(brillants)* glitter
pain [pɛ̃] *nm* bread; **un p.** a
loaf (of bread); **petit p.** roll; **p.
au chocolat** = chocolate-filled
pastry; **p. complet** wholemeal
bread; **p. grillé** toast; **p. de mie**
sandwich loaf
pair, -e [pɛr] **1** *adj (numéro)* even
2 *nm* **(jeune fille) au p.** au pair;
travailler au p. to work as an au
pair
paire [pɛr] *nf* pair **(de** of)
paisible [pɛzibl] *adj (vie, endroit)*
peaceful; *(caractère, personne)*
quiet
paix [pɛ] *nf* peace; **en p.** *(vivre,
laisser)* in peace **(avec** with)

Pakistan [pakistã] *nm* **le P.**
Pakistan • **pakistanais, -e 1** *adj*
Pakistani **2** *nmf* **P., Pakistanaise**
Pakistani
palais [palɛ] *nm (château)* palace;
P. de justice law courts;
pâle [pɑl] *adj* pale
Palestine [palɛstin] *nf* **la P.**
Palestine • **palestinien, -enne
1** *adj* Palestinian **2** *nmf* **P.,
Palestinienne** Palestinian
palette [palɛt] *nf (de peintre)*
palette; *(pour marchandises)* pallet
palier [palje] *nm (niveau)* level;
(d'escalier) landing
palissade [palisad] *nf* fence
palmarès [palmarɛs] *nm prize list*
palme [palm] *nf (de palmier)* palm
(branch); *(de nageur)* flipper
palmier [palmje] *nm* palm (tree)
pamplemousse [pɑ̃pləmus] *nm*
grapefruit
panaché, -e [panaʃe] **1** *adj*
multicoloured **2** *nm* shandy
pancarte [pɑ̃kart] *nf* sign, notice;
(de manifestant) placard
pané, -e [pane] *adj (poisson)*
breaded
panier [panje] *nm* basket
panique [panik] *nf* panic; **pris de
p.** panic-stricken
panne [pan] *nf* breakdown; **tomber en p.** to break down; **être en
p.** to have broken down; **p. d'électricité** blackout, *Br* power cut
panneau, -x [pano] *nm (écriteau)*
sign, notice; **p. d'affichage** *Br*
notice board, *Am* bulletin board

panoplie [panɔpli] *nf (jouet)* outfit; *(gamme)* set

panorama [panɔrama] *nm* panorama • **panoramique** *adj* panoramic; *Cin* **écran p.** wide screen

pansement [pɑ̃smɑ̃] *nm* dressing, bandage; **p. adhésif** *Br* sticking plaster, *Am* Band-aid®

pantalon [pɑ̃talɔ̃] *nm Br* trousers, *Am* pants

panthère [pɑ̃tɛr] *nf* panther

pantoufle [pɑ̃tufl] *nf* slipper

paon [pɑ̃] *nm* peacock

papa [papa] *nm* dad(dy)

pape [pap] *nm* pope

papeterie [papɛtri] *nf (magasin)* stationer's shop

papi [papi] *nm* = **papy**

papier [papje] *nm (matière)* paper; **un p.** a piece of paper; **p.-calque** tracing paper; **p. hygiénique** toilet paper; **papiers d'identité** identity papers; **p. à lettres** writing paper; **p. peint** wallpaper

papillon [papijɔ̃] *nm* butterfly; **p. de nuit** moth

papy [papi] *nm* grand(d)ad

paquebot [pakbo] *nm* liner

pâquerette [pɑkrɛt] *nf* daisy

Pâques [pɑk] *nm sing & nfpl* Easter

paquet [pakɛ] *nm* packet; *(postal)* package, *Br* parcel

par [par] *prép* **(a)** *(indique l'agent, la manière, le moyen)* by; **frappé p. qn** hit by sb; **p. mer** by sea; **p. le train** by train; **commencer p. qch** *(récit)* to begin with sth; **p. erreur** by mistake; **p. chance** by a stroke of luck **(b)** *(à travers)* through; **p. la porte** through the door; **jeter/regarder p. la fenêtre** to throw/look out (of) the window; **p. ici/là** *(aller)* this/that way; *(habiter)* around here/there; **p. les rues** through the streets **(c)** *(à cause de)* out of, from; **p. pitié** out of pity **(d)** *(pendant)* **p. ce froid** in this cold; **p. le passé** in the past **(e)** *(distributif)* **dix fois p. an/mois** ten times a *or* per year/month; **50 euros p. personne** 50 euros per person; **deux p. deux** two by two; **p. deux fois** twice

parachute [parafyt] *nm* parachute

parade [parad] *nf* parade

paradis [paradi] *nm* heaven

paragraphe [paragraf] *nm* paragraph

paraître* [parɛtr] **1** *vi (sembler)* to seem, to appear; *(apparaître)* to appear; *(livre)* to come out **2** *v impersonnel* **il paraît qu'il va partir** it appears *or* seems (that) he's leaving; **à ce qu'il paraît** apparently

parallèle [paralɛl] **1** *adj* parallel (**à** with *or* to) **2** *nm (comparaison)* parallel; **mettre qch en p. avec qch** to draw a parallel between sth and sth

paralyser [paralize] *vt Br* to paralyse, *Am* to paralyze

parapluie [paraplɥi] *nm* umbrella

parasite [parazit] *nm* parasite

parasol [parasɔl] *nm* sunshade, parasol

parc [park] *nm* park; **p. de stationnement** *Br* car park, *Am* parking lot; **p. naturel** nature reserve

parce que [parsəkə] *conj* because

parcourir* [parkurir] *vt (lieu)* to walk round; *(pays)* to travel through; *(distance)* to cover; *(texte)* to glance through; **il reste 10 km à p.** there are 10 km to go • **parcours** *nm (itinéraire)* route; **p. de golf** *(terrain)* golf course

par-dessous [pardəsu] *prép &
adv* underneath
pardessus [pardəsy] *nm* overcoat
par-dessus [pardəsy] 1 *prép* over;
p. tout above all 2 *adv* over
pardon [pardɔ̃] *nm* forgiveness;
p.! *(excusez-moi)* sorry!; **p.?**
(pour demander) excuse me?,
Am pardon me?; **demander p.** to
apologize (**à** to) ● **pardonner** *vt*
to forgive; **p. qch à qn** to forgive
sb for sth; **elle m'a pardonné
d'avoir oublié** she forgave me for
forgetting
pare-balles [parbal] *adj inv* **gilet
p.** bulletproof *Br* jacket *or Am*
vest
pare-brise [parbriz] *nm inv Br*
windscreen, *Am* windshield
pare-chocs [parʃɔk] *nm inv*
bumper
pareil, -eille [parɛj] 1 *adj* (**a**)
(identique) the same; **p. à** the
same as (**b**) *(tel)* such; **en p. cas**
in such cases 2 *adv* l'un the same
● **pareillement** *adv (de la même
manière)* in the same way; *(aussi)*
likewise
parent, -e [parɑ̃, -ɑ̃t] 1 *nmf (oncle,
cousin)* relative, relation 2 *nmpl*
parents *(père et mère)* parents
● **parenté** *nf* relationship; **avoir
un lien de p.** to be related
parenthèse [parɑ̃tɛz] *nf (signe)*
bracket, parenthesis; **entre
parenthèses** in brackets
parer [pare] *vi* **p. à toute
éventualité** to prepare for any
contingency
paresseux, -euse [parɛsø, -øz]
adj lazy
parfait, -e [parfɛ, -ɛt] *adj* perfect ●
parfaitement *adv* perfectly
parfois [parfwa] *adv* sometimes
parfum [parfœ̃] *nm (essence)*
perfume; *(senteur)* fragrance; *(de*

glace) flavour ● **se parfumer** *vpr*
to put perfume on
pari [pari] *nm* bet; **faire un p.** to
make a bet ● **parier** *vti* to bet (**sur**
on; **que** that)
Paris [pari] *nm ou f* Paris ●
parisien, -enne 1 *adj* Parisian 2
nmf **P., Parisienne** Parisian
parking [parkiŋ] *nm Br* car park,
Am parking lot; **'p. payant'** *Br* ≃
'pay-and-display car park'
parlement [parləmɑ̃] *nm* **le P.**
Parliament ● **parlementaire** *nmf*
member of parliament
parler [parle] 1 *vi* to talk, to speak
(**de** about *or* of; **à** to); **sans p. de...**
not to mention... 2 *vt (langue)* to
speak 3 **se parler** *vpr (langue)* to
be spoken; *(l'un l'autre)* to talk to
each other
parmi [parmi] *prép* among(st)
paroi [parwa] *nf* wall
paroisse [parwas] *nf* parish
parole [parɔl] *nf (mot, promesse)*
word; *(faculté, langage)* speech;
paroles *(de chanson)* words, lyrics;
adresser la p. à qn to speak to sb;
prendre la p. to speak
parquet [parkɛ] *nm (sol)* wooden
floor
parrain [parɛ̃] *nm Rel* godfather;
(de sportif, de club) sponsor
pars [par] *voir* **partir**
parsemer [parsəme] *vt* to scatter
(**de** with)
part¹ [par] *voir* **partir**
part² [par] *nf (portion)* share, part;
(de gâteau) slice; **prendre p. à**
(activité) to take part in; **faire p.
de qch à qn** to inform sb of sth;
d'une p.... d'autre p.... on the
one hand... on the other hand...;
d'autre p. *(d'ailleurs)* moreover;
de la p. de qn from sb; **c'est de
la p. de qui?** *(au téléphone)* who's
calling?; **pour ma p.** as for me; **à**

p. *(mettre)* aside; *(excepté)* apart from; **prendre qn à p.** to take sb aside

partager [partaʒe] *vt (avoir en commun)* to share (**avec** with); *(répartir)* to divide (up); **p. qch en deux** to divide sth in two; **p. l'avis de qn** to share sb's opinion

partenaire [partənɛr] *nmf* partner ● **partenariat** *nm* partnership

parti [parti] *nm (camp)* side; **p. (politique)** (political) party

participer [partisipe] *vi* **p. à** *(jeu)* to take part in, to participate in; *(bénéfices, joie)* to share (in) ● **participant, -e** *nmf* participant ● **participation** *nf* participation

particulier, -ère [partikylje, -ɛr] **1** *adj (propre)* characteristic (**à** of); *(remarquable)* unusual; *(soin, intérêt)* particular; *(maison, voiture, leçon)* private; **en p.** *(surtout)* in particular; *(à part)* in private **2** *nm* private individual; **vente de p. à p.** private sale ● **particulièrement** *adv* particularly; **tout p.** especially

partie [parti] *nf (morceau)* part; *(jeu)* game; **en p.** partly, in part; **en grande p.** mainly; **faire p. de** to be a part of; *(club)* to belong to ● **partiel, -elle** *adj* partial

partir* [partir] *(aux* **être**) *vi (s'en aller)* to go, to leave; *(se mettre en route)* to set off; *(s'éloigner)* to go away; **p. en voiture** to go by car, to drive; **p. en courant** to run off; **p. de** *(lieu)* to leave from; *(commencer par)* to start (off) with; **à p. de** *(date, prix)* from

partisan [partizã] *nm* supporter

partition [partisjɔ̃] *nf Mus* score

partout [partu] *adv* everywhere; **p. où je vais** everywhere *or* wherever I go; **un peu p.** all over the place

paru, -e [pary] *pp de* **paraître**

parvenir* [parvənir] *(aux* **être**) *vi* **p. à** *(lieu)* to reach; *(objectif)* to achieve; **p. à faire qch** to manage to do sth

pas¹ [pɑ] *adv (de négation)* **(ne...) p.** not; **je ne sais p.** I do not *or* don't know; **je n'ai p. compris** I didn't understand; **p. de pain** no bread; **p. du tout** not at all

pas² [pɑ] *nm* **(a)** *(enjambée)* step; *(bruit)* footstep; *(trace)* footprint; **p. à p.** step by step; **à deux p. (de)** close by; **faire un faux p.** *(en marchant)* to trip **(b)** **le p. de Calais** the Straits of Dover

passable [pɑsabl] *adj* reasonable

passage [pɑsaʒ] *nm (chemin, extrait)* passage; *(ruelle)* alley; *(traversée)* crossing; **être de p. dans une ville** to be passing through a town; **p. clouté** *ou* **pour piétons** *Br* (pedestrian) crossing, *Am* crosswalk; **p. souterrain** *Br* subway, *Am* underpass; **p. à niveau** *Br* level crossing, *Am* grade crossing; **'p. interdit'** 'no through traffic'; **'cédez le p.'** *(au carrefour) Br* 'give way', *Am* 'yield'

passager, -ère [pɑsaʒe, -ɛr] *nmf* passenger

passant, -e [pɑsã, -ãt] *nmf* passer-by

passé, -e [pɑse] **1** *adj (temps)* past; **la semaine passée** last week; **il est dix heures passées** it's after *or Br* gone ten o'clock; **p. de mode** out of fashion **2** *nm (temps, vie passée)* past; **par le p.** in the past

passeport [pɑspɔr] *nm* passport

passer [pɑse] **1** *(aux* **avoir**) *vt (pont, frontière)* to go over; *(porte, douane)* to go through; *(ballon)* to pass; *(film)* to show; *(vacances)* to spend; *(examen)* to take; **p. qch à qn** *(prêter)* to pass sth to sb; **p. son temps à faire qch** to spend one's time doing sth **2** *(aux* **être***) vi (se déplacer)* to go past; *(disparaître)* to go; *(temps)* to pass (by), to go by; *(film, programme)* to be on; **laisser p. qn** to let sb through; **p. de qch à qch** to go from sth to sth; **p. devant qn/qch** to go past sb/sth; **p. par Paris** to pass through Paris; **p. chez le boulanger** to go round to the baker's; **p. à la radio** to be on the radio; **p. pour** *(riche)* to be taken for; **p. sur** *(détail)* to pass over **3 se passer** *vpr (se produire)* to happen; **se p. de qn/qch** to do without sb/sth; **ça s'est bien passé** it went off well

passe-temps [pastɑ̃] *nm inv* pastime

passif, -ive [pasif, -iv] *adj* passive

passion [pasjɔ̃] *nf* passion; **avoir la p. des voitures** to have a passion for cars • **passionnant, -e** *adj* fascinating • **passionné, -e** *adj* passionate; **p. de qch** passionately fond of sth

passoire [paswar] *nf (pour liquides)* sieve; *(à thé)* strainer; *(à légumes)* colander

pastel [pastɛl] *adj inv & nm* pastel

pastèque [pastɛk] *nf* watermelon

pastille [pastij] *nf* pastille

patauger [patoʒe] *vi (s'embourber)* to squelch; *(barboter)* to splash about

pâte [pat] *nf (pour tarte)* pastry; *(pour pain)* dough; **p. d'amandes** marzipan; **p. feuilletée** puff pastry; **pâtes** pasta

pâté [pate] *nm (charcuterie)* pâté; **p. de maisons** block of houses

pâtée [pate] *nf (pour chien)* dog food; *(pour chat)* cat food

pathétique [patetik] *adj* moving

patience [pasjɑ̃s] *nf* patience; **avoir de la p.** to be patient; **perdre p.** to lose patience

patient, -e [pasjɑ̃, -ɑ̃t] **1** *adj* patient **2** *nmf (malade)* patient • **patienter** *vi* to wait

patin [patɛ̃] *nm (de patineur)* skate; **p. à glace** ice skate; **p. à roulettes** roller skate

patinage [patinaʒ] *nm Sport* skating; **p. artistique** figure skating • **patinoire** *nf* skating rink, ice rink

pâtisserie [pɑtisri] *nf (gâteau)* pastry, cake; *(magasin)* cake shop

patriote [patrijɔt] *nmf* patriot • **patriotique** *adj* patriotic

patron, -onne [patrɔ̃, -ɔn] *nmf (chef)* boss; *(propriétaire)* owner (**de** of); *(gérant)* manager

patrouille [patruj] *nf* patrol

patte [pat] *nf (membre)* leg; *(de chat, de chien)* paw • **pattes** *nfpl (favoris)* sideburns

paume [pom] *nf* palm

paupière [popjɛr] *nf* eyelid

pause [poz] *nf (arrêt)* break; *(en parlant)* pause

pauvre [povr] **1** *adj (personne, sol, excuse)* poor; **p. en** *(calories)* low in **2** *nmf* poor man, *f* poor woman; **les pauvres** the poor • **pauvreté** [-əte] *nf* poverty

pavé [pave] *nm* paving stone

pavillon [pavijɔ̃] *nm (maison)* detached house; *(d'exposition)* pavilion

paye [pɛj] *nf* = **paie** • **payement** *nm* = **paiement**

payer [peje] **1** *vt (personne, somme)* to pay; *(service, objet)* to pay for; **se faire p.** to get paid **2** *vi* to pay • **payant, -e** *adj (hôte, spectateur)* paying

pays [pei] *nm* country; *(région)* region; **du p.** *(vin, gens)* local

paysage [peizaʒ] *nm* landscape

paysan, -anne [peizã, -an] *nmf* farmer

Pays-Bas [peiba] *nmpl* **les P.** the Netherlands

P-DG [pedeʒe] *(abrév* **président-directeur général)** *nm Br* MD, *Am* CEO

péage [peaʒ] *nm (droit)* toll; *(lieu)* tollbooth

peau, -x [po] *nf* skin; *(de fruit)* peel, skin

péché [peʃe] *nm* sin

pêche¹ [pɛʃ] *nf (activité)* fishing; **aller à la p.** to go fishing • **pêcher** [peʃe] **1** *vt (attraper)* to catch; *(chercher à prendre)* to fish for **2** *vi* to fish • **pêcheur** *nm* fisherman

pêche² [pɛʃ] *nf (fruit)* peach

pédagogique [pedagɔʒik] *adj* educational

pédale [pedal] *nf (de voiture, de piano)* pedal

Pédalo® [pedalo] *nm* pedalo

pédiatre [pedjatr] *nmf* paediatrician

peigne [pɛɲ] *nm* comb; **se donner un coup de p.** to give one's hair a comb • **peigner 1** *vt (cheveux)* to comb; **p. qn** to comb sb's hair **2 se peigner** *vpr* to comb one's hair

peignoir [pɛɲwar] *nm Br* dressing gown, *Am* bathrobe; **p. de bain** bathrobe

peindre* [pɛ̃dr] *vti* to paint

peine [pɛn] *nf* **(a)** *(châtiment)* punishment; **p. de mort** death penalty; **p. de prison** prison sentence **(b)** *(chagrin)* sorrow; **avoir de la p.** to be upset; **faire de la p. à qn** to upset sb **(c)** *(effort)* trouble; *(difficulté)* difficulty; **se donner de la p.** *ou*

beaucoup de p. to go to a lot of trouble (**pour faire** to do); **avec p.** with difficulty; **ça vaut la p. d'attendre** it's worth waiting; **ce n'est pas** *ou* **ça ne vaut pas la p.** it's not worth it **(d) à p.** hardly, scarcely; **à p. arrivé, il... n...** sooner had he arrived than he...

peintre [pɛ̃tr] *nm* painter • **peinture** *nf (tableau, activité)* painting; *(matière)* paint; **'p. fraîche'** 'wet paint'

peler [pəle] *vt* to peel

pelle [pɛl] *nf* shovel; *(d'enfant)* spade

pellicule [pelikyl] *nf (pour photos)* film; **pellicules** *(de cheveux)* dandruff

pelote [pəlɔt] *nf (de laine)* ball; *Sport* **p. basque** pelota

peloton [p(ə)lɔtɔ̃] *nm (de ficelle)* ball; *(de cyclistes)* pack

pelouse [pəluz] *nf* lawn

peluche [pəlyʃ] *nf* **(jouet en) p.** soft toy

pénaliser [penalise] *vt* to penalize • **pénalité** *nf* penalty

penalty [penalti] *nm Sport* penalty

penchant [pãʃã] *nm (préférence)* penchant (**pour** for); *(tendance)* propensity (**pour** for)

pencher [pãʃe] **1** *vt (objet)* to tilt; *(tête)* to lean **2 se pencher** *vpr* to lean over; **se p. par la fenêtre** to lean out of the window

pendant [pãdã] *prép (au cours de)* during; **p. deux mois** for two months; **p. tout le trajet** for the whole journey; **p. que...** while...

pendentif [pãdãtif] *nm (collier)* pendant

penderie [pãdri] *nf Br* wardrobe, *Am* closet

pendre [pãdr] **1** *vti* to hang (à from); **p. qn** to hang sb **2 se**

pendre *vpr (se suicider)* to hang oneself; *(se suspendre)* to hang (**à** from) • **pendu, -e** *adj (objet)* hanging (**à** from)

pendule [pãdyl] *nf* clock

pénétrer [penetre] **1** *vi* **p. dans** to enter; *(profondément)* to penetrate (into) **2** *vt (sujet: pluie)* to penetrate

pénible [penibl] *adj (difficile)* difficult; *(douloureux)* painful, distressing; *(ennuyeux)* tiresome • **péniblement** [-əmã] *adv* with difficulty

pénicilline [penisilin] *nf* penicillin

péninsule [penẽsyl] *nf* peninsula

pensée [pãse] *nf (idée)* thought; **à la p. de faire qch** at the thought of doing sth

penser [pãse] **1** *vi (réfléchir)* to think (**à** of *or* about); **p. à qn/qch** to think of *or* about sb/sth; **p. à faire qch** *(ne pas oublier)* to remember to do sth **2** *vt (estimer)* to think (**que** that); *(concevoir)* to think out; **je pensais rester** I was thinking of staying; **que pensez-vous de...?** what do you think of *or* about...?; **p. du bien de qn/qch** to think highly of sb/sth

pension [pãsjõ] *nf* **(a)** *(école)* boarding school **(b)** *(hôtel)* **p. de famille** boarding house; **p. complète** *Br* full board, *Am* American plan **(c)** *(allocation)* pension • **pensionnat** *nm* boarding school

pente [pãt] *nf* slope

Pentecôte [pãtkot] *nf Rel Br* Whitsun, *Am* Pentecost

pépin [pepẽ] *nm (de fruit) Br* pip, *Am* seed, pit

perçant, -e [pɛrsã, -ãt] *adj (cri, froid)* piercing; *(vue)* sharp

perception [pɛrsɛpsjõ] *nf* perception

percer [pɛrse] *vt (trouer)* to pierce; *(avec une perceuse)* to drill; *(trou)* to make • **perceuse** *nf* drill

percevoir* [pɛrsəvwar] *vt (sensation)* to perceive; *(son)* to hear

perche [pɛrʃ] *nf (bâton)* pole

percher [pɛrʃe] *vi (oiseau)* to perch

perdant, -e [pɛrdã, -ãt] **1** *adj* losing **2** *nmf* loser

perdre [pɛrdr] **1** *vt* to lose; *(habitude)* to get out of; **p. qn/qch de vue** to lose sight of sb/sth **2** *vi* to lose **3 se perdre** *vpr (s'égarer)* to get lost; **se p. dans les détails** to get lost in details • **perdu, -e** *adj (égaré)* lost; *(gaspillé)* wasted; *(lieu)* out-of-the-way

père [pɛr] *nm* father

péremption [perãpsjõ] *nf* **date de p.** use-by date

perfection [pɛrfɛksjõ] *nf* perfection; **à la p.** to perfection

perfectionner [pɛrfɛksjɔne] *vt* to improve, to perfect • **perfectionnement** *nm* improvement (**de** in; **par rapport à** on); **cours de p.** proficiency course • **perfectionniste** *nmf* perfectionist

perforer [pɛrfɔre] *vt (pneu, intestin)* to perforate; *(billet)* to punch

performance [pɛrfɔrmãs] *nf* performance • **performant, -e** *adj* highly efficient

perfusion [pɛrfyzjõ] *nf* drip; **être sous p.** to be on a drip

péril [peril] *nm* danger, peril; **mettre qch en p.** to endanger sth

périmé, -e [perime] *adj (billet)* expired

période [perjɔd] *nf* period

périphérie [periferi] *nf (limite)* periphery; *(banlieue)* outskirts • **périphérique 1** *adj* peripheral **2** *nm & adj* **(boulevard) p.** *Br* ring road, *Am* beltway

périr [perir] *vi* to perish ●
périssable *adj (denrée)* perishable
perle [pɛrl] *nf (bijou)* pearl; *(de
bois, de verre)* bead
permanent, -e [pɛrmanã, -ãt] **1**
adj permanent **2** *nf* **permanente**
perm ● **permanence** *nf (salle
d'étude)* study room; *(service,
bureau)* duty office; **être de p.** to
be on duty; **en p.** permanently
permettre* [pɛrmɛtr] **1** *vt* to
allow, to permit; **p. à qn de
faire qch** to allow sb to do sth;
vous permettez? may I? **2 se
permettre** *vpr* **se p. de faire qch**
to take the liberty of doing sth;
je ne peux pas me le p. I can't
afford it
permis, -e [pɛrmi, -iz] **1** *adj*
allowed, permitted **2** *nm Br*
licence, *Am* license, permit; **p.
de conduire** *Br* driving licence,
Am driver's license; **passer son
p. de conduire** to take one's
driving test
permission [pɛrmisjɔ̃] *nf*
permission; **demander la p.** to
ask permission (**de faire** to do)
perpendiculaire [pɛrpãdikylɛr]
adj & nf perpendicular (**à** to)
perpétuel, -elle [pɛrpetɥɛl] *adj*
perpetual ● **perpétuité** *adv* **à p.**
in perpetuity; **condamnation à p.**
life sentence
perplexe [pɛrplɛks] *adj* perplexed
perroquet [pɛrɔkɛ] *nm* parrot
perruche [peryʃ] *nf Br* budgie,
Am parakeet
perruque [peryk] *nf* wig
persécuter [pɛrsekyte] *vt* to
persecute ● **persécution** *nf*
persecution
persévérer [pɛrsevere] *vi* to
persevere (**dans** in)
persil [pɛrs(l)] *nm* parsley
persister [pɛrsiste] *vi* to persist (**à**

faire in doing; **dans qch** in sth) ●
persistance *nf* persistence
personnage [pɛrsɔnaʒ] *nm
(de fiction, individu)* character;
(personnalité) important person
personnaliser [pɛrsɔnalize] *vt* to
personalize; *(voiture)* to customize
personnalité [pɛrsɔnalite] *nf (caractère, personnage)* personality; **avoir
de la p.** to have lots of personality
personne [pɛrsɔn] **1** *nf* person;
deux personnes two people;
p. âgée elderly person; **en p.**
in person **2** *pron indéfini (de
négation)* **(ne…) p.** nobody, no
one; **je ne vois p.** I don't see
anybody *or* anyone; **p. ne saura**
nobody *or* no one will know
personnel, -elle [pɛrsɔnɛl] **1** *adj*
personal **2** *nm* staff, personnel
perspective [pɛrspɛktiv] *nf
(de dessin)* perspective; *(idée)*
prospect (**de** of); *Fig (point de vue)*
viewpoint
perspicace [pɛrspikas] *adj* shrewd
persuader [pɛrsɥade] *vt* **p. qn
(de qch)** to persuade sb (of sth);
p. qn de faire qch to persuade
sb to do sth; **être persuadé
de qch/que…** to be convinced
of sth/that… ● **persuasif, -ive**
adj persuasive ● **persuasion** *nf*
persuasion
perte [pɛrt] *nf* loss; **une p. de
temps** a waste of time; **à p. de
vue** as far as the eye can see;
vendre qch à p. to sell sth at a
loss
pertinent, -e [pɛrtinã, -ãt]
adj relevant, pertinent ●
pertinemment [-amã] *adv* **savoir
qch p.** to know sth for a fact
perturber [pɛrtyrbe] *vt (trafic,
cérémonie)* to disrupt; *(personne)*
to disturb ● **perturbation** *nf*
disruption

pervers, -e [pɛrvɛr, -ɛrs] **1** *adj* perverse **2** *nmf* pervert ● **pervertir** *vt* to pervert

pesant, -e [pəzɑ̃, -ɑ̃t] *adj* heavy, weighty ● **pesanteur** *nf* heaviness; *Phys* gravity

peser [pəze] **1** *vt* to weigh **2** *vi* to weigh; **p. deux kilos** to weigh two kilos; **p. lourd** to be heavy; **p. sur** *(appuyer)* to press on; *(influer)* to bear upon; **p. sur qn** *(menace)* to hang over sb ● **pèse-personne** *(pl* **pèse-personnes)** *nm* (bathroom) scales

pessimiste [pesimist] **1** *adj* pessimistic **2** *nmf* pessimist

pétale [petal] *nm* petal

pétanque [petɑ̃k] *nf (jeu)* ≃ bowls

pétard [petar] *nm (feu d'artifice)* firecracker, *Br* banger

pétillant, -e [petijɑ̃, -ɑ̃t] *adj (boisson)* sparkling

petit, -e [pəti, -it] **1** *adj* small, little; *(taille, distance)* short; *(somme)* small; *(mesquin)* petty; **tout p.** tiny; **mon p. frère** my little brother **2** *nmf* (little) boy, *f* (little) girl; *(personne)* small person; **petits** *(d'animal)* young **3** *adv* **écrire p.** to write small; **p. à p.** little by little ● **petite-fille** *(pl* **petites-filles)** *nf* granddaughter ● **petit-fils** *(pl* **petits-fils)** *nm* grandson ● **petits-enfants** *nmpl* grandchildren

pétition [petisjɔ̃] *nf* petition

pétrole [petrɔl] *nm* oil, petroleum ● **pétrolier** *nm* oil tanker

peu [pø] **1** *adv (avec un verbe)* not much; *(avec un adjectif, un adverbe)* not very; *(un petit nombre)* few; **elle mange p.** she doesn't eat much; **p. intéressant/ souvent** not very interesting/often;

p. ont compris few understood; **p. de sel/de temps** not much salt/time, little salt/time; **p. de gens/de livres** few people/books; **p. à p.** little by little, gradually; **à p. près** more or less; **p. après/ avant** shortly after/before; **sous p.** shortly; **pour p. que...** *(+ subjunctive)* if by chance... **2** *nm* **un p.** a little, a bit; **un p. grand** a bit big; **un p. de fromage** a little cheese, a bit of cheese; **un (tout) petit p.** a (tiny) little bit; **le p. de fromage que j'ai** the little cheese I have; **reste encore un p.** stay a little longer

peuple [pœpl] *nm (nation, citoyens)* people ● **peuplé, -e** *adj (région)* inhabited **(de** by); **très/ peu p.** highly/sparsely populated

peur [pœr] *nf* fear; **avoir p.** to be afraid *or* frightened **(de qn/qch** of sb/sth; **de faire qch** to do sth *or* of doing sth); **faire p. à qn** to frighten *or* scare sb; **de p. qu'il ne parte** for fear that he would leave; **de p. de faire qch** for fear of doing sth

peut [pø] *voir* **pouvoir 1, 2**

peut-être [pøtɛtr] *adv* perhaps, maybe; **p. qu'il viendra, p. viendra-t-il** perhaps *or* maybe he'll come; **p. que oui/non** maybe/maybe not;

peuvent, peux [pœv, pø] *voir* **pouvoir 1**

phare [far] *nm (pour bateaux)* lighthouse; *(de véhicule)* headlight

pharmacie [farmasi] *nf (magasin)* *Br* chemist, *Am* drugstore ● **pharmacien, -enne** *nmf* pharmacist, *Br* chemist

phase [faz] *nf* phase

phénomène [fenɔmɛn] *nm* phenomenon

philosophe [filozof] **1** *nmf* philosopher **2** *adj* philosophical • **philosophie** *nf* philosophy • **philosophique** *adj* philosophical

photo [foto] *nf (cliché)* photo; *(art)* photography; **prendre une p. de qn/qch, prendre qn/qch en p.** to take a photo of sb/sth; **p. d'identité** ID photo • **photographe** *nmf* photographer • **photographie** *nf (art)* photography; *(cliché)* photograph • **photographier** *vt* to photograph; **se faire p.** to have one's photo taken

photocopie [fotokopi] *nf* photocopy • **photocopier** *vt* to photocopy • **photocopieur** *nm,* • **photocopieuse** *nf* photocopier

Photomaton® [fotomatɔ̃] *nm* photo booth

phrase [fraz] *nf* sentence

physique [fizik] **1** *adj* physical **2** *nm (de personne)* physique **3** *nf (science)* physics *(sing)*

piano [pjano] *nm* piano • **pianiste** *nmf* pianist

pic [pik] *nm (cime)* peak; *(outil)* pick(axe)

pichet [piʃɛ] *nm* pitcher, *Br* jug

picoter [pikote] *vt* **j'ai la gorge qui (me) picote** I've got a tickle in my throat

pièce [pjɛs] *nf (de maison)* room; *(morceau, objet)* piece; *(de dossier)* document; **p. (de monnaie)** coin; **p. (de théâtre)** play; **cinq euros (la) p.** five euros each; **p. d'identité** proof of identity

pied [pje] *nm (de personne, de lit, de colline)* foot *(pl feet)*; *(de verre, de lampe)* base; **à p.** on foot; **aller à p.** to walk, to go on foot; **au p. de** at the foot *or* bottom of; **avoir p.** to be within one's depth; **mettre qch sur p.** to set sth up

piège [pjɛʒ] *nm* trap • **piéger** *vt*

(animal) to trap; **voiture piégée** car bomb

pierre [pjɛr] *nf* stone; **p. précieuse** precious stone

piéton [pjetɔ̃] *nm* pedestrian • **piétonne, piétonnière** *adj f* **rue p.** pedestrian(ized) street; **zone p.** pedestrian precinct

pigeon [piʒɔ̃] *nm* pigeon

pile [pil] **1** *nf* (a) **p. (électrique)** battery (b) *(tas)* pile; **en p.** in a pile (c) *(de pièce)* **p. ou face?** heads or tails?; **jouer à p. ou face** to toss for it **2** *adv Fam* **à deux heures p.** at two on the dot

pilier [pilje] *nm* pillar

pilote [pilot] *nm (d'avion, de bateau)* pilot; *(de voiture)* driver • **piloter** *vt (avion)* to fly, to pilot; *(bateau)* to pilot; *(voiture)* to drive

pilule [pilyl] *nf* pill; **prendre la p.** to be on the pill

piment [pimã] *nm* chilli • **pimenté, -e** *adj (épicé)* spicy

pin [pɛ̃] *nm (arbre, bois)* pine

pince [pɛ̃s] *nf (outil)* pliers; *(de crustacé)* pincer; **p. à épiler** tweezers; **p. à linge** (clothes) *Br* peg *or Am* pin

pinceau, -x [pɛ̃so] *nm* (paint)brush

pincer [pɛ̃se] **1** *vt* to pinch **2 se pincer** *vpr* **se p. le doigt** to get one's finger caught **(dans** in); **se p. le nez** to hold one's nose • **pincée** *nf* pinch **(de** of)

ping-pong [piŋpɔ̃g] *nm* table tennis, Ping-Pong®

pioche [pjɔʃ] *nf (outil)* pick(axe); *Cartes* stock, pile • **piocher** *vt (creuser)* to dig *(with a pick)*; **p. une carte** to draw a card

pion [pjɔ̃] *nm Échecs & Fig* pawn

pipe [pip] *nf* pipe

piquant, -e [pikã, -ãt] *adj (au goût)* spicy; *(plante, barbe)* prickly

pique [pik] *nm Cartes* spades

pique-nique [piknik] (*pl* **pique-niques**) *nm* picnic

piquer [pike] **1** *vt (percer)* to prick; *(langue, yeux)* to sting; *(sujet: moustique)* to bite; **la fumée me pique les yeux** the smoke is making my eyes sting **2 se piquer** *vpr* to prick oneself; **se p. au doigt** to prick one's finger

piquet [pikɛ] *nm (pieu)* stake, post; *(de tente)* peg; **p. de grève** picket

piqûre [pikyr] *nf (d'abeille)* sting; *(de moustique)* bite; *(d'épingle)* prick; *Méd* injection; **faire une p. à qn** to give sb an injection

pirate [pirat] **1** *nm (des mers)* pirate; **p. de l'air** hijacker; **p. informatique** hacker **2** *adj* **radio p.** pirate radio; **édition p.** pirated edition ● **pirater** *vt (enregistrement)* to pirate; *Ordinat* to hack

pire [pir] **1** *adj* worse (**que** than); **c'est de p. en p.** it's getting worse and worse **2** *nmf* **le/la p.** the worst (one); **le p. de tout** the worst thing of all; **au p.** at (the very) worst; **s'attendre au p.** to expect the worst

piscine [pisin] *nf* swimming pool

pistache [pistaʃ] *nf* pistachio

piste [pist] *nf (traces)* trail; *Sport* track; *(de ski)* piste; **p. d'atterrissage** runway; **p. cyclable** *Br* cycle path, *Am* bicycle path; **p. de danse** dance floor

pistolet [pistɔlɛ] *nm* gun, pistol; **p. à eau** water pistol

pitié [pitje] *nf* pity; **avoir de la p. pour qn** to pity sb; **il me fait p.** I feel sorry for him; **être sans p.** to be ruthless ● **piteux, -euse** *adj* pitiful; **en p. état** in a sorry state ● **pitoyable** *adj* pitiful

pittoresque [pitɔrɛsk] *adj* picturesque

pizza [pidza] *nf* pizza ● **pizzeria** *nf* pizzeria

placard [plakar] *nm (armoire) Br* cupboard, *Am* closet

place [plas] *nf (endroit, rang) & Sport* place; *(lieu public)* square; *(espace)* room; *(siège)* seat; **à la p.** instead (**de** of); **à votre p.** in your place; **se mettre à la p. de qn** to put oneself in sb's position; **sur p.** on the spot; **en p.** *(objet)* in place; **mettre qch en p.** to put sth in place; **changer de p.** to change places; **faire de la p.** to make room (**à** for); **prendre p.** to take a seat; **p. de parking** parking space

placer [plase] **1** *vt* to put, to place **2 se placer** *vpr (debout)* to stand; *(s'asseoir)* to sit ● **placé, -e** *adj* placed; **bien/mal p. pour faire qch** well/badly placed to do sth

plafond [plafɔ̃] *nm* ceiling

plage [plaʒ] *nf (grève)* beach; *(surface)* area

plaider [plede] *vti Jur (défendre)* to plead; **p. coupable** to plead guilty

plaie [plɛ] *nf (blessure)* wound

plaindre* [plɛ̃dr] **1** *vt* to feel sorry for, to pity **2 se plaindre** *vpr (protester)* to complain (**de** about; **que** that); **se p. de** *(douleur)* to complain of ● **plainte** *nf* complaint; **porter p. contre qn** to lodge a complaint against sb

plaine [plɛn] *nf* plain

plaire* [plɛr] **1** *vi* **elle me plaît** I like her; **ça me plaît** I like it **2** *v impersonnel* **il me plaît de le faire** I like doing it; **s'il vous/te plaît** please **3 se plaire** *vpr (l'un l'autre)* to like each other; **se p. à Paris** to like it in Paris

plaisanter [plezɑ̃te] *vi* to joke (**sur** about) ● **plaisanterie** *nf* joke; **par p.** for a joke

plaisir [plɛzir] *nm* pleasure; **faire p. à qn** to please sb; **pour le p.** for the fun of it; **faites-moi le p. de...** would you be good enough to...

plan [plɑ̃] *nm (projet, dessin, organisation)* plan; *(de ville)* map; *Phot* **au premier p.** in the foreground; *Phot* **au second p.** in the background; **sur le p. politique, au p. politique** from the political viewpoint; **sur le même p.** on the same level; *Phot & Cin* **gros p.** close-up

planche [plɑ̃ʃ] *nf* board; **p. à voile** sailboard; **faire de la p. à voile** to go windsurfing

plancher [plɑ̃ʃe] *nm* floor

planète [planɛt] *nf* planet

planifier [planifje] *vt* to plan

plante [plɑ̃t] *nf* plant; **p. du pied** sole (of the foot)

planter [plɑ̃te] *vt (fleur, arbre)* to plant; *(tente)* to put up; *(mettre)* to put (**sur** on; **contre** against)

plaque [plak] *nf* plate; *(de verre, de métal)* sheet, plate; *(de verglas)* sheet; *(commémorative)* plaque; **p. chauffante** hotplate; *Aut* **p. minéralogique, p. d'immatriculation** *Br* number *or Am* license plate

plaquer [plake] **1** *vt (métal, bijou)* to plate; *(aplatir)* to flatten (**contre** against) **2 se plaquer** *vpr* **se p. contre** to flatten oneself against ● **plaqué, -e** *adj (bijou)* plated; **p. or** gold-plated

plastique [plastik] *adj & nm* plastic

plat, -e [pla, plat] **1** *adj* flat; *(mer)* calm, smooth; *(ennuyeux)* flat, dull; **à p. ventre** flat on one's face; **à p.** *(pneu, batterie)* flat; **poser qch à p.** to lay sth (down) flat **2** *nm (récipient, nourriture)* dish; *(partie du repas)* course;

p. de résistance main course ●
plate-forme *(pl* **plates-formes** *)* *nf* platform; **p. pétrolière** oil rig

plateau, -x [plato] *nm* tray; *Géog* plateau

platine [platin] *adj inv & nm (métal)* platinum

plâtre [platr] *nm (matière)* plaster *(de jambe cassée)* plaster cast

plausible [plozibl] *adj* plausible

plein, -e [plɛ̃, plɛn] **1** *adj (rempli, complet)* full; *(solide)* solid; **p. de** full of; **p. à craquer** full to bursting; **en pleine figure** right in the face; **en pleine nuit** in the middle of the night; **en p. jour** in broad daylight; **en p. soleil** in the full heat of the sun; **à la pleine lune** at full moon; **travailler à p. temps** to work full-time; **p. sud** due south; **p. tarif** full price *(de transport)* full fare **2** *adv* **de l'argent p. les poches** pockets full of money; **du chocolat p. la figure** chocolate all over one's face **3** *nm Aut* **faire le p. (d'essence)** to fill up (the tank)

pleurer [plœre] *vi* to cry

pleuvoir* [pløvwar] *v impersonnel* to rain; **il pleut** it's raining; *Fig* **il pleut des cordes** it's raining cats and dogs

pli [pli] *nm* **(a)** *(de papier, de rideau, de la peau)* fold; *(de jupe, de robe)* pleat; *(de pantalon)* crease **(b)** *(enveloppe)* envelope

plier [plije] **1** *vt (draps, vêtements)* to fold; *(parapluie)* to fold up *(courber)* to bend; **p. bagage** to pack one's bags (and leave) ● *vi (branche)* to bend **3 se plier** *vpr (lit, chaise)* to fold up; **se p. à** *(discipline)* to submit to ● **pliant, -e** *adj (chaise)* folding

plisser [plise] *vt (lèvres)* to pucker *(front)* to wrinkle; *(yeux)* to screw

up • **plissé, -e** *adj (jupe)* pleated
plomb [plɔ̃] *nm (métal)* lead; *(fusible) Br* fuse, *Am* fuze
plombage [plɔ̃baʒ] *nm (de dent)* filling
plombier [plɔ̃bje] *nm* plumber
plonger [plɔ̃ʒe] **1** *vi* to dive (**dans** into) **2** *vt (enfoncer)* to plunge (**dans** into) • **plongée** *nf* diving; *(de sous-marin)* dive; **p. sous-marine** scuba diving • **plongeoir** *nm* diving board • **plongeur, -euse** *nmf (nageur)* diver
plu [ply] *pp de* **plaire, pleuvoir**
pluie [plɥi] *nf* rain; **sous la p.** in the rain; **p. fine** drizzle
plume [plym] *nf* feather
plupart [plypar] **la plupart** *nf* most; **la p. du temps** most of the time; **la p. d'entre eux** most of them; **pour la p.** mostly
pluriel [plyrjɛl] *nm Gram* plural; **au p.** in the plural
plus¹ [ply] ([plyz] *before vowel,* [plys] *in end position) adv* **(a)** *(comparatif)* more (**que** than); **p. d'un kilo/de dix** more than a kilo/ten; **p. de thé** more tea; **p. beau/rapidement** more beautiful/quickly (**que** than); **p. tard** later; **p. petit** smaller; **de p. en p.** more and more; **de p. en p. vite** quicker and quicker; **p. ou moins** more or less; **en p.** in addition (**de** to); **au p.** at most; **de p.** more (**que** than); *(en outre)* moreover; **les enfants de p. de dix ans** children over ten; **j'ai dix ans de p. qu'elle** I'm ten years older than she is; **il est p. de cinq heures** it's after five (o'clock); **p. il crie, p. il s'enroue** the more he shouts, the more hoarse he gets **(b)** *(superlatif)* **le p.** (the) most; **le p. beau** the most beautiful (**de** in); *(de deux)*

the more beautiful; **le p. grand** the biggest (**de** in); *(de deux)* the bigger; **j'ai le p. de livres** I have (the) most books; **j'en ai le p.** I have the most

plus² [ply] *adv (négation)* **(ne...) p.** no more; **il n'a p. de pain** he has no more bread, he doesn't have any more bread; **il n'y a p. rien** there's nothing left; **elle ne le fait p.** she no longer does it, she doesn't do it any more *or* any longer; **je ne la reverrai p.** I won't see her again; **je ne voyagerai p. jamais** I'll never travel again

plus³ [plys] *conj* plus; **deux p. deux font quatre** two plus two are four; **il fait p. deux (degrés)** it's two degrees above freezing
plusieurs [plyzjœr] *adj & pron* several
plutôt [plyto] *adv* rather (**que** than)
pluvieux, -euse [plyvjø, -jøz] *adj* rainy, wet
pneu [pnø] *(pl* **pneus)** *nm (de roue) Br* tyre, *Am* tire • **pneumatique** *adj (gonflable)* inflatable
poche [pɔʃ] *nf* pocket • **pochette** *nf (sac)* bag; *(de disque)* sleeve
pocher [pɔʃe] *vt (œufs, poisson)* to poach
poêle [pwal] **1** *nm (chauffage)* stove **2** *nf* **p. (à frire)** frying pan
poème [pɔɛm] *nm* poem • **poésie** *nf (art)* poetry; *(poème)* poem • **poète** *nm* poet
poids [pwa] *nm* weight; **prendre/ perdre du p.** to gain/lose weight; **p. lourd** *(camion) Br* lorry, *Am* truck
poignard [pwaɲar] *nm* dagger • **poignarder** *vt* to stab
poignée [pwaɲe] *nf (quantité)* handful (**de** of); *(de porte, de*

casserole) handle; **p. de main** handshake

poignet [pwaɲɛ] *nm* wrist; *(de chemise)* cuff

poil [pwal] *nm* hair *(on body, animal)*; **poils** *(de brosse)* bristles • **poilu, -e** *adj* hairy

poinçonner [pwɛ̃sɔne] *vt (billet)* to punch

poing [pwɛ̃] *nm* fist

point [pwɛ̃] *nm (lieu, score, question)* point; *(sur i, à l'horizon)* dot; *(de notation)* mark; *(de couture)* stitch; **être sur le p. de faire qch** to be about to do sth; **à p.** *(steak)* medium; **déprimé au p. que…** depressed to such an extent that…; **mettre au p.** to perfect; **au p. où j'en suis…** at the stage I've reached…; **p. de côté** stitch; **p. de départ** starting point; **p. de vue** point of view, viewpoint; **p. faible/fort** weak/strong point

pointe [pwɛ̃t] *nf (extrémité)* tip, point; **sur la p. des pieds** on tiptoe; **en p.** pointed; **de p.** *(technologie)* state-of-the-art • **pointu, -e** *adj (en pointe)* pointed; *(voix)* shrill

pointure [pwɛ̃tyr] *nf* size

poire [pwar] *nf (fruit)* pear

poireau, -x [pwaro] *nm* leek

pois [pwa] *nm (légume)* pea; *(dessin)* (polka) dot; **à p.** *(vêtement)* polka-dot; **petits p.** *Br* (garden) peas, *Am* peas; **p. chiche** chickpea

poison [pwazɔ̃] *nm* poison

poisson [pwasɔ̃] *nm* fish; **les Poissons** *(signe)* Pisces; **p. d'avril** April fool; **p. rouge** goldfish • **poissonnerie** *nf* fish shop

poitrine [pwatrin] *nf* chest; *(seins)* bust

poivre [pwavr] *nm* pepper

poivron [pwavrɔ̃] *nm (légume)* pepper

pôle [pol] *nm Géog* pole; **p. Nord/ Sud** North/South Pole • **polaire** *adj* polar

poli, -e [pɔli] *adj* (a) *(courtois)* polite (**avec** to *or* with) (b) *(lisse)* polished

police [pɔlis] *nf* police; *Typ & Ordinat* **p. de caractères** font; **p. secours** emergency services • **policier, -ère 1** *adj* **enquête policière** police inquiry; **roman p.** detective novel **2** *nm* policeman, detective

polir [pɔlir] *vt* to polish

politesse [pɔlitɛs] *nf* politeness

politique [pɔlitik] **1** *adj* political **2** *nf (activité, science)* politics *(sing)*; *(mesure)* policy; **faire de la p.** to be in politics

pollen [pɔlɛn] *nm* pollen

polluer [pɔlɥe] *vt* to pollute • **pollution** *nf* pollution

Pologne [pɔlɔɲ] *nf* **la P.** Poland • **polonais, -e 1** *adj* Polish **2** *nmf* **P., Polonaise** Pole **3** *nm (langue)* Polish

polyester [pɔliɛstɛr] *nm* polyester

Polynésie [pɔlinezi] *nf* **la P.** Polynesia

polyvalent, -e [pɔlivalɑ̃, -ɑ̃t] *adj (salle)* multi-purpose; *(personne)* versatile

pommade [pɔmad] *nf* ointment

pomme [pɔm] *nf (fruit)* apple; *Anat* **p. d'Adam** Adam's apple; **p. de terre** potato; **pommes chips** *Br* (potato) crisps, *Am* (potato) chips; **pommes frites** *Br* chips, *Am* (French) fries; **pommes vapeur** steamed potatoes

pompe [pɔ̃p] **1** *nf (machine)* pump; **p. à essence** *Br* petrol *or* *Am* gas station; **p. à vélo** bicycle pump **2** *nfpl* **pompes funèbres** funeral parlour; **entrepreneur des pompes funèbres** *Br* undertaker, *Am* mortician

pomper [pɔ̃pe] *vt (eau, air)* to pump; *(faire monter)* to pump up

pompier [pɔ̃pje] *nm* fireman; **voiture de pompiers** fire engine

ponctuel, -elle [pɔ̃ktɥɛl] *adj (à l'heure)* punctual; *(unique) Br* one-off, *Am* one-of-a-kind

pondre [pɔ̃dr] *vt (œuf)* to lay

poney [pɔne] *nm* pony

pont [pɔ̃] *nm* bridge; *(de bateau)* deck; *Fig* **faire le p.** to make a long weekend of it

populaire [pɔpylɛr] *adj (personne, gouvernement)* popular; *(quartier, milieu)* working-class • **popularité** *nf* popularity (**auprès de** with)

population [pɔpylasjɔ̃] *nf* population

porc [pɔr] *nm (animal)* pig; *(viande)* pork

porcelaine [pɔrsəlɛn] *nf* china, porcelain

porche [pɔrʃ] *nm* porch

pornographie [pɔrnɔgrafi] *nf* pornography

port [pɔr] *nm* **(a)** *(pour bateaux)* port, harbour **(b)** *(d'armes)* carrying; *(du casque)* wearing

portable [pɔrtabl] **1** *adj (ordinateur)* portable; *(téléphone)* mobile **2** *nm (ordinateur)* laptop; *(téléphone)* mobile

portatif, -ive [pɔrtatif, -iv] *adj* portable

porte [pɔrt] *nf* door; *(de jardin, de ville)* gate; **mettre qn à la p.** to throw sb out; **p. d'embarquement** *(d'aéroport)* (departure) gate; **p. d'entrée** front door

portée [pɔrte] *nf (de fusil)* range; *Fig* scope; **à la p. de qn** within reach of sb; **à p. de la main** within

reach; **hors de p.** out of reach

portefeuille [pɔrtəfœj] *nm* wallet

portemanteau, -x [pɔrtmɑ̃to] *nm* coat stand

porter [pɔrte] **1** *vt* to carry; *(vêtement, lunettes)* to wear; *(moustache, barbe)* to have; *(trace, responsabilité)* to bear; **p. qch à qn** to take/bring sth to sb; **p. bonheur/malheur** to bring good/bad luck; **p. son attention sur qch** to turn one's attention to sth; **se faire p. malade** to report sick **2** *vi* **p. sur** *(concerner)* to be about **3 se porter** *vpr (vêtement)* to be worn; **se p. bien** to be well; **comment te portes-tu?** how are you?; **se p. candidat** *Br* to stand or *Am* to run as a candidate • **porte-bonheur** *nm inv* (lucky) charm • **porte-clefs** *nm inv* key ring • **porte-monnaie** *nm inv* purse • **porte-parole** *nmf inv* spokesperson (**de** for)

porteur, -euse [pɔrtœr, -øz] *nm/f (de bagages)* porter

portière [pɔrtjɛr] *nf (de véhicule, de train)* door

portion [pɔrsjɔ̃] *nf* portion

portrait [pɔrtrɛ] *nm (peinture, dessin, photo)* portrait; **faire le p. de qn** to do sb's portrait • **portrait-robot** *(pl* **portraits-robots)** *nm* identikit picture, Photofit®

Portugal [pɔrtygal] *nm* **le P.** Portugal • **portugais, -e 1** *adj* Portuguese **2** *nmf* **P., Portugaise** Portuguese *inv*; **les P.** the Portuguese **3** *nm (langue)* Portuguese

pose [poz] *nf (pour photo, portrait)* pose; **prendre la p.** to pose

poser [poze] **1** *vt* to put down; *(papier peint, rideaux)* to put up; *(moquette)* to lay; **p. qch sur qch**

to put sth on sth; **p. une question à qn** to ask sb a question; **p. sa candidature** *(à une élection)* to put oneself forward as a candidate; *(à un emploi)* to apply **(à** for) **2** *vi (modèle)* to pose **(pour** for) **3 se poser** *vpr (oiseau, avion)* to land; *(problème, question)* to arise; **se p. sur** *(sujet: regard)* to rest on; **se p. des questions** to ask oneself questions

positif, -ive [pozitif, -iv] *adj* positive

position [pozisjɔ̃] *nf* position; *Fig* **prendre p.** to take a stand **(contre** against)

posséder [pɔsede] *vt* to possess • **possession** *nf* possession; **en p. de qch** in possession of sth

possibilité [pɔsibilite] *nf* possibility; **avoir la p. de faire qch** to have the opportunity to do sth

possible [pɔsibl] **1** *adj* possible **(à faire** to do); **il (nous) est p. de le faire** it is possible (for us) to do it; **il est p. que...** *(+ subjunctive)* it is possible that...; **si p.** if possible; **le plus tôt p.** as soon as possible; **autant que p.** as far as possible; **le plus p.** *(quantité)* as much as possible; *(nombre)* as many as possible; **le moins de détails p.** as few details as possible **2** *nm* **faire (tout) son p.** to do one's utmost **(pour faire** to do)

poste¹ [pɔst] *nf (service)* mail, *Br* post; *(bureau)* post office; **la P.** the postal services; **par la p.** by mail, *Br* by post; **p. aérienne** airmail

poste² [pɔst] *nm* **(a)** *(lieu, emploi)* post; **être à son p.** to be at one's post; **p. de police** police station; **p. de secours** first-aid post **(b)** **p. (de radio/télévision)** radio/ television set

poster¹ [pɔste] *vt (lettre)* to mail, *Br* to post

poster² [pɔstɛr] *nm* poster

postuler [pɔstyle] *vi* **p. à un emploi** to apply for a job • **postulant, -e** *nmf* applicant **(à** for)

posture [pɔstyr] *nf* posture

pot [po] *nm* pot; *(en verre)* jar; *(de bébé)* potty; **p. d'échappement** *Br* exhaust pipe, *Am* tail pipe

potable [pɔtabl] *adj* drinkable; **eau p.** drinking water

potage [pɔtaʒ] *nm* soup

pot-au-feu [pɔtofø] *nm inv* = boiled beef with vegetables

pot-de-vin [podvɛ̃] *(pl* **pots-de-vin)** *nm* bribe

poteau, -x [pɔto] *nm* post; **p. électrique** electricity pylon; **p. télégraphique** telegraph pole

potentiel, -elle [pɔtɑ̃sjɛl] *adj & nm* potential

poterie [pɔtri] *nf* pottery

potion [posjɔ̃] *nf* potion

potiron [pɔtirɔ̃] *nm* pumpkin

pou, -x [pu] *nm* louse *(pl* lice)

poubelle [pubɛl] *nf Br* dustbin, *Am* garbage can; **mettre qch à la p.** to throw sth out

pouce [pus] *nm (doigt)* thumb

poudre [pudr] *nf (poussière, explosif)* powder; **en p.** powdered • **poudreux, -euse** *adj* powdery

poule [pul] *nf (animal)* hen

poulet [pulɛ] *nm* chicken

pouls [pu] *nm Méd* pulse; **prendre le p. de qn** to take sb's pulse

poumon [pumɔ̃] *nm* lung

poupée [pupe] *nf* doll

pour [pur] **1** *prép* for; **p. toi/moi** for you/me; **faites-le p. lui** do it for him, do it for his sake; **partir p. Paris/l'Italie** to leave for Paris/ Italy; **elle part p. cinq ans** she's leaving for five years; **elle est p. she's** all for it, she's in favour of it; **p. faire qch** (in order) to do sth; **p. que tu le voies** so (that) you may see it; **p. quoi faire?** what for?; **assez grand p. faire qch** big enough to do sth; **p. cela** for that reason; **p. ma part** as for me; **dix p. cent** ten percent **2** *nm* **le p. et le contre** the pros and cons

pourboire [purbwar] *nm* tip

pourcentage [pursɑ̃taʒ] *nm* percentage

pourquoi [purkwa] *adv & conj* why; **p. pas?** why not?

pourra, pourrait [pura, purɛ] *voir* **pouvoir 1, 2**

pourrir [purir] *vti* to rot • **pourri, -e** *adj (fruit, temps)* rotten

poursuite [pursɥit] **1** *nf (chasse)* pursuit; *(continuation)* continuation; **se lancer à la p. de qn** to set off in pursuit of sb **2** *nfpl Jur* **poursuites (judiciaires)** legal proceedings (**contre** against)

poursuivre* [pursɥivr] *vt (chercher à atteindre)* to pursue; *(continuer)* to continue, to go on with; *Jur* **p. qn (en justice)** to bring proceedings against sb; *(au criminel)* to prosecute sb

pourtant [purtɑ̃] *adv* yet, nevertheless; **et p.** and yet

pourvoir* [purvwar] *vt* to provide (**de** with); **être pourvu de** to be provided with

pourvu [purvy] **pourvu que** *conj* (a) *(condition)* provided (that) (b) *(souhait)* **p. qu'elle soit là!** I just hope (that) she's there!

pousse [pus] *nf* shoot, sprout

pousser [puse] **1** *vt (presser)* to push; *(moteur)* to drive hard; **p. qn à qch** to drive sb to sth; **p. qn à faire qch** *(sujet: faim)* to drive sb

to do sth; *(sujet: personne)* to urge sb to do sth; **p. un cri** to shout **2** *vi (presser)* to push; *(croître)* to grow; **faire p. qch** *(plante)* to grow sth; **se laisser p. les cheveux** to let one's hair grow **3 se pousser** *vpr (pour faire de la place)* to move over

poussette [pusɛt] *nf Br* pushchair, *Am* stroller

poussière [pusjɛr] *nf* dust; **une p.** a speck of dust • **poussiéreux, -euse** *adj* dusty

poussin [pusɛ̃] *nm (animal)* chick

poutre [putr] *nf (en bois)* beam

pouvoir* [puvwar] **1** *v aux (être capable de)* can, to be able to; *(avoir la permission)* can, may, to be allowed; **tu peux entrer** you may *or* can come in **2** *v impersonnel* **il peut neiger** it may snow; **il se peut qu'elle parte** she might leave **3** *nm (puissance, attributions)* power; **au p.** *(parti)* in power; **les pouvoirs publics** the authorities

poux [pu] *pl de* **pou**

prairie [preri] *nf* meadow

praline [pralin] *nf* praline

pratique [pratik] **1** *adj (méthode, personne)* practical; *(outil)* handy **2** *nf* practice; **mettre qch en p.** to put sth into practice; **dans la p.** *(en réalité)* in practice; **la p. de la natation/du golf** swimming/golfing • **pratiquement** *adv (presque)* practically; *(en réalité)* in practice

pratiquer [pratike] *vt (religion) Br* to practise, *Am* to practice; *(activité)* to take part in; *(langue)* to use; *(sport)* to play; **p. la natation** to go swimming • **pratiquant, -e** *adj* practising

pré [pre] *nm* meadow

préalable [prealabl] **1** *adj* prior, previous; **p. à** prior to **2** *nm* precondition **au p.** beforehand

précaire [prekɛr] *adj* precarious; *(santé)* delicate

précaution [prekosjɔ̃] *nf* *(mesure)* precaution; *(prudence)* caution; **par p.** as a precaution; **prendre des précautions** to take precautions

précédent, -e [presedɑ̃, -ɑ̃t] **1** *adj* previous **2** *nmf* previous one **3** *nm* precedent; **sans p.** unprecedented • **précéder** *vti* to precede

prêcher [preʃe] *vti* to preach

précieux, -euse [presjø, -øz] *adj* precious

précipice [presipis] *nm* chasm, abyss; *(de ravin)* precipice

précipiter [presipite] **1** *vt (hâter)* to hasten; *(jeter)* to hurl down **2 se précipiter** *vpr (se jeter)* to rush (**vers/sur** towards/at); *(se hâter)* to rush; **les événements se sont précipités** things started happening quickly

précis, -e [presi, -iz] **1** *adj* precise, exact; *(mécanisme)* accurate, precise; **à deux heures précises** at two o'clock sharp *or* precisely **2** *nm (résumé)* summary • **précision** *nf* precision; *(de mécanisme, d'information)* accuracy; *(détail)* detail; **donner des précisions sur qch** to give precise details about sth; **demander des précisions sur qch** to ask for further information about sth

préciser [presize] *vt* to specify (**que** that)

précoce [prekɔs] *adj (fruit, été)* early; *(enfant)* precocious

prédécesseur [predesesœr] *nm* predecessor

prédiction [prediksjɔ̃] *nf* prediction

préfabriqué, -e [prefabrike] *ad[* prefabricated

préface [prefas] *nf* preface (**de** to)

préfecture [prefɛktyr] *nf* pre‹ fecture; **la P. de police** polic‹ headquarters

préférable [preferabl] *ad[* preferable (**à** to)

préférence [preferɑ̃s] *nf* préfe‹ rence (**pour** for); **de p.** preferably **de p. à** in preference to

préférer [prefere] *vt* to prefer (à to); **p. faire qch** to prefer to do sth; **je préférerais rester** I woul‹ rather stay, I would prefer to stay **préféré, -e** *adj* & *nmf* favourite

préfet [prefɛ] *nm* prefect *(chie‹ administrator in a 'département')* **p. de police** = chief commissione‹ of police

préhistorique [preistɔrik] *ad‹* prehistoric

préjudice [preʒydis] *nm (à un‹ cause)* prejudice; *(à une personne‹* harm; **porter p. à qn** to do st‹ harm

préjugé [preʒyʒe] *nm* prejudice‹ **avoir des préjugés** to b‹ prejudiced (**contre** against)

prélèvement [prelɛvmɑ̃] *nn‹ (d'échantillon)* taking; *(de somme‹* deduction; **p. automatique‹** *Br* direct debit, *Am* automati‹ deduction

prématuré, -e [prematyre] *ad‹* premature

premier, -ère [prəmje, -ɛr] ‹ *adj* first; *(enfance)* early; *(qualité‹* prime; **le p. rang** the front row; **le‹ trois premiers mois** the first thre‹ months; **en p.** firstly; **P. ministr‹** Prime Minister **2** *nm (étage)* B‹ first *or Am* second floor; **le p‹ juin** June the first; **le p. de l'a‹** New Year's Day **3** *nmf* first (one)‹ **arriver le p.** *ou* **en p.** to arriv‹

first **4** *nf* **première** *(wagon, billet)* first class; *(vitesse)* first (gear); *Cin* première; *Scol Br* ≃ lower sixth, *Am* ≃ eleventh grade

prémonition [premɔnisjɔ̃] *nf* premonition

prendre* [prɑ̃dr] **1** *vt* to take (**à qn** from sb); *(attraper)* to catch; *(repas, boisson, douche)* to have; *(nouvelles)* to get; *(air, apparence)* to put on; **p. qch dans un tiroir** to take sth out of a drawer; **p. qn pour** to take sb for; **p. feu** to catch fire; **p. du temps/une heure** to take time/an hour; **p. de la place** to take up room; **p. du poids** to put on weight; **p. de la vitesse** to gather speed; **p. l'eau** *(bateau, chaussure)* to be leaking **2 se prendre** *vpr (médicament)* to be taken; *(s'accrocher)* to get caught; **se p. les pieds dans qch** to get one's feet caught in sth; **s'en p. à qn** to take it out on sb

prénom [prenɔ̃] *nm* first name • **prénommer** *vt* to name; **il se prénomme Daniel** his first name is Daniel

préoccuper [preɔkype] **1** *vt (inquiéter)* to worry **2 se préoccuper** *vpr* **se p. de qn/qch** to concern oneself with sb/sth • **préoccupation** *nf* preoccupation, concern • **préoccupé, -e** *adj* worried (**par** about)

préparatifs [preparatif] *nmpl* preparations (**de** for) • **préparation** *nf* preparation

préparer [prepare] **1** *vt* to prepare (**qch pour** sth for); *(examen)* to study for; **p. qch à qn** to prepare sth for sb; **plats tout préparés** ready meals **2 se préparer** *vpr (être imminent)* to be in the offing; *(s'apprêter)* to prepare oneself (**à**

ou **pour qch** for sth); **se p. à faire qch** to prepare to do sth; **se p. qch** *(boisson)* to make oneself sth

près [prɛ] *adv* **p. de qn/qch** near sb/sth, close to sb/sth; **p. de deux ans** nearly two years; **p. de partir** about to leave; **tout p.** nearby (**de qn/qch** sb/sth), close by (**de qn/qch** sb/sth); **de p.** *(suivre, examiner)* closely; **voici le chiffre à un euro p.** here is the figure, give or take a euro; **calculer à l'euro p.** to calculate to the nearest euro

présager [prezaʒe] *vt* **ça ne présage rien de bon** it doesn't bode well

presbyte [prɛsbit] *adj* long-sighted

prescrire* [prɛskrir] *vt (médicament)* to prescribe • **prescription** *nf (ordonnance)* prescription

présence [prezɑ̃s] *nf* presence; *(à l'école)* attendance (**à** at); **en p. de** in the presence of; **p. d'esprit** presence of mind

présent, -e [prezɑ̃, -ɑ̃t] **1** *adj (non absent, actuel)* present **2** *nm (temps)* present; **à p.** at present

présenter [prezɑ̃te] **1** *vt (montrer)* to show, to present; **p. qn à qn** to introduce sb to sb **2 se présenter** *vpr (dire son nom)* to introduce oneself (**à** to); *(chez qn)* to show up; *(occasion)* to arise; **ça se présente bien** it looks promising • **présentable** *adj* presentable • **présentateur, -trice** *nmf* presenter • **présentation** *nf* presentation; *(de personnes)* introduction; **faire les présentations** to make the introductions

préserver [prezɛrve] *vt* to protect, to preserve (**de** from) • **préservation** *nf* protection, preservation

président, -e [prezidã, -ãt] *nmf (de nation)* president; *(de société)* chairman, *f* chairwoman • **présidentiel, -elle** *adj* presidential

presque [prɛsk] *adv* almost, nearly; **p. jamais/rien** hardly ever/anything

presqu'île [prɛskil] *nf* peninsula

presse [prɛs] *nf Tech & Typ* press; **la p.** *(journaux)* the press

pressé, -e [prese] *adj (personne)* in a hurry; *(air)* hurried

pressing [presiŋ] *nm* dry cleaner's

pression [presjɔ̃] *nf* pressure; *(bouton)* snap (fastener); **faire p. sur qn** to put pressure on sb, to pressurize sb

prestation [prɛstasjɔ̃] *nf* **(a)** *(allocation)* benefit; **prestations** *(services)* services **(b)** *(de comédien)* performance

prestidigitateur, -trice [prɛstidiʒitatœr, -tris] *nmf* conjurer

prestige [prɛstiʒ] *nm* prestige • **prestigieux, -euse** *adj* prestigious

présumer [prezyme] *vt* to presume (**que** that); **p. de qch** to overestimate sth

prêt¹, -e [prɛ, prɛt] *adj (préparé)* ready (**à faire** to do; **à qch** for sth)

prêt² [prɛ] *nm (somme)* loan

prétendre [pretãdr] *vt (déclarer)* to claim (**que** that); *(vouloir)* to intend (**faire** to do); **à ce qu'il prétend** according to him

prétentieux, -euse [pretãsjø, -øz] *adj* pretentious

prêter [prɛte] **1** *vt (argent, objet)* to lend (**à** to); *(aide)* to give (**à** to); **p. attention** to pay attention (**à** to) **2** *vi* **p. à confusion** to give rise to confusion **3 se prêter** *vpr* **se p. à** to lend itself to

prétexte [pretɛkst] *nm* excuse, pretext; **sous p. de/que** on the pretext of/that; **sous aucun p.** under no circumstances

prêtre [prɛtr] *nm* priest

preuve [prœv] *nf* piece of evidence; **preuves** evidence; **faire p. de qch** to prove sth; **faire p. de courage** to show courage

prévenir* [prevnir] *vt* **(a)** *(mettre en garde)* to warn; *(aviser)* to inform (**de** of *or* about) **(b)** *(maladie)* to prevent • **prévention** *nf* prevention; **p. routière** road safety

prévisible [previzibl] *adj* foreseeable

prévision [previzjɔ̃] *nf* forecast; **prévisions météorologiques** weather forecast

prévoir* [prevwar] *vt (météo)* to forecast; *(difficultés, retard, réaction)* to expect; *(organiser)* to plan; **la réunion est prévue pour demain** the meeting is scheduled for tomorrow; **comme prévu** as planned; **plus tôt que prévu** earlier than expected

prier [prije] **1** *vi Rel* to pray **2** *vt (Dieu)* to pray to; *(supplier)* to beg; **p. qn de faire qch** to ask sb to do sth; **je vous en prie** *(faites-le)* please; *(en réponse à 'merci')* don't mention it • **prière** *nf Rel* prayer; *(demande)* request

primaire [primɛr] *adj* primary; **école p.** *Br* primary school, *Am* elementary school

prime [prim] *nf (sur salaire)* bonus; *(d'assurance)* premium

primitif, -ive [primitif, -iv] *adj (société, art)* primitive; *(état, sens)* original

primordial, -e, -aux, -ales [primɔrdjal, -jo] *adj* vital

prince [prɛ̃s] *nm* prince • **princesse** *nf* princess

principal, -e, -aux, -ales
[prɛ̃sipal, -o] **1** adj main, principal
2 nm (de collège) principal, Br
headmaster, f headmistress; **le p.**
(l'essentiel) the main thing

principe [prɛ̃sip] nm principle; **en
p.** theoretically, in principle; **par p.**
on principle

printemps [prɛ̃tɑ̃] nm spring; **au
p.** in the spring

priorité [priɔrite] nf priority (**sur**
over); Aut right of way; Aut **avoir
la p.** to have (the) right of way; Aut
p. à droite right of way to traffic
coming from the right; **'cédez la
p.'** Br 'give way', Am 'yield' •
prioritaire adj **être p.** to have
priority; Aut to have right of way

pris, -e[1] [pri, priz] **1** pp de
prendre 2 adj (place) taken; **être
p.** (occupé) to be busy; (candidat)
to be accepted; **p. de** (peur)
seized with; **p. de panique** panic-
stricken

prise[2] [priz] nf (action) taking,
(manière d'empoigner) grip; **p.
de sang** blood test; Él **p. (de
courant)** (mâle) plug; (femelle)
socket; Él **p. multiple** adaptor

prison [prizɔ̃] nf prison, jail;
(peine) imprisonment; **mettre qn
en p.** to put sb in prison, to jail sb
• **prisonnier, -ère** nmf prisoner;
faire qn p. to take sb prisoner; **p.
de guerre** prisoner of war

privé, -e [prive] **1** adj private **2**
nm **le p.** the private sector; Scol
the private education system; **en
p.** in private

priver [prive] **1** vt to deprive (**de**
of) **2 se priver** vpr **se p. de** to do
without, to deprive oneself of

privilège [privilɛʒ] nm privilege •
privilégié, -e adj privileged

prix [pri] nm (coût) price;
(récompense) prize; **à tout p.** at

all costs; **hors de p.** exorbitant

probable [prɔbabl] adj likely,
probable; **peu p.** unlikely •
probabilité nf probability,
likelihood; **selon toute p.** in all
probability

problème [prɔblɛm] nm problem
• **problématique** adj problematic

procédé [prɔsede] nm (technique)
process; (méthode) method

procéder [prɔsede] vi (agir) to
proceed; **p. à** (enquête, arrestation)
to carry out; **p. par élimination**
to follow a process of elimination
• **procédure** nf (méthode, règles)
(procès) proceedings

procès [prɔsɛ] nm (criminel) trial;
(civil) lawsuit; **faire un p. à qn** to
take sb to court

procession [prɔsesjɔ̃] nf
procession

processus [prɔsesys] nm process

procès-verbal [prɔsɛvɛrbal]
(pl **procès-verbaux** [-o]) nm
(amende) fine

prochain, -e [prɔʃɛ̃, -ɛn] adj
next; (mort, arrivée) impending •
prochainement adv shortly, soon

proche [prɔʃ] adj (dans l'espace)
near, close; (dans le temps) near,
imminent; (parent, ami) close; **p.
de** near (to), close to; **le P.-Orient**
the Middle East • **proches** nmpl
close relations

proclamer [prɔklame] vt to
proclaim (**que** that)

procuration [prɔkyrasjɔ̃] nf **par
p.** by proxy

procurer [prɔkyre] **se procurer**
vpr **se p. qch** to obtain sth

production [prɔdyksjɔ̃] nf
production; (produit) product •
producteur, -trice nmf producer
• **productif, -ive** adj productive

produire* [prɔdɥir] **1** vt to
produce **2 se produire** vpr

(événement) to happen, to occur • **produit** *nm* product; **p. de beauté** cosmetic; **p. chimique** chemical

professeur [prɔfɛsœr] *nm* teacher; *(à l'université)* professor; **p. principal** *Br* class *or* form teacher, *Am* homeroom teacher

profession [prɔfɛsjɔ̃] *nf* occupation, profession; *(manuelle)* trade • **professionnel, -elle 1** *adj* professional; *(enseignement)* vocational **2** *nmf* professional

profil [prɔfil] *nm* profile; **de p.** (viewed) from the side

profit [prɔfi] *nm* profit; **tirer p. de qch** to benefit from sth; **mettre qch à p.** to put sth to good use • **profitable** *adj* profitable (**à** to) • **profiter** *vi* **p. de** to take advantage of; **p. de la vie** to make the most of life; **p. à qn** to benefit sb, to be of benefit to sb

profond, -e [prɔfɔ̃, -ɔ̃d] **1** *adj* deep; *(joie, erreur)* profound; **p. de deux mètres** two metres deep **2** *adv* deep • **profondément** *adv* deeply; *(dormir)* soundly; *(triste, ému)* profoundly • **profondeur** *nf* depth; **faire six mètres de p.** to be six metres deep; **à six mètres de p.** at a depth of six metres

programme [prɔgram] *nm* *Br* programme, *Am* program; *Ordinat* program • **programmer** *vt* *Ordinat* to program • **programmeur, -euse** *nmf* (computer) programmer

progrès [prɔgrɛ] *nm & nmpl* progress; **faire des p.** to make (good) progress • **progressif, -ive** *adj* progressive • **progression** *nf* progression • **progressivement** *adv* progressively

proie [prwa] *nf* prey

projecteur [prɔʒɛktœr] *nm (de*

stade) floodlight; *Théât* spotlight; *Cin* projector

projet [prɔʒɛ] *nm (intention)* plan; *(étude)* project; **faire des projets d'avenir** to make plans for the future; **p. de loi** bill

projeter [prɔʒte] *vt (lancer)* to project; *(liquide, boue)* to splash; *(film)* to show; *(prévoir)* to plan; **p. de faire qch** to plan to do sth

prolonger [prɔlɔ̃ʒe] **1** *vt (vie, séjour)* to prolong; *(mur, route)* to extend **2 se prolonger** *vpr (séjour)* to be prolonged; *(réunion)* to go on; *(rue)* to continue • **prolongation** *nf (de séjour)* extension; **prolongations** *(au football)* extra time

promenade [prɔmnad] *nf (à pied)* walk; *(courte)* stroll; **faire une p.** to go for a walk; **faire une p. à cheval** to go for a ride

promener [prɔmne] **1** *vt (personne, chien)* to take for a walk **2 se promener** *vpr (à pied)* to go for a walk

promesse [prɔmɛs] *nf* promise; **tenir sa p.** to keep one's promise

promettre* [prɔmɛtr] **1** *vt* to promise (**qch à qn** sb sth; **que** that); **p. de faire qch** to promise to do sth; **c'est promis** it's a promise **2 se promettre** *vpr* **se p. qch** *(à soi-même)* to promise oneself sth; *(l'un l'autre)* to promise each other sth • **prometteur, -euse** *adj* promising

promotion [prɔmosjɔ̃] *nf* **(a)** *(avancement) & Com* promotion; **en p.** *(produit)* on (special) offer **(b)** *(d'une école) Br* year, *Am* class • **promouvoir*** *vt (personne, produit)* to promote; **être promu** *(employé)* to be promoted (**à** to)

prompt, -e [prɔ̃, prɔ̃t] *adj* prompt

prononcer [prɔnɔ̃se] **1** *vt* *(articuler)* to pronounce; *(discours)* to deliver **2 se prononcer** *vpr (mot)* to be pronounced • **prononcé, -e** *adj* pronounced • **prononciation** *nf* pronunciation

propagande [prɔpagɑ̃d] *nf* propaganda

prophète [prɔfɛt] *nm* prophet

propice [prɔpis] *adj* favourable (**à** to); **le moment p.** the right moment

proportion [prɔpɔrsjɔ̃] *nf* proportion; **en p. de** in proportion to; **hors de p.** out of proportion (**avec** to) • **proportionnel, -elle** *adj* proportional (**à** to)

propos [prɔpo] *nm (sujet)* subject; **des p.** *(paroles)* talk, words; **à p. de qn/qch** about sb/sth; **à p.** by the way

proposer [prɔpoze] **1** *vt (suggérer)* to suggest, to propose (**qch à qn** sth to sb; **que** + *subjunctive* that); *(offrir)* to offer (**qch à qn** sb sth; **de faire** to do); **je te propose de rester** I suggest (that) you stay **2 se proposer** *vpr* to offer one's services; **se p. pour faire qch** to offer to do sth; **se p. de faire qch** to propose to do sth • **proposition** *nf* suggestion, proposal; *(offre)* offer; **faire une p. à qn** to make a suggestion to sb

propre¹ [prɔpr] *adj* clean; *(soigné)* neat • **propreté** [-əte] *nf* cleanliness; *(soin)* neatness

propre² [prɔpr] *adj (à soi)* own; **mon p. argent** my own money; **être p. à qn/qch** *(particulier)* to be characteristic of sb/sth; **au sens p.** literally • **proprement** [-əmɑ̃] *adv (strictement)* strictly; **à p. parler** strictly speaking; **le village p. dit** the village proper

propriétaire [prɔprijetɛr] *nmf* owner; *(de location)* landlord, *f* landlady

propriété [prɔprijete] *nf (fait de posséder)* ownership; *(chose possédée, caractéristique)* property; **p. privée** private property

proscrire* [prɔskrir] *vt* to to ban

prospectus [prɔspɛktys] *nm* leaflet

prospère [prɔspɛr] *adj* prosperous

prostituée [prɔstitɥe] *nf* prostitute • **prostitution** *nf* prostitution

protection [prɔtɛksjɔ̃] *nf* protection; **assurer la p. de qn** to ensure sb's safety

protéger [prɔteʒe] **1** *vt* to protect (**de** from; **contre** against) **2 se protéger** *vpr* to protect oneself • **protégé, -e** *nmf* protégé, *f* protégée

protestant, -e [prɔtɛstɑ̃, -ɑ̃t] *adj & nmf* Protestant

protester [prɔtɛste] *vi* to protest (**contre** against); **p. de son innocence** to protest one's innocence • **protestation** *nf* protest (**contre** against); **en signe de p.** in protest

prothèse [prɔtɛz] *nf* **p. dentaire** false teeth

protocole [prɔtɔkɔl] *nm* protocol

prouver [pruve] *vt* to prove (**que** that)

provenance [prɔvnɑ̃s] *nf* origin; **en p. de** from

Provence [prɔvɑ̃s] *nf* **la P.** Provence • **provençal, -e, -aux, -ales 1** *adj* Provençal **2** *nmf* **P., Provençale** Provençal

proverbe [prɔvɛrb] *nm* proverb

province [prɔvɛ̃s] *nf* province; **la p.** the provinces; **en p.** in the provinces

proviseur [prɔvizœr] *nm Br* headmaster, *f* headmistress, *Am* principal

provision [prɔvizjɔ̃] *nf (réserve)* supply, stock; **provisions** *(nourriture)* shopping

provisoire [prɔvizwar] *adj* temporary; **à titre p.** temporarily

provoquer [prɔvɔke] *vt (incendie, mort)* to cause; *(réaction)* to provoke • **provocant, -e** *adj* provocative • **provocation** *nf* provocation

proximité [prɔksimite] *nf* closeness, proximity; **à p.** close by; **à p. de** close to; **de p.** local

prude [pryd] *nf* prude

prudent, -e [prydɑ̃, -ɑ̃t] *adj (personne)* cautious, careful; *(décision)* sensible • **prudence** *nf* caution, care; **par p.** as a precaution

prune [pryn] *nf (fruit)* plum

pruneau, -x [pryno] *nm* prune

pseudonyme [psødɔnim] *nm* pseudonym

psychanalyse [psikanaliz] *nf* psychoanalysis • **psychanalyste** *nmf* psychoanalyst

psychiatre [psikjatr] *nmf* psychiatrist • **psychiatrique** *adj* psychiatric

psychique [psiʃik] *adj* psychic

psychologie [psikɔlɔʒi] *nf* psychology • **psychologique** *adj* psychological • **psychologue** *nmf* psychologist

pu [py] *pp de* **pouvoir 1, 2**

public, -ique [pyblik] **1** *adj* public **2** *nm (de spectacle)* audience; **le grand p.** the general public; **en p.** in public

publication [pyblikasjɔ̃] *nf* publication • **publier** *vt* to publish

publicité [pyblisite] *nf (secteur)* advertising; *(annonce)* advertisement, advert; **faire de l** **p. pour qch** to advertise sth

puce [pys] *nf (insecte)* flea; *Ordina* (micro-)chip; **le marché au** **puces, les puces** the flea market

pudeur [pydœr] *nf* modesty; **pa** **p.** out of a sense of decency • **pudique** *adj* modest

puer [pɥe] **1** *vt* to stink of **2** *vi* t stink

puis [pɥi] *adv* then; **et p.** *(ensuite* and then; *(en plus)* and besides

puiser [pɥize] **1** *vt* to draw (**à** **dans** from) **2** *vi* **p. dans qch** t dip into sth

puisque [pɥiskə] *conj* since, as

puissant, -e [pɥisɑ̃, -ɑ̃t] *ad* powerful • **puissance** *nf (force* nation) & Math power; Math **di**: **p. quatre** ten to the power of fou

puisse(s), puissent [pɥis] *voi* **pouvoir 1**

puits [pɥi] *nm* well; **p. de pétrol** oil well

pull-over [pylɔver] *(pl* **pull** **overs), pull** [pyl] *nm* sweater, *B* jumper

pulpe [pylp] *nf (de fruits)* pulp

pulvériser [pylverize] *vt (vapor* ser) to spray; *(broyer)* to pulverize

punaise [pynɛz] *nf (insecte* bug; *(clou) Br* drawing pin, *Ar* thumbtack

punir [pynir] *vt* to punish; **p. q** **de qch** *(bêtise, crime)* to punish s for sth • **punition** *nf* punishment

pupille [pypij] *nf (de l'œil)* pupil

pupitre [pypitr] *nm (d'écolier* desk; *(d'orateur)* lectern

pur, -e [pyr] *adj* pure; *(alcool)* nea • **pureté** *nf* purity

purée [pyre] *nf* purée; **p. (d** **pommes de terre)** mashe potatoes, *Br* mash

purifier [pyrifje] *vt* to purify

pus¹ [py] *nm (liquide)* pus, matter

pus², **put** [py] *voir* **pouvoir 1**
puzzle [pœzl] *nm* (jigsaw) puzzle
pyjama [piʒama] *nm Br* pyjamas,
 Am pajamas; **un p.** a pair of
 Br pyjamas *or Am* pajamas

pyramide [piramid] *nf* pyramid
Pyrénées [pirene] *nfpl* **les P.** the
 Pyrenees

Qq

Q, q [ky] *nm inv* Q, q

qu' [k] *voir* **que**

quadrillé, -e [kadrije] *adj (papier)* squared

quadruple [k(w)adrypl] **1** *adj* fourfold **2** *nm* **le q. (de)** *(quantité)* four times as much (as); *(nombre)* four times as many (as)

quai [kɛ] *nm (de port)* quay; *(de gare, de métro)* platform

qualification [kalifikasjɔ̃] *nf (action, d'équipe, de sportif)* qualification; *(désignation)* description

qualifier [kalifje] **se qualifier** *vpr (équipe)* to qualify (**pour** for) ● **qualifié, -e** *adj (équipe)* that has qualified; **q. pour faire qch** qualified to do sth

qualité [kalite] *nf (de personne, de produit)* quality; **produit de q.** quality product; **de bonne q.** of good quality; **en q. de** in his/ her/*etc* capacity as

quand [kɑ̃] *conj & adv* when; **q. je viendrai** when I come

quant [kɑ̃] **quant à** *prép* as for

quantité [kɑ̃tite] *nf* quantity; **une q., des quantités** *(beaucoup)* a lot (**de** of)

quarante [karɑ̃t] *adj & nm inv* forty ● **quarantaine** *nf* (**a**) **une q. (de)** *(nombre)* (about) forty; **avoir la q.** *(âge)* to be about forty (**b**) *Méd* quarantine; **mettre qn en q.** to quarantine sb ● **quarantième** *adj & nmf* fortieth

quart [kar] *nm (fraction)* quarter; **q. de litre** quarter litre, quarter of a litre; **q. d'heure** quarter of an hour; **une heure et q.** an hour and a quarter; **il est une heure et q.** it's a quarter *Br* past *or Am* after one; **une heure moins le q.** quarter to one; *Sport* **quarts de finale** quarter finals

quartier [kartje] *nm* (**a**) *(de ville)* district, neighbourhood; **de q.** local; **q. général** headquarters (**b**) *(de fruit)* segment

quasi [kazi] *adv* almost ● **quasiment** *adv* almost

quatorze [katɔrz] *adj & nm inv* fourteen ● **quatorzième** *adj & nmf* fourteenth

quatre [katr] *adj & nm inv* four ● **quatrième** *adj & nmf* fourth

quatre-vingt [katrəvɛ̃] *adj & nm* eighty; **quatre-vingts ans** eighty years; **q.-un** eighty-one; **page q.** page eighty ● **quatre-vingt-dix** *adj & nm inv* ninety

que [kə]

que becomes **qu'** before a vowel or mute h.

1 *conj* (**a**) *(complétif)* that; **je pense qu'elle restera** I think (that) she'll stay; **qu'elle vienne ou non** whether she comes or not; **qu'il s'en aille!** let him leave!; **ça fait un an q. je suis là** I've been here for a year (**b**) *(de comparaison)* than; *(avec 'aussi', 'même', 'tel', 'autant')* as; **plus/moins âgé q. lui** older/younger than him; **aussi sage/fatigué q. toi** as wise/tired as you; **le même q. Pauline** the same as Pauline **(c) (ne...) que** only; **tu n'as qu'un stylo** you only have one pen **2** *adv* **(ce) qu'il est bête!** *(comme)* he's really stupid! **3** *pron relatif (chose)* that, which; *(personne)* that, whom; *(temps)* when; **le livre q. j'ai** the book (that *or* which) I have; **l'ami q. j'ai** the friend (that *or* whom) I have **4** *pron interrogatif* what; **q. fait-il?, qu'est-ce qu'il fait?** what is he doing?; **q. préférez-vous?** which do you prefer?

Québec [kebɛk] *nm* **le Q.** Quebec

quel, quelle [kɛl] **1** *adj interrogatif (chose)* what, which; *(personne)* which; **q. livre préférez-vous?** which *or* what book do you prefer?; **je sais q. est ton but** I know what your aim is; **je ne sais à q. employé m'adresser** I don't know which clerk to ask **2** *pron interrogatif* which (one); **q. est le meilleur?** which (one) is the best? **3** *adj exclamatif* **q. idiot!** what a fool! **4** *adj relatif* **q. qu'il soit** *(chose)* whatever it may be; *(personne)* whoever it *or* he may be

quelconque [kɛlkɔ̃k] *adj indéfini* any; **donne-moi un livre q.** give me any book

quelque [kɛlk] **1** *adj indéfini* some; **quelques** some, a few; **les quelques amies qu'elle a** the few friends she has **2** *adv (environ)* about, some; **q. peu** somewhat; *Fam* **100 euros et q.** 100 euros and a bit

quelque chose [kɛlkəʃoz] *pron indéfini* something; **q. d'autre** something else; **q. de grand** something big; **q. de**

plus pratique/de moins lourd something more practical/less heavy

quelquefois [kɛlkəfwa] *adv* sometimes

quelque part [kɛlkəpar] *adv* somewhere; *(dans les questions)* anywhere

quelques-uns, -unes [kɛlkəzœ̃, -yn] *pron* some

quelqu'un [kɛlkœ̃] *pron indéfini* someone, somebody; *(dans les questions)* anyone, anybody; **q. d'intelligent** someone clever

querelle [kərɛl] *nf* quarrel; **chercher q. à qn** to try to pick a fight with sb • **se quereller** *vpr* to quarrel

question [kɛstjɔ̃] *nf (interrogation)* question; *(affaire)* matter, question; **il n'en est pas q.** it's out of the question; **en q.** in question • **questionnaire** *nm* questionnaire

quête [kɛt] *nf* **(a)** *(collecte)* collection; **faire la q.** to collect money **(b)** *(recherche)* quest **(de** for); **en q. de** in quest *or* search of

queue [kø] *nf* **(a)** *(d'animal)* tail; **q. de cheval** *(coiffure)* ponytail **(b)** *(file)* *Br* queue, *Am* line; **faire la q.** *Br* to queue up, *Am* to stand in line

qui [ki] **1** *pron interrogatif (personne)* who; *(en complément)* whom; **q. (est-ce qui) est là?** who's there?; **q. désirez-vous voir?, q. est-ce que vous désirez voir?** who(m) do you want to see?; **à q. est ce livre?** whose book is this?; **je demande q. a téléphoné** I'm asking who phoned **2** *pron relatif* **(a)** *(sujet)* *(personne)* who, that; *(chose)* which, that; **l'homme q. est là** the man who's here or that's here; **la maison q. se trouve en face** the house which is or that's opposite (**b**) (sans antécédent) **q. que vous soyez** whoever you are (**c**) (après une préposition) **la femme de q. je parle** the woman I'm talking about

quiconque [kikɔ̃k] pron indéfini (sujet) whoever; (complément) anyone

quille [kij] nf (bowling) pin, Br skittle; **jouer aux quilles** to bowl, Br to play skittles

quincaillerie [kɛ̃kajri] nf (magasin) hardware shop; (objets) hardware

quinze [kɛ̃z] adj & nm inv fifteen; **q. jours** two weeks, Br a fortnight • **quinzaine** nf **une q. (de)** (about) fifteen; **une q. (de jours)** two weeks, Br a fortnight • **quinzième** adj & nmf fifteenth

quittance [kitãs] nf (reçu) receipt

quitte [kit] adj quits (**envers** with);

q. à... even if it means...; **en être q. pour qch** to get off with sth

quitter [kite] **1** vt (personne, lieu, poste) to leave; **ne pas q. qn des yeux** to keep one's eyes on sb **2** vi **ne quittez pas!** (au téléphone) hold the line! **3 se quitter** vpr to part; **ils ne se quittent plus** they are inseparable

quoi [kwa] pron what; (après une préposition) which; **à q. penses-tu?** what are you thinking about?; **après q.** after which; **de q. manger** something to eat; **de q. écrire** something to write with; **q. que je dise** whatever I say; **q. qu'il en soit** be that as it may; **il n'y a pas de q.!** (en réponse à 'merci') don't mention it!; **q.?** what?

quoique [kwak] conj (al)though; **quoiqu'il soit pauvre** (al)though he's poor

quota [kɔta] nm quota

quotidien, -enne [kɔtidjɛ̃, -ɛn] adj & nm daily

Rr

R, r [ɛr] *nm inv* R, r

rabais [rabɛ] *nm* discount

rabattre* [rabatr] **1** *vt (col)* to turn down; *(couvercle)* to close **2 se rabattre** *vpr (se refermer)* to close; *Fig* **se r. sur qch** to fall back on sth

rabbin [rabɛ̃] *nm* rabbi

raccommoder [rakɔmɔde] *vt (linge)* to mend; *(chaussette)* to darn

raccompagner [rakɔ̃paɲe] *vt* to take back

raccorder [rakɔrde] *vt*, **se raccorder** *vpr* to link up (**à** to)

raccourcir [rakursir] **1** *vt* to shorten **2** *vi* to get shorter ● **raccourci** *nm* short cut; **en r.** in brief

raccrocher [rakrɔʃe] **1** *vt (objet tombé)* to hang back up; *(téléphone)* to put down **2** *vi (au téléphone)* to hang up **3 se raccrocher** *vpr* **se r. à qch** to catch hold of sth; *Fig* to cling to sth

race [ras] *nf (ethnie)* race; *(animale)* breed; **chien de r.** pedigree dog ● **racial, -e, -aux, -ales** *adj* racial ● **racisme** *nm* racism ● **raciste** *adj & nmf* racist

racheter [raʃte] *vt (acheter davantage)* to buy some more; *(remplacer)* to buy another

racine [rasin] *nf* root

racler [rɑkle] **1** *vt* to scrape; *(peinture, boue)* to scrape off **2 se racler** *vpr* **se r. la gorge** to clear one's throat ● **raclette** *nf (outil)* scraper; *(plat)* raclette (*Swiss dish consisting of potatoes and melted cheese*)

raconter [rakɔ̃te] *vt (histoire, mensonge)* to tell; *(événement)* to tell about; **r. qch à qn** *(histoire)* to tell sb sth; **r. à qn que...** to tell sb that... ● **racontars** *nmpl* gossip

radar [radar] *nm* radar

radiateur [radjatœr] *nm* radiator; **r. électrique** electric heater

radiation [radjasjɔ̃] *nf* radiation

radical, -e, -aux, -ales [radikal, -o] *adj* radical

radio [radjo] *nf* **(a)** *(poste)* radio; *(station)* radio station; **à la r.** on the radio **(b)** *Méd* X-ray; **passer** une r. to have an X-ray ● **radio-réveil** (*pl* **radios-réveils**) *nm* radio alarm, clock radio

radioactif, -ive [radjoaktif, -iv] *adj* radioactive

radiographie [radjografi] *nf (photo)* X-ray ● **radiographier** *vt* to X-ray ● **radiologue** *nmf (médecin)* radiologist

radis [radi] *nm* radish

rafale [rafal] *nf (vent)* gust

raffermir [rafɛrmir] *vt (autorité)* to strengthen; *(muscles)* to tone up

raffiné, -e [rafine] *adj* refined

rafraîchir [rafreʃir] **1** *vt (rendre frais)* to chill; *(pièce)* to air; *(raviver)* to freshen up **2** *vi* to cool down **3 se rafraîchir** *vpr (temps)* to get cooler; *(se laver)* to freshen up ● **rafraîchissant, -e** *adj* refreshing ● **rafraîchissement** *nm (boisson)* cold drink

rage [raʒ] *nf (colère)* rage; *(maladie)* rabies

ragoût [ragu] *nm Culin* stew

raid [rɛd] *nm* raid

raide [rɛd] *adj (rigide, guindé)* stiff; *(côte)* steep; *(cheveux)* straight

raie [rɛ] *nf (motif)* stripe; *(de cheveux) Br* parting, *Am* part

rail [raj] *nm* rail; **le r.** *(chemins de fer)* rail

raisin [rɛzɛ̃] *nm* **raisin(s)** grapes; **r. sec** raisin

raison [rɛzɔ̃] *nf* (a) *(faculté, motif)* reason; **la r. de mon absence** the reason for my absence; **la r. pour laquelle…** the reason (why)…; **en r. de** *(cause)* on account of (b) **avoir r.** to be right (**de faire** to do *or* in doing)

raisonnable [rɛzɔnabl] *adj* reasonable

raisonnement [rɛzɔnmɑ] *nm (faculté, activité)* reasoning; *(argumentation)* argument

rajeunir [raʒœnir] *vt* **r. qn** to make sb look younger

rajouter [raʒute] *vt* to add (**à** to)

rajuster [raʒyste] *vt (vêtements, lunettes)* to straighten, to adjust

ralentir [ralɑtir] *vti* to slow down • **ralenti** *nm Cin & TV* slow motion; **au r.** in slow motion • **ralentissement** *nm* slowing down

rallonge [ralɔ̃ʒ] *nf (de table)* extension; *(fil électrique)* extension (lead) • **rallonger** *vti* to lengthen

rallumer [ralyme] *vt (feu, pipe)* to light again; *(lampe)* to switch on again

ramasser [ramase] *vt (prendre, réunir)* to pick up; *(ordures, copies)* to collect; *(fruits, coquillages)* to gather • **ramassage** *nm (d'ordures)* collection; **r. scolaire** school bus service

rame [ram] *nf (aviron)* oar; *(de*

métro) train • **ramer** *vi* to row • **rameur, -euse** *nmf* rower

ramener [ramne] *vt (amener)* tc bring back; *(raccompagner)* tc take back

rampe [rɑp] *nf (d'escalier)* banister; *(d'accès)* ramp

ramper [rɑpe] *vi* to crawl

rançon [rɑsɔ̃] *nf* ransom

rancune [rɑkyn] *nf* spite; **garde r. à qn** to bear sb a grudge • **rancunier, -ère** *adj* spiteful

randonnée [rɑdɔne] *nf* **(pédestre)** hike

rang [rɑ] *nm (rangée)* row *(classement, grade)* rank; **par r de taille** in order of size; **de haut r.** high-ranking; **se mettre en r** to line up (**par trois** in threes) • **rangée** *nf* row

ranger [rɑʒe] *vt (papiers, vaisselle* to put away; *(chambre)* to tidy (up) *(classer)* to rank (**parmi** among) • **rangé, -e** *adj (chambre)* tidy

ranimer [ranime] *vt (après éva nouissement)* to bring round; *(aprè arrêt cardiaque)* to resuscitate

râpé, -e [rape] *adj (fromage* grated • **râper** *vt (fromage)* tc grate

rapide [rapid] *adj* fast; *(progrès* rapid; *(esprit, lecture)* quick • **rapidité** *nf* speed

rappel [rapɛl] *nm* reminder **descendre en r.** *(en alpinisme)* tc abseil down

rappeler [raple] **1** *vt (pour fair revenir, au téléphone)* to call back **r. qch à qn** to remind sb of sth *vi (au téléphone)* to call back *se* **rappeler** *vpr* **se r. qn/qch** tc remember sb/sth; **se r. que…** tc remember that…

rapport [rapɔr] *nm* (a) *(lien* connection, link; **par r.** compared with; **rapports** *(entr* *personnes)* relations; **rapports (sexuels)** (sexual) intercourse **(b)** *(compte rendu)* report

rapporter [rapɔrte] **1** *vt (rendre)* to bring back; *(remporter)* to take back; *(raconter)* to report; **r. de l'argent** to be profitable; **on rapporte que...** it is reported that... **2 se rapporter** *vpr* **se r. à qch** to relate to sth; **s'en r. à qn/ qch** to rely on sb/sth

rapprocher [raprɔʃe] **1** *vt (objet)* to move closer **(de** to); *(réconcilier)* to bring together; *(comparer)* to compare **(de** to *or* with) **2 se rapprocher** *vpr* to get closer **(de** to); *(se réconcilier)* to be reconciled; *(ressembler)* to be similar **(de** to) ● **rapprochement** *nm (réconciliation)* reconciliation; *(rapport)* connection

raquette [rakɛt] *nf (de tennis)* racket; *(de ping-pong)* bat

rare [rar] *adj* rare; *(argent, main-d'œuvre)* scarce; **c'est r. qu'il pleuve ici** it rarely rains here ● **rarement** *adv* rarely, seldom ● **rareté** *nf (objet rare)* rarity; *(de main-d'œuvre)* scarcity

ras, -e [ra, raz] **1** *adj (cheveux)* close-cropped; *(herbe, barbe)* short; **à r. bord** to the brim; **pull (au) r. du cou** crew-neck sweater **2** *nm* **au r. de, à r. de** level with; **voler au r. du sol** to fly close to the ground

raser [raze] **1** *vt (menton, personne)* to shave; *(barbe, moustache)* to shave off **2 se raser** *vpr* to shave ● **rasé, -e** *adj* **être bien r.** to be clean-shaven

rasoir [razwar] *nm* razor; *(électrique)* shaver

rassembler [rasãble] **1** *vt (gens, objets)* to gather (together) **2 se rassembler** *vpr* to gather, to

assemble ● **rassemblement** *nm (action, groupe)* gathering

rassurer [rasyre] **1** *vt* to reassure **2 se rassurer** *vpr* **rassure-toi** don't worry ● **rassurant, -e** *adj* reassuring

rat [ra] *nm* rat

ratatouille [ratatuj] *nf Culin* **r. (niçoise)** ratatouille

râteau, -x [rato] *nm* rake

rater [rate] *vt (bus, cible, occasion)* to miss; *(travail)* to ruin; *(examen)* to fail ● **raté, -e** *nmf* loser

ration [rasjɔ̃] *nf* ration

rationnel, -elle [rasjɔnɛl] *adj* rational

rattacher [rataʃe] **1** *vt (lacets)* to tie up again **2 se rattacher** *vpr* **se r. à** to be linked to

rattraper [ratrape] *vt* to catch; **r. qn** *(rejoindre)* to catch up with sb; **r. le temps perdu** to make up for lost time ● **rattrapage** *nm Scol* **cours de r.** remedial class

rauque [rok] *adj (voix)* hoarse

ravages [ravaʒ] *nmpl* devastation; *(du temps, de maladie)* ravages; **faire des r.** to wreak havoc

ravi, -e [ravi] *adj* delighted **(de** with; **de faire** to do; **que** that)

ravin [ravɛ̃] *nm* ravine

ravir [ravir] *vt (emporter)* to snatch **(à** from); *(plaire à)* to delight; **chanter à r.** to sing delightfully ● **ravisseur, -euse** *nmf* kidnapper

ravitailler [ravitaje] *vt (personnes)* to supply ● **ravitaillement** *nm (action)* supplying; *(denrées)* supplies

rayer [rɛje] *vt (érafler)* to scratch; *(mot)* to cross out ● **rayé, -e** *adj (verre, disque)* scratched; *(tissu, pantalon)* striped ● **rayure** *nf (éraflure)* scratch; *(motif)* stripe; **à rayures** striped

rayon [rɛjɔ̃] *nm* **(a)** *(de lumière)*

ray; *(de cercle)* radius; *(de roue)* spoke; **dans un r. de** within a radius of; **r. X** X-ray; **r. de soleil** sunbeam **(b)** *(d'étagère)* shelf; *(de magasin)* department

rayonnant, -e [rɛjɔnɑ̃, -ɑ̃t] *adj (soleil)* radiant; *Fig (visage)* beaming **(de** with)

raz de marée [rɑdmare] *nm inv* tidal wave; **r. électoral** landslide

réacteur [reaktœr] *nm (nucléaire)* reactor

réaction [reaksjɔ̃] *nf* reaction

réagir [reaʒir] *vi* to react **(contre** against; **à** to)

réaliser [realize] *vt (projet)* to realize; *(rêve, ambition) Br* to fulfil, *Am* to fulfill; *(film)* to direct; *(comprendre)* to realize **(que** that) • **réalisateur, -trice** *nmf (de film)* director

réalité [realite] *nf* reality; **en r.** in reality

réanimation [reanimasjɔ̃] *nf* resuscitation; **(service de) r.** intensive care unit • **réanimer** *vt* to resuscitate

rebelle [rəbɛl] **1** *adj* rebellious **2** *nmf* rebel • **se rebeller** *vpr* to rebel **(contre** against) • **rébellion** *nf* rebellion

rebondir [rəbɔ̃dir] *vi* to bounce

rebours [rəbur] **à rebours** *adv* the wrong way

recensement [rəsɑ̃smɑ̃] *nm (de population)* census

récent, -e [resɑ̃, -ɑ̃t] *adj* recent

réception [resɛpsjɔ̃] *nf (accueil, soirée) & Radio* reception; *(de lettre)* receipt; *(d'hôtel)* reception (desk); **avec accusé de r.** with acknowledgement of receipt • **réceptionniste** *nmf* receptionist

recette [rəsɛt] *nf Culin* recipe **(de** for); **recettes** *(gains)* takings

recevoir* [rəsəvwar] *vt (amis, lettre, coup de téléphone)* to receive; *(gifle,*

coup) to get; *(client)* to see; **être reçu à un examen** to pass an exam

rechange [rəʃɑ̃ʒ] **de rechange** *adj (pièce)* spare

rechargeable [rəʃarʒabl] *adj* rechargeable • **recharger** *vt* to recharge

réchauffer [reʃofe] **1** *vt (personne, aliment)* to warm up **2 se réchauffer** *vpr (personne)* to get warm • **réchauffement** *nm (de température)* rise **(de** in); **le r. de la planète** global warming

recherche [rəʃɛrʃ] *nf* **(a)** *(quête)* search **(de** for); **à la r. de** in search of **(b)** *(scientifique)* research **(sur** into); **faire de la r.** to do research **(c) recherches** *(de police)* search, hunt; **faire des recherches** to make inquiries

rechercher [rəʃɛrʃe] *vt (personne, objet)* to search for; *(emploi)* to look for • **recherché, -e** *adj (très demandé)* in demand; *(rare)* sought-after; **r. pour meurtre** wanted for murder

récif [resif] *nm* reef

récipient [resipjɑ̃] *nm* container

réciproque [resiprɔk] *adj (sentiments)* mutual

récit [resi] *nm (histoire)* story; *(compte rendu)* account

réciter [resite] *vt* to recite

réclame [reklam] *nf (publicité)* advertising; *(annonce)* advertisement; **en r.** on special offer

réclamer [reklame] *vt (demander)* to ask for; *(exiger)* to demand; *(nécessiter)* to require • **réclamation** *nf* complaint; **(bureau des) réclamations** complaints department

récolte [rekɔlt] *nf (action)* harvesting; *(produits)* harvest; **faire la r.** to harvest the crops

recommandable [rəkɔmɑ̃dabl] *adj* **peu r.** disreputable

recommandation [rəkɔmɑ̃dasjɔ̃] *nf (appui, conseil)* recommendation

recommander [rəkɔmɑ̃de] *vt (appuyer)* to recommend (**à** to; **pour** for); **r. à qn de faire qch** to advise sb to do sth ● **recommandé, -e** *adj (lettre)* registered

recommencer [rəkɔmɑ̃se] *vti* to start again

récompense [rekɔ̃pɑ̃s] *nf* reward (**pour** *ou* **de** for); *(prix)* award ● **récompenser** *vt* to reward (**de** *ou* **pour** for)

réconcilier [rekɔ̃silje] **se réconcilier** *vpr* to become reconciled, *Br* to make it up (**avec** with) ● **réconciliation** *nf* reconciliation

réconforter [rekɔ̃fɔrte] *vt* to comfort

reconnaissable [rəkɔnɛsabl] *adj* recognizable (**à qch** by sth)

reconnaissant, -e [rəkɔnɛsɑ̃, -ɑ̃t] *adj* grateful (**à qn de qch** to sb for sth) ● **reconnaissance** *nf (gratitude)* gratitude (**pour** for); *(identification)* recognition; **r. de dette** IOU

reconnaître* [rəkɔnɛtr] *vt (identifier, admettre)* to recognize (**à qch** by sth)

reconstitution [rəkɔ̃stitysjɔ̃] *nf (de crime)* reconstruction

recopier [rəkɔpje] *vt* to copy out

record [rəkɔr] *nm & adj inv* record

recours [rəkur] *nm* **avoir r. à** *(chose)* to resort to; *(personne)* to turn to; **en dernier r.** as a last resort

recouvrir* [rəkuvrir] *vt* to cover (**de** with)

récréation [rekreasjɔ̃] *nf Scol Br* break, *Am* recess; *(pour les plus jeunes)* playtime

recroqueviller [rəkrɔkvije] **se**

recroqueviller *vpr (personne)* to huddle up

recrutement [rəkrytmɑ̃] *nm* recruitment ● **recruter** *vt* to recruit

rectangle [rɛktɑ̃gl] *nm* rectangle ● **rectangulaire** *adj* rectangular

recto [rekto] *nm* front; **r. verso** on both sides

reçu, -e [rəsy] **1** *pp de* **recevoir 2** *nm (récépissé)* receipt

recueil [rəkœj] *nm (de poèmes, de chansons)* collection (**de** of)

recul [rəkyl] *nm (en arrière)* retreat; *(déclin)* decline; **avoir un mouvement de r.** to recoil

reculer [rəkyle] **1** *vi (personne)* to move back; *(automobiliste)* to reverse, *Am* to back up; *(armée)* to retreat; *(diminuer)* to decline **2** *vt (meuble)* to move back; *(paiement, décision)* to postpone

reculons [rəkylɔ̃] **à reculons** *adv* backwards

récupérer [rekypere] **1** *vt (objet prête)* to get back, to recover; *(forces)* to recover **2** *vi (reprendre des forces)* to recover

recycler [rəsikle] *vt* to recycle ● **recyclage** *nm* recycling

rédacteur, -trice [redaktœr, -tris] *nmf* writer; *(de journal)* editor ● **rédaction** *nf (action)* writing; *(journalistes)* editorial staff

redemander [rədəmɑ̃de] *vt* to ask for more; **il faut que je le lui redemande** *(que je pose la question à nouveau)* I'll have to ask him/her again

rediffusion [rədifyzjɔ̃] *nf (de film)* repeat

rédiger [rediʒe] *vt* to write

redoubler [rəduble] **1** *vt* to increase; *Scol* **r. une classe** to repeat a year *or Am* a grade **2** *vi Scol* to repeat a year *or Am* a grade

redoutable [rədutabl] *adj* *(personne)* formidable; *(maladie)* dreadful

redresser [rədrese] **1** *vt* *(objet tordu)* to straighten (out); *(situation)* to put right; **r. la tête** to hold up one's head **2 se redresser** *vpr* *(personne)* to straighten up; *(pays, économie)* to recover

réduction [redyksjɔ̃] *nf* reduction (**de** in); *(rabais)* discount

réduire* [redчir] *vt* to reduce (**à** to; **de** by); **r. qn à qch** *(misère, désespoir)* to reduce sb to sth ● **réduit, -e** *adj* reduced

réécrire* [reekrir] *vt* to rewrite

rééducation [reedykasjɔ̃] *nf* *(de personne)* rehabilitation; **faire de la r.** to have physiotherapy

réel, -elle [reɛl] *adj* real

refaire* [rəfɛr] *vt* *(exercice, travail)* to redo; *(chambre)* to do up; **r. du riz** to make some more rice

référence [referɑ̃s] *nf* reference; **faire r. à qch** to refer to sth

refermer [rəfɛrme] *vt*, **se refermer** *vpr* to close *or* shut again

réfléchir [refleʃir] *vi* to think (**à** *ou* **sur** about) ● **réfléchi, -e** *adj* *(personne)* thoughtful; *(action, décision)* carefully thought-out; **tout bien r.** all things considered

reflet [rəflɛ] *nm* *(image)* & *Fig* reflection; *(lumière)* glint; **reflets** *(de cheveux)* highlights ● **refléter 1** *vt* to reflect **2 se refléter** *vpr* to be reflected

réflexe [reflɛks] *nm* & *adj* reflex

réflexion [reflɛksjɔ̃] *nf* *(d'image, de lumière)* reflection; *(pensée)* thought; *(remarque)* remark; **faire une r. à qn** to make a remark to sb; **r. faite, à la r.** on second *Br* thoughts *or Am* thought

réforme [refɔrm] *nf* reform

refrain [rəfrɛ̃] *nm* *(de chanson)* chorus, refrain

réfrigérateur [refriʒeratœr] *nm* refrigerator

refroidir [rəfrwadir] **1** *vt* to cool (down) **2** *vi* *(devenir froid)* to get cold; *(devenir moins chaud)* to cool down **3 se refroidir** *vpr* *(temps)* to get colder

refuge [rəfyʒ] *nm* refuge; *(de montagne)* (mountain) hut

réfugier [refyʒje] **se réfugier** *vpr* to take refuge ● **réfugié, -e** *nmf* refugee

refus [rəfy] *nm* refusal ● **refuser** *vt* to refuse (**qch à qn** sb sth; **de faire** to do); *(offre, invitation)* to turn down; *(proposition)* to reject

régaler [regale] **se régaler** *vpr* **je me régale** *(en mangeant)* I'm really enjoying it

regard [rəgar] *nm* *(coup d'œil, expression)* look; **jeter un r. sur** to glance at

regarder [rəgarde] **1** *vt* to look at; *(émission, film)* to watch; *(considérer)* to consider, to regard (**comme** as); *(concerner)* to concern; **r. qn fixement** to stare at sb **2** *vi* *(observer)* to look; **r. par la fenêtre** *(du dedans)* to look out of the window **3 se regarder** *vpr* *(soi-même)* to look at oneself; *(l'un l'autre)* to look at each other

régime [reʒim] *nm* *(politique)* regime; *(de bananes)* bunch; *(alimentaire)* diet; **suivre un r.** to be on a diet

région [reʒjɔ̃] *nf* region, area ● **régional, -e, -aux, -ales** *adj* regional

registre [rəʒistr] *nm* register

règle [rɛgl] *nf* **(a)** *(principe)* rule; **en r. générale** as a (general) rule **(b)** *(instrument)* ruler

règlement [rɛgləmɑ̃] *nm* **(a)**

(règles) regulations **(b)** *(de conflit)* settling; *(paiement)* payment; *Fig* **r. de comptes** settling of scores • **réglementaire** *adj* in accordance with the regulations

régler [regle] *vt (problème, conflit)* to settle; *(mécanisme)* to adjust; *(télévision)* to tune; *(payer)* to pay; **r. qn** to settle up with sb

réglisse [reglis] *nf Br* liquorice, *Am* licorice

règne [rɛɲ] *nm* reign • **régner** *vi (roi, silence)* to reign (**sur** over); **faire r. l'ordre** to maintain law and order

regret [rəgrɛ] *nm* regret; **avoir le r.** *ou* **être au r. de faire qch** to be sorry to do sth • **regretter** [rəgrɛte] *vt* to regret; **r. qn** to miss sb; **je regrette, je le regrette** I'm sorry; **r. que...** *(+ subjunctive)* to be sorry that...

regrouper [rəgrupe] *vt*, **se regrouper** *vpr* to gather together

régulier, -ère [regylje, -ɛr] *adj (intervalles, visage)* regular; *(constant)* steady; *(légal)* legal

rein [rɛ̃] *nm* kidney; **les reins** *(dos)* the lower back

reine [rɛn] *nf* queen; **la r. Élisabeth** Queen Elizabeth

rejet [rəʒɛ] *nm* rejection • **rejeter** *vt (relancer)* to throw back; *(offre, candidature, personne)* to reject

rejoindre* [rəʒwɛ̃dr] **se rejoindre** *vpr* to meet up

réjouir [reʒwir] **se réjouir** *vpr* to be delighted (**de** at; **de faire** to do)

relâche [rəlɑʃ] *nf* **sans r.** without a break

relâcher [rəlɑʃe] *vt (corde, étreinte)* to loosen; *(prisonnier)* to release

relais [rəlɛ] *nm (dispositif émetteur)* relay; *Sport* **(course de)** r. relay (race); **passer le r. à qn** to hand over to sb; **prendre le r.** to take over (**de** from); **r. routier** *Br* transport café, *Am* truck stop

relancer [rəlɑ̃se] *vt (lancer à nouveau)* to throw again; *(rendre)* to throw back

relatif, -ive [rəlatif, -iv] *adj* relative (**à** to)

relation [rəlasjɔ̃] *nf (rapport)* relationship; *(ami)* acquaintance; **être en r. avec qn** to be in touch with sb; **avoir des relations** *(amis)* to have contacts; **r. (amoureuse)** (love) affair; **relations internationales** international relations

relevé [rəlve] *nm* list; *(de compteur)* reading; **r. de compte** bank statement; *Scol* **r. de notes** list of *Br* marks *or Am* grades

relève [rəlɛv] *nf* relief; **prendre la r.** to take over (**de** from)

relever [rəlve] **1** *vt (ramasser)* to pick up; *(personne)* to help back up; *(copies)* to collect; *(faute)* to pick out; *(défi)* to accept; *(compteur)* to read; *(augmenter)* to raise; **r. la tête** to look up; **r. qn de ses fonctions** to relieve sb of his/her duties **2 se relever** *vpr (après une chute)* to get up

relief [rəljɛf] *nm (de paysage)* relief; **en r.** in relief; *Fig* **mettre qch en r.** to highlight sth

relier [rəlje] *vt* to connect, to link (**à** to); *(idées, faits)* to link together; *(livre)* to bind

religion [rəliʒjɔ̃] *nf* religion • **religieuse** *nf (femme)* nun; *(gâteau)* cream puff • **religieux, -euse 1** *adj* religious; **mariage r.** church wedding **2** *nm (moine)* monk **3** *nf* **religieuse** *(sœur)* nun

relire* [rəlir] *vt* to reread

reliure [rəljyr] *nf (de livre)* binding

reluire* [rəlɥir] *vi* to shine, to gleam; **faire r.** **qch** to polish sth up

remarier [rəmarje] **se remarier** *vpr* to remarry

remarquable [rəmarkabl] *adj* remarkable (**par** for)

remarque [rəmark] *nf* remark; **faire une r.** to make a remark

remarquer [rəmarke] *vt* (*apercevoir*) to notice (**que** that); (*dire*) to remark (**que** that); **faire r.** **qch** to point sth out (**à** to); **se faire r.** to attract attention

rembobiner [rãbɔbine] *vtvpr* to rewind

rembourser [rãburse] *vt* (*personne*) to pay back; (*somme*) to refund • **remboursement** [-əmã] *nm* repayment; (*de billet*) refund

remède [rəmɛd] *nm* cure, remedy (**contre** for)

remercier [rəmɛrsje] *vt* (*dire merci à*) to thank (**de** *ou* **pour qch** for sth); **je vous remercie d'être venu** thank you for coming • **remerciements** *nmpl* thanks

remettre* [rəmɛtr] **1** *vt* (*replacer*) to put back; (*vêtement*) to put back on; (*disque*) to put on again; (*différer*) to postpone (**à** until); **r.** **qch à qn** (*lettre*) to deliver sth to sb; (*rapport*) to submit sth to sb; **r.** **qn en liberté** to set sb free; **r.** **qch en question** to call sth into question; **r.** **qch à jour** to bring sth up to date **2** **se remettre** *vpr* **se r.** **à qch** to start sth again; **se r.** **à faire qch** to start to do sth again; **se r.** **de qch** to recover from sth

remise [rəmiz] *nf* (**a**) **r.** **en question** questioning (**b**) (*rabais*) discount

remontée [rəmɔ̃te] *nf* **r.** **mécanique** ski lift

remonter [rəmɔ̃te] **1** (*aux* **être**) *vi*

to come/go back up; (*niveau, prix*) to rise again, to go back up; (*dans le temps*) to go back (**à** to); **r.** **dans** (*voiture*) to get back in(to); (*bus, train*) to get back on(to); **r.** **à dix ans** to go back ten years **2** (*aux* **avoir**) *vt* (*escalier, pente*) to come/go back up; (*porter*) to bring/take back up; (*montre*) to wind up; (*relever*) to raise; **r.** **le moral à qn** to cheer sb up • **remonte-pente** (*pl* **remonte-pentes**) *nm* ski lift

remords [rəmɔr] *nm* remorse; **avoir des r.** to feel remorse

remorque [rəmɔrk] *nf* (*de voiture*) trailer • **remorquer** *vt* (*voiture, bateau*) to tow

rempart [rãpar] *nm* rampart; **remparts** walls

remplacer [rãplase] *vt* to replace (**par** with); (*professionnellement*) to stand in for • **remplaçant, -e** *nmf* (*personne*) replacement; (*enseignant*) substitute teacher, *Br* supply teacher; (*joueur*) substitute • **remplacement** *nm* replacement; **en r.** **de** in place of

remplir [rãplir] **1** *vt* to fill (up) (**de** with); (*formulaire*) to fill out, *Br* to fill in; (*promesse*) to fulfil **2** **se remplir** *vpr* to fill (up) (**de** with)

remporter [rãpɔrte] *vt* (*objet*) to take back; (*prix, victoire*) to win

remuer [rəmɥe] *vt* to move

rémunération [remynerasjɔ̃] *n* payment (**de** for)

renard [rənar] *nm* fox

rencontre [rãkɔ̃tr] *nf* (*de personnes*) meeting • **rencontrer 1** *v* (*personne*) to meet; (*difficulté*) to encounter; (*trouver*) to come across **2** **se rencontrer** *vpr* to meet

rendez-vous [rãdevu] *nm inv* (*rencontre*) appointment; (*amoureux*) date; (*lieu*) meeting place; **donner r.** **à qn** to arrange to meet sb; **prendre r. avec qn** to make an appointment with sb; **sur r.** by appointment

rendormir* [rɑ̃dɔrmir] **se rendormir** *vpr* to go back to sleep

rendre [rɑ̃dr] **1** *vt (restituer)* to give back (**à** to); **r. célèbre** to make famous; **r. la monnaie à qn** to give sb his/her change; **r. l'âme** to pass away **2 se rendre** *vpr (aller)* to go (**à** to); **se r. malade** to make oneself ill

renfermé, -e [rɑ̃fɛrme] **1** *adj (personne)* withdrawn **2** *nm* **sentir le r.** to smell musty

renforcer [rɑ̃fɔrse] *vt* to reinforce

renfort [rɑ̃fɔr] *nm* **des renforts** *(troupes)* reinforcements

renfrogner [rɑ̃frɔɲe] **se renfrogner** *vpr* to scowl

renifler [rənifle] *vti* to sniff

renne [rɛn] *nm* reindeer

renommé, -e [rənɔme] **1** *adj* famous, renowned (**pour** for) **2** *nf* **renommée** fame

renoncer [rənɔ̃se] *vi* **r. à qch** to give sth up, to abandon sth; **r. à faire qch** to give up doing sth

renouveler [rənuvle] *vt* to renew; *(expérience)* to repeat

rénover [renɔve] *vt (édifice, meuble)* to renovate • **rénovation** *nf (d'édifice, de meuble)* renovation

renseigner [rɑ̃seɲe] **se renseigner** *vpr* to make inquiries (**sur** about) • **renseignement** [-əmɑ̃] *nm* piece of information; **renseignements** information; **les renseignements (téléphoniques)** *Br* directory inquiries, *Am* information; **demander des renseignements** to make inquiries

rentable [rɑ̃tabl] *adj* profitable

rentrée [rɑ̃tre] *nf* **r. des classes** start of the new school year

rentrer [rɑ̃tre] **1** *(aux* **être)** *vi*

(entrer) to go/come in; *(entrer de nouveau)* to go/come back in; *(chez soi)* to go/come (back) home; **r. en France** to return to France; **en rentrant de l'école** on my/his/her/*etc* way home from school; **r. dans qch** *(pénétrer)* to get into sth; *(sujet: voiture)* to crash into sth; **r. dans une catégorie** to fall into a category **2** *(aux* **avoir)** *vt (linge, troupeau)* to bring/take in

renverser [rɑ̃vɛrse] **1** *vt (faire tomber)* to knock over; *(piéton)* to run over; *(tendance)* to reverse **2 se renverser** *vpr (récipient)* to fall over; *(véhicule)* to overturn

renvoyer [rɑ̃vwaje] *vt (lettre)* to send back, to return; *(employé)* to dismiss; *(élève)* to expel

réorganiser [reɔrganize] *vt* to reorganize • **réorganisation** *nf* reorganization

répandre [repɑ̃dr] **1** *vt (liquide)* to spill; *(odeur)* to give off **2 se répandre** *vpr (nouvelle, peur)* to spread; *(liquide)* to spill • **répandu, -e** *adj (opinion, usage)* widespread

réparer [repare] *vt (objet, machine)* to repair, to mend; **faire r. qch** to get sth repaired • **réparateur, -trice** *nmf* repairer • **réparation** *nf (action)* repairing; *(résultat)* repair; **en r.** under repair

repartir* [rəpartir] *(aux* **être)** *vi (continuer)* to set off again; *(s'en retourner)* to go back

répartir [repartir] *vt (poids)* to distribute; *(tâches, vivres)* to share (out); *(classer)* to divide (up)

repas [rəpɑ] *nm* meal

repasser [rəpase] **1** *vi* to come/go back; **r. chez qn** to drop in on sb again **2** *vt (examen)* to take again, *Br* to resit; *(film)* to show again; *(disque)* to play again; *(linge)* to iron • **repassage** *nm* ironing

repère [rəpɛr] *nm* mark; **point de r.** *(espace, temps)* reference point • **repérer 1** *vt (endroit)* to locate **2 se repérer** *vpr* to get one's bearings

répertoire [repɛrtwar] *nm (liste)* index; *(carnet)* (indexed) notebook

répéter [repete] **1** *vt* to repeat; *(pièce de théâtre, rôle)* to rehearse; **r. à qn que...** to tell sb again that... **2** *vi (redire)* to repeat; *(acteur)* to rehearse **3 se répéter** *vpr (radoter)* to repeat oneself; *(événement)* to happen again • **répétition** *nf (redite)* repetition; *Théât* rehearsal

replacer [rəplase] *vt* to put back

réplique [replik] *nf (réponse)* retort • **répliquer 1** *vt* **r. que...** to reply that... **2** *vi* to reply; *(avec impertinence)* to answer back

répondre [repɔ̃dr] **1** *vi* to answer, to reply; *(avec impertinence)* to answer back; *(réagir)* to respond (**à** to); **r. à qn** to answer sb, to reply to sb; *(avec impertinence)* to answer sb back; **r. à** *(lettre, question, objection)* to answer, to reply to; *(besoin)* to meet; **r. au téléphone** to answer the phone; **r. de qn/qch** to answer for sb/sth **2** *vt (remarque)* to answer *or* reply with; **r. que...** to answer *or* reply that... • **répondeur** *nm* answering machine

réponse [repɔ̃s] *nf* answer, reply; *(réaction)* response (**à** to)

reportage [rəpɔrtaʒ] *nm* report

reporter¹ [rəpɔrte] **1** *vt (objet)* to take back; *(réunion)* to put off, to postpone (**à** until); *(transcrire)* to transfer (**sur** to) **2 se reporter** *vpr* **se r. à** *(texte)* to refer to

reporter² [rəpɔrtɛr] *nm* reporter

repos [rəpo] *nm (détente)* rest; *(tranquillité)* peace

reposer [rəpoze] **1** *vt (objet)* to put back down; *(problème, question)* to raise again; *(délasser)* to rest, to relax; **r. sa tête sur** *(appuyer)* to lean one's head on **2** *vi (être enterré)* to lie (**sur** on) **3 se reposer** *vpr* to rest; **se r. sur qn** to rely on sb • **reposant, -e** *adj* restful, relaxing

repousser [rəpuse] *vt (en arrière)* to push back; *(sur le côté)* to push away; *(dégoûter)* to repel

reprendre* [rəprɑ̃dr] **1** *vt (objet)* to take back; *(activité)* to take up again; **r. de la viande** to take some more meat **2** *vi (recommencer)* to start again; *(continuer de parler)* to go on, to continue **3 se reprendre** *vpr (se ressaisir)* to get a grip on oneself

représenter [rəprezɑ̃te] *vt* to represent • **représentant, -e** *nmf* representative • **représentation** *nf* representation; *Théât* performance

répression [reprɛsjɔ̃] *nf (d'émeute)* suppression; *(mesures de contrôle)* repression

réprimander [reprimɑ̃de] *vt* to reprimand

reprise [rəpriz] *nf* **à plusieurs reprises** on several occasions • **repriser** *vt (chaussette)* to darn

reproche [rəprɔʃ] *nm* reproach; **sans r.** beyond reproach • **reprocher** *vt* **r. qch à qn** to blame *or* reproach sb for sth

reproduire* [rəprɔdyir] **1** *vt (modèle, son)* to reproduce **2 se reproduire** *vpr (animaux)* to reproduce; *(incident)* to happen again • **reproduction** *nf (d'animaux, de son)* reproduction; *(copie)* copy

reptile [rɛptil] *nm* reptile

république [repyblik] *nf* republic ● **républicain, -e** *adj* & *nmf* republican

répugnant, -e [repyɲɑ̃, -ɑ̃t] *adj* repulsive

réputation [repytasjɔ̃] *nf* reputation; **avoir la r. d'être franc** to have a reputation for being frank *or* for frankness

requin [rəkɛ̃] *nm (animal)* shark

rescapé, -e [rɛskape] *nmf* survivor

réseau, -x [rezo] *nm* network

réservation [rezɛrvasjɔ̃] *nf* reservation, booking

réserve [rezɛrv] *nf (provision, discrétion)* reserve; **en r.** in reserve; **r. naturelle** nature reserve

réserver [rezɛrve] *vt* to reserve; *(garder)* to save, to keep (**à** for) ● **réservé, -e** *adj (personne, place, chambre)* reserved

réservoir [rezɛrvwar] *nm (lac)* reservoir; *(cuve)* tank; **r. d'essence** *Br* petrol *or Am* gas tank

résidence [rezidɑ̃s] *nf* residence; **r. universitaire** *Br* hall of residence, *Am* dormitory ● **résident, -e** *nmf* resident ● **résidentiel, -elle** *adj (quartier)* residential

résigner [reziɲe] **se résigner** *vpr* to resign oneself (**à qch** to sth; **à faire** to doing)

résistance [rezistɑ̃s] *nf* resistance (**à** to); *Hist* **la R.** the Resistance

résister [reziste] *vi* **r. à** *(attaque, tentation)* to resist; *(chaleur, fatigue, souffrance)* to withstand ● **résistant, -e** *adj* **r. à la chaleur** heat-resistant

résolu, -e [rezɔly] **1** *pp de* **résoudre 2** *adj* determined (**à faire** to do) ● **résolution** *nf (décision)* resolution; *(fermeté)* determination

résoudre* [rezudr] **1** *vt (problème)* to solve; *(difficulté)* to resolve; **r. de faire qch** to resolve to do sth **2 se résoudre** *vpr* **se r. à faire qch** to resolve to do sth

respect [rɛspɛ] *nm* respect (**pour/de** for) ● **respectable** *adj (honorable)* respectable ● **respecter** *vt* to respect; **r. la loi** to abide by the law; **faire r. la loi** to enforce the law ● **respectueux, -euse** *adj* respectful (**envers** to; **de** of)

respirer [rɛspire] **1** *vi* to breathe **2** *vt* to breathe (in) ● **respiration** *nf* breathing; *(haleine)* breath

responsable [rɛspɔ̃sabl] **1** *adj* responsible (**de qch** for sth; **devant qn** to sb) **2** *nmf (chef)* person in charge; *(coupable)* person responsible (**de** for) ● **responsabilité** *nf* responsibility

ressembler [rəsɑ̃ble] **1** *vi* **r. à** to look like, to resemble **2 se ressembler** *vpr* to look alike

ressentir* [rəsɑ̃tir] *vt* to feel

ressort [rəsɔr] *nm (objet)* spring; **en dernier r.** *(décider)* as a last resort

ressortissant, -e [rəsɔrtisɑ̃, -ɑ̃t] *nmf* national

ressources [rəsurs] *nfpl* resources

restant, -e [rɛstɑ̃, -ɑ̃t] *adj* remaining

restaurant [rɛstɔrɑ̃] *nm* restaurant ● **restaurateur, -trice** *nmf* restaurant owner

reste [rɛst] *nm* rest, remainder (**de** of); **restes** remains (**de** of); *(de repas)* leftovers; **au r., du r.** moreover, besides

rester [rɛste] *(aux* **être***) vi* to stay, to remain; *(calme, jeune)* to keep, to stay; *(subsister)* to be left, to remain; **il reste du pain** there's some bread left (over); **il me reste une pomme** I have one apple left;

l'argent qui lui reste the money he/she has left; **il me reste deux choses à faire** I still have two things to do

restriction [rɛstriksjɔ̃] *nf* restriction

résultat [rezylta] *nm* result ● **résulter 1** *vi* **r. de** to result from **2** *v impersonnel* **il en résulte que...** the result of this is that...

résumer [rezyme] *vt* (*abréger*) to summarize; (*récapituler*) to sum up ● **résumé** *nm* summary; **en r.** in short

rétablir [retablir] **1** *vt* (*communications, ordre*) to restore **2 se rétablir** *vpr* (*malade*) to recover ● **rétablissement** *nm* (*d'ordre*) restoration; (*de malade*) recovery

retard [rətar] *nm* (*de personne*) lateness; (*sur horaire*) delay; **en r.** late; **en r. sur qn/qch** behind sb/sth; **avoir du r.** to be late; (*sur un programme*) to be behind (schedule); (*montre*) to be slow; **avoir une heure de r.** to be an hour late; **prendre du r.** (*personne*) to fall behind

retenir* [rət(ə)nir] **1** *vt* (*personne*) to keep; (*eau, chaleur*) to retain; (*larmes, foule*) to hold back; (*se souvenir de*) to remember; **r. l'attention de qn** to catch sb's attention; **r. qn de faire qch** to stop sb (from) doing sth **2 se retenir** *vpr* (*se contenir*) to restrain oneself; **se r. de faire qch** to stop oneself (from) doing sth; **se r. à qn/qch** to cling to sb/sth

retenue [rət(ə)ny] *nf* (*modération*) restraint; *Scol* (*punition*) detention

retirer [rətire] **1** *vt* (*faire sortir*) to take out; (*ôter*) to take off; (*éloigner*) to take away; **r. qch à qn** (*permis*) to take sth away from sb; **r. qch de qch** (*gagner*) to derive sth from sth **2 se retirer** *vpr* to withdraw (**de** from)

retouche [rətuʃ] *nf* (*de vêtement*) alteration ● **retoucher** *vt* (*vêtement, texte*) to alter; (*photo, tableau*) to touch up

retour [rətur] *nm* return; (*trajet*) return journey; **être de r.** to be back (**de** from); **à mon r.** when I get/got back (**de** from)

retourner [rəturne] **1** (*aux* **avoir**) *vt* (*matelas, steak*) to turn over; (*vêtement, sac*) to turn inside out **2** (*aux* **être**) *vi* to go back, to return **3 se retourner** *vpr* (*pour regarder*) to turn round; (*sur le dos*) to turn over

retrait [rətrɛ] *nm* withdrawal

retraite [rətrɛt] *nf* (*d'employé*) retirement; (*pension*) (retirement) pension; **prendre sa r.** to retire; **être à la r.** to be retired ● **retraité, -e 1** *adj* retired **2** *nmf* senior citizen, *Br* (old age) pensioner

retransmission [rətrɑ̃smisjɔ̃] *nf* broadcast

rétrécir [retresir] **1** *vi* to shrink **2 se rétrécir** *vpr* (*rue*) to narrow

rétrograder [retrograde] *vi* (*automobiliste*) to change down

retrouver [rətruve] **1** *vt* (*objet*) to find again; (*personne*) to meet again **2 se retrouver** *vpr* (*être*) to find oneself; (*se rencontrer*) to meet

rétroviseur [retrovizœr] *nm* rearview mirror

Réunion [reynjɔ̃] *nf* **la R.** Réunion

réunion [reynjɔ̃] *nf* (*séance*) meeting; (*d'objets*) collection, gathering; **être en r.** to be in a meeting

réunir [reynir] **1** *vt* (*objets*) to put together; (*amis, famille*) to get together **2 se réunir** *vpr* (*personnes*) to meet; **se r. autour**

de qn/qch to gather round sb/sth

réussir [reysir] **1** *(examen)* to pass **2** *vi* to succeed, to be successful (**à faire** in doing); **r. à un examen** to pass an exam • **réussi, -e** *adj* successful • **réussite** *nf* success; *Cartes* **faire des réussites** to play patience

revanche [rəvɑ̃ʃ] *nf* revenge; **prendre sa r.** to get one's revenge (**sur** on); **en r.** on the other hand

rêve [rɛv] *nm* dream; **faire un r.** to have a dream

réveil [revɛj] *nm (de personnes)* waking; *(pendule)* alarm (clock); **à son r.** on waking

réveiller [revɛje] **1** *vt* to wake (up) **2** **se réveiller** *upr* to wake (up) • **réveillé, -e** *adj* awake

réveillon [revɛjɔ̃] *nm (repas)* midnight supper; *(soirée)* midnight party *(on Christmas Eve or New Year's Eve)*

révéler [revele] *vt* to reveal (**que** that) • **révélation** *nf (action, découverte)* revelation

revendiquer [rəvɑ̃dike] *vt* to claim • **revendication** *nf* claim

revendre [rəvɑ̃dr] *vt* to resell

revenir* [rəv(ə)nir] *(aux être) vi* to come back, to return; **le dîner nous est revenu à 50 euros** the dinner cost us 50 euros; **r. cher** to work out expensive; **r. à** *(activité, sujet)* to go back to, to return to; **r. de** *(surprise)* to get over; **r. sur** *(décision, promesse)* to go back on; *(passé, question)* to go back over; **r. sur ses pas** to retrace one's steps

revenu [rəv(ə)ny] *nm* income (**de** from)

rêver [rɛve] *vti* to dream (**de** of; **de faire** of doing; **que** that)

rêverie [rɛvri] *nf* daydream

revers [rəvɛr] *nm (de veste)* lapel; *(de pantalon) Br* turn-up, *Am* cuff; *(au tennis)* backhand

revêtir* [rəvɛtir] *vt* to cover (**de** with)

rêveur, -euse [rɛvœr, -øz] **1** *adj* dreamy **2** *nmf* dreamer

réviser [revize] *vt (leçon)* to revise; *(jugement, règlement)* to review • **révision** *nf (de leçon)* revision; *(de jugement)* review

revoici [rəvwasi] *prép* **me r.** here I am again

revoilà [rəvwala] *prép* **la r.** there she is again

revoir* [rəvwar] *vt* to see (again); *(texte, leçon)* to revise; **au r.** goodbye

révolte [revɔlt] *nf* revolt • **révolter 1** *vt* to appal **2** **se révolter** *upr* to rebel, to revolt (**contre** against)

révolution [revɔlysjɔ̃] *nf (changement, rotation)* revolution

revolver [revɔlvɛr] *nm* revolver

revue [rəvy] *nf (magazine)* magazine; *(spécialisée)* journal; *(spectacle)* revue; **passer qch en r.** to review sth

rez-de-chaussée [redʃose] *nm inv Br* ground floor, *Am* first floor

Rhin [rɛ̃] *nm* **le R.** the Rhine

rhinocéros [rinɔserɔs] *nm* rhinoceros

Rhône [ron] *nm* **le R.** the Rhône

rhumatisme [rymatism] *nm* rheumatism; **avoir des rhumatismes** to have rheumatism

rhume [rym] *nm* cold; **r. des foins** hayfever

ri [ri] *pp de* **rire**

ricaner [rikane] *vi (sarcastiquement) Br* to snigger, *Am* to snicker; *(bêtement)* to giggle

riche [riʃ] **1** *adj (personne, pays, aliment)* rich; **r. en** *(vitamines)* rich in **2** *nmf* rich person; **les riches** the rich • **richesse** *nf (de personne,* de pays) wealth; (d'étoffe, de sol) richness; **richesses** (trésor) riches; (ressources) wealth

ricocher [rikɔʃe] vi to ricochet • **ricochet** nm ricochet

ride [rid] nf (de visage) wrinkle • **ridé, -e** adj wrinkled

rideau, -x [rido] nm curtain

ridicule [ridikyl] adj ridiculous

rien [rjɛ̃] **1** pron nothing; **il ne sait r.** he knows nothing, he doesn't know anything; **r. du tout** nothing at all; **r. d'autre/de bon** nothing else/good; **de r.!** (je vous en prie) don't mention it!; **ça ne fait r.** it doesn't matter; **pour r. au monde** never in a thousand years; **comme si de r. n'était** as if nothing had happened **2** nm **un r. de** a little; **en un r. de temps** in no time

rigide [riʒid] adj rigid; (carton) stiff; (éducation) strict

rigueur [rigœr] nf (d'analyse) rigour; (de climat) harshness; (de personne) strictness; **être de r.** to be the rule; **à la r.** if need be • **rigoureux, -euse** adj (analyse) rigorous; (climat, punition) harsh; (personne, morale) strict

rimer [rime] vi to rhyme (**avec** with)

rincer [rɛ̃se] vt to rinse

riposter [ripɔste] vt **r. que...** to retort that...

rire* [rir] **1** nm laugh; **rires** laughter; **le fou r.** the giggles **2** vi to laugh (**de** at); (s'amuser) to have a good time; (plaisanter) to joke; **pour r.** for a laugh

risque [risk] nm risk; **au r. de faire qch** at the risk of doing sth; **à vos risques et périls** at your own risk; **assurance tous risques** comprehensive insurance

risquer [riske] vt to risk; **r. de faire qch** to stand a good chance of doing sth • **risqué, -e** adj (dangereux) risky; (osé) risqué

rivage [rivaʒ] nm shore

rival, -e, -aux, -ales [rival, -o] adj & nmf rival • **rivaliser** vi to compete (**avec** with; **de** in) • **rivalité** nf rivalry

rive [riv] nf (de fleuve) bank; (de lac) shore

riverain, -e [rivrɛ̃, -ɛn] nmf (près d'une rivière) riverside resident; (près d'un lac) lakeside resident; (de rue) resident

rivière [rivjɛr] nf river

riz [ri] nm rice; **r. blanc/complet** white/brown rice; **r. au lait** rice pudding

RMI [ɛrɛmi] (abrév **revenu minimum d'insertion**) nm Br ≃ income support, Am ≃ welfare

RN (abrév **route nationale**) nf Br ≃ A-road, Am ≃ highway

robe [rɔb] nf (de femme) dress; (de prêtre, de juge) robe; **r. du soir** evening dress; **r. de chambre** Br dressing gown, Am bathrobe

robinet [rɔbinɛ] nm Br tap, Am faucet

robot [rɔbo] nm robot

roc [rɔk] nm rock

roche [rɔʃ] nf rock • **rocher** nm (bloc, substance) rock • **rocheux, -euse** adj rocky

rock [rɔk] **1** nm (musique) rock **2** adj inv **chanteur r.** rock singer

rognon [rɔɲɔ̃] nm kidney

roi [rwa] nm king; **fête des Rois** Twelfth Night

rôle [rol] nm role, part; **à tour de r.** in turn

romain, -e [rɔmɛ̃, -ɛn] **1** adj Roman **2** nmf **R., Romaine** Roman

roman [rɔmɑ̃] nm novel • **romancier, -ère** nmf novelist

romantique [rɔmɑ̃tik] ad

romantic

romarin [rɔmarɛ̃] *nm* rosemary
rompre* [rɔ̃pr] **1** *vt* to break; *(relations)* to break off **2** *vi (casser)* to break; *(fiancés)* to break it off
rond, -e¹ [rɔ̃, rɔ̃d] **1** *adj* round; *(gras)* plump; **chiffre r.** whole number **2** *adv* **10 euros tout r.** 10 euros exactly **3** *nm (cercle)* circle; **en r.** *(s'asseoir)* in a circle • **rond-point** *(pl* **ronds-points)** *nm Br* roundabout, *Am* traffic circle
ronde² [rɔ̃d] *nf (de policier)* beat; **faire sa r.** *(gardien)* to do one's rounds
rondelle [rɔ̃dɛl] *nf (tranche)* slice
ronfler [rɔ̃fle] *vi* to snore
ronger [rɔ̃ʒe] **1** *vt* to gnaw (at) **2 se ronger** *vpr* **se r. les ongles** to bite one's nails
ronronner [rɔ̃rɔne] *vi* to purr
rosbif [rɔzbif] *nm* **du r.** roast beef; **un r.** a joint beef
rose [roz] **1** *adj & nm (couleur)* pink **2** *nf (fleur)* rose • **rosé, -e** *adj & nm (vin)* rosé
rôti [roti] *nm* **du r.** roast meat; **un r.** a joint; **r. de bœuf** (joint of) roast beef • **rôtir** *vti* to roast; **faire r. qch** to roast sth
roue [ru] *nf* wheel
rouge [ruʒ] **1** *adj* red **2** *nm (couleur)* red; **le feu est au r.** the (traffic) lights are red; **r. à lèvres** lipstick
rougeur [ruʒœr] *nf* redness; *(due à la honte)* blush; **rougeurs** *(irritation)* rash
rougir [ruʒir] *vi* to blush (**de** with)
rouille [ruj] *nf* rust • **rouillé, -e** *adj* rusty
rouleau, -x [rulo] *nm (de papier, de pellicule)* roll; *(outil)* roller; **r. à pâtisserie** rolling pin; **r. compresseur** steamroller
rouler [rule] **1** *vt* to roll; *(crêpe,*

manches) to roll up **2** *vi (balle)* to roll; *(train, voiture)* to go, to travel
roulette [rulɛt] *nf (de meuble)* castor; *(jeu)* roulette
rousse [rus] *voir* **roux**
rousseur [rusœr] *nf* **tache de r.** freckle • **roussir** *vt (brûler)* to scorch, to singe
route [rut] *nf* road (**de** to); *(itinéraire)* way, route; *Fig (chemin)* path; **code de la r.** *Br* Highway Code, *Am* traffic regulations; **en r.** on the way, en route; **par la r.** by road; *Fig* **faire fausse r.** to be on the wrong track; **mettre qch en r.** to start sth (up); **se mettre en r.** to set out (**pour** for); **une heure de r.** *(en voiture)* an hour's drive; **r. départementale** secondary road, *Br* B road; **r. nationale** *Br* ≃ A-road, *Am* ≃ highway
routier, -ère [rutje, -ɛr] *adj* **carte/ sécurité routière** road map/ safety; **réseau r.** road network
routine [rutin] *nf* routine; **contrôle de r.** routine check
rouvrir* [ruvrir] *vti* to reopen
roux, rousse [ru, rus] **1** *adj (cheveux)* red, ginger; *(personne)* red-haired **2** *nmf* redhead
royal, -e, -aux, -ales [rwajal, -jo] *adj* royal
royaume [rwajom] *nm* kingdom • **Royaume-Uni** *nm* **le R.** the United Kingdom
ruban [rybɑ̃] *nm* ribbon; **r. adhésif** sticky *or* adhesive tape
rubis [rybi] *nm* ruby
rubrique [rybrik] *nf (article)* column; *(catégorie, titre)* heading
ruche [ryʃ] *nf* beehive
rude [ryd] *adj (pénible)* tough; *(hiver, voix)* harsh; *(rêche)* rough
rue [ry] *nf* street; **être à la r.** *(sans domicile)* to be on the streets • **ruelle** *nf* alley(way)

ruer [rɥe] **se ruer** *vpr (foncer)* to rush (**sur** at) • **ruée** *nf* rush; **la r. vers l'or** the gold rush

rugby [rygbi] *nm* rugby • **rugbyman** [rygbiman] (*pl* -**men** [-men]) *nm* rugby player

rugir [ryʒir] *vi* to roar

rugueux, -euse [rygø, -øz] *adj* rough

ruine [rɥin] *nf (destruction, faillite)* ruin; **en r.** *(bâtiment)* in ruins; **tomber en r.** *(bâtiment)* to go to ruin • **ruiner 1** *vt (personne, santé, pays)* to ruin **2 se ruiner** *vpr aussi Fig* to bankrupt oneself

ruisseau, -x [rɥiso] *nm* stream; *(caniveau)* gutter • **ruisseler** *vi* to stream (**de** with)

rumeur [rymœr] *nf (murmure)* murmur; *(nouvelle)* rumour

rupture [ryptyr] *nf* breaking; *(de couple)* break-up

rural, -e, -aux, -ales [ryral, -o] *adj (population)* rural; **vie rurale** country life

rusé, -e [ryze] *adj* cunning, crafty

Russie [rysi] *nf* **la R.** Russia • **russe 1** *adj* Russian **2** *nmf* **R.** Russian **3** *nm (langue)* Russian

rythme [ritm] *nm* rhythm; *(de travail)* rate; *(allure)* pace

Ss

S, s [ɛs] *nm inv* S, s

s' [s] *voir* **se, si**

sa [sa] *voir* **son³**

sable [sabl] *nm* sand

sablé [sable] *nm* shortbread *Br* biscuit *or Am* cookie

sablier [sablije] *nm* egg timer

sabot [sabo] *nm (de cheval)* hoof; *(chaussure)* clog

sabotage [sabɔtaʒ] *nm* sabotage

sabre [sabr] *nm* sabre

sac [sak] *nm* bag; *(grand, en toile)* sack; **s. à main** handbag; **s. à dos** rucksack; **s. de voyage** travel bag

sachant, sache(s), sachent [saʃɑ̃, saʃ] *voir* **savoir**

sachet [saʃɛ] *nm (small) bag*; **s. de thé** teabag

sacré, -e [sakre] *adj (saint)* sacred

sacrifice [sakrifis] *nm* sacrifice • **sacrifier 1** *vt* to sacrifice (**à** to) **2 se sacrifier** *vpr* to sacrifice oneself (**pour** for)

safari [safari] *nm* safari; **faire un s.** to go on safari

safran [safrɑ̃] *nm* saffron

sage [saʒ] *adj (avisé)* wise; *(tranquille)* good • **sage-femme** (*pl* **sages-femmes**) *nf* midwife • **sagesse** *nf (philosophie)* wisdom

Sagittaire [saʒitɛr] *nm* **le S.** *(signe)* Sagittarius

saigner [seɲe] *vi* to bleed; **s. du nez** to have a nosebleed • **saignant, -e** *adj (viande)* rare

saillant, -e [sajɑ̃, -ɑ̃t] *adj* projecting

sain, -e [sɛ̃, sɛn] *adj* healthy; **s. et sauf** safe and sound

saint, -e [sɛ̃, sɛ̃t] **1** *adj (lieu)* holy; **s. Jean** Saint John **2** *nmf* saint • **Saint-Esprit** *nm* **le S.** the Holy Spirit • **Saint-Sylvestre** *nf* **la S.** New Year's Eve

sais [sɛ] *voir* **savoir**

saisir [sezir] *vt* to take hold of; *(brusquement)* to grab; *(occasion)* to seize; *(comprendre)* to grasp

saison [sɛzɔ̃] *nf* season; **en/hors s.** in/out of season; **en haute/ basse s.** in the high/low season; **la s. des pluies** the rainy season • **saisonnier, -ère** *adj* seasonal

sait [sɛ] *voir* **savoir**

salade [salad] *nf (laitue)* lettuce; **s. verte** green salad; **s. de fruits** fruit salad

salaire [salɛr] *nm* salary

salarié, -e [salarje] *nmf (payé au mois)* salaried employee; **salariés** employees

sale [sal] *adj* dirty • **saleté** *nf* dirt; **saletés** *(détritus) Br* rubbish, *Am* garbage; **faire des saletés** to make a mess

salé, -e [sale] *adj (goût, plat)* salty; *(aliment)* salted

salir [salir] **1** *vt* to (make) dirty **2 se salir** *vpr* to get dirty

salle [sal] *nf* room; *(très grande, publique)* hall; *(de cinéma) Br* cinema, *Am* movie theater; **s. à manger** dining room; **s. de bain(s)** bathroom; **s. de classe** classroom; **s. de jeux** games room; **s. d'embarquement** *(d'aé-roport)* departure lounge; **s. d'opération** *(d'hôpital)* operating *Br* theatre *or Am* room

salon [salɔ̃] *nm* living room, *Br* lounge; **s. de coiffure** hairdressing salon; **s. de thé** tea room

salopette [salɔpɛt] *nf Br* dungarees, *Am* overalls

saluer [salɥe] *vt* to greet; *(en partant)* to say goodbye to; *(de la main)* to wave to; *Mil* to salute

salut [saly] *exclam Fam* hi!; *(au revoir)* bye!

samedi [samdi] *nm* Saturday

SAMU [samy] *(abrév* **service d'aide médicale d'urgence)** *nm* emergency medical service

sanction [sɑ̃ksjɔ̃] *nf (approbation, peine)* sanction

sanctuaire [sɑ̃ktɥɛr] *nm* sanctuary

sandale [sɑ̃dal] *nf* sandal

sandwich [sɑ̃dwitʃ] *nm* sandwich

sang [sɑ̃] *nm* blood • **sang-froid** *nm* self-control; **garder son s.** to keep calm; **de s.** in cold blood • **sanglant, -e** *adj* bloody

sanglier [sɑ̃glije] *nm* wild boar

sanglot [sɑ̃glo] *nm* sob • **sangloter** *vi* to sob

sanitaire [sanitɛr] *adj* sanitary

sans [sɑ̃] *(*[sɑ̃z] *before vowel and mute h) prép* without; **s. faire qch** without doing sth; **s. qu'il le sache** without him *or* his knowing; **s. cela, s. quoi** otherwise; **s. importance/travail** unimportant/unemployed; **s. argent/manches** penniless/sleeveless • **sans-abri** *nmf inv* homeless person; **les s.** the homeless • **sans-papiers** *nmf inv* illegal immigrant

santé [sɑ̃te] *nf* health; **en bonne/mauvaise s.** in good/bad health; **(à votre) s.!** *(en trinquant)* cheers!

saoul [su] *adj* = **soûl**

sapeur-pompier [sapœrpɔ̃pje] *(pl* **sapeurs-pompiers)** *nm* fireman

saphir [safir] *nm* sapphire

sapin [sapɛ̃] *nm (arbre, bois)* fir; **s. de Noël** Christmas tree

sardine [sardin] *nf* sardine

satellite [satelit] *nm* satellite; **télévision par s.** satellite television

satin [satɛ̃] *nm* satin

satire [satir] *nf* satire (**contre** on) • **satirique** *adj* satirical

satisfaction [satisfaksjɔ̃] *nf* satisfaction • **satisfaire*** *vt* to satisfy • **satisfaisant, -e** *adj (acceptable)* satisfactory • **satisfait, -e** *adj* satisfied (**de** with)

saturer [satyre] *vt* to saturate (**de** with)

sauce [sos] *nf* sauce

saucisse [sosis] *nf* sausage • **saucisson** *nm* (cold) sausage

sauf [sof] *prép* except

saumon [somɔ̃] *nm* salmon

sauna [sona] *nm* sauna

saupoudrer [sopudre] *vt* to sprinkle (**de** with)

saura, saurait [sora, sorɛ] *voir* **savoir**

saut [so] *nm* jump, leap; **faire un s.** to jump, to leap; **s. à la corde** *Br* skipping, *Am* jumping rope; **s. en hauteur/en longueur** high/long jump

sauter [sote] **1** *vt (franchir)* to jump (over); *(mot, repas, classe)* to skip **2** *vi (personne, animal)* to jump, to leap; **faire s. qch** *(exploser)* to blow sth up; **s. à la corde** *Br* to skip, *Am* to jump rope

sauvage [sovaʒ] *adj (animal, plante)* wild; *(tribu)* primitive; *(cruel)* savage; *(illégal)* unauthorized

sauvegarder [sovgarde] *vt* to safeguard; *Ordinat* to save

sauver [sove] **1** *vt (personne)*

to save, to rescue (**de** from) **2 se sauver** *vpr* (*s'enfuir*) to run away; (*s'échapper*) to escape ● **sauveteur** *nm* rescuer

savant, -e [savã, -ãt] *nm* (*scientifique*) scientist

saveur [savœr] *nf* (*goût*) flavour

savoir* [savwar] *vt* to know; (*nouvelle*) to have heard; **s. lire/ nager** to know how to read/swim; **faire s. à qn que...** to inform sb that...; **à s.** (*c'est-à-dire*) that is, namely; **pas que je sache** not that I know of; **je n'en sais rien** I have no idea, I don't know; **en s. long sur qn/qch** to know a lot about sb/sth ● **savoir-faire** *nm inv* know-how

savon [savõ] *nm* soap

savoureux, -euse [savurø, -øz] *adj* tasty

saxophone [saksɔfɔn] *nm* saxophone

scandale [skãdal] *nm* scandal ● **scandaleux, -euse** *adj* scandalous

Scandinavie [skãdinavi] *nf* **la S.** Scandinavia ● **scandinave 1** *adj* Scandinavian **2** *nmf* **S.** Scandinavian

scanner 1 [skanɛr] *nm* scanner **2** [skane] *vt* to scan

scénario [senarjo] *nm* script, screenplay

scène [sɛn] *nf* (**a**) (*de théâtre*) scene; (*plateau*) stage; **mettre en s.** (*pièce*) to stage; (*film*) to direct (**b**) (*dispute*) scene; **faire une s.** to make a scene

sceptique [sɛptik] *adj Br* sceptical, *Am* skeptical

schéma [ʃema] *nm* diagram

scie [si] *nf* (*outil*) saw

science [sjãs] *nf* science; **sciences naturelles** biology ● **science-**

fiction *nf* science fiction ● **scientifique 1** *adj* scientific **2** *nmf* scientist

scintiller [sɛ̃tije] *vi* to sparkle

scolaire [skɔlɛr] *adj* **année s.** school year

scooter [skutɛr] *nm* (motor) scooter

score [skɔr] *nm* score

scorpion [skɔrpjõ] *nm* scorpion; **le S.** (*signe*) Scorpio

Scotch® [skɔtʃ] (*ruban adhésif*) *Br* sellotape®, *Am* scotch tape® ● **scotcher** *vt Br* to sellotape, *Am* to tape

scout, -e [skut] *nmf* (Boy) Scout, *f* (Girl) Guide

script [skript] *nm* (*écriture*) printing; *Cin* script

scrupule [skrypyl] *nm* scruple; **sans scrupules** (*être*) unscrupulous; (*agir*) unscrupulously ● **scrupuleux, -euse** *adj* scrupulous

scrutin [skrytɛ̃] *nm* (*vote*) ballot; (*élection*) poll

sculpter [skylte] *vt* (*statue, pierre*) to sculpt; (*bois*) to carve; **s. qch dans qch** to sculpt/carve sth out of sth ● **sculpteur** *nm* sculptor ● **sculpture** *nf* (*art, œuvre*) sculpture

SDF [ɛsdeɛf] (*abrév* **sans domicile fixe**) *nmf* homeless person; **les SDF** the homeless

se [sə]

se becomes **s'** [s] before vowel or mute h.

pron personnel (**a**) (*complément direct*) himself; (*féminin*) herself; (*non humain*) itself; (*indéfini*) oneself, *pl* themselves; **il se lave** he washes himself; **ils** *ou* **elles se lavent** they wash themselves (**b**) (*indirect*) to himself/herself/itself/ oneself; **il se lave les mains** he washes his hands; **elle se lave les mains** she washes her hands (c) *(réciproque)* each other; *(indirect)* to each other; **ils s'aiment** they love each other; **ils** *ou* **elles se parlent** they speak to each other (d) *(passif)* **ça se fait** that is done; **ça se vend bien** it sells well

séance [seɑ̃s] *nf (de cinéma)* showing, performance; *(d'assemblée, de travail)* session

seau, -x [so] *nm* bucket

sec, sèche [sɛk, sɛʃ] **1** *adj* dry; *(fruits)* dried; *(ton)* curt; **frapper un coup s.** to knock sharply **2** *nm* **à s.** dry; **au s.** in a dry place

sécher [seʃe] **1** *vti* to dry **2 se sécher** *vpr* to dry oneself • **sèche-cheveux** *nm inv* hair dryer • **sèche-linge** *nm inv Br* tumble dryer, *Am* (clothes) dryer

sécheresse [seʃrɛs] *nf (d'air, de sol, de peau)* dryness; *(manque de pluie)* drought

séchoir [seʃwar] *nm (appareil)* dryer; **s. à linge** clothes horse

second, -e¹ [səgɔ̃, -ɔ̃d] **1** *adj & nmf* second **2** *nm (étage) Br* second floor, *Am* third floor **3** *nf* **seconde** *Rail* second class; *Scol Br* ≃ fifth form, *Am* ≃ tenth grade; *Aut (vitesse)* second (gear) • **secondaire** *adj* secondary; **école s.** *Br* secondary school, *Am* high school

seconde² [səgɔ̃d] *nf (instant)* second

secouer [səkwe] *vt* to shake; *(poussière)* to shake off; **s. qch de qch** *(enlever)* to shake sth out of sth; **s. la tête** *(réponse affirmative)* to nod (one's head); *(réponse négative)* to shake one's head

secours [səkur] *nm* help; *(financier, matériel)* aid; **au s.!**

help!; **porter s. à qn** to give sb help; **roue de s.** spare wheel

secousse [səkus] *nf* jolt, jerk

secret, -ète [səkrɛ, -ɛt] **1** *adj* secret **2** *nm* secret; **en s.** in secret secretly

secrétaire [səkretɛr] *nm* secretary; **s. d'État** Secretary of State • **secrétariat** *nm (bureau)* secretary's office; *(d'organisation internationale)* secretariat

secte [sɛkt] *nf* sect

secteur [sɛktœr] *nm (zone)* area; *Écon* sector

section [sɛksjɔ̃] *nf* section

sécurité [sekyrite] *nf (absence de danger)* safety; *(tranquillité)* security; **S. sociale** *Br* Social Security, *Am* Welfare; **en s.** *(hors de danger)* safe

séduire* [sedɥir] *vt* to charm; *(plaire à)* to appeal to; *(abuser de)* to seduce • **séduction** *nf* attraction • **séduisant, -e** *adj* attractive

ségrégation [segregasjɔ̃] *nf* segregation

Seigneur [sɛɲœr] *nm Rel* **le S.** the Lord

sein [sɛ̃] *nm* breast; **donner le s. à** *(enfant)* to breastfeed; **au s. de** within

Seine [sɛn] *nf* **la S.** the Seine

séisme [seism] *nm* earthquake

seize [sɛz] *adj & nm inv* sixteen **seizième** *adj & nmf* sixteenth

séjour [seʒur] *nm* stay; **s. linguistique** language-learning trip; **(salle de) s.** living room

sel [sɛl] *nm* salt

sélection [selɛksjɔ̃] *nf* selection **sélectionner** *vt* to select

self [sɛlf] *nm Fam* self-service restaurant

selle [sɛl] *nf (de cheval, de vélo)* saddle

selon [səlɔ̃] *prép* according to; **s. que...** depending on whether...

semaine [səmɛn] *nf* week; **en s.** in the week

semblable [sɑ̃blabl] *adj* similar (**à** to)

semblant [sɑ̃blɑ̃] *nm* **faire s.** to pretend (**de faire** to do)

sembler [sɑ̃ble] **1** *vi* to seem (**à** to); **il (me) semble vieux** he seems *or* looks old (to me); **s. faire qch** to seem to do sth **2** *v impersonnel* **il semble que...** it seems that...; **il me semble que...** it seems to me that...

semelle [səmɛl] *nf (de chaussure)* sole; *(intérieure)* insole

semer [səme] *vt (graines)* to sow

semestre [səmɛstr] *nm* half-year; *Univ* semester

séminaire [seminɛr] *nm* seminar

semi-remorque [səmirəmɔrk] (*pl* **semi-remorques**) *nm (camion) Br* articulated lorry, *Am* semi(trailer)

sénat [sena] *nm* senate • **sénateur** *nm* senator

sens [sɑ̃s] *nm* **(a)** *(faculté, raison, instinct)* sense; **avoir le s. de l'humour** to have a sense of humour; **bon sens** common sense **(b)** *(signification)* meaning, sense; **ça n'a pas de s.** that doesn't make sense **(c)** *(direction)* direction; **'s. interdit'** 'no entry'; **à s. unique** *(rue)* one-way; **dans le s. des aiguilles d'une montre** clockwise; **dans le s. inverse des aiguilles d'une montre** *Br* anticlockwise, *Am* counterclockwise

sensation [sɑ̃sasjɔ̃] *nf* feeling, sensation; **faire s.** to create a sensation

sensé, -e [sɑ̃se] *adj* sensible

sensible [sɑ̃sibl] *adj* sensitive (**à** to); *(douloureux)* tender, sore; *(progrès)* noticeable • **sensibilité** *nf* sensitivity

sentence [sɑ̃tɑ̃s] *nf Jur (jugement)* sentence

sentier [sɑ̃tje] *nm* path

sentiment [sɑ̃timɑ̃] *nm* feeling; **avoir le s. que...** to have a feeling that... • **sentimental, -e, -aux, -ales** *adj* sentimental; **vie sentimentale** love life

sentir* [sɑ̃tir] **1** *vt (douleur)* to feel; *(odeur)* to smell; **s. le moisi** to smell musty; **s. le poisson** to smell of fish **2** *vi* to smell; **s. bon/mauvais** to smell good/bad **3 se sentir** *vpr* **se s. humilié** to feel humiliated

séparation [separasjɔ̃] *nf* separation; *(départ)* parting

séparer [separe] **1** *vt* to separate (**de** from) **2 se séparer** *vpr (époux)* to separate (**de** from); **se s. de qch** *(donner, jeter)* to part with sth • **séparé, -e** *adj (distinct)* separate, *(époux)* separated (**de** from)

sept [sɛt] *adj & nm inv* seven

septante [sɛptɑ̃t] *adj & nm inv* *(en Belgique, en Suisse)* seventy

septembre [sɛptɑ̃br] *nm* September

septième [sɛtjɛm] *adj & nmf* seventh; **un s.** a seventh

séquence [sekɑ̃s] *nf* sequence

sera, serait [səra, sərɛ] *voir* **être**

serein, -e [sərɛ̃, -ɛn] *adj* serene

série [seri] *nf* series; *(ensemble)* set

sérieux, -euse [serjø, -jøz] **1** *adj (personne, doute)* serious; *(de bonne foi)* genuine, serious; *(fiable)* reliable **2** *nm* **prendre qn/qch au s.** to take sb/sth seriously

seringue [sərɛ̃g] *nf* syringe

serment [sɛrmɑ̃] *nm (affirmation solennelle)* oath; **prêter s.** to take an oath; *Jur* **sous s.** on *or* under oath

sermon [sɛrmɔ̃] *nm* sermon

séropositif, -ive [serɔpozitif, -iv] *adj Méd* HIV positive

serpent [sɛrpɑ̃] *nm* snake

serre [sɛr] *nf* greenhouse; **l'effet de s.** the greenhouse effect

serrer [sere] **1** *vt (tenir)* to grip; *(nœud, vis)* to tighten; *(poing)* to clench; **s. la main à qn** to shake hands with sb; **s. qn** *(sujet: vêtement)* to be too tight for sb **2** *vi* **s. à droite** to keep (to the) right **3 se serrer** *vpr (se rapprocher)* to squeeze up; **se s. contre** to squeeze up against • **serré, -e** *adj (nœud, vêtement)* tight; *(gens)* packed (together)

serrure [seryr] *nf* lock

serveur, -euse [sɛrvœr, -øz] *nmf* waiter, *f* waitress; *(de bar)* barman, *f* barmaid

service [sɛrvis] *nm* service; *(travail)* duty; *(d'entreprise)* department; **un s.** *(aide)* a favour; **rendre s.** to be of service (**à qn** to sb); **être de s.** to be on duty; **s. (non) compris** service (not) included

serviette [sɛrvjɛt] *nf (pour s'essuyer)* towel; **s. de bain/de toilette** bath/hand towel; **s. de table** napkin, *Br* serviette

servir* [sɛrvir] **1** *vt* to serve (**qch à qn** sb with sth, sth to sb) **2** *vi* to serve; **s. à qch/à faire qch** to be used for sth/to do *or* for doing sth; **ça ne sert à rien** it's useless, it's no good *or* use (**de faire** doing); **s. de qch** to be used for sth, to serve as sth **3 se servir** *vpr (à table)* to help oneself (**de** to); **se s. de qch** *(utiliser)* to use sth

ses [se] *voir* **son²**

session [sesjɔ̃] *nf* session

seuil [sœj] *nm (entrée)* doorway; *Fig (limite)* threshold; *Fig* **au s. de** on the threshold of

seul, -e [sœl] **1** *adj (sans compagnie)* alone; *(unique)* only; **tout s.** by oneself, on one's own, all alone; **se sentir s.** to feel lonely *or* alone; **la seule femme** the only woman; **un s. chat** only one cat; **une seule fois** only once; **pas un s. livre** not a single book; **seuls les garçons...** only the boys... **2** *adv* **(tout) s.** *(rentrer, vivre)* by oneself, alone, on one's own; *(parler)* to oneself **3** *nmf* **le s., la seule** the only one; **un s., une seule** only one, one only; **pas un s.** not (a single) one • **seulement** *adv* only; **non s.... mais encore...** not only... but (also)...

sévère [sevɛr] *adj* severe; *(parents, professeur)* strict

sexe [sɛks] *nm (catégorie, activité)* sex; *(organes)* genitals • **sexiste** *adj & nmf* sexist • **sexuel, -elle** *adj* sexual

shampooing [ʃɑ̃pwɛ̃] *nm* shampoo; **faire un s. à qn** to shampoo sb's hair

short [ʃɔrt] *nm* (pair of) shorts

si [si]

si becomes **s'** [s] before **il, ils**.

1 *conj* if; **si je pouvais** if I could; **s'il vient** if he comes; **si j'étais roi** if I were *or* was king; **je me demande si...** I wonder whether *or* if...; **si on restait?** *(suggestion)* what if we stayed?; **si oui** if so; **si non** if not; **si seulement** if only **2** *adv* **(a)** *(tellement)* so; **pas si riche que tu crois** not as rich as you think; **un si bon dîner** such a good dinner; **si bien que...** so much so that... **(b)** *(après négation)* yes; **tu ne viens pas? – si!** you're not coming? – yes (I am)!

SIDA [sida] (*abrév* **syndrome immunodéficitaire acquis**) *nm* AIDS

siècle [sjɛkl] *nm* century

siège [sjɛʒ] *nm* (a) *(meuble, centre)* & *Pol* seat; *(d'autorité, de parti)* headquarters; **s. social** head office (b) *Mil* siege

sien, sienne [sjɛ̃, sjɛn] 1 *pron possessif* **le s., la sienne, les sien(ne)s** *(d'homme)* his; *(de femme)* hers; *(de chose)* its; **les deux siens** his/her two 2 *nmpl* **les siens** *(sa famille)* one's family

sieste [sjɛst] *nf* siesta; **faire la s.** to have *or* take a nap

siffler [sifle] 1 *vi* to whistle; *(avec un sifflet)* to blow one's whistle; *(gaz, serpent)* to hiss 2 *vt* *(chanson)* to whistle; *Sport (faute, fin de match)* to blow one's whistle for; *(acteur, pièce)* to boo

sifflet [siflɛ] *nm* *(instrument)* whistle; **sifflets** *(de spectateurs)* booing

sigle [sigl] *nm* *(initiales)* abbreviation; *(acronyme)* acronym

signal, -aux [siɲal, -o] *nm* signal; **s. d'alarme** alarm signal; **s. sonore** warning sound

signaler [siɲale] *vt (faire remarquer)* to point out (**à qn** to sb; **que** that); *(par panneau)* to signpost

signature [siɲatyr] *nf* signature

signe [siɲ] *nm* *(indice)* sign, indication; **en s. de protestation** as a sign of protest; **faire s. à qn** *(geste)* to motion (to) sb (**de faire** to do); **faire s. que oui** to nod (one's head); **faire s. que non** to shake one's head

signer [siɲe] *vt* to sign

signification [siɲifikasjɔ̃] *nf* meaning

signifier [siɲifje] *vt* to mean (**que** that)

silence [silɑ̃s] *nm* silence; *Mus* rest; **en s.** in silence; **garder le s.** to keep quiet *or* silent (**sur** about) • **silencieux, -euse** *adj* silent

silhouette [silwɛt] *nf* outline; *(en noir)* silhouette; *(du corps)* figure

similaire [similɛr] *adj* similar

simple [sɛ̃pl] *adj (facile, crédule, sans prétention)* simple; *(fait d'un élément)* single; *(ordinaire)* ordinary • **simplicité** *nf* simplicity

simplifier [sɛ̃plifje] *vt* to simplify

simultané, -e [simyltane] *adj* simultaneous

sincère [sɛ̃sɛr] *adj* sincere • **sincérité** *nf* sincerity; **en toute s.** quite sincerely

singe [sɛ̃ʒ] *nm* monkey

singulier, -ère [sɛ̃gylje, -ɛr] 1 *adj (peu ordinaire)* peculiar, odd 2 *nm Gram* singular; **au s.** in the singular

sinistre [sinistr] 1 *adj (effrayant)* sinister; *(triste)* grim 2 *nm* disaster; *(incendie)* fire • **sinistré, -e** 1 *adj (population, région)* disaster stricken 2 *nmf* disaster victim

sinon [sinɔ̃] *conj (autrement)* otherwise, or else; *(sauf)* except (**que** that); *(si ce n'est)* if not

sinueux, -euse [sinɥø, -øz] *adj* winding

sirène [sirɛn] *nf (d'usine)* siren; *(femme)* mermaid

sirop [siro] *nm* syrup; *(à diluer)* (fruit) cordial; **s. contre la toux** cough mixture

site [sit] *nm (endroit)* site; **s. touristique** place of interest; *Ordinat* **s. Web** website

situation [sitɥasjɔ̃] *nf* situation, position • **situé, -e** *adj (maison)* situated (**à** in) • **situer** 1 *vt (placer)* to situate; *(trouver)* to locate; *(dans le temps)* to set 2 **se situer** *vpr (se trouver)* to be situated

six [sis] ([si] *before consonant*,

[siz] *before vowel) adj & nm inv* six • **sixième** [sizjɛm] **1** *adj & nmf* sixth; **un s.** a sixth **2** *nf Scol Br* ≃ first form, *Am* ≃ sixth grade

sketch [skɛtʃ] *(pl* **sketches**) *nm* sketch

ski [ski] *nm (objet)* ski; *(sport)* skiing; **faire du s.** to ski; **s. alpin** downhill skiing; **s. de fond** cross-country skiing; **s. nautique** water skiing • **skier** *vi* to ski • **skieur, -euse** *nmf* skier

slip [slip] *nm (d'homme)* briefs, underpants; *(de femme)* panties, *Br* knickers

slogan [slɔgã] *nm* slogan

SMIC [smik] *(abrév* **salaire minimum interprofessionnel de croissance)** *nm* = guaranteed minimum wage

smoking [smɔkiŋ] *nm (veston, costume)* dinner jacket, *Am* tuxedo

SNCF [ɛsɛnseɛf] *(abrév* **Société nationale des chemins de fer français)** *nf* = French national railway company

snob [snɔb] **1** *adj* snobbish **2** *nmf* snob • **snobisme** *nm* snobbery

sobre [sɔbr] *adj* sober

sociable [sɔsjabl] *adj* sociable

social, -e, -aux, -ales [sɔsjal, -o] *adj* social • **socialiste** *adj & nmf* socialist

société [sɔsjete] *nf (communauté)* society; *(compagnie)* company; **s. anonyme** *Br* (public) limited company, *Am* corporation

sociologie [sɔsjɔlɔʒi] *nf* sociology • **sociologue** *nmf* sociologist

sœur [sœr] *nf* sister; *(religieuse)* nun

sofa [sɔfa] *nm* sofa, settee

soi [swa] *pron personnel* oneself; **chacun pour s.** every man for himself; **chez s.** at home; **cela va de soi** it's self-evident (**que** that) • **soi-même** *pron* oneself

soi-disant [swadizã] *adj inv* so-called

soie [swa] *nf (tissu)* silk

soient [swa] *voir* **être**

soif [swaf] *nf* thirst (**de** for); **avoir s.** to be thirsty

soigner [swaɲe] *vt (enfant, malade)* to look after, to take care of; *(présentation, travail)* to take care over; **se faire s.** *(malade)* to have (medical) treatment • **soigné, -e** *adj (personne, vêtement)* neat, tidy; *(travail)* careful

soin [swɛ̃] *nm (attention)* care; *Méd* **soins** treatment, care; **avoir** *ou* **prendre s. de qch/de faire qch** to take care of sth/to do sth; **avec s.** carefully, with care

soir [swar] *nm* evening; **le s.** *(chaque soir)* in the evening(s); **à neuf heures du s.** at nine in the evening

soirée [sware] *nf* evening; *(réunion)* party

sois, soit¹ [swa] *voir* **être**

soit² [swa] *conj (à savoir)* that is (to say); **s.... s....** either... or...

soixante [swasãt] *adj & nm inv* sixty • **soixantaine** *nf* **une s. (de)** *(nombre)* (about) sixty; **avoir la s.** *(âge)* to be about sixty

soixante-dix [swasãtdis] *adj & nm inv* seventy • **soixante-dixième** *adj & nmf* seventieth

soixantième [swasãtjɛm] *adj & nmf* sixtieth

soja [sɔʒa] *nm (plante)* soya; **germes de s.** beansprouts

sol [sɔl] *nm* ground; *(plancher)* floor

soldat [sɔlda] *nm* soldier

solde [sɔld] *nm (de compte, à payer)* balance; **en s.** *(acheter)* in the sales, *Am* on sale; **les soldes** the sales

sole [sɔl] *nf (poisson)* sole

soleil [sɔlɛj] *nm* sun; *(chaleur, lumière)* sunshine; **au s.** in the sun; **il fait s.** it's sunny

solennel, -elle [sɔlanɛl] *adj* solemn

solidarité [sɔlidarite] *nf (entre personnes)* solidarity

solide [sɔlid] *adj (objet, état)* solid; *(amitié)* strong; *(personne)* sturdy

solitaire [sɔlitɛr] *adj (par choix)* solitary; *(involontairement)* lonely • **solitude** *nf* solitude; **aimer la s.** to like being alone

solution [sɔlysjɔ̃] *nf (de problème)* solution (**de** to)

sombre [sɔ̃br] *adj* dark; *(triste)* sombre, gloomy; **il fait s.** it's dark

sommaire [sɔmɛr] *nm (table des matières)* contents

somme [sɔm] **1** *nf* sum; **faire la s. de** to add up; **en s., s. toute** in short **2** *nm (sommeil)* nap; **faire un s.** to have a nap

sommeil [sɔmɛj] *nm* sleep; **avoir s.** to feel sleepy • **sommeiller** *vi* to doze

sommelier [sɔməlje] *nm* wine waiter

sommes [sɔm] *voir* **être**

sommet [sɔmɛ] *nm* top; *(de montagne)* summit, top

somnambule [sɔmnɑ̃byl] *nmf* sleepwalker; **être s.** to sleepwalk

somnifère [sɔmnifɛr] *nm* sleeping pill

somnoler [sɔmnɔle] *vi* to doze

son¹ [sɔ̃] *nm (bruit)* sound

son², sa, ses [sɔ̃, sa, se]

sa becomes **son** [sɔ̃n] before a vowel or mute h.

adj possessif (d'homme) his; *(de femme)* her; *(de chose)* its; *(indéfini)* one's; **s. père/sa mère** his/her/one's father/mother; **s. ami(e)** his/her/one's friend

sondage [sɔ̃daʒ] *nm* **s. (d'opinion)** opinion poll

songer [sɔ̃ʒe] **1** *vi* **s. à qch/à faire qch** to think of sth/of doing sth **2** *vt* **s. que...** to think that... • **songeur, -euse** *adj* thoughtful

sonner [sɔne] **1** *vi* to ring; **on a sonné (à la porte)** there's someone at the door **2** *vt (cloche)* to ring; *(l'heure)* to strike

sonnerie [sɔnri] *nf (son)* ring(ing); *(appareil)* bell; *(de téléphone) Br* ringing tone, *Am* ring

sonnette [sɔnɛt] *nf* bell; **s. d'alarme** alarm (bell)

sont [sɔ̃] *voir* **être**

sophistiqué, -e [sɔfistike] *adj* sophisticated

sorbet [sɔrbɛ] *nm* sorbet

sorcière [sɔrsjɛr] *nf* witch

sordide [sɔrdid] *adj (acte, affaire)* sordid; *(maison)* squalid

sort [sɔr] *nm (destin)* fate; *(condition)* lot; *(maléfice)* spell

sorte [sɔrt] *nf* sort, kind (**de** of); **toutes sortes de** all sorts *or* kinds of; **en quelque s.** in a way, as it were; **de (telle) s. que tu apprennes** so that *or* in such a way that you may learn; **faire en s. que...** *(+ subjunctive)* to see to it that...

sortie [sɔrti] *nf (porte)* exit, way out; *(action de sortir)* exit, departure; *(promenade)* walk; *(de film, de disque)* release; *(de livre)* publication; **s. de secours** emergency exit

sortir* [sɔrtir] **1** *(aux* **être**) *vi* to go out, to leave; *(pour s'amuser)* to go out; *(film)* to come out; **s. de** *(endroit)* to leave; *(famille, milieu)* to come from **2** *(aux* **avoir**) *vt* to take out (**de** of); *(film, livre)* to bring out **3 se sortir** *vpr* **s'en s.** *(malade)* to pull through

sosie [sozi] *nm* double

souche [suʃ] *nf (d'arbre)* stump; *(de carnet)* stub, counterfoil

souci [susi] *nm* worry, concern (**de** for); **se faire du s.** to worry, to be worried • **se soucier** *vpr* **se s. de** to be worried *or* concerned about • **soucieux, -euse** *adj* worried, concerned (**de qch** about sth)

soucoupe [sukup] *nf* saucer

soudain, -e [sudɛ̃, -ɛn] **1** *adj* sudden **2** *adv* suddenly

souffle [sufl] *nm (d'air, de vent)* breath, puff; *(respiration)* breathing; **reprendre son s.** to get one's breath back • **souffler** *vt (chuchoter)* to whisper; *(bougie)* to blow out

souffrance [sufrãs] *nf* suffering

souffrir* [sufrir] *vi* to suffer; **s. de** to suffer from; **faire s. qn** *(physiquement)* to hurt sb; *(moralement)* to make sb suffer • **souffrant, -e** *adj* unwell

souhait [swɛ] *nm* wish; **à vos souhaits!** *(après un éternuement)* bless you! • **souhaiter** *vt (bonheur)* to wish for; **s. qch à qn** to wish sb sth; **s. faire qch** to hope to do sth; **s. que...** (+ *subjunctive*) to hope that...

soûl, -e [su, sul] *adj* drunk • **se soûler** *vpr* to get drunk

soulager [sulaʒe] *vt* to relieve (**de** of) • **soulagement** *nm* relief

soulever [suləve] **1** *vt* to lift (up) **2 se soulever** *vpr (personne)* to lift oneself (up); *(se révolter)* to rise up • **soulèvement** [-ɛvmã] *nm (révolte)* uprising

soulier [sulje] *nm* shoe

souligner [suliɲe] *vt aussi Fig* to underline

soumettre* [sumɛtr] **1** *vt (pays, rebelles)* to subdue; *(rapport, demande)* to submit (**à** to); **s. qn à** *(assujettir)* to subject sb to **2 se soumettre** *vpr* to submit (**à** to) • **soumis, -e** *adj* **s. à** subject to

soupçon [supsɔ̃] *nm* suspicion • **soupçonner** *vt* to suspect (**de** of; **d'avoir fait** of doing) • **soupçonneux, -euse** *adj* suspicious

soupe [sup] *nf* soup

souper [supe] **1** *nm* supper **2** *vi* to have supper

soupir [supir] *nm* sigh

souple [supl] *adj (corps, personne)* supple; *(branche)* flexible • **souplesse** *nf (de corps)* suppleness; *(de branche)* flexibility

source [surs] *nf (origine)* source

sourcil [sursi(l)] *nm* eyebrow

sourd, -e [sur, surd] **1** *adj (personne)* deaf (**à** to); *(douleur)* dull; **bruit s.** thump **2** *nmf* deaf person

sourire* [surir] **1** *nm* smile; **faire un s. à qn** to give sb a smile **2** *vi* to smile (**à** at)

souris [suri] *nf (animal) & Ordinat* mouse (*pl* mice)

sournois, -e [surnwa, -waz] *adj* sly

sous [su] *prép (position)* under(neath); *(rang)* under; **s. la pluie** in the rain; **s. l'eau** underwater; **s. le nom de** under the name of; **s. peu** *(bientôt)* shortly

souscription [suskripsjɔ̃] *n* subscription

sous-développé, -e [sudevlɔpe] *(mpl* **sous-développés,** *fpl* **sous-développées)** *adj (pays* underdeveloped

sous-directeur, -trice [sudirɛk tœr, -tris] *(mpl* **sous-directeurs** *fpl* **sous-directrices)** *nmf* assistant manager

sous-entendu [suzãtãdy] *(pl* **sous-entendus)** *nm* insinuation

sous-estimer [suzɛstime] *vt* to underestimate

sous-marin, -e [sumarɛ̃, -in] (mpl **sous-marins**, fpl **sous-marines**) **1** adj underwater **2** nm submarine

soussigné, -e [susiɲe] adj & nmf undersigned; **je s.** I the undersigned

sous-sol [susɔl] (pl **sous-sols**) nm (d'immeuble) basement

sous-titre [sutitr] (pl **sous-titres**) nm subtitle

soustraire* [sustrɛr] vt to remove; Math to take away, to subtract (**de** from); **s. qn à** (danger) to shield or protect sb from • **soustraction** nf Math subtraction

sous-vêtements [suvɛtmɑ̃] nmpl underwear

soutenir* [sut(ə)nir] vt to support, to hold up; **s. que...** to maintain that... • **soutenu, -e** adj (attention, effort) sustained

souterrain, -e [suterɛ̃, -ɛn] adj underground

soutien [sutjɛ̃] nm support; (personne) supporter • **soutien-gorge** (pl **soutiens-gorge**) nm bra

souvenir [suvnir] **1** nm memory; (objet) memento; (pour touristes) souvenir; **en s. de** in memory of **2** se souvenir vpr se **s. de qn/qch** to remember sb/sth; **se s. que...** to remember that...

souvent [suvɑ̃] adv often; **peu s.** seldom; **le plus s.** usually

souverain, -e [suvrɛ̃, -ɛn] nmf sovereign

soyons, soyez [swajɔ̃, swaje] voir **être**

spaghettis [spageti] nmpl spaghetti

sparadrap [sparadra] nm (pour pansement) Br sticking plaster, Am adhesive tape

spécial, -e, -aux, -ales [spesjal, -o] adj special; (bizarre) peculiar

• **spécialement** adv (exprès) specially; (en particulier) especially

spécialiser [spesjalize] **se spécialiser** vpr to specialize (**dans** in) • **spécialiste** nmf specialist • **spécialité** nf Br speciality, Am specialty

spécifier [spesifje] vt to specify (**que** that)

spécifique [spesifik] adj specific

spectacle [spɛktakl] nm (**a**) (vue) sight, spectacle (**b**) (représentation) show • **spectateur, -trice** nmf spectator; (au théâtre, au cinéma) member of the audience; **spectateurs** (au théâtre, au cinéma) audience

spectaculaire [spɛktakylɛr] adj spectacular

spéculation [spekylasjɔ̃] nf speculation

spéléologie [speleɔlɔʒi] nf Br potholing, Am spelunking

sphère [sfɛr] nf sphere

spirituel, -elle [spirituɛl] adj (amusant) witty; (vie) spiritual

spiritueux [spirituø] nmpl (boissons) spirits

splendide [splɑ̃did] adj splendid

spontané, -e [spɔ̃tane] adj spontaneous

sport [spɔr] nm sport; **faire du s.** to do Br sport or Am sports; **voiture/terrain de s.** sports car/ground; **sports d'équipe** team sports; **sports d'hiver** winter sports • **sportif, -ive 1** adj (personne, allure) athletic **2** nmf athlete

spot [spɔt] nm (lampe) spotlight; **s. publicitaire** commercial

square [skwar] nm public garden

squash [skwaʃ] nm (jeu) squash

squelette [skəlɛt] nm skeleton

stable [stabl] adj stable •

stabiliser *vt*, **se stabiliser** *vpr* to stabilize ● **stabilité** *nf* stability

stade [stad] *nm Sport* stadium; *(phase)* stage

stage [staʒ] *nm (période)* training period; *(cours)* (training) course; **faire un s.** to train; **être en s.** to be on a training course ● **stagiaire** *adj & nmf* trainee

stand [stɑ̃d] *nm (d'exposition)* stand, stall

standard [stɑ̃dar] **1** *nm (téléphonique)* switchboard **2** *adj inv (modèle)* standard

standing [stɑ̃diŋ] *nm* **immeuble de (grand) s.** *Br* luxury block of flats, *Am* luxury apartment building

station [stasjɔ̃] *nf (de métro, d'observation, de radio)* station; *(de ski)* resort; *(d'autobus)* stop; **s. de taxis** *Br* taxi rank, *Am* taxi stand; **s. spatiale** space station ● **station-service** *(pl* **stations-service)** *nf* service station, *Br* petrol *or Am* gas station

stationnaire [stasjɔnɛr] *adj* stationary

stationnement [stasjɔnmɑ̃] *nm* parking

statistique [statistik] *nf (donnée)* statistic; *(science)* statistics *(sing)*

statue [staty] *nf* statue

statut [staty] *nm* status

steak [stɛk] *nm* steak

stéréo [stereo] *nf* stereo

stéréotype [stereɔtip] *nm* stereotype

stérile [steril] *adj* sterile; *(terre)* barren ● **stériliser** *vt* to sterilize

stéthoscope [stetɔskɔp] *nm* stethoscope

stimuler [stimyle] *vt* to stimulate ● **stimulation** *nf* stimulation

stock [stɔk] *nm* stock (**de** of); **en s.** in stock

stop [stɔp] **1** *exclam* stop! **2** *nm Aut (panneau)* stop sign

stratégie [strateʒi] *nf* strategy ● **stratégique** *adj* strategic

stress [strɛs] *nm inv* stress ● **stressant, -e** *adj* stressful ● **stressé, -e** *adj* stressed

strict, -e [strikt] *adj (principes, professeur)* strict; **le s. minimum** the bare minimum ● **strictement** [-əmɑ̃] *adv* strictly

structure [stryktyr] *nf* structure ● **structurer** *vt* to structure

studieux, -euse [stydjø, -øz] *adj* studious

studio [stydjo] *nm (de cinéma, de télévision, de peintre)* studio; *(logement) Br* studio flat, *Am* studio apartment

stupéfier [stypefje] *vt* to amaze, to astound ● **stupéfiant, -e 1** *adj* amazing, astounding **2** *nm* drug

stupeur [stypœr] *nf (étonnement)* amazement; *(inertie)* stupor

stupide [stypid] *adj* stupid ● **stupidité** *nf* stupidity

style [stil] *nm* style ● **styliste** *nmf (de mode)* designer

stylo [stilo] *nm* pen; **s. à bille** ballpoint (pen), *Br* biro®; **s. à encre, s.-plume** fountain pen

su, -e [sy] *pp de* **savoir**

subir [sybir] *vt* to undergo; *(conséquences, défaite, perte)* to suffer; **faire s. qch à qn** to subject sb to sth

subjectif, -ive [sybʒɛktif, -iv] *adj* subjective

submerger [sybmɛrʒe] *vt* to submerge; *Fig (envahir)* to overwhelm; *Fig* **submergé de travail** snowed under with work

submersible [sybmɛrsibl] *nm* submarine

subsister [sybziste] *vi (chose)* to remain; *(personne)* to subsist

substance [sypstãs] *nf* substance • **substantiel, -elle** *adj* substantial

substituer [sypstitɥe] **1** *vt* to substitute (à for) **2 se substituer** *vpr* **se s. à qn** to take the place of sb, to substitute for sb • **substitution** *nf* substitution

substitut [sypstity] *nm* substitute (**de** for)

subtil, -e [syptil] *adj* subtle

subvention [sybvãsjɔ̃] *nf* subsidy • **subventionner** *vt* to subsidize

subversif, -ive [sybvɛrsif, -iv] *adj* subversive

suc [syk] *nm (de plante)* sap

succéder [syksede] *vi* **s. à qn** to succeed sb; **s. à qch** to follow sth, to come after sth

succès [syksɛ] *nm* success; **avoir du s.** to be successful; **à s.** *(auteur, film)* successful

successeur [syksɛsœr] *nm* successor • **successif, -ive** *adj* successive • **succession** *nf* succession (**de** of, **à** to), *(série)* sequence (**de** of)

succomber [sykɔ̃be] *vi (mourir)* to die; **s. à** *(céder à)* to succumb to

succulent, -e [sykylã, -ãt] *adj* succulent

sucer [syse] *vt* to suck • **sucette** *nf* lollipop; *(tétine) Br* dummy, *Am* pacifier

sucre [sykr] *nm* sugar; *(morceau)* sugar lump; **s. en poudre, s. semoule** *Br* caster sugar, *Am* finely ground sugar • **sucré, -e** *adj* sweet, *(artificiellement)* sweetened • **sucrier** *nm (récipient)* sugar bowl

sud [syd] **1** *nm* south; **au s.** in the south; *(direction)* (to the) south (**de** of); **du s.** *(vent, direction)* southerly; *(ville)* southern; *(gens)* from or in the south; **l'Afrique du S.** South Africa **2** *adj inv (côte)* south(ern) • **sud-africain, -e** *(mpl*

sud-africains, *fpl* **sud-africaines)** **1** *adj* South African **2** *nmf* **S., S.-Africaine** South African • **sud-américain, -e** *(mpl* **sud-américains,** *fpl* **sud-américaines)** **1** *adj* South American **2** *nmf* **S., S.-Américaine** South American • **sud-est** *nm & adj inv* south-east • **sud-ouest** *nm & adj inv* south-west

Suède [sɥɛd] *nf* **la S.** Sweden • **suédois, -e 1** *adj* Swedish **2** *nmf* **S., Suédoise** Swede **3** *nm (langue)* Swedish

suer [sɥe] *vi* to sweat • **sueur** *nf* sweat; **(tout) en s.** sweating

suffire* [syfir] **1** *vi* to be enough (à for); **ça suffit!** that's enough! **2** *v impersonnel* **il suffit de faire qch** one only has to do sth; **il suffit d'une goutte/d'une heure pour faire qch** a drop/an hour is enough to do sth **3 se suffire** *vpr* **se s. à soi-même** to be self-sufficient

suffisant, -e [syfizã, -ãt] *adj (satisfaisant)* sufficient, adequate; *(vaniteux)* conceited • **suffisamment** [-amã] *adv* sufficiently; **s. de** enough, sufficient

suffoquer [syfɔke] *vti* to choke, to suffocate

suggérer [sygʒere] *vt (proposer)* to suggest (à to; **de faire** doing; **que** + *subjunctive* that) • **suggestion** *nf* suggestion

suicide [sɥisid] *nm* suicide • **se suicider** *vpr* to commit suicide

suis [sɥi] *voir* **être, suivre**

Suisse [sɥis] *nf* **la S.** Switzerland • **suisse 1** *adj* Swiss **2** *nmf* **S.** Swiss; **les Suisses** the Swiss

suite [sɥit] *nf (reste)* rest; *(continuation)* continuation; *(de film, de roman)* sequel; *(série)* series; *(appartement)* suite; **faire s. (à)**

to follow; **par la s.** afterwards; **à la s.** one after another; **à la s. de** *(derrière)* behind; *(événement, maladie)* as a result of; **de s.** *(deux jours)* in a row

suivant, -e [sɥivɑ̃, -ɑ̃t] **1** *adj* next, following; *(ci-après)* following **2** *nmf* next (one); **au s.!** next! • **suivant** *prép (selon)* according to

suivre* [sɥivr] **1** *vt* to follow; *(accompagner)* to accompany; *(cours)* to attend, to go to; **s. l'exemple de qn** to follow sb's example; **s. l'actualité** to follow events *or* the news **2** *vi* to follow; **faire s.** *(courrier, lettre)* to forward; **'à s.'** 'to be continued'

sujet¹, -ette [syʒɛ, -ɛt] *adj* **s. à** *(maladie)* subject to

sujet² [syʒɛ] *nm (question)* subject; *(d'examen)* question; **au s. de** about; **à quel s.?** about what?

super [sypɛr] *adj Fam* great

superbe [sypɛrb] *adj* superb

supérette [sypɛrɛt] *nf* convenience store

superficie [sypɛrfisi] *nf* surface; *(dimensions)* area

superficiel, -elle [sypɛrfisjɛl] *adj* superficial

supérieur, -e [sypɛrjœr] **1** *adj (étages, partie)* upper; *(qualité, air, ton)* superior; **à l'étage s.** on the floor above; **s. à** *(meilleur que)* superior to, better than; *(plus grand que)* above, greater than; **s. à la moyenne** above average; **études supérieures** higher *or* university studies **2** *nmf* superior • **supériorité** *nf* superiority

supermarché [sypɛrmarʃe] *nm* supermarket

superposer [sypɛrpoze] *vt (objets)* to put on top of each other; *(images)* to superimpose

superstitieux, -euse [sypɛrsti-sjø, -øz] *adj* superstitious • **superstition** *nf* superstition

supplanter [syplɑ̃te] *vt* to take the place of

supplément [syplemɑ̃] *nm (argent)* extra charge, supplement; *(de revue, de livre)* supplement; **en s.** extra • **supplémentaire** *adj* extra, additional

supplier [syplie] *vt* **s. qn de faire qch** to beg sb to do sth; **je vous en supplie!** I beg you!

support [sypɔr] *nm* support; *(d'instrument)* stand

supporter¹ [sypɔrte] *vt (malheur, conséquences)* to bear, to endure; *(chaleur)* to withstand; **je ne peux pas la s.** I can't bear her • **supportable** *adj* bearable; *(excusable, passable)* tolerable

supporter² [sypɔrtɛr] *nm (de football)* supporter

supposer [sypoze] *vt* to suppose, to assume (**que** that); *(impliquer)* to imply (**que** that); **à s.** *ou* **en supposant que...** *(+ subjunctive)* supposing (that)...

supprimer [syprime] *vt* to get rid of, to remove; *(mot, passage)* to delete

suprême [syprɛm] *adj* supreme

sur [syr] *prép* on, upon; *(par-dessus)* over; *(au sujet de)* on, about; **six s. dix** six out of ten; **un jour s. deux** every other day; **six mètres s. dix** six metres by ten; **s. votre gauche** to *or* on your left; **mettre/monter s. qch** to put/climb on (to) sth

sûr, -e [syr] *adj* sure, certain (**de** of; **que** that); *(digne de confiance)* reliable; *(lieu)* safe; **s. de soi** self-assured; **bien s.!** of course!

surcharge [syrʃarʒ] *nf (à payer)* surcharge • **surcharger** *vt (voiture, personne)* to overload (**de** with)

surchauffer [syrʃofe] *vt* to overheat

surcroît [syrkrwa] *nm* increase (**de** in); **de s., par s.** in addition

surestimer [syrɛstime] *vt* to overestimate

sûreté [syrte] *nf* safety; *(de l'État)* security; **être en s.** to be safe; **mettre qn/qch en s.** to put sb/sth in a safe place; **pour plus de s.** to be on the safe side

surexcité, -e [syrɛksite] *adj* overexcited

surf [sœrf] *nm Sport* surfing; **faire du s.** to surf, to go surfing

surface [syrfas] *nf* surface; *(étendue)* (surface) area; **(magasin à) grande s.** hypermarket

surgelé, -e [syrʒəle] *adj* frozen ● **surgelés** *nmpl* frozen foods

surgir [syrʒir] *vi* to appear suddenly (**de** from)

sur-le-champ [syrləʃɑ̃] *adv* immediately

surlendemain [syrlɑ̃dəmɛ̃] *nm* **le s.** two days later; **le s. de** two days after

surligner [syrliɲe] *vt* to highlight ● **surligneur** *nm* highlighter (pen)

surmener [syrməne] *vt* to overwork

surmonter [syrmɔ̃te] *vt (obstacle, peur)* to overcome

surnaturel, -elle [syrnatyrɛl] *adj & nm* supernatural

surnom [syrnɔ̃] *nm* nickname

surpasser [syrpase] *vt* to surpass (**en** in)

surpeuplé, -e [syrpœple] *adj* overpopulated

surplus [syrply] *nm* surplus

surprendre* [syrprɑ̃dr] *vt (étonner)* to surprise; *(prendre sur le fait)* to catch ● **surprenant, -e** *adj* surprising ● **surpris, -e** *adj* surprised (**de** at; **que +**

subjunctive that); **je suis s. de te voir** I'm surprised to see you ● **surprise** *nf* surprise; **prendre qn par s.** to catch sb unawares

surréaliste [syrrealist] *adj (poète, peintre)* surrealist

sursauter [syrsote] *vi* to jump

sursis [syrsi] *nm* **un an (de prison) avec s.** a one-year suspended sentence

surtout [syrtu] *adv* especially; *(avant tout)* above all; **s. pas** certainly not

surveiller [syrveje] *vt (garder)* to watch, to keep an eye on; *(contrôler)* to supervise ● **surveillance** *nf* watch (**sur** over); *(de travaux, d'ouvriers)* supervision; *(de police)* surveillance ● **surveillant, -e** *nmf (de lycée)* supervisor (in charge of discipline); *(de prison)* (prison) guard

survêtement [syrvɛtmɑ̃] *nm* tracksuit

survivre* [syrvivr] *vi* to survive (**à qch** sth); **s. à qn** to outlive sb ● **survivant, -e** *nmf* survivor

susceptible [sysɛptibl] *adj (ombrageux)* touchy, sensitive; **s. de** *(interprétations)* open to; **s. de faire qch** likely *or* liable to do sth

susciter [sysite] *vt (sentiment)* to arouse; *(ennuis)* to create

suspect, -e [syspɛ, -ɛkt] **1** *adj* suspicious, suspect; **s. de qch** suspected of sth **2** *nmf* suspect

suspendre [syspɑ̃dr] **1** *vt (accrocher)* to hang (up) (**à** on); *(destituer, interrompre)* to suspend **2 se suspendre** *vpr* **se s. à** to hang from ● **suspendu, -e** *adj* **s. à** hanging from

suspense [syspɛns] *nm* suspense

suspension [syspɑ̃sjɔ̃] *nf (d'hostilités, d'employé, de véhicule)* suspension

suspicion [syspisjɔ̃] *nf* suspicion

suture [sytyr] *nf Méd* **point de s.** stitch

SVP [ɛsvepe] (*abrév* **s'il vous plaît**) please

symbole [sɛ̃bɔl] *nm* symbol ● **symbolique** *adj* symbolic ● **symboliser** *vt* to symbolize

sympathie [sɛ̃pati] *nf (affinité)* liking; *(condoléances)* sympathy; **avoir de la s. pour qn** to be fond of sb ● **sympathique** *adj* nice; *(accueil)* friendly

symptôme [sɛ̃ptom] *nm Méd &* *Fig* symptom

synagogue [sinagɔg] *nf* synagogue

syndicat [sɛ̃dika] *nm (d'ouvriers)* (*Br* trade *or Am* labor) union; *(de patrons)* association; **s. d'initiative** tourist (information) office

syndiquer [sɛ̃dike] **se syndiquer** *vpr (adhérer)* to join a (*Br* trade *or Am* labor) union ● **syndiqué, -e** *nmf* (*Br* trade *or Am* labor) union member

syndrome [sɛ̃drom] *nm Méd &* *Fig* syndrome

synthétique [sɛ̃tetik] *adj* synthetic

système [sistɛm] *nm (structure, réseau)* system ● **systématique** *adj* systematic ● **systématiquement** *adv* systematically

Tt

T, t [te] *nm inv* T, t

t' [t] *voir* **te**

ta [ta] *voir* **ton**[1]

tabac [taba] *nm* tobacco; *(magasin) Br* tobacconist's (shop), *Am* tobacco store

table [tabl] *nf* (**a**) *(meuble)* table; *(d'école)* desk; **mettre/débarrasser la t.** to set *or Br* lay/clear the table; **être à t.** to be sitting at the table; **à t.!** food's ready!; **t. à repasser** ironing board (**b**) *(liste)* table; **t. des matières** table of contents

tableau, -x [tablo] *nm* (**a**) *(peinture)* painting; *(image, description)* picture (**b**) *(panneau)* board; *(graphique)* chart; **t. (noir)** (black)board

tablette [tablɛt] *nf (de chocolat)* bar, slab

tablier [tablije] *nm* apron

tabouret [taburɛ] *nm* stool

tache [taʃ] *nf* mark; *(salissure)* stain • **tacher** *vt (tissu)* to stain

tâche [tɑʃ] *nf* task, job; **tâches ménagères** housework

tâcher [tɑʃe] *vi* **t. de faire qch** to try *or* endeavour to do sth

tact [takt] *nm* tact; **avoir du t.** to be tactful

tactique [taktik] **1** *adj* tactical **2** *nf* tactics *(sing)*; **une t.** a tactic

Tahiti [taiti] *nf* Tahiti • **tahitien, -enne** [taisjɛ̃, -ɛn] **1** *adj* Tahitian **2** *nmf* **T., Tahitienne** Tahitian

taille [taj] *nf* (**a**) *(hauteur)* height; *(dimension, mesure)* size; **de t. moyenne** medium-sized (**b**) *(ceinture)* waist

taille-crayon [tajkrɛjɔ̃] *nm inv* pencil sharpener

tailleur [tajœr] *nm (personne)* tailor; *(costume)* suit

taire* [tɛr] **1** *vi* **faire t. qn** to silence sb **2** **se taire** *vpr (ne rien dire)* to keep quiet (**sur qch** about sth); *(cesser de parler)* to stop talking; **tais-toi!** be quiet!

talent [talɑ̃] *nm* talent; **avoir du t.** to be talented • **talentueux, -euse** *adj* talented

talkie-walkie [talkiwalki] *(pl* **talkies-walkies***) nm* walkie-talkie

talon [talɔ̃] *nm* heel; **(chaussures à) talons hauts** high heels

tambour [tɑ̃bur] *nm* drum • **tambourin** *nm* tambourine

tampon [tɑ̃pɔ̃] *nm* (**a**) *(marque, instrument)* stamp (**b**) *(bouchon)* plug, stopper; *(de coton)* wad, pad; **t. hygiénique** tampon

tamponner [tɑ̃pɔne] *vt (document)* to stamp; *(visage)* to dab

tandis [tɑ̃di] **tandis que** *conj (simultanéité, contraste)* while

tant [tɑ̃] *adv (travailler)* so much (**que** that); **t. de** *(pain, temps)* so much (**que** that); *(gens, choses)* so many (**que** that); **t. de fois** so often, so many times; **t. que** *(autant que)* as much as; *(aussi fort que)* as hard as; *(aussi longtemps que)* as long as; **en t. que** *(considéré comme)* as; **t. mieux!** so much the better!; **t. pis!** too bad!, pity!

tante [tɑ̃t] *nf* aunt

tantôt [tɑ̃to] *adv* (**a**) **t.... t....** sometimes... sometimes... (**b**) *(cet après-midi)* this afternoon

tapageur, -euse [tapaʒœr, -øz] *adj (bruyant)* rowdy

tape [tap] *nf* slap

taper [tape] **1** *vt (frapper)* to hit; **t. qch à la machine** to type sth **2** *vi* **t. à la machine** to type; **t. sur qch** to bang on sth

tapis [tapi] *nm* carpet; **t. roulant** *(pour marchandises)* conveyor belt

tapisser [tapise] *vt (mur)* to (wall)paper • **tapisserie** *nf (papier peint)* wallpaper; *(broderie)* tapestry

taquiner [takine] *vt* to tease

tard [tar] *adv* late; **plus t.** later (on); **au plus t.** at the latest

tarder [tarde] **1** *vi (lettre, saison)* to be a long time coming; **sans t.** without delay; **t. à faire qch** to take one's time doing sth; **elle ne va pas t.** she won't be long **2** *v impersonnel* **il me tarde de le faire** I long to do it

tardif, -ive [tardif, -iv] *adj* late; *(regrets)* belated

tarif [tarif] *nm (prix)* rate; *(de train)* fare; **plein t.** full price; *(de train, bus)* full fare

tarte [tart] *nf* (open) pie, tart • **tartelette** [-əlɛt] *nf* (small) tart

tartine [tartin] *nf* slice of bread • **tartiner** *vt (beurre)* to spread

tas [tɑ] *nm* pile, heap

tasse [tas] *nf* cup; **t. à thé** teacup

tasser [tase] **1** *vt* to pack (**dans** into) **2 se tasser** *vpr (se serrer)* to squeeze up

tâter [tate] *vt* to feel

tâtonner [tatone] *vi* to grope about • **tâtons** *adv* **avancer à t.** to feel one's way (along); **chercher qch à t.** to grope for sth

tatouer [tatwe] *vt (corps, dessin)* to tattoo; **se faire t.** to get a tattoo • **tatouage** *nm* tattoo

taudis [todi] *nm* slum

taupe [top] *nf (animal)* mole

taureau, -x [toro] *nm* bull; **le T.** *(signe)* Taurus • **tauromachie** *nf* bull-fighting

taux [to] *nm* rate; **t. d'intérêt** interest rate

taxe [taks] *nf (impôt)* tax • **taxer** *vt (produit, personne)* to tax

taxi [taksi] *nm* taxi

tchèque [tʃɛk] **1** *adj* Czech; **la République t.** the Czech Republic **2** *nmf* **T.** Czech **3** *nm (langue)* Czech

te [tə]

t' is used before a word beginning with a vowel or mute h.

pron personnel (**a**) *(complément direct)* you; **je te vois** I see you (**b**) *(indirect)* (to) you; **il te parle** he speaks to you; **elle te l'a dit** she told you (**c**) *(réfléchi)* yourself; **tu te laves** you wash yourself

technique [tɛknik] **1** *adj* technical **2** *nf* technique

technologie [tɛknɔlɔʒi] *nf* technology • **technologique** *adj* technological

tee-shirt [tiʃœrt] *nm* tee-shirt

teindre* [tɛ̃dr] **1** *vt* to dye; **t. qch en rouge** to dye sth red **2 se teindre** *vpr* **se t. (les cheveux)** to dye one's hair

teint [tɛ̃] *nm (de visage)* complexion

teinte [tɛ̃t] *nf* shade, tint

teinture [tɛ̃tyr] *nf* dyeing; *(produit)* dye • **teinturerie** [-rri] *nf (boutique)* (dry) cleaner's

tel, telle [tɛl] *adj* such; **un t. livre/homme** such a book/man; **de tels mots** such words; **t. que**

such as, like; **laissez-le t. quel** leave it just as it is; **en tant que t., comme t.** as such; **t. ou t.** such and such; **rien de t. que...** (there's) nothing like...; **t. père t. fils** like father like son

télé [tele] *nf Fam* TV, *Br* telly; **à la t.** on TV, *Br* on the telly

télécommande [telekɔmɑ̃d] *nf* remote control

télécommunications [telekɔmynikasjɔ̃] *nfpl* telecommunications

téléphérique [teleferik] *nm* cable car

téléphone [telefɔn] *nm* (tele)phone; **coup de t.** (phone) call; **passer un coup de t. à qn** to give sb a ring *or* a call; **au t.** on the (tele)phone; **t. portable** mobile phone • **téléphoner** *vi* to (tele)phone; **t. à qn** to (tele)phone sb, to call sb (up) • **téléphonique** *adj* **appel t.** telephone call

télescope [teleskɔp] *nm* telescope

télésiège [telesjɛʒ] *nm* chair lift

téléski [teleski] *nm* ski tow

téléspectateur, -trice [telespɛktatœr, -tris] *nmf* (television) viewer

télétravail [teletravaj] *nm* teleworking

téléviseur [televizœr] *nm* television (set) • **télévision** *nf* television; **à la t.** on television; **regarder la t.** to watch television; **programme de t.** television programme

telle [tɛl] *voir* **tel**

tellement [tɛlmɑ̃] *adv (si)* so; *(tant)* so much; **t. grand que...** so big that...; **crier t. que...** to shout so much that...; **t. de travail** so much work; **t. de soucis** so many worries; **tu aimes ça? – pas t.!** *(pas beaucoup)* do you like it?

– not much *or* a lot!; **personne ne peut le supporter, t. il est bavard** nobody can stand him, he's so talkative

témoigner [temwaɲe] *vi Jur* to give evidence, to testify (**contre** against) • **témoignage** *nm Jur* evidence, testimony; *(récit)* account; **en t. de qch** as a token of sth

témoin [temwɛ̃] *nm Jur* witness; **être t. de qch** to witness sth

tempérament [tɑ̃peramɑ̃] *nm (caractère)* temperament

température [tɑ̃peratyr] *nf* temperature; **avoir de la t.** to have a temperature

tempête [tɑ̃pɛt] *nf* storm

temple [tɑ̃pl] *nm (romain, grec)* temple; *(protestant)* church

temporaire [tɑ̃pɔrɛr] *adj* temporary

temps¹ [tɑ̃] *nm (durée, période, moment)* time; **avoir le t.** to have (the) time (**de faire** to do); **il est t.** it is time (**de faire** to do); **il était t.!** it was about time (too)!; **il est (grand) t. que vous partiez** it's (high) time you left; **ces derniers t.** lately; **de t. en t.** [dətɑ̃zɑ̃tɑ̃], **de t. à autre** [dətɑ̃zaotr] from time to time, now and again; **en même t.** at the same time (**que** as); **à t.** *(arriver)* in time; **à plein t.** *(travailler)* full-time; **à t. partiel** *(travailler)* part-time; **tout le t.** all the time; **t. libre** free time

temps² [tɑ̃] *nm (climat)* weather; **il fait beau/mauvais t.** the weather's fine/bad; **quel t. fait-il?** what's the weather like?

tenace [tənas] *adj* stubborn

tenailles [tənaj] *nfpl (outil)* pincers

tendance [tɑ̃dɑ̃s] *nf (penchant)*

tendency; *(évolution)* trend (**à** towards); **avoir t. à faire qch** to tend to do sth, to have a tendency to do sth

tendre¹ [tɑ̃dr] **1** *vt* to stretch; *(main)* to hold out (**à qn** to sb); *(bras, jambe)* to stretch out; *(muscle)* to tense; *(piège)* to set, to lay; **t. qch à qn** to hold out sth to sb; *Fig* **t. l'oreille** to prick up one's ears **2** *vi* **t. à qch/à faire qch** to tend towards sth/to do sth ● **tendu, -e** *adj (corde)* tight, taut; *(personne, situation, muscle)* tense; *(rapports)* strained

tendre² [tɑ̃dr] *adj (personne)* affectionate (**avec** to); *(parole, regard)* tender, loving; *(viande)* tender ● **tendresse** *nf (affection)* affection, tenderness

tenir* [tənir] **1** *vt (à la main)* to hold; *(promesse, comptes, hôtel)* to keep **2** *vi (nœud)* to hold; *(neige, coiffure)* to last, to hold; *(résister)* to hold out; **t. à qn/ qch** to be attached to sb/sth; **t. à faire qch** to be anxious to do sth; **tenez!** *(prenez)* here (you are)!; **tiens!** *(surprise)* well!, hey! **3 se tenir** *vpr (avoir lieu)* to be held; *(rester)* to remain; **se t. debout** to stand (up); **se t. droit** to stand up/sit up straight; **se t. par la main** to hold hands; **se t. bien** to behave oneself; **se t. à qch** to hold on to sth

tennis [tenis] **1** *nm* tennis; *(terrain)* (tennis) court; **t. de table** table tennis **2** *nmpl Br (chaussures)* tennis shoes

tension [tɑ̃sjɔ̃] *nf* tension; **t. artérielle** blood pressure; **avoir de la t.** to have high blood pressure

tente [tɑ̃t] *nf* tent

tenter¹ [tɑ̃te] *vt (essayer)* to try; **t. de faire qch** to try *or* attempt to do sth ● **tentative** *nf* attempt

tenter² [tɑ̃te] *vt (faire envie à)* to tempt; **tenté de faire qch** tempted to do sth ● **tentant, -e** *adj* tempting ● **tentation** *nf* temptation

tenu, -e¹ [təny] **1** *pp de* **tenir 2** *adj* **t. de faire qch** obliged to do sth; **bien/mal t.** *(maison)* well/badly kept

tenue² [təny] *nf* (**a**) *(vêtements)* clothes, outfit; **t. de soirée** evening dress (**b**) *(conduite)* (good) behaviour

ter [tɛr] *adj* **4 t.** ≃ 4B

terme [tɛrm] *nm* (**a**) *(mot)* term (**b**) *(date limite)* time (limit); **à court/long t.** *(conséquences, projet)* short-/long-term (**c**) **en bons/mauvais termes** on good/ bad terms (**avec qn** with sb)

terminal, -e, -aux, -ales [tɛrminal, -o] **1** *adj* final; *(phase de maladie)* terminal **2** *adj & nf Scol* **(classe) terminale** *Br* ≃ sixth form, *Am* ≃ twelfth grade

terminer [tɛrmine] **1** *vt* to end; *(achever)* to finish **2 se terminer** *vpr* to end (**par** with; **en** in) ● **terminaison** *nf (de mot)* ending

terminus [tɛrminys] *nm* terminus

terne [tɛrn] *adj* dull, drab

terrain [terɛ̃] *nm (sol) & Fig* ground; *(étendue)* land; *(à bâtir)* plot, site; *Géol* terrain; **un t.** a piece of land; **t. de camping** campsite; **t. de football/rugby** football/rugby pitch; **t. de golf** golf course; **t. de jeu(x)** *(pour enfants)* playground; *(stade) Br* playing field, *Am* athletic field; **t. de sport** *Br* sports ground, *Am* athletic field

terrasse [teras] *nf (balcon, plate-forme)* terrace; *(de café) Br* pavement or *Am* sidewalk area; **à la t.** outside

terre [tɛr] *nf (matière, monde)* earth; *(sol)* ground; *(opposé à mer, étendue)* land; **terres** *(domaine)* land, estate; *Él Br* earth, *Am* ground; **la t.** *(le monde)* the earth; **la T.** *(planète)* Earth; **à** *ou* **par t.** *(tomber)* to the ground; *(poser)* on the ground; **par t.** *(assis, couché)* on the ground; **sous t.** underground ● **terre-à-terre** *adj inv* down-to-earth

terreur [tɛrœr] *nf* terror ● **terrible** *adj* awful, terrible

terrifier [terifje] *vt* to terrify ● **terrifiant, -e** *adj* terrifying

terrine [terin] *nf (récipient)* terrine; *(pâté)* pâté

territoire [teritwar] *nm* territory

terroir [terwar] *nm (sol)* soil; *(région)* region

terrorisme [terɔrism] *nm* terrorism ● **terroriste** *adj & nmf* terrorist

tes [te] *voir* **ton**¹

test [tɛst] *nm* test ● **tester** *vt (élève, produit)* to test

testament [tɛstamɑ̃] *nm (document)* will; *Rel* **Ancien/ Nouveau T.** Old/New Testament

tête [tɛt] *nf* head; *(visage)* face; *(de lit, de clou, de cortège)* head; *(de page, de liste)* top, head; *(au football)* header; **à la t. de** *(entreprise, parti)* at the head of; *(classe)* at the top of; **de la t. aux pieds** from head or top to toe; **en t.** *(d'une course)* in the lead; *Fig* **perdre la t.** to lose one's head ● **tête-à-tête** *nm inv* tête-à-tête; **en t.** in private

téter [tete] *vt (lait, biberon)* to suck ● **tétine** *nf (de biberon) Br* teat, *Am* nipple; *(sucette) Br* dummy, *Am* pacifier

têtu, -e [tety] *adj* stubborn

texte [tɛkst] *nm* text

textile [tɛkstil] *adj & nm* textile

texture [tɛkstyr] *nf* texture

TGV [teʒeve] *(abrév* **train à grande vitesse)** *nm* high-speed train

Thaïlande [tailɑ̃d] *nf* **la T.** Thailand ● **thaïlandais, -e 1** *adj* Thai **2** *nmf* **T., Thaïlandaise** Thai

thé [te] *nm* tea ● **théière** *nf* teapot

théâtre [teatr] *nm (art, lieu)* theatre; *(œuvres)* drama; **faire du t.** to act

thème [tɛm] *nm* theme

théorie [teɔri] *nf* theory; **en t.** in theory

thérapie [terapi] *nf* therapy

thermomètre [tɛrmɔmɛtr] *nm* thermometer

thèse [tɛz] *nf* thesis

thon [tɔ̃] *nm* tuna (fish)

thym [tɛ̃] *nm* thyme

tic [tik] *nm (contraction)* twitch, tic

ticket [tikɛ] *nm* ticket

tiède [tjɛd] *adj* lukewarm, tepid; *(vent, climat)* mild

tien, tienne [tjɛ̃, tjɛn] **1** *pron possessif* **le t., la tienne, les tien(ne)s** yours; **les deux tiens** your two **2** *nmpl* **les tiens** *(ta famille)* your family

tiens, tient [tjɛ̃] *voir* **tenir**

tiercé [tjɛrse] *nm (pari)* place betting *(on the horses)*; **jouer au t.** to bet on the horses

tiers, tierce [tjɛr, tjɛrs] **1** *adj* third **2** *nm (fraction)* third; *(personne)* third party ● **Tiers-Monde** *nm* **le T.** the Third World

tige [tiʒ] *nf* stem, stalk

tigre [tigr] *nm* tiger

timbre [tɛ̃br] *nm (vignette)* stamp

timide [timid] *adj (gêné)* shy; *(protestations)* timid ● **timidité** *nf* shyness

tir [tir] *nm (sport, action)* shooting; *(au football)* shot; **t. à l'arc** archery

tirage [tiraʒ] *nm* **(a)** *Typ & Phot (impression)* printing **(b)** *(de loterie)* draw; **t. au sort** drawing lots

tirelire [tirlir] *nf Br* moneybox, *Am* coin bank

tirer [tire] **1** *vt* to pull; *(langue)* to stick out; *(trait, rideaux, conclusion)* to draw; **t. qch de qch** to pull sth out of sth; *(produit)* to extract sth from sth **2** *vi* to pull **(sur** on/at); *(faire feu)* to shoot, to fire **(sur** at); **t. au sort** to draw lots **3 se tirer** *vpr* **se t. de qch** *(travail, problème)* to cope with sth; *(danger, situation)* to get out of sth ● **tire-bouchon** *(pl* **tire-bouchons)** *nm* corkscrew

tiroir [tirwar] *nm* drawer

tisane [tizan] *nf* herbal tea

tisser [tise] *vt* to weave

tissu [tisy] *nm* material, cloth

titre [titr] *nm (nom, qualité)* title; *(diplôme)* qualification; **(gros) t.** *(de journal)* headline; **à t. indicatif** for general information; **t. de transport** ticket

tituber [titybe] *vi* to stagger

titulaire [titylɛr] *nmf (de permis, de poste)* holder **(de** of)

toast [tost] *nm (pain grillé)* piece or slice of toast; *(en buvant)* toast; **porter un t. à** to drink (a toast) to

toboggan [tɔbɔgã] *nm (d'enfant)* slide; *Can (traîneau)* toboggan

toi [twa] *pron personnel* **(a)** *(après une préposition)* you; **avec t.** with you **(b)** *(sujet)* you; **t., tu peux** you may; **c'est t. qui...** it's you who... **(c)** *(réfléchi)* **assieds-t.** sit (yourself) down; **dépêche-t.** hurry up ● **toi-même** *pron* yourself

toile [twal] *nf* **(a)** *(étoffe)* cloth; *(à voile, sac)* canvas; **une t.** a piece

of cloth *or* canvas; *Théât & Fig* **t. de fond** backdrop **(b)** *(tableau* painting, canvas **(c) t. d'araigné** (spider's) web, cobweb

toilette [twalɛt] *nf (action* wash(ing); *(vêtements)* clothes outfit; **faire sa t.** to wash (an dress); **les toilettes** *(W-C) Br* th toilet(s), *Am* the bathroom

toit [twa] *nm* roof

tôle [tol] *nf* sheet metal

tolérer [tɔlere] *vt* to tolerate ● **tolérance** *nf* tolerance ● **tolérant -e** *adj* tolerant **(à l'égard de** of)

tomate [tɔmat] *nf* tomato

tombe [tõb] *nf* grave; *(ave monument)* tomb

tomber [tõbe] *(aux* **être)** *vi* t fall; *(température)* to drop, to fal *(vent)* to drop (off); **t. malade** t fall ill; **t. par terre** to fall (down) **faire t.** to knock down; **laisse t.** *(objet)* to drop; *Fig* **laisser** qn to let sb down; **t. un lundi** t fall on a Monday; **t. sur qch** *(trou ver)* to come across sth ● **tombé** *nf* **la t. de la nuit** nightfall

tome [tɔm] *nm (livre)* volume

ton¹, ta, tes [tõ, ta, te]

ta becomes **ton** [tõn] before a vowel or mute h.

adj possessif your; **t. père** you father; **ta mère** your mother; **ami(e)** your friend

ton² [tõ] *nm (de voix)* tone; *(d couleur)* shade; *Mus (gamme* key; *(hauteur de son)* pitch ● **tonalité** *nf (de téléphone) B* dialling tone, *Am* dial tone

tondre [tõdr] *vt (gazon)* to mou ● **tondeuse** *nf* **t. (à gazon** (lawn)mower

tonifier [tɔnifje] *vt (muscles)* t tone up; *(personne)* to invigorate

tonique [tɔnik] *nm (médicament)* tonic

tonne [tɔn] *nf* metric ton, tonne

tonneau, -x [tɔno] *nm* barrel

tonner [tɔne] *v impersonnel* **il tonne** it's thundering • **tonnerre** *nm* thunder

torche [tɔrʃ] *nf (flamme)* torch; **t. électrique** *Br* torch, *Am* flashlight

torchon [tɔrʃɔ̃] *nm (à vaisselle)* dish towel, *Br* tea towel

tordre [tɔrdr] **1** *vt* to twist; *(linge, cou)* to wring **2 se tordre** *vpr* to twist; **se t. de douleur** to be doubled up with pain; **se t. (de rire)** to split one's sides (laughing); **se t. la cheville** to twist *or* sprain one's ankle • **tordu, -e** *adj* twisted; *(esprit)* warped

tornade [tɔrnad] *nf* tornado

torrent [tɔrɑ̃] *nm* torrent; *Fig* **un t. de larmes** a flood of tears • **torrentiel, -elle** *adj (pluie)* torrential

torse [tɔrs] *nm Anat* chest; **t. nu** stripped to the waist

tort [tɔr] *nm (dommage)* wrong; *(défaut)* fault; **avoir t.** to be wrong **(de faire** to do, in doing); **faire du t. à qn** to harm sb

torticolis [tɔrtikɔli] *nm* **avoir le t.** to have a stiff neck

tortiller [tɔrtije] **1** *vt* to twist **2 se tortiller** *vpr (ver, personne)* to wriggle

tortue [tɔrty] *nf Br* tortoise, *Am* turtle; *(de mer)* turtle

torture [tɔrtyr] *nf* torture • **torturer** *vt* to torture

tôt [to] *adv* early; **au plus t.** at the earliest; **le plus t. possible** as soon as possible; **t. ou tard** sooner or later; **je n'étais pas plus t. sorti que…** no sooner had I gone out than…

total, -e, -aux, -ales [tɔtal, -o] *adj & nm* total; **au t.** all in all, in total • **totalité** *nf* entirety; **la t. de** all of; **en t.** entirely

touche [tuʃ] *nf (de clavier)* key; *(de téléphone)* button; **une t. de** *(un peu de)* a touch *or* hint of

toucher [tuʃe] **1** *nm (sens)* touch; **au t.** to the touch **2** *vt* to touch; *(salaire)* to earn; *(émouvoir)* to touch, to move; *(concerner)* to affect **3** *vi* **t. à** to touch; *(sujet)* to touch on; *(but, fin)* to approach **4 se toucher** *vpr (lignes, mains)* to touch • **touchant, -e** *adj (émouvant)* moving, touching

toujours [tuʒur] *adv (exprime la continuité, la répétition)* always; *(encore)* still; **pour t.** for ever

tour[1] [tur] *nf (bâtiment)* tower; *(immeuble)* tower block, high-rise

tour[2] [tur] *nm (mouvement, tournure)* turn; *(de magie)* trick; *(excursion)* outing; *(à pied)* walk; *(en voiture)* drive; **t. (de piste)** *(de course)* lap; **de dix mètres de t.** ten metres round; **faire le t. de** to go round; **faire le t. du monde** to go round the world; **faire un t.** *(à pied)* to go for a walk; *(en voiture)* to go for a drive; **à t. de rôle** in turn; **t. à t.** in turn

tourbillon [turbijɔ̃] *nm (de vent)* whirlwind; *(d'eau)* whirlpool

tourisme [turism] *nm* tourism • **touriste** *nmf* tourist • **touristique** *adj* **guide t.** tourist guide; **route t.** scenic route

tourmenter [turmɑ̃te] **1** *vt* to torment **2 se tourmenter** *vpr* to worry

tournant [turnɑ̃] *nm (de route)* bend; *Fig (moment)* turning point **(de** in)

tournée [turne] *nf (de facteur, de boissons)* round; *(spectacle)* tour; **faire sa t.** to do one's rounds;

faire la t. de *(magasins, musées)* to go to, *Br* to go round

tourner [turne] **1** *vt* to turn; *(film)* to shoot, to make **2** *vi* to turn; *(tête, toupie)* to spin; *(lait)* to go off; **t. autour de** *(objet)* to go round; *(question)* to centre on; **t. bien/mal** *(évoluer)* to turn out well/badly **3 se tourner** *vpr* to turn (**vers** to, towards)

tournesol [turnəsɔl] *nm* sunflower

tournevis [turnəvis] *nm* screwdriver

tournoi [turnwa] *nm (de tennis)* tournament

tournure [turnyr] *nf (expression)* turn of phrase; **t. des événements** turn of events

Toussaint [tusɛ̃] *nf* **la T.** All Saints' Day

tousser [tuse] *vi* to cough

tout, toute, tous, toutes [tu, tut, tu, tut] **1** *adj* all; **tous les livres** all the books; **t. l'argent/le temps/le village** all the money/time/village; **toute la nuit** all night, the whole (of the) night; **tous (les) deux** both; **tous (les) trois** all three **2** *adj indéfini (chaque)* every, each; *(n'importe quel)* any; **tous les ans/jours** every *or* each year/day; **tous les deux mois** every two months, every second month; **tous les cinq mètres** every five metres; **t. homme** [tutɔm] every *or* any man **3** *pron pl* **tous** [tus] all; **ils sont tous là, tous sont là** they're all there **4** *pron m sing* **tout** everything; **t. ce qui est là** everything that's here; **t. ce que je sais** everything that *or* all that I know; **en t.** *(au total)* in all **5** *adv (tout à fait)* quite; *(très)* very; **t. simplement** quite simply; **t. petit** very small; **t. neuf** brand new; **t. seul** all alone; **t. droit** straight ahead; **t. autour** all around, right round; **t. au début** right at the beginning; **t. en chantant** while singing; **t. rusé qu'il est** *ou* **soit** however sly he may be; **t. à coup** suddenly, all of a sudden; **t. à fait** completely, quite; **t. de suite** at once **6** *nm* **le t.** everything, the lot; **un t.** a whole; **le t. est que...** *(l'important)* the main thing is that...; **pas du t.** not at all; **rien du t.** nothing at all

toutefois [tutfwa] *adv* nevertheless, however

tout-terrain (*pl* **tout-terrains**) [tuterɛ] *adj* **véhicule t.** off-road vehicle; **vélo t.** mountain bike

toux [tu] *nf* cough

toxicomane [tɔksikɔman] *nmf* drug addict

toxique [tɔksik] *adj* toxic

trac [trak] *nm* **le t.** *(peur)* the jitters; *(de candidat)* exam nerves; *(d'acteur)* stage fright; **avoir le t.** to be nervous

trace [tras] *nf (quantité, tache, vestige)* trace; *(marque)* mark; *(de fugitif)* trail; **traces** *(de bête, de pneus)* tracks; **traces de pas** footprints; **disparaître sans laisser de traces** to disappear without trace

tract [trakt] *nm* leaflet

tracteur [traktœr] *nm* tractor

tradition [tradisjɔ̃] *nf* tradition • **traditionnel, -elle** *adj* traditional

traduire* [traduir] *vt* to translate (**de** from; **en** into) • **traducteur, -trice** *nmf* translator • **traduction** *nf* translation

trafic [trafik] *nm (automobile, ferroviaire)* traffic; *(de marchandises)* traffic, trade • **trafiquant, -e** *nmf* trafficker, dealer

tragédie [traʒedi] *nf (pièce de*

théâtre, événement) tragedy • **tragique** *adj* tragic

trahir [trair] **1** *vt* to betray **2 se trahir** *vpr* to give oneself away • **trahison** *nf* betrayal; *(crime)* treason

train [trɛ̃] *nm* **(a)** *(de voyageurs, de marchandises)* train; **t. à grande vitesse** high-speed train; **t. corail** express train; **t. couchettes** sleeper **(b) être en t. de faire qch** to be (busy) doing sth

traîneau, -x [trɛno] *nm* sleigh, *Br* sledge, *Am* sled

traîner [trɛne] **1** *vt* to drag; *(wagon)* to pull **2** *vi (jouets, papiers)* to lie around; *(s'attarder)* to lag behind; *(errer)* to hang around; **t. par terre** *(robe)* to trail (on the ground)

traire* [trɛr] *vt (vache)* to milk

trait [trɛ] *nm* line; *(en dessinant)* stroke; *(caractéristique)* trait; **traits** *(du visage)* features; **d'un t.** *(boire)* in one go; **avoir t. à qch** to relate to sth

traité [trete] *nm (accord)* treaty; **t. de paix** peace treaty

traiter [trete] **1** *vt (se comporter envers, soigner)* to treat; *(problème, sujet)* to deal with; *(marché)* to negotiate; **t. qn de tous les noms** to call sb all the names under the sun **2** *vi* to negotiate, to deal (**avec** with); **t. de** *(sujet)* to deal with • **traitement** [trɛtmɑ̃] *nm* treatment

traiteur [trɛtœr] *nm (fournisseur)* caterer; *(magasin)* delicatessen

traître [trɛtr] *nm* traitor

trajet [traʒɛ] *nm* journey; *(distance)* distance; *(itinéraire)* route

trampoline [trɑ̃pɔlin] *nm* trampoline

tramway [tramwɛ] *nm Br* tram, *Am* streetcar

tranche [trɑ̃ʃ] *nf (morceau)* slice; *(partie)* portion; *(de salaire, d'impôts)* bracket

trancher [trɑ̃ʃe] *vt* to cut; *(difficulté, question)* to settle • **tranchant, -e** *adj* sharp

tranquille [trɑ̃kil] *adj* quiet; *(mer)* calm; *(esprit)* easy; **avoir la conscience t.** to have a clear conscience; **soyez t.** don't worry; **laisser qn/qch t.** to leave sb/sth alone • **tranquillité** *nf* (peace and) quiet; *(d'esprit)* peace of mind

transaction [trɑ̃zaksjɔ̃] *nf (opération)* transaction

transatlantique [trɑ̃zatlɑ̃tik] *adj* transatlantic • **transat** *nm (chaise)* deckchair

transcrire* [trɑ̃skrir] *vt* to transcribe • **transcription** *nf* transcription; *(document)* transcript

transférer [trɑ̃sfere] *vt* to transfer (**à** to) • **transfert** *nm* transfer

transformer [trɑ̃sfɔrme] **1** *vt* to transform, *(matière première)* to process; **t. qch en qch** to turn sth into sth **2 se transformer** *vpr* to change, to be transformed (**en** into) • **transformation** *nf* change, transformation

transfusion [trɑ̃sfyzjɔ̃] *nf* **t. (sanguine)** (blood) transfusion

transition [trɑ̃zisjɔ̃] *nf* transition • **transitoire** *adj (qui passe)* transient; *(provisoire)* transitional

transmettre* [trɑ̃smɛtr] **1** *vt (message, héritage)* to pass on (**à** to); *Radio & TV (émission)* to broadcast **2 se transmettre** *vpr (maladie, tradition)* to be passed on • **transmission** *nf* transmission

transparent, -e [trɑ̃sparɑ̃, -ɑ̃t] *adj* clear, transparent

transpercer [trɑ̃spɛrse] *vt* to pierce

transpirer [trãspire] *vi (suer)* to sweat, to perspire • **transpiration** *nf* perspiration

transplanter [trãsplãte] *vt (organe, plante)* to transplant

transport [trãspɔr] *nm (action)* transport, transportation (**de** of); **transports** *(moyens)* transport; **transports en commun** public transport; **moyen de t.** means of transport

transporter [trãspɔrte] *vt (passagers, marchandises)* to transport

trappe [trap] *nf* trap door

traquer [trake] *vt* to hunt (down)

traumatiser [tromatize] *vt* to traumatize • **traumatisant, -e** *adj* traumatic

travail, -aux [travaj, -o] *nm (activité, lieu, ouvrage)* work; *(à effectuer)* job, task; *(emploi)* job; *Écon & Méd* labour; **travaux** work; *(dans la rue) Br* roadworks, *Am* roadwork; *Scol & Univ* **travaux pratiques** practical work; *Scol & Univ* **travaux dirigés** tutorial

travailler [travaje] **1** *vi (personne)* to work (**à qch** on sth) **2** *vt (discipline, rôle, style)* to work on • **travailleur, -euse 1** *adj* hardworking **2** *nmf* worker

travailliste [travajist] *Pol* **1** *adj* Labour **2** *nmf* member of the Labour party

travers [travɛr] **1** *prép & adv* **à t.** through; **en t. (de)** across **2** *adv* **de t.** *(chapeau, nez)* crooked; **j'ai avalé de t.** it went down the wrong way

traverser [travɛrse] *vt* to cross; *(foule, période, mur)* to go through • **traversée** *nf (voyage)* crossing

trébucher [trebyʃe] *vi* to stumble (**sur** over); **faire t. qn** to trip sb (up)

trèfle [trɛfl] *nm (plante)* clover; *Cartes* clubs

treize [trɛz] *adj & nm inv* thirteen • **treizième** *adj & nmf* thirteenth

tréma [trema] *nm* di(a)eresis

trembler [trãble] *vi* to shake, to tremble; *(de froid, peur)* to tremble (**de** with); **t. pour qn** to fear for sb • **tremblement** [-əmã] *nm (action, frisson)* shaking, trembling; **t. de terre** earthquake

tremper [trãpe] **1** *vt* to soak, to drench; *(plonger)* to dip (**dans** in) **2** *vi* to soak

trente [trãt] *adj & nm inv* thirty; **un t.-trois tours** *(disque)* an LP; **se mettre sur son t. et un** to get all dressed up • **trentaine** *nf* **une t. (de)** *(nombre)* (about) thirty; **avoir la t.** *(âge)* to be about thirty • **trentième** *adj & nmf* thirtieth

très [trɛ] ([trɛz] *before vowel or mute* h) *adv* very; **t. aimé/ critiqué** *(with past participle)* much *or* greatly liked/criticized

trésor [trezɔr] *nm* treasure • **trésorier, -ère** *nmf* treasurer

tresse [trɛs] *nf (cordon)* braid; *(cheveux) Br* plait, *Am* braid • **tresser** [trese] *vt* to braid; *Br (cheveux)* to plait, *Am* to braid

tri [tri] *nm* sorting (out); **faire le t. de** to sort (out); **(centre de) t.** *(des postes)* sorting office • **triage** *nm* sorting (out)

triangle [trijãgl] *nm* triangle • **triangulaire** *adj* triangular

tribu [triby] *nf* tribe

tribunal, -aux [tribynal, -o] *nm Jur* court

tribut [triby] *nm* tribute (**à** to)

tricher [triʃe] *vi* to cheat • **tricheur, -euse** *nmf* cheat

tricolore [trikɔlɔr] *adj (cocarde)* red, white and blue; **le drapeau/ l'équipe t.** the French flag/team

tricot [triko] *nm (activité, ouvrage)* knitting; *(chandail)* sweater, *Br* jumper; **t. de corps** *Br* vest, *Am* undershirt • **tricoter** *vti* to knit

trier [trije] *vt* to sort

trilingue [trilɛ̃g] *adj* trilingual

trimestre [trimɛstr] *nm* quarter; *Scol* term; *Scol* **premier/second/ troisième t.** *Br* autumn *or Am* fall/ winter/summer term • **trimestriel, -elle** *adj (revue)* quarterly

trinquer [trɛ̃ke] *vi* to chink glasses; **t. à la santé de qn** to drink to sb's health

triomphe [trijɔ̃f] *nm* triumph (**sur** over) • **triomphant, -e** *adj* triumphant

triple [tripl] **1** *adj* treble, triple **2** *nm* **le t.** three times as much (**de** as) • **tripler** *vti* to treble, to triple • **triplés, -es** *nmfpl* triplets

triste [trist] *adj* sad; *(lamentable)* unfortunate • **tristesse** *nf* sadness

troc [trɔk] *nm* exchange

trois [trwa] *adj & nm inv* three; **les t. quarts (de)** three quarters (of) • **troisième 1** *adj & nmf* third; **le t. âge** *(vieillesse)* old age **2** *nf Scol Br* ≃ fourth year, *Am* ≃ eighth grade; *Aut (vitesse)* third gear

trombone [trɔ̃bɔn] *nm Mus* trombone; *(agrafe)* paper clip

trompe [trɔ̃p] *nf (d'éléphant)* trunk; *Mus* horn

tromper [trɔ̃pe] **1** *vt (abuser)* to fool (**sur** about); *(être infidèle à)* to be unfaithful to; *(échapper à)* to elude **2 se tromper** *vpr* to be mistaken; **se t. de route** to take the wrong road; **se t. de jour** to get the day wrong • **trompeur, -euse** *adj (apparences)* deceptive, misleading; *(personne)* deceitful

trompette [trɔ̃pɛt] *nf* trumpet

tronc [trɔ̃] *nm (d'arbre)* trunk

trône [tron] *nm* throne

trop [tro] *adv (avec adjectif,* *adverbe)* too; *(avec verbe)* too much; **t. dur/loin** too hard/far; **t. fatigué pour jouer** too tired to play; **lire t.** to read too much; **t. de sel** too much salt; **t. de gens** too many people; **du fromage en t.** too much cheese; **un verre en t.** one glass too many; **t. souvent** too often; **t. peu** not enough • **trop-plein** *(pl* **trop-pleins**) *nm (excédent)* overflow

trophée [trɔfe] *nm* trophy

tropique [trɔpik] *nm* tropic; **sous les tropiques** in the tropics • **tropical, -e, -aux, -ales** *adj* tropical

troquer [trɔke] *vt* to exchange (**contre** for)

trot [tro] *nm* trot; **aller au t.** to trot

trottoir [trɔtwar] *nm Br* pavement, *Am* sidewalk

trou [tru] *nm* hole

trouble [trubl] **1** *adj (liquide)* cloudy; *(image)* blurred; *(affaire)* shady **2** *adv* **voir t.** to see things blurred **3** *nm (désarroi)* distress; *(désordre)* confusion; **troubles** *(de santé)* trouble; *(révolte)* disturbances, troubles

troubler [truble] **1** *vt* to disturb; *(vue)* to blur; *(esprit)* to unsettle; *(inquiéter)* to trouble **2 se troubler** *vpr* to become flustered • **troublant, -e** *adj (détail)* disturbing, disquieting

troupe [trup] *nf (de soldats)* troop; *(de théâtre)* company

troupeau, -x [trupo] *nm (de vaches)* herd; *(de moutons)* flock

trousse [trus] *nf (étui)* case, kit; *(d'écolier)* pencil case; **t. à pharmacie** first-aid kit; **t. de toilette** toilet bag

trouvaille [truvaj] *nf* (lucky) find

trouver [truve] **1** *vt* to find; **aller**

t. qn to go and see sb; **je trouve que...** I think that...; **comment la trouvez-vous?** what do you think of her? **2 se trouver** *vpr* to be; *(être situé)* to be situated; **se t. dans une situation difficile** to find oneself in a difficult situation; **se t. petit** to consider oneself small **3** *v impersonnel* **il se trouve que...** it happens that...

truffe [tryf] *nf* truffle

truffer [tryfe] *vt (remplir)* to stuff (**de** with)

truite [trɥit] *nf* trout

truqué, -e [tryke] *adj (élections, match)* rigged; *(photo)* fake

tsar [dzar] *nm* tsar, czar

Tsigane [tsigan] *nmf* gipsy

tu¹ [ty] *pron personnel* you *(familiar form of address)*

tu², -e [ty] *pp de* **taire**

tuba [tyba] *nm Mus* tuba; *(de plongée)* snorkel

tube [tyb] *nm* tube

tuer [tɥe] **1** *vt* to kill **2 se tuer** *vpr* to kill oneself; *(par accident)* to be killed • **tueur, -euse** *nmf* killer

tulipe [tylip] *nf* tulip

tumeur [tymœr] *nf* tumour

tunique [tynik] *nf* tunic

Tunisie [tynizi] *nf* **la T.** Tunisia • **tunisien, -enne 1** *adj* Tunisian **2**

nmf **T., Tunisienne** Tunisian

tunnel [tynɛl] *nm* tunnel; **le t. sous la Manche** the Channel Tunnel

turban [tyrbɑ̃] *nm* turban

turbulent, -e [tyrbylɑ̃, -ɑ̃t] *adj (enfant)* boisterous

Turquie [tyrki] *nf* **la T.** Turkey **turc, turque 1** *adj* Turkish **2** *nm* **T., Turque** Turk **3** *nm (langue)* Turkish

turquoise [tyrkwaz] *adj in* turquoise

tuteur, -trice [tytœr, -tris] *nm (de mineur)* guardian

tutoyer [tytwaje] *vt* **t. qn** = to address sb using the familiar "tu" form • **tutoiement** *nm* = use of the familiar "tu" instead of the more formal "vous"

tutu [tyty] *nm* tutu

tuyau, -x [tɥijo] *nm* pipe; **t. d'arrosage** hose(pipe); **t. d'échappement** *(de véhicule)* exhaust (pipe)

TVA [tevea] *(abrév* **taxe à la valeur ajoutée)** *nf* VAT

type [tip] *nm (genre)* type **typique** *adj* typical (**de** of)

tyrannie [tirani] *nf* tyranny

Tzigane [tsigan] *nmf* = **Tsigane**

Uu

U, u [y] *nm inv* U, u
UE [yø] (*abrév* **Union européenne**) *nf* EU
ulcère [ylsɛr] *nm* ulcer
ultérieur, -e [ylterjœr] *adj* later, subsequent (**à** to)
ultimatum [yltimatɔm] *nm* ultimatum; **lancer un u. à qn** to give sb an ultimatum
ultime [yltim] *adj* last; (*préparatifs*) final
ultraviolet, -ette [yltravjɔlɛ, -ɛt] *adj & nm* ultraviolet
un, une [œ̃, yn] **1** *article indéfini* a; (*devant voyelle*) an; **une page** a page; **un ange** [œ̃nɑ̃ʒ] an angel **2** *adj* one, **la page un** page one; **un kilo** one kilo; **un par un** one by one **3** *pron & nmf* one; **l'un** one; **les uns** some; **le numéro un** number one; **j'en ai un** I have one; **l'un d'eux, l'une d'elles** one of them; *Journ* **la une** the front page, page one

unanime [ynanim] *adj* unanimous
uni, -e [yni] *adj* (*famille, couple*) close; (*couleur, étoffe*) plain
unième [ynjɛm] *adj* first; **trente et u.** thirty-first; **cent u.** hundred and first
unifier [ynifje] *vt* to unify
uniforme [ynifɔrm] **1** *adj* (*expression*) uniform; (*sol*) even; (*mouvement*) regular **2** *nm* uniform
union [ynjɔ̃] *nf* (*de partis, de consommateurs*) union, association; (*entente*) unity; **l'U. européenne** the European Union
unique [ynik] *adj* (**a**) (*fille, fils*) only; (*espoir, souci*) only, sole; (*prix, parti, salaire, marché*) single (**b**) (*exceptionnel*) unique; **u. en son genre** completely unique • **uniquement** *adv* only, just
unir [ynir] **1** *vt* (*personnes, territoires*) to unite; (*marier*) to join in marriage; (*efforts, qualités*) to combine (**à** with) **2 s'unir** *vpr* (*s'associer*) to unite; (*se marier*) to be joined in marriage; **s'u. à qn** to join forces with sb
unité [ynite] *nf* (*de mesure, élément*) unit; (*cohésion*) unity
univers [ynivɛr] *nm* universe • **universel, -elle** *adj* universal
université [yniversite] *nf* university; **à l'u.** *Br* at university, *Am* in college • **universitaire** *adj* **ville/restaurant u.** university town/refectory
urbain, -e [yrbɛ̃, -ɛn] *adj* urban
urgent, -e [yrʒɑ̃, -ɑ̃t] *adj* urgent • **urgence** *nf* (*de décision, de tâche*) urgency; (*cas d'hôpital*) emergency; **d'u.** urgently; (**service des) urgences** (*d'hôpital*) *Br* casualty (department), *Am* emergency room
urne [yrn] *nf* (*vase*) urn; (*pour voter*) ballot box; **aller aux urnes** to go to the polls
usage [yzaʒ] *nm* (*utilisation*) use; (*coutume*) custom; (*de mot*)

usage; **d'u.** *(habituel)* customary;
à l'u. de for (the use of); **hors
d'u.** out of order ● **usagé, -e** *adj
(vêtement)* worn; *(billet)* used ●
usager *nm* user

user [yze] *vt (vêtement)* to wear
out; *(personne)* to wear down;
(consommer) to use (up) ● **usé,
-e** *adj (tissu, personne)* worn out;
eaux usées dirty *or* waste water

usine [yzin] *nf* factory

ustensile [ystãsil] *nm* implement;
u. de cuisine kitchen utensil

usuel, -elle [yzɥɛl] *adj* everyday

utile [ytil] *adj* useful (**à** to)

utiliser [ytilize] *vt* to use ●
utilisateur, -trice *nmf* user ●
utilisation *nf* use ● **utilité** *nf*
usefulness; **d'une grande u.** very
useful

utopie [ytɔpi] *nf* utopia

UV [yve] *(abrév* **ultraviolet)** *nm
inv* UV

Vv

V, v [ve] *nm inv* V, v
va [va] *voir* **aller**[1]
vacances [vakɑ̃s] *nfpl Br* holiday(s), *Am* vacation; **partir en v.** to go on *Br* holiday *or Am* vacation; **les grandes v.** the summer *Br* holidays *or Am* vacation • **vacancier, -ère** *nf Br* holidaymaker, *Am* vacationer
vacant, -e [vakɑ̃, -ɑ̃t] *adj* vacant
vacarme [vakarm] *nm* din, uproar
vaccin [vaksɛ̃] *nm* vaccine; **faire un v. à qn** to vaccinate sb • **vaccination** *nf* vaccination • **vacciner** *vt* to vaccinate; **se faire v.** to get vaccinated (**contre** against)
vache [vaʃ] *nf* cow
vaciller [vasije] *vi* to sway; *(flamme, lumière)* to flicker
vagabond, -e [vagabɔ̃, -ɔ̃d] *nmf (clochard)* vagrant, tramp
vague[1] [vag] *adj* vague
vague[2] [vag] *nf (de mer)* & *Fig* wave; **v. de chaleur** heat wave
vaille, vailles *voir* **valoir**
vain, -e [vɛ̃, vɛn] *adj (sans résultat)* futile; *(vaniteux)* vain; **en v.** in vain • **vainement** *adv* in vain
vaincre* [vɛ̃kr] *vt (adversaire)* to defeat; *Fig (maladie, difficulté)* to overcome • **vaincu, -e** *nmf (perdant)* loser • **vainqueur** *nm (gagnant)* winner
vais [ve] *voir* **aller**[1]
vaisseau, -x [veso] *nm (bateau)* vessel; *Anat* **v. sanguin** blood vessel

vaisselle [vɛsɛl] *nf* crockery; **faire la v.** to do the washing up, to do the dishes
valable [valabl] *adj (billet, motif)* valid
valet [valɛ] *nm Cartes* jack
valeur [valœr] *nf (prix, qualité)* value; *(mérite)* worth; **avoir de la v.** to be valuable; **mettre qch en v.** *(faire ressortir)* to highlight sth
valide [valid] *adj (personne)* fit, able-bodied; *(billet)* valid • **valider** *vt* to validate; *(titre de transport)* to stamp
valise [valiz] *nf* suitcase; **faire ses valises** to pack (one's bags)
vallée [vale] *nf* valley
valoir* [valwar] **1** *vi (avoir pour valeur)* to be worth; *(s'appliquer)* to apply (**pour** to); **v. mille euros/cher** to be worth a thousand euros/a lot; **il vaut mieux rester** it's better to stay; **il vaut mieux que j'attende** I'd better wait; **faire v. qch** *(faire ressortir)* to highlight sth; *(droit)* to assert sth **2 se valoir** *upr (objets, personnes)* to be as good as each other
valse [vals] *nf* waltz
valve [valv] *nf* valve
vampire [vɑ̃pir] *nm* vampire
vandale [vɑ̃dal] *nmf* vandal • **vandalisme** *nm* vandalism
vanille [vanij] *nf* vanilla
vaniteux, -euse [vanitø, -øz] *adj* vain, conceited
vanter [vɑ̃te] **se vanter** *upr* to boast, to brag (**de** about, of)

vapeur [vapœr] *nf* steam; **cuire qch à la v.** to steam sth

vaporiser [vapɔrize] *vt* to spray

varappe [varap] *nf* rock-climbing

variable [varjabl] *adj* variable; *(humeur, temps)* changeable • **variation** *nf* variation

varicelle [varisɛl] *nf* chickenpox

varier [varje] *vti* to vary (**de** from) • **varié, -e** *adj (diversifié)* varied • **variété** *nf* variety

vas [va] *voir* **aller¹**

vase [vaz] *nm (récipient)* vase

vaste [vast] *adj* vast, huge

Vatican [vatikã] *nm* **le V.** the Vatican

vaut [vo] *voir* **valoir**

veau, -x [vo] *nm (animal)* calf; *(viande)* veal

vécu, -e [veky] *pp de* **vivre**

vedette [vədɛt] *nf (acteur)* star

végétarien, -enne [veʒetarjɛ̃, -ɛn] *adj & nmf* vegetarian

véhicule [veikyl] *nm* vehicle

veille [vɛj] *nf (jour précédent)* **la v.** the day before (**de qch** sth); **la v. de Noël** Christmas Eve; **à la v. de qch** *(événement)* on the eve of sth

veiller [veje] *vi* to stay up *or* awake; **v. à qch** to see to sth; **v. à ce que...** *(+ subjunctive)* to make sure that...; **v. sur qn** to watch over sb

veine [vɛn] *nf Anat* vein

vélo [velo] *nm* bike; *(activité)* cycling; **faire du v.** to go cycling

velours [vəlur] *nm* velvet; **v. côtelé** corduroy • **velouté** *nm* **v. d'asperges** cream of asparagus soup

vendange [vãdãʒ] *nf (récolte)* grape harvest; **faire les vendanges** to pick the grapes

vendre [vãdr] **1** *vt* to sell; **v. qch à qn** to sell sb sth, to sell sth to sb; **v. qch dix euros** to sell sth for ten euros; **'à v.'** 'for sale' **se vendre** *vpr* to be sold; **ça se vend bien** it sells well • **vendeur, -euse** *nmf (de magasin) Br* sales *or* shop assistant, *Am* sales clerk; *(non professionnel)* seller

vendredi [vãdrədi] *nm* Friday; **V. saint** Good Friday

vénéneux, -euse [venenø, -øz] *adj* poisonous

venger [vãʒe] **se venger** *vpr* to get one's revenge (**de qn** on sb; **de qch** for sth) • **vengeance** *nf* revenge, vengeance

venin [vənɛ̃] *nm* poison, venom • **venimeux, -euse** *adj* poisonous, venomous

venir* [vənir] *(aux* **être)** *vi* to come (**de** from); **v. faire qch** to come to do sth; **viens me voir** come and see me; **je viens/venais d'arriver** I've/I'd just arrived; **les jours qui viennent** the coming days; **faire v. qn** to send for sb

vent [vã] *nm* wind; **il y a** *ou* **il fait du v.** it's windy

vente [vãt] *nf* sale; **en v.** on sale; **v. par correspondance** mail order

ventilateur [vãtilatœr] *nm (électrique)* fan • **ventilation** *nf* ventilation • **ventiler** *vt* to ventilate

ventre [vãtr] *nm* stomach, belly; **à plat v.** flat on one's face; **avoir mal au v.** to have (a) stomach ache

venu, -e [vəny] **1** *pp de* **venir 2** *nmf* **le premier v.** anyone

ver [vɛr] *nm* worm; **v. de terre** (earth)worm

véranda [verãda] *nf* veranda(h); *(en verre)* conservatory

verbe [vɛrb] *nm* verb

verdict [vɛrdikt] *nm* verdict

verdure [vɛrdyr] *nf* greenery

verglas [vɛrgla] *nm Br* (black) ice, *Am* glaze

vérifier [verifje] *vt* to check, to verify; *(comptes)* to audit ● **vérification** *nf* checking, verification; *(de comptes)* audit(ing)

véritable [veritabl] *adj (histoire, ami)* true, real; *(cuir, or, nom)* real, genuine; *(en intensif)* real

vérité [verite] *nf (de déclaration)* truth; *(sincérité)* sincerity; **en v.** in fact; **dire la v.** to tell the truth

vernir [vɛrnir] *vt* to varnish ● **verni, -e** *adj* varnished ● **vernis** *nm* varnish; **v. à ongles** nail polish *or Br* varnish ● **vernissage** *nm (d'exposition)* opening

verra, verrait [vera, vɛrɛ] *voir* **voir**

verre [vɛr] *nm (substance, récipient)* glass; **prendre un v.** to have a drink; **v. de bière** glass of beer; **v. à bière** beer glass

verrou [vɛru] *nm* bolt; **fermer qch au v.** to bolt sth

verrouiller [vɛruje] *vt* to bolt

verrue [vɛry] *nf* wart; **v. plantaire** verruca

vers¹ [vɛr] *prép (direction)* to-ward(s); *(approximation)* around, about

vers² [vɛr] *nm (de poème)* line; **des vers** *(poésie)* verse

verse [vɛrs] **à verse** *adv* **il pleut à v.** it's pouring (with rain)

Verseau [vɛrso] *nm (signe)* Aquarius

verser [vɛrse] *vt* to pour (out); *(argent)* to pay **(sur un compte** into an account) ● **versement** [-əmɑ̃] *nm* payment

version [vɛrsjɔ̃] *nf* version; *Cin* **en v. originale** in the original language; **en v. française** dubbed *(into French)*

verso [vɛrso] *nm* back (of the page); **'voir au v.'** 'see overleaf'

vert, -e [vɛr, vɛrt] **1** *adj* green **2** *nm* green; *Pol* **les Verts** the Greens

vertical, -e, -aux, -ales [vertikal, -o] *adj & nf* vertical; **à la verticale** vertically

vertige [vɛrtiʒ] *nm (étourdissement)* dizziness; *(peur du vide)* vertigo; **vertiges** dizzy spells; **avoir le v.** to be *or* feel dizzy

vertu [vɛrty] *nf* virtue; **en v. de** in accordance with ● **vertueux, -euse** *adj* virtuous

vessie [vesi] *nf* bladder

veste [vɛst] *nf* jacket, coat

vestiaire [vɛstjɛr] *nm (de théâtre)* cloakroom; *(de piscine, de stade)* changing room, *Am* locker room

vestibule [vɛstibyl] *nm* (entrance) hall

vestiges [vɛstiʒ] *nmpl (ruines)* remains; *(traces)* relics

veston [vɛstɔ̃] *nm* (suit) jacket

vêtement [vɛtmɑ̃] *nm* garment; **vêtements** clothes; **vêtements de sport** sportswear

vétéran [veterɑ̃] *nm* veteran

vétérinaire [veterinɛr] *nmf* vet

veto [veto] *nm inv* veto; **opposer son v. à qch** to veto sth

vêtu, -e [vety] *adj* dressed **(de** in)

veuf, veuve [vœf, vœv] **1** *adj* widowed **2** *nmf* widower *f* widow

veuille(s), veuillent [vœj] *voir* **vouloir**

veut, veux [vø] *voir* **vouloir**

vexer [vɛkse] **1** *vt* to upset, to hurt **2 se vexer** *vpr* to get upset **(de** at)

VF [veɛf] *(abrév* **version française)** *nf* **film en VF** film dubbed into French

viande [vjɑ̃d] *nf* meat

vibrer [vibre] *vi* to vibrate ● **vibration** *nf* vibration

vice [vis] *nm (perversité)* vice; *(défectuosité)* defect

vice versa [vis(e)versa] *adv* vice versa

vicieux, -euse [visjø, -øz] *adj (pervers)* depraved; *(perfide)* sly

victime [viktim] *nf* victim; *(d'accident)* casualty; **être v. de** *(accident, attentat)* to be the victim of

victoire [viktwar] *nf* victory • **victorieux, -euse** *adj* victorious; *(équipe)* winning

vide [vid] **1** *adj* empty **2** *nm (espace)* empty space; *Phys* vacuum; **regarder dans le v.** to stare into space; **emballé sous v.** vacuum-packed; **à v.** empty

vidéo [video] *adj inv & nf* video • **vidéoclip** *nm* (music) video

vider [vide] *vt*, **se vider** *vpr* to empty • **videur** *nm (de boîte de nuit)* bouncer

vie [vi] *nf* life; *(durée)* lifetime; **en v.** living; **à v., pour la v.** for life

vieil, vieille [vjɛj] *voir* **vieux**

vieillard [vjɛjar] *nm* old man; **les vieillards** old people • **vieillesse** *nf* old age

vieillir [vjejir] *vi* to grow old; *(changer)* to age; *(théorie, mot)* to become old-fashioned • **vieilli, -e** *adj (démodé)* old-fashioned • **vieillissement** *nm* ageing

vieillot, -otte [vjɛjo, -ɔt] *adj* old-fashioned

Vienne [vjɛn] *nm ou f* Vienna

viens, vient [vjɛ̃] *voir* **venir**

vierge [vjɛrʒ] **1** *adj (femme, neige)* virgin; *(feuille de papier, film)* blank; **être v.** *(femme, homme)* to be a virgin **2** *nf* virgin; **la V.** *(signe)* Virgo

vieux, vieille, vieux, vieilles [vjø, vjej]

vieil is used before masculine singular nouns beginning with a vowel or mute h.

1 *adj* old; **être v. jeu** *(adj inv)* to be old-fashioned; **se faire v.** to get old **2** *nmf* old man, *f* old woman; **les vieux** old people

vif, vive [vif, viv] *adj (personne)* lively; *(imagination)* vivid; *(intelligence, douleur)* sharp; *(intérêt, satisfaction)* great; *(couleur, lumière)* bright

vigilant, -e [viʒilɑ̃, -ɑ̃t] *adj* vigilant

vigne [viɲ] *nf* vine • **vigneron, -onne** [-ərɔ̃, -ɔn] *nmf* wine grower • **vignoble** *nm* vineyard;

vignette [viɲɛt] *nf (de véhicule)* road tax sticker, *Br* ≃ road tax disc; *(de médicament)* label *(for reimbursement by Social Security)*

vigueur [vigœr] *nf* vigour; **entrer en v.** *(loi)* to come into force • **vigoureux, -euse** *adj (personne)* vigorous

vilain, -e [vilɛ̃, -ɛn] *adj (laid)* ugly; *(peu sage)* naughty

villa [vila] *nf* villa

village [vilaʒ] *nm* village

ville [vil] *nf* town; *(grande)* city; **aller/être en v.** to go (in)to/be in town

vin [vɛ̃] *nm* wine

vinaigre [vinɛgr] *nm* vinegar • **vinaigrette** *nf (sauce)* vinaigrette, *Br* French dressing, *Am* Italian dressing

vingt [vɛ̃] ([vɛ̃t] *before vowel or mute h and in numbers 22–29) adj & nm inv* twenty; **v. et un** twenty-one • **vingtaine** *nf* **une v. (de)** *(nombre)* about twenty • **vingtième** *adj & nmf* twentieth

viol [vjɔl] *nm* rape • **violer** *vt* to rape • **violeur** *nm* rapist

violent, -e [vjɔlɑ̃, -ɑ̃t] *adj* violent;
• **violence** *nf* violence; **acte de v.**
act of violence
violet, -ette [vjɔlɛ, -ɛt] **1** *adj &*
nm (couleur) purple **2** *nf* **violette**
(fleur) violet
violon [vjɔlɔ̃] *nm* violin •
violoncelle *nm* cello
virage [viraʒ] *nm (de route)* bend
virer [vire] **1** *vi* to turn; **v. au bleu**
to turn blue **2** *vt* Fin *(somme)* to
transfer (**à** to) • **virement** *nm* Fin
transfer
virgule [virgyl] *nf (ponctuation)*
comma; *Math* (decimal) point; **2**
v. 5 2 point 5
virtuel, -elle [virtɥɛl] *adj* virtual;
réalité virtuelle virtual reality
virus [virys] *nm* Méd & Ordinat
virus
vis¹ [vi] *voir* **vivre, voir**
vis² [vis] *nf* screw
visa [viza] *nm (de passeport)* visa
visage [vizaʒ] *nm* face
vis-à-vis [vizavi] *prep* **v. de**
(en face de) opposite; *(envers)*
towards
viser [vize] **1** *vt (cible)* to aim at;
(concerner) to be aimed at **2** *vi* to
aim (**à** at); **v. à faire qch** to aim
to do sth
visible [vizibl] *adj* visible •
visibilité *nf* visibility
visière [vizjɛr] *nf (de casquette)*
peak; *(de casque)* visor
vision [vizjɔ̃] *nf (conception,*
image) vision; *(sens)* sight
visite [vizit] *nf* visit; **rendre v. à**
qn to visit sb; **avoir de la v.** to
have a visitor/visitors; **v. médicale**
medical examination; **v. guidée**
guided tour • **visiter** *vt (lieu*
touristique, patient) to visit •
visiteur, -euse *nmf* visitor
visqueux, -euse [viskø, -øz] *adj*
viscous; *(surface)* sticky

visser [vise] *vt* to screw on
visuel, -elle [vizɥɛl] *adj* visual
vit [vi] *voir* **vivre, voir**
vital, -e, -aux, -ales [vital, -o]
adj vital • **vitalité** *nf* vitality
vitamine [vitamin] *nf* vitamin
vite [vit] *adv (rapidement)* quickly,
fast; *(sous peu)* soon
vitesse [vitɛs] *nf* speed; *(de mo-*
teur) gear; **à toute v.** at top speed
vitre [vitr] *nf* (window)pane;
(de véhicule, de train) window
• **vitrail, -aux** *nm* stained-glass
window • **vitré, -e** *adj* **porte**
vitrée glass door
vitrine [vitrin] *nf* (shop) window
vivant, -e [vivɑ̃, -ɑ̃t] **1** *adj (en vie)*
alive; *(récit, rue, enfant)* lively **2**
les vivants *nmpl* the living
vive¹ [viv] *voir* **vif**
vive² [viv] *exclam* **v. le roi!** long
live the king!
vivement [vivmɑ̃] *adv* quickly;
(répliquer) sharply; *(regretter)*
deeply
vivre* [vivr] **1** *vi* to live; **elle vit**
encore she's still alive or living;
v. de *(fruits)* to live on; *(travail)* to
live by **2** *vt (vie)* to live; *(aventure,*
époque) to live through
VO [veo] *(abrév* **version**
originale) *nf* **film en VO** film in
the original language
vocal, -e, -aux, -ales [vɔkal, -o]
adj vocal
vocation [vɔkasjɔ̃] *nf* vocation
vœu, -x [vø] *nm (souhait)* wish;
(promesse) vow; **faire un v.** to
make a wish; **meilleurs vœux!**
best wishes!
vogue [vɔg] *nf* fashion, vogue; **en**
v. in vogue
voici [vwasi] *prep* here is/are; **me**
v. here I am; **v. dix ans** ten years
ago; **v. dix ans que...** it's ten
years since...

voie [vwa] *nf (route)* road; *(rails)* track, line; *(partie de route)* lane; *(chemin)* way; *(de gare)* platform; **pays en v. de développement** developing country; **v. sans issue** dead end

voilà [vwala] *prép* there is/are; **les v.** there they are; **le v. parti** he has left now; **v. dix ans** ten years ago; **v. dix ans que...** it's ten years since...

voile¹ [vwal] *nm* veil ● **voilé, -e** *adj (femme, allusion)* veiled; *(photo, lumière)* hazy

voile² [vwal] *nf (de bateau)* sail; *(sport)* sailing; **faire de la v.** to sail ● **voilier** *nm* sailing boat; *(de plaisance)* yacht

voir* [vwar] **1** *vt* to see; **faire v. qch** to show sth; **v. qn faire qch** to see sb do/doing sth **2** *vi* to see; **fais v.** let me see, show me; **ça n'a rien à v. avec ça** that's got nothing to do with that **3 se voir** *vpr (soi-même)* to see oneself; *(se fréquenter)* to see each other; *(objet, attitude)* to be seen; *(reprise, tache)* to show

voisin, -e [vwazɛ̃, -in] **1** *adj (pays, village)* Br neighbouring, Am neighboring; *(maison, pièce)* next (**de** to) **2** *nmf* Br neighbour, Am neighbor

voiture [vwatyr] *nf* car; *(de train)* carriage, Br coach, Am car; **v. de course** racing car

voix [vwa] *nf* voice; *(d'électeur)* vote; **à v. basse** in a whisper; **à haute v.** aloud

vol [vɔl] *nm* **(a)** *(d'avion, d'oiseau)* flight; *(groupe d'oiseaux)* flock, flight; **attraper qch au v.** to catch sth in the air **(b)** *(délit)* theft; **v. à main armée** armed robbery; **v. à la tire** bag-snatching

volaille [vɔlaj] *nf* **la v.** poultry

volcan [vɔlkɑ̃] *nm* volcano ● **volcanique** *adj* volcanic

voler¹ [vɔle] *vi (oiseau, avion)* to fly ● **volant** *nm (de véhicule)* steering wheel; *(de badminton)* shuttlecock

voler² [vɔle] **1** *vt (prendre)* to steal (**à** from); **v. qn** to rob sb **2** *vi (prendre)* to steal

volet [vɔlɛ] *nm (de fenêtre)* shutter; *(de programme)* section

voleur, -euse [vɔlœr, -øz] *nmf* thief; **au v.!** stop thief!

volley-ball [vɔlebol] *nm* volleyball

volontaire [vɔlɔ̃tɛr] **1** *adj (geste, omission)* deliberate; *(travail)* voluntary **2** *nmf* volunteer ● **volontariat** *nm* voluntary work

volonté [vɔlɔ̃te] *nf (faculté, intention)* will; *(détermination)* willpower; **bonne v.** willingness; **mauvaise v.** unwillingness; **à v.** *(quantité)* as much as desired

volontiers [vɔlɔ̃tje] *adv* gladly, willingly; **v.!** *(oui)* I'd love to!

voltiger [vɔltiʒe] *vi (feuilles)* to flutter

volume [vɔlym] *nm (de boîte, de son, livre)* volume ● **volumineux, -euse** *adj* bulky, voluminous

voluptueux, -euse [vɔlyptɥø, -øz] *adj* voluptuous

vomir [vɔmir] **1** *vt* to bring up, to vomit **2** *vi* to vomit, Br to be sick ● **vomissements** *nmpl* **avoir des v.** to vomit

vont [vɔ̃] *voir* **aller¹**

vos [vo] *voir* **votre**

vote [vɔt] *nm* vote, voting; Br **bureau de v.** polling station, Am polling place ● **voter 1** *vt (loi)* to pass **2** *vi* to vote

votre, vos [vɔtr, vo] *adj possessif* your

vôtre [votr] **1** *pron possessif* **le ou la v., les vôtres** yours; **à la v.!** cheers! **2** *nmpl* **les vôtres** *(votre famille)* your family

voudra, voudrait [vudra, vudrɛ] *voir* **vouloir**

vouer [vwe] **se vouer** *vpr* **se v. à** to dedicate oneself to

vouloir* [vulwar] *vt* to want **(faire** to do); **je veux qu'il parte** I want him to go; **v. dire** to mean **(que** that); **je voudrais un pain** I'd like a loaf of bread; **je voudrais rester** I'd like to stay; **je veux bien attendre** I don't mind waiting; **voulez-vous me suivre** will you follow me; **si tu veux** if you like *or* wish; **en v. à qn d'avoir fait qch** to be angry with sb for doing sth

voulu, -e [vuly] *adj (requis)* required; *(délibéré)* deliberate

vous [vu] *pron personnel* **(a)** *(sujet, complément direct)* you; **v. êtes ici** you are here; **il v. connaît** he knows you **(b)** *(complément indirect)* (to) you; **il v. l'a donné** he gave it to you, he gave you it **(c)** *(réfléchi)* yourself, *pl* yourselves; **v. v. lavez** you wash yourself/yourselves **(d)** *(réciproque)* each other; **v. v. aimez** you love each other • **vous-même** *pron* yourself • **vous-mêmes** *pron pl* yourselves

voûte [vut] *nf (arch)* vault • **voûté, -e** *adj (personne)* stooped

vouvoyer [vuvwaje] *vt* **v. qn** = to address sb as "vous" • **vouvoiement** *nm* = use of the formal "vous" instead of the more familiar "tu"

voyage [vwajaʒ] *nm* trip, journey; *(par mer)* voyage; **aimer les voyages** to like *Br* travelling *or Am* traveling; **faire un v., partir en v.** to go on a trip; **être en v.** to be (away) *Br* travelling *or Am* traveling; **bon v.!** have a good trip!; **v. de noces** honeymoon; **v. organisé** (package) tour • **voyager** *vi* to travel • **voyageur, -euse** *nmf Br* traveller, *Am* traveler; *(passager)* passenger; **v. de commerce** *Br* travelling *or Am* traveling salesman, *Br* commercial traveller

voyant, -e [vwajɑ̃, -ɑ̃t] *adj (couleur)* gaudy, loud

voyou [vwaju] *nm* hooligan

vrac [vrak] **en vrac** *adv (en désordre)* in a muddle; *(au poids)* loose

vrai [vrɛ] *adj* true; *(réel)* real; *(authentique)* genuine • **vraiment** *adv* really

vraisemblable [vrɛsɑ̃blabl] *adj (probable)* likely, probable; *(crédible)* credible • **vraisemblablement** [-əmɑ̃] *adv* probably

vrombir [vrɔ̃bir] *vi* to hum

VTT [vetete] *(abrév* **vélo tout terrain)** *nm inv* mountain bike

vu, -e¹ [vy] **1** *pp de* **voir 2** *adj* **bien vu** well thought of; **mal vu** frowned upon **3** *prép* in view of; **vu que...** seeing that...

vue² [vy] *nf (sens)* (eye)sight; *(panorama)* view; **en v.** *(proche)* in sight; *(en évidence)* on view; **avoir qn/qch en v.** to have sb/sth in mind; **à première v.** at first sight; **de v.** *(connaître)* by sight

vulgaire [vylgɛr] *adj (grossier)* vulgar; *(ordinaire)* common

vulnérable [vylnerabl] *adj* vulnerable

Ww

W, w [dubləve] *nm inv* W, w
wagon [vagɔ̃] *nm (de voyageurs)*
carriage, *Br* coach, *Am* car;
(de marchandises) Br wagon,
Am freight car • **wagon-lit** *(pl*
wagons-lits) *nm* sleeping car,
sleeper • **wagon-restaurant** *(pl*
wagons-restaurants) *nm* dining
or restaurant car
wallon, -onne [walɔ̃, -ɔn] **1** *adj*

Walloon **2** *nmf* **W., Wallonne**
Walloon
watt [wat] *nm Él* watt
w-c [(dublə)vese] *nmpl Br* toilet,
Am bathroom
week-end [wikɛnd] *(pl* **week-
ends)** *nm* weekend; **partir en w.**
to go away for the weekend
whisky [wiski] *(pl* **-ies** *ou* **-ys)** *nm*
Br whisky, *Am* whiskey

Xx

X, x [iks] *nm inv* (*lettre, personne ou nombre inconnus*) X, x; **x fois** umpteen times

xénophobe [gsenɔfɔb] *adj* xenophobic • **xénophobie** *nf* xenophobia

Yy

Y, y¹ [igrɛk] *nm inv* Y, y

y² [i] **1** *adv* there; (*dedans*) in it/them; (*dessus*) on it/them; **elle y vivra** she'll live there; **j'y entrai** I entered (it); **allons-y** let's go **2** *pron* **j'y pense** I'm thinking about it; **je m'y attendais** I was expecting it; **ça y est!** that's it!

yacht [jɔt] *nm* yacht

yaourt [jaurt] *nm* yoghurt

yeux [jø] *voir* œil

yoga [jɔga] *nm* yoga; **faire du y.** to do yoga

Yo-Yo® [jojo] *nm inv* yo-yo

Zz

Z, z [zɛd] *nm inv* Z, z

zèbre [zɛbr] *nm* zebra

zéro [zero] *nm (chiffre)* zero, *Br* nought; *(de numéro de téléphone) Br* 0 [əʊ], *Am* zero; *(température)* zero; **deux buts à z.** *(au football) Br* two nil, *Am* two zero

zeste [zɛst] *nm* **un z. de citron** a piece of lemon peel

zigzag [zigzag] *nm* zigzag; **en z.** *(route)* zigzag(ging)

Zimbabwe [zimbabwe] *nm* **le Z.** Zimbabwe

zinc [zɛ̃g] *nm (métal)* zinc

zipper [zipe] *vt Ordinat* to zip

zodiaque [zɔdjak] *nm* zodiac; **signe du z.** sign of the zodiac

zone [zon] *nf* zone; **z. industrielle** industrial *Br* estate *or Am* park; **z. fumeurs/non-fumeurs** smoking/ no-smoking area

zoo [zo(o)] *nm* zoo ● **zoologique** *adj* zoological; **parc z.** zoo

zoom [zum] *nm (objectif)* zoom lens